REFERENCE

Cavaliers and Pioneers

CAVALIERS AND PIONEERS

Abstracts of
Virginia Land Patents and Grants

———

Abstracted by
NELL MARION NUGENT

———

Indexed by
CLAUDIA B. GRUNDMAN

REFERENCE

VOLUME TWO: 1666–1695

———

VIRGINIA STATE LIBRARY
RICHMOND
1977

Standard Book Number: 0–88490–009–6
Library of Congress Cataloging in Publication Data (revised)

Nugent, Nell Marion.
  Cavaliers and pioneers.

  Vol. 2 indexed by Claudia B. Grundman, and published
by Virginia State Library, Richmond.
    CONTENTS: v. 1. 1623–1666. v. 2. 1666–1695.
    1. Virginia—Genealogy. 2. Land grants—Virginia.
I. Title.
F225.N842   929'.3755   34–42407
ISBN 0–88490–009–6 v.2.

CONTENTS

INTRODUCTION

 I N 1934 volume one of *Cavaliers and Pioneers: Abstracts of Virginia Land Patents and Grants* was published in Richmond.[1] It was the first fruit of a plan encouraged and supported by Agnes Bernadine Sitterding. Abstracted and indexed by Nell Marion Nugent, custodian of the Land Office from 1925 to 1958, the book contained information from patent books 1 through 5. Mrs. Nugent had planned a series of five volumes to cover the seventeenth and eighteenth centuries. Her abstracts of patent books 6 through 14 were set in type for publication, but circumstances caused Miss Sitterding to abandon the project, and eventually the type was destroyed. Corrected page proofs of these abstracts survived, however, and were deposited in the Virginia State Library along with the records of the Land Office.[2] The library has had indexed the abstracts of patent books 6, 7, and 8, which appear in this volume, and intends in the future to have indexed and published those for patent books 9 through 14. These records present the best available chronicle of immigration of freemen, slaves, and indentured servants to colonial Virginia.[3]

As is evident from the lists of immigrants in the patent abstracts, the headright system was the major method of land acquisition in

1. Nell Marion Nugent, *Cavaliers and Pioneers: Abstracts of Virginia Land Patents and Grants, 1623–1800* (Richmond, 1934; reprint ed., Baltimore, 1974).

2. In 1948 the Land Office records were transferred from the capitol to the Archives Division of the Virginia State Library, and in 1952 the General Assembly transferred the duties of the register of the Land Office to the State Librarian. Daphne S. Gentry, comp., *Virginia Land Office Inventory* (Richmond, [1973]), xxx.

3. Studies based on the land records include Fairfax Harrison, *Virginia Land Grants: A Study of Conveyancing in Relation to Colonial Politics* (Richmond, 1925); Wesley Frank Craven, *White, Red, and Black: The Seventeenth-Century Virginian* (Charlottesville, 1971); and Edmund S. Morgan, "Headrights and Head Counts: A Review Article," *Virginia Magazine of History and Biography*, 80(1972):361–371.

seventeenth-century Virginia. The basic doctrine of English land tenure was that "all land whatsoever is held, mediately or immediately, of the Crown."[4] It followed that Virginia land was dispensed either by the Virginia Company of London under the authority of its various charters or, after the dissolution of the company, by the crown's own officials of the colonial government. "The Method settled by the king from the first seating of that Country," Henry Hartwell, James Blair, and Edward Chilton wrote in 1697, "was to allot 50 Acres of Land to every one that should adventure into that Country; which, if it had been punctually observed, would have been a lasting Encouragement to Adventurers, till the Country had come to be well peopled."[5]

The three authors complained to the Board of Trade, however, that the headright system had been abused. Although the distribution of the king's land ought to have benefited newcomers, the system tended to add available land to the holdings of already established planters rather than give it to the immigrants upon whom the rights to land were based. The county courts were generous with certificates to patent land. When the master of a ship "made oath that he had imported himself and so many Seamen and Passengers at divers Times into the Country, and that he never elsewhere made Use of those Rights; he had presently an Order granted him for so many Rights, (*i.e.*, so many Times 50 Acres of Land) and these Rights he would sell and dispose of for a small Matter. . . . The Masters likewise that bought the Servants so imported would at another Court make Oath that they bought so many Persons that had ventur'd themselves into the Country, and upon this so many Rights were order'd them: So that still the Land went away, and the Adventurers [i.e., immigrants] themselves, who remain'd in the Country, for whom it was originally designed, had the least Share."[6]

These abuses did not concern the crown immediately, for as long as land was being patented—regardless of who came to own it or whether it was settled and improved—the king could expect revenue from the rents, whereas land that was not patented paid him nothing. Crown

---

4. A.W.B. Simpson, *An Introduction to the History of the Land Law* (Oxford, 1961), 1.

5. Henry Hartwell, James Blair, and Edward Chilton, *The Present State of Virginia, and the College,* ed. Hunter Dickinson Farish (Williamsburg, 1940), 16. Written in 1697, the report was first published in London in 1727.

6. Ibid., 17.

officials, argued Hartwell, Blair, and Chilton, "little consider'd that the small Profit which comes by Quit-Rents, doth not ballance the great Damage of leaving the Country without Inhabitants," whose trade might have benefited both the English economy and the king's revenues. This careful description of existing abuses did not inspire imperial officials to act. Indeed, the revival of the treasury right in 1699—by which rights to land could be purchased without bringing settlers into the colony—and the opening of Northern Neck Proprietary lands about 1690 contributed to the formation of the huge estates characteristic of the eighteenth-century Virginia elite.[7]

Virginians were prompt to acquire land that previously had been patented, and the records show that much lapsed and escheat land was patented again. After patenting and surveying a tract of land a patentee was required to settle the land within three years of the date of the patent and to pay the annual rent of one shilling for every fifty acres. The title to lapsed land, as land was called that had not been settled within three years, returned to the crown, and could be claimed by the first person to petition the General Court. Without such petition, lapsed land would not have come to the attention of the court.[8]

Previously patented land could also return to the crown either when the landholder died without heirs or when he was convicted of a felony. Such land was called escheat land. In seventeenth-century Virginia most escheat land became available when persons died intestate; escheat for criminal offense was rare. Again, the legal process could be begun by a petitioner who requested "the Benefit of the Escheat." When the governor accepted a petitioner's request he issued a warrant "to the Escheator of the Precinct, who makes Inquisition, and finds the Office by a Jury of 12 men. Which Inquisition being return'd by the Escheator to the Secretary's Office, lies there 9 Months, that any Person concern'd

7. Ibid., 18; W. Stitt Robinson, Jr., *Mother Earth—Land Grants in Virginia 1607–1699*, E. G. Swem, ed., Jamestown 350th Anniversary Historical Booklets (Williamsburg, 1957), 48-74; Harrison, *Virginia Land Grants*, 42-51; "An Account of the Manner of Taking Up and Patenting Land in Her Majesty's Colony and Dominion of Virginia with Reasons Humbly Offered for the Continuance Thereof," *William and Mary Quarterly*, 2d ser., 3(1923):137-142.

8. Hartwell, Blair, and Chilton, *Present State of Virginia*, 19; William Waller Hening, ed., *The Statutes at Large; Being a Collection of all the Laws of Virginia, from the First Session of the Legislature in the Year 1619* . . . (Richmond, Philadelphia, and New York, 1809-1823), 1:468.

may come and traverse the Office, and if no body appears in that Time, a Patent passeth according to the Petitioner's Request." (Patents for escheat land abstracted in this volume may be located through the index, s.v., Deputy Escheator, Escheator, Inquisition, and Weir, Jno.) Whether acquired by original patent or by a successful petition for lapsed or escheat land, Virginia land was granted in free and common socage with an annual rent due on September 29, the day of Saint Michael and All Angels.[9]

The library is deeply indebted to the estate of Agnes Bernadine Sitterding for cooperation in bringing her project nearer to completion. Volume two of *Cavaliers and Pioneers*, which contains abstracts of patent books 6, 7, and 8, was indexed by Claudia B. Grundman, of Urbana, Illinois, a former member of the library staff. Printer's copy for the index was prepared from more than thirty-four thousand cards, and galley proof was read against the cards to insure the integrity of Mrs. Grundman's index. Throughout a long and often tedious process, all have been sustained by the recognition, in Fairfax Harrison's words, that these patent records represent one of "Virginia's most precious surviving muniment[s] of her past."[10]

JON KUKLA
Head, Publications Branch

9. Hartwell, Blair, and Chilton, *Present State of Virginia*, 20; Hening, *Statutes*, 2:56-57, 136-138; 3:304-329.

10. Harrison, *Virginia Land Grants*, 7.

ABBREVIATIONS

A., Acs., acres
Chs., chains
Cl., Clk., Clerk
Co., County
Cr., creek
Ct., court
Devdt., devident
Ewd., Ely., E.most, Eastward, Easterly, Easternmost
Esqr., Esquire
Genl., Generll, General
Gent., Gentleman
Govr., Governor
Mrs., Mistress (not always a married woman)

N., Nwd., Nly., North, Northward, Northerly
P., pole
Per., perches
Pers., persons
Per. adv., personal adventure
Riv., river
R., rod; rood.
S., Swd., Sly., South, Southward, Southerly
Servt., servant
Sw., swamp
Trans., transportation
W., Wwd., Wly., West, Westward, Westerly

( ) Indicates more than one spelling in the same record.
? Indicates uncertainty.
* Indicates that the list of headrights was omitted or incomplete in the patent book; names are given when they appear.

This list of abbreviations is based on the "Explanation" printed in volume one of *Cavaliers and Pioneers*, page xxxv.

CAVALIERS AND PIONEERS

PATENT BOOK NO. 6

By Sir Wm Berkeley, Knight, Governor &c.

(NOTE: The first four pages of this volume have so deteriorated it is impossible to give but *very brief* abstracts. It is apparent from many blank spaces this transcript was made from fragmentary records. One-quarter of the first two pages is entirely missing).

—— (Name blank), W'stmoreland Co., 22 Oct. 1666, p. 1. Trans. of: Wm. Milborn, Margtt. Green, Tho. Hull, Francis Dolphin, Richd. Parker, Alex. Gregory.

GEO. DAWSON & FRANCIS HAYDON, 1000 acs., 22 Oct. 1666, p. 1. Adj. Col. More Fantleroy's orphants, the Indian Path, line of *said* Randolph & Major Beale. Trans. of 20 pers: Thomas Poole, Alice Potter, Mary Meake, Jno. Little, Wm. Parker, Wm. Todd, Jno. Price, Sarah Price, Jno. Ellyson, Geo. Walker, Ann Leniton, Fra. Neson, Wm. Gilbert, Michael Short, Jno. Wormington, Richard Founding.

JNO. & THO. BOOCOCK, 750 acs., (Co. blank), 26 Oct. 1666, p. 1. Adj. Tho. Rowland, —— Vaughan, towards Wm. Freeke, Lt. Col. Pope, Appatamocks Cr. & Jno. Beard. 350 acs. as-signed by Lt. David Phillips to Lt. Col. Jno. Washington, who assigned to Nich. Saxton & by him sould to sd. Boocock, as by records of Westmoreland Co. may appear; 400 acs. for trans. of 8 pers: Francis Catwell, John Elliott, —— Cookindall (?), Margtt. West, Jno. Boocock, Anto. Boocock, Tho. Boocock, Alice Boocock.

RICHARD HEABERD, W'moreland Co., 26 Oct. 1666, p. 2. Mentions Mr.

Walter Broad—— (Broadhurst ?) & —— (Tho. ?) Pope.

ANDREW MONROWE, 920 acs. W'moreland Co., 26 Oct. 1666, p. 2. Mentions Potomack River, Thomas St——, John Hallowes, gent., Jno. Bear——. Part granted him by patent 8 Jan. 1651 & —— Mar. 1662; 280 acs. for trans. of 6 pers: Sarah Fanshaw, Margaret Bush, William Love, Sampson Wine, William Chase (?), Simon (?) Miller.

(NOTE: The first record on page 3 does not give the name of patentee, acreage or county; the date is 26 Oct. 1666. Mentions Puscaticon Creeke, an Indian Path, & —— Armestrong & Will Young.)

WILLIAM PEASLY, 390 acs. New Kent Co., S. side the freshes of Yorke Riv., p. 3, 26 Oct. 1666. Beneath land of Maj. Genll. Hammond, running to Henry Baxter, to Stones Swamp &c. Granted Jno. Moore & Wm. Peasly, 12 Oct. 1662 & due sd. Peasly as survivor.

WM. GREY & CHRISTOPHER BLACKBORNE, 775 acs., S. side of Rappa. Co. Upon James Gaynes, running to swamp at head of Occupasion Cr. &c. P. 3, 26 Oct. 1666. Trans. of 16 pers: Edward Berry, Kath. Berry,

Mas (or Mat.) Batten, Eliza. Berry, Eliz. Luggin, Mary Luggins, Ann Berry, Mary Berry, Mary Luggin, Danll. Lading, Prescilla Coding, Morgan Doll, Edwd. Kelly, James Greene; 2 Negroes.

WM. GREY, 363 A., 1 R., & 4 Per., Rappa. Co., Sittingborne Parish, S. side of Rappa. Riv., beg. on James Gaines &c., to main br. of sw. of Occapason Cr. &c., 26 Oct. 1666, p. 3. Trans. of 8 pers: Francis Coate, —— Runbridge, James Lodsey, Ann Simpson. (Record mutilated.)

JOHN PAINE, 1585 acs. Rappa. Co., p. 4, 26 Oct. 1666. (Mutilated.) (The following names appear under this record): Samll. Howard, Jno. Jnoson (Johnson), Wm. Cooke, Eliza. Smith, Jno. Warren, Francis James, Richd. Harman, Jno. Cotton, Ann Dunbar, Henry Mayes, James White, Wm. Evans, Rich. Symonds, Wm. Coppage, Stephen Sadl——, Mary Peny, Ellinor Day, Henry Thomas.

MAJOR JNO. WEIRE, 3000 acs., p. 4, 26 Oct. 1666. (Mutilated.) S. side Rappa. River, on S. E. point of a great Island; part of 2000 acs. granted Mr. Epaphroditus Lawson; mentions land of Coll. Jno. Catlett & Occupacon Cr. Trans. of 60 pers: Jno. Browne, Mary Gage, Tho. Webster, Wm. Thomas, Matthew Wms. (Williams, Jno. Short, Alex Davis, Charles Greene, Jno. Kippin, Wm. Sanders, Edwd. Frost, Wm. Jones, Tho. Carr, Isaac Ball, Tho. Leonard, Wm. Addison, Wm. Leech, Alice Goodale, Jno. Church, Charles Farthing, Richd. White, Abr. Iveson, Isaac Brumly, Jno. Rawlings, Fra. Fefs (Fess ?), Aug. Tomson, Wm. Tompson, Peter Francklin, Joseph Cort, Jno. Lancashiere, Jeremy Davis, Wm. Davis, Mary Swan, Char. Edward, Tho. Goulding, Wm. Harris, Cor. Williams, David Jones, Wm. Gatting, Saml. Corbett, John Gale, Wm. Peirce, Jno. Bell, Samll. Stanford, Wm. Everett, Margtt. Atkins, Tho. Peirce, Wm. Peirce, Jno. Yates, Tho. Gee, Fra. Wick.

JOHN WALTON, (WATTON), & ELIZABETH, his wife 450 acs. Isle of Wight Co., p. 5, 26 Oct. 1666. Beg. nere *Bennet's parke*, running to upper part of Goose hill Cr. &c. 350 acs. being half of 700 acs. granted unto Hugh Winn, dec'd., 3 Mar. 1640 & lately found to escheat & due sd. patentees, &c., & 100 acs. being marsh bet. the high land & Pagan Cr., & due for trans. of 2 pers: Jno. Watton & Francis Wren.

RICHARD BUTT, 200 acs. Low. Norf. Co., p. 5, 26 Oct. 1666. At the head of Robert Butt, beg. by the Cyprus Sw. & bounding on Anthony Benford. Trans. of 4 pers: Edward Holt, Edward Warding, Rich. Kee, Rice Dell.

ELIZABETH ORDELANT, Widdow, 650 acs. according to the ancient & lawfull bounds thereof, Nancimond Co., p. 5, 26 Oct. 1666. Part of 1650 acs. granted unto Cornelius Oudelant, dec'd. & lately found to escheat, as by an Inquisition recorded in the Secretaries office under the hands & seals of Coll Miles Cary, Escheator Generall for this country & the Jury sworne before him for that purpose, 17 Apr. 1666; now granted sd. Eliz., who hath made her composition to be paid according to Act.

MR. WM. BAUGH, 577 acs. Henrico Co., N. side of Appamattock Riv., p. 5, 16 Apr. 1668. (Mutilated). Beg. nigh Wm. Jeffry his house &c. to Perryes Stile feild &c. Trans. of 12 pers: Wm. Baugh, Senr., Wm. Baugh, Junr., Wm. Lewis, Wm. Nookes, Amie Read, Pennitt Jones, Sarah ——, Wm. Jefferies.

COLL. NATHLL. BACON, Esqr., 25 acs. Yorke Co., p. 6, 26 Oct. 1666. Granted unto Wm. Evans, dec'd., & now granted &c.

ELIZA. MEIGE, 50 acs. Yorke Co., p. 6, 26 Oct. 1666. Granted unto Henry Meige, dec'd. & found &c., & now due &c.

COLL. NATHANIELL BACON, Esqr., 700 acs., Nancimond Co., 26 Oct. 1666, p. 6. Part of 1650 acs. granted to Cornelius Oudelant, dec'd. & found to escheat &c., as by inquisition &c., now granted &c.

THOMAS FULCHER, 200 acs. Low. Norfolk Co., 26 Oct. 1666, p. 6. Granted unto Henry Wake, dec'd., & found to escheat &c., & now granted &c.

RICHARD PENNY, 300 acs., Nancimond Co., 26 Oct. 1666, p. 6. Part of 1650 acs. granted to Cornelius Oudelant, dec'd., found to escheat &c., & now granted &c.

JOHN PAINE, 542 A., & 82 P., S. E. of Pepetick Cr., Rappa. Co., 26 Oct. 1666, p. 7. 450 acs. beg. at cor. tree of Mr. Wm. Lane, where he now dwelleth & purchased of sd. Paine, &c. to N. E. br. towards land called *Ireland* &c., near land formerly David Warren's, dec'd; the residue on S. side of Rappa. Riv. in the freshes, opposite *Nanzemond*, beg. at Quiruck (or Quiunck) poynt &c. 450 acs. granted him —— of Feb. 1662; & 92 A. 82 P. for trans. of 2 pers: Wm. Boswell, Jno. Mathews.

THOMAS CEELY & JNO. NOBLE, 1000 acs. on N. side of Rappa. Riv., in the freshes nere the falls, 26 Oct. 1666, p. 7. Upon land of Coll. Clayborne. Trans. of 20 pers: Mary Gibbs, Robt. Peire, Ann Wilson, James Willms (Williams), Jonas Jnoson (Johnson), Andrew Ward, Wm. Robbinson, Jenkin Davis, Mary Watts, Tho. Couchman, Robt. Whitson, Thomas Hughes, Ri. Rumbridge, Dorothy Jones, James Ledsey, Thed. Paul, Ann Sampson, Sarah Cooper, George Gillins, Tho. Chouninge.

EDMD. COWLES, 125 acs. Chas. City Co., 29 Sept. ——, p. 7. Part of dev'dt. assigned by Jno. Stith to Ja. Hardway & by Jno. Hardway, his sonn & heire, sold to sd. Cowles, 3 June *1674*. (Badly mutilated.) Mentions Westover Path & Kemige's Creek.

THOMAS GOULDMAN, 1134 A. & 18 Po., on S. side of Rappa. Riv. on the back of a devdt. of Sir Henry Chicherly; 26 Oct. 1666, p. 8. Nere Ralph's Cr. running into Puscaticon Cr. &c. 650 acs. granted to Robt. Armstronge, 10 Sept. 1658 & by him (sold) to Coll. Tho. Goodrik by patent dated 20 Sept. 16——, deserted for want of seating & since petitioned to the Govr. & Councell by Thomas Gouldman & granted &c., & further due for trans. of 23 pers: Maurice Stubbs, Wm. Thompson, Danll Wallis, Mathias Adwell, David Jones, Tho. Salt, James Woodbery, Mary Dully, Jane Dempster, Henry Wood, Peter Spikes, Jonah Hart, Joseph Best, Wm. Turner, Ralph Dully, Peter Tomp. (Tompson ?), Robt. Haines, Wm. Harper, Jona. Davis, Martin Dye, David Idols, Walter Praton, Rich. Hopewell.

LT. COLL. THO. GOODRICH, 200 acs. on the head of Hoskins Cr., beg. by the Poquoson of sd. Cr., nigh Clemt. Thrush &c.; 29 Oct. 1666, p. 8. Granted to Anthony North, 18 Mar. 1662, deserted, & granted by order of the Genrll. Ct. & due for trans. of 4 pers: David Driver, Tho. Wmson (Williamson), Jno. James, Henry Jarman. (Mutilated).

LT. COLL. WM. KENDALL, 200 acs. N'ampton Co., 26 Oct. 1666, p. 9. At the seaboard side, beg. on Cedar Island, towards land of Mr. Neale, &c. Trans. of 4 pers: Mingo & Charles, Negroes; Henry Barnes, Walter Manington. (Mutilated)

JAMES GRAY, 900 acs. Accomack Co., 26 Oct. 1666, p. 9. A br. on the W. parting this & land that was Rich. Smith's in Capt. Tho. (Thomas) his Neck, running to land formerly Richard Bundocks, along Wm. Taylor's & a br. of Pocomock Cr. &c. Granted to Alphonso Ball & James Gray, 10 July 1664, & due sd. Gray as survivour.

RICHARD COXE, 809 acs. (300 acs. whereof Coxe sold unto Jno. Read), on a Sw. running downe Cow Cr. in Ware Riv., in Mockjack Bay, beg. at marked trees of Joseph Gregory on E. side of a br. &c., 26 Oct. 1666, p. 9. Granted sd. Coxe 5 —— 1657; and now renewed, etc. (Mutilated).

LT. COLL. WM. KENDALL, 1200 acs. at the head of Cherrystones Cr., where it divides itself into branches; 26 Oct. 1666, p. 10. Between 2 brs. of sd. Creek, the N. being Snaggy Pine br. & part of Hogg pen Cr. & the Southern being part of New Porte; beg. at 200 acs. formerly Major Wm. Andrewes'.

on N. side of New Porte Cr., to land of George Eveling, formerly Coll. Obedience Robins', to Tho. Harmanson, formerly Capt. Phillip Taylor's, to Capt. Jno. Savage, to the Rooty Br., along Francis Pettitt's 300 acs., and to the head of Snaggy Pine Br. 600 acs. granted to Capt. Jno. How, dec'd., found to escheat, & granted sd. Kendall, 11 Sept. 1663; 300 acs. granted him 1 Sept. 1664; 300 acs. due for trans. of 6 pers: Jno. Hawkins, Eliz. Merrick, Peter Gore, Tho. Hemence, —— Ridly, George Stanton.

MR. JOHN CAUTANCEAN, 461 acs. N'umberland Co., 29 Mar. 1666, p. 10. Beg. at S. S. W. side & at the head of a small cr. in Mr. Matrom's plantation, near land of Jacob & Wm. Cautancean, at head of a Cr. of Chikacone Riv., &c. 400 acs. granted Mr. Jno. Trussell, 14 Oct. 1649, assigned to Jacob Cautancean, dec'd., & due sd. patentee as son & heire; & 61 acs. for trans. of 1 pers.*

WM. & PETER PRESTLY, 2700 acs. N'umberland Co., 29 Mar. 1666, p. 11. Beg. at land of Mr. Jno. Matron, extending to a br. of Chickocone Cr., nigh horse path, land of Andrew Pettegrew, to Quioxters br., &c. Trans. of 54 pers: Peter Prestly, Wm. Bradly, Jon. Parke, Eliz. Smith, Ann Maide, Ann Petit, Margtt. White, Wm. Boswell, James Hoback, Wil. Prestly, Jone his wife, Joseph Benan (or Bevan), Jno. Lane, Roger Lane, Tho. Underhill, Wm. Baucroft (or Bancroft), Will. Booles (or Bootes), Hannah Newman, Wm. Harman, Margtt. Rayner, Wm. Ould, Ann Berry, Robt. Floring, Wm. Snerly, Wm. Milborne, Margtt. Greene, Tho. Hull, Fran. Dolphin, Rich. Parker, Alex. Gregory, Fran. Evans, Griffith Evans, Henry Wills, Wm. Blease, Tho. Poole, Alice Potter, Mary Meeks, Jno. Little, Wm. Baker, Wm. Todd, Jno. Price, Sarah Price, Jno. Ellyson, George Walker, Ann Lenniton, Francis Neson, Wm. Gilbert, Michaell Sherte (or Sherle), Jno. Wormington, Rich. Fownding, Mary Core, Edmond Herman (or Sherman), Gerrard Cresty, Grace Hill.

ROBERT MIDDLETON, 1120 acs. W'moreland Co., 21 May 1666, p. 11. At head of the main br. of Yeocomico Riv., &c., nigh Machotick Horse path, a br. dividing this & land of Francis Clay. 700 acs. granted him 26 Sept. 1665; & 420 acs. for trans. of 9 pers: George Gladwin, Joane East, John Sharpe, Robt. Tiverton, Andrew Mecollo, James Ocanula, Isabella Feshterton, Joane Gray, Robt. Fletcher. (Mutilated).

FRANCIS CLAY, 1480 acs. W'moreland Co., 21 May 1666, p. 12. On N. W. side & nigh head of Yeocomico Riv., 1000 acs. by former pattent, & 480 acs. for trans. of 10 pers: George Walker, John Clarke, Francis Read, Eliz. Snow, Wm. Cotton, Ed. Fownding, And. Barton, Joane Irish, Jno. Grimes. (Mutilated.)

MR. WM. LANE, 164 acs. in the freshes of Rappa. Co. on N. side the Riv., adj. plantation he lives on; 29 Oct. 1666, p. 12. Beg. at the mouth of a cr. near Mr. Charles Snead's clifts, &c., crossing Pepetick Cr. to his own & land of Mr. Jno. Paine. Trans. of 4 pers: Wm. Stratton (or Strutton), Geo. Ward Henry Harvy, Martha Watkins.

COLL. JNO. CATLETT, 150 acs. Rappa. Co., 6 Nov. 1666, p. 12. Upon the Riv. & Occupason Cr., adj. 400 acs. of, or called, Richard Lawson's. Trans. of 3 pers: Jno. Browne, Mary Gage, Tho. Webster.

THOMAS CREETON & HUGH ROYE, 2100 acs. New Kent Co., 6 Nov. 1666, p. 13. 1800 acs. bounded, viz: 400 acs. being marsh on the N. side of Yorke Riv., from Ash. Battent's marked trees, along Tho. Bell, to Cattaile Sw., to Capt. Chamberline, to Pepetico Sw. &c.; 300 acs. on sd. Chamberline, Tho. Davis, Jno. Durrett, Tho. Bell & land formerly Jno. Duncomb & Jno. Lewis'. 1400 acs. purchased of sd. Lewis & Duncomb; & 700 acs. for trans. of 14 pers: Wm. Windowe, Tho. Arnop (?), Wm. Tureton, Edward Larkin, Elinor Richardson, Mary Thorne, Joane Wild, Nan (a) Negro, Mathew Bradly, Val. Howell, Jno. Humphries, Henry Cooper. Thomas Bolton. An Meroin.

MAJOR JOHN WEIRE, 1770 A., 2 R., 10 po., Rappa. Co., Sittingborne Parish, on S. side of Rappa. Riv., on the head of Tignor's Cr. nere the Mill Cr., 24 Oct. 1666, p. 13. Beg. on a poynt bet. 2 branches &c., to Portobacco path &c., over the maine br. or poquoson of same to br. parting this & land of Tho. Rawson, to Jno. Smith, to Jno. Walker, dec'd. &c. Granted to Major Andrew Gilson, 27 June 16——, by him deserted & granted to. sd. Weire, & due for trans. of 36 pers: Jno. Davis, Mary Davis, Phill Wood, Wm. Scott, Fran. Norton, Sarah Phillips, Judith Stone, Jno. Wilcox, Ralph Harper, Geo. Dixon, Samll. Dowling, Jno. a frenchman, Nicho. Curtis, Danll. Watts, Alex. West, Tho. Wilmott, Wm. Welles, Peter Fareman, Joseph Stephens, Margtt. Palmer, James (or Jane) Batten, Fran. Porter, Martin Dye, Fred. Thompson, Ed. Horton, Robt. Parson, Danll. Hill, Tim. Wilson, Jno. Hart, Mary Hatton, Sam. Waterman, Rich. Holding, Jno. Collins, Roger Carter, Fran. Holland. Patriack Morgan.

SAME. 1800 acs. Rappa. Co., on S. side of sd. Riv., 6 Nov. 1666, p. 14. Beg. at S. E. poynt of a great Island, at 2000 acs. granted unto Ephaphroditus Lawson &c., to 304 acs. granted to Coll. Jno. Catlett, S. S. W. to Occupason Cr. &c. Trans. of 36 pers: Wm. Thomas, Mat. Williams, Jno. Short, Alex Davis, Charles Greene, Jno. Kippin, Wm. Sanders, Edward Frost, Wm. Jones, Tho. Carr, Ed. Cooper, Fran. Parker, Isack Ball, Tho. Leonard, Wm. Addison, Wm. Leech, Alice Goodale, Jno. Church, Charles Farthing, Rich. White, Abram Iveson, Isack Brumly, Jno. Rawlings, Fran. Fests, Aug. Tompson, Wm. Tompson, Nicholas Jnoson., Peter Franklin, Joseph Cort, Jno. Lancashire, Jeremy Davis, Wm. Davis, Mary Swan, Charles Edwards, Tho. Goulding, Wm. Harris.

EDWARD ROWZEE, Gent., & Wm. Harper, 200 acs. on S. W. side of Occupason Cr. above the narrowes of Lord (?) Neck, &c., being lower bounds of 400 acs. of land called Rich. Lawson's, &c; 6 Nov. 1666, p. 14. Trans. of 4 pers: Cor. Wms. (Williams), David Jones, Wm. Getting, Francis Wick.

WM. MOSELY, 520 acs. Rappa. Co., upon Occupason Cr., Sittingborne Parish, 1 Nov. 1666, p. 15. Beg. at Tho. Page &c. 360 acs. granted unto Tho. Page, deserted & granted unto Jno. & George Mott, deserted, & upon petition &c. granted unto sd. Mosely; 160 acs. residue for trans. of 4 pers: Jno. Dennett, Wm. Alder, Samll. Francis, Jno. Johnson, Mary Wotton, Nicholas Spicer, Henry Tarett (?), James Potts, Stephen Baker, Nich. Baker, Samll. Carbett (or Carbelt).

RICHARD STURMAN, 1004 acs. W'moreland Co., 26 Oct. 1666, p. 15. 826 acs. upon branches of Nomany, beg. at Katharine Brent, nere Hackett's feild, along Major Lewis & Mr. Jno. Lord, Maj. Peirce's line &c., & 178 acs. beg. at cor. of Mr. Hardiches, on line of Katharine Brent, to br. of Corrotoman &c. Trans. of 21 pers: Robt. Rachaell, Roger Cocshell, Jno. Ludlow, Jno. Hopkins, Tho. Butler, Jno. Gall, Jno. Lining, Wm. Cross, Edm. Poole, Sarah Jackson, Wm. Frizell, Tho. Cross, Tho. Read, Jno. Read, Tho. Lane, Wm. Coale, Tho. Read, Wm. Smith, Rich. Sturman. Wm. Robbinson, Peter Wyth.

JOHN BEARD, 250 acs. W'moreland Co., 24 Oct. 1666, p. 16. Upon Andrew Monrowes Cr., & land pattented from Wm. Bothum, now in possession of Rich. Heabeard &c. Granted sd. Heabeard 27 Mar. 1658, deserted, & upon petition &c. granted sd. Beard; trans. of 5 pers: David White, Wm. Whitecroft, Jno. Lewellin, Mary Soane, Wm. Gilbert.

LESTRANGE MORDANT, 450 acs. N'umberland Co., S. side Potomack Riv. nigh Nomeny; 24 Oct. 1666, p. 16. Beg. at Danll. Hutt, Merchant, along line of Wm. Overedd &c. Granted unto Tho. Dios, 9 Apr. 1663, deserted &c., trans. of 9 pers: Wm. Beale, Wm. Jones, Morgan Kenott, James Stephen, Tho. Page, Sarah ——, Robt. Rose, Henry ——, An Smith.

MR. THOMAS BALLARD, 800 acs. Rappa. Co., on S. side & in the freshes of Rappa. Riv., 6 Nov. 1666, p. 16. Beg. on a Cr. dividing this & land of

Jno. Weire &c. Granted to Robt., Thomas & Wm. Mosse by severall pattents, deserted, granted by order &c., & due for trans. of 16 pers: Mat. Wilkenson, John Smith, Rich. Curteen, Nathll. Nash, Tho. Marshall, Jno. Hall, Rich Ceely, Wm. Davis, James Stadling (?), Rich. Stramford, Mary Right, Faith Thrift, Jane, Bishop, Elinor Carpenter, Alice Hammond; Toney (a) Negro.

COLL. NICHOLAS SPENCER, 500 acs. in Potomack freshes, 6 Nov. 1666, p. 17. N. E. upon a cr. above Coll. Speaks land, S. E. upon Gosnells Land &c. Granted to Peter Smith 15 July 1657, deserted; granted unto Mr. Isaak Allerton, 6 Apr. 1662, deserted; upon petition &c. granted sd. Spencer & further due for trans. of 10 pers: Tho. Mathews, 3 times, 4 Negroes; Toby Plator (?), John Jones, Ann James, Mary Wms. (Williams).

MATHEW JENNINGS, 500 acs. New Kent Co., bet. branches of Harquack Swamp; 9 June 1666, p. 17. Beg. on lower side of sd. branch, bounding on land of Jno. Garrett & Edward Carbenbrocke &c. by his own house, to land of Jno. James, Peter Ford, Jno. Haines, Wm. Henderson & Coll. Wm. Clayborne. Granted to Ralph Mazey & purchased by sd. Jennings.

JOHN JAMES, 259 acs. New Kent Co., upon br. of Hartquack Sw., 9 June 1666, p. 17. 100 acs. purchased of Ralph Mazey, beg. at the mouth of Hawkes nest br., by sd. James' house &c., by land of Mr. Mathew Jennings, &c. Trans. of 3 pers: Jno. Browne, Mary Gage, Tho. Webster.

ROBERT JARRATT, 284 acs. in a necke bet. Yorke & Chikahomani Rivers, adj. Jonathan Hughes, Wm. Mosse & nere Mosses Sw. &c; 9 June 1666, p. 18. Trans. of 6 pers: Wm. Thomas. Mathew Wms. (Williams), Jno. Short, Alex. Davis, Charles Green, Jno. Kippin.

JOHN GLEN, 65 acs. New Kent Co., 9 June 1666, p. 18. Adj. land of Capt. Barnehouse & by a branch of Warrani Sw. Trans. of 2 pers: Wm. Saunders, Edward Frost.

JOHN POUNCY, 800 acs. New Kent Co., 9 June 1666, p. 18. Upon the lowerside of Mattadecon Cr. & by land of Jno. Garraway. Trans. of 16 pers: Wm. Jones, Tho. Carr, Ed. Cooper, Fran. Parker, Isaak Bell, Tho. Leonard, Wm. Addison, Wm. Leech, Alice Goodale, Ann Church, Charles Farthing, Rich. White, Abram Iveson, Isaak Bumly, Jno. Rawlings, Fran. Jeffts.

CHARLES LOVEING, 350 acs. New Kent Co., 29 Mar. 1666, p. 18. Adj. Richard Littlepage & James Turner, Capt. Langstone's back line &c. Trans. of 7 pers: Jno. Bowre, Michaell Trott, Mary Ratcliffe, Wm. Ralph, Ann Francklin, Margtt. Ashborne, Jno. Jones.

MOYSES DAVIES, 220 acs. New Kent Co., 18 Feb. 1666, p. 19. Beg. in Henry Goodgaine's line nere a br. of Skiminoe Sw., upon Richard Price, by the Road &c. to Mr. Arthur Price, William Morgan & Thomas London &c. Trans. of 5 pers: Jno. Browne, Mary Gage, Thomas Webster, Wm. Thomas, Mathew Williams.

MOYSES DAVIES, Gent., 1450 acs., same Co. & page, 19 Mar. 1666. S. side of Yorke Riv. over against *Manskin*, beg. at the mouth of Tottopottomoyes Cr. &c. to tree in sight of Capt. Anthony Langstone's plantation, crossing the Road, &c., below the mountaines, to Robt. Anderson's land &c. Trans. of 29 pers: Jno. Short, Alexander Davies, Charles Greene, Jno. Kippin, Wm. Sanders, Jno. Rawlings, Peter Francklin, Wm. Davies, Edward Frost, Wm. Jones, Thomas Carr, Edward Cooper, Francis Parker, Francis Jeffs, Joseph Cort, Isaak Ball, Tho. Leonard, Wm. Addison, Wm. Leech, Alice Goodale, Aug. Thomson, Jno. Linconshire, Ann (?) Church, Charles Farthing, Richard White, Abram Iveson, Isaak Brumly, Nich. Johnson, Jeremiah Davies.

WILLIAM ONOUGHTON, 500 acs. Accomack Co., at the head of the N. br. of Hunting Cr., 9 Nov. 1666, p. 20. Trans. of 10 pers: German Gilliot, Sarah Gilliott, Tho. Gilliot, Germon Gilliot, Wm. White, Wm. Stoling, Francesco a Turke, Edmond Bland, Xtopr. Layton, Eliz. Lawson.

NATHANIELL, JNO. & GEORGE RADCLIFFE, 1200 Accomack Co., nere Potomack Riv., on S. side of a crooked cr., 9 Nov. 1666, p. 20. Adj. land of John Renny, &c. Trans. of 24 pers: Mary Blento, Jno. Mundy (?), Jno. Barwis (?), Xtopr. Potter, Neh. Carlington, John Smith, Antho. Bouch, Jno. Warwick, Wm. Boothby, Mary Germon, Edward Wrath, James Roxford, Roger Lasingby, Edward Jones, Row. Nurse, Lewis Wright, Michaell Worrall, Jno. Ross, Robt. Want, Owen Lawthern, Jeffrey Hall, Morgan Evans, Will Thorpe, George Darby.

JNOA. RUE (or Rice), 300 acs. Accomack, 9 Nov. 1666, p. 20. S. side of the S. br. of Hunting Cr., on land of James Atkinson & Xtopr. Thompson. Trans. of 6 pers: Jane Summers, Joan Gwin, Lewis Stedman, Samll. Dyers, Humphrey Alston, Henry Charwick (or Charnock).

(NOTE: Pages 21-22 missing from this book have been inserted in old Vol. 5, between pages 64 and 65. See photographic reproduction in Vol. I of C. and P., page 288.)

MR. PETER JETT, 600 acs. Rappa. Co., N. side of sd. Riv., in the freshes about 3 mi. from the river side; 21 Jan. 1666, p. 23. Beg. at the E'wd. cor. tree of a peice of land called the forrest, *alias* Coleman's, nigh Major Underwood &c., by a horse road goeing up Potomack Riv. &c. Trans. of 12 pers: Francis Triplett, Alice Triplett, John Deane, Paul Woodbridge, Jno. Symmons, Walter Hart, Francis Curtis (or Custis), Josias Welding, Thomas Larthrop, James Foster, Will Maggott, Samll. Goodman.

CAPT. ALEXANDER FLEMING, 200 acs. on S. side of Rappa. Co. & in the freshes, 21 Jan. 1666, p. 23. Beg. at land formerly Walter Dickenson's, adj. Lt. Coll. Toby Smith, with land of Mr. Jno. Hull, nere the Road &c. Trans. of 4 pers: Jno. Davies, Tho. Hooton, Dorothy Hart, David Parker.

JOHN BENSON, 140 acs. Gloster Co., at the head of the beach swamp;

15 Mar. 1666, p. 23. Adj. lands of Lawrence Smith & Will. Ironmonger. Trans. of 3 pers: Eliz. Gilbert, Rich. Wingate, Stephen Cotswood.

ROBERT TOWNSEND, 650 acs. Chas. Riv. Co., 16 Apr. 1667, p. 24. Bet. Marteaw's & Townsend's Creeks. (Record badly mutilated.) Mentions Capt. Marteaw, & Will. Prior. Granted unto Francis Townsend, sonn & heire * * * of —— Townsend, by pattent dated 10 M—— * * *, now of right descends unto sd. Robt. as the true & lawfull heire of sd. Francis, dec'd.

MRS. ELIZABETH OUDELANT, 1500 acs., parte in Isle of Wight Co. & part in Nancimond Co., 26 Oct. 1666, p. 24. Beg. on a poynt belonging to a branch of Beverly Cr. crossing same, to Mr. Marshall's cornefeild &c., by the Otterhole br. &c. to an Island nere the mouth of a Cr. &c. 1400 Acs. granted unto Moore Fantleroy, 20 Feb. 1643 & purchased by Cornelius Oudelant, husband of sd. Eliz., & since his death escheated to the King; & 100 acs. for trans. of 2 pers: Tho. Ward, Jno. Deoorett (Devorett ?).

MR. THO. BEALE, Junr., 929 acs. neer head of Rappa. Cr., 28 May 1673, p. 24. Beg. neer the mouth of Herring Cr. that empties into Rappa. Cr. &c. Trans. of 19 pers: Andrew Canidge, James Lovestone, Jno. Richardson, Ja. Foster, Geo. Hilliard, Andrew Molten, Ja. Davies, Ann Child, Eliz. Wilkinson, Tho. Clark, Wm. Taught, Elias Johnson, Ja. Ballum, Tho. Long, Ja. Chaddock, Emma. Halderson, Lewis Hollis, James King. (Mutilated.)

MRS. ELIZABETH OUDELANT, 300 acs., Nancimond Co., 26 Oct. 1666, p. 25. Beg. in Chuckatuck Cr., by the side of a br. & Lawsons land &c. 280 acs. granted to Moore Fantleroy, 20 Feb. 1643, & purchased of him by Cornelius Oudelant, her husband, & since his escheated to his Majesty; 50 acs. due for trans. of: James Arnoll.

EDWARD TEALE (or Trate), 276 acs. Gloster Co., adj. the devdt. he lives upon, 6 Mar. 1666, p. 25. Beg. at the mouth of a small br. deviding this from land of Mr. Oliver Green &c. to *old line* of his own land. Trans. of 6 pers: Tho. Chamlis (or Chambrs), Jno. Settle, Tho. Cox, Henry Smith, Jno. Cocke, Jno. Davies. (Note: The general & county indices carry this name as *Trate,* as does the record from which this abstract was copied, however, examination of an earlier patent indicates this name should be Teale. See *Vol. I C. and P.* p. 488, for 180 acs., 27 Jan. 1663. N. M. N.)

ANN HACK, GEORGE, NICHOLAS HACK & PETER HACK, 1000 acs., according to the ancient & lawfull bounds thereof, Accomack Co., 22 Mar. 1666, p. 25. Granted unto Doctor George Hack, lately found to escheat, as by inquisition &c., dated 7 Aug. 1665 & now granted sd. Ann Hack, George, Nicholas & Peter Hack, who have made their composition &c.

MR. OLIVER GREEN, 770 acs. Gloster Co., N. side of Ware Riv. swamp, 16 Mar. 1666, p. 26. (Mutilated.) Mentions lands of Edward Teale (or Trate) & James Bradbery. 400 acs. by patent dated 30 Mar. 1657; 370 acs. for trans. of 8 pers: Jno. Collins, Tobias Hurst, Anna Ashby, Jno. Calvert, Robert Henly, Eliz. Thomasett, Stephen ——, Henry ——.

DAVID BRAND, 1178 acs. New Kent Co., on S. side of the Dragon Swamp, 16 Mar. 1666/7, p. 26. Mentions Mr. Light & Spencer's branch. (Mutilated). Trans. of 24 pers: Eliz. Gilbert, Rich. Wingate, Rich. Prior, Margtt. Prigett, Susan Joyce, (a) Negro, Sarah Bew, Jeffery Bew, Jno. Grimes, Tho. West, Will Clarke, Jno. Benson, Tobias Sely, Tho. Boone, Ambrose Hamond, George Walker, Rich. Mould, Samll. Baker. (Note: The surnames of the following have been obliterated: Jno., Christopr., James, Jno. Ogd.——, Eliz., Jno. M——.

CAPT. JNO. HULL, 7100 A., 2 R., 13 P., Rappa. Co.; 30 Sept. 1663, p. 27. 5798 A. 2 R. 13 P. *in* Farnham Parish, on N. side of sd. Riv., beg. Michaell Hugill, &c. to Tho. Robinson & Edward

Lewis; 664 acs. in sd. parrish, on N. side sd. Riv., beg. at the head of Totoskey Cr., running to head of Sellevants gutt, S. nere an Indian path &c; 650 acs. beg. where sd. Cr. devides into 2 maine branches &c. to land of sd. Hugill & Dennis Swillivant &c. 5798 A. 2 R. 13 P. granted sd. Hull & Mr. Will Mosely, 20 Feb. 1662, which sd. Mosely sold to sd. Hull; 664 acs. granted sd. Hugill the same date & sold to sd. Hull; 650 acs. granted sd. Hull 18 Mar. 1663.

JOHN MEDERS & HENRY PETERS, 4200 acs., on S. side & aboute 3 mi. from the Riv. upon Pwomansend (Powmansend) Cr., Rappa. Co., 17 Apr. 1667, p. 28. Beg. nere the run next to land of Mr. Silvester Thatcher, &c., over a br. to Quarter br. &c. Trans. of 84 pers: Jo. Webb, Will Jones, Samll. Jnoson (Johnson), Jno. Manning, Edward Anderson, An Anderson, Mary Lancaster, Will Holt, Rich. Willis, Susan Price, Margtt. Winch, Patriak Mason, Jno. Hart, Tho. Bentloe, Mary Bentloe, Tymothy Ball, Wm. Cochard, Ed. Drason (or Deason). Mar. Foster, Ralph Burts, Alex Palmer, Henry Short, Nicho. Cooper, Walter Howard, John Davies, Will Moore, Martin Barnes, Tho. Allen, Edward Ells, Samll. Farmar, Mary Goslick, Wm. Howsford, Jno. Jenkins, Xtopr. Keible, George Keible, Wm. Lambert, Robt. Mossey, Rice, Milton, Nath. Milton, Tho. Evans, Susan Parson, Jno. Cocke, Oneal (an ?) Ireshman, Francis Veale, Tho. Phips, Antho. Patridge, Nathanll. Swift, James Shadd, David Turner, Katharine Timple, Gilbert Grimes, Roger Webber, Ralph Dike, Phillip Peters, Henry Peeters, Mary Peters, Jno. Peeters, Eliz. Peters, Tho. Smith, Jno. Smith, James Horton, Wm. Booth, Jno. Holland, Tho. Frampitt, Henry Brock, Jno. Mories, Francis Straid, Jno. Goad, Wm. Finch, Nicholas Medway, Thomas Stone, Jno. Grave, Wm. Heath, Samll. Medford, Gabriel Dudley, Thomas Harris, Silvester Mathews, Jno. Bowen, Martin Reynolds, Henry Wilkenson, Tho. Fleet, Ralph Sawer, Thomas Brent, Wm. Hollis.

MR. FRANCIS TRIPLETT, 1050 acs. Rappa. Co., on N. side & in the freshes of same. 21 Jan. 1666, p. 29. Beg. at land formerly Samll. Nicholls', dec'd., S. on line of Thatcher's otherwise Mr. Jno. Hull's, nere land of Mr. Toby Smith, dec'd., &c. to the forrest land otherwise Coleman's, &c. to land of Major Underwood, dec'd. &c. Trans. of 21 pers: Xtopr. Hard, Mine James Robt. Fletcher, Tom a Scott, Tom a boy, a maid servant, James Hunt, Peter Jett, Will Jett, Peter, Junior, (Jett ?), Mary Jett, Mary Jett, Martha Jett, Jno. Taylor, Francis Sanders, David Jones, Patriack Horton, James Dukeman, Wm. Hanson, Charles Stepler (?), Lewis Baniton (or Barriton).

JOSEPH NEWTON, 400 acs. according &c., Accomack Co., 17 Apr. 1667, p. 29. Granted to Francis Sherwood, dec'd., found to escheat &c., under Col. John Stringer, Esch'r., 20 Dec. 1666, & now granted &c.

LT. COLL. WILLIAM KENDALL, 350 acs. N'ampton Co., 1 Nov. 1666, p. 29. Beg. at head br. of Hungars Cr., S. to Will Jones his br., & N. towards Richard Jacobs &c. Granted to Jno. Vines, 20 Oct. 1661, deserted, & granted by order &c., & further due for trans. of 7 pers: Wm. Kendall, Wm. Lewis, Ann Bishop, Miles Craves, Michaell Frost, Mary Knight, An Norgood.

THOMAS HARMANSON, 800 acs. N'ampton Co., 17 Apr. 1667, p. 30. (Being more than his 1000 acs. granted to Phillip Taylor, dec'd., 19 Dec. 1643, conteyned within the bounds layed claime to for sd. 1000 acs.). On the N., S., & W. sides of 1000 acs. & bounded on S. partly by Mountnes Cr. &c., running to land of Capt. Jno. Savage &c. Trans. of 16 pers: Edward Gable, James Greenwood, Rich. Robbins, Wm. Sharpe, Nan a Negro, Daniell Cadd, John Marayne, Ellenor Due, Geo. Jenkins, Jud a Negro, Wm. Biggs, Jno. Abraham, Tho. Somersett, Jno. Watts, Tho. Coleman, Danll. Donaushan.

COLL. JNO. STRINGER, 1050 acs. Accomack Co., at *Occocomson*, 1 Apr. 1667, p. 30. Bounded on E. by the seaboard side, S. by Will Taylor, N. by

Thomas Rideing &c. Trans. of 21 pers: Edward Stanly, Rich. Allen, Robt. Bindlos, Jno. Molinax, Ed. Fleetwood, George Watson, Mordica Edwards, Wm. Howe, Wm. Beare, Eliz. Peacock, Jno. Rimington, Jno. Hutchenson, Nath. Taylor, Jone Burt, Robt. Browne, Jno. Knott, Robt. Wapall (or Worpull), Washpate (?) Jones, Rich. Wyar, Oliver Atkins, Robt. Ware.

MR. HENRY FILMORE, 360 acs., Warwick Co., 20 Mar. 1666/7, p. 30. Granted unto Anthony Barnham, dec'd., found to escheat &c. by inquisition under Coll. Myles Cary, Esqr., his Majestie's Escheator Genll. for this country &c., 23 Feb. 1666.

WILLIAM SCOTT, 100 acs., Nancimond Co., in Chuckatuck Cr., 4 Mar. 1666/7, p. 31. Granted to Moreine Delamundaies, dec'd., lately found &c., as by inquisition under Col. Miles Cary. Esch'r. Gen'll., &c.

PATRIACK BARTLEY, 100 acs., Surry Co., 20 Mar. 1666/7, p. 31. Granted to Henry Meadowes, dec'd., lately found &c., as by inquisition under Col. Miles Cary, etc.

JOCIAS MODEY, 300 acs., Yorke Co., 1 Apr. 1667, p. 31. Granted unto Giles Modey, dec'd., lately found &c. (As above).

RICHARD BONNY, 660 acs., Low. Norf. Co., 4 Mar. 1666, p. 31. Granted unto Wm. Jacob, dec'd., lately found &c. (As above).

HENRY BISHOP, 2300 acs. Accomack Co., 9 Nov. 1666, p. 32. On the N. side of Bockatenock Cr. & bay, E. on the deviding Cr. & partly by the entrance into Selbyes bay &c. Trans. of 46 pers: Samll. Evins, Jno. Colan, Tho. Castle, Tho. Hobson, Rich. Porter, Tho. Treman, Jno. Digory, Tho. Peirce, Joseph Sawle (or Sawte), Richard Hawke, Hump. Arscott (or Hescott), Jno. Thomas, Tho. Hickes, Bath. White, Bernard Kendall, David Moyle, Francis Hearle, Nath. Lugger, Rich. Ersly, Edward Hearle, Jno. Cerly, Rich. Carter, Georg Fletcher, Wm. Dalston, Wm.

Hudleston, Jane Wilford, Mary Musgrave, Jno. Milward, Gilbert Thacker, Henry Wilmot, Godfrey Clarke, Symon Degg, Wm. Wolley, Jno. Wright, Francis Barker, Jane Bamfeild (or Barnfeild), Jno. Roll, Peter Ball, Jno. Skelton, Wm. Jennings, Charles Grills, Will Webber, Jno. Edwards, Stephen Wheeler, Peter Jenkens, Charles Bacawen.

DANIELL SELBY, 600 acs. Accomack Co., at *Mattapony*, 9 Nov. 1666, p. 32. Adj. Jno. & Edward Smale (or Smate). Trans. of 12 pers: Tho. Dacer, Phil. Howard, Fran. Salked, Kath. Fleming, George Denton, Margtt. Briscoe, Jane Richmond, Jno. Stenhouse, Jno. Carson, Jno. Harper, Henry Poole, George Vernon.

EDWARD SMALE & JNO. SMALE (or SMATE), 500 acs. Accomack Co., att *Mattapony*, 9 Nov. 1666, p. 33. On N. side of Tho. Purnell. Trans. of 10 pers: Walter Horton, Wm. Herbert, Robt. Eyre, Susan Bullock, Roger Elestree, Jno. Donage, Tho. Piler (?), Edward Seymore, Jno. North, Will Madox.

EDWARD SMITH, 700 acs. Accomack Co., 9 Nov. 1666, p. 33. On N. side of Robt. Richardson S. upon the Bevor Dam & its branches, &c. Trans. of 14 pers: Peter Heymon, Jno. Barrell, Thomas Manly, George Wooger, Jno. Knathbull, Robt. Davell, James Austin, Jno. Ford, Will Man, Will Stoakes, Henry Matson, Jeffery Wells, Robt. Vivell, Tho. Chalcot.

JNO. PARAMORE, 1500 acs. Accomack Co., 9 Nov. 1666, p. 33. S. side of Paramores Cr., running to Herren Cr. mouth &c. Trans. of 30 pers: James Upton, Godfrey Martin, Rich. Hoshton, Edward Mosly, Rich. Kerkby, Henry Banister, Roger Willis, Arthur Brockly, Jno. Kett, James Symonds, Edwd. South, Tho. Forge, Jno. Samon, Oliver Chichester, Joan Hill, Jno. Dalton (or Datton), Jno. Spencer, James Whiting, Lewis Aleberry (?), Jno. Ashew (or Ashen), Oliver Atkens, Robt. Ware, Ralph Gosber (?), Abram Atkins, Robt. Murrey, Tho. Felding, Constantine Lee (or Ler), Rowland Light, Jno. Blacketer (?), Edw. Croome.

JNO. PIKE, 400 acs. Accomack Co., at *Mattapany*, 9 Nov. 1666, p. 34. N. side of land of Danll. Selby. Trans. of 8 pers: Mary Stotwell, George Taylor, Jno. Brodway, Jno. Davy, Mary Stuckly (?), James Bond, Jno. Camon (or Carson), Ztopr. Bills.

STEPHEN BARNES, 600 acs. Accomack Co., at Bockatnoctun bay, & adj. Johnson's bay, 9 Nov. 1666, p. 34. Running to N. side of Johnsons bay &c. Trans. of 12 pers: Wm. Sprey, Jno. Mahen, Sam. Gully, Jno. Williams, Edward Phillips, Tho. Chikester, Rich. Vivian, Jno. Croiton (or Croston), Bernard Grinvill, Charles Trevanion, Walter Langden, Rowland Eyre.

CHRISTOPHER THOMPSON, 500 acs. Accomack Co., 9 Nov. 1666, p. 34. S. side of the S. br. of Hunting Cr., adj. land of Jon. a (or Jona.—Jonathan ?) Rue (or Rice), &c. Trans. of 10 pers: Jno. Young, James Court, Nicholas Staning, James Smith, Jeff. Balcott, Owin Morris, Robt. Shipp, Mathew Gore, Tho. Hoard, Miles Frost.

ROBT. COLEMAN, 200 acs. Gloster Co., 18 Mar. 1672/3, p. 34. Beg. at a small swamp deviding this from land of Danll. Clark, adj. Richd. Foster, running S'ly. by W. &c. to said swamp, being a S. br. of Severne. Trans. of 4 pers: Wm. Stirke (?), Jno. Leetch, Francis Bishopp, Laureline (?) Walke.

ROBT. RICHARDSON, 2000 acs. Accomack Co., nere *Bockanoctun*, 9 Nov. 1666, p. 35. Trans. of 40 pers: Jno. Ferress, Rich. Cooke, Charles Agard, James Cotton, James Bany, Sarah Shelling, James Ouldcastle, Alice Okeland, Jane Taylor, James Ashton, Joan Limes, Thomas May, Henry Mastin (or Maslin), Robt. Weaver, Arthur Wren, Thomas Roxford, Tymothy White, Rowland Mercer, Miles Lackland, Jno. Butler, Edwar. Boscay, Jno. Harris, Tho. Reynolds, Jno. Tanner, Edw. Nasworthy, Tho. Hearle, Jno. Moile, Oliver Sawle, Jno. Nicholls, Ezekiell Arundell, Wm. Painter, Tho. Tunill (or Turrill), Rich. Holland, Jno. Lamphlugh (?), Rich. Tolson, Mary Atkins, Tho. Denton, Edward Stanly, Henry Every, Samll. Fleigh.

THOMAS SELBY, 1250 acs. Accomack Co., at *Bockatenoctun*, on N. side of Henry Bishop's land, bet. Selbyes bay & the sea, 9 Nov. 1666, p. 35. Trans. of 25 pers: Nicholas Hany, Jno. Kellegrew (or Kellegrene), James Smith, Tho. Perrey, Andrew Cory, Francis Burgess, Wm. Mohun, Nicho. Sawle, James Crocker, Regnald Harkey, Tho. Wadden, Edward Elliott, Edward Hendor, Jno. Conock, Edward Musgrave. Wm. Charlton, Robt. Watby, Judith Stone, Wm. Thomas, Thomas (a) Welchman, James Collins, James Huntly, Jonah Walbrocke, Mathew Gross, Robt. Smith.

ALEXANDER WILLIAMS, 600 acs. Accomack Co. at *Bockatenoctun*, bet. Robt. Johnson on the N. & Tho. Selby on the S., & adj. Richardson's line; 9 Nov. 1666, p. 35. Trans. of 12 pers: James Yeamans, Henry Rouse, Andrew Roberts, James Harris, Robt. Long, Tho. Langly, Jno. Willoughby, Tho. Standfold, Jno. Priduex (?), Jno. Molsworth, Francis Jones, Anthony Chinow (?).

ROBT. JOHNSON, 600 acs. Accomack Co., N. side of Paramores Cr. on Johnson's bay &c., 9 Nov. 1666, p. 36. Trans. of 12 pers: George Heale, Hugh Trevenion, Hugh Pomroy, Tho. Willis, Nath. Mohun, Jno. Blish, James Lear, Jno. Webster, Thomas Newton, James Johnson, Susan Johnson, Joane Strinder.

JOHN JENKINS, 1200 acs. Accomack Co., formerly N'ampton Co., parte bet. 2 maine br. of Accomack Cr. which makes Egg Neck, &c., 9 Nov. 1666, p. 36. 400 acs. parte granted sd. Jenkins, 3 Nov. 1660, & 800 acs. for trans. of 16 pers: Kath. (?) Hodkins, Joane Long, Jno. Meredith, Jno. Pannull, Ed. Jenkins, Edgar Hine, Rob. Hillar, Edward Smith (?), Jeff. Waringham, Jno. Taylor, Tho. Winn, Eliz. Reynolds, Joseph Harris, Nicholas Smith, Myles Gray, Jane Willand (or Willard).

RICHARD KELLUM, 850 acs. Accomack Co., N. side of Occahanock Cr., adj. Jno. West & Jno. Waltham, 9 Nov. 1666, p. 36. 300 acs. granted him 24 July 1651, & 200 acs. 10 June 1654: 350 acs. for trans. of 7 pers: Margtt. Barton, Eliz. Johnson, Jno. Knight,

Robt. Wright, Lydia Elerfeild (?), Robt. Fowler, Jno. Verier (or Vercer).

MAJOR JNO. TILLNEY, 350 acs. Accomack Co., N. side of Nuswadox Cr., 9 Nov. 1666, p. 37. Along the bay side to the Muddy br., & adj. lands of Jno. Robbins & Samll. Jones. 200 acs. granted Jno. Major, 30 Jan. 1640, & by Will. Major, his son & heire, assigned to Will Bosman, 28 Jan. 1662, who assigned to sd. Tilney 28 Apr. 1663; 150 acs. for trans. of 3 pers: Thomas Thabarne, Stephen Brent, Jno. Salmon.

OWIN HAIES, 400 acs. Low. Norf. Co., 4 Mar. 1666, p. 37. Granted unto Thomas Bullock, dec'd., lately found to escheat &c., as by inquisition under Col. Myles Cary, Esch'r. Gen'll., dated 16 May 1666 &c.

PLUMMER BRAY, 350 acs. Low. Norf. Co., 4 Mar. 1666, p. 37. Granted unto John Kemp & lately found to escheat &c. (As above).

THO. PELLS, 400 acs. Rappa. Co., S. side of Gilsons Cr., 22 Apr. 1670, p. 37. Beg. at Geo. Morris & Mr. Tho. Button &c. Parte of 2,000 acs. granted to Robt. Beverley, 20 Apr. 1670 & by him assigned to sd. Pells.

MR. FRANCIS HAMMOND, 2000 acs. Yorke Co., 17 Apr. 1667, p. 38. Mattapony Riv. on the N. N. E. & lands of Maj. Will. Lewis on the E. S. E. Renewal of patent dated 1 Nov. 1654.

EDWARD ISON, 300 acs. Nancimond Co., 17 Apr. 1667, p. 38. Adj. his own & lands of Wm. Denson, Anthony Branch, Symon Symoonds & Jno. Crewdon. Trans. of 6 pers: Thomas Spicer, Jno. Hewes, Wm. Bourer, Robt. Jarras, Henry Clutterbrock, Will Watkins.

EMANUELL CAMBOW, Negro, 50 acs. James Citty Co., 18 Apr. 1667, p. 39. Parte of a greater quantity granted to Will Davis, lately found to escheat &c., as by inquisition dated 12 Apr. 1664 & now granted &c.

ROBERT BURGESSE, 343 A., 108 po., Chas. Citty Co., on S. side of Appomattox Riv., 12 Nov. 1666, p. 39. Beg. at Gilbert Platt, running to lines of Robt. Coleman, Sr. & Jr., his own land &c. Trans. of 7 pers: George Armestrong, Mathew Jones, Robert Terrill, Anth. Gardner, Eliz. Colesy, Wm. Satterwaite, An Marble.

THOMAS JORDAN, 550 acs. Nancimond Co., 22 Oct. 1666, p. 39. Adj. lands of Jeremiah Rutter & Hopken Howell. Trans. of 7 pers: Roger Logmore, Jno. Laycock, Jno. Rogers, Robt. Bateman, Jno. Penny, Alice Perry, Sarah Johnson, oseph Phillips, Dorman King, Robt. Goffe, Edmond Morgan.

NORTH FLEETE, 300 acs. in the S. br. of Nancimond Riv., on the N. side, 22 Oct. 1666, p. 40. Granted unto John Skerrott, 17 Mar. 1654 & assigned to sd. *Northfleete*. (Note: The name is omitted in the body of this patent; marginal notation gives it as North fleete & the genrl. index lists it as 2 names.)

GEORGE SPIVY, 150 acs. Nancimond Co., 22 Oct. 1666, p. 40. Nere head of the S. br., beg. at his own land &c. Trans. of 3 pers: Jno. Clay, Margarett Iresh, Will Patrick.

JOHN GATLEN, 425 acs. with 28 acs. of marish, Nancimond Co., 22 Oct. 1666, p. 40. Beg. at a poynt of marsh of Chuckatuck Cr. over against Major Davis' landing, up the cr. N. N. W., adj. land of Giles Laurence & Mrs. Oudelant. Trans. of 9 pers: Samuell Daues (or Daves), Emanuell Abson (or Alson), Francis Young, Tho. English, Eliz. Holman, Margtt. Mathews, Robt. Bach, Wm. Gwin, Tho. Everad.

MR. LAWRENCE SMITH, 807 acs. Gloster Co., 18 Mar. 1666/7, p. 41. Beg. in the N. br. of Seavern Riv:, dividing this & land of Coll. Augustine Warner, Esqr. &c. to Thomas Graves' land, to Tymberneck Cr. main swamp &c. to Mr. Burwell's line &c., to br. parting this & land of Wm. Rawlings. 80 acs. granted to sd. Warner in 1653; 148 acs. granted to him 11 Feb. 1657, both of which he used to sd. Smith, & 579 acs. for trans. of 12 pers: Tho. Cooke, Geo. Ballentine, Jno. Cannida,

Rich. West, Elizab. Lettsom, Elizab. Pain, Wm. Prickett, Mary Cooke, Rich. Tucker, Fran. Brion, Ann Brown, Elizab. Giles.

JOHN WRAY, 240 acs. Gloster Co., Kingstone Parrish, upon head of Queens Cr., 15 Mar. 1666, p. 41. Beg. Richard Carey, adj. land formerly granted to Edward Welch &c. Trans. of 5 pers: Tho. Miles, Tho. Chambers, Jno. Settle, Jno. Cox, Mary Sharpe.

DAVID MUNORGON, 696 acs. Gloster Co., 2 Feb. 1666/7, p. 42. Upon head br. of Ware riv. swamp, beg. at Will Culman's land nere Thomas Royston's, by Bryery br. &c. & along Rich. Renshaw. Trans. of 14 pers: Jno. Davies, Tho. Hoton, Doro. Hart, David Parker, Rich. Hickson, James Ambrose, Jane Tredings, Nath. Lember, Wm. Wood, Barth. Clarke, Jno. Collins, Jno. George, Jno. West, Wm. Lewis.

MR. WILLIAM MAY, 100 acs. of marish land in James Citty Island, below *Goose Hill*, 15 Apr. 1667, p. 42. N. on land of Maj. Holt, now in possession of Jno. Barbar, N'ly. on Jno. Pinhorne, N. E. on Parchmores Cr., S. E. on the maine river, S. E. & S. W. on Will Sarsnett. Granted to Thomas Woodhouse & Wm. Hooker, 21 July 1657, deserted, & granted sd. May &c. Trans. of 2 pers: Charles Greene, Wm. Sanders.

HENRICK FORSAN VAN DEAVORACK, Senr., 214 A. 64.4 chs., in the Pecosan Parrish, Yorke Co., 14 Nov. 1666, p. 43. On W. side of a swamp, adj. Mr. Rooksbyes line, the head of the Gleab line, over Christopher Gullington's line, to E. side of the Ridge path &c. Trans. of 5 pers: Jno. Kippin, Edward Frost, Wm. Jones, Tho. Carr, Edward Cooper.

ROBT. HOWSE, 250 acs. Surry Co., 14 Mar. 1666, p. 43. On S. side of Bland's path, adj. Mr. Simonds land, &c. Trans. of 5 pers: George Jordan, 2, Mary Jordan, Alice Miles, Jno. Clarke.

MR. THOMAS HUNT, 836 acs. Surry Co., 14 Mar. 1666, p. 44. Beg.

where the path goes over the main black water swamp somewhat below the feild commonly knowne by the name of the *King of Weynocks old feild. &c.* Trans. of 17 pers: Tho. Shutwell, Isaak Tatum, Eliz. Williams, Tho. Bavy (or Bany), Fran. Mason, Hanah Quelch, Robt. Thompson, Margtt. Baum, Jno. Felton, Phill. Felton, Eliz. Williams, Hanah Poland, Eliz. Mathewes, Edward Shelton, Margtt. Parkinson, Margtt. Upealaum (?), Mary King.

RALPH CREED, 750 acs. Surry Co., side, adj. George Jordan, a run deviding this from plantation whereon Capt. Thomas Flood now liveth &c. 150 acs. parte of a devdt. granted unto Coll. Jno. Flood, dec'd., & by Thomas Flood, his lawfull heire, sould to sd. *Creeke* (Creed), & due for trans. of 12 pers: Will Jordan, et uxor, Charles Greene, Jno. Kippin, Wm. Sanders, Edw. Frost, Wm. Jones, Edward Carr, Tho. Cooper, Francis Parker, Isaak Ball, Tho. Leonard.

THOMAS WOODWARD, JUNR., 1100 acs. Isle of Wight *or* Nansimond Co., 17 Apr. 1667, p. 45. Upon the black water or toward the head of Chawon or Chawonock Riv., includ. an old Indian feild called *Mountsack.* Trans. of 22 pers: Wm. Addison, Wm. Leech, Alice Goodale, Ann Church, Charles Farthing, Rich. White, Abram Iveson, Isaak Brumley, Jno. Rowlings, Francis Jeffts, Aug. Thompson, Wm. Thompson, Nicholas Johnson, Peter Francklin, Joseph Court, Jno. Lincolnshire, Jeremiah Davies, Wm. Davies, Mary Swan, Charles Edwards, Thomas Golding, Wm. Harris.

ROBT. WHITEHAIRE, JOHN BOWLER & CHARLES EDMONDS, 3000 acs. New Kent Co., upon N. side of Riv., 25 Apr. 1667, p. 45. Trans. of 60 pers: Robt. Armestrong, Jno. Johnson, Alexr. Brue (or Brice), James Henderson, Andrew Mailer, Charles James, James Feild, Charles Davison, Patrick Watson, James Browne, James Soruter, Tho. Hamilton, Henry Sinker, Aug. Orum, David Salmon, Tho. Wilson, George Wilson, James Fargeson, Jno. Meeke, Jno. Fargeson, Jno. Mauer,

James Arthur, Robt. Lundsdale (or Lonsdale), Alex. Browne, Eliz. Burwell, Mary Tailer, James Canner, Mary Mackham, Mary Lyon, Katharine Loird, Mary Johnson, Anis Sherer, Jno. Wilson, James Berkeley, Jane Addis, Francis Oberton, James Gerry, James Thompson, Danll. Pepper, Wm. Sayer, Henry Wethred, Hollis Usald (?), Rich. Powell, Robt. Whitaker, Mary Claber, Jno. Roberts, Jno. Ward, Tho. Greene, Wm. Gravener, Henry Collett, Jno. Reynolds, Robt. Smith, Thomas Parker, Charles Blake, Mary Hall, Eliz. Guildford, Jno. Cumbell (or Cambell), Jno. Griffeth, Jno. Mackey, Francis Baulden.

JNO. CLEMENS, 350 acs. Surry Co., 30 Mar. 1667, p. 46. Upon a main br. of Crowches Cr. nere the head, nere severall lands of Jno. Fry & Edward Pittaway, to Maj. Will. Marriott. Trans. of 7 pers: Phillip Howard, Roger Plumer, Tho. Panton, Jno. Wray, Robt. Salter, Edw. Place, Ed. Browne.

MR. NICHOLAS MEREWETHER, 651 acs. Surry Co., 25 Apr. 1667, p. 46. 175 acs. upon land he bought of Wm. Seward, beg. by the white marish, upon the Indian Spring Sw; 240 acs. on W. side of Cyprus Sw. &c; 236 acs. on E. side of the maine Black Water Sw. &c. Trans. of 14 pers: Jno. Coates (or Coales), Margtt. Long, Lewis Wilkenson, Ed. Johnson, Phillip Ashley, Tho. Preston, Tho. Wareham, Will. Gayler, Wm. Lancaster, James Beare, Abram Johnson, Jno. Spire, Jno. Facknham (?), Symon Salter.

SAME. 850 acs., same Co. & date, p. 47. On- Black Water *alias* Cyprus Sw., beg. on the E'wd. side, adj. land of Anthony Spiltimber &c., a br. dividing this & land of George Blow, &c. to Capt. Corkers land &c. Trans. of 17 pers: Tho. Giles, Henry Sterne, Roger Symons, Jno. Phillpott, Tho. Kentley, Jno. Tyler, Morgan Lewis, Mathew Hughes, James Roberts, Roger Clayton, Robt. Herne, Wm. Strood, Symon Allin, Jeremiah Ward, Richard Cord, Richard Smith, Samll. Warrin.

WILLIAM PORTEN, 449 A., 12 P. on N. side of the E. br. of Eliz. Riv.,

Low. Norf. Co., 21 Aug. 1667, p. 47. Adj. land of Arthur Tappin. Trans. of 9 pers: Rich. Smith, Samll. Warrin, James Bird, Tho. Davies, Edw. Sneath, Wm. Tanner, Robt. Wheler, Henry Weston, Isaak Scott.

THOMAS GAINES, 1030 acs. Rappa. Co., 27 Feb. 1665/6, p. 48. S. side of Rappa. Riv. upon the maine Pocoson of Piscataway Cr. above land of Hutson & Holt, opposite to land of James Vaughan, running over branches of Hoskins Cr. &c. Trans. of 21 pers: William Blaze, Kath. Royner, Margtt. Royner, Robt. Flewelling, Francis Evans, Alice Potter, Wm. Milborne, Elinor Parker, Wm. Ould, Robt. Flory, Alexr. Berry, Mary Weekes, George Poole, Rich. Evans, Ann Leson, Elianor Fishmay, James Williamson, Thomas Lynard, Thomas Hackett, Robt. Hogg, Jno. Lucas.

JAMES BOUGHAN, 150 acs. Rappa. Co., upon the maine sw. of Piscataway Cr., 27 Feb. 1665/6, p. 48. Beg. by the maine sw. &c, to branches deviding this from land of Thomas Harper & Robt. Clemonds &c. Trans. of 3 pers: Eliz. Pettus, Eliz. Edom. Jno. Roakes.

WILL. AIRES, 592 acs. Rappa. Co., upon main br. or sw. of Piscataway Cr., above land of Mr. Jno. Gregory, 27 Feb. 1665/6, p. 48. Trans. of 12 pers: Jno. Watson, Robt. Bryan, Thomas Morice, Henry Boswell, Mary Berry, Moses Rabbitt, Arthur King, James Johnson, Jno. Berry, Ruth Mason, Mathew Jennings twice.

THO. HARPER & ROBT. CLEMONDS, 700 acs. Rappa. Co., upon Piscataway Sw., bet. James Boughan & Francis Browne &c; 27 Feb. 1665/6, p. 49. Trans. of 14 pers: Jno. Atkins, Jno. Sheffeild, Mich. Wilson, Ralph Sharpe. Will. Bateman, Mich Wills, Alexr. Mount, Marke Alester, George Rayman, Samll. Burton, Ephrim Parker, Edward Milton, Mary Fisher, Jno. Ransforth.

MAJOR WM. PEIRCE, 4310 acs., W'moreland Co. & Rappa. Co., 3 Oct. 1666, p. 49. 1810 acs. due by pattent,

22 Mar. 1665/6, & 2500 acs. newly taken up; beg. in line of Mr. Jno. Lordd & Wm. Horton &c. 2500 acs. for trans. of 50 pers: Richd. Sawer. Jno. Crompton, Robt. Knight, Henry Clarke, Jno. Smith, Giles Collins, Samll. Swan, Jane Coy, Joane Whiteing, Jno. Gilder, Wm. Staremore, Robt. Bradley. Eliz. Wms. (Williams), Fran. Painter, Jno. Browne, Jona. Saul, Jno. Smith, Abram Harlock, Jno. Palmer, Tho. Land, Rich. Keene. Robt. Lucas, Eliz. Chapman, Wm. North, Wm. Chiper, Mary Parey, Eliz. Côwell, Henry Beard, Jno. Henton, Wm. Davies, Joane Scott, John Whiston, Ralph Creeder, Grace his wife, Jno. Clarke, Tho. Shartwell, Isak Tatem, Eliz. Williams, Eliz. Maudlin, Joane Maudlin, Tho. Cary, Tho. Wall, Senr., Tho. (Wall) Junr., Tho. Bany (or Bavy), Francis Mason, Hanay Quelch, Robt. Thomson, Mary Bavin (?), Jno. Felton, Phill Fellow.

WM. LLOYD & JNO. BIDDLE, 4750 acs. W'moreland Co., 17 Apr. 1667, p. 50. Beg. a mile from Nomany Riv., adj. land of Jno. Wood. Granted unto Wm. Drummond, Esqr., 10 Sept. 1661, deserted, now granted by order &c., & further due for trans. of 95 pers: Phill Harwood, Roger Plumer, Thomas Panton, Jno. Wray, Robt. Salter, Edw. Place, Edw. Bourne, Jno. Coales, Margtt. Long, Lewis Wilkenson, Phill Ashby, Tho. Preston, Tho. Wareham, Wm. Lancaster, James Beare, Abram Jnoson., Jno. Spire, Tho. Faukham, Symon Salter, Edward Jnoson., Robt. Thomson, Margtt. Bauin (?), Jno. Felton, Phill Felton, Will Gayler, Thomas Gilles, Henry Stearne, Roger Symons, Jno. Philpott, Jno. Tyler, Morgan Lewis, Mathew Hughes, James Roger, Roger Clayton, Tho. Kentby, Robt. Herne, Wm. Strood, Symon Allin, Jeremy Ward, Rich. Cord, Rich. Smith, Samll. Warrin, James Bird, Tho. Davies, Eliz. Williams, Hanah Palmer, Eliz. Mathews, Edward Shelton, Edward Sneath, Wm. Tanner, Robt. Wheeler, Henry Weston, Isaak Scott, Jno. Atkins, Tho. Sheffeld, Nich. Wilson, Ralph Sharpe, Wm. Bateman, Mathew Wills, Alexr. Mont, Marke Abster (or Alester), George Roymon, Samll. Burton, Cutch Butler, Fred Downes, Wm. Downes, Isaak Gibson,

Robt. Read, Margtt. Parkinson, Marg. Upsalarum, Mary King, Wm. Jordan, Henry Harper, Tho. Dannings, Tho. Beale, Jno. Marston, Roger Gray, Mary Talbott, Mich. Orton, James Neale, Tho. Murry, Luke Bayly, Tho. Beale, Mary Jordan, Alice Miles, Jno. Clarke, Tho. Shutwell, Isaak Tatem, Eliz. Williams, Tho. Bauy (Bany-Bavy ?), Francis Mason, Henry Quelch, Cor. Obreeman, Jno. Pew, Tho. Edridge.

CUTHBERT POTTER, Gent., 3672 acs. Lancaster Co., on Sanderland *alias* Boswell's Cr., & br. of the greate swamp on S. side of Rappa. Riv., 20 Sept. 1661, p. 51. (*By Francis Moryson.*) 442 acs. beg. at a poynt of marish, nere land of Tho. Williams &c. to Mr. Barnhams Cr.; 1200 & 600 acs. backing sd. tract &c., to Mimcock Cr; 50 acs. beg. on sd. 600 acs. along an Indian path that crosseth the line leading over the head of the Cr. to the house of Thomas Pattison &c., to land sd. Potter purchased of Evan Davies; & 1380 acs. aboute 2 mi. above the horse path & nigh Mattapony path that goeth from plantation of Mr. Jno. Curtis &c., to Mr. Charles Grimes, &c. 442 acs. parte of patent to Henry Nicholls & Evan Davies, 19 Oct. 1653 & by sd. Davies assigned to Potter; 1200 acs., 600 acs., & 50 acs. by patents to sd. Potter dated 14 Dec. 1655, 7 Oct. 1658 & 20 Aug. 1660, respectively; the last due for trans. of: Edw. Ramsey.

THOMAS TAYLOR, 631 acs. Henrico Co., N. side of James Riv., commonly called *Harrahadockes*. over against *Kingsland;* 23 Sept. 1667, p. 52. 281 acs. from the riv. a little below the Orchard from Mr. Arthur Bayly's land, &c. to the lower side of Harrahattocks Cr. mouth, &c. 350 acs. on N. side of the *Rowndaboute* &c., to S. side thereof at a cor. of Jno. Cox, &c., to 4 Mi. Cr. old path, &c. 281 acs. granted sd. Taylor 25 Sept. 1663, & 350 acs. for trans. of 7 pers: Francis Taylor, Dorothy Taylor, Jno. Young, Jno. Bell, Jno. Steward, Symon Balms (or Balono), Will. Stanaway.

SOLLOMAN KNIBB, 710 acs. Henrico Co., N. side James Riv., 24 Sept.

1667, p. 52. Beg. on the E'ly. run of Baylyes Cr. &c. to Coll. Stegg's path, &c. Trans. of 15 pers: Solomon ——, Jno. Carter, Jno. Hartwell, Edward Good, Edward Currell, Eliz. Russell, Alice Atkenson, Jno. Worth, Robt. Davis, Phill. Sherringham, Alice Harris, Mary Piggott, Mary Glas, Wm. Atkenson, Vincent Shuttleworth.

FRANCIS PERCE & WM. PERCE, 350 acs., Henrico Co., N. side of James Riv., 24 Sept. 1667, p. 53. N. N. W. on 2 Mi Cr., S. S. W. against *Varina,* E. S. E. upon 3 Mi. Cr. swamp, taking in the sw., N. N. E. towards 4 Mi. Cr. & bounded with a running brooke called the Rowndaboute. Granted to Seath Ward, viz: 150 acs., 13 Sept. 1635; 50 acs. purchased from Jno. Baker, last of May 1636, & 150 acs. 17 Nov. 1643, for trans. of 3 pers: Jonathan Blanshard, Eliz. Gibbin, Henry Chaddocke.

JNO. LEAD, 75 A., 24 P., 24 Sept. 1667, p. 53. 50 acs. parte granted to Wm. Bayly, who assigned to Thomas Taylor, who assigned to sd. Lead; beg. on E. side of 4 Mi. Cr., along the river S. E. by S. &c. to the Southern run by Baylie's feild &c. Trans. of 2 pers: Edward Underhill, Iz. Vinter.

GEORGE POOLE, RICHD. FARTHINGALE, RICHD. BARRINGHAM & JAMES FORSITH, 800 acs. Gloster Co., Ware Parish, 7 Apr. 1671, p. 53. Beg. at a Black stump, accounted Hen. Corbill's cor. tree &c. 600 acs. granted sd. Corbill, 6 Mar. 1653, who assigned to the abovenamed; & 200 acs. overplus found within sd. bounds is now due to them severally for trans. of 4 pers.* (Marginal note: This patt. recorded in folio 352.)

JOHN WILSON, 100 acs. Henrico Co., N. side of Appomattox Riv., 24 Sept. 1667, p. 54. Beg. at the riv. side, W. by N. N'ly., along an old known fence, being the line parting this & Orphants of George & Will Worsnam, &c., adj. his own land &c. Due for trans. of 7 pers.* "dated 6 May 1638 & the other 25 Sept. 1663." Sd. 100 acs. being parte of a dvdt. purchased by Wm. Clarke conteyning 1100 acs, granted him by Sir Jno. Harvey, late Jovr., 6 May 1638; sould to Leonard Langton 29 Oct. 1638, who sould to Seath Ward 3 Jan. 1639, as by record of sd. deed at James Citty 24 Sept. 1640 & assignment thereon endorsed may appear & for better confirmation the Widdow Dorothy Clarke did afterwards surrender same to Seath Ward at a court held at *Varina*, 25 Mar. 1640, who at a Ct. held at *Varina* 9 Nov. 1640 assigned to Wm. Worsnam 200 acs. parte of 300 acs. lying at the Old Towne Cr., by deed dated 2 Nov. 1640, endorsed &c; Sd. Ward for good consideration assigned the other 100 acs. to Michaell Masters 28 Oct. 1642 at a Ct. held at *Varina*, at which Ct. sd. Masters surrendered up sd. 100 acs. to Henry Rowen, who in like manner at the same Ct. surrendered same to Peter Feepond, who at same Ct. surrendered to sd. Wilson.

THOMAS DYAS & RICHARD GRANGER, 1350 acs. upon branches of Nomeny River betwixt Potomack & Rappa. Rivers, 15 Apr. 1667, p. 55. Beg. at Mr. Jno. Whetstone &c. to Will Bayly & Edward Halley, &c. Trans. of 27 pers: Tho. Bevington (or Berington), Peter Dunken, Jno. Moore, Margtt. Gosnoll, Eliz. Gosnoll, Eliz. Ireland, Martha Magnett, Eliz. Scarfe, Will. Bryant, Josyas Mills, James Ireland, Mary Powell, Edward Pith (or Pitts), Tho. Spinny, Richard Spinny, Dorothy Spinny, Robt. Whiting, Henry Vincent, Isabell Channey, Tho. Dutton, Jane Raven, Peter Handy, Well the Negro, Jno. Evans, Jno. Newman, Wm. Cuningham, Ann Thornton.

ROBT. KING, 500 acs. Stafford Co., 15 Apr. 1667, p. 55. S. side upper Machoatick Beavor Dam &c., along land of Edward Hewes &c. to Mr. Robt. Howsing by a horse bridge &c. Trans. of 10 pers: Tho. Rea, Geo. Smither, Geo. Swan, Tho. Childres, Jno. Clemons, Ann Powell, —— Smith, Wm. Storke 4 times.

MR. JNO. WHETSTONE, THOMAS DYAS & PATRIACK SPENCER, 1050 acs. W'moreland Co., in the freshes betwixt Potomack & Rappa. Rivs., 15 Apr.

1667, p. 55. Upon S. E. side of the maine run of Gr. Rappa. Cr., beg. nere another tract of sd. Dyas, &c. to small br. & horse path &c. Trans. of 21 pers: Richard Corbin, Wm. Safe, Edmd. Sippins, Rich. Hopkins, Henry Miller, James Greene, Marma. Dennis, Wm. Browne, Tho. Storke, Richard Holland, Peter Spicer, Edw. Lanaster, Meane Broddreck (or Brodduck), Tho. Broadhurst, Hoell Windoe, Wm. Berry, Jno. Farrell, Mary Baker, Jane Baker, Antho. Holburd, Eliz. Smith.

MR. JNO. WHETSTONE, 2430 acs. W'moreland Co., 24 Sept. 1667, p. 56. N. E. side of E.most Herring Cr. of Nomeny Riv., beg. by the maine br. in line of Coll. Nicholas Spensor, &c. 1000 acs. granted him 9 Apr. 1663 & 1430 acs. due for trans. of 29 pers: Wm. Gray, Charles Turner, Mary Sandy, Jno. Leake, James Laske (or Laeke), Tho. Evans, Robt. Crane, Henry Davies, Adam Toold, Tho. Wall, Jno. Smith, Faith Flood, Xtoper. Foster, Tho. Flood, Wm. Thompson, Kath. Thomson, William, Samuell, John Katharine (Thompson ?—no surnames), Wm. Bett, Henry White, Robt. Short, Fran. Lewis, Tho. Allen, Joseph Gregory, Peter Hill, Mary Shaw, Jonathan Barbar.

EDWARD HUMSTON, 337 A., 80 P., Staff. Co., 15 Apr. 1667, p. 56. S. side up. Machotick Riv., upon Mr. Robt. Howsen's &c. Trans. of 7 pers: Susan Woodward, Kath. Griggs, Xtoper. Bell, Jno. Harvey, Alexr. Pate, Math. Hogson. Henry Clarke.

MR. WM. STORKE, 600 acs. bet. Potomack & Rappa. Rivs., on branches of Appomattox Cr., 24 Sept. 1667, p. 56. S. by a br. devideing this & land of Mr. Jno. Washington, N. by a br. devideing this & land of Capt. Ashton & Jno. Alexander &c. Trans. of 12 pers: Eusebius Kemp, Dorathy Godfrey, Sarah Greene, Eliz. Lluellin, Jno. Davies, Will. Kippin, Mathew Cole, Henry Haines, Fran. Gouldsmith, Tho. Mathewes, Mary Maning, Ezekiell Francis.

ROBT. HOWSON, 450 acs. Staff. Co., 15 Apr. 1667, p. 57. S. side of Up. Machotique Riv. damm, beg. by his corne feild. fence, to land of Jno. & Thomas Palmore, crossing the Horse path &c. to N. side of the Horse bridge &c. Trans. of 9 pers: Danll. Long, Susan Mathew, Rich. Corbin, Abigall Watkins, Wm. Safe, Robt. Rowlins, Sarah Tenn (or Fenn), Joseph Dunn, Edm. Sippins.

WM. SAVIDGE, 152 acs. Chas. Citty Co., 10 May 1667, p. 57. N. side of the western br. &c. Trans. of 4 pers: Arthur Norwood, Jno. Redman, Luke Peirce, George Matterson.

GEORGE WATKIN, 200 acs. Surry Co., 23 Apr. 1667, p. 57. Trans. of 4 pers: Wm. Jellett, Rich. Booth, Jno. Booth, Ann Jenuary.

WM. THOMSON, 230 acs. Surry Co., 1 Mar. 1666, p. 57. Beg. at Francis Sowerbye's land, thence upon a swamp &c. Trans. of 5 pers: Alice Price, Henry Stevens, Susan Mathew, 2 Negroes.

JNO. RAWLINS & MICHAELL METTANEY (Mettany), 332 acs. Surry Co., 10 May 1667, p. 58. At the head of Up. Chipoakes Cr., beg. on S. side of the W. br., &c. to Mr. Stephens' land, upon the S. br. until it meets with the W. br. &c. Trans. of 7 pers: George Leads, Hum. Watkins, Robt. Breed, Ed. Taylor, Mary Brett, Ambrose Taylor, Tho. Dutton.

RICHARD DREW, 800 acs. Surry Co., 24 Apr. 1667, p. 58. Beg. nigh Mr. Allin's path, S. upon land of Richard Harrison &c. Trans. of 16 pers: Francis Phillips, Nich. Peirce, Wm. Herbert, Tho. Morgan, Arthur Sands, Geo. Low, Saml. Potter, Giles Walker, Jno. Tomkins, Rich. Seaborne, Wm. King, Martin Parry, Joseph Edgcume, Ralph Poole, Mary Evans, Susa. Holladay.

FRANCIS SOWERBY, 80 acs. Surry Co., 1 Mar. 1666, p. 58. Beg. at corner betwixt Ralph Creed & Coll. Jordan's land, E. by S. upon Woodhouse land, &c. Trans. of 2 pers: Mary Spicer, Jno. Bruton.

DANIELL REGANT, 200 acs. Surry Co., 23 Apr. 1667, p. 58. Beg. opposite to land of Coll. Jordan, to the Cyprus Sw. &c. Trans. of 4 pers: Roger Parsons, Rich. Atkins, Arthur Stephens, Robt. Surbett.

CAPT. THOMAS BUSBY, 1170 acs., in Surry Co. & Chas. Citty Co., 10 May 1667, p. 59. 650 acs. on both sides the S. br. of Upper Chipoakes Cr., along Mudgett's line to the Carte path, to Jno. Baker, &c; 520 acs. upon the W. br. of sd. Creek, to head of George Burcher's land, nigh the spring bottome &c., which tract was granted to Thomas Mudgett 19 Dec. 1663 & assigned to sd. Busby; 650 acs. for trans. of 13 pers: Wm. Southcott, Jno. Jennings, Tho. Garrett, Wm. Copeman, Morgan Osborne, Tho. Bliss, Wm. Lee, Tim Cardish, Mary Cardish, Stephen Hopewell, Jno. Davis, Mary Davis, Phi. Wood.

EDWARD BUSHELL, 400 acs. Surry Co., 1 Mar. 1666, p. 59. On W. side of Bevor Dam Swamp, parting this & land of Mr. Barker, &c. to the maine Black Water Sw. &c. Trans. of 8 pers: Will Scott, Fran. Norton, Sarah Phillips, Judeth Stone, Jno. Wilcox, Ralph Harper, Geo. Dixon, Samll. Dowling.

WM. PORTER, 600 acs. Surry Co., 23 Apr. 1667, p. 59. Beg. at cor. tree of Huniford's land, to Robt. Huckes' cart path, &c. Trans. of 12 pers: Jno. (a) frenchman, Nicholas Custis, Danll. Watts, Alex. West, Tho. Wilmott, Wm. Wells, Peter Jarman, Jo. Stephens, Marg. Palmer, Jane Batten, Fran. Porter, Martin Due.

MR. LAURENCE WASHINGTON & MR. ROBT. RICHARDS, 700 acs. Staff. Co., 27 Sept. 1667, p. 60. Beg. ½ mile from land of Jno. Walton, surveyed by Mr. Sampson, next to Mr. Turney &c. Granted to Richard Turney 10 Sept. 1656, assigned to David Phillips, who sould to Thomas Broughton. & by him reassigned to sd. Phillips, who assigned to sd. Richards & James Harris; Harris sould his parte to Richards, who assigned one-halfe to sd. Washington, as doth appear by records of W'moreland Co.

WILL. ADOLPHUS, 300 acs., N'-ampton Co., 15 Apr. 1667, p. 60. Granted to Wm. Adolphus, Senr., lately found to escheat, as by inquisition under the hand of Coll. Jno. Stringer, Escheator, &c., 19 Aug. 1665, & now granted &c.

MR. ALEXR. MURRAY, 704 acs. Gloster Co., 13 Nov. 1672, p. 60. Neer Chescake Path beside the Beech Br. that falleth into Ware Riv., beg. at his own, running to Tho. Colle's land, Major John Smith's, Mr. Cooke's, Mr. Campfeild's &c. Trans. of 14 pers: Winifred Alfred, Peter Stout, Ann Scott, Ja. Whitteker, Wm. Garland, Agnis Rose, John Seaward, Nicholas Harper, Peter Loyd, Jeff. Bewston, Jno. Atkins, Jno. Skinner, Tho. Stroud, Jno. Ashby, Mary Fry, James Trott (?).

FRANCIS TRIPLETT, 1050 acs. on N. side of Rappa. Riv. in the freshes, 21 Jan. 1666, p. 61. Beg. at land of Mr. Samll. Nicholl's, deserted, to land of Mr. Thaicker alias Capt. Jno. Hull's, nere Coll. Toby Smith, deserted, &c. to the forrest alias Coleman's &c. to land of Mr. William Underwood, deserted, &c. Trans. of 21 pers: Xtopher. Hard, Mine James, Robt. Fletcher, Tom a Scott, Tom a boy, Wm. Jett, a maid servant, James Hunt, Peter Jett, Peter (Jett ?) Junior, Mary Jett, Mary Jett, Martha Jett, Jno. Taylor, Fran. Sanders, David Jones, Pat. Horton, James Dukeman, Wm. Hanson, Charles Stephens, Lewis Bainton (or Baniton).

JAMES COGHILL (also written Cogbill), 1050 acs. in the freshes of Rappa. Co., on the S. side, beg. aboute a mile from the head of the E'wd. br. of Potobaco Cr., in a line of Mr. Robt. Paine, Clarke, over severall paths to Potobaco Towne, to Potobaco Run, next to Mr. Silvester Thatcher, &c. to the Indian line &c. 17 Apr. 1667, p. 61. Trans. of 21 pers: Wm. Thompson, Isaak Rose, Patriak Weekes, Jno. Hobbs, Mary Hart, Samll. Davis, Tho. Portman, Nich. Smart, Danll. Willis, Rich. Forrest, Jno. Rock, Jane Willis, Timothy Salter, Robt. Datrill, Phill. Woodford, Wm. Garrett, Tho. Johnson, Ralph Mathew, Henry Batts, Mary Bateman, Wm. Worden.

ALEXANDER FLEMING, 2750 acs. in the freshes of Rappa. Co., S. side the river, aboute 2 mi. up Pwomansend Cr. &c., crossing severall paths to Nanzatico &c., to land of Will. White, to Mr. Robt. Paine &c., to maine run of Potobacco Cr., over severall paths to Nanzaticon, thence on maine run of Powmansend &c. 17 Apr. 1667, p. 62. Trans. of 55 pers: Margtt. Rawlins, Geo. Howlett, Samll. Harford, Robt. Floring, Jno. Greene, Tho. Wood, Rich. Parker, Francis Willis, Henry Mills, Benjamin Daniell, Lawrence Hooker, Michaell Wadloe, Robt. Spurtin (or Spurlin), Alice Potter, Mary Hunt, Danll. Williams, Dennis Shorpe, James Adkins, Silvester Thatcher, Dorothy Thatcher, Jno. Deane, Wm. Hope, Fran. Jones, Wm. Crofts, Samll. Welch, Nich. Spruce, Elinor Woodbridge, Jno. Worlock, Nich Spensor, Rich. Spicer, Math. Haines (or Harris), Wm. Thomson, Jane Saltir, Mary Wood, Daniell Parker, Walter Williams, Gartreed Sparkes, Jno. Huchenson, Dennis Watkins, Mary Spruce, James Bruce, Francis Pye, Martin Woodliffe, Robt. Savin, Rich. Palmer, Samll. Prince, Nicholas Willis, Grace Andrewes, Symon Grey, Jno. Sexton, Stephen Michaell, Jno. Mullis, Danll. Dickins, Hen. Vandulett, Henry Sanders.

LT. COLL. JOHN EPES, 2550 A., 3 R., 16 P., S. side James Riv., Chas. Citty Co., comonly knowne by the name of Cha. Cytty, 30 Sept. 1674, p. 62. Beg. at the mouth of Gravelly Cr., up the riv. to the Cytty landing, &c. to Causon's Cr. &c. to John Howell &c., to Michill's corner, to Gower's corner &c., night Cattaile br., along Mr. Whittington's line &c. nigh Bare Creek, to br. at Coleman's field &c. to mouth of Baylyes Cr. 1700 acs. granted to Capt. Fra. Epes 29 May 1638 & due sd John as son & heire; 280 acs. granted sd. Francis 17 Mar. 1663, & due as above; 572 acs. for trans. of 11 pers: Robt. Bennett, Elin. Frith, Hump. Ferick, Jno. Lewis, Peter Seaman, Sarah Smith, Sarah Richards, Wm. Brush, Richd. Wright, Richd. Crawshaw, John Maide.

MR. SILVESTER THATCKER, 1050 acs. Rappa. Co., S. side the Riv. in the freshes, aboute 2 mi. from *Potobacco Towne*, beg. next to land of James Cog-&c. 17 Apr. 1667, p. 63. Trans. of 21 pers: Jno. Goose, Wm. Snip, Nich. Holmes, Robt. Arnall, James Darby, Walter Dixon, Mary Wood, Jeffrey Fletcher, Tim Wallis, Jane Powell, Jno. Savidge, Wm. Harte, Tho. Parsons, Mary Hart, Samll. Price, James House, Walter Haines, Ralph Holt, Jno. Watkins, Tho. Footer (or Foster), Will. Davis.

JAMES COGHILL, 600 acs. Rappa. Co., S. side the Riv., in the freshes, 17 Apr. 1667, p. 63. 3 mi. from the river beg. nere Mattapony path at land of Xtoper. Blackborne & Wm. Gray, &c. to Occupason run, to Henry Jarman & Tho. Page, &c. Trans. of 12 pers: Tho. Griffin, Den. Magrath, Ed. Power, Jno. Edwards, Tho. Kely, Ed. Follett, Jno. Poore, James Man, Eras. Pewry (or Perry), Mary Smith, Wm. Cooke, Sam. Hayward.

MR. BEHETHLEM GILSON, JUNR., 1050 acs. Rappa. Co., 27 Sept. 1667, p. 64. On S. side about 2½ mi. from the Riv., beg. about 100 po. from a path to *Potobaco* from *Mattapony Indian Towne* or *Chikahomani*, cor. of Mr. Robt. Paine & Mr. Thomas Page, nere a run of Mr. Lucas' Cr., crossing a path & severall branches to line of Valentine Allen &c. Trans. of 21 pers: 15 Negroes; Samll. Howard, Jno. Thompson, Wm. Cooke, Eliz. Smith, Jno. Warren, Francis James.

MAJOR JNO. WEIRE & MR. ROBT PAINE, 1185 acs., N. side of Rappa. Riv., nere *Nanzaticon*, beg. about half a mile from the river on the W. side of a Cr. nere a path, nere an Isle of sunken land on the mouth of a valley &c. 27 Sept. 1667, p. 64. Trans. of 24 pers: Rich. Harman, An Cotten, Jno. Dunbar, Henry Mayes, James White, Wm. Evans, Rich. Symmonds, Wm. Coppage, Stephen Sadler, Mary Perry, Eli. Day, Jno. Savage, Wm. Harte, Tho. Parsons, Mary Harte, Saml. Price, James House, Walter Haines, Ralph Holt, Jon. Wil-

kins, Tho. Footer, Wm. Davis, Symon Croft, Martin Hide.

COLL. JNO. STRINGER, 1050 acs. Accomack, on lands of *Occacomson* & *Assawomen;* 6 Nov. 1673, p. 64. Beg. at the head of a br., Coll. Kendall, to Henry Smith, along Edward Smith's line to Mr. Mackeel's, along Mr. Rideing's, &c. Trans. of 21 pers: Robt. Chine (or Chue), Marth. Addams, Tho. Mathewes, Jno. Ennes (or Ems), Wm. Addams, Susan Haman, David Evans, Wm. Strepe (?), Jno. Smith, —— Williams, Edwd. Perkenson, Rich. Thomas, Eliza. Carew, Jno. Hulford, Tab., Peter. Mingoe: Negroes; Hen. Rawlins, Lamb. Groton, Richd. Robins, Diana Fraime (?).

COLL. JNO. WALKER, 900 acs. Rappa. Co., E. side of Rappa. Cr., 27 Sept. 1667, p. 65. Nere land of Jasper Griffin, to cor. of Mathew Barrett's land, &c. Trans. of 18 pers: Jno. Russell, Robt. Sutton, Rich. Wharton, Tho. Roe, Wm. Vaughan, Henry Burcher, Wm. Davies, George Proched (?), Phill. Snead, Robt. Hunt, Edward Turner, Rich. Harding, Walter Smith, Jno. Hatton, Tho. Dutton, James Hide, Francis White, Nich. Hill.

ZEROBABELL WELLS, 500 acs. N'umberland Co., S. side of Armebyes Cr., 27 Sept. 1667, p. 65. Granted to Richard Wells, 1 Aug. 1653 & assigned to the above, his son & heire.

GEORGE WATKIN, 917 acs. Surry Co., 1 Mar. 1666, p. 65. Betwixt Austin Hunicut & Sunken Marish Mill, upon Wm. Carter & Harris' land. Trans. 19 pers: Redrick Thomson, Edward Horton, Robt. Purson, Danll. Hill, Tim. Wilson, Jno. Hart, Mary Hatten, Samp. Waterman, Rich. Holding, Jno. Collins, Roger Carter, Fran. Holland, Patria Morgan, Wm. Sutton, George Ward, Henry Harvy, Martha Watkins, Jno. Russell, Robt. Sutton.

JNO. CATLETT, Gent., 4506 acs. Rappa. Co., Sittingborne Parish, 27 Sept. 1667, p. 66. 1850 acs. bet. Rappa. Riv. & Occopason Cr., beg. below a parcell of marish called the *Thickett*, to *Pigg Poynt* & is the lower end of land of

Thomas Hawkins, Gent., &c. to *Light Wood poynt;* 1542 acs. thereof granted to John Catlett & Ralph Rowzee, dec'd., 20 Feb. •1662; 304 acs. of which was first granted to George Eaton, dec'd., 18 June 1651 & for sometime holden by sd. Catlett & Rowzee, now found to escheat, & granted to sd. Catlett 13 Apr. 1664 &c; 792 acs. thereo f called the forrest, beg. on E. side of a gr. branch falling into Occupason maine run, thence to Mattapony path &c. 1864 acs. purchased, viz: 1364 acs. from Jno. Prosser, 17 Jan. 1665, 200 acs. from Jno. Spereman, 24 Aug. 1666 & 300 acs. from Jno. Lampart 21 Jan. following; the whole being parte of a greater devdt. granted to sd. Prosser, 8 Oct. 1665, beg. by the mouth of Golden Vale Cr. on the S. side &c., nere Pwomunzeene Cr. &c. to land of Roger Richardson &c.

MAJOR WILLIAM BALL, 240 acs. on N. side of Rappa. Riv., upon David Fox, land of Grimes, a Cr. devideing this & land of Tho. Harwood. Granted unto Edward Grimes, 21 May 1651, deserted, & now granted, &c. 30 Sept. 1667, p. 67. Trans. of 5 pers: Wm. Jeffres, Abram Jackson, Tim White, Bernard Moore, Mary Feild.

MAJOR WM. BALL & MR. THOMAS CHETWOOD, 1600 acs. Rappa. Co., N. side of Rappa. Riv., 17 Apr. 1667, p. 68. Trans. of 32 pers: Will. Ball, his son, Hanah Ball, Her daughter, Mary Jones, Martha Jones, Ran. Gwill, Jos. Haseldowne, Joseph Foster, Ralph Gath, George Comes, Yarrett Williams, Henry Scoller, Will. Higgins, Edward Wagg, Dorothy Wells, Wm. Morris, Joshua Greene, Jno. Chandler, Wm. Harloe, Nath. Freeman, Tho. Harris, George Martin, Jno. Bridgman, Eliz. Smith, Grace ———, Edward Salter, Richard Blackman, Robt. Sanders, Tho. Bowles, Tho. Dickins, Robt. Ambrose.

VINCENT COX, 665 acs. W'moreland Co., 27 Sept. 1667, p. 68. Beg. at Robt. Selfe, to a br. falling into Nomeny Riv., &c. to Mr. Francis Clay &c., to head of a br. falling into Yeocomico Riv. 346 acs. parte granted sd. Cox 20 Oct. 1661; 319 acs. due for trans. of 7 pers: Waltron Morgan, Will. Smith,

Dorcas Houghton, Eliz. Fisher, Eliz. Bakehouse, Rowland Morgan, Jno. Davis.

LT. COLL. JNO. GEORGE, 360 acs. at Castle Creek, in *Warrisquick,* Isle of Wight Co., 17 Apr. 1667, p. 69. Upon land of Francis Place, Robt. Lawrence, S. upon George Cobiroe (?) devided from same by a Cyprus Swamp, & E. upon James Riv. 200 acs. purchased of Justinian Cooper, & 160 acs. for trans. of 4 pers: Tho. Ward, Jno. Devorett, James Arnold, Jno. Allin. (Marginal note: There was a mistake in this patt. & is recorded in folio 151.)

RICHARD JARRATT (Jarrett), 345 acs. Surry Co., 7 Aug. 1667, p. 69. Beg. at the head of Richard Drew's land, along Watkins' land, upon Capt. Baker's line &c. Trans. of 7 pers: Will. Bett, Henry White, Robt. Short, Fran. Lewis, Thomas Allen, Joseph Gregory, Peter Hill.

WILL. PORTER, 432 acs. Surry Co., 7 Aug. 1667, p. 69. Beg. at Wm. Huniford's line on E. side of the 3rd Sw. of black water, &c., upon Capt. Cockerham & Mr. Bareham's line, &c. Trans. of 9 pers: Mary Shaw, Jno. Barbar, Susan Woodland, Katharine Griggs, Christopher Wells, Jno. Harvey, Alexr. Pate, Mathew Hogson, Henry Clarke.

JNO. DAVIS, 1000 acs. New Kent Co., S. side of Tottopottomoyes Cr., 27 Feb. 1666, p. 70. Beg. at Cornelius Debany, &c. Trans. of 20 pers: Wm. Alford, Jno. Battin, Dor. Hughes, Rob. Incherson, Jno. Bayly, Sarah Incherson, Dany (or Davy) Price, Sarah Hull, Edw. Perkins, Wm. Stanford, Marke Waters, Wm. Brice, Mary Stanford, And. Hillier, Tho. Dowes (or Dewes), Will. Carr, Mary Bowes, Richard Symmons, Tho. Barker, David Griffeth.

ANN REYNOLDS, 238 acs. N'umberland Co., 8 Nov. 1666, p. 70. At the head of Mattaponie Riv., on land of Jno. Kent &c. 92 acs. granted sd. Ann 9 Feb. 1663 & residue for trans. of 5 pers: Euse. Kemp, Dor. Godfrey, Sarah Jrime, Eliz. Luellin, Jno. Davies.

CAPT. WM. NUTT, 253 acs. N'umberland Co., 8 Nov. 1666, p. 70. Beg.

in Roger Waters line, to Chicacone path &c. 200 acs. by purchase of sd. Waters & residue for trans. of 2 pers: Wm. Kippin, Math. Cole.

THOMAS TOWERS, 720 acs. N'umberland Co., 8 Nov. 1666, p. 71. Beg. at the head of the Bevor Dam Sw., S. to br. of Chicacone Riv. &c. to maine br. of Kings Cr. &c. 450 acs. granted him 4 July 1664 & residue for trans. of 6 pers: Henry Haines, Francis Gouldsmith, Thomas Mathewes, Mary Manning, Ezekiel Francis, Daniell Long.

MR. JAMES GAYLARD, of Staff. Co., 1000 acs. 8 Nov. 1666, p. 71. Beg. at Coll. Peter Ashton, to W'wd. side of an Indian Marish deviding this & land of Mr. Robt. Ausborne, &c. Trans. of 20 pers: Francis Peirce, Rich. Flud, Hugh Owin, Ralph Edwards, Will. Smitton, Jno. Owin, James Rowkins, Jno. Moore, Alice Powell, Jno. Streete, Arthur Figes, Tho. Bagwell, Jno. Belson, Jno. Peare, Henry East, Tho. Kendall, Wm. Cocke, Jno. Russell, Jane. Young, Phill Hamlin.

JOHN BRASSEUR, 400 acs. Nancimond Co., 17 Apr. 1667, p. 72. Butting on land of Mr. Francis Spight. 300 acs. granted Robt. Brasseur & Peter Rey, 24 Feb. 1638, by patt. for 600 acs., which moiety is due sd. John as his son & heire; & 100 acs. for trans. of 2 pers: Richard Kingsbury, Alice Whitaker.

JNO. BENSON, 366 acs. Gloster Co., in Mockjack Bay, on the head of Ware Riv., 10 Apr. 1667, p. 72. Beg. at Mr. Francis Camfeild (or Cawfeild) by the Indian path to Chescake, to Mr. Thomas Colles &c. Trans. of 8 pers: Jno Dunbar, Ed. Freman, Edward Jennings, Jno. Gatton, Will. Grimes, Jno. Cooper, Jno. Harris.

THOMAS WISDOME, 127 acs. Gloster Co., 10 Apr. 1667, p. 72. Upon N. side of Tho. Deacons Mill Sw., beg. at the mouth of a br. deviding this from land of Tho. Miller &c. to Mr. Tho. Vicars line, &c. Trans. of 3 pers: Jno. Reeve, Judith Knight, Mary Godfrey.

JNO. & GEORGE MOTT, 1200 acs. on the N. side & in the freshes of Rappa. Riv., 23 Sept. 1663, p. 73. Beg. on S. E. side of Muddy Cr., &c. Granted to Tho. Paine & Cyprian Bishop, deserted, &c. Trans. of 24 pers: Jno. Cocke, Su. Lodge, Wm. Hence (or Henie), Wm. Smith, Jno. Banting, Alex. Smith, Francis Wright, Wm. Bellingham, Tho. Coft, Isaak Mathewson, Tho. Ford, Jno. Jones, David Sommerfeild, Dorcas Barrow, Samll. Prickloe; Hanah Rosier, Jeffrey Graves, Jno. Thomas, Nich. Menler, Tho. Johnson, Ann Greene, Tho. Barnett, Jacob East, Wm. Kirkeham.

HENRY CORBIN, Esqr., 350 acs. Rappa. Co., 1 Aug. 1667, p. 73. Granted unto James Bagnall, dec'd., found to escheat &c., as by inquisition under Major Jno. Weir, Escheator for sd. County, &c. 1 May 1667, & now granted &c.

WM. HORTON & FRANCIS KIRKMAN, 3500 acs. in the freshes of Petomacke Riv., on W. side of a Cr., deviding this & land of Capt. Gyles Brent, opposite to that part of *Annocoston Indian Towne* called *Aquakick*, etc. 3 Sept. 1669, p. 73. Trans. of —— pers.*

THOMAS JONES, 74 acs. Gloster Co., 10 Apr. 1667, p. 74. Upon branches of Tottopotomoyes Sw., beg. in Michaell Graffton's (Crafton's) line, to Saml. Sallis' line, to Mr. Edward Corderoy, &c. Trans. of 2 pers: Mary Stoakes, Rebecca Shatten.

JNO. BENSON & JNO. WALLER, 423 acs. in Ware Parish, Gloster Co., 10 Apr. 1667, p. 74. Beg. at Mr. Talifro, along Wm. Peach, to Xtopher. Grinawaye's land, to Edward Teale's line nere the Hollybush pond, &c. Trans. of 9 pers: Eliz. Higgenson, Wm. Hughes, Wm. Johnson, Mary Blury, Jeremiah Upshaw, Jno. Tilson, Tho. Stephens, Robt. Smith, Rebecca Toppin (or Tappin).

CAPT. JNO. LORD, 1667 acs. W' moreland Co., at the head of Mr. Pope's Cr., 29 Sept. 1667, p. 75. 600 acs. N. upon sd. Cr., E. upon Mr. Arthur Terrill &c; 600 acs. bounded N. with the aforesaid 600 acs., S. with branches of the

Bevor Dam, with land of Abram Feild & Christopher Butler & land of Danll. Swillivant; 467 acs. on the back line of sd. 1200 acs., crossing a br. of Rappa. Cr. &c. 600 acs. granted to Richard Walker 16 July 1654 & assigned to Samll. Bonum, who assigned halfe to Jno. Bocock, who assigned to sd. Lord; the other halfe sd. Bonam assigned to sd. Lord; the other 600 acs. granted sd. Lord the same time by pattent dated 18 Mar. 1662; & 467 acs. for trans. of 9 pers: Tho. Basington (or Barington), Peter Dunken, John Moore, Marg. Gosnoll, Eliz. Gosnell, Eliz. Ireland, Martha Magnett, An Thornton, Eliz. Scarfe.

MR. JOHN KERBY, 130 acs. in Ware Parish, Gloster Co., 22 Apr. 1671, p. 75. Beg. at land he lives on, &c. Trans. of 3 pers: Wm. Fleet, Jno. Turrett, Peter Spraggy.

CAPT. JNO. LORD & MR. WM. HORTON, 1544 acs. W'moreland Co., 17 Apr. 1667, p. 76. 800 acs. upon lands of Major Lewis, & Thomas Dyas, &c. 744 acs. upon land surveyed for Henry Durant and land of Major Peirce. Trans. of 31 pers: Wm. Bryant, Josyah Mills, James Ireland, Mary Powell, Edward Pith, Tho. Spinny, Rich. Spinny, Dorothy Spinny, Robt. Whiting, Isa. Chamney (or Chainney), Tho. Dutton, Jane Raven (?), Peter Handy, Will (a) Negro, Jno. Goods, Wm. Spyre, Michaell Holmes, Robt. Ascall (?), James Darby, Walter Dixon, Mary Wood, Jeffery Fletcher, Tim Wallis, Jane Powell, Rich. Corbin, Wm. Safe, Edm. Sipkins, Rich. Hopkins, Henry Miller, James Greene, Mar. Dennis.

WILL. SMITH, 590 acs. W'moreland Co., 17 Apr. 1667, p. 76. At the head of Hollowes Cr., 400 acs. beg. at a poynt called the wading place opposite Capt. Jno. Washington, to land formerly Thomas Moulten's, crossing br. of Bevor Dams of sd. Cr. & another run belonging to Mr. Pope &c; 90 acs. bounded with sd. 400 acs., &c; 100 acs. beg. on E. side of sd. Dams & N. side of sd. 400 acs., &c. 400 acs. being parte of a former grant; & 190 acs. for trans. of 4 pers: Wm. Browne, Tho. Storke, Rich. Holland, Rich. Lancaster.

MAJOR JOHN WEIRE, 150 acs. Rappa. Co., 2 Oct. 1667, p. 77. Beg. by a little cr. of Occupason Cr., upon land surveyed for Richard Coleman & land of Wm. Hall, &c. Granted to Wm. Harper, 20 Feb. 1662, deserted, &c., & further due for trans. of 3 pers: Teage Okey, Rice James, Ann Jones.

THOMAS BRERETON, 40 acs. N'umberland Co., 29 Oct. 1666, p. 77. W. N. W. & N. E. on Yeocomico Riv., upon land of Wm. Warder, & upon a Cr. deviding this & land of Mr. Charles Ashton. Granted Jno. Hoskins (or Haskins) 4 June 1663, deserted, &c., & further due for trans. of: Thomas Wilkenson.

RICHARD LAWRENCE, 2000 acs. Rappa. Co., on N. side of sd. Riv., 13 Oct. 1665, p. 77. On Ewd. side of Rappa. Cr., sometimes called Fleets Cr., bounded S. E'ly. by Manokin Cr. &c. Granted sd. Lawrence & Capt. George Bryar by joynt tenure by 2 pattents each dated 26 Sept. 1664, but now solely & entirely belonging to sd. Lawrence, as Survyvour of sd. Bryar.

COLL. EDMOND SCARBURGH, 3000 acs. Accomack Co., at Pockomoke Riv., 9 Oct. 1667, p. 78. Beg. below Hogg Quarter, up sd. river & including all necks & branches to the uppermost extent of this devdt., S'ly. to severall extents as by the swamp & unhabitable parts admitts this. Trans. of 60 pers: Thomas Hobbs, Arthur Tomlin, Timo. Heldersby, Godfrey Nowell, Jno. Walsington, Jno. Wrath, Mathew Bishop, Henry Shirly, Edward Sadler, Owen Lewis, Edmond Hollis, James Golding, Ja. Whitehead, Lewis Ball, Arth. Williams, Edmd. Hungarth, Ja. Gollington, Margaret Smith, Jeffrey Hollingsby, Hen. Chishester, Mary Chandler, Jane Moseley, John Dole, Tho. Carpenter, Micha. Rouse, James Gray, Joseph Cox, Jane Murry, Joane Kettlesby, Lewis Washford, Tho. Crosse, Morris Jones, Natha. Blackleigh, Lewis Roe, Rowland Monke, Edmd. Holt, James Bagnall, Mathew Foreland, Simon Orthar, Rowld. Oxley, Jeffry Ryland, Godfrey Bewfield, Hen. Cooper, Jno. Winsley, Tho. Yeamans, Rowland House, Jno. Denbigh,

Wm. Richley, Joseph Nurse, James South, John Lewin (or Lewiss), Morgan Lewis, Mary Esterfield, Joane Roberts, James Rowles, John Fowler, Hen. Warren, Maurice Vaughan, Hutchfeild Beechan, Magl. Southfeild.

SAME. Co., acreage, date & page the same as above. Bounded by his own severall devidents on the seaside, bet. Gr. & Little Matomkin Crks. & the great white marsh, &c. Trans. of 60 pers: Robert Farlow, Rebecca Wrath, Wm. Fortescue, James Forrest, Jeffry Newington, Isaak Bullard, John Radnock, Robert Meakes, Morris Curwethy, Tho. Loath (or Loach), James Killingsworth, Lewis Axton, Rowland Meeres, Richard Chandler, Mathew Tomlinson, Richard Blewfield, Robt. Redland, John Barnefield, Lewis Joanes, Tho. Heath, Saml. Willis, Rich. White, Tho. Rollington, Robt. Weaver, Mathew Rivers, Susan Scarlett, Tho. Helford, James Sadler, Jno. Horsington, Tho. Chesterfeild, Rowland Ribraud (?), Eliza. Colt, Robt. Pond, Sisley Ranger, Edgar Sutton, Natha. Holt, Adam Rouse, Tho. Nurse, Edward Hamar, John Rouse, James Graves, Edward Bastable, James Watts, Arthur Frost, Oliver Atkins, Miles East, Nehemiah Gold, Mary Edgarton, Wm. Blue, Joan Wollerton, Roger Grimes, Morgan Evan, James Halser, Joab Huntley, John Hoile, Jeane Lawrey, Jno. Stapleton, Nich. Hollis, Robert Wielding, Ralph Hedgar.

MR. JOHN HAYMAN, 463 acs. James Citty Co., 19 July 1667, p. 79. 413 acs. being high land & 50 acs. marsh; beg. at the head of a br. neare a Spring by his house, to Kethes Cr., to Nathll. Hunt's corne field. &c. to Wm. Hudson's fence &c. to a br. of the Bavor Dams, &c. to Mr. Litlers Spring &c. 330 acs. included in a patt. to Thomas Smith, 21 Aug. 1637, who sold to Peter Ridley & by him sold to sd. Hayman; 100 acs. by patt. to sd. Ridley 23 Sept. 1639 & sold to sd. Hayman; & residue for trans. of Theo. Hone.

NATHANAELL BRADFORD, 400 acs. Accomack Co., 9 Oct. 1667, p. 79. On the head of Mr. Edward Revell, & Jonas Jackson at *Watchapreag*, N. by

the main S. br. of Nichowomson (Niccowomson) Cr. Trans. of 8 pers: Edward Waller, Tho. Gibbons, Gideon Hayden, James Finsh, Jno. Tregon, Margaret Strede, Robt. Culliford, James Gold.

ARTHUR ROBINS, 1000 acs. Accomack Co., 9 Oct. 1667, p. 80. W. side of Nathanael Bradford's 400 acs. & sd. Bradfords devdt. at *Watchapreag*, bounded on S. by land of Richard Kellum & Bartholomew Meares, N. by Niccowomson maine S. br. &c. Trans. of 20 pers: Edward Mosse, James Heyton, John Long, Sarah Carter, Judeth Small, Rich. Dix, Jno. Washford, Edgar Glascocke, Tho. Standard, Miles Fortesque, James King, Joseph Dun, Joane Oxford, Tho. Murley, Eliza. Tailor, Martha Wont, Tho. Billington, James Scott, Abigail Barnhouse, Tymothy Champion.

MRS. ANNE TOFFT, 2600 acs. Accomack Co., 9 Oct. 1667, p. 80. Bounded on W. by a cr. formerly called Muddy Cr., now Guilford's, &c., to the utmost maine br. of Arathusa, formerly Kecqotank, Cr. extending to her own 1250 acs. &c. Trans. of 52 pers: Rich. Sandis, Bernard Hide, Ano. Bateman, Robert Burneham, Tho. Lambert, Jno. Polchill, Robt. Heath, Ja. Culpepper, Wm. Leonard, Tho. Crispe, Wm. Boyes, Jno. Head, Rich. Duke, Edw. Flinch, Jno. Horseman, John Radley, James Hodgskins, Natha. West, Jeffry Riston, Rich. Penington, Jno. Light, Tho. Kirland, Jno. Halstead, Robt. Heywood, John Ewtis, Hen. Slayter, Cutbert Ogle, George Hutton, Roger Kenion, Jno. Ainsly, Jas. Blathurst, Alexander Wood, Wm. Pearepoint, Wm. Wall, Jno. Walpoole, Rich. Brownlow, Ralph Aston, Nich. Townley, Jno. Girling, Ralph Aston, Jno. Parker, Rich. Standish, Tho. Nolres, Alexander Rigby, Robt. Ireland, Nich. Moseley, Jno. Ducken, Tho. Cutler. Wm. Bankes, John Birom, Wm. Fisse, Tho. Long.

JNO. GORING, 1000 acs. belonging to Edmond Scarburgh, by him assigned to sd. Goring, Accomack Co., at Timber Cr., 9 Oct. 1667, p. 81. Trans. of 20 pers: John Ramsey, Jean Norwich, Martha Clowes, Margaret Roach, Rowland Cheap, Edwd. Bankes, Jno. Perry,

Wm. Serjeant, Thomas Weaver, Joseph Crosfield, Abraha. Branch, Sarah Cuningsby, Edward Haines (or Homes), James Cutwright, Obediah Ebington, Richard Aymes, Rowland Nexford, Michael Rye, Jane Collings, Susan Rowley.

MR. HENRY SMITH, 1000 acs. Accomack Co., being part of an island where the E. & W. line from Smith's Island intersect, &c., & bounded by parte of Chesepaik Bay &c. Trans. of 20 pers: Jno. Smith, Hen. Smith, Margery Smith, Saml. Holbrooke, Joan Holbrooke, Rich. Webb, Wm. Nock, Eliza. Nock, Roger Mills, Rachell Moodey, Rich. Chambers, Jane Powell, Wm. Turner, Roger Burkum, Judith Godfrey, Wm. Underwood, Joseph Morley, Michael Frost, Mary Slingsby, Jasper Marding.

WM. WHITE, 400 acs. Accomack Co., 9 Oct. 1667, p. 81. At the head of Hunting Cr., bounded on W. by land of John Carew &c. Trans. of 8 pers: George Potter, Wm. Bogan, Nicholas Ducke, Thomas Stafford, John Harris, Thomas Berry, Josias Calmady, Edmond Fowell.

WILLIAM HICKMAN, 1000 acs. Accomack Co., at *Arcadia,* 9 Oct. 1667, p. 82. Bounded on E. by land of George Watson &c. Trans. of 20 pers: Jno. Morton, Hen. Henly, Jno. Winston, James Bullen, Susan Hooper, Thomas Freake, Tho. Trenchard, George Fulford, Robert Napfield, Thomas Baynard, George Gray, Robert Tider, Robt. Fortesque, Edw. Tremain, Rich. Cabell (or Caball), Tho. Carter, Jno. Tanner, Robt. Walker, George Howard, Jonathan Sparke.

MR. ROBERT HUTCHINSON, 1250 acs. Accomack Co., 9 Oct. 1667, p. 82. 1200 acs. being halfe of a necke of land formerly elected by Lt.Coll. William Waters & assigned to sd. Hutchinson; at great Matomkin, bounded on E. by the Seaboard, on S. by a right line which divides this necke into 2 equal parts; beg. at a stake in the marsh, runing to the bridge at Matomkin br. &c. Trans. of 25 pers: Robert Hutchinson,

James Lipscombe, Gabriel Littleton, George Jenkins, Hugh Meares, Leonard Powell, Dorcas Woodford, Mary Ridge, Henry Lurton, Mountjoy (?) Evelling, Jane Evelling, Rebecca Evelling, Rowld. Rolley, Grace Deneare, Ellinor Meridath, John Blackborne, Moses Bently, George Evelling, Thomas Pittman, Fra. Pittman, Joseph Pittman, Robert Woodford, Rowland Hudson, Anne Ridge, Susan Tessero (?).

THOMAS MOORE, 520 acs. (*with the consent of the adjoyning neighbors*), N'ampton Co.; at Magette Bay, 8 Oct. 1667, p. 83. Running to land whereon Jno. Knight liveth &c. Trans. of 11 pers.* (Only these names appear: Patrick, Manuell, Phillip.)

MICHAELL CRAFTON, 720 acs. Gloster, E. side of Poropotanke Cr., 8 Oct. 1667, p. 83. Beg. at the mouth of a br. deviding this & land of Oliver Greene &c. to br. deviding this & land of Mr. Jno. Pate &c. 614 acs. granted to Mr. Nich. Jernew 3 July 1652, who sold to sd. Crafton; & 106 acs. for trans. of 3 pers: John Banckes, James Winch, Robert Collet (?).

THOMAS HANKES, 300 acs. on branches of Peanketanke Swampe & Poropotanke, 8 Oct. 1667, p. 84. Beg. at his other devdt. in the line of Coll. Lee's land, S. to Rapahanock path, &c. Trans. of 6 pers: Edward Roe, 2 tymes, Hannah Wilson, John Law, Edward Roper, Francis Tersell.

ROBERT BOWMAN, Junr., 250 A., 8 P., Henrico Co., on S. side of James Riv., 28 Sept. 1667, p. 84. Adj. Robt. Bowman, Senr., &c. to lower side of Sir John Zouche's bottome, &c. Trans. of 5 pers: Peter Proud, Alice Genner, Joane Cary, Thomas Lisborne, Richard Verlin.

WILLIAM WILKINS, 472 A., 3 R. 1 P., Chas. Citty Co., S. side of James Riv., 13 Mar. 1665, p. 85. On the head of Flowerdee hundred Cr., on E. side of the S. run joyneing to Wm. Harris &c. Trans. of 10 pers: Teage Okey, Rice Joanes, Ann Joanes, Francis Chandler, Tho. Grice, Edward Allester, Gerard

Greene, Francis Oateley, Zach. Ellmer, Richard Smith.

SAME. 308 A., 3 R., 31 P., same location, date & page. 200 acs. purchased of Richard Pace, as by records of sd. county will appeare; & residue for trans. of 3 pers: Samll. Warren, James Bird, Thomas Davis.

MAJOR GENLL. MANERING HAMOND, 4610 acs. New Kent Co., S. side of Yorke Riv., on E. branch of Black Cr., 1 Nov. 1667, p. 86. Including on the other side of the Bay a neck conteyning 350 acs., 3760 acs. called *Fort Royall,* granted to him 15 Mar. 1649; & 850 acs. by pattent 1. May 1661.

WM. HARRISON, Junr., 368 A., 3 R., 37 P., Chas. Cytty Co., S. side of James Riv., 5 Apr. 1667, p. 86. Beg. in a line of Capt. David Peoples, to Robt. Jones, down the Pyny Sw. to the old Towne Bridge, to James Jones, to line of Mr. Richd. Tye, &c. Trans. of 7 pers.*

MR. WILLIAM FOGG, 650 acs. Rappa. Co., S. side the river, 18 Feb. 1666, p. 87. Beg. at S.most end of a line deviding this & land formerly Rich. West's, to land of Nicholas Burt &c., to Popcman br. &c. to land of Thomas Page & Jno. Watson, over a great br. &c. to topp of hills deviding this & land of Jno. Catlett, Gent. &c. 222 acs. being parte of 444 acs. granted sd. Fogg & Richard West, 28 July 1663; 428 acs. for trans. of 9 pers: Henry Knowles, Edmund Bird, Richard Badger, Willm. Baseley, James Lee, Elizabeth Clampe, Thomas Fogg, Edward Smith, Wm. Tanner.

ENOCH DOUGHTY, 500 acs. on N. side of Rappa. Riv., above *Nanzemone Towne,* 8 Nov. 1667, p. 88. Beg. next to land of Mr. Charles Grimes, dec'd., &c. crossing main br. of Doughties Cr., &c. Sd. land granted sd. Doughty by Govr. & Councell &c., as deserted by Robert Pollard, in the Nov. Genll. Ct. 1664; sd. Doughty entered rites accordingly & in Apr. 1667 he obtained their order for further time to save & seate the sd. 500 acs., but he finding no record of Pollard's grant by vertue of his former rights resurveyed the sd. land &c. Due for trans. of 10 pers: Margarett Davis, Elizabeth Harris, Richard Haveacre (or Haneacare), Jno. Bowcher, Wm. Rawnall, David Bram, Jno. Beacell, a Negroe, Jno. Smith, Wm. Muskett.

GEORGE BROWNEING, 103 A., 38 P., 14 Nov. 1667, p. 88. Bet. his own & land of Thomas Gagecome &c. to John Howell's field &c. Granted by order of Genrl. Ct. &c. (County not mentioned.)

MR. THOMAS PATTISON, 400 acs. S. side of Rappa. Co., upon branches of Killman's Cr., 8 Nov. 1667, p. 89. By land of Evin Davis & Thomas Williams. Trans. of 8 pers: Rich. Kathericke, Wm. Clubbs, Alice Long, Edward Joanes, Joane Hannock, Jno. Gillam, John Norton, Margaret Vackham.

RICE JONES, 1300 acs. S. side of Lancaster Co., 8 Nov. 1667, p. 89. Beg. at land formerly Haward's, by the Draggon Sw., &c. to his own former devdt. &c. 1000 acs. granted to Mr. John Appleton, 15 May 1661, who sold to Henry Ward, marryner, 11 Nov. 1663, who sold to sd. Jones, 10 May 1664; upon resurvey 300 acs. overplus was found within the old bounds, which is due for trans. of 6 pers: Edward Greene, Willm. Lawrence, Saml. Wood, Jno. Lovejoy, Xtopher. Fallingbee, Mary Salvage.

DAVID CRAFFORD, 86 A., 29 Chs., James Citty Co., Martins hundred Parish, 7 Aug. 1667, p. 90. Beg. on the S. side of the Church path in Mr. Richard Whittacre's lyne, &c. to the Dead man's Stake, &c. to Wm. Bedford's lyne, to the run of Greene's Sw., &c. Part of 1500 acs. granted to Mr. Tho. Loveing, dec'd., 14 Oct. 1643 & became due to Mrs. Anne Loveing, as heire of sd. Thomas, & purchased of her by sd. Crafford.

To the PARRISH OF MARTYNS (Martins) BRANDON, 200 acs. *for a Gleebe belonging to their Church in the* Co. of Chas. Citty, 5 Dec. 1667, p. 90.

Lying betwixt Capt. Johnson's land & the Marchants (Merchants), beg. at a marked oake standing on the banke by the watering place, thence S. E. E'ly. along Capt. Johnson's lyne 320 pole thence N. E. E'ly. 100 po. thence paralell to the first lyne 320 po. upon the River, thence S. W. W'ly. along the River side to the first station.

THOMAS BELL, 160 acs., New Kent Co., being surplusage of the marsh belonging to Hugh Roy & Thomas Creeton, being done by order &c. upon petition of sd. Bell; 11 Dec. 1667, p. 91. Beg. at a small gutt 128 po. above the mouth of the *thorowfare* in sd. marsh &c. to Mattasack Cr. & the river. Trans. of 4 pers: Joane Mills, John Horseman, Tho. Leamond, Thomas Dandy (or Daudy) .

THOMAS COLLES, Merchant, 200 acs. Gloster Co., on the head of the North Riv. in Mockjack bay, 17 Dec. 1667, p. 91. Beg. at Coll. Elliott, to land of Andrew Careles, &c. Trans. of 4 pers: Arthur Griggs, Morgan Joanes, Samll. Spendlow, Wm. Calver.

ABRAHAM FLOOD & RICH. CARTER, 150 acs. Staff. Co., 31 Dec. 1667, p. 92. Adj. land of Mr. Robert King. Part of land granted to Mr. Andrew Pettigrew, 28 Jan. 1662, who sold to Robert Houseing, by him sold to Richard Ayliff, who sold to the above patentees, as by bill of sale recorded in sd. county, 18 Apr. 1666.

MR. RICHARD HILL, 212 acs. (Co. not given), 31 Dec. 1667, p. 92. Beg. at land formerly belonging to sd. Hill, now in tenure of Lt. Coll. John Washington, &c. to the horse path, to land of Mr. John Foxhall &c. 100 acs. parte granted sd. Hill 14 Feb. 1661; & 112 acs. for trans. of 2 pers: Wm. Territt, Margarett Basse.

MARTHA LUDFORD, Widdow, 300 acs. Middlesex Co., 29 Mar. 1672, p. 92. Granted to William Ludford & lately found to escheat &c. & by inquisition under Henry Corbyn, Esqr., Deputy Escheator, &c., 30 Apr. 1670 may appear, & now granted sd. Martha &c.

MR. ROBERT KING & ANTHONY HOGGARD, 737 acs. Staff. Co., upon branches of Up. Machotick Riv., 31 Dec. 1667, p. 93. A branch dividing this from land of Edward Hewes, to N. W. side of the horse bridge dividing this & land of Mr. Robert Hewson &c. Trans. of 15 pers: Mr. John Lord, 3 tymes; John Bennett, Thomas Gibbins, James Goodacre, James Winterbottome, John Thompson, David Chitby, John Marshall, Minion Younge, Anne Young, Robert Whitehead, Tho. Smith, James Valience (or Dalience).

MR. JOHN FOXHALL, 640 acs. bet. the Rivers Potomack & Rappahannock, 31 Dec. 1667, p. 93. Beg. at land pattented by Rich. Coleman called *the forrest,* across branches of the E.most dams of Apomatickes Cr. to N. side of Westmoreland horse path, &c. to Major Wm. Underwood, dec'd. &c. Trans. of 13 pers: Andrew Hanson, James Colstreame, John Small, Capt. Tho. Allen, Henry Smith, John Brookes, Francis Harper, Wm. Falkner, John Cave, Gilbert Cooper, Charles Coggan, Mary Spensax, Sam boy a Negro.

MR. ROBERT KING, 395 acs. Staff. Co., bet. Rappa. & Potomack Rivs., 31 Dec. 1667, p. 94. Beg. at land surveyed for Henry Perry (Berry), Robert Peck & Jno. Welch &c. to Mr. Francis Hale his cart path &c. Trans. of 7 pers: Thomas Grooby, Margarett Woory, Mary Smith, Edmond Westborne, Tho. Bressey, Lawrence Caps, Davy Herbert.

HENRY BERRY, ROBT. PECK & JOHN WELCH, 550 acs. Staff. Co., betwixt Potomack & Rappa. Rivs., 31 Dec. 1667, p. 94. Trans. of 11 pers: Leonard Tucker, and his wife, Nicho. Mires, John Moore, John Kendall, Ann Wilson, John Crock. Note: The remainder of these rights being transferred from a pattent of Vincent Young's, dated 18 Mar. 1662 for 200 acs., being surveyed out by an ancient pattent.

MR. JONATHAN NEWELL & MR. AMBROSE CLARE, 2500 acs., New Kent Co., S. side & in the freshes of

Yorke Riv., 3 Jan. 1667, p. 95. Beg. at Mr. Francis Burnell's land, &c. Trans. of 50 pers: Ralph Spier, Paul Graves, Alice Waterman, Bartho. Dobson, Hannah Worsely, Edmond Bell, Nicho. Cobb, Wm. Causon, Avis Witing (?), Wm. Hopkins, Anne Gower, Nichol. Payne, Jonathan Hobdy, John Slater, John Rogers, Robt. Hardy, Edw. West, James Egg, Judith Jennings, Walter Holsted, Samll. Bradshaw, Joseph Fowler, Eliza. Page, Mr. Jonathan Newell, 2 tymes, James Old, Edmond Stephens, Wm. Russell, David Skidmore, Walter Morgan, Josh. Porten, Jacob Merick, Wm. Radge, James Partrige, Wm. Tomblins, Edward Love, Lawrence James, Rich. Millard, Benjam. Bedoes, Wm. Watkins, Giles Rawlins, Stephen Deswell, Rich. Woodward, Wm. Delamaine, Hugh Rodd, Andrew Rowton, Paul Booth, Wm. Alford, John Battin, Dorothy Hughes, Robert Incherson.

MR. JNO. DUNCOMB (Duncombe), 600 acs. New Kent Co., N. side of Mattapony Riv., ½ mi. above *Mattapony New Indian Towne;* 3 Jan. 1667, p. 95. Beg. at Mr. Leonard Clayborne's, &c. Trans. of 12 pers: John Bayly, Sarah Incherson, Davy Jrice, Sarah Hull, Edward Perkins, Wm. Stanford, Marke Waters, Wm. Bryce, Mary Stanford, Andrew Hellyer, Tho. Bowes, Wm. Carr.

JOHN CAPE, 650 acs., S. side Yorke Riv., New Kent Co., on a br. of Chiccahomony Sw. called Muschmino (?), 3 Jan. 1667, p. 96. Beg. on S. side of Westifer (Westover) path &c., to path from Westifer path to Rich. Bullock's house, &c., to line that divides New Kent from James Citty County, &c. Trans. of 13 pers: Mary Bowes, Rich. Symonds, Tho. Barker, David Griffith, Francis Peirce, Rich. Flyde, Hugh Owen, Ralph Edwards, Wm. Snitton (or Sintton-Suitton), Jno. Owen, James Rawlins, Jno. Moore, Alice Powell.

JOHN PIGG, 600 acs. New Kent Co., N. side of Mattapony Riv., 3 Jan. 1667, p. 96. Adj. his own & land of Mr. Mody. Trans. of 12 pers: John Street, Francis Taylor, Jno. Peirce, Tho. Harden. Jno. Adams, Wm. Davis. Wm.

Wood, David Jones, Eliz. Smith, Tho. Maine, Joseph Ball, Tho. Warden.

JOHN TALBOTT & ELIAS DOWNES, 1600 acs. New Kent Co., S. side of Mattapony Riv., 18 Dec. 1667, p. 97. Beg. a little below sunken grownd &c., to forkes of Fawnes br., to land of Edward Holmes &c. Trans. of 32 pers: Wm. Clayborne, Wm. Harris, Wm. Morris, Jno. Pipps, Tho. Story, Rich. Petonere (?), Jno. Palmer, Roger Sadler, John Wilson, Roger Barloe, Wm. Dawson, Jno. Swift, Rich. Evans, Peter Jennings, Arthur Grymes, Jno. Willett, Wm. Cawsey, Daniel Haddock, Jno. Fox, Tho. Cox, Francis Jones, Hugh Evans, Rich. Thompson, Tho. Varnall, Jno. King, Wm. Roberts, Jno. Griffen, Hugh Meredith, Robt. Sowersby, Margarett Woodward, John Gates, Jno. Gardner.

MR. GEORGE CURTIS, 1100 acs. upon black water Cr., in Mockjack bay, Gloster Co., 20 Dec. 1667, p. 97. Beg. on the white marsh Cr. &c. down the Deviding Cr. &c. 700 acs. granted him 20 Sept. 165— & 400 acs. due for trans. of 8 pers: Leonard Baxter, Wm. Beard, Simon Gold, Patrick Forgeson, Sander Murray, Mary Rownd, Rich. Gibbs, Anne a Negroe.

WM. FRISWELL, 600 acs. Lancaster Co., S. side of Rappa. Riv., 20 Dec. 1667, p. 98. Beg. at Charles Hill &c. to Mr. Edmond Kempe &c. Trans. of 12 pers: John Hudson & his wife, Robt. Hill, Jno. Fisher, Anne & Mary Hudson, Xpher. Keeble, Henry Organ, Tho. Elgar, Wm. Chapman, Francis & Mary Smith.

THOMAS COLLES, 137 acs., Gloster Co., 20 Dec. 1667, p. 98. Beg. at Coll. John Walker, to N. E. side of the Deepe br., &c. Trans. of 4 pers: Tho. Colles, & Sarah his wife, Wm. Porbeney (?), George Anderson.

WALTER WHARTON, 425 acs. N. side of Lancaster Co., at the head of the branches of the Sw. of Morattico Cr., 30 Dec. 1667, p. 98. Beg. at Edward Riley, to land of Abraham Bush. to path leading towards *Chiccacoane* to land of Doctor Sanders &c. Trans. of 9 pers: Rich. Guysick, Henry Prise, Tho.. Knight,. Wm. Johnson, Rich. Woodcock, Tho. Butterfield, Stephen Wileman, John Hobbs, Jeremy Sackeridge.

STEPHEN PETTUS, 350 acs. New Kent Co., upon branches of Ware Cr., 8 Jan. 1667, p. 99. Beg. at John Basbye's standing by Ashwell patch, &c. to land whereon he now liveth & upon land of Wm. Allen &c. 250 acs. granted Lazarus Thomas, 12 Oct. 1655, since sold to Nicho. Bond, who sold to sd. Pettus; 100 acs. newly taken up, & due for trans. of 2 pers: Stephen Pettus, John Hinde.

LT. JOHN NEEDLES, 550 acs. Lancaster Co., N. E. side of Peanketanke Riv., opposite to the Store point devident; 20 Dec. 1667, p. 99. Running to Barbeque Cr. & land of Capt. Brocas &c. 220 acs. granted to Alexander Read & John Needles, 23 Feb. 1663, & by sd. Read assigned to sd. Needles; 280 acs. newly taken up & due for trans. of 5 pers: Wm. Pettitt, James Johnson, Alex. Sanhough, Doro. Boswell, Elizabeth Davis.

WM. MORGAN, 50 acs. on E. side of Mockjack bay, running to land of Walter Morgan &c. 20 Dec. 1667, p. 99. Trans. of: Anne Disford.

ROGER LEONARD, 300 acs. Gloster Co., in Mockjack bay, upon E. side of the E.most river, 20 Dec. 1667, p. 100. Bounding upon land of Adam Bennett, Henry Prouse, &c. Trans. of 6 pers: Elizabeth Lay, Isaak Remnant, Jno. Booth, John Morgan, Wm. Combes, Mary Harwood.

ANNE BORAM, 148 acs. Gloster Co., on *Horne Harbor,* beg. 100 po. from sd. Cr., 20 Dec. 1667, p. 100. Trans. of 3 pers: Rose Davys, Payne Harvy, Mary Bryden.

WM. GARRETT, 100 acs. Lancaster Co., in Fleet's bay, on S. side of Tabb's Cr., 20 Dec. 1667, p. 100. Part of 400 acs. granted to George Thompson, 11 Mar. 1657, who sold to Wm. Angell, &

by Uriah Angell, his heire sold unto sd. Garrett.

MAGN. BARRETT, 100 acs. Lancaster Co., in Fleet's Bay, on N. side of Tabb's Cr., adj. land of Wm. Garrett, 20 Dec. 1657, p. 100. Part of 400 acs. &c. as above.

PATRICK MILLER, 120 acs. Lancaster Co., S. side of Rappa. Riv., 20 Dec. 1667, p. 101. Beg. at Capt. Wm. Brocas, running to land of Wollerton & to N. side of Barbeque Cr. Part of 300 acs. granted sd. Miller, 20 Aug. 1655.

SAME. 1000 acs., same Co., date & page. Beg. at a small gutt parting this & land of James Bonner, up the Riv. to land of Mr. Parrott &c., to land of Charles Hill, deserted, &c. to land of Rowland Marke Rowle, &c. 400 acs. parte granted sd. Miller, 18 Mar. 1663, & 600 acs. now taken up & due for trans. of 12 pers: Hannah Leigh, Widdow, Hanna & her daughter, Isaak Tillison, Katherine Shaw, Alice Rippon, Margarett Hamersly. Note: Remainder of these rights taken from a patt. of sd. Miller dated 20 Aug. 1655.

ROWLAND MACKROREE (Mackrore), 300 acs. Lancaster Co., S. side of Rappa. Riv., 20 Dec. 1667, p. 101. Beg. at George Wadding &c. 200 acs. parte granted to James Bonner, 19 Oct. 1653, sold to James Mackman, who sold to Wm. Frisell & by him sold to sd. Mackrore, 8 Oct. 1659; 100 acs. for trans. of 2 pers: Sarah Younge, Ellenor Browne.

HENRY PROUSE, 200 acs. Gloster Co., 20 Dec. 1667, p. 102. Upon E.-most Riv., beg. at a cr. parting this & land of Roger Leonard &c. Trans. of 4 pers: Roger Williams, George Hill, Tho. Hunter, Cornel. Luglee.

WM. ROBERTS, 170 acs. Gloster Co., 20 Dec. 1667, p. 102. In the North River in Mockjack Bay, beg. next to land of Mr. Richard Bayly, along the Riv. to Mr. Dedman &c. Trans. of 3 pers: John Boteley, Edward Williams, Anthony Sharpeley.

DUNKIN BOHONO (Bohonno), & JNO. MECHEN, 220 acs. Gloster Co., upon the head of the E.most Riv. in Mockjack Bay; 20 Dec. 1667, p. 102. Adj. lands of Mr. Armestead & Capt. Dudley. Trans. of 4 pers: Tho. Arnis (or Amis), John Blan, Roger Shackleford, John Thomas.

MR. JAMES RANSOME, 300 acs. Gloster Co., upon E. side of the N. Riv. in Mockjack Bay, 20 Dec. 1667, p. 103. Adj. Capt. Rich. Dudley. Trans. of 6 pers: Wm. Sanders, Anne Dutton, Anne Gwyn, Tho. Bidell, Mary Lename, Theo. Pendesey.

HUMPHRY JONES, 100 acs. Lancaster Co., S. side of Rappa. Riv., 20 Dec. 1667, p. 103. Beg. at Peter Mountague, to land of Jno. Phillips on Parrott's Cr., & to land of Oliver Seater. Trans. of 2 pers: Margaret Field, Wm. Robinson.
HENRY SINGLETON, 300 acs. Gloster Co., neare mouth of the E.most Riv. in Mockjack Bay, adj. his own land., 20 Dec. 1667, p. 103. Granted to Thomas Morgan, who sold to sd. Singleton, 25 Oct. 1660.

CAPT. RICHARD DUDLEY, 300 acs. Gloster Co., on *Gwin's Ridge*, 20 Dec. 1667, p. 103. Trans. of 6 pers: Jane Bartlett, Issabell ——, Tho. Cobb, Jno. Bolton, Jno. Cooper, Edward Smith.

SAME. 300 acs., same Co. & date, p. 104. On N. Riv. in Mockjack Bay, beg. at a cr. deviding this & land of Edward Welch, dec'd., &c. Trans. of 6 pers: John Mechan, John Snow, Rich. Phillipps. Saml. Powdry, Jno. Walton, Jno. Whaley.

JOHN SANDERSON, 300 acs. Gloster Co., 20 Dec. 1667, p. 104. Adj. Mr. Cooke, running to a br. of Ware Riv. &c. Trans. of 6 pers: Rowland Prince, Wm. Frees, Alexander Smith, Rich. Badger, Jno. Smith, Joane Sandwicke.

DAVID BARRICK, 220 acs. Lancaster Co., S. side of Rappa. Riv., 20 Dec. 1667, p. 104. Beg. at Mr. Leache's land, running to Frisell's lands, &c.

Trans. of 4 pers: Peter Smalwood, James Speareman, John Due, Rich. Motley.

WILLIAM CLAW & CORNELIOUS MATHEWES, 320 acs. Gloster Co., 20 Dec. 1667, p. 104. (Note: Marginal reference give this as *Colawne* & *Collawine*, instead of Claw. Does not appear in county index to patents.) On branches of Peanketanke, beg. at land of Coll. Warner, running to land of Thomas Royston &c. Trans. of 6 pers: Leonard French, Jonathan Catford, Martin Godwyn, Saml. Sparkes, Tho. Jart, Tho. Delume.

LANCASTER LOVETT, 700 acs. Low. Norf. Co., Lyn haven Parrish, 9 Dec. 1667, p. 105. Upon a former devdt. of sd. Lovett, comonly called the *Labor in vayne*, upon lands of Renatus Land & Jno. Martin, & upon land of Francis Land, comonly called *Poultryes hall*. 500 acs. part granted him 20 Oct. 1661, & 200 acs. for trans. of 4 pers: Rich. Farrell, Tho. Stanbridge, Elizabeth Paul & Elizabeth Thornedon.

MILES LEWIS & RICHARD LEWIS, orphants of Rich. Lewis, 400 acs. in Chuckatuck Parrish, 29 Jan. 1667, p. 105. Adj. lands of Tho. Jordan & Jeremy Rutter. Trans. of 8 pers: Henry Johnson, Mary Elmes, John Jones, Peeter Strong, Theo. Brent, Peter Thurston, Robt. Thurston, Peter Stacy.

THOMAS GOLDMAN, 1200 acs. Rappa .Co., S. side the Riv., upon the maine pocoson of Hodskins Cr., 4 Apr. 1667, p. 105. Trans. of 24 pers: Jonath. Webb, Wm. Jones, Sam Johnson, Jno. Maning, Ed. Anderson, Amy Anderson, Mary Lancaster, Wm. Holt, Rich. Willis, Susan. Price, Margt. Winch, Patrick Mason. Jno. Hart. Rich. Benslow, Mary Benslow (or Bentlow), Tymothy Ball, Wm. Conchant, Ed. Deacons. Mar. Foster, Ralph Birch, Hen. Short, Nich. Cooper, Walter Howell, Jno. Davis.

THOMAS BUTTON, 404 acs. Rappa. Co., upon the head of Hodgkins Cr., 4 Apr. 1667, p. 106. Beg. at a path by land of Lt. Coll. Goodrich, by lands of

Hodgskins & White, &c. Granted to John Gillett, now newly measured & due for trans. of 8 pers: Wm. Moore, Mr. Ty. Barne (?), Tho. Allen, Ed. Ells, Saml. Fanne (?), Mary Gossicke, Wm. Houseford, Jno. Jenkins.

MR. THOMAS WARREN, 200 acs. Surry Co., on the Black Water Sw., 22 Sept. 1667, p. 106. Beg. at a br. deviding this & land of Martyn Sheppard &c. Trans. of 4 pers: Alice Atkinson, John Wench (or Worth), Robt. Davis, Phillipp Sheringham.

MR. EDWARD PETTAWAY, 700 acs. Surry Co., on E. side of the maine br. of Crowche's Cr., 13 Dec. 1666, p. 107. Beg. at the Mill path, &c. to lands of Jno. Twye & George Foster. Trans. of 14 pers: Geo. Coney, Jno. Markle, Owen Ridley, Arthur Harris, James a Negro, Margery Ashton, Isaiah Delaman, Jacob Fisher, Phill Hall, Anthony Black, Nich. Merry, James Persey, Anne Howell, Mary Sheppard.

MRS. ANNE BRETT, 300 acs. W'moreland Co., S. side of Potomak Riv., 1 Oct. 1667, p. 107. N. W. on the head of Corawoman Cr., & adj. land of Walter Broadhurst, & Wm. Harditch, &c. Granted to Mr. Walter Broadhurst, 4 Sept. 1655, derserted, & now granted by order &c. (Note: The following names appear under this record:) Simon Ticknor, Joan Thomas, Wm. Ratliff, Jno. Stone, Peter Gill, Eliz. Cary.

MR. JOHN PAGE, 1900 acs. New Kent Co., S. side of Yorke Riv. & freshes thereof, 14 Mar. 1672, p. 107. Beg. at upper bounds of Mr. John Winsloe's land &c. Trans. of 28 pers: Wm. Betts, Mary Worley, Eliz. Cane, Jno. Flowers, Nich. Hammer (or Hamner), Edmond Almond, Hanah Millington, Hester Wensworth, Wm. Edenborough, Eliz. Winstopher, Wm. Pestell, Arth. Price, 2, Rich. Russell, Wm. Cooke, Eliz. Russell, Henry Sheriff, Tho. Teale, Wm. Cooke, Margaret Scott, Tho. Sloper, Jno. Palmer, Xtopher. Linkton, Wm. Ruttledge, Ben. Galattby, Fra. Williams, Tho. Batts, Sara Gillifer. Jno. Jaques. Mary Bretty, Eliz. Townsend, Tho. Cotton, Edwd. Cox, Allice Penny, Saml. Crabtree, Jno. Dunkley.

SAME. 1700 acs., same Co. & date, p. 108. S. side Yorke Riv. on both sides of Totopomoyes Cr., beg. in line of Mr. Moses Davis, over Powhite path &c. Trans. 34 pers: Joseph Teterson (or Teverson), Joseph Davis, Edwd. Berry, Robt. Goodman, Tho. Caplin, Wm. Grant, Joseph Mounford, Geo. Frowd, Robt. Griffith, Wm. Batod (?), Jno. Dyer, Cha. Wood, Geo. Nuccles, Ann Standige, Wm. Ruggle, Eliz. Griffith, Mary Johnson, Elenor Brotherhood, Mary Sherman, Samll. Seane (or Seare), Jno. Johnson, Jno. Davis, Fran. Fisher, Joseph Carpenter, Edwd. Eglestone, Dorothy Browne, Richd. Davis, Jno. Fossett, Mary Hunt, Sara Yates. Barbary Abbot, Richd. Drury, Edwd. Newton, Ann Langley.

RICHARD TUNSTALL, 1368 acs. New Kent Co., N. side of Mattapony Riv., 25 Apr. 1667, p. 108. 500 acs. knowne by the name of *Aquintenockco* & formerly granted to Robert Abrahall; 200 acs. lying on land of Rich. Barnehouse, beg. at the N. of Aquintenocco Cr., down the Riv. to mouth of Apostecoake, joyning upon land of Barnes, &c. 700 acs. granted Coll. Robt. Arahall, who assigned to sd. Tunstall; & 668 for trans. of 14 pers: Abraham Harman, Jno. Blackstock, Saml. Harrison, Jno. Whitlyn, Joane Barrett, Jno. Miller, Anne Collins, Jno. Waller, Rich. Parkson, Antho. Wells, Tho. Smurford, Kath. Davys, Jno. Rice, Edw. Nicholls.

JOHN WINSLOE, Gent., 600 acs. New Kent Co., S. E. side of Mattapony Riv., (date blank), p. 109. 500 acs. upon a br. of sd. Riv. &c. to br. of a swamp deviding this & a lower devdt. of Mr. Wm. Wyatt &c; 100 acs. over against the S. of sd. Winsloe, against the house of Thomas Soanes &c., by the house of James Coale &c. 500 acs. part granted Coll. Robert Abrahall, 20 Feb. 1654 & assigned to sd. Winsloe; & 100 acs. for trans. of 2 pers: Phillip Purlon (or Purton), Mary Bristoll.

MR. CHARLES ROANE, 401 A. & 40 Ch., Chas. Citty Co., 7 Aug. 1667, p. 109. Beg. upon N. side of Kittawan Cr. &c. to the Oystershell Landing in Moyses Cr. &c. Trans. of 9 pers.*

SAME. 50 acs., same Co., date & page. S. side Kittawan Cr., beg. upon lowermost end of Weyanock upon James Riv., down same to the mouth of sd. Cr., up the same to Andrew Milderum's Landing &c. Trans. of 1 pers.*

THOMAS NORCOTT, 472 acs. in the W. br. of Eliz. Riv., adj. lands of James Harris, Thomas Wright & Richi Starnell; 30 Aug. 1665, p. 110. 200 acs. granted to Jno. Dereard (Debar ?— See Vol. I, pp. 228-234) & assigned to sd. Norcott, & 272 for trans. —— pers.*

MR. ROBERT FLACKE, 2400 acs. Isle of Wight Co., on branches of the black water, (date blank), p. 110. Beg. on W. side of the 2nd swamp by Jno. a Pounch (or Jnoa. Pounch), his quarter &c. to the 3rd sw. &c., to Jno. Oliver & Thomas Wombwell &c. 1970 acs. by former patt. to sd. Flacke & 430 acs. for trans. of 9 pers.* (Re-recorded on p. 273).

CAPT. THOMAS GODWIN (Godwyn), 179 acs. in Chuccatuck Parrish, adj. lands of Hopkin Howell, Jeremy Rutter, Jno. Dukes, Tho. Beest & Jno. Thomas. 6 Feb. 1667, p. 111. Trans. of 4 pers: Mary Yates, Mary Eggleston, Henry Holt, John Price.

GILES WEBB, 681 acs. Lancaster Co., N. side of Rappa. Riv., & running to E.most br. of Richards Cr., 18 Feb. 1667, p. 111. Granted to Toby Smith, Gent., 10 Mar. 1652 & sold to sd. Webb 5 Feb. 1653.

MR. WILLIAM TRAVERS, 2650 acs. N. side of Rappa. Co., 27 Feb. 1667/8, p. 112. 2250 acs. granted to Mr. Thomas Chetwood & George Hasellock & by them assigned to sd. Travers; 400 acs. for trans. of 8 pers: Wm. Travers, Rebecca Travers, Rich. Harris, James Benning, Lancelott Fletcher, James Bird, Jno. Arler, Joane Claydon.

PARRISH OF SOUTHWARKE, Surry Co., 200 acs. for a Gleebe, 1 Dec. 1666, p. 112. N'ly. by land of John Watkins, Mr. Thomas Woodhouse & Francis Sowerby, E'ly. by land of Thomas Grey & S'ly. & W'ly. by the maine woods.

RICHARD YEATES, 450 acs. in S. br. of Eliz. Riv., bet. lands of Francis Sawyer & his own, 13 Mar. 1667/8, p. 112. 300 acs. granted to Capt. Tho. Willoby, 28 Feb. 1636, assigned to Jno. Yeates & due sd. Richd. as heire of Jno., & 150 acs. for trans. of 3 pers.* Note: Rights out of a relinquished patt. dated 4 May, 1636, granted to Rich. Yeates the elder.

JOHN CHYNN, 370 acs. upon a br. of Moratico Cr., adj. land of Edward Miles; 17 Mar. 1667/8, p. 113. Granted to David Fox, Gent., assigned to Lambeth Lambethson, who assigned to Alexander Portus, by him assigned to Thomas Williams, who assigned to John Chynn & Henry Davis, & sd. Davis assigned his title to sd. Chynn.

JOHN CHYNN & JOHN GIBSON, of Lancaster Co., 550 acs. in Rappa. Co., 17 Mar. 1667/8, p. 113. Beg. by the Draggon Swampe & adj. land of John Colles, &c. Trans. of 11 pers: John Johnson, James Johnson, Henry Woodbridge, Anne Wilson, Wm. Harman Robt. Flering, Francis Dolphin, Rich. Mills, Jno. Medler (?), Wm. Baker, Rich. Parker.

JOHN SEXTON, 1000 acs. New Kent Co., N. side Yorke Riv., 16 Mar. 1667/8, p. 114. Beg. in line of Mr. Woodward & adj. lands of Mr. Arnold & Mr. Sneade. Trans. of 20 pers: Wm. Ashley, Nicho. Coote, Amy Spratt, Eliz. Holmes, Geo. Winter, Wm. Fox, Abram Vickers, Wm. Carey, Peter White, Susan Swann, Wm. Thomas, Susan White, Wm. Ivey, Grego. Rawlins, James Wilson, Edw. Smith, Alex. Gardner, Jno. Mathewes, Fran. Cox, James Collis.

CORNELIOUS DABONY (Debany), 300 acs. New Kent Co., S. side Yorke Riv., above Totopotomoyes Cr., beg. at the mouth of same; 16 Mar. 1667/8, p. 114. 200 acs. granted to him 27 Sept. 1664; & 100 acs. due for trans. of 2 pers: Joane Winter, Besse an Indian.

MR. WILLIAM WOODWARD & JOHN BORRAS, 179 acs. New Kent Co., N. side of Yorke Riv., 17 Mar.

1667, p. 115. On Mr. Woodward's land, beg. by Mr. Johns Cr. &c., to Manskin Path, &c. (Note: the following names appear hereunder;) Wm. Sheppard, Emanuel Mason, Rich. Scondrett, Edward Howard; Wm. Donn, James Goffe (or Gosse), Jacob Parry, Kathe. Whitney. Note: "Last 4 rights due to Mr. Clayborne."

MAJOR GENERALL ROBERT SMITH, 550 acs., Lancaster Co., S. side of Rappa. Riv., & formerly in possession of Edward Bosswell. 29 Nov. 1667, p. 115. S. W. upon Obert's Cr., Sunderland Cr. on N. W., Henry Nicholls land on the W. & running to Thompson's Swamp, a br. of Obert's Cr. Granted to Sir William Berkeley & by him assigned to sd. Smith, 12 Nov. 1666.

SAME. 1900 acs. Rappa. Co., in the freshes & S. side the river, about a mile from the river or bay side of *Potobago*, 20 Mar. 1667, p. 116. Beg. neere the head of the Eastermost br. of Potobago Cr. Trans. of 38 pers: Wm. Danyell, Tho. Dawkins, Roger Shawcocke, Rich. Bostocke, Tho. Sealeby, Abra. Lawes, Jno. Kirke, Wm. Skelton, Jno. Godfrey, Jno. Blasson, Tho. Wingate, Geo. Davyes, Pet. Bennett, Wm. Hill, Wm. Lacy, Fra. Street, Robt. Lee, Jno. Brownen, Hen. Ball, Tho. Rapier, Tho. Wroth, Rich. Thompson, Robt. Whitehorn, Mathew Stevenson, Xpofer. Jeames, Tho. Browne, Wm. Worrell, Wm. Chapman, Geo. Breeding, Charles Chipp, Mary Turner, Anne Lynbey, Eliz. Clarke, Jno. Morgan, Eliz. Pellington, German Gillott & 2 Negroes.

JOHN WAKEFIELD & JOHN SHERER, 1050 acs. Isle of Wight Co., on branches of the first Sw. of the Black Water, 5 Apr. 1668, p. 116. Adj. Cooke's lyne & their own land. 700 acs. granted to Xpofer. Lewis 26 July 1652 & by him sold to the above; & 350 acs. for trans. of 7 pers: Tristram Eaton, Luke Mansens, Merrick Edwards, Robert Sampson, Merlin Cant, Joseph Baker, Francis Rippington.

HENRY CORBYN, Esqr., 5776 acs. Rappa. Co., S. side sd. Riv., 29 Nov. 1667, p. 117. Beg. at the mouth of

Weire Cr. on the E. side, adj. land formerly Richard White's, now Mr. Robt. Talliferoe's, crossing the mouth of Pasabetank Cr., with lyne of Abraham Moon, dec'd., &c. to a hill nere a valey called *Solomons Garden* &c. 4000 acs. by purchase of the right formerly John Gillett's, dec'd., etc. 1776 acs. by order of the Gov'r. &c. as wast land & due by & for the charge of shipping 36 pers. aboard the *Virga. Merchant,* Mr. Buley, Comander, who was cast away comeing for this country Coll. Lee haveing had the benefitt in the like kind by order of the Quarter Court, dated 18 Oct. 1660.

MR. HENRY KING, 1000 acs. Isle of Wight Co., on the first br. of the black water, 18 Apr. 1668, p. 117. 900 acs. beg. in the Swampe, a br. parting this from land of Phill. Hunniford &c. 750 acs. granted to Jno. Sweet, 26 Sept. 1643 & by' sd. King's father long since purchased of sd. Sweet; 100 acs. purchased of Francis England & 250 acs. for trans. of 5 pers: Cutbert Fletcher, Ferdinando Downe, Wm. Edmonds, Joshua Gibson, Robt. Read.

MR. WM. LOYD, 2467 acs., 18 Apr. 1668, p. 118 Beg. at a main run of Rappa. Cr., along Coll. Peyton's marked trees &c. Payment to be made from the first entry of survey dated 29 Oct. 1666. Due for trans. of 49 pers: John Smith, Anne Smith, Giles Smith, Tho. Duke, Bridgett Edwards, Math. Stakes, Key Kelley, Mary Blunt, Mary Usher (?), Ann Jones, Frances Priest, Wm. Rosse, Hen. Martyn, Tho. Just, Phill, Flowre, Wm. Raydon, Rachell Williams, Margaret Williams, Bridgett Batchellor, August Wickey, Wm. Lewis, Jno. James, Eliz. Wood, Lydia How, Wm. Badger, Jno. Badger, Jno. Gaffer (or Gasser), Danl. Merricke, Tho. Jones, Ed. Seare, Ed. Ramsey, Anne Ramsey, Wm. Garrett, Wm. Thornebery, Abra. Woodward, Jno. Hart, Alex. Spencer, Eliz. Dely, Thomas Palmer, Wm. Proctor, Mihill Withers, Tho. Collins, Mary Gissell, Patience Rouse, Wm. Paulett, Tho. Bird, Wm. Allett, Tho. Perry, Jno. Please, Eliz. Cooper.

SAME. 1300 acs., Rappa. Co., same date & page. Beg. at land of Major

Peircyes (Piercys), to main br. of Rappa. Cr., S. upon Mr. Lord &c. Trans. of 26 pers: Bernard Winefry, Anne Wood, Tho. Small, Wm. Carr, Rich. Grimston, Avered Danl. (Daniel), John Fish, Ellenor Parker, Geo. Parker, Step. Pinder, Jo. Miller, Jno. Gregory, Jermar. Hopkins, Rebecca Parry, Julyan Crow, Tho. Coggan, Eliz. Willett, Jno. Harwell, Jno. Paider, James Moore, John Waddell, Wm. Lenox, Andrew Marshall, Wm. Read, Robt. Duckett, David Sadler (?).

DAVID JENINGS, 320 acs., N'umberland Co., at the head & on the S. side of Gr. Wiccocomico Riv., 18 Apr. 1668, p. 119. Beg. on the N. side of a br. or sw. of sd. river called Pope's Sw. dividing this & land of Dr. Edwd. Saunders, & adj. James Pope &c. to S. side of Machoatick horse path &c. Trans. of 7 pers: Wm. Tippett, Jno. Hilliard, Peter Rogers, Jno. Gibbs, Wm. Pitt, Robt. Williams, Jno. Thistletoe.

JAMES POPE & JAMES HILL, 790 acs. N'umberland Co., on S. side of the main br. of Gr. Wiccocomico Riv., 18 Apr. 1668, p. 119. Beg. at land of Rich. Iliffe &c., to a br. of Corotomon Riv., nigh Machoatick path &c. to their other lands. Trans. of 16 pers: Jno. Goosy, Boaz Hollis, Ann Owen, Tho. White, Ann White, Edwd. White, Tho. White, Ann White, Wm. Fowler, Jos. Draper, Tho. Draper, Joan White, Hanna White, James Hill, James Lucer (or Lucas), Wm. Smart. Note: 10 acs. due.

MR. JOHN BARKER, 916 acs. Surry Co., 7 May. 1667, p. 119. 600 acs. on the N. side of James Riv. about 7 or 8 mi. from the head of Up. Chipoakes Cr., beg. on the E. side of the maine br. of Black Water called the Beavor Sw., over a br. of same to the Division Sw., & 316 acs. adj. same, beg. on the E. side of Bevor Dam Sw. &c. 600 acs. granted sd. Barker 20 Oct. 1661, & 316 acs. for trans. of 6 pers: Jno. Barker, Tomson Wood, Jno. Gilbert, 3 Negroes: Frank, Cube & Bab.

PETER SMITH, 400 acs. Low. Norf. Co., in a br. of the W. br. of Eliz. Riv., 19 Apr. 1668, p. 120. 200 acs. beg. on

the E. side of Loyd's Cr., by Edmond Bowman, running to mouth of Reedy Br., through the Swampe &c. 200 acs. beg. by the Cr. side, adj. his own land &c. 200 acs. granted sd. Smith 9 Dec. 1665, & 200 acs. for trans. of 4 pers: Hen. Harper, Tho. Dunning, Tho. Beale, John Marston.

HENRY CORBIN, Esqr.; 1390 acs. on N. side of Rappa. Co. in the freshes, about 550 po. from the river side; 25 Mar. 1667/8, p. 120. Beg. at a beavor dam at land surveyed for Sir Henry Chichly, Knight, next Gingoatege Cr., by the main run of same &c., crossing severall branches of Poetris Cr., &c. Trans. of 28 pers.*

JAMES JOPE, 150 acs. N'umberland Co., on S. side of the main br. of Gr. Wiccocomico Riv., 18 Apr. 1668, p. 121. Beg. in a br. of Pope's Sw. dividing this & land of Mr. Edward. Saunders, &c. Trans. of 3 pers: James Hill, James Luker, Wm. Hobson.

PHILLIP LUDWELL, 200 acs. Rappa. Co., on Gilson's Cr., 17 Apr. 1667, p. 121. Part of 1000 acs. granted to John Pate, who sold to Isaac Matheson, who lost for want of seating & now due by order &c., for trans. of 4 pers: Tho. Wattson, Jacob Henson, Peter Prow, Jno. Triggs.

CAPT. CHRISTOPHER WORMLY, 800 acs., Rappa. Co., on S. side of the main sw. of Mr. Andrew Gilson's Cr., 22 Apr. 1668, p. 121. Part of 1000 acs. taken up by Mr. Jno. Pate, by pattent dated 31 Dec; 800 acs. sold by sd. Pate to Capt. Rich. Hobbs, who lost for want of seating & now due sd. Wormly by order &c., & for transs. of 16 pers: Jno. Snow, Jno. Smoole, Wm. Tuck, James Winter, Robt. Fowler, Peter Perton, Jno. Hockly, Tho. Quigg, Peter Rutt, Jno. Sprigg, Ann House, James Taylor, Jno. Trelany, Wm. Petterson, Henry Howell, Tho. Poole.

MR. PETER MELLS, 450 acs. Rappa. Co., on N. side the river, 17 Apr. 1667 p. 121. Beg. opposite a gr. mare down the river &c. to land of Tho. Hopkins, dec'd. &c. 400 acs. due in right of his father, as by patent dated 6 Sept. 1654; & 50 acs. for trans. of: Jno. Phillipps.

MR. FRANCIS HAILE, 1865 acs. Rappa. Co., in the freshes on N. side the Riv., 17 Apr. 1668, p. 122. 565 acs. beg. on E. side of the mouth of Pye Cr., adj. land he now lives upon; 1300 acs. granted sd. Haile & Mr. Wm. Heabert, 9 Feb. 1663 & now assigned to sd. Haile; beg. on W. side of a small run, crossing the Doegs Path &c. 565 acs. due for trans. of 12 pers: Jno. Holt, Ralph Eckston, Ellinor Paige, Jno. Richardson, Nich. Parker, Mary Sanders, Tho. Hart, Jeter Penington, Seth Mason, Danll. Potts, Wm. Palmer, Robt. Maw.

MR. JAMES YATES, 300 acs. Rappa. Co., in the freshes & on N. side the Riv., 17 Apr. 1668, p. 122. Beg. on the S. W. side of the maine br. of Perpetick (or Propetick) Cr., N. of land of Mr. George Baley, to land of Wm. Mills &c. Trans. of 6 pers: Jno. Phillipps, Jno. Wood, Mary Dawfeild, Tho. Barber, Daniell Thorne, Jno. Burtt.

MATHEW BARRATT, 300 acs. Rappa. Co., 17 Apr. 1668, p. 122. Beg. on E. side of Rappa. Cr., next below the horse bridge or roade, &c. Being part of a greater tract belonging to Jasper Griffin & purchased by sd. Barratt of Jno. Sibly & Antho. Garratt, who bought of sd. Jasper

MR. DANIELL WILD, 1484 acs. York Co., 19 Mar. 1662, p. 123. 795 acs. beg. at Tho. Smith's land on the main sw. br. of the old Mill Sw. on Queens Cr., to Skimino Sw., up the same athwart Rickahock Path, to W.most br. of Skimino Cr., along the Hott Water Path &c; 669 acs. 47 chs. beg. on W. of a br. of said Sw., in line of Tho. Smith, by Rich. Ford's land, along Warranie Path &c; 64 acs. 149 po. beg. on W. side of a br. dividing this & land of Tho. Meekins, neer the cart path, by land of Alex. Walker &c. 750 acs. granted to sd. Wild & Phillip Chesly 10 June 1654 & by sd. Chesly & Margarett, his wife, assigned to sd. Wild; 669 acs. 47 chs. assigned by Francis Kirkman; & 64 acs. 149 po. assigned by James Harris.

WM. LIGHT, Marrinor, 812 acs. Henrico Co., S. side of James Riv., commonly called St. Kitts, 23 Apr. 1668, p. 123. 172 acs. assigned by Col. Tho. Stegge, 8 Feb. 1664; 640 acs. newly taken up, beg. on the Riv. side, running into two slashes which run into trampling place run, which goes into Stony Cr., & adj. his own & land of Robt. Huson. Sd. land due for trans. of 13 pers.*

MR. THOMAS TOOKE, 1228 acs. Isle of Wight Co., 9 May 1667, p. 124. Beg. in the maine swamp, adj. his 800 acs., down the Ashen Swamp &c. 800 acs. granted to his father; 178 acs. granted him 9 Mar. 1662; & 250 acs. for trans. of 5 pers: Jno. Walton, Francis Wren, Eliz. Brumidge (or Brunridge), Ralph Harton, Abram Harmon.

JNO. BOWEN & GEORGE SOONES, 689 acs. Rappa. Co., on head branches of Rappa. Cr., neer Mr. Wm. Laine, 17 Apr. 1668, p. 124. Trans. of 14 pers: Wm. Horne, Jno. Harper, Peter Hartly, Tho. Petty, Wm. Draper, Wm. Smith.

JOHN MATHEWES, 1050 acs. Stafford Co., formerly part of W'moreland, 25 Apr. 1668, p. 125. 550 acs. beg. on the W.most side of the S. W. br. of Pasbetansey Cr., opposite land of David Anderson, formerly Abraha. Rouse; 500 acs. adj. same. 550 acs. granted to John Dainely, Merchant, 4 Sept. 1661, who sold to Tho. Pritchett & Francis West, 5 Mar. 1661, who sold to David Anderson, 3 Feb. 1662, who sold to sd. Mathewes 25 Mar. 1668; 500 acs. granted to Xpofer. Lunn, 18 Mar. 1662, who sold to Wm. Horton 24 Feb. 1663, who assigned to sd. Mathewes 17 Dec. 1667.

HENRY COSSUM, 450 acs. W'moreland Co., 17 Apr. 1668, p. 125. 550 acs. on the Bever Damms a br. of Up. Machotike, beg. upon Tho. Davys &c. 100 acs. beg. in a fork of Herring Cr., to land of John Bruton &c. 350 acs. granted to Arthur Shoare, dec'd. & sd. Cossum, 4 Sept. 1661 & now due him as survivor; & 100 acs. being all that is to be found of a pattent of 543 acs. to Capt. Jno. Ashton, 16 Nov. 1664 by whom it was let fall & now granted by order &c., for trans. of 2' pers.* *Note:* These rights transferred from a patt. of Jno. Ashton's, dated 16 Nov. 1668.

THOMAS & HENRY BATTS, sonns of Mr. Jno. Batts, dec'd., 5878 A., 2 R. 8 Po., S. side James Riv., in *Appomatock,* Chas. City Co., 29 Apr. 1668, p. 126. Beg. at the heads of Jordan's land & Mirchants Hope, &c. to the head of Chas. City Cr. &c. Trans. of 118 pers: Jno. Grace, Nich. Thetcher, Tho. Bridge, Tho. Stephenson, Jno. Whitfeild, Tho. Overton, Danll. Scott, Antho. Foxcroft, Thristrum Knowles, Abra. Drure, Tho. Lake, Alice Lake, Roger Mallory, Ed. Eslome, Joan Thomas, Mary Ireland, Wm. Bate, Jun. 2 times, Martha Bate, Dr. Samll. Sickleman (?), Jno. Bate, Senr., Jno. Batte, Junr., Wm. Batte, Tho. Batte, Hen. Batte, Phillip Mallery, Nath. Mallery, Sen., Nath. Mallery, Junr., Wm. Mallorv, Tho. Mallory, Eliz. Mallary, Xpher. Denby, Jno. Denbeigh, Tho. Holford, Anne Holford, Jno. Adams, Hen. Doughty, Timothy Doughty, Rich. Oldfeild, Jno. Chiloe, Francis Terringham, Deverell (Averell) Franke, Edmund Key, Robt. Pollard, Ed. Scofeild, Jervis Kitson, Jno. Carter, Ed. Bryan, Ri. Bigland, Mary Key, Eliz. Key, Anne Pollard, Ellen Harris, Luce Crosland, Wm. Wood, Jno. Millicent, Jno. Morrell, Tho. Walker, Jno. Vickars, Danll. Foxcroft, Pare Fereman, Jno. Amanson, Tho. Harris, Sebrough Stringer, James Strettell, Nich. Poole, Tho. Wise, Tho. Hanson, Rich. Horsfall, Tho. Pollard, Jno. Key, Senr., Wm. Key, Rich. Wood, James Barron, Senr., Tho. Colebeck, Grace Horsfall, Eliz. Preistley, Eliz. Key, Dorothy Key, Susan Key, Eliz. Key, Judith Horsfall, Jane Watson, Margaret Newis, Jennet Hoyle, Dorothy Kennersly, Jno. Key, Junr., Abraham Kay, Jno. Moore, James Barron (or Barrow), Junr., Anne Taylor, Susannah King, Anne Tutin, Antho. Pursley, John Tagger, Roger Speake, Wm. Watson, Jno. Watson, Robt. Stocks, Robt. Crowder, Jno. Wood, Arthur Shoore, Hen. Preistley, Wm. Sickes, Fra. Greathead, Geo. Dawson, Jno. Fowler, Jno. Smeale, Marke Waterson, George Greene, Fra. Cartwright, Fra. Bell, Wm. Banks, Susanna Craven, Anne Kirkby, Hugh Boyd, Jno. Kinnersley, Margery Lambert, Agnes Taylor, Samll. Jrice.

MR. ROBERT PAYNE (Paine), 3141 acs., in the freshes of Rappa. Co., & River on the S. side. 27 Apr. 1668, p. 127. 179 acs. beside land of Jno. Meader, formerly Robert Thomlyn, &c. to a *pignutt tree* dividing this & land of Willm. Wilton, thence to Henerick Lucas &c., being part of a pattent to Alex. Fleming & John Ayres, 13 Jan. 1661 & sold to sd. Paine; 378 acs. adj., which was taken up by John Eyres, but never patented, & due him for trans. of 8 pers., & by him sold to sd. Payne; 2164 acs. beg. at land of Peter Cornwell, running to a white oak dividing sd. Cornewell & Mr. Danll. Gaines' land neare Cattayle Br. made by Mr. Tho. Lucas, Senr. Creeke, crossing Cockle Cr., thence neare Chickahominy Path &c; 416 acs. nere the 378 acs., running to land of Henry Lucas, James Coghill, Potobago Path &c. 2164 acs. taken up by sd. Payne & Wm. Hodgson, but not pattented, & by sd. Hodgson & Onah (?), his wife, assigned to sd. Payne; 416 acs. taken up by sd. Payne; the sd. 2580 acs. *granted sd. Payne by the name of Davis,* 25 Sept. 1665. (*Note:*) The following names appear under this record: Jno. Ayres, Fran. Tunning, Marmaduke Short, Ed. Holdip, Mary Bell, Wm. Frith, Jane Day, Martyn Wood.

JNO. PALMER, 500 acs. Staff. Co., on a br. of Up. Machotick Dam, 17 Apr. 1668, p. 128. Granted unto Robt. Alexander, 23 Mar. 1664, assigned to Robert King & Jno. Parbin (or Parkin), deserted & upon petition granted to sd. Palmer, & due for trans. of 10 pers: Tho. Burton, Hen. Gottell, Mary Story, Wm. Sattaway, Ed. Burr, Eliz. Sanders, Jno. Sorrell, Wm. Burr, Tho. Ratting, Hump. Tolwood

DAVID ANDERSON, 800 acs. Staff. Co., 27 Apr. 1668, p. 130. 400 acs. bounded with w'most br. of Pasbetancy Cr., beg. on lyne of Wm. & Jno. Habeard; & 400 beg. at S. E. cor of sd. land, &c. 400 acs. granted unto Tho. Friswell, 19 Aug. 1659, assigned to Abra. Rouse, who assigned to Mr. Gerrard Fouke, who assigned to Wm. Tilt, who assigned to sd. Fowke, who assigned to sd. Anderson; & 400 acs. for trans. of 8 pers.* "The rights due to this patt. is Transfer'd from a patt. of Jno. Ashtons Dated 16th November 1664."

MR. FRANCIS CAMPFEILD, 314 acs. Gloster Co., 10 Apr. 1668, p. 130. Beg. in Mr. Cooke's line, to head of Crabbtree Br., to the head of the broad br., to the W. side of the Indian path road &c. Trans. of 6 pers: Wm. Harvy, Jno. Roberts, Rich. Peake, Nic. Reinolds, Stephen Pore, Cha. Gualter.

MR. WILLIAM BOWLIN, 807 acs., Abington Parrish, Gloster Co., 14 Apr. 1668, p. 131. Beg. at a small cr. dividing this & land of Coll. Augustine Warner, to Edwd. Wills, to Kerbye's w.o., to swamp dividing this & land of Mr. Law. Smith, &c. 750 acs. granted Mr. David Fox, in 1648 & assigned to sd. Bowlin; & 137 acs. for trans. of 3 pers: Jno. Cheney, Peter Hicks, Wm. Preston.

JOSEPH BAYLEY, 1215 acs. N. side of Lancaster Co., 7 June 1666, p. 131. Upon a main br. of Corrotoman. Trans. of 25 pers: Geo. Hearne, Jane Steddick, Ann Lorkin, Robt. Medcalfe, Angell Sanderson, Jno. Russell, Robt. Sutton, Rich. Wharton, Tho. Roe, Wm. Vaughan, Henry Burcher, Wm. Davies, Geo. Brockes (or Broches), Phill Snead, Robt. Hunt, Edward Turner, Rich. Harding, Walter Smith, Jno. Hatton, James Hide, Fran. White, Nich. Hill, Geo. Leads, Robt. Bread, Mary Brett. Marginal Note: "This pattent false drawne & rights made use of."

ROBT. JEFFERSON, 92 acs. Gloster Co., 10 Apr. 1668, p. 131. N. side of Crane Neck Cr. Sw., beg. at Mr. Regault's (Rigault), land, by the Bay path &c. Trans. of 2 pers: Wm. Powell, Martha Cookett, Tho. Killerson.

JAMES HAWLEY, 700 acs. N'umberland Co., 7 June 1666, p. 132. On S. side of Potomack & head br. of Machoatick Riv., beg. at George Watts. Trans. of 14 pers: Tho. Dutton, Hump. Watkins, Edward Taylor, Ambrose Taylor, Fran. Phillips, Nich. Price, Wm.

Herbert, Tho. Morgan, Arthur Sands, Geo. Loe, Saml. Porter, Giles Walker, Jno. Tomkins, Rich. Seaborne. Marginal Note: "In this patt. there was errors & is amended & recorded in folio 152."

RICH. RICE, 188 acs. N'umberland Co., 7 June 1666, p. 132. Upon a devdt. of sd. Rice's & Tho. Addams' upon branches of Chickacone; &c. Trans. of 4 pers: Wm. King, Martin Parry, Joseph Edgrome (or Edgcome), Ralph Poole.

ABRAM JOYCE & RICH. THOMPSON, 200 acs. N'umberland Co., 7 Mar. 1666, p. 132. Upon land of Tho. Adams & Phillip Carpenter, Henry Roach & Geo. Courtney & Walter Weekes. Trans. of 4 pers: Mary Evans, Susan Hollady, Mary Spicer, Jno. Britton.

THO. CHETWOOD & WM. THOMAS, 176 acs. N'umberland Co., 7 Mar. 1666, p. 133. Upon Cowpen Cr., beg. at a cr. parting this from land of Capt. Rogers where hee now liveth. Trans. of 4 pers: Roger Parsons, Rich. Atkins, Robt. Stevens, Robt. Surbett (or Sarbett).

THOMAS ADDAMS & RICHARD RICE, 700 acs., (Co. not given) 7 Mar. 1666, p. 133. 400 acs. betwixt 2 maine branches at the head of Chickacone Riv., &c. & 300 acs. by the maine br. called Tuckahoe Sw. Trans. of 14 pers: Wm. Southcott, Jno. Jennings, Thomas Garratt, Wm. Copeman, Morgan Osborne, Tho. Bliss, Wm. Lee, Tim Cardis, Mary Cardiff (or Cardiss), Stephen Hopwell, Jno. Bennett, Jno. Carter, James Blackmore, Robt. Clarke (or Clanke).

WM. GRAY & XTOPR. BLACKBORNE, 775 acs. S. side Rappa. Co., 29 June 1666, p. 134. Adj. James Gaynes & a sw. at the head of Occupacon Cr. Trans. 16 pers: Ed. Hill, Wm. Hackney, Vall. Wallis, Saml. Clanke (or Clarke), Jno. Peteridge, Robt. Norris, Wm. Ram, Geo. Baker, Wm. Miller, Ri. Wells, Geo. Dyer, Eliz. Wood, Mary Martin, James Potter, Jno. Scollding, Rich. Parrott.

HENRY LEADBEATER (Ledbetter), 224 acs., S. side of Appomatock Riv., 29 Apr. 1668, p. 134. Adj. land of Robt. Coleman at head of land where he now liveth. 125 acs. part of 250 ac. patt. sould by Ed. Tunstall to sd. Leadbeater's father; 99 acs. for trans. of 2 pers: Margery Lucas, Mary House.

JOHN MAYES (Maies), sonne of Wm. Maies, dec'd., 293 A., 2 R., 33 P., Chas. City Co., S. side of Appomatock Riv., 29 Apr. 1668, p. 134. 125 acs. part of 250 ac. patt. sold by Ed. Townstall to sd. Wm., & adj. Maies land, along Samll. Woodward's line &c. to lower end of the gr. Sw. 168 acs. part for trans. of 4 pers:. Jno. Bird, Sazel Berry (?), Jeremy Right, Wm. Belvett (or Beloett).

GEO. WORSNAM (Worsam), sonne of Geo. Worsnam, dec'd., 399 A., 10 P., Henrico Co., Bristow. Parish, N. W. side of Apomatock Riv., 29 Apr. 1668, p. 135. 200 acs. part of 1100 acs. granted to Wm. Clarke, 6 May 1636, who sold to Leonard Laughton, 29 Oct. 1638, by him to Seath Ward as deed at James Citty, 24 Sept. 1640;. & for better confirmation the widow Dorothy Clarke surrendered sd. land to sd. Ward at a court held at Verina 23 Mar. 1640, who assigned 200 acs. part & 300 acs. to Wm. Worsnam, &c. Sd. 200 acs. beg. at the Old Towne & Cr., to land of John Wilson, along an old known fence to outside bounds of the grand pattent; 199 acs. from sd. 200 acs., towards Swift Cr., downe old Towne Cr. &c. 199 acs. for trans. of 4 pers: Sarah Ashpoole, Thos. Ellett, Elizabeth Idering, Mary Records.

HEN. REEVES, 150 acs. Nancemond Co., 17 Mar. 1672/3, p. 135. At the head of Chuckatuck Cr., adj. Richd. Lewis, John Howell & his own land. Trans. of 3 pers: John Ellin, Katherine Kately, Elizabeth Hill.

COL. JOHN CARTER, Esqr., of Rappa., 6160 acs. Lancaster Co., N. side Rappa. Riv., 27 Apr. 1668, p. 136. Beg. at the mouth of Corotoman Riv., down Rappa. Riv. to mouth of Slaughters alias Johns Cr. & now known as Coll. Carter's Cr., to Mr. Ironmonger's land, to mouth of Hutchins' Cr., along Wm. Hutchins' & John Meredith's lands to Sw. dividing this & land of Wm. Clapham, Senr. &c. 1600 acs. granted him 6 Sept. 1654; 560 acs. granted to Jno. Meredith, who sold to Mr. Geo. Marsh, by whom it was sold to sd. Carter, both of which parcells were put into one patt. 24 Jan. 1663; 4000 acs. being deserted by Samll. Mathews, Senr., Esqr., by order &c. granted sd. Carter 12 Oct. 1665.

MR. PETER KNIGHT, 574 acs. Gloster Co., E. side of Poropatanck Cr., 3 Apr. 1668, p. 137. Beg. at Tottapotamoyes Cr., adj. Mr. Fra. Ironmonger's Plantation, along Mr. Fra. Morgan's line to tancks Poropotanck (Cr.), to cor. of Purton dividend, &c. The sd. land pattented by sd. Knight 16 July, 1652 for 1000 acs., & on resurvey found to be 574 acs.

MR. WILLIAM HAWARD, 164 acs Gloster Co., in Petsoe Parrish, 1 Apr. 1668, p. 137. Beg. at path from Haward's house to Mr. Forsith's, by Rappa. Road, along Mr. Robert Lee's land &c. along land he lives upon, &c. Trans. of 4 pers: Joseph West, John Gunson, Eliz. Browne, Jno. Fryer.

TOBIAS HANSFORD, 324 acs. Gloster Co., Ware Parrish, 8 Jan. 1666, p. 138. Beg. at the mouth of Deepe Cr. in Mockjack Bay, along Christop. Robins, to the old feild, to mouth of Finches Cr., &c. Trans. of 7 pers: Richd. Jones, Tho. Dowler, Samll. Colebrook, Jno. Bennett, Tho. Brumfeild, Susan Titele, Jno. Newell, Jno. Yewin (or Pewin).

NATH. BROWNE, 500 acs. N. side Rappa. Riv., upon Deepe Cr., adj. land of Mr. Tho. Powell; 28 Apr. 1668, p. 138. 250 acs. part granted Geo. Vizee, & sd. Browne, 16 Mar. 1662, who assigned to sd. Browne; 250 acs. for trans. of 5 pers: Rich. Robinson, Eliz. his wife, Mr. Jno. Rayne, Sarah Grimsted, Jno. Norton.

JNO. NEWMAN & WILLIAM FITCHARBETT (Fitzharbett), 320 acs.

Rappa. Co., upon br. of Moratico, 28 Apr. 1668, p. 138. Adj. Mr. Glascocke, Mr. Travers & devdt. of sd. Newman & Paule Woodbrige, & land of Mr. Stephens. Trans. of 7 pers: Charity Winter, Lewis Thomas, Jno. Grange, Tho. Gandy, Tho. Archer, Eliz. Jacob, Anne Payne.

GEORGE SEATOUNE (Seatonne), 300 acs. Gloster Co., 16 Apr. 1668, p. 139. 200 acs. part granted to Geo. Thompson, 26 Nov. 1653, lying on the head of 1000 acs. formerly known as Coll. Hugh Gwynn's devdt. in the maine upon S. side of Peanketank Riv., adj. land surveyed for Coll. Humphrey Higginson; which sd. Thompson assigned to Edward Jelfe, who assigned to sd. Seatonne 2 May, 1659; 100 acs. by bill of sale from Oliver Bolfe to sd. Jelfe 19 Jan. 1653, who assigned to sd. Seatoune, running from the old man's Cr. at Peanketanke, unto William Lewis', &c.

CAPT. JOSIAS PICKUS, 420 acs. Rappa. Co., S. side sd. Riv., behind land of Sir Henry Chickley; 28 Mar. 1667, p. 139. Nigh the ridge path from Jno. Lacye's to Dr. Goodson's (Godson), by sd. Lacy's plantation to land of James Ellison, dec'd., over brs. of the Green Sw. of Killman Daynes (or Dayves), &c. Trans. of 9 pers: John Dix, Senr., John Dix, Junr., Hester Dix, Jno. Mitchill, Tho. Hynes, Grace Huball, Arthur Parker, Susan Walden, Mary Ansell.

THOMAS BLAND, MARY his wife, & to the heirs of the said Mary, 750 acs. Up. Par. of Is. of Wight Co., 1 June 1664, and recorded 21 May, 1668, p. 140. Beg. nere James Riv. on land in the tenure of Willm. Lewer, by Filgate's Island, &c. to Pollington's poynt, by Mr. Taberer, to Peter Hull, to br. of Hutchinson's Cr. to land of Major Nicho. Hill. Part of 1500 acs. granted to Rich. Bennett, Esqr., who assigned to sd. Hill as properly belonging to Mary Bland & Silvester the wife of sd. Hill, as by deed of partition 8 Apr. 1663, bet. Theo. Bland, Esqr., Atty. of Thomas Bland & sd. Mary his wife, & sd. Major Hill & Silvester his wife, now belonging to sd. Thomas & Mary, &c.

JOHN LACY, 370 acs. Rappa. Co., behind land of James Ellison, dec'd., above land of Tobias Smith, & adj. land sold to Capt. Josias Pickus; 28 Mar. 1667, p. 140. Beg. nigh the Ridge path from sd. Lacye's to Dr. Goodson's, by Kilman's Sw. &c. 100 acs. granted sd. Lacy & Roger Overton, 18 Mar. 1663/4; & 270 for trans. of 6 pers: Robert Marshall, Robert Newton, Mary Smart, Obadiah Sprouson, Rich. Vezey, Marmaduke Jones.

JOHN COLE, 287 acs. Rappa. Co., upon Peanketanke Sw., some 2 mi. from Capt. Clayborne's quarter, opposite land formerly John Maddison's; 28 Mar. 1667, p. 141. Trans. of 6 pers.* Note: The rights transferred from a patt. of Wm. Burford's for 640 acs., dated 3 Feb. 1663, & by him relinquished.

MR. ROBERT GRIGGS, 800 acs. Lancaster Co., N. side Rappa. Riv., at head of Col. Carter's Cr., 1 June 1668, p. 141. 160 acs. adj. 640 acs. granted him 24 Mar. 1664, lands of John Cone, Abia Bonyson, the Gleebe Land, &c. Trans. of 4 pers: James Johnson, Alex. Sansought, Doro. Boswell, Elizabeth Davys.

MR. ELIAS OSBORNE, 200 acs. Chas. Citty Co., S. E. side of Ward's Cr., 1 June 1668, p. 142. Beg. at the mouth of Hancock's bottome, along Mr. Bird's lyne, to the Mushell Shell banke, &c. Trans. of 4 pers: John Osborne, Wm. Osborne, Elias Osborne, Joseph Osborne.

CHRISTOPHER GREENAWAY (Grenaway), 370 acs. Gloster Co., 28 Oct. 1665, p. 142. Adj. Mr. Rigault, in Peaches Sw. Trans. of 8 pers: Alexander Anderson, Jno. Horne, Edward Hawkins, Jno. Heyward, Robt. Fargar, Hen. Browne, Francis Sterne, David Sterne.

MR. XPOFER. RIGAULT, 770 acs. Gloster Co., N. E. side of Crane Neck Cr. Swampe, 10 Apr. 1668, p. 142. Adj. Mr. Bew & Willm. Peach. 600 acs. part granted sd. Rigault 6 Mar. 1654; & 170 acs. found within, & due for trans. of 4 pers: Lambe & Maria, Negroes; John Twyney, John Kelley.

MR. JEFFRY BEW, 620 acs. Gloster Co., Ware Par., 4 Apr. 1668, p. 143. Beg. at cor. of a grand pattent of 3500 acs., neere Rich. Traherne's house, up Ware Riv. Sw., & adj. Wm. Peach & Xpofer. Rigault. Trans. of 13 pers.*

MR. JOHN LEWIS, 100 acs. New Kent Co., N. E. side of Cainhoe's Sw., 22 Apr. 1668, p. 143. Beg. at John Leviston's land next Edward Watkins', along sd. Sw. to the head spring deviding this & land of John King. Trans. of 2 pers: Tho. Crues. Peter Marshall

GODFREY HUNT, 320 acs. Nancemond Co., 18 Mar. 1672/3, p. 143. Adj. William Pope, John Rodes' & Richd. Webb. Trans. of 6 pers: Wm. East, Richd. Willett, Tho. Price, Jno. Durley (or Dudley), Danll. Markes, Danll. Faine (?).

MR. LAWRENCE SMITH, 170 acs. Gloster Co., 20 Apr. 1668, p. 144. Adj. Xpofer. Robins, beg. at the head of a cr. or bay that runs to the N. side of Turtle poynt, crosse a cr. to Mockjack Bay side, &c. Trans. of 4 pers: Wm. Davis, Tymothy Sisse, Edward Brookman, Ed. Preafe (or Prease).

MR. THO. VICARS & MR. JOHN BUCKNER, 517 acs. Gloster Co., Petsoe Par., 19 Feb. 1667, p. 144. On N. side of the br. dividing John Day & Isack Richardson, adj. Oliver Green, Edw. Teale, Xtofer. Greenaway, Tho. Wisdom, Tho. Miller, & neere Rappa. path. Trans. of 10 pers: Wm. Thompson, Math. Jackson, Anne Gulley, Eliz. Suckery, Gutt. (or Griff.) Andrew, Phillip. Buckner, Rich. Node, Debery Hicks, Jno. Cotgrave, John Clarke.

MR. JOHN BUCKNER, 194 acs. Gloster Co., 19 Feb. 1667, p. 145. Beg. nere the plantation he lives upon, to Francis Ironmonger, by an arbour in Mr. Barnard's lyne, by Rappa. path, along Isack Richardson, to Mr. Talliferoe's, &c. Trans. of 4 pers: Wm. Watson, Edward Teale, Tho. Vickers.

THOMAS ROYSTON, 608 acs. Gloster Co., Petsoe Par., 6 Feb. 1667, p. 145. Adj. Davyd Monorgond's land

nere Royston's plantation, down Briery Br. to Ware Riv. Sw., by Rappa. Road path, &c. Trans. of 12 pers: Anth Ashly, Robt. Frey, Jno. Franklyn, Jno Fryer, Peter Craven, Francis Cole, Nich. Thompson, Francis George, Steph. Title, Humphry Goodman, Tho. Stephens, Edward Greene.

MR. WILLIAM WILLIS, 250 acs. Gloster Co., 'upon a branch of Crane neck Cr., 20 Oct. 1665, p. 146. Adj. Mr. Ralph Harwood, Coll. John Chessman & his own land. Trans. of 5 pers: Wm. Wilkinson, Danl. Miles, Walter Barefoot, Walter Croop, Wm. Hawkins.

JAMES GAYNES, 519 acs. Rappa. Co., S. side sd. Riv., 11 Mar. 1667, p. 146. Beg. nigh the head of Popomons Br. to Occapason Cr. 386¼ acs. part granted to Capt. Tho. Hawkins, 20 Sept. 1661, who assigned to sd. Gaynes; & 132¾ acs. for trans. of 3 pers: James Roberts, Jone Roberts, Anne Roberts.

MR. THO. JERMINGAN (or Jerningan), 250 acs. Nanzemond Co., at a place called Somerton, 18 May, 1668, p. 146. Adj. lands of Aylington & Wm. Moore. Trans. of 5 pers.*

COLL. JOHN WALKER, 1030 acs. Rappa. Co., 16 Apr. 1668, p. 147. Beg. on E. side of the maine run of Rappa. Cr. at a poynt next below the Briggs or road, nere Pantagh (or Perantagh) Br. to Apamatike path, nere Rappa. Run, &c. Trans. of 21 pers: John Moulden, Jno. Bartlett, Rich. Fox, Jno. Neale, Nico. Goodwood, Robt. Holloway, Jno. Chambers, Robt. Shoult, Franc. Downer, Abra. Warren, Rich. Ford, Hen. Reynold, Judith Clerke, Mary Haynes, Mary Garrett, Amy 'Load, Ann Towers, John Shepheard, Geo. Fermer, Jno. Ashborne, Tho. Collins.

LT. COLL. CUTBERT POTTER, 270 acs. Lancaster Co., S. side Rappa. Riv., bet. his 2 former devdts., 14 Mar. 1667, p. 147. Beg. by Mattapony Path, over the King's road, through Mr. Wm. Gourden's Orchard, by his pasture fence, &c. Trans. of 6 pers: Tho. Chewning, Symon Nesum, Mary Coulton, Alice Bancroft, Rachell Packett, Wm. Netherton.

MR. RICH. CHURCH, 550 acs. Low. Norf. Co., S. side the E. br. of Eliz. Riv., 20 Apr. 1668, p. 148. On E. side of Billingsgate Cr., adj. Willm. Joyce, Rich. Whitbye, & Nehuntrees Cr. 500 acs. purchased of Tymothy Ives: & 50 acs. for trans. of: Robert Tirrell.

MAJOR EDWARD HILL, 2544 acs. Chas. Citty Co., in *Shirley Hundred*. 28 Mar. 1664, p. 148. Adj. Joseph Royall, S. to Sw. parting Shirley Hundred from Shirley Hun. Island, & on land of Mr. Walter Aston. 2476 acs. part granted to Coll. Edward Hill, his father, 18 Dec. 1660; 68 acs., overplus found within, for trans. of 2 pers: Sarah Plasted, Samll. Grey.

MR. THOMAS EDMONDSON, 513 acs. Rappa. Co., S. side the Riv., upon a br. of Puscatwa Cr. called Mr. Perrye's Swamp, 27 Sept. 1667, p. 149. Adj. Mr. Robert Payne, over the King's road, to Mattapony Indian Path &c. Trans. of 10 pers: Peter Helcott, Mary Angell Robt. Spirman, Wm. Peareman, Jno. Hull, Barth. Daw, Hen. Sparrow, Robt. Jones, Henry Archer, Anne Wingate.

JOHN BROWNE, 600 acs. Surrey Co., 1 Mar. 1666, p. 149. E. side the maine Black water Sw., along Thomas Gaultney &c. Trans. of 12 pers: Willm. Pendeston, Jno. Ashfield, Jno. Williams, Eliz. Collier, Walter Catford, Maurice Broadstreet, Rich. Kakett, Jno. Goddin, Jno. Collins, Wm. Bayley, Robt. Crawley, Wm. Satergood.

JOHN SEXTON, 700 acs. New Kent Co., S. side Yorke Riv., 8 Apr. 1668, p. 150. Beg. by Mattadckon Cr. Trans. of 14 pers: James Rushing, Edw. Cennett, Wm. Martyn, Jno. Taylor, Mary Kepax, Tho. Hoggs, Jno. Watkins, Jno. Littlehart, Stephen Willis, Edward Crop, Marey Turner, Eliz. Hudson, Tho. Perrey, Jno. Pryer.

WILLM. FUZEY, 1000 acs. New Kent Co., N. side Mattapony Riv., 8 Apr. 1668, p. 150. Adj. Mr. John Duncombe. Trans. of 20 pers: Edw. Halley, Mahalael Browdo (?), Ed. Peets, Robt. Woodall, Edw. Garr (or Gurr), Geo. Jackson, Tho. Pead, Su. Snoswell,

Eliz. Tomlyn, Ed. Harfrey, Tho. Tiller, Hump. Haynes, Judith Edgar, Tho. Blowes, Wm. Bankes, Pet. Herring, Jeffry Stone, Lawrence Alsop, Tho. Frise, Alex. Pewett.

SAME. 600 acs., same Co., date & page. N. side sd. Riv., at the mouth of Deep run above the *Mattapony Towne*, along path to *Nangatico Towne*, &c. Trans. of 12 pers: Rich. Stedman, Robt. Norris, Andrew King, Ed. Taylor, Willm. Goodale, James Driver, Fran. Fawe, Jno. Legg. Josias Wheeler, Mary Smith, Robt. Strowd, Jo. Keate.

MAJOR JOHN SMITH, 500 acs. Gloster Co., 1 Apr. 1665, p. 151. Beg. nigh the head of Tanks Poropotanke Cr., to an old field, parallel with *Purton Dev'dt.*, over good luck br., to Totopotomoyes Sw., along Mr. Peter Knt. (Knight) &c. 300 acs. granted to Mrs. Anna Bernard, 2 July 1652; & 200 acs. for trans. of 4 pers: Francis Bernard, Mary Mynns, John Reeves, Elias Frenchman. (A frenchman ?).

LT. COLL. JOHN WALKER, Esqr., 1200 acs. on E'wd. side of a run of Ware Riv., 14 Oct. 1663, (& recorded 25 July, 1668) p. 151. Adj. land of Mr. Mordecai Cooke & Zachary Cripps. Renewal of his pattent dated 9 Oct. 1658.

LT. COLL. JOHN GEORGE, 360 acs., Is. of Wight Co., 17 Apr. 1667, p. 151. E. upon the maine river, S. upon Ciprus Sw. & N. upon land of Francis Place, now in possession of Mr. Isacke George. Trans. of 8 pers: Tho. Ward, Jno. Devoratt, James Arnold, Jno. Allam, Jno. Blast, Clause Couse, Jno. Hoborough, Tho. Jones.

JAMES HAWLEY, 700 acs. W'moreland Co., nere head of Nomeni Riv., 26 June 1666, p. 152. Beg. at Herring poynt & adj. his own land. Trans. of 14 pers: Tho. Dutton, Hump. Watkins, Ed. Taylor, Ambrose Taylor, Fran. Phillips, Nich. Peirce, Wm. Herbett, Tho. Morgan, Arthur Land, Geo. Loe, Samll. Porter, Giles Walker, Jno. Tompkin, Rich. Baborne (or Bakorne).

JNO. SIMPSON, 650 acs. in the freshes of Rappa. Riv., adj. Mr. Hawkins; 26 June 1666, p. 152. Trans. of 13 pers: Geo. Hearne, Jane Steddick, Ann Lodekin (or Lovekin), Robt. Medcalfe, Angell Sanderson, Jno. Russell, Robt. Sutton, Rich. Wharton, Tho. Roe, Wm. Vaughan, Henry Burcher, Wm. Davis, Geo. Broches.

MR. GILES CALES (Cale), 120 acs. Warwicke Co., 26 Sept. 1667, p. 153. Beg. at a Bever Dam, over Scoones Dam, to land of Robert Gillett, &c. Due by inheritance from Tho. Stephens, to whom it was granted 5 Mar. 1652, & now renewed.

SAME. 150 acs., same Co., date & page. In Nutmeg Quarter. Due as above.

MR. RICHARD WHITTACRE, 135 A. 66 chs., James City Co., 28 Oct. 1666, p. 153. 120 A. 66 chayne beg. in a br. of Greene Sw. by Capt. Ramsye's corne field fence, down the Riv., to point of marsh next the house, &c; the residue bet. James Riv. & Mr. Tho. Loveing, &c. 100 acs. part given him by Major Wm. Whittaker, his dec'd. father, & 40 acs. for trans. of: Peter Johnson.

MAJOR DAVID CANT, 542 acs. Gloster Co., on the br. neare head of Peanketank Riv., 15 Mar. 1663, p. 154. Beg. on W. side of the Store br., to Gill's corner, adj. Mr. Ludlowe &c. Trans. of 11 pers.*

MR. JOHN BUCKNER & MR. THO VICARS, 122 acs. Gloster Co., 16 June 1668, p. 154. Beg. by Rappa. Path, opposite to James Bradburye's plantation, to Ginsye's corner, &c. Trans. of 3 pers: John Morryson, Tho. Johnson, Augustin Cobham.

MR. THOMAS VICARS, 20 acs. Gloster Co., 16 June 1668, p. 154. On N. W. side Totopotamoyes Sw., by Mr. Wm. Corderoye's plantation, &c. Trans. of: Neale Cobley.

MR. THOMAS FOGG & HENRY LUCAS, 397 acs. Rappa. Co., bet. land formerly Tho. Page's & the now land of Mr. Tho. Lucas, Senr., 18 Feb. 1666, p. 155. Beg. upon the River, nigh the Comon road, &c. Trans. of 8 pers: James Leveston, An Canadge, Tho. Featly (or Fently), Robt. Rouse, Hen. Martyn, Mary Crosse, John Johnson, Eusebius Long.

WILLIAM HARRIS, sonn & heire of Thomas Harris, 850 acs., Surry Co., S. James Riv., on N. W. & S. E. sides of the Sunken Marsh above & below the mill; 2 June 1668, p. 155. Adj. the Rich Neck, Robt. Webb, Mr. Edwards, Wm. Carter, Chipoakes path & Mr. Green. Granted sd. Thomas 13 Feb. 1657 & due said Wm. as sonn &c.

WILLIAM BLAIKE, 97 acs. Rappa. Co., N. side the Riv., nere the head of Richards Cr., 20 Apr. 1668, p. 155 Nere land of Mr. Giles Webb & Miles Hugill. Trans. of 2 pers: Willm. Williams, John Jeffryes.

MR. WILLIAM HOSKINS, 350 acs S. side of Rappa. Co., 18 Apr. 1668, p. 156. Adj. land of Lt. Coll. Smith's Orphants, land formerly belonging to Mr. Anthony Stephens & land of Lt. Coll. Guttridge. Trans. of 7 pers: Jno. Cheny, Jane Bishop, Susan Fisher, Sarah Parsons, Ann Beard, Wm. Talbutt, Edward Williams.

MR. THOMAS PHILPOTT, 307 acs. W'moreland Co., 14 Aug. 1668, p. 156. Beg. at his plantation seated at the head of a small cr. falling into Potomack Riv., &c. to a sw. falling into Roatanke Cr., &c. 100 acs. by pattent in 1652, & 207 acs. in 1662

JAMES FULLERTON, 700 acs. Rappa. Co., S. side Rappa. Riv., 29 Sept. 1667, p. 156. Adj. Wm. Aires upon the maine pocoson of Puscattwa Cr. Trans. of 14 pers: James Pope, Wm. Hare, Geo. Strong, Danll. Peck, Wm. Stanly, Rich. Hobbs, Xpofer. Child, Tho. Stenton, Ann Thorowgood, Ed. Palmer, Lewis Watts, Samp. David, Robt. Rowle, Jno. Thompson.

MR. TOBIAS HANDFORD, 320 acs. Gloster Co., on the E'wd. side at the mouth of Deepe Cr., 8 Jan. 1666, p. 157. Adj. Xpofer. Robins, to marsh dividing this & Coll. Augustine Warner Esqr., to Rich. Field, to Finches Cr., &c. 150 acs. granted Coll. Jno. Walker, Esqr., 15 Mar. 1651; & 174 acs. due for trans. of 4 pers.*

COLL. PETER ASHTON, CAPT. JNO. ALEXANDER, MR. WM. HORTON & ROBT. STREET, 2000 acs. Staff. Co., at the head of upper Machoticke Riv., 6 Aug. 1668, p. 157. Nigh Robert King's plantation. Surveyed by order of Staff. Court & due for trans. of 40 pers.*

GEORGE MORRIS & JOHN LONG, 1600 acs., upon branches of Major Andrew Gilson's Cr., 29 Sept. 1667, p. 158. Adj. land formerly belonging to Mr. John Pate, & Mr. Tho. Button, an Indian path, &c. Trans. of 32 pers: Hen. Tirrell, Jonath. Morcott, Charles Manford, Wm. Tucker, Ann Green, Robt. Tirrell, Hen. Tirrell, Wm. Tirrell, Mary Wakeman Math. Bayer, Jno. Lane, Ed. Foster, Hen. Creyton, Tho. Button, Mary Gill, Jno. Owen, Jno. De Rouse, Roger Perry, Wm. Warman, Jno. Dean, Xpofer. Chant, Tho. Blunt, Mary Burges, Eliz. Pride, Francis Hunt, Tho. Long, Jno. Davis, Wm. Preckfield, Nich. Harding, Alice West, Ralp. Hopkins, Dennis Astris. (or Ascris).

COLL. AUGUSTINE WARNER, Esqr., 1224 acs. Gloster Co., Abington Par., 20 Jan. 1666, p. 158. On N. E. side of a peninsula, adj. Xpofer. Robins, Wm. Bowlin, Dry Poynt, &c. 600 acs. part granted to him 18 Jan. 1642; & 624 acs. for trans. of 13 pers.*

MR. THOMAS MILLER, 390 acs. Gloster Co., Petsoe Par., 28 Oct. 1665, p. 159. On S. side of a sw. dividing land of Isaak Richardson & Jno. Day, nere Rappa. Road, to Mr. Richard Barnard, Tho. Vicars & a br. dividing this from land of Tho. Wisdom. Trans. of 8 pers: Tho. Beale, Senr., Tho. Beale, Junr., twice, Alice Beale, thrice, Jno. Pope, Jno. Temple.

JNO. WALLER, 126 acs. Gloster Co., Ware Parish, 20 Feb. 1667, p. 159. Adj. Edward Teale & his own land. Trans.

of 3 pers: Rich. Slater, Mary Humphrves Sarah Hopkins.

DOMINGO MEDERIS & JAMES JOHNSON, 1000 acs. New Kent Co., bet. Dragon Sw. & Axells Br., 8 Apr. 1668, p. 160. 500 acs. part granted to Tho. Clayborne in 1662, who assigned to the abovenamed; 500 acs. for trans. of 10 pers: Roger Tomson, Rich. Arton, Peter Grange, Ann Denew (?), Robt. Fuller, Mary Ingerston, Rice Jervis, Absolon Stringer, Morris Avery, Jno. Carter.

RICH. DAVIS, 700 acs. New Kent Co., N. side Mattapony Riv., 16 Mar. 1667, p. 160. Beg. by Tomonocorocon Sw., adj. Lewis Adkins, by Mr. Poteet's Quarter, &c. 660 acs. granted sd. Davis 25 June 1660; & 40 acs. for trans. of: Abraham Morris.

EDWARD BOMPAS, 280 acs. New Kent Co., S. side of York Riv., 8 Apr. 1668, p. 161. Beg. at Cornelius Debany, above Manskin. crosse to Totopotomoyes Cr. to Mr. Moses Davis, &c. Sd. land granted to Edmond Machyn 20 July, 1662, conteyning 1000 acs., assigned to sd. Bompas, & upon resurvey there is found but the contents of this patent.

RICHARD BULLOCK, 100 acs. New Kent Co., S. side Yorke Riv., 8 Apr. 1668, p. 161. Beg. at head of a br. of Muschimino, &c. Trans. of 2 pers: Robert Bogas, Sarah Mynns.

GABRIELL MICHELL (Mitchell), 182 acs. New Kent Co., N. side of Mattapony Riv., 8 Apr. 1668, p. 162. Beg. at John Durwood, up the Sw., &c. Trans. of 4 pers: Henry Mason, Jeffry Marble, Roger Strong, Arthur Peirce.

MR. ROBERT POLLARD, 65 acs. New Kent Co., N. side of Mattapony Riv., 16 Mar. 1667, p. 162. Beg. at Simpson's Cr. parting land of Edward Simpson from land on which sd. Pollard now liveth, a br. dividing this & Mr. Edw. Booker, &c. Trans. of 2 pers: Robert Collier, Elias Paine.

JEREMIA CLEATON, 13 acs. New Kent Co., N. side Mattapony Riv., 8 Apr. 1668, p. 162. Upon a br. of

Aquicke Sw., adj. Lewis Adkins, Mr. Poteet, &c. Trans. of: Tho. Descon (or Deston).

MR. WM. DUDLEY, 3000 acs. Lancaster Co., on N. side of the great Sw., called Peanketanck or Dragon Sw., 13 Mar. 1667, p. 163. Beg. at an Indian bridge; adj. Cutbert Potter, Mr. Batchellor's fence, Mr. Willis' land, &c. 2000 acs. granted him 2 June, 1657, & 2000 aes. 24 Sept. 1659; but the courses of both of these pattents not agreeing with the naturall *scittuacond* of the place, & 1000 acs. found to belong to Mr. Cuth. Potter, by survey of Coll. Jno. Cattlett & Mr. Geo. Morris, Surveyors, with a jury of the neighbourhood appointed by order of the Genll. Ct. for decideing a difference between them, etc.

MR. WM. DOWNEING, 1570 acs. N'umberland Co., N. side of Gr. Wiccocomico (Riv.), 28 Apr. 1668, p. 164. Adj. Henry Bradley, Mr. Wildey, & a br. falling into Chetanck Cr., &c. 700 acs. granted to him 24 June 1664; & 870 acs. for trans. of 18 pers: Anne Ayliffe, Wm. Downeing, twice, Edward Lugg, Wm. Jones, Eliz. Horne, Wm. Reynolds, Mary Lewis, Tho. Sharpe, Tho. Reeves, Abrahed Tod, Nich. Hadcocke, Arthur Grant, Robt. Fowkes, Millicent Johnson, Jno. Archer, Mary Horne, Alice Humphry.

MR. EDWARD SANDERS, 207 acs. N'umberland Co., S. side Gr. Wiccocomico Riv., 28 Aug. 1668, p. 164. On N. side of a br. dividing this & land of Thomas Sallisbury, on S. side of a br. dividing this & land of Tho. Lane, &c. Trans. of 4 pers: Mary Morgan, Mary Walker, Jno. Brookes, Leo. Sotherby.

MR. JOHN HANEY, 1250 acs. N'umberland Co., N. side Gr. Wiccocomico Riv., 28 Apr. 1668, p. 165. On E. side of Whickars Br., to br. dividing this from land of Jno. Hughlett, adj. Mr. Jno. Mattrom, Mr. Wm. & Mr. Peter Presley, nigh Chiccacone horse path, adj. Rich. Nelmes, Jervice Dodson, dec'd., &c. 350 acs. part granted to him 10 Mar. 1662; 400 acs. from Jno.

Hughlett & conteyned in part of 900 acs. granted sd. Hughlett in June 1663; 500 acs. for trans. of 10 pers: Tho. Lane, Eliz. his wife, Wm. Molins, Val. Menstoe (or Mensloe), Anne Morgan, Jane Le Bay, Jno. Barber, Jno. Howlett, Edw. Morris, Mary Cloud.

WILLIAM PEIRCE (Peirse), 100 22 Apr. 1668, p. 166. Beg. nigh the mouth of Scott's Cr., along Mr. Harwood's lyne &c. Granted Jno. Rolfe, Wm. Peirce, Tho. Peirce & Willm. Spenser, & now due by order of the Gov'r. &c., at a Genll. Ct. held at James Citty, 24 Apr. 1667.

MR. THO. PATTISON & MR. RICH. BREDGATT, 220 acs., S. side Rappa. Riv., upon a maine br. of Dragon Sw., 24 Apr. 1668, p. 166. Beg. by the sd. pocoson side, adj. Jno. Chyn, Jno. Gibson & Jno. Mayo. Trans. of 4 pers: Tho. Coker, Tho. Spencer, Jno. Richards & 1 Negro.

RICHARD AUSTEN, 300 acs. New Kent Co., on S. side Yorke Riv. 7 mi. up the narrowes, 5 Aug. 1668, p. 166. Adj. Mr. Thomas Vaulx, Mr. Lewis Burwell & Mr. Tho. Broughton. Granted to Francis Flood, 19 Apr. 1648, who sold to Thomas Austen, father of the abovenamed, who bequeathed to sd. Richd. & Jno. his brother, & now due sd. Richd. entirely as survivour.

CAPT. LAWRENCE BAKER, 2050 acs. Surrey Co., 24 Apr. 1667, p. 167. Nigh James Keddickes, upon Rich. Drewe's lyne &c. 500 acs. part granted Mr. Tho. Stamp 12 May, 1640, who assigned to sd. Baker & Mr. James Taylor, joynt tenants, 18 Dec. 1649, & due sd. Baker by survivourship & soe resolved by Coll. Miles Carey, Escheator Gen., upon inquisition &c; 500 acs. more granted joyntly to sd. Baker & Taylor 6 Mar. 1644, confirmed by new patt. 11 June 1650, which alsoe became due by survivourship, &c. 1050 acs. for trans. of 21 pers: Capt. Law. Baker, twice, Eliz. his wife, Jno. his sonne, James his sonne, Jane Rich, Anne Reeve, Alice Lee, Anne Millington, Jno. Macom James Wilson, Robt. Bruce, Jno. Sloope, Jno. Phillips, James Clarke,

Andrew Overing, Wm. Hart, Tho. Powell, Henry Rigg, Jane Downes.

WILLIAM CARNEY, 100 acs., in western br .of Eliz. Riv., by Clarke's Cr., 17 Mar. 1667, p. 167. Granted to Rich. Starnell, 11 Jan. 1652, who bequeathed to sd. Carney.

MR. FRANCIS KIRKMAN, 747 A., 68 Chs. & 64 decimall parts, James Citty Co., upon Archers Hope Cr., 6 Jan. 1666, p. 168. 590 A. 20 Chs. & 8 primes beg. nere head of the maine br. of the E'most. Gleebe Cr., &c. to the *old ferry place,* up James Riv. & the back river &c. 109 A. &c., & 47 A. 28 chs. 64 dec. parts &c. adj. the Gleebe land &c. 500 acs. part granted to Lucy, Judith & Jane Webster 20 July 1646, & sd. Jane dying, sd. land became wholly due to sd. Lucy & Judith; which Lucy, marrying with Capt. John Sheppard, sold 150 acs., more or lesse, unto Major Joseph Croshaw; sd. Judith marrying Jno. Hudson, sd. Kirkman purchased the whole patt. of sd. Croshaw, Jno. & Lucy Sheppard & Jno. & Judeth Hudson; 90 acs. 20 chs. & 8 primes of high land & 100 A. 59 ch. & 2 pr. of marsh land, being surplus upon a resurvey, was granted sd. Kirkman by order &c. & due for Trans. of 4 pers.* 47 A., 28 ch. 64 dec., granted him by order &c. 31 Oct. 1666 & due for trans. of 1 per.*

THOMAS MAPLES & WILLIAM HITCHMAN (Hichman), 200 acs. James Citty Co., on branches of Warrany Cr., 10 Sept. 1668, p. 169. Beg. on Burchen Sw. & standing in Sir John Ayton's lyne, alongst the horse path, along Tymber Sw., &c. Trans. of 4 pers: Teage Okey, Rice James, Anne Jones, Francis Chandler.

SAME. 536 acs., same Co. & date, p. 170. On the Tymber Sw., adj. Wm. Elcome, nere Mr. Sorrell's path, Warreny Sw., nere an Indian field, to Mr. Burnell, Sir John Ayton &c. Trans. of 11 pers: Tho. Grymes, Gerard Green, Edward Allester, Fra. Oatley, Charles Forbody, Mary Watts, Hump. Clarke, Geo. Bayley, Wm. Payne, Jno. Light, Anne Barber.

GEORGE BROWNEING, 189 A., 1 R., 11 Po., Henrico Co., S. side of James Riv., 18 May. 1668, p. 170. Beg. by a path from *Coxendale* to Powells, adj. Tho. Ligon, &c. Trans. of 4 pers: Geo. & Margarett Browneing, Wm. Burrowes, Rich. Edwards.

MR. JOHN LEWIS, 2600 acs. New Kent & Gloster Co.'s, upon both sides of Poropotanke Sw., beg. at the mouth of a gr. branch next below his plantation by the *old womans poynt*; 16 Aug. 1667, p. 171. Adj. Tymothy Lowdell. John Leviston, Mattapony Sw., Richd. Major, Junr., Geo. Major, Popetico Sw., Jno. Chamberline, to br. dividing this from land of John Fox, to John Nettle. Geo. Austin, Cole's Br., & br. dividing this from land of Mr. Rich. Lee, to the bridge Sw., to the Mill, &c. 80 acs. purchased of sd. Lowdell; 1000 acs. of Mr. Hoel Prise; 600 acs. granted sd. Lewis 23 Nov. 1663; & 920 acs. for trans. 19 pers: Wm. Jones, Morgan Kennett, James Stephens, Tho. Page, Sarah ——, Robt. Rosse (or Resse), Henry ——, Ann Smith, Robert Wilson, Issabell Wilson, Mary Berly (or Benly), Jeremy Norton, Israel Jermy, Peter Armstrong, Mary Meredith, Tho. Brough, Tho. Meese, Roger Ingerson, Robert Morris.

MR. RICH. DUDLEY, 944 acs. Gloster Co., upon branches of Poropotank Cr., 28 Oct. 1665, p. 172. Adj. Mr. John Green by Mr. Pate's Sw., along Mr. Peter Knight, by Spence's lyne to Parradise Path, to Chiscaike Path, to Mr. John Pate, &c. 400 acs. granted Wm. Armfield 24 Nov. 1663, purchased by Mr. Pate, who assigned to sd. Dudley; 544 acs .for trans. of 11 pers: Edw. Holland, Rich. Perkins, Jno. Dance, Jno. Holmes, James Griffin, James White, Wm. Evans, Margaret Milburne, Franc. Hilyard, Mary Wilson, Francis Sale.

MR. GERRARD BROADHURST. 500 acs. Staff. Co., S. Potomack Riv. & N. E. side of Chapawansick Cr., 20 Sept. 1668. p. 172. Adj. Mr. Nath. Pope. Granted to Coll. Peter Ashton, 16 Oct. 1665, who sold to Anne Brett *alias* Broadhurst, & given to sd. Gerrard.

MR. WILLIAM DUDLEY, 1750 acs. Lancaster Co., N. side of Peanketank Riv., 16 Aug. 1667, p. 173. N. upon Gleab Land Cr. to Mr. Edmond Kemp, crossing the damms to Wm. Frissell, to David Barwicke, to Mr. Wm. Leach & Mr. Kible, to *Mount Folly* land &c. 92 acs. granted to Mr. Geo. Kible, who assigned to Mr. Rigby & by him to sd. Dudley; 1658 acs. for trans. 33 pers: Jno. Sparkes, Robt. Car, Mary Britton, Wm. Shatterill, Edwd. Parker, Obadia Jones, Wm. Archer, Hen. Foster, Robt. Porter, Luke Shartick, Mary Elmer "& 1000 acs. by a relinquished patt. of sd. Dudley, dated 2 June 1657."

WM. DANGERFIELD, 64 acs. Rappa. Co., S. side Rappa. Riv., upon Gilson's Cr., 4 Apr. 1667, p. 173. Beg. in sight of Anth. North's house, through the old field to Cooper's point, to the old house &c. Trans. of 2 pers: Xpofer. Kible, Joseph Kibble.

MR. GILES CALE (Cales), 1400 acs. Lancaster Co., but now called Rappa., on S. E. side of Farnam Cr., 26 Sept. 1667, p. 174. Adj. lands of Leroy Griffin, & Mr. Thomas Griffin, &c. Due by inheritance from Tho. Stephens, to whom it was granted 2 Sept. 1652.

JOHN AXOLL (Axton), 600 acs. Staff. Co., S. side of Potomack Cr., 23 Sept. 1668, p. 174. On W'wd. side of Weepsiwasson Cr., adj. Mr. Henry Meese, Mr. Wm. Horton, Mr. Willm. Haberd &c. Granted unto Capt. David Mansfield, who assigned & made over in marryage unto Mr. Henry Blagrove & Mary his wife, daughter of sd. David, who sold to Edward Carey, dec'd.. & sd. *Axton*.; & now due said *Axton* by survivorship.

WM. HODGSON, 25 acs. S. side of Rappa. Co., in the freshes. about ½ mi. up Lucas Cr., 24 Sept. 1668, p. 175. Beg. on S. side of the horse path, to plantation he lives upon, &c. Trans. of: John Withers.

JOHN BRAWTHERT, 76 acs., Rappa. Co., about a mi. from Rappa. Cr., 25 Sept. 1668, p. 175. Beg. neer a run of water called Manoikin; adj. Fra.

Settell; cutting a path to sd. Cr., &c. Trans. of 2 pers: Jno. Brawthert, Mary Brawthert.

MR. NATHANIELL BENTLY, 395 acs. in the freshes of Rappa., about 4 mi. from the River, 24 Sept. 1668, p. 175. Beg. next to Willm. Hodson, to path to *Potobago*, to John Ames, &c. Due sd. *Brently* for trans. of 8 pers: Symon Dennett, Patrick Mason, Danll. Smart, Wm. Price, Jane Hooker, Martyn Woodhouse, Robt. Parsons, Tymothy Jackson.

MR. JOHN WISE, 1060 acs. Accomack Co., bet. Chickanesseks & Anancock Creeks, 24 Sept. 1668, p. 176. N'wd. upon Chiccanessecks. E'wd. by a gutt parting this from land of Mr. Jno. Michell, to br. of Ekeeks Cr. &c., by Kings Cr., to Parker's back Cr., &c. Granted to Willm. Waters 20 Feb. 1661, & assigned to sd. Wise.

THO. TEAKEL (Teackle), 350 acs. Accomack Co., bet. Cradock & Nondui Creeks, 25 Sept. 1668, p. 176. Adj. Jno. Milboy, the main bay of Chesepiack & his own land. Trans. of 7 pers:, Samll. Trian, Tho. Smith, Wm. Hickes, Robt. Kemp, Tho. Fanshaw, Cha. Mainard, Jno. Shaw, Jno. Bendish, Tho. Argall, James Silvercock.

LT. COLL. THOMAS BEALE & RANDOLPH KIRK (Kirke), 1500 acs. W'moreland Co., bet. Potomeck & Rappa. Rivers, neer branches of Nominy Riv., 25 Sept. 1668, p. 176. Nere land of Andrew Read, adj. Wm. Basbey (or Basley) & Edwd. Hally. Trans. of 30 pers: James Foster, Geo. Hilyard, Andrew Melton, James Davis, Anne Chile, Eliz.Wilkinson, Tho. Clarke, Wm. Toft, Elias Johnson, James Balam, Tho. Long, James Caddock, Edw. Halderson, Lewis Hollis, James Syms, Wm. Bandall, Jo. Lee, Ja. Chambers, Eliz. Phillips, Ann Fanebee (?), James Wood, Wm. Crumbe, Jno. Hill, Eliz. Moxom, Saml. Horrid, Jone Briggs, James Brand (or Brawd), Wm. Smith, Mary D—— Abrah. James.

THO. MAIDSTAIRD (Meadstaird), 1136 acs., about 10 mi. up the N. side of Rappa. Riv., 26 Sept. 1668, p. 177. 1000 acs. granted to Mr. Epa. Lawson, 22 May 1650 & sold by his heires-to sd. Maidstaird, 11 Sept. 1666, as by records of Lancaster Co., beg. by the river side, adj. land of Slawter, &c; 136 acs. beg. a mile from the Riv., adj. sd. 1000 acs., neer br. of Johns Cr. & land of Griggs, &c. sd 136 acs. for trans. of 3 pers: Robt. Cage, Wm. Ellis, Tho. Taylor.

CAPT. JOHN HULL, 1400 acs. Rappa. Co., N. side Rappa. Riv., 23 Sept. 1668, p. 177. 1100 acs. granted to Miles Riley 12 Oct. 1665 & given by will to sd. Hull. 200 acs. adj. Thomas Robinson; 300 acs. adj. Coll. Fanteleroye's Orphts., & a sw. dividing this & land of Geo. Bryer's Orphts. Trans. of 28 pers.*

THO. PAWELL (or Panell), 646 acs. in Rappa. on S. side the river in the freshes, about 4 mi. from the water side, 26 Sept. 1668, p. 178. Adj. Mr. Robt. Bently, cutting a path to Potobago, adj. Mrs. Bethlm. Gillson, John Amis & Nath. Bently. Trans. of 13 pers: David Salt, Marmaduke Wicks, Eliza. Hopkins, Nich. Walters, Jane Coventry, Wm. Haines, Ralph Smith, Cornelius Nowell, Jon. Biss (?), Mary Hart, Samll. Dennis, Peter Wood, Jane Salt.

JOHN SHERLOCK, Junr., 426 acs in Rappa. on N. side of Totoskey Cr. 26 Sept. 1668, p. 178. Adj. land formerly Hugell's now Capt. Jno. Hull's, cutting a path to Tuffleyes, adj. Denis Swillevant, &c. Sd. land formerly taken up by John Sherlock, Sehr., for 600 acs. & on resurvey found to be but 426 acs.

JOHN WITHERS, 320 acs. W'moreland Co., 20 July 1662, p. 179. Adj. Mr. Tho. Fowkes at the head of a creek of Potomac Cr. Granted to sd. Withers 18 Dec. 1658.

JOHN PEIKE, 1450 acs. Staff. Co., upon maine run of Potomack Cr., 26 Sept. 1668, p. 179. Adj. plantation formerly Jno. Mathewes'. Part of patt. to Thomas Wilkinson dated 10 June 1658, who sold to Robt. Warren, Edw. Warren & sd. Peike, & due him by sur-

vivorship. (Note: Marginal notation gives this as 1250 acs.)

GERRARD FOWKES, WM. HORTON, RICH. GRANGER & THO. GRIGG, 2000 acs. W'moreland Co., upon branches of Up. Machotike, 4 Sept. 1661, p. 179. Adj. land formerly in possession of Gervis Dodson, dec'd., & to Mr. Peter Ashton. Trans. of 40 pers.*

WILLM. WEBB, 400 acs. W'moreland Co., upon N. side of a maine br. of Attapin Cr. Dam, 26 Sept. 1668, p. 180. Adj. Mr. John Bruton. Trans. of 8 pers: Charles Jones, Tho. Jones, Wm. West, Wm. Robinson, Dennis Belony, Edith Jackson, Mihill. Connaway, Wells a Negro.

COLL. PETER ASHTON, 485 acs. N'umberland Co., 26 Sept. 1668, p. 180. 400 acs. granted sd. Ashton 17 Nov. 1654; S'ly. upon Wiccocomico Riv., E'ly. upon a cr. devideing this & land of Capt. Wm. Clayborne, Esqr., &c. 85 acs. granted to John Johnson 4 June 1655, who assigned to sd. Ashton; on N. side of Gr. Wiccocomico Riv., betwixt Mr. James Hawley & Wm. Betts, &c.

WM. GREY & CHRISTOPHER BLACKBOURN, 1138 acs. Rappa. Co., on the S. side, 28 Sept. 1668, p. 181. 775 acs. part. adj. Mr. James Gaines; 363 acs. 4 perches adj. sd. Gaines on Ocupaseth Cr. &c. Both tracts granted them 26 Oct. 1666

MR. ROBT. COLEMAN, 634 acs., Is. of Wight Co., 25 Sept. 1667, p. 181. Beg. in the Cyprus Br., to Mr. Driver's new land, by Rutter's land, by a pocoson to Mr. Ruffin, to Bennett & Smith, to a great Cyprus Sw., &c. 300 acs. purchased of Ambrose Bennett, & 334 acs. for trans. of 7 pers: David Jones, Samll. Fuller, Robt. Coleman, Peter Frenchman (a frenchman ?), Rich. Atkins, Jno. Sellaway, Samll. Dutton.

THO. CHETWOOD & JNO. PROSSER, 5275 acs. on N. side of Rappa. Co., in the freshes, 28 Sept. 1667, p. 182. Beg. at Tacopacon spring, to an

Indian tree, to Simpson's oake, &c. Trans. of 106 pers: Jno. Amis, Mary Amis, Robt. Allen, Danll. Dolby, Wm. Hutt, Fran. Parrott, Margtt. Gruntell, Samll. Watts, John Jones, Tho. Wood, Nich. Harris, Walter Price, James Wells, Rich. Smith, Mary Palmer, Margtt. Palmer, Redrick Thompson, Edw. Horton, Rich. Holding, John Collins, Martha Watkins, Jno. Carter, Robt. Clanke, Will. Hackney, Vall. Wallis, Rich. Parrott, Jon. Hart, Peter Worley (or Worsley), Mar. Skinner, Hans Peterson, Robt. Martin, Stephen Tuke, Joseph ——, Geo. Andrews, Rich. Burton, David Nicholls, Eliz. Smart, Wm. Tuftley, Henry Elliott, Edw. West, Jno. Blake, Jane Batten, Robt. Parson, Danll. Hill, Roger Carter, Fran. Holland, Jno. Bennett, James Blackmore, Edward Hill, Samll. Everton, Jno. Cutteridge, 3 Negroes; Samll. Pryse, Joane Wilkinson, Fran. Sanderor (?), An Thrash, Susan Lucas, An Stoaks, Obedia Evans, James Price, And. Ward, Mary Page, Will Cooke, Jno. Davis, Mary Davis, Phillip Wood, Will Scott, Fran. Porter, Tim Wilson, Jno. Hart, Patriak Morgan, Will Strutton, Robt. Norman, Will Ram, Geo. Baker, Will Miller, Rich. Wells, Jno. Russell, Francis Morton, Sarah Phillips, Judith Stone, Jno. Wilcockes, Ralph Harper, Geo. Dixon, Samll. Dowling, Jno. (a ?) Frenchman, Nich. Custis, Danll. Watts, Alex. West, Tho. Wilmott, Will Wells, Peter Jearman, Joseph Stevens, Martin Dye, Mary Hatten, Samp. Waterman, George Ward, Henry Harvy, Geo. Dyer, Eliz. Wood, Mary Marty, James Porter, Jno. Scolding, Robt. Sutton.

THE PARISH OF CHRIST CHURCH, Lancaster Co., N. side of Rappa. River, 839 acs. *for a Glebe*, 29 Sept. 1668, p. 182. At head of Coll. Carter's Cr., formerly called Slaughter's Cr. 500 acs. part granted to Wm. Chapman, last of May 1657 & by him sold to the parish to make a *Glebe;* 330 due by order of the Genll. Ct., 1 Nov, 1666. Beg. at Blunt poynt, running to the head of Blunt poynt Cr., to land of Coll. Carter, &c.

THO. PAGE, WM. HODGSON & SAMLL. WEILDING, 3075 acs. Rappa.

Co., about 1½ mi. from the Riv. on the S. side; 3 Apr. 1667, p. 182. Nere land of Peter Cornehill, adj. Tho. Lucas, Senr., crossing Chikahomani Path, adj. Robt. Price, &c. Trans. of 62 pers: Rich. Wharton, Tho. Roe, Wm. Vaughan, Henry Burcher, Wm. Davis, Geo. Broach, Phill Snead, Robt. Hunt, Ed. Turner, Rich. Harding, Walter Smith, Jno. Hatton, James Hide, Fran. White, Nath. Hill, Geo. Leads, Robt. Breed, Mary Brett, Tho. Dutton, Hump, Watkins, Ed. Taylor, Ambrose Taylor, Fran. Phillips, Nich. Price, Wm. Herbert, Tho. Morgan, Arthur Sands, Geo. Low. Samll. Porter, Giles Walker, Jno. Jenkins, Rich. Seaborne, Will King, Martin Pary, Jos. Edgcome, Ralph Poole, Mary Evens, Susan Holladay, Mary Spicer, Jno. Burton, Roger Parsons, James Bayly, Rich. Atkins, Arthur Stevens, Robt. Surbett, Wm. Southcott, Jno. Jenning, Tho. Garrett, Wm. Copeman, Morgan Orborne (or Ozborne), Tho. Bliss, Will Lee, Tim. Cardiff, Stephen Hopewell, Eliz. Parker, Jno. Sexton, Job Thomas, Jos. Finch, Jno. Bradford, Mary Bradford, Rich. Harris.

WM. PEBLES, 862 A., 2 R., Chas. City Co., S. side James Riv., 3 Nov. 1673, p. 182. 473 A., 3 R., 24 Po., beg. on Tho. Newhouse, to Birchen Sw., &c. 388 A., 2 R., 16 Po., nigh the *old Towne Land,* &c. The first tract by patt. dated 30 July 1670; & residue for trans. of 7 pers: Hen. Makeley, Roger Cooke, Mary Bennet, Jno. Traharne, Eliz. Jettly, Mary Gibbonss, Tho. Anderson.

CAPT. ALEX. FLEMING, 560 acs. in the freshes of Rappa. Co., about 2 mi. from the river, 4 Sept. 1667, p. 183. Beg. at Cockill Cr., which issues into Mr. Lucas' Cr., adj. Mr. Beth. Gilson & Mr. Robert Paine. Trans. of 12 pers: Law. (or Lanc.) Fletcher, James Bird, Jno. Aster, Joane Claydon, Alice Ayers, Eliz. Clayton, Marmaduke Harwar, Samll. Briggs, An Smith, An Loud (?), Ant. Champion, Henry Hasser.

THO. PAGE, 783 acs. Rappa. Co., in the freshes about a mile from the Riv. on the S. side, 3 Apr. 1667, p. 183. Beg. about 2 perches from the Roade, adj. Will. Hodgson, Mr. Thomas Lucas, Senr., &c. Trans. of 16 pers: Wm. Shore (or Shone), Jacob Gower, Edwd. Wise, Esop Archer (or Anber), Dorothy Browne, Tho. Webb, Roger Jones, Hugh Williams, Eliz. Whithead, Geo. Cussall, Tho. Button, Nath. Busterd, Susan Haven, Hump. Jordan, Margtt. Johnson, Law. Monke.

LT. COLL. JNO. WASHINGTON, 560 acs. in the freshes of Rappa., aboute 2 mi. from the river, 3 Nov. 1673, p. 183. Beg. neer Cockill Cr. issuing into Mr. Lucas' Cr., adj. Mr. Beth. Gilson, Mr. Robt. Paine &c. Granted to Capt. Alex. Fleming, 4 Sept. 1667, who sold to Elizabeth Hoskins, by her deserted, & now granted by order &c., dated 2 Oct. 1671, & further due for trans. of 11 pers: Wm. Gerley, Mary Jones, Wm. Grant, Geo. Grigory, Grace Langby, Wm. Gray, James Bryant, Tho. Gresham, Martin Gardiner, Wm. St. Jno., Antho. Glover, Jno. Thorpe.

GEORGE FRESHWATER, 400 acs. N'ampton Co., at Magette Bay, 26 Sept. 1668, p. 184. Part being the Peyney point betwixt Craddock Cr. & Fishermans Cr. The other part adj. Peter Walker, Wm. Harper, the bay & sd. creeks. 200 acs. part granted John Neale & by conveyance come to sd. Freshwater; & 200 acs. for rights produced &c: Nich. Roades, Jno. Copeman, Audrey Angell, Jno. Humble.

LT. COLL. WILLM. KENDALL, 289 acs. N'ampton Co., neare Magette bay & N. side of Craddock Cr., 26 Sept. 1668, p. 184. Trans. of 6 pers: Anne Beetle, Tho. Hey, Joseph Jepson, Jno. Burthwell, Andrew Abrega, Wm. Hopers.

JOHN EYRE, 240 acs. N'ampton Co., at Magettee Bay, 26 Sept. 1668, p. 185. W'wd. by the bay, beg. where the halfe way tree stood, &c. Said land was purchased from the lawfull proprietor by Mr. Tho. Eyre, dec'd., & by him possessed, & now for more security pattented by sd. John Eyre, as sonne & heir to sd. Tho. Eyre.

LT. COLL. WILLM. KENDALL, 502 acs. N'ampton Co., at Magette Bay,

26 Sept. 1668, p 185. On S. side of Jonas Dixon's land. Due for rights &c: Wm. Berefield, Jno. Underwood, Eliz. Turfitt, Tho. Sanders, Jno. Howker, Rich. Ridge, Ann Man, Tho. Lucas, Jno. Simpson, Hen. Hawley, Mordecay Evens.

MAJOR JNO. TILNEY, 1000 acs. Accamack Co., 26 Sept. 1668, p. 186. Bounded on N. by a br. of Nusswadox Cr. & the freshwater br., W. by land of Jno. Hinman &c. 800 acs. granted to Willm. Berryman 2 Mar. 1640, & assigned by Jonah Jackson son & heire of Jane Berryman, sole sister & heire to sd. Wm. Berryman, 16 July 1663; 200 acs. for rights produced: Robt. Watby, Judith Stowe (or Stone), Wm. Collins, Tho. a Welshman.

SAME. 1100 acs., same Co., date & page. On W'n. part of Machepungo Cr. &c., and on part of land formerly belonging to Mr. Stephen Charleton, adj. Danl. Quillion, the head of Browne's Br., & Jno. Prettyman. 550 acs. granted to Mr. Charles Scarburgh 23 Nov. 1647 & assigned to sd. Tilney; 550 acs. due by rights &c: Jno. Parker, Jno. Mocelest, Jno. Coll, Joseph Dergell, Danll. Till, Anne Shaw, Tho. Wyn, Eliz. Reynolds, Joseph Harrey, Nich. Smith, Margarett Burton.

COLL. NICH. SPENCER, 1200 acs. W'moreland Co., S. side Potomack Riv., upon branches of Apomattox, 22 Sept. 1668, p. 187. Adj. Mr. Nathaniel Pope, to E'most. side of run falling into Rappa. Riv. &c., crossing branches of the Beaver Dams of Appomatox &c. Granted to Jno. Washington & Tho. Pope, 14 Sept. 1661, deserted, & now granted by order &c. & further due for trans. of 24 pers: Andrew Thomson, Mary Floyd, Jno. Malum, Wm. Stith, Robt. Phebe, Jane Smith, Peter Lockett, Samboy a Negro, Toney a Negro, Constaine (or Constance) Moore, Wm. Pretty, Peter Freborne, Hen. Lambert, Wm. Price, Jno. Martyn, Tho. May, Jno. Wells, Alex. Rosse, Jno. Elmore, Ralph Landford, Peter Phepond, Symon Tucker, Margaret Popeley, Tho. Symonds.

MR. PETER RICHARDSON & THE HEIRES OF JAMES ROE, dec'd., 1500

acs. Gloster Co., 17 Mar. 1672/3, p.
127. Beg. in a plantation seated by Mr.
Sawyer, dec'd., along Mr. Burwell's line
to the White Marsh, to Coll. Francis
Willis, to Wm. Debnam, by the path
from the Mill to the Gleab Land, to
Mr. Cheesman's land, &c. Granted to
Mr. Stephen Gill in 1649, sold to Mr.
Peter Richardson & James Roe.

MR. WM. WOODWARD, 640 acs.
New Kent Co., N. side of Mattapony
Riv., some 4 mi. from same upon
branches of Apastenock Cr., 29 Sept.
1668, p. 188. Granted to Coll. Robert
Abrall, 9 Mar. 1660, assigned to Major
Wm. Wyatt, deserted, & now granted
by order &c., further due for trans. of
13 pers: Jno. Hart, Rich. Bentloe,
Mary Bentloe, Tymothy Winch, Patrick
Mason, Jno. Hart, Wm. Ball, Wm.
Couchard, Nich. Cooper, Edw. Deacons,
Marmaduke Foster, Ralph Burts, Henry
Short.

MAJOR WM. FERRER & LT. COLL.
THO. LIGON, 300 acs. Henrico Co.,
S. side of James Riv., 29 Sept. 1668,
p. 188. Beg. in *Mt. Mount my ladyes
field,* at a place where an *old oven* had
stood, to the faling ground of Proctor's,
to the Reedy Br. &c. Trans. of 6 pers:
Walter Felkes, Samll. Rigoll, James
Hicton, Ann Armstrong, Tho. Poldon,
Wm. Dodson.

JOHN BROWNE, 110 acs. Henrico
Co., N. side of James Riv., 29 Sept.
1668, p. 189. Adj. Seath Ward, Radford's lyne, &c. Trans. of 3 pers:
Ellenor Willis, Jone Davis, Phillis ——.

ROBERT COLEMAN, Senr., 283 A.,
14 P., Chas. City Co., S. side Appamattox Riv., 29 Sept. 1668, p. 189. 207
acs. granted to Mr. Walter Chiles, who
sold to sd. Coleman; 2 acs. at the head
thereof granted to Henry Leadbeater,
who sold to sd. Coleman; the residue
lately taken up; beg. at the river, adj.
sd. Leadbeater, sd. Coleman's house,
along the Cart path, the slash, the
Peirtey Sw., the Inland Pattent, &c. 75
acs. for trans. of 2 pers: Tho. Tampin
(or Pampin), Wm. Jenkins.

JNO. TAYLOR, 699 acs., 26 June
1666, p. 190. 450 acs. runing up a Sw.

of Wiccocomico & adj. his own land;
249 acs. runing up a Sw. & adj. Rich.
Iliff (?). Trans. of 14 pers: Phill
Snead, Robt. Hunt, Ed. Turner, Rich.
Harding, Water (or Waler), Smith,
Jno. Haddon, James Hide, Francis
White, Nich. Hill, Geo. Lead, Robt.
Bear, Mary Brett, Wm. Clarke, Jno.
Sop (?).

THOMAS NORTHFLEETS, 300 acs.
on N. side of the S'n. br. of Nancemond Riv., 30 Sept. 1668, p. 190.
Granted to Jno. Skerrott, 17 Mar. 1654
& assigned to sd. Northfleetes.

THO. COWLING, 650 acs. Up. Par.
of Nancemond Co., 22 Sept. 1668, p.
191. 350 acs. part granted him 5 July
1653, & 300 acs. for trans. of 6 pers:
Jane Hely, Robt. Hely, John Rash, Thomas Browne, John Preminter, Thomas
Boane.

MR. JOHN NEEDLES, 128 acs. Lancaster Co., in Rappa. Riv., on E'wd.
side of Barbacue Cr., 1 Oct. 1668, p.
191. Adj. Sir Henry Chickley & Edw.
Webb. Granted to Mr. Robt. Wollerton, 3 Sept. 1658, deserted, & due Mr.
Robt. Beverley by order &c., 24 Oct.
1666, who assigned to sd. Needles; due
for trans. of 3 pers: Rich. Mounts,
Samll. Cox, Elias Robinson.

JNO. SHAPLEY, 350 acs. Gloster
Co., in the narrowes of Milford Haven,
1 Oct. 1668, p. 191. Beg. at cr. divid-
ing this & land of Mr. English, adj.
Mr. Peter Arnold &c. 200 acs. granted
George Cabell, who assigned to Mr.
Abraham English & by him to sd. Shap-
ley; residue for trans. of 3 pers: Jno.
Pratt, Wm. Thomas, Antho. Perin.

THOMAS BRERETON & AN-
THONY ARNELL (Arnold), 1700 acs.
New Kent Co., S. side of Pomonkey
Riv. & part upon branches of Chickahominy Sw. & upon Westover Path behind Rice Hughes & land formerly Capt.
Anthony Langstone's; 2 Oct. 1668, p.
191. Adj. John Jackson. 500 acs.
granted sd. Arnell 25 Oct. 1657; 1200
acs. entered in the office 26 Sept. 1661,
& due for trans. of 24 pers: Jno. Cawsey, Katherine Aires, John Gage, Eliz.

Mallard, Rich. Harvey, John Bradley, Peter La:pero (or La:peur), John Brigsby, John Simpson, Wm. Barker, John Lewis, Eliz. Bandy, Robt. Atkins, Mary Willinson, John Whitcroft, Wm. Aldridge, Eliz. Price, Will Loveday, Robt. *ap* Thomas, Margt. Phillipps, Tho. Cockett, Jane Cubb (or Cobb), Wm. Wheeler, Jno. Mercer.

CAPT. JNO. HULL, 1200 acs. Rappa. Co., N. side of Rappa. Riv., & E. side of Totaskey Cr., 25 Sept. 1668; p. 192. Adj. Tho. Robinson, Edw. Lewis, & Crosse Cr. &c. 800 acs. granted to Quintillian Sherman & Thomas Robinson, 3 Nov. 1664; 400 acs. granted to Miles Reyley 3 Oct. 1664; all which land was deserted for want of seating & now granted by order &c. at James Citty 21 Apr. 1668; & further due for trans. of 24 pers: Jno. Heres (or Leres ?), Jno. Dunn, John Hart, Wm. Searby, Jno. Reader, Mat. Tickner, Jno. Aldridge, Tho. Cox, Cha. Cupper, Wm. Hanch, Wm. Loveridge, Jno. Critchett, Tho. Willyson, Wm Powell, Jno. Seaton, Mary Cencer, Phill. Boadman, Julyas Hall, Tho. Shelton, Wm. Strang, Wm. Haydon, Tho. Harper; Cevilian, Fiedaseth (?) servants.

LUKE LUNN, 450 acs. Nancimond Co., Up. Parish, 22 Apr. 1667, p. 193. Adj. land of Symon Symmonds, Evan Griffith, Griffin's land, Will Poope, Isaraell Johnson, &c. Trans. of 9 pers: Wm. Stephens, et uxor, Tho. Phillips, Jam. Welding 3 times, Lucy his wife, Tho. Walker, John Nash.

MICHAELL KING, 300 acs. Up. Par. of Nancimond Co., 5 Oct. 1667, p. 193. Adj. Robt. Brasseur. Trans. of 6 pers: Tho. Milner 4 tymes, David Bevin, Danll. Beaven.

JNO. COOPS, 800 acs. Nancimon Co., 5 Oct. 1667, p. 193. At the head of Mill Cr. falling into the S'n. br. of Nancimond Riv., & adj. Mr. Francis Spight. Trans. of 16 pers: Dorathy Beaven, Will Hollowell, Ann Feild, Tho. Bones (or Bours), his wife, Hump. Jennings, Jno. Wells, Jno. Ford, Rich. Rogers, Nich. Browne, Francis Barry, Will Cowcomb, Benj. Beale,

Ralph Emery, Jno. Francis, Will Lambert.

WILL. SMELY, 300 acs., at head of Queen's Cr., a br. of the W'n. br. of Nancimond Riv., 5 Oct. 1667, p. 194. Adj. Hugh Sanders & Jno. Moore. Trans. of 6 pers: Wm. Lift, Ri. Burte, Joane Richards, Rich. Day (or Vay), Jno. Steedman, Joane Smith.

MR. RAWLEIGH TRAVERS, 580 acs. S. side Rappa. Co., aboute 3 mi. from the Riv., 12 Sept. 1668, p. 194. Beg. nere a run of Occupaso Cr., adj Cornelius Nowell, & Vall. Allin, to E'wd. of Chickahomani Path, towards *Potobaco Towne* &c, Trans. of 12 pers: Eliz. Hall, Geo. Hearne, Jane Strydick, An Lorkin, Robt. Metcalfe, Aug. Sanderson, Geo. Spivy, James Young, Eliz. Jones, Eli. Uty, Jane Blundall, Eliz. Plume.

MORRIS FEGARRELL, in the rite of Katherine his wife, who was the relict of Roger Howard, 200 acs. Low. Norf. Co., 26 Apr. 1670, p. 194. Granted to sd. Howard & found to escheat as by inquisition &c. under Mr. Wm. Alford, Depty. Escheator &c., now graunted &c.

RICH. PARROTT, Gent., 1300 acs. Lancaster Co., S. side Rappa. Riv., 21 Aug. 1666, p. 195. 740 acs. at the mouth of Wading Muddey Cr; 450 acs. granted him in 1649; 290 acs. being surplus within the bounds; 300 acs. adj. same, upon Parrott's Cr. Said land granted sd. Parrott 6 Oct. 1657, assigned to Minor Minson, who died without heire & land found to escheat; 300 acs. adj. Robert Prise & above the said 740 acs. Trans. of: Mr. Rich. Parrott, Rich. his sonne, David Salisbury, Tho. White, Hen. Bowser, Saml. Eldridge, Jno. Rosse, Jno. Curtys, Ellen Burton, James Wilson, James Grandee, Wm. Mason.

SAME. 950 acs. Lancaster Co., N. side Peanketank Riv., 20 Nov. 1665, p. 196. E. side of Haddawaye's old field, adj. Doctor Whittaker, Gleebe Land Cr. &c, including an island in a gr. bay. 850 acs. part of 1900 acs. granted Mr. John Matrom; & 100 acs. for trans. of 2 pers: Tho. Waldon, Sarah Briggs.

MR. ROBERT HORSINGTON, 2000 acs. Staff. Co., S. side Potomack, S. W. side of Yosockcocomocoe Cr., 29 Oct. 1668, p. 196. Granted to Xpofer. Harris, 7 Oct. 1658, deserted, & granted to Mr. Danl. Wild & Mr. Francis Kirkman, by order &c. 21 Sept. 1663 & patt. 27 Oct. 1663, who transferred their title to sd. Horsington, the land being in W'moreland Co. now called Staff., the Co. being since divided, as alsoe the Cr. called Yeocomico in sd. Wild & Kirkman's patt. which was a mistake being called Yosockcocomocoe.

JOHN LEE, Esqr., 3100 acs. W'moreland Co., 18 Oct. 1668, p. 197. 2600 acs. granted to him 1 Dec. 1654; 500 acs. adj. land of sd. Capt. John Lee, Mr. Tho. Philpott, nigh Machoticke Path, &c., & is due for trans. of 10 pers: Tymothy Freeman, Wm. Bell, Jno. Way, Rich. Sharp, Tho. Sparrow, Tho. Woodward, Stephen Aday, Gawen Kenneday, Jno. Wilson, Jenkin Thomas.

DENNIS EYS (Eyes), 460 acs. N'umberland Co., N. side of the main br. of Gr. Wiccocomoco Riv., & nigh the Cove (or Cone) path, &c., 8 Oct. 1668, p. 197. 270 acs. granted 1 Mar. 1662; & 190 acs. for trans. of 4 pers: Henry Maunder, Alex. Fleming, Xpo. Saveytayle (?), Rich. Williams.

MR. AMBROSE FIELDING, 190 acs. N'umberland Co., N. side Gr. Wiccocomoco Riv., 8 Oct. 1668, p. 198. Adj. John Southerland & Adam Yarrett. Trans. of 4 pers: Tho. Forsith, Lewis Beard, Wm. Osmotherly, Peter Waterson.

PHILLIP EVANS & HUGH HARRIS, 600 acs. N'umberland Co., at head of Mattapony Riv., 8 Oct. 1668, p. 198. Adj. Machotick Path & land of Tymothy Green. Trans. of 12 pers: Tho. Gregson, Tho. Hutchinson, Jno. Butcher, Wm. Battin, Jno. Griffin, Jno. Hemerson, Rich. Lentall, Wm. Morris, Wm. Hill, Rich. Chapman, Jno. Fish, Jno. Buxton.

DENNIS CONWAY, 670 acs. N'umberland Co., N. side of the maine br. of Gr. Wiccocomoco Riv., 8 Oct. 1668,

p. 199. 390 acs. part granted to him 14 Aug. 1664; & 280 acs. for trans. of 6 pers: Jno. Thompson, Robt. Thickes, Tho. Price, Math. Meriox (or Mercox), Geo. Creedwell, Math. Bently.

MR. EDWARD COLES, 626 acs. N'umberland Co., S. side of little Wiccocomoco Cr., 8 Oct. 1668, p. 199. Beg. at the head of Coles Cr., opposite plantation of Tho. Dorrow, to Cr. dividing this & land of Coll. Wm. Clayborne, &c. 494 acs. granted to him 20 Dec. 1650; & 132 acs. for trans. of 3 pers: Robt. Greene, Rich. Fortice, Tho. Swan.

MR. RICH. NELMES, 1200 acs. N'umberland Co., N. side Gr. Wiccocomoco Riv., 8 Oct. 1668, p. 200. Nigh a br. of Chingohan, to br. of the Scotts Cr. &c. 500 acs. assigned from Abraham Moon, 23 Feb. 1653; 525 acs. granted him 4 Feb. 1662; & 175 acs. for trans. of 4 pers: Robt. Pimar, Ed. Fanning, Ellinor an Irish wench, Hugh Mongomery.

JONATHAN HOWES, 589 acs. N'umberland Co., at the head of the broad cr. falling into Yohocomoco Riv., (no date), p. 200. (Note: The following names are listed and it is assumed this land was given for transportation): Jno. Oliver, Eliz. Stafford, Jno. Bell, Edw. Samson, Jno. Ashwith (or Askwith), Wm. Segar, Wm. Hancock, Peter Colvyn, Edw. Knight, Tho. Arsbridge, Jno. Mophatts, Tho. Browne.

JOHN CAPES, 650 acs. New Kent Co., S. side of Yorke Riv., on a br. of Chiccahominy Sw. called Musshunmo (?), 8 Oct. 1668, p. 201. Beg. on S. side of Westover Path, from sd. path to Rich. Bullock's house &c. to lyne that divides New Kent Co. from James Citty Co., &c. Trans. of 13 pers: Mary Bowes, Rich. Simonds, Tho. Barker, David Griffin, Francis Peirse, Rich. Flyde, Hugh Owen, Ralph Edwards, Wm. Smitton, Jno. Owen, James Rawkins, Jno. Moore, Alice Powell.

MR. EDWARD SANDERSON, Merchant, 3500 acs. James Citty Co., 7 Oct. 1668, p. 201. 2715 acs. part surveyed by order of the Gen. Court 25 Sept

1667 by Major Tho. Ligon, on E. side of Chiccahominy Riv., N. on Sanderson's Cr., S. upon cr. parting land of John Felgate & Coll. Robert Holt from his own, &c., crossing the path from sd. Holt to sd. Sanderson, to land of Phillip Chesley & sd. Holt, since purchased by sd. Sanderson, to maine br. of Checkatus Cr., to Sir Wm. Berkeleye's lyne which crosses sd. br. & Ridge from Hotwater Sw. &c., upon poyny point Cr. & his own Cr. which is opposite & against his islands &c; 26 May 1668 surveyed by Mr. Rich. Lawrence, presidt. to Coll. Edmond Scarburgh, Surveyor Genll., for sd. Sanderson, 3 islands in sd. Co., on E. side of sd. Riv., called: Hope alias Morgan's Is., conteyning 107 acs; great Is., 239 acs. & little Is. 89 acs. &c. 2200 acs. granted him Jan. 1650; 400 acs. granted to Phill. Chesley 7 June 1650; 200 acs. for trans. of 4 pers; sd. Wm. Morgan's Island was purchased by John Browneing & sold to James Cockett & sd. Sanderson, who seized upon as his right from Cockett for debt, being 150 acs. & since Sanderson added another right making it 200 acs. & due for trans. of 1 pers. & 500 acs. more adj. the whole devdt., due for trans. of 10 pers: Tho. Webber, Eliz. Blackley, Edward Fellowes, Jo. Carpenter, Owen Evans, Jno. Allen, Robt. Hen (?), Kath. Hudson, Alex. Bugden (or Brigden), Winch Bedford.

CAPT. FRANCIS EPPS, 1980 acs. Chas. Citty Co., S. side James Riv., S. side of Appamattox Riv., 4 Oct. 1668, p. 203. 280 acs. adj. Capt. Batts, Walter Brookes ,Nich. Tatum, Jno. Baker, & his own land. 1780 acs. granted him 23 Jan. 1653 & renewed 17 Mar. 1663; 1700 acs., granted him 29 May 1638, bounding upon Bayly's Cr., Cason's Cr., &c.

MR. THOMAS BRERETON, 3000 acs. New Kent Co., upon branches of Ashiamanscott *alias* Whorecock Sw., & adj. John Pigg. 3 Nov. 1668, p. 203. 1500 acs. granted Mr. Geo. Chapman, 1 Sept. 1658 & 1500 acs. granted sd. Brereton 28 Nov. 1662.

MRS. ELIZABETH CLAYBORNE, Junr., 1000 acs. New Kent Co., on the freshes of Yorke Riv., (date blank), p. 204. On N. side the Riv., against plantation of Charles Edmonds, aboute ½ mi. below the landing, &c. Trans. of 20 pers: Robert Beachman, Arabella Shingleton, Mary Warkeing, Geo. Marshall, Jno. Busby, Wm. Sheares, Tho. Hick, Hen. Robinson, Isabella ———, Wm. Yeos, Jno. Mitchell, Wm. Selamy, Tho. Tucker, Wm. Whitaker, Jno. Probe, Ed. Kettleboy, Kath. Harman, Jno. Thorowgood, & 2 Negroes.

JOHN SMITH & FRANCIS HAYDON, 1000 acs. in Potomack freshes, 20 Nov. 1668, p. 204. Extending to the mouth of the 2nd Cr. above *Puscatna*, along Mr. Randolph, &c. Granted to Francis Carpenter, 5 June 1658, assigned to Weilkes Manders, as by records of N'umberland may appeare, who sold to the abovenamed.

MR. JOHN FLOWRE (or Floure), 750 acs., Chas. Citty Co., bet. *Shirly Hundred* & Turkey Island Cr., 24 Nov. 1668, p. 205. Formerly possesst by Robt., Playne, dec'd., granted to Eliz. Grayne, widdow, & by her (by the name of Heyman) transferred to sd. Playne & lately found to escheat as by inquisition &c. under Thomas Ludwell, Esqr., Escheator Genrll., &c., dated 15 Aug. 1667 & now granted &c.

THOMAS HARWARR (Harwar) & NICH. COX. 922 acs. Rappa. Co., S. side the Riv., 7 Dec. 1668, p. 205. 867 acs. adj. John Chyn, Tho. Pattison & Rich. Bredgatt, Jno. Sharpe, Jno. Mayo, & Lt. Coll. Tho. Goodrich; 55 acs. adj. Rich. Spurlong, & purchased from him; 867 acs. for trans. of 18 pers: Nich. Cox, Wm. Crosse, Hen. Battle, Jno. Williams, Jno. Jones, Bethell Garland, Rich. Brookes, Eliz. Chamberlen, Rich. Knowles, Wm. Crosse, Jno. Loxley, Wm. Chambers, Jno. Stock, Patrick Cookman, Charles Thomas, Tho. Harwarr, Hugh Lee, Sampson Cooper.

MR. THOMAS HOBSON, 660 acs. N'umberland Co., 14 Dec. 1668, p. 206. 550 acs. E'ly. towards the *Gleebe Land*, N. upon the head of Mattapony, &c. 116 acs. upon Mattapony Riv. &c. Granted to John Kent, 20 Nov. 1656, deserted, & now granted &c., & due for trans. of 13 pers: Jno. Jackson, Wm. Smith, Wm. Boharry, Jane Fuller. Jno. Smithson, Joseph Hartington, 1 maid servt., Tho. Spilman, Mary Spilman, Wm. Blake, James Jackson, Evan Johnson, Willm. Colyer. (Note: Marginal notation: 666acs.).

MR. DANLL. CHANDLER, sonne & heire of Mr. Jno. Chandler, dec'd., 350 acs. N'umberland Co., S. E. side of Chickacone Riv., 6 Jan. 1668, p. 206. Adj. Mr. Cortan (or Corsan). & the bridge Cr. Granted sd. John 28 Jan. 1656, renewed 11 Jan. 1663, & due sd. Dan'l. as above.

CAPT. JOSEPH BRIDGER, 1000 acs. Is. of Wight Co., on a Sw. running into the W. br. of Nanzemond Riv., 21 Sept. 1668, p. 207. Including 2 Indian fields. Granted to Thomas Harris 2 Mar. 1658, renewed 18 Mar. 1662, deserted, & now granted by order &c., & further due for trans. of 20 pers: Tho. Key, David Anderson, Peter Loe, Jane Edwards, Mary Rose, Peter Symonds, Grace Dyer, Ann Sculler, Francis Everett, Willm. Thomas, Isaak Stone. Danl. Roberts, Alice Johnson, Susan Howard, Rich. Stroud, Tho. Jones, Willm. Jacob, Giles Drinkert. *Water* Taylor, Symom Franklyn. Marginal Note: It appears there is but 500 acs. of land in this patt. & Mr. Bridger assigned ten rights to Mr. Wm. White. Only the 3 last of these rts. due to the sd. White.

MR. DANL. CHANDLER, sonne & heire of Mr. John Chandler. dec'd., 1500 acs. N'umberland Co., upon branches of Wiccocomoco & Chickacone Rivs.. on the left hand of path from *Chickacone* to *Moraticon;* 6 Jan. 1668. p. 207. 800 acs. part upon Moraticon Path; 600 acs. crossing Snake Sw., a gr. br. of Chiccacone & adj. Mr. Fra. Clay; & 100 acs. adj. Granted sd. John 28 Jan. 1656, renewed 11 Jan. 1663, & now due as above.

MIHILL. GOWREE, 30 or 40 acs. James Citty Co.. *Merchants Hundred* Par., 8 Feb. 1668, p. 208. Formerly belonging to John Turner, dec'd., who purchased of Capt. Rich. Barnehouse; lately found to escheat by inquisition &c., under Coll. Miles Carey. Esch., 20 Dec. 1666, & now due &c.

CURTIS LAND. 457¾ acs., by supposition part in Chas. & James City Co.'s, as yet undetermined. 20 Apr. 1667, p. 208. Adj. Joseph Fry, Dockman's run, John Hickes. Mr. Bromefield & by land of Torry Hamm & Torry Ham Run (?). Trans. of 9 pers: Robt. Thorne, Peter Maborne, John Hollady. Wm. Browne, Roger Waterson, Hen. Glead, Alice Pinson (or Pinton), Wm. Richards. Abra. Kirke.

STEPHEN DURDEN. 250 acs. Up. Par. of Nanzemond Co., 1 Mar. 1668, p. 208. Adj. Robert Hookes, Israel Johnson. Thomas Powell, Tho. Galle & his own land. Trans. of 5 pers: Alex. Camwell. Peter Colgrane (or Colgrave), Jno. Humen, Ann Shara, Peter Starke.

MR. JOHN & GEORGE MOTT, 3700 acs. on N. side in the freshes of Rappa. Co., 10 Sept. 1668, p. 209. Beg. at E'most side of Mundy Cr. &c. nere Beech Br., Wilton's Cr., & adj. Wm. Wilton, &c. 1200 acs. granted them 23 Sept. 1663; & 2500 for trans. of 50 pers: David Browne, Nath. Evatts, Jno. Vyney, Jno. Rotheram, Geo. Mott, Jno. Mott, Ann Mott, Roger Omalong, Ellen Eauks (or Eanks), Tho. Barnes, Wm. Barwick, Tobias Craford, Tho. Cooper. Da. Thomas, Jno. Harris, Ann Williams, Roger Williams, Geo. Hill, Tho. Hunter. Cor. Luglee, Roger Fowler, Issabell Cooke, Christian Benstead, Mary Symkin. (Note: Other names not given.)

MR. JOHN OVERSTREET, 37 A., 77 Ch. 69 dec., Yorke Co., Hampton Par., 7 Sept. 1667, p. 209. Adj. Jeffry Moor, Tho. Dennett, Zachary Padrie, Edward Wade, the horse path & his own land. Trans. of: Margaret Webster.

JOHN ATKINS, sonne of Lewis Atkins, dec'd., 650 acs. S. side Mattapony Riv., 14 Sept. 1668. p. 210. Adj. Edward Diggs. Esqr., Wm. Goffe &c. Granted to Mr. Antho. Stephens, 11 Mar. 1659, renewed 12 Oct. 1662, & by him sold to sd. Lewis 29 May. 1663. & now due sd. John, as heire &c.

THOMAS SALISBURY, 312 acs. N'umberland Co., at the head of Dennis' Cr., 11 Sept. 1666, p. 210. Beg. on N. side of a sw. dividing this from land of Doctor Edward Sanders; adj. Willm. Griffin & Thomas Lane. Trans. of 6 pers: Robt. Lee, James Martyn, Ann Lawson, Jno. Lawson, Eliz. Lawson, Edwd. Raccle (or Rattle).

GODFREY HUNT, 100 acs., in Chuckatuck Cr., 18 Nov. 1668, p. 210. Adj. John Barrett, Tho. Benbridge & Mr. Wm. Burgh. Trans. of 2 pers: Susan Jannah, Robert Newton.

GODFREY RAGSDALE, 450 acs. Henrico Co., N. side Appomattox Riv., 13 Jan. 1668, p. 211. 300 acs. part granted to Tho. Causey 10 Apr. 1641, who sold to John Butler 6 Oct. 1641 & by him sold to Godfry Ragsdale, father of the present possessor (in whose right he holds) as may appeare by an other writeing under the hand of sd. Butler dated 25 Feb. 1642; & 150 acs. by a former grant.

MR. JOHN BEAUCHAMPE, 82 A., 2 R. & 24 Po., Henrico Co., N. side of James River., adj. Barrow plantation; 17 Aug. 1668, p. 211. Trans. of 2 pers: Jno. Beauchamp, John Waylett.

THOMAS PURNELL & JOHN BENSON, 950 acs. Gloster Co., on brs. of the N. Riv. in Mockjack bay, 1 Oct. 1668, p. 211. Adj. Lt. Coll. Elliott. Trans. of 19 pers: Susan Joyce, Sarah Bew, Dorothy Browne, Jeffry Bew, Jno. Wells, Jno. Grymes, Tho. West, Mary Andrewes, Wm. Clarke, Wm. Portis, John Bennett, John Whitmore.

JOHN BRADY, 380 acs. Surry Co., at head of brs. of Graye's Cr., 7 Oct. 1668, p. 212. Beg. by the Mill Sw. side, to br. of Besses Sw., to the maine sw. &c. 180 acs. by his patent. 18 Mar. 1662, & 200 acs. for trans. of 4 pers: Rich. Core, Jeremy Ward, Symon Allen, Wm. Stroud.

WILLM. PULHAM, 311 acs. New Kent Co., N. side Black Cr. on the W'wd. br., 10 Dec. 1668. p. 212. Adj. Willm. Stone, Robert Harman, Wm.

Owen, James Evans, &c. Trans. of 6 pers: Tho. Hales, James Juarles, John Nicholls, Wm. Harris, Eliz. Slade, Tym. Tovey (or Torey).

WILLM. ANDERSON, 437 acs. New Kent Co., Stratton Major Par., 10 Dec. 1668, p. 213. On branches of Poropotanke, beg. on N. side of plantation of Capt. John Fox, to S. side of road to Rappa. &c. 64 acs. purchased of Tho. Hanks; & 373 acs. for trans. of 8 pers: Jane Goffe, Mary Goffe, Aaron Goffe, Jane Jenkins, Roger Jones, Wm. Bengee. Edwd. Kempe, Ann Peper.

ROBERT BLACKWELL & JAMES BLACKWELL, 700 acs. being the upper part of 1350 acs. taken by Major Joseph Croshaw in New Kent Co., S. side of Yorke Riv. in the freshes; 10 Dec. 1668, p. 213. Running to a br. over against Poropotank Cr., to Whiteing's Br., to Arthur Price & to Stretching Sw. Granted Major Croshaw, 27 Feb. 1649, & given by deed of guift to the abovenamed, as by records of Yorke Co. Ct. may appeare.

WILLM. OWEN & JAMES EVANS, 334 acs. New Kent Co., N. side Black Cr., 10 Dec. 1668, p. 213. Towards land of Rebecca Harman, adj. Wm. Stone, to Mattadequne Cr. & land of Wm. Pulham. Trans. of 7 pers: Jno. Davenport, Edwd. Hall, Edward Reeve, Robert Whitton, Geo. Legatt, Tho. Gardiner James Thomson.

MR. JOHN WINSLOE & RICHARD AWBORNE, 2000 acs. New Kent Co., S. side & in the freshes of Yorke Riv., 12 Feb. 1667. p. 213. Adj. Mr. Jonathan Newell. Trans. of 40 pers: Thomas Chowning. Symond Nesome, Mary Coulton, Alice Bancroft, Rachell Puckett, Wm. Netherton, Duke Hornesby, Do. Hall, Ellen Barnbridge. Hen. Bedford, John Mosse, Jo. Talling. Rich. Thaxton, Ed. Docker, Tho. Bond, Edward ———, Mrs. Mary Potter, Ester Bristoe, Jno. Blankett. An. Deluke (or Delux), Ellen Hudson, Fra. Knitter, Xpof. Hall, Jno. Lee. Andr. Vincent, Ed. Poole, Rich. Batting, Rich. Broome, Sarah Mould, Rowland Jones, Steph. Rudwell, Jno. Osborne, Eliz. Jackson, Wm. Hunley,

Wm. Oliver, Wm. Rose, Xpof. Harrum, Danll. Tugg, Margaret Hall; & 1 bought of Mr. Richards.

MR. SAML. SWANN, 248 acs., part of patt. of 540 acs., Surry Co., about 3 mi. W'wd. from John Brady; 18 Dec. 1668, p. 213. In a Reedy br. of Ciprus Sw., by the path to Capt. Corker's, to S. side of Pigeon Sw., &c. Granted to Mr. Tho. Swann, Junr., 28 Sept. 1664, & due the sd. Sam'l. as brother of sd. Thomas, who is now dec'd.

THOMAS SWANN, Esqr., 500 acs. James Citty Co., N. side of James Riv., 18 Dec. 1668, p. 214. Part of a devdt. of Mr. Rice Hoe, next above Thomas Scott's leased land, sold by sd. Hoe to James Warradine. Sd. land purchased by Capt. Edward Hill of James Warradine, who purchased of sd. Hoe, & due sd. Swann by purchase from sd. Hill.

JOSEPH BAYLY, 517 acs. N. side Lancaster Co., upon maine br. of Corotoman Riv., 18 Sept. 1668, p. 214. Adj. John Taylor, Domine Theriott &c. Trans. of 11 pers: James Lawrence, Jane Johnson, Edwd. Digby, Mathew Merriett & his wife, Jno. Kent, Antho. Thompson, Tymothy Swinyell (?), Jno. Peters, Mary Gardner, Hen. Simpkin.

MR. THOMAS SPENCER, 334 acs. & 28 po., New Kent Co., N. side Yorke Riv., adj. plantation whereon he lives, 20 Aug. 1668, p. 214. Being a surplus of land & granted out of Capt. Underwood's clayme; running through the meadow of Mattaquince, &c. Due by order &c., 25 Sept. 1667, & for trans. of 7 pers: Tho. Batten, Anne Batten, Andrew Gill, Jno. Daniell, Mary Duram, Hanna Love (or Lowe), Wm. Stenton.

CAPT. ANTHO. FULGHAM, 150 acs. Is. of Wight Co., 18 Mar. 1668, p. 215. 100 acs. upon Pagan point Bay, land of Mr. Thomas Davis & Mr. Jno. Mohoone; 50 acs. of marsh adj. land he bought of Mr. Silvester Thatcher on Pagan Cr. 100 acs. granted sd. Thatcher & Fulgham, 22 Oct. 1643, & by Thatcher assigned; & 50 acs. for trans. of: Robt. Hare.

MR. THOMAS CULLEN, 400 acs. Up. Par. of Nanzemond Co., 20 Sept. 1668, p. 215. Adj. Jno. Moore, Jno. Garrett & Francis Hutchens. Trans. of 8 pers: Tho. Cullen, his wife & 6 children.

ROBERT SMITH, Esqr., 550 acs., Lancaster Co., in Sunderland Cr., 17 Apr. 1669, p. 215. Granted to Edward Boswell, dec'd., lately found to escheat as by inquisition &c., under Henry Corbyn, Esqr., Dep. Eschr., 5 May 1668, & now granted &c.

MR. THO. WOODWARD, 100 acs. marsh land in the Low. Par. of Is. of Wight Co., on Pagan Cr., 17 Apr. 1669, p. 216. Adj. Willm. Parrot, by Capt. Anth. Fulgham & lands in possession of Rich. Maddison, to place called the *Iron point*, &c. Trans. of 2 pers: Margaret Peacock, Edwd. Davys.

HAMOND WOODHOUSE, 341 A., 3 R., 7 P., Chas. Citty Co., N. side James Riv., 20 Apr. 1669, p. 216. At the head of his own & land of Jno. Warrener, nigh the Seller run, &c. Trans. of 7 pers: Robt. Jervis, Amy Sparson, Pet. Gill, Robt. Derrick, Wm. Mason, Patrick Izard, Mary Cole.

THOMAS WEBSTER, 115 acs. Henrico Co., N. side of Appamattox Riv., 20 Apr. 1669, p. 216. Adj. Geo. Archur, along the Old Towne run, the old towne cr., &c. Trans. of 2 pers: Mary Clatan, Nich. Bishop.

WILLIAM MATHEW, 1148 acs., called *Lilly*, Rappa. Co., upon brs. of Totoskey, 18 Nov. 1668, p. 217. Adj. Mr. Wm. Travers, a hucklebury pond, &c. Trans. of 23 pers: Rich. Mountey, James Morris, Wm. Jones, Ralph Staynes, Jno. Warren, Abrahd. Shaw, James Watson, Anth. Hartup, Mary Cremer, Eliz. Williams, Andrew Johnson, Wm. Joyner, Barth. Painter, Fra. Clarke, Geo. May, Jno. Buck, Jame Acton, Kath. Head, Jno. Ward, Geo. Rivers, Ann Wilson, Wm. Clarke, Andrew Phenice (?).

ARTHUR ETTY, 491 acs., called *Wachford*, Rappa. Co., 19 Apr. 1669,

p. 217. Adj. Willm. Mathew & a br. of Totaskey Cr. Trans. of 10 pers: Mary Leechman, Arth. Johnson, Mary Thetford, Wm. Stephens, Tho. Greene, Robt. Owen, Jno. Grant, Andrew Thompson, Marke Jackson, Fran. James.

MR. THO. IKEN, 1350 acs. Warwick Co., Mulberry Island Par., 14 May 1669, p. 218. Beg. at the mouth of a cr. nere his now dwelling house, formerly the dwelling house of Capt. Wm. Peirce, which cr. divides this from Baker's neck *where the Church formerly stood,* along James River & the gr. marsh dividing this from Mulbury Is., nere George Harwood, John Basse, to an old field nere the Cart path, along Brewer's & Pawle's (Paulle's) land on the side of Bedlam Marsh, up Warwick Riv., nere the mouth of Butler's Bridge Cr., up N. br. of same dividing this & land of Capt. Tho. Flynt, to Butler's Cr. Sw., along Mr. Henry Filmer, &c. Part of 2100 acs. granted sd. Wm. Peirce 16 Dec. 1643, etc. 400 acs. overplus found herein, due in right of his wife Elizabeth, late wife to Mr. Edward Griffith, dec'd., for trans. of 8 pers: Wm. Wharton, Theo. Potter, Rich. Foxhall, Wm. Whitaker, Henry Morgan, Mary Lord, Tho. Needles, Thomas a Negro.

ROBERT BEVERLEY, 6000 acs. on both side of one of Mattapony runns, 12 July 1669, p. 218. Neere the Indian Path betwixt *Mattaponie* & *Port Tobacco,* &c. Trans. of 60 pers.*

MR. THOMAS HAYNES, 1300 acs. Lancaster Co., 20 July 1669, p. 219. Beg. at a point in the forke of Indian Cr., formerly called Coratomen Cr., out of Fleet bay, bet. Mr. George Wale & Mr. Robert Jones, adj. sd. Haynes' Mill path where it crosses the road from *Rappa.* to *Wiccocomoco,* &c., by an Indian path in sight of Haddawayes Cr., dividing this from land of Simon Sallard, &c. 450 acs. part granted Jervas Dodson 3 Mar. 1656, who assigned to sd. Wale, who assigned to sd. Haynes; 500 acs. granted sd. Dodson 29 Nov. 1658; both tracts included in one patt. & granted sd. Wale 10 Feb. 1662 & assigned to sd. Haynes; 160 acs.

granted Mr. Robert Jones 28 June 1664, & since to Capt. Edmd. Lister as deserted land, who assigned to sd. Haynes 12 Oct. 1668; 190 acs. for trans. of 4 pers: James Day, Joan Stroud, Edwd. Ellis, Judith Rogers.

MR. JOHN HERBERT, 1227 acs. Low. Norf. Co., upon W. side of the S'n. br. of Eliz. Riv., 21 July 1669, p. 220. Up Deepe Cr. to Goose Cr., to land of John Manning, by Dueling Cr. &c. 350 acs. by his patt., 1 Oct. 1661; 350 acs. 11 Mar. 1664; 527 for trans. of 11 pers: Jno. Horrod, Eliz. Bankes, Jno. a Scott, Geo. Green, Mary Goodrich, Susan Poole, Wm. Green, Jno. Waller, Jno. Clarke, Mary Jones, James Harlow.

MR. JOHN MANING (Manning), 300 acs. Low. Norf. Co., E. side of the S'n. br. of Eliz. Riv., 14 Sept. 1667, p 220. Upon Gatters Cr. & his own land. 200 acs. granted him 25 Oct. 1648, & 100 acs. for trans. of 2 pers: Jno. Carpenter, Luke White.

WM. CHICHESTER, 220 acs. Low. Norf. Co., on N. side of Danll. Tanners Cr., 14 Sept. 1667, p. 220. Trans. of 5 pers: James Garland, Marke Tomlyn, Tymothy Rice, John Seaborne, Mary Ringly.

HENRY HOLSTEAD, 58 acs., Low. Norf. Co., S. side of the E'n. br. of Eliz. Riv., at the head of Indian Cr., 14 Sept. 1667, p. 221. Adj. Thomas Richardson, Wm. Whitehurst & his own land. Trans. of: Eliz. Bright.

RICHARD NICHOLLS, 320 acs. Low. Norf. Co., S. side of the E'n. br. of Eliz. Riv., 14 Sept. 1667, p. 221. Adj. Moses Lynton, Adam Dollard & his own land. 120 acs. part of 250 acs. granted Robt. Martyn 12 Oct. 1638, who sold to Tho. Miles 4 June 1645, who sold to sd. Nicholls 8 Sept. 1649; 200 acs. for trans. of 4 pers: Tho. Eastfeild, Peter Martyn, Rowld. Marke, Owen Hetland.

JOHN SLOW, 640 acs. Low. Norf. Co., W. side of the S'n. br. of Eliz. Riv., on N. side of Deepe Cr., 14 Sept.

1667, p. 221. Beg. at his father's cor. tree. Trans. of 13 pers: James Endfield, Mathew Frith, Robt. Dallison, Jeremy Neeve, Tymothy Ware, Rowland Meeres, Jno. White, James Allington, Arthur Hickman, Mary Hart, Wm. Haynes, Jacob De Hay, Bruce Matrom.

THOMAS FENFORD, 50 acs. Low. Norf. Co., on W. side of the S'n. br. of Eliz. Riv., 14 Sept. 1667, p. 222. Adj. his own land. Trans. of: Richard Morris.

THOM. HARRIS, 97 acs. Low. Norf. Co., N. side of Danll. Tanner's Cr., 14 Sept. 1667, p. 222. Adj. Mr. Tho. Fulcher. Trans. of 4 pers: Wm. Mosse, Robt. Taunton, Peter Abram, Hen. Lownd.

NICHOLAS WILLIAMS, 200 acs. Low. Norf. Co., N. side of Danll. Tanner's Cr., 14 Sept. 1667, p. 222. Trans. of 4 pers: Herbert Emmett, George Jones, Hanna Emmerson, Roger Thornley.

JOHN CORPOREW, 200 acs. Low. Norf. Co., S. side of the E'n. br. of Indian Cr. in Eliz. Riv., adj. Wm. Morrys & Moses Linton. Trans. of 4 pers.*

MR. GEORGE MOORE, 1400 acs. Is. of Wight Co., on the 2nd Sw. of Black Water, 12 May 1669, p. 223. Adj. Capt. Wombrell, Hull's br., Beaver Dam br., &c. Trans. of 28 pers: Tho. Walter twice, Jane Walter, Jno. Holly, Jno. Collins, Rich. Bennett, Jno. Henkens, Robt. Scott, Marth. Farloe, Alice Moore, Jno. Dunkin, Jno. Beddins, Wm. Powell, Rich. Lyne, Robt. Bennett, Rich. Lowden, Richard Beedle, Wm. Kill, Hanna Woodriff, Tho. Elmes, Jno. Whitby, Tho. Whitby, Tho. Williams, Jno. Shells, Jone Rugg, Hen. Darsy, Mary Jones, Pedro a Negro.

THOMAS LUDWELL & THOMAS STEGG, Esqrs., ½ acr. James Citty, on the Riverside & adj. to the W'most of those 3 houses all which joyntly were formerly called by the name of the *old State House;* 1 Jan. 1667, p. 223. Due for building of a house in James Citty.

MR. WILLM. OLDIS & MR. ROBERT RUFFIN, 2050 acs. Is. of Wight Co., bet. brs. of the Blackwater, 11 June 1669, p. 224. Adj. Coll. Pitt, Math. Tomlin & Capt. Fulgham. Trans. of 41 pers: Tho. Nayes, Rich. Hatton, Jno. Morgan, Wm. Hindge, Rich. Hindge, Jane Hindge, Rich. Hindge, Junr., Jane Hindge, Junr., Wm. Oldis 2 tymes, Mr. Da. Leare (?) 3 tymes, Stephen Pinke, Wm. Pinkeney, Wm. Elliott, Susan Elliott, Saml. Duke, Mildred Nicholls, Tho. Austen, Mary Jones, Jno. Poe, Wm. Peirce, Robt. Pawlett, Wm. Grigg, Jno. Arthur, Petr. Strange, Hen. Long, Robt. Rouse, Jno. Peterson, Hen. Thompson, Tho. Hill, Richd. Loyd, Wm. Green, David Milton, Sara. Wilkins, Ben. Burton, Charles Balam. Hugh Hartley, Phill. Bond, Robert Duglas.

MR. HEN. RANDOLPH, 961 acs., 1 furlong, 26 perches, Henrico Co., known as *Tymber Slash,* 23 Oct. 1666, p. 224. Bet. Mr. Cock & Mr. Crewe's yard by a Cart path, by E'ly. run of 4 Mi. Cr., adj. Tho. Taylor, Bryan Smith &c. Granted to Tho. Ludwell, Esqr., 16 June 1663, deserted; now granted by order &c. & due for trans. of 19 pers.*

MR. JOHN PATE & MR. ROBERT BEVERLY, 6000 acs. upon N. side of Mattapony mayne run, adj. sd. Beverly's land, 15 July 1669, p. 225. Trans. of 120 pers: Jno. Pate, Tho. Fitts, German Hall, Wm. Kenon, Saml. Dunning, Mary Dunning, Hen. Dunning, Jno. Carter, Mary Carter, Morgan Treson (or Trelow), Edwd. Dyer, Eliz. Jones, Susan Martyn, Tho. Fryer, Wm. Allen, Tho. Allen, Jeremy Taylor, Jno. Parker, Hen. Leroy, Patrick Mahoon, Wm. Hare, James Parland, Tho. Starling, Tho. Gardner, Sy. Eldridge, Geo. Longer, Joan Sanderson, Jno. Johnson, Fra. James, James Jackson, Tho. Williams, James Jordan, Reyn. Patterson, Tho. Oliver, Jno. Betters, James Belt, Jere. Draper, Tho. (an) Indian, Mary Thompson, Walter Light, Wm. Paine, Edwd. Evens, Jno. Ward (or Ware), Tho. Harwood, Robt. Allen, Jno. English, Jonas Summer, Do. Bywater, Nich. Dance, Geo. Windul (?), Wm. Alexander, Math. Cotton, Wm. Kelham, Isack

Oliver, Jno. Coughland, Jno. Smith, Math. Jones, Jno. Sowell, Jno. Rivers, Marth. Hubard, Azarius Robinson, Ma. Davis, Tho. Gurnett (or Garnett), Tho. Starkey, Jno. Turwyn, Ja. Frynd (or Fryer), Tho. Ferris, Tho. Read, Foster Frank, Eldred Payne, Tho. Cumton, Mary Putterhall, Freeman Farmer, Theodras Mucarter, Toby Fryer, Eliz. Coney, Lath. Harford, Jno. Dixon, Talor Foster, Jno. Cooke, Ja. Talbott, Xpo. Charlton, Ja. Turner, Tho. Jones, Robt. Whiteing, Rich. Taylor ,Eliz. Barker, Hugh Davis, Jno. Cooke, Tho. Lee, Theo. Jones, Tho. Farthingale, Tho. Ball, Jno. Beedell, Jeremy Aldridge, Mary Aldridge, Hen. Johnson, Tho. Raylan (or Raylard), Wm. Ferris, Tempus Milner, Dor. Bridges, Tho. Taylor, Alexd. Stanton, (or Hunton), Wm. Bernett, Wm. Hayward, Anth. Hawley, Dorothy Stanly; & 13 Negroes.

MR. JOHN PATE, 1200 acs. Rappa. Co., N. side Gilson's Cr., adj. Robert Beverley & Tho. Button; 15 July 1669, p. 226. Trans. of 24 pers.*

MR. THOMAS PATTISON, 1626 acs. Rappa. Co., on the S. side, 12 June 1669, p. 226. Beg. on Ralph's Cr. or Kilman's Beavor Dams, down Tom Browne's Sw. &c. 400 acs. granted him 8 Nov. 1667; & 1226 acs. for trans. of 25 pers: Tho. Hudson, Jno. Richman, Patrick Duelling, Hen. Morgan, Robt. Baker, Danl. Cutler, James Hooper, Symon Dorrell, Wm. Burton, Nich. Bead, Rich. Bayly, Hen. Haselwood, Robert Weekes, Jane Pigg, Edwd. Pigg, Lucy Perry, Robt. Cade, Edwd. Newberry, Jno. Grymson, Robt. Bryon, Mary Norton, Jeffry Moore, Jno. George, Peter Nevill, John Foard.

MR. THO. NEWHOUSE, 1050 acs. Chas. Citty Co., S. side James Riv., 15 July 1669, p. 227. Adj. Mr. Sparrow, Burchen Sw. &c. Trans. of 21 pers: Edward Ellis, Roger Reese, Hugh Barrow, Judith Avery, Fra. Poyters, Wm. Hind, Jno. Ward, Ellenor Fowle, Tho. Mallory, Jno. Barloe, Ja. Cabbock, Samp. Ellis twice, Jno. Ball, James Okeldry, Tho. Fitchett, Danl. Sawman, Ann Danby (or Dauby), Jno. Cromwell,, Jno. Yapp, David a Scotchman.

MAJOR WM. PEIRSE (Peirce), 3110 acs. W'moreland Co., 14 Aug. 1669, p. 227. Adj. 600 acs. purchased of John Wood, land of Katherine Brent; nere the horse path, his own land &c. 600 acs. granted him 22 Mar. 1665/6, & 2500 granted him 3 Oct. 1666 & now joyned into one patt.

THOMAS ROBINSON, 1000 acs. N'umberland Co., on the head of Yohocomoco Riv., & adj. Antho. Linton; 18 Aug. 1669, p. 228. Granted to sd. Robinson 24 July 1664 by name of *John*, which was a mistake & now granted in his proper name.

MR. BENJAMIN HOWARD, 700 acs. New Kent Co., S. Yorke Riv., 23 Aug. 1669, p. 228. On lower side of Cowcansick Br., crossing Wm. Swinburne, adj. Jno. Waddell, Jno. Jackson, Westover Path, Major Genll. Hamond, &c. 325 acs. part he lives upon, purchased of Capt. Anth. Langston; & 475 acs. for trans. of 10 pers: Jno. Arson, Geo. Parker, Wm. Benson, Ann Grange, Hen. Peters, Anth. Hurd, Abra. Brocas, Arthur Brett, Wm. Pratt, Jno. Pratt.

PETER FOARD, 300 acs. New Kent Co., 23 Aug. 1669, p. 228. At the mouth of Massicooke Cr. on N. E. side of Mattapony Riv. & adj. Capt. Richard Barnehouse. Trans. of 5 pers: Jno. Gilson, Geo. Gunt, Abigal Gaylar, Peter Sprout (or Spront), Nath. Frances, John Shoare.

JOHN CAPE, 639 acs. New Kent Co., on brs. of Chickahominy Riv., 23 Aug. 1669, p. 229. Adj. Mr. Tho. Mitchell's land that crosses Towincke Br., to Rich. Scrugg & Mr. Tonnsey, Wm. Mosse, Jonathan Higgly; &c. 122 acs. purchased of sd. Mitchell; 200 acs. of sd. Scrugg, & 316 acs. of Robert Garrett, & now bounded with entire bounds.

SAME. 830 acs. Same Co., date & page. On N. W. side of Westopher Path, adj. Mr. Math .Hill, to dividing line bet. this & James Citty Co., crossing a br. of Musciminoe (?), along Mr. Thomas Marstson, Mr. Booth, Lt. Coll. Hen. Gooch, the Rumney Marsh, Mr.

Tho. Brereton & Anth. Arnold; 30 acs. on E. side of sd. Marsh, adj. Brereton & Wm. Griffin. Trans. of 17 pers: Jno. Petigrew, Roger Marston, Amy Amys, Robt. Thorowgood, Hen. Rouse, Jno. Andrewes, Ambrose Field, Anth. Brewster, Tho. Toft, Arthur Hildbrand, Ann Mitton, Wm. Bruce, Archabold Harris, Margart. Neave, John Grere, David Duglas, Robt. Williams.

RICH. SCRUGG, 400 acs. New Kent Co., W. side of Towincke Br., a br. of Chickahominy Riv., 23 Aug. 1669, p. 230. Adj. Edwd. Price, Mr. Mitchell, Tho. Morley & Jno. Cape. 300 acs. part of 1000 acs. granted sd. Scrugg & Geo. Gilbert in 1662; 100 acs. part of 1000 acs. granted sd. Scrugg & Charles Woodington.

MR. AMORY BUTLER, 280 acs. New Kent Co., upon head br. of Hartquake Sw., on N. side of Mattapony Riv., 17 Apr. 1669, p. 230. Running to Bridge Sw., a br. of Peanketank Sw. Trans. of 6 pers: Geo. Upton, Willm. Groves, Arth. Bromley, Ambro. Bingham, Wm. Raven, Susan Dodd.

MR. THOMAS EDMONDSON, 220 acs. Rappa. Co., at Relph's Cr. issuing from Puscaticon, 16 Apr. 1667, p. 231. Adj. Kilman's (Sw.), Burchen Br., Beavor Dam Br. & the Green Sw. Granted to Neile Peterson, 2 Dec. 1663, deserted, & now granted by order &c. (Note: The following names appear:) Jno. Richards, Wm. Prouse, Hen. Row, Peter Ayres, Robt. Wilson.

GEORGE PEAD, 150 acs. Gloster Co., 25 Sept. 1671, p. 231. Adj. Wm. Bearline & S. side of *Winter Harbour.* Granted to John Pead, his father, 21 Sept. 1652 & now due as sonn & heire.

GILBERT ELAM, 867 A., 3 R., 24 P., Henrico Co., S. side James Riv., 25 Sept. 1671, p. 231. 503 acs. granted sd. Elam 18 Mar .1662; above *Bermuda Hundred,* bet. Tho. Shippy & Richd. Johnson; the residue adj. sd. tract, Henry Lowin, Mr. Wm. Hatcher, Tho. Wells' new plantation, nigh the Fox Slash, Martin Elam, Roxdale Sw., Robt. Bowman, Junr., Robt. Elam, &c. 503

acs. granted to Robt. Elam, 20 Nov. 1662 & due sd. Gilbert as marrying his daughter; the residue for trans. of, 7 pers: Eliza. Elam, Martha Elam, Richd. Simmes (?), Francis Martin, Jno. Griffith, Martha Elam, Eliza. Elam.

ROBERT FLACK (Flake), 2400 acs. Is. of Wight Co., on brs. of the Blackwater, 20 Aug. 1666, p. 232. W. side of the 2nd Sw., by *John a pouch* quarter; below the bridge, to 3rd Sw. &c. adj. Jno. Oliver, Tho. Wombell &c. 1970 acs. due by his former patt., & 430 acs. for trans. of 9 pers: Mary Jenkens, Jno. Bettey, Jane Eason (or Eaton), Robt. Loafes, Geo. Johnson, Jno. Colwall, Geo. Toods, Geo. Morrison, Tho. Anmors (?).

SAME. 450 acs., Same Co. & page; 10 Sept. 1669. Adj. the above, lands of Phill. Hanniford, Wm. Porter & Mr. Allen. Trans. of 9 pers: Joan Coale, James Anderson, Wm. Friswell, Robt. Furgue, Jno. Melligine (Melligue ?), Walter Fleming, Jno. Wattson, Jno. Mackes, Wm. Simpson.

MR. THO. ATKINSON, 600 acs. Is. of Wigh tCo., on the 3rd Sw. of Blackwater, 10 Sept. 1669, p. 233. 300 acs. granted to Robert Flack (Flake), who gave to the wife of sd. Atkinson; 300 acs. for trans. of 6 pers: Tristram Eason, Luke Mausen (or Mansen), Merick Edwards, Robt. Sampson, Merlyn Cant, Joseph Baker.

WM. RICHARDSON & THOMAS ATKINSON, 230 acs. Is. of Wight Co., S. W. side of the 3rd Sw. of Blackwater, 10 Sept. 1669, p. 233. Adj. Robt. Flake. Trans. of 5 pers: Wm. Agg, Wm. Musgrove, Jno. Bush, Eliz. Morgan, Jno. Griffice.

MR. ROWLAND PLACE, 1228 A., 1 R., 26 P., Henrico Co., N. side James Riv., at. Almond's Cr., 25 Aug. 1669, p. 233. 600 acs. granted to Humphry Lister in 1650, given to John White, as by records of James Citty, who sold to Mr. Tho. Hunt, who sold to sd. Place; 628 acs. for trans. of 13 pers: Wm. Jeffries, Abra. Jackson, Tim. White, Bernard Moor, Jaques Johnson, Peter

Ellet, Edwd. Hinton, And. Beale, Robt. Cary, Robt. Haines, Wm. Jarrett, Tho. Yates, Rich. Harwood.

JOHN WINBORNE, 500 acs. Nanzemond Co., by Somerton Marsh, 22 Apr. 1669, p. 234. Trans. of 10 pers: Jno. Winborne & his wife, Hanah Davis & Sister, Morris Hoper, Fran. Williams, Rich. Travis, Jno. George, Jno. Law (or Land), Peter Arrow.

MR. THO. BRIDGE, 750 acs. Low. Norf. Co., Lynhaven Par., 10 Aug. 1669, p. 234. Adj. Lt. Col. Lambert; by a path from Mr. Hoskins to said Bridges, &c. 256 acs. granted him 25 Mar. 1655; 150 acs. purchased of Henry Snaile; & 344 acs. for trans. of 7 pers: James Toolton, Sarah Edick, Richard & Nich. Williams, Ann Beales, Robt. Speed.

JOHN LAWRANS, 50 acs. in the Western Br. of Nanzemond Riv., adj. Jno. Crewden & Henry Lawrens 22 Apr. 1669, p. 234. Trans. of 1 pers.*

CHARLES ROANE (Rone), 761 acs. Gloster Co., S. side of the gr. sw. on head of Peanketank Riv., 26 Dec. 1669, p. 235. Beg. neare the Road path crossing the Gr. Sw. from Mr. Partridge's house, &c. Trans. of 15 pers.*

SAME. 150 acs. Same Co., date & page. Adj. Gill's land. Trans. of 3 pers.*

MR. RICH. SEARLES, 345 acs. W'moreland Co., S. E. side of Nominy Riv., 2 July 1669, p. 235. Adj. Mr. Tho. Bushrod & a pond dividing this & land of Wm. Spence. 150 acs. by patt. 10 Apr. 1665; & 195 acs. for trans. of 4 pers: Rich. Searles, Tho. Read, Wm. Harris, Mary Middleton.

SAME. 278 acs., same Co. & date, p. 236. Flood's Cr. dividing this & land of Peter Dunken. Assigned by Rich. Kennor & Eliz. his wife, 26 Feb. 1667.

MR. THO. YOWELL, 780 acs. W'moreland Co., S. E. side of Nominy Riv., 2 July, 1669, p. 236. Above Flood's Cr., adj. Peter Dunken & Coll.

Nich. Spencer. 500 acs. granted Mr. Tho. Vaulx, 18 Oct. 1650, who with Eliz. his wife sold to sd. Yowell; 150 acs. granted sd. Yowell, 19 Oct. 1653; & 130 acs. for trans. of 3 pers: Jno. Warren, Ann Wells, Phillip Flowe.

JOHN PIPER, 400 acs. W'moreland Co., upon branches of Appomattox Cr., 2 July 1669, p. 236. Adj. Mr. Jno. Washington, Mr. Robt. Nurse & Mr. Jno. Watts. Trans. of 8 pers: Tho. Carrock, Sarah Newman, Ann Marshall, Henry (?) Ward, Jno. Yates, Ellenor ——, Eliz. Hutson, David Darling.

PETER DUNKEN, 140 acs. W'moreland Co., S. E. side Nominy Riv., 2 July 1669, p. 237. N. E. side of Flood's Cr., a cr. dividing this & land of Tho. Yowell. Sold to him by Rich. Kenor (Kennor) & Elizabeth his wife, 6 Oct. 1665.

GERRARD MASTERS & WILLM. WALLER, 800 acs. Staff. Co., S. W. side Ocquia Cr., 2 July 1669, p. 237. Adj. Mr. Rich. Fossiker (Fossaker), near head of Hope Cr., on a Ridge, along the Hope line, &c. Trans. of 16 pers: Jno. Roberts, Jno. Windell, James Corroff (or Corross), Mary Cell, Wm. Grinsley, Eliz. Willis, Robt. Jones, Jno. Sanders, Hen. Butler, Rich. Thorne, Sarah Bower, Wm. Martyn, Jno. Graves, Jo. Wilson, Wm. Watson, Jno. Harvy.

WM. SPENCE, 180 acs. W'moreland Co., S. E. side of Nominy Riv., 2 July 1669, p. 237. Adj. Rich. Searles. Sold by Rich. Kenner to Rich. Searles, re-purchased by Kennor, who with Eliz. his wife sold to sd. Spence, 2 Oct. 1665.

JOHN MATHEWES, 1567 acs., in the freshes & on N. W. side of Potomack Riv., on S. W. side of Mussell Cr., & adj. land of Mr. Tho. Bunberry; 2 July 1669, p. 238. Trans. of 31 pers: Mary Loaton, Danl. Laury, Cornel. Crehon, Jno. Cullis (or Collis), Mary James, Jno. Smith, Robt. Wright, Geo. Hill, Rich. Meredith, Eliz. Burnett, Steph. James, Phl. Chambers, Tho. Cooke, Edwd. Plunkett, Jno. Scott, Mary Starky, Rothell Nelmes, Tho. Mallard, Eliz. Harrison, Margt. Latham, Robt.

Lynn, Wm. Lynn, Fra. Waddington, Alice Hitchin, Tho. Hatchaway, Jno. Meredith, Grace Roberts. Jone Dorne, Geo. Crouch, Jno. Alexander, Wm. Kirkeman.

JOHN CLARKE, 600 acs. Yorke Co., at the New Pocoson Riv., 10 Aug. 1669, p. 238. 500 acs. at the head of a br. parting it from 100 acs. pattented by Wm. Clarke, his father; running to Deadman's brooke &c. 100 acs. upon sd. river & Oyster Cr. 350 acs. purchased by his father of Joseph Jolly; 150 acs. of Jno. Watkins; 100 acs. by patt. to said Wm. 21 Aug. 1637. & due the above as heire, &c.

CAPT. EDMOND LISTER. 435 acs. N'umberland Co., 20 Apr. 1669, p. 239. Adj. Mr. John Chandler, Adam Yarrett & Rich. Rice. Trans: of 9 pers.*

RICHARD JONES. 200 acs. upon branches of Puscataway Cr., 24 Apr. 1669, p. 239. Adj. Mr. Tho. Brereton on E. side of Whorecock Sw. Trans. of 4 pers.*

WILLM. BRYNN, 200 acs. Nanzemond Co., adj. Charles Camell; 22 Apr. 1669, p. 239. Trans. of 4 pers: Mary Grady, Mary Bayly, Ann Wahan, Wm. Brynn.

MR. LAWRENCE SMITH, 75 acs. Gloster Co., Abington Par., betwixt land of Wm. Alsop, dec'd., Mr. Tho. Graves, Senr. & his own land; 15 Mar. 1668/9, p. 240. Nere the head of Timber Neck Cr. Trans. of 2 pers: John Fletcher, Jno. Winterbottome.

MR. JOHN BUCKNER & THOMAS ROYSTON, 1000 acs. Gloster Co., in Chiscake branches, 12 Oct. 1668, p. 240. Beg. nere Chiscake Path, along Rappa. Path &c. Trans. of 20 pers: Jno. Buckner, Eliz. Williams, Valentine Smith, Abr. Smith, Jno. Falkner, Tho. Royston. Robt. Haniger, Jno. Clay, Edwd. Hewes, Hen. Glover, Jno. Demott, Ann Steed (or Sleed), Jno. Colt, Peter Johnson, Jno. Willis, Edward ———, Wm. Crump, Henry Nelson, Peter Barton, Abr. Harman.

JNO. CURTIS, 160 acs. Gloster Co., adj. Tho. Purnell, Jno. Benson, & Col. Elliott; 27 Oct. 1668, p. 241. Trans. of 3 . pers: Tho. Williams, Griffith Hewes.

JNO. HOWELL, 203 A., 32 po., comonly called Bakers, Chas. Citty Co., at the mouth & on S. side of Appamattox Riv., 18 Aug. 1669, p. 241. A gutt parting this & land of Nath. Tatum, running to Cawson's Cr. &c. Granted sd. Howell for a greater quantity but upon resurvey but the quantity above found.

FRANCIS REDFORD, 254 A., 3 R., 8 P., Henrico Co., on N. side of James Riv., 5 Aug. 1659, p. 241. Nigh the Round about Slash; adj. his own land &c. Trans. of 5 pers: Rich. Gerrard, Nath. Pertue (or Perlue), Wm. Stile, Jno. Milner, Marke Carter.

ROBER (Robert ?) TUCKER, 100 acs. in the Western br. of Eliz. Riv., adj. land of the Widdow Jennings & Jno. Ellott, &c; 22 Apr. 1669, p. 242. Trans. of 2 pers: Rich. Murffee, Nath. Dibble.

HEN. GAY, 400 acs. Up. Par. of Nanzemond Co., adj. James Collins & Phillip Dewell; 22 Apr. 1669, p. 242. Trans. of 8 pers: 4 children assigned by Tho. Cullen; Andrew Clawson, Edwd. Jones, Wm. Lucorkle, Sarah Wake.

MR. ROBT. BEVERLY, 116 acs. Gloster Co., Petsoe Par., on a path from Mr. Wm. Howard towards Mr. Forsith's; 22 Apr. 1669, p. 242. Trans. of 3 pers.*

MR. RICHARD LEE, 450 acs. Gloster Co., Petsoe Par., 29 Jan. 1668, p. 243. Beg. in the Beach Spring Valley, to the bridge Sw., by the Rich land br., to Mr. Charles Roane, Coles branch &c. Trans. of 9 pers: Rich. Lee, Wm. Winfeild. Abra. Good, Math. Dent, Silvester Ison, Sarah Ingram, Geo. Jennings, Geo Henry. Jno. Horton.

WILLM. BROWNE & WM. BALTROPP. 744 acs. W'moreland Co., be-

Rappa. & Potomack Rivers, 7 Aug. 1669, p. 243. Adj. Hen. Pate. Granted sd. Brown, Danl. White & sd. Baltrop 3 Mar. 1664. & by White sold to the abovenamed, 20 Aug. 1668.

MR. JAMES FORSITH, 116 acs. Gloster Co., Petsoe Par., 13 Apr. 1669, p. 243. Beg. at the path from his land to Mr. Howard's &c. Trans. of 3 pers: Tho. Hill, Jno. Phillipps.

WM. YOUNG, 1000 acs. Staff. Co., in the freshes of Potomack Riv., 6 Oct. 1669. p. 244. At the mouth of Island Cr. being the N. br. of Poehick Cr., &c. Trans. of 20 pers: Abell Swale (?), Jno. Smalboard, Eliz. Crouch (or Crench), Hen. Bayly, Nevet Howlet, Jno. Savage, Joseph Thomas, Geo. Ambrose, Ja. Reynolds, Tho. Reynolds, Danl. Browne, Tho. Sheere, Ana. Burson, Saml. Sadler, Jno. Oneale. Rich. Owen, Jno. Johnson, Isabell Spencer. Eliz. Florey, Geo. Benson.

MR. ROBT. KING, 850 acs. bet. Potomack & Rappa. Rivers, Staff. Co., 18 May 1669, p. 244. Adj. S. side of Mr. Haile's Cart Path, land surveyed for Hen. Berry, Peck & Welch, &c. to land surveyed for said King & Hoggard. Trans. of 17 pers: Wm. King, Elizabeth King, Jno. Nibbs, Edward Willis, Robt. Jones, Jno. Palmer, Tho. Overill, Wm. Bennett, Wm. Edwards, Jno. Austen, Eliz. Walkett, Jno. Browne, Stephen Jackson, Jno. Norton, Hen. Bruce, Peter Ayres, Hen. Coulson.

MR. JNO. WINSLOE, 600 acs. New Kent Co., S. side Peanketank Sw., 7 Aug. 1669, p. 245. Adj. David Bramm. Trans. of 12 pers: Fra. Constab 2 tymes, Wm. Merith 4 tymes, Jno. Hancock, Abra. Curber twice, Eliz. Browne, Tho. Symon twice.

HEN. AWBERRY, 480 acs. Rappa. Co., adj. his own land & neare the road path to Puscaticon Cr., 3 Sept. 1669, p. 245. Trans. of 10 pers: Robt. Rowles, Jno. Thompson, Wm. Amys, Geo. Barker, Rich. Blake, Ann Thruson, Mary Norman, Tho. Bridge, Jno. Awberry, Charles Owen.

CAPT. THO. BRERETON, 600 acs New Kent Co., N. side of Mattapon Riv. upon branches of Ashnawayman scott Sw. & adj. his own land; 14 Aug 1669, p. 245. Trans. of 12 pers: Wm Clayborne, Robt. Tayler. Tho. Burgis Jane Flood, Alice Alwood. Rich. Morley Robt. Abbott, Andre. Barry. Wm. Gunn, Lot Went, Jno. Clayborne, Wm. Perkins.

MR. FRANCIS SANDERS, 130 acs. James Citty Co., at the head of Jones Cr. of Chickahominy Riv; a little above the Mill, 7 June 1669, p. 246. 100 acs. part sold by Honble. Sir Wm. Berkeley unto Wm. Dubosse, who assigned to Mr. Edward Gunnell & by him to sd. Sanders; 30 acs. for trans. of: Hen. Muston.

EDWARD SIMPSON, 84 acs. New Kent Co, N. side Mattapony Riv., 24 Apr. 1669. p. 246. 14 acs. adj. his own, & Popetico cr. dividing this from land of Robert Pollard.' 14 acs. on N. side of Yorke by Popetico Cr. Trans. of 2 pers: Tho. Smith, Geo. Reeves.

MR. WM. HARRISON, 300 acs. Chas. Citty Co., 24 July 1669, p. 246. Part hereof granted to Jno. Freeme & found to escheat by inquisition, dated 18 June 1668 under Mr. Hen. Randolph, Eschr. &c; formerly granted to Tho. Calloway, &c.

MR. ANTHO. WYATT, 398 acs. Chas. Citty Co., 24 July 1669, p. 247. Granted to Geo. Potter, dec'd. & found to escheat, etc., (as above).

MR. MORRIS ROSE, 300 acs. Chas. Citty Co., 24 Apr. 1669, p. 247. Granted to Tho. Cole, & found, &c. (as above.)

MR. VINCENT YOUNG, 443 acs. Staff. Co., N. side of Machotick Riv., 25 July 1669, p. 247. Granted to Stephen Norman, dec'd. & by inquisition dated 9 Sept. 1668 under Col. Peter Ashton, Depty. Eschr., found, etc.

GEO. CHAPMAN, 400 acs. New Kent Co., 10 Nov. 1669, p. 247. Granted to Rich. Jackson, dec'd., & by inquisition dated 21 Apr. 1669 under Mr. Tho. Hall, Depty. Eschr. found &c.

MR. JAMES WALLACE, 990 acs. Chas. Citty Co., 24 July 1669, p. 248. Granted to Tho. Wheeler, dec'd., & by inquisition dated 18 June 1669, under Mr. Hen. Randolph, Depty. Eschr., found &c.

JOHN WEST, 100 acs. Chas. Citty Co., 24 July 1669, p. 248. Granted to John Pratt, dec'd., & by &c. (as above).

MR. ARTHUR ALLEN, 350 acs. Surry Co., 12 May 1669, p. 248. Granted to Willm. Thomas, dec'd., & by inquisition dated 10 Oct. 1668 under Tho. Ludwell, Esqr., Eschr. Genrll. for this country, found &c.

JOHN BOUGEE (or Bongee), 50 acs. New Kent Co., 20 Nov. 1669, p. 248. granted to Jno. Broccus, dec'd., & by inquisition dated 21 Apr. 1669 under Mr. Tho. Hall, Depty. Eschr., found &c.

CAPT. WILLM. BASSETT, 1800 acs. New Kent Co., 10 Nov. 1669, p. 248. Granted to Jno. Broch, dec'd., & by inquisition &c. (as above).

MRS. ELIZABETH BOUCHEIR (Boucher), daughter of Mr. Danl. Boucheir, 200 acs. Isle of Wight Co., 24 July 1669, p. 249. Granted to her father, & by inquisition dated 5 Nov. 1668, under Capt. John Jenings, Depty. Eschr., found &c.

HONOR BONISON (Bonyson), 1300 acs. Lancaster Co., 24 July 1669, p. 249. Granted to Eppia. Bonyson, who was an alien, & by inquisition dated 5 Nov. 1668 under Capt. Phill. Ludwell, Depty. Eschr., found &c.

DOCTOR FRANCIS HADDON, in right of the heires of GILES MOODEY, dec'd., 1000 acs. New Kent Co., 24 July 1669, p. 249. Granted to sd. Moodey, an alien, & by inquisition dated 10 Sept. 1668 under Thos. Ludwell, Esqr., Eschr. Genrll., found &c..

MR. GEO. ENGLISH, 300 acs. Staff. Co., 24 Apr. 1669, p. 249. Granted to Roger Petfitt. dec'd., & by inquisition dated 9 Sept. 1668 under Col. Peter Ashton, Depty. Eschr., found &c.

MR. THOMAS ROBERT, 300 acs. Yorke Co., 24 July 1669, p. 250. Granted to Gerrard Weyts, dec'd., an alien, & by inquisition dated 3 Aug. 1666 under Coll. Miles Cary, Esqr., Eschr. Genrll., found &c.

DIANA MOORE, relict of JNO. AXFORD, dec'd., 100 acs. Gloster Co., 24 Oct. 1669, p. 250. Granted to Jno. Axford (first written Axoll), dec'd., & by inquisition dated 24 Oct. 1668 under Capt. Phill. Ludwell, Depty. Eschr., found &c.

SARA LONG & MARY SHIPLEY, daughters to MR. ABRHAM ENGLISH, dec'd., 350 acs. Gloster Co., 4 July 1669, p. 250. Granted to their father, an alien, & by inquisition dated 9 Nov. 1668 under Capt. Phill. Ludwell, found &c.

CAPT. CHARLES MORRYSON, 350 acs. Eliz. Citty Co., 24 July 1669, p. 250. Granted to Rich. Hull. dec'd., & by inquisition dated 31 Oct. 1667 under Mr. Wm. Alford, Depty. Eschr., found &c.

WILLM. MORRIS, 50 acs. Eliz. Citty Co., 24 July 1669, p. 251. Granted to Hen. Hawley, dec'd., & by inquisition dated 5 Mar. 1667, &c. (as above).

ANN WILSON, relict of JOHN WILSON, 75 acs. Eliz. Citty Co., 24 July 1669, p. 251. Being the moyety of 150 acs. granted to Jno. Gundry, dec'd., & after several alienations sold to sd. Jno. Wilson; by inquisition dated 7 March 1667, &c. (as above).

GEORGE FRISSELL, 150 acs. N'ampton Co., bet. the Seaboard side & Maggetty Bay, 18 Oct. 1669, p. 251. Adj. Francis Harper & land called Drakes. Trans. of 3 pers: Geo. Hasfoot, Danll. Windall, Tho. Joanes.

WILLM. MELLING, Gent., 655 acs. N'ampton Co., 17 Sept. 1669, p. 252. Adj. Kings Cr., Nath. Wilkins, John Robins & Jno. Waterson. 450 acs. granted him 30 May 1663; 160 acs. from sd. Waterson out of his devdt. of 444 acs; & 65 acs. out of Jno. Wilkins' patt. of 500 acs., dated 19 Apr. 1638.

FRANCIS HARPER, 150 acs. N'ampton Co., bet. the Seaboard & Maggetty Bay & adj. his own land; 18 Oct. 1669, p. 252. Trans. of 3 pers: Jno. Johnson, Judith Liest (?), Ellinor Mitchell.

STEPHEN COSTEN, 200 acs. N'ampton Co., 18 Oct. 1669, p. 252. Bet. the Seaboard & Maggetty Bay, adj. Francis Harper, &c. Trans. of 4 pers: Jno. Johnson, Minefred Wilson, Jno. Million, James Falkner.

HENRY CORBYN, Esq., 500 acs. Lancaster Co., N. side of the freshes of Rappa. Riv., about 14 mi. above *Nanzemond Towne*, 25 Sept. 1669, p. 253. A gutt dividing this from 1000 acs. surveyed for Jno. Weire. Granted to Jno. Phillips & John Butts (or Batts), 7 Sept. 1654, deserted, & now granted by order &c. Trans. of 10 pers: Adry Henderson, Jno. Clarke, Robt. Utich, Wm. Johnson, Giles Gardner, Griffin Roberts, Allen Fullerton, Ralph Henderson, Jno. Johnson, Dunkin Robinson.

MRS. ANN JOANES, relict of CAPT. WM. JONES, 300 acs. N'ampton Co., near the head of Hongers Cr., 23 Oct. 1669, p. 253. Granted to sd. Wm., deserted, & now due for trans. of 6 pers: Eliza. Hickman, Henry Wilkinson, Henry Trading, Edward Evens, Alice Morgon, Jams Stamp.

NATHAN FLETCHER, 240 acs. & 80 acs. of marsh, Gloster Co., on the North Riv. & Ware Riv., 22 Apr. 1670, p. 253. Adj. Tho. Boswell, Senr., Augustine Horth &c. 200 acs. granted to Lt. Col. Antho. Elliott 29 Mar. 1651 & assigned to sd. Fletcher; & the residue being overplus, is due for trans. of 2 pers.*

LT. COLL. THO. GOODRICH, 1800 acs. Rappa. Co., S. side the River, upon brs. of Puscatna Cr., 15 Oct. 1659, p. 254. Trans. of 36 pers: Susanna Skeife, Tho. Crew, James Hill, Rich. Jones, Jno. James, Fra. Dawson, Tho. Pritchard, Rich. Turner, Jno. Davyis, Walkin Bowin, Wm. Goulson, Tho. Barrington, Margt. Williams, Susan Ward, Paul Hutt, Mary Webb, Jno. Good, Saml. Daugly, Tymothy Porter,

Wm. Hoe, Nath. Wareman, Robt. Sly, James Crofts, James Martyn, Rich. Hooper, Rich. Paggett, Wm. Harman, Susa. Dedman, Tho. Hobbs, Jon. Payne, David Worth, Judu. Smart, Peter Frith, Obadi. Ruth, Teigh Marrah, Mary Good.

SAME. 2876 acs. Same Co. & page, 24 Oct. 1669. 2000 acs. Adj. Jno. Mills, Thomas Rayson, Anthony North, & orphant of Clement Thrush; 876 acs. adj. Hoskins Cr., Edward Pagett, Gilson's Cr., Major Andrew Gilson, & Mr. Pate. 2000 acs. granted him 28 May 1664; & 876 acs. since added, due for trans. of 18 pers: Wm. Langley, Nich. Constable, Robt. Badley, Jno. Sherman, Tho. Crew, Joseph Moore, Elisha Fisher, Robt. Ellis, Wm. Richards, Geo. Murrell, Alex Robins, Joseph Spring, Jno. Parr, Edwd. Williams, Mary Briggs, Wm. Norton, David M——.

NATH. HICKMAN, 450 acs. N'umberland Co., N. E. upon Mattapony Riv., adj. Jno. Bennett & Mr. Newman; 31 Dec. 1662, p. 255. Trans. of 9 pers.* Granted him 1 Aug. 1653, & now renewed.

WM. WHITE, 150 acs. Rappa. Co., 21 Sept. 1667, p. 255. Adj. Jno. & Geo. Kilman upon Piscataway Cr., land of Neale Peterson, over the Beaver Dam Sw. to W. side of Kilman's Sw. & nigh land of Young, dec'd. Granted to Jno. Kilman 2 Dec. 1663, deserted, & now granted by order &c. (Note: The following names appear hereunder:) Isaak Stone, Danll. Roberts, Alice Johnson.

MR. WM. CODOGAN (Cadogan). 50 acs. in the W'n. br. of Nancemond Riv., lying bet. 2 creeks which makes it an island; adj. Stephen Durden & his own house; 23 Mar. 1666, p. 255. Trans. of: Susan Howard.

Same. 150 acs. in W'n br. of Nancemond Riv., adj. Michael Brinkley, Henry Plumton & his own land; 23 Mar. 1666, p. 256. Trans. of 3 pers: Richd. Stroud, Tho. Jones, Wm. Jacob.

MR. WM. WHITTINGTON, 3600 acs. N'ampton Co., 29 Oct. 1669, p. 256. Bet. the Seaboard & 1800 acs. sold by Capt. Stone to Capt. Wm. Whittington, dec'd., his father; from the freshwater br. of Matawoms Cr. to Mountneyes Cr., including two hummocks known as Oake Island & Pond Is., & 200 acs. belonging to Wm. Satchell; 750 acs. being part of 950 acs. granted to sd. Stone 30 Jan. 1640, sold to sd. Wm. dec'd., 800 acs. granted the abovenamed 20 Oct. 1661, which was grounded on a patt. granted 11 Mar. 1653 to his father; 2050 acs. for trans. of 41 pers: Danll. Peper, Wm. Sawyer, Henry Wethered, Hollis Uszald, Richd. Powell, Robt. Whiteacre, Mercy Clator, Jno. Roberts, Jno. Ward, Tho. Green, Wm. Gravener, Henry Collet, Jno. Reynolds, Robt. Smith, Tho. Parker, Cha. Blake, Mary Hall, Eliza. Guildford, Jno. Cumbell, Jno. Griffith, Jno. Mackey, Fran. Brauldon, Mary Anderson, Mary Pemble, Fran. Sanders, Robt. Brett, Abra. Hullings, Tho. Wilkinson, Ja. Bullock, Geo. Bradshaw, Tho. Parker, Edwd. Floyd, Jno. Bond, Ben. Daniell, Robt. Whitehair 7 tymes.

THO. HUNT, 900 acs. N'ampton Co., 28 Oct. 1669, p. 256. 600 acs. W'wd with Old Plantation Cr., a cr. parting this & land of Wm. Walton now in possession Richd. Whittmarsh, & from land of John Bagwell; 50 acs. granted Thos. Hunt, dec'd., his father, 8 Sept. 1638; 350 acs. granted Wm. Berryman 20 Feb. 1638 & assigned to Tho. Hunt, dec'd; 200 acs. to Henry Williams, dec'd., 20 Feb. 1638 & by his heires sold to sd. Tho. 28 Oct. 1667; 300 acs. for trans. of 6 pers: Richd. Whitemarsh, Robt. Hollyday, Jno. Powell, Samll. Emat (?), Richd. Curtis, Mary Hubbert.

MR. RICHARD HEABEARD (Habeard), 1539 acs. Staff. Co., 29 Oct. 1669, p. 257. 480 acs. nigh Pasbetan Cr., adj. Tho. Frizle, Jno. & Wm. Heabeard & Roger Perfitt; due by his patt. dated 31 Mar. 1660; 1059 acs. divided by a br. from sd. Jno. & Wm., adj. plantation of Richard Rosier, land of Wm. Green & near Rappa. branches. Trans. of 21 pers: Jno. Dawson, Wm. Waters, Robt. Hobley, Jno. Wells, Henry Browne, Seth Joslin, Rich. Coulton, Tho. Morris, Rich. Jennings, Jone

Judd, Hen. Boswell, Jno. Powell, Robt. Raker, Tho. Williamson, Phillip Rowby (or Rowly), Rich. Angell, Timothy Butler, Jno. Broome (or Breeme), Mary Yapp, Wm. Hemly, Jno. Groves.

RICHD. WHITEMARSH, 458 acs. N'ampton Co., 30 Oct. 1669, p. 257. 158 acs. due by purchase from Wm. Walton, son & heire of Jno. Walton, who purchased of Tho. Gaskins, to whom it was granted 9 Sept. 1636; 300 acs. adj. Tho. Hunt att Old Plantation Cr; Trans. of 6 pers: Peter Constable, Isaack Harmon, Peter Derrick, Jno. Baker, Antho. Pace (or Place), Tho. Sand.

THOMAS TUNNELL, 700 acs. at Accocompson, adj. Jno. Watts; 30 Oct. 1669, p. 258. 400 acs. part of Southby Littleton's 850 acs. pattented 12 Sept. 1664; 300 acs. for trans. of 6 pers: Tho. Tunnell, Tho. Beare, Richd. Holland, Phill. Shapcott, Jno. Strangwaies, Mary Napper.

THOMAS LEATHERBURY (Letherbury), 1400 acs. Accomack Co., near the head of Anancock Cr., 30 Oct. 1669, p. 258. Part being a neck on the S. side of Jno. Jenkins' land bet. 2 salt & freshwater brs. of sd. Cr. 1200 acs. granted Jno. Ebsey (or Elsey), 3 Nov. 1660; & 200 acs. for trans. of 4 pers: Jno. Turner, Tho. Peake, Robt. Legg, Samll. Plumb, Danll. Smith.

GEO. JOHNSON, 950 acs .Accomack Co., N. side of the N'n. br. of Muddy Cr., 30 Oct. 1669, p. 258. 400 acs. granted Jno. Raney 10 Jan. 1662 & assigned to sd. Johnson; 550 acs. for trans. of 11 pers: Geo. Pitt, Tho. Chard, Mary Reymes, Jane Napier, Robt. Coker, Jno. Fownes, James Holland, Ja. Holt, Tho. Rutland, Arth. Wolfe, Augustine Hurle.

SAME. 400 acs., same location; 28 Oct. 1669, p. 259. Granted to John Renny 10 Jan. 1662, & assigned to sd. Johnson.

WM. SENIOR. 300 acs. N'ampton Co., 28 Oct. 1669, p. 259. Adj. Wm. Satchell, by Scott's Quarter Br., &c.

Granted to Mr. Wm. Whittington, & assigned &c

LT. COLL. WM. KENDALL, 1300 acs. N'ampton Co., bet. lands of *Hungars* & the Seaboard side, 28 Oct. 1669, p. 259. Beg. by Thos. Smith's branch; by Tho. Dunton, to Billioate's cor., unto Jno. Stockley & along Wm. Whittington, &c. 350 acs. by order &c., 1 Nov. 1666 & since purchased of John Vines, who had a former right; 950 acs. for trans. of 19 pers: Kath. Legardo, Jno. Daniell, Wm. Shore, Jno. Shellivan, Jude Bernard, Ann Hodge, Judge (a) Negro, Wm. Biggs, Jno. Abram, Tho. Sumersett, Jno. Watts, Tho. Coleman, Danll. Donahan, Rebec. Cole, Tho. Smith, James Burketan, Samll. Grinnall, Wm. Kenede (or Lenede), Rich. Whitehair.

MR. NICHOLAS HEALE, 365 acs. Lancaster Co., 13 Oct. 1669, p. 260. Adj. lands of Mich. Miller, John Symmons, Joseph Bayly & a br. of Coretoman Riv. Trans. of 8 pers: Mathew Hodge, Joane Williams, Eliz. Harris, Jasper Lewis, Jno. Sloe (or Store), Tho. Roberts, Mathew Smith, Jno. Johnson.

ROBT. BULLINGTON, 100 acs. Henrico Co., N. side of James Riv., adj. Mr. Jno. Farrer & Francis Radford; 26 Oct. 1669, p. 260. Trans. of 2 pers: Jno. Richardson, Wm. Merritt.

LT. COL. WM. KENDALL & CAPT. WM. SPENCER, 600 acs., N'ampton Co., 26 Oct. 1669, p. 260. Granted to Elias Hartrey, dec'd., & by inquisition &c. under Col. Jno. Springer, Depty, Eschr., 26 Feb. 1666, &c.

GEO. ARCHER, 784 A. 3 R. 10 P. Henrico Co., Bristore (Bristol) Par., N. side of Appamattock Riv., next above the *old Towne Land*, 25 Sept. 1671, p. 260. 500 acs. running from the *Old Towne* at the mouth of *Tunstall's Neck*, &c. to the *poynt landing* neer the dwelling house sold by Wm. Ridley to John Mudgett, &c. to Major Wm. Harris' survey, &c; 50 acres at the foot hereof called *Tunstall's Neck*, where Mudgett formerly & Archer now liveth, to Godfrey Ragsdale, &c. to Tho. Webster, the

Old Town Creek, &c. 550 acs. granted to sd. Archer June 2 1665; & the residue for trans. of 5 pers: Wm. White, Tho. Atkins, Sara Poole, Jno. & Dunge, Negroes.

ARTHUR UPSHOTT, 335 acs. N'ampton Co., at the head of Broad Cr., a br. of Muswadox Cr., 30 Oct. 1669, p. 261. Adj. Jno. Dolby, formerly Tolson's, &c. 250 acs. granted to Roger Johns 28 Nov. 1645, assigned to Rich. Allen, who assigned to Jno. Coleston (Couleston), by him assigned to Rich. Jacob, who by will gave to Edward Hamond, who sold to sd. Upshott; the residue for trans. of 2 pers: Edwd. Grant, Wm. Smalby.

EDWARD BRANTLY, 675 acs. Is. of Wight Co., 30 Oct. 1669, p. 261. Neer Mr. England & the *Dancing place*, through a pocoson, by Mr. Tookes to the Ashen Sw., neer Hen. White's old Cart Path to the Mill &c. Trans. of 14 pers: Fra. Hobbs, his wife, Eliz. Williamson, Richd. Lewis, Robt. Suite, Jno. Bleto, Eliz. Chittin, Wm. Bilbey, Oliver Williams, Tho. Sore, Austin Battin, Eliz. Fowler, Eliz. James, Eliz. Smith, Robt. Hall.

MR. SAML. BONAM, 400 acs. Lancaster Co., in the freshes of Rappa. Riv., about 14 mi. above *Nanzemond Towne*, 29 Oct. 1669, p. 262. Beg. at a cr. dividing this from land of Jno. Batt & Jno. Phillips &c. Granted to John Sharp 14 June 1655, deserted, & since granted to Jno. Appleton 2 June 1664, deserted, & now granted by order, &c. Trans. of 8 pers: Adam Robinson, Katherine Adams, Mary Fawkett, Jno. Achill, Susan Bradley, Tho. Johnson, Nath. Watridge, James Ausley (or Ansley).

MR. ROBT. HOWSING (Houseing), 6000 acs. on the W. side in the freshes of Potomack Riv., above the dividing branches, 21 Oct. 1669, p. 262. Opposite *my Lord's Island*, &c. to N. point of a Cr. *named by the English* the Indian Cabin Cr., dividing this & land surveyed for Jno. Mathewes. Trans. of 120 pers: Mr. Houseing 4 tymes, Giles Cable, Robt. Young, Lucas (?) Gardner,

Ezekell Willin, Petr. Slaseby, Mary Plum, Wm. Price, Tho. Davis, Jno. Sprart, Tho. Draper, Edwd. Kent, Jeremy Pibold, Jno. Leake, Jo. Truman, Lan. Mosely, Tho. Thruston, Jno. Hudson, Hen. Lupton, Josias Franklin, Hen. Pratt, Jno. Bates, Mary Standly, Ed. Seaman, Wm. Hobson, Row. Lawson, Jno. Porks, Evan Pressey, Ja. Towne, Robt. Dooeby, Pet. Skinner, Xpo. Dunford, Eliz. Burton, Nich. Whitehead, Rich. Day, Robt. Young, Jno. Suttle, Jo. Newberry, Rich. Freman, Theo. Griffin, Tho. Cooke, Jno. Lane, Robt. King, Ja. Moss, Rich. Norton, Miles Gray, Jno. Hughill, Lott Richeson, Tho. Suckett, Wm. Cox, Mary Wilkinson, Geo. Hollis, Jeff. Wormely, Sym. Harper, Susan Wappin, Mar. Preston, Morris Dixon, Sam. Pike, Fran. Trotter, Jno. Holmes, Alex. Fisher, Tho. Palmer, Wm. Salmon, Phill. Watson, Sam Gipson, Jno. Porter, Tim Shelly, Ra. Hopkins, Tho. Fletcher, Sy. Haynes, Jno. Wells, Patrick West, Ja. Hunter, Bar. Boucher, Rich. Carter, Ed. Bostock, Jo. Dew, Saml. Farmer, Jno. Norris, Ed. Norris, Ro. Stapler, Jo. Stapler, Mar. Copeland, Mary Potter, An. Barber, Susan Phelps, Do. Hobson, An. Percott, Ma. Herbert, Cisly Serby, Reb. Parker, Sara Knowles, Ma. Edwards, Fra. Worstly, Kath. Smith, Jone Messell, Tho. Killip, Jno. Mapes, Fra. Cogan, Tho. Shereman, Jno. Allen, David Taylor, Geo. Green, Hum. Wilson, Tho. Lawrenson, Cha. Hudson, Robt. Foster; & 10 Negroes.

MR. THO. WARREN, 450 acs. Surry Co., 1 Nov. 1669, p. 263. Trans. of 9 pers: Arthur Grant, Mary Spue, Wm. Dix, Roger Browne, Henry Neeve, Tho. Rogers, Abra. Hart, Mary Wilson.

MR. JNO. LEVISTON, 780 acs. New Kent Co., 5 Nov. 1669, p. 263. 380 acs. on N. E. side & neare the road to the mill, adj. Mr. Jno. Lewis, by Cattaile br., a br. of Mattasup Cr., to Mr. Jno. Major, adj. Andrew Cotton, along Kings Sw., & adj. land where sd. Leviston now liveth; crossing path to the church, &c. 400 acs. on N. W. side of Poropotanck Cr. behind land of Jno. Thomas. 400 acs. granted him 16 Dec. 1653; & 380 acs. for trans. of 8 pers: Jno. Freegrave, Geo. Hunt, Abra. Mayes,

Wm. Turner, Jone Wilkins, Peter Arrowes, Mary Wise, Jno. Neaves.

RICHARD COLEMAN, 380 acs. W'moreland Co., 13 Dec. 1665, p. 264. 300 acs. adj. plantation of Mr. Wm. Presley, a cr. of Yeocomoco Riv., &c; granted to Tho. Sheppard & James Claughton 6 May 1652; sold to Rich. Flint, who sold to Willm. Coleman & Robt. Baynam & by Baynam transferred to sd. Coleman 12 July 1658; 80 acs., granted sd. Wm. 20 Aug. 1661, adj. sd. Sheppard, John Tingey, Martyn Cole, Howett & Cawsey; on land of Tho. Philpott, John Powell & John Ward; all of which is due sd. Richd. as heire of his brother, the sd. Wm. Coleman.

WM. NEWSOME & GERRARD REYNOLDS, 400 acs. N. side Rappa. Riv., Lancaster Co., upon the head of Coretoman Riv., adj. Mr. Conaway; 20 Dec. 1669, p. 264. Trans. of 8 pers: Edwd. Huntly, Wm. Battin, Tho. Collins, Robt. Broome, Ann Hall, Jacob Stanford, Joane Howard, Elias Land.

MR. CORNELIUS REYNOLDS, 180 acs. Gloster Co., adj. Mr. Williams, Xpofer. Abbott, the Road path, &c; 15 Oct. 1669, p. 264. Trans. of 4 pers: Saml. Franks, Mary Goden, Danl. How, Eliz. Vase.

MRS. ANNE TOFT, 2000 acs. Accomack Co., 30 Oct. 1669, p. 265. 300 acs. nere the Seaboard, bet. 1450 acs. of Col. Edmond Scarburgh & the main br. of Gargaphia Cr; 1700 acs., being 2 necks, on the Seaboard, adj. Swanscutt Cr., Matappany Cr. & part of the *Maryland lyne* &c. Trans. of 40 pers: Ann Toft, Ed. Little, Sara Hewett, Jane Gestling, Jno. Atkinson, Tho. Cubb, Nich. Mellickhopp, Jno. Wickecage, Wm. Abchurch, Jno. Beare, Tho. Davis, Jno. Davis, Mary Dekins, Rich. Lawrence, Bar. Watson, Hum. Atkins, Jno. (a ?) Spainard, Amos Cooke, Jno. Sparkes, Wm. Gardner, Fra. Talcoate, Ann Carpenter, Roger Hodge, Robt. Parker, Wm. Litchfield, Patrick Eaton, Tho. Bell, Osmond Deereing, Mich. Ward, Owen Murphey, Mary Barton, Tho. Mitchell, Cha. Stephens, Marrian Frane, Joseph Lifegar, Ralph Justice,

Ambrose Archer, Eliz. ———, Jno. Fletch, Joseph Hulett.

MR. WILLM. CUSTIS, 300 acs. Accomack Co., S. side of Mesangoe Cr., 30 Oct. 1669, p. 265. Granted to John Wallop *alias* Wadlow, assigned to Wm. Walton, deserted, & now resurveyed for sd. Custis; trans. of 6 pers: Edmd. Euedall (?), Jno. Jeffryes, James (?) Miller, Jno. Still, John Dellin, James Ironsides.

WM. TAYLOR, 1000 acs. Accomack Co., bet. Occohanock Cr. & Matchepungoe, 30 Oct. 1669, p. 266. Adj. Edward Hitchkin & Barth. Meares, Rich. Hill, Arthur Upshott & Mr. Potts. Trans. of 20 pers: Edwd. Herdson, Tho. Powell, Ja. Bricklock, Xpofer, Person, Robt. Francis, Jno. Litler, Wm. Hutton, Wm. Ebruck, Hen. Martyn, Geo. Alsop, Anne Power, Allen Moore, Robt. Hill, Marga. Tunck, David Cave, Thorowgood Pate, Tho. Prosser, Jno. Summers, Cornel. Harrison, Tho. Bagley.

JOHN WALTER, 200 acs. Accomack & N'ampton Co.'s, on N. side of S'n. br. of Broad Cr., on E. side of land lately in possession of Nicholas Hudson now claymed by Arthur Upshott, & on Balliott & Bell's land; 30 Oct. 1669, p. 266. Trans. of 4 pers: Henry Wright, Jno. Stephens, Charles Cox, Tho. Morgan.

TEAGE MISKETT, 300 acs. Accomack Co., nere Gullford Cr., adj. land of Lawrence Robinson, formerly Robt. Hill's, & land of Martyn Moore; 30 Oct. 1669, p. 266. Trans. of 6 pers: Edward Pine, Amos Pollard, Jno. Tuckfield, Jno. Kellam, James Clifford, Math: Halls.

MR. DANL. FOXCRAFT, 600 acs. Accomack Co., S. side Pocomoke Riv., adj. Wm. Chafe (Chase ?), over the Cattaile pond, &c; 30 Oct. 1669, p. 267. Trans. of 12 pers: Humphry Bishop, Joane Tregon, Jno. Roxby, Tho. Moore, Robt. Lawrence, Geo. Hussey, Wm. Long, Ja. Floyer, Math. Davis, Grego. Gibbs, Jno. Hoskins, Geo. Stile.

THO. GITTINS, 450 acs. Accomack Co., neare *Husswadox*, adj. land former-

ly Stephen Charleton's, Major Tilney & Danl. Quillory; 30 Oct. 1669, p. 267. Trans. of 9 pers: Peter Hoskins, James Smith, Jeffry Williams, Jane Barrenton, Ben. Cawfield, Jane Sutt, Robt. Thompson, Aron Hester, Hugh Ligon.

WILLM. BLAKE, 300 acs. Accomack Co., S. side Mesangoe Cr., adj. Wm. Aleworth; 30 Oct. 1669, p. 267. Trans. of 6 pers: Hen. Norley, Tho. Gibbons, Math. Heale, Mary Walder, Margaret White, Jone Wilding.

JOHN STOCKLEY, 200 acs. N'ampton Co., adj. Robert Foster, sonne of John Foster, dec'd; 30 Oct. 1669, p. 268. Trans. of 6 pers: Tho. Gwyn, Owen Morris, Edgar Powell, Mich. Leigue.

MARTYN MOORE, 400 acs. Accomack Co., near Guilford Cr., adj. Teage Miskett; 30 Oct. 1669, p. 268. Trans. of 8 pers: Jno. Holt, James Rye, Tho. Other, David Gosse, Hugh Owen, Ann Corker, Ed. Singen (or Lingen), Wm. Hepton, Herbert Price.

ROGER TERNON, 300 acs. Accomack Co., on Hunting Cr., 30 Oct. 1669, p. 268. ½ of 600 acs. granted to Tho. Orily 23 Feb. 1663 & assigned to sd. Ternon; adj. sd. Orily & Wm. Onoughton.

THOMAS ORILY, 300 acs. Accomack Co., adj. Roger Ternon & John Lewis; 30 Oct. 1669, p. 268. ½ of his patent dated 23 Feb. 1663.

HENRY SCOTT, 400 acs. Accomack Co., adj. Jno. Williams & Jno. Johnson; 30 Oct. 1669, p. 269. Granted to Jno. Johnson, 3 Mar. 1658.

MR. JOHN CARY, 230 acs. Surry Co., adj. Capt. Thom. Flood, Ware Sw., near Getting's house, & along the Cart path to Arthur Jordan's, &c; 27 Dec. 1669, p. 269. Part of 1100 acs. granted to Coll. Jno. Flood & purchased of his relict & overseers of his will, &c.

RICKETT BURKE, 408 A., 8 primes, Rappa. Co., N. side of the river in Sittenburne Par., & on N. W. side of the main br. of Rappa. Cr., adj. Richd. Coleman, near the horse path; 30 Oct. 1669, p. 269. Trans. of 9 pers.*

MR. EDWARD SANDERS, 3747 acs. bet. Lancaster & N'umberland Co.'s, upon Dameron's Cr., 14 Dec. 1669, p. 270. Adj. land sold by John Hopper to sd. Sanders; on a br. of Coretoman Riv., E'wd. from Machotick foot path, &c; 207 acs. on N. side of a br. dividing this from land of Thomas Salisbury, Tho. Lane & his own; 640 acs. on S. side of Gr. Wiccocomico Riv. 2900 acs. granted him 5 Mar. 1662; 207 acs. granted him 28 Aug. 1668; 640 acs. for trans. of 13 pers: Jno. Richard, Jno. Brookes, Susan Wheritt, Edwd. Jacob, Wm. Batts, Eliz. Couchanshaw (?), Rich. Otter, James Allen, Tho. Walterman, Tho. Harris, Sara ——, Eliz. Jermin, Tho. Prescott.

WILLM. TIGNOR, 550 acs. N'umberland Co., N. siide of Gr. Wiccocomoco Riv., 4 Jan. 1669, p. 271. Upon Mr. Ashton's Cr., dividing this from John Johnson & Willm. Betts, & towards Tho. Gerrard. Granted to James Hawley 2 June 1657, assigned to Willm. Leech, who sold to sd. Tignor.

THOMAS COLLINS, 165 acs. New Kent Co., on lower side of branches of Ware Cr., 8 May 1669, p. 271. A br. divid. this & land of John Brocas, adj. Thom. Williams & Edward Ashwell. Trans. of 4 pers: Hen. Brewster, Roger North, Amy Stratford, Willm. Wareing.

THOMAS SLOE (Slow), 640 acs. Low. Norf. Co., in Eliz. Riv., on N. side of Deepe Cr., adj. Jno. Chyreys (Chyregs (?), 30 Oct. 1669, p. 271. Trans. of 13 pers: Tho. Senior, Eliz. Senior, Jno. Sloe, Tho. Sloe, Robt., Jacob. Isack. Ann, Susan, Eliz. Slow, Geo, Rookins, Mary Darlin.

MR. THOMAS HOBSON, 1000 acs. Staff. Co., on E. side of Hopkins Cr., in Potomack freshes; 27 Apr. 1668, p. 272. Granted to Wm. Wildy, deserted, & granted to Major Colclough, deserted, & now granted by order &c. Trans. of 24 pers.*

THOMAS STEGG, Esqr. 2773 A., 32 P., Henrico Co., S. side James Riv., adj. his own land at the falls; 27 Oct. 1669, p. 272. 1850 acs. granted him 29 Dec. 1663; & residue for trans. of 19 pers: Robt. Chambers, Tho. Carver, Edwd. Rycroft, Tho. Hambleton, Jeffry Mumfort, Hen. Greene, Mawrice Lenox, Jno. Olton, Tho. Palman, Rowland Dewson, Rich. Hamond, Jno. Brathwhaite, Silvester Ward, Rich. James, Tho. Robinson, Jno. Parker, Mary Symonds, Andrew Morris, Hum. Chapman.

CAPT. JNO. CUSTIS, 200 acs. N'ampton Co., near head of Pimmenoe Br., 7 Feb. 1669, p. 273. Trans. of 4 pers: Jno. Willett, Sam. Bennett, James Duninge, Peeter Vicary; Eliz. Mings, land due for.

MR. THO. BUSBY, 194 acs. Chas. Citty Co., by the W'n. br. of Up. Chipokes Cr., 16 Apr. 1669, p. 273. 95 acs. granted to Jno. Rawlins & Mich. Mittaine, 10 May 1667, & assigned to sd. Rawlins; 90 acs. for trans. of 2 pers: Robt. Busby, Wm. Emms.

MR. EDMOND CHESMAN, 300 acs. N. side Chesman's Cr., on Bay tree neck, adj. Jno. Adleston, bet. Lt. Col. Jno. Chesman, Mr. Beale & Jno. Clarketon &c; 20 Sept. 1668, p. 273. Granted Col. Jno. Chesman & sd. Adleston 13 May 1654, renewed 18 Mar. 1662, deserted, & now granted by order, &c. Trans. of 6 pers: Jno. Benson, Margaret Nixson, Jane Constable, Hen. Stevens, Rich. Ham, Robt. Westwood.

MAJOR WILLM. MARRIOTT, 1460 acs. Surry Co., known as Ware neck, neare the Divills Wood Yard Sw. adj. Mr. Rolph, the cart path to Mr. Warren's, to Ware Neck, to Spiltimber's, to Blands path, along Besses Sw., along path to Mirells, &c. 1150 acs. granted Mr. John Corker 20 Oct. 1661 & by him & his son Wm. sold to sd. Marriott; 310 acs. now added & due for trans. of 7 pers: Wm. Jellett, Rich. Booth, Jno. Booth, Ann Jenoway, Alice Prise, & a Negro man & woman.

MR. GEORGE MORRIS, 860 acs. New Kent Co. Stratton Maior Par., on

N. side of Mattapony Riv., 29 Apr. 1668, p. 274. By an Indian Path to Jno. Maddison's house, adj. Anth. Arnell, &c; along John Exoll's path, now the road to Chiscake Path, nigh head of the Woolfe Pitt Br., to the Cart path and King's road, to Anth. Haynes, over the head of the green br. & Mantepike Path, dividing this from land of Jno. Hill, &c. 640 acs. granted to Col. Robt. Abrahall & Jno. Pigg, 10 July 1658; residue within sd. bounds purchased of sd. Abrahall, who purchased of sd. Haynes, who purchased of Capt. Wm. Clayborne, the first proprietor thereof.

MAJOR WILLM. MARRIOTT (Marryott), 414 acs., Surry Co., adj. Robert Lane; 22 Oct. 1669, p. 275. Trans. of 9 pers: Jno. Lewlyn, Abr. Mosse, Wm. Oldis 2 tymes, David Lee 3 tymes, Stephen Spinke, Wm. Pickney.

DAVID MURRAY, 600 acs. Low. Norf. Co., S. side of the E'n br. of Eliz. Riv., adj. Willm. Whitehouse; 29 Oct. 1669, p. 275. 400 acs. by former patt., & 200 for trans. of 4 pers: Jno. Knowles, Jno. Browne, Mary Gage, Tho. Webster.

MR. RICH. WHITTAKER, 158 acs., Middlesex Co., bet. head brs. of Parrotts Cr. & Mr. Burnham's Cr; 5 Feb. 1669, p. 275. Part of devdt. bought by Wm. Copeland of Danl. Welch & alsoe the sd. land whereon sd. Copeland liveth, &c., on the lower side of Huckleberry Sw., &c. Trans. of 3 pers: Tho. Mann, Wm. Dyer, Sara Johnson.

MR. JNO. FOXHALL, 314 acs. W'moreland Co., bet. Potomack & Rappa. Rivers; 23 Oct. 1669, p. 276 Adj. Lt. Col. Jno. Washington, Jno. Piper, Mr. Jno. Watts, near Ned the Indians path, &c. Trans. of 7 pers: Jno. Foxhall, Marth. Foxhall, Mary Foxhall, Sara Foxhall, Sara Taylor, Kath. Hine, Senr., Kath. Hine, Junr.

MAJOR WILLM. WYATT, 2240 acs. New Kent Co., 17 Apr. 1669, p. 276. 1940 acs. adj. Rich. Barnehouse; including the whole marsh adj. being 850 acs., &c. to Portcock Sw., John Cosby; 300 acs. adj. Mr. Henry Soane

&c. 1940 acs. granted him 24 May 1664, & 300 acs. 28 June 1664 & now joyned into one pattent.

MR. THOMAS WRIGHT & JOHN CHYNN, 220 acs. N. side of Rappa. Co., near the head of Moratticoe Cr., by the Mill Dam, &c; 26 Apr. 1670, p. 276. Trans. of 5 pers: Ralph Hall, Ben. Davis, Cutberth Taylor, Lyddia Gates, Edward Jones.

MR. WM. PEACH, 570 acs. Gloster Co., Ware Par., upon the Gr. Sw., & brs. of Ware River, 7 May 1669, p. 277. By plantation of Mr. Rigault comonly called Bradford's Quarter &c., opposite Greenwayes plantation, near Tho. Purnell's plantation, near Mr. Toliferoe's quarter, &c. 300 acs. granted to Capt. Tho. Breman 11 Mar. 1653, sold to Mr. Tho. Peach, & now due sd. Wm as sonne & heire; 270 acs. found within & due for trans. of 6 pers: Margarett Overdell Sara Baxter, Robt. Greenaway, Alice Bradshaw, Eliz. Banckes, Hen. Gibbs.

MR. THO. TUGWELL, 210 acs. Middlesex Co., upon brs. of the Dragon Sw., 30 Oct. 1669, p. 277. 100 acs. purchased of Rich. Lewis, adj. Mr. Potter's Quarter, Mr. Hen. Thacker &c. Trans. of 3 pers: Jane Stoakes.

MR. WM. BLACKEY, 1300 acs. New Kent Co., S. side of Yorke Riv., 23 Oct. 1669, p. 278. Beg. at Tankes Queenes Cr., to mouth of br. bet. this & land of Geo. Gill, by the Ridge Path. &c. 900 acs. granted Tho. Gibson, found to escheate, & granted to sd. Blackey; 400 acs. within the old bounds, due for trans. of 8 pers: Tho. Bushell, Jno. Burgis, Eliz. Fritch, Jno. Nelson, Wm. Sanders, Jno. Elkinson, Alice Symonds, Edwd. Goodson.

MR. THOMAS CHETWOOD & MR. WALTER WHARTON, 490 acs. Lancaster Co., N. side of Rappa. Riv., being part of a neck comonly called Steven's Neck, lying bet. 2 main brs. of Col. Carter's Cr; 28 Feb. 1669, p. 278. Adj. Stephens' (Steven's) land, Mr. Robert Griggs & the Gleebe land. Trans. of 10 pers: Wm. Purston, Hen.

Weekes, Jno. Bilson, Jno. Besouth, James Mingay, Obadiah Wright, Jno. Isenson, Mary Peterson, Judith Avery, Jacob Nerford.

DAVID FULLER & EDWARD WETHERBORNE, 165 acs. Rappa. Co., adj. Mr. Saml. Griffin & the Bryery Sw; 26 Apr. 1670, p. 278. Trans. of 4 pers: Fran. Jordan, Eliz. Mason, Tho. Bulfinch, Joseph Evans.

MR. THO. CHETWOOD, 150 acs. Lancaster Co., 28 Sept. 1669, p. 279. Adj. Mr. Tho. Haynes, on E. side of the Road way from Col. Carter's to *Wiccomoco,* &c. Trans. of 3 pers: Wm. Gibson, Tho. Greere, Peter Plumton.

MR. RICHARD PARKER, 350 A., 3 R., 16 P., Henrico Co., S. side James Riv., on the head of the 4 Mi. Cr., beg. at Harrowhaddox Path; 28 Oct. 1669, p. 279. Trans. of 7 pers: Gilbert Platt, Jno. Norris, Jno. Harding, Ellenor Creed, Joan Snelling, & 2 Negroes.

NATH. FLETCHER, 320 acs., Gloster Co., neare *Ware Point;* 12 Aug. 1669, p. 279. Adj. Mr. Tho. Boswell, Augustine Horth, &c. 200 acs. granted to Col. Anth. Elliott 29 Mar. 1651 & assigned to sd. Fletcher; 120 acs. overplus now added & due for trans. of 3 pers: Gilbert a Dutchman, James Draper, Joan Fletcher.

JOHN CONE, 470 acs. Lancaster Co., 20 Sept. 1669, p. 280. Adj. Abra. Bonnison (Bonyson), neare the head of Tabb's Cr., to Sw. of Nantipoyson Cr., both Crks. issuing out of Fleet's Bay, to land of Rowland Lawson, to Mr. Robert Griggs, by Mr. Tho. Chetwood, &c. Trans. of 10 pers: Abraham Johnson, Wm. Worts, Henry Jenny (?), Roger Abrall, Jno. James, Eliz. Richards, Henry Norton, Peter Wiston, Jno. & James Norgrave.

JOHN ASHLY, 137 acs. Lancaster Co., 20 Dec. 1669, p. 280. On run of the maine Sw. of cr. formerly called Haddawaye's Cr. out of Fleet's bay, adj. Mr. Robt. Griggs, Abia. Bonyson, the *Gleebe Land,* &c. Trans. of 3 pers: Jno. Huggins, Ralph Mayes, George Gibbs.

JNO. HOWELL, 274 acs. N'umberland Co., bet. Gr. Wiccocomoco & Chickacone Rivers, adj. land of the orphants of Mr. John Chandler, &c; 20 July 1669, p. 280. Trans. of 6 pers: Roger Thomas, Maudlyn Valsey. Mordecay Evans, Nich. Brookes, Jno. Terry, Tho. Holwood.

MR. WALTER WHARTON, 226 acs. Lancaster Co., nigh head of cr. formerly called Haddawayes Cr., 16 Oct. 1669, p. 281. Adj. Mr. Tho. Haynes, by an Indian Path from Wiccocomoco to Rappa. Riv., Abia Bonnyson, the *Gleebe Land,* Col. Carter, &c. Trans. of 5 pers: Robt. Peirson, Armiger North, Hen. Brease, Rich. Earle, Ann Howson.

MRS. ELIZ. BYNNS, 777 acs. Surry Co., Lawnes Cr. Par., adj. Geo. Blowe, along Poeaketinke Sw., & a sw. of the Bridge Sw; 18 Oct. 1669, p. 281. Trans. of 16 pers: Arch. Mulliball, Wm. Bunge, Berry ——, Tho. Lovejoy, Kath. Symms, Hen. Lee, Wm. Gibson, James Hibley (or Hikley), Hanna Cooper, Tho. Grace, Jno. Allin, Obedience Merrick, Hanna Warwick; Dick, Peter, Hector: Negroes.

RICH. AWBORNE, 605 acs. Surry Co., Lawnes Cr. Par., adj. land of Blow, Robt. Laine & Mrs. Bynns; 18 Oct. 1669, p. 281. Trans. of 12 pers: Jonath. Smalley, Rich. Bennett, Rich. Felkes, Margaret Roberts, Robert Smyth, Rebecca Tappin, Alice Whittaker, William Reems (or Reeve), Jno. Stareman, Wm. Hunt, James Scott, Thomas Pratt.

MR. JOHN SANDERS, 650 acs. Warwick Co., Mulberry Is. Par., on Skiffes Cr., 5 July 1669, p. 282. On E. side of a Spring called *Jacob's Well,* a gutt dividing this from land of Capt. Robt Pyland, adj. Mr. Hely, Alsupp's fence near the Cart path, &c. 500 acs. part leased to Jacob Avery 2 Feb. 1630 for 21 yrs., afterwards granted to Wm. Ravenett by 3 patents: 150 acs. 21 Nov. 1635; 250 acs. 23 Sept. 1636; 100 acs. 20 Feb. 1638, who gave to his daughter Susanna now wife of sd. Sanders by his will dated 20 Mar. 1656; 150 acs. for trans. of 3 pers: Tho. Dowin, Edw. Hoard (or Heard), Cisley Jorden.

RICH. SHEWELL, 200 acs. near head of the S'n. br. of Nanzemond Riv; 30 Oct. 1669, p. 282. Trans. of 4 pers: Robert Williams, Jno. Edwards, Tho. Alcock, Peter Wicks.

EDWARD REYLEY & JNO. KILL-INGHAM, 500 acs. N. side Rappa. Co., adj. Mr. Merryman; 26 Apr. 1670, p. 282. Trans. of 10 pers: Wm. Stevens, Tho. Greene, Robt. Owen, Jno. Grant, Adry Thompson, Marke Jackson, Fra. James, Humfry Bayly, Ann Clarke, Wm. Light.

PHILLIP BROWNE, of W'moreland Co., 200 acs. in sd. Co. bet. Potomack & Rappa. Rivers, adj. Jno. Willis, Mr. Jno. Foxhall, neare Ned the Indians path & Lt. Col. Jno. Washington; 30 Oct. 1669, p. 283. Trans. of 4 pers: Steven Nicholas, Ann Groves, Tho. Bennyton Jno. Maycrop (or Maycron).

MR. JNO. WILLIS, 261 acs. W'more-land Co., upon brs. of Appomattox Cr., bet. Potomack & Rappa. Rivs., adj. Lt. Col. Jno. Washington; 21 Oct. 1669, p. 283. Trans. of 6 pers: Jno. Temple, Simon Bird, Tho. Parrott, Jane Davys, Fra. King, Oliver Thomas.

JNO. POTTER, 150 acs. Lancaster Co., adj. Jno. Newman, a br. of Morat-tico Cr. &c; 20 Dec. 1669, p. 283. Trans. of 3 pers: Jno. Mercer, Geo. Row, Peter Bridge.

ROBERT JOHNSON, 300 acs. Up. Par. of Nancemond Co.. 30 Oct. 1669, p. 283. Trans. of 6 pers: Charles Duthkaies (?), Jno. Turley, Jane Cres-dall, Ann Williams, Tho. Russ, Susan Broughton.

MR. THOMAS VICCARS & ROBERT LITTLEFIELD, 550 acs. Glos-ter Co., bet. branches of Chiscake & Ware Riv., 16 Aug. 1669, p. 284. Adj. David Monorgond (Monorgon), Rich. Renshaw, John Saunders, or Tho. Chenye's, the Indian Path, Lawrence Smith, Col. Warner, & a br. of Peanke-tanke &c. Trans. of 11 pers.*

THOMAS COLLINS, 250 acs. Glos-ter Co., Kingston Par., upon *Peanke-*

tanke Ridge, 19 July 1669, p. 284. Up-on main br. of Wadeing Cr., adj. Mr. Elliott's Quarter, Mr. Warkeman & Mr. Kemp. Trans. of 5 pers: Wm. Sea-man, Eliz. his wife, Jno. his sonne, Jno. Lee, Samll. Drewer.

JAMES ENNIS & HIS SONNE JAMES, 200 acs. Low. Par. of Is. of Wight Co., upon the mayne br. of Pagan Cr., adj. land of Capt. Jno. Upton, now in Jno. Wheatelye's possession. & the *Batchellors plantation,* now in possession of Peter Garland; 2 Apr. 1670. p. 285. Granted to Mr. Peter Knight 13 Mar. 1638, who sold to sd. Ennis last day of Jan. 1665.

MR. MOSES DAVYS (Davis), 400 acs. New Kent Co., bet. Totopotomoyes Cr. & brs. of Yorke Riv., 6 Dec. 1669, p. 285. Beg. by upper Powhite Path, by Nickahooke br., to Mr. Jno. Page & his own land. Trans. of 8 pers: Robt. Freston, Amy Marygold, Jno. Lemort, Isaak Stremor, Jeremy Syms, Jacob Millecent, James Mercombe. Tho. Smith.

MR. WM. BATT, 700 acs. Chas. Citty Co., toward head of the S. side of Baylie's Cr., adj. James Warrendine's land comonly called *High Peake* now in the occupation of Mr. Wm. Ditty & Robt. Langram; 22 Apr. 1670. p. 285. Granted to Robt. West. 2 Aug. 1652 for trans. of 14 pers., & by surrender in Chas. Citty Ct., 3 Aug. 1653, renewed in the name of sd. Batt.

JAMES THWEATE, 600 acs. Chas. Citty Co., S. side Appamattox Riv., on W'wd. run of Baylye's Cr., adj. Robt. Coleman. Junr; 22 Apr. 1670. p. 286. Trans. of 12 pers: Willm. Williams, Sara Leage. Geo. Davis. Rachell Wil-liams. Eliz. Williams, Jno. Edwards, James Thweat. Jno. Lawrence. Jno. Hob-son, Mary Hobson, Wm. Noting, Ed-ward Price.

JNO. WALLOP *alias* WADLOW, 3050 acs. Accomack Co., on S. side of Gingoeteage Cr., a br. thereof which has a bridge over it neer the freshwater, to the 2nd. bridge from the *fort neck.* &c. to Cedar Br. which is the N. E. side of land of Samll. Taylor &c; 20 Apr. 1670,

p. 286. 700 acs. granted him 5 Apr. 1666; 1350 acs. granted to Lt. Col. Wm. Waters 12 June 1664, who sold to sd. Wallop 14 Jan. 1666.

ROBERT BEVERLEY, 2000 acs. Rappa. Co., S. syde of Gilson's Cr. & N. & S. syde of Hoskins Cr., 20 Apr. 1670, p. 286. Adj. George Morris, Mr. Thomas Button, &c. Trans. of 40 pers: Thomas Mould, Grace Wilson, Anne Crouch, Wm. Buedle, Robt. Harrison, Andrew Grove, Capt. Robt. Bristow twice, "A woman servt. dyed at sea," Phillip White, Thomas Wright, Thomas Ames, Jon. Heyley, Jon. Vaddall, Wm. Bell, Jon. Parramoore, Jon. Wilkinson, Niccolas, Baldwinne, Marmaduke Moore, Rich. Knight, Robt. Goffe, Edwd. Osborne, Sarah Marsh, Anne Frawlin, Henry Ellis, Samll. Acklestone, Tho. Wetherstone, Jon. Eadall, Fr. Mavill, Ralph Clifford, Jon. Fox, James Greene, James Curder, Anne Walter; & 6 Negroes.

MR. WARWICK CAMMOCK, 1923 acs. Rappa. Co., in the freshes on S. side of the Riv., & on S. side the maine run of Puemondsem Cr., adj. Hen. Peters & Jno. Mader; 22 Apr. 1670, p. 286. Trans. of 39 pers: Joseph Cornish 6 tymes, Jno. & Wm. Blake, each 6 tymes, Tho. Sheppard 6 tymes, Mary Fletcher, Geo. Hollis, Fra. Pitman, Edwd. Swift, Tho. Palmer, David Holt, Geo. Haynes, Rich. Markham Wm. Dyer, Mary Dyer, Alice Hobbs, Jane Dennett, Emanuel Talbott, & his wife Rebecca, his daughter.

JNO. MEADER, 625 acs. Rappa. Co., on the S. of the Riv. in the freshes in the run of Puesmonseen (Cr.), & adj. Mr. Camock; 22 Apr. 1670, p. 286. Trans. of 13 pers: Emanuel & Rebecca Talbott, Fra. Wood, Wm. Wilson, Eliz. Gilbert, Rich. Smith, Tho. Kirkeley, Wm. Scott, Edwd. Peckett, Hugh Lewis, Edwar Staller, Edwd. Russell, Margarett Butcher.

MR. THOMAS HOLMES, 575 acs. New Kent Co., S. W. side Peanketanke Sw., 27 Mar. 1667, p. 287. Beg. where he now liveth, down Holmes' br. to John Roberts' land, to Exalls Sw. &c.

Trans. of 12 pers: Jno. Winsloe, 5 tymes, his wife once, Job. an Indian, Berryman Winsloe, Ephraim Parker, Sara Gray, Ben. Hoodall, Samll. Carter.

JOHN TWYNNY, 300 acs. Gloster Co., on E'most side of a run of Ware Riv., at the head of Mockjack bay, & adj. land of Jno. Walker; 16 Apr. 1669, p. 287. Said land granted to Henry Palme & John Swingleton, deserted, & granted sd. Twynny by order, &c. Trans. of 6 pers.*

MR. ROBERT WOODSON, 1192 A., 3 R. 32 P., Henrico Co., N. side James Riv., 26 June 1670, p. 287. Adj. Tho. Ludwell, Esqr., Tho. Ligon, Jno. Woodson, Col. Stegg & Mr. Ballard. Trans. of 24 pers: Wm. Marsh, Jno. Yeates, Wm. Newton, Peter Allerton, Jno. Amys, Hen. North, Amy Joanes, Jeremy Norton, Marg. Burch, Jno. Lestrange, Abr. Bennett, Robt. Wilkes, Jno. Porter, Susan Greere, Robt. Bowman, Wm. Arton, Hen. Brutons, Mary Evelyn, Tho. Philpott, Hugh Wright, Abra. Sproson, Marg. Henrick, Tho. Hewes, Rich. Hyres (or Hyves).

HENRY CORBYN, Esqr., 250 acs. N. side of Rappa. Riv., upon a place formerly knowne by the name of the Deep Creeke, & adj. Mr. Tho. Powell; 21 June 1670, p. 288. Granted to Geo. Vezey & Nath. Browne, deserted, & now granted by order, &c. Trans. of 5 pers: Adrie Henderton, Wm. Johnson, John Clark, Giles Gardiner, Robt. Utick, Griffin Roberts.

EDMOND CHISMAN, JR., 202 A., 60 chs., Yorke Co., on W. side of the run of the main br. of Mill Sw., above the mouth of Cod Run, near the Wolfe trap Br., &c; 8 July 1670, p. 288. Trans. of 4 pers: Jno. Benson, Margarett Nickson, Jane Constable, Hen. Stephens.

¶JOHN JAMES, 500 acs. Staff. Co., N. E. side of Poehick Cr., in the freshes of Potomack Riv., 20 July 1670, p. 288. Adj. Will. Greene, Mr. Rich. Normansell, &c. Trans. of 10 pers: Frances Dade, Christ. Dade, Fran. Dade, Junr., Mary Dade, Margarett Frankling, Eliz.

Stittin, Mathew Bennett, Danill Gaines, Rob. Jackson, Edw. Crissell (or Grissell).

JOHN WHITT & JOHN WOORMAN (Worrnam), 600 acs. Staff. Co., N. E. side of Occkaquon bay or river, beg. at a neck opposite to Dogges Iland, a cr. dividing this & land of Will. Harriss & Tho. Bartar, adj. Robert Collingwood, &c; 20 July 1670, p. 289. Trans. of 12 pers: Rich. Hunt, John Phillips, Jone Holland, John Browne, Hen. Godfrey, Thô. Williams, Jone Tharpe, Tho. Tomson, Will. Harding, Rich. Martin, James Claw (or Clare). John Nagro (a Negro ?).

WILLIAM PEBLES, 473 A., 3 R., 24 P., Chas. Citty Co., S. side of James Riv., adj. Mr. Tho. Newhouse, the Burchen Sw. &c; 30 July 1670, p. 289. Trans. of 10 pers: James Durant, John Minter, Fra. Hawgood, Tho. Tomlinson. James Dent, John Grimshaw, Christo. Brown, Catharin Jenken, Giles Wright, Will. Langland.

JOHN GOREINGE, 574 acs. Surry Co., Lawnes Cr., Par., adj. the green swamp, along Mr. Awborn's line, &c; 8 Aug. 1670, p. 289. Trans. of 11 pers: John Twyford, Mary Row, Ann Weston, Alise Farley, John Morse, John Rogers, Fran. Taylor, Elinor Barrett, said Goreing's wife, John Tomson, Will. Duke.

JAMES TURNER, 786 acs. New Ken: Co., upon both sides of the Horse path to *Mahexem* (or *Matrexem*) & upon upper side of Whyting's Br., 17 June 1670, p. 290. Trans. of 16 pers: Sarah Bridges, Eliz. Burnett, Edw. Owen, Charles Rawlins, Rob. Warren, Rich. Jones, Joseph Palmer, John Gill, Tho. Moreman, Hen. Price, Will. Sweetewood, Joseph Beard, Ellen Jackson, Margery Hopkins, Patrick Sackfeild, Margarett Sackfeild.

GEORGE CHAPMAN, 1900 acs. New Kent Co., in *Permunckey Necke,* by Permunckey path, neer Cohoake Sw., adj. Major Croshaw, crossing the path from Capt. Mallory to Mr. Woodward, &c; 4 Sept. 1670, p. 290. Trans. of 38 pers: Rich. Bayly & wife 2, Tho.

Grant, Peter Hunt, Wm. West, Wm. Taylor, Rich. Spurding, Geo. Lenox, Jno. Jennings, Robt. Tibolts, Elias Degarris, Tho. Tabb, Fra. Cherry, Joan Hobbs, Danl. Thrap, Theo. Moyses, Jno. Weekes, Nath. Wilson, Jno. Jones, Jno. Hutchinson, Rich. Cooke, Geo. Wharton, Rich. Thornebury, Robt. Wilson, Robt. Grixson (or Grigson), Ed. Hilyard, Jno. Goodwinch, Wm. Thornebury, Robt. West, Hum. Briggs, James Hart, Tho. Hind, John Ludford, Hen. Weekes, Marth. Hixon, Wm. Barnett, Tho. Winter, Wm. Willis.

MR. THO. PARKER, 120 acs. Rappa. Co., Sittingborne Par., N. side the River, adj. John Jenings, Major John Weire & Tho. Ervin, Mr. John Paine, &c; 30 Oct. 1669, p. 291. Trans. of 3 pers: Robt. Frissell, Jno. Ruth, Mary Dunwell.

MR. WILL. LANE, 1438 acs. Rappa. Co., on the run of Rappa. Cr., N. side the Riv., adj. Rich. Colman; 30 Oct. 1669, p. 291. Trans. of 29 pers.*

RICH. HOULT, 600 acs. Rappa. Co., S. side the Riv., upon Pascattaway Cr., & the main pocoson thereof, beg. at Kings Sw., to the horse path, along Tho. Gaines & John Moraine (?), by James' land to James Booughan, &c; 25 Oct. 1669, p. 291. Part granted to Will. Denby 1 Aug. 1661; 200 acs. for trans. of 4 pers: John Brett, Wm. Mayes, Hen. Goose, Saml. Strong.

WILL. BRUSE, of Rappa. Co., Sittingborne Par., 250 acs. in sd. Co. & Par., 30 Oct. 1669, p. 292. Nigh a path to the Indian Sw. & adj. his own land. 50 acs. made over to him by Henry Creeton 3 Nov. 1668; 200 acs. for trans. of 4 pers: Mary Warrin, Darby Cleymond, Penelope his wife, Jno. A Taylor (John a tailor ?).

RICH. KING, 300 acs. Low. Norf Co., S. syde of the E'n. br. of Eliz. Riv., adj. Will Rogers; 1 Nov. 1669, p. 292. Trans. of 6 pers: Michael Finders, Jno. Farthing, Tho. Morse, William Coock, Hen Foster, Rich. Crane.

WILLI. HEATH, 378 acs. Surry Co. & Chas Citty Co., S. side of the head of up. Chipoakes Cr., adj. Tho. Stephens & on N. side of a great swamp; 23 Oct. 1669, p. 292. 250 acs. purchased of Will. Lee; 50 acs. purchased of Will. Shorte; 78 acs. for trans. of 2 pers: Himselfe & Sarah Killetts.

- MRS. ANNE BARNETT, 1500 acs. W'moreland Co., S. side Potomack Riv., upon E. side of Matchotick Cr., adj. Tho. Peake; 6 Sept. 1654, p. 293. 1000 acs. granted her 3 Apr. 1651; & 500 acs. for trans. of 10 pers.*

MR. LUKE BILLINGTON, 679 acs. Co. of Rappa. & in the parish Ternham Creek (Farnham ?), a br. dividing this & land of Mihill Hugill, adj. Bayley's line &c; 30 Oct. 1669, p. 293. 329 acs. part granted him 18 Mar. 1663; & 350 acs, for trans. of 7 pers: Jno. Webster, Tho. Adams, Wm. Nightingale, Hen. Googe, Rich. Young, Eliz. Stafford, Tho. Whittingaine.

MR. HENRY CLARKE, of Rappa. Co., 1495 acs., 30 Oct. 1669, p. 293. Adj. land of Tho. Goose, given to by George Brayer by will, running to N. side of the Mirey Br. 1400 part granted to Capt. John Hull 23 Sept. 1668 & sold to sd. Clarke; 95 acs. for trans. of 2 pers: Jno. Field, Wm. Rogers.

WILLIAM GREEN, 1150 acs. Staff. Co., N. W. side of Potomack Riv., at N. E. poynt of Pohick Cr; 25 Oct. 1669, p. 294. Trans. of 23 pers: Jacob Mickleson, Wm. Browne, Eliz. Baker, Nich. Brookes, Sym. Sampson, James Derrick, Jon. Motershed, Ralph Eversley, Tho. Walter, Eliz. Willimott (or Willicott), Joane Cresse, Hanna Felcher, Wm. Waven, Ben. Fish (?), Edwd. Fuller, Tho. Lepper, Wm. Greene, Jno. Read, James Harris, Tho. Melvyn, Sym. Embert, Saml. Lane, Rich. Smith.

GEORGE CHAPMAN, 4150 acs. New Kent Co., in *Pamunkey Necke*, 22 Apr. 1670, p. 294. Beg. by Pamunkey Path, nere Cohookoke Cr., along the roade from Capt. Mallory to Mr. Will Woodward, adj. John Rawhan & Major Joseph Croshaw. Being surplus within bounds of sd. Crowhaw's 5500 acr. patt., granted sd. Chapman by order, &c;

Trans. of 83 pers: Rich. Pinkenett, James Trenon (or Treven), Wm. Spence, Jno. Wilkins, Anne Mosse, Wm. Atkeson (or Acheson), Jno. Wiston; 3 Negroes; Edwd. Mullins, Sym. Rosse, Morris Swiliver (?), Jno. Cooper, Jno. Bransis (?), Kath. King, Robt. Burrs, Danl. Meekes, Wm. Drew, Nich. Bagar, James Boteman, Jno. Seawell, Rich. Cooke, Robt. Anderson, Jeffry Heddon, Tho. Holder, Wm. Chapman, Arth. Wright, Geo. Hobson, Robt. Foster, Wm. Williams, Jno. Yatebey, Saml. Furbush, Eliz. Mason, Phill. Drake Tho. Pinke, Thom. Drayes, Ann Bruster Wm. Norton, Nich. Stoke, Eliz. Smith, 2 Negroes; Hen. Sinkeler, John Hume, Hen. Trowell, John Brett — 8, from Jno. Capes patt. in fol. 96 —— 13, Wm. Rogers, Hen. Best, Tho. Rowley, Peter Nelson, Jno. Decart, Wm. Rosse, Hen. Thornton, Tho. Grosse, Hen. Greene, Tho. Prouse, Tho. Neale, Jno. Cales, Jno. West, Robt. Prouse, Hen. Inge.

CAPT. JOHN HULL, of Rappa. Co., 650 acs., *Fernham* (Farnham) Parish, N. side Rappa. Riv., adj. Henry Austin, Tho. Freshwater, Robt. Sissen, Tho. Goose & near the road to the *Court house*; 30 Oct. 1669, p. 295. Granted to Milles Reyley, dec'd., of sd. Co., & given by will to sd. Hull.

MR. WILL. HARRYS, THO. BAXTER & BURR HARRYS, 1200 acs. Staff. Co., upon W. side of Potomack Riv., upon main run of a cr. of Oquaquon Riv; 25 Oct. 1669, p. 295. Trans. of 24 pers: Roger Harding, James O Leslony (?), Math. Watkins, James Humfry, Susan Darby, Joseph Taylor, Wm. Angett, Jno. Somers. Jno. Whithers, 2 tymes, Anna Withers, Hanna Hall, Wm. Thomson, Wm. Hitchins, Jno. Bryant, Mary Harris, Walter Johnson, Wm. Richards, Ann Martyn, Jno. Arkill, Robt. Grittin, Wm. Rolt, Ellen Golsby, Paul Leech.

MR. WILL MOSELEY, 427½ acs Rappa. Co., S. side the Riv., on branches of Ekepaco Cr., adj. Col. Cattlett, Richard Goode, & Robt. & Tho. Mose of 9 pers: Jno. Teage, Hen. Barloe. (Moss ?); 18 Apr. 1670, p. 296. Trans.

Rog. Tyne, Wm. Short, Ann Jackson, Tym. James, Tho. Pratt, Rich. Albane, Mary Sparrow.

MR. JOHN BUTLER, of W'moreland' Co., 597 acs. in Rappa. Co. & W'moreland Co., adj. his own, & land of Mr. John Lord & near Pritchett's Br. & the maine sw. of Rappa. Cr; 18 Apr. 1670, p. 296. Trans. of 12 pers: Jno. Godwyn, Greg. Dixon, Wm. Sharp, Robt. Spence, Abr. Dix, Rich. Porter, Anth. Tilney, Robt. Dowty, Mary Newell, David Fossaker, Wm.. Leech, Marg. Purton.

MR. CHRISTOPHER BUTLER, of W'moreland Co., 339 acs. Rappa. Co., on brs. of Pepetick Cr., N. side of Rappa. Co; adj. Major Weire & Tho. Ervin, Mr. John Paine, Col. Will. Underwood, near brs. of Pope Cr., &c; 18 June 1670, p. 297; Trans. of 7 pers: Jno. Thomas, Roger Worts, Mary Neave, Tho. Turkey, Wm. Hix, Mary Dill, Robt. Greene.

MR. JOHN WITHER, 512 acs. Staff. Co., S. side of Patomack Cr., near land of John Martin & Col. Yoe; 25 Oct. 1669, p. 297. 300 acs. by assignment of Will. Northall 25 July 1667; & 212 acs. for trans. of 5 pers:* (Note: "The rights of this patt. are recorded to Rogers & Hoyles patt. in folio 97."

HENRY NICHOLAS, 300 acs., S. side of the E'n. br. of Eliz. Riv., 30 Oct. 1669, p. 297. 100 acs. by patt., 22 Nov. 1651; & 200 acs. for trans. of 4 pers: John Wright, Mary Lawrence, Rob. Luellin, Jno. Leggatt.

MR. MATHEW PAGGE, 1250 acs. James Citty Co., adj. *Neck of Land,* upon Mr. Batt's, the Gleab Land Cr. & the back Cr; 19 Mar. 1662, p. 298. Granted to John Crump, 29 Nov. 1654; by sd. Crump's will equally divided bet. his wife Elizabeth & his daughter Elizabeth; which sd. daughter dieing sd. land by the will was given to his wife, now wife of sd. Pagge; by deed dated 2 Dec. 1657 sd. Eliz. freely gave same to sd. Mathew.

MR. THO. GOOSE & the Orphant of GEORGE BRAYER (Breyer), 750 acs. Rappa. Co., 30 Oct. 1669, p. 298. 500 acs. granted sd. Breyer 20 Feb. 1663: & 250 acs. granted sd. Breyer 24 Aug. 1664 & by him given to sd. Goose & his orphant.

MR. JOHN HEABEARD & WILL. HEABEARD, 530 acs. Staff. Co., W. side of Pasbetanzy Cr., opposite land formerly Lunsford's, adj. Mr. David Anderson, a br. dividing this & land of Mr. Richard Heabeard; 25 Oct. 1669, p. 298. Part hereof by their patt. dateed 18 Mar. 1662; 180 acs. for trans. of 4 pers: Mary Sanders, Tho. Boreman, Jno. Barber, Solom. Johnson.

EDWARD ROGERS & CHARLES HOYLE, 1500 acs. Staff. Co., N. side Potomack Cr., adj. Mr. Walton, Charles Wood, on S. side of Aquokeeke maine run,. &c; 25 Oct. 1669, p. 299. Part granted sd. Rogers 14 Oct. 1665; & 900 acs. for trans. of 18 pers: Jno. Jones, Peter Ashborn, Robt. Prise, Ann Thruson, Tho. Nelmes, Wm. Giles, Marg. Rix, Thom. Bruce, Aswell North, Hen. Thorne, Percivall Burton, Robt. Ferne, Abr. Shurd, Hen. Parry, Tho. Sturdevant, John Green, Hen. Hunt, Rich. Brent, Tho. Moore, Hen. Walker, Tho. White, Peter Gibson, Tomazine Grigson, Ann Borny, Tho. Preston, Sym Wharton, Ann Fish, Jno. Good, Ellen Drew, Jeffrey Smith.

MR. JOHN JARRAT & THO. JOANES, 450 acs. New Kent Co., Stratton Major Par., N. side of Mattapiony, & adj. Edward Cardingbrooke: 18 Apr. 1670, p. 299; Trans. of 9 pers Tho. Turner, Fra. Fretwell, Eliz. Burkeley, James Smithers (Smithers ?), Mary Beard, Jno. Thomson, Wm. Richards, Tho. Bryan, Mary Gwyn.

MR. THO. JOANES, 289 acs. New Kent Co., Stratton Major Par., N. side Mattapony Riv., by the King's Road, adj. Tho. Hickman & Mr. Cardenbrook; 18 Apr. 1670, p. 299. Trans. of 6 pers: Mary Winter, Susan Island, Wm. Mallace, Mary Salter, Jno. Edwardson, Wm. Simpson.

MR. THOMAS MOORE, 2400 acs. Is. of Wight Co., on 3rd Sw. of the Black Water, at Tho. Atkins' Br., on Clarke's Br., adj. Christop. Holleman, Tho. Atkinson & Coppahunk Sw; 10 May 1670, p. 300. 400 acs. granted him 6 June 1666; & 2000 acs. for trans. of 40 pers: George Knight, George Lodge, Rich. Jones, Sarah Sparks, Hannah Gettings, Tho. Ely, Mary Warthington, Rich. Breed, Ed. Bushell 3 times & one Man, Thomas Willinge, John Shell, Jone Rogers, Tho. Towlt, Tho. Underwood, Eliz. Underwood, Eliz. Underwood, Eliz. Broadwether. (Note: Other names not given.)

MR. JOHN DORWOOD, 68 acs. New Kent Co., N. side Mattapony Riv., adj. Tho. Hickman, Junr., Major Will. Wyett, & land of Mr. John Winslow, formerly Col. Robt. Abrall's; 18 Apr. 1670, p. 300. Trans. of 2 pers: Wm. Bolter, Joseph Almond.

MR. GILES ROGERS, 400 acs. New Kent Co., Straton Major Par., upon the Road Pascataway, at cor. of Francis Craine's, along Capt. Tho. Brereton, by a br. of Whore Cock Sw., by Bestland Sw., by Morley's path, &c; 18 Apr. 1670, p. 300. Trans. of 8 pers: Jno. Evans, Tho. Clinker, Fra. Milburne, Jane Swann, Tym. Swart, Gabr. Morton, Tho. Smith, Hanna Clarke.

HENRY BATTLE, 170 acs. Rappa. Co., S. side the Riv., adj. land of Sharpe, in Yorke Sw., Chiscaiack Path, Bridge's corner, Hill's howse, & Mrs. Johnson's land; 18 Apr. 1670, p. 301. Trans. of 4 pers.*

MR. HENRY TROWELL, 120 acs. New Kent Co., near the house of John Collet, to main Sw. of Hokadaye's Cr., & adj. George Chapman; 27 Apr. 1670, p. 301. Trans. of 3 pers: Rich. Bundall, James Stock, Barsheba Shaw.

MR. JAMES PARRY, 107 acs. New Kent Co., above *Mahixeen;* on Tinsleyes br., adj. Mr. Moses Davis' land by upper Powhite Path; 27 Apr. 1670, p. 201. Trans. of 2 pers: Hen. Sucklyn, Mary Palmer.

HENRY TROWELL, 500 acs. New Kent Co., S. side York Riv., opposite mouth of Mattapainy Riv., at Trowell's Cr., along the road to Cataill Br., a br. of Brushes Sw., adj. Rich. Barnett, a cr. dividing this from the *Bricke house dividend,* &c; 18 Apr. 1670, p. 302. 200 acs. by purchase from Mr. Tho. Holmes, as by patt. dated 12 Oct. 1647; & 300 acs. for trans. of 6 pers: Jno. Cheston 2 tymes, Sara Palmer, Edwd. Rawlyns, Rich. Forshaw, Bryan Hazleworth.

MR. WILL OWIN & JAMES EVENS, 350 acs. New Kent Co., upon brs. of Mattadequn Cr., adj. John Garraway; 27 Apr. 1670, p. 302. Trans. of 7 pers: Jno. Redman, Lewis Bevyn, Tho. Davis, Kath. Arcome, Tho. Atkinson, Hen. Davys, Jno. Jackson.

MRS. EME JOHNSON, 286 acs. Rappa. Co., S. side sd. Riv., adj. land formerly Hill's & Sharpe's; up Yorker br., &c; 18 Apr. 1670, p. 302. Trans. of 6 pers: Jno. Dilyard, Robert Warren, Peter Higgins, Robt. Taylor, Harry England, Peter Rombolt.

SIR WILLM. SKIPWORTH, Knt., Barronet, 545 acs. New Kent Co., some 4 mi. from Capt. Will. Claiborne's Quarter called *Best Land,* adj. Jno. Richards, & the maine sw. of Pianketanck Riv; 16 Apr. 1670, p. 303. Granted to Sir Gray Skipwith, deserted, & granted to Major Genrll. Robert Smith, by order &c. who assigned to to sd. Sir Willm. Trans. of 11 pers.*

MR. JOHN FLEMING & MR. THO. GLASS, 900 acs. New Kent Co., 27 Apr. 1670, p. 303. Bet. Totopotomoyes & Matadequin Crks., adj. Charles Loving, Cornelius Dabany, Rob. Anderson, John Sexton, Mr. Moses Davis & *Tobtopultamoyes* (?) Cr. Trans. of 18 pers.*

ROBERT BEVERLEY, 6000 acs. upon the N. & S. syde of Mattaponie maine run, neere the Indian path bet. *Mattaponie & Port Tobacco;* 20 Apr. 1670, p. 303. Due by his patt. dated 12 July 1669.

MR. GODFREY HUNT, 1000 acs.
Nancemond Co., 18 Apr. 1670, p. 304.
600 acs. granted 5 Apr. 1664, adj. John
Turner, Andrew Coalwood, Ralph Ellis
Will. Poop (Pope ?), Richard Staple,
& Hopkin Howell; 400 acs. adj. Samuel
Farmer, his own land, &c. Trans. of 8
pers: Edward Thorneton, Jno. Tillett,
Tho. Wright, Wm. Williams, Sarah
Liddiott, James Risden, Jno. Hall, Fra.
Ellett.

MR. HUMPHRY HARWOOD, 2644
acs. Warwick Co., on E. side of Skeaths
Cr., 18 Apr. 1670, p. 304. On Motte's
poynt, near Will. Murdaye's plantation,
an Indian feild, near fence of Hen.
Charles, adj. Owen Morris, Capt. Na-
thaniell Hurd, neare the Mill, &c.
Granted to Capt. Tho. Harwood 26
Nov. 1652 but the courses not agreeing
&c; 575 acs. being overplus, due for
trans. of 12 pers: John Berrow, Rob.
Perry, Will. Lambemott, John Webster,
Ann Burgesse, Tho. Scott, Rich. Smith,
Tho. Hudson, Baptist Starr, Tho. Squier
(or Esquier), Hen. Stockman, Tho.
Scotch.

MR. AMBROS CLEARE, 1155 acs.
Rappa. Co., N. side sd. Riv., near head
of Fernanan Cr., 26 Sept. 1667, p. 305.
By an Indian feild near the head of a
br. of Marratecoe. Granted to Capt.
Phillip Luddwell, deserted, & granted
sd. Cleare by order &c. Trans. of 23
pers: Tho. Nicholas, Alce Aldgie (?),
George Davyd, Tho. Clarke, Sam. Fish,
James Bennett, Will. Mercer, Judith
Thompson, Ann Askew, Mark Sanders,
Marey Beadle, Tho. Joanes, Alix Tho-
mas, Andrew Cock, Elias Warren,
Jonath. Baldwich, Nich. Willson, Tho.
Dematy, Sam. Willson, Minifield Wilks,
Joan Wallys, Margrett Wallys, Dorothy
Wassell.

MR. THO. BLAKE, 400 acs. Is. of
Wight Co., in a br. of the Black Water,
adj. Henry King (or Knight altered) &
Mr. Tooke's land; 18 Apr. 1670. p.
305. 240 acs. by patt. dated 8 June
1664; & 160 acs. for trans. of 3 pers:
Edwd. Lane, Jno. Rookes, Edwd.
Phillips.

MR. GEORGE DURANT, 700 acs.
Low. Norf. Co., on E. side of the N.
River falling into Corotoke; a cr. divid-
ing this from land of Mr. Thomas
Tulies, a br. dividing this from land
called Matsepunge, etc; 30 Sept. 1670,
p. 306. Trans. of 14 pers: Tho. Brad-
shaw, Robt. Brush, Hen. Macra, Rich
Williams, Peter Belson, Jno. Fox,
Robert Wilkinson, Ann Douse, Rich.
Read, Hump. Townsend, Hen. Thacker,
Robt. Duceing, Peter Robinson, Jeffry
Snead.

MR. JOHN WHEATLY, 100 acs., Is.
of Wight Co., 14 Sept. 1670, p. 306.
Granted to John Wheatly, Senr., dec'd.,
found to escheat as by inquisition &c.,
under John Jenings, Depty. Esch'r., &c
& now granted, &c.

MR. RICHARD MADISON, 200 acs.
Is. of Wight Co., 14 Sept. 1670, p. 306.
Granted to Richard Madison, dec'd.,
lately found to escheat &c. (As above.)

MICHAELL FULGHAM, in right of
his wife, 100 acs. Is. of Wight Co., 15
Sept. 1670, p. 307. Granted unto John
Feneryeer (?) dec'd., found to escheat
&c. (as above.)

JOHN GUDEREG (GUDERIDGE),
200 acs. Is. of Wight Co., 15 Sept.
1670, p. 207. Granted to John Stiles,
dec'd., &c. as above.

JOHN VICARIS, in behalf of JAMES
BENN, Orphant, 276 acs. Is. of Wight
Co., 15 Sept. 1670, p. 307. Granted to
Christopher Benn, dec'd., &c. as above.

THOMAS CLARKE, 300 acs. Surry
Co., 14 Sept. 1670, p. 307. Granted to
William Gapin, dec'd., found to escheat
&c., under Lieut. Coll. George Jordan,
Depty. Esch'r., &c.

ROBERT NURSE, 189 acs. W'moreland Co., 15 Sept. 1670, p. 307. Granted to John Stowker, dec'd., found to
escheat &c., under Lt. Coll. John Washington, Depty. Eschr. &c.

MISTRIS REBECKA IZARD, 250
acs. in behalfe of her 2 daughters
MARY & MARTHA IZARD, Is. of

Wight Co., 14 Sept. 1670, p. 308.
Granted to Richard Izard, dec'd., found
to escheat &c., under John Jenings,
Depty. Eschr. &c.

MR. PATRICKE WHITE., 160 acs.
Low. Norf. Co., 30 Sept. 1670, p. 308.
West side of the N. River falling into
Corotoke, Trans. of 3 pers: Jno. Morse,
Rebecca Farnefeild, Sampson Kirby.

MR. DANIELL HARRISON, 200 acs.
Lancaster Co., 28 Oct. 1669, p. 308.
Upon W. side of Corrotoman, adj. William White, upon the hills, Mr. ——
Hacker & upon a br. dividing this &
land formerly William Clapham's, Junr.
Granted to William Wroughton & Richard Flint, deserted, & 'now granted by
order, &c. Trans. of 4 pers: John Diamond, Elizabeth Garret, Abigall May,
Richard Richledge.

SAME, 88 acs. Same Co., date &
page. N. side Rappa. Riv., adj. Edward
Harris, dec'd., a cr. dividing this & land
of Richard Colman. Granted unto Richard Joans, deserted, & now granted by
order, &c. Trans. of 2 pers: Timothy
Symson, Andrew James.

MR. JOHN BLAGRAVE, 800 acs.
Staff. Co., S. side of Oquia Cr., adj.
Mr. Edward Sanders, the maine run of
Aquokeeke Cr., Mr. Rowland Travers,
&c; 25 Oct. 1669, p. 309. Trans. of 16
pers: Ann Chapman, James Gregory,
Tho. Gibson, Morris Filcher, Hen. Lee,
Jno. Bright, Tho. Allen, Alice Hamford,
Dorothy Rowles, Mich. Hollis, Robt.
Humfryes, Jno. Pell, Jno. Watts, Rich.
Jones, Rich. Watts, Sara Beverly.

MR. ROBERT COLLINGWOOD,
640 acs. Staff. Co., N. E. side of Oquaquon Riv., a cr. of same dividing this
& land formerly William Bourne's, &c;
25 Oct. 1669, p. 309. Trans. of 13
pers: Ann Bell, Tho. Dyas, Wm.
North, Solom. Pinchlitton, Jane Jones,
Tho. Harris, Jno. Meredith, Sebill
Brady, Joane Tulley, Tho. Hunt, Wm.
Browne, Jno. Walter, Jno. Andrew.

MR. JOHN ALEXANDER, Senr.,
1285 acs. Staff. Co., N. side of Potoa-
mack Cr., adj. Edward Rogers, Charles

Heyle, Henry Bayle, John Peeke, Mr.
Walton, &c; 25 Oct. 1669, p. 309.
Trans. of 26 pers: Robert Dent, James
Foard, Rich. Lewis, Mary Lewis, Symon
Rowland, Jno. Lenthall, Eliz. Garland,
Ann Harloe, Tho. Jenkin, Wm. Hum-
fry, Jno. Somerly, Ralph Beylyn, Hen.
Davys, Tho. Waters, Jer. Morly, Sara
Whitty, John Grymes, Robt. Salvey,
Hen. Thomlyn, Jno. Holmes, Mary Day,
Wm. Teddar, Jno. Collett, Eliz. Fowler,
Jno. Grigson, Robt. Waller.

COLL. JOSEPH BRIDGER, 800 acs.
Is. of Wight Co., 20 Nov. 1674, p.
309. Formerly in possession of Capt.
Jno. Upton, dec'd., found to escheat
&c., & by inquisition of Capt. Jno.
Jenings, Depty. Esch'r. &c., there being
a dispute bet. Coll. Robt. Pitt & sd.
Bridger in the Genrll. Ct., as to who
the best right to the escheat, &c., &
confirmed to said Bridger, &c.

MR. RICHARD WEBLY, 480 acs.
N. side of Rappa. Co., adj. his own
land; 10 Mar. 1664/5, p. 310. Trans.
of 10 pers: John Wilson, Robt. Sharpe,
Hen. Walpoole, Peter Dobbs, Tho.
Staples, Hen. Newton, Susan Collins,
Jno. Baker, Tho. Dowley, Mary Darby.

MR. ROBERT BRACEWELL, 800
acs. Up. Par. of Nancimond Co., adj.
his own & land of James Long; 22 Apr.
1670, p. 310. Trans. of 16 pers: Mary
Greene, Tho. Mekins, Wm. Croach,
Hump. Thorne, Wm. Mingay, Peter
Gregory, Rich. Roberts, Charles Grig-
son, Marg. Rayson, Jno. Thornape (?),
Wm. Jones, Robt. Best, Hugh Green,
Abr. Kimberly, Jno. Dayves, Dorot.
Parsons.

MR. JONATHAN ROBBINSON
(Robinson), 100 acs. Up. Par. of Nanze-
mon Co., adj. Francis Maldin, Mr.
George Ludlow & Mr. Brise; 22 Apr.
1670, p. 310. Trans. of 2 pers: Jno.
Dearing, Mary Hewes.

MR. ANTHONY BRANCH, 133
acs., in the W'n. br. of Nanzimon River,
adj. Symond Symons & his own land;
22 Apr. 1670, p. 310. Trans. of 3 pers:
Hen. Watts, Wm. Tully, Mary Hix.

JOHN MEDFORD, 300 acs. Rappa. Co. on N. side of sd. Riv. in Fernam (Farnham ?) Parish; adj. John Williams, Luke Billington & Mr. Griffin; 23 Apr. 1670, p. 311. Granted to John Sucket, 20 Feb. 1662, deserted & since granted to sd. Medford by order &c. Trans. of 6 pers: Geo. Sessale, Wm. Drew, Robt. Heale, Morg. Jones, Wm. Major, Robt. Griggs.

MR. WILLIAM MOORE, 800 acs. Nanzimond Co., at Somerton Sw; 22 Apr. 1670, p. 311. Trans. of 16 pers: Ben. Stone, Tho. Gully (or Tully), Tho. Meese, Wm. Ripley, Geo. Baker, Wm. Townely, Jo. Bird, Fra. Neeve, Jacob Sanderson, Tho. Richards, Sara Reynolds, Sam. Gray, Jono. Bonner, Robt. House, Wm. Clay, Miles Atleston (or Alleston).

ALEXANDER ANDERSON, 300 acs. Up. Par. of Nanzemond Co., adj. James Long & Hugh Sanders; 22 Apr. 1670, p. 311. Trans. of 6 pers: Jno. Dickeson, Wm. Harris, Hen. North, Anth. Keen, Wm. Randall, Geo. Bayfeild.

MR. JAMES LONGE, 200 acs. Up Par. of Nanzimond Co., adj. his own land; 22 Apr. 1670, p. 311. Trans. of 4 pers: Jno. Jacob, Wm. Andrewes, Symon Meredith, Susan Nalpar.

LT. COLL. WILLIAM KENDALL, 200 acs. Accomacke Co., bet. Broad Cr., freshwater br. & Bell's Br., adj. John Walter, Thomas Bell & Major John Tilney; 6 Oct. 1670, p. 312. Trans. of 4 pers: Anth. Gold, Rich. Mosse, Judith Baker, Geo. Risdell.

MR. THOMAS MOORE, of N'ampton Co., Planter, 90 acs. knowne as *Sandy Island,* on the S. end of sd. County, adj. W. side of Smithe's Island River; 6 Oct. 1670, p. 312. Trans. of 2 pers: Peter Derrick, Jno. Baker.

SAME. 80 acs., known as *Racoone* Island with a ceder hummocke & sunken Marsh thereunto belonging, adj. Smith's Is. Riv. & Sandy Is; same Co., date & page. Trans. of 2 pers: Peter Constable, Isack Harman.

MR. DANIELL NEECH, 250 acs. N'ampton Co., bet. head of Magetty Bay Pond & the Seaboard side, at N. bounds of land of Francis Harper; 5 Oct. 1670, p. 313. Trans. of .5 pers: Jane Edwards, Mingoe a Negro, Sara Olive, Jeffry an Indian, Geo. Williams.

JOHN EYRE, THOMAS EYRE. DANIELL EYRE, sons of Mr. Thomas Eyre, dec'd., 1600 acs. N'ampton Co., adj. S. E. upon Smith's Is., land of Lt. Col. William Kendall in possession of Neale Mackmillon; 6 Oct. 1670, p. 313. 1500 acs. called *Goulden Quarter,* granted to John Neale, Merch't., dec'd., 18 June 1636, assigned to Thomas Deacon & Morris Tomson & Companie of the Ship *Rebecca,* & by Mr. William Whitby & Thomas Platt, Attys. of sd. Deacon, Tomson & Co., assigned to Capt. Francis Pott 2 June 1646 & ack. & by George Fletcher before the Gov'r. & Counsell 9 Dec. 1652, & by sd. Pott divised by will unto Susana his relict, mother of sd. John, Thomas & Daniell Eyres, now the wife of sd. Kendall & by the joynt & severall consents of Kendall & wife granted to the above-named patentees 31 Mar. 1662, & since that released & confirmed to them by William Foster & Margaret his wife, sole daughter & heire of sd. John Neale, 9 July 1668; 100 acs. due sd. Kendall for trans. of 2 pers., & assigned to sd. patentees above, viz: Ann Stacye, Tho. Sans (?)

MR. WILLIAM BRITTINGHAM, 450 acs. Accomacke Co., N. side of Kings Cr. & E. side of Pokamocke Riv., adj. N'ly. upon line bet. Virginia & Maryland, N. E. upon land of John Williams; 5 Oct. 1670, p. 313. Trans. of 9 pers: William Green, Thomas Larford, Robert Burly, Joan Broadway, Abraham Mackington, Joan Roxford, Edward Hart, Robert Hull, James Grimes.

SAME. 150 acs., same location, date & page. Trans. of 3 pers: John Brickhill, Henry Monke, Edward Breame.

LT. COL. WILLIAM KENDALL, 10,500 acs. Accomacke Co., from the N. Gr. freshwater br. of Crooked Cr. unto land of Mr. Henry Smyth, adj. John Stokeley, land formerly John Wallop's, along Robert Johnson, to Massango Cr., along Assowam freshwater Br., to land that was Nicholas Lawler's, to the Ratcliffes, &c; (date blank), p. 314. 200 acs. part granted to Jerman Gilliot, 9 Nov. 1666, assigned to Daniell Foxcroft, 16 Nov. 1668; 6000 acs. granted to David Williamson 5 Apr. 1666 & sold to sd. Kendall 12 Mar. 1669; 300 acs. being excepted from sd. deeds assigned to Daniell Foxcroft 30 Mar. 1669, by him assigned to sd. Kendall 21 June 1670; 4,370 acs. due for trans. of 86 pers: Robert Hockett, John Brinford, Ralph Deoge, Thomas Pawting, Jethro Parker, Izabell Carabley, Phillip Courtine, George Fountain, John Marrer, Robert Mawer, Christopher White, Augustin Beanhim (?), Rowland Murry, Ralph Geralld, Tho. Mosse, Aron Goudmy (or Gouding), John Spitte, John Bennell, Jane Berry (or Beny), La. Chonch a frenchman, Jacob Durring, Thomas Blackleach, Brayant Nyne, Robert Merry, John Noode, Peeter Hemlocke, John Flint, Will. Neale, Patricke Denis, Roger Lee, James Sanderson, Thomas Tocker, Rebecca Tucker, Mary Williams, Charles Metsaese, John Walker, Jane Fulcher, Michaell Smith, Michaell O Nys, John Bowne, Arthur Dennis, Will. Steward, Thomas Hog (or Heg) Joseph Ipson, John Butterworth, Andrew Abrega, William Hopers, William Benifield, John Underwood, Elizabeth Turfitt, Thomas Sanders, John Howker, Richard Ridge, An. Man, Thos. Lucas, Joh. Simpson, Henry Hawle, Mordica Evens, Pattrick, Phillipe, Manuell, (no surnames), Robert Armestrong, John Johnson, Alex. Bruce, James Henderson, Andrew Miller, Clarke James, James Field, Charles Davison, Pattrick Watson, James Browne, James Soruter, Tho. Hamlington, Henry Sinkler, Arch. O ruin, David Salmo (or Salino), Thomas Mison, Geo. Wilson, James Furgeson, John Meeke, John Forgeson, John Mauor, James Arthur, Robert Landsdal, Alex Browne, Elizabeth Burnell. *Marginal Note:* This patent is mistaken and is recorded in fol. 316.**

RICHARD KING, 240 acs. Rappa. Co., E. side of Puscattaway Cr., adj.

John Bebey, land of Cable & the Loggwood Sw; 16 Aug. 1670, p. 315. 100 acs. by patt. 18 Sept. 1663 & 140 acs. for trans. of 3 pers: John Warner, Eliz. Peterson, Edward Joans.

MR. PETER GODSON, 309 acs. Rappa. Co., S. side sd. Riv., adj. lands of Kilman, John Bebey & King; 16 Aug. 1670, p. 315. Part of 410 acs. granted to Francis Overton & William Charlton, 21 Aug. 1663, & assigned to sd. Godson.

MR. FRANCIS FURMES, 150 acs. Rappa. Co., S. side sd. Riv., adj. lands of Kilman, John Bebey, Capt. Pickett, &c; 16 Aug. 1670, p. 315. 100 acs. granted to Francis Overton & William Charleton & assigned to Peter Godson, who assigned to sd. Furmes; 50 acs. for trans. of: John Burton.

MR. ANTHONY BRIGGS (Bridgges) & HENRY BAYLY, 640 acs. Staff. Co., N. side Potomack Cr., on brs. of Aquakeeke Cr., adj. Edward Rogers & Charles Hoyles; 22 Apr. 1670, p. 315. Trans. of 13 pers: Wm. Greene, Jno. Biggs, Steven Sandy, Wm. Bowles, Rich. Perkes, Sara Holt, Edwd. Horner, Ja. Carey, Ann Horner, Rich. Brady, Jno. Rowsell, Tho. Smith, Jno. Griggs.

**NOTE: Because of the length, only names that differ from the list given in Kendall's patent, referred to in 4th *Abstract* above, will be repeated, viz: John Bramford, Ralph Degoe, Thom Powting, Izabell Carabey, Phillip Courtin, Augustin Beauham (or Beanham), Ralph Gerald, Aron Goodmy, John Spit, John Benell, Jane Benny, Laurance Chouch a frenchman, Brayan Nine, John Nod, George Fountin, Robert Merry, James Landerson, Thom Toucker, Rebeca Toucker, Charles Masease, Michael Ony, Arthur Denis, Willi. Bennefield, Jo. Symson, Hen. Howle, Hen. Skiner, John Mavor, Robert Lansdell. 6 Oct. 1670, p. 316.

MR. WILLIAM LANE, 1438 acs. Rappa. Co., N. side sd. Riv., adj. Herman Shelderman & Richard Colman; 30 Oct. 1669, p. 317. Trans. of 29 pers: Jno. Webster, Tho. Adams, Wm.

Nightingale, Alex. Googe, Rich. Young, Eliz. Stafford, Tho. Whittingham, Robt. Fristow, Jno. Ruth, Mary Dunnell (or Dimwell), Steph. Slaughter, Peter Farmer, Hen. Wood, Sara Smith, Jon. Darby, Ralph Harris, Jno. Wallis, Nich. Brett, Phill. Hart, Jno. Sterman, Phill. Shaw, Rich. Davys, Robt. Musgrove, Tho. Lane, Eliz. Wison, Hen. Price, Rich. Carter, Eliz. Harris, Stephen Wild.

WILLIAM PEBLE, 473 A., 3 R., 24 P., Chas. City Co., S. side James Riv., adj. Mr. Thomas Newhouse, Burchen Swamp, &c; 30 July 1670, p. 317. Trans. of 10 pers: James Durant, Jno. Minter, Fra. Hawgood, Tho. Thomlyn, James Dent, Jno. Grimshaw, Xpofer. Browne, Katherine Jenkin, Giles Wright, Wm. Langlaid.

MR. JOHN KINDRED, 554 acs. Surry Co., adj. Capt. Coskerham; 19 Oct. 1670, p. 317. Trans. of 11 pers: David Jones, Saml. Fuller, Robt. Coleman, Peter a frenchman, Rich. Atkins, Jno. Sellaway, Saml. Dutton, Jno. Rice (or Kite), Bridgett Balam, Tristrum Easton, Luke Meinesens (?).

GEORGE WATKINS, 105 acs. Surry Co., adj. the Sunken Marsh & land of William Nusam; 19 Oct. 1670, p. 317. Part of 275 acs. found to escheat by inquisition taken before Thomas Ludwell, 22 June 1668, &c.

BRYAN STOTT, 640 acs. Lancaster Co., E. side of Morattecoc Cr., bet. John Symson & land on which he dwelleth, on N. side of Mr. Chitwood's Swamp; 16 Aug. 1670, p. 318. Renewal of patt. granted to him 24 Aug. 1664.

MR. ROBERT GRIGGS, 373 acs. Lancaster Co., E. side of the mouth of Slaughter's Cr., parting this & land of Col. John Carter, adj. land of Mr. John Madestard; 16 Aug. 1670, p. 318. Part of 700 acs. granted to Epaphroditus Lawson, 3 Sept. 1649, & assigned to sd. Griggs.

MR. ROBERT PRICHARD, 218 acs. Lancaster Co., E. side of a sw. of a br.

of Corotoman Riv., at the head of which he now dwells, adj. land of Charles Grims, dec'd., & by John Walker & William Pughe; 16 Aug. 1670, p. 318. Trans. of 5 pers: Jno. Holdersbye, Mary Melling, Jno. Wilson, Robt. Henrick, Peter Denby.

COL. NICHOLALL (Nicholas) SPENCER, 900 acs. W'moreland Co., in Nominy Bay, E. N. E. upon Potomack Riv., a gr. pond dividing this & land of Mr. Richard Wright, adj. line of John Armesby, dec'd; 6 Oct. 1670, p. 319. Part of 963 acs. granted to Col. John Matrome, dec'd., 13 Aug. 1650, & due sd. Spencer by deed from Mr. Richard Wright & Ann his wife, the naturall daughter of sd. Col. Matrome, dated 18 Aug. 1662, & recorded in sd. Co., etc.

MISTRESS ANN WRIGHT, daughter of Mr. Richard Wright, 1100 acs; in Potomack freshes above Puscatua, adj. Mr. John Ashton; 7 Oct. 1670, p. 319. Granted to Robert Bradshaw & James Claughton & deserted; 500 acs. granted to Edward Williams, & deserted; & granted to Coll. Nicholas Spencer & Mr. Richard Wright by patt. & order of the Gen'l. Ct. dated 28 Sept. 1661, recorded 6 Sept. 1665; & now intirely due sd. Spencer as survivor; and by him out of his love and affection given to sd. Mistris Ann as by conveyance recorded &c., 6 Sept. 1665.

MAJOR JOHN WEIRE, 522⅓ acs., in Sittenbourn Par., N. side of Rappa. Riv., adj. Charles Sneed (Snead), by main br. of Irland Sw., Mattox Path, &c; 8 Oct. 1670, p. 319. Trans. of 11 pers: Wm. Cooper, Rich. Price, Wm. Lawrence, Symon Snead, Jno. Harris, Wm. Cooke, Symon Carpenter, Ralph Ingram, Edmd. Baxter, David Browne, Wm. Smith.

MR. WILLIAM MOSELEY & NICHOLAS CATTLET, 646 acs. Rappa. Co., S. side sd. Riv., N. side the Mill Cr., adj. Willard's line, Thomas Button, &c; 7 Oct. 1670, p. 320. Trans. of 13 pers: Lewis Jones, Ann Reyney, Jno. Barnett, Fra. Collett, Edwd. Jones, Jno. Burnett, Alex. Fulton, Edward James,

James Black, David Ennis, James Nesbett, Alex. Webster, Peter Edwards.

MR. RICHARD GOODE, 256 acs. S. side of Rappa. Riv., E. side of Ohcapce (or Chcapce) Creeke, adj. Mr. William Moseley; 15 Oct. 1670, p. 320. 195 acs. purchased of sd. Moseley; & 61 acs. for trans. of: Dowgell Mackmillion.

THOMAS FRESHWATER, 279-1/5 acs., Rappa. Co., Fernham Par., neare Totoskey Cr., adj. Robert Sisson; 6 Oct. 1670, p. 320. Formerly granted sd. Freshwater, but not fairly marked &c. Trans. of 6 pers.*

CAPT. JOHN HULL, 1200 acs. Rappa. Co., N. side sd. Riv., E. side of Totoskey Cr., 10 Oct. 1670, p. 321. 800 acs. granted to Quintillian Sharman & Thomas Robinson, 3 Nov. 1664; 400 acs. granted to Miles Reley 3 Oct. 1664 all of which was deserted, & petitioned by sd. Hull, to whom it was granted at a court held at James Citty 21 Apr. 1668; formerly granted to sd. Sharman, but upon triall in the Gen'l. Ct. found to belong to sd. Hull. Sd. land adj. Thomas Robinson, Edward Lewis & Crosse Cr. Trans. of 24 pers.* Note: The rights for this patent are recorded in this booke Fol. 192 under Capt. Jno. Hull's patt.

LANCASTER LOVETT, 1200 acs. Low. Norf. Co., Linhaven Par., on S. E. side of a br. of Bennett's Cr. parting this & land of John Martin, dec'd; another br. parting this & lands of Thomas Goodacre, William Goodacre, Thomas Davis, Benony Burrows & Major Adam Thorowgood's called *Timber Neck;* 10 Oct. 1670, p. 321. Beg. at a peninsula called *Little Island* where Benet's Cr. divides into 3 branches, to land of Richard Poole, to Renatus Land, &c. 700 acs. granted him 9 Dec. 1667; 500 acs. for trans. of 10 pers: Robert Glascock, Deborah Glascock, Elizabeth Bray, Robert Bird, Francis Bright, Thomas Shepard, William Filman (?), John Bigg, John Wilkinson, Mathew Read.

SAME. 300 acs., same Co. & date, p. 322. Beg. at the Sandy bankes by *Lincolne,* adj. Plumer Bray & the maine

Ocean; Trans. of 6 pers: Richard Farmer, Thomas Stanton, John Abrell, Nicholas Willis. John Gibson, Mathew Danett (or Darcott).

MR. WILLM. WYATT, JUNR., 500 acs. New Kent Co., N. E. side of Mattapony Riv., behind Mr. Barnehouse & Major Wm. Wyatt, Senr., adj. Coll. Robert Abrahall, &c. Granted to Peter Foard, deserted, & now granted by order &c. Trans. of 10 pers: Roger Cannon, Herbert Johns, Wm. Snowden, Mary James, Tho. Grant, Michell Ward, Seth Hunt, Greg. Rawles, Robert Barnes, Priscila Thomson. 20 June 1670, p. 322.

MR. JOHN BOOCOCK, 600 acs. W'moreland Co., S. side of the main br. of Attappin Cr., above 100 acs. of John Hiller's; 10 Oct. 1670, p. 322. Granted to Jno. Vaughan, assigned to Mr. Jno. Watts, assigned to Boocoocke, who deserted; granted to Mr. Geo. Morris, deserted, & granted to Mr. Anth. Boocock, lately dec'd., by order &c., & due sd. John his brother & heire. Trans. of 12 pers: Edward Dutcheley, Tho. Whatly, Phineas Powell, Kather. Williams, Jasper Bennett, Mary Hamond, Mary Newman, Rich. Melcham (or Welcham), Margaret Cooley, Tho. Redd, Kath. Butler, Jane Godwyn.

MR. JOHN MEDFORD, 250 acs. Rappa. Co., N. side sd. Riv., Fernam Par., adj. Thomas Robinson on N. E. side of Totoskey Cr., & James Samford; 21 June 1670, p. 323. Granted to John Suckett 20 Feb. 1662, deserted, & now granted by order &c. Trans. of 5 pers: Henry Cutbone (or Cutbore), Robt. Gunn, Danll. Lyddall, Rich. Hardwood, John Hares.

COLL. THOMAS DEW, 750 acs. Up. Norf. Co., on E'wd. sid of the S'n. br. of Nanzemond Riv., S'wd.' side of Crany Cr., opposite Crane & Nehokin Islands; & adj. Mr. Randall Crew; 10 Oct. 1670, p. 323. Granted sd. Dew 8 Jan. 1643.

JOHN MARTYN, 268 acs. Rappa. Co., 11 Oct. 1670, p. 324. Granted to Jno. Martyn, dec'd., 26 June 1667, found to escheate, by inquisition 4 Nov.

1668 under Major John Weire, Depty. Esch'r. &c.

WILLIAM HARRIS (HARIS), & THOMAS BAXT0R, 3000 acs. Staff. Co., S. W. on Occoquon Riv., adj. Mr. Dreaton, neare the falls, & upon a sw. dividing this & land of Col. Humphrey Higginson; 10 Oct. 1670, p. 324. Granted to Lt. Coll. Miles Cary, 5 Oct. 1654; renewed, & taken up by new rights for trans. of 60 pers., 7 Oct. 1657; deserted for want of seating; & now granted by order, &c. Trans. of 60 pers: Peter Elumme (?), Tho. Eving, Jno. Brent, Edward Wood, James Burton, Wm. Williams, Fra. Loveden, Dennis Muckama, Hen. Stoner, Robt. Merriott, Wm. Rachell, Jno. Burch, Roger Marshall, Tho. Haris, Wm. Wood, Jno. Thomas, Geo. Stone, Tho. Winder, Robt. Stoker, Jno. Rowle, Jno. Watts, Tho. Lane, Rich. Thompson, Wm. Bankes, Clemt. Holder, Tho. Watts, Hump. Peele, Phill. Stevenson, Cha. Hill, Tho. Hunt, Jno. Wilkinson, Adrian Perry, Mary King, Jno. Butler, Tho. Olevant, Rich. Ellett, Wm. Wilson, Xpian. Michell, David Jones, Xpofer. Lowne, Fra. Beele, Ann Keeling, Ann Taller. *Marginal Note:* The residue of these rights being taken from a patt. of Willm. Boren's 5 June 1666 being for 1000 acs.

ROBERT LOVELL, 500 acs. W'moreland Co., N. E'ly. upon Potomack Riv., adj. Jno. Lancelott & Samll. Bonam; 14 Oct. 1670, p. 324. Granted to Wm. Botham 24 Oct. 1655, assigned to Richd. Heaberd 25 Aug. 1656, assigned to Wm. Peirce 2 Oct. 1660, who assigned to sd. Lovell 7 July 1670.

DAVID FALKENER, 342 acs. Rappa. Co., 11 Oct. 1670, p. 325. 142 acs. purchased of Jno. Burkett, who purchased of Richard West; 200 acs. adj., granted to Nich. Burket, dec'd., found to escheate by inquisition Major Jno. Weire, Depty. Esch'r., 4 Nov. 1668, & now granted &c.

WILLM. LANE, 200 acs., Rappa. Co., 11 Oct. 1670, p. 325. Granted to John Greene, dec'd., found to escheate &c.

MR. JOHN BERRIMAN (Berryman), MR. WM. HARTON & JOHN PALMER, 1227 acs. W'moreland Co., on Rowlers Cr., neer the horse path, adj. Mr. Robert Howson, Mr. Robt. King & Antho. Hoggerd, Mr. John Bruton, Wm. Webb, &c; 14 Oct. 1670, p. 325. Trans. of 25 pers: Alice Tanner, Wm. Oldfeild, Jno. Tappin, Richd. Thompson, Samll. Hayles, Henry Pratt, David Jones, Mary Warner, Jno. Rumbolt, David Susannah, Hugh Billingsley, Josiah Dolling, Jno. Thorp, Mary Gildimore, Jno. Wyatt, Wm. Gillett, Peter Dunkin, Jno. Cassinett, Joseph Aldrige, Jno. Harbington, Jno. Raymund, Symon Williams, Ralph Henderson, John Fleet, Robt. Flowers.

MR. HENRY RANDOLPH, 1185 acs. N. side Rappa. Riv., neare *Nanzaticon.* near Poyestes (?) Cr. &c; 13 Oct. 1670, p. 326. Granted to Major Jno. Weir & Mr. Robt. Paine 26 Sept. 1667, deserted, & now granted by order &c. Trans. of 24 pers: Jno. Dick, Tho. Wells, Martyn Hollis, Ed. Palmer, Jo. Payne, Nich. Collis, Jacob Allin, Robt. Haynes, Fra. Wallis, Mary Holmes, Wm. Hooper, Jno. Davis, Mary Wootton, Jam. Rouse, Margery Allen, Jno. Drewett, Wm. Holmes, Hen. Porter, Walter Strunt, Dennis Olman, Obadia Peterson, Sam. Stevenson, Nich. Mackinny, Arth. Powell.

THOMAS REYNOLDS, 50 acs. Chas'. City Co., Martyn Brandon Par., 14 Oct. 1670, p. 326. By deed of guift from Marke Avery 8 Apr. 1660, ac'k. in sd. Ct., 3 Oct. 1660, &c.

JOHN BARROW, 1500 acs. in the freshes & on S. side of Rappa. Riv., adj. Tho. Lucas, Junr. & Clemt. Herbert; 13 Oct. 1670, p. 326. Granted to Henry Berry & assigned to sd. Barrow 14 Mar. 1662 & confirmed to him by order &c. 23 Mar. 1665.

THOMAS LUDWELL, ESQR., 1432 acs. W'moreland Co., bet. Potomack & Rappa. Rivs., neare brs. of Nominy Riv., adj. Col. Thomas Beale & Randall Kirke, Mr. Wm. Bazeley & Edward Hally, &c; 16 Apr. 1670, p. 327. Granted to Mr. Henry Tyler, deserted, & now granted by order &c. Trans. of

29 pers: James Allen, Robert Fowles, Mary Billett, Ann Sherring, Morris Herd, Rich. Elwood, Jno. Miller, Saml. Mason, Jane Tyler, Thomas Shoare, Wm. Winson, Charles Old, Jno. Holland, Jno. Williams, Jno. Boredey, Roger Connond, Wm. Scott, Sara Smith, Robt. Johnson, Jane Johnson, Jno. Turkinton, Jno. Hayman, Tho. Williamson, James Hallowell, Ja. Arkehill, Arnold Man, Jno. Jennings, George Atkins, Robert Thomson.

MR. MICHAEL HILL, 220 A., 1 R., 16 P., Chas. City Co., S. side of Appomattox Riv., adj. Walter Brookes & John Sturdevant; 15 Oct. 1670, p. 327. Trans. of 5 pers: Jno. Armstrong, Wm. Duke, Mary Greene, Robt. Dyamond, Darcy Grymes.

NICHOLAS RENN, 100 acs. Gloster Co., N. side of Yorke Riv., adj. Mr. Fossaker, 3 Feb. 1664, p. 327. Trans. of 2 pers: Math. Fenney, Wm. Totman.

MR. RICHARD PARROTT, 158 acs. Middlesex Co., bet. Parrott's Cr. & Mr. Burnham's Cr., 5 Feb. 1669, p. 328. Near Willm. Copeland's plantation, &c. Part of devdt. bought by sd. Copeland of Daniel Welch. Trans. of 3 pers: Thomas Mann, Willm. Dyer, Sara Johnson.

WM. CRADDOCK, 560 acs. W'moreland Co., down the maine Sw. to Jaspers; 18 Oct. 1670, p. 328. Granted to Henry Durant 22 Oct. 1666, deserted, & now granted &c. Trans. of 11 pers: Fra. Wild, Alice Plant, Peter Stiff, David Sands, Elinor Thorowgood, Wm. Craddock, Mary Marshall, Jno. Thomas, Jno. Evans, Jane Goodwin, Jno. Blade.

JOHN & GEORGE MOTT, 15,654 acs. on N. side & in the freshes of Rappa. Riv., 17 Oct. 1670, p. 329. Adj. Wm. Wilton, Mr. Wm. Ball, Richard Heabeard, & over hrs. of Potomeck Riv., &c. Trans. of 313 pers: John Hartry, Tymothy Kidd, Robt. Harken (?), Annie Durkin, John Spillcott, Tho. Caduggan, Robt. Spencer, William Jenings, Robt. Grey, Robt. Lilbourn, John Tilney, Peter Foord, Jane Hardy, Alexr.

Noble, Peter Hackett, John Tuck, Peter Webb, Hen. Crasier, Joseph Peters, Wm. Prouse, Tho. Hartley, To. Jenkins, Phill. Wilcott, George Philpott, Peter Derick, Mary Piggott, Arthur Powell, John Creed, Hum. Lucas, Tho. Stoute, Hen. Pede, Tho. Lockner, Sarah Whitloe, John Johnson, Jeremie Hatterscy, Josua. Crasby, Nath. Upshott, Peter Royston, John Speedwell, Anthony Crafford; 26 Negroes by assignment from Coll. Warner; Jno. Simson, Jno. Watkins, Jno. & Wm. Smith, Tho. Smith, Wm. Johnson, Jeremie Wilson, Geo. Hobbs, Jno. Cranes, Geo. James, Wm. Tibbo (or Tibbs), Jno. & Tho. Stevens, Roger Blackwell, Tho. Charley, Richd. James, Richd. Layton, Abell Williams, Henry Stubbs, Matt. Samper, Jno. Jones, James Martin, Andrew Todd, Jno. Ireland, Tho. Fisher, Danll. Doe, Mary Harris, Wm. Morgan, Ann Morgan, Jno. Burcks, Richd. & Elizab. Whitehead, Eliz. Mathewes, Mary Marty, Fran. Boyer, Robert ——, Wm. Day, Hen. Morgan, Jno. Webb, Mary Herbert, Tho. Dyall, John Cadde, Robt. Hill, Randall Smith, Wm. Covington, Jno. Mannell (or Manuell), Rich. Elliott, Alexr. Reed, Tho. Foley, Tho. Heywarton, Symon Wells, Jno. Peters, Fra. Hattfeild, Wm. Taylor, Wm. Griffin, Sebastian Adough, Josias Pickes, Erick Everson, Hance (?) Patterson, Jno. Beoperts (?), Jno. Tomson, Xpofer. Benland, Richd. Williams, Jno. Derrell, Jno. Dawson, Ames Wolme (or Woline), Richd. Rayman, Tho. Parsons, Jno. Pannell, Symon Wedge, Robt. Holt, Jno. Danjell, Wm. Parsons, James Palmer, Jno. Farrell, Ed. Tydy, Nic. Burton, Winnifred Holmes, Ju. Parker, Robt. Matly, Jno. Jones, Patrick Cosins, Hen. Stafford, Fra. Cox, Hen. Honywood, Lewis Price, Ester Watson, Tho. Paggitt, Robt. Collins, Ed. Fibbs, Mary Ford, Cha. Marshall, Ja. Boswell, Tho. Grey, Sam. Gregorie, Danll. Pearman, Nic. Adkins, Ann Porter, Eliz. Boston, Hanna Blackwell, Silvanus Wood, Jno. Snell, 9 Negroes; Wm. Brown, Jno. Dorodey, Row. Prince, Wm. Freech (or Freez), Alexr. Smith, Richd. Whitehead, Wm. Austin; Tho. Watkins, Arthur Allen, Jno. Thomas, Simon Felcham, Mary Jones, Elenr. Vaughan, Simon Bird, Michaell Atkins, Geo.

Brown, Matt. Hudson, Jno. Lomax, Ja. Mills, Tho. Hudson, Matt. Wilkinson, Jane Hancock, Mary Rodes, Tho. Hawkins, Jno. Lawrence, Tho. Stubbs, Tymo. Grasin, Joyce Warner, Eliza. & Tho. Browning, Jno. Custis; 24 rites transferd from a patt. in foll. 209 in this book, that patt. being part of this land; 24 rites more transferd from another patt. in this booke in fol. 73 being alsoe a part of this land. P. L. (Phil. Ludwell) Cl.

JOHN WALTER, 400 acs. N'ampton Co., 18 Oct. 1670, p. 330. 200 acs. granted 10 Oct. 1664 to Nich. Hudson, assigned to Cornelius Berry, who assigned to sd. Walter; 200 acs. in Accomack & N'ampton Co.'s, N. side of the S'n. br. of Broad Cr., adj. Nich. Hudson, Billiot & Bell & Major John Tilney. Trans. of 8 pers: Alex. Chambers, Robt. Hambleton, Tho. Scott, Wm. Jones, Jane Abram, Tymo. Steere, Jasper Ellett, Seth Stevens.

COL. NICH. SPENCER, 3250 acs. W'moreland Co., at the head of Nominy Riv., S. E. of Herring Cr., by br. of Machotick Riv., opposite Tho. Yowell; 14 Oct. 1670, p. 330. 2500 acs. granted to Thos. Hawkins & by Thomas Hawkins, Jr. ,sonne & heire, sold to sd. Spencer; upon resurvey found to be 3250 acs. 750 acs. for trans. of 15 pers: Jno. Tanner, Ralph Greene, Robt. Watkins, And. Seymore, Eliz. Thurlow, Mary Carver, Tho. Williams, Jno. Atkinson, Steph. Plummer, Lawrence Fox, Wm. Goffe, Edward Ratcliffe, Jno. Jennings, Edw. Place, Tho. Corbett.

RICHARD COX, 1052 acs. Gloster Co., upon brs. of North Riv. Mill Damm; 19 Oct. 1670, p. 331. 809 acs. granted him 26 Oct. 1666; 253 acs. adj. same, land of John Benson, John Reed, Col. Anth. Elliott, dec'd. &c., & due for trans. of 5 Negro servts. by assignment of Jno. Carver, Atty. of Mr. Gilbert Metcalfe.

JOHN REED, 385 acs. Gloster Co. at the head of Cow Cr; 19 Oct. 1670, p. 331. 300 acs. purchased of Richard Cox; 85 acs. adj. Anthony Gregory, sonne of Joseph Gregory; Thomas Purnell, John Benson, & land Thomas Price

purchased of Jno. Benson; 85 acs. for trans. of 2 Negroes, by assignment, as above.

WILLIAM COVENTON, 20 acs. S. side of Rappa. Co., adj. land on which he lives. 19 Oct. 1670, p. 331.
SAME. 300 acs., same Co. & date, p. 332. On a br. of Dragon Sw., adj. John Cole. Trans. of 6 pers: Ann Bygott, Eliz. Pickett, Mary Long, Mary Pearman, Jane Prince, Fra. Enugge (?).

MR. AMBROSE WHITE, 400 acs. Accomack Co., upon the W'n. island of Chesepiake Bay; 10 Oct. 1670, p. 332. Beg. at Sandy Bay, WNW from the 'S'n. part of Wat Taylor's island, &c. Trans. of 8 pers: Ambrose White, Robt. Mason, Wm. Williams, Tho. Sheppard, Xpofer. Roberts, Jno. Glost, Tho. Barton, John Lanes.

MR. GRIFFIN SAVEDGE (Savage), 2000 acs. Accomack Co., neare Guilford Cr; 10 Oct. 1670, p. 332. Trans. of 20 pers: Edwyn Catesby, Roger Isham, Math. Somers, Tho. Audly, Wm. Hart, Jno. Broughton, Morris Rottoman, Robt. Chechister, Tho. Lownes, Edgar Feilding, Abra. Young, Tho. Smith, Joseph North, Tho. Rabley, Jane Walling, Wm. Eagerly, Robt. Wilford, Godfry Warrington, James Roxburry, Ann Beanely.

EDMOND BELSON, 100 acs. Nancemond Co., 26 Apr. 1670, p. 333. Granted to Nich. Cornwall, dec'd., & by inquisition &c., under Mr. Willm. Alford, Depty. Esch'r., 11 Aug. 1669, &c.

MR. SAMUEL GRANDBURY, 125 acs. Nancemond Co., 26 Apr. 1670, p. 333. Granted to Ralph Broadhurst, dec'd., & by inquisition &c. under Mr. William Alford, Depty. Esch'r. &c.

WILLIAM BLAIKE, 97 acs. Rappa. Co., N. side sd. Riv., neare head of Richards Cr., neare Mr. Giles Webb & adj. Miles Hugill; 22 Apr. 1668, p. 333. Trans. of 2 pers: Jno. Wilson, Rebecca Newman.

MR. PETER KNIGHT, 400 acs. Gloster Co., a mile below Olliver Green, by a Great Sw., by Mr. Cooke's land, &c; 2 Mar. 1668, p. 333. Granted to Wm. Newman 20 Apr. 165—, part of which he sold to Elias Cobson, who assigned to sd. Knight.

MR. FRANCIS BURNELL, 2000 acs. New Kent Co., S. side & in the freshes of Yorke Riv., adj. Capt. William Bassett & Capt. Phillip Ludwell; 16 Sept. 1666, p. 334. Trans. of 40 pers: Math. Ower. Senr., Eliz. Ower, Math. Ower, Junr., Wm. Corteene, Jno. a french boy, Moses Baker, Jno. Ower, Math. Baker, Marth. Ower, Joseph Leducke, Edwd. Ower, Tho. Curson, Edwd. Minton, Wm. Bland, Geo. Hunt, Wm. Thrashall, Edwd. Spencer, Ellinor Williams, Joan Watkins, Rich. Vincent, Ambrose Kerry, David Powell, Walter Higgins, Rice Evans, Edwd. Williams, Rich. Wroughton, Phill. Prosser, Geo. Hughes, Alice Hughs, Robt. Hooper, James Spiritts, Ed. Lambert, Jno. Bell, Ambr. Parry, Ann James, Blanch Powell, Wm. Twyford, Rich. Grase, Rich. Holland, Rich. Pryce.

MR. ARTHUR MOSELEY, 540 acs. (or 550), Low. Norf. Co., Lynhaven Par., on a br. of the broad creek; 20 Oct. 1670, p. 334. Granted to Willm. Moseley, his father, 17 Feb. 1652 & bequeathed to sd Arthur.

THOMAS MAIDESTARD, 350 acs. Lancaster Co., neare *Musketo point*, 20 Oct. 1670, p. 334. Granted to Rice Jones, 18 Apr. 1650, assigned to Ever (?) Peterson, who being an alien sd., land escheated, as by inquisition under Capt. Phillip Ludwell, Depty. Esch'r., 29 Jan. 1669, & now granted &c.

CAPT. JOHN WEEST, 200 acs. Accomack Co., bet. Andin & Corotocks Crks., adj. Richard Johnson & Willm. Waller, along Milboyes line &c; 21 Oct. 1670, p. 335. Trans. of 4 pers: Xpofer. Cleverly, Robert Taylor, Isaak Brandon, Jno. Littleton.

THOMAS GILSON, 1050 acs. Rappa. Co., about 2½ mi. from sd. Riv. on the S. side, near a path to *Portabacco* from *Mattapony Indian Towne*, or *Chickahominy*. adj. Mr. Robert Payne & Mr. Thomas Page, to Mr. Lucas' Creek, &c.

to Valentine Allen, &c; 20 Oct. 1670, p. 335. Granted to Bethlehem Gilson 27 Sept. 1667, by her deserted &c., & granted sd. Thomas by order &c. Trans. of 21 pers: Robert Jones, Alex. Story, Wm. Peirce, James Phillips, Saml. Welstead, Humphry Hatch, Hugh Jones, Jno. Temple, Jno. Griggs, Roger Lee, Jacob Dempster, Sara Newman, Isabella Williams, Grace Bigott, Ann Thomp (?), Peter Paley, Rice Griffin, Paul Richards, Nath. Butler, Symon Rogers, Mary Goodson.

WILLM. RUFFIN, 758 acs. Is. of Wight Co., 4 May 1666, p. 335. Adj. Ambrose Bennett, the Corne Sw. &c. Trans. of 16 pers: Jonathan Dollattry, Mary Drinkwater, Jno. Moone, Dorothy Davies, Evan Evans, Elenor Murray. *Note:* The 16th March 1676/7 The Rt. Honoble. the Governor doe Promise to make good the Rights Wanting. Test, Hen. Hartwell, Cl.

HUMPHRY MARSHALL, 1300 acs. Is. of Wight Co., 5 Apr. 1667, p. 336. Adj. Mr. Fulgham, Tho. Harris *or* John Nevell & Mr. Hardy. 700 acs. granted Jno. Marshall 12 July 1665, assigned to sd. Humphry his son; & 600 acs. for trans. of 12 pers: Wm. Serjeant, Jno. Rice, Susan Ward, Jno. Greenwood, Jno. Warner, Mary Warner, Rachel Simpson, Wm. Grimble, Ann Browne, James Nicholas, Tho. Taylor, Toby Rogers.

WM. RUFFIN & ROBT. COLEMAN, 938 acs. Is. of Wight Co., adj. Tho. Harris, 4 May 1666, p. 336. Trans. of 19 pers: Wm. Bright, Sarah Mead, Jno. Kemp, Judith Olive, Luke Raben (or Raven), Mary Hopkins, Sara Milbridge, Roger Waterford, James Love, Jno. Swifft, Patrick Love, Symond Grey, Edith Tyler, Morgan Jones, Susan Ripley, John Bacon (or Baron ?), Jno. Staples, Jno. Rawly, Lawrence Fault.

JANE BROOKES, Relict of Henry Brookes, 280 acs. W'moreland Co., S. E. side of Appomatox Cr., adj. Col. Jno. Washington, Rich. Higden, Lawrence Abington, &c; 16 Oct. 1670, p. 337. Being the surplus of 1020 acs. granted sd. Henry 14 Oct. 1657, & granted sd.

Jane by order, &c. 23 Oct. 1669. Trans. of 6 pers: Tho. Johnson, James Wells. Martyn Jones, Wm. Davys, Mary Bonner, Wm. Mallard.

MR. ISAAK ALLERTON & MR. THO. BUNBARY, 880 acs. Staff. Co., in the freshes of Potomack Riv., adj. John Mathewes; 22 Oct. 1670, p. 337. Trans. of 18 pers: Roger Pye, Ja. Tenet, Agnes Dyell, Peter Stamford, Jno. Browne, Jno. Baker, Phill. Newman, James Wells, Mary Spencer, Hen. Griffith, Jno. Dangerfeild, Geo. Phillips, Saml. Greene, Wm. Bendry, Wm. Smith, Jno. Peather, Wm. Miller, Tho. Hall.

HENRY & ELIZABETH LAWRENCE, 350 acs. in the N. W. br. of Nancemond Riv., 19 Oct. 1670, p. 337. 250 acs. adj. Mr. Robert Lawrence, & an Island by the Cr., &c. 100 acs. on an island, adj. a Cr., &c. 250 acs. granted to Humphry Edey 27 Dec. 1652 & 100 acs. purchased by sd. Edey of Jno. Loyd 28 Mar. 1652; both parcels given by will of sd. Edey to sd. Henry & Eliz.

THOMAS CHETWOOD & JNO. KILLINGHAM, 600 acs. Rappa. Co., 26 Apr. 1670, p. 338. Trans. of 12 pers.* Beginning by "R. L." path, &c.

EDWARD WETHERBORNE. 150 acs. Rappa. Co., by the Bryery Swamp, 17 Nov. 1670, p. 338. Trans. of 3 pers: Mich. Jones, Marke Makins, Ambrose Palmer.

JNO. CARPENTER, CHARLES CARPENTER & WILLIAM WEST, 800 acs. N'umberland Co., at the head of a br. of the maine br. of Gr. Wiccocomoco Riv., nigh Machoticke Path, adj. Mr. Wm. Hall, to N. side of a br. of Moraticoe, &c; 24 Nov. 1670, p. 338. Trans. of 16 pers: Jno. Foster, Jno. Hilyard, Fra. Moulton, Wm. Davys, Mary Child, Sara Wilkinson, Geo. Clarke, Hum. Taught, Edwd. Johnson, Edwd. Ballum, Wm. Long, Geo. Chaddock, Ann Halderson, Obadia Hollyes, Isaak Syms, Hugh Lee.

HENRY WOODNOT & THOMAS SMITH, 456 acs. Rappa. Co., S. side

sd. Riv., along Wm. Talbott & Jno. Lacy to Lt. Col. Goodrich, by the White Marsh, Mrs. Smith, &c; 17 Nov. 1670, p. 339. Taken up by Mr. Anth. Stephens, deserted, & granted to Jno. Carpenter by order &c., assigned to the abovenamed 25 Jan. 1667. (Note: The following names appear under this patent:) Sampson Cooper, Wm. Smith, Wm. Allen, Hanna Loe (or Lee), Saml. Cooper, Hen. Smith, Eliz. Francisoys, Mary Brickfield, Edwd. Templer, Tho. Gilbert.

MR. THOMAS MADDYSON (Maddison), 1198 A., 3 R., 9 P., Rappa. Co., by the mayne br. of Moratico; 5 Apr. 1670, p 339. Sold to sd. Maddison by Jno. Carpenter, Mihill. Miller & Charles Carpenter, 4 Apr. 1670. Trans. of 24 pers: Tho. Prescott, Wm. New, Peter Bull, Robert Nuce, Wm. Porter, Jeffry Bun, Ann Wilson, Tho. Powell, Robert Willis, Henry Bryant, Robert Thacker, Isaak Paul, Ralph Grymes, Rachell Griggs, Robert & Thomas Potter, Amy Goodson, Tho. Warren, Thomazine Temple, Robt. Rich, Tho. Towers, Alex. Mackwilliams, Tho. Williamson, John Mynns.

THO. MADDISON (Madison), 200 acs. Rappa. Co., 17 Nov. 1670, p. 340. Trans. of 4 pers: Xpian. Holladay, Wm. Nicholls, Peter Gibbs, Rowland Hudson.

SAME. 180 acs., same Co., date & page. Trans. of 4 pers: Robert Greene, Mary Rose, Morris Green, Hen. Groves.

SAME. 250 acs., same Co., date & page. Trans. of 5 pers: Tho. Preston, Wm. Morgan, Mary Senior, Jane Lassers, Tho. Jarvis.

RICHARD GOODMAN, 424 acs. Rappa. Co., N. side sd. Riv., by the Bryery Sw., up the road path, along an old path called Chickacone Path, by the Turkey br., &c; 20 Nov. 1670, p. 341. 300 acs. granted to Edward Wetherborne & Gerrard Reynolds, who sold to sd. Goodman; 124 acs. for trans. of 3 pers: Jno. Marsh, Peter Gobson, Wm. Nicholls.

MR. GEORGE HEALE, 710 acs. Lancaster Co., 17 Nov. 1670, p. 341. Adj. Dominick Theriott on E. side of Mount Noddy Sw. at the head of Corotomen, on land of Joseph Bayly, Mihill Miller & Jno. Symonds, by Pope's land &c. 365 acs. granted him 13 Oct. 1669; & 355 acs. for trans. of 7 pers: Jno. Mohun, Robert Brett, Saml. Greene, Mary Edwards, Rich. Johnson, Wm. Harris, Martyn Dallyson.

MR. THOMAS HARWAR & NICH. COX, 922 acs. Rappa. Co., S. side sd. Riv., 17 Nov. 1670, p. 342. 867 acs. adj. Jno. Chin. Tho. Pattyson, Rich. Bredgar, Jno. Sharp, Jno. Mayo & Lt. Col. Tho. Goodrich; 55 acs. adj. Rich. Spurland & purchased of him. 867 acs. for trans. of 18 pers.* Note: This patent is recorded in this booke in folio 205.

HENRY WOODNUTT, 602 acs. Rappa. Co., adj. Lt. Col. Goodrich; 17 Nov. 1670, p. 342. Trans. of 12 pers: Alice Streete, Tho. Parker, Cassandra Sheppard, Peter Powell, Walwyn Hannus, Mary Norman, Tho. Thruston, Edwd. Hayes, Humphry Thaxter, Ambrose North, Marg. Pendexter, Thomas Bendister (or Bendish).

THOMAS ELVAR, 303 acs. Rappa. Co., adj. David Birke; 17 Nov. 1670, p. 342. Part of 606 acs. granted sd. Elvar & Tho. Maddison, 8 July 1663, which is now divided.

DAVID BIRKE, 303 acs. Rappa. Co., adj. Tho. Elvar; 17 Nov. 1670, p. 343. Formerly taken up by Tho. Elvar, Tho. Maddison, who sold his part to sd. Birke 24 July 1664.

MR. THOMAS HARWAR, 70 acs. Rappa. Co., adj. land of Mr. Smith & Jno. Lacy; 17 Nov. 1670, p. 343. Trans. of 2 pers: Peirce Monyon, Jno. Mathewes.

MR. RICHARD BULLER & MR. THO. BATTS (Batt), 378 A., 1 R., 24 Po., Henrico Co., N. side of Appomattock Riv., against the middle of the *Indian* towne; beg. at a Spring bottome, adj. George's field at the river, &c; 3

Feb. 1670, p. 343. Trans. of 8 pers: Jno. Stephens, Ann Williams, Margaret Bumpas, Joan Bishop, Hen. Bennett, Robt. Luddington, Jno. Ellis, Jno. Rosser.

MR. JNO. BUCKNER & MR. THOMAS ROYSTON, 2000 acs. Rappa. Co., on S. side & in the freshes of sd. Riv., adj. Mr. Lawrence Smith. 2 May 1671, p. 343. Trans. of 40 pers: Tho. Hix, Jno. Busby, Geo. Young, Geo. Barker, Mary Parker, Robt. Beecham, Hen. (?) Hardacres, Jno. Davis, Dorcas Young, Danll. Grouch, Eliz. Sharpes, Wm. Gradwich, Geo. Brooke, Hen. Castell, John Hayward, Ja. Barkehust, Hen. Powell, Humphrey Thomas, Wm. Greene, Jno. Hunt, Peter Cosens, Tho. Cheyney, Mary Cheyney, Robt. Edwards, Blanch Harding, Xper. Edee, Arrabella Singleton, Mary Greeford, Ann Townesend, Jno. Friswell, Muscuff Scilly, Jno. Jones, Marg. Tompson, Jno. Wery, Wm. Wright, Robt. Rate (or Race), Jno. Kelley, Jno. Farrell, Robt. Thurston, Robt. Hull (or Hall).

JNO. CHADWELL, 650 acs. Low. Norf. Co., E. side of Ridgeford Sw. a br. of Eliz. Riv., 25 Nov. 1670, p. 344. Trans. of 13 pers: Wm. Thomas, Math. Williams, Jno. Short, Alex. Davis, Cha. Green, Jno. Kippin, Wm. Sanders, Edwd. Frost, Wm. Jones, Tho. Carr, Edw. Cooper, Fra. Barber, Isaac Ball.

MR. ROBERT BULLINGTON, 150 acs. Henrico Co., 6 Apr. 1671, p. 344. Granted to Wm. Dawker, dec'd., & by inquisition under Mr. Henry Randolph, Depty. Esch'r., 7 Oct. 1669 &c. and now granted &c.

MR. CHARLES BRYAN, 800 acs. New Kent Co., 6 Apr. 1671, p. 344. Granted to Wm. Plumtree, dec'd., & by inquisition under Mr. Tho. Hall, Depty. Esch'r., 3 Oct. 1670 &c.

EDWARD ISAN, 400 acs. Nanzemond Co., 6 Apr. 1671, p. 345. Granted to Jno. Garrett, dec'd., & by inquisition under Mr. Wm. Alford, Depty. Esch'r., 7 June 1670 &c.

THOMAS GARRETT, 150 acs. Nanzemond Co., 6 June 1671, p. 345.

Granted to Rich. Russell, assigned to Edward Dence, dec'd., & by inquisition &c. (as above).

WIDDOW HARRIS, 300 acs. Nanzemond Co., 6 Apr. 1671. p. 345. Granted unto Margaret Rogers, wife of Willm. Rogers, dec'd., 14 Aug. 1637; by inquisition &c. (as above).

MR. JOHN BRASEUR (Brasure), 300 acs. Nanzemond Co., 6 Apr. 1671, p. 346. Granted to Peter Johnson. dec'd., assigned to Peter Rey, who sold to Robert Braseur, dec'd., & by inquisition &c. (as above).

JOHN PETERS, 250 acs. Nanzemond Co., 6 June 1671, p. 346. Granted to Mr. Jno. Googins, dec'd., assigned to Lawrence Peterson, dec'd., & by inquisition &c. (as above).

MIHILL HUGHILL & THOMAS SHORT, 1000 acs. on the N. side & in the freshes of Rappa. Riv., 26 May 1666, p. 346. Trans. of 20 pers: Harman Ford, Hen. Kilderkin, Rich. Bartlett ,Abra. Packford, Rich. Downer, Fra. Clifton, Robt. Clifton, Fra. Conniers, Tymothy Holt, Rich. Hudson, Robt. Chambers, Rich. Ellis, James Clawson, Tho. Portman, Jno. Bawdon, Giles Burd, Tho. Moon, Jesper Arnold, Jonath. Dew, Joseph Axon.

WILLIAM THATCHER, 300 acs. Lancaster Co., E. side of Corotoman Riv; adj. his own, land of Tho. Steed & Mr. Robt. Jones. 24 Mar. 1664, p. 347. Trans. of 6 pers: Tho. Carile, Wm. Lampert, Wm. Roberts, Wm. Courte, Jno. Foreman, Tho. Cocken.

TYMOTHY GREENE, 445 acs. N'umberland Co., upon the head of Mattapony Riv., adj. Jno. Kent's land, Nath. Hickman, James Clawton, James Johnson; 3 Feb. 1664, p. 347. Trans. of 9 pers: Jno. Ashford, Geo. Ferrer, Jno. Sharpman, Amy Tawked, Amy Collins, Mary Gartricke, Mary Harper, Judith Trackby, Tho. Tart.

JAMES HILL, 100 acs. N'umberland Co., upon the head of Wiccocomoco

Riv., 26 June 1666, p. 347. Trans. of 2 pers: Jno. Cale. Emy Portey.

WM. MAJOR. 200 acs. Accomack Co., bet. Nusswadox & Ockahannock Crks., adj. Tho. Johnson, land formerly Nicholas Waddiloe's now belonging to one Teage an orphan. & in possession of Tymothy Coe, adj. John Cuttin, & Jno. Evence (?), 26 May 1673. p. 347. Trans. of 4 pers: Abraham Buckley, Wm. Morgan, Joseph Clarke, Geo. Hasleup (?).

MR. JOHN PROSSER & HENRY CREIGHTON, 4246 A., & 8 Primes, Rappa. Co., on S. side & in the freshes of sd. Riv., adj. Mr. Talliferoe his lyne called Nicaponckes. over Snow Cr., &c; 14 Mar. 1670/1. p. 348. Trans. of 85 pers: Tho. Colly, Rich. Pantry. Geo. Signe. Geo. Powell. Geo. Glasse, Geo. Geinkes, Geo. Smith. Wm. Colt. Jno. Williams. Nich. Rawlyns. Jno. Chamberlain, Fra. Symons Wm. Abram, Hen. Joanes, Jno. Joanes, Jno. Gosling, Hum. Joanes, Edwd. Prichard, Tho. Griffith, Wm. Downes, Tho. Smith. Jno. Brydon (or Boydon), Mr. Robt. Williams. 9 tymes, Tym. Johnson, Mary Bennett, Ann Joanes, Alice Eston. Phill. Flowe. Tho. Watts, Robt. Mercer, Patience Darkwell, Obadia Robins, Jno. Elton, Tho. Newcock, Rich. Wooton. Barth. Field. Ellen Wescott, Eliz. Cofield. Jno. Bramlyes, Jno. Baker. Fra. Peterson. Ralp Hopkins, Saml. Glover, Jane Standfast, Wm. Porter, Nath. Gardford (or Gareford). Joseph Copton, Wm. Brumwell, Wm. Bowleware, Jno. Leatherland, Tho. Strange, Rebecca Browne, Wm. Landale. Ja. Bush. Mich. Parramore, Tho. Hoskins. Tho. Skory. Mary Benner, Marth Pallett. Mary Potts. Saml. Johnson, Walter Price, Edward Munt, Saml. Parrott. Jo. Parrott, Fra. Parrott, Ja. Culpeper, Roger Baynard, Su. Mason, Tym. Johnson. Judith Sanford, Robt. West, Jno. Fish. Marmaduke Pickman, Geo. Parsons, Fra. Purtyn; 1 Negro.

RICHARD IVESON, sonne of Abraham Iveson, dec'd., 2200 acs. Staff. Co., upon the maine run of Quantiqunt Cr.. & adj. Christopher Lund; 29 Mar. 1671, p. 348. Granted to Wm. Beach & Richard Hattoll 22 Mar. 1665, assigned to Richard Normansell, who assigned to sd. Abraham & by Abraham his sonne given to sd. Richard his brother.

LT. COL. JOHN WASHINGTON, 450 acs. N'umberland Co., S. side Potomack Riv., nigh *Nominy;* adj. Danl. Hutt, merchant, & Wm. Overed; 10 Oct. 1670, p. 349. Granted to Le Strange Mordaunt 24 Oct. 1666, deserted & now granted by order, &c. Trans. of 9 pers: Nicho. Joanes, Alice Little, Joan Norwood, Jno. Nicholls, Tho. Goose, Jno. the frenchman, Rowland Davys, Tho. Knapton, Anth. Dodson.

WILLIAM GREENE, 250 acs. W'moreland Co., on a br. of Oquia Riv., opposite Saml. Mottershead & adj. Thomas Hyatt; 17 Jan. 1670, p. 349. Trans. of 5 pers.*

RICHARD GROSE, 200 acs. Is. of Wight Co., 6 Apr. 1671, p. 349. Escheat land, as by inquisition under Jno. Jenings, &c.

DOROTHY BARTELEY, 100 acs. Surry Co., 6 Apr. 1671, p. 350. Granted to Patrick Barteley, dec'd., & by inquisition &c. under Mr. George Watkins, Depty. Eschr., 31 May 1669, granted &c.

DAVID ANDREWES, 200 acs., Surry Co., 6 Apr. 1671, p. 350. Granted to Nich. Williams, dec'd., & by inquisition &c. under Richard Awborne, Depty. Esch'r., 26 Sept. 1670, granted &c.

RICHARD MOORE, 112 A., 3 R., 18 P., Chas. City Co., S. side Appomatock Riv., 7 Apr. 1671, p. 350. Adj. Maj. John Epes, nigh Michaell Hill, adj. Mr. Whittington, the *Spring Garden patt.,* John Sturdevant, &c. Trans. of 2 pers: Tho. Belcher, John Learewood.

MARTIN ELAM, 287 acs. Henrico Co., S. side James Riv., 7 Apr. 1671, p. 350. Beg. nigh the Blind Slash, along Flinton's Slash to Tho. Wells, & adj. Robt. Bowman. Trans. of 6 pers: John Rosser, Tho. Hollins, Jane Prout, Kath-erine Powell, Nicholas Ellis, William Ricketts.

THOMAS WEBSTER, 442 A., 1 R. 15 P., Henrico Co., N. side of Apomattox Riv., at the heads of the *Old Towne lands,* on the Old Towne Run & Cr. & adj. Geo. Archer. (In 3 tracts.) Trans. of 10 pers.*

CAPT. JOSIAS PICKES, 3500 acs. New Kent Co., N. side Mattapony Riv., 7 Apr. 1671, p. 351. Neare the mouth of a Slash at the upper end of the Banke where the Monsy (or Mongy) (?) did formerly live, adj. a levell neare (the) Moratticoe Indians, &c. Trans. of 70 pers: Jacob Limken, Jno. Dalton, Owen Prester, Wm. Clarke, Jno. Snackwell, Step. Annis, Jno. Batts, Jno. Lugger, Hen. Sternhold, Joseph Lambe, Jno. Betten, Wm. Fluellen, Peter Succott, Josias Pickes, Rich. Byron, Jno. Deheld (?), Jno. Dunston, Jac. Burrage, Ann Hodges, Mary Hodges, Mary Nixon, Mary Lord, Mary Williamson, Eliz. Bowney, Sara Sarckell, Hanna Humphry, Peter Nutt, Jno. Holloway, Mich. Thornbury, Hen. Tally, Edwd. Traveller, Chester Bredley (or Bradley), Sym. Reddey, Tho. Grose, Rich. Ridley, Wm. Baker, Tho. Browne, Edwd. Rives, Tho. Baker, Danl. Merritt, Jo. Pickes, Senr., Jo. Pickes, Junr., Jno. Devy, Jac Burrage, Eliz. Perry, Tho. Eaton, Sampson Gull, Tho. Rudey, Eliz. Cuddy, Ellenor Barwell, Eliz. Richards, Ann Stacey, Dor. Proctor, Rich. Bredgar, Alex. Fisher, Rachell Appleton, Greg. Goodwyn, Robt. Willowby, Jno. Small, Jno. Fife, Wm. Gold, Jno. Hart, Antho. Sparks, Wm. Allan, Xtophr. Buckle, (or Huckle), Stephen Huckle, Tho. Fisher, Tho. Harper, Jno. Trice, Tho. Dyer.

MR. GEORGE POOLE, RICH. FARTHINGALE, JAMES BARNINGHAM & JAMES FORSITH, 800 acs. Gloster Co., Ware Par., adj. corner tree *accounted* Henry Corbell's &c. 600 acs. granted sd. Corbell 6 Mar. 1653 & assigned to sd. Poole, et als; 200 acs. overplus due them severally for trans. of 4 pers: Charles Hatcome, Charles Bastock (or Bostock), Jno. Gregory, Eliz. Wood. 7 Apr. 1671, p. 352.

THOMAS LUDWELL, Esqr., 2994 A., 2 R., 35 P., on S. side of Chickahominy Swamp, 7 Apr. 1671, p. 352. 2093 A. 1 R. 25 P. at a run called Col. Wynn's Quarter, to a run above Pomonkey Path, over Cowtayle quarter run, &c; 901 A., 1 R. in Henrico Co., on N. side of James Riv., at the forkes of the cattayle run; at head of Mr. Rich. Cock, Senr., to Mr. Green, &c. Surveyed for sd. Cock & Mr. Jno. Beauchamp, deserted, & now due by order &c., & trans. of 60 pers: Tho. Moss, Jno. Grout (or Gront), Jno. Brewer, Jarvis Rogers, Roger Mekes, Jno. Skittlethorpe, Jno. Scott, Jeremie Everingha (?), Jno. Heper (?), Eliz. Lasher, Peter Sides, Jno. Steer, Wm. Withington (or Wilkington), Jno. Fisoll, Eliz. Osburn, Jno. Carpenter, Beata Fowler, Mary Bolton, Rebecka Bough, Francis Robinson, Robt. Hart, Mary Pickiner, Wm. Evans, Robt. Write, Robt. Littlefeild, Richd. Marsh, Tho. Hutton, Nic. Corben, Sara Mesem, Fran. Cary, Sara Clement, Wm. Waites, Symon Benford, Addam Rose, Jno. Symons, Jno. Grimston, Jno. Ladrick, Jno. Stringer, Ester Marshall, Rich. Bridges, Nic. Martin, Wm. Bagshaw, Eliz. Truelove, Barbara Corderoy, Danll. Ridely, Tho. Burroughs, Abraham Allen, Margery Rose, Richd. Clark, Humphry Elliot, Jno. Hunt, Jno. Wortham, Jno. Gaineford, Wm. Shirley, Gilb. Makevary (?), Jno. Mackargoe, Jno. Cotton, James Bowlin; 2 Negroes.

LIEUT. COL. THO. LIGON (Liggon), 387 A., 1 R., 32 P., Henrico Co., N. side of Appomatock Riv., bet. a small island on the W'wd. & a gr. island on the E'wd., neigh Major Genll. Wood's trees on Fleete's land, nigh a path, to the old towne Run &c., over against the middle of the Appomatock Indian Towne at a spring bottom, by a feild &c; 7 Apr. 1671, p. 353. Trans. of 7 pers: Roger Bridges, Arnol Mouse, Garrett Lidwith, Henry Cole, Oswell Osborne, James Barnell, Anthony Little.

MR. LEONARD CLAYBORNE, 3000 acs., N. side of Mattapony Riv., on upper side of Doctor Moody, &c., 1 Apr. 1671, p. 353. Trans. of 60 pers: James Taylor, Tho. Thomson, James

Taylor, Sanders Allin, Jno. Burnum, Jno. Ring, Tho. Hopkins, Tho. Wright, Rivers Burr, Wm. Freeman, Jno. Napp, Jno. Engrum, Rich. Ashton, Robt. Murrley (or Marrley), Christopher Awrkon (?), Tho. Hinton, Martin Hill, Margreett Buttey, Tho. Seawell, Samll. Dainne, Susan Hall, Wm. Pallmor, Tho. Poule, Alce Wilson, Tho. Hunlocke, Tho. Turrnor, Rich. Lethersell, Margery Backer, Denby Ray, Alex. Oriell, Ann Underwood, Jno. Thickepeney, Tho. Williames, Christin Demadgetts, Jno. Cumpton, Rich. Bruster, Robt. Rigbey, Petter Rickett, Edw. Welch, Raulph Browne, Joane Isame, Jno. Branch, John Meeke, Rich. Carter, Robt. Persifield, Nath. Chapman, Edw. Hill, Jno. Norton, Rich. Young, Mary Purfing (?), Rich. Hall, Jno. Fowler, Mary Brenthall, Thomas Twy, Wm. Neck, Robt. Poole, Jeremiah Bunch, Jno. Fosque, Tho. Mekin, Mary Sanders.

RICHARD WHITE & GEORGE VINCENT, 425 acs. N. side of Lancaster Co., at the heads of the branches of the Sw. of Marattico Cr., adj. Edwd. Riley, Abraham Bush, by the path towards Chicacone, to Doctor Saunders (Sanders), &c; 4 Apr. 1671, p. 354. Granted to Whalter Wharton, deserted, & now granted by order &c. Trans.. of 9 pers: John Shaxton, Wm. Michaell, Rob. Rowse, Nich. Cox, Wm. Crosse, Hen. Battle, John Williams, Jno. Jones, Bethel Garland.

THOMAS HARWAR, 200 acs. Rappa. Co., S. side sd. Riv., adj. Rob. Armstrong, & on a br. of Ralphs Cr. running into Piscaticon; 21 Sept. 1668, p. 354. Granted to William Williamson, assigned to John Webb, deserted, & now granted by order &c., & for trans. of 4 pers: Rich. Brookes, Eliza. Chamberlyn, Edw. Berry, Kath. Berry.

MR. WILLM. WHEELER, 110 acs. on N. side of Rappa. Co., towards head of Farneham Cr., adj. Mr. Billington & land formerly Coll. Fonteleroy's; 28 Mar. 1671, p. 355. Trans. of 3 pers: Margar. Battle, Eliza. Berry, Eliza. Suggins.

MR THOMAS CHETTWOOD (Chetwood), 482 A., 3 R., 12 P., Lancaster Co., bet. branches of Corotoman & Marattico, adj. Thomas Chatwin; 28 Mar. 1671, p. 355. Trans. of 10 pers: Anne Berry, Mary Berry, Danll. Lading, Prescilla Cadding, Mary Suggins, Ben. Stepman (or Shepman), Wm. Roberts; 2 Negroes.

MR. JOHN THOMAS, 1000 acs. upon a br. of Potomack freshes beyond land of Col. Speake, upon the Island Cr. & by land of Mr. Jernew; 4 Apr. 1671, p. 355. Trans. of 20 pers: Peter Hardgray, Wm. Wilson, Robt. Lawton, John Thompson, Mary Newton, Peter Gill, Jno. Jones, Mary Jones, Tho. Turtyn, Hen. Morley, Wm. Mallers, James Bray, Anne Hunt, Tho. Coghill, Jno. Powler (?), Nicholas Carew, Jno. Rancher, Jno. Ricks, Peter Turner, Jeffry Mosse.

SAME. 1000 acs., p. 355. At the head of a Cr. in Potomack freshes beyond the Doegs Island & land of Col. Speake, adj. Robert Lord & James Magregory & another seate of John Woods. (Note: Record unfinished.)

MR. LAWRENCE SMITH, of Gloster Co., 4972 acs., Rappa. Co., S. side & in the freshes of sd. Riv., on lower side of Nusaponocks Cr., adj. land granted sd. Smith & Mr. Robt. Talliafero; 25 May 1671, p. 356. Trans. of 99 pers: By assignment of Col. Warner 26 Negroes; Jno. Johnson, Jno. Watkins, Jno. Smith, Wm. Smith, Tho. Smith, Wm. Johnson, Jeremie Wilson, Geo. Hobbs, Jno. Crame (or Craine), Geo. James, Wm. Tibbs, Jno. Stevens, Wm. Stevens, Roger Blackwell, Xtophr. Denny, Cornelius Mathews, Wm. Collawn; 12 Irish servts; Jno. Knowles, Wm. Denington, Geo. Brookes, Samll. James, Symon Kingley, Xtophr. Dickens, Thomas Wheatly, Jno. King, Jno. Sampson, Lawrence Smith twice, Tobyas Cely, Thomas Bood, Ambrose Hammond, Geo. Walter (or Walker), Richd. Mold, Samll. Baker, Jno. Ashton, Xtopher. Adly, James Corveen, Jno. Oyden, Eliz. Sharp, Jno. Read, Arth. Read, Alexr. Hall, Cuth. Davies, Simon Eliott, Margat. Parland, Wm. Cary, Ja. Scott, Rich. Taylor, Elizb. Spencer, Ellen Harris, Stephen Smith, Richd. Danes (or

Daves), Jno. Browne, Eliz. Harwood.

SAME. 719 acs. Gloster Co., 22 July 1662, p. 357. 119 acs. upon a br. of Ware Riv. in Mobjack Bay, adj. Lt. Col. Jno. Walker; 600 acs. on Beech Sw., neere Mr. Cooke's quarter, along Robin hoods Spring Br., &c. 119 acs. granted him 11 Feb. 1657; & 600 acs. for trans. of 12 pers: Edwd. Bewitt (or Bearitt), Jno. Goss, Nath. Mott, Susanna Jones, Mary Thwait, Jno. Lee, Jno. Pratt, Wm. Derrick, Peter Spray, Hannah Gold, Jo. Harbinger, Antho. Yates.

MR. HENRY WOODHOUSE, 740 acs. Low. Norf. Co., in Lynhaven. 3 Apr. 1670, p. 357. 500 acs. at the mouth of the Little bay; 200 acs. adj. same; 25 acs. adj. land of Jno. Woodhouse; 15 acs. adj; 500 acs. granted him 22 May 1637; 200 acs. part of patt. to John Moy 5 May 1638 & purchased by sd. Henry; 45 acs. for trans. of: Thomas Creed.

MR. JOHN THOMAS, 1000 acs. at the head of a Cr. in Potomack freshes beyond the Doegs Is. & land of Col. Speake, adj. land of Robert Lord & James Magregory & a seate of John Woods; 4 Apr. 1671, p. 358. Trans. of 20 pers: Jno. Gregory, Henry Neale, John Brigges, Wm. Thurstone, Jno. Carner, Mary Meriwether, Thomas Dunstone, Anne Gundwile (or Gundivile), Jno. Moody, Anne Cooke, Rob. Thorowgood, Tho. Lawrence, Susan Freeman, Tho. Portris, Tho. Appleton, Rich. Brewton, Mary Brussells, Henry Dod, Mary Cole, Jno. Rosse.

MAJOR WILLM. MARRIOTT, 408 acs., Surry Co., nigh Mr. Bins' Cart path, by a Reedy Sw., & the foote path to Southwarke. &c; 27. June 1670, p. 358. Trans. of 8 pers.*

TIMOTHY TURTONS, 900 acs., New Kent Co., on S. side of Yorke Riv., below Waire Cr., & below Little Cr., &c; 24 Aug. 1670, p. 358. Trans. of 18 pers: Martyn Skinner, Tho. Barnett, Tho. Vintner, Tho. Fletcher, Alex. Nash, Rich. Long, Jno. Rawlins, Xpofer, Wooton, Edwd. Spicer, Rich. Chestowne, Wm. Edwards, Tho. Carpenter, Tho. Horecroft, Jno. Howell, Jone

Glanfeild, Edwd. Eabury, Robt. Reynolds, Jno. Gaines.

JOHN DORWOOD & NICHOLAS WAIRE (Ware), 536 acs., New Kent Co., between branches of Piankatank Sw. & Matapony Riv; 16 June 1671, p. 359. 300 acs. for sd. Dorwood, & 200 acs. for sd. Ware; adj. Gabrill Michill; & Griffin Lewis. Trans. of 11 pers: Peter Dihald (or Divald), Robt. Thompson, Hen. Jones, Mary Hatloe, Jno. Morgan, Robt. Neale, Tho. Davis, Charles Hallife, Abigall Neale, Rich. Beauport, Ja. a frenchman, David Stever. (NOTE: *This record crossed out.*)

NICHOLAS KING, 100 acs., New Kent Co., N. side of Mattapany Riv., on N. side of Asetyomps Sw., at the mouth of a br; 20 Nov. 1670, p. 359. Trans. of 2 pers: Sander Murray, Wm. Blare.

DAVID PRICHARD, 900 acs., New Kent Co., bet. branches of Piankatank & Arakiaco; adj. Thomas Langford where he liveth, crossing Capt. Jeames' meadow br., by a slash above the Path to Stringers; over the *forte:* to Thomas Hawkes, & adj. sd. Prichard & Charles Roames, &c; 16 June 1671, p. 360. Trans. of 18 pers: Hen. Barkeham, Mathew Roden, Fra. Boyce, Saml. Woodward, Davy Phillips, Edmd. Parry, Tho. Orly, Edmd. Deremy (?), Samll. Scofeild, Tho. Street, Hen. Hunt, Roger Baxter, Original Browne, Jno. Morgan, Vincent Mansfeild, Jno. Askew, Howel Morgan, Jno. Heasard (or Heaford).

CAPT. EDMUND BOWMAN & MR. SOUTHY LITTLETON, 2264 acs., N'ampton Co., on N. side of Swansicutts *alias* great Matapany Cr., & W'wd. on the divisional line bet. Va. & Maryland, &c; 23 May 1671, p. 360. Trans. of 46 pers: Southy Littleton, Mary Holt, Jno. a servt; Tho. Kester, Rich. Atkinson, Rowland Savage, Gumstead a Negroe, Jno. Edgscome, Hen. Roberts, Jno. Rosier, Jno. Armell, Wm. Bosca, Wm. Pedarmis, Ja. Jellett, Hugh Hesca, Jno. Penrose, Ja. Prade, Rich. Rowse, Jno. Rash (or Rush), Nich. Burland, (or Burlace), Tho. Tresey, Jno. Carusey (or Carnsey), Rich. Pendarvis, Hanibal

Buggins, Jno. Bowthen, Tho. Blacll (or Bladle), Hugh Courtney, Mich. Hill, Wm. Trevisa, Hen. Spur, Jno. Walbrooke; Ja. Warren, Edwd. Elsemon (?), Roger Jones, Math. Carter, Hump. Garland, Edwd. Ragner (or Raguer), Jno. Moore, Lewis Wilford, Math. Johnson, Tho. Warner, Ja. Whaley, James White, Arth. Grimes, Wm. Wray, Tho. Hartcoate.

WILLM. ROGERS, 100 acs. on S. side of the E'n. br. of Eliz. Riv., adj. James Whitehurst; 24 May 1671, p. 361. Trans. of 2 pers: Jno. Thomson, Wm. Dix.

MR. ARTHUR SMITH & JOSIAH HARISON, 1250 acs., Is. of W. Co., on Seaward's br. of the black water; adj. Mathew Tomlin; & Anthony Mathewes; 2 Jan. 1670, p. 361. Trans. of 25 pers.*

SAMUELL PEACHY, 190 acs., Rappa Co., on N. side the Riv., adj. John Williams, Giles Webb, John Sucket, Mr. Giles Cale, Francis Slaughter & Mr. William Hodgkins; 10 Dec. 1670, p. 361. Trans. of 4 pers: Jno. Crowcher, Ralph Gaydon, Robt. Duckeree (or Duckeen), Jennett Mynes.

MR. EDWD. GUNNELL, 1426 acs., Surry Co., by the Beavor Dam Sw. & Black Water Sw; 8 Nov. 1670, p. 362. Trans. of 20 pers: Ursala Day, Mathew Walton, Laurence Ash, Geo. Morgan, Mathew Barten, Mary Haynes, for his (Gunnell) transportation 4 times, Geo. Gunnell, Hen. Dam (?), Wench (?) Bedford, Rich. Hunington, Sarah Newman, Eliz. Robinson; & Marke, Robert, Joane & Ammun, Negroes.

MR. JAMES BRAY & MR. THOMAS HANCOCK (Hancox), 376 acs., James City Co., adj. Mr. Rob. Sorrill & Mathew Collins; neere a br. of Warrany (Creek); on W. side of old Rockahock Path, &c; 18 Apr. 1671, p. 362. Trans. of 7 pers: Margerett Bunbas, Isaac Bishopp, Henry Bennett, Robt. Luddington, Jno. Ellis, Jno. Bunbas, Jno. Roster, Tho. Hollings.

MR. THOMAS BUNBURY (Bunberry), 250 acs., Staff. Co., at a br. of

Oquia Riv., opposite Samuell Mottershead; nigh Tho. Wyatt, &c; 10 Feb. 1671, p. 362. Trans. of 5 pers: Jno. Sturrett (or Sturrell), Mary Williams, Tho. Grant, Wm. Burton, Arthur Davis.

SAME. 640 acs., Staff. Co., on branches of upper Mechotick Riv., bet. Potomacke & Rappa. Rivers; adj. Mr. Rob. Howson; 5 Apr. 1671, p. 363. Trans. of 13 pers: Tho. James, Edmond Ward, Tho. Gibbs, Tho. Bunbury, Jane Benning, Eatey Reading, Edwd. Sale, Jno. Kent, Jno. Simpson, Jos. Pile, Natha. Oxwich, Edmond Shelton, Rowland Peirce.

* MR. WILLM. THOMPSON, Minister, 630 acs., Surry Co., adj. Fra. Sothersby; 16 Mar. 1670, p. 363. Trans. of 13 pers: Wm. & Kather. Thompson, Wm., Saml., Jno. & Kath. Thomson, their children; Eleazer Thompson, Jno. Allen, Margt. Thomas.

THOMAS RICHARDSON, 50 acs., Low. Norf. Co., by the Deep Neck, near mouth of Goose Cr., & adj. his own & land of John Cherry; 25 July 1671, p. 363. Trans. of: Tho. Prescoate.

MAJOR WILLM. WYATT, 1900 acs., New Kent Co., on N. E. side of Mattapony Riv; adj. Rich. Barnhouse; crossing the Road, to Wm. Henderson; to island at the upper end of a marsh, &c; 21 Oct. 1670, p. 364. 400 acs. granted him 27 Apr. 1653; 350 acs. purchased of Tho. Plucknett; 100 acs. granted him 24 May 1664; & 1050 for trans. of 21 pers: Jno. Scott, Jno. Owen, Hen. Browne, Jno. Burke, Tym. Carter, Rich. Holloway, Mary Field, Bridgett Usher, Jno. Camell, Wm. Jessiott, James Bell, Margery Ram, Easter Ram, Jno. Alwood, Ann Bedinn, Jno. Phillips, Jno. Holsworth, James Day, Ashwell Batten, Ann Batten, Andrew Gill.

MR. HENRY LEE, sonne of Henry Lee, dec'd., 350 acs., Yorke Co., in Hampton Par., adj. Francis Morgan & Wm. Sawer's plantation; 22 Mar. 1670, p. 364. Granted Henry Lee, 5 July 1653, who bequeathed to his sd. sonne.

JAMES COLLINS, 164 acs., in the Up. Par. of Nanzemond Co., adj. his own & land of Francis Wells; 29 July 1671, p. 364. Trans. of 4 pers: Martha Wisdome, Tho. Pilman, Tho. Good, Edwd. Sedle.

MR. CHARLES ROANE, 451 A., 40 chs., Chas. Citty Co., upon N. side of Kittawan Cr., on the Oystershell landing in Mapscoe Cr., adj. Andrew Mildrum's landing; up James River, to *Wyanoake*, &c; 7 July 1671, p. 265. 320 acs. purchased of Mr. Rice Hoe; & the residue now taken up & added. Trans. of Robert Roane, & Cha. Roane.

MR. CHARLES CAMMELL (Camell), 250 acs., Nanzemond Co., 25 July 1671, p. 365. Adj. Robert Riddick, Mr. Wm. Wright, & his own land, in a gr. arrowread pocoson. Trans. of 5 pers: Jno. Hart, Wm. Edsell, Jno. Jenkins, Tho. Eldridge, Jno. Jenkinson.

MR. ROBERT RIDDICK, 100 acs., Nancemond Co., 24 July 1671, p. 365. Adj. Cammell's land; crossing a gr. white marsh, &c. Trans. of 2 pers: Mary Rich, Hanna Evans.

WM. BENSTON, 1000 acs., N'ampton Co., neer *Pocomoke* at the unpassable branch, adj. his own & land of his brother, & the bounds bet. Virga. & Maryland; 26 Nov. 1671, p. 365. Trans. of 20 pers: Wm. Yeo, Xtoph. Mathewes, Wm. Chapman, Tho. Wingood, Richd. Gibbs, Katherine Thomson, Mary Turner, Richd. Southern, Michll. Harrison, Margery Ames, Grace Tomlinson, Elinor Finner, Ja. Davies, Robt. Heckfeild, Robt. Barnett, Rebecka Knight, Wm. White, Wm. Willett, Walter Taylor, Tho. Thomas.

CAPT. WM. CORKER, 1850 acs., Surry Co., on S. side the Sipres Sw., 6 Aug. 1671, p. 366. Trans. of 37 pers: Jno. Sturman, Hen. Bridges, Robt. Nixon, Peter Spinx, Rich. Gwilliams, Jno. Beach, Robt. Prouse, Tho. Norton, Jno. Hix, Wm. Dixon, Mary Rose, Xpofer. Roades, Jno. Shaxton, Alice Edwards, Jno. Sparrow, Andrew Barnes, Hellena Bynns, Margt. North, Tho. Rands, Jno. Batts, Wm. Morecock, David Biggs, Jno. Rogers, Alice Sampson, Tho. Turner, Ambr. Loyd, Tho. White, Mary Whittaker, Tho. Bradshaw, Lawrence Bird, Abraha Winter, James Syms, Thomaz. Boston, Hanna Logg, Susan Basse, Thom. Wilkinson, Jno. Wimblethorp.

MR. ALEXANDER MURRAY, 1250 acs., Gloster Co., on E. side of Beach Br. of Ware River; adj. Col. Walker; 14 June 1671, p. 366. 200 acs. deserted by Col. John Walker & granted sd. Murray; 1000 acs. for trans. of 20 pers: Jno. Trott, Wm. Phillips, Peter Crow, Alex. Whitloe, James Barkin, Tho. Prim, Jeffery Miller, Tho. Fisher, Tho. Hill, Jno. Cradock, Humphry Hellier, Richd. Johnson, Wm. Penroe (or Penrose), Jno. Skeat, Hen. Hockley, Mary Dumond, Elener Salter, Jno. Hart, Wm. Symes, Tho. Briddy.

THOMAS BLAKE, 400 acs., Isle of Wight Co., in a br. of the black water, adj. Henry King; & Mr. Tookes; 20 Oct. 1670, p. 366. 240 acs. part granted him, 8 June 1664; & 160 acs. for trans. of 3 pers: Edward Love, Jno. Rookes, Edwd. Phillipps.

WILLM. PORTER, 30 acs., Henrico Co., on N. side of James Riv., beg. at Mr. Ballard his out seat at the Poplar Brooke; adj. Mr. Rich. Cock, &c; 7 Apr. 1671, p. 367. Trans. of: Jane Christy.

WM. PORTER, 58 A., 3 R., Henrico Co., N. side James Riv., adj. devdt. granted to & lost by Mr. Jno. Beauchamp, which was granted to Honble. Tho. Ludwell, Esqr., Secretary, &c; 7 Apr. 1671, p. 367. Trans of Lyddia Drunkard.

WILLM. RICKETTS, 350 acs., New Kent Co., on N. side of Mattapony Riv., upon Assamanket Sw., 19 Sept. 1667, p. 367. Trans. of 7 pers: Jno. Camell, Wm. Jeffiat (?), James Bell, Margery Ram, Ester Ram, Jno. Alwood, Ann Bedum.

MR. JNO. RISLEY, 12 A., 39 Chs., Yorke Co., adj. land of Lt. Coll. Wm. Barber, dec'd., Robert Jones, Walter

Wood, orphant, & near the head of Black Sw., 6 Feb. 1670, p. 367. Trans. of: Wm. Reeves.

MR. EDWARD THELWELL, 250 acs., near head of the S'n. br. of Nansemond Riv., adj. Thomas Mason, & Fra. Wells; 14 Apr. 1670, p. 368. Trans. of 5 pers: Gabriel Norton, Edwd. Thomas, Jno. Tomes, Mary Pynes, Tho. Edmonds.

MR. JNO. SUMNER, 67 acs., in the Up. Par. of Nancemond Co., adj. Henry Coopeland; Tho. Norfleet; & Wm. Moore; 14 Apr. 1670, p. 368. Trans. of 2 pers: Wm. Patten & his wife.

JAMES MONROW, 300 acs., Nancemond Co., adj. Richard Slaughter; & Jno. Jolley; 14 Apr. 1670, p. 368. Trans. of 6 pers: David Mudroyn, Wilson Pervin, Rich. Jennings, Jno. Jnoson (Johnson), Jno. Mattagett, Eliz. Langston.

MR. WM. CODOGAN, 800 acs., Nansimond Co., upon Somerton Sw., adj. Thomas Mulford; 10 Oct. 1670, p. 368. Trans. of 16 pers: Jno. Bagworth, Eliz. Tindall, Steph. Key, Fra. Archer, Wm. Clarke, Amy Bethlehem, Tho. Jackson, Rich. Dickeson, Tho. Cockerell, Jane ' Snayle, Edwd. Dudley, Jno. Thomas ,Wm. Hall, David Evans, Dorothy Davys, Jane Morris.

RICHMOND TIRRELL, 600 acs., New Kent Co., upon branches of Chickahominy Sw., adj. Thomas Meredith; & Mr. George Smith; 8 Feb. 1670, p. 369. Trans. of 12 pers: Wm. Loveday, Jno. Mercer, Wm. Jackman. Dan'l. Gaynes, Margt. Hollyer, Jno. Clarke, Joseph Alman, Andr. Hogg, Johana Jackson, Mary Savage, Wm. Tyrrell, Hanna Gundry.

COL. JNO BLAKE, 2400 acs., Nancemond Co., running to the head of Knotty Pine Cr. &c; 10 Oct. 1670, p. 369. Trans. of 48 pers: Jane Darby. Nich. Holmes, James Wilson, Tho. Hobbs, Mark Tomlyn, Prist. Morgan, Mar. Mallages, Mary Bridges, Jno. Cordwell, Jno. Bowles, Hen. Stephens, Wm. Goldstone, Jno. Kidwell, Eliz.

Brigg, Rich. Collins, Hen. Grymes, Jno. Walker, Rich. Duffeild, Rebec. Balls, Jno. Deare, Wm. Gray, Rich. Glay, Eliz. Shellon, Roger Gun, Tho. Jones, Fra. Keyes, Hen. Keyes, Ann Clarke, Wm. Gould, Jno. Withrid, Tho. Price, Walter Curtis, Robt. Roberts, Lewis Davys, Issabell Lewis, Edwd. Phillips, Jno. Roates, Edwd. Land, Edwd. Davis, Margt. Peacock, Mihill Goodale, Wm. Whitlock, Jno. Evans, Jno. Harrison, Martha Evans, Hen. Short, Tho. Pack, Roger Everett.

JAMES PETERS, 900 acs., Nancemond Co., 6 Apr. 1671, p. 369. Granted to Lawrence Peterson, dec'd., 14 Oct. 1650; & escheated by inquisition, &c. under Mr. *Wm. Alford, Depty. Esch'r., 7 June 1670, &c.

NICHOLAS PERRETT (Perrott-Perriott), 150 acs., Nancemond Co., 6 Apr. 1671, p. 369. Granted to Francis DeGregory, found to escheate &c. (as above).

THOMAS BEST, 300 acs., Nanzemond Co., 6 Apr. 1671, p. 370. Granted to Peter Johnson & Jno. Carter; by them sold to Peter Rye, dec'd., & lately found to escheate &c., by inquisition under Mr. Wm. Alford, &c.

MR. GEORGE WEBB, 50 acs., Eliz. Citty Co., 6 Apr. 1671, p. 370. Escheated from David Poole, by inquisition &c., under Mr. Wm. Alford, Depty. Esch'r. &c.

MRS. JANE POOLE, 474 acs., Eliz. Citty Co., 6 Apr. 1671, p. 370. Granted to Jno. Poole, dec'd., found to escheate, &c. (as above).

WILLIAM MORRIS, 150 acs., Eliz. Citty Co., 6 Apr. 1671, p. 370. Granted to David Poole, dec'd., found to escheate, &c. (as above).

HENRY BRIGGS & MARY, his wife, in right of THOMAS BLUNT & RICHARD WASHINGTON, Orphants, 250 acs., Surry Co., 6 Apr. 1671, p. 371. Granted to Charles Foard, dec'd., & escheated by inquisition, &c. under Richard Awborne, Depty. Esch'r., &c.

EDWARD HOLLYER, 200 acs., Low. Norf. Co., in Lynn Haven Par., at the head of Lynn Haven River, on the W. side, neare a place called the hollow poplar: 9 Feb. 1670, p. 371. Trans. of 4 pers: Robert Rosse, Mary Mynns, Peter Rans (or Raus), Hen. Clay.

COL. WM. KENDALL, 12,200 acs., in that part of N'ampton formerly called Accomack Co., 25 Sept. 1671, p. 371. 10,500 acs. granted him by the name of Lt. Col. Wm. Kendall, 6 Oct. 1670; 1700 acs. granted Mr. Henry Smith, 5 Apr. 1666, who assigned to sd. Kendall, 19 July 1661.

WM. JOHNSON, sonne of Wm. Johnson, dec'd. 550 acs. on N. W. side of Puscatna (Puscatakon) alias Coxes Cr., parallel to land of Robert Young; & adj. Randall Chamlett, &c; 25 Sept. 1671, p. 371. Granted his father 6 Oct. 1656, & given by will to sd. Wm.

ARTHUR UPSHOTT, 200 acs., Accomack Co., in Matchapungo Neck: N. E. towards Machapreage, to N. E. side of Ann Dymon's feild; including all the farme & parsonage marsh, &c; 28 Sept. 1664, p. 372. 1000 acs. part of a greater devdt. belonging to & deserted by Capt. Pott: 1000 acs. formerly belonging to & deserted by Mr. George Marsh, being part of 3500 acs. taken up & deserted by sd. Capt. Pott: by order of Court 18 Oct. 1660 confirmed to Wm. Kendall, who assigned to sd. Upshott.

MR. DEVORAX BROWNE, 850 acs., N'ampton alias Accomack Co., on Mondui Cr., alias Gr. Nuswattox Riv., from Arrocoke Cr. mouth to Mussatanzick Cr., along line of Dorman Swellevan, to Jno. Faucett; along Jno. West, &c; 27 Sept. 1671, p. 372. Granted to Ralph Barloe, 5 Oct. 1649, who bequeathed to Jno. Elsey, who assigned to Maj. Wm. Waters 14 Oct. 1658, who assigned to sd. Browne, 26 Mar. 1660. (Marginal notation gives this as 750 acs).

AMBROSE WHITE, 1300 acs., N'ampton Co., on S. side of Pungateage

Riv., Wly. on Pocomoke Cr., & adj.
Jno. Robinson, &c; 21 Sept. 1671, p.
373. Granted to Nich. Waddilow, ·2,
Apr. 1655, deserted, & now granted by
order, &c. Trans. of 26 pers: Ambrose
White, Robt. Mason, Wm. Williams,
Tho. Sheppard, Xpofer. Roberts, Jno.
Glose, Tho. Burton, Jno. Lawes, Ambrose White, Jno. Glasse (or Glosse),
Tho. Fuller, Ja. Roberts, Sara Jones,
Hugh Butler, Sara Jackson, Joan Smith,
Wm. Miller, Mary Hall, Jno. Townshend, Mary Harvy, Roger Edwards,
Jno. Thomson, Tobias Browne, Rachell
Browne, Hen. Plunkett.

MR. WILLM. WHITTINGTON,
600 acs., N'ampton Co., on N. & S
sides of Lovelong br., adj. Richard
Bundock & Mary Lewis; 28 Sept. 1671,
p. 373. Granted to Geo. Watson, 9
Nov. 1666, deserted, & now granted by
order, &c. Trans. of 12 pers: Lawrence
Gery, Mary (or Marg.) Gery, Edwd.
Gery, Ellenor Gery, Jno. Bayley, Tho.
Beard, Ann Thompson, Geo. Font, Rich.
Lynch, Robt Adkins, Reynold Sadler,
Tho Jones.

MR. EDWARD REVELL, 1000 acs.,
N'ampton Co., at little Matomkin Cr.,
& towards Gr. Matomkin Cr; 29 Sept.
1671, p. 373. Granted to Col. Edmond
Scarburgh, 12 Nov. 1664, deserted, &
now granted, &c. Trans. of 20 pers:
Mary Buck, Mary Atkinson, Isabell
Smith, Isaak Broadly, Tho. Barton,
Wm. Williamson, Wm. Symonds, Susan
·Bateman, Andrew Price, Jno. Hogshead,
Jeremy Hooke, Rich. Greene, Math.
Browne, Jno. Dawkes, Mary Symonds,
Roger Thrower, Margt. Bisse,. Sara
Richards, Hary Moore, Robt. Kirke.

THOMAS FALKENER, 140 acs.,
Gloster Co., on the Easterne River; 29
Sept. 1671, p. 374. Granted to Thomas
Todd, who dying without an heire, or
otherwise disposing thereof by will, said
land escheated, by inquisition, &c., 9
Nov. 1668, &c.

MR. WILLIAM PLUMMER, 150
acs., Gloster Co., on N. side of Pepper
Cr. in Mockjack Bay; 29 Sept. 1671, p.
374. Granted to Nich. Boates, who
dying without heire or otherwise disos-

ing thereof by will, said land· escheated,
by inquisition taken 22 Dec. 1669, &c.

MAJOR GEORGE PARKER, 50 acs.,
N'ampton Co., 2 Oct. 1671, p. 374.
Granted to Anthony Johnson, dec'd., &
by inquisition under Col. John Stringer,
Depty. Esch'r., &c., 18 Aug. 1671 &c.

WM. WILTON. 300 acs., on N. side
& in the freshes of Rappa. Riv., about
10 mi. above Nanzemund Towne; adj.
Nicholas Merriwether; on the maine br.
of Divideing Cr., &c; 3 Oct. 1671, p.
374. Granted to Fra. Place, 7 Sept.
1658 & assigned to sd. Wilton.

MR. ROBERT PRICE, 300 acs.,
Middlesex Co., 3 Oct. 1671, p. 375.
Escheated from Robert Kemp, dec'd., by
inquisition under Henry Corbyn, Esqr.,
Depty Esch'r., 24 Apr. 1671, &c.

WILLM. BROCK, 350 acs., Low.
Norf. Co., in Lynn Haven Par., at head
of the fresh ponds in Dam Neck: 3 Oct.
1671, p. 375. Trans. of 7 pers: Morris
Fegarrell, James Thomas, Rich. Welch,
Mary Hems (?), Ann House, Danl.
Magrock, Hanna Keyes.

MORRIS LISSON, 400 acs., N'ampton Co., adj. Francis Benston; 3 Oct.
1671, p. 375. Trans. of 8 pers: Cornelius Swillivan, Robt. Brinson, Susanna
Milse, Wm. Lawrence, Mary Daniell,
Geo. Brookes, Margt. Barr, Tony a
Negroe.

EDMOND MOORE, 400 acs., Low.
Norf. Co., in Lynn Haven Par., at the
4th run from the mouth of Lyn haven
Riv., 3 Oct. 1671, p. 375. Trans. of 8
pers: Wm. Jeller (or Teller), Tho.
Hall, Ann Bishop, Olive Hale, Wm.
Studs, Tho. Apslands (?), Ellinor
Smith, Terlock Crage.

WILLIAM CORNIX, 1736 acs., Low.
Norf. Co., in Lynn Haven Par., part
being the Chinkapen ridge, the Grassey
ground, & Salisburg Plaine: on N. E.
side of the Beavor Damms, neare
Thunder bolt pine Br., by the Cipres
Sw., &c; 3 Oct. 1671, p. 376. 890 acs.
granted sd. Cornix by 2 patents, 25
Nov. 1657; & 846 acs. for trans. of 17

pers: Jno. Lawrence, Rich. Davys, Mary Edwards, Arrable Martyn, Ann Bowler, Alex. Daniel, Ben. Councell, Wm. Newport, James Slevan, Jno. Axstead, Margt. Heath, Edwd. Leath, Oliver Hall, Ellen Johnson, Ann Sadler, Tho. Lambert, Ann Williams.

CAPT. RICHARD HILL, 600 acs., N'ampton Co; being a neck on the N. side of Gingoeteage Cr. & the middle br. thereof, bounded on E. by the br. of the first bridge from the fort hills, &c; 3 Oct. 1671, p. 376. Trans. of 12 pers: Wm. Willett, Tho. Best, Ja. Fowkes, Jno. John, Xpofer. Judson, Mich. Thomas, Dorothy Cowden, Ruth Shelly, Ann Aubv (or Anby), Ja. Bowles, Jno Whiten, Rich. Lewis.

MR. HENRY SPRATT, 1100 acs., Low. Norf. Co., in Lyn Haven Par., on N. side of broad Cr., by *young* Geo. Fowler's land, &c; 3 Oct. 1671, p. 377. 800 acs. granted to Barth. Hoskins, 10 Mar. 1662, who sold to sd. Spratt; 300 for trans. of 6 pers: Hen. Spratt, Hen. Spratt, Issabella Spratt, Sara Sworten, Jno. Gold, Geo. Farnell.

JOHN STOKELEY, 200 acs., N'ampton Co., on the Seaboard side, between his own & land of Billiott; 3 Oct. 1671, p. 377. Trans of 4 pers: James Outhery (?), Geo. Hudson, Peter Welding, Rich. Bytoge.

PLOMMER BRAY, 150 acs., Low. Norf. Co., on N. side of Broad Cr., a br. parting this from land of Richard Hargrove; 3 Oct. 1671, p. 377. Trans. of 3 pers: Wm. Jells, Tho. Hall, Ann Bishop.

THOMAS WOLSTON (WOOLSTON), 450 acs., Low. Norf. Co., bet. *Rooded* & *Curratuck:* 100 acs. part being *Patience Island,* in the fresh ponds, comonly called Woolston's Is; 3 Oct. 1671, p. 377. Trans. of 9 pers: Tho. Woolston, his wife, his 5 sons, his 2 daughters.

HENRY SMITH, 300 acs., Low Norf. Co., in Lyn haven Par., on S. side of the broad run & E. side of Cipres Sw; 3 Oct. 1671, p. 378. Trans. of 6 pers:

Wm. Gold, Dudly Keale, Jno. Nash, Evan a frenchman, Sara Porter, Mary Welch.

WILLIAM EDWARDS, 200 acs., Low. Norf. Co; at a path from the E'n. br. of Eliz. Riv. to the North Riv; 3 Oct. 1671, p. 378. Trans. of 4 pers: Fra. Pomroy, Jno. Jackson, Fra. Henshaw, Florence Pomroy.

REBECCA STEREMAN, 1050 acs., W'moreland Co., 3 Oct. 1670, p. 378. Escheated from Edmond Brent, dec'd., by inquisition, &c., under Major Jno. Washington, Depty. Esch'r., 19. Nov. 1669; now granted, &c.

WILLM. CLEMENTS, 100 acs., W'moreland Co., formerly N'umberland Co; E. on Potomack Riv., S. upon Jno. Earle, &c; 3 Oct. 1671, p. 378. Escheated from Jno. Hewett, dec'd., & by inquisition &c. (as above.)

JANE BOAZ, 300 acs. Staff. Co., 4 Oct. 1671, p. 379. Granted to Xpofer. Boaz, dec'd., by inquisition, &c., under Major Jno. Washington, Depty. Esch'r. 24 Feb. 1670, &c.

BENONY BOURROUGH (Burrough), 944 acs., Low. Norf. Co., in Lyn Haven Par., near head of Bennett's Cr., N. of Adam Thorowgood, on the N. side of a Beavor pond, formerly called Needham's Marsh; adj. Lambert & land that was sd. Thorowgood's & now Wm. Smith's, &c; 3 Oct. 1671, p. 379. 590 acs. part granted to Fra. Yardly, 28 July 1648, sold to Christopher Burrough, 1 June 1652, & due sd. Benoni as heire to his dec'd, father, 354 acs. granted sd. Christopher 7 Nov. 1651, & due, etc.

REBECCA STEREMAN, 300 acs., W'moreland Co., on S. side Potomack Riv., E'ly. & S'ly. upon Nominy Riv., W. on Rich. Hawkins, & N. upon Kings Cr. which divides this & land of Mr Speake; 3 Oct. 1671, p. 379. Escheated from Edmond Brent, dec'd., & by inquisition under Major Jno. Washington, granted &c.

WM. HANCOCK, 700 acs., Low. Norf. Co., in Lynn Haven Par., on N.

side of the E'n. br. of Eliz. Riv; S. on Hoskins Cr. parting this & land of Mr. Wm. Moseley; 3 Oct. 1671, p. 379. 100 acs. granted to Geo. Fowler 6 Nov. 1663, who sold to sd. Hancock; 600 acs. for trans. of 12 pers: Mary & Henry Slade, Charles Baker, Eliz. Vouse, Jno. Rees, Jno. Quelch, Jaques Joslin, Charles Regarall, Wm. Richardson, Jno. Cooke, Barth. Shoare, Teage at Dovell.

MR. JOHN FOXHALL, 150 acs., W'moreland Co., 3 Oct. 1671, p. 379. Down a br. & sw. of Pope's Cr., to land of Xpofer. Butler & Abraham Feild, &c. Granted to Robert Porter, dec'd., & escheated by inquisition under Maj. John Washington, &c.

JOHN DEANE, 400 acs., on S. side of Rappa. Riv., on branches of Kilman's Cr., adj. Evan Davys & Tho. Williams, &c; 3 Oct. 1671, p. 380. Granted to Tho. Pattison 8 Nov. 1667, deserted, & granted sd. Deane by order &c. Trans. of 8 pers: Wm. Ashly, Abrah. Rolt. James Ellis, Robt. Willett, Maudlya Poynter, Rich. Jones, Ann Wood, Jane Forrest.

CHARLES GRUNDY (Gundry), 366 acs., Low. Norf. Co., on N. side of Danl. Tanner's Cr., 4 Oct. 1671, p. 380. Adj. Col. Mason, Hugh Purdy & Mich. Lawrence. Trans. of 8 pers: Wm. Chichester, his wife, 4 children; Jno. Reese, Tho. Leonard.

MR. HENRY RANDOLPH, 335 acs. 25 po., Henrico Co., on S. side of James Riv., 6 Oct. 1671, p. 380. Beg. in Mount my Ladyes feild against a place where an old oven had stood &c., to the red water slash, to falling ground of Procters, &c. Granted to Lt. Col. Tho. Ligon & Capt. Wm. Farrar 3 Oct. 1664, deserted & now granted by order &c. Trans. of 7 pers: Donoge Hickcene (?), Teage Mackermore, Donoge Macye, Donoge Ch—, Teague Steneholme, Wm. White, Tho. Atkins.

MR. THO. DEACON, a parcell of land in Gloster Co., 5 Oct. 1671, p. 381. Given by Mr. Tho. Bremoe to Margarett, his wife, by will; from

whom it escheated by inquisition under Miles Cary, Esqr., Esch'r., 4 July 1665 &c.

EDWARD ROWZEE & JAMES GULLACK, 460 acs., Rappa. Co., 6 Apr. 1671, p. 381. Granted to Rich. Morley, & escheated by inquisition under Major Jno. Weir, Depty. Esch'r., 4 May 1670 &c.

JOHN DANGERFEILD, 560 acs., Rappa. Co., 6 Apr. 1671, p. 381. Granted to Frances Dangerfeild, wife of Wm. Dangerfeild, dec'd., from whom it escheated by inquisition, &c. (as above.)

THOMAS SALISBURY, 540 acs., N'umberland Co., on S. side of Gr. Wiccocomoco Riv., adj. Mr. Christopher Garlington & land of Doctor Sanders; 27 Oct. 1670, p. 381. Trans. of 11 pers: Jonath. Parker, Nich. Claughton, Jno. Holland, Fra. Gilbert, Barth. Yeomans, Fra. Hill, Charity Hayter, Sara ————, Robt. Pennell, Ann Mosse, Wm. Gosse.

JAMES POPE, 70 acs., N'umberland Co., at the head of Gr. Wiccocomocoe Riv., & adj. his own land; 27 Oct. 1670, p. 382. Trans. of 2 pers: Wm. Herbert Jno. Dew.

GEORGE COURTMELL, 220 acs., N'umberland Co., at the head of Mattapony Riv., adj. Robt. Sech (or Seth); 27 Oct. 1670, p. 382. Granted to Jno. Kent, 500 acs. & by will given to his wife Phebe, with whome sd. Courtmell hath marryed; upon perambulation in the Parish of Chickacone the bounds of the patt. are found to have incroached upon land of Robt. Sech (?) & soe there remaines cleare noe more than 220 acs. remaines, &c. Trans. of 5 pers: Tho. Mash, Tho. Vaughan, Hen. Blarke, Hide Williams, Rich. White.

WM. CORNISH, 550 acs., N'umberland Co., adj. Danl. Holland, Chickacone Cr., & land of Robert Newman, & brs. of Hull's Cr; 27 Oct. 1670, p. 382. 400 acs. being the moyety of 800 acs. granted sd. Cornish & Danl. Holland 9 Dec. 1662, to them assigned by Rich.

Gibble & granted 1 Dec. 1656; 150 acs. for trans. of 3 pers: Saml. Webb, Rich. Jackson, Wm. Smith.

DANIEL HOLLAND, 550 acs., N'umberland Co., adj. Wm. Cornish, on Andrewes' br. of Hull's Cr., &c; 27 Oct. 1670, p. 383. 400 acs. being the moyety, &c. (as above.) 150 acs. for trans. of 3 pers: Erasmus Withall, Philemon Patten, Geo. Whitehorne.

SAML. MAYHANE, 300 acs., N'umberland Co., adj. land of Corderoy Ironmonger, by him bought of Thomas Lane; & adj. Mr. Edwd. Sanders; 27 Oct. 1670, p. 383. Trans. of 6 pers: Mary Peirce, Ann Higham, Mary Vizzard, Jane Bolt, Rich. Gold, Saml. Churrell.

MR. PETER PRESLEY, 500 acs., N'umberland Co., at the head of Chickacone Riv., adj. Richard Rice, Jno. Robinson, Machotick Path & land of Richard Cox; 27 Oct. 1670, p. 383. Trans. of 10 pers: Hugh Harris, Rich. Johnson, Mary Jones, Marth. Cornell, Sara Francis, Tho. Symonds, Jone Middleton, Saml. Glynn, Prudence Edwards, Ann Middleton.

HUGH NEVETT, 1170 acs., Gloster Co., in Mobjack Bay, at the forke of a br. of White Marsh Cr; to the head of Dividing Cr., to the Blackwater, &c; 6 Oct. 1671, p. 383. 940 acs. purchased of Mr. Geo. Curtis 16 Feb. 1668; 230 acs. for trans. of 5 pers: Robt. Ballard, Martha Brentford, Ann Hartwell, Jonath. King; 1 Negro.

MR. WM. MOSELEY & NICH CATLETT, 1730 acs., Rappa. Co., on S. side sd. river & on the N. side of Mill Cr; adj. Mr. Tho. Button, lands of Mr. Pate, Dangerfeild, Moncaster, Capt. Hump. Booth, Nich. Willard, & Gaynes, &c., over Bryces Sw., &c; 29 Sept. 1671, p. 384. 646 acs. granted them 17 Oct. 1670; 1084 acs. for trans. of 22 pers: Peter Dyas, Sara. Warner, Tho. Hill, Nath. Burthenhod, Margart Meene, Darby Driscoe, Tho. Hurston; & 15 Negroes.

THOMAS RAWSON, 591 acs., on S. side of Rappa. (Riv.), adj. Jno.

Mills neare the flood gate of Major Jno. Weire's Mill on S. side the creek; adj. Henry Moncaster, &c; 29 Sept. 1671, p. 384. Trans. of 12 pers: Math. Lewis, Jno. Luke, Robt. Young, Judith Abbett, Rich. Deaprise, Wm. Joyner, Wm. Cade, Eliz. Cade, (or Cadd), Wm. Atkin, Cha. Selch, (or Letch), Anth. Sheppard, Margt. Hutchins.

CHRISTOPHER BUSTIAN, 660 acs., Low. Norf. Co., in the S'n. br. of Eliz. Riv., 5 Nov. 1671, p. 385. Adj. land of Markham, now in possession of George Vallentine; & Capt. Wm. Carver, &c. 450 acs. granted John Yates who sold to James Warner, who sold to sd. Bustian; 210 acs. for trans. of 5 pers: Jno. Lawson, Mary Bruce, Wm. Lennidge, Robt. Benns, Geo. Johnson.

THOMAS HARDING, 525 acs., N'umberland Co., at the head of Broad Cr. of Yeocomocoe Riv., 27 Oct. 1670, p. 385. 500 acs. adj. James Claughton & James Johnson, Machotick Path, &c; 25 acs. at the head of Mattapony Riv., adj. sd. Clawghton & Johnson & Thomas Harding. Trans. of 11 pers: David Lynsay, Jno. Sympson, Wm. Thomas, Ben. Johnson, Robt. Aldage, Saml. Syms, Tho. Quick, Hen. Walden, Jno. Thomas, Jno. Lane, Anth. Lancaster.

JOHN WARREN, 180 acs., Surry Co., purchased of Thomas Webb, dec'd., on W. side of the Deep Spring Sw. adj. Capt. Baker's old feild, a br. parting this & land of Mr. Hardy; 3 Oct. 1671, p. 386.

RICHARD SKYNNER, 50 acs., Surry Co., at the head of Lawnes Cr., adj. land formerly Doctor Pawlyes, S. upon land formerly of Wm. Traledor, &c; 6 Oct. 1671, p. 386. Sd. land formerly in possession of Robt. Parkes; purchased by sd. Skynner from Jno. Bacon. Trans. of: Merrick Edwards.

RICHARD BRADFORD, 1197 acs. Chas. Citty Co., bounded on 2 sides with the Old Tree Run & the Fishing Run; 27 Nov. 1671, p. 386. Due sd. *Radford* by 2 conveyances from Hoel Prise & of record in sd. Co. Court.

PHILL. WATKINS, 650 acs. New Kent Co., N. side of Mattapanie Riv., adj. a Pine neck; part of a great devdt. of Mr. Edward Diggs', Esqr; 23 May 1673, p. 386. Sd. land granted to Will. Goffe 22 July 1659, assigned to John Maddison, who assigned to Martha Goffe, relict of Wm. Goffe; by her deserted, & now granted by order, &c. Trans. of 13 pers: Jno. Fransham, Katherine Paine, Wm. Webb, James Minster, Tho. Fresh, Tho. Wells, Jeff. Hawkins, Jno. Blewitt, Jno. Curle (?), Wm. Thweat, Arthur Pinner,Isabell. Jackson, James Toler. Marginal ·notation: This land deserted by Watkins & the rites transferd, Teste, P. L. Clk. (Note: This record has been crossed out, but is here given because of the numerous names it contains.)

MR. HENRY RANDOLPH, 1254 acs., Henrico Co., 27 Nov. 1671, p. 387. 600 acs. beg. at Hatcher's Run, towards the Swift Cr., towards the Ashen Sw. &c; 650 acs. upon the E. run of the Swift Cr. & next above land of Xpofer. Robinson & John Sturdevant, towards sd. Sw., &c. 600 acs. granted sd. Robinson & Sturdivant 23 Feb. 1652, deserted, & granted sd. Randolph by order, &c., for trans. of 12 pers; 654 acs., now joyned, & due for trans. of 14 pers: Wm. Hunt, Ja. Scott, Tho. Pratt, Jno. Berchard, Rich. Preston, Jno. Robts. (Roberts ?), Jno. Matram, Wm. Ward, Nich. Moore, Walter Chapman, Geo. Prichey, Jno. Basse, Ann Davenport, Rose Allen, Sara Williams, Jno. Mathewes, Ewsebius Williams, Jno. Sparke, Teo. Rennson (or Remison), Robt. Jones, Robt. Batteresse (?), Ellen Robinson, Tho. Blanchett, Hen. Brotherton, Jno. Lawrett, Robt. Harman.

MR. BARTHOLOMEW CHANDLER, 1238 A., 2 R., 36 P., Henrico Co., on N. side of Appamattock Riv. & on S. side of Swift Cr., 27 Nov. 1671, p. 387. Nigh Mr. Chandler's cleare ground, by Mr. Henry Randolph, to the Old Towne run &c; to Powatan Path, &c. Trans. of 16 pers; & by purchase of 400 acs. from sd. Randolph; in 1662: Bridget Chandler, Phill. Jones, Geo. Worsley, Solomon (?), Wm. Chandler, Rich. Jacob, Rich. Dobbs,

Ann Turberfeild, Jno. Hentland, Randall Burne. Fra. Miller, Geo. Lee, Rich. Racheley, Wm. Norroot, Rich. Hunt. Alice Walden.

ESSEX BEVILL & AMY, his wife, 600 acs., Henrico Co., on N. side of Appamattox Riv., near mouth of the Old Towne Cr., 27 Nov. 1671, p. 388. 400 acs. part of pattent granted to Jno. Cookeney in 1638, who bequeathed to Richard Skiddey, who dying without heire,- the land escheated & was by a former patt. granted to Amy Butler, now wife of Essex Bevill; 200 acs. adj. alsoe granted sd. Amy 29 Sept. 1664, & now by her consent, renewed in the joynt name of her husband & herselfe.

DANIEL JENNIFER & ANNE, his wife, lately called ANNE TOFT, 5,000 acs. in N'ampton, alias Accomack, Co. being a large neck of land bet. Gingoteak Cr. & Swansicuts Cr., adj. part of line dividing Virginia & Mary Land (Maryland); 12 Feb. 1671/2, p. 388. 3000 acs. part granted Col. Edmond Scarborough & by him legally conveyed to sd. Anne Toft 15 Mar. 1668; 2000 acs. due for trans. of 40 pers, by sd. Jennifer: Paul Size, Wm. Latom, Jno. Jaekson, Jno. Richardson, Tho. Saunders, Tho. Waterton, Jno. Harris, Wm. Bunne, Wm. Saintclear, Richd. Lee, Jane Davison, Elizab. Scott, Michaell Scott, Jno. Hunter, Jno. Findall, John Machall, Richd. Morrison, Richd. Millett, Agnes Niccoll, John Carlile, Gilbert Creder, Tho. Jacob, Charles Clark, Jennet Cornway, Wm. Hartwell, Franc. Kirkman, Wm. Bradley, Henry Hartwell, Xpian. Wilson, Wm. Anderson, Wm. Birne, Wm. Synn; Tom, Moll, Frank, Rose, Tom Jack, Will, Nan— Negroes.

SAME. 11,300 acs., same Co., date & page. On Stokeley's Branch, & Bundick's Br. 1450 acs. part granted to Col. Edmond Scarborough 29 Sept. 1662; 1400 acs. more also granted sd. Scarbrough 20 June 1664, both of which legally conveyed by him & Mary his wife to sd. Anne Toft 17 Aug. 1668; 1200 acs. granted sd. Anne 23 Feb 1663; 7,350 acs. due sd. Jenifer for trans. of 145 pers: Jno. Stevens, Tho

Hollings, Ann Williams, Jane Pratt, Margt. Bumpas, Kath. Powell, Joan Bishopp, Nic. Ellis, Hen Bennett, Wm. Ricketts, Robt. Luddington, Arnold Prouse (or Mouse), Jno. Ellis, Garret Lodgwick, Jno. Bumpas, Henry Cole, Jno. Rosser, Oswall Osbourne, James Barnes, Antho. Little, Jane Arbrey, Kath. Little, Toby Pitt, Ann Green, Obadia Butler, Lewis Williams, Wm. Jeffs, Owen Nazerene, Tho. Fowler, Tho. Mason, Archib. Turner, Fran. Bumpas, Ann Saunders, Margat. Grimley, Tho. Stafford, Margerie Woodward, Margt. Jeffreys, Tho. Richards, Jno. Write, Jno. Butler, Wm. Potter, Martha Neale, Jno. Reeve, Sara Dowman, Wm. Pemberton, Jno. Penny, Jno. Bates, Jno. Bellen (or Bellew), Hen. Hurst, Fra. Gillam, Hen. Downing, Jno. Galopper, Ann Winnell, Peter Roche (or Rocke), Jno. Bess, Jno. Trusser, Fra. Boucher, Wm. Dugdall, (or Dugdale), Henry Smith, Hen. Revill, Wm. Foxcreep, Jno. Whithurst, Jno. Withers, Marmad. Grey, Jno. Washington, Jno. Temple, Hen. Melton (or Molton), Owen Lloyd, David Fluellen, Oliver Cratts, Antho. Grosier, Patrick Isickle, Jeffrey Jefferson, Wm. Cronley, Jno. Finley, Hen. Ackworth, Jno. Vines, Wm. Pittegree, Tho. Hartloe, Seth Harloe, Hump. Hare, Enock Burrough, Jno. Swinerton, Wm. Bateman, Wm. Coleman, Mary Tralaine, Wm. Collavine (?), Trist. Twiford, Mark Davidson, Hen. ——, Peter Purfroy, Jno. Collison, James Hatt (or Start), Wm. Lee, Tho. Penny, Robt. Colls, Jno. Hancock, Peter Peterson, Miles Eversham, Willm. Williams, Jno. Terrill, Jno. Corne, Tho. Mackwms. (Mackwilliams), Tho. James, Wm. Palsgrave, Wm. Jenkinson, Tho. Dillin, Tho. Cobson, Eliza. Cobson, An. Pigrim, Job. Harvey, Tho.Thurloe, James Pepper, Jno. Thorogood, Wm. Harmer, Jno. White, —— Wheatly, Overton Manly, Peter Spraggen, Jno. Tenderby, (?), Henry Woodcot, Grace Marven, Jane Ferrell, Tho. Woodcock, Jno. Haddock, Wm. Peckstone, Jno. Pheasant, Tho. Alfred, Hen. Speedwell, Josias Thetcher, Wm. Pinchman, Jno. Trinkill, Alexr. Hull, Wm. Pettit, Jno. Symons, Wm. Tilbury, Fran. Harbert, Wm. Stone; Hector, Mingoe, Tonie, Doll, Nancie, Marie—Negroes.

MR. WM. DRUMMOND, 1442 A., 1 R., James Citty Co., in Chickahominy Riv., 167——, (date blank), p. 389. 1200 acs. granted him 26 Mar. 1662; beg. at the next point above Warrany Landing place; on Warrany Cr., &c. Granted William Taylour, 9 Nov. 1638; 242 A., 1 R., granted Edmond Cowles & Phillip Charles, 6 Aug. 1666, & assigned to sd. Drummond 29 Sept. 1668; being a neck in sd. river on N. side of James Citty, adj. Gregory Wells, & next towards Ould feild; due sd. Cowles & Charles for trans. of 5 pers.*

SAME. 200 acs., James Citty Co., in Pashehayes; adj. William Drewet, Mr. John White, Daniel Liell & Sir Francis Wyat. 167—(date blank), p. 389. Lease: for term of 99 years. Annuall Rent: 8 bbls. merchantable Indian corne shelled, to be paid at the dwelling house of sd. Drummond, upon sd. land, &c. Provided he, his heirs &c., shall not plant or seat upon sd. land within 6 months next ensuing, it shall be (lawful) for any other person to procure a lease for same. Granted by Act of Court 25 Nov. 1671, in consideration of his great charge in building & other improvements thereon &c. Note: By Act of Court 12 June 1638 for the better strengthening of James Citty, it was ordered, that the mayne land in Passbehayes on this side Powhetan Swamp should bee leased into parcells & divisions during the terme of 21 years, reserving to the Gov'r. &c. the annuall rent of 2 bushells of Indian corne for every 50 acs. with further proviso that such Leasees do plant and seat upon their land, &c.

WILLIAM SHORT, Planter, sonne & heire of William Short; 1100 acs. Surry Co., above the head of Up. Chippoakes Cr. about 1½ mi. up the W'most br., &c; 167— (date blank) p. 390. Granted to Robert Moseley, Gent., 7 Jan. 1649, who assigned to his father, 28 Oct. 1657.

ELIZABETH, SARAH & MARGARET DYE, children of —— Dye, dec'd., 690 acs. Accomack, alias N'ampton, Co., at Matomkin; 23 Mar. 1671/2, p. 390. Beg. at Dye's Bridge; down

Matomkin Cr., &c. 600 acs granted them 5 Apr. 1666; 90 acs. for trans. of 2 pers: Jno. Fletcher, Wm. Peregrine.

LAURANCE ROBINSON, 1350 acs., N'ampton Co., on a br. of Muddy Cr., parting this & land of Griffin Savage; lying bet. Martin Moore & Wm. Hickman; adj. Wm. O Noughton & on a br. of Hunting Cr; 23 Mar. 1671/2, p. 390. Trans. of 27 pers: James Latterell, Wm. Peterson, Jno. Joy (or Ivy), Jeffery Grigson, Ferdinand Hawker, Ben. Finch, Tho. Tupe (or Tripe), Sara Pink, Hum. Hawthorn, Eliza. Male, Jno. Dickason, James Davison, James Cobman, Jacob Jefferson, Peter Peterson, Wm. Thomson, Wm. Baker, Jno. Wheally, Jno. Drye, Ann Macklin, Hump. Lloyd, Wm. Swepston, Jno. Moodery, Jno. Philps, Hen. Sowerby, John Mackoine, Wm. Wheally.

CAPT. JNO. WEST, 1750 acs., N'ampton Co., S. W. side of Deep Cr., 23 Mar. 1672, p. 390. Sd. land is half of 3500 acs. granted to Tabitha & Matilda Scarborough 27 Mar. 1656, by them deserted, & now due by order, &c. Trans. of 35 pers: Patrick Mason, Jno. Hart, Richd. Bentloe, Mary Bentloe, Tymothy Ball, Wm. Couchard, James Shadd, Edwd. Deacons, Marmaduke Foster, Ralph Burts, Hen. Short, Nich. Cooper, Walter Howard, Nathan Swift, Jno. Davies, Wm. Moore, Marten Barnes, Tho. Allen, Edwd. Ells, Samll. Farmer, Anth. Patridge, Mary Gossick, Wm. Howsford, Jno. Jinkins, Xtopher. Keebles, Joseph Keebles, Wm. Lambert, Thomas Phipps, Robt. Mosely, Richd. Milton, Matt. Milton, Tho. Evans, Susan Parsons, O Neale (an) Irish man, Fran. Veale.

SAME. 3650 acs., same Co. & date, p. 391. 2650 acs. bet. Chickanessex Cr. on the S. W. & lands of Deep Cr. on N. E. &c; 1000 acs. bet. little Cr. & the Bay &c; 1500 acs granted sd. West 10 Aug. 1664, & deserted; 800 acs. granted Mrs. Ann Toft 25 Mar. 1665 & assigned to sd. West; 800 acs. granted Robert Brace 12 Apr. 1661 & assigned to sd. West; 550 acs. for trans. of 11 pers: Mary Lee, Jno. Babtista, Elias Johnson, Tho. Lucas, Tho. F——.

Ann Parre, Mary Wheeler, Law. Robinson, Alice Rewkerry, Jno. Robinson, Jno. Slater.

HENRY AWBERRY, 1530 acs. Rappa. Co., S. side sd. Riv., 23 Mar. 1671/2, p. 391. 1050 acs. on S. side of Hoskins Cr., adj. Thomas Browning; by Nanzatico (?) Path &c., granted him 9 Apr. 1664; 480 acs. adj., neere the road path to Puscaticond Cr., &c., granted him 3 Sept. 1639.

CAPT. JNO. WEST, MR. CHARLES SCARBOROUGH & MR. DEVEREUX BROWNE, 1400 acs., N'ampton Co., N. on Stockleys Cr., S. on Arethusa Cr, & main br. formerly called Kicotanke Cr., &c; 26 Sept. 1671, p. 392. Granted to Col. Edmond Scarborough, 20 June 1664; deserted, & now granted by order, &c. Trans. of 28 pers.* Marginal Note: This land lett fall by the abovesd. West, Brown & Scarburgh & is pattented by Mr. Dahll. Jenifer. Test. P. L. Clk. "Noe patt. but Mr. Jenifers is Issued out of the office for this Land" Test, Phill. Ludwell, Clk.

CAPT. JNO. WEST, MR. CHARLES SCARBOROUGH, MR. DEVEREUX BROWNE & MR. EDMOND SCARBOROUGH, 3000 acs., N'ampton Co., 26 Sept. 1671, p. 392. Bounded on S. by Gingo Teage & a gr. branch thereof, N. by Swansine (?) Cr., &c. (Granted as above.) Trans. of 60 pers.* (Marginal Note: as above.)

EDWD. REVELL, 1950 acs., N'ampton Co., *the great neck of the Matomkins,* on the Seaboard side bet. the creeks of Gr. Matomkin on the N., & a middle cr. of same on the S., &c; 23 Mar. 1671/2, p. 392. Trans. of 39 pers: Tho. Locker, Richd. Robins Joseph Hall, Wm. Denny, Xtoher. Buck, Jno. Cutter, Jane Broad, Sara Sentill, James Scott, Ann Prinn, Jno. Shutt, Samll. Butt, Fra. Sayther, Tho. Pickman, Nicho. Saiwell, Nicho. Beere, Ralph Cock, Jeffery Bourne, Richd. Roe, Ann Pege, Geo. Day, Edwd. Hackish, Tobias Blackwell, Wm. Young, Joseph Sennor (or Seamor), Hump. Waick (or Traick), Tho. James, Roger Carde, Antho. Lather, Richd. Pott, Wm. Batter,

Mary Waye, Barth. Edwards, Symon Mullins, Sarah Jefferey, Nathll. Labor, Hen. Derrick, Rachell Dickins, Eliz. Savage (or Swaye).

JNO. KENDALL, 700 acs., Accomack Co., in the head of Crooked Cr., 23 Mar. 1671/2, p. 393. 500 acs. adj. John Renny; 200 acs. S. on Mesangoe Cr., W. on Charles Ratcliff, &c. 500 acs. granted to sd. Rattcliff 5 Apr. 1666, deserted, & granted sd. Kendall by order, &c; 200 acs. granted to Nicholas Layler 5 Apr. 1666, deserted, &c. Trans. of 14 pers: Alexr. Chambers, Robt. Hambleton, Tho. Scott, Wm. Jones, Jno. Knight, Jame Abraham, Tymothy Steere, Jasper Elett, Seth. Stevens, Edward Herdson, Mary Gore, Allice Morgan, James Emeratt, Wm. Allan.

AMBROSE WHITE, 2150 acs., N'ampton Co., at *Matompkin,* on the Seaboard side; adj. Jno. Baggwell; Mr. Revell in the Great Neck; the Middle Cr; & Gr. Matompkin Cr; 25 Mar. 1672, p. 393. Trans. of 43 pers: Wm. Burst, Andrew Swaine, Peirce Dilling, Tho. Farnell, Hugh Meare, Fra. Curline. Ann Woodyer, Ann Hanger, Rebecka Hunton, Mary Loe, Ja. Fowkes, twice; Mary Peale. Tho. Williams, Roger Buckum, Wm. Turner, Ambrose White, Roger Mason, Wm. Williams, Tho. Sheapheard, Christo. Roberts, Jno. Glass, Tho. Barton, Jno. Land, Wm. Thackray, Mary Thackray, Ann Thackray, Wm. Thackray, Junr., Tho. Poole, Jno. Whiskin, Wm. Frett, Jno. Battersea, Jno. Pattison, Wm. Fillpott, Hen. Cush, Jno. Symkin, Wm. Tomlinson, Ja. Claiter, Wm. Overbury, Jno. Scott, Wm. Stapleton twice, Jane Stapleton.

HUBERT PETTY, 73 acs., Lancaster Co., on a br. of Morattico Cr., adj. land sould to Jno. Mott, by Col. Corbyn; 25 Mar. 1672, p. 394. Trans. of 2 pers.* Marginal Note: "Not granted lying on the North side of Rappa. River."

THO. DUNTON, 600 acs., N'ampton Co., at *Hungars;* W. on land that was Mr. Hollowaye's; N. by the Divells Ditch, a br. of Hungars Cr; 22 Mar. 1671/2, p. 395. 300 acs. granted to Jno. Vines 20 Oct. 1661, & sold to sd. Dunton; 300 acs. for trans. of 6 pers: Xtopher. Perkinson, James Brigstock, Robt. Francis, Elizabeth Normore, William Hatton, Wm. Elrocke (?).

LT. COL. WM. KENDALL, 1700 acs., N'ampton Co., 26 Mar. 1672, p. 395. 1300 acs. bet. the land of *Hungars* & the seaboard, on N. side of Hungars Cr., on a freshwater br. called Tho. Smith's br., along his land to Billiope's corner; to Jno. Stokeley; to Wm. Whittington, &c. (which is due by patt. recorded in the 259 page of this booke); 400 acs. N. on Mountney's Cr., to Henry Feild's old house, &c., which 400 acs. granted to Capt. Wm. Whittington, who sold to Jno. Stokeley, 30 July 1655, who assigned to sd. Kendall 17 Jan. 1670.

DANLL. PENSAX (or Pensal), 600 acs., N'ampton Cr., near a Gr. White Marsh, bet. *Pungoteag & Matompkins;* adj. Capt. Jno. West; 26 Mar. 1672, p. 395. Trans. of 12 pers: Cha. Scarburgh 6 tymes; Dorothy Davies, Margarett Barton; Mary, sold to Ja. Barnaby; Jno. Cole, Wm. Hopkins, Abraham Jack.

ROBERT DAVIS, 350 acs., N'ampton Co., at the head of brs. of Muddy Cr., (by some called Guilfords Cr.) adj. John Parker of *Mattapony;* Thomas Nixon (Nickson); Miles Gray; & Griffin Savage; 26 Mar. 1672, p. 396. Trans. of 7 pers: Wm. Price, Paule Scrick, Mary Trotman, Jno. Watts, Miles Grany, John Ramsey, Fra. Wright.

EDWD. MOORE, (or Moone) JUNR., 200 acs. N'ampton Co., S. side Mesangoe Cr., adj. Mr. Aleworth & land formerly Jno. Wallop's; 26 Mar. 1672, p. 396. Trans. of 4 pers: Danll. Woodgate, Peter Yorke, Wm. Goodale, Katherine Nordige. *(Note:* Indexes give this name as *Moore.)*

WM. NOCK, 400 acs., in the Up. part of N'ampton Co., on S. side of a freshwater br. of a Cr., by some called little Matompkin, by others Watcha-

preag. & by others Nickowomsim; adj.
Arthur Robbins; 26 Mar. 1672, p. 396.
Trans. of 8 pers: Edwd. Dale. Jno.
Powell, Xtopher Peters, Jno. Rickards.
Eliz. Flite, Thos. Banick, Sara Varlett.
Geo. Nicholls.

NICHOLAS MILLECHOP, 300 acs.,
N'ampton Co., at the head of a br. of
Mesangoe (Cr.); adj. Robt. Hill; 26
Mar. 1672, p. 396. Trans. of 6 pers:
Wm. Stevens, Roger Dixon, Jno.
Castellin, Jno. Crane, Sara Poole, Jane
Coward.

JNO. PARKER, of *Mattapanie*. 400
acs., N'ampton Co., bet. *Gargaphya* &
Muddy Cr; adj. Capt. Danll. Junifer;
by the Cart Path from *Gargaphya* to sd.
Cr; 26 Mar. 1672, p. 397. Trans. of
8 pers: Jno. Parker, Jno. Fording,
Francisco a Turk; Alexr. Cooper, Jno.
Lawes, Barbara Howard, Peter Elsie,
Tho. Davies.

SAME. 885 acs., same location, date
& page. Adj. land of Geo. Johnson,
formerly of Alexr. Massey; to Nicholas
Millechop &c. Trans. of 18 pers: Alice
Clason, Jacob Brown, Jno. Harrison,
Jno. Long, Hen. Carter, Samll. Gold-
smith, Johanna Goldsmith, Susanna
Goldsmith, Tho. Fookes, Amy Fookes,
Isaac Hamond, David Wmson. (Wil-
liamson), Nicholas Newman, Edwd.
Lemon, Tho. Butler, Hen. Selman,
Edwd. Brown, Jno. Clark.

MILES GRAY, 400 acs., N'ampton
Co., N. on a br. of Gr. Mattapanie Cr.,
by some called Swansicutts. & E. on
Mattapanie Neck; 26 Mar. 1672, p.
397. Trans. of 8 pers: Danll. Fox-
craft 3 tymes: Patrick Atkins. Ann
Poury. Eliz. Harwood, James Brown.
Wm. Holesteed.

CHA. SCARBURGH, DEVORAX
BROWN & CAPT. JNO. WEST, 4500
acs., N'ampton Co., bet. Muddy Cr. &
Hunting Cr., adj. Law Robinson, Robt.
Hill, Teag Miscoll & Martin Moore;
lands of Wm. Onoughton, Roger Tern-
old (or Terrold), Tho. Orely & Jno.
Lewis; 23 Mar. 1671/2, p. 398. Trans.
of 90 pers: Jno. Stewer, Wm. Pride,
Tho. Taylor, Jno. Williamson. Jno.

Start, Mary Start, Wm. Start, Mary
Start, Wm. Cotterell, Jno. Buffkin,
Henry Hoskins ,Jno. Creed, Edward
Green, Fra. Hacker, Jno. Porter, Tho.
Philpott, Jno. Trevett, Wm. Nowell,
Tho. Webb, Jno. Rose, Baus Markes,
Tho. Wms. (Williams), Wm. Wms.,
Alexr. Knishman (or Kirshman), Richd.
Feild, Tho. Palmer, Barbara Batty,
Nicho. White, Richd. Coward, Jno.
Sexton, Owen Colona, Pattrick Hayes,
Edwd. Cooke, Jno. Roode, Edwd.
Prestidge, Wm. Williams, Elizabeth
James, Christopher Strobing, Wm.
Palmy, Jno. Furbush, Edwd. Cock, Robt.
Ester, Eliz. Furnace, Wm. Williams.
Stephen Tilby, Fra. Chambers, Wm.
Pallma (?), Edwd. Presley, Elinor
Ferrell, Nich. John, Jno. Lidleton, Jno.
Whittowne, Great Mary, Wm. Ferne
(or Herne), Ogen Colonan, Isaac
Brandell, Constant Cliaverley, Xtopher.
Dey, Darby Ogrohor, Patrick Hayes,
Boy James Xtopher, Strobridge, Robt.
Bee, Tho. Jones, Wm. Morris, Wm.
Ellis, Jno. Spicknell, Edwd. Harlington,
James Loe, Mary Upton, Roger John-
son. Theoderick Long, Jno. Bill, Mary
Mathewes, Jean Lardovs, Hopkin Mor-
ris, Owin Neale, Edwd. Robinson.
Joane Nossere, Johanna Webb, Wm.
Jones, Samll. Johnson, Jno. Maning.
Edwd. Anderson, Amy Anderson, Mary
Lancaster, William Holt, Richd. Willis.
Susanna Price, Margarett Winch.

CAPT. JNO. WEST, 1000 acs.,
N'ampton Co., adj. Tho. Letherbery.
(Letherberry); Jno. Jinkins (Jenkins)
& Wm. Benson (Benston), at *Anan-
cock*; 14 Jan. 1671, p. 398. Trans. of
20 pers: Peter Fiford, Elizabeth Wheel-
er, Jno. Webb, Henry Cobb, Jno.
Whistler, Antho. Martin, Wm. Stubbs,
Jno. Frith, Jno. Fish, Peter Gurnett,
Mathew Bennett, Jno. Juell, Giles
Boones. Jno. Wilton, Jno. Stevens.
Teage Mocarta, Wm. Abdell, Christo.
Moses, Jno. Say, Tho. Bell.

GEO. PARKER, 1650 acs. N'ampton
Co., on N. E. side of Anancock Cr.,
N. W. on the Bay, S'ly. on Elkes Cr.
& Back Cr; 26 Nov. 1671, p. 399.
1300 acs. granted him 26 Sept. 1661 &
350 acs. for trans. of 7 pers: Tho

Davies, Andrew Price, Jno. Parker, Robt. West, Barbery Green, Richd. Parnell, Katherine Silver.

ROBT. BOWMAN, JUNR., 557 A., 2 R., 22 P., Henrico Co., on S. side James Riv., 29 June 1671, p. 399. Adj. Henry Lower (?); above Packers (or Parker's) Gutt, along the sw., nigh Possums meadoe, to upper landing at the house; to land given him by his father Robt. Bowman, dec'd; along Martin Elam; to Joseph Tanner's orphants, to Coles Cr., to the landing &c. 100 acs. part given him by his father 10 Jan. 1661; 215 A., 8 P., by patt. 28 Sept. 1667; 242 A., 2 R., 14 P., for trans. of 5 pers: Wm. Thomas, Mary Rowland, Ann Townsend, Wm. Rider, Peter Madland.

JOHN BAGWELL, 600 acs., N'ampton Co., at the head of Gr. Matomkin Cr., 25 Mar. 1672, p. 400. Trans. of 12 pers: David Turner, Katherine Temple, Gilbert Grimes, Roger Wilton, Ralph Dike, Phillip Peartree, Jno. Robinson, Nicho. Watson, Wm. Peters, Tho. Collins, Wm. Write, Fra. Taylor.

CAPT. DANIELL JENNIFER, 5000 acs., N'ampton Co., 12 Feb .1671/2, p. 400. 3000 acs. comonly called *Gingoteage*, granted to Col. Edmond Scarburgh 22 June 1664, & by him conveyed to Mrs. Anne Toft, now wife of sd. Jennifer, 16 Mar. 1668; 2000 acs. called *Mattapony Neck*, bet. Gingoteag Cr. & Swansicuts Cr. &c. Due by order of court, &c., & trans. of 40 pers.* *Note:* The rights due are recorded under a patt. in folio 388 for 5000 acres, there being a mistake for 2000 acres of land in that pattent. Test, Phill Ludwell, Cl.

RICHARD WHITEHEAD, 812¼ acs., on S. side of Rappa. Riv., beg. at the lower fall; 15 Mar. 1672/3, p. 400. Granted to Capt. Thomas Hawkins 2 June 1666; deserted, & now granted by order, &c. Trans. of 16 pers: Jno. Hedley, Zupere Hawboro, Robt. Edgerton, Tho. Beverlev, Wm. Bargeman, Margartt Perry, Mary Duck, Jno. Wms. (Williams), Tho. Hanlett (or Haulett), Jno. Heanes, Ja. Langley, Tho. Gouge, Jno. Brookes, Rich. Hill, Jno. Man, twice.

DEVORAX BROWN, 3600 acs., N'ampton Co., on N. E. side of Deep Cr. & Drummonds Cr., adj. land formerly Wm. Gower's, to land formerly James Atkinson's, along land that was Jno. Arnes (?), to Xtopher. Thomson, *the father, to the maine freshwater br. of sd. Cr.*, &c; 27 Mar. 1672, p. 401. 1750 acs. part of 3500 acs. granted Tabitha & Matilda Scarburgh 27 Mar. 1656; 1000 acs. granted Tabitha Smart 10 July 1664; which 2 tracts were deserted, & granted by order, &c. 26 Sept. 1671; 850 acs. newly taken up; & all due for trans. of 84 pers: Wm. Collier, Eliz. JaGold, Jno. Hart, Robt. Roe, Ruben Preston, Jno. Foxland, Nody Jonson, Jno. Read, Joseph Wells, Hen. Harvy, Peter Tomson, Tho. Strong, Ja. Carpenter, Jno. Hutton, Richd. Sceneall (?), Roger Carrick, Richd. Cockhead, Tho. Penfold, Jno. Haverly, Abra. Nailer, Samll. Pumford, Jno. Pen, Richd. Wood, Tho. Strange, Jno. Danll. (Daniell), Tho. Gibbs, Ambrose Everett, Hugh Thomas, Ralph Sawyer, Paule Booth, Jno. Freind, Symon Higgins, Tho. Jones, Jno. Sumers, Wm. Shepherd, Tho. Qualler, Oliver Serjant, Symon Lane, Jno. Townsend, Hum. Lansford, Michaell Brookin, Abraham Green, James Dawsey, Wm. Knt. (Knight), Jno. Whitmore, Fra. Davies, Fra. Toune, (?), Ann Sumers, Katherine Auborley, Phill. Scanderell, Richd. Arlington, Hugh Heyward, Robt. Dawson, Wm. Knight, Samll. Davies, Cha. West, Richd. Hyatt, Wm. Cooper, Wm. Sabine, Jno. Norris, Wm. Peircey, Jane Ashly, Tho. Abraham, Fran. Pembore, Wm. Duckett, Jone Lock, Mary Woolfe, Tho. Fopall, Mary Evans, Eliz. Howell, James Meredith, Tho. Smith, Ellex. Sharpboord (or Sharpboorne), Tho. Hopwood, Wm. Pagler, Ja. Boles, Hum. Wheeler, Walter Frislier (?), Robt. Woodhouse, Jno. Mulbery, Tho. Towen, Fran. Orland, Tho. Moore (or Moon), Richd. Grunsell.

JOHN PARKER, of *Mattapony*, 200 acs., N'ampton Co., 29 Mar. 1672, p. 402. Part Between *Pokeamoke* & *Mesango;* Near the W. end of St. George's Island. Trans. of 4 pers: John Clarke, Jane Niccoles, Elizab. Gilman, Peter an Indian.

THOMAS NICKSON (Nixson), 850 acs., N'ampton Co., bet. *Gargahia* & brs. of Muddy Cr., adj. Capt. Daniell Jennifer; & John Parker; 29 Mar. 1672, p. 402. Trans. 17 pers: Capt. Jno. Custis 8 tymes transported; Alice ———, Dorothy Bowle, Mary Humfrey, Charles Crosse, Rich. Aldridge, Barthew. Hearné, Hescot Trissell; Joane & Isabella, Negroes.

EDWARD MOORE, JUNR., 400 acs., N'ampton Co., on N. side Mesango Cr., adj. land formerly Charles Ratcliff's; 29 Mar. 1672, p. 402. 200 acs. granted to James Taylor (Taylour), 5 Apr. 1666 & assigned to sd. Moore; 200 acs. for trans. of 4 pers: ·Phillip White, James Puntin, Katherine Maize, Joane Birch.

MILES GRAY, 620 acs., N'ampton Co., bet. Wm. Whittington, land formerly Richard Bundick's & land of Jóhn Parker (&) Robert Davis; adj. Capt. Daniel Jennifer & Laurance Robinson; 29 Mar. 1672, p. 402. Trans. of 13 pers: Cesar Wheeler, Wm. Boone, Tho. Lucar, Tho. Favours (or Havours) Jno. Holstead, Mary Wheeler, Charles Trissell, Jno. Elsye, Anne Shaa, Arnold Elsye, Daniel Mickeley; Aron & Jone, Negroes.

CAPT. RICHARD HILL, 100 acs., N'ampton Co., being a hummock called Half Moone Island; on S. side of Hunting Cr.; 29 Mar. 1672, p. 402. Trans. of 2 pers: Edward Brewerton, Peeter Bouten.

CAPT. WM. CLEYBOURNE, 1400 acs., New Kent Co., 28 Mar. 1672, p. 403. Granted to Mr. Henry Soames; sould to Raph Mazey; & escheated by inquisition &c. under Mr. Thomas Hall, Depty. Esch'r., &c.

MARGARET & MARY WILLIAMSON, Coheirs of James Williamson, 350 acs. in Rappa. Riv., about 39 miles up on the N. side, on E'wd. of the mouth of Willing Cr; 1 May 1665, p. 403. Granted to Mr. Edward James 22 May 1650 & also by patt. 4 Jan. 1653; assigned to Thomas Best 5 Sept. 1654.

who assigned to Thomas Williams & Alexander Porteus 6 Feb. 1654, who assigned to sd. Williamson 6 Aug. 1656.

JNO. DAVIES & CHARLES DUCHACE, *in right of their wives,* 100 acs., Surry Co., 15 Apr. 1672, p. 403. Granted to Thomas Boswell, Junr., & escheated by inquisition, &c., under Richard Awborne, Depty. Esch'r., &c.

JOHN ROLLES, 200 acs., N'ampton Co., 17 May 1672, p. 403. Granted to Antonio Johnson, *Negro.* & escheated by inquisition, &c. under Col. John Stringer, Esch'r. &c.

JOHN BOWMAN, 108 A., 3 R., James Citty Co., on N. side of James Riv., & W. side of Chickahominy Riv., adj. Thomas Tinsley; on the Ridge Path, to a forke of Móses Run, &c; 15 May 1672, p. 403. Trans. of 3 pers: Bryan Rooke, Wm. Taylour, Anthony Johnson.

MAJOR JOHN TILNEY, 100 acs., N'ampton Co., 17 May 1672, p. 404. Granted to Thomas Clifton, dec'd., & afterwards remayning in possession of Jno. Johnson; escheated by inquisition, &c. 28 Mar. 1663, under Col. John Stringer, &c; granted to sd. Stringer, 24 Dec. 1663, & assigned to sd. Tilney 16 Jan. 1665.

EDWARD GREENWOOD, 281 acs., Chas. Citty Co., on N. side of Up Chipoakes Cr., against Swan Bay; 25 Apr. 1672, p. 404. Trans. of 5 pers., mentioned under his patt., dated 19 Nov. 1651.

LT. COL. WILLIAM WATERS, 700 acs., N'ampton Co., on the Eastern Shore of Va., in the *old plantation Neck,* on S. side of Kings Cr., against the *Church poynt;* along the Bay, to land formerly holden by James Jackson; to Mr. John Michaell, &c; 26 May 1671, p. 404. 450 acs. granted him by escheat patt., 24 Oct. 1665; 100 acs. granted to Wm. Andrewes; 50 acs. to Francis Martin; & 100 acs. to James Pteine, all of which was purchased by sd. Waters.

CAPT. ROBERT SPENSER, 300 acs., Surry Co., 15 May 1672, p. 404. 150 acs. on S. side of James Riv., about a mile up Crouches Cr., to the Reedy Sw. & Cr; 150 acs. at the head thereof. Granted to Henry Meadowes 28 Sept. 1649, & assigned to sd. Spencer as by patt. dated 24 Aug. 1666.

DEVEREUX BROWNE, 3700 acs., N'ampton Co., in Jolles Neck at *Pocomoke:* adj. 2000 acs. that was Edmond Scarburgh's, &c., to 600 acs: called *Oken hall.* formerly Henry Smyth's land, &c; 16 May 1672, p. 405. Trans. of 74 pers: Edward Greenly, Jdia. Francklyn, Elizab. Grimes, Winifred Brothers, Mary Rogers, Suzan Wyn, Elizab. Suckler, Robt. Grice, Jno. Barrow, Geo. Signett, Tho. Parsons, Humfry Evans, Tho. Sorre, Jno. Stapley, Jno. Thomas, Jno. Shadwell, Edmond Barriell, Thomas Forson, Edwd. Penlast, Jno. Sutton, Wm. Leverack, Franc. Quinch, Edw. Barriff (or Barriss), Wm. Crane, Franc. Williams, Jno. Sandes, Jno. Salter, Henry Beale, Anne Draper, Jno. Evinson (or Ewinson), Geo Granger, Wm. Key, Geo. Eagres, Elias Bucker, Mary Wells, Daniell Baker, John Lovens, Isaac Dix, Wm. Clavell, Thomas Foster, Elizab. Chautress (or Chantress), Samuell Jones, Senr., Sam. Jones, Junr., Jno. Jones, Mary Jones, Jasper Jones, Sarah Turnor, Kather. Fisher, Henry Permaine, Xpofer .Thompson, Wm. Foord, Abralom Gandy, Jonath. Eaton, Elidey Blunt, Anto., a boy, Tho. Greene, Jno. Beale, Arthur Edwards, Jno. Read, Elias Verginia, Roger Ware, Peter Presly, Wm. Neworth, Timothy Love, Wm. Jones, Wm. Smyth, Wm. Goodchild, Griffin Savage, Samll. Capmaker, Arthur Bradley, Wm. Foard, Jno. Hamond, Jno. Lloyd, Ruth Colledge.

CAPT. DANIEL JENNIFER, 1500 acs., N'ampton Co., called Gingoteage Island; parted by sunken marshes & creeks from Gingoteag Neck; N. E. on the Maryland line; 1 Apr. 1671, p. 405. Trans. of 30 pers: James Draper, Jno. Orbald (or Ozbald), Vincent Barry, Anto. Libb, Robert Parrior, Jno. Machin, Henry Silvester, Richd. Miller, Roger Griffin, Richard Wing, Abell Barker, Walter Acton, Thomas Whitmore, Jno. Weld, Jno. Charlton, Ann Phillips, Richd. Lister, Tho. Morefeild, Geo. Ludlow, Tho. Jones, Francis Smyth, Mary Feild, Jno. Whittaker, Richd. Rivers, Jno. Harding, James Dudley, Tho. Wells, Henry Lee, Thomas Fleetwood, Wm. Morton. *Marginal Note:* These 30 rights were taken from a pattent granted to Ann Toft 2nd Aprill 1664 and in regard this land was within the bounds off Mary (Maryland?) the Governor ordered the said rights to stand good for so much land to be pattented in Virginia.

COL. HENRY CORBYN, Esqr., 550 acs., Rappa. Co., on S. side sd. Riv., 15 May 1672, p. 406. 350 acs. granted to Mr. Robert Eyres 1 Feb. 1648, & assigned to Mr. Oliver Sprey 28 May 1649, who sould to Mr. James Bagnall, dec'd., whose heyres sould to sd. Corbyn 23 Oct. 1666; 200 acs. granted to John Bell dec'd., 14 June 1655; adj. Cyprian Bisshop & sd. Bagnall; due by escheat &c., inquisition 1 May 1667 under Mr. Thomas Bowler, Depty. Esch'r. &c.

RALPH RACHELL, 200 acs., Chas. City Co., on S. E. side of Wards Cr., at the mouth of Hannocks bottom, adj. Mr. Bird; along the Mussell Shell banck, &c; 28 Jan. 1670, p. 406. Granted to Elias Osborne 1 June 1668, who assigned to sd. Rachell.

JOHN BAILEY, 300 acs., Nansimond Co., 28 Oct. 1672, p. 406. Granted to Robert Brassiere, & escheated, by inquisition, &c. under Wm. Alford, Depty. Esch'r. &c.

WM. BLECHINDEN, 150 acs., Nansimond Co., 28 Oct. 1672, p. 406. Granted to Thomas Bailey, & escheated, etc. (as above.)

JOHN GATLYN, 250 acs., Nansamond Co., 28 Oct. 1672, p. 406. Granted to John Briggs, & escheated, &c. (as above.)

ROBERT BUNCKLEY, 100 acs., Nansamond Co., 28 Oct. 1672, p. 407. Granted to Thomas Brice & John Addice, & escheated, &c. (as above.)

JOHN CRUEDEN, 200 acs., Nansamond Co., 28 Oct. 1672, p. 407. Granted to Robert Brassiere, &c. (as above).

GEORGE & HENRY BILLINGSLEY, 500 acs., Nansimond Co., in *Chuckatuck;* 28 Oct. 1672, p. 407. Granted to John Billingsley, &c. (as above.) *Saving & forever reserving out of the sd. 500 acs. 1½ acs. granted to the parishioners of Chuckatuck for erecting a Church upon & for a buriall place belonging to the sd. parish for ever.*

JOHN EWENS, 50 acs., Nansimond Co., 28 Oct. 1672, p. 407. Escheat land of Wm. Ward, &c.

CAPT THOMAS FULCHER, 60 acs., Lower Norf. Co., 28 Oct. 1672, p. 407. Escheat land of Capt. Robert Page, &c.

MALACHY THRUSTON, 100 acs., Low. Norf. Co., 28 Oct. 1672, p. 408. Escheat land of William Holley (or Halley), & escheated by inquisition under Wm. Alford, Depty. Esch'r., &c.

BARTHOLOMEW WILLIAMSON, 110 acs., Low. Norf. Co., 28 Oct. 1672, p. 408. Escheat land of Robert Worster.

MRS. KATHERINE LAWRENCE, 160 acs., Low. Norf. Co., 28 Oct. 1672, p. 408. Escheat land of Thomas Gregory.

ROBERT BLAKE, 200 acs., Low. Norf. Co., 28 Oct. 1672, p. 408. Escheat land of Wm. Smyth.

AUGUSTINE MOORE, 225 acs., Eliz. Citty Co., 28 Oct. 1672, p. 408. Escheat land of Thomas Shirley; inquisition under William Alford, &c.

THOMAS TABB, 300 acs., Eliz. Citty Co., 28 Oct. 1672, p. 408. Escheat land of John Gibbs.

FRANCIS RADFORD, 629 A., 3 R., 8 P., Henrico Co., on N. side of James Riv., 1 July 1672, p. 409. 375 acs. at the Roundabout Slash, adj. Morgan Peirce; granted to Capt. Wm. Farrar & Tho. Liggon, who assigned to Francis Radford, 12 Oct. 1665; 254 A., 3 R., 8 P., granted sd. Radford 5 Aug. 1669.

RICHARD JONES, (Joanes), Mariner, 680 acs., on E. side in the S'n. br. of Eliz. Riv; 1 July 1672, p. 409. 400 acs. taken up Mr. Wm. Julyan, & by several conveyances due sd. Jones; 280 acs. adjoining, granted him 8 Apr. 1665.

FRANCIS SOWERSBY, 666 acs., Surry Co., 1 July 1672, p. 409. 455 acs. adj. Mr. Thompson; & his own land; 211 acs. granted him 21 May 1666. 455 acs. for trans. of 10 pers.*

COL. AUGUSTINE WARNER, 10,-100 acs., in Rappa. & New Kent Counties, on the maine Sw. of Mattapony, opposite land of Mr. Laurance Smyth & some 12 mi. from the falls of Rappa. Riv., 8 Oct. 1672, p. 410. Beg. at the mouth of a br. dividing this & land of Mr. John Prosser & Thomas Pannell; along brs. of Nussaponocks Cr. &c. Trans. of 202 pers: John Glover, Jno. Sharp, Mary Sharp, Ann Steele, Jno. Bradford, Mary Withton, Dorothy Pope, James Okey, Edw. Symonds, Francis Powell, James Wright, Henry Starr, Geo. White, Samll. White, Tho. Frost, Tho. Cole, Wm. Frith, Edward Carey, Arthur Wilson, Toby Adcock, Tho. Manns, Wm. Gwynn, Henry Tocker, Franc. Tocker, Jno. Scott, Symon Hind, Phill. Butler; a french man; Toby Golding, Toby Willoughby, Jno. Starling, Aug. Leech, Wm. Fletcher, Jno. Jakes, Samuell Hide, Jno. Skynner, Robert Bryan (or Brynn), James Winney, Arthur Stokes, Samll. Mathewes, Ralph Morton, Ann French, Arthur Surley, Charles Gibbon, Jno. Stoner (or Stover), Wm. Holty (?), Henry Syrott, Roger Green, Jno. Hind, Humfry Herring, George Nettle, Margt. Hathaway, Geo. Swann, Wm. Grimes, Ann Fleet, Roger Barfoot, Stephen Hubert, Mary Hubbard, Laur. Townley, Margt. Finchinbrook, Eliz. Barnett, Alice Powell, Margt. Child, Jno. Forbus, Mary Finch, Wm. Rogers, Jno. Black, Mathias Cutbert, Crow ——, Geo. Grimes, Jno. Steele, Jacob Warner, Jno. Wheatly, Robert Perry, Phillip Strainge, Charles Deane, Tho. Crafton, Wm. Marrow,

Joseph Cottington, Watkin James, Edw. Johns, James Dedman, Jno. Locker, Samll. Storey, Franc. Coney (or Coury) Jno. Newark, Anth. Pratt, Jenkin Morris, Henry Tockworth, Mary Grainger, Jno. Grainger, Ralph Hutton, Stephen Goffer, Maurice Presser, Ann Cullam, Saml. Wild, Geo. Bancroft, Wm. Windebanck, Wm. Amcock, Franc. Armestead, Sith Forster, Scarlett Bayes. Samuell Wallington, Ambrose Kelk, Jno. Kelk, (or Keck), Tho. Brackwell, Henry Hearne, Tho. Butler, Ambrose Dudley, Jno. Watson, Jeffry Cobbs, Edmond Thursby, Augustine Warner Junr., Jno. Melton, Wm. Borning, Franc. Hathaway, Tho. Wallington, Geo. Kelk, Henry Cherarsell, Andrew Charersell (?), Sam. Stephens, Jno. Day, Franc. Walton, Wm. Gyton, Katherin Browne, Tho. Thorpe, Geo. Spirage, Wm. Turner, Stephen Hind, Rich. Grey, Jno. Baker, Wm.* Baker, Joane Wheatley, Roger Whaley, Jno. Bradford, Franc. Wheeler, Walter Jones, Daniel Jones, Henry Joyner, Humfry Lobe, James Allerton, Daniel Graves, Margery Woodbridge, Henry Thacker, Geo. Bray, Jno. Brundell, Franc. Osey, Jno. Constable, Tho. Hocker, Daniell Paget, Robte. Crawley, Alex. Wyatt, Xpofer. Towers, Xpofer. Hill, Adam Swyne, Gregory Lloyd, Samll. Austin, Tho. Wilson, Edw. Wilford, Isaac Bright, Wm. Adkins, Geofry Dowdy, Sander Simes, Wm. Hutchinson, Tho. Rolfe, Wm. Uggins, Laur. Prosser, Tho. Partlett, Jno. Oxbrow, James Olsley, Oswald Staines, Peter Hide, Geo. Groome, Rich. Baily, Isaac Ambrose, Henry Somers, Peter Peares, Jno. Watkans, Wm. Wilcox, Andrew Leaver, Samll. Duckenfeild, Wm. Grimes, Anne Falkner, Wm. Payne, Jno. Baxter, Henry Heyward, Wm. *Many-Crafts,* Arthur Fowler; *"and twelve Irishmen but I have not their names in memory but some of them are alive."*

WILLIAM HOWARD, 108 acs., Gloster Co., in Petsoe Par., bet. Bennet's Cr. & his own land; 14 Aug. 1672, p. 411. At the pitch of the Oystershell poynt, by Oystershell banck little Cr., to Cappahoshack *als.* Capt. Jenings' Path. Trans. of 3 pers: William Powell, Martha Cockett, Tho. Killerson.

JOHN DICK, 278 acs., Rappa. Co., on S. side of sd. Riv., 8 Oct. 1672, p. 411. 250 acs. on brs. of Pascataway Cr., adj. Capt. Josias Pickeye's (or Pickneye's), & John & Geo. Kilman; down the half mile sw. to Kilman's Beaver dams; up the green br., &c. 220 acs. granted Neale Peterson 2 Dec. 1663; deserted, & granted to Mr. Tho. Edmonson 15 Apr. 1667, who assigned to sd. Dick; 30 acs. for trans. of 1 pers.* 28 acs. granted to Wm. Lacey, 18 Sept. 1665, & granted sd. Dick by order, &c.

WM. WATSON, 750 acs., New Kent Co., upon brs. of Mattadequn Cr., adj. David Craford, near Westover Path; 8 Oct. 1672, p. 411. Trans. of 15 pers: Capt. Robert Bristow twice; "a woman died at Sea"; Phillip White, Tho. Wright, John Amey, John Heley, Jno. Woodale, Wm. Bell, Jno. Paramour, John Wilkinson, Nich. Baldwin, Marmad. Moore, Rich. Knight, Robert Goffe.

ROLAND HORSELEY & ROBERT LANCASTER, 473 acs., New Kent Co., on S. side of Mattadequn Cr., on little Cr., adj. Charles Bryan, &c; 8 Oct. 1672, p. 412. Trans. of 10 pers: Edward. Osborne, Sarah Marsh, Ann Frawlin, Hen. Ellis, Samll. Acklester, Tho. Weatherston, Jno. Edall. Franc. Manuall, Ralph Clifford, John Fox.

JAMES MOORE, 78 acs., New Kent Co., in a br. of Mattadequn Cr., & a br. of Wionoke Sw., adj. Wm. Basset's & his own land; 8 Oct. 1672, p. 412. Trans. of 2 pers: William Maybanck, John Seed.

WILLIAM OWEN, 938 acs., New Kent Co., bet. brs. of Black & Mattadequn Creeks; adj. Roland Horseley & Robert Lancaster; & William Pullam; 8 Oct. 1672, p. 412. 350 acs. granted him 27 Apr. 1670; & 588 acs. for trans. of 12 pers: Geo. Plumtree, Ellis Pawlett, Oliver Clarkson, George Yorke. Betty an Indian, Ann Waters, Leonard Cleybourne, Ann Eaton. Geo. Hull, Sara Poole, William Beadle, Betty, (an) Indian.

EDMOND GROSSE, 1300 acs., New Kent Co., upon mayne sw. of Chickahominy Riv., next above Phillip Freeman, & adj. his own land; 8 Oct. 1672, p. 413. Trans. of 26 pers: Magnus Miller, Elizabeth Robbins, Wm. Hannah, James Makellow, Kather. Karrington, John Hatton, Elizab. Lane, John Lee, Edward Love, Nicholas Tompson, Nicholas Tompson, Nicholas Miller, John Mault, David Smyth, Tho. Goodgame, Wm. Steele, Thomas Moore, Bridget Price, Wm. Richardson, Mathew Izard, Capt. Robt. Bristoll 2; a woeman servt. dyed at sea; Phill. White, Tho. White Jno. Amey, Jno. Hely.

MATHIAS MARRIOTT & THOMAS HART, 338 acs., Surry Co., adj. George Blowe on N. side of Blackwater Sw; 14 Aug. 1672, p. 413. Trans. of 7 pers: William Jellett, Richd. Booth, John Booth; a Negro man & woman; Ann Jenuary, Alice Price.

MR. WALTER CHILES, 70 acs. in James Citty Island called *Black Poynt:* 20 May 1670, p. 413. Granted to his father, Walter Chiles, & due him as sonne & heyr.

JNO. KENDALL, 200 acs., Accomack (Co.), bet. Broad Cr., freshwater run & Bell's Br., adj. Jno. Walter; Tho. Bell; Major Tylney, &c; 28 Oct. 1673. p. 413. Granted to Col. Wm. Kendall 6 Oct. 1670, deserted, & now granted by order, &c. Trans. of 4 pers: Robt. Armstrong, Jno. Johnson, Alexr. Bruce, Ja. Henderson.

COL. JOHN STRINGER, GEORGE BRIGHOUSE & ROBERT FOSTER, 2100 acs., N'ampton Co., in *Foster's Neck;* adj. sd. Foster & Billioat; on S. side of Browne's Marshes; by Mountney's Cr. &c., including all hummocks, islands & marishes unto low water mark, &c; 14 Aug. 1672, p. 414. Trans. of 41 pers: John Browne, Henry Godfrey, Tho. Williams, John Thorp, Tho. Thompson, Wm. Harding, Richard Martin, James Clare, Roger Crainby, David Williams, Mary Sommers, Sarah Bonner, Humfry Dowley, Miles Adder, Suzan Richards, Robert Johnson, Mary Griffin, John Sampson, Thomas Jones, Dorothy Willis, George Atkins, Wm. Billing, Thomas Alderly, John Sanson, Tho. Rogers, Grace Worseley, Timothy

Collins, Mary Yapp, Elizab. Winter, Joseph Barker, Suzan Hobbs, John Bell, Thomas Cole, Wm. Bird, Joseph Carrill, Kather. Dowly, Robert Baker, John Watts, Richard Booker, William Tully, James Sands, Ezekiell Poynter.

PHILLIP HUNLEY, 460 acs., Gloucester Co., in Kingston Par., upon Pudding Cr., 19 Aug. 1672, p. 414. Beg. at his landing place on sd. Cr., adj. Richard Long; & Marke Foster, &c. 300 acs. granted him 20 Nov. 1661; 160 acs. for trans. of 4 pers: Thomas Garwood, Edward Hayes, Thomas Haverfinch, Bridgett Derrell.

CHARLES FETHERSTON, 700 acs., Henrico Co., on N. side of Appomatock Riv., 30 Sept. 1672, p. 414. Adj. orphans of Mr. Wm. Walthall; along Timsberry's Runn, &c. Trans. of 14 pers: Edward Roddom, John Crabb, Charles Fetherston, Wm. Fraviles (?), Tho. More, Xpofer. Renings, Richd. Read, Robert Grimley, Benja. Jabin, Tho. Chamberlaine, twice, Jone Crosse, Wm. Cooke, Wm. Poyne (or Payne).

THOMAS BUSBY, 760 acs., Surry Co., in the main Blackwater Sw., (date blank) 1672, p. 415. Trans. of 16 pers: Peter Phillips, Jno. Huson, Elianor Gorton, Alex. Dunbarr, Jennet Davison, Mary Briggs,Cesar Briggs, Ann Armitage.

WM. DANIELL (Daniel), 115 acs., Middlesex Co., 5 Oct. 1672, p. 415. Indian Bridge Br. dividing this & land of Alex. Morray; adj. Mr. Alexander Smyth, along the run of the great *als.* Dragon Sw. Part of 190 acs. granted Lieut. Col. Cutbert Potter, by order of the Genrl. Court, 21 Apr. 1668, who sould to sd. Daniell. Trans. of 3 pers: John Russell, Wm. Cock, Joane Younge.

DAVID CRAFORD, 1000 acs., New Kent Co., in brs. of Mattadequn Cr., 8 Oct. 1672, p. 415. Adj. Jno. Pounce's land; crossing Little Cr., &c. Trans. of 20 pers: John Ambrose, Tho. Chowning, Symon Neesom, Mary Colton, Alice Bancroft, Rachell Packett, Wm. Netherton, Duke Hornsby, Dorothy Hall, Ellen Bainbridg, Henry Bedford, Jno.

Mosse, Joseph Talling, Richd. Thaxton, Edw. Docker, Tho. Bond, Edward ———, Mrs. Mary Potter, Ester Bristoe (or Briscoe), Jno. Blankett.

THOMAS BROOKES, 600 acs., Nansimond Co., 8 Oct. 1672, p. 416. Trans. of 12 pers: Anne Deluke, Ellyn Hudson, Franc. Knitter, Xpofer. Hall, Jno. Lee, Andrew Vincent, Edward Poole, Rich. Batten, Rich. Broome, Sara Mould, Roland Jones "*brickle* & another bought of Mr. Richards."

MR. JOHN BRYANT, 350 acs., at the head of the S'n. br. of Nansimond (Riv.); adj. Robert Johnson; 8 Oct. 1672, p. 416. Trans. of 7 pers: Stephen Rudwell, John Osborne, Elizabeth Jackson, William Whinsley, William Oliver, Wm. Rose, Xpofer. Harrison. (*Note:* Marginal notation gives this name as *Bryan.*)

ROBERT LASSISTER, 400 acs., Up. Par. of Nansimond, 8 Oct. 1672, p. 416. In a gr. Arrow red (reed) Pocoson, & adj. John Ellis. Trans. of 8 pers: Daniel Trigg, Margt. Hall, Barbados Mary, Giles King, Margt. Atkins, Blith ———, Jno. Stanford & his wife.

JOHN COPELAND, 600 acs., Nansimond Co., upon Somerton Run; adj. John Winborne; & William Moore; (date blank) 1672, p. 416. Trans. of 12 pers: William Stringer, Margt. Stocks, Richd. Jenkins, Robert Spenser, Joyce Spencer, Anne Spensor, Robert Spensor, Herbert Williams, Tho. Sanders, William Wonter, Jane Jones, Jonas Bennett.

WM. JONES, 800 acs., Nansimond Co., adj. John Copse; 8 Oct. 1672, p. 416. Trans. of 16 pers: John Goodwin, Francis Davies, John Gunson, Joseph West, John Frayer, Eliz. Browne, Henry Randall, John Pettiford, Walter Callowhill, Eliz. Frayer, John Farnham, Richd. Mayvill, John Perkins, Geo. Wood, Jno. Fox, John Trowell.

JOHN BAREFEILD, 450 acs., Nansimond Co., by Somerton Sw., adj. John Odium (?); 8 Oct. 1672, p. 417. Trans. of 9 pers: Sarah Needham,

Margt. Needham, Elizab. Needham, Mary Batten; Maria & Diligence—Negoes; Francis Harris, Robert Pagett, James Lensey.

MR. EDWARD THELOALL, 400 acs., Nansimond Co., adj. Tho. Mason; Mr. Jno. Blake; &c; 8 Oct. 1672, p. 417. Trans. of 8 pers: Mary Taylour, Mary Gipson, Robert Short, Jno. Collis, Tho. Britton, Jno. Stephens, John Oakes, Nicholas Carter.

JEREMY ORLEY (Orly), 100 acs., Nansimond Co., by a fresh run side; 8 Oct. 1672, p. 417. Trans. of 2 pers: Charles Chambers, John Winter.

THOMAS BROOKES, 100 acs., Nansimond Co., by Somerton Sw., 8 Oct. 1672, p. 417. Trans. of 2 pers: Joane Tricken (or Fricker), & Edward Fricker.

THOMAS COTTELL, 50 acs., in the western br. of Eliz. Riv., adj. his own & land of Robert Grymes; 8 Oct. 1672, p. 417. Trans. of: Elizabeth Hide.

NICHOLAS KING, 531 acs., New Kent Co., at the head of Kings Cr., in Poropotank Cr., beg. at the landing point; on Cainhooe's (or Cainhowe's) Swamp to the head spring; along Jno. Levingston's, &c; 8 Oct. 1672, p. 418 Trans. of 11 pers: Robert Wateman, Margt. Hillman, Samll. Upter, Jane Hammond, Mary Middleton, John Mayres, Wm. Browne, John Hills, Elizabeth Westifer, William Barsett, Elizabeth Laslev.

JAMES BAUGHAN & THOMAS HARPER, 1000 acs., Rappa. Co., upon Pascataway Pocoson; 8 Oct. 1672, p. 418. Beg. at a small island; to the Towne Marsh; through Musketo feild, to the maine sw. & another island, &c. Trans. of 20 pers: Edward Morris, Richard Kellett, Mary Woolsley, Mary Stack (or Slack), Mary Wood, Sam. Maynard, John Dowglas, Wm. Sperry, Robert Willow, Robert Lestrow, William Seymor, Geo. Morris, William Nelson, Thomas Bodurda, Tho. Ennis, Elizab. Day, Bathsheba Lambert, John Jolley, Wm. Sincleer, John Minos.

RICHARD JONES & GEORGE TURNER, 1000 acs., Rappa. Co., on S. side sd. Riv., upon branches of Pascataway. Pocoson & Mr. Perrye's Sw., 8 Oct. 1672, p. 418. Adj. Lt. Col. Goodrich; Mr. Brereton, the horse path, &c. Trans. of 20 pers: Mary Browne, Elizab. Farnell (or Farrell), Elianor Guttridg, Anne Marven, Joseph Beckley, Jno. Simrell, St. John Hall, William Blake, William ——, John Price, Franc. Rice, Elizab. Parr, Margaret Lightfoot, William Locken, Edmond Whitney, James Greening, Martha Grigs, Peter Ball, Charles Bleige, Hester Bacchus.

JOHN COLE (Coale), 214 acs., Rappa. Co., on N. side the Dragon Sw., opposite land he lives upon; up the maine Sw., &c; 8 Oct. 1672, p. 419. Trans. of 5 pers.*

DENNIS DALLEY (Dally), 200 acs., Low. Norf. Co., in *Lynhaven;* adj. land of Capps'; & Capt. Laurance; 1 Oct. 1672, p. 419. Trans. of 4 pers: Elizabeth Watkins, Ellenor Edwards, Wm. Davison, Daniell Frizell.

SAME. 600 acs., same Co., date & page. At head of the eastern shore of Lynhaven; on the Short Ridge, adj. Edmond Moore; & Wm. Brock. Trans. of 12 pers: Robert Bray, 3 tymes; John Kines, Mary Wood, Roland Rabey, Morgan Bryan, Walter Powell, Elizabeth Smyth; & 3 Negroes.

WILLIAM NICCOLLS, 350 acs., Low. Norf. Co., on S. side of the E'n. br. of Eliz. Riv., called *Lyons quarter;* 29 Sept. 1672, p. 420. Trans. of 7 pers: Richd. Barrett; & 6 Negroes: Jone, Mary, Katherin, Thomas, Peter Ellen.

THOMAS WELLS, 560 A., 2 R., 24 P., Henrico Co., on N. side Appamatock Riv., 28 Sept. 1672, p. 420. 200 acs. beg. at Conecock brooke; adj. his own, & land of Col. Wood; 100 acs. adj. on Col. Wood's, to the *rock:* towards Flinton's Sw; &c; 260 A. 2 R. 24 P. adj. his own & James Ekins, &c. 300 acs. granted to Henry Lowne 23 Mar. 1652, assigned to, & pattented by sd. Wells 25 Sept. 1663; residue by

patt. 24 Mar. 1665. Marginal Note: "Treble Pattent."

ALEX. GWYN, 186¾ acs., Low. Norf. Co., in Daniel Tanner's Cr; 1 Oct. 1672, p. 420. Trans. of 4 pers: Tho. Lambert, Ann Williams, Robert Harper, James Eamman.

ARGOLL YARDLEY, 500 acs., in the Up. part of N'ampton Co., at Chickanessex Cr., adj. Lt. Col. Waters; & S'ly. towards *Onancock;* 3 Oct. 1672, p. 420. Part of 1000 acs. granted to John, Sarah & Margaret Michaell & due sd. Yardley in right of his wife the sd. Sarah by guift from the sd. John, her father, who gave his part as part of his daughter's portion, &c. Also due by order &c. Trans. of 10 pers: Herman Johnson, John Robins, John Bullock, Evan Lloyd, Mary Mosse, Jone (or Jane) Hill, John Michaell, Senr., Roger Davis, Thos. Webster, Ann Atkins.

THOMAS TITUS & NICHOLAS DIXON, 1000 acs., Nansimond Co., 1 Oct. 1672, p. 421. Trans. of 20 pers: Robert Bickford, Constant Belore, Phillip Burke, Eliz. Biggfeild, James Kinkead, Symon Prickyard, John Tayton, Alex. Aylin (or Aytin), Ann Snoell (?), Richard Coker, Margaret Vartrill, James Evans, Anne Thornton, Oliver Normond, John Taylour, James Perry, Richd. Ratclift, Anthony Powell; Narcey & Peter—Negroes.

MR. WM. WHITTINGTON, 5800 acs. on the upper part of N'ampton Co., all of *Jengoteag Iland,* being the next island to the N'wd. of Kekotanck Is., *als.* Occocomson Is., 2 Oct. 1672, p. 421. Trans. of 116 pers: Jno. Fort, Jno. Magoome, August. Haire, David Walker, Kath. Bromfeild, William Wright, Margery Dee, Jno. Hadson, Amos Bowell, Wm. Elven (or Elben), Matt. Pope, Hen. Swart, Law. Roe, Wm. Lee, Michaell Roxby, Jane Marry, Mary Cadger, Lettice Long, James Griffin, Mathew Blore, Thomas Lewis, Edwd. Brookes, Jane Byford, Robt. Jones, Jno. Onglitred (or Ouglived), Isaac Blades, Jeffry Baldwin, Tho. Ross, Lewis Morris, Ellenor Collen, Margarett Charve (or Charte), Mary Surnell (or Surrell),

Antho. Rullo, William Shane, John Abbot, Tho. Wisk, Tho. HeathCock, Richd. Grinnell, Tho. Moore, Jno. Oakly, Caleb Gravener, Tho. Pilgrim, Stephen Spicer, William Whiteing, Geo. Hancock, Tho. Cooper, Jno. Renniston, Edwd. Merlin (or Mertin), Tho. Baker, Geo. Kemp, Isaac Morgan, Theoph. Parsons, Tho. Bishopp, Eliza. Trew, Tho. Hawkins, Jno. Coplestone, Jno. Hilton, Tho. Evesham, Fra. Orland, Rowld. Maldin, Richd. North, Rebecka Billingley, Henry Tomlin, Richd. Martin, Jno .Wood, Arth. Bishopp, Mary Wrath, Tho. Blake, Robt. Willington, Robt. Cross, Mary Engham, Walter Williamson, Kath. Jordan, David Mackmillion, Antho. Leonardy, Luke Hambleton, Alexr. Logon, Jeane Shalling, Danll. Ross, Jno. Mackbane, James Newitt, Stephen Mannering, Michaell Taylor. Samll. Pensal (or Pensax), Tho. Hustings, Antho. Newport, Jno. Walker, Wm. Baldry, Jno. Hogg, Jonath. Tigg, Jno. Strong, Mathew Coome, Henry Morgan, Guidoe Valence, Miles Courtney, James Roe, Roger Holt, Edwd. Goslin, Jeffery Rowse, Jno. Upton, Danll. Bird, Robt. Askin, Jno. Neeve, Robt. Armestrong, Jno. Johnson, Alexr. Bruce, James Hinderson, Andrew Nailer, James Clarke, James Field, Cha. Davison, Patrick Watson, Ja. Bourne, Ja. Soruter, Tho. Hamilton; Hector a Negroe.

ROBERT YOUNG, of Eliz. Riv., in Low. Norf. Co., 250 acs., in Lynn haven Par., on Broad Cr., 30 Sept. 1672, p. 422. Granted to Tho. Browne 9 Mar. 1652, & after severall assignments due sd. Young.

AMBROSE WHITE, 1300 acs., N'-ampton Co., neer *Pungoeteage;* adj. 1300 acs. of Nicholas Waddiloe; 22 Sept. 1671, p. 422. Granted sd. Waddiloe 2 Apr. 1655, deserted, & now granted by order, &c. Trans. of 26 pers: William Hoskins, Peter Stower, Jno. Stoner, Mary Bonner, Jno. Bonner, Tho. Pluver, Jno. Fitchett, Tho. Perry, Jno. Lowry, Wm. Killagre, Tho. Falconer, Steven Johnson, Robt. Malum, Jno. Oliver, Ben. Lewis, Harbert Brush, Tho. Fison, Will. Piper, Alexr. Fisher, Jno. Harper, Mary Swart, Jno. Lipcott,

Wm. Coleburne, Antho. Everet; Tomboy & Franck—Negroes.

CAPT. JNO. WEST & MR. CHARLES SCARBROUGH (Scarburgh), 2500 acs., N'ampton Co., bet. Crooked Cr. & Pokomock Riv., on N. (side of) Mesangoe Cr., W. upon Chesapiack Bay; adj. John Renney, William Chase, William Wallis, formerly surveyed for James Jolly; on the lands of Mesangoe, viz: Charles Ratcliff; land formerly James Taylor's, & Edwd. Moore (or Moone), Junr., on St. George's hummock or island, & Jno. Parker's 200 acs., &c. Trans. of 50 pers: Edwd. Moss, Peter Butler, Jno. Strashley, Edward Vaughan, Tho. Starr, Jno. Hauthorne, Mary Ripley, Ann Billipps, Tho. Philpott, Jno. Ashton, Wm. Huddy, Tho. Patterson, Tho. Oversea, Tho. Wilsheir, Wm. Middleton, Henry Packer, Jno. Bateman, Edwd. Parker, Jno. Loyd, Mary Pritchett, Tho. Forsith, Peter Prigg, Arthur Willett, Jno. Miller, Eliza. Miller, Mary Miller, Tho. Hancoke, Joseph Jonson, Wm. Hicman, Hen. Ludford, Wm. Williams, Jno. Sparkes, Jno. Driver, Wm. Baker, Tho. Collier, Tho. Harper, Jno. Flint, Tho. Meceney, Wm. Conaway, Hun. Floyd, James Jasper, Hen. Rolph, Jno. Davie, "Will the Smith," Ben. Rowland, Geo. Fipps, Jno. Skittle, Wm. Horsey, Owin Jones, Mary Jones. 3 Oct. 1672, p. 423.

CAPT. JOHN WEST, 1000 acs., N'ampton Co. at *Gingoteage;* adj. Capt. Richd. Hill & Capt. Danll. Jenifer; 3 Oct. 1672, p. 423. Trans. of 20 pers: Wm. Hampton, Tho. Draiton, Jno. Wigg, Hen. Wageman, Peter Plover, Arth. Brightwell, Mary Phillis, Ann Tracey, Geo. Trigg, Peter Hacker, Jno. Thackray, James Veysey, Peter Hardman, Tho. Fisher, Jno. Randall, Alexr. Crafton, Nic. Trevitt, Jno. Armorer, Jno. Brooman, Edward Coomes.

SAME. 500 acs. Same Co., date & page. N. side Pungoteage Cr., adj. Cha. Scarburgh, the maine Bay & N'ly. towards *Matchotanck.* Granted Matilda Scarburgh 20 Oct. 1661, deserted, & now due by order, &c. Trans. of 10 pers: Robt. Pitt, Danll. Oneale, Jno. Middleton, Hen. Peirce, Antho. Fowler,

Hen. Spittless, Jno. Rodes, Tho. Gamon, Tho. Jones; Will (a) Negroe.

ROBERT PARKER, 150 acs., in Rappahannock; bet. Mill Cr. & the River; adj John Smith; Nicholas Cattlett; Henry Munkaster or Tho. Munday, &c; 14 Oct. 1672, p. 424. Trans. of 3 pers: Roger Smith, James Jones, Widdoe Huderson.

COL. THO. GUTTERIDGE, 4626 acs., Rappa. Co., on S. side sd. River; 4 Oct. 1672, p. 424. 2876 acs. granted him 24 Oct. 1669; 1200 acs. granted Thomas Goldman, 4 Apr. 1667, & sould to sd. Gutteridge; 550 acs., adj. this & land of Graves; & Mr. Beverley; by Rappa. Indian Path neer the Pocoson; &c; due for trans. of 93 pers: (Note: Others not named.) Richd. Hall, Robt. Rite, Geo. Flint, Elizabeth Barker, Jno. Wagoner, —— Morgan & his wife, Robt. Shereman, Wm. Peeters, —— Marsy, Jno. Collins.

COL. JOHN STRINGER, 400 acs., N'ampton Co., on S. side of Savage's Cr., on Chisapeiacke Bay, & Jackson's Gutt; 4 Oct. 1672, p. 424. Granted to Daniell Cugley 27 June 1635, & sold to sd. Stringer by Capt. John Savage, heyr to sd. Cagley.

COL. THOMAS LIGGON, 1468 A., 1 R., 28 P., Henrico Co., on S. side of James Riv., 28 Sept. 1672, p. 425. 167 A., 1 R., 12 P., being half of a devdt. granted Thomas Liggon & Major Wm. Farrar 2 Oct. 1664; adj. to the lower of Mount my Lady Feild, &c., & Major Harris, &c; 1301 A. 16 P. adj. same; up the Ashen Sw., to old Powhetan Path, &c. Trans. of 13 pers: John Rosser, Tho. Hollins, Jane Prout, Katherine Powell, Nich. Ellis, Wm. Ricketts, Roger Bridges, Arnold Mouse, Garrett Ledwith, Henry Cole, Oswald Osborne, James Barnes, Anth. Little, Katherin Little, Anne Green, Lewis Williams, Owen Margaren (or Margarett), William White, Thomas Atkins; John & Dimgoe—Negroes; Sarah Poole, Mary Browne, Francis James, Tho. Morton, Henry Knighton.

COL. THOMAS GOODRICH, 2200 acs., New Kent Co., 5 Oct. 1672, p. 425. Nere the N. side of the Indian Path from Matopony towne that was att the head of Piscataway Cr. unto the new towne now planted by those Indians on Matapony Riv., &c., adj. Capt. Brewerton nere the head of Hashwamankcott (?) Sw., &c. Trans. 44 pers: Wm. Claibourne, William Harrise, William Morrise, John Pipe, Thomas Story, Richard Pettener, John Palmer, Roger Sadler, John Willson, Roger Barlow, William Dawson, John Swith, Richard Evans, Peter Jenins, Arther Grime, John Willett, William Kirtley, Daniell Haddock, John Fox, Francis Jones, Hugh Evans, Tho. Fox, Richard Tomson, Thomas Varnall, John Kinge, William Roberts, John Griffin, Hugh Meridith, Robert Southerby, Margolld (?) Woodall (or Woodart), John Jatts, John Gardiner, William Richardson, John Homen, John Ashly, John Callise, Rowland Garrett, Sam. Wetherington, Henery Burkett, Isaac Thatcher, Robert Barrington, John Abott, Henery William, Cuthbert Barrow.

PHILLIP WATKINS, 500 acs., New Kent Co., 5 Oct. 1672, p. 426. Granted to Mr. George Morris, deserted, & now granted by order, &c. Trans. of 10 pers: Richd. Smith, Robt. Peirson, Robt. Kewe (or Krewe), Phill. Ellis, Andrew Dunn, Richd. Clark, Jonathan Hopkins. Wm. Crewes, Jno. Turnwood (?) William Harrow. Note: This land deserted by Phill. Watkins & the rites made use of. Test P. L. (Note: This record crossed out, but inserted because of names.)

SAME. 500 acs., same Co., date, & page. Upon Assacamanscocke branch, about 3 mi. from the river; adj. land supposed to be surveyed for George Chapman. Granted to John Petit 5 Mar. 1658, deserted, & now granted by order &c. Trans. of 10 pers: Arth. Howse, Tho. Johnson, Tho. Priddy, Antho. Tayler (or Sayler), Peter Goold, John Wiggon, Lancelott Vowell, Peter Harpyer. Jno. Griffin, Peter Lloyd.

JOHN DAVIS (Davies), 500 acs., Henrico Co., 1 Oct. 1672, p. 426. 300

acs. adj. John Burton; includ. nigh half the long feild, over the *brass* Spring, &c; half of patt. granted Robert Cradock, & by Howell Price, Atty. of sd. Cradock, sould to John Cox, who assigned to sd. Burton; 300 acs. due sd. Davis a ssonn & heire of his father, John Davis; 200 acs. for trans. of 4 pers: Abell Gower, Wm. Gower, John Clarke, Ann Malby.

THOMAS STEVENS (Stephens), 175 acs., Gloucester Co., 7 Oct. 1672, p. 426. Granted to Elias Wigmore & by inquisition, &c. under Peter Jennings, Depty. Esch'r., 4 July 1665, &c. Sd. land was part of 1050 acs. on the head of Clay branch Cr., adj. Capt. Gill.

HENRICO PARISH, 198 A., 3 R., 16 P., in sd. Co., *being a Gleab,* at V*arina,* on N. side of James Riv., on the 16 Apr. 1666, and by the ancient neighbourhood shewed bounded, viz: beg. at the River side at a small oake & running NW by N 320 W 100 po. along Capt. Davies' slash SE by S ½ S'ly. 300 po. to a pohickery standing about two Poles above the *Court house,* then Ea. 136 pole to the place aforementioned. (Recorded) 7 Oct. 1672, page 427.

ELIZABETH NEWET (Nevet-Newett), now wife of Wm. Newett, late Elizabeth Jones; 170 acs., Surry Co., in Lawnes Cr. Par., above George Harris' Path; upon the Deep Sw., &c; 8 Oct. 1672, p. 427. Part of a greater tract of escheated land.

JOHN BAUGH, 200 acs., Henrico Co., on S. side of James Riv., 7 Oct. 1672, p. 427. Adj. the orphants of Joseph Tanner; Major Wm. Harris; & James Atkins. Trans. of 4 pers: John Tirrell, John Curten, Mathew Spinkes, Joane Ruggells.

COL. WILLIAM KENDALL, 2050 acs., N'ampton Co., on N. side of Tom Smith's (Smyth's) br., adj. Thomas Dunton; land of Billiot; Jno. Stokeley; along Mountney's Cr., including Oke Island & adj. land formerly Capt. William Jones': 8 Oct. 1672, p. 427. 1700 acs. granted sd. Kendall 26 Mar. 1672;

200 acs. part of 3600 acs. granted to Wm. Whittington 29 Oct. 1669, who sould to sd. Kendall 31 July 1672; 150 acs. for trans. of 3 pers.*

SIR WM. SKIPWITH, Knight, sonne & heire of Sir Grey Skipwith, Knt., 400 acs., in Middlesex Co., upon Mill Cr. *alias* Glebe land Cr., 8 Oct. 1672, p. 428. Adj. William Frizell; Mr. Edmd. Kemp, dec'd., &c. Said land formerly surveyed by Sir Grey Skipwith Knight in his life time & the survey together with Rights for the same returned into the Secretaries Office the 20 Mar. 1665 that patent might thereon issue forth, but the said survey being by casual accident lost in the office, & Wm. Dudley makeing clame to the said land by an after graunt, & the same being brought before the Right Honorble. the Gov'r. & Councell by Dame Anne Skipwith, Mother of the sd. Sir Wm., in behalfe of her said sonne, who humbly prayed the Right Honorble. the Gov'r. & Councell that they would please to determine in whose right the land lay, and the said Dudley makeing all arguments possible for himselfe, it pleased the Right Honorble. the Gov'r. & Councell, by there order bearing date the 27 of Sept. 1671, to adjudge & declare that the right of the said land is and was in the sd. Sir Wm. Skipwith, &c. And that the said Wm. Dudley should emediately deliver up the possession of the sd. land to the use of sd. Sir Wm.

WM. ELLIOTT, Senr., Planter, of Kingstone Par., Gloucester Co., 1100 acs. neere the head of Queen's Cr., in sd. Co., 8 Oct. 1672, p. 428. Adj. Richard Carev; the Shakeing Bridge; on head of the Dirty Br., through the Sw., to Mr. John Armstead, neere the sand (or saw) pitts; along Mr. George Seaton; to a br. dividing this & Thomas Sellers' land, &c. 900 acs. granted Edward Welch 1 Aug. 1654; assigned to Thomas Boswell, Senr. & againe granted sd. Boswell 14 Oct. 1663, who assigned to sd. Elliott; 200 acs. due for trans. of 4 pers: Joseph Fellowes, Danll. Ware. Richard Browne, Ellinor Anderson.

LAMBERT MOORE & BARTHOLOMEW RAMSEY, 350 acs., Gloucester

Co., 8 Oct. 1672, p. 429. Betwixt land of David Cant, dec'd., & Tho. Dawkins. Trans. of 7 pers: Ellin Forman, Jon. Savage, John Norrick, Elias Paine, Jon. Howard, Robt. Lane, Joane Philpott.

MATHEW GAYLE, 284 acs., Glost. Co., in Kingstone Par., 8 Oct. 1672, p. 429. Adj. Phillip Hunley. Trans. of 6 pers: Wm. Blake, James Paine, Mary Bullock, Tho. Harwood, Anne Hertford, John Arthur.

MR. THOMAS MILNER, 350 acs., Nansimond Co., against Dumplin Island; 9 Oct. 1672, p. 429. Beg. at *Troublesome poynt* upon Nansimond Riv., to land of Richard Hyne; adj. Mr. Christopher Achelley; land of John White, dec'd., now in possession of Wm. Gatlyn. 200 acs. part of a greater devdt. granted to Francis Malden 16 May 1638, & by Francis, his sonne & heyre, assigned to sd. Milner; 150 acs. for trans. of 3 pers: Wm. Wimberley, Peter Wimberley, Katherine Barstable.

JOHN WALLOP *alias* WALLOW, 1550 acs., in Up. part of N'ampton Co., 9 Oct. 1672, p. 430. 450 acs. being all of *Kekotank Island* alias *Accocomson Is.*, the next Is. to *Gingoteag* als. *Chincoteag Is;* 100 acs. N. on line bet .Va. & Md., adj. 1700 acs. in Mattopony Neck & S. on a freshwater br. of Gr. Mattapony Cr. Trans. of 35 pers: John Wallop, Rebecca Wallop, Wm. Wallop, Joane Rosser, Cornell Ross, Jermon Jones, Elizab. Playfire, Elizab. Miner, Wm. Watts, Tho. Eldridge, Jno. Tomkins. Franc. Webster, William Elder, Jno. Jacob, Isaac Read, Edmond Parrish (?). Jone Chaney, Miles Feilding, James Trowton, Jno. Cracherly, James Mitten. Richard Dawloop, Tho. Lazenby, Tho. Lyner, Margery Mosse, Rebecca Wigg, Meredith Evans, Jno. Hereford; Maria & Mattara Negroes.

SAME. 650 acs., Same Co., date & page. At *Gingoteag;* adj. Mr. Nichool, formerly sd. Wallop's; land formerly Samuell Taylor's; & land of Richd. Hill. Trans. of 13 pers: Ambrose White, Jno. Glasse, Tho. Fisher, James Roberts, Sarah Jones, Hugh Butler, Sara Jackson, Joan Smyth, Wm. Miller, Mary Hall.

James Temenson, Peter Harvy, Wm. North.

WILLIAM WOULDHAVE, 100 acs., N'ampton Co., bet *Accohannock* & *Mathapungo;* adj. Robert Watson, John Savage, Wm. Taylor, & land formerly belonging to Potts; 9 Oct. 1672, p. 430. Trans. of 2 pers: Roger Edwards, John Townsend.

ELIZABETH MARSH, wife of Paul Marsh, eldest dau. of Phillip Meredith; MARY HINMAN wife of Richard Hinman, 2nd dau., & ELIANOR TREWET wife of George Trewet, the 3rd dau., 350 acs., N'ampton Co., at Accohannock Cr., 9 Oct. 1672, p. 430. Adj. land of Ralph Doe (Dow), & Jno. Hammaren, formerly Jno. Baldwin & Robert Marriot's; 300 acs. granted to Nicholas Waddilow 15 Sept. 1649, who sould to sd. Phillip; & in partnership is due the abovenamed as heyres, &c. 50 acs. for trans. of: Tobias Browne.

NATHANIEL BRADFORD, 400 acs., N'ampton Co., near *Mathapungo;* adj. Wm. Nock; Barthew. Meares; & Arthur Robins; 9 Oct. 1672, p. 430. Trans. of 8 pers: Miles Roxell, James Hoxley, Richard Webster, Tho. Bossington, John Lovelock, Mathew Kele, Anne Eaton, Elizabeth Abbott.

SAME. 2800 acs., same Co. & date, p. 431. At *Watchapreag* near *Matchapungo Neck;* beg. at Mr. Kendall, at Matchapungo Cr., to Richard Kellam; on a fresh water br. of Nicowomson, by some called little Matomkin Cr., to Edward Revell & Jonah Jackson, &c; 1400 acs. granted him 26 Sept. 1664; 1400 acs., which was deserted, granted him in 2 patts., viz: 1000 acs. 26 Mar. 1662, & 400 acs. 9 Oct. 1667, & by order &c. is regranted him; due for trans. of 28 pers: Edgar Lowderell, Geo. Outrell, Tho. Clarke, Rob. Dorrington, Nehemiah Blake, Maurice Pembrooke, Jno. Moore (?), Richd. Wiggon, Samuell, Taylor, Robert Adkins. Jno. Medcalf, Mary Meares, Katherin Sherley. Sybill Bullock, Wm. Fetherston, Robt. Paine, Samll. Thurston, Elizab. Jenkins, Tho. Williamson, Jno. Reeves; Sandela & Joan Negroes. (Note: The following names have been crossed out: Edwd. Demstall, Richd. Beare, Joshua Rounder, Adam Rinch, Edgar Onley (?), Margar ——.)

BARTHOLOMEW MEARES, 500 acs., N'ampton Co., on E & W sides of Matchapungo Bever dam Br., 9 Oct. 1672, p. 431. Adj. Richard Kellam. 200 acs., part of 500 acs., granted sd. Meares & William Taylour 26 Mar. 1662; by them divided, &c., by deed 4 Oct. 1668, recorded in Accomack; 300 acs. granted sd. Meares 5 Apr. 1666, deserted, & regranted by order, &c. Trans. of 6 pers: George Roe, Robert Hemmens, James Okeley, Jane Lewis, Joan Smyth, Rebecca Long.

GEORGE JOHNSON, 300 acs., N'ampton Co., being hummocks of trees & marsh, on N. side of the N. br. of Muddy Cr., toward Cattayle Cr.; 9 Oct. 1672, p. 431. Trans. of 6 pers: Ann Lazing, Morgan Jones, Rachell Browne, John Ferres, Richard Cooke, Charles Agore.

CHRISTOPHER THOMPSON. 600 acs., N'ampton Co., 9 Oct. 1672, p. 432. At the head of the neck made by the N br. of Deep Cr. & the S. br. of Hunting Cr; adj. land formerly John Arnes (?), now Mr. Browne's; running to Dye's br. & land of Capt. John West. 500 acs. by a former patt., & 100 acs. for trans. of 2 pers: Xpofer Thompson, twice.

ROBERT BRACEY (Brace), 650 acs., N'ampton Co., on S. side of Messango Cr., adj. Wm. Aldworth; 9 Oct. 1672, p. 432. 300 acs. granted to William Blake 30 Oct. 1671, who sould to sd. Brace 5 Jan. 1671; 350 acs. for trans. of 7 pers: Robert Bracey, Senr., Robert Bracey, Junr., Elizabeth Bracey, Edward Smallee, Tho. Cunningham Elizab. Everett.

ROBERT HILL, 400 acs., N'ampton Co., at Messango br., adj. Col. William Kendall; 9 Oct. 1672, p. 432. Trans. of 8 pers: Tho. Willy, Ann Willy, Rebecca Townsend, Uriah Cummin, Grace Cumin, James Cotton, James Banny, James Old Castle.

RICHARD BUNDICK, 600 acs., N'ampton Co., 9 Oct. 1672, p. 432. Being the surplus within bounds of his 1400 acs. at Arcadia; adj. Geo. Watson. Trans. of 12 pers: Alice Oakeland, Jane Taylour, James Ashton, Jeremy Stullins (or Shillins), Jane Limes, Thomas May, Henry Maselin, Robert Weaver, Arthur Wrenn, Tho. Roxford, Timothy White, Rowland Mercer.

THOMAS NICKSON, 400 acs., N'ampton Co., at Gingoteag; adj. Jno. Wallop; Capt. Hill & Capt. West; 9 Oct. 1672, p. 433. Trans. of 8 pers: Michael Lackland, Jno. Butter, Edmond Baskey, Jno. Harris, Tho. Reignolds, Jno. Tanner, Edw. Nayworthy, Tho. Heart.

EDWARD HITCHIN, 340 acs., N'ampton Co., neere Matchapungo; 9 Oct. 1672, p. 433. A br. dividing this from land of Barthew. Meares; along Richard Hill, Junr., to William Taylour; to Richard Kellam, &c; 300 acs. granted Wm. Taylour & Barthew. Meares, 26 Mar. 1662, by them divided &c., by deed 4 Oct. 1668, recorded in Accomack; sould by Taylour to sd. Hitchin, 16 June 1671; 40 acs. for trans. of John Male.

NICHOLAS MILCHOPP, 550 acs., N'ampton Co., on a br. of Muddy Cr., 9 Oct. 1672, p. 433. Trans. of 11 pers: John Male, Oliver Sawte, John Niccolls, Hezekia Arundell, William Painter, Tho. Tunnell, Richard Holland, Jno. Lamplash, Richd. Toleson, Mary Atkins, Tho. Dinton.

JNO. AYRES & XPOFER. THOMPSON, 600 acs., N'ampton Co., adj. Capt. Richard Hill's land in forker neck at head of Hunting Cr; 9 Oct. 1672, p. 433. Trans. of 12 pers: John Eyres 8 tymes; Robert Davis, Edward Broadway, Richard Lewis, George Youngman.

JOHN AREW, 300 acs., N'ampton Co., at Hunting Cr., 9 Oct. 1672, p 434. Being the NW half part of Wm. Gowers' 600 acs., granted 23 Feb. 1663, & by him bequeathed to sd. Arew (?).

CHARLES & MARY CALVERT, 800 acs., part being a neck in N'ampton Co., bet. the N. br. of Anancock & a br. dividing this & land of John Jenkins; part being out of the neck; 9 Oct. 1672, p. 434. Granted to Xpofer. Calvert, 2 Oct. 1655, & assigned to sd. Charles & Mary.

RICHARD BAILY, sonne of Richard Baily, dec'd., 1200 acs., N'ampton Co., on the N & S sides of the head of Cradocks Cr., dividing this & land of Edmond Scarburgh, & land formerly Richd. Hill's, &c; 9 Oct. 1672, p. 434 700 acs. granted his father 15 Sept. 1649, & due sd. Richard as heire; 500 acs. granted Toby Norton 24 July 1651, assigned to his father, &c.

RICHARD KELLAM, 1850 acs., N'ampton Co., at Matchapungo Cr., 9 Oct. 1672, p. 434. 1700 acs. by former patent; 150 acs. being surplus, &c. Trans. of 3 pers: Phillip White, Jane Pantin (or Partin), Katherin Mayze.

HENRY TRUETT (Trewett), 350 acs., N'ampton Co., at *Anancock;* 9 Oct. 1672, p. 434. Being half of the neck facing the mouth of the maine Cr., adj. John Williams; sd. Anancock Cr., &c. Sd. land after elder Pattents are surveyed is all that can be found of 500 acs. granted his father George Truett, 3 Nov. 1660, which is due him as sonn & heyre.

CAPT. THOMAS HAWKINS, 812¼ acs., on S. side of Rappa. Riv., at the lowest fall; 9 Oct. 1672, p. 435. Granted him 2 June 1666; not seated, & now regranted, having entered new rights. Trans. of 17 pers.*

MR. JOHN ROBINS, 500 acs., N'ampton Co., at *Gingoteag.* at the Seaboard; adj. Southey Littleton; & N. upon line bet. Va. & Maryland; 7 Oct. 1672, p. 435. Trans. of 10 pers: John King; Cosango, Philassa, great Tony, Peter. Hannah, Robin. & James— Negroes.

COL. JNO. BLAKE. 200 acs., Nansimond Co., adj. William Eson; 7 Oct. 1672, p. 435. Trans. of 4 pers: Mary

Blenly, Jeremy Upshaw, John Tilson, Tho. Stevens.

MR. EDWARD ROWSEY, 400 acs., in Sittingborne Par., on S. side Rappa. Riv., & S. E. side of Ocapaceo Cr., &c; 10 Oct. 1672, p. 436. Trans. of 8 pers: William Dane, Tho. Watson, Rich. Nellen, Elizab. Clecke (or Clerke) Alice Decone, Henry Lea (or Rea) Timothy Douty, Jno. Kates.

ROBERT CARDIN, 46 acs. in Sittingborne Par., on S. side of Rappa. Riv., near Chestucson Cr., on line of Mr. John Cox, facing Ocapacee (?) Cr. &c; 10 Oct. 1672, p. 436. Trans. of: Laurence Mount Stephory.

FRANCIS GRAVES, 714 acs., Rappa. Co., on S. side sd. Riv., part on branches of Gilson's Cr. & part in Hodgkins Cr; adj. Mr. Beverley, near Button bridge; over the new Road &c., 20 Oct. 1672, p. 436. Trans. of 15 pers: John Oldis, Tho. Knott, Tho. Ichady (?), Peter Dyos, Sarah Warner, John Miles, John Cooper, John Dearing, Thomas Hill, Mathew Lewis, Jno. Luke, Robert Young, Henry Milby, Judith Abbott, Rich. Deprize. (Note: The following names have been crossed out: Alice Huflow, Mary Sheeres, Tho. Davies, Tho. Batts (or Botts-Butts).

ROBERT MOSS (Mosse), 944½ acs., Rappa. Co., in Sittingborne Par., on S. side sd. Riv; 10 Oct. 1672, p. 436. A branch dividing this from land Mr. Wm. Moseley lives upon; & adj. Mr. John Cox. 331 acs. purchased of sd. Moseley; 613 acs. for trans. of 16 pers: Arthur Gosling, Peter East, John Bliss, Elizab. Webster, Roger Morgan, Alice Williams, Michael Mogley, Richd. Fuzzey, Mary Martin, John Chatfeild, Tho. Strathling, Henry Kerson, Henry Newton

JOHN WILLIAMS, 149½ acs., Rappa. Co., on S. side of Rappa. Riv., near plantation of John Cooke; adj. Wm. Spicer; on branch of Ocapesee Cr., cor. to Vincent Stanford. &c; 10 Oct. 1672, p. 436. Trans. of 3 pers: Tho. Davy, Elizabeth Weeden, Dorothy Wilkinson.

HENRY TANDYS, 868 acs., in Farnham Par., Rappa. Co., on S. side sd. Riv., 10 Oct. 1672, p. 437. On N. & S. side of the Mill Cr., being part of land granted Mr. Andrew Gilson, deserted, & granted to Major John Weyr, who sould to John Dangerfeild, who sould to sd. Tandy. Trans. of 7 pers.*

COL. THOMAS STEGG, Esqr., 2773 A., 32 P., Henrico Co., on S. side of James Riv., 27 Oct. 1669, p. 437. At the head of his old patt. at the falls &c; to Powhite runn; &c. 1880 acs. part granted him 29 Dec. 1663; & 923 A., 32 P., for trans. of 19 pers.

CONQUEST WYATT, sonne & heire of Edward Wyatt, 530 acs., on NW side of Hoccadies (Hoccadayes) Cr; 10 Oct. 1672, p. 437. Beg. neere Wyatt's old plantation; adj. Robert Elliott; Mary Kibble; George Harper; &c. 480 acs. assigned by Lt. Col. Anthony Elliott, dec'd., to Jon. Snelling, dec'd., who assigned to Erasmus Withers, who assigned to sd. Edward Wyatt; & due sd. Conquest by will; 50 acs., being overplus adj., due for trans. of: John Rivers.

GEORGE HARPER, 133 acs., Gloucester Co., bet. the Chescake Indians' land & Conquest Wyatt; 10 Oct. 1672, p. 438. Trans. of 3 pers: George Anderton, Dorothy Jones, Simon Stacey.

ROBERT BEVERLEY, 500 acs., Gloucester Co., upon brs. of Hoccadaye's & Chiescake Crks., adj. Robert Elliott, youngest sonne of Lieut. Col. Anthony Elliott, dec'd., neere Noakes' plantation, where he now lives, adj. his own & land of Conquest Wyatt; &c; 10 Oct. 1672, p. 438. Trans. of 10 pers: Richard Mounts, Mathew Jones, Samll. Cox, Simon Stacey, Elias Robinson, Sara Howard, Wm. Allexander, Henry Herbert, Will. Allen, Jno. Gibson.

MARY KIBBLE, dau. of Geo. Kibble, dec'd., 500 acs., Gloucester Co., on brs. of Hoccadaye's Cr., adj. Robert Elliott, sonne of Anthony Elliot, decd., neere Noakes' (or Stoakes') plantation; & Conquest Wyatt; 11 Oct. 1672, p. 438. Granted to Robert Beverley the day

before these presents, & assigned by deed the same day, &c.

RICHARD BAILEY, 882 acs., Gloucester Co., upon brs. of Hoccadaye's Cr., & North Riv. Mill runn; adj. Robert Elliott, & Thomas Gaunt's land, lately purchased of Mr. William Elliott; beg. upon a path by maine br. of sd. Cr., at the usuall place of going over sd. branch to plantation of Conquest Wyatt; &c; 11 Oct. 1672, p. 439. Trans. of 18 pers: Margrett Clarke, James Meridine, Henry Hebe, Solomon Blake, Wm. Harris, Tho. Simson, Richard Hussey, Jon. Pratt, Issabell Collier, Rich. Bailey, Jon. Mavell (?), Sara Howard, Henry Herbert, Jon. Gibson, Geo. Anderson, Jon. Arthur, Anne Hetford (or Herford), Tho. Harwood.

WM. WHITTINGTON, 2850 acs., N'ampton Co., att Hungers; W'wd. with a bloofe povnt faceing the Bay & 110 acs. sold by Capt. Stone to James Davis; S'wd. by Mattawoms Cr., & 300 acs. sold by Capt. Stone to Winstone (?) Foster, &c; adj. land formerly Capt. Jones' in a forke of a freshwater br. of Hungers Cr. &c; 11 Nov. 1672, p. 439. 1390 acs. part of 1800 acs. granted Mr. Wm. Stone 4 June 1635, & sold to Capt. Wm. Whittington 3 Oct. 1653, & now descended to sd. Wm. his son & heire; 1460 acs. for trans. of 30 pers: Richd. Beere, John Collins, Tho. Wms. (Williams), Tho. Midleton, John Wells, Robert Hamleton, Hump. Davis, Richd. Henderson, Gilb. Flemon, Hen. Tyman, Richd. Roberts, Richd. Alworth, Cha. Woodhowseton, Rowland Peirce, Chr. Denham, Jane Cuttey, Wm. Thomson, Geo. Anderson, Jon. Littlehowse, Cha. Burston, Tho. Bissaker, Hen. Peck, Mary Baker, Fra. Russell, Wm. Roebanck, Dolloe Thomas, Tho. Northey, Amm Poore, Jane Vaughan, Edwd. Hooke.

AMBROSE WHITE, 450 acs., in Accomack, bet. land of Occahanock & Machepungo; 11 Nov. 1672, p. 439. Adj. land now or late of Dorothy Jordan; Arthur Upshott, John Salvage; John Storyie; Edmd. Smith & Henry Bishop. Granted to Cornelius Watkinson 10 Sept. 1664, who defaulted in planting &c. & granted sd. White by order, &c. Trans. of 9 pers: Ja. Collison, John Trott, Wm. Pascall, John Penny, Peter Loveless, John Windle, Tho. Miller Ja. Cattle, John Hardy, Winifred Alfred, Peter Stout, Ann Scott, Ja. Whitteker, Wm. Garland. Note: The overplus of these Rites being five are recorded under a patt. in this Book, fol. (60). Teste P. L. Clk.

BENJAMIN HARRISON, 1240 acs Surry Co.; 12 Nov. 1672, page 440. 600 acres on S. side the Riv., about 1½ mi. up Upper Chipokes Cr., upon the E. side, neere land formerly Jeremy Clements; upon E. side or a Sw., against Sandy point; granted 18 May 1637 to Benja. Harrison, his father, & due him as heire; 140 acs. in sd. Co., from the Sunken Marsh neere Up. Chipokes; adj. lands formerly Henry Neale's & Henry White's; granted Wm. Gapin 22 Aug. 1645, sold to his father, & descended to him, &c; 500 acs. in sd. Co., on S. side James Riv., upon a br. of Sunken marsh; on S. side the round Island Sw; granted his father 9 Oct. 1649, & due, &c. 12 Oct. 1672, p. 440.

JOHN MOHUN, 720 acs., New Kent Co.; S. side Yorke Riv., 25 Oct. 1672, p. 440. A cr. dividing this & land of Lt. Col. Hockady, now belonging to his son John Hockady; up Trowell's Cr. to its main br. by the Roade; neere John Collett, &c. 400 acs. granted to Geo. Chapman 10 Nov. 1669, assigned to Mr. Richd. Whittaker, who assigned to sd. Mohun; 120 acs. granted Hen. Trowell 27 Apr. 1670, who sold to sd. Mohun; 200 acs. for trans. of 4 pers: Bryan Henly, John Mohun, Warwick Mohun, Mary Capel.

DANIEL CLARKE, 500 acs., Chas. City Co., side Jas. Riv., 25 Nov. 1672, p. 441. Beg. at the head of the Gr. Meddow; by E. br. of Herrin Cr. &c. Trans. of 10 pers: John Petty, Alice Crank, Ann Warren, Wm. Stephens, Roger Hall, Wm. Lowder, Eliz. Michell, Geo. Butler, James Rumsy, Tho. Shecket.

MR. DANIEL HARRISON, 220 acs., Rappa. Co., in Sittingborne Par., 1 Nov.

1672, p. 441. S. W. side of Rappa. Riv., on the head of Occupacon Cr; adj. Wm. Spicer. Trans. of 5 pers: Tho. Harwood, Rich. West, Mary Hunter, Eliz. Wright; & 1 Negro woman.

JAMES BESOUTH, 176 acs., & 59.28 chs., Yorke Co., 15 Dec. 1672, p. 441. 98 acs. on S. W. side of Briery Sw., adj. Tho. Shaw & Rich. Harris; to the Indian Spring Path; to Rich. Joanes, neere the White Marsh; 78 A. 59.28 chs. adj. his own, neere Capt. Tayler; over a br. of the Gr. Sw. &c., to N. side of the Gr. High Roade, &c. 50 acs. granted to Jno. Hartwell 25 Aug. 1642; 48 acs. to sd. Besouth 18 Oct. 1662; 78 A. & 58.28 Chs. for trans. of 2 pers: Augustin Shelborne, Jno. Blackcocke.

MR. RICH. DUDLEY, 944 acs., Gloster Co., on brs. of Porpotancke Cr., 1 Dec. 1672, p. 442. Beg. at Mr. John Greene, by Mr. Pate's Sw., along Mr. Peter Knight, to Spence's line; to Paradice Path; to Chescaiack Path; to Mr. John Pate, &c; 400 acs. granted Wm. Armefeild 24 Nov. 1663; sold to Mr. John Pate, who assigned to sd. Dudley; 544 acs. granted sd. Dudley 28 Oct. 1665; deserted, & granted to Peyton, who assigned to Dudley. Trans. of 11 pers: John Prichard, Rich. Preston, Jno. Roberts, John Mathram, Wm. Ward, Rosse Allen, Nich. Moore, Walter Chapman, Geo. Pritley, Jno. Basse, Ann Devenport.

RICHARD HOLDER, 80 A., 1 R., 5 P., in James Citty, 28 Jan. 1672, p. 442. On James Riv., &c., near the Orchard, &c. Due by order &c., for trans. of 1 per.*

MORRIS PRICE, 100 acs., Yorke Co., in Pecoson Par., 28 Jan. 1672/3, p. 443. In a br. on W. side of Woolfe Trap Ridge belonging to Edmund Hudson; towards Enos Macletoch, (?), & towards Henrick Van Doverach. Trans. of himselfe twice.

EDMUND PALMER, 2800 acs., Is. of W. Co., 5 Feb. 1672, p. 443. Adj. his own, & lands of Anthony Mathews;

& Jno. Portis; bet. Sheeres & Clarke; & Mathews & Aires; to Arthur Smith; Mr. Bressie; Mr. Bodie; &c. Trans. of 56 pers: Hen. Madockes, Wm. Haies, Math. Fones (or Jones), Jno. Rice, Rich. Dale, Jonas Jones, Wm. Prosier, Jane James, Ann Toleson, Ann Kater, Ann Browne, Jno. Devenham, Wm. Butwell, Tristram- Easton, Luke Mansens, Merrick Edwards, Robt. Sampson, Merlin Cant, Joseph Baker, Fra. Rippington, Escott Ann, Robt. Smith, Ambrose Sadly, Robt. Hues, Jno. Harris, Ellinor Tewe, Owen Griffin; his owne person; Dan. Sam—, Jno. Granger, Jno. Williams, Jeremy Callaway, Rich. Smokam, Tho. Clarke; Rich. Bee, Eliz. Collings, Sara Miles, Mary. Embry, Peter Prescot, Fra. Nickolls, And. Stanford, Wm. Harding, Ann Fowler, Robt. Harris, Antho. Williams, Hen. George, Alce Howse, Marg. Howse, Robt. Norton, Jno. Fisher, Geo. Smith, Moses Dirham, Robt. Clarke, Mihill Fox, Nehemiah Davis, Eliz. Strange.

JOHN HUMES, 300 acs. New Kent Co., on N. side of Mataponie Riv., 28 Feb. 1672/3; p. 444. Adj. Jno. Kea; Wm. Burch; the maine br. of Mastico; & Major Wm. Wyatt. Trans. of 6 pers: Hen. Stalker, Mary Hamond, Mary Ports, Jno. Barnhouse, Edward Marson, Betritia Walcot.

WM. DROMMOND, 960 acs., Low. Nof. Co., on E. side of brs. of the N. river of Coratocke; 5 Mar. 1672/3, p. 444. Trans. of 20 pers: Ja. Bishop, Ealis Samond, Jno. Crewes, Richd. Mumpson, Mary Cossins, Sam. `Haliot, Jno. Hall, Wm. Duncon, Math. Wilkinson, Jno. Smith, Wm. Dawby, Rich. Ceely, Ja. Stradling, Math. Nash, Wm. Davis, Wm. Grace; Tom, Jacob, Gregory—Negroes.

MR. LAWRENCE SMITH & ANTHO. BUCKNER, 716 acs., Rappa. Co., S. side the Riv., adj. Capt. Tho. Hawkins; 17 Mar. 1672/3, p. 444. Trans. of 14 pers: Richd. Gower, John Delton, Jno. Brookes, Hen. Hodges, Nich. Bennett, Fra. Cosbrook; & 8 Negroes.

ROBT. TALIAFERO, sonn of Robt. Taliafer, 739 acs., Rappa. Co., in the freshes & on S. side Rappa Riv., adj. Hen. Corbyn, Esqr., & Mr. Grimes; 17 Mar. 1672/3, p. 445. 100 his due as Grandchild of sd. Grimes; 639 acs. for trans. of 14 pers: Tho. Dowler, Patrick the Irishman, Isaack Johnson, Geo. Flower, Richd. Beale, Lewis Davis, Jacob Plower, John Pettit, Pestee Sutton, James Bromfeild, Robt. Franckland, Tho. Brumfeild, Elinor Foord, Edwd. Starke.

RICHARD PERRIN, 740 A., 1 R., 24 P., Henrico Co., N. side James Riv., 15 Mar. 1672, p. 445. 474 acs. called the Worlds End; from John Burton's house down; the Riv. 12 ft. below Cornelius' Cr; granted to Capt. Mathew Edloe 2 Oct. 1656 & sould to sd. Perrin; 266 A., 1 R., 24 P., at the head &c; trans. of 5 pers: Steven Lewin (or Lewis), Tho. Stanbrig, Nan the Maide, Jona. Fish, Tho. Mason.

JOHN STUARD, 600 A., 3 R., 32 P., Henrico Co., N. side Appomatock Riv., 15 Mar. 1672, p. 446. Beg. at a gr. br. of the Ashen Sw., adj. Orphants of Will. Walthall; & John Puckett; against place called the Cowpens, in possession of Tho. Ligon, Sr., on Powatan Path, &c. Trans. of 12 pers: Sanders Davis, John Hiselfe (?), Evan Owen, Henry Jame (?), William Pattison, Will. Bond, Richard Moore, Martha Benn, Elizabeth Drewry, John Renolds, Mary Armstid, Christopher Webb.

EDWARD BIRCHETT, 351 A., 32 P. Chas. Citty Co., S. Appomatock Riv., 15 Mar. 1672/3, p. 446. Adj. Mr. Henry Batts', next to James Thweate &c. Trans. of 7 pers: Alis Mobell, Ellinor Bottomly, George Mercer, Elinor Woodcock, Catherine Crosse, Mary Davis, George Bankes.

CAPT. JOHN KNOWLES, 793 A., 2 R., 2 P., Henrico Co., N. side James River, 15 Mar. 1672, p. 446. Adj. Henry Bayly; Mr. John Beauchampe; Cornelius' Run; &c. Trans. of 16 pers: Brick Wife (or Wise), Rich. Robison, Jano. Deckson, Giles Grooms, An. Wife (or Wise), Margery Robison, John Surley, Will. Fenley, Will. Lambert. Mary (a ?) woman, John Watts,

Obedem (?) Gearles (?), Eliza. Wilden, Eliza. Harris, Ralph Parry, Tho. Fourehands.

RICHARD WOMACK, 450 A., 3 R., 8 P., Henrico Co., N. side Appomatock Riv., 15 Mar. 1672/3, p. 447. At a br. of Ashen Sw., adj. John Puckett; the Spring Run, Mr. Baugh; nigh the Round Slash; to Major Harris, &c. Trans. of 9 pers: Sarah Johnson, John Adams, Mary Cooke, Jane Hayes, Jane Barrett, Tho. Browne, Joan Grigory, Jane Treble, An. Percer.

JAMES THWEATE (Thweat), 650 acs., Chas. City Co., S. side Appomatock Riv., 15 Mar. 1672/3, p. 447. Adj. Robt. Coleman; along the Blackwater, to the Gr. Meddow; along Baylie's run, &c. Trans. of 13 pers: Hercules Flood, Edward Young, An. Faulkner, Tho. Hopp, James Thweate, Roger Jones, Margarett Mathewes, Mary Bonner, Rebecca Robinson, Peeter Jones, Winifrid Price, James Farloe, John Throer.

MR. THO. LIGON, SR., 340 acs., Henrico Co., N. side Appomatock Riv., at head of Ashen Sw., knowne by the name of the *Cowpens;* adj. his land at *Mount Malada;* 18 Mar. 1672/3, p. 447. Beg. at sd. Sw; to the W. of New Powatan Path, &c. Trans. of 7 pers: Robert Chaplin, Edward Penny, Robt. Perry, Richard Collins, Tho. Bizence (?), George Harris, Sarah Hinds.

LT. WM. GORDON, 245 acs., Middlesex Co., 19 Mar. 1672, p. 448. Adj. land he puchased of Col. Cuth. Potter; on Mr. John Sheapherd (Sheppard); land of John Cant, sonn of Major David Cant; upon Mr. Alex. Smith; neer the Road Path, &c. Trans. of 5 pers: Jno. Sampson, Jone Griffe, Hannah Comy (or Coury), Dorothy Prosser, Elias Paine.

WM. HUST (or Herst), 363 acs., Gloster Co., in Petsoe Par., 18 Mar. 1672/3, p. 448. Adj. Tho. Royston; by Rappa. Path; neer plantation of Richd. Ireland, to David Monorgan; up Bryery Br., &c. Part of devdt. granted sd. Royston 6 Feb. 1667, who sold to said Hust or Herst.

EDMD. PORE (Poore), 77 acs., Gloster Co., in Kingstone Par., neere Richard Long; & adj. Phillip Hunley; 18 Mar. 1672 p. 448. Trans. of Elizabeth Scroope, (or Stroope) twice.

JOHN GYTON (or Gylon), 188 acs., Gloster Co., upon the Green Br., a br. of Milford Haven; neer Peter Arrundell; adj. Thomas Puttman; &c; 19 Mar. 1672/3, p. 449. Trans. of 4 pers: Ann Ellis, Nathanll. Giles, Jno. Jackson, Richd. Mounts.

CHRISTOPHER ACHELLES, 300 acs., Nansimond Co., adj. Wm. Burhle (?); 11 Apr. 1673, p. 449. Trans. of 6 pers.* (This record crossed out.)

RICH. DREW, 250 acs., Surry Co., 1 Mar. 1672, p. 449. By the Sw. bet. Mr. Davis & sd. Drew; by the old feild side where Mr. Cullmer lived. Purchased of Wm. Butler, 14 Apr. 1664.

WM. BUTLER, 590 acs., Surry Co., in Lawnes Creek Parish 1 Mar. 1672/3, p. 449. At the mouth of a Sw. on N. side of the old feild where Major Butler formerly lived; by a Spring on S. side the old feild where Rich. Skener formerly lived; &c. 500 acs. granted his father, Wm. Butler, 29 Aug. 1643; 90 purchased of Roger Delke.

CHARLES BLANKEVILE (Bankevile), 440 acs., Warwick Co., 8 May 1673, p. 450. Neare James Riv., adj. Mr. Stratton's land in tenure of Mr. Tho. Merry; land of Symon Daniells' orphan, in possession of Jno. Jackson; &c. Said land formerly in possession of Hen. Moore, whose relict he married; & for trans. of 9 pers.*

ARTHUR FRAME, 300 acs., Accomack Co., S. side of the S. br. of Hunting Cr., adj. James Atkinson; & Xpofer. Thompson; &c; 8 May 1673, p. 450. Granted to Jno. Rice, 9 Nov. 1666, deserted, & now granted by order, &c. Trans. of 6 pers: Samll. Michell, Richard Robins, Alice Michell, Stephen Avis, Jno. Margritts, Rich. Fregott. *(Note:* This patent crossed out.)

EDMUND SCARBROUGH, 2350 acs., N'ampton Co., on E'wd. side of an old Indian feild; down Occohanock Cr., unto Craddocke Cr., &c; 13 May 1673, p. 450. 2000 acs. granted Edmund Scarbrough 12 Aug. 1649; & 350 acs. found within, &c. Trans. of 7 pers: His owne trans. 3 times; Ursila Scarbrough, Ursila Scarbough, Junr., Robt. Peirce, Robt. Lewis. (Note: This patent crossed out.)

JOHN HATTON, 240 acs., Low. Norf. Co., in W. br. of Eliz. Riv., at the mouth of a sw. of Langlie's Cr., adj. Stephen Markes; a cr. parting this & land late Col. Brone (Browne ?). &c; 13 May 1673, p. 451. Part of 300 acs granted him, 11 Jan. 1652, & now renewed.

FRANCIS RADFORD, 93 A., 2 R., 8 P., Henrico Co.; N. side James Riv., 13 May 1673, p. 451. On line of the Orphans of Garrett, at the Roundabout; on John Browne, & his own land, &c. Trans. of 2 pers: Richard Gerrard, John Milner.

JAMES TRICE, 226 acs., New Kent Co., adj. Mr. John Winsloe; Capt. Thomas Ramsey, &c; 13 May 1673, p. 451. Trans. of 3 pers: Robt. Bristow, twice; & "a woman died at Sea."

JOHN DUKE, 486 acs., James City Co., E. side of Chickahominie Riv., 13 May 1673, p. 452. N. W. upon Tyascun Sw., adj. land formerly Wm. Dormer's; on lines of David Newell; Robert Hubert, &c. Trans. of 10 pers: Phill. White, Tho. Wright, Jno. Amey, John Haley, John Vordale, Wm. Bell, John Pocamow (or Paramore), John Wilkison, Nich. Baldrin, Mar. More.

BARTHO. OWEN, 648 acs., Surry Co., 14 May 1673, p. 452. On S. W. side of John Chewakins Sw., & upon Mr. Corker. Granted to John Vincent, deserted, & now granted by order, &c., 20 Sept. 1671. Trans. of 13 pers: Robt. Prouse, Mary Ransome, William Taylor, Robert Greene, Tho. Wilkins, Tho. Taylor Ann Stock, Elinor Edwards, Sym. Corlile; "for Importation of himself."

HEN. RANDOLPH, 244 A., 3 R., 8 P., at the head of land surveyed for John Strudivant (Sturdivant?); 17 May 1673, p. 452. Granted to John Gillam, 5 Sept. 1663, deserted & granted sd. Randolph 21 Sept. 1671. Trans. of 5 pers: Geo. Huntt, Law. Pitt, Eliz. Gurton (or Garton); Tom & Maria Negroes.

WM. WILSON, 300 acs., Low. Norf. Co., at the head of a br. of Eliz. Riv., 28 Mar. 1672, p. 453. Granted to Rich. Jones 28 Apr. 1665, deserted, & now granted by order, &c. Trans. of 6 pers: Mathew Bently, Rich. Fortice, Jno. Oliver, Robert Greene, Thos. Swann, Eliz. Stafford.

WM. THATCHER, 434 acs., Lancaster Co., N. side Rappa. Riv., 9 May 1673, p. 453. Adj. Mr. Thomas Haynes; Wickacomico Path; Col. Carter; Walter Heard, &c., to Pewem's popler, &c. Trans. of 9 pers: Edw. Huntly, Wm. Batting, Tho. Collins, Robt. Broome, Ann Hall, Jacob Stanford, Joane Howard, John Wigmore, Elias Lane.

THO. RYLAND, 120 acs. Gloucester Co., in Kingstone Par., 23 May 1673, p. 453. Beg. at cor. belonging formerly to sd. Ryland; adj. Caleb Helder; Major Robt. Bristowe, &c. Trans. of 3 pers: Alice Ryland, Tho. Rush, Rich. Lake.

EDWD. MATHEWES, sonn of Edwd. Mathewes, dec'd., 1536 acs., Henrico Co., on N. side of James Riv., 26 May 1673, p. 454. Near the head of a Deep Bottome on W. side of the 4 Mi. Cr., nigh a path, below the Wading place; to a br. of Grindall's run; to John Lead; on division bet. Tho. Ludwell, Esqr., Secretarie, & Capt. Mathewes, &c. 600 acs. granted to Mr. Walter Aston 20 Dec. 1651, who sold to Mr. John Dibdell, who sold to Ellis Else, who sold to Jno. Waterridge; & by Robt. Wild, who married the relict & admx. of Wateridge, sold to Capt. Edwd. Mathewes, his father. The residue for trans. of 19 pers: John, Elizabeth, Mary, Sarah, Joseph, & Wm. Fisher; Mary Drury, Sarah Carter, Wm. Fisher, Wm. Flesh, Ruth Hewanno (?), Wm. Fisher, James & John White, Tho.

Edmonds, Rich. Foster, Wm. Bridger, Jno. Lad, Rich. Tunstall.

JAMES AKIN & RICHD. WO-MACK, 335 acs., Henrico Co., N. side Appamattock Riv., 26 May 1673, p. 454. At the head of Tho. Wells; to Flinton's run, &c. 250 acs. granted sd. Akin 20 Oct. 1665; 85 acs. due them for trans. of 2 pers: Phillip Childers, Ann Dally.

ELIZABETH LANG (Lange), Relict of Peter Lange, ELIZABETH & JOANE LANGE, daughters to sd. Peter; 400 acs. N'ampton Co., 27 May 1673, p. 455. Granted sd. Peter, & escheated by inquisition, &c. under Col. Jno. Stringer, Depty. Esch'r., &c., & now granted sd. Elizabeth & her 2 daughters, &c.

ROBT. BAGGBE (Baggby), 80 acs., New Kent Co., 27 May 1673, p. 455. Beg. at his own land, on N. side of Matapanie Riv; Adj. Mr. Lockie, &c. Trans. of 2 pers: Samll. Hoskins, Thomas Else.

SAME. 100 acs., Same Co. & page, 28 May 1673. N. side sd. Riv., adj. George Wesren (Weston); Sir Grey Skippwith; & Mr. Geo. Chapman. Trans of 2 pers: Wm. Warrington, David Randoll.

THO. MOSEIER (Moyser-Moyseir), 1100 acs., in up. part of N'ampton Co., neare *Gingotake;* on a br. of Gingotake Creek; 27 May 1673, p. 456. 650 acs. granted Jno. Wallop 9 Oct. 1672, & assigned to sd. Moyseir; 450 acs. for trans. of 9 pers: Eliz. Mantoone, John Tanner, John Jacob, Wm. Upton, Thom. Eliot, Andrew Were, Jno. Eldish, Ja. Wakefeild, Eliz. Andrewson.

MATHEW SHIPP (Ship), 400 acs., Low. Norf. Co., being a neck whose point shoots against the uper landing of the North River; 27 May 1673, p. 456. Trans. of 8 pers: Edw. Smith, Jno. Smith, Jno. Spratt, Tho. Richardson, Marie Fox, Edw. Stiles, Eliner Hall, Ja. Coleman.

JOHN LADD, 700 acs., Low Norf. Co., Linhaven Par; on both sides of Linhaven Riv., & on Beaver Dam Cr;

27 May 1673, p. 456. 600 acs. granted Mr. Edw. Hall 30 June 1661; 300 acs. of which he assigned to Savell Gaskins, 16 May 1667, & by Job Gaskin, his sonn & heire, assigned to sd. Ladd 10 May 1671; 300 acs. part of sd. 600 acs., assigned 5 Jan. 1663 by sd. Edw. Hall to Roger Fountaine, who assigned, 28 Aug. 1665, to Jno. Boring, who, 11 Oct. 1670, sould to sd. Ladd; 100 acs. for trans. of 2 pers: James Kines (or Kirnes), & Tho. May.

HEN. SMITH, 2600 acs., N'ampton Co., adj. *Oken Hall Land:* 27 May 1673, p. 457. At Ewemus' (or Eresmus') branch, at land of sd. Smith; along Morris Liston, &c. Trans. of 52 pers: Miles Feilding, Ja. Trowton. Jno. Cracherly, Ja. Mittus, Jno. Lovelock, Mathew Steele, Marg. Welch, John Moore, Robt. Hommens, Jam. O'Keley (or Oreley), Jane Lewis, Ann Eaton (?), Jane Brookes, Rich. Dawloop (?), Tho. Lasingby, Tho. Lynn, Marg. Mosses, Edgar Lauderell, Geo. Outrell, Edw. Domstall, Rich. Beare, Joane Smith, Rob. Long, Ann Lazing, Eliz. Abott, Grace Powell, Rebecca Wigge, Merideth Evans, Jno. Hereford, Wm. North, Tho. Clarke, Robt. Borrington, Josa. Rownder, Adam Finch, Morgan Jones, Tho. Willy, Ann Willy (or Wiley), Nehi. Black, Hen. Robts. (Roberts), Miles Roxell, James Roxell, Rich. Webster, Tho. Bossinton, ——— Pembrooke, Edgar Oxley, Rich. Wiggon, Geo. Roe, Reb. Townsend, Uriah Cuenin, (?) Grace Cuenin (or Cudrin), Jno. Brookes, Xper. Roberts.

JACOB JOHNSON, 600 acs., Low. Norf. Co., at a br. of little Cr., in Linhaven Par., 27 May 1673, p. 457. Adj. Mr. Guggins; Lt. Col. Addam Thorowgood; &c. 400 acs. part of 500 acs. granted Robert Hayes 22 Nov. 1648, & by Nathaniell & Addam, his sons, sold to Mr. Symon Cornix, dec'd, & by Wm. Cornix, his sonn & heire, sold to Mr. Robt. Bray, who sold to sd. Johnson; 100 acs. granted Rowland Morgan 8 Nov. 1651, who sold to Wm. Fann, who sold to sd. Johnson, & by him sold to Mr. Symon Cornix, whose son Wm. sold to sd. Bray, who sold to

Johnson; 100 acs. for trans. of himselfe twice.

FRANCIS SHIPP, 550 acs., Low. Norf. Co., being a neck made by the turnings of a Cyprus Sw., 27 May 1673, p. 458. Trans. of 11 pers: Jacob Johnson, for transporting himselfe 4 tymes; John Symons, Tho. Burnett, Jonathan Garnett, ——— Burfeild, James Kir' wood, Rose Russell, Sara Owin.

BENONIE BORACE, 994 acs., Low. Norf. Co., in Linhaven Par., on Bennett's Cr., 27 May 1673, p. 458. On N. side of land formerly Addam Thorrogood's: beg. at Needam's Marsh neer Tho. Davis' fence; to land that was Mr. Guggins', land that was Mr. Lambert's; to land formerly sd. Thorowgood's & now Wm. Smith's; &c. 944 acs. granted him 30 Oct. 1671; & 50 acs. for trans. of: Tho. Ivy.

JOHN TAYLOR, 34 acs., Accomack, called *Watts Island,* S. of *Watts Gr. Is.,* by some called *Gabriell's Is.;* 27 May 1673, p. 458. Trans. Tho. Ivy the 2nd tyme.

RICHD. FOUNDER, 100 acs., Low Norf. Co., at Little Cr., bet. a br. o same on the E., & the line comonl: called Mr. Thorrogood's Grand Pattent on the NW., adj. land formerly Robt Hayes on S., it being the land he lives on; 27 May 1673, p. 458. Trans. of 2 pers: Jno. Lestrange, Wm. Arton.

WM. WEST, 400 acs., Low. Norf. Co., neer the north Riv., on W. side of a ~r. Poruoson; 27 May 1673, p. 459. Trans. of 8 pers: Jno. James, Peter Norton, Wm. Neeve (?), Robt. Wills, Abraham Johnson, Jeffry Ayres, Alice Moone, Wm. Duke.

FINLAW MACKWILLIAM, 400 acs., N'ampton Co., at the head of a freshwater br. of Hunting Cr., adj. land formerly Wm. White's; on Gargaphia Path; &c. Trans. of 8 pers: Jno. Ayers 8 times.

JOHN WALTHAM, 700 cs., N'ampton Co., N. side of Accohanock Cr. adj. Rich. Vahan; Rich. Kellum; &

Rich. Bayly; 27 May 1673, p. 459. 450 acs. granted him 15 Sept. 1649, 250 acs. for trans. of 5 pers: Robt. Davis, Edw. Broadway, Rich. Lewis, Geo. Youngman, Robt. Youngman.

WM. BENSTON, 300 acs., N'ampton Co., on S. side of a S. br. of Anancock Cr., parting this & Tho. Letherbery's 1200 acs; a br. parting this & the plantation formerly in possession of John Dye, now claymed by sd. Letherbery; 27 May 1673, p. 459. Trans. of 6 pers: Eliz. Gord, Jno. Semans (?), Joseph Heard, Hen. Lange, Peter Lapthorne, Geo. Trais (?).

ISAAC DICKS (DIX), 1000 acs., N'ampton Co., being a neck bet. 2 brs. of Nuswatocks Cr., 27 May 1673, p. 460. 400 acs. granted to Mary Lewis 12 Sept. 1664, deserted, & now granted by order, &c. Trans. of 20 pers: Jno. Husbands, Peter Pagett, Hugh Vines, Tho. Davmard, Tho. Baggell, Law. Attkins, Wm. Bunn, Anth. Denis, Jno. Barber, Barth. Cooke, Geo. Sharpe, Rich. Peirce, James Tucker, Peter Waade, Tho. Holdman, Jno. Glagdon, Tho. Preist, Jane Cleverdon, Jno. Crowg (or Croney), Wm. Younge.

GEO. PARKER, 374 acs., N'ampton Co., at *Pungat,* on SW side of Pokomock Cr., adj. land of John Williams; land formerly Nich. Wadalow's; & land of Antonia Johnson, Negro; 27 May 1673, p. 460. 100 acs. granted to Francis & Mary Vincent 20 Mar. 1660 & by one of them her moyety assigned to the Husband of the other & by the other & her husband; sd 100 acs. assigned to Wm. Chase, who assigned to sd. Parker; 274 acs. for trans. of 6 pers: Anth. Price, Fra. Sittering (or Littering), Jno. Dorgon, Geo. Hellard, Mary Heard, Jno. Deckan.

RICH. KELLUM, 1000 acs., N'ampton Co., on N. side of Accahanock Cr; adj. Mr. Jno. West; & Rich. Bayly; 27 May 1673, p. 460. 850 acs. granted him 9 Nov. 1666; 150 acs. for trans. of 3 pers: Eliz. Teag, James Varnett, Tho. Bellarmin

SAME. 1850 acs., same Co., & date, p. 461. At Matchapungo Cr., 400 acs.

granted to Jno. Ewens 11 Mar. 1655, & sold to sd. Kellum; 400 acs. granted sd. Kellum 26 Mar. 1662; 900 acs. granted him 10 May 1664; 150 acs. being surplus within the bounds, & due for trans. of 3 pers: Phill White, Jane Patten, Kath. Mayes.

WM. HARPER, 100 acs., N'ampton Co., on the easterne shore; 27 May 1673, p. 461. Granted to Mathew Wardall, & escheated by inquisition, &c., under John Stringer, Depty. Esch'r. &c; now granted &c.

ROBT. LAWRANCE, Junr., 600 acs., Nansemond Co., by a Beaver Dam Sw., 28 May 1673, p. 461. Trans. of 12 pers: Aron Loveringe, Stephen Hicks, Wm. Wickall (or Nickall), Peter Humphrys, Eliza. Hales, Susan Elliott, Arthur Figgs, Tho. Bagnall, John Belson, John Peare, Henry East, Tho. Kendall.

CHRISTOPHER T H O M S O N (Thompson), 800 acs., N'ampton Co., neare Matomkin, adj. lands of Isaac Dix; Geo. Watson, Hickman; Laurence Robinson; Finlaw Mackwilliam; & Tho, Lewis; 28 May 1673, p. 461. Trans. of 16 pers: Tho. Tarris, Jane Browne Tho. Talye, Rich. Kelly, Hen. Flowers. Jno. Munrow, Jno. Currin, Fra. Tally Nich. Baskewell, Tho. Cox, Jno Browne, Wm. Wayne, Geo. Peirce, Oliver Haley, Wm. Poyle, Edm. Kelly

SAME. 600 acs., Same Co., date, & page. At Matomkin; called the Great Neck; at the head of Nuswatox Cr., bet. 2 branches: one parting this & land of Isaac Dix, & the other on land of Wm. Marshall; Trans. of 12 pers: Andrew Dent, Jno. Lewis, Jno. Pearse, Tho. Wood, Jno. Jeffers, Rich. Cooke, Charles Agard (?), James Cotton, Ja. Banny, Ja. Oldcastle, Alex. (or Alice) Oakland, Jane Taylor.

RICH. BONNE, 1300 acs., Low. Norf. Co., including the Vally (?) Quarter & part of Cow Quarteridge; 28 May 1673, p. 462. Trans. of 26 pers: Jno. D'Jane, Jno. Matetoone (?), Eliz. Tam, Robt. Trayle, Wm. Russell, Eliz. King, Tho. Vince, Edw. George, Jeff.

Beake, Hugh Ofirgison, Hugh Crooke, Penolepe Cane (or Cace), Thrustan Mayo, Jno. a French boy; Patrick a Irish boy; Hannah Vincle (?), Ja. Hartlesse, James Morrill, Tho. Rustell, James Ashton, Sarah Hulling, Nich. Lackland, Jno. Butter, Edm. Baskey, Jno. Harris, Tho. Reignold.

DEARMAN MACKELL, 100 acs., Low. Norf. Co., neare Rudee; bet. the salt ponds & the sand banks; 28 May 1673, p. 462. Trans. of 2 pers: Tho. Deane, Tho. Bench.

JNO. FRIZLE, 100 acs., Low. Norf. Co., to the N'wd. of Rudee; adj. Dearman Mackele; 28 May 1673, p. 462. Trans. of 2 pers: Owen Wiles (or Wilis), Brigett Jerome.

RICHARD JONES, 240 acs., Eliz. City Co., 30 May 1673, p. 462. 147 acs. adj. Rich. Allen; & Rich. Thomas; & neere the Drinking Place; 93 acs. adj., part of a greater patt. of Major Tho. Cely, who sold to sd. Jones. Trans. of 3 pers.*

THO. BARBER & SAM OUSTIN, 4000 acs., New Kent Co., S. side Mattaponie Riv., 15 May 1670 p. 463. Neere Mr. Hen. White; & adj. John Talbott. 1000 acs. purchased of Col. Manoring Hamond, heire to Fra. Hamond; 3000 acs. being surplus, &c., & due for trans. of 60 pers.*

HEN. CORBYN, ESQR., 1959½ acs., Rappa. Co., on S. side & in the freshes of sd. Riv., 8 July 1673, p. 463. Adj. Prosser & Creighton on upper side of Swann Cr., over brs. of Weire Cr., adj. his own land called Naemcock. 725 acs. granted to Tho. Ballard, Esqr., who sould to sd. Corbyn; 1234 acs. for trans. of 23 pers: Eliz. Homes, Jane Holmes, Rich. Randall, Jane Wilson, Ann Richardson, Rich. Ware, Pred. Reynolds, Rich. Powell, Eliz. Robinson, Geo. Springfeild, Jno. Gascoigne, Adam Theo., Walter Tompson, Tho. Hilton, Elinor Julyan, Eliz. Mathes, Ann Warberton, James Dier 2, Eliz. Wormell, Arthur Mitchell, Robt. Williams, Zach Newman, Stephen Hunt.

COLL. JOSEPH BRIDGER, 432 acs., Surry Co., adj. Phillip Huniford on E. side of the 3rd Sw. of the Blackwater; Capt. Cockram & Capt. Barham; 18 July 1673, p. 464. Granted to Wm. Porter 11 Aug. 1667, deserted & now due for trans. of 9 pers: Hester House, Eliz. Sidney, Tho. Baker, Mary George, Abra. Evans, Wm Browne, Mary Woodard, Eliz. Sutton, Tho. Snow.

WARWICK MOHUN, 350 acs., New Kent Co., upon brs. of Black & Mattadqun Crks., adj. Charles Bryan; Rowland Horsely; 8 July 1673, p. 464. Trans. of 7 pers: James Mason, Andr. Banckes, James Huchins, John Cawdwell, Eliz. Cramer, Tho. Jordan, James Terrick (or Terruk).

JOHN CORPORYON (or Corporyou), 100 acs., Low. Norf. Co., in Linhaven Par., 14 July 1673, p. 464. Bet. E. & S. brs. of Eliz. Riv., adj. David Murrow; Michaell Meckay; & land of the Whitehusts. Trans. of 2 pers: Elinor Edwards; a Trumpeter.

JOHN CORPREW, 500 acs., Low. Norf. Co., 14 July 1673, p. 464. By Ridgeford Sw. on the head of the S. br. of Eliz. Riv., at a place called the Beare Spring; Trans. of 10 pers: Elinor Dike, Daniel Sulivant, Jno. Norris, David James, Daniell Persons, a Dutch body, Wm. Paugborne; 3 Negroes.

JOHN GORING, 974 acs., Surry Co., 1 July 1673, p. 465. 574 on E. side of the Greene Sw., along Mr. Awborn's land, &c; granted sd. Goring 8 Aug. 1670; 400 acs. granted Charles Amry, who assigned, &c; trans. of 8 pers: Edw. Amry, twice; John Towers, Tho. Walker, Wm. Rickitts, Eliz. Odioum, Charles Amry, twice.

JOHN WILLIAMS, 444½ acs., Low. Norf. Co., S. side Daniell Tanner's Cr; adj. Abraham Ellett & Richd. Joanes; his own, & land of Wm. Cooper; 24 Aug. 1673, p. 465. Trans. of 9 pers: Phillip Hamblin, Robt. Halsey, John Dunn, Henry Ewbance, Christopher Fleming, Edw. Becheler, Jno. Butler, Tho. Tripla, Willm. Callup.

EDWARD FOLLIOTT, 1700 acs., New Kent Co., N. W. side of the main br. of Ware Cr., 12 July 1673, p. 465. Beg. by Rickahoc Path; nere path to Tho. Mattins; by the Roade to *James Towne*, &c. Surveyed in name of Mr. Edwd. Overman for 1000 acs., 9 Nov. 1652, & assigned to sd. Folliott; 700 acs. found within, &c. Trans. of 14 pers: Danll. Renist, Wm. Owen, Jane Knowles, Pet. Stubbins, Lion. (?) Cocks, Wm. Raveale, Jer. Farland, Susa. Lewis, Eliz. Fenuson (or Fennson), Ollive (or Allice) Beate, Jno. Carlett, Ja. Wood, Wm. Fenton, Hen. Lemmon, Mary Nickolls.

CAPT. SOUTHEY LITTLETON, 2800 acs., N'ampton Co., at Nandin (or Nandui) Cr., on the main Bay of Chesepiake; on Arracocke Cr., a br. parting this & land formerly Geo. Trewett's; includ. *Cherry Island;* 7 Oct. 1672, p. 465. 2340 acs. granted him 25 Mar. 1656; renewed 26 Nov. 1661; 200 acs. granted John Wise 24 Mar. 1655; renewed 20 Oct. 1661, & sold to sd. Littleton 16 Sept. 1672; 260 acs. for trans. of 6 Negroes: Long James, Black Jack, Paul, Jone, Johannocke, & Congo.

PARISH OF WESTOPHER, Chas. Citty Co., 93 A., 1 R., 8 P., on N. side James River, for a *Gleabe;* 8 Aug. 1673, p. 466. Beg. at a bottome parting Capt. Southscott & this survey, along the Riv. to extreame of bottom next Mr. Bland; to head of the Hogpen bottom, &c. Due sd. Parish for trans. of 2 pers.*

JAMES WESHARD (Wishard), 200 ac., Low. Norf. Co., nere the pyne Neck Dams of Little Cr., adj. Ann Bennett, neare the High Roade, &c; 8 Aug. 1673, p. 466. Trans. of 4 pers: Ambros Curtis, Nich. Huggens, Florence Carter, Willm. Griffin.

JOHN PORTIS & HEN. WEST, 900 acs., Is. of Wight Co., upon brs. of the Blackwater; adj. John Sherer; 25 Sept. 1673. p. 466. Trans. of 18 pers: Peter Viccaridge, Edw. Abdam, Danll. Jones, Ahrm. Burwicke, Sam. Starms, Math. Blake, Nora Cornelius, Eliz. Tucker, John Treven, Cornelius Tanner, Jno. Dalby, Richd. Herman, Eliner Beate

Abrm. Bradly, Joane Dorman, Wm. Charles; Isa. Horsham, Jane Clarke.

PHILLIP LUDWELL, TOBIAS HANDFORD & RICHD. WHITE-HEAD, 20,000 acs., New Kent Co., or S. side of Mattapony Riv., in *Pomunkey Neck;* 24 Oct. 1673, p. 467. Trans. of 400 pers.*

EDMOND SCARBROUGH, JUNR., 2350 acs., N'ampton Co., 13 May 1673, p. 467. On E. side of an old Indian feild; down Occahanock Cr., by the maine bay; on Craddock Cr., formerly called *Nondue*, &c. 2000 acs. granted him 12 Aug. 1649; & 250 acs. for trans. of 7 pers: Edmond Scarbrough 3 times Delila Scarbrough, (Ursila ?), Delila (Ursila) Sarbrough, Junr., Jno. Peirce, Robt. Lewes.

THOMAS WOODWARD, JUNR., 1600 acs., Is. of Wight Co., 5 Oct. 1673, p. 467. At mouth of a br. of the Blackwater; adj. Mr. Newman; Hugh Latimore, Tho. Tookes; Anthony Mathews; Edm. Palmer; Jno. Portis & Henry West; a br. parting John Sherer & Jno. Clarke from Mr. Sweete; &c. 1200 acs. purchased from Sweete's patt., Wm. Cooke's (or Tooke's) & a parcell of Sherer's land; 400 acs. for trans. of 8 pers: Paul Seise, Wm. Latten, Jno. Jackson, Jno. Richardson, Tho. Sannders (or Saunders), Tho. Waterton, Jno. Harris, Wm. Dunn.

MR. AMBROSE LOYD (Lloyd), 700 acs., New Kent Co., W. side of Assawaymanscott Sw., 4 July 1673, p. 468. Adj. Wm. Gosse (or Goffe), &c. 640 acs. granted to Mr. Anthony Haynes 5 Oct. 1658; assigned to sd. Lloyd as by conveyance in Warwick Co. Ct., 21 Jan. 1672; 60 acs. found within; & due for trans. of 2 pers: Martin Skiner, Jno. Barnett.

SAME. 650 acs., same Co., date & page. In the forke of Whorecocke Sw.; adj. Mr. Robt. Rowles' land bought of Mr. Martyn Palmer, neare main run of Assawaymanscott Sw., to land Robt. Baylye bought of John Pigg; to Mr. Lockye's line, &c. 500 acs. granted sd Haynes 5 Sept. 1658 & sold &c., (as

above); 150 acs. found within, & due for trans. of 3 pers: Tho. Vintner, Tho. Fletcher, Alexander Nash.

JNO. MOLTON (or MELTON), 400 acs., Up. Par. of Nansemond Co., 2 June 1673, p. 468. Adj. Jno. Poole & Walter Beasley (Bestey). Trans. of 8 pers: Richd. Long, Robt. Rollings, Christopher Wootten, Edwd. Spicer, Richd. Cheston, Wm. Edwards, Tho. Carpenter, Tho. Horecraft.

THO. BROOKES, 200 acs., Nansemond Co., 2 June 1673, p. 468. Adj. Jno. Odrum; 2 June 1673, p. 468. Trans. of 4 pers: Jno. Hewitt, Joane Glandfeild, Edwd. Erbury, Robt. Reynolds.

WM. BREEME, 600 acs., Nansemond Co., 2 June 1673, p. 469. Trans. of 12 pers: Jno. Graynes (or Grayves), Sanders Allen, Sanders Murrey, Jno. Burnham, Wm. Blare, Jno. King, Ja. Taylor, Tho. Hopkins, Tho. Thompson. Tho. Wright, Jno. George, Rivers Burr (or Furr).

AMBROSE BOSEMAN, 300 acs., at the head of Queen's Cr., a br. of the W. br. of Nansemond Riv., adj. Hugh Sanders & Jno. Moore; 2 June 1673, p. 469. Granted to William Smeley 5 Oct. 1667, & by sd. Smeley & Ellenor, his wife, sold to sd. Boseman.

FRA. SPIKES, 150 acs., Nansemond Co., adj. Jno. Taylor; Tho. Cowling; & Mr. Jno. Blake; 2 June 1673, p. 469. Trans. of 3 pers: Phebe Carver, Mary Yeoman, Jno. Belcher.

JNO. BALLARD, 300 acs., Nansemond Co., 2 June 1673, p. 469. Trans. of 6 pers: His owne person, & Besheba his wife, Jno. & Joseph his sons, Wm. Freeman & Jno. Napp.

HUMPHRY GRIFFIN, 200 acs., Nanzemond Co., adj. his own & land of James Younge; 2 June 1673, p. 469. Trans. of 4 pers: Lawrence Berry, James Cole, Fra. Cooke, Jno. Ingram.

CHARLES ROAN, 100 acs., Glouster Co., upon brs. of the Dragon Sw; adj.

Jno. Wittmore; & land supposed to belong to Col. Lee's children, &c; 20 Oct. 1673, p. 470. Trans. of 2 pers: Jno. Jones, Wm. Kellam.

JOHN GOODSON, 100 acs., Glouster Co., S. side the North Riv. Mill Run, adj. his own & Hen. Jeffs land; nere Goodson's Plantation, corner of Mr. Abraham Judson's Juarter, &c; 20 Oct. 1673, p. 470. Trans. of 2 pers: Dorothy Bywater, Jno. Jones.

DANIELL MACOY, 189 acs., Low. Norf. Co., E. side of the S. br. of Eliz. Riv., 23 Oct. 1673, p. 470. On N. side of the Little Cr., adj. Alexr. Rosse; & the Path that goes to old Butts; &c. 100 acs. granted to Tho. Hall. about 30 yrs. since, & by severall conveyances made over to sd. Macoy; 89 acs. for trans. of 2 pers: Geo. Ivey, Hanna Ivey.

MR. RICHD. JONES, Senr., 400 acs., Low. Norf. Co., by Bowman's Runn; 23 Oct. 1673, p. 471. Trans. of 8 pers: Elinor Harrington, Jno. Moss, Katherine Wood, Ja. Codder, Modling Burrow, Owen Dogharty, Nich. Gilline, Robt. Smart.

DENNAS MACOY, 160 acs., Low. Norf. Co., E. side of the S. br. of Eliz. Riv., 23 Oct. 1673, p. 471. 60 acs. granted to Tho. Everidge 10 Nov. 1649, & by severall conveyances made over to sd. Macoy; 100 acs. trans. of 2 pers: Tho. Jenkins, Jno. Chapman.

JNO. WALLIS, 330 acs., Low. Norf. Co., W. side of the S. br. of Eliz. Riv., at the mouth of Julians Cr., adj. Edwd. Davis; 23 Oct. 1673, p. 471. 200 acs. granted to Capt. Wm. Carver, part of 500 acs., 5 June 1659, renewed 4 July 1664, & sold to sd. Wallis 15 June 1666; 130 acs. trans. of 3 pers: Jsepher & Potter, Indian; & a Negro.

WARREN GODFRY & ISAAC BARRENTON, 204 acs., Low. Norf. Co., being part of the Ridge bet. the E. & S. brs. of Eliz. Riv; nere Anthony Benford; & adj. Evan Williams; 3 Oct. 1673, p. 471. Trans. of 5 Negroes: Bess, Sambo, Mingo, Jack, Betty.

THO. HANCKS, 264 acs., in Glouster & New Kent Co.'s; 23 Oct. 1673, p. 472. By Samuell Huckstep's branch & a br. in Peanketank or Dragon Sw., neere Jon. Stringer's Plantation. Trans. of 6 pers: Robt. James, James Buglasse, Mary Huttson, Wm. Smeton, Jno. Ward.

HENRY SPRATT, 1800 acs., Low. Norf. Co., 23 Oct. 1673, p. 472. Being a Neck in Curratuck below Tarrer's Cr., & Little Cr; Trans. of 36 pers: Himself 6 times; Tho. Rogers, Bridger Millcahy, Richd. Pledg, Tho. Nash; Cate, Grace, Jack, Little Jack, Indians; Hanna, Mereia & a child; Negroes; Jno. Chamberlin, his wife & child; Eliz. Carver, Rose Carver, "fine Nan," Richd. Pajne, Richd. Taylor (or Laylor), Edwd. Shoulder, Eliz. Garland, Mary Parr, Wm. Smith, Tho. Whittby, Wm. Jonson, Nich. Nicholson, Han. Spicer, Herman Maire, Cor. Johns, Paule Raniers (or Rainers), Peter Limhall.

MICHAELL FENTRIS, 450 acs. Low. Norf. Co., S. side of the E. br. of Eliz. Riv., 23 Oct. 1673, p. 472. Adj. Tho. Cartright, Wm. Nicklis, Evan William & Henry Nicklis. 300 acs. granted to Manasseth Porter 13 Jan. 1661, & descended to his brother & heire Jno. Porter, Senr., who sould to sd. Fentris, 28 Sept. 1672; 150 acs. for trans. of 3 pers: Wm. Elis, Eliz. Fookes; & 1 Negro.

JNO. THROWER, 100 acs., Low. Norf. Co., upon Col. Mason Little Cr., adj. Capt. Tho. Fulcher; 23 Oct. 1673, p. 472. Granted Tho. Ivey 22 Aug. 1648, & since his decease by Tho. & Geo., his sons, sould to Wm. Richardson, who sold to sd. Thrower.

ANTHONY LAWSON, 490 acs., Low. Norf. Co., at the E. br. of Eliz. Riv., neare Broad Cr., 23 Oct. 1673, p. 473. Adj. Mr. Wm. Mosley, Wm. Hancock; Mr. Fowler; Robt. Young; & Wm. Martin. Trans. of 10 pers: Himself twice, Jno. Baxter, Wm. Church, Garrett Really, Eliz. May, Wm. Cooke, Edwd. Stanley; Sambo & Marea Negroes.

THOMAS VICESIMUS IVEY, 620 acs., Low. Norf. Co., at the head of the

E. br. of Eliz. ʀɪv., 23 Oct. 1673, p.
473. 170 acs part of 200 acs. granted
Col. Jno. Sidney, who sould to Geo.
Kemp, & by severall assignments be-
longs to sd. Ivey; 450 acs. bet. sd. br.
& Samll. Bennett's Cr., adj. Wm. Han-
cock; trans. of 9 pers: Tho. Vicesimus
Ivey, Alice Ivey, Mary Ivey, Mary Edon,
Jno. Paine, Wm. Edwards, Grace Dunn;
1 Negro: & an Indian.

MORGAN MOORE, 135 acs., Low.
Norf. Co., S. side the E. br. of Eliz.
Riv., adj. Richd. King; & Tho. Watkins;
23 Oct. 1673, p. 473. 75 acs. part of
150 acs. ranted Hen. Nicklis, who
sould to sd. Watkins, who sould to sd.
Moore; 50 acs. granted sd. Watkins 5
July 1653; entered in the Treasurer's
office 15 Aug. 1661; & sould to sd.
Moore.

WM. WATKINS, 225 acs., Low.
Norf. Co., S. side of E. br. of Eliz. Riv.,
23 Oct. 1673, p. 474. 75 acs. part of
150 acs. granted Hen. Nicklis; by severall assignments due Tho. Watkins,
dec'd.; & due sd. Wm. as his heire.
150 acs. adj. Matha. Mathias; Wm.
Whitehust; Wm. Rogers; & David
Marro; trans. of 3 pers: Jno. Davis,
Griffin Gwyn, Robt. Dunston.

GEO. FOWLER, 550 acs., Low.
Norf. Co., in Linhaven Par., at the head
of Cornix Dam; adj. Moseley's land;
Wil. Hancock, &c; 23 Oct. 1673, p.
474. 150 acs. part of 750 acs. granted
Lt. Col. Tho. Lambert, dec'd., comonly
called *Puckett's Neck;* sould to sd.
Fowler by Lewis Bandermull, as marrying one of the coe-heirs of sd. Lambert,
8 Mar. 1669; 400 acs. for trans. of 8
pers: Edwd. Abbott, Grace Arnold,
Alice Ellis, Ann Stegg, Jno. Wells, Hen.
Selby; & 2 Negroes.

JAMES WHITEHUST, 400 acs.,
Low. Norf. Co., at the 3 runns of the
Easterne Ridges.; adj. Wm. Nicklis'
land; 23 Oct. 1673, p. 474. Trans. of
8 pers: Fra. Christopher, Amey Edcarr,
Hen. Gardner, Robt. Bowers, Peter
Riglesworth; & 3 Negroes.

LT. COL. PHILLIP LUDWELL, 400
acs., New Kent Co., on brs. of Hore-

cock Sw., upon the King's Road to
Piscattaway in sd. Co., according to
survey made by Capt. Wm. Clayborne;
adj. Mr. Tho. Brereton; Francis Craine
(?); & Wm. Ball. 22 Oct. 1673, p.
474. Granted to Giles Rogers, who sold
to Walter Carradine, who lost same for
want of seating, & now granted by
order, &c. Trans. of 8 pers: Jno. Lid-
cott, Jeffry Ames, Ann Creed, Tho.
Burridge, Jno. Tuttle, Jno. Wheatly,
Owin Loyd, Winifred Croy (or Cross),
Tho. Frizell. 1 Right due.

RICHD. SHAPLEY (Shapely), sonne
of Jno. & Mary Shapley, 130 acs.,
Glouster Co., in *Milford Haven,* 23 Oct.
1673, p. 475. Neare head of a cr. parting this & land of Rich. Long; by Guy
Knight, &c. Part of a devdt. granted to
Mr. Abraham English, who bequeathed
to his dau., Mary Shapely, & given to
her sd. sonne, his heirs & assigns forever; to ratifie which she hath caused
the sd. patt. to be drawne, which tract
was surveyed by the appointment & consent & in the presence of Richd. Long
& Mary Shapely, by Robt. Beverly, Sur-
veyer of sd. Co., in the presence of
divers witnesses.

MR. WM. ELLIOT, sonn of Lt. Col.
Anthony Elliot, dec'd., 340 acs., Glou-
cester Co., N. side of North Riv. Mill
runne; 23 Oct. 1673, p. 475. Neare
head of sd. runne belonging alsoe to
Mr. Peter Starling (Sterling), dec'd.,
adj. Mr. Richd. Bailie; on a br. of
Hoccaday's Cr; along Thos. Guant (or
Gaant); neere Mr. Iveson's Quarter; &c.
Trans. of 7 pers: Wm. Alexander, Wm.
Allen, Mathew Jones, Simon Stacy, Sara
Howard, Henry Herbert, Jno. Gibson.

WM. TAYLOR, 1000 acs., Accomack
Co., bet. Accohanock Cr. & *Matchapongo;* 25 Oct. 1673, p. 475. Adj. 500
acs. of Edwd. Hitchin & Bartho. Meeres;
land of Richd. Hill; 600 acs. of sd.
Taylor; lands of Arthur Upshott; trees
marked by Col. Scarbrough for Potts'
land; &c. Regrant of his patt. dated
30 Oct. 1669.

THO. HANCKS (Hanks), 500 acs.,
Gloucester Co., upon head brs. of Poropotank Sw., 23 Oct. 1673, p. 476. Beg.

at his own land; to Cha. Roane's line, neere the Roade; by Tho. Dawkins; & Lambert Moore; adj. Huckstep's land, xc. Due by patt. dated 8 Apr. 1663, part of which being surveyed away by a more ancient pat., & now on the other side augmented to make the same 500 acs.

JOHN SHAPELY (Shapley), 430 acs. Gloucetser Co., in the narrowes of Milford Haven, 23 Oct. 1673, p. 476. Beg. at *Hollowing Point* at mouth of 3rd Neck Cr., along the waterside of the Thorough faire from Mobjack Bay to Pianketank Riv., to cr. at the narrowes parting this & land of Peter Arrundell, by Jno. Guiton(?); by Jno. Gytont's line, to Jno. Guyton; to Tho. Putnam; to Guy Knight; to Mr. English, by Englishes' Cr., *alias* 3rd Neck Cr., &c. 300 acs. granted him 1 Oct. 1668; 80 acs. now surveyed & due for trans. of 2 pers: James Forland, Roger Peirce.

GUY KNIGHT, 423 acs., Gloucester Co., on Milford Haven & the W. branch, 23 Oct. 1673, p. 476. Nere head- of a br. parting this & land of Abraham English, dec'd.; by the haven or bay; to Tho. Putnam's land, & Jno. Shaple's land, &c. 400 acs. granted him 27 Aug. 1666; 23 acs. found within &c., & due for trans. of: Geo. Anderson.

NICHOLAS MILLECHOP, 400 acs., N'ampton Co., on NE side of the maine N. freshwater br. of Muddy Cr., adj. his own & land of John Parker; 25 Oct. 1673, p. 477. Sd. 400 acs. is all that can be found of his patt. for 550 acs. dated 9 Oct. 1672.

GRIFFETH SAVAGE, 700 acs., N'ampton Co., bet. the heads of Assawom brs. & Messango; adj. Capt. Daniell Jeniffer; Stockley's land, & 300 acs. of Nicholas Millechop; 25 Oct. 1673, p. 477. Trans. of 14 pers: Ambrose White, Jno. Fisher, James Roberts, Sara Jones, Hugh Butler Sara Jackson, Joane Smith, Wm. Miller, Mary Hall, Ja. Tomenson, Peter Harby, Roger Edwards, Jno. Townsend.

SAME. 230 acs. Same Co., date & page. S. side of N. br. of the forked brs.

of the Middle br. of Muddy Cr., adj. his own; Robt. Davis & Thomas Nickson's land. Trans. of 5 pers: Tobias Browne, Rachell Browne, Phill. White, Jane Puntin (or Purtin), Katherine May.

THO. GOODACRE, 125 acs., Low. Norf., on Saml. Bennett's Cr., bet. Rowland Morgan & Tho. Davis; 25 Oct. 1673, p. 477. Part of 500 acs. granted John Langfeild 10 Feb. 1637, & by sd. *Langstone* assigned to Will. East, who bequeathed to John Straton, & by Hen., his brother & heire, sould to sd. Goodacre.

JOHN AXTELL, 400 acs., Low. Norf. Co. to the S'wd. of *Roodee;* adj. Wm. Brock; 25 Oct. 1673, p. 478. Granted to Jno. Poore 25 Feb. 1664, who assigned to Richd. Bonny 15 Nov. 1665, & by him assigned to sd. Axtell 15 June 1666.

CHARLES RATCLIFF, 1300 acs., in Accamack, 27 Oct. 1673, p. 478. 600 acs. on N. side of Messangoe Cr., N'ly. towards *Pokomocke;* 700 acs. at the head of Crooked Cr. in Accamack; 500 acs. part of sd. 700 acs. adj. John Renney &c; 200 acs. part S. on sd. Cr. & adj. his own land. 600 acs. granted him 10 Sept. 1664; 700 acs., viz: 500 granted him 5 Apr. 1666, deserted, & by order &c. granted to John Kendall 12 Oct. 1670, assigned to sd. Ratcliff 6 Apr. 1672; 200 acs. granted Nicholas Layler, deserted, & granted sd. Kendall, & assigned as above.

PETER ARRUNDELL, 350 acs., Gloucester Co., in Kingston Par., in Pyanketanck Bay; 23 Oct. 1673; p. 479. Beg. at the mouth of a cr. at the narrowes of Millford Haven parting this from Jno. Shapely (Shapley), adj. Jno. Guyton (or Gayton), &c., a cr. parting this & Caleb Holder, &c. 200 acs. granted Jno. Coungden 1 July 1642 & now properly belonging to sd. Peter; 150 acs. now taken up & due for trans. of 3 pers: Rebecka Motly, Samll. Cox, Elias Robinson.

MAJOR ROBT. BRISTOW, 930 acs., Golucester Co., in Kingston Par., on NE side of Mobjack Bay, nere mouth of North Riv; adj. Tho. Ryland; & Mr. Tho. Preston; 23 Oct. 1673, p. 479. 700 acs.

granted Wm. Ap Thomas 16 Nov. 1652; renewed 28 Oct. 1662; sould to Capt. Tho. Todd, who sould to sd. Bristow; 230 acs. newly taken, & due for trans. of 5 pers; Wm. Fisher, Wm. Carter, Jno. Whetstone, Henry Charles, & Barnaby a Negroe.

MICAELL (Michael), KING, 600 acs., Nansemond Co., 18 Sept. 1671, p. 479. Granted to Robt. Brashure, dec'd., & escheated by inquisition, &c., under Mr. Wm. Alford, Esch'r. &c; now granted &c.

MR. JNO. NEWTON, 600 acs., Nansemond Co., 23 Oct. 1673, p. 480. Granted to Robt. Brashure, &c. (as above.)

HUGH LEE, 1374 A., 2 R., Chas. Citty, on S. side of Appomatock Riv., running to the Black Water, 28 Oct. 1673, p. 480. Trans. of 27 pers: Richard Cutson, Andrew Rudenford (?), Elizabeth Rugles, Francis Riggs, Jeremiah Hutt, John Burrage, Margett Edwards, Martha Hiatt, Simon Harrwood, John West, Katherin Fry, Hugh Lee, Ann Lee, Johan Davis, Tho. Williams, Hugh Lee 7 times, Elizabeth Downing, Elizabeth Downing, Will Downing his son and daughter, Mary Samper.

MAJOR FRANCIS EPES, 927 A., 2 R., 16 P., Henrico Co., N. side of Appomatock Riv., on Swift Cr., 27 Oct. 1673, p. 480. Trans. of 20 pers: · Paul Vandin, Clare his wife Richd. Flaskett, Rowland Peirce, Ann Wells, Peter Prior, Tho. Nickolas, Henry Clearke, Geo. & Marg. Browneing, Wm. Buroughs, Richd. Roberts, Richd. Edwards, Rowland Bell, Phill Ibell, Ann Darnell (or Darrell), Jno. Alworth, Cha. Woodhuston, Jno. Hobby, Jno. Highly (?).

HENRY BATTS & MR. JNO. STURDIVANT, 3528 acs., Chas. City Co., S. side Appomatock Riv., on 2nd br. of the Black Water; 28 Oct. 1673, p. 480. Trans. of 71 pers; Tho. Williams, John James, Richd. Dearelove, Wm. Dobson, Geo. Gee, Jno. Barlow, Jno. Tovey, Joseph Tovey, Ran. Birchinhead, Phill. Bowles, Chris. Hinton, Han. Barlow, Ja.

Cappoke, Kath. Huson, John Lee, Edwd, the Shomaker; Susanah Mallory, Edwd. Hanakin, Tho. Mallory twice; Griffeth Evans, Ja. Crewes 4 times; Wm. Hurdings, David Anderson, Patrick Jorden, Jno. Burgamed (or Burgained), Morice George, Ja. Marchant, Wm. Crowder, Mary Hust, Eliz. Dyer, Moll Browne, Eliz. Arnold, Wm. Barnnard, Jno. Steridge, Phill. Gledger, Tho. Holmes, John Thompson, Walter Gay, Robt. Turvon (or Jurvor), Jeffrey Nash, Theod. Moore, Dan. Carr, Hugh Griffin, Wm. Browne, James Atkins, Ja. Alder, Rich. Brise, Ed. Ladd, Robt. Haley, Hen. Bedford, Ja. Bradshaw, Wm. Barker, Godfry Wynn, Jno. Hughes, Gabriell Jones, Sus. Edwards, Prisscilla Lane, Mich. Tallman, Chris. Peike, Tho. Waller, Wm. Howard, (or Haward), Chas. Mason, Wm. Brett, Phill. Anderson, Rebecca Salter, Fra. Reynolds; Mingo a Negro.

HEN. FILMER, 360 acs., Warwick Co., 27 Oct. 1673, p. 481. Granted to Anthony Barnham, dec'd., & escheated by inquisition, &c., dated 23 Feb. 1666, &c., & now granted &c.

WILL. BOBBETT, 96 A., 3 R., 24 P., Chas. City Co., S. side Appomatock Riv., neigh Mr. Whittington; on Major Epes' line; & the Cattale Br., 27 Oct. 1673, p. 481. Trans. of 2 pers: John Lead, Richard Tonstall.

JOHN MAIES, 89 A., 23 P., Chas. City Co., S. side Appomattock Riv., at E'ly. end of the long slash, neigh Samuell Woodward; neigh Maies' tobacco field; along the gr. sw., &c; 27 Oct. 1673, p. 481. Trans. of 2 pers: Philemon Childers, Thos. Crompton.

MARTIN ELAM (Ellam), 453 acs., Henrico Co., S. side James Riv., on Proctor's Run; adj. Mr. Christopher Branch, &c; 27 Oct. 1673, p. 481. Trans. of 9 pers: Margaret & Michaell Whitty, John Stuard, Michaell Adkins, Edward Nellei (?); Mongo, Longo, Hongo, Ambo Negroes. (Marginal notation: 463 acres.)

WM. & MARY KENDALL, sonn & dau. to Wm. Kendall, 6000 acs. Acca-

mack Co., 27 Oct. 1673, p. 482. From
Crooked Cr., alongst Col. Edmund Scar-
burgh; to Mr. Henry Smith; W. by the
Ratcliffs' & Nicholas Layler; S. on Mes-
angoe Cr., lands of Robt. Johnson &
Germane Gilliott; to Mr. Jno. Stockly;
sd. land first sold by David Williamson
to Wm. Kendall, found to be deserted by
sd. Williamson, & on petition of sd.
Kendall, granted by order, &c. to sd.
Wm. & Mary, 18 Apr. 1670. Trans. of
120 pers: James Gerey, Fra. Obertson,
Ja. Ardis, Ja. Berkly, Jno. Wilson, Peter
Vicarige, Samll. Staren, Jno. Trever,
Oliver Beale, Wm. Charles, Edwd. Ab-
don, Math. Bleake, Corn. Tenner, Abra.
Bradly, Isaac Forsham, Danll. Jones,
Noah Cornelius, Jno. Dolby, Joane Dor-
man, Jane Clark, Abra. Barwick, Eliz.
Tucker, Rich. Harman, Bryan Dayly,
Water (Walter ?) Read, Edwd. Thomas,
Andrew Hambleton Tho. Jagby, Robt.
Wiggon, Jno. Smithers, Lettice Clark,
Tho. Ockford, Jno. Wilson, David Mak-
hane, Joane Dornan (?), James Tomson,
Alexr. Chambers, Robt. Hambleton, Tho.
Scott, Wm. Jones, Wm. Alarine (or
Alarme), James Garratt, Tho. Powell
(?), Eliz. Robins, Bryan Okeham, Cor-
nelius Harman, Wm. Russell, Jno. Dear-
ing, Wm. Batts, Ja. the Scotchman, Nich.
Nash, Samll. Tucker, Peter Gore, Geo.
Stanton, James Abraham, Tymoth, Steere,
Jaspar Ellett, Seth. Stevens, Mary Gore,
Alice Morgan, William Erbrack, Marg.
Best, Elinor Burrell, Dea. Minell, Geo.
Lucas, Eliz. Loyd, Jno. Stanford, Peter Lee,
Eliz. Watson, Jno. Keeper, Corn. Wallis,
Jno. Frost, Jno. Gabree, Jno. Knt.
(Knight), Edwd. Herdson, Xtopher.
Perkinson, James Brigstock, Robt. Francis,
Eliza. Nermore (?), William Hatten,
James Scott Joseph Ipson, Jno. Butter-
worth, Andrew Abegar (?), Wm. Hoperd,
Wm. Benefeild (or Berefeild), Jno.
Underwood, Eliza. Turfitt, Tho. Sanders,
Jno. Howker, Rich. Ridge, Anna Man,
Mary Greenwell, Joane White, Eliz.
Emma (or Ennus), Wm. Kreven, Ann
Poare, Wm. Ought, James Kerneston,
Thomas Lucas, Jno. Symson, Henry Haw-
ley, Mordica Evens; Patrick, Phillip,
Manuell (Note: surname not given)
Mary Tayler, Jane Kanere, Mary Makean,
Mary Lygon, Katherine Laird, Mary

Johnson, Agnes (or Aynnes) Sherer,
Wm. Bond, Samll. Tackfeild, Wm. Ab-
bott, Jno. Littler, Xtopher. Barrett,
Cornelius Andrewes.

GEO. FRESHWATER, 50 acs., N'ampton Co., 27 May 1673, p. 482. Escheat
land of Robt. Wardall, dec'd., Inquisition, &c. under John Stringer, Depty.
Esch'r., &c.

WM. HARPER, 100 acs., N'ampton
Co., 2 Nov. 1673, p. 482. Escheat land
of Robt. Wardall. (As above.)

CAPT. DANLL. JENIFER & Ann his
wife, lately called Ann Toft, 2350 acs.,
N ampton Co., 30 Oct. 1673, p. 483. Adj.
part of 2600 acs. granted said Ann Toft;
bet. 2 brs. of Muddy Cr., now called
Guilford; &c. to br. of Arathusa, form-
erly Keokotanck; towards Gorgaphie
Br., which lyeth next S'wd. to Gorgaphie
house, 200 acs. part of 2600 acs. granted
sd. Ann Toft 9 Oct. 1667; 2150 acs.
part of surplus within sd. bounds; due
by order &c. Trans. of 43 pers: Wm.
Mills, Wm. Prichard, Robt. Boyston,
Wm. Barrett, Alice Staples, Alice Alepp,
Jno. Powell, Gilbert Coalinge, Hugh
Eglstone, Cha. Hollingworth, Marryn
Cole, Tho. Poynder, Tho. Pecke, Richd.
Baker, Diana Mallery, Robt. Thwait,
Edwd. Bishopp, Robt. Dollyson, Tho.
Strange, Joane Quicksall, Jno. Durman,
Gyles Dowlass (?), Richd. Tatlock, Jno.
Alvon (or Albon), Mary Peircely, John
Luke, Dorras Grinsden, Joseph Ames,
Hen. Pecke, Jno. Maucke, Roger Wol-
ford, Richd. Niblett, James Sanson,
Honor. Rugg, Edwd. Brockhouse, Geo.
Russell, Margerett Martin, Rosse Gussiso
(?), Wm. Bromfeild, Dorothy Olive,
Jno. Waford, Martha Ellett, Hen. Gib-
bons, Sam, Poncey.

THO. WEBSTER 754 A., 1 R., 3 P.,
Henrico Co., N. side of Appomattock
Riv., 28 Oct. 1673, p. 483. 251 A., 28
P., granted him 20 Oct. 1665; beg. at the
old Towne Land; 76 A., 27 P., by second
fall of the Old Towne Cr. &c; 115 acs. at
the head of same, adj. Geo. Archer;
along the Old Towne Run &c., as by
patt. 7 Apr. 1671; 311 A. 3 R. 28 P. adj.,

beg. at land of Jno. Fowler; along Batt. Chandler; nigh the Indian Path, to mouth of the gr. branch, &c. Sd. lands granted by former pattents. 300 A., 1 R. 3 P. for trans. of 6 pers: Dermond Mack Daniell, Robert Lewis, Martin Paine, Elinor Norton, Jno. Langford, Edwd. Averrett.

TYMOTHY ALLEN, 681 A., 3 R., 24 P., Henrico Co., S. side James Riv., 30 Oct. 1673, p. 484. Bet. the head of Proctor's & the redd water, where they close; to the head of *Fearing pattent*, to Jefferson & Hancock's land, &c. 350 acs. granted Tho. Osburne 20 Aug. 1642, & by Tho. Osburne, his lawfull heire, sold to Essex Bevell & Tho. Grundy, last of July 1666, & by them sold to sd. Allen; 331 A., 3 R., 24 P., for trans. of 7 pers: Joseph Nottingham, Tho. Williams, Matthew Whittington, Jane Watts, Katherine Huckson, Fra. & Peter Martin.

FRANCIS WHITTINGTON, 1200 acs., Chas. City Co., S. side Appomattock Riv., at the head of Baylye's Cr., 30 Oct. 1673, p. 484. 900 acs. granted Tho. & Henry Batts, who sold to sd. Whittington; 300 acs. for trans. of 6 pers: Barth. Batts, Jno. Cumber, Robt. Mevill (?), Jno. Collins, Mary Mahanes, Elizab. Wood.

MR. JOHN PORTER, SENR., 3000 acs., Low. Norf. Co.; nere the Path from the E. br. of Eliz. Riv. to the North Riv., 28 Oct. 1673, p. 485. Adj. 300 acs. granted him 16 Mar. 1663; lands of James Whitehust; Wm. Edwards; the Ashen Sw., a Cyperus Sw. to Fra. Ship's land at the foote of Godfrey's runn; &c. Trans. of 60 pers: Joane Burch, Eliz. Stratford, Danll. Coalstone, Nich. Tyler, Ann Goedby, twice, Jane Jacobe, Eliz. Chamberlen, Lewis Coner, Jno. Tanner, Tho. Tunnell, Abigall Sellwood, Wm. Deridge, Jno. Molleene, Robt. Burgess, Rich. Blewett, Mary Owen, Wm. Painter, Rich. Holland, Jno. Lamplaph, Rich. Tolson, Mary Atkins, Tho. Dinto, Edw. Stanley, Hen. Juery (?), Ja. Fleig, Tho. Pickin, Cha. Gandy, Jno. Stroud, Ann Fisher, Jno. Weden, Patrick Kyte (or

Kyle), Ann Clarke, Cha. Belvin, Jno. Pearse, Corn. Mackenney, Tho. Winch, Samll. Palmer, Wm. Beverly, Hen. Blunden, Oliver Ozborne, Fra. Taylor, Ja. Cotton, Jno. Role, Robt. Crumpton, Jno. Ventris, Ja. Eveling, Jno. Low, Rich. How, Hen. Bainton Tho. Wankling, Will. Kub, Tho. Kent, Mary Petthouse, Peter (an) Indian; Doll, Mary, Besse, Mingo, Rose, Negroes.

JNO. FOWLER, 398 acs., Henrico Co., N. side Appomatocks Riv., 30 Oct. 1673, p. 485. 200 acs. adj. his own land; along the Old Towne run; 198 acs. on N. side of old towne Cr., neigh the Stony point, &c. Trans. of 8 pers: Jno. Baxter, Mary Peelam, Robt. C. . ., Tho. Wooles, Mary his wife, Paul Vandin (or Vaudin), Clare Vaidin, Ann Wells.

RICHD. WILLIAMS, 176½ acs., Low. Norf. Co., in Danll. Tanner's Cr., 29 Oct. 1673, p. 485. To head of the Little Cr., along land of Jno. Ozborne, &c. Trans. of 4 pers.*

CAPT. WM. BIRD, 1280 acs., on N. side of James Riv., 27 Oct. 1673, p. 486. Beg. on the River about a mile above the falls, N by E to a slash named *Woodards Labour;* &c. Granted to Col. Stegg 25 Jan. 1663, deserted, & granted to Wm. Woodard by order, &c., 10 Oct. 1670, who assigned to sd. Bird. Trans. of 26 *pers:* Ann Robyson, Eliz. Vauken, Tho. Mechell, Ann Bomly, Henry Capel, Eliz. Morten, Ja. Piggott, Robt. Martin, Rich. Archer, Abra. Law, Godfry Ragsdale, Walter Brokes, Bartho. Chandler, Tho. Boott, Ja. Hector, Joell Burgalle, Jno. Clengsen.

MARY, JOSEPH, EDWD. & MARTHA TANNAR, 650 A., 2 R., 8 P., Henrico Co., S. side James Riv., 30 Oct. 1673, p. 486. At the Middle Spring bottome; nigh Mr. Baugh; to mouth of *Hell Garden* Bottome, at the Landing, at the house, &c. 450 acs. granted Joseph Tannar, dec'd., 24 Mar. 1662, & given to his children, above-named. 200 A., 2 R., for trans. of 4 pers: Eliz. Rogers, Christ. Hatton, Math. Linsley, Norgs (?).

EDWARD BIRCHETT, 551 A., 32 P., Chas. City Co., S. side of Appomatock Riv., 31 Oct. 1673, p. 486. 351 A., 32 P., adj. Hen. Batts; & James Thweate; on the Blackwater, &c; 200 acs. adj. runn of Baile's Cr., &c., granted him 15 Mar. 1672; 200 acs. part of *Spring Garden Patt.* bought of Hen. Batts, as by records of *Bristoll Court* may appear.

GEORGE ARCHER, 1395 A., 3 R., 2 P., Henrico Co., in Bristoll Par., N. side Appomatock Riv., next above the *old town land;* 31 Oct. 1673, p. 487. For brcdth, running from the *Old Towne* at the mouth of Tonstoll's Neck, SSW along the Riv., to path at the Point Landing, below dwelling house formerly sould by Wm. Ridly to Jno. Mughett, directly as the Path now is, through the meddow to the foot of the hill, &c., to Maj. Wm. Harris; &c; 50 acres at the foote hereof & called *Tonstoll's Neck* where Mudgett formerly & Acher now liveth, &c; along Godfry Ragsdall; to Thomas Webster to the Old Towne Cr., &c; 784 A., 3 R., 10 P., granted sd. Archer 25 Sept. 1671; 387 A., 1 R., 32 P., purchased of Col. Tho. Liggon 27 Aug. 1673, as by records of Bristoll Court may appear; beg. on the river bet. a small Island on the W'wd. & a Gr. Island on the E'wd., at the head of a meddow, nigh Maj. Genrl. Wood, his marked trees of Fleets Land; nigh a Path to Old Towne Runn; over against the middle of the *Appomatock Indian Towne,* &c. 223 A., 2 R., bet. land pur- chased of Col. Liggon & the sd. Archer, makeing all to joyne; 223 acs. for trans. of 5 pers: William Fravills, Xtopher Jennings, Tho. Moore, Richd. Lead (or Read), Robt. Grimebey.

SUSANNAH HUFFLER, 200 acs., Low. Par. of Nansimond Co., 3 Nov. 1673, p. 488. Granted to Mr. Wm. Bur- bage & sould to George Sheares, dec'd; escheated by inquisition, &c., under Mr. Wm. Alford, Esch'r., 11 Aug. 1669, & now granted, &c.

THOMAS SCUTCHINS, 150 acs. in *Chuckatuck,* Nansemond Co., called by the Indian name of *Husquaking;* bet. 2 small creeks of Chucktauck Cr., adj.

Maj. Tho. Davies, &c; 3 Sept. 1673, p. 488. Granted to Richard Preston 22 Dec. 1636, who sold to Edward Keyser 19 Jan. 1645; the same day Gyles Webb, his Atty., assigned to Thomas Cliffe, who conveyed to sd. Scutchins 14 Oct. 1661.

THOMAS MERSER, 200 acs., in Pusell Poynt Cr., a br. of the S. br. of Eliz. Riv., 3 Oct. 1673, p. 488. Granted to Richd. Starnell, who sould to Mich. Waybourne, who sould to sd. Merser.

ROBT. LUCY (Lewcy), 1000 acs., Chas. City Co., S. side James River, on the Blackwater, at a place called *Saw Tree;* adj. Richd. Taylor; 3 Nov. 1673, p. 488. Trans. of 20 pers: Jno. Butler, Steph. Ryland, Phill. Jerman, Mary Sawer, Roger Poynton, Eliz. Strickland, Tho. Butler, Mary Doer, Susan Marsh, Richd. Combs, Riddy Ashday, Rob. Hyatt, John Derrell, Roger Mills, Wm. Walker, John Shelly, Prisscila Chena (?), Richd. Taylor, Ann Godfry, Richd. Taylor.

RICHARD TAYLOR, 1000 acs., Chas. City Co., S. side James Riv., on the Black- water; behind *Merchants Hope,* at a place called *Saw Tree;* 3 Nov. 1673, p. 488. Beg. at a swamp nigh the house, &c. Given him by will of Richd. Taylor, his father, 15 July 1672. (*Note:* The fol- lowing names appear hereunder:) Tho. Mayson, Pollidor Richd., Richd. Putman, Jo. Davis, Jno. Adams, Eliz. Seabrook, Hen. Roberts, Tho. Hudson, Oliver Davenport, Eliz. Wise, Ellen Faircloth, Aylse Asley, Anne Towsing, Richd. Staf- ford, Tho. Jones, Eliz. Herd, Wm. Hew- gille, Susan Fairbrother.

JOHN GAMMON, 500 acs., Low. Norf. Co., neare the parting of Ridgford & Cyprus Swamps; 4 Nov. 1673, p. 489. Trans. of 10 pers: James Gainerell (or Gamerell), Mary Creed, Jone Jennings, Pres. Dorrington, Mary Cooper, Math. Albots, (Abbots ?), Jno. Low, Elinor Nash, Lazras Jenkins, Theod. Taylor.

JNO. PROSSER & THO. PANNELL, 5200 acs., New Kent Co., bet. the maine run of Mattapony & Rappa. Riv; 4 Nov.

1673, p. 489. Trans. of 104 pers: Jno. Greene, Peter Himon, Mary Pym, Jane Drury, Simon Radford, Grace Hutchinson, Wm. Sampson, Tho. Dutton, Jno, Elkin, Francis Ticknor, Moses Ticknor, Francis King, Ezekiah Grigg, Jno. Peters, Sarah Hull, Tho. Cuff, Tho. Upton, Joane Thomas, Jno. Cushin, Jno. Duke, Alexander Frizell, Peter Smith, Restitute Jennings, Robt. Yeomans, Mary Richards, Jno. Franklin, Edith Staple, Tobiah Richards, Humphrey Lyddington, Jno. Thomas, Wm. Knight, Simon Williams, Mary Franklin, Jeremiah Pyborne, Tho. Addams, Geo. Dixon, Daniell Oneale, Anne Butcher, Sarah Turner, Wm. Patchell, Wm. Shippey, Jno. Smith, Ric, Duke, Ralph Elkin, Jno. Gale Tho. Churnell, Mary Simpkin, Patrick Lidumes Hugh Douding, Abigall Leviston, Jno. Temple, Sam. Broudribb, Ralph Eddleston, Jonas Arutcklie, Wm. Thomas, Tho. Butler, Jno. Lucie, Wm. Durrant, Simon Wilsford, Wm. Bush, Tho. Nicholson, Jno. Seegood, Geo. Cooper, Dorithy Readeing, Marg. Emett, Neald Cobley, Jno. Morrison, Tho. *Jno.* Jnoson, Austin Cobham, Jno. Clarke, Tho. Vickers, Jno. Whittnorth, Ric. Serrey, Tho. Lambert, Wm. Franklin, Wm. Cocke, Jno. Jnoson, Joane Pitts, Tho. Preston, Ed. Noble, Wm. Baker, Jno. Gray, Ralph Peck, Jno. Edwards, Ellinor Williams, Ann Wood, Rose Whitehead, Hen. Neidum, Tho. Hia, Edw. May, Tho. Osborne, Rich. Turner, Ann Stevens, Susanna Marshall, Anthony Jeffordson, Jno. Lewis, Adren Gardiner, Margaret Middleton Alice Simpson, Tho. Bradborne, Jno. Sinckler; & 3 Negroes.

THO. PANNELL, 2400 acs., Rappa. Co., S. side the Riv., about 3 mi. from same, on brs. of Occopace Cr., adj. Tho. Page; Bethl. Gilson; & Cornelius Noell; 4 Nov. 1673, p. 489. Trans. of 48 pers: Robt. Smith, Wm. Clarke, Wm. Newman, James Browne Geo. Tompson, Wm. Cooke, Jno. Turner, Jno. More, James Browne, John Walker, Tho. Newsom, Rich. Dun, Jno. Dennis, Robt. Bayly, Tho. Overy, Abbigall Smith, Wm. Butler, Tho. Crow, Ric. Coleman, Rich. Cooke, Antho. Edge, Rice Corbett, Wm.

Land, Wm. T..., Hen. Jones, Edmund Dobson. Ann Due, Tho. Dane, Wm. Alliott, Fran. Page, Jno. Stringer, Wm. Morris, Hum. Dale, Tho. Lack, Jere. Trent, Robt. Carr, Geo. Dawson, Nico. Hunt, Ralph Cole, Walter Curby, Roger Williams, Rice Legg, Antho. Ball, Natl. Cooke, Ann Baker, Elize. Staines, Dori. Simpson, Matilda Leele.

SIMON MILLER, 817 acs., Rappa. Co., in the freshes & on S. side the Riv., on the head of Pewamanesee Cr., adj. Cadw. Jones; lands of Talliaferro, Buckner, Prosser & Royston; 5 Nov. 1673, p. 490. Trans. of 17 pers: Eliz. Bryant, Jane Andrewes, Joseph Tooth, Ann Sucklin, Jno. Goose, Ric. Glover, Ellin Clarke, Hen. Smith, Wm. Ayliott, Tho. Dane, Wm. Dally, Geo. Suckett, Tho. Hudry, And. Rider, Hen. Rider, Dor. Brookes, Sarah Short.

JNO. BURTON & JNO. AUSTINE (Austin), 2172 acs., Rappa. Co., S. side the Riv., in the freshes, about 4 mi. back in the woods; adj. Jno. Bowsey; & by a br. of Nusaponnocks, &c; 5 Nov. 1673, p. 490. Trans. of 43 pers: Wm. Jewell, Jona. Turner, Sarah Lambert, Sarah Clarke, Jno. Jacus, Ric. Grimbell, Mary James, Tho. Worback, And. Gibson, And. Heart, Wm. Newman, Tho. Shory, Rach. Eldred, Antho. Davis, Alice Elliott, Fran. Amis, Tho. Jnoson, Eliz. Boateright, Antho. Addlstone, Tho. Andrewes, Jane Bullock, Jacob Allem, Tho. Buck, Joseph Piccus, David Thomas, Jacob Oldman, Jno. Smith, Ralph Goldman, Wm. Woodlad, Sarah Gifford Eliz. Kendall, Robt. Smith, Ric. Duncombe, Mary Andrewes. Jno. Williams, Wm. Tickener, Tmo. Tertman, Jno. Bates, And. Richardson, Amy Jnoson, Jane Ellin, Tho. Sosbie (?), Kath. Smith.

ROBERT BEVERLEY, 1500 acs., Gloster Co., S. side Pieanketanck Riv., neere Noakes' Plantation, adj. Mr. Robert Elliott, sonne of Anthony Elliott, dec'd., Conquest Wyatt; Geo. Harper; Hoccadaye's Cr., Cheescake Cr., & his own 500 acs.; 6 Oct. 1673, p. 490. 500 acs, granted 11 Oct. 1672; 1000 acs. for trans. of 20 pers: Jon. Ward, Jon.

Rivers, Robt. Clarke, Wm. Finnis, Anne Lister, Ann Barr, Jon. Arthur, Ann Herford, Tho. Harwood, Robt. Peters, Geo. Grave (or Grand), Rich. Long, Tho. Lewis, Tho. Mayes, Anth. Beale, Wm. Roberts, Robt. Molton, Geo. Diamond, Phill. Surgeon, Peter Russl. (Russell ?).

HENRY BENSON, 1071 acs., Rappa. Co., on S. side the river in the freshes above the falls; beg. at Jno. Bowzee; to Ewe tree Poynt by Motts' falling br., &c; 5 Nov. 1673, p. 491. Trans. of 22 pers: And. Hubbert, Ed. Andrew, Joane Willcocks, Antho. Harper, Jno. Watts, Jno. Gibson, Tho. Cole, Tho. Jnoson, Ellen Crump, Susan Harper; Tho. Burton, James Sharp, Ed. Dickason, Wm. Sterne, Sarah Baughan, Dor. Jenkins, James Scott, Jno. Jones, James Thorp, Jno. Triplitt, James Cooper, Sarah Simpkins, Ed. Ryly.

JOHN BOWSEY, 1465 acs., Rappa. Co., S. side & in the freshes of sd. Riv., on the head of Nussaponaxe Cr., 5 Nov. 1673, p. 491. Trans. of 30 pers: Ric. Jones, Jno. Croftes, Jane Hugall, Jno. Short, Jno. Gowrie, Sarah Smith, James Brench, Martha Clarke, Amy Crosse, Antho. Jackson, Sarah Heires, Alice Short, James Fisher, Antho. Jacob, Jno. Simpson, Sarah Joice, Silvester Jacob, Mary Jackson, Alice Gourden, James Gower, Alice Blake, Robt. Brimstone, Wm. Greene, James Tune, Susan More, Jno. Butch, Wm. Gowrie, Susan Jones, Leonard Gullock, Jno. Kendall.

SAME, 1668 acs., in the freshes & on S. side of Rappa. Riv., opposite the falls; adj. Capt. Laurence Smith in the line of Capt. Hawkins; land of sd. Smith & Anthony Buckner, &c; 5 Nov. 1673, p. 492. Trans. of 34 pers: Gilbert Hancock, Jona. Grantam, James Strong, Jno. Roberds, Ric. Groves, Jno. Gray, Grace Trent, Robt. Blissed, Abra. Jnoson, Jno. Sturrop, Mary Grantam, Geo. Robbins, Ric. Griffin, Rachell Groves, Antho. Fristoe, Jacob Massy, James Trencher, Ric. Hayes, Roger Smith, Sam. Cheney, Ram. (?) Nurse, James Foster, Sarah Winter, Jonat. Turner, Wm. (a) french-

man, Volen. (?) Ostler, Oliver Sergeant, Jesper Elvin, Ben. Finch, Jonah. Jervis, Sam. Johnson, Susan Turner, Xpher. Gosbin, Francis Wix.

CADWLL. (Cadwallader ?) JONES, 1443 acs., on S. side & in the freshes of Rappa. Riv., adj. Warwick Camock (Cammock); 5 Nov. 1673, p. 492. 625 acs. granted Symon Miller, who sould to sd. Jones; 818 acs. for trans. of 17 pers: Abra. Vintner, Sarah Cooke, Wm. Sanders, Tho. Page, Curby Clerke, James Heart, James Scott, Eliz. Giles, Mary James, Marg. Jenkins, Anth. Hanford, John Whitehead, Wm. Rider, James Nevett, Eliz. Byant, James Phillips, James Williams.

SOUTHEY LITTLETON, 1200 acs., N'ampton Co., 27 May 1673, p. 492. Escheat land of Robt. Barrington; inquisition under Col. Jno. Stringer, Depty Esch'r. &c.

ALEXANDER ROBBINS, 650 acs., Rappa. Co., upon brs. of Gilson's Cr., adj. Mr. Robt. Pley; 5 Nov. 1673, p. 493. Trans. of 13 pers: Wm. Gray, And. Jnoson, Jno. Street, Joane Glover, Wm. Clopton, Susan Hant James Druett, Jno. Jackson, Jno. Blunt, James Gyllett, Jno. Little, Ciprian Bishop, Geo. Birt.

THO. PARKER, 73½ acs., Rappa. Co., in Sittingbourne Par., S. side the River, adj. Robt. Gaines; & Wm. Moseley; 5 Nov. 1673, p. 493. Trans. of 2 pers: Robt. Sisson, Mary Sisson.

ROGER MICHAELL, 1500 acs., N'ampton Co., commonly called by the Indian name Romagstuck; on N. side of Onancocke Cr., running to a freshwater br. of Chickanessex Cr.; &c. to Ekeek's branch; 4 Nov. 1673, p. 493. Trans. of 30 pers: Hugh Martin, Xtoph. Gettings, Richd. Adkinson, Rowld. Savage, Jno. Edgcomb, Hen. Robts. (Roberts), Hugh Biscall, Jno. Rosko, Wm. Pendarvis, Jno. Arundell, Wm. Posca, Jno. Penross, Ja. Billet, Ja. Pradd, Richd. Rouse, Jno. Rush, Nic. Burlace (?), Tho. Trefy, Jno. Carusue (?), Richd. Pendarvis, Hanniball Bugin (?), Jno. Bouthen, Tho. Blaite, Hugh Courtney, Michll. Hill, Wm. Trevisa, Hen. Spurr; Ann & Geo., Negroes.

ROBERT BEVERLEY, 150 acs., Gloster Co., S. side of Garden Cr., 6 Nov. 1673, p. 493. Granted to Edward Lucas 17 July 1655, deserted, & since granted to Charles Hill by order &c., 15 Mar. 1658, & since claimed by Major Tho. Celie, but never seated; granted sd. Beverley by order &c. Trans. of 3 pers:' Wm. King, Isaac Steene, Ralph Armstead.

ROBERT HODGE, 280 acs., Low. Norf. Co., in Linhaven Par., on W. side of Saml. Bennett's Cr., beg. at the head of Cattayle br., 6 Nov. 1673, p. 494. 250 acs. granted Savill Gaskin 20 Oct. 1661, & sold to Wm. Hodge, 29 Oct. 1662; 30 acs. part of one Lancfeild's pattent, sould to sd. Wm., & the whole due sd. Robert, his brother & heire.

THOMAS PUTNAM, 333 acs., Gloster Co., upon brs. of Milford Haven; neere Mr. Richd. Long; adj. Jno. Guyton & Jno. Shapley; 23 Oct. 1673 p. 494. Due by his patt. dated 19 Apr. 1662.

ROBERT BEVERLEY, 920 acs., Gloster Co., upon Poropotanck Cr., 24 Oct. 1673, p. 494. 720 acs. on E. side of sd. Cr., beg. at the mouth of a br., dividing this & land of Oliver Green; to a br. dividing this & land of John Pate; &c; granted to Michaell Crafton 8 Oct. 1667 & sold to sd. Beverley; 200 acs. upon E. side of sd. Cr., adj. sd. 720 acs. & land of William Ginsey; granted sd. Crafton, deserted; granted unto Mr. John Pate, & deserted; granted to John Okeham 22 Mr. 1665 & deserted; granted sd. Beverley by order, &c. Trans. of 4 pers: Thomas Martin, Katherine Pawer (or Power), Joseph Poore (?), Mathew Tubb.

SAME. 150 acs., same Co. & page; 6 Nov. 1673. Bet. Garden Cr. & the E'most River. Granted to Jon. Hampton 14 July 1655, & deserted; to Charles Hill 15 Mar. 1658, & deserted; claimed by Maj. Tho. Celie, but not seated; now

granted by order, &c. Trans. of 3 pers: Thomas Bramley, John Lane, John Poland.

HENRY TRENT, 200 acs., Henrico Co., N. side James River, 7 Nov. 1673, p. 495. Beg. at Mr. Place, halfe a mi. from the river, at the head of Coleson's. Trans. of 4 pers: Charles Tyre Henry Trent, Margarett Rayes, Alice Sleek (?).

.HENRY SHEREMAN, 228 acs., Henrico Co. S. side James Riv., beg. at a sw. next to Peter Lee; 7 Nov. 1673, p. 495. Part of devdt., knowne by the name of Warwick, pattented by Capt. Mathew Gough, & escheated in name of sd. Shereman.

CAPT. JOHN SAVAGE, 9000 acs., N'ampton Co., 8 Nov. 1673, p. 495. W. upon Chisepiack Bay, E. upon the maine ocean, S. upon Cherryston Cr., formerly called Accomack Cr., N. on Savage's Cr., formerly called Wiscoponson. Granted to Hannah Savedge, 24 Aug. 1635; renewed 21 Nov. 1637; renewed 28 Nov. 1664 to the abovenamed, & due for trans. of 122 pers.,* & for trans. of 58 pers., whose names are mentioned under patt. to Col. John Stringer 13 Mar. 1661, who with Anne, his wife, assigned to sd. Savedge, 11 Aug. 1663.

MR. WM. DROMMOND, 461 A., 1 R., 4 P., James City Co., N. side James Riv., 19 Oct. 1674, p. 495. Bet. the Orphant of Edloe, & 700 acs., "belonging to the Orphant purchased of Young"; beg. at the Round about Sw., at the corner parting the Orphant of Math. Edloe & land of Capt. Hubert Farrell; to the Hoggpen Neck gutt; to Barker's House; down line of John Edloe, &c. Trans. of 10 pers: Robt. Farrar, Jno. Allen, Jno. Gammon, Geo. Row, Wm. Hearne Susan Chiles, Susan Cutts, Jno. Cresam, Wm. Michell, Lawrence Cewch; & Mingo a Negro.

WM. BLAKE, 300 acs., Accomack Co., on E. side of Capt. Southey Littleton's land at Accocomson; adj. Samll. Tayler; Col. Jno. Stringer; & NW towards Oake Hall Land; 7 Nov. 1673, p. 496.

Granted to Tho. Tunnell 30 Oct. 1669, deserted, &' now granted by order, &c. Trans. of 6 pers: Richd. Marriner, Phill. Wheeler, Sarah Miles, Jno. Wheler, Peter Watkison, Richd. Horchings (?).

ABELL GOWER, 501 A., 1 R., 24 P., Henrico Co., S. side James Riv., 7 Nov. 1673, p. 496. "Nigh the Swamp side neigh a Remarkeable Greate Stone", along Sheffeild's Sw., to Mr. Branche's corner, &c., 101 A., 1 R., 24 P., bought of Mr. Richd. Word at the date hereof, & belonging to Sheffeild's patt; 400 acs. for trans. of 8 pers: Richd. Word, Tho. Wood, Hen. Sherman, Jno. Homes, Tho. Hemings, Ewin Wricraft, Wm. Ballad, Isabell Walding.

MAJOR WM. HARRIS, 1202 A., 2 R., 4 P., Henrico Co., N. side James Riv., 7 Sept. 1671, p. 496. Beg. at the Middle Spring bottome, adj. Orphants of Tanner; Mr. Wm. Baugh; to the Ashen Sw., along the maine Sw., to the head of the Red Water, to the head of the Dry bottome, &c., adj. Tho. Liggon & Wm. Farrar, over mouth of the Ware bottome, &c. Trans. of 24 pers: Morgan Williams, Adam Rosse, Mar. Horgott, Mary Brone, (Browne), Tho. Deer, Wm. Blackman, Wm. Linney, Marg. Floyd, Ann Guy, Wm. Ascott, Ell. White, John Jones, Hugh Leading, Nich. Chiles, Mathew Allen, Wm. Butler, Jno. North, Nice. Moore, Edwd. Evans, Jno. Edwds. (Edwards), El. Manaclith Deborah Corey, Wm. Jones, Wm. Battersee.

WM. JERMAN, 300 acs., Accomack Co., S. side Menssongo Cr., 7 Nov. 1673, p. 497. 300 acs. granted Wm. Custis, deserted, & now granted by order, &c. Trans. of 6 pers: Robt. Harrison, Wm. Abram, Edmd. Wood, Kath. Worthon, Wm. Collins, Jno. Cardy.

JOHN ROGERS & JOHN LEWIS, 400 acs., Henrico Co., N. side James Riv., adj. Wm. Humphries, on E. side of the Mill Run; 7 Nov. 1673, p. 497. Trans. of 8 pers: Wm. Wilkins, Michaell Trencham, Edwd. Nicholas, Tho. More, Jno. Steward, Gerratt Warren, Nicholas ...., Will Richards.

WM. COOKE, 800 acs., Is. of W. Co., on 2nd br. of the Black Water; adj. Capt. Baker; & Wm. Myles; 10 Nov. 1670, p. 497. Trans. of 16 pers: Eliza. Beale, Wm. Langford, Peter Bedford, Jon. James, Richd. Ames, Jon. Vicars, Richd. Vicars, Mary Cooke 3 severall passages, Lettice Powell; 3 Negroes, John Beefe's wife & 1 Childe.

WILLIAM MACON, 100 acs., Nanzemond Co., 7 Nov. 1673, p. 498. Formerly granted to Henry Rey (a frenchman), who purchased of Anthony Oger (?); afterwards was in possession of Thomas Bullerd, who sold to sd. Macon; escheated by inquisition, &c., under Mr. Wm. Alford, Depty. Esch'r., 7 June 1670, &c.

ARTHUR FRAME, 500 acs., Accomack Co., att Hunting Cr.; upon land of Finlaw Mackwilliam & John Corey; 10 Nov. 1673, p. 498. Granted to Jno. Lewis 9 Nov. 1666, deserted, & granted by order, &c. Trans. of 10 pers: Alice Michell, Jno. Margritts, Richd. Robins, Stephen Avis, Dick Frigott, Long James, Paul, Johanock Jone, Congo, Negroes.

ROBT. DRAPIER, 50 acs., Yorke Cr., in Pocoson Par., adj. Edmd. Hudson, & his own dwelling house; 10 Nov. 1673, p. 498. Part of 200 acs. granted Edmd. Watts 29 Nov. 1637, who sould to Robt. Drapier, 9 Mar. 1653.

WALTER KIBLE (Kibble) & Margaret Kibble, son & dau. of Geo. Kibble, dec'd., 14 Jan. 1673, p. 498. 2500 acs. on the maine or Gr. Sw. or runs of Mattapony River; part of 6000 acs. granted Mr. Jno. Patte & Robett Beverly, 15 July 1669; 1500 acs. due by "assignment of their father in law Capt. Robert Beverly & by himself putt into this pattent," 1000 acs. for trans. of 20 pers: Tho. Humphry, Jno. French, Barbery Smith Geo. Tacker, Math. Tubb, Ann Kemp, Sarah Greene, Mary Salman, Daniell (an) Irish boy, Thomas Brantly (or Brambly), Lambert More, Eliz. More, Danll. More, Tho. Gowldin, Antho. Beale, Tho. Mertin (or Martin), Eliz. Pinck, Kath. Power, Joseph Pore, Will Roberts.

CAPT. ROBERT BEVERLY, 8200 acs. 24 Jan. 1673, p. 499. 7000 acs. on both sides of the Gr. Sw. or maine run of Mattaponié Riv., neere the Indian Path, from *Mattapony Indian Towne* to *Port Tobo. Indian Towne*, &c; 1200 acs. adj. same. 6000 acs. granted him 20 Apr. 1671; 1000 acs. pattented by sd. Beverly & Mr. Jno. Pate in a patt. of 6000 acs. 16 July 1669; 1200 acs. included in his patt. of a greater quantity, dated 20 Apr. 1670.

HOELL PRICE & JOHN UNDER-HILL, 3409 acs., 123 poles, in New Kent Co., on N. side of the main Sw. of Chickahominy; over Powhite Sw., to Powhite Path including an Island of 50 acs. &c; 20 Sept. 1661, p. 499.

COL. JOHN BLAKE, 450 acs., Nanse-mond Co., 25 Feb. 1673/4, p. 500. 100 acs. on the W. br. of Nanzemond Riv., on S. side some 2½ mi. up the br., adj. Geo. Ludlow; Fra. March, &c; 200 acs. adj. Tho. Babb; 150 acs. adj. Titus Car-line; Wm. Moore; Mr. Hen. Plumton; & Mr. Wm. Codogan, along line of *old battle*, etc.; 100 acs. granted sd. Babb. 12 Dec. 1641, sold to Johna. Robinson, who sold to John Battle, & by him sold to sd. Blake; 200 acs. granted Jno. Battle 14 Dec. 1653, & sold to Blake; 150 acs. added, due for trans. of 3 pers: Richd. Angell, Jno. Barber, Joane Wanell (or Warell).

SAME. 800 acs., on Mathewes Cr., a br. of the S. br. of Nanzemond Riv.; adj. Col. Tho. Dew; & Geo. Spyvey; same date & page. 300 acs. granted him 30 Oct. 1662; 500 acs. for trans. of 10 pers: Xper. Hoare, Mary Neale, Robt. Pom-prett, Fra. Lane (of Land), Jno. Hart, Wm. Edson, Tho. Eldridge, Jno. Jenkins, Jno. Jenkinson, Martha Wisdom.

MR. JOHN HAWKINS, 600 acs., Up. Par. of Nanzemond Co., 25 Feb. 1673/4, p. 500. Trans. of 12 pers: Tho. Pil-man, Tho. Good, Edwd. Solday, Mary, Rich, Hen. Evens, Ann Edwin, Mary Edwin, Tabitha Towers, David Price,

Edwd. Burson, Randall Barecott, Joane Wyatt.

COL. JOHN BLAKE, 1050 acs., in Mathewes Cr., a br. of the S. br. of Nanse-mond Riv., 25 Feb. 1673/4, p. 501. 400 acs. granted him 30 Oct. 1662; 650 acs. now added, due for trans. of 13 pers: Tho. Colling, his wife, 10 children, & Andrew Clayton.

COL. JOHN BLAKE 2000 acs., & MR. WM. CODOGAN, 1000 acs., Nanzemond Co., at a place called *Wick-ham*, hard by So. Key; 25 Feb. 1673/4, p. 501. Trans. of 60 pers: Edwd. Jones, Wm. Lewcorkell, Sarah Wake, Jno. Bell, Edwd. Samson, Aswit & Wm. Seagar, Wm. Hancock, Peter Colvin, Edwd. Kight, Tho. Asbridge, Jno. Mofatts, Tho. Browne, Francis Wood, Wm. Wilson, Eliz. Gilbert, Richd. Smith, Tho. Curt-ly, Wm. Scott, Edwd. Peckitt, Hugh Lewis, Edwd. Staller, Edwd. Rusell, Mar-gerett Butcher, Eliz. Focke, Jno. Barnes, James Swoyle, Wm. Fitcherbert, Richd. Samuell, Wm. Buckler, Tho. Hayward, Wm. Hickoson, Even Jones, Wm. Brocke, Tho. Dasse, Jno. Smith, Tho. Cullin 3 times, Jno. Cullin, & 20 Negroes.

JNO. BURNELL & EDWD. PIGG, 920 acs., New Kent Co., N. side Matto-pony Riv., adj. Tho. Hall & Jno. Pigg's 3831 acs.; & Robt. Bagby & Wm. Hern-den's 1800 acs. &c. 18 Feb. 1673/4, p. 501. Said land taken up by Jno. Pigg & assigned to sd. Burnell & Edw. Pigg; trans. of 19 pers: Jonathan (?) Male, Tho. Leister, Jane Qually, Tho. Youall, Edwd. Tompson, Robt. Lake, Anth. Mary, Robt. Cooper, Jno. Pinnell (?), Fra. Havercup, Richd. Powell, Wm. Lant, Geo. Perkins, Nicho. Polentine, Edwd. Blunt, Edwd. Hall, WHlm. Jacson, Mary Martyn, Joyce Davis.

WM. HURT, 213 acs., New Kent Co., in St. Stephen's Par., adj. Pecke's land; by the Mill path, &c; 18 Feb. 1673/8 (1673/4), p. 502. Trans. of 3 pers: Hen. Trowell twice; Lamboe (a) Negroe.

MR. THO. HALL & JNO. PIGG, 3831 acs., on NE side of Mattopony Riv.

above the tides flowing, in New Kent Co; about 40 paces above an Indian Weire, &c; 18 Feb. 1673/4, p. 502. Trans. of 77 pers: James Meate, Hen. Jack, Ann Akin, Alexdr. Logan, Cha. Jack, And. Jack, Ja. Coggill, Mary Coggill, Jno. Russell, Tho. Shory, Eliza. Gray, Sa. Williams Wm. Thorne, Samll. Peachy, Jno. Sheppard, Abra. Robinson, Jno. Jones, Mary Smith, Sarah Smith, Jno. Overbury, Wm.Clopton, Hen. Rider, Fra. Hatton, Samll. Moody, Hum. Moody, Math. Huberd, Sarah Fenn, Jno. Gillett, Robt. Shokey, Richd, Price (or Prin), Robt. Purvis, Tho. Parker, Wm, Daniell, Mary Daniell, Ann Cowthorne, Rich. Simins, Robt. Bishope, Wm. Gray, Susan Smith, Jennett Bough, Hen. Turner, Samll. Talke, Jno. Hawford, Tho. Conny (?), Jno. Underhill, Tho. Smith, Jno. Dowglas, Daniell Frizell, Danll. Sanders, Mary Bough, Jno. Gilam, Robt. Holme, Eliz. Montague, Wm. a boy; Wm. Brate; Eliz. Parr, Mar. Luckett, Rowland Graham, Richd. Fitzee, (or Fichee), Tho. Browne; Mary Hayes, Edwd. Drapier, Richd. Reade, Robt. Jennings, Robt. Lee, Abra. Browne, Robt. Prior, Robt. Lambo, Ingoe . . . . . . ; & 8 Negroes,

ROBT. BAGBY & WM. HERNDEN, 1800 acs., New Kent Co., N. E. side of Mattopony Riv., about 40 paces above an Indian Weire, adj. Mr. Hall & Mr. Pigg, &c; 18 Feb. 1673, p. 502. Trans. of 36 pers: Mich. Edmonds, Timothy Key, Geo. Landell, Margerett Plumton, Wm. Mercer, John French, Wm. Carter, Nich. Potter, Wm. Kirby, Geo. Randell, Nich. Peirceson, Wm. Cutler, Margt. Wmson. (Williamson), Geo. Turner, Nich. Kirby, Freemon, Wm. Sheeres Benj. Sheeres, Wm. Dawson, Tim. Wittingham, Antho. Thompson, Xpefer, Mickleton, Geo. Barker, James Jones, Marg. Nicholls, Cuthbert Tunstall, Theo. Whitney, Randall Morecroft, Fra. Barnett, Xper. Morline, Geo. Ridley, Tho. Butlesby, Nich. Smith, Geo. Drumond, Wm. Netherby, Tho. Throgmorton, Wm. Sanders.

WM. HERNDEN, 64 acs., New Kent Co., in St. Stephen's Par., adj. land he now lives upon, & along land of Wm.

Hurt, &c; 18 Feb. 1673/4, p. 502. Trans. of: Xper. Arson.

WM. HERNDEN & ROBT. BAGBY, 1000 acs., New Kent Co., N. side Mattopony Riv., adj. Mr. Tho. Hall & Mr. Jno. Pigg's 3831 acs., & 920 acs. of sd. Pigg, &c; 18 Feb. 1673/4, p. 503. Trans. of 20 pers: Wm. Simpson, Geo. Stradling, Anth. Jefferson, Wm. Bilkinson, Wm. Ambrey, Wm. Conway, Eliz. Clarke, Const. Hewett, Jno. Symons, Robt. Wells, Robt. Chickester, Cha. Price, Tho. Davis, Jno. Ward, Ja. Smith, Jacob Stringer, Ann Trowell, Eliz. Crowder, Eliz. Beare, Alice Coffe.

WM. HERNDEN, 430 acs., New Kent Co., N. side Mattopony Riv., adj. Mr. Morrice; Richd. Davis & Robt. Jones; by the roade to Dennis' plantation; to Tomocoricon (?) Sw., &c; 18 Feb. 1673/4, p. 503. Trans. of 9 pers: Tho. Warr, Hen. Bonskin, Tho. Coocke, Richd. Owen, Wm. Hawley, Jno. Ashington, Alice Lameham, Mathew Thomas, Bridgett Crosst (or Crafft.)

WM. WATTS, 270 acs., New Kent Co., upon brs. of Aquintanocoke Sw., adj. land he lives upon, on NE side of Mattopony Riv; by Cheese Cake Path dividing this & land of Mr. Carleton; along Mr. Holmes' (Home's) path; to Major Wyatt's &c; 18 Feb. 1673/4, p. 503. Trans. of 5 pers: Moses Godden, Sarah Rosse, Thomas Griffin, Ellen Michell, John Moore.

RICHARD DAVIS, 250 acs., New Kent Co., upon NW side of Tomocoricon Sw., at mouth of a br. dividing this & Mr. Geo. Morrice; by the roade to Dennis' plantation, &c; 18 Feb. 1673/4, p. 503. Trans. of 5 pers: Cornelius Danaway, Eliz. Warren, Susan Warren, Benja. Dards, Ralph Bolton.

JOHN DUKE, 136 acs., in *Chickahominy*, upon Tiaskun Sw., adj. Mr. Jos. Wadd; & Edwd. Gyllie's land; to land where he now lives, &c; 15 Dec. 1673, p. 504. Trans. of 3 pers: Edwd. Griffith, Jno. Glantin, Robt. Turtle.

JOHN DORWOOD, 380 acs., New Kent Co., upon brs. of Tassatiumps (?) Cr., upon the Indian Cabbin Br., to Ralph Greene, &c; 15 Dec. 1673, p. 504. Trans. of 8 pers: Henry Hawly, Mathew Price, Fra. Brookes, Wm. Westley, Henry Hewitt, Richd. Smith, Francis Warr, Mary Jolly. Marginal Note: This land entered with Mr. Kirkman in the office 7 Oct. 1665 as appears by his receipt, but the survey being lost, noe patt. issued till now, however it is thought fitt the man have a rite from the entry, haveing always paid the King's rents. Teste P. L. Clk.

ANDREW DAVJS, JNO. WEBB & JOHN LANGWORTHY, 1900 acs., New Kent Co., on S. E. side of Machumps Cr., on S. side of Yorke Riv., above Mahaxeenes; &c; 15 Dec. 1673, p. 504. Trans. of 38 pers: Ann Mathewes, Wm. Tabor, Tho. Kidd, Hen. Barkham, Martha Rodon, Fra. Boyse, Samll. Woodward, David Phillips, Edwd. Parry, Tho. Orly (or Orby), Samll. Scofield, Tho. Street, Hen. Hunt, Roger Baxter, Originall Brown, Jno. Morgan, Vincent Mansfeild, Jno. Askew, Howell Morgan, Jno. Heskard, Robt. Turreton, Antho. Wardman (or Waneman), Samll. Boyse, Wm. Edwards, Tho. White, Antho. Lucy, Jno. Ustrill, Tho. Symons, Jno. Bennett, Tho. Woodhouse, Richd. Hill, Richd. Hobarne, Wm. Ellin, Jno. Redding, Wm. Freeman, Richd. Rayman, Joan Visard, Edmd. Deerling.

WM. MOORE, 400 acs., Nancemond. Co., 16 Dec. 1673, p. 504. Beg. at his own Mills; adj. Francis Benton, Wm. Ward, & Richd. Winshew; 300 acs. granted him 30 Oct. 1662; 100 acs. for trans. of 2 pers: Eliz. Gale, Jno. Broade.

JOHN WIMBERLY, 400 acs., Nanzemond Co., by the W. branch; adj. Robt. Gooks; 16 Dec. 1673, p. 505. Trans. of 8 pers: Richd. Arme, Hester Jones, Wm. Elsey, himselfe twice, Mr. Peter Feild, 3 times.

WM. PHILLIPS, 3000 acs., New Kent Co., upon both sides of Totopoto-moys Cr., adj. Mr. Jno. Page; 18 Feb. 1673/4, p. 505. Trans. of 60 pers: Tho. Williams, Joseph Tovy (or Tery), Jno. Jones, Phill. Bowles, Ra. Barkenhead, Richd. Dearelove, Jno. Tery (or Tovy), Kath. Hewson, Tho. Mallory, Tho. Hatford, Jno. Gallamore, Tho. Watton, Naz. Hooke, Gab. Harrison, Jacob Flepo, Eliz. Finch, Jno. Davis, Mary Durham, Hanah Love Wm. Stinton, Tho. Forger, Ann Searle, Wa. Thomas, Wm. Wood, Fra. Whetherbone, Jer. Jerram, Edwd. Lewis, Richd. Carter, Abra. Mihilmay, Jno. Smith, Tho. Hooks, Jos. Humphreys, Ja. Cunlock, Mary Rosse, Mary Whittington, Richd. Pratt, Wm. Bivin (?), Griff. Evans, Wm. Davis, Rich. Morland, Sar. Carter, Eliz. Williams, Ja. Scott, Kath. Penn, Jane Grey, Fra. Woodward, Wm. Fisher, Jno. Seabright, Ad. Bolton, Rich. Thomas, Geo. Sumnerside, Robt. Heatly, Jno. Curry, Ja. Hambleton, Robt. Breedwood, Tho. Williams, Hen. Denman; John Hill; Palmena, Peter, Robt., Negroes.

MR. CHARLES SCARBURGH, 4350 acs., Accomack Co., at Pungoteag Cr., 18 Feb. 1673/4, p. 505. Beg. at the back Cr., to head of Revell's, by some called Randolpf's, branch; to land claimed by Mr. Edwd. Revell; &c. 3050 acs. granted him 10 May 1650; renewed 12 Nov. 1664; 1300 acs. for trans. of 26 pers: Charles Scarburgh, twice; Wm. Baldry, Jno. Evans, Jno. Eves, Jno. Newell, Brid. Clare, Tho. Jones, Jno. Jones, Kath. Newjat, Henry Wheler, Humphry Joanes, Sus. Jones, Edwd. Norris, Richd. Hayes, Eliz. Franke, Geo. Wilson, Jones Terry, Sarah Ives, Wm. West: Dick, Mary, Jno. Joane, Tom, Mafana, Negroes.

RICHD. PARKER, 314 acs., Surry Co., upon the maine Blackwater Sw., adj. Mr. Jno. Barker; 20 Dec. 1673, p. 505. Trans. of 7 pers: Jasper Grantum, David Phillips, Evan Davis, Wm. Marriott, Richd. Parker, twice; Jno. Watrin.

MR. THO. PEIRCE, 155 acs., Warwick Co., in Mulbery Island Par., 2 Mar. 1673/4, p. 506. Beg. on a point neare Warwick Riv., near Geo. Harwood's house. &c. Trans. of 3 pers: Wm. Foard, Joseph Huberd; Jno. Mills.

MR. PHILL. WATKINS, THO. WATKINS & WM. RICKETTS, 850 acs., New Kent Co., on NE side of Mattaponie; 6 Mar. 1673/4, p. 506. Adj. Mr. Watkins, & Mr. Richd. Davis; the head of Brewerton's br., &c. Trans. of 17 pers: Jno. Derham, Eliz. Jones, Aron Powell, Paule Millington, Jno. Peasely, Isabell Burton, Jno. Scealy, Wm. Bewe, Jno. Wheeler, Hercu. Price, Martha Bealton, Jno. Ridon, Robt. Wms. (Williams), Richd. Frift, Jno. Godfry, Stephen Heath, Jno. Halings (or Stalings).

SAME. 900 acs., same Co., date & page. By Mattapony Indian Path &c., to Mr. Thomas Brewerton, &c. Trans. of 18 pers: Mary Barly, Ja. Steward, Jno. Copres, Tho. Gales, Mary Symonds, Cha. Barwell, Jno. Elwood, Rich. Jones, Robert Parsons, Phill. Ellis, And. Dunn, Richd. Clarke, Joha. Hopkins Wm. Jeoffery, Richd. Cole, Edwd. Heath, Tho. Belt, And. Carlton.

MAJOR NICHOLAS HILL, 670 acs., Is. of W. Co., at the Blackwater; 26 Mar. 1674, p. 506. Beg. neare Parson's Bridge on the Beverdam br., in George More's line, by Miles & Cooke's land, by Edward Jones, to England's cor.; up Hull's br., to Geo. Branch, &c. Trans. of 14 pers: John Munke, Margerett Lewis, Edwd. Wood, Katherine Wood, Joane ......, Richd. Okes, Jno. Prehowse, Ralph Answorth, ... Graves & Rachell his wife, Richd. Priden, Rowland Davis, Margerett & Joane ....

MR. DANIELL WYLDE, 100 acs., Yorke Co., 26 Mar. 1674, p. 507. Escheat land of Cornelius Johnathan, dec'd. Inquisition under Tho. Ludwell, Esqr., Eschr's. Genl. of Va., &c.

CHARLES EDMONDS, THO. HANCOCK & RICHD. TAYLOR, 3000 acs., New Kent Co., on the North River where sd. Edmonds liveth; 7 Apr. 1674, p. 507. Trans. of 60 pers: Tho. Evans, Eliza. Day, Barsheba Lambert Jno. Jolly,

Wm. Smiley, Jno. Mins. (or Mint), Mary Browne, Eliza. Farnell, Ellenor Gutheridge, Ann Warren, Joseph Beckley (or Berkley), Jno. Simerell, St. Jno. Hall, Wm. Blake. Jno. Price. Fra. Price, Eliz. Parr, Margaret Lightfoot, Wm. Locker, Edmund Whitney, James Greening, Martha Griggs, Peter Ball, Cha. Bleige, Hester Baccus, Wm. Sanders, Phill. Harwood, Robt. Salter, Margaret Long, Tho. Waram, Jno. Speed, Wm. Gailer, Jno. Tyler, Roger Plumer, Edwd. Place, Edwd. Wilkins, Wm. Lancaster, Tho. Panton (?), Edwd. Bourne, Phill. Ashley, Ja. Bare, Symon Salter, Tho. Giles, Henry Sterne, Roger Symons, Jno. Philpott, Richd. Card, Richd. Smith, Samll. Warren, Ja. Bird, Tho. Shepherd, Jno. Bishop, Susana Smith, Ann Smith, Richd. Jones, Eliz. Massey, Jno. Wms. (Williams), Dorothy Smith, Ellinor Blackell, Tho. Wye.

HENRY READER, 450 acs., New Kent Co., 7 Apr. 1674, p. 507. Adj. Charles Edmonds, Richd. Taylor & Tho. Hancock. Trans. of 9 pers: Robt. Frizell, Robt. Rouse, Geo. Bostock Edwd. Bostock, Eliza. Lasher, Tho. Cannon, Mathew Walton, Henry Godwin, Geo. Meckton (?)

CAPT. MARTIN PALMER, 1152 acs., New Kent Co., S. side Mattapanie Riv., in Pamunkey Neck; 7 Apr. 1674, p. 507. At mouth of Hollowing poynt Cr., adj. land formerly Joseph Croshaw's; land of Col. Wm. Claibourne; & Ralph Graves, &c. 400 acs. granted Major Joseph Croshaw, & sold to sd. Palmer; 700 acs. granted to Jno. Exoll & Anth. Haines; sold to Tho. Jones, who sold to sd. Palmer; 52 acs. for trans. of: Jno. Botie.

CHARLES HAWLY, 250 acs., New Kent Co., on brs. of Tassantium Sw., on N. E. side of Matapanie Riv., adj. Jno. Dorwood; by a path that goeth to the flaxmans; &c; 7 Apr. 1674, p. 508. Trans. of 5 pers: Edwd. Bockman (or Buckman), James Lord, Peter Chesrim, Robt. Forsey, Tho. Robinson.

JOHN HUME, 523 acs., New Kent Co., NE side of Matapanie Riv., upon

Masticock Swamp; on the run of Pesti-
cock Sw., &c; 7 Apr. 1674, p. 508. Trans.
of 10 pers: Josias Hingstone, Jno. Wans-
ley, Ja. Elliott, Eliz. Badmore, Joane
Fardle, Robt. Toone (?), Jno. Blake,
Wm. Cox, Richd. Barnard, Samll. Ridley.

JOHN KEY, 370 acs., New Kent Co.,
NE side of Matapanie Riv. adj. Major
Wm. Wyatt; Wm. Burch, Jno. James;
& Jno. Hanies (or Haines); &c; 8 Apr.
1674, p. 508. (*Note:* The following
names appear hereunder:)' Jno. Key,
Edmd. Key, Wm. Brookes, Mary Douglas, Cha. Cock, Wm. Black, Jno. Oliphant

MR. RICHD. WHITEHEAD, 2000
acs., Rappa. & New Kent Co.'s; on W.
side Portobago Path; 8 Apr. 1674, p. 508.
Trans. of — . pers: Major Robt. Bristow,
twice; a woman servt. dyed at sea; Phill.
White, Tho. Wright, Tho. Amye, Jno.
Halley, Jno. Vindall, Wm. Bell, Jno.
Paramore, Jno. Wilkinson, Nich. Bald-
win, Marmaduke More, Richd. Knight,
Robt. Goffe, Edwd. Osborne, Sara Marsh,
Ann Frawlin, Henry Ellis, Samll. Ackles-
ton, Tho. Wetherstone, Jno. Edall,
Francis Manvill, Ralfe Clifford, John
Fox, James Green, James Carder, Ann
Walker, Tho. Mold, Grace Wilson, Ann
Crouch, Wm. Budle, Robt. Harrison, An-
drew Groine (or Grove); 6 Negroes.

MR. THO. BATTS, 1862 A., 1 R., 32
P., Henrico Co., N. side Apamattock
(Riv.); 8 Apr. 1674, p. 509. Adj. his
land above the falls, above the *Appamat-
tock Indian Towne;* against an island;
running to the old Towne Cr., nigh land
of Jno. Fowler, &c. Trans. of 37 pers:
Tho. Nixon, Tho. Partridge, Ja. Balli-
corne (or Ballitoune), Marmaduke
Browne, Wm. Harroge, Jonas Right, Al-
lice Beinns, Wm. Morter, Ja. Cragoe,
Jno. Wells, Catwin Foster, Hen. Kent,
Robt. Bowlin, Sara Godwin, Jno. the (?)
Grecian, Jno. Beacham, Jno. Waitell,
Wm. Bobett, Wm. Kindells (?), James
Gent, Tho. Stubbs, Jno. & An Clarke,
Tho. Cleere, Robt. Bookseller, Richd.
Deerton, Mathew Sheers, Jno. Hobson,
Tho. Meriton, Jno. Peo, Wm. Hobson;

Joseph & Hector Negroes; Sacco & Moll
Indians; Eliza & Joane woemen.

JAMES HALL, 302 A. 3 R. 12 P.
Chas. Cytty Co., on S. side of Appamat-
tock Riv; beg. at mouth of a Cr. parting
Mr. Wm. Farrar & Xtopher. Woodward;
8 Apr. 1674, p. 509. Trans. of 6 pers:
Ja. Wasbrooke, Robt. Ward, Ja. Hall,
Cha. Stuard, Tho. Hind, Samll. Moyson
(or Mayson).

WM. WILLIAMS, 331 acs., Chas.
Cytty Co., S. side Appamattock Riv., 8
Apr. 1674, p. 509. Beg. at Samll. Woodward; to Cr. parting Mr. Farrer & sd.
Woodward, along Jno. Maise (Maies),
&c. 291 acs. sold by Samll. Woodward
to Mr. Antho. Wyatt 8 Oct. 1650, who
sold to Robt. Burges 23 Jan. 1655, who
sold to sd. Williams 20 Sept. 1660, as
by (records of) *Bristow Cort* may appear; 40 acs. for trans. of: Richd. Wright.

HERCULES FLOOD, 470 A., 1 R.,
Chas. City Co., S. side Appamattock Riv.,
8 Apr. 1674, p. 510. Adj. his own land
& Wm. Jones'; along the Blackwater,
&c. Trans. of 9 pers: Sara Hill, Senr.,
Sara Hill, Junr., Mihill Hill, Junr., Robt.
Richardson, Jno. Hobson, Jno. Addams,
Ann Thomas, Wm. Hotting, Tho.
Gregorie.

WM. JONES, 470 A., 1 R., Chas. City
Co., S. side Appamattock Riv., adj. Her-
cules Flood; down the Blackwater, &c;
8 Apr. 1674, p. 510. Trans. of 9 pers:
Tho. Killdells, Wm. Butler, Richd. Wat-
son, Ann Peterson, David Goodale, David
Good, Mihill Jackson, Ann Moone, Wm.
Jones.

HUGH LEE, 2000 acs., named *Abex-
conaway,* Chas. City Co., S. side Appa-
mattock Riv. on N. side the 3rd br. of the
Black Water; nigh Warrick Path, &c;
8 Apr. 1674, p. 510. Trans. of 40 pers:
Richd. Sparkes, Hen. Neale, Jno. Crew,
Andr. Crew, Richd. Dennis, Wm. Marsh,
Morris Joyce, Hen. Allaman, Jno. Browne,
Wm. Bernard, Tho. Clark, Tomasin Har-
ris, Jno. Browne, Phill. Pledge, Mary
Browne, Jno. Cox, Richd. Warren, Tho.

Michell, Jno. Drennett, Barbara Petingall, Cha. Bartlett, Wm. Taylor, Jno. Floyd, Tho. Stanley, Joan Liswell, Sara King, Rebecka Love (?), Sara Swetland, Jacobus Jonson, Eliz. Cooper, Tho. Woods, Tho. Dance, Jno. Burges, Tho. Ory (?), Addam Bradshaw, Robt. Fydoe, Martha Gibbs, Robt. Hicks, Jno. Allen, Tho. Alford.

COL. WM. KENDALL, 268 acs., Accomack Co., near *Matchepungoe;* bet. Col. Edmd. Scarburgh & Capt. Fra. Potts, along land of Edwd. Hitchins to lines of Wm. Wouldhave; &c. 8 Apr. 1674, p. 510. Trans. of 5 pers: Wm. Morgan, Tho. Peirce; Bess, Kate, Wm., Tom,— Negroes.

THOMAS HANCKES, & CORNELIUS CHEESMAN, 260 acs., in Gloster & New Kent Co.'s; 8 Apr. 1674, p. 511. Adj. land whereon sd. Hanckes liveth. Trans. of 5 pers: Tho. Jenkins, Peter White, Wm. Coachman, Mary Haines, Marv Card.

HENRY WRIGHT, sonne & heire of Jon. Wright, 140 acs. Gloster Co., adj. Robert Beverley; & Mr. Robt. Elliott; 8 Apr. 1674, p. 511. Trans. of 3 pers: Jane Davis, Tho. Richards, John Beeve (or Beene.)

SAMLL. CLERKE, 700 acs., Gloster Co., E. side Poropotanck Cr. & maine Sw; 8 Apr. 1674, p. 511. Granted Mr. Peter Knight, dec'd., 25 Aug. 1652 & due sd. Clerke *as heire & next of kinne.*

MR. THOMAS WARWICK, 600 acs., Middlesex Co., upon branches of Perrot's Cr., adj. Jeremiah O'bere; & Thomas Low; 8 Apr. 1674, p. 511. 200 acs. granted him 19 Apr. 1664; 400 acs. for trans. of 8 pers: Joan Bishop, Jon. Rosser, Roger Bridges, James Barnes, Owen Mageine-(or Mageire), Tho. Stafford, Jon. Wright, Sara Downham.

THOMAS LOE, 1200 acs., Middlesex Co., on head brs. of Perrot's Cr., 9 Apr. 1674, p. 512. Adj. *Jaimaica land;* Mr. Thomas Warwick; & Jeremiah Obere; 300 acs. granted Martha Ludford, Widdow, now wife of sd. Loe, 29 Mar, 1672; 900 acs. for trans. of 18 pers: Wm. Pigeon, Nathaniell How, Henry Locker, Wm. Justen, Benjamin Palmer, Jon. Perry, Jon. Duckenhead, Humphrey Jarvis, Samll. Curson, Tho. Davis, William Cleavers, Jon. Doblander, Eliz. Sope, Tho. Prigg, Anne Gibbs, Jon. Rogers, Tho. Oakeham, Edward Cornith.

CAPT. RICHARD DUDLEY, 980, acs., Gloster Co., upon brs. of Poropotanck Cr., 9 Apr. 1674, p. 512. Adj. Mr. Pate; land of John Greene, dec'd., Mr. Peter Knight, dec'd. now Samuell Clarke's; & Spence's land; by Daunceing Valley, by Curle's path & br., by Rappa. Path, &c. 944 acs. granted him 28 Oct. 1665; 36 acs. found within & due for trans. of: Robert Yellow.

JOHN MASTERS, 550 acs., Rappa. Co., upon brs. of Gilson's Cr., adj. Capt. Beverly; Elick Robins; & Theo. Wale (Whale); 8 Apr. 1674, p. 513. Trans. of 11 pers.*

WM. TABBUTT (Tabott), 114 acs., Rappa. Co., adj. Col. Goodrich; in Holly Sw. belonging to Ralph Cr., adj. Hen. Woodnoll; by Jno. Stanford's fence; & land formerly Thomas Paddison's; 8 Apr. 1674, p. 513. Trans. of 2 pers.*

MR. RICHARD CLARKE, 206 acs., Rappa. Co., 4 mi. in the woods, bet. Hodgkins Cr. & Gilson's (Cr.); adj. Col. Goodrich; over the mouth of Mr. Pate's Sw., along Francis Graves to Mr. Tanges; 8 Apr. 1674, p. 513. Trans. of 4 pers.*

EDWD. CORDENBRACKE (Cordenbruck), 900 acs. New Kent Co., S. side Mattapony Riv., behind Thomas Hickman; on N. side of a br. of Hartquake Sw., &c; 8 Apr. 1674, p. 513. 800 acs. granted to Martin Palmer & Geo. Chapman 16 Dec. 1661 & assigned to the abovenamed; 100 acs. for trans. of 2 pers: Edmd. Jenkins, Ellinor Crackrell.

GEORGE BILLIPPS, 500 acs., Gloster Co., on Garding Cr., 9 Apr. 1674, p. 514. S. side sd. Cr., opposite land of Forrester; along the Bever Dams, &c. 250 acs.

granted him 27 Jan. 1663; 250 acs. for trans. of 5 pers: Ann Crouch, Wm. Budle, Robt. Harrison, Andrew Grone (or Grove), Richd. Crittendon.

JNO. WALLOP, als: WADDILOW, 450 acs., Accamack Co., N. side of a freshwater br. of Gr. Matapanie Cr., by some called Swansieutts; E'wd. upon 1700 acs. called *Matapanie Neck* granted to Mrs. Ann Toft, bet. Miles Grey & Capt. Danll. Jenifer, & the line bet. Va. & Md. on the N; 9 Apr. 1674, p. 514. 100 acs. granted him 9 Oct. 1672; 350 acs. for trans. of 7 pers: Samll. Taylor, Jno. Medcalfe, Katherine Shirly, Wm. Fetherstone, Robt. Atkins, Mary Meeres, Sibbilla Bullock.

SAMUELL TAYLOR, 700 acs., Accomack Co., E. upon Gingoetege Cr., adj. land formerly Wallop's; Col. Jno. Stringer; & Wm. Blake; 9 Apr. 1674, p. 514. 300 acs. part of 950 acs. granted him 5 Apr. 1668; 400 acs. for trans. of 8 pers: Robt. Paine, Samll. Hurstone, Eliz. Jenkins, Tho. Wmson. (Williamson), Jno. Reeves, Jno. Bisby; Sandilo & Jone, Negroes.

WILLIAM SNAPES, 110 acs., Gloster Co., adj. Spence's land; Major Richard Lee; & Capt. Richard Dudley; in Daunceing Valley & Beach Spring Valley; 9 Apr. 1674, p. 514. Trans. of 3 pers: Thomas Hollins, Arnall Mouse, Anthony Little.

ALEXANDER SNELLING, sonn of Wm. Snelling, dec'd., 43 acs., Glocester Co., 1½ mi. from the North River side; at head of land of Tho. Chapman, dec'd., & adj. Abraham Ivison; 8 Apr. 1674, p. 515. Granted sd. Wm. 11 Oct. 1659, & due sd. Alexr. as his sonn.

MR. GEO. MORRIS, 2100 acs., Rappa. & New Kent Co.'s; adj. Col. Thomas Goodrich; along an Indian Path, over a redy br., to an Indian feild; &c; p. 515. (Unfinished—no date.)

MR. GEO. MORRISE (Morris), 434 acs., New Kent Co., adj. land of Richd. Davis on Esqr. Digges' Creek called *Clēmacoraton;* by Edwd. Dennis' path; downe Tomacoracon Sw., &c; 16 Nov. 1673, p. 515. Trans. of 8 pers.*

SAME. 3000 acs., Rappa. & New Kent Co.'s, bet. Rappa. Riv. & Mattapony; adj. Col. Goodrich & Mr. Henry Aubrey, bet. 2 pocosons of Pascataway & Jelson's Cr; 8 May 1674, p. 516. By the Indian Path; to a br. of Tuckahow Sw. or Beaver Dam Sw., &c. Trans. of 60 pers: Tho. Diston, Jno. Barthelson, Jno. Wagh, Eliz. Doglas, Tho. Webster, Alexander Webster, Pomp. (?) Moncreife, Ja. Wood, Tho. Lugg, Robt. Lindsey, David Richardson, Luke Hanilton (or Harilton), Edwd. Jones, Wm. Key, Tho. Barber, James Barber, Dugell Camell, Morgan Morehead, Jno. Maddison, Danll. Wilky, Edwd. Keely, Da. Camerin, Davd. Allison, Wm. Hartwell, Jno. Herring, Ja. Goodry, And. Halliburton, Tho. Catherwood, Alexr. Porteus, Jno. Porteus, Sarah Smith, Wm. Dennis, Roger Overton, Tho. Smith, Wm. Greane, Jno. Paterson, Tho. Cockin, And. Hambleton, Danll. Camell, Jno. Margregor, Richd. Rice, Jno. Mathews, Robt. Smith, Hu. Morris, Timo. Davis, Tho. Wagnall, Edwd. Solders (?), Nich. Burras, Tho. Hill, Edwd. Wheeler, Tho. Berkler, Tho. Harper, Wm. Durham, Math. Jones, Jno. Katherin, Nich. Lee, Sar. Dido (?), Tho. Spencer, Jno. Royston, Wm. Young.

SAME. 1190 acs., Rappa. Co., 8 Apr. 1674, p. 515. On brs. of Jelson's Cr., adj. Mr. Pley (Mr. Ply); & Mr. Button, &c. 800 acs. granted sd. Morris & Jno. Long, 29 Sept. 1667; 390 acs. for trans. of 7 pers: Richd. Davies, Wm. Freeman, Edwd. Gerriah (?), Mary Tite, Wm. Case, Nich. Cocks, Daniel Dobins.

CAPT. LAURENCE SMITH, 4600 acs., New Kent Co., on both sides of the redy br. belonging to Mattapony, &c; 13 Dec. 1673, p. 516. Trans. of 92 pers: Wm. Webly, Salam. Jones, Jno. Browne, Rog. Adley, Ja. Moore, Edwd. Mosse, Ralph Adkins, Ro. Rouse, La. Austin, Hugo Meakings, Jno. Watts, Jno. Morpus, Wm. Smith, Jno. Dues, Richd. Jones, Robt. Wms. (Williams), Phill.

Watts, Jno. Greene, Wm. Grindon, Geo. Pollard, Wm. Thomas, Mary Marey, Jno. Hutchingson, Jno. George, Jno. Kingly, Geo. Genkins, Wm. Langstaffe, Hen. Wormeston, Will. Cranidge, Lidia Franklin, Eliza. Grymes, Winifd. Brothers, Mary Rogers, Susan Winn, Eliz. Sackler, Robt. Grice, Jno. Barrow, Geo. Signett, Tho. Parsons, Hum. Evans, Tho. Sorre, Jno. Staples, Jno. Thomas, Jno. Shadwell, Edmd. Barrnell, (or Barriell), Tho. Forsan, Edwd. Carlest, Jno. Sutton, Wm. Levorack, Fran. Quinch (?), Edwd. Barriff, Wm. Crane, Fra. Williams, Jno. Sanders. John Driver, Jno. Salter, Henry Beale, Ann Draper, Jno. Empson, Geo. Granger, Wm. Key, Geo. Eagres, Elias Bucker, Mary Wells, Danll. Baker, Jno. Jno. Lorem (or Loveing), Isaack Dix, Wm. Clavell, Jno. Penney, Jno. Morrine, Wm. Wilkins, Tho. Phipp, Tho. Foster, Eliz. Chartris, Jno. Pettigree, Jno. Perry, Wm. Dulake, Geo. Fish, Tho. Whidbee, Alexr. Hill, Geo. Till, Jno. Pittman, Hen. Stafford, Giles Bryer, Jeff. Thornton, Jno. Bruster, Jno. Lippincott, James Lesher, Mary Holdfast, Johana. Withers; 2 Negroes.

MR. JOHN BUCKNER, MR. ROBT. BRYAN, & MR. THO. ROYSTON, 3553½ acs., Rappa. Co., in the freshes of sd. Riv., on the S. side; adj. land of Jno. Prosser called the *Golden Vale;* ๅeare the new roade to Mr. Taliaferro, land of Moone——, over br. of a sw. running into Pewomenseen (?), &c; 19 Sept. 1671, p. 518. Trans. of 71 pers: Em. Ratclife, Nath. Mott, Wm. Lobb, Dan. Anderton, Robt. Thruston, Tho. Morgan, Samll. Bargess, Mary Williams, Ja. Barkhust, Robt. Edwards. Jno. Jones, Tho. Kings, Tho. Ramsey, Edwd. Sadler, Tho. Hix, Dor. Young, Hen. Powell, Blan. Harding, Jno. Warry, Edwd. Kerrick, Reynold Robinson, Edwd. Graves. Jno. Busby, Dan. Grouch, Hump. Thomas, Xper. Eddy. Marg. Tompson, Jno. Jones, Jno. Robinson, Jno. Senecay, Geo. Young, Eliz. Sharp, Wm. Greene, Arb. Singleton, Wm. Wright, Wm. Alexander, Isabell Tompson, Geo. Barker, Wm. Geadwith, Jno. Hunt, Mary Grefor, Robt. Rayt, Richd. Bradshaw, Anna Pat-

tison, Wm. Travis, Mary Parker, Geo. Brooke, Peter Cosens, Ann Townesend, Jno. Kelly, Tho. Hall, Robt. Hull, Robt. Beecham, Hen. Castell, Tho. Chainy, Jno. Frissell (Frisprell ?), Jno. Farrell, Jno. Tuty, Rich. Clay, Arthur Powell, Ann Hardacres, Jno. Hayward, Mary Chainy, Mus. Silly (or Lilly), Jno. Davis; Negro Tom.

JOHN LINDSEY, 700 acs., Middlesex Co., upon Dragon Sw., betwixt White Oke Sw. & Bryery Br., adj. Tho. Kidd, Tho. Cordwell, Mr. Hen. Niccolls; & Robt. Aldin; 10 June 1674, p. 518. (*Note:* The following names appear under this:) Owen Lindsey, Andrew Rosse, John Hallett, Cha. Robinson, Jane Edwards, John Lindsey, George Harper, Willm. Seale, Robt. Wilkison, Jno. Thomas, Edwd. Bowman, Jno. Benham, Martha Gibson; & a Negro.

LT. COL. JNO. SMITH, MR. JOHN BUCKNER, MR. PHILL. LIGHTFOOT, MR. THO. ROYSTON & MR. JOHN LEWIS, 10.050 acs., New Kent Co., on Mattapony Riv; adj. Mr. Tho. Hall & John Pigg, & Hernden & Bagby.; 25 Feb. 1673/4, p. 518. Trans. of 201 pers: J. Hollaway, Tho. Egleston, Tho. Humphrys, Alexdr. Olivant, Peter Hacker, Tho. Harris, Lewis Williams, M. Grimson, Tho. Richards, Jno. Reeve, Ow. Mageron, F. Windebanck, Peter Marsali, Ch. Pryor, Math. Pew, David Streton, Wm. Garlin John Moncke, Peter Amkett, Ann Sape, Jno. Connadra (?) Tho. Garnett, Wm. Brookes, Tho. Royston, Wm. Mason, Alice Seate (or Seale), Tho. Stanton, Mary Birch, Pen. Jnoson (Johnson), Jno. Jones, Wm. Rickutts, Joane Bishopp, Jno. Rosser, Rodger Bridges, Ja. Brims, Tho, Stafford, Jno. Bennor, Mathew Watson, Jno. Bray, Richs. Wees, Mary Blany, Danll. Salt. Jno. Milles, James Greene, Ann Royston, Jno. Herbert, Nich. Howse, Wm. Davis, David Jones, David Price, Jno. Speede, Jno. Wright, Hen. Bennett, Jane Brent, Garrett Hedwith (or Tredwith), Antho. Little, Tho. Mason, Anth. Sheppard, Rich. Lord, Robt. Mayden, Kath. Miles, Robt. Douglas, Samll. Rosier (or Ros-

ser), Hen. Isaak, Tho. Chalky, Richd.
Thompson, Ralph Butter, Jno. Hodgston,
Sus. Bishop, Wm. Morden, Ann Daniell,
Roger Hayward, Elias Cobson, Mary
Grome, Robt. Cooper, Sarah Dowman,
Tho. Hollings, Arn. Mouse, Kath. Little,
Fra. Bumpas, Ann Sanders, Nich. Carry,
Tho. Aldree, Geo. Pinhorne, Wm. Hutt
(or Hust), Zach. Jackson, Tho. Clarke,
Jno. Bosslingham, Tho. Ryle, Jno. Lin-
sey, Tho. Wildham, Richd. Sime, Ann
Strinn, Mary Middleton, Tho. Hill, Wm.
Johnson, Hen. Chitty, Jno. Barnaby,
Symon Debins, Robt. Huddington, Jno.
Ellis, Kath. Powell, Nich. Ellis, Hen.
Cole, Ann Greene, John Rodes, Jno.
Creamer, Eliz. Doughlty, Tho. Smith,
Jno. Willis, Jno. Browne, Edwd. Ware,
Robt. Yallop, Robt. Hodsden, Richd.
Wms. (Williams), Wm. Tibbalds, Fra.
Hords, Edw. Cantram, Wm. Anderson,
Tho. Cordewell, Robt. Strong, Geo.
Strong, Ma. Prickett, Marg. Jefferies,
Wm. Butler, Jno. Potter, Marth. Neale,
Jno. Orbry, Obediah Pitt, Yart Mourty,
Clemt. Onely, Wm. Clavator, Susan
Berry, Edwd. Steward, Peter Baxton,
Paul Lambert, Ann Ford, Kath. Paine,
Peter Marshall, Mary Chapman, Ann
Dennis, Danll. Mackdougall, Kath. Higgs,
Jno. Drapier, Jno. Pate, Tho. Hix, Tho.
Allen, Wm. Young, Debias Butler, Hum.
Hunt, Xper. Hunt, Jno. Mandy, Judy
Lewis, Mary Chapman, Jno. Spilman,
James Cooke, Morrice Neave, Fra. Cole,
Richd. Bennett, Mary Nettle, Rich.
Bookes, Mary Sampson, Nathan. (?)
Sides, Capt. Lightfoote twice, Eliz.
Tucker, Tho. Jones, Robt. Colle, Jno.
Gunter, Roger Price, Geo. Page, Ja.
Bradberry, Lancett Ready, Wm. Lodge,
.... Reade, Ja. Heates, Wm. Laurence,
Tho. Plowman, Jno. Bennett, Jno. Mandy,
Jno. Tistaile, Grace Smith, Wm. Giat
(?), Sim. Sacre, Jno. Berry, Jerm. Dicke,
Pawle Ramsey, Tho. Wilson, Fra. Foxell;
Angelo (a) Negro, & 4 Negroes.

MR. GEO. MORRICE (Morris), 1190
acs., Rappa. Co., on brs. of Gelson's Cr.,
adj. Mr. Button; & Mr. Ply; 8 Apr.
1674, p. 519. 800 acs. granted sd. Morris
& Jno. Long 29 Sept. 1667; 390 acs.

trans. of 7 pers.* *Marginal Note:* Recorded in Folio 515.

SAME. 434 acs., New Kent Co., 16
Nov. 1673, p. 519. Adj. Richd. Davis
on Esqr. Digges Cr. called *Tomacoracon,*
along Edwd. Dennis' path, downe Tomacoracon Sw., &c. Trans. of 8 pers.*
Marginal Note: Recorded in folio 515.

PHILLIP FREEMAN, 650 acs., James
City Co., upon maine Sw. of Chickahominy Riv., above Westham Path, adj.
Tho. Meredeth & Tho. London; 10 Mar.
1673/4, p. 519. Granted him 2 May
1661.

GEO. PEARCE, 2100 acs., Nanzemond
Co., by a br. of the Blackwater; adj. Col.
Pitts & Col. Bridger; 21 Sept. 1674, p.
519. Trans. of 42 pers: Joseph Woors,
Tho. Seawell, Tho. Turner, Tho. Wil-
liams, Ed. Wessell, Nath. Chapman,
Richd. Mathews, Samll. Daines, Rich.
Lenersell, Xpian. Demacketts, Ralph
Broune, Ed. Hull, Tho. Griffin, Susan
Hall, Mar. Baker, Jno. Compton, Joan
Estham (?), Rand. Delarge, Wm. Palmer,
Darby Ray, Gerard Wakeham, Jno.
Branch, Tho. Poole, Alexdr. Orrell,
Richd. Bruster, Richd. Carter, Martin,
Hynton, Marg. Butty, Alice Wilson, Tho.
Hunlock, Ann Underwood, Tho. Thick-
penny, Robt. Regly, Peter Kickett, Robt.
Percivall, Jno. Meeks; 6 Negroes.

ROGER TARLETON, 50 acs., Nanzemond Co., adj. Wm. Smealy & Ralph
Boseman; 21 Sept. 1674, p. 520, Trans.
of: Robert North.

MR. GYLES DRIVER, 930 acs., Is. of
W. Co., 21 Sept. 1674 p. 520. 580 acs.
granted him 26 Oct. 1662; on the Cyprus
Sw., adj. Ambrose Bennett's heirs; 380
acs. part of sd. 580 acs. nigh unto Parson
Bracewell, &c; 200 acs. granted him 12
Mar. 1657, renewed 13 Jan. 1661; 350
acs. newly taken up; nigh the Gr. freshet;
nere the Towering tubb pond &c. Trans.
of 7 pers: Will. Howle, Phillip Seargent,
Wm. Phillips, Jno. Driver, Moses Seargant, Ann Bradford, Eliz. Seargent, & 1
Negro.

MR. HENRY APPLEWHAITE, 300
acs., Is. of W. Co., 21 Sept. 1674, p. 520.
Adj. Robt. Edwards, Wm. Bodie, Roger
Davis, Roger King & Paul Luke. Part
of 700 acs. granted to Edmund Palmer,
& sold to him, 9 Jan. 1668.

JOHN TAYLOR, 200 acs.. Up. Par.
of Nanzemond Co., adj. Thomas Cowting; & John Ballard; 21 Sept. 1674, p.
520. Trans. of 4 pers: Margerett Johnson, Ann Spencer, Ann Greene, Pope
Oliver.

MR. JOHN HARDIE, 1390 acs., Is.
of W. Co., 21 Sept. 1674. p. 521. Adj.
Mathew Tomlin; Wm. Westray; & land
of Fulgham & Bressie, &c. 1150 acs.
granted him 5 June 1666; 240 acs. for
trans. of 5 pers: Izabell Jones, Tho. Fore,
Mary Wilkinson, Phillip Wrayford, Phillip Mutis.

MR. JOHN PORTIS. 376 acs., Is. of
W. Co., 21 Sept. 1674, p. 521. Adj. Mr.
Nich. Smith; a br. of Seaward's Cr; Mr.
Cobb; Mr. Tuck; Anthony Mathews; &
Burnett's land, now in tenure of sd.
Portis; &c. 200 acs. granted Robert
Burnet 19 Sept. 1643 & assigned to sd.
Portis 9 Apr. 1664; 120 acs. purchased
of Edmund Palmer, 18 Aug. 1673; 56
acs. for trans. of: Mark Wood.

MR. ROBERT HOLDEN, 250 acs., in
Martins Hundred Parish; 21 Sept. 1674,
p. 521. Beg. at a point where Skiffes'
Cr. & Mr. Hayman's Cr. joynes; upp
Beaver Dam Gut, to Proctor's Spring;
down a br. of Shipp's (or Skipp's) Cr.;
&c. 150 acs. purchased of Mr. Fra. Kirkman; 100 acs. for trans. of 2 pers: Himselfe twice; Nath. Crosse.

WM. WALTON, 200 acs., Accomack
Co.; bet. Gr. & Little Matomkin Creeks;
adj. James Walke; &c; 21 Sept. 1674, p.
521. Trans. of 4 pers: And. Michells,
Danll. Selby, Samll. Michell, Alice
Michell.

MAJOR EDMUND BOEMAN, 250
acs., Accomack Co., neere *Matomkin;* W.
upon Gargatha Path; 21 Sept. 1674, p.

522. Trans. of 5 pers: Hen. Jones, Mary
Bayley, Tho. Wilson, Wm. Hine, Jno.
Wheeler.

MR. CHRISTO. CHARELTON
(Charleton). 836 acs:, New Kent Co.,
upon lower side of Aquintanocoke Sw.,
on NE side of Mattapony Riv., adj. Mr.
Dunston; Major Wyatt, & by Mr. Homes'
path, & Cheesecake Path, &c; page 522.
(*Unfinished*—no date.)

MR. GEO. HOOPER, 346 acs., Middlesex Co., joyneing on *Jaimaica Land:*
21 Sept. 1674, p. 522. Neere the Path
from *Jaimaica* to the *Towne;* to Mr.
Cocke & John Jadwin; &c. Trans. of 7
pers: Peter Rusell, Eliz. Harding, Griffin
Roberts, Allen Fullerton, Ralph Henderson. Jno. Jnoson, Wm. Robinson.

JOHN RICHENS & GEO. HOOPER,
1100 acs., Middlesex Co.. 21 Sept. 1674,
p. 522. Adj. Wm. Blaze; Jno. Jadwin,
by the Path from the Roade to Mr. Rice
Joanes, &c. Trans. of 24 pers: Jno. Pot-
ter, Martha Neale, Jno. Ellis, Kath.
Powell, Jno. Land, Jno. Poeland, Wm.
King, Isaac Stern, Ralph Armestead, Hen.
Petman, Jno. Wilcocks. Jno. Turner.
Gregory a boy, & Jno. Man's trans. 3
times; Barbery Abbot, Eliz. Williams,
Jane Edwards, Ja. Stubbins, Eliz. Dad-
more, Robt. Molton. Geo. Diammond,
Phillis Sergant.

GEO. GILL. 3000 acs., New Kent Co.,
S. side Tatapotomoys Cr., 21 Sept. 1674,
p. 523. Adj. Mr. Jno. Page. Doctor Phil-
lips; Jno. Davis; a br. of Chickahominy;
&c. Trans. of 60 pers: Jno. Telley. Geo.
Price, Jno. Peacock, Ralph Cox, Wm.
Barrett, Jno. Secke (Lecke). Hause Hor-
son, Jno. Waite. Abra. Rax (?), Edwd.
Newby, Alice Range, Eliz. Burnett, Gome
Reeves, Alice Staples, Robt. Markason.
Ra. Brighton, Hen. Underhill. Elinor
Jones, Ja. Hooke, Samll. Meedle, Jentt,
Wynn, Jos. Longe, Susan Darmand,
Math. Collins, And. Lerture, Is. Webster,
Richd. Watson, Edwd. Lacy, Isabell
Darby, Tom. Godfrey, Steph. Sarles, Ann
Deere, Richd. Hull, Robt. Waller. Jno.
Byke, Arthur Crampton (or Crumpton),
Jno. Bradle, Suke (or Luke) Harper,

Hen. Wilde, Wm. Robottom, Wm. Hunter, Izabell Webster, Wm. Ball, Edwd. Brisle, Tho. Scott, Margy. Graves, Margt. Freele (or Breele), Hen. Longman, Geo. Long, Walter Peirce, Jno. Criton, Jno. Cohon, David Logon, Richd. Hodkin, Tom. Boyer, Mary Remaller, Jone Elles, Elenor Dogin, Jno. Hasell.

MAJOR RICHARD LEE, 1140 acs., Gloster Co., knowne by the name of *Paradise;* 22 July 1674, p. 523. Beg. at the Bridge br., issueing out of Poropotank maine Sw., to the Spring br. or valley; by the Beach Spring; to the Bridge Sw., by the Rich Land br. or sw; to S. side of Cole mire br., mere Mr. Jno. Lewis; to main br. of Poropotanke Sw., to Mr. Lee's Horsepasture Br; &c. 1000 acs. granted sd. Lee by 2 pattents; 140 acs. betwixt sd. tracts, for trans. of 3 pers: Tho. Mason, Mary Woodward, Wm. Butler.

JOHN PHIPPS, 1100 acs., James Citty Co., uppon NE br. of Pohatan Sw., 21 Sept. 1674, p. 524. Adj. Sir Wm. Berkeley; Mr. Greene; Mr. Wild, Mr. Udall; & land of Page; &c. Granted to Mr. Fra. Wheeler, 20 Sept. 1661 which patt. expressed 679 acs. only, & sold to sd. Phipps by Mr. John Page, his Atty; 421 acs. for trans. of 9 pers.*

JNO. RICHENS, 400 acs., Middlesex Co., part of an old devidend known by the name of *Jamaica;* on SW side of one of the forkes of Bryery Br., 21 Sept. 1674, p. 524. Part of 1200 acs. taken up by Mr. Jno. Curtis, dec'd., assigned to Jno. Harris, who bequeathed to sd. Richens.

ROBT. ALDIN, 100 acs., Middlesex Co., upon Dragon Sw., on both the Bryery Br., adj. Tho. Cordwell; 21 Sept. 1674, p. 524. Trans. of 2 pers: Arthur Bruse, Ann Bruse.

MR. JNO. LEEKE, 83 A., 34 P., Gloster Co., at *Tindall's point;* adj. Robt. Todd; by the Roade; to Furbush's fence, adj. on Yorke Riv., &c; 21 Sept. 1674, p. 524. Due by purchase from Alexander Hussie.

MR. ALEXANDER SMITH, 110 acs., Middlesex Co., adj. land whereon he lives; land of Major David Cant, dec'd., Mr. Wm. Gordon, the *Gleabe Land,* by the Roade, &c; 21 Sept. 1674, p. 525. Trans. of 3 pers: Eliz. Royland, Phillip Powell, Jno. Day.

CAPT. ROBERT BEVERLY, 3000 acs., Rappa. Co., S. side sd. River, 21 Sept. 1674, p. 525. S. side the maine Sw. of a Mill formerly Mr. Andrew Gilson's. 2000 acs. bounded as in a patt. granted sd. Beverley 20 Apr. 1670; 1000 acs. adj. & due for trans. of 20 pers: Nath. Symonds, David Thomas, Lewis Dennis, Jo. Williams, Jno. Brooke, Antho. Paydon, Edwd. Loyd, Cha. Steward, Robert Leath, Mich. Basse, Jno. Burnett, Jno. Woody, Eliz. Morris, Jano. Morris, Jane Wilkinson, Mary Hambleton, Jno. Johnson, Jacob Didley, Tho. Ellis, Robt. Hunt.

SAME. 600 acs., New Kent Co., same date & page. N. side Mattapony Riv., on back of Mr. Mady (or Mody) & his own land. Granted to John Pigg 3 Jan. 1667, deserted, and granted sd. Beverley by order, &c. Trans. of 12 pers: Samll. Taylor, Jno. Must, Jane Clarke, Edwd. Shippard, Richd. Toldicdy (?), Stephen Millner, Mary Jones, Robt. Bevyns, Eliz. Stiles; 3 Negroes.

WM. HAVERCOMB. 905 acs., Low Norf. Co., S. side the E. br. of Eliz. Riv., 23 Sept. 1674, p. 526. Adj. Mr. Jno. Porter, Senr., in the Ashen Sw., to James Josling; to head of the little Cipriss br., nigh James & Jno. Kemp; to land of Isack Hocker, &c. Trans. of 18 pers: Jno. Custis, unr., Mary Robinson, Eliza. Ayre, Gabriell Jacob, Rich. Walpoole, Teage Odale, George Inch (?), Jno. Alford, Jno. Marshall, Mary Conton, Jno. Broader, Jno. Tillery, Sam. Hearing (?), Owen Tews (?), Jno. Brook (?); 2 Indians; Jone a Negro. (*Note:* Marginal note: 950 acs.)

JAMES HANDSON, 158 acs., Low Norf. Co., at head of the Indian Cr. in Eliz. Riv., adj. Richard Whitehurst &

Henry Holstead; 23 Sept: 1674, p. 526.
58 acs. granted sd. Holstead 14 Sept.
1667. 100 acs. for trans. of 2 pers:
Mathew Wilson, Wm. Wilson.

THOMAS GOULDMAN, 2200 acs.,
in Rappahannocke (Co.), on brs. of Hoskings Cr., below an Indian Path; to Porttobacco Path; to Elick Robins; over
Hoskins' pecoson; to Col. Goodrich, &c;
23 Sept. 1674, p. 526. Trans. of 44 pers:
Robert Cardin, James Wolverige, Richard
Beatly, Daniell Leaty, Leanord Dent,
Thomas Werlett, George Webber, Sum-
mersett Haughton, Thomas Willson,
John Poole, Mary Pendelton, George
Denny, Amey Johnson, Christian Ellen,
Sarah Hibbles, George Browning, Wil-
liam Smyth, Sarath Smyth, John Betton
(or Belton), Joane Biny, Amy Jackson,
Edward Wiett, Richard Grimsted, Thomas
Hart, Ben. Dalifeild, John Haslelock,
Will. Bunt, John Jones, Thomas Wat-
kins, Griffin Jones, Elisabeth Sinering-
ton, Thomas Wood, Dies Come, Richard
Cauthorn, Ann Cauthorne, Aurelia Cau-
thorn, Henery Cox, William Smyth, Ann
Hasellwood, Elizabeth Herbett, Will,
Blackford, John Roberts, Richard Lifton,
Mary Wiatt.

THEOPHILUS WALE & DANIELL
SWILLIVANT, 450 acs., Rappa. Co., 23
Sept. 1674, p. 527. Adj. Elick Robins &
Mr. Thomas Gouldman; by an Indian
Path; on lines of John Masters; & Capt.
Beverly. Trans. of 9 pers: John Langly,
Tho. Jones, Will. Young, Sam. Thorpe,
George Willkinson, Tho. Godwin, Rich-
ard Godwin, Lawrance Smyth, John
Armested.

EDMUND PAGITT, 1019 acs.,
Rappa. Co., S. side Rappa. River; on
SW side of Mill Cr., formerly Tignor's;
23 Sept. 1674, p. 527. Adj. John Weire,
Gent; on SW side of the Backe Roade;
adj. Thomas Rawson, &c. 707 acs. granted
sd. Pagitt & William Shargaint 20 Oct.
1666; 312 acs. for trans. of 7 pers: John
Banester, John Gardnar, Mary Cox, Will.
Sommefeild, Arthur Green, Tho. Green,
Mary White.

GEO JOHNSON, 1100 acs., Acco-
mack Co., bet. N. br. of Muddy Cr. &
Cattaile Cr; 25 Sept. 1674, p. 527. 300
acs. granted him 9 Oct. 1672; 800 for
trans. of 16 pers: Wm. Rust, Tho. Harris,
Jonas Motts, Steph. Boner, Jno. Cooke,
A Smith, Will ...., Betty Ayris (or
Ayers), Persillia Blake, Jone ..... Betty
Browne, Margerett Jon, Jno. Smith, Sam.
Hall; 2 Negroes.

MR. THOMAS WOODWARD,
SENR., 1300 acs., Is. of W. Co., on the
Blackwater; 25 Sept. 1674, p. 527. Adj.
Capt. Antho. Fulgham; lands of Oldis
& Ruffin; Col. Pitt & his Partners, &c.
Trans. of 26 pers: Isabell Lewis, ...
Davis, Robt. Roberts, Walter Curtis, Tho.
Price, Jno. Withridge, Wm. Gould, Ann
Clarke, Hen. Keys, Fra. Keys, Tho. James
Roger Gunn, Eliza. Shellam, Richd. Clay,
Wm. Geer, Jno. Deane, Rebecca Balt,
Richd. Duffeild, Jno. Walker, Hen,
Grimes, Richd. Collins, Eliz. Grigg, Jno.
Kidwell, Wm. Golston, Hen. Stevens,
Jno. Boales.

THOMAS GRIFFIN, 250 acs., Low.
Norf. Co., called Surrey Plantation; by a
cr. running N'ly. out of Curratuck Bay;
including Piney Island; 26 Sept. 1674,
p. 528. Trans. of 5 pers: Jno. Ashworth
himselfe, & 3 Negroes: Besse, Nan, Dick
Morris Fitzgarrall.

HUGH FORGISON, 69 acs., Low
Norf. Co., 26 Sept. 1674, p. 528. Trans.
of 2 pers: Jno. Buttler, Daniel Akerson.

JOHN WHITE, 195 acs., Low. Norf.
Co., in the N. br. of Curratuck; a marsh
dividing this & Mr. Basnett's land; &
Thomas Pitt's land; 26 Sept. 1674, p
528. Trans. of 4 pers: Jno. White, Susan
White, Jno. White, Junr., Solomon
White.

PETER MALBONE, 250 acs., Low.
Norf. Co. called by the name of Long
Island; on Curratuck Bay, including a
small island on the seaboard E'ly. from
Long Is; 26 Sept. 1674, p. 528. Trans.
of 5 pers: Peter Malbone, Margery
Ward, Elizabeth Thompson, James Hogg,
Jno. Mills.

ROBT. SYMMONDS (Symonds), 74 acs., Low. Norf. Co., called *Cedar Island;* S'ly. from Long Is,. & W. upon Curratuck Bay; 26 Sept. 1674, p. 529. Trans. of 2 pers: Edward Price, Tassell Shaw.

LT. COL. JNO. TILLNE, 1600 acs., Accomack Co., bet. Messongo & Cattaile Cr., adj. Robt. Brace & Col. Wm. Kendall; 25 Sept. 1674, p. 529. Trans. of 32 pers: Edwd. Dakes, Miles Hubberd, Tho. Blake, Tho. Williams, Jno. Betts, Ambrose Archer, Jno. Freeman, Richd. Cutler, Jer. Dickes, Jno. Bloxam, Ralph Sadberry, Ann Clifford, Amos Cooke, Roger Kanie, And. Hoope, Fra. Waller, Han. Leech, Amos Cooke, Ben. Salt, Ralph Justis, Robt. Lowe, Isaac Dutchman, Ja. Pryer, Wm. Turner, Wm. Litchfeild, Mary Johnson, John Hayes, Jno. Sands, Jo. Linoke; Tongo, Mingo, & Mass, Negroes.

MR. WILL. HATCHER, 227 acs., Henrico Co., S. side James Riv., 26 Sept. 1674, p. 529. Bet. Gilbert Elam & Henry Lown. Trans. of 5 pers: Tho. Childers, Sarah Poynter, Hen. Davernett, Edwd. Stringer, Ann Fryer.

EDWARD RICHARDS, 1528 acs., Chas. Citty Co., S. side James Riv., 26 Sept. 1674, p. 529. Below the Ponds nigh head of Ward's Cr., adj. Thomas Morgan & his own land, down the Boggy Br., nigh a small Indian feild, &c. 750 acs. granted Jno. Westrope 30 Aug. 1650 & sold to John Graves & Tho. Morgan 29 July 1653, & by sd. Morgan sold to sd. Richards 10 Jan. 1654. 778 acs. for trans. of 16 pers: Wm. Jones, Tho. Alford, Richd. Verdin, Wm. Browne, Ann Browne, Tho. Browne, Richd. Right, Tho. Trainer, Hugh Moganhoragon, Christopher Garry, Fran. Bird, Hannah Townesend, Mary Druwell, John Martin, Tho. Cooper, Inghambred Anderson.

NICHO PERKINS, 537 acs., 3 R., 20 P., Henrico Co., N. side James Riv., adj. Richard Parke; 26 Sept. 1674, p. 530. Trans. of 11 pers: Hackalia Harner, Margaret Harner, Hen. Flegg, Margat. Flegg, Robt. Day, Jane Scott, Mary Diggs,

Jno. Browne, Jno. Hall, Eliz. Drummer; Scipio, Negro.

HENRY LOWNE, 516 acs., Henrico Co., S. side James Riv.; 26 Sept. 1674, p. 530. Running to his Landing; beyond the mouth of Usher's Cr., to Mr. Wm. Hatcher, above Packers Gutt, &c. 350 acs. granted to Richd. Johnson 20 June 1639 & sold to sd. Lowne 1 May 1655; 100 acs. granted to James Usher in 1620 & by Ann Gates (or Gales), dau. & lawful heire of sd. Usher, with her husband, sold to sd. Johnson in 1638, & by him sold to sd. Lowne 16 Apr. 1655, as by Henrico Court may appeare; 66 acs. for trans. of 2 pers: Grace Savage, Tho. Clare.

JOHN KEMP, 500 acs., Low. Norf. Co., in Linhaven Par., N'wd. from the E. br. of Eliz. River; adj. Wm. Edwards; 25 Sept. 1674, p. 530. Trans. of 10 pers: Arthur Tappin himselfe 5 times, & his wife once, Isaac Hocker, Mary his wife, Susanna Hocker, Mich. Clare (or Clarie)

MICHAEL MACOY, 150 acs., Low. Norf. Co., in Linhaven Par., on the head of the S. side of the E. br. of Eliz. River; adj. David Murrow; 28 Sept. 1674, p. 530. Trans. of 3 pers: William Lampert, Edward Davis, Rachell Wetherly.

MR. THO. BOWLER, 504 acs., Rappa. Co., on S. side by the river, 28 Sept. 1674, p. 531. Adj. Mr. Tho. Paine; line of James Bagnall, dec'd., Mr. Tobyas Smith; & land of John Sharpe. Granted to Tho. Pattison & Wm. Denby 3 Dec., 1663 & sold to sd. Bowler.

AMBROSE WHITE, 2000 acs., called *Comforts Quarter,* Accomac Co., bet. *Gingoteag, Accocomson & Pokomoke;* 28 Sept. 1674, p. 531. Adj. Samll. Tayler; Col. Jon. Stringer; Mr. Henry Smith; Capt. Southy Littleton; Wm. Benston; Capt. Danll. Junifer; Capt. John West; Thomas Nickson; & Thomas Moysier. Trans. of 40 pers: Wm. Jones, Sara Turner, Jane Simson, Wm. White, James Smith, Roger Smart, Eliza. Nuttall, Garrett Townesend, Hen. Patten, Robt. Russell, Edwd. Smart, Milles Williams,

Peter Pritchard, Griffin Ellis, Samll. Attkins, Robt. Harrison, Fra. Doughty, Eliza. Roberts, Jane (or James) White, Barnard Tanner, Oliver Tompkins, Jno. Webb, Sara Jones, Hen. Plunkett, Cicely Burk, Mary Burk, Mary Atkinson, Eliz. Smith, Isaac Bradly, Tho. Barton, Wm. Williamson, Wm. Symons, Susan Bateman, Andrew Price, Jno. Hogshead, Jer. Hook, Richd. Green, Mathew Browne, Jno. Burford, Jno. Harryson.

GEORGE GOODLOE, 250 acs., Middlesex Co., S. side of Rappa. Riv., 29 Sept. 1674, p. 532. Adj. land of Henry Corbyn, Esq., now Major John Burnham's; Wm. Copeland; & Robt. Price. Granted to Mr. Jno. Curtis, dec'd., 8 Mar. 1665/6, deserted, & granted sd. Burnham by order, &c., 7 Apr. 1674, which order he assigned to sd. Goodloe 29 May 1674. Trans. of 5 pers: Wm. Pidgeon, Nath. How, Hen. Locker, Wm. Justen, Benj. Palmer.

CORNELIUS ELLIS, 82 acs., Low. Norf. Co., on E. side of the S. br. of Eliz. Riv; on Norgrove's (?) land; 29 Sept. 1674, p. 532. Trans. of 2 pers: Jno. Addams, Tymothy Harra.

RICHD. GOODE, 220 acs., Rappa. Co., S. side sd. river; on branches of Occapacee; 29 Sept. 1674, p. 532. Adj. Wm. Moseley; to Coghill's line; adj. Wm. Gray, &c. Trans. of 4 pers: Sam Fenn, Fran. Hatton, James Moody, Jno. Griffin.

NICHOLAS COPELAND & JAMES ANDREWS, 567 acs., Rappa. Co., S. side the River; on brs. of Occapacee Cr., on S. side the maine swamp; 29 Sept. 1674, p. 532. Adj. land of Tho. Button; Barber's line; neare the Indian Path, &c. Trans. of 12 pers: Sarah Griffin, Jane Chambers, Giles Elliot, Wm. Sterne, Tho. Greene, Geo. Grant, Henry Clerke, Henry Clerke, Junr. Joane Clerke, Jno. Clerke, Jno. Degg, Rich. Spurr.

SCARBURGH, CAPT. EDMUND SCARBURGH & MRS. TABITHA BROWNE, 8000 acs., Accomacke Co., bet. Gr. & Little Matomkin Creeks;

29 Sept. 1674, p. 533. Beg. neere the Roade to *Gargaphya;* by the Middle br. or cr. to Wm. Waltham; to Capt. Wm. Custis; to Wm. Burton, &c. Said land contained within bounds of a patt. for 3000 acs. granted Col. Edmund Scarburgh 9 Nov. 1667; & by order &c., 30 Sept. 1672, the overplus granted to sd. West & Scarburgh; 5000 acs. for trans. of 100 pers: Tho. Ellis, Robt. Hunt, Samll. Taylor, Jane Clarke, Ann Winnell, Richd. Swann, Richd. Mathewes, Wm. Blossom, Hen. Hornbuckle, Jno. Scott, Patrick Tripp, Dennis Waughall, Jno. Obryon, Tho. Pickman, Wm. Poore, Wm. Petty, Tho. Holdfast, Jno. Weaver, Tho. Stacy, Willi. Pickerin, Richd. Cox, Jno. Debruish, Wm. Pidgeon, Jno. Bird, Jno. Duckenhead, Nathall. How, Hen. Locker, Richd. Wine, Wm. Justin, Benja. Palmer, Jno. Perry, Jno. Jeffry, Hum. Jarvis, Samll. Curson, Tho. Davis, Wm. Cleveat, Jno. Dobland, Ja. Harvey, Jno. Hartrey, Tho. Webb, Wm. Davis, Jno. Rowell, Eliz. Sope, Jno. Ellis, Tho. Mogg, Tho. Prigg, Ann Gibbs, Mary Pulman, Jno. Rogers, Tho. Oakeham, Edwd. Cornith, Robt. Yellow, Senr., Robt. Yellow, Junr., Jno. Breeke, Edwd. Thomas, Tho. Sidner, Jeffry. Davis, Will. Scrivener, Jno. Tapper, David Thomas, Jno. Koone, Wm. Gardner, Lewis Dennis, Antho. Peydon, Edwd. Loyd, Robt. Seath, Michaell Bass, Jno. Burnett, Jno. Williams, Cha. Stowverd, Jno. Woody, Eliz. Morris, Jane Moone, Jno. Moone, Jane Wilkinson, Mary Hambleton, Jno. Johnson, Phillip How, Jno. Murphy, Tho. Norris, Will. Gill, Jno. Creed, Hen. Whiffler, Jacob Didley, Jno. Checkford, Tho. Sawyer, Tho. Carwright, Wm. Shelly, Antho. Ruther, Job. Ashley, Wm. Tymson, Christopher Shapley, Arthur Kelley, Robt. Holloway, Ben. Teacle, Wm. Mabry, Hugh Houson; Tomboy Martha & Delitia, Negroes.

ROBERT TODD, 380 acs., at *Tindall's Point;* 21 Sept. 1674, p. 534. Beg. at a cove parting this & land of Mr. John Leeke; upp Yorke River; adj. Edwd. Mumford; by John Bell's path; downe Tindall's Cr; to Chesnutt Br., to W. syde of the Gr. Roade, &c. 250 acs.

granted his father, dec'd., 7 May 1666; 130 acs. overplus, & due for trans. of 3 pers: Edw. Cornick, Robt. Yellow, Senr., Robt. Yellow, Junr.

MR. WILLIAM RANDOLPH, 591 A., 2 R., 20 P., Henrico Co., N. side Appamatock River; on N. side of Swift Cr., 1 Oct. 1674, p. 534. Adj. the upper Saw Mill Dividend; nigh the Indian Cabbins at the dividing falls bet. his land & Eusebius King, &c. Trans. of 12 pers.*

MR. EUSEBIUS KING, 507 A., 2 R., 8 P., Henrico Co., N. side Appamatock Riv; & on N. side of Swift Cr., 1 Oct. 1674, p. 534. Adj. Mr. William Randolph at the divideing fall, &c; to the point of rocks; &c. Trans. of 10 pers.*

DANLL. EIRE, sonne or Mr. Tho. Eire, dec'd., 1650 acs. Accomake Co., on the Swamp bet. land of Massongo & Muddy Cr., 29 Sept. 1674, p. 535. Adj. Capt. Danll. Jenifer; Robt. Brace; Wm. Alworth; land formerly John Wallop's; land of Geo. Johnson, &c. Assigned him by Col. Wm. Kendall & further due for trans. of 33 pers: Ann Tomkins, Geo. Font, Richd. Syuch, Robt. Adkings, Jno. Frankling, Wm. Warren, Ren. Sadler, Tho. Jones, Hen. Layton, Danll. Harwood, Ann Teagle, Richd. Ladbroke, Tom. Pead, Honor Dudly, Tho. Clifton. Johna. Owen, Mary Warren, Jno. Everatt, Ja. Robinson, Edwd. Wright, Edwd. Dinot (or Diccot), Richd. Husbands, Geo. Cooke, Alice Lander (or Lauder), Morg. Wilson, Math. Bradwell, Alexdr. Swann, Jno. Clarke, Richd. Cox, Jno. Carter, Jno. Stevens; Mingo & Charles, Negroes.

COL. WM. KENDALL, 239½ acs., N'ampton Co., at Maggaty Bay; adj. Xper. Dickson; 29 Sept. 1674, p. 535. Trans. of 5 pers: Hen. Barnes, Walter Manington, Jno. Hawkins, Tho. Hemins, Eliz. Merrick.

MR. JOHN KENDALL, 400 acs., N'ampton & Accomack Co.'s; 29 Sept. 1674, p. 535. Adj. Thomas Bell, & land formerly Wm. Roberts' now Robt. Foster's; land of Tho. Browne; Lt. Col. Jno.

Tillne, now in possession of Jno. Mackeel, Junr., by land formerly of Danll. Quillian. &c. 200 acs. granted him 28 Oct, 1673; 200 acs. for trans. of 4 pers: Hester Ridgsey, Wm. Morgan, Tho. Pearie (or Pearce), Wm. Trott.

HEN. PLUMPTON, 500 acs., Nansemond Co., 29 Sept. 1674, p. 535. At a place formerly called now (or new) Plumpton Parke, near the place called Keepers Lodge; adj. Mr. Lear; by Bare Quarter; over the white marsh; &c. Trans. of 10 pers: Jno. Heath, Richd. Gardner, Wm. Dyer, Geo. Williams, Dva (?) Druit, Mary Creeke, Richd. Ozborne, Alice Gwillin, Step. Gaile, Sym. Preachett.

MR. WM. OLDIS & MR. ROBT. RUFFIN, 2050 acs., Is. of W. Co., bet. branches of the Blackwater, 21 Sept. 1674, p. 536. Adj. Col. Pitt, Westray's land; to line bet. Tomlin & Fulgham's land, &c. Trans. of 41 pers.* Note: The rights belonging to this pattent recorded under patt. in this booke in folio 224

JNO. SEXTON, 900 acs., New Kent Co., S. side Yorke Riv., 2 Oct. 1674, p. 536. By Madadecums Cr. 700 acs. granted him 8 Apr. 1668; 200 acs. for trans. of 4 pers: Joh a boy, Phillip Butler, Eliz. Balaer, Roger Albin, Samll. Moore.

EDWD. PORE, 150 acs., Gloucester Co., Kingston Par., neere Marke Foster; 21 Sept. 1674, p. 536. Trans. of 3 pers: Ann Gibbs, Jno. Rogers, Tho. Okeham.

CAPT. JNO. ARMESTEAD, 440 acs., Gloucester Co., Kingstone Par., neare head of a Cr. of the Eastermost river, adj. Xper. Dicken; 21 Sept. 1674, p. 536. Trans. of 9 pers: Jno. Perry, Jno. Ducken, Humph. Jarvis, Samll. Carson, Tho. Davis, Wm. Cleavers, Jno. Doblander, Eliz. Sope, Tho. Prigg. (Marginal note: 450 acres.)

MR. FRANCIS BRIDGE, 300 acs., Middlesex Co., 21 Sept. 1674, p. 537. W'wd. of Mr. Richd. Parriott's branches, beg. at an Oke belonging to the Montagues' at a dry valley issueing out of Mr.

Nich. Cocke's upper Cr., heere Jamaica Path; crosse the Doggwood Valley; a br. parting this & land of Tho. Low; &c. Trans. of 6 pers: Xper. Copeland, Wm. Hall, Tho. Robinson, Wm. Lenam, Mary Nuttbrowne, Mary Merfy.

JA. STUBBINS, 450 acs., Gloster Co., upon brs. of Poropotanke; adj. Capt. Richd. Dudley; in Danceing Valley; to Curle's Path & Br., to br. of the Rich Land Sw., to Mr. Richd. Lee; adj. Geo. Haynes & Spency's land, &c; 21 Sept. 1674, p. 537. Trans. of 9 pers: Jno. Nicholas, Jno. Westone, Jonas Rice, Wm. Bryan, Tho. Glover, Richd. Davis, Cha. Parsons, Tho. Cooper, Tho. Goose.

JNO. BILLIOT, sonne of Jno. Billiot, dec'd., 1050 acs., in N'ampton (Co.); on a br. of Forked Cr., parting this & land of Tho. Bell; & adj. Robt. Foster; 23 Sept. 1674, p. 537. Granted to his father 9 Oct. 1656; renewed 20 Oct. 1661; due him as heire, &c; petitioned for by Mr. Edmund Scarburgh as deserted land, but his order dated 21 Dec. 1673 was reversed & land confirmed to sd. John.

WM. TIGNOR, 550 acs., N'umberland Co., on N. side of Gr. Wiccocomico Riv., 23 Oct. 1674, p. 538. Upon a cr. dividing this from Jno. Johnson; E. upon Mr. Ashton's Cr. & land; towards land of Wm. Bitt; & Tho. Garrard, &c. Granted Mr. Ja. Hawly, 2 June 16..; assigned to Wm. Leach 14 Oct. 1661, who assigned to sd. Tignor 10 Apr. 1666.

CAPT. SOUTHY LITTLETON, 4250 acs., N'ampton Co., bet. Maggettey Bay & the Seaboard side; from the sandy point of Old Plantation Cr. mouth to the *Divell's Ditch*, &c; adj. 400 acs. called Gogges (?) land; to land formerly Wm Ennis', &c; 5 Oct. 1674, p. 538. 1050 acs. granted to Mr. Charles Harmer 4 June 1635; 150 acs. granted to Elizabeth Harmer 17 Sept. 1644, to which was added the sd. 1050 acs., as being the dau. & heire of sd. Charles; by deed of sale dated 1 May 1654 assigned by Thomas Harmer, son & heire of Doctor John Harmer, heire to sd. Charles Har-

mer & Elizabeth, his dau., made over & assigned to Nathaniell Littleton, Esqr., & againe granted to Edwd. Littleton, his son & heire, 25 Mar. 1656, & renewed by order of the Quarter Court 26 Nov. 1661; decendeth to sd. Southy, as bro. & heire of sd. Edward. 800 acs. more granted to sd. Nath'l., 20 Sept. 1644 & descended to sd. Southy, &c; 1200 acs. granted to Robt. Barrington 17 Sept. 1644, & found to escheat by inquisition, &c., before Col. John Stringer, Depty. Esch'r., 24 Oct. 1672, & regranted to sd. Southy, 27 Mar. 1673, &c; 250 acs. within the bounds of the sd. 1200 acs., was granted to sd. Barrington; & of the aforesd., 800 acs. was granted to Danll. Neach 5 Oct. 1670, by him deserted, & granted sd. Southy, by order, &c., 9 Apr. 1674. 800 acs. for trans. of 16 pers: Jno. Dabridcourt, Jno. Sims, Edw. Parle, Jno. Browsgrove, Eliz. Peacock, Amos Bonfeild, Math. Pope, Wm. Elvin, Mary Aldrige, Jno. Harris, Jo. Billeter, Jno. Brookes, Jno. Cooke, Samll. Carter, James Harloe, Tho. Blackhall. *Note:* Rights for the 250 acs. laps't by Danll. Neach. (*Note:* The following names appear:) Jno. Moore, Eliz. Moore, Eliz. Moore, Sarah Moore & Jno. Hansson.

CAPT. WM. MOSELEY, CAPT. ROBERT BEVERLEY & NICCOLAS CATTLETT, 1200 acs., Rappa. Co., S. side Rappa. Riv., on N. or N. E. side of Gilson's Cr., 21 Sept. 1674, p. 539. Beg. at Robt. Beverley's in line of Mr. Tho. Button, &c. Granted Mr. John Pate, dec'd., 15 July 1666; deserted, & now granted by order, &c. 646 acs. granted sd. Moseley & Catlett 7 Oct. 1670, being within sd. 1200 acs; 460 acs. for trans. of 9 pers: Wm. Freeman, Wm. Spinly, Richd. Jasper, Eliz. Kerneys, Dunken Robinson, Ja. Everatt, Jno. Holland, Isaac Woods, Wm. Jones.

JOHN BRYANT (Bryon), 81 acs., Nanzemond Co., 6 Oct. 1674, p. 540. Adj. his own; land of Mr. William Denson, & Henry Gaye. Trans. of 2 pers.* NOTE: "These Rights were in the office before the Removeall of the office from Laurences which said Rights by order of the Genll. Court are Good." (*Note:* The following has been crossed out: "as allowed by the order of the Governor & Councell".)

MICHAELL TUCKER, 200 acs., New Kent Co., on NW br. or forke of Black Cr., 9 Sept. 1674, p. 540. Adj. William Townsend; Mathew Hubbert; by *pough-white path*, &c; Trans. of 4 pers: Samll. Moore.*

MR. HUGH YEO, 2050 acs., Accomack Co., at Matchapongo Cr. & River; 5 Oct. 1674, p. 540. Beg. at a cr. parting this from Nevell's Neck; big Matchapongo Cr. parting this from land of Major Jno. Tilne; over the Back Cr; &c. 1000 acs. granted to Stephen Charleston 29 Aug. 1650 & 700 acs. granted him 16 Mar. 1653, both of which sd. Charleton gave to his dau. Eliz. by deed dated 17 Oct. 1654, with the provisor if she died without issue the land should belong & appertaine unto her sister Bridgett Charleton; now the sd. Eliz. being dead without issue & sd. land belonging to sd. Bridgett, who is now the wife of Capt. Isaac Foxcraft, was by them sould to sd. Yeo, 16 June 1668; 350 acs. for trans. of 7 pers: Richd. Chambers, Jno. Meekes, Antho. Hardy, Eliz. Michell, Laurence Atkins, Jno. Beare, Tho. Colwell.

MR. JNO ROBINS (Robbins), 950 acs., N'ampton Co., S. side Cherrystone Cr., bet. Drew's Cr. & the *Secretaries Land;* 5 Oct. 1674, p. 541. Beg. on N. side of Vaughan's *alias* Montnues (?) Cr., to Nath. Wilkins land &c. 100 acs. granted Col. Obedience Robbins 18 Oct. 1647 & descended to sd. John as his sonne & heire; 292 acs. granted his sd. father 30 Mar. 1643, & descended, &c; 100 acs. granted Capt. Clemt. Dilke 12 Dec. 1627 & found to escheat as by inquisition before Col. Jno. Stringer, &c., 8 May 1663; regranted to Mrs. Grace Robbins, Widdow, 3 Sept. 1663; &c; 100 acs. granted Wm. Williams, dec'd., & found to escheat, & granted as aforesaid; both of which were made over to sd. Jno. by deed from said Grace, dated 10 Mar. 1673; 100 acs. granted Jno.

Little 20 Sept. 1647, who assigned to Jno. Derman 16 Jan. 1650, & by Jno., his sonne & heire, conveyed to sd. Jno. Robbins 28 Nov. 1667; 258 acs. for trans. of 5 pers: Jno. Robins, Wm. Clements, Joane Frankling, Wm. Savage, Jno. Symonds.

MRS. ANN BOATE, 1350 acs., Accomack Co., on S. side of Pungoteage Cr., 8 Oct. 1674, p. 541. W. upon the Bay & Arrakokes Cr., E. upon Wanstansick Br., &c. 900 acs. being part of 1000 acs. granted her by the name of Ann Hack, Widdow, & to Geo. Hack & Peter Hack, 11 Sept. 1665; 450 acs. for trans. of 9 pers: Jno. Freeze, Benock Freeze, Kath. Varlett, Wm. Varlett, Sus. Cox, Nich. Brett, Nich. Hart, Marg. Harmon, Mary Tomson.

MAJOR EDMUND BOEMAN & CAPT. SOUTHEY LITLETON, 2264 acs., Accomack (Co.), on N. side of Swansicutts, otherwise called, Gr. Mattapony Creeke; N. upon the line bet. Va. & Md; 5 Oct. 1674, p. 542. Granted to them, 23 May 1671, by which patt. the land was falsely bounded, & by order, &c., 8 Apr. 1674, granted according to the true bounds.

MAJOR EDMD. BOEMAN, 600 acs., Accomack Co., at Messongo Cr., 9 Oct. 1674, p. 543. Granted to Robert Johnson 5 Apr. 1666, deserted, & regranted sd. Boeman by order &c., 9 Apr. 1674, & due for trans. of 12 pers: Jno. Trelany, Wm. Gosling, Jno. Arundell, Samll. Gosworth, Wm. Terdin, Wm. Loyn, Wm. Paggett, Jno. Wottors, Corn. Morrice, Christopher Nutter; & And., & Donor., Irishmen.

CAPT. SOUTHEY LITTLETON, 600 acs., Accomack Co., at *Pocamoke;* on land formerly of Morris Liston; bet. Wm. Benston & Mr. Henry Smith; & adj. Mr. Ambrose White; 8 Oct. 1674, p. 543. Trans. of 12 pers: Jno. Martin, Jno. Barnes, Jno. Robinson, Jno. Brewer, Geo. Grey, Edwd. Jones, Jno. Carr, Fra. Allen, Margt. Mathews, Wil. Collhart, Alexr. Allen.

JONAH JACKSON, 500 acs., Accomack Co., at Accohanock Cr., 8 Oct.
1674, p. 543. Near land formerly Phillip'
Meredeth's; to land of Alexdr. Adison;
to lands of Nuswadocks; to Edwd. Moore,
&c. 300 acs. granted him 24 July 1651;
200 granted Edwd. Moore 20 Oct. 1661,
deserted, & now granted by order, &c., for
trans. of 4 pers: Jno. Jaspher, Richd.
Wood, Jacob Fowkes, Jonas Backman.

CAPT. ROBERT BEVERLY & RICH-
ARD BARBER, 600 acs., Rappa. Co., S.
side Rappa. Co. or River; 21 Sept. 1674,
p. 544. Adj. Henry Jermaine, Wm. Gray
& Tho. Page; beg. about 3 mi. from the
river neere Mattapony Path; cor. to Xper.
Blackburn & Wm. Gray; to Occapation
runn, &c. Granted to James Coggill 17
Apr. 1667, deserted, & now granted, &c.
Trans. of 12 pers: Geo. Jeffers, Jo.
Feild, Wm. Nicholas, Jno. Bywater, Jno.
Pearson, Jno. Fugill, Tho. Hallat, Michll.
Hurst, Jno. Johnson, Hugh Hughson,
James Jackson, Amy Blissard.

KATHERINE LOWDELL, 150 acs.,
New Kent Co., 12 Oct. 1674, p. 544.
Granted to Wm. Owen, who dying without heires, was found to escheat, by inquisition, under Mr. Tho. Hall, &c.

PETER RICH, 350 acs., Nanzimond
Co., in a Gr. Arrow Read Pocoson; 14
Oct. 1674, p. 544. Trans. of 7 pers.*
Note: "These Rights were in the office
before the office was removed from
Laurences, which said rights by order of
the Genll. Court are good, there appear-
ing a Certificate for them under the hand
of Wm. White then Clerke dated" (Note:
No date.) Test, P. L. Cl.

CAPT. SOUTHY LITTLETON, 1500
acs., Accomack Co., bet. brs. of Pungotege & Matchepungoe Bever dam Br: 5
Oct. 1674, p. 545. Beg. at the head of
the S'most maine freshwater br. of Pokomoke Cr., which is a br. of Pungotege
Cr., to land of James Grey & Alphonse
Ball; to Richd. Hill, Junr., to Barthol.
Meares; along Nathll. Bradford to Wm.
Nock; to Mr. Cha. Scarburgh; to Revell's
alias Randall's Br., to Mr. Hugh Yeo; to

land formerly Nicolas Waddilow's, &c.
Trans. of 30 pers: Joan Constable, Mr.
Green, Ann Cowdrip, Eliza. Cowdrip,
Claus Tusan, Tho. Cullen, Nicho. Broad,
Gellion Vanplancks, Fran. Runshoute,
Derick Vessell, Peter Peterson, Mary
Constable, Dun. Superion, Susanah Su-
perion, Sarah Superion, Henrick John-
son, Tho. Crabb, Derick Johnson, Walter
Broad, Richd. Lovegrove, Robt. Watson,
8 times, Rebecka Superion, Tho. Black-
hall.

THO. FENFORD, 300 acs.; Low.
Norf. Co., W. side of the S. br. of Eliz.
Riv., adj. his own land; 21 Sept. 1674, p.
545. Trans. of 6 pers: Tho. Culson, Jno.
Morfeild, Jno. Bray, Bartho. Bee, Jno.
Robardson, Wm. Morgan.

MR. JAMES HARRISON, JOHN
BOWZEE; & ELIZ., MARGERETT,
ANN & ELIN MOTT, the 4 Orphans of
Mr. Geo. Mott; 9019 acs., on S. side of
Rappa. Riv., about 6 mi. up the falls;
29 Nov. 1674, p. 546. Trans. of 180
pers: Jno. Gaile, Tho. Buckler, Edith
Stable, Hen. Vincent, Tho. Bell, Wm.
West, Eliz. Howell, Tho. Pittman, Jno.
Frazell, Elin Thomas, Lewis Boyse, Jno.
Williams, Jud. Cooper, Jno. Stephens,
Wm. Williams, Jno. Fisher, Peter
Holmes, Jno. Chase, Jno. Starky, Jno.
Wilson, Robt. Sands, Jno. Vickers, Henry
Long, Wm. Smith, Ann Crowch, Fowler
Phillips, Doroth. Newcome, Jno. Ward,
Jno. Dunn, Bartho. Chandler, Danll.
Oneale, Jno. Sampson, Jno. Wiseman,
Tho. Eliston, Wm. West, Jno. Sumner,
Edwd. Parker, Wm. Steedman, Tho.
Nowell, Adam Hill, Robt. Davis, Jno.
Witchell, Mary Knowles, Tho. Butler,
Al. Jones, Theo. Piles, Jno. Lucy, Jno.
Dugard, Rich. Wakelynn, Jno. Howard,
Tho. Warner, Wm. Crostie (?), Wm.
Wakelynn, Wm. Jordan, Jno. Bell, Tho.
Bunting, Mary Wakelynn, Alice Ran-
dolph, Alexdr. Frizell, Wm. Staples,
Mary Pettitt, Susan Cooke, Ralph Cole,
Mary Williamson, Tho. Watts, Peter
Chirpett (or Chripett), David Jnoson,
Richd. Webly, Ja. Montron, Sym. Jer-
mans, Rebecca Smith, Tho. Padge, Judeth
Jones, Jno. Trelony, Antho. Peterson,

Jno. Bickner, Francis Holmwood, Jno. Temple, Jno. Williamson, Robt. Young, Richd. Bickner, Peter Ridley, Rebecca Smith, Wm. Semons, Robt. Readman, Simon Willæms, Jno. Paulin, Dorothy Stoakes, Eliz. Watkins, Sampson Eliott, Wm. Hewes, Susan Steele, Jno. Drayton, Hellen Thomas, Jno. Clarke, Mary Price, Peter Rogers, Richd. Hogsdon, Jno. Knowles, Simond Bland, Ralph Eliott, Tho. Averie, Tho. Wood, Ja. Price, Cha. Cox, Tho. Darnell, Wm. Lambe, Jea. Reanold, Darby Swillivant, Robt. Mosse, Tho, Jones, Tho. Well, Tho. Cox, Margerett Humstead, Abra. Moore, Sar. Wild, Jno. Snow, Thó. Duke, Lidia Dix, Fra. Smith, Robt. Howkes, Jno. Thomas, Jno, Chiles, Dixy Hare, Andrew Greene, Wm. Wilson, Canute Williamson, Peter Peterson, Wm. Sherman, Stephen Meadows, Jo. Roberdson, Edwd. Travers, Timothy Wallington, Eliz. Sackler, David Marriott, Tho. Tunill, Stephen Fewell, Solom. Martin, Wm. Donolye (?), David Anderson, Hanna Knight, Eliz. Wilson, Jannett Brice, Tho. Reade, Wm. Harris, Susan Wells, Geo. Searles, Ann Middleton, Jno. Wood, Tho. Cadger, Alice Gardner, Mary Pope, Jno. Yates, Tho, Franklynn, Jno. Hannah, Tho. Hudson, Mary Collomb, Tho. Jnoson, Adam Fryer, Antho. Williams, Peter Mills, Peter Gray, Ad. Turner, Jno. Carter; & 16 Negroes.

MR. RICHD. BAILY, 1875 acs., Gloucester Co., S. side of Peanketank River, beg. at mouth of Hoccady's Cr; 16 Nov. 1674, p. 547. By the Beaver Dams, to the goeing over of Snelling's Path; adj. Mr., Robt. Elliot; Tho. Gaunt; Mr. Wm. Elliot; his own land at the head of a valley of Allin's Cr; & downe a br. dividing this & land of Robt. Beverly, formerly Col. Elliot's; &c. 600 acs. purchased of Col. Antho. Elliott; 882 acs, granted sd. Baily; 393 acs. now found adj., due for trans. of 8 pers.*

CAPT. LAURENCE SMITH & CAPT. ROBT. BEVERLY, 6500 acs., Rappa. & New Kent Co.'s; adj. 4600 acs. of sd. Smith; beg. by the Beaver Dams or near head of the Ready Br., &c; 16 Nov. 1674.

p. 547. Trans. of 130 pers: Hen. Bry, Math. Towers, Edwd. Gittes, Wm. Rowland, Jno. Conmark, Richd. Shay, Eliz, Harwood, Fra. Fox, Jerm. Parsons, Jno. Hall, Math. Robinson, Tho. Knight, Tho. Hopkins, Wm. Givor (or Guyor), Jno. Linkehorne, David Bourne, Xper Bicks, Wm. Holliday, Mich. Hookam, Jo. Ecale (or Erale), Ja. Couch, Jno. Yarrow, Hen. Chapman, Geo. Hawsone, Jno. Boyce, Jno. Smith, Rich. Williams, Jno. Gores (or Goods), Jno. Patten, Steph. West, Robt. Elson, Wm. Birdloe, Eliz. Knight, Elen Hitch, Ann Syra, M. Hutchson, Tho. Knell, Sam. Orkney, Geo. King, Richd. Presly, Tho. Mady, Susan Kerne, Eliz. Newty, Wm. Fuller, Ja. Newton, Oliver West, Edwd. Strong, Ja. Linsey, Jno. Perry, Arth. Wright, Jane Luse, Wm. Roberts, Amb. Neale, Phillip Carey, Jno. Douding, Ann Wheatly, Wm. Howell, Xper. Lewis, Joane Maynards, Rich. King; 4 Negroes.

GEO. BATES, 412 acs., (Co. not given), .. Nov. 1674, p. 548. Granted to James Smith, dec'd., & escheated by inquisition, &c., under Tho. Ludwell, Esqr., Esch'r., &c. ..

THOMAS GRAVES & JEFFERY GRAVES, sonnes of Tho. Graves, dec'd., 440 acs., Gloucester Co., in Abbington (Par. ?), 6 Mar. 1674/5, p. 548. Adj. Mr. Robt. Coleman, neere dwelling house of Jeffry Graves; neere the Gr. Roade to Tindall's point, &c. 200 acs. purchased by Thomas Graves, Senr., of Danll. Clarke; 240 acs. granted him 20 Nov. 1661, & the whole now due the above under the will of their father; & according to sd. will at their request & in their presence devided by Capt. Laurence Smith & Capt. Robt. Beverly.

DUNKEN BOHANNAN, 340 acs., Goulcester Co., in Kingstone Par., upon the E'most River; 6 Mar. 1674/5, p. 548. Beg. at gutt parting this & land of Jno. Nevell; &c. Part of a gr. devdt. granted to Mr. Wm. Armestead & due sd. Bohannon by assignment.

STEPHEN FENTRY, 300 acs., Gloucester Co., Kingston Par., 6 Mar. 1674/

5, p. 549. Beg. uppon Queen's Cr., adj. Mr. Jno. Curtis & James Lindsay. Part of a gr. devd.t pattented by Mr. Ja. Cary, & assigned by him.

DANLL. LANGHAM, 350 acs. Gloster Co., Abbington Par., neere Mr. Robt. Coleman; 6 Mar. 1674/5, p. 549. Granted to Xper. Abbott 20 Jan. 1657, & due sd. Danll. by marrying Mary, the dau. of sd. Abbott.

JNO. GUYTON. 313 acs., Gloster Co., Kingston Par., 6 Mar. 1674/5, p. 549. 188 acs. as expressed in his former pattent; 125 acs. adj. & adj. Mr. Jno. Armestead. Trans. of 3 pers.*

JAMES LINDSAY (Lindsey), 390 acs., Gloster Co., Kingston Par., 6 Mar. 1674/5, p. 549. On Queen's Cr., adj. Jacob Johnson; & Stephen Fentry. Part of a gr. devdt. granted to Richd. Cary, who assigned to sd. Lindsey.

JNO. NEVELL. *Infant*. 100 acs., Gloster Co., Kingston Par., 6 Mar. 1674/5, p. 549. Adj. Dunkin Bohannan, on W. side of the E'most river; & adj. lands of Richd. Cary & Mr. Jno. Armestead. Due sd. Bohannan by purchase from Mr. Armestead, & due sd. Nevell as sonne & heire of his dec'd. father.

MR. MATHEW KEMP. JUNR., 229 acs., Gloster Co., Kingston Par., 6 Mar. 1674/5, p. 550. Beg. at the mouth of a br. devideing this & land of Mr. Tho. Palliser (or Talliser) ; by Col. Mathew Kemp's feild close by the fence, & down Peanketanck River, &c. Trans. of 5 pers: Jno. Stephens, Eliz. Packwood, Ann Sargant, Margrett Banks, Jno. Greene.

CAPT. LAURENCE SMITH, 330 acs., Gloster Co., Abbinton Par., 6 Mar. 1674/5, p. 550. Adj. Col. Ludlow, dec'd., Mr. Jno. Banister, Abbott, Coleman & Edwd. Foster &c. to the hernes nest Pine, &c. Trans. of 7 pers.*

GABRIELL HILL, 250 acs., New Kent Co., (date blank), p. 550. Beg. in the forke of a br. of Axoll's (or Exoll's), Br., &c. 134 acs. granted sd. Hill 29

Nov. 1665; 116 acs. adj. sd. land which he lives uppon; beg. by Cole's Br., upp the Spring Br., neere his plantation; to Sorrell's Br., by Axoll's Sw., &c. Trans. of 3 pers: Wm. Greenefeild, Eliz. Lankford, Rich. Malloone.

JOHN GREENE, 600 acs., Gloster Co., Petsoe Par., uppon brs. of Poropotank Cr., 1 Mar. 1674/5, p. 551. Adj. Mr. Dudley's line; his own; Samll. Clarke; Henry Hubert, &c. 350 acs. granted him 25 Aug. 1655; renewed 13 Jan. 1661; & 250 acs. found within, &c., due for trans. of 5 pers.*

JACOB JOHNSON, 740 acs., Gloster Co., Kingston Par., uppon Queen's Cr., 6 Mar. 1674/5, p. 551. Adj. James Lindsey; along line made by Mr. Jno. Curtis; along the Roade to Mr. Wm. Elliott, Senr.,, to the Dirty Br., to Rich. Carey's; &c. 440 acs. purchased from Rich. Cary; 300 acs. for trans. of 6 pers.*

COL. MATHEW KEMP, 573 acs., Gloster Co., Jingstone Par., 26 Jan. 1674/5, p. 551. Adj. Mr. Palliser. neere Col. Kemp's Quarter; to Joanna Pounall (or Tounall ?) &c; 400 acs. granted to Jno. Chapman 15 Sept. 1658 & sold to sd. Kemp; 173 acs. for trans. of 4 pers.*

MR. GEO. CURTIS, 800 acs., Gloster Co., Kingstone Par., on S. side Peanketank River, bet. Peanketank Cr., *alias* Col. Kemp's Cr., & Wadeing Cr., 26 Jan. 1674/5, p. 552. Adj. Col. Kemp, neere Wm. Marloe's fence; land of Mr. Tho. Palliser; by Lady Skipwith's land, &c. Purchased of Mr. Edwd. Wyatt, & further due for trans. of 16 pers.*

RICHARD DAVIS, 370 acs., New Kent Co., in Stratton Major Par., 1 Mar. 1674/5, p. 552. Adj. land he lives uppon; beg. in Arakieco Sw., adj. Leonard Chamberlin; by David Prichard's Path; to Jno. Stringer, &c., 256 acs. adj. Capt. Jones; along Hanks' line, &c. Trans. of 7 pers: Richd. Davis, Tho. Burger, Jno. Waters, Izarell Wrenn, Barbara Hargrave, Jno. Williams, Xper. Hudson, Laurence Morton.

JNO. WILLIAMSON, JUNR., 758 acs., Low. Norf. Co., in Tanner's Cr. precincts, 22 Jan. 1674, p. 553. Nere head of the fresh runn branch; at head of Lazarus Jenkin's land; adj. Richard Jones; bet. the Black Walnutt Neck & the Long Neck; to Gater's Cr., &c. 644½ acs. granted him 16 Mar. 1655; 113½ acs. granted 24 Aug. 1660; for trans. of 3 pers: Danll. Negletine (?), Jno. Moore, Mary Williams.

CAPT. DANLL. JENIFER, 1680 acs., Accomack Co., in Messango Sw., 26 Jan. 1674/5, p. 553. Adj. Col. Wm. Kendall; land formerly granted to Jno. Wallop; by Jno. Parker's; to land formerly Alexdr. Massie's; to N. maine freshwater br. of Muddy Cr., & along Geo. Johnson, &c. Trans. of 34 pers: Wm. Bromfeild. Dor. Olive. Jno. Waford. Math. Elliot, Wm. Anzer (or Arecher), Hen. Gibson, Sam. Ponvoy (or Ponroy), Jane Dylera, Rich. Williams. Nath. Barton, Geo. Foard. Ger. Lee, Ja. Boyd, Jno. Juler. Sus. Martin, Xper. Jackson, Rich. Greinall (or Greivall), Tho. Capp, Derman Cavine, Marg. Sumers. Tho. Shelite, Tho. Blake, Joane Scott, Ma. Knight, Ed. Bishopp. Nath. Darchartie, Jno. Manzo (or Manro), Hen. Flower. Sar. Cutts, Eliz. Mouth. Tho. Cunningham; & 3 Negroes.

JAMES WALLACE, 738 acs., Chas. City Co., S. side James River, 26 Feb. 1674/5, p. 553. On the Black water, at land of Robt. Lucy; over the Cattaile branch, &c. Trans. of 15 pers: Tho. Taylor, Jno. Wood, Benj. Poore (or Good ?), Jno. Nicholas, Phill. Paites, Mary Kennon, And. Peck, Rich. Cake. Edd. Averett, Jno. Langford, Elinor Norton, Robt. Lewis, Martin Paine, Dermmat Donnell, Sarah Hind.

ROBT. BENNETT, 330 acs., Gloster Co., Kingstone Par., 26 Jan. 1674/5, p. 554. Beg. at his own & land of Jno. Guyton; along James Bealy (Beale), &c. Granted to Capt. Jno. Armestead 21 Sept. 1674 & assigned to sd. Bennett & his heires for ever (alwaies provided that he die with issue of his body lawfully begotten, otherwise to returne to the said Armestead & heires & to their only use and behoofe) which assignment is for & in consideration that the said land formerly belonged to his father Adam Bennett & the pattent thereof lost as by the said assignment uppon the said pattent will appeare. (Note: The following names appear under this record:) Tho. Newbery, Jno. Wooderoff, Jno. Hardy, Jno. Hadaway, Symon Hobson, Jone Fellps.

200 acs., for a GLEEBE, in the Parish of Southwork, (Surry Co.), 26 Jan. 1674/5, p. 554. Uppon a Gr. Swamp parting Jno. Watkins' land. & uppon a br. of same parting Graves' land & the Gleebe. & uppon Mr. Thomson's land, &c.

COL. ROBT. ABRAHALL, 350 acs., New Kent Co., 2 Mar. 1674/5, p. 554. Granted to Wm. Moore, & escheated by inquisition, &c., under Tho. Hall, Depty. Esch'r., &c.

JOHN PIGG, 280 acs., Rappa. Co., upon N. side of a gr. br. of Peanketank Sw., 2½ mi. from Capt. Claiborne's. Quarter; 10 June 1675, p. 554. Over the Path leading to Mr. Paine's, of Rappa., &c. Granted to Jno. Paddison 18 Feb. 1663, deserted, & granted to Edwd. Hudson, & by him deserted; granted sd. Pigg, by order &c., 21 Sept. 1671 & due for trans. of 6 pers: Tho. Culson, Jno. Bray, Wm. Morgan, Jno. Robardson, Jno. Morfeild, Barth. Bee.

MR. GEO. LEE. 300 acs., Surrey Co., 10 June 1675, p. 555. Granted to Jeremiah Dickeson, & escheated by inquisition &c., under Tho. Ludwell, Esch'r. Genr'l. of Va., 22 June 1668; granted to Mr. Geo. Watkins. who assigned to sd. Lee.

JOHN ADAMS. 160 acs., Low Norf. Co., on N. side of Eliz. River, 10 June 1675, p. 555. Adj. his own land. Trans, of 3 pers.*

ROGER SMITH, 100 acs., Rappa. Co., some 3 mi. back into the woods; beg. at Col. Goodrich; adj. land of Randolph Curtis, formerly Hodgkins' land;

to line of Woodnot & Smith; 10 June 1675, p. 555.

MR. JOHN STITH, 636 A., 1 R., 24 P., Chas. Citty Co., N. side James River; 11 May 1675, p. 555. Beg. on N. side of the Easterne Runn Br., niegh Martiall's Path; down the westerne Gr. Branch to the Indian Cabbin point, being the forke of the branches, &c. Trans. of 13 pers: Tho. Boone, Jno. Arrow, James Sparkes, Jno. Burnett, Tho. Herring, Wm. Rogers, Jno. Hond, Mary Bates, Jno. Clarke, Alice Roberts, Symond Gibson, Water Baux (or Banx) Nich. Wiskin.

EDWD. GRESHAM, 111 acs., New Kent Co., N. side of Axoll's Sw., 10 June 1675, p. 556. Adj. Col. Claiborne, &c. Trans. of 3 pers.*

JOHN & GEO. KILLMAN, 920 acs., Rappa. Co., on Ralph Cr., a br of Pascutway Cr., 10 June 1675, p. 556. By land of Greene, nye the Greene br; joyning Capt. Jno. Duke; to Braye's corner; to Beaver Dam Cr. or Ralph Cr., to land of Coggall, &c. Trans. of 19 pers.* Note: "This pattent of noe force. H. Hartwell, Cl.'

WM. BALL, 370 acs., New Kent Co., on branches of Ashawaymankirth; 10 June 1675, p. 556. Beg. at land of Jno. Pigg, next to Mr. Rowle; adj. land of Rogers; & Jno. Maddison; along Mr. Lockey's, &c. Trans. of 8 pers.*

MR. PHILLIP LIGHTFOOT, 150 acs., Gloster Co., Abbinton Par., 15 June 1675, p. 557. Adj. Edwd. Momford (Mumford) on one side, & Yorke River upon another; on Mr. Richd. Booker's land, lately Mr. Reynold's; & on Mr. Jno. Banister, &c. 90 acs. due unto Capt. Jno. Lightfoot by purchase from the Widdow Fleet & Jno. Cooper & his wife, & since that for a debt due from sd. Capt. Lightfoot to Mr. Phillip Lightfoot extended to the use of sd. Phillip; 60 acs., being overplus adj., due for trans. of 2 pers.*

LEWIS DAY, 400 acs., Gloster Co., Petsoe Par., adj. Tattapotomoys Sw., 15 plantation, &c. Granted to Jno. Day 24

July 1653 & due sd. Lewis as his sonne & heire.

CAPT. ROBT BEVERLEY, 698 acs., Gloster Co., Ware Parish; 15 June 1675, p. 558. Betwixt & adj. Mr. Wm. Elliott, Junr., & his brother Mr. Tho. Elliot; land of Mr. Marke Warkeh. dec'd. land of Mr. Wm. Marloe, formerly pattented by Tho. Collins; and of the Chiescake Indians; & of Mr. Richd. June 1675, p. 557. Neere Jno. Boothe's Bailey, & by him purc f Lt. Col. Anthony Elliot, dec'd. P. one Warner's marsh; to the land remoely leased by Mr. Wm. Elliot to Geo Wolley (Woolley), &c., by the path to Hoccadayes Cr., formerly called Snelling's path, &c. to a br. of Wadding Cr., &c. 500 acs. purchased of Wm. Elliott, Junr., 14 Sept. 1672; 198 acs., being overplus, &c., due for trans. of 4 pers.*

FRANCIS BROUGHTON, 170 acs., Gloster Co., Ware Par., 15 June 1675, p. 559. Adj. land he lives upon; beg. at a br. of Craney Cr., cor. of Wm. Roberts', late dec'd., to Burches' branch, to runn of Geo. Poole's br; by Jordan's lines, &c. Trans. of 4 pers.*

LEONARD AMBROSE, 60 acs., Gloster Co., Ware Par., 15 June 1675, p. 559. Betwixt land of Humphry Meed, dec'd., & Jno. Wells, dec'd; Mr. Ja. Clarke; & Morgan Lewis. Trans of 2 pers: Richd. Blackwell, Fra. Palmer

DAVID CANT, sonn of Major David Cant, dec'd., 1400 acs., Gloster Co., S side of Peanketanck Riv., 15 June 1675, p. 559. Jeg. upon S. side of Store branch neere the dwelling house of sd. Major Cant; by plantation of Geo. Haynes; to Lambert Moore, to Walter Cant's, formerly Knoxe's land; &c, 600 acs. granted Mr. Tho. Ballard 15 Oct. 1657 & sold to sd. Major Cant, who bequeathed to sd. David; his sonn; 500 acs. granted to —— Gill, & since purchased by Col. Augustin Warner, who bequeathed to his grandsonn, the sd. David; 300 acs. being overplus adj. due for trans. of 6 pers.*

WALTER CANT, sonne of Major David Cant, dec'd., 500 acs., Gloster

Co. ,15 June 1675, p. 560. S. side
Peanketanck & the Dragon Sw., &c.
Due unto —— Knoxes by patt. (date
blank); purchased by sd. Major Cant
& bequeathed to sd. Walter.

THO. SEWELL, 150 acs.,, Gloster
Co., Abbington Par., 15 June 1675, p.
560. Adj. Danll. Langham, Robt. Coleman, Tho. & Jeffrey Graves & Capt.
Laurene Smith, &c. Trans. of 3 pers.*

BRYAN SMITH, 2200 acs., betweene
New Kent & Rappa. Co.'s; 10 June
1675, p. 560. Beg. neere the Indian
Path from Matapony Towne that was at
the head of Piscataway Cr. to the new
Towne planted by those Indians on
Mattapony River; to land of Capt.
Brewerton near head of Hashwamaci-
kers (?) Sw., &c. Trans. of 44 pers:
Tho. Johnson, Jo. Barloe, Wm. Ag-
newes, Jno. Ratlett, Jno. Heath, Wm.
Powell, Wm. Davis, Cha. Dabell, Jno.
Lane, Sus. Gentle, Elin. Todkin, Elin.
Ovell, Danll. Parke, Esqr., Samll.
Browne, Thos. Child, Edw. Mattox,
Samll. Richeson, Mich. Emott (or
Emett), Corn. Hall, Phill. Cotton, Job.
Cooking, Jno. Wilkins, Richd. Sandely,
Propter Bohomini, Tho. Leonard, Tho.
Elliot, Jo. Waterer, Jno. Peirce, Wm.
Willis, Edwd. Snouing, Ja. Merifeild,
Corn. Degon, Geo. Southerland; 6
Negroes.

THOMAS JOYNER, 1300 acs., Is.
of W. Co., uppon the Cypruss Branch,
15 June 1675, p. 561. By Knowles'
land; Blythe's land; unto Mr. Bodye's
land; to a point where Elme Sw. falleth
into the Cypresse Sw; along Jno. Garner; &c. 1200 acs. by a former pattents,
& 100 acs., now added, for trans. of 2
pers: Helie Corbutt, Ann Bell.

ENOCH DOUGH1Y, 4763 acs.,
Rappa. Co., S. side sd. River; 15 June
1675, p. 561. Beg. at cor. tree of
Warwick Cammock on S. side of a br.
of a Beaver Damm; to Jno. Meader &
Hen. Peters; to the Doge's Path, to a
br. called Tuckquako Sw., &c. Trans.
of 97 pers: Wm, Dennett, Sarah Mills,
Alice Bedford, Edwd. Grimes, Tho.
Dynars, Jane Potts, Robt. Smart, David
Holt, Peter Wilmott (or Wiltnott),

Jno. Tew, Jno. Holt, Evan Parnam,
Arthur Skew (?), Edwd. Froth, Mary
Waines, Jo. Parker, Wm. Clefton,
Danll. Paine, Samll. Holmes, Wel.
Honywood, Kath. Weeks, Fra. Symons,
Eliz. Wood, Xpr. Lightfoot, Howell
Watkins, Dennis Wood, Nich. Wallace,
Paul Hart, Robt. Marke, Wm. Sayer,
Wm. Kellick, Mary Palmer, Ma.
Haimes, Walter Marsh, Fra. Dougty
(?) & wife, Enoch Doughy, & wife,
Jno. Caster, Ros. Delaroy, Rich. Bray
4 times, Peter Malary, Danll. Grey,
Mich, Yardly, Jno. Wilard, Jno. Weadle,
Gyles Mathews, Tho. Powell (or
Powdle), Tho. Barrow, Allen Mackbeth
(or Mackbech), Kath Jones, Richd.
Klesby, Dennis ——, Jane Ginhorne,
Jo. Clerk, Tho. Hancock, Ann Webb,
Timo. Sendall, Hen. Long, Tho. Tun-
nell, Jno. Benn, An (?) Jones, Fra.
Bestall, Hen. Jones, Ja. Steward, Wm.
Benck (or Jerck), Tho. Tucker, Cha.
Crosse, Mary Charles, Cho. Hoell (?),
Ja Masingam, Tho. Edwin, Jno. White,
Samll. Smith, Wm. Trowell, Ja. Foster,
Gra. Newardo (or Stewarde), Rich.
Jones, Jno. Rumball, David Manseli,
Wm. Wilcocks, Ja. Turner, Wm. Bush-
rodd, Edwd. Stewarder (or Newarder),
Nan Russell, Sarah Jenkins, Tho. Wood-
bridge, Mary Turner, Peter (?) Sudden,
Edwd. Rutlage.

GEO. CHAPMAN, 608 acs., New
Kent Co., on branches of Black Cr., 19
June 1675, 562. Adj. Capt. Richd.
Barnham; Geo. Smith & Edmd. Price;
neere Westham Path; to Capt. Lydall,
&c. Granted to Capt. Martin Palmer
21 Aug. 1665, deserted, & by order, &c.,
granted sd. Chapman, for trans. of 12
pers: Margt. Lyddall, Ja. Baily, Robt.
Abbott, Wm. Skeale, Edwd. Loe (or
Lee), Wm. Beadle, Geo. Plumtree,
Rich. Byton, Jer. Cleaton, Jno. Dowish;
Mingo & Sue Negroes.

CUTHBERT WILLIAMSON, 144 A.,
32 P., Chas. Citty Co., N. side James
Riv., 16 June 1675, p. 562. Beg. 2 ft.
of Berkeley's line, nigh head of the
Ashen Sw; to Kemeges (?) Runn, &c.
Trans. of 3 pers: Ben. Davis, Jesse
O'dunn (or Odum), Richd. Locksley,
Tho. Cleed (or Clood).

HANNAH TOMKINS, 200 acs. Gloster Co., 4 Oct. 1675, p. 562. Granted to Abraham Turner, dec'd., & escheated by inquisition, &c. under Jno. Baskervile, Depty Esch'r. for York Co; &c.

JNO. & GEORGE KILLMAN, 920 acs., Rappa. Co., S. side sd. Riv., & on Pascattaway Cr., 10 June 1675, p. 563 Beg. at the old feild; to Tho. Greene; by Dr. Goodson's fence; by Jno. Dybly; to Capt. Josias Pickis; by the Greene br; to land formerly Neele Peterson's; to the Beaver Dam Sw., to Mr. Coggall's land, &c. 550 acs. granted them 4 Oct. 1655; 150 acs. granted Mr. Wm. White & purchased by sd. Jno.. & George as appeares by patt. 21 Sept, 1667; 220 acs. for trans. of 5 pers.*

MR. THO. COCK, 1983 A., 3 R., in Chas. Citty Co., on N side James Riv., 4 Oct. 1675, p. 563. Beg. uppon Gyllie's (Gilles) path neare Merridaes path; over Mongoies Run, to W. br. of Herring Cr; to a run of Chickahominy, &c. Trans. of 40 pers: Dorcas Young, Ann Chandler, Ralph Jenings, Hugh Jones, Robt. Mercer, Robt. Grey, Math. Terrell, Ja. Wragg, Jone Harrison, Jno. Edwards, Jno. Almand, Hen. Tyre, Wm. Baker, Marg. (or Mary) Smith, Mary Sly, Rebecca Jackson, Rich. Beake, Jno. Glover, Hen. Peterson, Isaac Warren, Danll. Hugh, Morris Neale; 4 Irishmen; Bridgett Carter, Walter Floyd, Jane Alder, Tho. Mann, Bernard Winn, Tho. Castle, Edwd. Richardson, Hen. Hicks, Marg. Swann, Tho. Cary, Jno. Caddy, Eper. Packenton, Roger Dornan, Richd. Clerke.

RICHARD BLOW, 635 acs., Surry Co., 4 Oct 1675, p. 563. On E. side of the maine Black Water Sw. Granted to Geo. Blow, his father, 9 Aug. 1664, & due him as heire.

MR. THO. COCK, 3087 A., 3 R., Henrico Co., N. side James Riv., 4 Oct. 1675, p. 564. Beg. on S. side of Chickahominy Sw., at land taken up by Mr. Beachamp. Trans. of 62 pers: Jno. Smith, Sarah Carter, Jno. Robinson, David Williams, Jno. Lamber, Jno. Watts, Tho. Webb, Mary Webb, Jno.

Fisher, Eliz. Hames (or Haines), Joane Ashbrooke, Tho. Mory, Ann Gray, Ja. Wile, And. More, Jno. More, Cath. Kyte, Abell Davis, Tho. Sorrell, Xper. Bobblett, Jno. Bayly, Tho. Spring, Jno. Garrett, Jeffery Harris, Wm. Storey, Godfrey Bayly, Tho. Hewes, Cha. James, Tho. Everton, Jno. Henry, Wm. Alaman, Tem. Waker, Herc. Baker, And. Floide, Sar. Jackson, Alice Petercue (?), Corn. Yeurnon, Jno. Peterson, Abig. Thomas, Peter Rudds, Jo. Mason, Tho. Wild, Mathew Wild, Abra. Goose, Andrew Sheeres, Joane Marston, Wm. Richards, Sara Carter, Mary During, Tho. Foster, Geo. Ashbrooke, Tho. Winter, Wm. Johnson; Bungo, Sante, Hector, Hercules, Tomeline,* Sancha, Sallo, George, Toney.

NICHOLAS & WM. COX, 273 acs., Chas. Citty Co., N. side James Riv., 4 Oct. 1675, p. 564. Adj. Mr. Jno. Stith; nigh a br. of Herring Cr., &c. Trans. of 6 pers.*

EDWD. GILLY (Gilley), 146 A., 3 R., Chas. Citty Co., N. side James Riv., 4 Oct. 1675, p. 564. Beg. on the Easterne branch; along land of Mr. Danll. Clarke; to Mr. Dibdall's path, &c. Trans. of 3 pers.*

HENRY BUTT, 320 acs., Low Norf. Co., 4 Oct. 1675, p. 564. Adj. Robt. Butt. Granted to Antho. Benford 6 Nov. 1665, deserted, & now granted by order, &c. Trans. of 7 pers: Tho. Culson, Jno. Bray, Wm. Morgan Jno. Richardson, Jno. Morfeild, Batt. Bew, Edw. James.

MR. HENRY AUBERY, 5100 acs., Rappa. Co., bet. brs. of Pascattaway & Hodkins Creeks & br. of Mattapony River; 4 Oct. 1675, p. 565. Beg. by an Indian Path nigh the new Roade to Gellon's Mill; to land of Paggett & Gouldman; to sd. Aubery's Quarter; &c. Trans. of 102 pers: Jno. Turner, Wm. Dally, Jno. More, Junr., Jno. More, Senr., Jno. Wisdom, Wm. Heath, Geo. Tomson, Wm. Vier, Geo. Bryan, Rich. King, James More, Jno. Clerke, Jno. Taylor, Ann Taylor, Tho. Thorpe, David Flack, Jno. Austin, Tho. Temple, Ann Smith, Alice Page, David Filford,

Samll. Johnson, Wm. Trowell (?), Tho. Cotton, Tho. Warren, Peter Taylor, Geo. Blace (or Blane), Mary Thorpe; a child; Jno. Jeoford, Wm. Blace (or Place), Tho. Cooper, Wm. Vincent, Tho. Simkins, Mary Simkins, Cha. Gray, Ellen Smith, Wm. Jnoson, And. Rider, Wm. Rider, Tho. Buck, Wm. Tauty (or Tanty), How. Appowell, Robt. Sisson, Tho. Joyner, Wm. Newman, Edw. Bray (?), Jno. Smith, Benj. Buck, Rich. Newman, Wm. Feild, Morris Fitzgarrell, Jno. Austin, Tho. Suckett, Wm. Thorneton, Robt. Ayloffe, Sar. Smith, W.m. Gower, Jno. Cheany, Wm. Gauler, Peter Jenkinson, Ann Salter, Wm. Tyfard, Tho. Morgan, Richd. Senior, Tho. Fitz Randolph, Jam. Sherlock, Rich. Nangle, Tho. Frost, Robt. Shiply, Jno. Williams, Jno. Parker, Mary Jervis, Sam. Goldsmith, Jno. Day, Sus. Marvell, Robt. Feilding; Richd. Graves, Mordecay Jnoson, Abigall Elliott, Eliz. Huggett, Samll. Jnoson, Richd. Bates, Jno. Jates, Fra. Bateman, Sallam Williams. Hugh Martin, Jno. Jones, Morris Heard, Jno. Merriott, Jno. Jacques, Arthur (or Archer) Price, Samll. Sorrell, Wm. Sorrell. Wm. Butler, Robt. Jones, An. Golding, Robt. Peake, Jno. Butler.

HENRY WOODNETT (Woodnott), 750 acs., Rappa. Co., S. side Rappa. Riv., some 4 mi. into the woods; 4 Oct. 1675. p. 565. In a forke of the Beaver Dam Sw., by Goodman Spurtin's plantation; over the Roade to Mrs. Emy Johnson; to Mr. Harwarr & Cox; to Mr. Bowler, to Randall Curtice (Curtis). &c. 460 acs. granted Mr. Tho Harwarr & Nich. Cox, & sold to sd. Woodnott; 290 acs for trans. of 6 Negroes.

MR. JNO. GREGORY & HUGH MEAD, 200 acs., Rappa. Co., betwixt both their devidents, 4 Oct. 1675, p. 565. Adj. Richd. Hoult, by the horse path, to the Church path; to Mr. Hen. Aubery, &c. Trans. of 4 pers: Tho. Edmunson; Alice Asely, Jno. Gufford, Jo. Eglestone

HENRY GREENE & CHA. CHAIRE, 180 acs., Rappa. Co., on Dragon Sw., opposite Col. Wm. Claiborne & Jno. Richards; 4 Oct. 1675, p. 566. 110 acs.

granted Tho. Pattison & Richd. Bridgett 24 Apr. 1668; 70 acs. for trans. of 2 pers.*

NICKOLAS & WM. COX, 220 acs., Chas. Citty Co., N. side James Riv., 4. Oct. 1675, p. 566. Beg. in the forkes of the Broad Run which runs into Chickahominy Sw., &c. Trans. of 5 pers.*

THOMAS WOOD, 400 acs., Rappa. Co., upon brs. of Pascattaway Cr., 4 Oct. 1675, p. 566. Beg. at the horse path on the Dragon (Sw.) to Pascattaway; on land of Richd. Jones & Geo. Turner; along land of Fra. Browne, &c. Trans. of 8 pers: Ed. Bland, Wm. Binks (or Burks), Wm. Hinsly, Jno. Paggett, Hugh Hanna, Mary Jnoson, Ann Helding, Benj. Fanskith.

MAJOR JNO. LEWIS & MR. JNO. LANE, 43 A., 20 P., New Kent Co., Stratton Major Par; on NW side of Assatiam Sw. & Cr., 4 Oct. 1675, p. 566. Adj. Nicholls' land; Jas. Trite's (?); & land of Mr. Hen. Briggs, &c. Trans. of 1 pers.*

MR. HENRY SMITH, 1826 acs., Rappa. Co., S. side sd. Riv., 22 Sept. 1674. p. 567. Oppossett Totoskey Cr., & along ancient line of Sir Henry Chickeley; by the new roade, to land of Jno. Lacy (Lacey); to Randall Curtis; down the Beaver Dam Sw., to land formerly Jno. Paine's, &c. 1350 acs. granted to Mr. Tobias Smith; 200 acs. purchased of Sir Hen. Chickeley, both of which parcells are joyned in a patt. dated 24 Sept. 1657; 276 acs. for trans. of 6 pers: Jno. Ma Bryan (?), Jno. Key, Geo. Plinton, Wm. Hutchinson, Math. Smith, Geo. Taylor.

RICH. TAYLOR, 642 acs., New Kent Co., at head of Ware Cr., 4 Oct. 1675, p. 567. Beg. at Mr. Folliott on NW side of the maine br. of sd. Cr., neare the house of Mr. Boaterite; to Col. Pettus' land, &c; 200 acs. granted Geo. Browne & purchased of Henry Reader, who escheated it in 1673; 442 acs. found within, & due for trans. of 9 pers: Jno. Lanhorne twice, Henry Hart, Jno. Gultumnee, Eliz. Wells, Wm.

Wesberry, Matth. Phillips, Elinor Smith, Jno. Stone. (*Rich. Parker* crossed out.)

MR. THOMAS BOWLER, 1460 acs., Rappa. Co., some 3 mi. in the woods behind Mr. Henry Smith; 4 Oct. 1675, p. 567. Beg. by a br. of Ralph's Cr. &c., by Tho. Crowe's fence; crossing the white marsh, &c. 650 acs. granted Robt. Armestrong 10 Sept. 1658., who sold to Col. Tho. Goodrich; 484 acs. pattented by sd. Goodrich, with sd. 650 acs., 20 Sept. 1661, which he sold to sd. Bowler; 326 acs. found within; the whole added together & now by him nominated & called *The Mary Gold*; 326 acs. for trans. of 7 pers: Peter Deane, Jno. Hooper, Hannah Comes, Edwd. Clarke, Jone Sheares, Ja. Bartlett, Jno. Reade.

MR. WM. CLAPHAM, 200 acs., Rappa. Co., S. side sd. Riv., 4 Oct. 1675, p. 568. Adj. his other 200 acs., lately belonging to Jno. Crimp, who was seized thereof in fee & soe dyed without heire or disposing of sd. land, the same was found to escheat, by inquisition, &c. under Capt. Robt. Beverley, Depty. Esch'r., & a jury of 12 sufficient able men, as appeares by sd. inquisition now lying in the Secretarie's office; with Mr. Danll. Gaines, foreman of sd. jurie, &c.

RICHARD BARBER, 550 acs., Rappa. Co., S. side sd. Riv., upon S. side of Occupation runne; 6 Oct. 1675, p. 568. Part of a gr. tract granted to Henry Jerman, Jno. Powell, William Coppin & Cornelius Nowell. & by sd. Jerman & Powell devided & sett apart, &c; & assigned to sd. Coppin & Nowell for their halfe part; & since found to escheate, by inquisition &c. under Capt. Robert Beverley, &c; Mr. Robt. Mosse, foreman of sd. jurie; now due by order &c. (*Note:* Firsts spelt *Barker* & altered).

ROBT. HUSON, 200 acs., Henrico Co., S. side James Riv., 6 Oct. 1675, p. 568. Adj. land of Edwd. Dely; along Mr. Light; &c. Trans. of 4 pers: David Martin, Hen. Heynes (or Heapes), Edmd. Peters, Elizab. Howard (or Havard).

CAPT. THOMAS HAWKINS, 2611 acs., in 2 tracts, Rappa. Co., S. side sd. Riv., 6 Oct. 1675, p. 569. 1677 acs. lately belonging to Mr. Tho. Lucas, Senr. & Mr. Tho. Lucas, Junr. his sonne, where they both lived & dyed; beg. at a cr. dividing this & land of Col. (?) Page &c.; to cr. dividing this from land of Vallentine Allen, &c; 934 acs. on E. side of a cr. about 2 mi. above *Port Tobacco* Indian Towne, &c. Both of which lately belonged to sd. Lucas, Junr., whereof he dyed seized in fee & leaveing noe issue nor disposed of same by will or otherwaies, both of sd. tracts escheated; by inquisition, under Capt. Robt. Beverley, Depty. Esch'r., & a jury, with Mr. Danll. Gaines, foreman, &c.

MR. THO. MOSSE, 375 A., 25 Per., Rappa. Co., S. side of Rappa. River; 6 Oct. 1675, p. 569. Being land whereon he liveth, formerly belonging to Augustine Bladenburgh, & by him sold to sd. Mosse; but by reason of sd. Bladenburgh being an alien & neither naturalized nor denizised he could make hoe title in fee to sd. Mosse. & sd. lands escheated, by inquisition under Capt. Robt. Beverley. Esch'r., &c; Mr. Jno. Bagwell, foreman of the jury, &c.

EDWD. HATCHER, 1300 acs., Henrico Co., N. side James Riv., 6 Oct. 1675, p. 570. Next to Lilley Valley; nigh Cornelius' Cr., over Mr. Beauchampts path, &c. Trans. of 26 pers: Jno. Scutfeild (or Stutfeild), Mary Gage, Eliz. Richards, Jno. Smith, Eliz. Haward, Jno. Cleer, Samll. Greene, Hopkin Powell, Susa. Wilshire, Marg. Browneing, Jno. Hosock, Tho. Filbrough, And. Martin, Ben Salt, Eliz., Curtin, Peter South (or Souch), Morris Mathews, Tho. Watson, Jno. White, Kath Fossett, Geo. Croker, Jno. Hosock, Cha. White, Benja. Salt, Tho. Deacon, Peter Souch (?), Morris Mathew, Hen. Hatcher.

ROBT. HUSON, 126 acs., Henrico Co., S. side James Riv., 6 Oct. 1675, p. 570. In Grindall's run, & adj. Henry Sherman's land. Trans. of 3 pers: Jno. Huffeild, Hopkin Powell, Mary Gage,

MR. THO. MEAD, 640 acs., New Kent Co., N. side Mattapony Riv., upon branches of Peanketank maine Sw., about 2 mi. from Mr. Tho. Holmes; 6 Oct. 1675, p. 570. On Timber Br., along land of John Pigg & Jno. Maddison. Granted to Cornelius Reynolds 6 June 1664, assigned to Richd. Sankey, who assigned to sd. Mead, 8 Jan. 1673.

EDWARD OWLD, 452 acs., Lower Norf. Co., Low. Par. of Lynhaven, 9 Oct. 1675, p. 570. Beg. on the Middle Neck; to Brushy Neck; by the horse path, & adj. Mr. Basnett, &c. Trans. of 9 pers: Tho. Sampson, Jno. Hewes, John David, John Cabidge, Edwd. Stenton, Richard Knight, Philip Williams; Negro boy Jack, & Negro woman Jone.

(Note: Mistake in pagination.)
THOMAS BENSON, 100 acs., Low. Norf. Co., Lynhaven Par., 9 Oct. 1675, p. 580. Trans. of 2 pers: Alice Morton, John Uhle.

JOHN VAUGHAN. 221 acs. Low. Norf. Co., S. side Black Water Cr:, 9 Oct. 1675, p. 580. Trans. of 5 pers: John Vaughan, Wm. Conner, Charles Cornelius, James Smother, Elizabeth Ruff.

THOMAS TOOLEY, 150 acs., Low. Norf. Co., N. side Black Water Cr., 9 Oct. 1675, p. 580. Trans. of 3 pers: Tho. Tooley & his wife, Tho. Tooley.

. MR. WM. CORNICKS (Cornix), 238 acs., Low. Norf. Co., Lynhaven Par., 9 Oct. 1675, p. 580. Beg. on Chincopin Ridge iin his old line; by the Brushy Ridge; to the Poplar ridge; &c. Trans. of 5 pers: An Harris, Elizab. Davis, Mary Hill, Margret Jones, Idith (Judith ?), Warner.

JOHN GRIFFIN, 179 acs., named *Griffin's Points*, Low. Norf. Co., on E. side of the north River; 9 Oct. 1675, p. 580. Adj. Col. Mason & Mr. Fowler's line. &c. Trans. of 4 pers: Thomas Owens, Thomas Hill, Jno. Pead; Hannah Snead (or Snowe).

MR. HENRY WOODHOUSE, 441 acs., Low. Norf. Co.; being part of the Long Ridge; 9 Oct. 1675, p. 581. S'ly. from Richard Bonnie's land, through a pocoson, &c. Trans. of 9 pers: Daniel Anderson, Edward Oulds, Ursla Thornton, Edward Stringer, Charles Hendley, Robt. Richmond, Patrick Anguis (?): Roger & Bess, Negroes.

ROBT. SYMONDS. 100 acs., called the *good land*, Low. Norf. Co., 9 Oct. 1675, p. 581. On a marsh on Curretuck Bay, &c. Trans. of 2 pers: Tho Pitts, Jno. Beck.

WILLIAM LANGLEY, 829 A., 3 R., 14 P., Low. Norf. Co., in Tanner's Cr., 9 Oct. 1675, p. 581. Beg. on the maine cr., to Horner's gutt; to mouth of Crab point Cr., by the Dirty br. &c. 200 acs. granted him 21 Nov. 1625; 629 A., 3 R., 14 P., for trans. of 13 pers: Andrew White, Wm. Hadley, Jno. King, Tho. Atkins, Michael Wade (?), Phillip Browne, Tho. Harding, Wm. Rosse, Hugh Jones, Robt. Brooks; 3 Negroes.

MR. WM. WEST, 656 acs., Low. Norf. Co., on E. side of the N. river; 9 Oct. 1675, p. 582. 400 acs. granted him 27 May 1673; 256 acs. for trans. of 5 pers: Wm. West, Wm. West, Lawrence Boucher, Richard Haudick (or Handick), Henry Southerne

JOHN ADAMS, 170 acs., Low. Norf. Co., Eliz. Riv. Par., 9 Oct, 1675, p. 582. Bet. 2 small crks. in Ellett's Cr:, to the *Glebe Land*, &c. Trans. of 4 pers: Jno. Cleare, Andrew Martin, Samuel Green, Elizab. Richards.

ROBT. HARPER, 220 A., 1 R., 24 P., Low Norf. Co., Lynhaven Par., towards the head & on W. side of Lynhaven Riv., called the Aishin Swamp; 9 Oct. 1675, p. 582. Adj. Renatus Land, &c. Trans. of 5 pers: Giles Collins, Edward Rogers, Peter Millett, Lidia Allen, Christopher White

MR. WM. NEWMAN, 184 acs., Low. Norf. Co., in Tanner's Cr. Precincts; 9 Oct. 1675, p. 582. Adj. Abrah. Ellett; Richard Jones; John Williamson, &c. Trans. of 4 pers: Wm. Palmer, Thomas Drape, Wm. Cordridge, Tho. Hewes.

MR. WM. BASNETT, 1150 acs., Low. Norf. Co., in the N. branches of Curretuck Bay called *Colchester:* 9 Oct. 1675, p. 583. Beg. at George. Indian Quarter; along a marsh dividing John White's this land, & Dancing ridge; to *frank* Indian Quarter; along the Green Br., &c., includ. a ridge dividing this & land of Thomas Griffin. 510 acs. granted him 10 Sept. 1664; & 640 acs. for trans. of 13 pers: Jno. Morris, Jno. Wright, James Skerrer, David Freeman, Richard Jones, Sarah Willoughby, Robt. Darby, Jno. Boulton, Jno. Scott, Tho: Jones, Robt. Nowell, Arthur Maquin, Elizabeth Twist.

CAPT. WM. CARVER, 784 acs., Low. Norf. Co., Lynhaven Par., called *Brinson's Quarter:* 9 Oct. 1675, p. 583. Beg. by the Broad ridge; to the Reedy Sw; &c. Trans. of 16 pers: Jno. Dattee, Mary Carvett (or Carnett), Nora Briant, Rich. Hudson, Benja. Pickworth, Wm. Beverley & his wife. Jone Getterey. Christian Bruce, Edw. Holloway, Clemt. Harrison, Honour Norton, Elizab. Barton, Tho. Wakefield, An Sommerhill, James Harrold.

JOHN KEELING, 537 acs., Low. Norf. Co., Lynhaven Par., 9 Oct. 1675, p. 583. Beg. in his old. survey; neare Thorowgood Keeling; on land of Lt. Tho. Keeling, dec'd., to the road path; by a br. of Lynhaven Riv., to a marsh neare the bridge, &c. 150 acs. granted him 9 Oct. 1665; 387 acs. for trans. of 8 pers: George Minchin, Susan his wife, Richard Parsons, Wm. Garrett, Henry Barnard, Charles Miclere, James Snowe, Mathew Dennis.

EDMUND MOOKE, 400 acs., •Low. Norf. Co., 9 Oct. 1675. p. 584. On the Negro Sw., the Piney Sw., & the Cyprus Sw. Trans. of 8 pers: Francis Dun, Margaret Motley, Tho. Evans, James Shepheard, Nicholas Dugras (?), Jno. Guydon, Benedict Lewis.

COL. LEMUEL MASON & MR. GEORGE FOWLER, 670 acs., called *Matchepongo,* Low. Norf. Co., lying E'ly. from the north River; 9 Oct. 1675, p. 584. Trans. of 14 pers: John Smith, Richard Kemp, John Wolfe, Richard

Ward, Mary Wormwell, Owen Morgan, Wm. Pincks, Jno. Baynam, Edward Rogers, Wm. Trumball, Jno. Richardson, Robt. Davis, Wm. Tanner, Riehd. Bailey.

RICHARD JONES, 709 acs., Low. Norf. Co., E'wd. side of Eliz. River; 9 Oct. 1675, p. 584. S. side of Lambert's Cr; N. side of the mouth of Ellett's Cr., over the mouth of Sandy Br. Cr., to the Brushy Neck; to cr. dividing this & land of Abraham Ellett, &c. 680 acs. granted him 1 July 1672; & 29 acs. for trans. of: Mary Filks.

CAPT. RALPH WORMELY, 2870 acs., Middlesex Co., S. side of Rappa. Riv., & on both sides of Rosegill Creek *alias* Nimcocke Cr.; 12 Sept. 1675, p. 585. 2400 acs. on the lower side of Nimcocke Cr., beg. at the mouth; neare fence of the plantation where Jno. Allen lately lived; to Timber Neck Sw; to Major Genll. Robt. Smith, &c; 450 acs. on up. side of Nimcocke Cr., from the mouth; to head of Vause's Cr., &c. Due Capt. Ralph Wormely, dec'd., by 2 patents for a greater quantity, but by exact survey not found to exceed the above quantity; due the abovenamed as being the onely sonne & heire.

COL. ROBERT ABRAHALL, 1200 acs., Gloster Co., NE side of Mattopony Riv., 20 Oct. 1675, p. 585. Beg. at Mr. Holland's; along Mr. Sandford's (Handford's), &c. Granted to Wm. Lewis 25 May 1654; assigned to Jonath. Parson, & by him lapsed for want of seateing; & now granted by order, &c. Trans. of 24 pers: Marg. Williams, Arther Parker, Abra. Karr (?), Jno. Symonds, Sarah Hawman, Rich. Twinson, Patrick Cossell, Samll. Cellinger, Wm. Bray, Der. Johnson, Robt. Lee, Edw. Gogson, Wm. Boulton (or Boalton), Fra. Wood, Fra. Lacy, Eliz. Westbrook, Eliz. Hooke, Rosamond Pruett (or Brett), Ra. Harding, Wm. Smith, Wm. Brand, Martin Norris, Tho. Wheeler, Sa. Johnson.

THEO. HONE, JUNR., & THO. HONE, 736 acs., James Citty Co., 5 Oct. 1675, p. 586. 200 acs. on brs. of Warrany Cr., on the Burchen Sw., in Sir Jno. Ayton's lyne; on the Horse path; to the Timber Sw., &c; 536 acs.

on sd. Creek brs., beg. neere Mr. Sorrell's, path; neere Warrany Sw., by an Indian feild; by Mr. Burnell; & land of Wm. Elcom, &c. Granted to Tho. Maples & Wm. Hitchman by 2 pattents, 10 Sept. 1668, & lapsed for want of seating; granted Jno. Wright, -2. Apr. 1674 & assigned to sd. Theo. & Tho. Hone. Trans. of 15 pers: Jno. Tallon, Marg. Lewis, Sarah Burdett, Wm. Moyle. (Other names not given.)

MR. RICHD. THREADER, 2300 acs., in Rappa. & New Kent Co.'s; bet. Mattapony & Rappa. Rivers; 24 Feb. 1675/6, p. 586. Adj. Col. Tho. Goodrich. 2100 acs. granted to Geo. Morris; 200 acs. newly taken up. Trans. of 46 pers.*

WM. ATKINS, 280 acs., New Kent Co., on brs. of Mattadegun; & adj. Wm. Watson; 24 Feb. 1675/6, p. 588. Trans. of 6 pers: Jno. Salter, Wm. Barrington, Jo. Seare, Eliz. Bulman, Eliz. Banford. (Note: Error in pagination—p. 587 not mentioned).

MARY PIRON, 345 acs., New Kent Co., 24 Feb. 1675/6, p. 588. Adj. Mr. Whitehaire, on Crump's Cr., to Mathump's Cr., & by a slash to Capt. Bassett's. Trans. of 7 pers: Rich. Wilson, Jane Williams, James Parry, Theop. Whale, Mich. Robinson, Edw. Linsey.

WM. PULLUM, 260 acs., New Kent Co., on NW br. of Black Cr., 24 Feb. 1675/6, p. 588. Beg. at Mic. Tucker's corner; to Hubard's land; along Will. Oens (?) line; to Mr. Mohun; to Jno. Boughan, on Cattaile Br., &c. 70 acs. taken up by his father & is the remainder of that grant; 190 acs. now taken. Trans. of 4 pers.*

ROW. HORSLY (Horsely) & ROBT. LANCASTER, 767 acs., New Kent Co., 7 Mar. 1675/6, p. 589. At lower side of the mouth of the little Cr., to Cha. Bryan; along Wm. Owens'; near the Holly Spring; along David Crafford; to Jno. Pouncy; by Mattadegun Cr., &c. 473 acs. granted 8 Oct. 1672; 294 acs. now taken on N. side of the Little Cr. is Lancaster's part, &land on the S. side is Horsely's. Trans. of 6 pers: Rich.

Corley, Eliz. Sutton, Jno. Coleman, Wm. Wood, Giles West, Richd. Norcot (?).

JAMES WILSON, 700 acs., New Kent Co., on the head of Ware Cr. on the E. side; 24 Feb. 1675/6. p. 589. Beg. at Mr. Stanaway's on Mount Folly Path; down the Cowpen Sw; to Robt. Harris; along a br. of the Reedy Sw; to Gillman's land, &c. Renewal of his patt. dated 29 Jan. 1661.

MATHEW MORGAN, 136 acs., New Kent Co., 24 Feb. 1675/6, p. 589. Granted to Wm. Owen, & found to escheat by inquisition under Tho. Hall, Esch'r., &c.

ROWLAND PLACE, Esqr., 5579 A., 3 R., Chas .Citty Co., on E'ly. & W'ly. sides of the Oldman's Cr., & E'ly. side of Herring Cr. till it joyneth Mr. Bland; to Balistans Path; to the head of the Ridges; to the Cattailes; to Marshall Path; along Mr. Clarke; to Cellar Runn, to the horse path at Turner's corner; along the heads of Buckland; to Herring Cr., &c; 24 Feb. 1675/6, p. 590. Trans. of 112 pers: Guy, George, Tho., Laurence; Caser, Dick, Gilla, Besse, Maria, Agbo, Killa, Assa; Guy, Geo., Ramis, Abasse, Cokee; Ja. Minge; Edwd. Jones; Eliz. Tattle; Alexdr. Rosse; Tho. Haye; Tho. Muns; Hanebak, Anth., Susan Basse, Han. Basse, Eliz. Basse, Samll. Basse, (28); (Note: As written, the punctuation used makes it difficult to discriminate between single and full names). Theo. Bland, Richd. Stanton, Jno. Hill, Fran. (a ?) Frenchlad, Nich. Cock, Tho. Walls, Robt. Spencer, Tho. Darling, Charles Bechet (or Prechet), Jno. Girling, Edwd. Beasley, Tho. Buttler, Math. Ruffin, Samll. Temple (or Semple), Samll. Additt, Wm. Aldrith (?), Fra. Aldwith (?), Jno. Crabb, Fra. Crab, Geo. Ledger, Tho. Howlett, Jane Thompson, Doro. Stockett, Jno. Elson, Wm. Aldwith (?), Jno. Clemance, Tho. Gold, Robt. Freland, An. Hoer (?), Tob. Wilson, Wm, Burk, Elinor Boyce, Arth. Ball, Mich. Stephens, Tho. Brush, Geo. Wallace, Thomas ——, Tho. Picknor, (an) Irish boy, Jno. Robinson, And. Cann, Tho. Marsh, Wm. Dowglas, Jno. Smart, Jas. Sumerpall (or Simmerpall ?), Jno. Pryce, Roger Beard, Rich. Newton, Sara Jewitt, Wm. Hardey, Jno. Judgner (?), Hen. Wilson, Robt. Millard, Tho. Gold, Eliz. Pryce, Jno., an Indian; Benj. Champion, Walter Steward, Tho. Wilson. Margarett Cornall, Eliz. Cornell, Amb. Towlady, Ebott Neale, Eady Neale, Eliz. Askew, Wm. Wigg, Jno. Wall, Rowld. Place, Rich. Welbeck, Josua Adams, Wm. Brexton, Ann Holden, Jno. Barnett, Jno. Berch, Eliz. Sayre (or Fayre), Rich. Basker, Toby an Indian, Jno., Edw., Maria, Media, Peter, Geo., Negroes.

MR. DAVID CRAFFORD, 1350 acs., New Kent Co., on the Little Cr., a br. of Mattadegun Cr., 24 Feb. 1675/6, p. 591. Adj. Wm. Owens, in Owens' br., to head of a br. of Chickahominy (Sw.); near head of a br. of Black Cr., by Powhite Path, &c. Trans. of 27 pers: Robt. Smith, Tho. Hollaway, Jno. Trower, Ja. Hutton. Ja. Rice, Robt. Glide, Wm. Bivian, Jno. Elliott, Danll. Tunstill, An Jones, Jno. Travers (or Traven), Richd. Sale, Robt. Morris, Jno. Trevers, Ann Chandler, Rich. Hewling, Sarah Brown, Wm. Liford, Tho. Winch, Robt. Bennett, Ben, Ash, Robt. Rosse, An. Burtock (or Burcock), Abigall Sewell, Tho. Thompson, Wm. Daniell, Tho. Okey.

SAME. 375 acs., same location, date & page. Trans. of 8 pers: Tho. Grimes, Ed. Allester, Tho. Greene, Ja. Oatly, And. Almer, Jno. Miller, Jno. Dixon, Lidia How.

MARY DICKESON, 930 acs., Gloucester Co., 24 Feb. 1675/6, p. 591. Granted to Edwd. Titterton; found to escheat as by inquisition, &c., under Col. Phill. Ludwell, Esch'r., &c.

WM. THOMPSON, 150 acs., Gloucester Co., Petsoe Par., 24 Feb. 1675/6, p. 592. Adj. Mr. Fawcett; Mr. Wm. Howard; E. side of Rappa. Path; Mr. Robt. Lee; Mr. Thorneton; Mr. Tho. Viccars; Mr. Rich. Farthingall; & Mr. Ja. Forsyth. Assigned by Mr. Jno. Buckner & Mr. Tho. Viccars, 25 Nov. 1673; trans. of 3 pers: Edwd. Best, Tho. Jones, Tho. Browne.

LT. COL. GEO. JORDAN, 690 acs., Up. Par. of Surry Co., at the mouth of a Reedy Marsh, neare an Indian Path; along the Cyprus Sw., a br. of the maine Black Water; to Mr. Arther Jordan, neere head of the Little Marsh; to the Middle Marsh; along the White Marsh, &c. Trans. of 14 pers: Wm. Jordan, Ar. (?) Jordan, Mary King, Robt. Shoutwell, Robt. Blackston, Jno. Felton, Wm. Thomson, Fortune Flood, Geo. Jordan, 2, Jea. Shoutwell, Jno. Clerke, Rich. Felton, Tho. Backey.

HENRY FRANCIS, 150 acs., Surry Co., 24 Feb. 1675/6, p. 592. Granted to William Gappin, & escheated by inquisition, &c., under Wm. Edwards, Depty. Esch'r; now granted to said Edwd. Francis, &c. (Note: Marginal notation gives this name as Henry.)

MICH. ROBINSON, 200 acs., New Kent Co., upon Axolls Sw., cor. of Mr. Black; 24 Feb. 1675/6, p. 593. Trans. of 4 pers: Arth. Wright, Robt. Foster, Robt. (?) Buroughs, Rich. Blackman.

JNO. GARRETT. 204 acs., New Kent Co., Stratton Major Par., adj. Mr. Cardingbrook, near a br. of Hartquake Sw., to Jennings' line; by the path to Spencer's; to Assatiams Meddow; along Rawlins' line; &c; 24 Feb. 1675/6. p. 593. Trans. of Wm. Merrith, 4 times.

MR. ROBERT HUBBERD (Hubert), 168 A., 27 chs., 2 primes, in Warwick Co., 7 Feb. 1675/6, p. 593. Adj. Mr. Humphry Harwood; the horse path. Mr. Townesend; bounded by Hawford's land; Westen's dividend; Mr. Wolfe's orphants', &c. Trans. of 4 pers: Fra. Allett, Robt. Greene, Mary Newman, Kath. Boker.

WM. BLECHENDEN. 50 acs., Nanzemond Co., 24 Feb. 1675/6, p. 593. Granted to Michaell Carrinton, & escheated by inquisition, under Jno. Lear, Depty. Esch'r., &c.

MR. GEORG GWILLINS. 300 acs., Nanzemond Co., 24 Feb. 1675/6, p. 594. Part of 400 acs. granted to James Cannaday, & found to escheat by inquisition under John Lear, Depty. Esch'r., &c.

MURCY BAKER, relict of Silvester Baker, 200 acs., Nanzemond Co., 24 Feb. 1675/6, p. 594. Escheat land of sd. Silvester, by inquisition under John Lear, Depty. Esch'r., &c.

WILLIAM CLEYBORNE, JUNR., 1000 acs., New Kent Co., in the forkes of Pamunkey Riv; beg. at mouth of same & upwards to land of Charles Edmonds; 24 Feb. 1675/6, p. 595. Trans. of 20 pers.*

JOHN LEE, 100 acs., Up. Par. of Nanzemund Co., 24 Feb. 1675/6, p. 595. Adj. sw .or br. dividing this & land formerly Micah. Hill's, now seated by Francis Sanders; adj. Mr. James Peeters & Capt. John Mason, neare the Cart path to Isen's Mill, &c. Trans. of 2 pers.*

JOHN HARRIS, 300 acs., Up. Par. of Nanzemond Co., 24 Feb. 1675/6, p. 595. Adj. William Brin; & Georg Spivey; Col. Blake; & neare a little howse belonging to sd. Spivey. Trans. of 6 pers: Tho. Pryor; Mathew, Franciscoe, Richard, & Ned, Negroes.

MR. EDWARD THELWELL, 150 acs., Up. Par. of Nanzemond Co. 24 Feb. 1675/6, p. 595. At land of Mr. Walter Bazeley's orphts., now in possession of Thomas Holder; adj. Thomas Mason & his own land; upp the Beaver Dam Sw; &c. Trans. of 3 pers: Tony, Isabell & Bastian, Negroes.

RICHARD PARKER, 100 acs., Nanzemond Co., at a place called Hoods Neck, in the Southern br., 24 Feb. 1675/6, p. 596. Adj. his own land; beg. at the mouth of a cr. or gutt below a small island; to land Tho. Parker lives on, &c. Trans. of 2 pers: Tho. Coward, Mary Benny.

WM. SPEIGHT, 137 acs., Nanzemond Co., joyneing on N. side of his father's land, in the upper parish, now called Tho. Speight's land; beg. by a muddy br. deviding this & land of Jno. Ballard; to his father's als. Brother's line; to line of John Battle, Junr; &c; 24 Feb. 1675/6, p. 596. Trans. of: Osman Crabb, 3 times.

RICHARD BAKER, 400 acs., Up. Par. of Nanzemond Co., 24 Feb. 1675/6, p. 596. Near Mr. Winborn's cor., by the High Way to Somerton; adj. his own land, &c. Trans. of 8 pers: Alexdr. Frizell, Jno. Rich. Ja. Cressee, Geo. Glidden, Robt. Whittle, Mary Crosse, Sara Stiles, Geo. Walker.

WM. JONES, 100 acs., Nanzemond Co., in Old Battle's line; & adj. Mr. Hinton's land; 24 Feb. 1675/6, p. 597. Trans. of 2 pers: Arthur Holder, Peter Bleem.

HUMPHRY GRIFFIN, 750 acs., Up. Par. of Nanzemond Co., 24 Feb. 1675/6, p. 597. Beg. by the Crosse Sw. that goes out of Barbaicue (Sw.?), &c. Trans. of 15 pers: Hester Yarde, Steph. Powell, Symon Preacher, Ann Snowe, Eliz. Williams, Jno. Lea, Wm. Rich, Wm. Wallis (or Vallis), Ja. Vulgar, Denis Gresson, Jo. Ramsell, Wm. Prince, Elinor Kerbye; Tony & Mary Negroes.

MICHAELL KING, 900 acs., Up. Par. of Nanzemond Co., in the way to South Key, at a place now called Kingston; 24 Feb. 1675/6, p. 597. Near head of a br. from Somerton Sw; adj. lands of Jno. Winborne; Bream; & Robinson; &c. Trans. of 18 pers: Wm. Smeberland (?), Marg. Ferrell, Hen. Hicks, Ja. Stroud, Pers. Floyd, Jno. Okey (or O'Key), Marg. Stepton, Mary Neckunun, Robt. Short, Samll. Dines, Em. Obsolon, Fra. Young, Thoma. Inglish, Eliz. Holman, Margt. Mathews, Robt. Batch, Wm. Gwinn, Tho. Ererard (or Everard ?).

WM. SPEIGHT, 117 acs., Up. Par. of Nanzemond Co., adj. his own; & land of Mr. Hinton; near path to Humphry Griffin's; &c; 24 Feb. 1675/6, p. 597. Trans. of: Osman Babb, twice.

RICHARD JONES, Senr., (?), 200 acs., Low. Norf. Co., upon Ridgford's Sw. at the head of the S. br. of Eliz. Riv., 15 Mar. 1675, p. 598. Beg. at John Chadwell; adj. Jno. Corperhew, &c. Trans. of 4 pers: Math. Bow, Tho. Lodimore, Herbert Jones, Marge. Browne.

WM. WHITEHURST, 459 acs., Low. Norf. Co., on W. side of the Indian Cr., 15 Mar. 1675, p. 598. Beg. at James Handson's; to Henry Holstead; to Richard Whitlye's; to Thomas Alexander; to Fading Sw; &c. Trans. of 9 pers: Wm. & Mary Serson, Jno. Pittman, Tho. Watts, Hanna Ward, Elinor Ward, Lucy Twigar; Lucy & Tony, Negroes.

JNO. PRESCOTT, 787 acs., Low. Norf. Co., 15 Mar. 1675, p. 598. 400 acs., due by patt. dated 6 Nov. 1665; on E. side of the S. br. of Eliz. Riv., adj. Edmond Crickman (or Crickmore); & Jno. Biggs; &c; 387 acs. beg. at Prescott's point; to Roule's (?) point; to Chincopine Ridg; by the Long Ridg; &c. Trans. of 8 pers: Eliz. Harris, Ann Curtis, Jno. Shard, Danll. Negelture, Jno. Moore, Mary Wms. (Williams), Mary Felcks (?) & Ben, a Negro.

EDWARD HASTELL, 367 acs., Low. Norf. Co., W. side of the S. br. of Eliz. Riv., 15 Mar. 1675, p. 598. At Joseph Mulder'ss land; up Deepe Cr; to Francis Fleetwood; &c. Trans. of 7 pers: Jno. Stone, Ben. Brambury, —— Marshall, Jno. Bright, Jno. Crosse, Wm. Cooke, Will. Payne.

TIMOTHY IVES, JUNR., 270 acs., Low. Norf. Co., W. side of the S. br. of Eliz. Riv., 15 Mar. 1675, p. 599. Beg. upon the Road point neere mouth of Guillam's Run; to a marsh against old Butts' (or Britts') Cr., &c; 200 acs. granted to Mr. Richard Jones, Senr., 28 Apr. 1665; assigned to Timothy Ives, Senr., 15 Feb. 1671, who assigned to the abovenamed, his son; 70 acs. for trans. of 2 pers: Wm. Lodimore, Eliz. Ketcher.

ROBT. BURGESSE (or Burgeste), 332 acs., Low. Norf. Co., on W. side of the S. br. of Eliz. Riv; 15 Mar. 1675, p. 599. 250 acs. granted to Joseph Mulder 28 Apr. 1665, & assigned to the above, 15 Nov. 1672; 82 acs. for trans. of: Wm. Greene, twice.

THOMAS MERCER, 602 acs., Low. Norf. Co., in Pussell point Cr., of the S. br. of Eliz. Riv., 15 Mar. 1675, p. 599. 200 acs. granted to Richard Starling, the elder, 20 Apr. 1653; & by Joseph Newton & Denis Morris, who marryed the coe-heyres of sd. Starling, conveyed to Michaell Wayburne, 16 Oct. 1671, who conveyed to sd. Mercer, 17 Feb. 1672; 4$2 acs. for trans. of 8 pers: Anth. Reboone, Jno. Greygoose, Lor. Baker, Peter Porter, Jno. Simonds, Alexr. Rosse, Rich. Harper, Mark Lenear (or Lescear?).

RICHARD WHITLY, 220 acs., Low. Norf. Co., in the S. br. of Eliz. Riv., on E. side of Pustell (or Pussell) point Cr., & adj. Thomas Mercer; 15 Mar. 1675, p. 599. 100 acs. granted to Bartholomew Ingoebritson 18 Oct. 1664, who assigned to Capt. Nicho. & Robt. Jordan, 10 Feb. 1664, & by sd. Capt. Robt. Jordan assigned to sd. Whitly 18 Jan. 1669; 120 acs. for trans. of 3 pers: Eliz. Whitby, Tho. Banks, Mary Allen.

THEODOR TAYLOR, 150 acs., Low. Norf. Co., in the S. br. of Eliz. Riv., neere the head of Julian's Cr., & adj. John Wallis; 15 Mar. 1675, p. 600. Being part of a patt. granted Richard Taylor & Tho. Nash, 6 Nov. 1665, & due sd. Theodor by order of the Co. Court of Low. Norf., 17 Aug. 1669.

RICHARD BACHELOR, 700 acs., Low. Norf. Co., neere the head of Deepe Cr., in the S. br. of Eliz. Riv., adj. Edward Browne; 15 Mar. 1675, p. 600. 300 acs. part of 1200 acs. granted Edward Browne & Richard Starnell, 9 Mar. 1658, & due sd. Bachelor by several assignments; 400 acs. for trans. of 8 pers: Sara Needham, Eliz. Needham, Jno. Thomas, Margt. Needham, Fra. Harris, Mary Batten; & 2 Negroes.

MR. WM. HARRISON, 600 acs., Up. Par. of Nanzemond Co., 11 Mar. 1675/6, p. 600. Adj. Mr. Tho. Francis; & his owne land. Trans. of 12 pers: Neddy, Yanke, Capt. Dick, Hana, Nany; Negroes; Jno. Hopkins, Hannah Smith, Geo. West, Peter Aldwick, Eliz. Anny, Jno. Harris, Jno. Morgan, Jno. Bullock.

COL. WM. KENDALL, 100 acs., N'ampton Co., at Nunswattocks Cr., at the head of the N. E. br., 11 Mar. 1675/6, p. 600. Adj. Stephen Horseley; & on a Ridge by Occahanoke Path, &c. Granted to Rich. Bayly 17 Mar. 1655; renewed; & assigned to Phill. Fisher, who lapsed same for want of seateing; & now due by order, &c; trans. of 2 pers.*

WM. ANDERSON, 60 acs., Gloucester Co., in Petsoe Par., 11 Mar. 1675/6, p. 601. Adj. his owne; Major Lewis; land of Nettle;& Jno. Jebell's, neere the five Springs, &c. Trans. of 2 pers: Ja. Bartlett, Jno. Read.

JAMES REYNOLDS, 140 acs., Gloster Co., in Petsoe Par., 11 Mar. 1675/6, p. 601. Adj. Walter Cant, sonn of David Cant, dec'd.; land formerly called Knoxe's; land of Tho. Dawkins & Samll. Patridge; by the Dragon Sw. runne, &c. Trans. of 3 pers: Ja. Clarke, Robt. Dyer, Robt. Cannon.

SUSANNA WELLS, Infant, only child & heire of Jno. Wells, dec'd., 50 acs. Gloster Co., Ware Par., 11 Mar. 1675/6, p. 601. And to the heirs of her body lawfully begotten & for default of such issue or heirs of her body, &c., then to her mother Grizell, late wife & widdow of sd. Jno., & to her heires & assigns for ever. Adj. devdt. of sd. John, which was surveyed by Mr. Jno. Lewis, Surveyor, at the instance & for the use of Edwd. Wells, father of sd. Jno., & Grandfather of sd. Susanna, but to this day never pattented. Sd. land adj. Mr. Clarke; Humphry Mead; & Col. Willis. Due by order, &c., & alsoe for trans. of 2 pers: Edwd. Clarke, Joane Sheares.

DAVID MURRAY, the younger, 113 A., 1 R., 6 P., Low. Norf. Co., Lynhaven Par., called the *Piney thicknetts;* on S. side Lyon's quarter run; 15 Mar. 1675/6, p. 602. Trans. of 3 pers: Emanuell Delannero (?), Robt. Davison, Antho. Alanson.

MARY JOSLEN, 28 A., 1 R., 1 P., Low. Norf. Co., Lynhaven Par., 15 Mar. 1675/6, p. 602. Towards the head of a br. of Broad Cr., adj. Wm. Martin & Robert Young. Trans. of Theodore Floyd.

THOMAS MORRIS, 200 acs., Low. Norf. Co., 15 Mar. 1675, p. 602. On S. side of the mouth of Nonneys Cr., on Curretuck Bay, &c. Trans. of 4 perss: Tho. Morris, Josias Morris, William Johnson, Samll. Browne.

JANE BOULTON, relict of Wm. Boulton, 350 acs., Low. Norf. Co., at the path from the E'n. br. of Eliz. Riv. to the North River; 15 Mar. 1675/6, p. 602. Trans. of 7 pers: Hannah White, Tho. Browne, Jacob. Johnson, twice; Wm. Carly, Mary Mount, Walter Hannard (?).

SARAH RUSSELL, 70 acs., Low. Norf. Co., in the N. brs. of Curretuck, 15 Mar. 1675/6, p. 603. Beg. on the green Br., to marsh dividing this & land of Thomas Griffin; Mr. Basnett. Trans. of 2 pers: Nicholas Fossen (or Foster), Howell Cannard.

THOMAS MOYSER, 485 acs., Low. Norf. Co., towards head of Lynhaven Riv., 15 Mar. 1675/6, p. 603. Adj. Henry Smith; neare the broad run; to John Bowrin, &c. Trans. of 10 pers: Tho. Browning, Richd. Richards, Tho. Green, Alex. Martin, Peter Edmonds, Symon Porter, Roger Cardin, Thos. Attwood, Henry Smith.

HENRY SPRATT, 351 acs., Low. Norf. Co., Lynhaven Par., 15 Mar. 1675/6, p. 603. Adj. Henry Smith on the Cyprus Sw; & land of Edm. Moore, &c. Trans. of 7 pers: Tho. Wentworth, Richd. Jackson, Joseph Oliver, Walter Hannard, Jno. Wood, Jno. Powell, Jno. Shaw (or Shair).

MR. JOHN TOWNELY (Townly), 1100 acs., New Kent Co., Stratton Major Par., 17 Mar. 1675/6, p. 604. Beg. at a forke of Arrakeco Sw., next below his house, by Jones' pond, &c. 640 acs. purchased of Mr. Ralph Green; & 460 acs. for trans. of 9 pers.*

CAPT. WM. BIRD, 7351 A., 2 R., 24 P., Henrico Co., N. side James Riv., 15 Mar. 1675/6, p. 604. Beg. (at) Shoccores Cr. mouuth, up the river bet. W & NW &c. 1280 acs. granted him 27 Oct. 1673; the residue for trans. of

122 pers: Jno. Willoughby, - Mary Stringer, Tho. Huccoby (?), Tho. Browne, Eliz. Pirnell (?), Wm. Branard, Wm. Whittingam, Tho. Lowder, Abra. Hodkins, Antho. Wheeler, Wm. Howard, Tho. Kyte, Arth. Miles, Jno. Dacres, Tho. Ardell, Peter Simonds, Robt. Ball. Jno. Gardner, Anth. Strange, Jno. Bull, Tho. New, Robt. Penfather, Wm. Key (?), Roger Keniston, Wm. Miller, Jno. Pick, Wm. Harding, Jno. Parsons, Robt. Temple, Darby Enroty, Jno. Beck, Ja. Beck, Eliz. Hollinsby, Mary Carter, Rich. Fossell, Xper. Meads, Jno. Lilley, Jno. Wallis, Wm. Wile (or Wild), Jno. Wittin, Peter Merie (?), Jno. Warren, Hana. Goodwin, Ben. Bean, Doro. Willimph, Mary Thornehill, Esther Jnoson, Mary Cooke, Jno. Drury, Tho. Chapell, Wm. Drowgen, Mary Cox, Ma. Shorter, Wm. West, Jno. Hedgpath, Tho. Wharton, Tho. Hayles, Wm. Lovedere, Cha. Pistore, Isa. Bates, Jno. Smith, Geo. Toppin, Hugh Buckins, Jane Haydens, Jane Laurence, Alex. Mackwell, Othelr. Wright, Barba. Hath. Eliz. Hollinsby, Eliz. Archer, Wm. Wheeler, Wm. Stith, Eliz. Crispin, Tho. Davis, Hen. Barnard, Ja. Mackary, Wm. Elam, Ja. Thompson, Ben. Hudson, Wm. Bird, Jno. Hampton, Hen. Harman, Robt. Estly (?), An. Simson, Sara Browne, Rich. Terrell, Jno. Dawby (or Dawly), Wm. Orme, Hen. Parsons, Jno. Ternden, Geo. Lisse, Cha. Cooper, Obed. Bay, Eliz. Page, Samll. Welch, Robt. Stock, Fra. Leech, Tho. Dicer, Bry Booden (or Prooden), Ja. Howard, Wm. Stanard, Mary Wakam, Wm. Holden, Ma. Johnson, Geo. Sharpnells, Wm. Palmer, Jno. Harrinton, Wm. Gyles, Isac Creswell, Wm. Waters, Jno. Coulchester, Jas. Shippy, An. Duncum, Jno. Seabrite Phill. Dyer, Jno. North, Nath. Shurbun, Tho. Hales, Francis (?) Dixon; Jack, Torfy, Cate, Negroes.

MR. EDWD. JONES, 600 acs., Is. of W. Co., on W. side of the 1st gr. br. of the Blackwater; beg. at the mouth of the Orpts. (Orphants ?) Br., downe Hull's Br., &c; 21 Mar. 1675/6, p. 605. Purchased of Mr. Fra. England 3 Jan. 1670, out of his patt. dated 29 Sept. 1664.

JNO. GRIMES, 200 acs., Low Par. of Nanzemond (Co.,) 21 Mar. 1675/6, p. 605. Beg. by a smale Lodge point within Pigg Point, &c. Part of a patt. of 800 acs. granted Mr. Fra. Hough 17 May 1637; sd. land after several assignments & conveyances gradually from sd. Hough comeing & decending & now being in possession of sd. Grimes.

RICHARD THOMAS, sonn & heire of John Thomas, 174 acs., Nanzemond Co., 21 Mar. 1675/6, p. 605. 150 acs. on E. side of New Towne Haven Riv; adj. Humphry Scoen &c; the residue bounded with his owne; land of Mr. Jordane; & Tho. Best. Granted to sd. John Thomas, 19 Nov. 1654.

MR. ROBT. PRICE, 450 acs., Middlesex Co., 21 Mar. 1675, p. 606. Beg. at Major Burnham; to his owne plantation; by Joshua Smith; to Mr. Humphry Jones; to land of the orphans of Mr. Richd. Lewis, &c. 300 acs. granted him 3 Oct. 1671; & 150 acs. for trans. of 3 servants: Peter Deane, Jno. Hooper, Hanna Cones (or Cowes).

MR. JAMES BAGNALL, 300 acs., Is of W. Co., 22 Mar. 1675/6, p. 606. Granted to Capt. Jno. Upton, who assigned to Mr. Robert Bracewell; by him given to his son Robt., who assigned to sd. James Bagnall; found to escheate as by inquisition, under Capt. Jno. Jennings, Depty. Esch'r., &c.

MR. THO. ADDISON, 200 acs., Low. Par. of Nanzemond Co., on E'wd. side of White's Cr., bet. Wm. Stephens & Wm. Knott; 22 Mar. 1675/6, p. 606. Part of 1300 acs. granted to Jno. Wilkins, 10 May 1673; sd. 200 acs., after severall assignments, &c. now in possession of sd. Addison.

JNO. SMITH, 50 acs., Nanzemond Co., at the head of Chuckatuck, 24 Feb. 1674/5, p. 607. Granted to Stephen Deford, & escheated, by inquisition under Jno. Lear, Depty. Esch'r., & granted to Tho. Parker, who assigned to sd. Smith, 19 Sept. 1674.

EDWD. ROBINS, 680 acs., at *Jingoteige*, in Accomack Co., 22 Mar.

1675/6, p. 607. Beg. where the line bet. Va. & Md. intersecteth with the salt water of the sea side;· to Capt. Southy Littleton, &c. 500 acs. granted to Jno. Robins, by him deserted, & now granted, &c; trans. of 10 pers; & 180 acs. for trans. of 4 pers: Jno. Haning, Jno. Hawkins, Jno. America, Step. Gossins, Kath. Whelply, Margt. Richardson, Margt. Price, Wm. Browne, Jno. Smith, Samll. Hall, Tho. Cooper, Jno. Tharry, Martin Johnson; Tom a Negro.

THO. HEADY, 475 acs., Accomack Co., on W. side of the forked Cr; & N. upon Phillips' Cr., 22 Mar. 1675/6, p. 607. 450 acs. granted to Edward Harrinton 4 July 1653, assigned to Robt. Watson, & renewed by order, &c., 20 Oct. 1661; by him assigned to Edwd. Hammond 17 Sept. 1665, who assigned to William Roberts 15 May 1669, & by him assigned to Robert Foster, who assigned to sd. Heady 29 Apr. 1672; 25 acs. for trans. of: Rich. Williams.

JNO. THOMPSON, 300 acs., Accomack Co., bet. Nasswattux & Ochahannocks Creeks; 22 Mar. 1675/6, p. 608. Beg. at land of Thomas Savage; to Nico. Tubbins (or Stubbins); to Obed. Johnson; along Jno. Smith, &c. Trans. of 6 pers: Wm. Lawrence, Tho. Braston, Richd. Beare (or Beard), Rich. Wood, Mordecay Edwards, Angus Powell.

HIOREM GRIFFETH, 345 acs., N'ampton Co., at *Pimeno;* 23 Mar. 1675/6, p. 608. Adj. Capt. Southy Littleton; to the maine br. of Pemino Cr., &c. Being ½ of 400 acs. granted Xper Kirke 11 Nov. 1642, who assigned to Wm. Ennis 21 Mar. 1642, who assigned to sd. Griffeth 11 Sept. 1673; 145 acs. within sd. bounds, due for trans. of 3 pers: Rich. Dicks, Mary Davis, Jno. Tillery.

WM. ANDERSON, 450 acs., Accomack Co., bet. lands of *Occohanock* & *Matchepungo;* 26 Mar. 1676, p. 609. Bounded by lands that now are or of late were Dorothy Jordan's; Arth. Upshore's; Jno. Savage; Jno. Sturges; Edwd. Smith & Hen. Bishop's. Granted to Cornelius Watkinson 10 Sept. 1664, who made default of planting or seate-

ing, &c; granted to Amb. White by order, &c., at James Citty 8 Nov. 1672, who likewise defaulted, &c; granted sd. Anderson by order &c. & for trans. of 9 pers? Richard Williams, Robt. Jones, Agnes Powell, Eliz. Wood, Jno. Ricks, Geo. Hudson; & 3 Negroes.

ANTHONY FULGHAM, 780 acs., Is. of W. Co., upon branches of Chawanoke Riv., called the Black Water; 6 June 1676, p. 609. Beg. upon Seaward's br., by Doct. Williamson's land; to Mr. John Fulgham, by Tomlin, &c. 400 acs. granted John Seaward 15 Apr. 1648; 380 acs. for trans. of 8 pers: Tho. Craddock, Wm. Johnson, Ja. Reese, Jno. Eanig (?), Robt. Smith, Edith Smith, Will. Price, Jno. Jacob.

JOHN FREEMAN, 400 acs., Low Norf. Co., neare head of the W'n. br. of Eliz. Riv., 6 June 1676, p. 609. Adj. land surveyed by William Defnall (?) & Thomas Lovell; to the *inchaunted ridge;* &c. Trans. of 8 pers: Jane Williams, Jno. Tutte, Cha. Morgan, Mary Cutter, Rich. Reynolds, Edwd. Browne, Mary Hartly, Jno. Freeman.

RICHARD WHITAKER, 600 acs., Warwicke Co., 1 June 1676, p. 610. Beg. at mouth of Deviding Br. issuing out of back Cr., a br. of Warwick River, &c.; Mr. Robert Crew; neare the maine Road; upon land of Henry Coney (?) &c. 450 acs. part of 1050 acs. granted Thomas Bernerd, gent. 10 Dec. 1642 & purchased by sd. Whitaker; 150 acs. overplus within &c., & due for trans. of 3 pers.*

MAJOR JOHN WEST, 1000 acs., N'ampton Co., 1 June 1676, p. 610. Adj. Thomas Letherby (Letherbery); John Jenkins, & William Benson, at *Accomack;* N'wd. on the S. br. of Letherberys Br., &c. Granted him 14 Jan. 1671, & being lapsed for want of seating &c., was granted to Capt. Southy Littleton by order, &c., 21 Mar. 1675/6, who assigned to sd. West 26 Mar. 1676; further due for trans. of 20 pers: Robt. Smith, Jno. Trower, Robt. Glide, Jno. Eliott, Jno. Traven, Tho. Holloway, Ja. Hutton, Wm. Bivian, Danll. Tunstall, Richd. Sale, Jno. Meeres, Jno. Arnold,

Sara Bremy, Wm. Ludington, Bennett Winch, Ren. Ash, Jno. Rosse, An. Burtock, Ezek. Sewell, Tho. Thompson.

CAPT. ANTHONY ARMESTEAD, 928 acs., Eliz. Citty Co., on NW side of the back river, 1 June 1676, p. 611. Adj. land of Marke Morgan's orphts., now in possession of Abraham Woodwerd; adj. Richard Symons & severall lands of Xpher. Thomas, Moses Baker's Orphts., & Orpht. of Anthony Tilly & land of Marke Parish (?); to Deepe Sw. neare Burton's quarter; adj. land of Phillip Johnson, in possession of Thomas Jenkins; to Gullett Cr. issuing out of the broade Cr., &c. 353 acs. due by 2 pattents, viz: 100 acs. granted Thomas Keeling 28 Nov. 1635; & 300 acs, granted to William Armstead, his father, 16 May 1638; 450 acs. granted sd. William 7 July 1636; 125 acs., within sd. bounds, due for trans. of 3 pers:. Hugh Jones, Jane Jones, Tho. Bowden.

JOHN WELLS & EMANUELL WELLS, 400 acs., Warwick Co., in Mulbery Island Par., 6 June 1676, p. 611. Granted to Thomas Iken, & escheated by inquisition, under Lt. Col. William Cole, Depty. Esch'r; now granted sd. John & Emanuell *Wills,* &c.

WILLIAM PROSSER, 50 acs., Surry Co., 6 June 1676, p. 612. Granted to Richard Stephens, found to escheate, by inquisition under Henry Hartwell, Depty. Esch'r., &c.

MRS. KATHERIN LOWDALL, Exix. to Mr. Tymothy Lowdall, 150 acs., New Kent Co., 6 June 1676, p. 612. Granted to John King; found to escheate, by inquisition under Thomas Hall, Depty. Esch'r., &c.

EDMD. MOORE, 134 acs., Low. Norf. Co., Lynhaven Par., 12 June 1676, p. 612. Trans. of 3 pers: Wm. Cooper, Jno. Mauden, Eliz. Wallent.

ELIZ. BRANCH, 140 acs., Low. Norf. Co., on N. side of Danll. Tanner's Cr., 12 June 1676, p. 612. Beg. on a point deviding this & land of Robt. Woodie; & land of Wm. Crouch, &c. Trans. of 3 pers: Jno. Guin, Timothy Holmes, Kath. Low.

ALICE PETERS, 698 acs., Low. Norf. Co., in Danll. Tanner's Cr., 12 June 1676, p. 613. Adj. Samll. Roberts; up Boughs Br; on the Indian Towne Cr; along Queen Grave Cr., &c. 500 acs. granted Symon Peters 20 Oct. 1661; 198 acs. for trans. of 4 pers: Leonerd Wagener, Jno. Barnes, Kath. Wells, Tho. Pomfrett.

JOHN STOAKELY, 370 acs., called *Dunn,* in N'ampton Co., 13 June 1676, p. 613. N. upon Dunn Cr. 200 acs. granted Capt. Edmd. Scarburgh 28 Nov. 1635 & assigned to Alice Wilson, to whom it was granted 11 May 1639; by her assigned to Fra. Stoakely & Tho. Ward, & by Ward assigned to said Francis; due sd. John as sonn & heire of sd. Francis; 170 acs. within the bounds, due for trans. of 4 pers: Margtt. Harmanson, Robt. Gimbalson, Jno. Wayre, Tho. Taylor.

ROBERT NETHERLAND, 490 acs., Chas. Citty Co., on N. side of Flower de hundred Cr., 15 June 1676, p. 613. Adj. land of Mr. Pace upon sd. Cr., NE upon Snow Cr., &c. Granted to Tho. Drew, Gent., dec'd., 4 June 1657, & being not seated, &c., granted sd. Netherland by order. &c. Trans. of 10 pers: Jno. Wilson, Tho. Hilliard, Robt. Susser, Tho. Arth. (Arthur ?), Negro Thoms. (Others not mentioned.)

ALEXDR. FOREMAN, 415 acs., Low. Norf. Co., 19 June 1676, p. 614. Beg. at his 400 acr. patt., dated 18 Oct. 1664; adj. Mr. Richd. Jones; along Gillam Neck Sw; down the Cyprus Sw., &c. Trans. of 8 pers: Jno. Clerke, Richd. Tayler, Richd. Foreman, Samll. Johnson, Eliz. Mathews, Peter Dawkes, Jno. Martin, And. Packly.

AUGUSTINE MOORE, 285 acs., Eliz. Citty Co., at head of little Poquoson Cr., 19 June 1676, p. 614. Adj. Mr. Tho. Wyth; William Up (ap) Thomas; Tho. Prittiman; Tho. Tabb; &c. 200 acs. granted to John More, his father, 3 July 1635; 85 acs. found within, for trans. of 2 pers: Wm. Wms. (Williams), Morph. Berry.

CAPT. DANIELL JENIFER, 5800 acs., Accomack Co., knowne by the

name of *Gentgoteage,* on the upper part
of the Co., being the next island to the
N'wd. of Kekotank Is. *alias* Occocomson Is., 27 Mar. 1677, p. 615. Granted
to Mr. William Whittington 2 Oct.
1672, deserted &c. & now granted by
order, &c. Trans. of 116 pers.*

By Herbert Jefferys, Esqr., Governor &c.

COL. NICHOLAS SPENCER & LT.
COL. JOHN WASHINGTON, 5000
acs., Staff. Co., in the freshes of Potomacke Riv., near apposite to *Puscataway
Indian Towne in Maryland* & near land
of Capt. Giles Brent, on the No. side,
& neare land surveyed for Mr. William
Green & Mr. William Dudly & others
on the So. side; being a neck of land
bet. 2 crks. & the maine river on the
E., sd. maine river of Potomack on the
N., a Cr. by the English called Little
Hunting Cr. on the S. by a Cr. called
by the Indians Epsewassen Cr., &c; ....
of .... 1677, p. 615. Trans. of 100
pers.*

HENRY BERRY, 550 acs., Staff. Co.,
bet. Rappa. & Potomack Rivers; beg. at
William Lippitt's cor; to Symons' oake;
to Arnold's; & adj. Mr. James Key; &
his own land. (*Note:* Record unfinished.) Page 616.

HENRY BERRY, 428 acs., Rappa.
Co., adj. Mr. Robert King; Mr. Bun-
berey; Mr. Francis Hales; & Mr. James
Keyes land; by a Cart path at end of
Mr. Robert King's head line; to Mr.
Howsend's line; to Hayles; &c. (*Rec-
ord unfinished.*)

ANDREW WATSON, 260 acs. Staff.
Co., on NE side of Quanticott Cr., adj.
John Jeames. &c; 15 Jan. 1677, p. 617.
Trans. of 3 pers: Jon. Tomes, Alice
Andrews, Willi. Seawell.

HENRY WALKER, 2150 acs., Staff.
Co., on both side the maine run of
Yeoassacomico Cr; —— of —— 1677,
p. 617. Trans. of 43 pers: Henry Mar-
tin, Tho. Davis, Roger Cocksell, Jo.
Hopkins, Ambrose Thomas, Jo. Gold-
worthy, Jo. Loudloe, Jos. Read, Jos.
Dyer, Tho. Watkins, Will. Lewis, Tho.
Foster, Grace Adams, Anne Fleete, Jo.

Smith, Tho. Lewis, Will. Dyer, Jeptha
Parker, Anne Jones, Will. Cole, Willi.
Martin, Joane Hohen (?), Jo. Boy,
Richard White, Tho. Read, Tho. Ackly,
James Langly, Eliz. Pickeren, Sarah
Yard, Georg Berkeley, Willi. Merry-
feild, Mary Branch, Tho. Giddons, Sam,
Sims, Jo. Harris, Rich. Gold, Jo. Car-
penter, Jo. Holt, Jane Charles, Tho.
Floyd, Jone Powell, Sibbill Press, Mary
Smith.

SAME. 2960 acs., Staff. Co; —— of
—— 1677, p. 618. On Yeosiocomico
Runn; adj. his own; Thomas Baxter,
Thomas Gregg; & land of Major An-
drew Gilson. Trans. of 59 pers: John
Greene, Thomas Big, Martin Fisher,
Charles Perkes, Jo. Ellis, Robt. Franck,
Cornelius Chreman (?), Tho. Eldrige,
Rich. Sawyer, Jo. Compton, Robt.
Knight, Henry Clarke, Jo. Smith, Giles
Collins, Sam Siscan, Joane Eagle, Henry
Jones, Alice Homes, Robt. Betts, Willi.
Smith, Bridgett Futer, Tho. Godfry,
James Bides, Owen Williams, James
Morris, Math. Hardige, Abr. Willoby,
Jo. Spaine, Eliz. Wilsonn, Sarah Harris,
Rand. Mathews, Jo. Farrer, Jo. Skitton,
Miles Thomas, Tho. Steply, Jeffery
Johnsons, Franck Rowland, Ellen Lard-
ing, Symon Cander, Joane Rowles,
Richd. Harvy (or Harby), Tho. Sands,
Jo. Moss, Mary Hiibbs, Math. Roads,
Hanah Kemp, Rowland Bankes, Willi.
Barber, Robt. Carpenter, Jos. Daniell,
Sarah Madder, James Baker, Willi.
Helliard, Eliz. Lutes (or Kates), Willi.
Bussee, Jo. Maynard, Jo. Dabny.

SAME. 550 acs., Staff. Co., —— of
—— 1677, p. 619. N.E. side of Quan-
ticock Cr., adj. lands of Mr. Richard
Boughton & Samuell Spooner. Trans.
of 11 pers: Nicolas Jones Alice Little
Joanna Norwood, Jo. Nickolls, Tho.
Gauge, Jo. an Irishman. Rowland Davis,
Tho. Knapton, Antho. Dodson, Jo.
Rosse, William Lane.

JOHN WEBB & JOHN REA. 700
acs., in Up. part of New Kent Co., on
S. side of land formerly taken up by
Andrew Davis on Machumps Cr; ——
of —— 1677, p. 619. 500 acs. belonging to sd. Webb & 200 to sd. Rea.
Trans. of 14 pers: Thomas Davis,

Charles Halsy, Abigall Neale, Rich. Davenport, James the frenchman; Daniell Steere, Tho. Turpin, Tho. Barber, Amor (or Amos) Via, Fr. Derige, Tho. Wallbrooke, Jo. Bird, Morrice Thomas, Deborah Buncks.

MATHEW JENINGS (Jennings), 600 acs., New Kent Co., bet the 2 maine brs. of Hartquake, upon N. side of Mattapony Riv; —— of —— 1677, p. 620. By the house of John James; adj. lands of Peter Ford & John Hands; William Henderson; Col. William Cleyborne; &c. 500 acs. purchased of Ralph Massey; 100 acs. of sd. Cleyborne, & now included in one pattent.

GEORG WOODWARD, 2000 acs., James Citty Co., in Wimbleton Par., & upon Tyascum Sw., p. 620. (*Date blank*). Adj. William Elcones (?) land, &c. Sd. land granted to sd. Woodward by Sir John Ayton as by patt. dated 15 Oct. 1653, &c.

JAMES JACKSON, 200 acs., Low. Norf. Co; 1677; p. 621. Adj. land of Alex. Gwyn; to Gates Cr., &c. Part of a patt. belonging to John Godfry. Trans. of 4 pers: Thomas Turpin, Tho. Barber, Tho. Walbrooke, Jo. Brice. (*Date blank*).

GEORG MORRIS, 2300 acs., in the Counties of New Kent & Rappa; bet. Rappa. & Mattapony Rivers; 1677, (*date blank*), p. 621. Beg. at land of Col. Thomas Goodrich; &c. 2100 acs. Part formerly taken up by patt. Trans. of 5 pers: John Butler, Jon. Taylor, Anne Taylor, Thomas Thorpe, Mary Thorpe.

GEORG JONES & HENRY CLARKE, 1261 acs., Rappa. Co., N. side the river; 27 Feb. 1677/8, p. 621. Beg. in a white *martish* Sw. on N. side the roade; adj. Major John Weire; Robt. Tomlin; William Moss; Richard Burke; cor. tree of Coleman or Patrick Norton; land of Mr. William Lane, &c. Trans. of 26 pers: Georg Jones twice, Jon. Skinner, Tho. Searle, Willi. Hill, Jon. Chapman, Isaac Bucher, Tho. Hamond, Barth. Marriott, Jon. Roumble (?), Jon. Jeffrey, Georg Smith; Teag; Darby; & Denby, Irish boys; Jon.

Grover, Susan (a ?) Kinsman, Anne Cumber, Eliz. Rich. Christ. Sherbrooke, Kate Lothlen (or Lochlen), Tho. Barker, Anne Rayney, James Loyd, Leonard Gill. NOTE: "Is truly dated accord. to the pattent. Hen. Hartwell).

WARREN GODFREY (Godfry), 148 acs., called the Dam necks; Low. Norf. Co., 1677; p. 622. Beg. at David Murray, Junr; to the Cyprus Sw., &c. Trans. of 3 pers: Sarah Hodwood, Georg Turly, Thomas Taylor.

COL. WILLIAM TRAVERSE (Travers), 780 acs., Staff. Co., at the head of Doegs Cr; adj. Mr. Wells; & Mr. Jon. Thomas; 22 Mar. 1677/8, p. 622.Trans. of 16 pers: Joseph Smith, Richard Hatter, Tho. Sampson, Patrick Nicolls, Tho. Todd, Tho. Clarke, Marvell Mosely, Giles Baines (or Bames), James Johnson, Henry Shares, Jon. Butcher, Peter Legray, Mary Wood, Margery Holland, Joane Wade, Jon. Stretchly.

EDMUND GWINN, 80 acs., Gloster Co., 4 Apr. 1678, p. 622. Granted to Capt. Tho. Bremore, dec'd., & afterwards to William Court; found to escheate by inquisition, under Col. Phillipp Ludwell, Depty. Esch'r. Genrll., &c.

MARY TITTERTON (Tytterton), 930 acs. Gloster Co., 4 Apr. 1678, p. 623. Granted to Edward Titerton, & escheated by inquisition, &c., under Col. Philip Ludwell, Depty. Esch'r., &c.

THOMAS VICKARS (Viccars), Clerke, 1260 acs. Rappa. Co., N. side the River, above & below the falls; 10 Apr. 1678, p. 623. Opposite Mr. John Buckner; adj. Mr. Mott, &c. Trans. of 26 pers: John Hill, Alex. Forbush, James Martin, Richard Hambleton, Richard Nixon, Tho. Crandell. Robt. Thripy (?), Thomas Moore, Christ. Ward, John Punsley, Elix. Foxon, Hester Harrison, John Chapman, Tho. Ingle, Robt. Griffith, Faith Beard, William Hasell, Georg Courtman, James King, Sam. Thurwell, Sam. Hill, Mary Baker, Nich. Arrundell, Henry Exodus, Elias Nicholls, Symon Moyfer (or Moyser).

WARREN GODFRY (Godfrey), 106 acs., Low. Norf. Co., adj. the tract called *the New Discovery*, 20 Oct. 1677, p. 624. Beg. at a line tree of the old patent & cor. of William Nichols, &c. Trans. of 2 pers: Warren Godfry, John Adkis.

THOMAS FENFORD, 797 acs., Low. Norf. Co., on the W. side of the S. br. of Eliz. River; 10 Oct. 1678, p. 624. Beg. at the mouth of Smith's Cr., to Fenford's Cr; to Timothy Ive (or Jue); by Gwilliams' runn; by Jacob Smith, &c. 200 acs. granted to Rich. King 20 Sept. 1664 & assigned to sd. Fenford, 16 Nov. 1665; 300 acs. granted sd. Fenford 21 Sept. 1674; 50 acs., by patt. 14 Sept. 1667; 247 acs. for importation of 5 pers.* Marginal Note: Truely recorder according to the pattent. H. H. Cl.

MR. GEORG BRENT, 584 acs., Staff. Co., on N. side of Little Hunting Cr., 14 Dec. 1677, p. 625. Beg. neare mouth of sd. Cr., to Mr. James Clifton & his own land, &c. Trans. of 12 pers: Georg Brent, John Fitzherbert, Anth. Williams, Anne Brent, Dorithy Fitzherbert, Georg Mallett, Eliz. Brent, Mary Brent, Edwd. Barton, Tho. Bird, Rich. Netherton, Elianor Veale. (Truely dated, &c.)

SAME. 1143 acs., 7 Nov. 1677, p. 625. On NW side of Mr. Mathews' land; upp the runn of Gr. Hunting Cr. &c. Trans. of 23 pers: William Turner, Willi. Sexty, Tho. Hix, Henry Tindall, John Jones, James Katherine, Georg Brent, Henry Brent, Henry Mildmay, John Simpson, Anthny Shelton, Rich. Hudman, Mary Hudman, Georg Wilkes, James Clifton, Edmd. Fitzherbert, Eliz. Greene, John Adams, Charles Baker, Mathew Davis, Evan Jones, Ralph Fleet, John Hoskins. (Note: "The true date. H. Hartwell.")

SAME. 555 acs., within the forke of little Hunting Cr., on S. side of the howse, &c; 3 Nov. 1677, p. 626. (The True date. H. H.) Trans. of 11 pers: Willi. Stephens, William Smith, John Busby, Franc. Powell, Jos. Pitts, Jon. Lightwade, Sarah Pye, Mary Warrington, Mary Newell, Rich. Mildmay, William Burly.

SAME. 1391 acs., on N. br. of the forke of little Hunting Cr., at the head of Mr. Mathews' land, &c; 6 Nov. 1677, p. 626. (The true date according, &c.) Trans. of 28 pers: James Glavis, Thomas Strickland, Noell Whaley, Willi. Whaley, James Levans, William Tompson, Peter Penion, Jo. Almond, Willi. Davis, Thomas Bortering, Andrew Williams, Willi. Sims, Jon. Archer, Thomas Lightwood, John Tomson, Eliz. Cherrington, Eliz. Winsell, Georg Brent, James Ashton, Thomas Lewis, Edmund West, Jon. Sallen, Anne Woollen, Tho. Perce, Ralph Deane, Jon. Wilks, Thomas Dunn.

JOHN CARPENTER & JOHN MOTT, 245 acs., Lancaster Co., 5 Jan. 1677, p. 627. Adj. Joseph Bayly; Georg Hale; Thomas Chetwood; & Thomas Chatwin. Trans. of 5 pers: Susanna Newman, Mary Pammer, Mary Treene (or Greene), Penelope Mason, Eliza Mason.

JOHN CARPENTER, 100 acs., upon Morattico Cr., 5 Jan. 1677, p. 627. Adj. land of Thomas Stephens, dec'd., the Ouldman's Cr. & Sw., & land that did belong to William Fittsherbert. Trans. of 2 pers: Mary Davis, John Potterell.

ABRAHAM BUSH, 35 acs., Lancaster Co., in a br. of Morattico Cr., adj. land of Patrick Grimes & Abraham Bush; 5 Jan. 1677, p. 627. Trans. of: John Moulten.

MR. OLIVER BOUSSER, 200 acs., Lancaster Co., upon Morattico Cr. & Rappa. Riv., 5 Jan. 1677, p. 628. Adj. lands of Thomas Stephens, dec'd., & Mr. John Chinn. Trans. of 4 pers: Tho. Davis, Tho. Wright, John Palmer, Tho. Goldfinch.

THOMAS DRAPER, of Lancaster Co., 120 acs., at a pond on the NW side of Washington's run; on Col. Carter's lline; a little above the roade; & adj. land formerly James Gates'; 5 Jan. 1677, p. 628. Trans. of 3 pers: John Sell, William Nelmes, Thomas Smith.

ELIAS WEBB, 140 acs., W'moreland Co., 5 Jan. 1677, p. 629. Adj. Andrew

Marrow; Mr. Peale; & Mr. Freake; &c.
Trans. of 3 pers: William Evans,
Joseph Parke, Anne Taylor.

RICHARD MERRYMAN & ABRA-
HAM BUSH, 437 acs., 5 Jan. 1677, p.
629. Beg. by Chichacone Path; adj.
James Pope & James Hill; upon land
of Bennitt; Georg Hall, & Henry Hartly.
Trans. of 9 pers: Thomas Smith,
Daniel Pell, John Williams, John
Evañs, Tho. Spelman, Daniell Rose,
Anne Martin; James & Agnis, Negroes.

JOHN ELDER, 72 acs., Low. Norf.
Co., Eliz. Riv. Par., 18 May 1677, p.
629. Beg. at his ancient survey; & adj.
John Osborne, &c. Trans. of 2 pers:
Rose Russell, Sarah Owen. (Note: "The
true date. Hen. Hartwell.")

THOMAS GLASCOCK, 280 acs., on
N. side of Rappa. Co., on the head of
Morattico Cr., 4 Apr. 1678, p. 630.
Adj. Nicholas Farmer & Thomas Ste-
phens. Transs. of 6 pers: Joane Wade,
John Butcher, Richard Vessi, Edmond
Symons, Anthony Billington, John
Sharpe.

JAMES KEYES, 2000 acs., Rappa.
Co., on N. side & in the freshes of the
river, 3 Apr. 1678, p. 630. Beg. neare
the mouth of the Doegs Cr., on the N.
side, to head of Machowateg bever dam;
& adj. Mr. Hales' linc, &c. 1680 acs.
granted to Col. Gerrard Fowke & Richard Heybeard 28 Mar. 1664 & by the
latter, the survivor, sould to sd. Keyes;
320 acs. for trans. of 7 pers: Jon
Palmer, Jane Norway, Anne Feilding,
Thomas Arnold, Tho. Richards, Willi.
Delfe, Jon. Cross.

ORIGINALL BROWNE, 200 acs.,
W'moreland Co., bet. Potomacke &
Rappa. Rivers, 4 Apr. 1678, p. 631.
Beg. at land of John Willis; along Mr.
John Foxhall; to Ned the Indians path;
along Lt. Col. John Washington, &c.
Trans. of 4 pers: William Browne,
Robert Midleton, Jos. Rogers, Willi
Morgan.

MATHEW TOMPSON, 1906 acs.,
Staff. Co., on N. side of Potomack Riv.,
on SW. side of the So. branch of little

Hunting Cr., neare land of John
Mathews; 12 Jan. 1677, p. 631. Trans.
of 38 pers: Henry Tostin, Susan Todd,
Jon. Sorrell, Robt. Harding, Tho. Yapp,
Tho. Chadwell, Jon. Kinderdine, Jon.
Bowles, Jon. Orgin, Thomas Day, Mary
Symons, Anne Champe, Margarett John-
son, Mary Wilsonn, Jon. Wilton, Jos.
Blowd, Robert Sanders, Sarah Hatton,
Mary Tinting, Jon. Coner, William
Davis, Jon. Loyd, Jon. King, Eliza.
Wilsonn, Willi. Moble, Mary Oldten,
Mary Norwich, Georg Russell, Willi.
Willett, Henry Fain (?), Georg Eaxle,
Willi. Morrison, Rich. Finch, Eliz. Poy-
ner, Rich. Ustead, Tho. Whithdy, Mary
Andrews, John Peare.

JOHN WATTSON, 478 A., 3 R., 1
P., Henrico Co., on N. side of James
Riv., at White Oake Br. or Sw., which
falleth into Chichahominy (Sw.); 2
Jan. 1677, p. 632. Adj. Mr. Thomas
Cocke (Cock); over New Kent Roade,
&c. Trans. of 10 pers: Eliza. Dormer,
Jon. Cole, Robt. Day, William Cleft,
Willi. Milner, Willi. Howard, Jon.
Hunt, Anne Adams, Anne Nobles,
Grace Savage.

THOMAS WELLS, 296 A., 3 R., 19
P., Henrico Co., N. side James Riv.,
3 Jan. 1677, p. 632. Adj. Mr. Thomas
Cocke & Mr. John Wattson; neare
Cedar Br., which falleth into White
Oake Br; neare New Kent Roade, &c.
Trans. of 6 pers: William Randolph,
William Seawell, Tho. Edwards, Elianor
Butler, Peter Dangerfeild, John Lawne.

WILLIAM YOUNG, 240 acs., Rappa. Co., towards the head of Ralph's
Cr., which issueth out of Puscattocon;
date blank, p. 632. Adj. land pattented
by his father, Robt. Young, dec'd., 20
Sept. 1661, & due him as sonne & heire.

CAPT. JOHN TONGE, 500 acs.,
New Kent Co., on SE side of Black Cr.,
dividing this & land of Richard Side-
well; &c; 30 June 1677, p. 633. Said
land lately purchased of Major Georg
Lyddall.

THOMAS SEAWELL, 500 acs., New
Kent Co., on N. side of Mattapony Riv.,
upon Assanamyuscock Br; 20 Feb. 1677,

p. 633. Adj. land supposed to bee surveyed by Georg Chapman, &c. Granted to John Potteet 10 May 1668, after whose decease one John Hethersall, whoe married his widdow, escheated the sd. land, in that sd. Potteet was an allien; & afterwards Phillipp Watkins purchased sd. Hethersall's right to same, &c., which sd. Phillipp & Elizabeth his wife, sould to sd. Seawell 10 Jan. 1675.

RICHARD DAVIS, 370 acs., New Kent Co., Stratton Major Par., 23 Oct. 1677, p. 634. Beg. at Leonard Chamberlaine; by Prichard's line; to Hankes' line, &c. Trans. of 8 pers: Henry Leirs (or Lewis), Jonathan King, Peter Lewellin, Robt. Parsons, David Morgan, Rees Morgan, Dorothy Lewis, Peter Sandifer. (The true date, &c.)

THOMAS CLAIBORNE, 1500 acs., New Kent Co., in the upper forks of Yorke Riv., 25 Oct. 1677, p. 634. Beg. on upper side of falling Cr. at the mouth; opposite Charles Edmunds, &c. Trans. of 30 pers: Georg Humphrys, Mary How, Stephen Pond, Peter Breton, Alice Francis, Anne Smith, Henry Bevan, Anthony Symons, Grace Parsons, Julian King, William Owens, Henry Marr, Joane Watkins, Tho. Clarke, Eliz. Hunt, Hugh Powell, Jon. Awbry, Peter Person, Hugh Oliver, Dorothy Vincent, Mary Scragg, Jon. James, Thomas Milles, Anne Broughton, Tho. Harris, Mary Dale, Willi. Russell, Mary Bodin, Timothy Rogers, Peter Anderson.

EDWIN CONWAY, 1650 acs., in Lancaster & N'umberland Co.s; on SE side of W'wd. br. of Currotoman Riv. &c., adj. Col. Cod's line; 26 Sept. 1678, p. 635. Granted to Edwin Conway, dec'd., 30 Nov. 1659, & due the abovenamed as son & heire. (Note: This name first spelt Connaway.)

RICHARD HARGRAVE, JUNR., 109 acs., Low. Norf. Co., 5 June 1678, p. 635. Beg. in Cockroft's line; neare land of Alexander Gwyn; to line of the Orphans of Harding, &c. Trans. of 2 pers: Richard Buck, Jane Johnson.

RICHARD STANLEY, 142 acs., Low. Norf. Co., 5 June 1678, p. 636. Beg. by land of Owen Willis; to the green sea, &c. Trans. of 3 pers: Peter Nevell (or Newell), Jno. Goring, Tho. Duke.

MR. JOHN EDWARDS, 200 acs., Low. Norf. Co., E. side of the S. br. of Eliz. Riv.; 5 June 1678, p. 636. Adj. Thomas Alexander; & James Hanson. Trans. of 4 pers: George Horne, Alexander Gethings, Richard Tidborne, Ellinor Barne.

WILLIAM COCKROFFT, 510 acs., Low. Norf. Co., 5 June 1678, p. 636. Beg. at a point dividing this & land of Charles Egerton; between the 2 orphans of Tho. Harding; on Broad Cr; &c. 390 acs. granted to Tho. Harding, dec'd., 20 Oct. 1661, & due sd. Cockrofft by marrying one of the orphans; 120 acs. for trans. of 2 pers: Arthur Moseley, An. Moseley.

THOMAS WELLBORNE, 83 acs., Accomack Co., on Fox Island, in Chesipeacke Bay, 4 Apr. 1678, p. 637. Being the N. island to Watts' Is; beg. at S'most side of a little Cedar Hamocke on S. end of Fox Is., &c. Trans. of 2 pers: Thomas Welborne, John Welborne.

MR. CHARLES SCARBURGH, 2100 acs., Accomacke Co., at Gr. Matomkin Cr., 4 Apr. 1678, p. 637. Granted to Col. Edmund Scarburgh, his father, for trans. of 42 pers.* & given to sd. Charles; by him deserted, & regranted to him by order &c; and due by the first rights, &c.

COL. SOUTHY LITTLETON, 1000 acs., Accomack Co., at Gingoteag, 4 Apr. 1678. p. 637. Adj. Capt. Richard Hill; &, Capt. Daniell Jennifer; &c. Granted to Major Jon. West 3 Oct. 1672, by him deserted, & regranted to sd. Littleton by order, &c; trans. of 21 pers: William Cill, Benj. Ayre, John Smith, Samuell Hall, Thomas Cooper, John Tirry, Martin Johnson, Richard Dicks, Mary Davis, John Moore, Eliz. Moore, Eliz. Moore, Sarah Moore, John Daybridg Court, John Hanson, John Broomesgrove, Eliz. Peacock, Amos Bonville, Mathew Pope, Wiilliam Elvin.

MAJOR EDMUND BOWMAN, 300 acs., Accomack Co:, in Mosango Cr., 4 Apr. 1678, p. 638.- Granted to William Jemin (Jerman ?), 7 Nov. 1673; deserted, & regranted to sd. Bowman by order, &c. Trans. of 6 pers: John Haning, John Hokins, John America, Stephen Causins (or Cousins), Katherine Whelply, Margarett Richards.

RICHARD HOLLAND, 600 acs., Accomack Co., near a gr. marsh bet. *Pongoteige* & *Motompkin;* adj. 1000 acs. surveyed by Capt. John West; 4 Apr. 1678, p. 638. 300 acs. granted to Daniell Pensax 26 Mar. 1672; deserted, & condemned by sd. Holland, & due him for trans. of 12 pers: Margarett Price, William Browne, Mary Aldrig, Jos. Bellaser, Edward Parle (or Parke), John Harris, John Brookes, John Coke, Samuell Carter (or Carver), James Harlo (?), Tho. Blackhill.

ANDREW ANDREWES, 650 acs., N'ampton Co., at Hungers Cr., 4 Apr. 1678, p. 639. Beg. on N. side sd. Cr; to a br. of same called Wilcock's gutt; unto Mr. William Westerhowse; along the bay, &c. 200 acs. granted to William Andrews, dec'd., 25 June 1635; 400 acs. granted sd. William 10 Feb. 1637; & given to his 2 sons John & Andrew by deed dated 4 Jan. 1653; & wholly due to sd. Andrew by survivor shipp; 50 acs. for trans. of: John Barnes.

CAPT. CHARLES SCARBURGH & MAJOR JOHN WEST, 400 acs., Accomack Co., on the Westerne island of Chesipeacke bay; 4 Apr. 1678, p. 639. Beg. at a sandy bay WNW from the S. part of Watt Taylor's island; by a gr. sound bet. the E'most & W'most island. Granted to Ambrose White 10 Oct. 1670; deserted & regranted the above-named by order, &c. Trans. of 8 pers: James Foster, Roger Dorthyon, Jon (a) Welchman, Jane Hunt, Margt. Evesham Jon. Robinson, Georg Gray, Edward Jones.

CAPT. DANIELL JENNIFER, 1680 acs., Accomack Co. in Messango Sw., 4 Apr. 1678, p. 640. Adj. Col. William Kendall; John Wallop; John Parkes; & land formerly Alexander

Massey's; to northerne maine freshwater br. of Muddy Cr; to Georg Johnson's land, &c. Granted to sd. Jennifer 26 Jan. 1674/5, deserted, & by order, &c., granted to Henry Hartwell, whoe in court relinquished his right to sd. Jennifer. Trans. of 34 pers: Henry Gibbins, John Bellmaine, Rich. Williams, Edward Hughes, Jon. Barker, William Blumfeild, Dorothy Oliver, Jane Diton, Georg Flood, Sam. Pomroy, Geo. Archbold, Edw. Williams, Jon. Wafers, Pale Sayes, Willi. Latmer, Jon. Jackson, Jon. Richardson, Tho. Sanders, Tho. Waterton, Jon. Harris, Willi. Burny, Willi. Sinclare, Rich. Lee, Jane Davidson, Eliz. Scott. Mich. Scott, Jon. Hunter, William Anser (or Auser) Nath. Barton, Susan Martin, Margt. Sumers, Edith Bishopp, Sarah Cutts, Eliz. Mouth (or Month).

COL. WILLIAM KENDALL, 100 acs., N'ampton Co., neare *Gogs,* 4 Apr. 1678, p. 640. E'ly. on 200 acs. called *Gogs* belonging to Thomas Mackmillion, sonne & heire of Neale Mackmillion; &c. Trans. of 2 pers: John Carr, Francis Allen.

THOMAS TOMPSON, lawfull bro. & heire of Robert Tompson, 700 acs., N'ampton Co., 4 Apr. 1678, p. 641. Beg. at Harloe's Holes neer head of Old Plantation Cr; &c. Granted to William Watters 10 May 1652, assigned to Robt. Tompson the elder, dec'd., & renewed by sd. Robert, his sonne & heire, by pattent, 26 Mar. 1662.

MR. JOHN MATHEWS, 2944 acs., Warwick Co., Denbigh Par., 29 Mar. 1678, p. 641. Beg. on NW side of Deepe Cr; by an old feild where Jno. Lewis lived; to an old feild called *Shottholt;* to a white oake in a flashett; adj. Jno. Lewis; downe Pottash Cr. to the mouth; downe Warwick River, &c. Granted to Samll. Mathews, Esqr., & due sd. John as being his Grandsonn & heire.

HODGES COUNCEILL, 941 acs., Is. of W. Co., on head brs. of the Beavor Dams, adj. Robt. Lawrence; 20 Mar. 1677/8, p. 641. Adj. his own; & land of Wm. Collins. Trans. of 19 pers:

Wm. Russell, Ann Parr, Edwd. Thomas, Jno. Gibbs, Tho. Prittis (or Peittis), Arth. Spencer, Arth. Davis, Ann Cooke, Ja. Manning, Geo. Martin, Hodges Councill, Wm. Clent, Allexdr. Mathews, Kath. Thomas, Jno. Drake, Rebecca Fee, Chris. Elson, Tho. Davis, Law. Blandett.

WM. THERRIAT, 3500 acs., Lancaster Co., adj. to head of Corotoman River, 1 May 1678, p. 642. Beg. at mouth of Clapham's Cr; adj. Mr. Edwin Conaway, &c. 1600 acs. granted to Dom. Therriatt 18 Apr. 1662; 1900 acs. surveyed in the name of sd. Dom. Therriatt, dec'd., but by reason of the patt. granted to the *Lords Proprietors* noe patt. hath issued; which sd. land is confirmed to sd. Wm., as being his sonn & heir, & haveing found rights for sd. 1900 acs. (*Note:* The following names appear:) Wm. Ball, Wm. Ball, Han. Ball, Han. Ball, Mary Jones, Martha Jones, Randolph Civill, Jos. Halsdownes, Jos. Foster, Ra. Goch, Geo. Coomes, Yar. (?) Williams, Hen. Scholler, Wm. Higgins, Edwd. Vagg (or Dagg), Ja. Crosse, Peter Eversham, Ack Ogum (or Oquin), Car Kath (?), Alexr. Harkin, Sar. Wilkinson, Eliz. Stephens, Isaac Sims, Alexr. Hart, And. Lately (or Lateby), Wm. Horsly, Wm. Heavell, Alice Stedwell, Eliz. Bell, Tho. Whitticar, Isaac Citizen, Wm. Cooper, Jno. Kemp, Antho. Thompson, Owen Thomas, Tim. Swinall, Jno. Lee, Jno. Reader, Ja. Elder, Wm. Jones.

SAME. 27 acs., same Co., date & page; SE upon the mouth of Corotoman Riv., SW upon Island Neck Cr., & NE upon land of Edwd. Grimes, dec'd. Granted to Jno. Woddington 15 Jan. 1658 & sould to Wm. Vaughan, & by said *Vaugh* sold to Dominick Therriatt, tather of sd. Wm., & due him as sonn & heire.

ROBT. BULLINGTON, 244 A., 1 R., 4 P., Henrico Co., N. side James River, 10 May 1678, p. 642. At head of Capt. Jno. Farrar's land; along Capt. Davis' to Jno. Cox at the path goeing to *Harrahadox* neigh the Spring; neare Baily's path; to the *Roundabout*, &c. Trans. of 5 pers: Richd. Page, Morris

Akeron (or Aheron), Jane Case, Ben. Adams, Ann House.

JOHN TURNER, 1036 A., 2 R., 32 P., Chas. Citty Co., in Waineoke Par., N. side James River, bet. Sellat Runn & Fishing Run; 20 May 1678, p. 643. Adj. Lt. Col. Clarke; Major Edloe; Mr. Bradford; to a place called the *Arrow Reads;* by Chickahominy Path to Major Edlow's; over Collenses Run; to Mr. Rowld. Place, &c. Trans. of 21 pers: Ann Batters, Jno. Price, Marg. Elmes, Sar. Ashell (?), Eliz. Allen, Ann Rider, Jno. Davis, Gris. Marleur, Mary Yates, Ja. Toms, Ja. Power, Robt. Webb, Noria Bristoll, Tho. Barton, Alexr. Stinton, Ed. Picost (?).

MR. HENRY APPLEWHAITE, 925 acs., Is. of W. Co., 30 May 1678, p. 643. Upon head of the Black Water branches, beg .at Col. Pitts'; to Capt. Oldis; by Wm. Westraye's; to Mr. Hardy; adj. Am. Bosman; & Jno. Williams; &c. Trans. of 19 pers: Hen. Hackley, Jo. Albert, Jonas Crossland, Jon. Cockett, Richd. Ware, Danll. Steph (Stephens ?), Tho. Pinckney, Wm. Bane, Mary Perry, Mary Birch, "& six times his selfe."

JOHN WILLIAMS, 925 acs., Is. of Wight Co., at the head of Black Water Sw., 30 May 1678, p. 644. Adj. Ambrose Bosman & Mr. Applewhaite; along Hugh Sanders; towards Col. Pitt, &c. Trans. of 19 pers: Jno. Macksell, Mary Lawrence, Math. Culling, Fra. Turley, Mary Burlington, Davd. Spencer, Wm. Vincent, Ann Hamond, Elin. Toper, Wm. Harbert, Ja. Piddin, Er. Green, Tho. Thurrell, Nich. Wilson, Tho. Short, Symond Peeters, Wm. Mansell (Stansell), Antho. Clubb, Hen. Jarman.

JNO. WRAY, 1200 acs., New Kent Co., S. side Yorke River, on branches of Matchumps & Crumpe's Cr., 31 May 1678, p. 645. Assigned to him by Jno. Webb, who entered same with Col. Wm. Clayborne, then Surveyor, who died before finishing the survey. Beg. in James Piron's line, where John Longworthy's line cutts sd. line; on Steven Tarton (Tarleton); to Fleman's on up. side of Matchumps Cr., crossing same, &c. Trans. of 24 pers: Jno. Claiborne, Jane Claiborne, Jno. Claiborne, Hen. Claiborne, Jane Claiborne, Job. Hews, Wm. Sedwick, Wm. Scotcher, Nicho. Dimer (or Dimes), Wm. Constable, Richd. Green, Rebecca Argoe, Wat. Upton, Geo. Heriot, Brid. Killington, Ann Terrill, Eliz. Downeman, Sar. & Jos., Indians; Tho. Rebells; Mingo, Jack, Guy, Negroes. *Note:* "Whereas I am informed that Col. Wm. Claiborne, late Surveyor in New Kent did not long before his death *beging* a Survey of a parcell of 1d. on the S. side the narrowes of Yorke River for one Jno. Webb but leaveing it imperfect for want of one line being run & soe dying & being obliged to the sd. Webb for the finisshing thereof he refuses to pay for what is done, I doe therefore hereby License Capt. Tho. Claiborne to finish the said survey on his brother Wm. Claibornes behalfe wch. survey shall be good & vallid. In witness whereof I have hereto sett my hand this 21st March 1677/8. Phill Ludwell, Depty. Survr. Genll. to Capt. Tho. Claiborne."

MR. WM. CRIMES, 450 acs., Gloster Co., on brs. of Poropotank, adj. Capt. Richd. Dudley, Geo. Haynes, & Spencer's land; 5 June 1678, p. 646. Beg. at Capt. Richd. Dudley's in Danceing Valley; to Curtis Path & Br; to br. of the Rich Land Sw; to Major Richd. Lee, &c. Granted to Mr. Ja. Stubbins 21 Sept. 1674, deserted, & now due by order, &c. Trans. of 9 pers: John Hill, Jno. Dyer, Joane Homes, Ann Roberts, Jno. Spragg (?), Robt. Hall, Nich. Glasse, Abra. Page, Mary Seagres (or Seäyres).

DANLL. LONG, 100 acs., Middlesex Co., bet .Robt. Beverley & Mr. Christo. Robinson; up a runn of the Bryery Br., &c; 5 June 1678, p. 646. Trans. of 2 pers: Jasper Guonshott (?), Jno. Smith.

MR. CHRISTO. ROBINSON, 300 acs., Middlesex Co., bet. Daniell Long, Henry Niccolls, Thomas Cordwell & the Bryery Br., 5 June 1678, p. 646. Trans. of 6 pers: Edwd .Andrews, Ad. Armestrong, Samll. Carriadge, Eli. Taylor; Antho. & Coebarrow, Negroes.

ROBERT BEVERLEY, 50 acs., Middlesex Co., 5 June 1678, p. 647. Adj. land surveyed the same day for Danll. Long; adj. Randolph Seagres, on the Bryery Br., by sd. Long's house; &c. Trans. of: Kebo, a Negro .

WILLIAM COOPER, 142 A., 1 R., 18 P., Low. Norf. Co., S. side of Daniel Tanner's Cr., beg. on a br. called the fresh runn; adj. Lazarus Jenkins; 5 June 1678, p. 647. 42 A. 1 R. 18 P. part of patt. granted to Samuel Robbarts, 28 Sept. 1661, & assigned to sd. Cooper; 100 acs. for trans. of 2 pers: Mary Parr, Eliz. Allier.

JOS. WATTFORD, 97 A., 3 R., 11 P., Low Norf. Co., on S. side of the Broad Cr. of the W. br. of Eliz. Riv., 5 June 1678, p. 647. Adj. Robt. Bowers; Jno Wattford; & land of Richard Eastwood. 50 acs. granted to Thomas Meares 1 June 1649, assigned to John Wattford, long deceased, & due sd. Joseph as heire at law. The remainder due for trans. of: Mareo, a Negroe.

JOHN WATTFORD, 97 A., 3 R.,. 11 P., Low Norf. Co., on N. side of the W .br. of Eliz. Riv., 5 June 1678, p. 647. Adj. land of Robert Bowers; Jos. Wattford; & Richard Eastwood. 50 acs. granted to Tho. Meares 1 June 1649 & assigned to John Wattford, long since deceased, & due sd. John as heire at law; the remainder due for trans. of: Sambo, a Negro.

WILLIAM POWELL, 130 acs., Low. Norf. Co., at the head of a br. of Langley's Cr., on NW side of the W, br. of Eliz. Riv., 5 June 1678, p. 648. Bounded on the old pattent; neare Carter's land, &c. Trans. of 3 pers: Tho. Harding, Henry Pullen, Margaret Prichard.

NICHOLAS HUGGINS, 450 acs., Low. Norf. Co., in Lynhaven Parish; 5 June 1678, p. 648. Up the little Cr., against Hog Island; beg. at Great Neck Br; neare Collins' Br. head; etc. Granted to Jno. Cubbige & Henry Brakes, 13 Mar. 1649. (*Note: This record has been crossed out.*)

WILLIAM BROTHWAIT (Broth-wett) & JOSEPH MUNS, 212 acs., Low. Norf. Co., 5 June 1678, p. 648. Beg. below Mary Lowe; to the long pine creeke; on Church Cr; including land of the Orphans of Lowe, which is to bee excepted. Trans. of 5 pers: Geo. Parmeter, Tho. Peck, Jno. Salmon, Senr., Kath. Salmon, Jno. Salmon, Junr.

JAMES WISHARD, 200 acs., Low. Norf. Co., neare the pine neck dams, which belong to Little Cr., 9 June 1678, p. 648. Beg. at land of Anne Bennett; neare the high road, &c. Granted him 8 Aug. 1673, deserted, & since con-demned in the Genrl. Court, & now due for trans. of 4 pers: Mary Michell, Jno. Holden, Jno. Morle (or Morler), Jno. Watkins.

MR. THO. VICCARIS, 190 acs., Gloster Co., Ware Par., 5 June 1678, p. 649. Beg. neer head of the Bryery Br; adj. Major Lawrence Smith, Mr. Mordecay Cooke; land of Rich. Wrent-shaw, dec'd; land formerly taken up by himselfe & Robt. Littlefeild; & land of Col. Aug. Warner. Trans. of 4 pers: Ed. Best, Tho. Jones, Tho. Browne, Richd. Bironton (?).

EDMUND DOBSON, WM. DOB-SON & JNO DOBSON, sonns of Mr. Edward Dobson, late of Gloster Co., dec'd., 1150 acs., in sd. Co., in Abinton Par., 5 June 1678, p. 649. Bounded by Mobjack Bay, Severne River & Burnt Creek, & on SE side of Seader Island. 920 acs. Granted to their father 4 Apr. 1653; renewed 20 Nov. 1661 & dis-posed among his sons by will; 230 acs. within sd. bounds & due as above. Trans. of 5 pers: Ed. Linkill, Davd. Woolly, Ann Gwyn, Abra. Amiss, Jno. Rogers.

MR. AUG. CANT, 750 acs., Middle-sex Co., upon Pieanketanck Riv., 5 June 1678, p. 650. Beg. at the mouth of the Beavor Dams &c; below planta-tion of Erasmus Withers, formerly Tho. Hixon's, &c. Granted him 12 June 1665 & now measured, surveyed & pattented, &c.

MR. ARTH. ALLEN, 350 acs., Surry Co., Lawnes Cr. Par., 14 June 1678, p. 650. In a br. of the Black Water Sw. Granted to Capt. Lawrence Baker 11 Dec. 1665, deserted, & granted by order &c., for trans. of 7 pers: Tho. Godd-liffe &wife, Jno. Marriell, Robt. Pitt, Ja. Hayes, Tho. Waller, Ni. Sessums.

MR. ROBT. RUFFIN & MR. WM. NEWSAM, 850 acs., Surry Co., on E. side of the 3rd Sw. of the Black Water, 14 June 1678, p. 650. Granted to Capt. Wm. Cockerham & Mr. Cha. Barham 14 May 1666, deserted, & granted the abovenamed by order, &c., for trans. of 17 pers: Hen. Reynolds, Lett. Powell, Steph. Hartly, Kath. Longford, Cha. Dennis, Ja. Loyd, Herbt. Richardson, Wm. Carpenter, Wm. Kitto, Mary Way-man, Hen. Barker, Pet. Jno. Lafeeter, Richd. Inkins (or Jukins), Jno. Shep-pard, An North; Simon & Emanuell, Negroes.

COL. JOSEPH BRIDGER, 850 acs., Is. of W. Co., 22 July 1678, p. 650. Granted to Nath. Floyd (or Loyd), & escheated by inquisition, &c. under John Jennings, Depty. Esch'r. &c.

WM. EDWARDS, 605 acs., Surry Co., Lawnes Cr. Par., 14 July 1678, p. 651. Beg. at Blowe's & Robert Laine's land; along Mr. Bynns, &c. Granted to Richd. Awborne 18 Oct. 1669, by him lapsed; granted to Mr. Fra. Kirkman & Mr. Wm. White; deserted; & by order, &c. granted to sd. Edwards. Trans. of 12 pers: Wm. Edwards, Barnaby Goffe, Teige Oswillan, Dor. Moul, Sara New-ton, Fra. Warne, Walter Rouse, Wat. Resly, Jane Watkins, Antho. Evans, Eliz. Blackwell; Kath. (a) Negro.

TIMO. CARTER, 1000 acs., New Kent Co., St. Stephen's Par., 1 June 1678, p. 651. Part of branches of Apostecoque Cr. & part on Timber Br. head; beg. in line of Mr. Richardson by Cheescake Path; in sight of Abbott's Plantation; by Gizage's line; to Major Wm. Wyatt, to Mr. Bird's path; &c. Trans. of 20 pers: Rich. Evans, Clemt. Sampson, Mary Barnes, Jno. Chandler, Wm. Venderhill, Jno. Wilson, Wm. Loyd, Ja. Winchcomb, Pet. Simons,

Tho. Barlow, Jno. Fillpott, Hen. Moore, Robt. Smith, Jno. Jenkins, Wm. Morgan, James Canaday, Elice Pate (or Pace), Jno. Irish, Geo. Crump, Mary Green.

MR. RICHD. BROOKES & MR. FRA. STAFFORD, 168 acs., Rappa. Co., adj. Esqr. Bowler's Quarter devdt., 5 June 1678, p. 651. Adj. Mr. Brookes' plantation; along Mr. Harwood's line, &c. granted Roger Smith 10 June 1675 & assigned to sd. Brookes; 50 acs. purchased of Tho. Smith, to whom it was granted with Hen. Woodnott 17 Nov. 1670; the residue newly taken up.

JOHN LAWRENCE, 530 acs., Is. of W. Co., upon the maine Black Water, 5 June 1678, p. 651. Trans. of 11 pers: Davd. Scott, Jno. Strowd, Jno. Read, Robt. Wilch, Wm. Brookman, Danll. Rashlup, Alexdr. Currigan, Jno. Adookhart, Jno. Rice, Tho. Dellin, Jno. Dugall.

MR. GABRILL HILL, 630 acs., New Kent Co., St. Stephen's Par., 25 May 1678, p. 652. 514 acs. beg. by Colacke Br., through his plantation; adj. Mr. Jno. Broach, over Cole's Br; by the Ridge Path to John Richards'; to Jno. Exall's Sw., &c; 114 acs. by the Spring Br., down Sorrills Br; &c. 514 acs. granted to Ja. Cole 15 Mar. 1660; 116 acs. granted sd. Hill 6 Mar. 1674/5.

THOMAS ST. JOHN & JNO. HAILES, 140 acs., Rappa. Co., 5 June 1678, p. 652. Adj. Wm. Young on Pascataway Cr. Trans. of 3 pers: Eliz. Rogers, Mary Jenkins, Tho. Greenwood

MR. ARTH. ALLEN & MR. WM. NEWSAM, 550 acs., Surry Co., (date blank), p. 652. Beg. in Capt. Cockerham's line, &c. Granted to Jno. Kindred 19·Oct. 1670, deserted, & granted by order, &c. Trans. of 11 pers: Ja. Weekes, Jno. Story, Fra. Nims. Rog. Cooke, Ja. Jones, Ja. Fry, Rich. Spight, Jno. Fulks, Geo. Yeomans, Tho. Hurlstone, Nicho. Stringer.

JOHN COLE, 650 acs., Accomack Co., 26 Sept. 1678, p. 652. Escheat

land of Jno. Flack; inquisition under John Stringer, Depty. Esch'r., &c.

MR. FRA. MASON, 300 acs., Surry Co., at the head of Tappahanock or Crouche's Cr., 26 Sept. 1678, p. 653. Betwixt Mr. Mason & Crouche's land, now in possession of Capt. Robt. Spencer; by the Cart path being the roade to Mr. Wm. Edwards, &c. Granted to Mr. Bishop, dec'd., 4 July 1641 & after his decease held by his son, John Bishop, as being his heire; & sd. John being likewise dec'd., sd. land discends to sd. Mason as heire to sd. Jno. Bishop.

WM. GREY & JNO. GREY, 800 acs., Surry Co., S. side James Riv., at head of Smith's Fort Cr., 26 Sept. 1678, p. 653. Adj. John Kemp. Granted to Thomas Grey, their father, 14 Mar. 1652, & due the abovenamed by will, & now confirmed & renewed.

MATHEW STRICKLAND, 902 acs., Is. of W. Co., bet. maine Sw. of *Ring Sale* (King Sale ?), & the Beavor dams Br., 26 Sept. 1678, p. 653. Beg. by the maine sw. at Wm. Collins. &c. Trans. of 18 pers: Ja. Lee, Rich. Mathews. Mary Lee, Rich'd. Feild, Richd. Strickland 5 times, Tho. Poole. Wm. Blare, Do. Campinn, Wm. Genly, Nico. Taylor, Wm. Prigin, Jno. Howell, Tho. Match, Wm. Symonds.

REBECCA GYLES, 162 A., 2 R., Henrico Co., N. side James Riv., 26 Sept. 1678, p. 653. Beg. at Capt. Jno. Knowles', on Cornelius' Run; to Cornelius Cr., &c. Trans. of 4 pers: Hen. Harman, Jno. Emerson, Tho. Carmell.

MR. HENRY HAYWARD, 216 acs., Yorke Co., New Pocoson Parish, 28 Sept. 1678, p. 653. On N. side of Cheesman's Mill; adj. his own land, &c. Trans. of 5 pers: Samll. Mann, Dennis Conyard, Benj. Vincent, Tho. Strange, Eliz. Williams.

ALEXANDER NEWMAN, 810 acs., Lancter Co., 26 Sept. 1678, p. 654. 560 acs. upon a maine br. of Marrattico, parting this & land of Tho. Chitwood; adj. John Custis; & Jno. Newman; 560 acs. granted Jno. Newman 22 Oct.

1663; 252 acs. granted Tho. Chitwood 9 July 1663; both of which were deserted & afterwards granted to Mihell. Miller, by order, & sould to John Newman, who deserted; by order, granted to Wm. Mathews 25 Sept. 1677, who sould to sd. Alexdr., 25 Oct. 1677; further due for trans. of 17 pers: Jane Robinson, Eliz. Vaughan, James Kent, Mary Coock, Jno. Bayly, John Brookes, Richd. Archer (or Arther), Mary Young, Tho. Martin, Edwd. Harey (or Hardy), Wm. Gulin, Row. Ward, Symo. Wood, Wm. Jarrett, Nath. Spencer, James Man.

MR. ARTHUR ALLEN & MR. WM. NEWSAM, 432 acs., Surry Co., p. 654. Beg. at Wm. Huniford's line, on E. side the 3rd Sw. of Black Water; adj. Capt. Cockerham & Mr. Barham; &c. Granted to Wm. Porter 7 Aug. 1667, deserted, & now granted by order, &c. Trans. of 9 pers: Samll. Lovejoy. Robt. Littleton, Fra. Dodkin, Abra. Hodge. Wm. Snow, Rich. Bright; Tony, Comsee, Stephen Negroes. (*Note:* The Governor's name, & date left blank.)

COL. ROBT. ABRAHALL, 1000 acs., New Kent Co., NE side of Mattapony Riv. 26 Sept. 1678, p. 654. Behind land of Major Wm. Taylor & Mr. Edwd. Diggs. Granted to Tho. Peck 8 June 1658 .deserted, & now granted by order, &c. Trans. of 20 pers: Fra. Wood, Fra. Lacy, Eliz. Westbrooke, Eliz. Hooke. Rosamond Brett, Rachell Hardine. Wm. Smith, Wm. Brand, Martin Morris. Tho. Wheeler. Margtt. Wms. (Williams), Arth. Parker. Ara. Carr, Jno. Simonds, Sarah ——, Rich. Swinson, Pat. Cassell, Samll. Sallenger, Wm. Bray.

MR. ANTHO. BUCKNER, 2506 acs. Staff. Co., upon branches of Acquia Run, 26 Sep. 1678, p. 655. Part of 15,750 acs., taken in partnership by sd. Buckner, Renett, Bowly, Colticoate & Morris; upon the head of a valley, near the Ridge, on NNW side of the maine runn of Acquia, &c. Trans. of 50 pers: Jno. Barton, Hen. Forrest, Tho. Morris, Jno. Waters, Wm. Salley, Robt. Collis. Robt. Cole, Antho. Buckner, Geo. Carpenter, Ja. Bardall, Mart. Ingram, Peter

Groves, Cha. Coltrop. Mary Salter. Wm. Rogers, Robt. Frale (or Frald), Mary Buttler, Hen. Coltrop. Sit. Buttrum, Jno. Wilford. Tho. Willis, Jno. Stratton, Ra. Engell (or Angell), Adam Curtis, Wm. Simpson, Tho. Bray, Ric. James, Hum. Brett, Sara Martin, Samll. Kenly, Robt. Chambers, Samll. Pollard. Hen. Walton, Marta Orange, Hen. Dabson, Ja. Landall, Han. Sanders. Tho. Rivers, Jno. Cogan, Jno. Rivers, Rog. Massey, Abra. Harwood, Jone Stokes, Mary Jones, Ja. Goffe, Ja. Baker, Tho. Lambert, An Nevett (?), Edwd. Brookes, Wm. Graves, Jone Fuch. (*Note:* Governor's name omitted.)

MR. ROBT. EVERETT, 147 acs., Yorke Co., New Poquoson Par., p. 655. S. of Cheesman's Mill; adj. line of Mr. Edmd. Cheesman, dec'd; by Denbigh Path, &c. Trans. of 3 pers: Ann Taylor. Geo. Sexton, Mary Clarke. (*Note:* Name of Gov'r. & date omitted.)

MRS. JUDITH RANDOLPH, 690 A., 14 P; in Bristoll Par., on N. side of Swift Cr; 28 Sep. 1678. p. 655. Being all the land bet. her now (or new) dwelling house & *Timbusbery*, the Saw Mill dev'dt. & Hatcher's run; to head of Mr. Randolph's patt., &c. Trans. of 14 pers: Wm. West, Jno. West, Jno. Smith, Tho. Mason, Fra. Bumpas. Ann Sanders, Margtt. Grimley. Tho. Stafford. Mary Woodward, Magtt. Jeffrys, Tho. Richards, Jno. Wright, Wm. Buttler. Jno. Potter. (*Note:* Gov'r's. name omitted.)

HUGH WILLIAMS & JOHN OWIN, 298 & 153 Acs., bet. Rappa. & Potomeck Rivers; adj. Richd. Rosser, &c; by a br. of Paspatancy &c; along Fra. Hayls' land, &c. 26 Sept. 1678. p. 656. Trans. of 6 pers: Edwd. Bell. Jos. Porten, Jno. Rogers, Wm. Radge, Jno. West. Ja. Old.

WM. SEARGANT & JOANE CLARKE. 1585.3 acs., Rappa. Co., on NE side of Rappa. Riv., 26 Sept. 1678, p. 656. Beg. by a Cart Path; nye Mattox Path, to Capt. Lord; to Jno. Buttler upon a br. of Rappa. Sw; to Jno. Bowin; to Cha. Snead; by Capt. Wm. Mosely, &c. Trans. of 32 pers: Tho.

Ford, Jone Thresore, Ph. Pender, Wm. Broadstreet, Gid. Frith, Eliz. Blumfeild. Richd. Jnoson (Johnson), Jno. Thomson, Fra. Cellby, Ann Compton, Jno. Roberts, Tho. Jones, Wm. Gear, Fra. Simonds, Wm. Bayly, Tho. Buck, Ben. Buck, Geo. Smith, Eliz. Jones, Ma. Sutton (?), An Graves, Wm. Clifton, Jno. Ford, Edwd. Lewis, Tho. Gollies, Mary Tompson, Ja. Gresham, Jno. French, Za. Eldritt, Tho. Fryon, Wm. Segior ,Jno. Apleby.

MR. JNO. BURCKETT & MR. DAVID STERNE, 853.111 acs., Rappa. Co., NE side sd. River, 26 Sept. 1678, p. 656. Beg. at land of Tobias Smith. in possession of Richd. Bray, to Pepetick Cr; to line of Tho. Hopkins, dec'd., &c. Due as marrying the sisters & heirs of Peter Mills, dec'd., to whom 400 acs. was granted 30 Sept. 1665; the residue for trans. of 9 pers: Paull Seize, Wm. Latnett, Jno. Jackson, Jno. Richardson. Tho. Sanders, Tho. Waterton (or Waterson), Jno. Harris, Wm. Birny, Wm. Sinckler.

EDWIN THACKER & CHICHELEY CORBIN THACKER. 844-3/8 acs., bet. Rappa. & Potomeck Rivers; on a gr. sw. of Rappa. Cr; 26 Sept. 1678, p. 657. Beg. at John Buttler, Wm. Seargan & Joane Clarke; &c. Trans. of 16 pers: Eliz. Larrett, Seayward Bearfeild. Jno. Goodman, Jos. Rutford, Reb. Yates, Tho. Cooper. Jno. Oxly, Margtt. Massey, Jno. Dully, Wm. Hunt, Isa. Davis Mary Straton, Fran. Bryant, Geo. Palmer, Alice Hall, Roger Bagwell.

LT. COL. JNO. ARMESTEAD, 220 acs., Gloster Co., upon the head of the E'most Riv. in Mobjeck Bay. 21 Sept. 1678, p. 657. Adj. Capt. Dudly (Dudley). Granted to Dunkin Bohonno & John Mekin 20 Dec. 1667, who assigned to sd. Armestead; deserted, & granted to Geo. Seaton ,who neglected the pattenting thereof, & by order granted sd. Armestead; trans. of 5 Negroes:–Jack, Nancy, Enah, Manell, Hannell.

WM. PORTEN. 200 acs., Low. Norf. Co., 27 Sept. 1678, p. 657, Beg. at John Gater's; to Mr. Egerton; neare Gwyn's land; by Newman's land; &

including 34 acs. bet. Mr. Egerton & Math. Godfry; &c. Trans. of 4 pers: Hum Smith, Elinor Smith, Wm. Westbrooke, Tho. Sandwich.

JOHN DEGGE, 1800 acs., Gloster Co., Kiingston Par., 26 Sept. 1678, p. 658. Bounded by lands of Smithers, Greggs, Ja. Foster. Wm. Smith. Pet. Sterling, Mr. Hampton, & Mathew Gayle; at the head of the Beavor Dams; including 150 acs. called Lucas' Neck & granted to Robt. Beverly 6 Nov. 1673. Trans. of 36 pers: Jno. Williams, Mary Supon (?), Rich. White, Mary Webb, Eliz. White, Anna Gibson, Martha Hunt, Sus. Powell, Rach. Powell, Mary Benbridge, Ja. Turner, Jos. Maninton, (or Manniton), Tho. Counlow, Tho. Clements, Wm. Moore, Wm. Anson, Wm. Baker, Wm. Davidson, Margtt. Osborne, Jona. Tucker (or Tasker), Jno. Harris, Zach. Deserson, An. Anington (or Arington), Samll. Verdy, Robt. Packer, Wm. Davise, Jno. Munn. Rich. Young; Joseph & Richard Negroes; Margtt. Davis, Howell Jones, Robt. Bunbury, Tho. Gardner, Jno. Smith, Fra. Smith.

ARCHABELL BROMLEY, 500 acs., Gloster Co., Kingston Par., 26 Sept. 1678, p. 658. 150 acs. granted to Wm. Bedlam 1 July 1653, & bounded as in that pattent & a deed of sale from Coll. Christ. Wormely & Frances his wife to sd. Bromley; 350 acs. bet. Winter Harbour & Horne Harbour & the maine bay; beg. at Geo. Peed's land; to John Tillitt, & Gyles Vandecasteell. &c. Trans. of 7 pers: Tho. Burnett, Jno. Dicks, Elinor Weavor, Phill. Stephens, Jno. Craddock, Wm. Thompson, Hester Buckinham.

JOHN TILLETT & GYLES VANDE-CASTEELL, 25 acs., Gloster Co., Kingstone Par., 26 Sept. 1678, p. 658. Running from Archabell Bromley to Horne Harbour; along the maine bay, &c. Trans. of: Hum. Gwynn.

WILLIAM BEARD (Berd), 380 acs., Gloster Co., Kingstone Par., 26 Sept. 1678. p. 659. Beg. at Richard Longest, neer sd. Berd's house; to Col. Dudly; neer Jno. Waters' plantation; to C---

Armestead, &c. Trans. of 8 pers: Cha. Stafford, Wm. Farrar; & 6 Negroes.

MR. CHRISTOPHER DICKINS, 160 acs., Gloster Co., Kingstone Par., 26 Sept. 1678, p. 659. Beg. at Humphry Toy; near Dickins' plantation; by new line of young Phill. Hunley, &c. Trans. of 3 pers: Jno. Hill, Jno. Dyer, Jone Holmes.

JOHN DEGGE, 200 acs., Gloster Co., Kingstone Par., 26 Sept. 1678, p. 659. Beg. at Rich. Ripley; along Marke Thomas; to Henry Siingleton; to Mr. Plummer's line; &c. Trans. of 4 pers: Jno. Degg, Abra. Buckley, Edwd. Davis, Ja. Bradock.

JOHN COLLIS, 620 acs., Gloster Co., Kingstone Par., 26 Sept. 1678, p. 659. From head of the Beavor Dams to Math. Gayle, &c. Trans. of 12 pers: An. Roberts, Jno. Spragg, Robt. Hall, Nich. Glasse, Abra. Page Samll. Carriage, Mary Seayres, Jas Grencill, Jno. Smith, Edwd. Andrews, Adam Armestrong, Eli. Taylor.

RALPH ARMESTEAD, 48 acs., Gloster Co., Kingstone Par., 26 Sept. 1678, p. 660. Beg. at a path by Tho. Dyer's land; to Dyer's Cr., &c. Trans. of 1 Negro.

JOHN WATERS, 140 acs., Gloster Co., Kingstone Par., 26 Sept. 1678, p. 660. Beg. at Mr. Wm. Elliott; to Col. Dudley; to Rich. Longest, &c. Trans. of 3 pers: Edwd. Best; & 2 Negroes.

LAWRENCE PERROTT, 137 acs., Gloster Co., Kingstone Par., 26 Sept. 1678, p. 660. Beg. at Col. Richd. Dudley; to Capt. Armestead & Wm. Beard. Trans. of 3 pers: Tho. Jones, Tho. Browne, Richd. Byronton.

PHILL. HUNLY, JUNR., 200 acs., Gloster Co., Kingstone Par., adj. his father's land on Pudding Cr; along Mr. Dickins' line; to Hump. Toy; &c; 26 Sept. 1678, p. 660. Trans. of 4 pers: Mary Bald, Joyce Gwynn, Hum. Gwynn, Geo. Buckingam.

RICHARD LONGEST, 680 acs., Gloster Co., Kingstone Par., 26 Sept.

1678, p. 661. Beg. at Jacob Johnson; along Capt. Armestead; by Wm. Beard's plantation; by Col. Dudley; along John Waters' plantation; to Mr. Wm. Elliott; &c. Trans. of 14 pers: Jno. Terrett, Alice Baserman, Mary Bridge, Eliz. Alliborne, Jno. Sheppard, Jane Bedy (or Body), Jno. Lacy, Rich. Whitehead, Jno. Whitehead, Jno. Wright, Abra. Copin, Wm. Paine, Walter Harris, Geo. Wilcock.

ROBERT LENDALL, 150 acs., Gloster Co., Kingstone Par., 26 Sept. 1678, p. 661. Adj. Hum. Toy, formerily Mr. Armestead's land; by the E'most river; &c. Granted sd. Lendall 18 Oct. 1652; renewed; & now resurveyed, &c.

MR. RICHD. ROBINSON, 200 acs., Middlesex Co., 26 Sept. 1678, p. 661. On the run of the Gr. Swamp; adj. Wm. Daniell & land of John Smith, dec'd; David Allison & Wm. Downing &c; near the Dragon Sw; adj. Alexdr. Smith, &c. Trans. of 4 pers: Ja. Navell, Benj. Wagg, Jno. Deffant, Ja. Legiatts.

MR. ROBT. BEVERLEY, 300 acs. Midlesex Co., 26 Sept. 1678, p. 662. W'wd. of Mr. Rich. Perrott's branches; beg. at the Montagues, at the side of a Dry Valley, out of Mr. Nicho. Cock's upper creeke; neer Jaimaica Path; neer the Dogwood Valley; a br. parting this & land of Tho. Low; &c. Granted to Mr. Fra. Bridge 21 Sept. 1674, & sold to Ja. Bateman 14 Aug. 1675, who deserted; now granted by order. &c. Trans. of 6 Negroes.*

MR. EDWD. OLIVER, 57 acs., Nansemond Co., 28 Sept. 1678, p. 662. Escheat land of John Lock; inquisition under John Lear, Depty. Esch'r., &c.

DOCTOR JOHN SPEIR, 600 acs., Nanzemond Co., 28 Sept. 1678, p. 662. Escheat land of Thomas Hunson; inquisition under John Lear, Dept'y. Esch'r., &c.

EDWIN CONWAY, 400 acs., Middlesex Co., 26 Sep. 1678, p. 663. On the head of Mrs. Brocas' land. Granted to Abraham Moone 2 Jan. 1652, who sold to Capt. Wm. Brocas, who made over to sd. Conway as by conveyance, &c.

JNO. GREENHAUGH, 446 acs., Henrico Co., knowne by the name of Smith's bay; 26 Sept. 1678, p. 663. E side of James Riv; by land of Thom. Markham; W. by the gr. River; N. by land of Soloman Knibb, & E. on lands of Mr. Richd. Cocke. 400 acs., granted him 6 Dec. 1652; renewed 5 Aug. 1665; & renewed & included in this present patt; 46 acs. by order of the Gen. Ct., 26 Oct. 1666, & due for importation of: Jno. Greenhaugh.

LIEUT. COL. CAD. JONES & MR. DAVID JONES, 14,114 acs., Staff. Co., upon both sides of Accotynk & Pohick Rivers, upon Mr. Normansell's land; 29 Dec. 1677, p. 663. Beg, in a valley about 4 mi. from the Doeges Run on SW side; by an Indian Path; to br. of Occaquon, &c. Trans. of 282 pers: Jno. Dawson, Len. Sheldon, Wm. Peirce, Fra. Terston, Ja. Peirce, Hum. Larkey, Elinor Duke, Wm. Mallory, Jno. Woodson, Wm. Watson, Cad. Jones, Phill. Buraways, Jona. Burasse, Wm. Bugg, Jno. Boyston, Nath. Dodson, Wm. Terry, Hen. Burgaine, Wm. Blear, Hen. Bedison, Amy, Rich. Burden, Phill Boway, Rich. Caper, Tho. Craford, Hen. Jnoson, Wm. Peterfeild, Phill. Jnoson, Jonas Clinch, Jno. Saw, Tho. Crostell, (?), And. Marsh, Tho. Classe, Rich. King, Jno. Benett, Wm. Bideson, Jno. Booker, Jno. Bevin, Jos. Blayton, Wm. Boome (or Boonie), Tho. Bart, Tho. Barrow, Wm. Bonoroell, Jno. Boyer, Jno. Cattrickle (?), Jno. Caterch, Edwd. Cutts, Cha. Clay, Tho. Cooper, Rich. Bishop, Jno. Berry, Rich. Baker, Jno. Buttler, Tho. Aldridge, Jno. Atweeke, Walter Atkinson, Cad. Jones, Jno. Ashton, Hen. Johnson, Cher. Amy, Abra. Cason, Tho. Carpenter, Cha. Coxon, Gilb. Cox, Gilb. Crafts, Jno. Collier, Jno. Downason, Wm. Daniell, Wm. Daine, Jno. Dawson, Wm. Digby, Jno Drysand, Math. Dyer, Jno. Davis, Tho. Dawham, Row. Farmar, Tho. Gilron, Wm. Griffeth, Geo. Hincks, Margtt. Wittin, Jno. Howell, Wm. Harison (or Hartson), Robt. Hancock, Tho. Hackett, Robt. Hayes, Jno. Herne, Tho. Jenings, Cha. King, Eliz. Lodder, Wm. Tooth,

Wm. Lawrenc, Allen Minott, Tho. Milton, Wm. Miles, Wm. Markeham, Jno. Noble, Cha. Oddway, Jno. Prick, Ja. Powell, Jno. Farmar, Fra. Patch, Jno. Robinson, Jno. Russell, Tho. Reade, Eliz. Stanton, Hen. Eddes, Wm. Green, Wm. Guy, Digby Habeck, Wm. Haslipp, Rich. Hodcins, Jno. Hancock, Ma. Harrison, Eliz. Rudiford, Math. Howard, Tho. Halfhide, Wm. Jones, Tho. Jenkins, Jno. Knight, Tho. Lachett, Lud. Williams, John Maine, Edmd. Tooth, Wm. Moore, Robt. Catle, Jno. Beind, Geo. Potter, Jno. Jones, Tho. Shalley, Tho. Bamly, Even Hopkins, Wm. Hill, Samll. Hues, Ed. Hanston, Per. Told, Ric. Lee, Cha. Loveday, Jno. Figo (?), Wm. Merriday, Ester Smith, Tho. Peeters, Wm. Marshall, Wm. Maine, Jno. Newmar (or Newman), Phill. Pollard, Jno. Page, Wm. Roberts, Jos. Tryman, Jno. Fox, Ja. Gasrill, Rich. Herbert, Jno. Hall, Hen. Hayes, Jno. Jewigg (?), Wm. Jones, Ja. Loyd, Jero. Murring, Jno. Meekins, Jno. Mountstephen, David Owen, Nath. Pile, Fra. Peirce, Ja. Pallin, Jno. Robinson, Robt. Redman, Jno. Smith, Rich. Smith, Rich. Simons, Samll. Shefeild, Tho. Hanby, Alexr. Scofield, Jno. Gossling, Wm. Stillen, Rich. Toms, Tho. Waldron, Edwd. Wight, Hen. Worsay, Jno. Williams, Jno. Wilson, Tho. Weeks, Hum. Wheeler, Rich. Booth, Rich. Peese, Ed. Randall, Tho. Groves, Alexr. Kemp, Peter Smith, Robt. Leeper, Wm. Wilmore, Bar. Watson, Tho. Philpaine, Robt. Salisbury, Jno. Weeright, Wm. Ward, Mary Brighouse, Wm. Green, Roger Beaman, Tho. Franckleyn, Jno. Rone, Jno. Watton, Samll. Burgis, Edwd. Hobbs, Wm. Marshall, Wm. Cadwell, Ben. Banfeild, Fa. Peirsons, Jone Driner (or Driver), Benj. Manering, Jno. Smith, Rich. Facom (?), Ja. Wilson, Ja. Jemerson (?), Jno. Chamberlaine, Tho. Salvine, Fra. Whitacar, James Waters, Jno. Thedam, Tho. Sawgood, Geo. Peirson, Ann Spaines, Wm. Woodland, Ja. Townesman, Rich. Watts, Tho. Lewis, And. Thomson, Hen. Dible, Ja. Williams, Ann Furbush, Jno. Birch, Rich. Seldon, Math. Turpin, Wm. Walker, Mich. Leech, Ja. Johnson, Roger Sparkes, Wm. Thornehall, Hen. Wiggin, Edwd. Wood, Martin Redband,

Jno. Rock, Solamon Tranter, Tho. To-good, Corn. Rosse, Jno. Seamatoe, Rich. Pallison, Tho. Merty, Hen. Batts, Wm. Baker, Jone Green, Ja. Atkins, David Jones, Robt. Sanderson, Jno. Collier, Jno. Web, Nico. Barons, Wm. Smith, Robt. Vasser, Ed. Prichett, Abell White, Alexdr. Ling, Mary Weavor, Jacob Read, Geo. Goodlaw, John Browne, Jno. Powell, Robt. Russell, Cha. Kilpond, Ja. Griffin, Ann Atkins, Rich. Davenport, Alexr. White, Robt. Bryan; & 2 Negroes.

WM. BAYLY, 458 acs., Rappa. Co., on the N. side; 28 Sept. 1678, p. 664. Adj. lands of Mr. Geo. Taylor; Mr. Geo. Jones; Mr. Robt. Tomlin; Mr. Wm. Mosse; &c. Trans. of 9 pers: Jos. Hoe, Robt. Bushare, Mary Harris, Jno. Weston, Jno. Trulove, Mich. Lock; & 3 Negroes.

HANCOCK LEE, Gent., 268 acs., Accomack Co., 3 Oct. 1678, p. 664. Escheat land of Col. Wm. Kendall. Trans. of 5 pers: Wm. Robinson, Pat. Morgan, Robt. Munck, Jno. Lovett, Jno. Jewett.

THO. KENDALL, 400 acs., N'ampton Co., 3 Oct. 1678, p. 664. Escheat land of Jno. Kendall. Trans. of 8 pers: Jno. Tomlin, Hen. Newton, Jno. Jones, Eliz. Steward, Mary Gale, Tho. Barrowes, Mary Hill, Alice Meeres.

MALAG. PEAL (Peale), 843 acs., W'moreland Co., upon branches of Pope's Cr., 20 Nov. 1678, p. 665. Adj. lands of Mr. Pope & Mr. Vaughan; Mr. Robt. Vaulx; & John Buttler; &c. Trans. of 17 pers: Geo. Bladgon, Jno. Tucker, Doro. Mather, Richd. Middleton, Richd. Drake, Roger Dunn, Rich. Bunn, Jno. Davis, Wm. Maston, Susana Lee, Mary Weall, Geo. Weal, Ja. Falwood, Ja. Gill, Wm. Barker, amll. Swallow, Mary Bryan. (Note: Geo. Blackdon crossed out.)

COL. THO. PATE, 200 acs., Gloster Co., N. side Yorke Riv., & E. side of Propotank Cr., 10 Oct. 1678, p. 665. Adj. Mr. Jarnew; Wm. Ginsey & his own land. Granted to Mr. John Pate 21 Dec. 1662, deserted, & upon petition of John Okeham, granted by order, 22

Mar. 1665/6, who pattented the same day, but was by him deserted, & upon petition of sd. Col. Pate it was granted to him, &c. Trans. of 4 pers.*

ROGER SHACKLEFORD (SHAKLE-FORD), 313 acs., Gloster Co., 20 Nov. 1678, p. 665. Neer Mattapony old path; by Edwd. Parker's path, to Mr. Patridge's whole devdt., made by Robt. Beverley; to his own plantation; adj. William Norman & Thomas Amies' land; &c. Said land due by two purchases from Mr. Samll. Patridge & Thomas Hancks (or Haucks), who are now both deceased.

THOMAS AMIES (Amis), 295 acs., Gloster Co., 20 Nov. 1678, p. 666. On the Dragon Sw., adj. land of Samll. Patridge, dec'd., now claimed by Mr. John Carver as haveing purchased the same; on Roger Shackleford; Wm. Norman, Charles Roane, &c. Said land purchased of sd. Patridge.

CAPT. JOHN ARMSTEAD (Armestead), 550 acs., Gloster Co., Kingston Par., on E. side of the E'most river, 20 Nov. 1678, p. 666. Adj. Mr. Dickins' plantation. Granted to Mr. Wm. Armestead for 600 acs., 1 July 1651 & due sd. John as his brother & heire.

WILLIAM NORMAN, 177½ acs., Gloster Co., 20 Nov. 1678, p. 666. Adj. Thomas Amies' land; Ricd. Credendine's line, now John Kellie's line, &c. Due by 2 purchases from Roger Shackleford & Richd. Holloway.

ROBT. BEVERLEY, 300 acs., Gloster Co., bet. Major David Cant & Thomas Dawkiins; 20 Nov. 1678, p. 666. Granted to Robt. Moore & Bartholomew Ramsey 20 Nov. 1675, & now renewed, &c.

THOMAS MATTHEWS (Mathews), 300 acs., in *Cherry Point Neck*, N'umberland Co., 27 Nov. 1678, p. 667. Adj. his own & lands of Mr. Wm. Keen; Capt. John Rogers; Mr. John Rogers, Junr., Mr. Henry Mettcalfe; Col. Samll. Griffin; Mr. John Ashton; Mr. Nicholas Owens; Mr. Francis Little, & Mr. Robt. Bryerley; lands of 2 last mentioned formerly belonged to Francis Symons, dec'd. Trans. of 6 pers: William Blake, James Johnson, Evan Johnson, William Collier, John Vaughton, Matthew Beale.

MAJOR ANDREW GILSONN (Gilson), 6710 acs., Staff. Co., 10 Oct. 1678, p. 667. Beg. on SSW. side of Iverson's land; adj. Henry Walker; David Jones; Dixy (or Disey) Ward; on SSW side of Powell's runn, &c. Trans. of 134 pers: Jno. Thomas, Tho. Thrift, Wm. Loram, Jno. Stainey, Peet. Fry, Eliz. Jones, Abra. Richards, Jno. Sampson, Ann Lany (or Lacy), Geo. Griffin, Wm. Houseden, Tho. Hocknott, Wm. Hawkins, Edwd. Sparrow, Mich. Ford, Jno. Amy, Wm. Carew, Jno. Crips, Jno. Crips, Wm. Parker, Sar. Rose, And. Wilson, Mary Taylor, Antho. Gibson, Robt. Smithby, Steph. Rider, Alice Farloe, Tho. Sands, Tho. Cooke, Wm. Davis, Tho. Howgate, Alex. Lowner, Win. Cargrave, Isa. Markes, Jno. English, Alic. Simonds, Eliz. Edwards, Robt. Broxo (?), Pet. Taylor, Wm. Denby, Robt. Prichard, Welch Williams, Alex. Camwell, And. Hewen, Hen. Barnard, Rich. Gilbert, Tho. Taylor, Jno. Fly, Robt. Brown, Wm. Digby, Samll. Melony, Jer. Johnson, Steph. Dick, Ja. Pybourn, Jno. Naylor, Jud. Church, Geo. Jenkins, Tho. Powell, Samll. Andrews, Row. Tench, Samll. Howell, Mary Wilkes, Adam Strong, Jno. North, Robt. South, Jno. Stephens, Symon Clay, Tho. Deareing, Jno. Jones, Abell Smith, Edwd. Carlton, Jno. Masters, Han. Mason, Symon Flew, Jno. Andrews, Tho. Golding, Abra. Loyd, Mary Pratt, Lid. Jaxon, Anth. Rich, Jno. Franklin, Mary Morgan, Ra. Warren, Rob. Hopkins, Jno. Darby, Pet. Williams, Jno. Bishop, An Nilkick, Ja. Nelson, Jno. Ratliff, Gilbert Dawson, Jno. Williams, Mary Jenkins, Jno. Burton, Mary Williams, Jno. Cooke, How. Price, Jno. Mathews, Wm. Howell, Jno. Barton, Jno. Francklin, Tho. Thomplin, Jno. Brush, Jno. Tomkin, Corn. Floyd, Jno. Newman, Mary Jenkins, And. Fleming, Wm. Darby, Math. Crox, Tho. Phillips, Wm. Price, Ja. Blunt, Nath. Phillips, An Jenkins, Wm. Hill, Jno. Franklin, Wm. Price, Wm. Price, Jos. Nelson, Pet. Taylor, Mary Crips, Tho. Liewell (or Lidwell), Mary Taylor. Jno. Bruer-

ton, An Williams, Pet. Dunbar, Jno. Washer, Hugh Morgan, Wm. Jenkins, Tho. Powell, Jno. Gilbert, Fra. Crew, Wm. Powell; Jo a Negro.

MR. GEO. HAILE, 1950 acs., Lancaster Co., on NW br. of Corotoman Riv; adj. John Nickols; 6 July 1678, p. 668. 1000 acs. granted to En. Hocker & Anto. Dony, 29 July 1652; 500 acs. of which was purchased by Nick Haile of En. Hocker; 452 acs. formerly taken up by sd. Nick Haile within 500 acs. bought of sd. Hocker; 500 acs. which belonged to sd. Hocker's patt., & taken up by Col. Math. Kemp & Capt. Jenings, & sould by sd. Kemp to Geo. Haile; Col. Kemp's right of the overplus within bounds of sd. 500 acs. is 472 acs. Trans. of 10 pers: Eliz. Turner, Xper. Adams, Jno. Stephens, Wm. Barnes, Sa. Barbar, Elnor May, Sam. Bexby, Jno. Miller, Tho. Collins, Tho. Phillips.

THOMAS HAYNES & ROBT. GRIGG, 210 acs., Lancaster Co., 20 Nov. 1678, p. 668. Part supposed to be deserted by Mr. Tho. Chitwood; & granted them by order, &c. On E. side of Slauter's Cr; in line of land formerly Epaphd. Lawson's, &c. Trans. of 5 pers: Wm. Dew, Eliz. Walker, Mary Baxter, Rich. Sampson, Clary Woodnutt.

MR. JNO. WRIGHT, 1040 acs., Nanzemond Co., 10 Nov. 1678, p. 669. Beg. on S. side Dumplin Island Cr. mouth; to an old feild about the Landiing, formerly belonging to Capt. Francis; behind Sapcoates; along line formerly of Steph. Garey; to Cr. parting Powell's Neck from Norris' *alias* Garey's land; to Powell's point, &c. 350 acs. due by patt. last of May 1636; 350 acs., 18 June 1638, both granted to Wm. Parker & by him conveighed to sd. Wright's father; 100 acs. by patt. 10 June 1637 to Tho. Powell, who assigned in like manner; 240 acs. found within, &c. Trans. of 5 pers: Tho. Idens, Jno. Fear, Jno. Mackgiblin, Margtt. Roberts; & 1 Negro.

WM. SPEIGHT, 176 acs., Up. Par. of Nanzemond Co., at a place called *Barbica;* adjoyning Humphrey Griffin;

10 Nov. 1678, p. 66y. Neer the Crosse Sw; along Barbaca Sw; &c. Trans. of 2 pers: Wm. Russell, Jos. Smith.

JAMES PETERS (Peeters), 400 acs., Up. Par. of Nanzemond Co., 10 Nov. 1678, p. 669. Beg. by Syprus Sw., near a Reedy white marsh, &c. Trans. of 8 pers: Robt. Martin, Alice Hill, Fra. Synock, Diana Seayres, Tho. Langdell, Danll. Horton, Rich. Stiball, Fra. Whitwell.

WILLIAM MAJOR, 130 acs., Yorke Co., in Yorke Par., 20 Nov. 1678, p. 670. Beg. by a swamp parting this & land of Owen Morris; along Mr. Henry Clarke; to land of John Hill, dec'd., &c. Due as son & heir to Wm. Major; & for trans. of 3 pers: Ja. Stringfellow, Isah. Tull, Mary Tony.

MR. THO. HARWOOD, 206 acs., Yorke Co., New Pocoson Par., 20 Nov. 1678, p. 670. Beg. on S. side the Mill Dam of Major Edmd. Chesman, dec'd., & nere the sd. mill; &c. Trans. of 4 pers: Wm. Green, Wm. Glover, Jno. Robinson, Ann Jackson.

EDWARD MOSSE, 115 acs., Yorke Co., New Pocoson Par., 20 Nov. 1678, p. 670. Beg. in line of John Jackson, dec'd. &c. Trans. of 3 pers: Tho. Moore, Jos. Blunt, Fra. Loyd.

THOMAS CHESMAN, 175 acs., Yorke Co., New Pocoson Par., 20 Nov. 1678, p. 670. Adj. land of Col. Jno. Chesman, dec'd., &c. to head of Blackkoon (or Rackkoon) Brooke, &c. Trans. of 4 pers.*

SAME. 420 acs., in Yorke Co. & Par., 20 Nov. 1678, p. 671. Beg. by the maine Road, & adj. Mr. Tiplady; & Mr. Peter Temple; &c. Trans. of 9 pers.*

ROBERT HALL & EDWD. THOMASON, 12 acs., Staff. Co., with a small point of marsh adj., in Ocquia Cr., E'ly. from their dwelling house; 20 Nov. 1678, p. 671. Trans. of: Ja. Clifton.

JOHN CARR & JOHN SIMSON, 627 acs., on NW side of Gr. Hunting Cr; 20 Nov. 1678, p. 671. Trans. of 13 pers: Jno. Simson, Mary Simson, Rich. Owen, Eliz. Ball, Mary Thomas, Geo. Cittwood, Jos. Pitts, Hanna Barnes, Ja. Harmesby (or Harmesly), Tho. Smith, Mary Mosse, Giles Brent.

ROBT. HALL & EDWD. THOMASON, 104 acs., Staff. Co., W. side of Ocquia Cr; on S. side of Austin's Run; 20 Nov. 1678, p. 671. Beg. at the Bridge going over Austin's Run to their own Landing; to line of Simon Bowling; &c. Trans. of 2 pers: Rowld. Throckburgh, Mary Smith.

CAPT. JOHN QUIGLEY, 80 acs., W'moreland Co., on NW side of Appamatocke Cr., 20 Nov. 1678, p. 671. Adj. land in tenure of Elias Webb; &c. Trans. of 2 pers: Honer Cofferon, Wm. Rayner.

JOHN WELLS & THOMAS DERRICK, 363 acs., Staff. Co., on SW side of the Dogs (Doegs) Cr., on NE side of Mr. Green; beg. at head of sd. Cr., opposite a gr. branch, &c; 20 Nov. 1678, p. 672. Trans. of 7 pers: Wm. Smith, Tho. Marshall, Tho. Terrill, Geo. Smith, Amos Burgiss, Jane Frizell, Jone Sanders.

RICHARD CURTIS, 296 acs., Lancaster Co., 20 Nov. 1678, p. 672. Beg. at Mr. Tho. Haynes, on E. side of the Roadway from Col. Caters (Carter's) to Wickocomoco; to E. side of a Sw. whiich goes (out) of Hugh Brent's Sw., &c. 150 acs. granted Mr. Tho. Chitwood 28 Sept. 1669, who sould to sd. Haynes, & by him to sd. Curtis; 146 acs., overplush now taken, due for trans. of 3 pers: Roger Chee, Susan Loce. Jno. Hill.

FRANCIS EMANUELL, 210 acs., Lancaster Co., 20 Nov. 1678, p. 672. Beg. at Richd. Curtis, in Col. Carter's line, on E. side of Hugh Brent's Sw; to Abia. Bonnison; to W. side of the Indian Path; along Mr. Thos. Haynes; &c. Trans. of 5 pers: Rowld. Vaughan, Jno. Spratt, Geo. Heal, Richd. Parnell, Ann Lambert; Dica a Negro.

HENRY CLARKE, 355 acs., on N. side the river; (County not given.) adj. Mr. Tho. Beal; Lt. Col. Jno. Hull (?); Tho. Short & his own land; 20 Nov. 1678, p. 673. Trans of 7 pers: Tho. Williamson, Davd. Morris, Robt. Arch, Mary Arch (or Arsh), Hen. Porter, Tho. Jones, Richd. Russell.

By Sir Henry Chicheley, Deputy Gov'r.
CAPT. JOHN ARMESTEAD, 550 acs., Gloster Co., Kingston Par., upon E. side of the E'most river; 31 Jan. 1678, p. 674. (*Note: "Ut in alys"*—as *in other (patents).* Adj. Mr. Christo. Dickins' plantation, &c. Trans. of 11 pers: Jno. Wright, Abra. Copin, Wm. Paine, Walt. Haris, Jno. Roberts, Mary Bradford, Mary Elliott, Ma. (a) Dutch woman, Han. Waldridge, Margery Brookes, Mary Hare.

RICHARD DUKE, 400 acs., New Kent Co., 23 Apr. 1679, p. 674. *"Ut in alys".* On branches of Horocock Sw., & upon the King's Road to *Pascataway,* according to survey by Capt. Wm. Claiborne; adj. Mr. Thomas Brewerton; Francis Craine; & land of Wm. Ball. First granted to Giles Rogers, who assigned to Walter Caradine, who lost for want of seateing; granted unto *said Ludwell* by order, 21 Oct. 1673, who assigned to sd. Caradine, who lost, &c; granted sd. Duke by order, & for trans. of 8 pers: Rich. Duke, Ma. Duke, Geo. Duke, Edmd. Crisp, Ann Tyler, Edwd. Wood, Ann Wood, Wm. Sherwood.

COL. LEMUELL MASON, 1250 acs., 24 Apr. 1679, p. 674. Beg. at the *Hogpen point* on SW side of Cr. deviding this & land of Mr. Tho. Willoughby, near the house of Marrace; to a Gr. Pinie Sw; to land of Downeman, in the tenure of Lt. Fra. Mason; &c. Granted to Lt. Fra. Mason, his father, last of August 1642, & now new pattented.

BENJAMINE VANLANDINGHAM, 160 acs., Rappa. Co., 30 Apr. 1679, p. 674. Adj. Wm. Mathews; by *"R. L." path;* by Col. Travers; &c. Trans. of 3 Negroes: William, Bando, Symon.

MR. EDWARD COLES, 148 acs., N'umberland Co., 1 May 1679, p. 675.

On the N .side of Gr. Wiccomoco Riv., adj. his own; Richard Smith; Richard Way; William Tignoll; Jno. Motley; & land of Major Tho. Brereton. Granted to Wm. Thomas; deserted, & granted sd. Coles 18 Oct. 1670. Trans. of 3 pers: Mary (a) Dutchwoman, Hana. Waldridge, Mary Brookes.

WILLIAM CHANEY (Cheney), 550 acs., Rappa. Co., 3 May 1679, p. 675. Beg. by the Dragon Sw; adj. Jno. Colle's, &c. Formerly taken by William Matthewes, being deserted by John Chymm (Chynn ?) & John Gibson, & granted sd. Chany, by order, &c. Trans. of 11 pers: Joseph Askew, Jno. Thompson, Hen. Starkes, Elizabeth Merr, William Terry, Rose Streake, William Carter, Elizabeth Watson, Ann Duttenfield, Francis Harbour.

JOHN FRANCIS, & RICHARD VANLANDINGHAM, 293 acs., 2 R., 20 P., Rappa. Co., 30 Apr. 1679, p. 675. Beg. by the Ridge Path; along Mathew Wilcocks; by Mr. Samll. Griffin, &c. Trans. of 6 pers: Jacob Lawrence, Wm. Wood, John Morgan, Robt. Irish, Mary Green, Roger Williams.

DAVID FOX, 178 acs., Lancaster Co., 30 Apr. 1679, p. 676. Adj. Henry Davis on S. side of a Sw. of the NW br. of Corotomen Riv; to Capt. Fox; along John Davis; to Henry Davis' line just by his corne feild, &c. Trans. of 4 pers.*

JOHN WASHBOURNE, 600 acs., Accomack Co., at *Pokamock;* on land formerly Morris Liston's; bet. Wm. Benton & Mr. Hen. Smith; adj. Mr. Amb. White, &c; 30 Apr. 1679, p. 676. Granted to Col. Southy Littleton 8 Oct. 1674, deserted, & granted sd. Washbourne by order, &c. Trans. of 12 pers: Richd. Sanders, Mary Savage, Jno. Perofrack, Tho. Davis, Sar. Watson, Jno. Dowman, Fran. Baines, Rich. Cooper, Ja. Norris, Mary Dobbins, Jno. Borrick, Richd. White.

COL. SOUTHY LITTLETON, 2800 acs., Accomack Co., bet. branches of Pongotege & the seaside, 30 Apr. 1679, p. 676. Beg. neer head of Pocomoke

Br., being the S. bounds of 1300 acs. formerly Nich. Waddlow's; adj. James Grey; Richd. Hill; to Watchaprege Br; to Barth. Meeres; to Nath. Bradford; to Wm. Nocke; unto Capt. Cha. Scarbrough; near head of Randall's Br; to land formerly Mr. Antho. Hodgskins'; to Mr. Hugh Yeo, &c. 1500 acs. granted him 5 Oct. 1674; & 1300 acs. granted Mr. Ambrose White 27 Sept. 1671, deserted, & regranted sd. Littleton by order, &c. Trans. of 26 pers: Jno. Coke, Samll. Carver, Ja. Harloe, Tho. Blackhill, Jno. Barnes, Jno. Robinson, Geo. Grey, Edwd. Jones, Jno. Carr, Fra. Allen, Mary Mathews, Wm. Coltwit (Coulturt ?), Jno. Brewer, Alex. Allen, Jno. Sims, Jno. Martin, Ja. Hews, Ruth Rogers, Elth. Howard, Cha. Roberts, Jno. Crabtree, Su. Shell, Mary Waterland, Margtt. Cooper, Ann Meares, Walter Steventon.

SAME. 150 acs., same Co., date & page. In the _Forehead neck_ on N. side of King's Cr. at _Pocamoke;_ on Williams' gutt or cr., & bet. bounds between Virga. & Maryland. Granted to Wm. Brittingham 1 Oct. 1675, deserted, & granted sd. Littleton by order, &c. Trans. of 3 pers: Jos. Billeser, Jno. Brookes, Edwd. Parke.

JAMES MURDAH, 280 acs., Up Par. of Nansemond Co., 30 Apr. 1679, p. 677. Part of 500 acs. granted to Argall Yardley, Esqr., 6 Feb. 1637. Upon Dumplin Island Cr., which divides this & Wm. Sanders; to house of Thomas Pearce, &c. (Note: "Which Land being due by & for Transportation of Six Person", crossed out. The following names appear under this record: Sa. Magleen, Jno. Okey.)

WM. GRANBERRY, 85 acs., Nansemond Co., at head of Bennett's Cr., 30 Apr. 1679, p. 677. Beg. upon the Mill Run, near an old _still house;_ by Col. Edwd. Carter; to Robert Peele; &c. Trans. of 2 pers: Margtt. Farlie, Eliz. Blake.

WM. SANDERS, 175 acs., in the Up. Par. of Nansemond Co., by Dumplin Island Cr., at the head of Mr. Jno. Wright's land; neere the Ridge; by

John Murdah; &c; 30 Apr. 1679, p. 678. Being part of 500 acs. granted to Argall Yardley, Esqr., 6 Feb. 1637, which, after severall sales, &c., from diverse persons, descended to & is in possession of sd. Sanders.

EDMUND BELSON & ROBERT MOUNTGUMERY, in behalfe of themselves & diverse inhabitants resideing from Cowards Creeke downwards to said Belson's; & from Belson's to Robert Peel's, by the Mill at the head of Mr Bennett's Cr; 850 acs. of swamp land in Nanzemond Co., by or near the boundarye of sd. Inhabitants; beg. at corner of the _Parish_ land N. to Wm. Staples; by Wm. Carter; by the Widdow Smith; by Capt. Jeffrys' fence; &c; 30 Apr. 1679, p. 678. Trans. of 17 pers: Wm. Waylett, Isabell Waylett, Tho. Waylett, Abigall Waylett, Jno. Sawyer, And. Mills, Ann Waylett, Sar. Waylett, Jno. Hay, Sar. Spilman, Abr. Feethwell (?), Tho. Alles, And. Gray, Robt. Allett, Tho. Clarke, Robt. Peeters, Samll. Lichinges (?).

ROBT. PEELE, Senr., & Robt. Peele, Junr., 175 acs., Nanzemond Co., at head of Mr. Bennett's Cr., 30 Apr. 1679, p. 678. Beg. by the Mill Run; to the _Parish land:_ by sd Peele's house & orchard; &c. 125 acs. being halfe of an ancient (patent) granted to one More & Welton; escheated to Samll. Granberry, & conveyed to sd. Peele; 50 acs. due for trans. of: Tho. Coterell.

DANILL GOHON, 100 acs., Gloster Co., Kingston Par., 1 May 1679, p. 679. Adj. his plantation; & line of Mr. Hen. Preston. Trans. of 2 pers: Mary Hare, Raiph Rand.

JOHN PICKERING, 197½ acs., Gloster Co., Kingston Par., 1 May 1679, p. 679. Adj. land of Mr. Mark Warkman, dec'd; land of Joanna Careless, now Charles Jones; & Mr. Wm. Marlow, &c. 110 acs. purchased of Mr. Jon. Carver; 87½ acs. being King's land. Trans. of 2 pers: Math. Woodnott, Charles ——.

THOMAS RYLAND, 240 acs., Gloster Co., Kingston Par., 1 May 1679, p.

679. Beg. at his own corner; adj. Caleb Holder; & Major Bristow. Trans. of 5 pers: Mary Higgins, Wm. Burdon, Geo. Thacker, Jno. Wood, Eliz. Holder.

MR. GEORGE AXE, 157½ acs., Gloster Co., Kingston Par., upon Queen's Cr., 1 May 1679, p. 679. Betwixt lands of Mr. Wm. Elliot, Senr., Mr. Geo. Seaton, dec'd., & Capt. Jno. Armestead. Trans. of 3 pers: Ja. Filder, Geo. Gill, Sar. Carter.

MR. EDWD. DORRELL, 205 acs., New Kent Co., S. side Yorke Riv. in the narrows; 1 May 1679, p. 680. Beg. at James More's; down a gr. br. of Mattedequin Cr. to the forke; by the Rowling Path nere head of Boar Sw; by Waineoake Sw; & bounded on all sides by sd. Mors & Thomas Genes (?). Trans. of 4 pers: Jno. Trumpier, Wm. Lambert, John Beamount, Han. Wilkinson.

JOHN HALL, 345 acs., N'amptn Co., 1 May 1679, p. 680. Adj. lands of Jeremiah Griffith; & Southey Littleton; &c. 200 acs. granted Phill. Watkins, & escheated, as by inquisition under Col. Jno. Stringer, Esch'r., &c., 10 July 1665; granted to Marke Manlow, 24 Oct. 1665, who made over to Manuell Hall, 6 Nov. 1665, & due sd. John, as his sonn & heire; 145 acs. within, &c., due for trans. of 3 pers: Geo. Parker, Alice Turbett (or Tarbett) ; Rose, a Negro.

RICHARD HEYNES, 400 acs., neere head of the S. br. of Nanzemond Riv; 6 May 1679, p. 680. Granted to Richard Heynes, his father, 12 Apr. 1653 & now new pattented.

THOMAS PARKER, 600 acs., neer head of the S. br. of Nanzemond Riv., 25 Apr. 1679, p. 681. Granted to Francis Wells 20 Oct. 1665 & purchased by sd. Parker of Symon Irons, who married Dorothy, the dau. & sole heire of sd. Wells.

HUMPHREY GWYN (GWYNN), 250 acs., N'ampton Co., N & W upon Nusswattux Cr., & S. upon land of Capt. Steph. Carleton; 1 May 1679, p.

681. Trans. of 5 pers: Tho. Chapman. Fra. Evans, Wm. Allan, Ann Armstead, Margtt. Norris.

FRANCIS JARVIS, 150 acs., Gloster Co., Kingston Par., on E. side of the E'most River, 1 May 1679, p. 681. Adj. Robert Lendall; Hen. Prouse's plantation, &c. Trans. of 3 pers: Margtt. Ashon, Hen. Webb, Sar. Muskett.

ADAM WOFFENDALL, 783 acs., W'moreland Co., 8 May 1679, p. 681. Granted to Capt. Jno. Ashton 16 Nov. 1664, deserted, &c. N. upon the Beaver Dams of Atopian Cr., S. (upon) Nansatico Path, &c. Trans. of 16 pers: Tho. Green, Jno. Staves (or Stanes), Jone Abbe, Wm. Loyd, Wm. Stoell, Mary Tiler, Jas. Turner, Samll. Jones, Mas. Johnson, Tho. Fletcher, Timoth. Staves (or Stanes), Wm. Knitt, Bridges (or Bridget) Brone (?), Nich. White, Nath. Bridge, Geo. Hanes.

JOHN WATERS, 500 acs., Gloster Co., Kingstone Par., 1 May 1679, p. 682. Adj. Col. Dudley, Law. Perrott, Charles Jones, Col. Kemp, Mr. Wm. Elliott, Richd. Longest, &c. 140 acs. granted sd. Waters 26 Sep. 1678; 360 acs. for trans. of 7 pers: Jonas Vernoy, Jno. Morgan, Fra. Javis, Ann Jarvis, Math. Gale, Margt. Gale, Eliz. Gale.

JOHN HULETT (Hughlett), 400 ·s., N'umberland Co., at the head of Gr. Wicocomoco River, 1 May 1679, p. 682. N. upon Wickars Br., dividing thiis from 400 acs. surveyed for him & Tho. Salisbury, SSW upon a path out of Budde's Neck. crossing Macholtick foot path; adj. Robt. Wilson & Robt. King. Granted sd. Hughlett 1 Sept. 1662 & now new pattented.

MRS. MARY TOWNESEND, 2532 acs., Staff Co., S. side Potomack Riv., bet. Little Hunting Cr. & Doges Cr. 1 May 1679, p. 682. Trans. of 51 pers: Rich. Mason, Jno. Stone, Tho. Sanders, Sar. Knight, Tho. Withy, Jno. Knapp, Jno. Richason, Tho. Roberts, Mary Folliott, Jno. Steele, Han. Franke, Robt. Parr, Ja. Langhorne, Marth. Snow, Alice Rivers, Jno. Beamount, Tho. Cox.

Pet. Sly, Ma. Forbish, Jno. Norton, Robt. Wilson, Jno. Frost, Wm. Knott, Wm. Farlowe, Darby Hare, Ma. Hare, Su. Loyd, Jno. Hart, An. Firth, Wm. Andrews, Tho. Smart, Adam Long, Ja. Edwards, Timo. Cox, Paul Arnold, Jno. Stainey, Jno. Lawrance, Pet. Clave, Sa. Rich, Robt. Forth, Tho. Church, Jno. Jenings, Samll. Smith, Tho. Hoare, Rich. Dixon, Jno. Williamson, And. Steele, Rig. Wilsons twice, Ed. Corbin, Mary Turnagen.

MR. ROBT. HUTCHINSON, 1125 acs., Accomack Co., in Gr. Mattomkin (Cr.), 1 May 1679, p. 683. Beg. at Mattomkin bridge; up Hutchinson's Cr. to the maine horse rode called Gargatha Path; to corner of Ayres & Thompson's land, &c. 925 acs. granted him 9 Oct. 1667; being part of patt. for 1250 acs. "noe more being to be found within the bounds thereof" &c; 200 acs. being due for the residue of the rights of 1250 acs., &c.

LT. COL. ARTHUR SMITH, 2275 acs. in the Low. Par. of Is. of W. Co; on W. side of the lower Bay Cr., 10 May 1679, p. 683. Beg. at the mouth of Seaward's Cr; along land of Pharo. Cobb; bet. his own & Hen. Wiggs; to Capt. Hen. Applewaight; along Mathew Walkely; to Mr. Gyles Drivers; to Richd. Reynolds, Senior. 1500 acs. granted to Mr. Arth. Smith, dec'd., his father , 21 Mar. 1643; 775 acs. for trans. of 16 pers: Jno. Pollintine, Hugh Mathews, Jno. Crosland, Tho. Hampton, Marg. Any, Pet. Barnes, Wm. Walker, Ra. Mathews, Jno. Drake, Richd. Ferne, Tho. Drake, Conogh Handland, Mary Wilson, Robt. Horsley, An. Bell, M. Golding.

MR. RICHARD JORDANE. Senr., of Is. of W. Co., 363 acs., in the Low. parish of sd. Co., on NW side of the head of the Low. Bay Cr. & mouth of the maine Cyprus Sw., 10 May 1679, p. 684. Beg. at a small island surrounded by marsh; cor. of Richd. Reynolds, Junr., along Christo. Bly; along Mr. Tho. Pitts. &c. 250 acs. granted him 18 Mar. 1662; 113 acs. being waste; due for trans. of 3 pers: Jno. Williams, Herbt. Lawrence, Mary Gante.

MR. WM. SMELLY, 480 acs., Is. of W. Co., in the Westerne branch parish; 10 May 1679, p. 684. 400 acs. being half of patt. to Wm. Hunt. late of Nanzemond Co., 14 Dec. 1653, who conveighed to Simon Irons, late of Nanzemond Co., 30 Dec. 1653, who assigned to sd. Smelly 23 Mar. 1667; 80 acs. being waste, &c; beg. at Mr. Hen. Plompton; to Mr. Denson; along Tho. Markes, &c; 80 acs. for trans. of 2 Negroes: Mingo & Mathew.

RICHARD REYNOLDS, the younger, of Is. of W. Co., 566 acs., in the Low. Par. of sd. Co., on NW side of the head of the low. Bay Cr; 10 May 1679, p. 684. Beg. at an island near head of sd. Cr; to Chr. Bly's line; along Hen. King; to Col. Smith, & Mr. Driver; to head of West freshett or swamp, &c. 241 acs. part of 450 acs. granted Mr. Chr. Reynolds. late of sd. Co., 15 Sept. 1636. & by will given to his eldest sonn Chr., & his heires forever ,who bequeathed to sd. Richard, his onely sonn & heire; 100 acs. part of 350 acs. granted to Mr. Richd. Jordan. Senr., 18 Mar. 1662, who conveighed to sd. Chr. Reynoldes 17 May 1658, who bequeathed to sd. Richards; 225 acs. being waste, together with sd. 341 acs., due for trans. of 12 pers: Danll. Hennon (or Herron-*altered*), Jno. Champion. Lewis Davis, Edwd. Goodson. (*Note:* Conveyance from Jordan to Reynolds *antedates* his pattent.)

MARY HARRISON, Widdow. 280 acs., Lancaster Co., 10 May 1679, p. 685. 200 acs. W'most of Corotomen Riv., adj. Wm. White; land of Hacker; & E. upon a br. deviding this & land formerly of Wm. Clapham, Junr; 88 acs. on N. side of Rappa. Riv., adj. land of Edward Harrison, dec'd; a Cr. deviding this & land of Richd. Coleman. Granted to Danll. Harrison 28 Oct. 1669, & deserted; &c. Trans. of 6 pers: Kath. Moone, Jane Wilson, Jeremiah Thorneton. Richd. Assale, Richd. Lambert, Jno. Miller.

MR. RICHD. JOHNSON, 270 acs., New Kent Co., on NE side of Matapony Riv., on br. of Aqumtanacock Sw; joyninig Wm. Watts' land that he lived

upon; 13 May 1679, p. 685. Beg. at
Chees Cake path, deviding this & land
of Mr. Carleton; by Mr. Homes
(Holmes) path; to Maj. Wyatt, &c.
Granted to Wm. Watts, 18 Feb. 1673/4,
deserted, & granted sd. Johnson by
order, &c. Trans. of 6 pers: Richd.
Stone, Math. Stroud, Margtt. Bath,
Math. Roe, Wm. Effinges, Tho. Evings.

MR. THO. HOBSON, 70 acs., N'um-
berland Co., S. side Gr. Wicocomoco
Riv., 13 May 1679, p. 685. Adj. Mr.
Wm. Wildey; land belonging to heires
of Jno. Mosely, & land of the heires of
Roger Walter. Trans. of 2 pers: Henry
Sanders, Wm. Leach.

MR. RICHARD JOHNSON, 523
acs., New Kent Co., on NE side of
Matapony River, 13 May 1679, p. 686.
Beg. at Mastecock Sw; to runn of Pesti-
cock (Sw.), &c. Granted to John Hume
17 Apr. 1674, deserted, & granted sd.
Johnson, for trans. of 11 pers: Jno.
Vaughan, Moses Davis, Jno. Russill,
Jno. Chandler, Tho. Williams, Eliz.
Knowles, Eliz. Mitchell, Godfrey Cutler,
Wm. Tong (or Tony), Jos. Sleeper,
Jacob Butler.

MR. JOHN WASHBOURNE, 644
acs., N'ampton Co., on S. side of Pungo-
tege River, 13 May 1679, p. 686. Adj.
Cha. Scarbrough's 400 acs. purchased of
Mr. Hugh Yeo, Merchant; land of Mr.
Antho. Hoskins; Jno. Robinson; &
Nich. Waddilow. Granted to Hugh
Yeo 2 Oct. 1655, deserted, & granted
by order, &c. Trans. of 13 pers: Jno.
Moore, Eliz. Moore, Eliz. Moore, Sar.
Moore, Jno. Dabridgcourt, Jno. Hanson,
Jno. Bromsgrove, Eliz. Peakock, Amos
Bonville, Math. Pope, Wm. Elvin,
Mary Aldridge, Jno. Harris.

COL. ROBT. ABRAHALL, 250 acs.,
New Kent Co., 30 May 1679, p. 686.
Lyeing on branches of Tansantium Sw.,
on NE side of Matapony Riv; beg. at
Jno. Dorwood; by a path that goeth to
the *Flaxmans;* &c. Granted to Charles
Hawly 7 Apr. 1674, deserted, &c. Trans.
of 5 pers: Wm. Foard, Wm. Street,
Robt. Reagland, John Rogers.

BENJA. HATCHER & JOHN MIL-
NER, 350 A., 2 R., & 14 P., Henrico
Co., N. side of James River, in the
forke of Cornelius Run; 30 May 1679,
p. 687. Neare the maine branch; along
Beauchamp's path, &c. Trans. of 7
pers: Wm. Stanley, Edwd. Fernett, Mary
Gay, Jno. Leath (or Leach), Rich.
Cooper, Robt. South, Jno. Lantthorpe.

MR. RANDALL HOLT, 1450 acs.,
Surry Co., Lawnes Cr. Par., comonly
called *Hog Island,* 30 May 1679, p.
687. Beg. at Rumney Marsh Point to
mouth of Dunstan's Cr; to mouth of
Caesar's hole Cr; to Black Walnutt
point; to Persimon point, to mouth of
Chuck Cr; to Rumney Marsh point, &c.
Granted to —— Holt, his father, 1
Aug. 1643 & due him as heire.

HENRY BIGGS, 321 acs., New Kent
Co., on head branches of Assatians Sw.,
30 May 1679, p. 687. Beg. at Robert
Hill; to William Rogers, by a Cattayle
meadowe, &c. Trans. of 6 pers.*

WILLIAM UNDERWOOD, 2784
acs., Rappa. Co., 13 May 1679, p. 688.
Upon S. side of a Beaver Dam; parallel
to land of Thomas Whitlocke; cor. to
Richard Coleman; by a path to *Nan-
satticcoe,* &c. Due William Underwood,
his father, viz: 1400 acs. granted William Smart 15 Mar. 1657, assigned to
William Clapham, Junr. (?), who assigned to sd. William the father; 1384
acs. for trans. of 28 pers.*

MR. WILLIAM EDWARDS, 605
acs., Surry Co., Lawnes Cr. Par., 16
Apr. 1679, p. 688. Beg. at cor. pine of
Blows & Robert Lane's land; along
Mr. Binns'; &c. Granted to Richard
Awborne, 18 Oct. 1669, lapsed, &
granted to Mr. Fra. Kirkman & Mr.
William White; deserted, & by order
granted to sd. Edwards, & by him pattented 14 July 1678, & is now truly
bounded.

NICHOLAS SESSUMS, 550 acs. in
the Low. Par. of Surry Co., on the
Bridge Sw., a br. of the Black Water
Sw., 30 May 1679, p. 688. Beg. bet.
Richard Blow & Mr. William Edwards;
to Mrs. Marriott's line, &c. Trans. of

11 pers: Richd. Jorden, Kath. Smellie, Wm. Cregord, Robt. Hobbs, Eliz. Ash, Rich. Jordane & wife; Dongo, Hector, Frank, & Marea, Negroes.

THOMAS BINNS, 974 acs., Surry Co., 30 May 1679, p. 689. 574 acs. beg. on E. side of the Greene Sw; along Mr. Awborne's line, &c; which was granted to John Goring 8 Aug. 1670; 400 acs. on SW side of sd. Sw; which was granted to Charles Armery, who assigned to sd. Goring & due him by rights; which sd. tracts of land were pattented by sd. Goring 1 July 1673, but deserted &c; granted sd. Binns by order, &c. Trans. of 21 pers: Cha. Ranger, Géo. Green, Ja. Scott, Eliz. Johnson, Wm. Wells, Mary (or Marg.) Rose, Kath. Avecromy (?), Jno. Hawkins, Toby Davies, Jno. Hewlett, Mary Marcey, Ursley Hemett, Tho. Watson, Jno. Cooper, wife, Bartho. Bee, Edwd. Jones, Mary Linn; Peter & Jeny Negroes.

GEORG MORRIS, 700 acs., Rappa. Co., 4 mi. into the woods, 13 May 1679, p. 689. Beg. by the maine Sw. of Peanketancke; adj. land formerly John Coale's; by the horse path; land of Stanfast, dec'd., & by Thomas Crow & Samuell Green; &c. Trans. of 14 pers.*

MR. HENRY HARTWELL, 736 acs., James Citty Co., 30 May 1679, p. 690. 200 acs. beg. on branches of Warrany Cr; on Burchen Sw., in line of Sir Jon. Ayton; by the horse path; on the Timber Sw; &c. 536 acs. in brs. of Warrany Cr; beg. on Timber Sw., adj.

William Elcombe, - neare Mr. Sorrill's path; neare an Indian feild; adj. Mr. Burnell & sd. Ayton; &c. Granted to Thomas Maples & William Hitchman by pattents dated 10 Sept. 1668; by them lapsed, & granted William Hitchman by pattents dated 10 Sept. 1668; by them lapsed, & granted to John Wright by order, &c., who assigned to Theophilus & Thomas Hone, who pattented the same but never prosecuted the same according to the provisoe in the pattent; granted by order, to sd. Hartwell, & due for trans. of 15 pers.*

MR. DANIELL WHITE, 600 acs., W'moreland Co., 30 May 1679, p. 691. Adj. William Courts; & Francis Gray; on the W'wd side of Machotocke River. Granted to Georg Weading 23 Mar. 1664, deserted, & granted sd. White by order, &c. Trans. of 12 pers.*

GEORG WEEDON & DANIELL WHITE, 483 acs., W'moreland Co., 30 May 1679, p. 691. On head branches of Attopin Cr., bet. same & Storks Bridge Sw., a br. of Appamattocke Cr; adj. land of Mr. Wm. Stork (or Stock); nigh a bryery thickett on N. side of NonJottico Path; adj. Capt. John Alexander & William Browne. Trans. of 10 pers.*

WILLIAM HARRIS, 1600 acs., Staff. Co; at head of the main runn of Niobscoe (Nyobscoe) Cr., 20 May 1679, p. 691. Beg. by an Indian Path dividing this & land of Mr. Nathan Barton; along the Ridge Path; to Mr. Robert King; along Burbridge's land, &c. Trans. of 32 pers.*

PATENT BOOK NO. 7

By Sir Henry Chicheley, Knight, Deputy Governor, &c.

MR. GEORGE BURGH, 170 acs., Gloster Co., Abington Par., 5 Sept. 1679, p. 1. Adj. the Old feild; Charles Jones; John Waters; Gwynn's Ridge, &c. Trans. of 4 pers: Samll. Wheeler, Samll. Chapman. *(Note:* Record mutilated & torn from book.)

RICHARD CREEDLE, 220 acs., Gloster Co., on the North Riv., p. 1. Adj. Mr. Tho. Tabb; land of Tompkins, formerly Turner's; to br. by *the Chappell.* Granted to his father, Richard Creedle, 8 June 1643 (?) *(Record as above).*

MR. JOHN ARMESTEAD, 500 acs., S. side of Peanketank Riv., near Gwynn's Ponds; along Queen's Cr., to King's Cr; &c., 25 Sept. 1679, p. 2. Granted to —— Burton, 15 Sept. 1651, assigned to Mr. Wm. Armestead & due sd. John, as sonn & heire. Re-surveyed by Robt. Beverley, Surveyor of sd. Co., 22 July 1679. *(Record as above.)*

CHARLES ROANE, 700 acs., Gloster Co., upon Dragon Sw., p. 2. Adj. John Cant, Thomas Dawkins, Roger Shackleford, Jno. Davies, Mr. Jno. Carver, James Reynolds &c. *(Record as above.)*

MRS. ELIZTH. BANISTER, 1600 acs., Gloster Co., Abington Par., 25 Sept. 1679, p. 3. Adj. land of Maj. John Scarsbrooke, dec'd; Edwd. Allin; Mr. Wm. Craine's plantation; Mr. John Debnam; Mr. Stoakes; Cha. Smith; along the Gr. Roade; adj. Robt. Todd; Edward Munford; Jno. Williams; to house & plantation formerly leased by Jno. Banister to John Bell; by Tindall's Cr; &c. For & dureing her naturall life, & after he decease to her sonn John, sonn & heire of John Banister, dec'd. & in case of his decease without heires of his body lawfully begotten, then to his surviving sisters &c; 465 acs. granted to Peter Rigby, 12 Feb. 1651, & sold to sd. John; 1145 acs. by vertue of a bill of sale from Coll. Geo. Ludloe to sd. John, dec'd; due unto sd. Eliz. & her son for trans. of 23 pers: Jer. Wood, Tho. Toles, Wm. Davis, Jno. Hyne, Samll. Mott, Xpr. Deins, Fra. Browne, Mary Coleman, Xpr. Leucas, Danll. Oliver, Tho. Mampry, Griff. Loyd, Chas. Gallis, Jos. Oliver, Sa. Swanson, Eliz. Jones, Nat. Spencer, Ja. Fisher, Robt. Walker, Job. Whitnell, Rich. Bardly, Sam Ba——, Hen. Waad. Tho. Susan (?).

EDW. MUNFORD, 80 acs., Gloster Co., 25 Sept. 1679, p. 4. 12 acs. being an island about a mi. above Tindall's point; 68 acs. upon Fishing pt., by Yorke Riv., by the Roade Path, to Robt. Todd. 68 acs. due in right of his wife Mary daughter of Jos. Watkins, who purchased of John Fleete; the island was this day taken up by Mrs. Eliz. Banister, widdow &c., who immediately sould to sd. Munford; further due for trans. of 1 per: Jack.

MAJOR ROBT. BEVERLEY & HENRY HARTWELL, 346 acs., Middlesex Co., 25 Sept. 1679, p. 4. Adj. on *Jamaica Land;* John Jadwin; neer the path from *Jamaica* to the *Towne:* Mr. Cock's. &c. Granted to Geo. Hooper, 21 Sept. 1674, deserted, & upon petition granted the abovenamed. Trans. of 7 pers: John Lee, Richd. Mathews. Nicho. Taylor, Mary Lee, Peter Sims, John King, Elizth. Oxford.

MR. GEO. GOODLOE, 60 acs., Middlesex Co., 25 Sept. 1679, p. 5. N.W. side of Bryery Br., adj. Mr. Rand. Seager (Segar), & Mr. Abra. Weekes. Trans. of 2 Negroes: Sarah & Moll.

MR. THOMAS WOOMBWELL, sonn & heire to Mr. Tho. Woombwell, Gent., late of Isle of Wight Co; 650 acs., in the Up. Par. of sd. Co., 25 Sept. 1679, p. 5. In the forke of the 1st & 2nd br. of the maine Black Water, comonly. known by the name of Timber Neck; part of 1050 acs. granted to Mr. George Hardy, Mr. Tho. Wombwell & Peter Hull Orphane, 15 July 1651, viz: 400 acs. to sd. Hull; & the residue betweene sd. Woombwell & Hardy, who assigned his whole right to sd. Woombwell, 20 Nov. 1654.

WM. PHILLIPS, 3000 acs., New Kent Co., 25 Sept. 1679, p. 5. Upon both sides of Totopotomows Cr; & along Mr. John Page. Granted to him 18 Feb. 1673/4, & *by reason of the Late Troubles* the pattent is lost & now confirmed.

ARTHUR DAVIES, of Surrey Co., 461 acs., in Surrey & Is. of Wight Counties; 25 Sept. 1679, p. 6. On both sides of the first br. of the maine Black Water Sw; adj. Mr. Fra. Reynolds (or Raynors) line; Mr. John Gutheridge, Senr; to a gr. Pocoson, &c. 250 acs. granted to Mr. Thomas Taberrer & Fra. Higgins, of Is. of Wight Co., 14 Aug. 1652, who, on 1 May 1655, in sd. court, surrendered to Richard Williamson, Orpht. of Richd. Williamson, who sold to sd. Davies, 24 Oct. 1672; 211 acs. for trans. of 5 pers: Tony, Mingo, Mathew, Negroes; Mary Estwood, Edwd. Robinson. (Marginal notation gives this as *561* acres).

EDWD. THOMAS, 286 acs., Rappa. Co., on S. side of Rappa. Riv., 25 Sept. 1679, p. 6. Adj. land formerly Hill's & Sharpe's; up Yorke Br. & Sw; &c. Granted to Emd. Johnson, 18 Apr. 1670, deserted, & now due for trans. of 6 pers.*

SAME. 1100 acs., Middlesex Co., same date; p. 7. On land of Wm. Blaze; adj. John Jadwin; the path from the Road to Mr. Rice Jones; to Geo. Hooper, &c. Granted to Jno. Richins & Geo. Hooper, 21 Sept. 1674, deserted, & now due for trans. of 22 pers.*

ELIZTH. WEBB, 100 acs., Up. Par. of Nanzemond Co., behind *Tucker's Neck;* 25 Sept. 1679, p. 7. Corner to Wm. Tucker; to w.o. standing in sight of the *Church path,* &c. Surveyed for her father, James Webb, & left to her by his will; & further due for trans. of 2 pers.*

WM., HUMPHRY & JOHN TOMKINS, sons of Humphrey Tomkins, dec'd., 217½ acs., Gloster Co., upon the North Riv., 25 Sept. 1679, p. 8. Adj. Wm. Debnam; Mr. Tho. Tabb; & Richard Creadle. 200 acs. granted Abra. Turner, 10 Oct. 1642; the residue found within the bounds, & due for trans. of 1 pers: James ——— .

JOHN CARAWAY, 190 acs., Low. Norf. Co., on the N. side of the E'n. br. of Eliz. Riv., 25 Sept. 1679, p. 8. Adj. Wm. Hancock; Bartho. Williamson; &c. 90 acs. part, escheat land, pattented by Geo. Fowler, who sold to sd. Caraway; 100 acs. part of 300 acs. granted to Richard Worster, 22 May 1637 & sould to sd. Caraway, dec'd., & now due the above, as his son & heire at law.

NICH. HUGGINS, 450 acs., Low. Norf. Co., Lynhaven Par., against Hogg Island; 29 Sept. 1679, p. 9. Beg. at the Gr. Neck Br. mouth, against sd. Is., neer Collins' Br; &c. 200 acs. granted to John Cabbidge (?), 13 Mar. 1649, & left by will to Hen. Breakes; 250 acs. granted sd. Breakes, 13 Mar. 1649, all of which he left to Alice, his wife, & Phillis, his daughter, to be equally divided betwixt them; sd. Huggins purchased the part belonging to sd. Phillis from her husband Thomas Workeman, by her consent; & the other part due sd. Huggins as marrying the sd. Alice.

JOHN FEREBY (Ferebee), 69 acs., Low. Norf. Co., 29 Sept. 1679, p. 9. Granted to Hugh Forgison, 26 Sept. 1674; deserted; & now due for trans. of 2 pers: Elizth. Newton, Edwd. Ruch. (?).

MR. MATHEW KEMP, 640 acs., New Kent Co., N.E. side Mattapony Riv., 1 Oct. 1679, p. 10. Adj. Mr.

Diggs. Granted Mrs. Elizth. Kemp for a greater quantity, 24 Mar. 1664, & now resurveyed by Coll. Jno. Lewis; & due for trans. of 13 pers: Pat Morgan, Wm. Coalson, Rich. Snead, Geo. Coxson, Jno. Cloud, Wm. Carmiel, Jno. Roe, Tho. Jones, Jona. Knt. (Knight), Geo. Harwick, Wm. Munford, Samll. Hunt, Tho. Hayward.

MR. CHA. EGGERTON, 563 acs., being the plantation he lives on; Low. Norf. Co.; N. side of the E'n. br. of Eliz. Riv; 1 Oct. 1679, p. 10. Adj. Croxcroft's corner; to mouth of Broad Cr; Moseley's Neck Cr. mouth; to Orchard point; to Long point; &c. 419 acs. granted to Wm. Porter (or Porten), 9 May 1666; assigned to Arthur Tompkins for 500 acs; & by his will left to his wife Ann Tompkins, & now due sd. Eggerton by marrying sd. Ann; together with 144 acs. enlarged on 'the water side, which is due for trans. of 3 pers: Jane Hewitt, Susan Goodlin, Tho. Clutton.

GEORGE MORRIS, 700 acs., Rappa. Co., some 4 mi. back into the woods; 1 Oct. 1679, p. 11. Beg. by the main sw. of Peanketank; to land formerly John Cole's; by the horse path; by land of Standfast, dec'd; adj. Tho. Crow; & Samll. Green. Trans. of 14 pers: Edwd. Morris, Rich. Collit, Mary Woolsey, Mary Stock, Mary Wood, Samll. Mainerd, Jno. Duglis, Wm. Spery (or Speny), Robt. Willone, Robt. Lessrone (?), Wm. Sen. (Senior), Geo. Morris, Wm. Nelson, Tho. Bedusey (?).

MR. FRA. WARREN, 647 acs., upon S. side of the main run of Chickahominy, Henrico Co., 1 Oct. 1679, p. 11. Adj. Mr. Wyatt; to Oughnom brook, &c. Trans. of 13 pers: Eliz. Thrift, Jacob Wareing, Ja. Daniell, Richd. Jones, Margtt. Jones, Tho. Cooper, Robt. Haborne (?), Ja. Morant, Jno. Davies, Fra. Bankes, Eliz. Broadrib, Mill. Bleize, Mary Cock.

JOSEPH BROOKES, 300 acs., New Kent Co., Stratton Major Par., 1 Oct. 1679, p. 11. Near the heads of some brs. of Pianketank Sw; adj. Mr. Brookes & Mr. Burges' (Burgis') land, &c.

Trans. of 6 pers: Mary Ring, Jno. Stubbins, James Hurst, Wm. Knight, Abra. Smith, Symond Long.

HENRY WYATT, 900 acs., Henrico Co., S. side Chickahominy, 1 Oct. 1679, p. 12. Upon the maine run of Chickahominy; to the Cattaile br. forke; &c. Trans. of 18 pers: Richd. Sorrell, Jno. Tarr, Wm. Wells, Math. Stroude, Wm. Streater, Cha. Scrugg, Bar. Wyatt, Alice Milson, Laur. Bathurst, Edmd. Tony, Peter Tony, Mar. Jones, Ja. Goslin, Em. Hurst, Jone Curtis, Geo. Wms. (Williams), Corn. Lowers (or Lowes), Tho. Dowers.

JOHN PLEASANTS & JNO. HADDELLSEY, 548 A., 3 R., & 20 P., Henrico Co., N. side of James Riv., 1 Oct. 1679, p. 12. On the maine brooke of 4 Mi. Cr; adj. Capt. Mathews, &c. Trans. of 11 pers: Melch. Richardson, Math Mock, Fra. Mawbury, Mary Clarke, Samll. Anderson, Hen. Turncy (or Turner), Jos. Wells, Susan Perrott, Jno. Kempton, Abra. Goff.

JNO. PIGG, 760 acs., New Kent Co., St. Stephen's Par., 1 Oct. 1679, p. 12. Neer Jno. Bremer's land. Trans. of 15 pers: Wm. Neaves, Tho. Hill, Eliz. Pritty, Fra. Ring, Mathew Hattissill, Wm. Smith, Sar. Smith, Jno. Betton, Jone Biney, Mary Jackson, Edwd. Wyatt, Rich. Grimstead, Tho. Hart, Benj. Dollifeild, Jno. Haslock.

MR. MARKE WARKEMAN, a devdt. of land called *Pamptike*, containing 918 Acs., in New Kent Co; N. side of Pamunkey Riv., in *Pamunkey Neck;* 1 Oct. 1679, p. 13. Beg. at mouth of Goodin's (Goodwin's) Cr. or Sw. a little below Goodin's (Goodwin's) Island; to Pamptike Cr., dividing this & land of Mr. Wm. Woodward &c. Trans. of 18 pers.*

JOHN PIGG & FRANCIS CRANE, 800 acs., New Kent Co., N. side of Mattapony Riv., 1 Oct. 1679, p. 13. Behind land of Anthony Arnold, before land of Wm. Hurke (or Harke) & Wm. Herne; beg. by the Mill Path, to Mill Cr. Sw; to Cattaile Br., to Jno

Maddison's Spring Br., &c. Trans. of 16 pers: Robt. Cordin, Ja. Woolveridge, Richd. Beateby, Danll. Leasy, Leo. Denly, Tho. Useletts, Geo. Wilber, Somersett Haughten, Tho. Wilson, Jno., Poole, Mary Pendleton, Geo. Denn, Amy Johnson, Christr. Ellen, Sar. Hibbles, Geo. Browning.

WM. COLLINS, 1313 acs., Is. of Wight Co., on the maine br. of King Sale; 22 Nov. 1679, p. 14. Trans. of 27 pers: Isaac Tull, Mary Tony, Jno. White, Jno. Arnold, Wm. Woodley, Wm. Butler, Tho. Hollins, Steph. Fullerton, Susa. Fullerton, Robt. Johnson, Jno. Potter, Ja. Garrett, Symond Pitt, Jno. Rosser, Roger Bridges, Mary Wood, Tho. Stafford, Lewis Williams, Jno. Owen, Tho. Mason, Ann Green, Edwd. Ellis, Nich. Powell, Hen. Bennett; & 3 Negroes.

LT. COLL. JOHN WEST, 2500 acs., Accomack Co., bet. Crooked Cr. & Pocomoak Riv., 25 Nov. 1679, p. 14. Mesango Cr. & the Bay on the S; & Cheespiack Bay on the W; on Crooked Creek, adj. John Renney, Wm. Chase, & Wm. Wallis, formerly surveyed for James Jolley; on lands of Messango, adj. Cha. Ratcliffe, land formerly James Taylor's, & 200 acs. of Edw. Moore, Junr; & Jno. Parker & St. George's Humock or Island. Granted sd. West & Mr. Charles Scarburgh, 3 Oct. 1672; deserted; & granted bv order, &c: & further due for trans. of 50 pers: Tho. Butler, Ja. Arbery, Jno. Reeve, Mary Linn, Jno. Hobbs, Jno. Weekes, Nath. Wilson, Obed. Pitt, Sa. Dowman, Martha Neal, Edw. Jones, Danll. Thorp, Jno. Jones, Jno. Hutcheson, Ann Watts, Jno. Baskett, Tho. Wilkins, Bar. Beech, Theo. Moyses, Rich. Cooke, Geo. Wharton, Jno. Merfeild, Jno. Robart, Wm. Morgan, Jno. Bray, Ma. Fowler, Ed. Fisher, Robt. Gould, Tho. Culson, Richd. Bayly, Eliz. Bavly, Wm. West, Ed. Hudson, Jno. Goodin, Wm. Thompson, Wm. Taylor, Richd. Spurlin, Geo. Lenett, Jno. Jenings, Ed. Marshall, Hen. Godfry, Jno. Hodvn, Robt. Tibalts, Eli. Degrane, Tho. Tabh (?), Fra. Cherry, Hen. Thomas, Jno. Thompson, Hum. Gunn, Mart. Skinner.

NATHANIEL BRADFORD, 644 acs., Accomack Co., S. side of Pungoteage Riv., 25 Nov. 1679, p. 15. Adj. Charles Scarburgh's 400 acs. purchased by Hugh Yeo; land of Mr. Anthony Hoskins; John Robinson; & Nicholas Waddilow. Granted to Hugh Yeo 2 Oct. 1655, deserted, & granted by order; &c. Trans. of 13 pers: Tho. Vinter, Jno. Barnet, Tho. Fletcher, Alexr. Nash, Richd. Long, Jno. Rawlins, Xper. Wooton, Ed. Spicer, Rich. Clefton, Wm. Edwards, Tho. Carpenter, Tho. Harcroft, Jno. Howill.

PETER WHITE, 350 acs., Gloster Co., 26 Nov. 1679, p. 15. Formerly taken up by Lambert Moore & Bartho. Ramsey; deserted; & since granted to Robt. Beverley, & by him sold to sd. White. Adj. Tho. Dawkins; neer Richd. Hollowaye's plantation; neer Walter Cant's Quarter; &c.

HUMPHREY TOY, 10 acs., in Kingston Parish; on E'most river; adj. his own 550 acs; 26 Nov. 1679, p. 15. Beg. neer the mouth of Benetts Cr; &c. to Dennetts Cr; &c. Due for 1 right.*

ARTHUR ALLEN, of Surrey Co., **EDWD. THELWELL & ROBT. HORNEING,** of Nanzemond Co., 337 acs., S. side of Beavor Dam Br., a br. of the S'n. br. of Nanzemond Riv; part in Is. of Wight & Part in Nanzemond Co., 29 Nov. 1679, p. 16. Beg. at land of Tho. Mason, now in passession of John Dotery. 200 acs. part granted to Richd. Showell, 30 Oct. 1669; deserted, & granted to the abovenamed, with 137 acs. adj. waste land; further due for trans. of 7 pers: Robt. Ruffin, Rich. Lanham, Geo. Adwell, Mar. Whitehead, Tho. Futerell, Lewis Williams, Edwd. Davis.

ROGER TARLETON, 167 acs., Is. of Wight Co., on br. of the W'n. br. of Nanzemond Riv., 29 Nov. 1679, p. 16. Adj. Henry Plumton, Tho. Markes, Wm. Smelly; Ra. Boozeman & his own land, by a former purchase. 50 acs. granted him 21 Sept. 1674; & 117 being waste land adj. Trans. of 3 pers: Jone (or Jane) Davison, Wm. Barton, Margtt. Gregory.

WM. POWELL, of Is. of Wight Co., 257 acs., in sd. Co., on head br. of the W'n. br. of Nanzemond Riv., 29 Nov. 1679, p. 16. Adj. Mr. Tho. Pitt, & Francis Bridle; &c. Trans. of 6 pers: Jno. Davies, Eliz. Breslv. Edwd. Welbank, Tho. Davies, Robt. Lancaster, Richd. Miller.

HEN. WATKINSON, 170 acs., Henrico Co., N. side of James Riv., in Verina Parish; 29 Nov. 1679, p. 17. Adj. John Lewis, near a br. of three (mile) run; & lands of Mr. Cock & Bechamp. Trans. of 4 pers.*

WILLIAM SAWYER, of Gloster Co., Planter, son & heir of Wm. Sawyer, late of sd. Co., Planter; 850 acs., New Kent Co., S. side of the Dragon or Peanketank Sw; 3 Jan. 1679/80, p. 18. Some 2 mi. below the mouth of the br. (where) Jno. Exoll hereto(fore) lived, & some 4 mi. from Mr. Tho. Holmes' Quarter; lyeing abrest with the gr. dam, &c. Granted to Jno. Pigg & Evan Davies, 20 July 1661, for trans. of 17 pers; & by sd. Pigg, the surviv. joynt tenant, & Jane, his wife, conveyed to sd. Sawyer, 24 July 1662; & by order of the Gen. Ct. at James Citty, 23 Sept. last past, in a suit between Wm. Sawyer, Plaintiff, & Amb. Clare, defd., the sd. land is confirmed to sd. Wm.

THOMAS PARNELL, of Is. of Wight Co., 150 acs. in sd. County; bet. the 2nd & 3rd Sw. of the maine Black Waters; 21 Jan. 1679, p. 18. Adj. land of Robt. Flake, in possession of Peter Hayes; & land of John Richardson. Trans. of 3 pers: Danll. Bayly, Tho. Morton, Jeffrey Cooke.

WILLIAM SCOTT, Junr., of Is. of Wight Co., 24 acs., on N. side of the Indian Cr. Sw., in sd. Co; 21 Jan. 1679, p. 18. Adj. John Garwood. Trans. of: Ann Okey.

MR. ROBT. KING, the elder, of Is. of Wight Co., 200 acs., near Tapsters, alias the long pond, Cr., in the Low. Par. of sd. Co; 21 Jan. 1679, p. 19. On W. side of High's Island, upon Mr. Thomas Parker; adj. Major Geo. Narsworthy, &c. 150 acs. granted Mr. Trustram Norsworthy, 3 May 1643 & willed

to his son Thomas, who sold same, 12 July 1670; 50 acs., being waste land adj., due for trans. of: Wm. King.

FRANCIS BRIDLE, of Is. of Wight Co., 422 acs., in sd. Co., on head of the br. of the W'n. br. of Nanzemond Riv., 21 Jan. 1679, p. 19. Adj. Tho. Powell; Richd. Hutchins; Tho. Pitt; & Wm. Smelly. Trans. of 9 pers: Jno. Reeve, Jno. Garrett, Mary Sanders, Peter Buttler, Wm. Ellis, Jno. Owen, Wm. Rose, Ann Cole, Jeffry Stafford.

MATHEW STRICKLAND, 1803 acs., Is. of Wight Co., on the maine Black Water; 20 Apr. 1680, p. 20. Adj. Col. Pitt; George Peirce; Col. Bridgers, &c. Trans. of 36 pers: Tho. Culson, Jno. Bray, Wm. Morgan, Bar. Bee, Darby Ray, Edwd. Jones, Jno. Morfeild, Jno. Robison, Mary Lyn, Alex. Onell (or Oneel), Margt. Bomps, Jone Bishop, Henry Benett, Robt. Huddington, Ann Underwood, Richd. Ashton, Robt. Murley, Xper. Raughan, Tho. Hinton, Tho. Williams, Martin Hinton, Margtt. Butty, Tho. Seawell, Samll. Dames, Rich. Bruster, Eliz. Hall, Wm. Palmer, Tho. Poole, Alice Wilson, Edwd. Walsh, Robt. Regly, Tho. Hurlock, Tho. Turner, Rich. Lennersell, Mar. Barker, Ra. Browne.

MR. GILES LIMSCOTT, 1411 acs., Is. of Wight Co., on the maine Black Water, 20 Apr. 1680, p. 20. Adj. Robt. Lawrence & John Lawrence. Trans. of 28 pers: Edwd. Hill, Symon Wilson, Alice Warkman, Pet. Hatcher, Jone Isham, Jno. Branch, Rich. Carter, Edwd. Mason, Wm. Chapman, Jno. Hoskins, Antho. Meekes, Jno. Taylor, Tho. Elbury, Ja. Spicer, Wm. Potter, Sym. Buttler, Jno. Green, Hen. Davies, Tho. Richards, Wm. Wright, Hen. Cole, An Sanders, O (?) Morgan, Lewis Williams, Ed. Rogers, Jno. Maccall, Wm. Shard, Antho. Bishop.

MR. JOSIAH HARRISON, 750 acs., Is. of Wight Co., on br. of the Black Water, 20 Apr. 1680, p. 21. Adj. lands of Seaward, Smith, Fulgham & his own. Trans. of 15 pers: Wm. Tuller, Jno. Arnold, Roger Deale, Peter White, Jno. Isaac, Edwd. Sampson, Antho. Thompson, Margtt. Illam, Jno. Davis, Richd.

Peacock, Jone Morris, Josep. Newman, Richd. Niccolls, Wm. Ford.

THOMAS PARNELL, 1100 acs., Low. Par. of Is. of Wight Co., on S. side of Currawaugh Sw., 20 Apr. 1680, p. 21. Adj. land formerly taken up by sd. Parnell & Limscott; Robert Lawrence, Junr., Hodges Councill's line; & Col. Jos. Bridger's line. Trans. of 22 pers: Wm. Howell, Phill. Sergant, Wm. Phillips, Jno. Driver, Mo. Sergant, Ann Bedford, Eliz. Sergant, Jno Francis, Ja. Madro, Jno. Hatton, Hub. Pettys, Ann Baylie, Jno. Crowder, Ann Pilgrim, Eliz. Weston, Lucy Holt, Jno. Corbit, Eliz. Brogen, Morris Wms. (Williams), Jno. Sneath, George Turner; 1 Negro.

ISAAC COATES, 418 acs., N. side of James River, S. side of the run of Moses Cr., 20 Apr. 1680, p. 21. Adj. Mr. Bishop. Granted to Bartho. Knipe, 6 Oct. 1652; deserted; & granted by order, &c. Trans. of 9 pers: Tho. Moor, Jno. Hoskins, Tho. Sadler, Arthur Mandy, Peter Long, Henry Mayden, James Mason, Jone Miles, Sara Morris.

DAME FRANCES BERKELEY, 285 acs., James City Co., 20 Apr. 1680, p. 22. From the head of the Long Meadow to Coll. Holt's land; to her Ladyship's devdt. called the *Hotwaters;* &c. Trans. of 6 pers.*

WILLIAM SOANES, 420 acs., James City Co; N. side of Chickahominy Riv., 20 Apr. 1680, p. 22. Beg. below the mouth of a slash on Tyescun Sw., to Dormer's old line; to Mr. Wade's land; along Edwd. Gilles, &c. Part of 450 acs. assigned to sd. Soanes, & further due for trans. of 8 pers: Tho. North, Geo. Morse, Ann Poor, Robt. Davies, Jone Vahan, Mary Swann, Edmd. Huck, Law. Bromfeild.

GARRARD ROBERT ELLYSON, 577 acs., 20 Apr. 1680, p. 22. 377 acs. in New Kent Co., in the narrows of York Riv., by land of George Chapman; adj. Wm. Cox & John Hope; 200 acs. in James City Co., on N.E. side of a br. of Burchen Sw. Granted to Capt. Robt. Ellyson, 5 Mar. ——, & due him as sonn & heire,

RICHARD GISZARD (GIZZARD), 337 acs., New Kent Co., St. Stephen's Par., adj. Mr. Holmes; 20 Apr. 1680, p. 23. Trans. of 7 pers: Hugh Hayly, Tho. Roberts, Joane Roades, Eliz. Rider, Jos. Jeffreys, Jno. Huggis (or Huggins), Alexr. Camell.

MR. JOHN LANE, 540 acs., New Kent Co., Stratton Major Par., on the head br. of Arrakieco Sw., 20 Apr. 1680, p. 23. Adj. Mr. John Townby; Sparkes' path; the flaxmans path; along Green's line, &c. Trans. of 11 pers: Ja. Fleming, Wm. Newland, Jno. Belman, Mary Fleming, Tho. Williams, Ann Dennis, Tho. Williams, Jno. Canedy, Alexr. Christian, Richd. Chapman, Hen. Cox.

BARTHOLOMEW RAMSEY, 590 acs., New Kent Co., St. Stephen's Par., 20 Apr. 1680, p. 23. Adj. land that was John Roberts; adj. Sawyer's cor; down the Miery Br., up Timber Br., to Burford's cor; to Wells' & Reade's lines. Trans. of 12 pers: Alexr. Camell, Jos. Pighill, Sus. Dickson, Jno. Flowers, Is. Jaques, Mary Davies, Jno. Paveat, Wm. Jenkins, Mar. Fisher, Jno. Woster, Ja. Upton, Edwd. Hoskins.

SAMUELL WOODWARD, 870 acs., upon Appamatuck River, 20 Apr. 1680, p. 24. 600 acs. pattented by Chr. Woodward, 24 Aug. 1637, & due sd. Samll. as his heir, which is renewed & included in this pattent; bounding N. upon the river, E. upon land lately belonging to Wm. Farrar, Gent., W. upon the Winding River; lying in Bristoll Par., Chas. City Co., on S. side of sd. river; containing all the waste lands bet. sd. Chr. on the river & lands called Bayly's; on head of land of Mr. John Mayes on the S'wd., & lands in possession of Ja. Hall; to Henry Newcomb; near plantation called *Hoffords;* to Hofford's run; the Kings Road, &c.Imp. of 6 pers: Robt. Stanly, Wm. Corbutt, Ellen Roach; 3 Negroes.

CAPT. WM. RANDOLPH, MR. FRA. EPPS & MR. JOS. ROYALL, 580 acs., commonly called Capt. Martin's Swamp, S. side of James River, Henrico Co., 20 Apr. 1680, p. 24. Adj. land of sd. Royall & Capt. Henry Isham. Trans. of 12 pers: Richd. Kennon 8 times; Jno. Cornwall, Edwd. Oliver, Wm. Suttle, Jno. Hardiman.

WILLIAM WHITTACAR, 400 acs., in James City & Yorke Co.'s; 20 Apr. 1680, p. 25. Near Wm. Paulett's land; adj. Tho. Buck; Robt. Harris; Mrs. Higgenson; & Col. Tho. Pettus. Trans. of 8 pers: Wm. Whittacar, twice, Jno. Conyers, twice, Eliz. Langley, & 3 Negroes.

JOHN FLEMING & ANDREW DAVIES, 1000 acs., New Kent Co., 20 Apr. 1680, p. 25. Adj. devdt. of Andrew Davis, on br. of Matchumps Cr. Trans. of 20 pers: Jno. Wms. (Williams), Mary Wilson, Walter Coale, Jno. Ivey, Jno. Cooper, Wm. Lott, Geo. Leach, Tho. Warren, Sar. Martin, Eliz. Jones, Jno. Read, Wm. Jackson, Mary Carter, Hen. Tilney, Edwd. Carter, Tho. Carey, Wm. Clarke, Edwd. Land, Fra. Strong, Hen. Jones.

RICHARD BOOTH, of Is. of Wight Co., 560 acs., in the Low. Par. of sd. Co., on both sides the br. & near the head of Curawaugh Sw., 20 Apr. 1680, p. 25. Near Col. Jos. Bridger's line. Trans. of 12 pers: Wm. Harris, Tho. Gulls Geo. Goodman, Antho. Watts, Tho. Hodson, Jno. White, Wm. Floyd, Edwd. Barton, Jno. George, Hen. Aylett, Ja. Hall, Tho. Barker. (Note: Marginal notation mentions Hen. Hartwell, Clk.)

MR. THO. BENBRIDGE, 210 acs., Nanzemond Co., S.E. side of Chuckatuck Cr., 20 Apr. 1680, p. 26. Beg. at a br. dividing this & land of Edwd. Cowan; near the Indian path; to Mr. Godfry Hunt. 170 acs. part of an ancient patt. for 500 acs. granted to Geo. Salesbury, which after several conveyances, &c., belongs to sd. Benbridge; the remainder part of 100 acs. granted to sd. Hunt Nov. 18, 1668 & surrendered to sd. Benbridge.

MAJOR GENERAL JNO. CUSTIS, an island, in Accomack Co; 100 acs., in Pocomoke Riv., called *Cobhams Island*, near the Back Cr., dividing *Jollies*

Neck from land of Robt. Pitts; 20 Apr. 1680, p. 26. Trans. of 2 pers: Edwd. Custis, Walter Young.

PATRICK COWAN, 180 acs., Nanzemond Co., S.E. side of Chuckatuck Cr., 20 Apr. 1680, p. 27. Just above Long point; near land of Major Davis, dec'd., to point above the Landing place; by the old Indian path, &c. Part of 500 ac. patt. of Georg Salesbury, which became the right of Edwd. Cowan & descended to sd. Patrick, his son & heir.

WM. GRAY, of Surrey Co., 680 acs., in sd. Co., on both sides of the head of the Lower Sunken Marsh, 20 Apr. 1680, p. 27. 494 acs. part of 850 acs. granted to Wm. Harris, 2 June 1668, who sould to sd. Gray, 2 Sept. 1679; 186 acs. being waste land; adj. Mr. Richd. Briggs; Mr. Edwards; the Cart path; Mr. Robt. Ruffin; &c. 186 acs. for trans. of 4 pers: Symond Prouts, Arth. Denis, Robt. Winch, Peter South.

THOMAS SENIOR, 113 acs., Surrey Co., 20 Apr. 1680, p. 28. Bet. lands of Mr. Fra. Mason. Mr. Jno. & Tho. Edwards & Mrs. Mary Marriott, on lower side of Crouche's Cr; beg. near Mr. Bins' Cart path; on Bishop's line, &c. Trans. of 3 pers: Wm. Shoreing, Tho. Tindall, Wm. Carpenter.

HENRY WIGGS, 20 acs., Low. Par. of Is. of Wight Co., on S. side the head of Vasser's Cr., 20 Apr. 1680, p. 28. Adj. land he now lives upon; a br. dividing this from land of Col. Arthur Smith; by Mr. Pharo Cobb, &c. Trans. of 1 per.*

HUGH LEE, 400 acs., on the Black Water, called *Rownam*, Chas. City Co., in Bristoll Par., 20 Apr. 1680, p. 28. Trans. of 8 pers: Tho. Chamberlaine, twice: Israel Horty, Wm. Howard, Tho. Watson, Wm. Sidnam, Mary Gay, Cha. Roberts.

MR. ROBT. TUCKER, 172 A., 2 R., 24 P., Chas. City Co., on N. side of the Black Water, 20 Apr. 1680, p. 29. Adj. Wm. Jones; Jordan's path, Edwd. Bircherd; the Reedy Br; Baylie's path, &c. Trans. of 4 pers: Jno. Tucker, 3 times; Sar. Twill.

HENRY CROWTHER, 349 acs., 3 rood & 32 poles, Chas. City Co., Bristoll Par., S. side of Appamatuck Riv., 20 Apr. 1680, p. 29. Adj. Mr. Hugh Lee; Chohuncock Br; &c. 149 A., 3 R., & 32 P., purchased of Georg Downing; & 149 acs. for trans. of 3 pers: Richd. Bayly, Eliz. his wife, Wm. West, Wm. Taylor.

JOHN SOMERS, 100 acs., N'ampton Co., 20 Apr. 1680, p. 29. On the seaboard side; bounded S'ly. by Dun Cr; E'ly. by Macon Riv., N'ly. by a cr. parting Joseph Warren & land sd. Somers bought of Jno. Penell, & land of Wm. Goldin. Trans. of 2 pers: Tho. Taylor, Wm. Upton.

WM. VAUGHAN, 1225 A:, 32 Po., Chas. City Co., on S. side of Appamatuck Riv., 20 Apr. 1680, p. 30. 100 acs. part of 150 acs. purchased of Hugh Lee; adj. Tho. Lowe; 100 acs. purchased of Robt. Burges (Burgis), along Mr. Robert Coleman, & Hen. Chanus (?), &c: 720 acs. adj. Jno. Ewens; Wm. Johnson; the Ballows; lines of Colson, Lear, &c; which 720 acs. was assigned to sd. Vaughan by Hugh Lee, Wm. Ballow & Gilb. Pratt; the residue on the S. side the river from his old land; downe the Black Water, to sd. Lee; on line of Henry Chumings, &c. Trans. of 7 pers: Jno. Peterson, Tho. Stroud, Susan Holsworth, Richd. Spewlyn, Geo. Levett (or Lovett), Jno. Jenings, Robt. Tybaulds, Elias Degarris.

THOMAS BUTT & THOMAS MILNER, 3000 acs., Low. Norf. Co., upon a br. of the S'n. br. of Elizabeth Riv. & called by the name of Sturchcomb (or Stinchcomb); 20 Apr. 1680, p. 31. Near head of Burchen Sw., adj. Richd. Butt; the Gum Sw., Cyprus Sw; &c. Trans. of 60 pers: 5 by cert.(ificate); Riich. Birley, Wm. Fox, Marv West, Mary Extell; Amy; Nan; Richd. Hamlin, Rich. Church, Walter Makeady, Jno. Daws, Giles May, Jno. Pearse, Wm. Leach (or Leath), Rich. Senders. Tho. Wilson. Geo. Sharp, Rich Niccolls: 13 by Certificate; Jno. Buttock. And. Reeven, Edmd. Nichols, Jno. Warham, Jno. Thomas, Tho. West. Wm. Dennis, Th. Martin; 14 by Certificate; Reb.

Wheeler, Giles Randle, Jno. Edmonds, Cha. Shaw, Sar. Anderson, Mary Lambert, Math. Elmes.

THOMAS BUTT & ROBT. BUTT, 514 acs., Low. Norf. Co., on E'wd. side of the S'n. br. of Eliz. Riv., 26 Apr. 1680, p. 31. Near Robt. Butt's old line; adj. Walter Costen; Thomas Etheridge, on the Green Sea, &c. 380 acs. granted to Robt. Butts, Senr., 20 Oct. 1661, & left to the abovenamed by will. (Note: the following names, without explanation, appear under this record) Wm. Wm., David Board, Mary Formby, Ja. Daws, Math. Sanderson.

MAJOR WM. WYATT, 850 acs., New Kent Co., N.E. side of Mattapony Riv., 26 Apr. 1680, p. 32. Beg. at the mouth of Mathapungo (Matchapungo) Cr., which divides this & land of Mr. Arthur Price; to Mr. Jno. Winsloe's (Winslow) line; near John Jarratt, &c. 400 acs. part by patt., 16 Mar. 1663; & 450 acs. adj. for trans. of 9 pers: Samll. Creff (or Cress), Robt. Anderson, Jno. Lithorn, Jo. Mesam, Jo. Dukely, Wm. Mines, Jo. Hetherly, Tho. Michells, Tho. Haid (or Haies).

THOMAS HICKMAN, 1000 acs., New Kent Co., S.E. side of Matapony Riv., 26 Apr. 1680, p. 32. Adj. Mr. Wm. Wyatt. Granted to Thomas Ballard, 16 July 1655; deserted; & by patt., dated 6 Oct. 1658, granted to Thomas Hickman, father of the above, & is now renewed.

JOHN JARRATT, 204 acs., New Kent Co., Stratton Major Par., 26 Apr. 1680, p. 33. Adj. Mr. Cordenbrook's land, near br. of Hathquake Sw; along Jenings' line; by Spencer's line; to Assatiams Meadow; on Mr. Rawlins' line, &c. Granted sd. Jarratt 24 Feb. 1675/6 & now renewed. (Note: This name altered—& appears to be Garratt.)

RALPH WORMELEY, ESQR., 740 acs. Middlesex Co., comonly called Timber neck land; near plantation of Thomas Lee; adj. plantation of Mr. Georg Reeve; by head lines of Nincocke or Rosegill; by the old feild where Mr. Maximillian Pettus now lives, &c; 26

Apr. 1680, p. 33. 700 acs. granted Sir Henry Chickeley 24 Dec. 1663; formerly due Capt. Brocas 2 Feb. 1653; & due sd. Wormeley by assignment of sd. Chicheley 2 Dec. 1678; 40 acs., within sd. bounds, due for trans. of: Tho. Horseley.

SAME. 2200 acs. Rappa. Co., N. side Rappa. Riv., bet. Portus' Cr. & Chingatague Cr., *being formerly an Indian habitation called Nanzattico, &c*; 26 Apr. 1680, p. 34. Granted sd. Chicheley, 8 Dec. 1656, & now due by assignment dated 25 Dec. 1674.

JOSHUA STORY (Storey), 850 acs., New Kent Co., N. side Mattaponie (Riv.); adj. Mr. Watkins; Mr. Richard Davis; the head of Brewerton's branch; &c; 26 Apr. 1680, p. 34. Granted to Phillipp Watkins, Thomas Watkins & William Ricketts, 6 Mar. 1673/4; deserted; & now due by order, &c. Trans. 17 pers: Samll. Tayle, Jno. May, Pet. Mealy, Ann Chillingsworth, Grace Feild, James Taberer, Wm. Payne, Reb. Black, Tho. Feild, Hen. Heath, Jno. Collins, John Brice, Wm. Wood, Jos. Storey, Tho. Bray, Steph. Goodin, James Fry.

SAME. 600 acs., same Co., & date; page 35. N. side Mattapony Riv., adj. Mr. Mody. Granted to John Pigg 3 Jan. 1667; deserted; granted to Robert Beverly 21 Sept. 1674; deserted, & now granted by order, &c. Trans. of 12 pers: Sus. Seares, Tho. Green, Wm. Eabank, Ed. Hudson, Tho. Warkin, Wm. Turner, Rice Thomas, Tho. Swearn, Law. Patrick, Nich. Weekes, Step. Sikes, Corn. Taylor.

WM. SNAPES, 75 acs., Gloster Co., Petsoe Par., adj. Col. John Lewis; Saml. Clarke; & James Dudley; 26 Apr. 1680, p. 36. Trans. of 2 pers: Tho. Wright, Jno. Carpenter.

By Thomas Lord Culpeper, Baron of Thorsway, Lieut. Gov'r., &c.

JAMES COLLINS, Senr., 450 acs., Up. Par. of Nanzemond; adj. land of David Loyd, now Samuell Watson's; & adj. Thomas Parker; 10 July 1680, p. 36. Trans. of 9 pers: Folke Adams,

Nich. Lux, Tho. Skews, Jno. Lafull, Jno. Cotton, Owen Jones, Wm. Walbank, Samll. Waldridge.

JOHN MURFRYE (Murfrey), 160 acs., Lower Par. of Nanzemond; at mouth of Browne's Br., neare his now dwelling house; adj. the Glleab Land; nigh the Shoemaker's Br., by Nanzemond River; a cr. parting this & land of Capt. Edward Streater, &c; 10 July 1680, p. 37. 100 acs., part of 200 acs., granted Mathew Adkinson 18 Aug. 1637 & now due after several sales, &c; 60 acs. being overplus, due for trans. of: Jno. Murfrey.

JOHN BABB, 80 acs., of marsh land in the W'n. br. of Nanzemond Riv., adj. his own land & *where the Church now stands;* opposite to Capt. Oldis' Landing; to Babb's upper landing, &c; 10 July 1680, p. 37. Trans. of 2 pers: Jno. Catlock, Margtt. Harford.

COL. JOHN LEAR, 900 acs., in Nanzemond & Is. of Wight Co.'s; on Indian Cr., a br. of Nanzemond Riv; adj. 700 acs. of Audry Bonny which was the upper side of land held by Francis Wells, dec'd., now sd. Lear's; running to the reedy sw. or flatty poquoson; through Richard Barber *alias* Thomas Gale's Orchard, &c; 10 July 1680, p. 38. 650 acs. granted Richard Saven 11 June 1653; renewed by Symon Iron 18 Mar. 1662, &c; 250 acs. for trans. of 5 pers: Mary Harrdy, Richd. Stubb, Walter Stafford, And. Hare, Isaac Ellis.

HENRY PLUMPTON, 200 acs., Nanzemond Co., near head of the S'n. br; by John Maccallum's land; adj. Mr. Acthell (?); & opposite Richard Heynes; 10 July 1680, p. 38. Trans. of 4 pers: Jno. White, Tho. Bushell, Barb. Thompson, Jno. Waldrone.

GEORG LAWRANCE, 120 acs., at the head of his father's line, in the W'n. br. of Nanzemond; adj. land of his brother John Lawrance; Mr. Isen & sd. *old* Mr. Lawrance; 10 July 1680, p. 39. Trans. of 3 pers: Jno. Eaton, Edwd .Read, Richd. Houndson.

RICHARD SANDERS, 300 acs., in the Up. Par. of Nanzemund; at the head of Capt. John Mason, in the W'n. br; adj. Michaell Hill, now sd. Sanders', land; John Wallis; & Thomas Garnygan; &c; 10 July 1680, p. 39. Trans. of 6 pers: Wm. Baker, Wm. Trueman, Steph. Seagood, Richd. Reynolds, Jone Seabrooke, Jno. Geab (?).

JANE STOAKES, Widdowe, 800 acs., Up. Par. of Nanzemond Co., adj. Robert Brasewell & James Long; 10 July 1680, p. 40. Granted sd. Brasewell 22 Apr. 1670, deserted; & now granted, &c. Trans. of 16 pers: Thomas Williams, James Harris, Jno. Walker, Wm. Tanner, Wm. Gore, Mary Fish, Tim. Good, Eliz. Edwards.

WILLIAM OLDIS & WILLIAM GATLIN, (Gattlin), 650 acs., at a place called *Adderbury*, in Nanzemond Co., neare the side of King sale Sw; a br. dividing this & land of William Collins; 10 July 1680, p. 40. Trans. of 13 pers: Ja. Scot, Tho. Jones, Bar. Barnes, Eliz. ——, Jno. Solder (?). Ann, Deb., Wm. Ramsey, Roger Monteague, Edwd. Morraw, Eliz. Robinson, James Patridge, Steph. Luch (or Luck).

MR. ROBERT KAE, 170 acs., Up. Par. of Is. of W. Co., on S.E. side of Lawnes Cr., & running to mouth of a small cr., knowne as Speckman's folly; &c; 10 July 1680, p. 41. Trans. of 4 pers: Thomas Royall, Jno. Trueweck, Jno. Evens, Wal. Hopton.

MR. HENRY BIGGS, 321 acs., New Kent Co., on head brs. of Assatians Sw; adj. Robert Hill; & William Rogers; a Cattaile meadowe, &c; 10 July 1680, p. 41. Trans. of 7 pers: Wm. Rowse, Ann Strange, Edwd. Archer, Danll. Meekes, Jno. Alwood (or Atwood), Loud Dennis, Eliz. Davis. (Marginal notation: 320 acres.)

RICHARD CLARKE, 736 acs., New Kent Co., S. side of Yorke Riv., at the mouth of little cr., where it falls into Skimino Cr; adj. William Whitmore; land formerly Arthur Price's, neare the Labour in Vaine Path, &c; 10 July 1680, p. 42. Trans. of 15 pers: Samll. Higins (or Stigins), Walter Patso, Nich. Young, Ben. Heath, Tim. Boyter, Tim.

Hatches, Ed. Keeling, Rich. Gregory, Rob. Smith, Jno. Hailes, Antho. Beeland, Jno. Cooke, Danll. Ware, Jos. Fellowes; "one more."

MOSES DAVIS, 400 acs., New Kent Co., bet. Totopotomoyes Creekes & branches of Yorke Riv; beg. by uper Powhite Path; by Nickahooke branch; adj. his own & land of Mr. John Page; 10 July 1680, p. 42. Granted sd. Davis 6 Dec. 1669, deserted; & by order, granted to John Fleming, who assigned to sd. Davis. Trans. of 8 pers: Edwd. Newton, And. Smith, Symon Miller, Tho. White, James Nurse, Jno. Knight, James New, Tho. Wells.

GARRETT JOHNSON, 1140 acs. James Citty Co., N. side of the head of Chichahominy Riv; on the upper side of Barbadoes runn; through Chichahominy Sw., &c; 10 July 1680, p. 43. Formerly granted to sd. Johnson & now due for trans. of 23 pers: Wm. Beavin, Nich. Pryor, Ja. Varney.* Note: "The Records have bin Exactly Searched for the date of the originall pattent but by the miscarraige of some part of the Records in the late Troubles many matters are missing of which this canot be found." Nicho. Spencer, Secty. Recorded by Hen. Hartwell, Clk.

THOMAS SORESBY, 620 acs., Up. Par. of Surry Co; neare Mr. William Symons' Cart path, bet. sd. Symons, Mr. Allen & William Scarbrough; 10 July 1680, p. 43. Trans. of 13 pers: Ann Donn, Fra. Sumner, 2, his wife & 2 children, Wm. Burgh, Wm. Elliott, Kath. Church, Wm. Mandy, Tho. Carter, Jno. Shepard, Robt. Aylett.

THOMAS BURTON, 350 acs., Henrico Co., upon Appamattocke Riv; adj. Mr. John Baugh, & Mr. Abraham Wood; 10 July 1680, p. 44. Granted to Ambrose Cobb, 20 July 1639, & by several assignments now due sd. *Barton*.

MR. ALEXANDER WALKER, 10 acs., James Citty Co; beg. on Richahoc Path; & adj. Col. Holt's line; 10 July 1680, p. 44. Trans. of 1 pers.*

THOMAS WARBERTON, Senr., 430 acs., James Citty Co; beg. at the mouth of a small slash of Pagan Cr. Sw; including 40 acs. purchased of John Knight, dec'd; 10 July 1680, p. 44. Formerly granted, & now new surveyed, &c.

MAJOR GENERLL. ABRAHAM WOOD, .1304 acs., Chas. Citty Co., Bristoll Par., on S. side of the runn of Appamattuck Riv., adj. his own land, neare the Indian Towne Cr; opposite Mr. Thomas Batts; 10 July 1680, p. 45. Trans. of 27 pers: Fr. Conaway, Jno. Bevens, Hen. Manering, Susan Leach, Margtt. Farrar, Nich. Brooke, Nich. Overbee, Jno. Jacob, Robt. Harrison, Tho. Edwards, Rich. Phillips, Benno. Blake, Ed. Peasock, Wm. Fleming, Jno. Blacksha, Anth. Thiskett (or Huskett), Tho. Benington, Tho. Moore, Rebecca Sandy, Sanders Bruse, Ed. Savage, Mary Flood, Fra. Child, Mary Green, Edw. Prichett (or Birchett), Ann Grant, Mart Trydon.

HENRY NEWCOMBE, 549 A., 4 R., 22 P., Chas. Citty Co., S. side of Appamattux; 10 July 1680, p. 45. 387 A., 2 R. beg. at Citty Cr. Sw; adj. Samuell Woodward; nigh W'n. br. of Bayly's Cr., to a sw. called the head of the Citty Cr; 162 A., 2 R., adj. John Mayse; Bayly's path; Mr. Robert Coleman; Mr. Henry Batts; &c. 387 A., 2 R., granted sd. Newcombe 15 Feb. 1663; residue for trans. of 4 pers: Tho. Withrington, Dorothy Egdole, Jno. Garill (or Gavill).

MR. ROBERT EVARETT, 280 acs; the greatest part in the New Poquoson Parish in Yorke Co., & part in Warwick Co; 10 July 1680, p. 46. Bet. his own & land of Mr. Thomas Harwood. Trans. of 6 pers: Bridge Sperring, Arra. Mann, Margtt. Hunter, No. (an) Irish maide, Fra. Ridley, Sar. Taylor.

MR. THOMAS CHEESMAN, 550 acs., Yorke Co., New Poquoson Par., & part in Warwick Co., 10 July 1680, p. 47. Beg. neare land of Col. John Cheesman, dec'd; Mr. Wild, dec'd; & Thomas Harwood; &c. Trans. of 11 pers: Jno. Parker, Jno. Parsons, Fra. Raymon, Wm. Green, Tho. Welson, Jno. Leasson, Mary Vinson, Mary Hilliard, Mary Whitmor, Mary Pole, Judith Walker, Jane Constable.

MR. HENRY AWBERY, 6630 acs., Rappa. Co., 10 July 1680, p. 47. 1050 acs. on S. side of Hoskins Cr; adj. Thomas Browning; by Nanjattico Path; by maine run of Hoskins Cr; as appeares by patt. of sd. Awbery 9 Apr. 1664; 480 acs. adj. same; neare the road path that goes to Puscatecon Cr; granted him 3 Sept. 1669 & since granted him 23 Mar. 1671/2; 5100 acs. bet. brs. of Piscataway Cr., Hodgskins Cr. &br. of Mattapony Riv; beg. by an Indian path; nigh the new road by Gillsonn's Mill; to the head of Paggett & Gouldman, &c; granted sd. Awberey 19 Mar. 1677/8.

WHEREAS the Gingas King Indians hath made verry often repeated complaints and hath troubled the Governor & Councell about their land they have possessed at the Sea side on the Easterne shore ever since the yeare 1641 as appears by an Ancient Pattent on record in the same yeare notwithstanding which the said Indians complained they were still disturbed by John Kendall lately deceased which was there seated by Capt. John Savage whoe alsoe pretended a claime to said land and for as much as at a Court held at James Citty by the Honoble. Gov'r. Sir William Berkeley and Councell of State bearing date the 28 Sept. 1674 then the said Govr. & Councell tooke the case of the said Indians (whoe have ever beene in Amity with us) into serious consideration and graunted order that fower of the Gentlemen of that place should goe upon the said land and make enquiry into the bounds of the said John Kendall did at that present possesse and doe cause as much in leiu thereof to bee layd out convenient for the said Indians out of Capt. Savages land which is to be freely possessed by the said Indians without disturbance of any person or persons whatsoever as by the said order may appeare. In obedience to which said order of the Generll. Court Coll. John Stringer, Coll. John Custis, Capt. Southy Littleton & Major Edmund Bowman, Gentlemen, elected for the said purpose have with all vigilance and care made such inspection into the said land as by the report of the same under their hands and at the instance of the said Gentlemen Capt. Southy Littleton made Survey of the said land of the Indians which may alsoe appeare by his plott given under his hand dated the second of September 1675. Now know yee that I the said Thomas Lord Culpeper, &c., give and grant unto the GINGAS KING INDIANS 650 acs. of land lying & being in N'ampton Co., begining & bounded N'ly. upon Angoods (or Augood) Cr., thence to a marked tree SW by S ½ W to a markt corner tree thence NW by N ½ W 172 poles to another markt tree thence N 74 degs. W. 200 po. to a markt red corner tree thence S 3 degs. E 310 po. by a line of markt trees by Capt. Savages his land to a markt corner tree of the said land thence by a line of markt trees by Coll. Kendalls land to a markt tree there standing thence all along E. 8 degs. N. by a direct line of markt trees by Mr. Thomas Harmansons land to the sea side thence bounded by the Marshes to the first bounds of the said Angoods (or Augood) Cr. The said land being due to the said Gingas King Indians as by Antient Pattent doth & may appeare. To have and to hold, &c. To bee held, &c. Yeilding and paying, &c. Provided, &c. Dated the 10 July, 1680. Page 49.

By Sir Henry Chicheley, Depty. Govr. &c.
MR. THOMAS TODD, 1084 acs., New Kent Co., St. Stephen's Par; upon Peanketanke or Dragon Sw; neare Sawyers Br., &c; 26 Sept. 1680, p. 50. 850 acs. purchased of William Sawyer; 234 acs. for trans. of 5 pers: Tho. Gunston, John Clarke, Wm. Neale, Nich. Parke (or Sparke—altered), En. Foreman.

RALPH GREENE, SENR., 179 acs., New Kent Co., Stratton Major Par., on branches of Arrakico Sw; by the path from his quarter to Sheers; by path to John Parkes; & adj. land of said Henry Greene; 26 Sept. 1680, p. 51. Trans. of 4 pers: Danll. Macy, Allen Magrey, Nath. Thornton, Edwd. Jones.

JOHN BREMER, 600 acs., New Kent Co; N. side Mattapony Riv; adj. Mr. Moody, & John Pigg; 26 Sept. 1680, p. 51. Granted to John Pigg, assigned in Sept. 1673 to Edward Cooke, who assigned to Lt. Coll. John Smith 10 Dec. 1673, who assigned to sd. Bremer 10 Nov. 1675, who assigned to Georg Ballenden 6 Dec. 1675 & by him assigned to sd. Bremer 17 Jan. 1678/9.

MR. ABRAHAM WEEKS (Weekes) & MR. HUGH WILLIAMS, 1091 acs., 26 Sept. 1680, p. 52. On back of land purchased by Henry Corbyn, Esqr. & another taken up by sd. Corbyn, dec'd; crossing the main br. of Ware Cr. &c; crossing a gr. br. of Tasating Cr; by a valne (?) called Solomons garden &c. Trans. of 22 pers: Jno. Chedle, Wm. Niccolls, Wm. Stokes, Ben. Clarke, Jona. Smith, Jno. Thruston, Abr. Baker, Jno. Colston, Jno. Oldis, Rich. Goodman, Tho. Deadman, Hen. Griffin, Jno. Houge (or Hoage), Richd. Osborne, Mary Baker, Eliz. Keble, An. Smith, Julan Niccolls; 4 Negroes.

GILBERT ADDAMS, 150 acs., Low. Par. of Is. of W. Co., on brs. of the Blackwater, 26 Sept. 1680, p. 52. Adj. Mr. Nicholas Cobb; Mr. Thomas Tooke; by a cart path; &c. Trans. of 3 pers: Mary Kent, Jno. Brown, Tho. Clarke.

GEORG MORRIS, 3000 acs., in Rappa. & New Kent Co.'s; bet. Rappa. Riv. & Mattapony; adj. Col. Gooderich & Mr. Henry Awbry lying bet. the 2 pocosons of Pascataway & Gilson's Cr; by an Indian path, to a br. of Tuckahoe Sw. or Bever dam Sw; to the Maine Sw; &c; 26 Sept. 1680, p. 53. Granted to sd. Morris 8 May 1674, & now new pattented.

SAME. 1190 acs., Rappa. Co; on brs. of Gilson's Cr; adj. Mr. Pley's & Mr. Butten's lands, &c; same date & page. 800 acs. part granted sd. Morris & John Long 29 Sept. 1667; & 390 acs. granted sd. Morris 8 Apr. 1674, & now new pattented.

JOHN SIVILL, 100 acs., Low. Norf. Co., in the northerne brs. of Curretuck adj. John White & Mr. Wm. Basnett & Georges quarter; 27 Sept. 1680, p. 54. Trans. of 2 pers: Jno. Steward, Jno. Gray.

HENRY PLATT, 250 acs., Low. Norf. Co., towards head of the S'n. br. of Eliz. Riv; a br. dividing this & land of Walter Costen; & adj. Richford Sw; 27 Sept. 1680, p. 54. Trans. of 5 pers: Wm. Hayly, Wm. Poore, Edwd. Raning (?) 3 times.

WILLIAM WOODHOUSE, 28 acs., Low. Norf. Co., Lynhaven Par; adj. his own land; 27 Sept. 1680, p. 54. Trans. of: Tho. Brinson.

DENNIS DALLEY, 50 acs., of broken land, marsh & sandbanks going by the name of the *Indian Landing;* Low. Norf. Co., in the northerne brs. of Curretuck; 27 Sept. 1680, p. 55. Running N'ly. from the house to the maine ocean, &c. Trans. of: Wm. Griggs.

RGER HODGIS, 242 acs., Low. Norf. Co; neare the Roadway & neare Henry Dale; by Goose Cr; to Herbert's corner; neare John Manning; on Julyan's Cr; to Nash's corner; &c; 27 Sept. 1680, p. 55. Trans. of 5 pers: Jno. Nickolls 3, Wm. Ownes, Jno. Snow.

PETER CRASHLOE, 150 acs., Low. Norf. Co; on N. brs. of Curretuck; opposite Georges Quarter; a br. dividing this & land of John Brookes, a marsh dividing this, Mr. Basnett's & Georges quarter; &c; 27 Sept. 1680, p. 55. Trans. of 3 pers: Nich. Repar; Henry & Jack, Negroes.

THOMAS SMITH, 173 acs., Low. Norf. Co; on N. brs. of Curratuck; adj. John Brookes; & Mr. Basnett, &c; 27 Sept. 1680, p. 56. Trans. of 4 pers: 2 Negroes, Tony, Sambo.

RICHARD BONNEY, 200 acs., Low. Norf. Co; called by the name of *Turky quarter;* adj. Mr. Henry Woodhouse; 27 Sept. 1680, p. 56. Trans. of 4 pers: Eliz. Medcalfe, Edwd. Farnswill, Bryan Carter, Jno. Gisbone.

MARMADUKE ETHERIDGE, 250 acs., Low. Norf. Co; adj. land he lives on, called *Mannings Ridges;* towards land of John Etheridge, &c; 27 Sept. 1680, p. 56. Trans. of 5 pers: Jone ——, Jno. Scrubby (?), Geo. Harme, Richd. Titibury, Alex. Gittins.

PETER POYNER, 350 acs., Low. Norf. Co; by the broad cr. issuing from the southern br. of Eliz. Riv; neare Edward Davis; 27 Sept. 1680, p. 56. Trans. of 7 pers: Peter Poyner, Tho. Bell, Jno. Blandall, Wm. Brackett, Jone Morgane, Mary Jone Bonnell (?), Phill. Lee.

JOHN JAMES, 1000 acs., Low. Norf. Co., 27 Sept. 1680, p. 57. A swamp parting this & the long ridge; by the road; to Richard Bonney's, line &c. Trans. of 20 pers: Bet servt., Jane Beag, Hector Pings (-), Pet. Boward, Jane Butler, Isac Britt; Jno., Quan, Mich., Dego, Mark Ducum, Ja. Thomas, Pet. Mason, Jno. Britoon, Jno. Deane; Taffy, Dick, Tom, Ann, Pegg.

MR. JOHN SANDFORD, 1680 acs., Low. Norf. Co., on Corretuck Bay; adj. Thomas Morris; a cr. dividing this & land called the *good land;* 27 Sept. 1680, *p.* 57. Trans. of 34 pers: Robt. Bell, Wm. Green, Jona. Geo: (George ?), his wife, Jno. Semell, An. Patridge, Geo. Green, En. Tart, Eliz. Ash, Jno. Petart, Ja. Edwards, Danll. Edwards, Jno. Holliday, Rich. Morman, Edwd. (an ?), orphant, Samll. Scapman (?), Samll. Wheeler, Robt. Positon, Tho. Chapman, Ja. Bendall, Danll. Pecort, Wm. Former (or Forcer), Tho. Pecort, Brid. Prichett, Mary Wakely, Wm. Holliday, Jno. Sandford; 4 Negroes.

WALTER COSTEN, 50 acs., Low. Norf. Co., towards the head of the S'n. br. of Eliz. River, called *Costen's Island;* at the mouth of Hiccory Noll Cr. of sd. branch; 27 Sept. 1680, p. 57. Trans. of: Ann Jones.

JOHN BROOKES, 206 acs., Low. Norf. Co., in the northerne brs. of Corretuck; E'ly. on Franks quarter, &c; 27 Sept. 1680, p. 58. Trans. of 4 pers: Abra. Potts; & 3 Negroes.

DENNIS DALLEY, 1235 acs., Low. Norf. Co; in the N. brs. of Corretuck, neare the mouth of little Cr., by the Oyster Cove in Piney Point bay & adj. land of John White; 27 Sept. 1680, p. 58. Trans. of 25 pers: Tho. Vinsy, Tho. Deane, Tho. Benns, Jno. Norman, Jno. Atterson, Mary Watts, Mary Briggs, Mich. Hurstead (or Hunstead), Edwd. Remington, twice; Jno. Hodge, 6 times; Jeff Winston, twice; Her. Gun, Jos. Lake, Sar. Argill, Tho. Flute. Cha. Thomas, Dor. Revell (or Revett), Wm. Sadler.

MR. ANTHONY LAWSON & MR. ROBERT HODGE, 1250 acs., Low. Norf. Co., going by the name of *Chester Forrest;* adj. Mr. Wm. Basnett; the salt pond branches; Edward Owld; to the Thunder bolt pine; to line of Cornix; a br. dividing this & land of William Brock; neare Swillivan's or Ward's land, &c; 27 Sept. 1680, p. 58. Trans. of 25 pers: Ben. Johnson, Debr. his wife; Deb., Jane, Eliz., 3 children; Jonas Eyres; Zambo, John, Catalina, Negroes; James (a ?) Boy, Jno. Lewis, Jos. Pitts, Hester Smith, Robt. Hodge 12 times.

THOMAS HOLLOWELL, SENR., 634 acs., Low. Norf. Co., on N. side of the W'n. br. of Eliz. Riv; upon Broad Cr; adj. land of Richard Jones, &c; 27 Sept. 1680, p. 59. 450 acs. granted him, 18 Mar. 1662; residue for trans. of: Jno. Frost 4 times.

JOHN FEREBEE, 485 acs., Low. Norf. Co., towards the head of Lyn haven Riv; adj. Henry Smith, John Bowrin, &c; 27 Sept. 1680, p. 59. Granted to Thomas Mosier 15 Mar. 1675; deserted; & now granted by order, &c. Trans. of 10 pers: Math. Atkinson, Wm. Car, Rich. Bacon, Ra. Carr, Hen. Chaun (?), Hen. Bill, Edwd. May, Wm. Wry, Steph. Arfirt (?).

WILLIAM BROCK, 1000 acs., Low. Norf. Co., Lynhaven Par., at the fresh ponds, to the S'wd. of *Rudee;* 27 Sept. 1680, p. 60. In the dam neck; adj. William Basnett; from the Thunder bolt pine; next to Dennis Dolley, &c. 350 acs. granted sd. Brock 3 Oct. 1671;

350 acs. 1 Oct. 1661; 100 acs. 25 Feb. 1664; 200 acs. for trans. of 4 pers: Robt. Bray twice; Peter & Nan Negroes.

JAMES JACKSON, 200 acs., Low. Norf. Co., N. side Daniell Tanner's Cr., adj. James Symons; 27 Sept. 1680, p. 60. Trans. of 4 pers: James Jackson twice, Tho. Twiner, Wm. Jones.

SAME. Same acreage, Co., & date; page 61. At the White oak Br., adj. Alexander Gwynn; to Gater's Cr; being part of patt. belonging to John Godfrey. Trans. of 4 pers: John Folke, Thomas Many, Jno. Mason, Edward Carpenter.

MR. JOHN WRIGHT, 84 acs., in Yorke Co. & Par; adj. Mr. Edward Mosse; 28 Sept. 1680, p. 61. Trans. of 2 pers: Edward Algood, Joseph Sutton.

JAMES BAUGHAN, 150 acs., Rappa. Co; upon the maine Sw. of Piscatoway Cr; certaine branches dividing this & land of Thomas Harper & Robt. Clements; 29 Sept. 1680, p. 61. Granted to Thomas Batts; deserted; & now due by order, &c., at James Citty, 16 Apr. 1680.

RALPH ARMESTEAD, 150 acs., Gloucester Co., Kingston Par; adj. his own land; by Dyer's Cr; &c; 29 Sept. 1680, p. 62. 48 acs. granted him 26 Sept. 1678; & 102 acs. of sw. land added, due for trans. of 2 pers.*

MARK FOSTER, 475 acs., Gloster Co., Kingston Par., on Pudding Cr; adj. Phillip Hundley; 29 Sept. 1680, p. 62. Renewal of patt. dated 13 Feb. 1661.

THOMAS CHEESMAN, 530 acs., Gloster Co., in *Milford Haven.* 29 Sept. 1680, p. 62. Near head of Lilley's Cr., adj. land of —— Forrest; by Garden Cr. marsh; the garden patch; along the maine Bay; to Rigbye's point, &c. 450 acs. granted Peter Rigby 16 Aug. 1640, & sold to Edmd. Cheesman, his father; the residue, being overplus within the bounds, due for trans. of 2 pers.*

FRANCIS JARVIS, 130 acs., Gloster Co., Kingston Par; adj. Humphrey Toy

& Mr. Christopr. Dickins; 29 Sept. 1680, p. 63. Part of 200 acs. granted Henry Prouse 20 Dec. 1667 & purchased by sd. Jarvis.

MORDECAI COOKE, 1000 acs., Glost. Co., Ware Par; within which survey is 140 acs. belonging to Mr. Tho. Colles, dec'd; 29 Sept. 1680, p. 63. Beg. on S side the path to Mr. Francis Campfeild's plantation, neer Cooke's devdt., whereon he now dwells; by Colles Br; by Price's land, to NE side of the rowling path; by North Riv. Path; along Mr. Ironmonger; & Mr. John Smith's lines, &c. Trans. of 20 pers.*

MAJOR LEWIS BURWELL, 3400 acs., Glos. Co., 29 Sept. 1680, p. 64. Beg. at Mirtle Pt. on Carter's Cr; through John Creed's old field & part of his Orchard; by Peter Garland's plantation; by Dr. Clarke; to Mrs. Bowlin's; by the path to the old quarter field; along Maj. Lawrence Smith; by maine br. of Tymber Neck Cr., to spring by end of Mixons Seller; along Minnifred's line, &c. 3200 acs. granted him 26 Apr. 1654; 200 acs. within, due for trans. of 4 pers.*

JOSEPH STYLE & JOSHUA STORY, 200 acs., New Kent Co., N. side Mattapony Riv., 2 Oct. 1680, p. 65. Adj. Mr. John Bruch (Brouch), by Axoll's Sw; &c. Surveyed by Michaell Robinson & by him never pattented, & now due for trans. of 4 pers: Geo. Street, Tho. Lanceley, Frances Style, Jos. Styles.

JOSEPH STYLE, 430 acs., New Kent Co., N. side Mattapony Riv., 2 Oct. 1680, p. 65. Adj. Mrs. Morris, Richard Davis & Robert Jones; down Tomocoricond Sw; &c. Granted to Willm. Herndon 18 Feb. 1673/4; deserted; & granted by order, &c., for trans. of 8 pers: Edwd. Fanherty, Danl. Scanland, Den. Scanland, Jno. Wood. Robt. Matchett, Jno. Tremer, Tho. Ellitt, Tho. Wingfeild.

CAPT. DANIELL JENIFER, 2500 acs., N'ampton Co., bet. Crooked Cr. & Pokomoke Riv. on Mesangoe Cr., & Chesepiack Bay; 2 Oct. 1680, p. 66.

Adj. John Renny; Willm. Chase; William Wallis', formerly survey'd for James Jolly; Charles Ratcliffe; land formerly James Taylor's; & Edward Moore, Junr; on St. George's Hummocks, or Islands; & land of John Parker. Granted to Capt. John West & Mr. Charles Scarburgh 3 Oct. 1672, & deserted; Lt. Col. John West, one of the pattentees, upon petition, did get a grant & tooke out a patt. 25 Nov. 1679; sd. Jenifer petitioning the court this day that grant of sd. West was contrary to law, prayed hee might have a grant, & that West's patt. might be vacated; & the Court having judged the patt. granted contrary to law, did make same null & void & did grant that sd. Jenifer might have a patt., &c. Trans. of 50 pers: Richard Ashton, John Murley, Tho. Rohan, John Hinton, William Man, Margarett Bowtell, Thomas Seawell, Sam. Danes, Willm. Bray, William Robertson, Susannah Hall, Willm. Palmer, Tho. Poole, Alice Wilson, John Hunlock, Tho. Turner, Rich. Lencell, Mary Baker, John Joanes, John Lynzey, John Fulke, Alexander Anvill, John Wood, Anne Penny, Tho. Williams, Symon Markett, John Compton, Grace Wakham, John Wild, Arthur Peter, Rich. Bruester. Robt. Rigbey (or Rigley), Peter Hickley, Edw. Walch, Ralph Browne, Joan Elume, Jo. Branch, Jo. Meeks. Beni. (a) Negro: Susan Balley, Rich. Carter, Robt. Percy, Willm. Chapman, John Hill, John Austin, Willm. Culson, James Blackey, John Thomas, Willm. Woodley, Tho. Roaper.

JOHN TANKARD, 2000 acs., called Comforts Quarter, Accomack Co., bet. Gingoteag, Accocomson & Pocomocke, 2 Oct. 1680, p. 66. Adj. Saml. Taylor; Col. John Stringer; Mr. Henry Smith; Capt. South. Littleton; William Benston, Capt. Danl. Jenifer; Capt. Jno. West; Tho. Nickson; Tho. Moyster (or Moyser); &c; Granted to Ambrose White 28 Sept. 1674; deserted; & granted sd. Tankard by order, &c. Trans. of 40 pers: Tho. Dicks, Ja. Hamett (or Harnett), Wm. Raylett, Jno. Standy, Ja. Throyton, Wm. Morlyn, Jane Carter, Mrs. Waad (?), Jno. Pavy, Jane Foreman, Wm. Andrews, Tho. Lockey, Eliz.

Scearle, Marm. Surbe, Jno. Lambeck, Tho. Morry (or Morris), Antho. Munday, Robt. Church, Jno. Morris, Tho. Yeoman, Ja. Corbett, Wm. Paine, Peter Turner, Symond Long, Jno. Foster, Tho. Oneall, Jno. Williams, Tho. Peterson, Jacob Johnson, Wm. Jackson, James Harris, Mary Wright, Tho. West, Jone Harty, Mich. Thompson, Isaac White; & 4 Negroes.

GREGORY BARNETT, 73 acs., New Kent Co., Blissland Par., S. side Yorke Riv., 20 Apr. 1680, p. 67. Adj. land of Col. Hamond; crossing Roccohock Path, &c. Trans. of 2 pers: Jno. Hicks, Math. Pyland.

MR. WM. EDWARDS, 590 acs., Surry Co. over against *James Citty*, 2 Oct. 1680, p. 67. 380 acs. granted to Mr. Wm. Edwards, dec'd., of sd. Co., who by will, 8 Mar. 1665, gave to his son, the abovenamed; 180 acs. purchased of Thomas Senior, son & heir of John Senior, late of same Co., adj. sd. 380 acs., & known by name of *Mathewes Mount;* 30 acs. adj., granted sd. Edwards 6 June 1678; the whole devdt. beg. at mouth of Tappahannah or Crouche's Cr., down James Riv. to Baynham's, at the mouth of a gr. Sw. &c. (*Note:* 1 name appears under this record, which is evidently the headright for the above 30 acs.) Jno. Richards.

RICHARD BOOTH, of Is. of W. Co., 465 acs., on W. side of Mr. Lawrence's Beaver Dam, a br. of the maine Blackwater; in sd. Co; neer Robt. Lawrence, Junr; 23 Apr. 1681, p. 68. Trans. of 10 pers: James Carter, Mary Symond, Jno. Wells, Peter Wright, Tho. Jackson, Jno. Waad, Tho. White, Wm. Long, Saml. Poynte (or Poynter), Jane Humphry.

JOHN MOORE (Moor), Shoemaker, of Is. of W. Co., 300 acs., in sd. Co., on brs. of Blackwater; adj. Phill Wrayford; & George Peirce's gr. pattent; &c; 23 Apr. 1681, p. 68. Trans. of 6 pers: Jone Jeffreys, Tho. Johnson, Eliz. Hardy, Jno. Manor, Henry Waters, Wm. How.

WM. POWELL, of Is. of W. Co., 400 acs., in sd. Co., on brs. of the Blackwater; adj. John Watkins; 23 Apr. 1681, p. 68. Trans. of 8 pers: Thomas Ely, Symond Keeper, Wm. Harty, Tho. Ellam, Ja. Mason, Mary Wells, Elinor Hardy, Ann Moore.

JOHN BYNEHAM, of Surry Co., 215 acs., in the Low. Par. of sd. Co; adj. Rich. Jordan, Junr; down the Mill br; neer Mr. Warren, &c; 23 Apr. 1681, p. 68. Trans. of 5 pers: Jona. Warry, John Morkeday (?), Wm. Wood, Susane Datty, And. Charway.

THOMAS HOLDER, 470 acs., Is. of W. Co., N. side of Corowaugh Sw; adj. Richd. Booth; Robt. Johnson; Col. Bridger; &c; 23 Apr. 1681, p. 69. Trans. of 10 pers: Hopkin Howell, Mardy Moner (?), Jonas Carter, Tho. Shutter, Wm. Levett, An. Avery, Jno. Otterham, Moses Williams, Morris Mackadum, Theo. Bearey (or Beardy).

PHILL. WRAYFORD, 350 acs., Is. of W. Co., on brs. of the Blackwater; beg. at Mr. Acheley's corner; adj. Col. Bridger; &c; 23 Apr. 1681, p. 69. Trans. of 7 pers: Marke Horpu (?), Jona. Moore, Tho. Norton, Wm. Darby, Pers. Eldy, Ja. ONakerby (or Makerby), Tho. Doubty.

ROBT. JOHNSON, of Is. of W. Co., 2150 acs., in sd. Co., neer the head of Corowaugh Sw., 23 Apr. 1681, p. 69. Adj. Arth. Allen, & Robt. Horneing; the *county line;* Rich. Booth; Tho. Holder; & John Bryan. Trans. of 23 pers: Alexr. Steners (or Stevers), Wm. Quick, Nico. James, Wm. Sanckey, Ja. Harris, Hen. Hunt, Jno. Blinam (?), Ed. Hopkins, Nath. Pitman, Jno. Hutson, Ja. Catch, Tho. James, Saml. Davis, Tho. Baskerfeild, Nath. Rawn, Ann Atwood, Margt. James, Jno. Farrell, Br. Clemens, —— Armestrong, Margtt. Carmell, Bl. Jarvis, Wm. Wichell, Susan Elliott, Eliz. Scott.

MR. ARTHUR JORDAN, 150 acs., Up. Par. of Surry Co; on Stoney Runn Br., neere the Roade, &c; 23 Apr. 1681, p. 70. Trans. of 3 pers: Geo. Hackey, Henry Woody, Tho. Maundy.

GEORGE PEIRCE, 2500 acs., Is. of W. Co., on brs. of the Blackwater, 23

Apr. 1681, p. 70. 2100 acs. by former patt; 400 acs. being waste land adj; on N. side the Cyprus Sw., adj. Col. Bridger, &c. 400 acs. for trans. of 8 pers: Jno. Williams, Edwd. Wilks, Antho. Ward, Mary Warker, Edwards Atly (or Acly), Tho. Moor, Toby Smith, Tho. Paine.

JOHN WATKINS, 400 acs., Is. of W. Co., on Blackwater brs; betwixt Col. Bridgers, Mr. Acheley & his own land; 23 Apr. 1681, p. 70. Trans. of 8 pers: John Paully, Tho. Joyner, Wm. Crock, Noa Lurcher, Sampson Lardy, Ja. Thomason, Sar. Ratly (or Racly), John Young.

RICHARD REYNOLDS, SENR., 380 acs. in the Low. Par., Is. of W. Co., NW side of the Lower Bay Cr; 23 Apr. 1681, p. 71. 209 acs. part of 450 acs. granted Chr. Reynolds, dec'd., 15 Sept. 1638, who gave by will to his sonn John, who bequeathed to sd. Richard; 171 acs. within the bounds; adj. Col. Arth. Smith, &c; due for trans. of 4 pers: Jno. Dale, Tho. Leese, Tho. Otly, Mary Howly.

MAJOR THO. TABERER, 400 acs., Up. Par. of Is. of W. Co., & comonly called *Bassetts Choice*, neer mouth of Pagan Cr., 23 Apr. 1681, p. 71. 150 acs. granted Mr. Peter Knight in 1640, who sold to Mr. John Bland, merchant, of London, & by Mr. Giles Bland, his sonn & Atty., conveyed to sd. Taberer 4 Dec. 1675, together with a confirmation of the sale & a relinquishment of dower by Mrs. Sar. Bland, wife & Genl. Atty. of sd. John, 6 Oct. 1679; 250 acs. adj; the whole beg. at mouth of Palentines Sw., dividing this & Mr. James Day; adj. John Mungoe; Taberer's Cr., Hutchin's Cr; the Crosse Cr; & Jones hole Cr; &c. 250 acs. for trans. of 5 pers: Tho. Mordy, Wm. Savage, Tho. Lurdin (or Lundin), Wm. Hankine, Jno. Norton, Jane Vardy, Eliz. Kerby, James Young.

GEORGE PEIRCE, 400 acs., Is. of W. Co., on brs. of Blackwater; adj. Mr. Asheley; Phill. Wrayford; & his own land; 23 Apr. 1681, p. 71. Trans. of 8 pers: Jno. Sands, Abr. Barnes, Chr.

Jones, Tho. Brown, Wm. Moon, And. North, Jno. King, Fard. Stamp.

JONATHAN ROBINSON, RICHARD THOMAS & JOHN SANDERS, 1650 acs., in Is. of W. & Nanzemond Co.'s; S. side King Saile Sw; adj. Tho. Titus & Nico. Dickson; 23 Apr. 1681, p. 72. Trans. of 33 pers: Rand. Hill, Richd. Allen, Jno. Golley (or Gollry), Math. Foster, Bar. Holland, Ja. Gilfred, Wm. Taylor, Jno. Rossier, Jos. Wigmore, Peter Stone, Wm. Mansfeild, Jno. Simons, Jno. Taylor, Ja. Perry, Marg. Curtell, An. Thorne, Ja. Evins, Jno. Bevin, Wm. Nash, Wm. Nodedge, Jno. Ford, Lan. Plumer, Robt. Relph, Cha. Alden, Phill. Pope, Jeffry Pittman, Jno. Critchell, Godf. Davis, Simon Collier, Hugh Edwards, Ja. Peacock, Tho. Blith, Wm. Nash.

JOHN ROBERTS, 1450 acs., Is. of W. Co., on head brs. of Indian Cr; 23 Apr. 1681, p. 72. 800 acs. granted Mr. Robt. Brockwell, dec'd., 22 Apr. 1670; deserted, & by order, &c., granted to Jane Stoakes, widdow, who hath intermarried with sd. Roberts, & in her name pattented 10 July 1680; 650 acs. adj., being waste; the whole beg. at Mr. Edwd. Goodwin's; adj. Symon Iron's land, in possession of Col. Jno. Lear, &c. 650 acs. for trans. of 13 pers: Wm. Snead, Jno. Forst, Sy. Wheeler, Els. Grant, Kath. Snelly, Ja. Morton, Esk. Snout (?), El. Graves, Edwd. Snuggs (or Scruggs), Mil. Cooke, Th. Southwell, Ab. Hatcher.

MOSES SPRING & AARON SPRING, 100 acs., Low. Norf. Co., at head of the W. br. of Eliz. Riv., adj. Rigglesworth's pattent; Jno. Freeman; &c; 23 Apr. 1681, p. 72. Trans. of 2 pers: Edward Fry & 1 Negro.

WILLIAM KERNEE, 100 acs., Low. Norf. Co., N. side W. br. of Eliz. Riv; adj. Robert Loveday & land of Buckmaster; & S.E. on Clarke Cr; 23 Apr. 1681, p. 73. Trans. of 2 pers: Lewis Conner, Thomas Ward.

MAJOR ANTHO. LAWSON, 762 acs., Low. Norf. Co., 23 Apr. 1681, p. 73. Beg. at Mr. George Fowler; adj.

Wm. Hancox; Chapman's land; Mr. Henry Spratt's, formerly Haskins' corner; land Lawson sold to Henry Snaile; through a Sw. to Bridge's cor; adj. land of Lambert, &c. 420 acs. part of 750 acs. granted to Thomas Bridge, & assigned to sd. Lawson; 342 acs. part of his own patt. of 490 acs.

ALEXANDER GWYN, 197 acs., Low. Norf. Co., upon ·S. side of a br. of Tanner's Cr; 23 Apr. 1681, p. 73. Adj. Mr. Porten; Mr. Egerton; & Cockrofft's lines; &c. Trans. of 4 pers: William Morgan, Samuell Houlden, Jno. Collins, Charles Griffin.

BENJAMIN HARGRAVE, 250 acs., Low. Norf. Co., 23 Apr. 1681, p. 74. Beg. by Broad Cr., cor. of Richard Hargrave, Sr; & adj. Richard Hartwell. 150 acs. part of 250 acs. granted Richard Hargrave, Sr., in Mar. 1652; renewed 18 Dec. 1662; 100 acs. for trans. of 2 pers: William Bamton, David Varding (or Vurding).

MR. JAMES KEMPE, 180 acs., Low. Norf. Co., Lynhaven Par., 23 Apr. 1681, p. 74. Adj. Jno. Kemp & Job Kemp. Trans. of 4 pers: Tho. Moore, Richard Well, John Lee, George Martin.

MR. PHILLIP HOWARD, 200 acs., Low. Norf. Co; S. side of the W. br. of Eliz. Riv., at head of Green's Cr., 23 Apr. 1681, p. 74. Beg. at a br. dividing this, land of Katherine Green. & John Whinfield; by an Oyster sheld point; adj. Thomas Green; br. dividing Johnson's & land of the Orphants of William Green; &c. Trans. of 4 pers: Wm. Andrews, Sarah Goddin, Wm. Potter, Wm. Swetman.

MORRIS LOYD, 489 A., 2 R., 10 P., Chas. City Co., 23 Apr. 1681, p. 75. 200 acs. part on Turkey Island Cr., opposite the gr. meadow; which land was pattented by William Humphrys, 18 Mar. 1662, who sould to sd. Loyd; 289 A., 2 R., 10 P., on N. side of James Riv., in Westopher Parish; adj. John Lewis; Madame Bland; & Col. Edward Hill. Trans. of 6 pers.*

MR. GEORGE BROWNING, 37 A., 2 R., 8 P., Henrico Co., in Varina Par.,

23 Apr. 1681, p. 75. Adj. Mr. Liggon; Abraham Womacke; Thomas Sheppey; Thomas Jones; &c. Trans. of 1 pers.*

EDWARD EASTHAM, 280 acs., New Kent Co., in St. Stephen's Par., 23 Apr. 1681, p. 76. Beg. near path to Maj. Morris' house; on Mantepike Jath, to Blanckett's line; neare Peter Deshasero's plantation; to Mattison's devidend; &c. Part of patt. granted to John Mattison, & sold to sd. Eastham 8 Apr. 1680.

NICHOLAS WARD, 536 acs., New Kent Co., in Stratton Major Parish, 23 Apr. 1681, p. 76. Upon Assatiams branches, according to bounds formerly made by Col. William Cleyborne; beg. in Michell's line; adj. John Durwood; Griffin Lewis, &c. Trans. of 11 pers.* "Eleven Rights recorded under Jno. Dorwoods & Nico. Wards old pattent is good to Richd. Ward & used for this pattent."

MARMADUKE MARRINTON, 250 acs., Low. Norf. Co., on a br. of the S. br. of Eliz. Riv., 23 Apr. 1681, p. 77. Granted him 20 Oct. 1661, & now new pattented.

MR. MATHEW JENNINGS, Chirurgion, 760 acs., New Kent Co., in the freshes of Yorke Riv., 23 Apr. 1681, p. 77. Adj. land Peter Ware bought of Col. William Cleyborne, dec'd; land of Mr. Edward Cardingbrooke; the E'wd. br. of Hartquake Sw; running to head of Hawkesneast Br; land of John James, dec'd., 500 acs. whereof granted him by William Berkeley, late Gov'r., 9 June 1666; & 100 acs. being the free guift of Col. William Clayborne, Senr., out of his devdt. purchased of Mr. Frederick Fortson, dec'd; 160 acs. purchased of William Henderson, 22 Feb. 1666. Trans. of 16 pers.*

WM. WRIGHT, 200 acs., Low. Norf. Co., at head of Craney Is. Cr., adj. Capt. Sibsie; 30 Sept. 1681, p. 78. Due by will of his father, Thomas Wriight, dated 10 Jan. 1654.

WILLIAM OVERTON & EVAN JONES, 4600 acs., New Kent Co., S.

side Pomunky Riv., 23 Apr. 1681, p. 78. Beg. at mouth of the falling creek. Trans. of 92 pers: Wm. Overton, Law. Hardwick, Alice Ashly, Walter Pilgrim, Jane Blackburn, Tob. Peckett, Ja. Letherland, Ann Burlison, Geo. Glasse, Tho. Britton, Davd. Boore, Eliz. Shaw, Jno. Norman, Richd. Sampson, Hen. Floyd, Tho. Neale, Ann Robinson, Wm. Fuller, Sus. Browne, Tho. Pearson, Wm. Nelson, Ann Cole, Edwd. Viccars, Jno. Coole, Edwd. Berry, Richd. White, Nath. Peirson, Barbary Evans, Jno. Jorne, Tho. Jones, Mary Dalling, Tho. Dunkeston, Wm. Beech, Mary Adkins, Ja. Ralph, Wm. Wheeler, Saml. Watts, Sar. Dunham (or Durham), Rich. Arnall, Ed. Whicker, Han. Whitaker, Jerom Creed, Richd. Wood, Bar. Raby (?), Ed. Leeds, Tho. Steele, Edmd. Gills, Hen. Wakefeild, Eliz. Howard, Rich. Walker, Jas. Farwell, Ann Coole, Ti. Peely, Jno. Fitt, Phil. Moolen, Mary Thorp, Eliz. Cooper, Rich. Lusher, Wm. Heasell, An. Burlinton, Fra. Stringer, Geo. Harper, Eliz. Martin, Richd. Franklin, Jno. Snellen, Ra. Bell, Samll. Wenn, Margtt. Green, Jno. Loote, Phil. Page, Geo. Stocken (or Storken), Marth. Tudny, Robt. Beecraft, Tho. Sims, Fra. Dissen, Wm. Burkitt, Hen. Larby, Rice Jones, Rich. Eleatherell, Dennis Marson, Robt. Griffin, Wm. Iron, Mary Gurgrave (or Gargrave), Eliz. Overton, Edmd. Foard, Jno. Richardson, Ob. Hone, Jno. Jones, Saml. Jones, Eliz. Jones, Eliz. Jones, Junr., Sar. Jones.

ROBERT JONES, 250 acs., New Kent Co., NE side of Mattapony Riv., 23 Apr. 1681, p. 79. On back of Esqr. Diggs' land; beg. by side of Weesockan Branch, &c. Trans. of 5 pers.* "Five Mr. Claibornes Rights assigned."

ELIZABETH OTEY, 91 acs., New Kent Co., S. side Yorke Riv., 23 Apr. 1681, p. 79. Beg. by the Spring Br; by James Wilsonn's; by the ridge path; by Mr. John Davis' Spring runn; &c. Said land belonging to Elizabeth Sherly, dec'd., by vertue of the will of her father, Richard Sherley, & dew Elizabeth Otey as being heire of the whole blood to said Eliz. Sherly, Junr.

CAPT. WILLIAM JONES, 495 acs., New Kent Co., Straton Major Par:, 23 Apr. 1681, p. 80. "Reputed by some to bee parsons land and graunted said Jones", &c; beg. in Arrackico Sw., above Thomas Dorby's howse; by the old feild in Mr. Sheares line; by path to Mr. Greene's quarter called the *Horne tree;* &c. Trans. of 12 pers: Nath. Barnister, Rich. Smith, Jno. Ousman, Rich. Stenton, Jno. Stinton, Jno. Hamilton, Rich. Stinton, Richd. Arkill, Edwd. Froster, Jane Ward, Robt. Peircy, Robt. Peircy.

CHARLES TURNER, 2400 acs., New Kent Co., S. side Yorke Riv. in the freshes; 23 Apr. 1681, p. 80. Beg. at Doct. William Phillipps' on S. side of Tottopotomoyes Cr., on Mr. Georg Gill's line; by br. of Chichahominy Sw., called White Oake Quarter Sw; &c. Trans. of 48 pers: Symon Floyd, Humph. Davies, Ja. Metcalfe, Richd. Read, Ja. Reeves, Mich. Singclear, Tho. Roundtree, Wm. Roundtree, Nath. Moody, Tho. Taylor, Lettice Smith, Robt. Turton, Martin Craddock, Rich. Makepeace, Nath. Eaton, Rich. Hutchins, Samll. Clements, Oliver Jolliff (?), Wm. Painter, Mich. Peasly, Tho. Bitting, Richd. Shermon, Wm. Skerrott, Peter Wilmott, Rich. Keely, Tho. Filpott, Robt. Shaw, Samll. Talbott, Jno. Winsper, Tho. Cox, Cha. Warden, Andrew Dutton, Samll. Pattle, Tho. Choakly, Kath. Blake, Danll. Jones, Mary Bates, Fra. Orgen, An. Rouse, Cha. Turner, Eliz. Moor, Robt. Blake, Danll. Meakey, Jacob Morris, Mary Dunn, Jno. Cooke, Nath. Roe, Tho. Colclough.

MAJOR ROBERT PAYTON, 1000 acs., New Kent Co., St. Stephen's Par., 23 Apr. 1681, p. 81. By order of Col. John Lewis, part of 900 acs. granted to Thomas Watkin & William Rickett, & part of a devdt. of 600 acs. adj; Beg. by sd. Rickett's path, formerly an Indian Path, adj. Mr. Brereton; cross the Ridge Path, to Tommacorcon Sw; &c. Trans. of 20 pers.*

WILLIAM SKELTON, 150 acs., Gloster Co., 23 Apr. 1681, p. 82. Part of a great devident sold to him by Tho. Dawkins. Beg. at sd. Dawkins; neer

John Whittamore's plantation; to Richard Holloway's corne field fence; to land formerly Knoxes', now Walter Kant's, surveyed by order of Col. Augustin Warner, dec'd; by the great Road; to James Reynalds; in old line of Edwd. Roe; &c. Due by deed from Tho. Dawkins & Anne his wife, 15 Oct. 1673, &c; surveyed by Robt. Beverley, Surveyor of sd. Co., 29 Oct. 1680, in the presence, of sd. Dawkins, Charles Roane, Edwd. Waller, & other neighbours, witnesses.

HENRY PRESSON, 100 acs., Eliz. City Co., upon Patchtree Damme; N. towards the long pond; 23 Apr. 1681, p. 82. Due as sonne & heire of Thomas Presson, to whom it was granted 19 Dec. 1650.

CHARLES ROAN, 700 acs., Gloster Co., upon the Dragon Swampe, 23 Apr. 1681, p. 83. Adj. James Reynalds, Thomas Dawkins, Richd. Holloway, Roger Shackleford & Mr. John Carner, formerly Mr. Samll. Patridge's land; line of sd. Dawkins, formerly Edward Roe's; & John Whittamore's plantation. Granted him 25 Sept. 1679 & by misunderstanding of Dawkins' true line, resurveyed, &c.

LYONELL MORRIS, 860 A., 20 P., Henrico Co., Varina Par., S. side Chichahominy Maine Sw., 23 Apr. 1681, p. 84. Beg. at Mr. Henry Wyatt; to Powhite Path; to Reedy Br., &c. Trans. of 18 pers: Jane Cox, Nich. Bardy, Hum. Robinson, Jno. Ellitt, Rich. Gitting (or Gilling), Jno. Spearman, Ed. Boomer, Reb. Rickason, Tho. Weare, Jos. Trowell, Alice Carles, Jno. Cole, Samll. Bugge, Isabell Rite (or Rice), Edwd. Finch, Fra. Caretope, Peter Crosse.

MR. JAMES MINGE, 571 acs., New Kent Co., 23 Apr. 1681, p. 84. Escheat land of Richard Stock; inquisition under Thomas Hall, Depty. Esch'r., 14 Sept. 1674.

CHRISTOPHR CHARLETON, 836 acs., New Kent Co., lower side of Aquitanocke Sw., on NE side of Mattapony Riv., 23 Apr. 1681, p. 85. Beg.

at Mr. Dunston; to Major Wyatt; by Mr. Homes' path; by Cheesecake Path; &c. Trans. of 17 pers: Wm. Snelling, Sar. Lyon, Wm. Seager, Mich. Frost, Geo. Ward, Tho. Swinburn, Juda Perry, Margtt. Fleet, Tho. Gwynn, Wm. Fitz William, Max Robinson, Rich. Knowles, Jno. Searjeant; 4 Negroes.

JOHN DICKESON, 263 acs., New Kent Co., S. side *Matte de quin* Cr., 23 Apr. 1681, p. 85. Beg. neare head of a br. of Chichahominy Sw., neare Capt. Underhill's line; to land of William Owen, &c. Trans. of 6 pers: Eliz. Hurly, Jno. Court, Robt. Frizell, Edwd. Taylor, Jno. Harlick, Wm. Skinner.

MRS. FRANCES IZORD, 1036 A., 5 P., Henrico Co., Varina Par; on S. side of Chichahominy maine Sw., 23 Apr. 1681, p. 86. Beg. upon Uffenum brooke; crossing Widdows runn, &c. Trans. of 21 pers: Jno. Starling, Tho. Ware, Eliz. Fisher, Tho. Meeler, Rich. Brooke, Eliz. Brock, Geo. Alees, Geo. Base, Rebecca Niccols, Fra. Little, Eliz. Rogers, Tho. Stanly, Robt. Spinlugg, Jno. Oakely, Wm. Rogers, Tho. Boeman, Nath. Jones, Nedd ——, Gunny ——, Tho. Worly; Pegg a Negro.

MR. HENRY TURNER, 712 A., 1 R., 24 P., Henrico Co., Varina Par., S. side Chichahominy Sw., 23 Apr. 1681, p. 86. Beg. at Mrs. Izard's line; to Whimsicull runn; &c. Trans. of 15 pers: Tho. Auborne, Tho. Drake, Rich. Norden, Seth. Rouch, Izraell Pye, Hum. Strange, Mary Beven, Wm. Lawrence, Cha. Hooke, Jno. Evans, Tho. Fead, An Balding, Wm. Green, Wm. Milson; Jno. a Negro.

MR. HENRY CARY, 670 acs., Warwick Co., comonly called the forrest, 23 Apr. 1681, p. 87. Beg. side of the Back Cr. runn, neare the foote bridge; upon Capt. Richard Whittaker; to the little oaken sw; parallel to land of Benjamine Brock & Mrs. Elizabeth Read; through the Briery Sw., along Mrs. Read's land purchased of James Hayly; by a sw. falling into Cleyborne's Neck; &c. 300 acs. part of 1050 acs. granted to Zachariah Cripps, & purchased by Col. Miles Cary, dec'd., father of sd. Henry; 370 acs. within the bounds, etc. Trans. of 7 pers.*

THOMAS TILLEY, 130 acs., in Low. Par. of Nanzemond; 23 Apr. 1681, p. 87. Beg. by the river side; adj. land of Edmund Welch, &c. Part of an ancient pattent of 800 acs., granted to John Parrott, of *Pigg Point,* which, after severall descents, &c., now due sd. Tilley.

JOHN CHILCOTT, 650 acs., Up. Par. of Nanzemond; neare the maine runn of Barbicue Sw., 23 Apr. 1681, p. 88. 600 acs. part granted to John Hawkins, 25 Feb. 1673/4 & by deed surrendered to sd. Chilcott; 50 acs. for trans. of: Ja. Arnott.

THOMAS DUKE, 430 acs., Up. Par. of Nanzemond; 23 Apr. 1681, p. 88. Neare Thomas Harrell; adj. Thomas Parker; the Cross Sw; & 200 acs. formerly belonging to William Wright, &c. 200 acs. granted sd. Wright 18 Mar. 1662, who conveyed to sd. Duke; 230 acs. for trans. of 5 pers: Tho. Duke, Tho. Duke, Fra. Marr, Jno. Deverett, Wm. Harring.

GEORG SPIVIE, JUNR., 400 acs., Up. Par. of Nanzemond; 23 Apr. 1681, p. 89. Beg. at Mr. James Peters on Cypresse Sw., &c. Trans. of 8 pers: Mary Harmon, Benja. Vickers, Wm. Collins, Ja. Yeomans, Sar. Harper, Richd. Porter, Jno. Annis, Jno. Allin.

THOMAS HARRELL, 150 acs., in Nanzemund, at head of Parker's Cr., 23 Apr. 1681, p. 89. Part of 250 acs. granted Silvester Baker 1 Apr. 1658; renewed in 1662, & now in possession of the abovesaid Thomas, as heire of his father, Thomas Harrell, who purchased from sd. Baker.

COL. THOMAS DEWE, 450 acs., in Uper. Par. of Nanzemund, at head of Crany Cr., issuiing out of the Southard br., 23 Apr. 1681, p. 90. Beg. in line of *Hood's neck pattent,* now Francis Parker's; to Georg Spivey, Senr., crossing the Beavor Dam, into the maine Pocoson; &c. Granted to Randall Crew 13 Nov. 1640, which, after severall surrenders & discent, is in possession of sd. Col. Dewe.

WILLIAM GATTLIN, 280 acs., in Nanzemund Up. Par., at *Kingsale;* 23 Apr. 1681, p. 90. Beg. in Adderberry pattent belonging to sd. Gattlin; adj. William Collins; neare Meadow branch; through a pocoson &c. Trans. of 6 pers: Tho. Ward, Is. (or Js.) Dyway, Wm. Williams, Edwd. Cooke, Jno. Lercock, Cha. Harris.

MATHEW SPIVIE, 86 acs., in Up. Par. of Nanzemond; 23 Apr. 1681, p. 91. Beg. behind Edward Holmes' now dwelling howse; in line of *Jericoe;* &c. Trans. of 2 pers: Eliz. Johnson, John Rickason.

RICHARD TAYLOR, 200 acs., in Up. Par. of Nanzemund, neare head of Corawaugh Sw., a little to the E'wd. of the County Line; along a gr. pocoson &c., 23 Apr. 1681, p. 91. Trans. of 4 pers: Susana ———, Geo. Floyd, Jno. Lentland (or Loutland), Mary Edwards.

THOMAS PARKER, 700 acs., Up. Par. of Nanzemund, neare head of the Southerne br., 23 Apr. 1681, p. 92. By the *County Line;* & adj. William Bush, &c. Part of 600 acs. granted to Francis Wells, 20 Oct. 1665, & surrendered to sd. Parker. 200 acs. for trans. of 4 pers: Samll. Golderott, Ja. Mashell (or Maskell), Jno. Sherly, Mathew White.

DANIELL HINDE, 150 acs., Up. Par. of Nanzemond Co., 23 Apr. 1681, p. 92. Beg. at Jeremiah Orley; to James Canneday, &c. Trans. of 3 pers: Margtt. Farlie, Eliz. Blake, Richd. Hardman.

JOHN JOHNSON, 350 acs., Nanzemond Co., at *Sommerton,* 23 Apr. 1681, p. 93. Trans. of 7 pers: Jno. Culpepeer 6 times; & Curtis Land.

THOMAS, RICHARD & FRANCIS PARKER, the 3 sons of Richard Parker, dec'd., 1420 acs., in the S. br. of Nanzemund (Riv.); beg. N. of Crany Cr. mouth, opposite Crany Island, *alias Crains Ehancing* (?) a little above Parker's Cr. mouth; to the *Crosse Sw. Pattent;* adj. John Small; to the *Hood Neck Pattent,* &c. 300 acs. granted to William Hatfeild, by 2 pattents for

200 acs. & 100 acs., dated 24 Aug. 1638; 460 acs. granted to Randall Crews 9 Sept. 1648; all of which by deeds became the proper right of sd Richard Parker, Senr; 400 acs. granted him 18 Mar. 1662; 100 acs. granted Richard, Junr., 24 Feb. 1675/6; 160 acs. being overplus; due for trans. of 4 pers: Ann Crosdell, Geo. Dobson, Wm. Handly, Tho. Northon.

JOHN NORRIS, in the right of his wife Mary, 112 acs., in the Up. Par. of Nanzemund Co., 23 Apr. 1681. p. 94. Beg. towards head of Savage's Cr; along John Garey. &c. Part of 700 acs. granted John Gary, who sould to Richard Savage, dec'd., & is now in possession of sd. Norris in right of his wife, the sole heirisse of sd. Savage.

RICHARD TAYLOR & GEORG CORPES, 400 acs., Up. Par. of Nanzemund, at *King sale*, 23 Apr. 1681, p. 95. Adj. William Gattlin & line of Adderbry pattent. &c. Trans. of 8 pers: Antho. & Jno. Warren, Robt. Owen, Leo. Strong, Jno. Brown, Alexr. Flemin, Mary Owen, Dorothy Hall.

THOMAS BOBBY, 500 acs., *"wanting three"*, James City Co., on W. side of Chichahominy River, 23 Apr. 1681, p. 95. Adj. Humphrey England & Thomas Warden. Granted to William Fry 29 Aug. 1643, & by Lydia Noell & Elizabeth Jones, by deed duely executed, 7 Aug. 1680, assigned to sd. Bobby.

NICHOLAS BUSH, 317 acs., James City Co., N. side James Riv., E. side of Chichahominy Riv., 23 Apr. 1681, p. 95. Beg. on W. side of Jones' Swamp, to *old* Mr. Knight's line: to John Merryman, &c. Granted to Nicholas Bush, his father, 6 Apr. 1655; renewed 21 Oct. 1662, & due him as heir &c.

WILLIAM BROWNE. 970 acs., James City Co., N. side Chichahominy Riv., comonly called the *Fort land*, formerly belonging to Mr. Thomas Rolfe, dec'd; 23 Apr. 1681. p. 96 Beg. at mouth of *Nanteboy Neck*: to Nantepoy runn; to William Webb's plantation; to Richard New: to a br. of Ravennett's runn; along Esqr. Diggs'

line, to Webb's Spring branch, &c. 525 acs. granted to Thomas Rolfe, gent., 8 Aug. 1653; 300 acs. granted him 25 Apr. 1656; 50 acs. 16 Oct. 1658; & 95 acs. being within the bounds alwayes accounted part of sd. *Fort land*, & due sd. Browne for trans. of 2 pers.*

COL. EDWARD HILL, 2200 acs., New Kent Co., 23 Apr. 1681, p. 96. Beg. neare N. side of the Indian Path from *Mattapony Towne* that was at the head of Piscattaway Cr. unto the *New Towne* now planted by those Indians on Mattapony River; on line of Capt. Brereton neare head of Hashwamackott Sw; &c. Granted to Col. Thomas Goodrich; deserted; & granted sd. Hill by order, &c. Trans. of 44 pers: Tho. Wilks, Edwd. Mayer, Tho. Hagard (or Hayard), Walt. Sansum, Joan Benson, Jno. Smead, Jno. Allen, Mary Morris, Richd. Harp, Jno. Hide, Robt. Jones, Mary Jones, Robt. Cloid, Tho. Bothomly, Hum. Clayden, Ja. Hall, Hul. Speed, Ja. James, Geo. Marlor, Wm. Phillips, Edwd. Robinson, Mary Young, Wm. Morley, Tho. Calling, Mary Dobson, Wm. Hollyman, Eliz. Dame, Darcas Joanes, Fra. Helle (or Hille), Joa. Reams, Roger Norton, Wm. Rogers, Tho. Penton, Jno. Lawrence, Geo. Day, Mar. Wright, Her. Margerum, Alice Fuller, Eliz. Stephens, Jno. Huson, Wm. Burnett, Alexr. Nicholson, Mar. Rookesby, Mun. Macklemore.

MR. WILLIAM SHERWOOD, 28½ acs., at the mouth of James City Island, 23 Apr. 1681 p. 97. Beg. at James Riv., at the head of a gr. slash issuing into the back river; to Block Howse Hill point; to Mr. Richard James; to a br. of Pitch & Tarr Sw; &c. Granted to John Baldwyn 4 Oct. 1656 for 15 A., 59 P., & now found to conteyne 28½ acs. Given by will of Baldwyn to John Fulcher, who sould to sd. Sherwood 22 Oct. 1677.

SAME. 1 acr. in James Citty "on which formerly stood the brick howse formerly called the Country howse which said howse and land formerly belonged to the Country, and by the Honoble., The Grand Assembly was sould and assigned to Major Richard Webster", who assigned to Richard Ricks, dec'd., & by order, &c., 17 Oct. 1660 was sould to John Phipps, whoe amongst other lands sould to John Knowles 5 Oct. 1661, who conveyed said howse & acre of land to Jonathan Newell 23 Apr. 1667, whoe dying without issue the same descended & came to David Newell, his bro. & heire at law, whoe sold *the ruins of the sd. howse* & the acre to sd. Sherwood, 6 Feb. 1677, whoe hath built a faire howse & appurtenances on the same; which acre begins at a stake before Col. White's dore, running towards his howse WNW, &c. 23 Apr. 1681, p. 98.

MAJOR FRANCIS POYTRES (Poytheres), 609 A., 2 R., 9 Po., Chas. City Co., on S. side of the Black Water, on S. side of James Riv., 28 Sept. 1681, p. 99. Running to the Nottaway Path; to the black water Spring; to the black water maine Sw; nigh Capt. Robert Lewcy; to br. that comes by Townes quarter; to line of Hercules Flood, &c. Trans. of 12 pers.*

RICHARD THREDER, 243 acs., New Kent Co., on N. side of Mattapony (Riv.), 28 Sept. 1681, p. 99. Beg. at Robert Hill; by Cow meadowe; down the Sw. to mouth of Cattaile meadowe; &c. Trans. of 5 pers.*

SAME. 258 acs., in same Co; Stratton Major Par; same date; p. 100. Adj. John Garrett & Mr. Carding Brooke, (Cardingbrooke); &c. Trans. of 5 pers.*

SAME. 195 acs; same location; same date, & page. By the Ridge Path in a pondie branch; adj. John Garrett & Rogers' corner; &c. Trans. of 4 pers.*

SAME. 242 acs., Same Co; St. Stephen's Par; same date & page. Beg. by John James' Spring, in Burche's line; adj. Abbott's line, & Bray's line, &c. Trans. of 5 pers.*

MR. JOHN SMITH, 306 acs., Chas. City Co., Bristall Par., on S. side of the Blackwater, at a place called *Worrockhocke;* 28 Sept. 1681, p. 101. Beg. in the 2nd br. of the Blackwater; along line of Hugh Lee; crossing Worrock-

hocke maine br; crossing horse path br., &c. Trans. of 6 pers.*

ISAAC BATES, 261 A., 3 F., 24 P., Chas. City Co., Wyanoake Parish, S. side James Riv., 28 Sept. 1681, p. 101. Adj. John Hobbs; nigh land of Richard Warthen, &c. Trans. of 6 pers.*

MR. ROBERT WOODSON, MR. JOHN WOODSON, MR. THOMAS EAST, MR. ROBERT CLARKE & MR. WILLIAM PORTER, 531 A., 1 R., 4 P., Henrico Co., S. side of the White Oake Sw., in Verina Par., 28 Sept. 1681, p. 102. Adj. Mr. Thomas Cocke; Madam Bland; Thomas Wailes; &c. Trans. of 11 pers.*

RICHARD HURSTLY, 94 acs., Eliz. City Co., neare head of Hampton Riv., 28 Sept. 1681, p. 102. Beg. at mouth of Baldwyn's Cr. falling into sd. river; adj. Charles Blangevile; near the road & bridge; &c. Granted to Thomas Sally 30 Nov. 1628, from it descended to Adam, his son & heire, whoe bequeathed gave to Elizabeth his wife & her heires forever, whoe devised to sd. Richard Hurstly.

THOMAS GLOSE (Gloss), 900 acs., New Kent Co., 28 Sept. 1681, p. 103. Adj. Mr. Tarleton & Robert Hughes by a forke of Chichahominy Sw., &c. Trans. of 18 pers.*

RINGING GARDNER, 350 acs., New Kent Co., St. Stephen's Par., upon branches of Tymber Br., 28 Sept. 1681, p. 103. Beg. at Tymothy Charter's on Cheesecake Path & running by sd. Carter; by Nicholas Abbott's plantation, adj. William Burford; Mr. William Richardson; &c. Trans. of 7 pers.*

JAMES CATHOME, 120 acs., Warwicke Co., 28 Sept. 1681, p. 103. Beg. at Capt. Langhorne; adj. Zachariah Chappell; &c. Trans. of 3 pers.*

MR. WILLIAM CRUMP, 1015 acs., New Kent Co., on S. side & in the narrowes of Yorke Riv., 28 Sept. 1681, p. 104. Beg. by the Mill roade neare Stephen Crump's fence; by a Spring; by Westover Path; upon land of Mr. Jones

& Jonathan Higly; to William Mosse; crossing the Ridge Path, to Col. Georg Lyddall (Liddall), by S'wd. br. of Black Cr; to Mr. Nappier, &c. 933 acs. granted to Mr. Georg Morris 19 July 1663 & conveyed to sd. Crump, 10 Nov. 1669; 82 acs. newly taken, & due for transs. of 2 pers.*

HENRY PRICE, 97 acs., Warwick Co., 28 Sept. 1681, p. 104. Beg. neare Waters' Cr. Mill dam, &c. Trans. of 2 pers.*

MR. SAMUELL RANSHAW, 136 acs., Warwick Co., 28 Sept. 1681, p. 105. Beg. in the Pyny Sw. neare James Cathom; to Harwood's. Neck reeds; &c. Trans. of 3 pers.*

WILLIAM NORWOOD, 70 acs., Warwicke Co., in pinye Sw., 28 Sept. 1681, p. 105. Adj. Mr. Samuell Ranshaw by the plaines; bv the old James Towne road heading Waters' Cr., &c. Trans. of 2 pers.*

MR. THOMAS WATKINS, 420 acs., Rappa. Co., upon a br. of Piancketancke Riv., 28 Sept. 1681, p. 105. Beg. by a path; to br. deviding this from land of John Cole, dec'd; to White Marsh, &c. Trans. of 9 pers.*

JOHN DANGERFEILD, 680 acs.. Rappa. Co., S. side the river, 28 Sept. 1681, p. 106. Beg. on Cooper's point; to Mr. Reeves; to Pickner's Cr; adj. Mr. Benjamine Goodrich; Mr. Robert Tomlin; Mr. Anthony North; downe Gilson's Cr., &c. 560 acs. granted 6 Apr. 1671; & 64 acs. 4 Apr. 1667; 60 acs. now taken, & due for trans. of 2 pers.*

MR. THOMAS MERRY, 200 acs., Warwicke Co., Denbigh Par., 28 Sept. 1681, p. 106. Beg. at Capt. John Langhorne near Kirby's pine; to Whitby's Sw; to Samuell Groves, &c. 150 acs. granted Mr. Giles Cale 26 Sept. 1667 & assigned to sd. Merry; 50 acs. found within, & due for trans. of 1 pers.*

CAPT. JOHN LANGHORNE, 1990 acs., Warwick Co., Denbigh Par., 28 Sept. 1681, p. 107. Beg. on point at mouth of Waters' Cr; down James River, to a small swash; adj. Mr. Thomas Merry; Mr. Hatton; the *Parish land;* neare Kirbie's pine; to Whitbye's Sw; adj. Robert Groves' land, held in right of the heires of —— James, dec'd; along land to bee surveyed for James Cathome; also Mr. Samuell Ranshaw's new devdt; adj. William Norwood; downe the Mill Damme, &c. 1300 acs. granted to William Whitby 2 July 1652 & by William, his son & heire, sold to sd. Langhorne, 24 Jan. 1675/6, & confirmed by order, &c., 27 Nov. 1679; 690 acs., found within, due for trans. of 14 pers.*

RICHARD GOODWIN, 100 acs., Nanzemund Co., 28 Sept. 1681, p. 108. Escheate land of William Kinsey; inquisition under William Byrd, Esch'r., &c.

WILLIAM GILES, 100 acs., Henrico Co., 28 Sept. 1681, p. 108. Escheate land of Henry Alford; inquistion under William Byrd, Esch'r., &c.

JOHN LANGSTON, 1300 acs., New Kent Co., (date blank), 1681, p. 108. Escheate land of Hannah Clarke; inquisition under Marke Warkeman, Depty. Esch'r., &c.

GEORGE NELSON, 500 acs., New Kent Co., 28 Sept. 1681, p. 109. Escheate land of John Rahan; inquisition under William Leigh, Depty. Esch'r. &c.

SAMUELL BOND, 290 acs., James City Co., (date blank), p. 109. Escheate land of Margarett Pond, *alias* Morley; inquisition under Mathew Kemp, Esch'r., &c.

MAJOR ARTHUR ALLEN, 200 acs., Surry Co., 28 Sept. 1681, p. 109. Escheate land of Edward Oliver; inquisition under William Byrd, Esch'r., &c.

BARTHOLOMEW RAMSEY, 400 acs., New Kent Co., 28 Sept. 1681, p. 110. Escheate land of John Roberts; inquisition under William Leigh, Depty. Esch'r., &c.

WILLIAM WHITE, 800 "or" 900 acs., Chas. City Co., (date blank), 1681, p. 110. Escheate land of Dorothy Drew; inquisition under Henry Hartwell, Depty. Esch'r., &c.

WILLIAM ARCHER, 600 acs., Chas. City Co., 28 Sept. 1681, p. 110. Escheate land of William Duke; inquisition under Henry Hartwell, Depty. Esch'r., &c.

SION HILL, 420 acs., Surry Co., 28 Sept. 1681, p. 111. Beg. on E. side of the Holly Bush Sw. in or neare Mr. Warren's line; to head of Hull Cabin branch; to John Clements, &c. Trans. of 9 pers.*

COL. ROBERT ABRAHALL, 1000 acs., New Kent Co., St. Stephen's Par., on both sides of Whorecock Sw., 28 Sept. 1681, p. 111. Beg. at Arnold's land; crossing the Mill Sw; to Bayly's Spring Br; &c. Granted to Thomas Peck, 8 June 1658 & purchased of his heire by Col. Thomas Swann, who sould to sd. Abrahall.

EDWIN CONWAY, 900 acs., Rappa. Co., 28 Sept. 1681, p. 111. Att Tacopacon Spring, the beg. of patt. for 5275 acs. granted Thomas Chetwood (Chitwood), & John Prosser; running to an Indian tree mentioned in their pattent; along Rappa. River & Pocoson, &c. Trans. of 18 pers: Thomas Gordon & Jane his wife, Ann Simpson, Mary Butcher, Tho. Dennis. Geo. Ware. Fran. Dellaway. Wm. Makenzie, Sary. (?) Fillips. Eliza. Karre, Wm. Karre, Elo. Nest, Fran. Brookes. Ja. Simpson, Tho. Spencer, Nicho. White; Judeth, a Negro, & a Negro man.

SAME. 1200 acs., Rappa. Co., Cittinebourne Parish, 28 Sept. 1681, p. 112. Beg. on NW side of the mouth of Prosser's Cr. out of Rappa. Riv., on the SW side, right against plantation of Mr. Anthony Savage; &c. Trans of 20 pers: Henry White Ino. Sharp, Phillip Sherwood, Ann Blake, Henry Blake, Martin Groves, Willm. Johnson, Ino. Tomson, Tho. Deame. Wm. Frith, Walker Smith, Lawrance Barker. Tho. Short, Alice Bridges, Mary Greene,

Eliza. Browne, Jo. Bridges, Sarah Smith, Lawr. Browne, Samll. Thorp, Phill. Fen, Jno. Best, Tho. Smith, Jonathan Banks.

SAME. 200 acs., Middlesex Co., 28 Sept. 1681, p. 112. Adj. the runn of the Cr. Sw; & lands of William Daniell & John Smith, dec'd., David Allison, William Downing, & Alex. Smith, by the Dragon Sw; &c. Granted to Mr. Richard Robinson, at James City 28 Sept. 1678; deserted, & granted sd. Conway by order, &c. Trans. of 4 pers: Ann Cross, Mary Lforth (?), James Martin, Marke La:feavour.

MR. JOHN LANGSTON, 1316 acs., New Kent Co., 28 Sept. 1681, p. 113. Beg. at mouth of a small sw. on S. side of Yorke Riv., dividing this from land of Sir Phillip Honywood (Honnywood); cor. to Moses Davis; neare the horse road; below the mountaines; adj. John Fleming, Thomas Glass, & James Turner. 1300 acs. granted to Mrs. Hannah Clarke, found to escheate by inquisition under Mr. Marke Warkeman, Depty. Esch'r., & granted sd. Langston by order, &c; 16 acs. due for one right whose name is entered, &c.*

THOMAS HUNT, JOHN FLOYD, EDMUND BIBBY & GEORG CLARKE, 2200 acs., called *Hog Island*, alias *Shooting Beach Is.*, in Accomack & N'ampton Co.'s; 28 Sept. 1681, p. 113. S. on inlett bet. this & Prouts Is., N. on inlett bet. this & Feakes' Is., &c. Trans. of 44 pers: Jon. Patrick, Jon. Starbush, Wm. Catton, Tho. Cadby, Jon. Baker, Matt. Morgan, Ja. Harrison, Tho. Hewes, Tho. Trotter, Elias Trotter, Richd. Bayly, Wm. Bannister, Jon. Cory, Wm. Lethermore, Grace Minter, Richd. Hyde, An. Emmerton, Hen. Patrick, Ed. Young, Jon. Cooper, Jon. Hacker, Abra. Hill, Xpher. Holt, Robt. Swet, Robt. House, Hen. Middow, Geo. Griffin, Jon. Hatherne, Phill. Sheringham, Jer. Bridges, Jo. Spring, Wm. Taylor, Jon. Parson, Danl. Walton; Bess, Wm., Mary, Jon. Antho., Jacob, Negroes.

THOMAS FENWICK, 3000 acs., Low. Norf. Co., W. upon a runn of

Ashen Sw., neare path from E. br. of Eliz. Riv. to the North River; 28 Sept. 1681, p. 114. Adj. 300 acs., part of 350 acs. granted to John Parker, Senr., 16 Mar. 1663; adj. James Whithurst; William Edwards; the Cypress Sw; land of Francis Shipp, at foot of Godfreese runn, &c. Granted sd. Parker 28 Oct. 1673; deserted; & now granted sd. Fenwick for trans. of 60 pers: Cha. (a) Scotchman, Amb. Strugwell, Eliz. Ayres, Wm. Adam, Jno. Sway, Martha Young, Susan Knewby, Jno. Shurly, Jno. Keene, Euse. Walter, Hen. Heymore, Robt. Britt, (or Brill), Kath. Steward, Tho. Husse, Jone Turley (or Turby), Tho. Pawlett, James Buckley, Wm. Norton, Symon Norton, Elinor Newton, Ed. Jenkins, Jno. Coper, Eliz. Rice, Jno. Langford, Eliz. Pallty, Edw. Williams, Sar. Jacob, Tho. Symon, Eliz. Milton, Jane Sands, Steph. Coleman, Mary Feild, Eliz. Board, —— Levall, Wm. Edly, Edwd. Bower, Ell. Heymore, Eliz. Floyd, Fran. Chees (?), James French, Tho. Luck, Edwd. Manly, Ja. Shirly, Wm. Gouch, Jane Good, Math. Mason, An. Bower, Geo. Cox, Sampson Power, Tho. Lamb, Jno. Lyn, Mary Edwards, James Norris, Thomas Williams, Hen. Roberts; Tony, Mingo, Sango, Ben, Judith Negroes.

CAPT. ADAM KEELING, 578 acs., Low. Norf. Co., in Linhaven River, 28 Sept. 1681, p. 114. 200 acs. N'ly. upon the little creek; 378 acs. by the long creek; N. to Chesapeax Bay, &c. 200 acs. sold by Adam Thorowgood to Thomas Keeling, who assigned to the abovesaid Adam, his son, 15 Aug. 1659; 378 acs. newly taken, & due for Imp. of 8 pers: Hen. Barnett, Rich. Bartho. (Bartholomew ?), Eliz. Midleton, Tho. Legg, James Jones; Fra. Dom., Mary Negroes.

ROBERT HARMON, 4920 acs., New Kent Co., S. side of Totopotomoyes Cr., 28 Sept. 1681, p. 115. Beg. at land of John Davies; by br. of Mattadequm; by a br. of Chichahominy Sw; adj. Doctor William Phillips; Mr. John Page; & John Davies. 3000 acs. granted Georg Gill 21 Sept. 1674, who assigned to sd. Harmon 28 May 1681; 1920 acs. for trans. of 39 pers: Jon. Beene, Wm.

Jones, Wm. Williams, Wm. Audwell (or Andwell), Robt. Redmore, Anne Bartholomew, John Cotton, Rich. Jones, Samll. Long, Eliz. Archer, Tho. Wiilliams, Mary Ponton (or Pouton), Nich. Myall, Tho. Tucker, Wm. Newell, Robt. Foster, Jon. Hasse, Mary Walsor, Jno. Anselle, Mary Barnet, Mary Collen, Willi. Williams, James Canaday, Tho. Heming, Jon. Fowler, Wm. Norman, Wm. Showell, Barth. Themyer (or Hemyer ?), Justinian Hill, Nich. Lancaster, Cornelius Carvell, James Rayman, Rich. Showell, Tho. Armstrong, Grace Wilson, Jon. Wilson, Jon. Morgan, Sarah Steward, Rich. Crane, Eliz. Dane.

MR. JOHN BUCKNER, 300 acs., Gloster Co., Petsoe Parish; 28 Sept. 1681, p. 115. Adj. & betwixt land pattented by Major John Smith 1 Apr. 1665 on the back of *Purton* old devidend & land of Mr. Francis Ironmonger, (on ?) Totapatomie Sw; & 300 acs. granted to Mrs. Ann Bernard 2 July 1652; beg. at sd. Smith, dec'd., on NW side of Goodluck branch; to Totapotomie Cr; &c. Trans. of 6 pers.*

ROBERT BEVERLY, 300 acs., Middlesex Co., 28 Sept. 1681, p. 116. Betwixt lands of Daniell Long, Henry Nicholls, & Thomas Cordwell; & the Bryery Br; & adj. Mr. Linsey's line. Granted to Christopher Robinson, & lost for want of seating; now granted, &c. Trans. of 6 pers.*

JOHN SYMONS, 377 acs., in W. br. of Nanzemund (Riv.), 28 Sept. 1681, p. 116. Beg. at James Colding; to a br. deviding this & land of Stephen Dorden; &c. 200 acs. granted to Georg Ludloe in a patt. for 500 acs., dated last of August 1638, which, after severall surrenders, descended to sd. Symons; 177 acs. granted to the father John Symons the elder, 30 Oct. 1662.

JAMES COLDING, 168 acs., in the W. br. of Nanzemund Riv., 28 Sept. 1681, p. 117. Running down the Sw. to a gr. white oak against John Wain's howse, &c. 150 acs. being part of 500 acs. granted Mr. Georg Ludlow, Merchant, the last of Aug. 1638, which, after severall conveyances & descents is now in fee belonging to sd. Colding; 18 acs. being marsh, due for trans. of 1 pers.*

MR. WILLIAM BURTON, of Accomack Co., 500 acs., being a Cedar Island on the seaboard side, in sd. Co; on S. on end of a ridge neare mouth of Codd Cr; 28 Sept. 1681, p. 117. Trans. of 70 pers: John How, Joan Resha, Elizabeth Brown, Martha Short, George Davis, Tho. Jenkins, Francis Crosson, Griffith Evans, Dayved Even (?), Fran. Smith.

ROBERT SPENCER, 650 acs., New Kent Co; N. side of Mattapony Riv., 28 Sept. 1681, p. 118. Beg. a mile from sd. river, backing a piney neck, part of a gr. devidend of Edward Diggs, Esqr; &c. Granted to William Goffe 22 July 1659, assigned to John Maddison, who assigned to Martha Goffe & by said Martha, John, & William deserted; by order dated 22 Sept. 1662, patt. thereon grounded graunted to John Prosser; deserted; & sold to sd. Spencer, whoe finding the same not duely seated, according to law, by any of sd. persons, on 3rd Dec. 1679, after hee had in his owne right for many yeares made his dwellinig plantation & lived thereon, entered his claim &c; & now due unto himi by making choice thereof & seating thereon as deserted land; &c. Trans. of 13 pers: Tho. Mason, Wm. Jones, Edwd. Newby (or Newly), Jño. Long, Mary Evan, Eliz. Thomas, Wm. Awbery, Tho. Elliot, Fra. Hunt, Eliz. Strong, Sus. Whally, Jos. Ewe, Adam Johnson.

WM. COX, 551 acs., New Kent Co; upon branches of Skimmeno, 20 Apr. 1682, p. 118. Beg. on W. side of a runn in Mr. Martin Baker's line; to the gr. swamp; to Collins' runn; &c. 334 acs. part purchased by Henery Goodgame, dec'd., of Wm. Pullam, & left to his son, Ephraim Goodgame. who sould to sd. Cox; 217 acs. for trans. of 5 pers: Thomas Webster, Elizabeth Blacksley, Edward Fellows, Joseph Carpenter, Owen Evans.

ROBERT BIRD, 234 acs., New Kent Co., 20 Apr. 1682, p. 119. Neer

Holmes' plantation. Trans. of 5 pers: Geo. Harland, Richd. Hawkins, Edwd. Clement, Mary Gardner, Sarah Killick.

CAPT. HENRY APPLEWHAITE, 1260 acs., Low. Par. of Is. of Wight Co., on the Blackwater branches; 20 Apr. 1682, p. 119. Beg. at George Peirce; adj. Col. Joseph Bridger; neer Burgh's Sw; on land of John Williams; &c. Trans. of 26 pers: John Macksell, Wm. Vincent, Wm. Herbert, Nicholas Wilson, Mary Burlington, Francis Turley, James Tiddin, David Spencer, Mary Lawrence, Ann Hamond, Erasmus Green, Henry Tooker, Matt. Culling, Elinor Cooper, Thomas Thursell. "Eleven due by Clerks Certificate."

THOMAS GRANT (Graunt), 111 acs., Low. Norf. Co., at head of Tanner's Cr., 20 Apr. 1682, p. 119. Beg. at Samuel Roberts; on Peters' line; to head of Bogg's br; &c. Trans. of 3 pers: Nora Bryant, Riichard Hudson, Benjamin Pickworth.

CAPT. MARTIN PALMER, 1500 acs., New Kent Co., in *Ramoncock Neck;* being part of the surplus within bounds of Major Joseph Croshaw's dividend; 20 Apr. 1682, p. 120. Beg. at sd. Croshaw's on N. side of Bull Sw., the maine br. of Hollowing Point Cr; crossing same to main sw. of Cohoak Cr; to land of John Hume; by road to Mr. Woodward; to Capt. Roger Mallory; &c. Granted to Mr. George Chapman, who, with Abigail his wife, sold to sd. Palmer.

MR. THOMAS LOW, 674 acs., Chas. City Co., S. side of Appamattux Riv., Bristoll Par., at a place called *Moncusenecke;* 20 Apr. 1682, p. 120. Crossing the 1st & 2nd branch; Persimond br; to Moncusenecke main Sw; &c. Trans. of 14 pers: Samll. Fluid (or Floid), Walter Piggett, Thomas Taylor. Richd. Cooke, Thomas Pritchett, John Marshall, Wm. Kerby, John West, Thomas Chappell, Wm. Stalyard, John Hardway, Richard Younge, Peter Moyle, George Knighton.

MR. ROBERT KAE, 300 acs., Low. Par. of. Surry Co; on E. side of the 3rd

Sw. of the main Blackwater; 20 Apr. 1682, p. 120. Beg. in Mr. Robert Flake's line; to Arthur Allen; &c. Trans. of 6 pers: John Whitaker, Daniel Rowland, James Bird, Margarett Hutchins, James Edwards, Hannah Erre.

CAPT. JACOB LUMKIN (Lumpkin), 565 acs., New Kent Co., St. Stephen's Par., on N. side of Mattapony Riv., 20 Apr. 1682, p. 121. Beg. in the Spring Br; by br. of Hellicon Sw; to Col. William Claibourne's line of *Bestland* dividend; by the Horse Path; to forke of Tussuckey Br; &c. 115 acs. purchased of Stephen Benbridge, who purchased of Col. William Claibourne, Junr; 450 acs. for trans. of 9 pers: Dorothy Bankes, Richard Hawkins, Rose Aldridge, John Knight, Mary Trott, Jos. Townly, Giles Harman, Thomas Parker, Thomas Porter.

MR. MARKE WARKEMAN, 918 acs., called *Pampertike*, New Kent Co., N. side Pamunkey Riv., in *Pamunkey Neck;* 20 Apr. 1682, p. 121. Beg. at mouth of Goddin's (Goodin's) Cr. or Sw. below Goddin's Island; up the Cr. about 1½ mi; to head of a br. of Pampertike Cr; to Mr. William Woodward; &c. Purchased by one —— Booth of the Queen of Pamunkey, after whose decease the land was granted to his sonn, Robert Booth, by order of Assembly, 25 Apr. 1679, & by him assigned to sd. Warkeman.

MR. EDWARD MOSS (Mosse), 759 acs., in theCo. & Parish of Yorke, 20 Apr. 1682, p. 122. Beg. on NE side of Cheesman's Cr., parting this from land of Argoll Blackstone; neer Esqr. Wormeley's old line; to John Wright; along Jackson's line; &c. 400 acs. granted Mr. John Chew, 18 Feb. 1638; 115 acs. granted sd. Mosse 20 Nov. 1678; 244 acs. for trans. of 5 pers: Ephraim Adams, Edward Gill, Robert Lammerton, Robt. Traveller, Teague Dawling.

JOSHUA MEATCHAM, 292 acs., Chas. City Co., N. side of the Blackwater; Westover Parish; 20 Apr. 1682, p. 122. Adj. Mr. James Wallis; by the gr. meadow; along Capt. Busbie; &c.

Trans. of 6 pers: Wm. Tatersone, Richd. Owneley, Tho. Stevens, John Edloe, Katherine ——, Mary Ellis.

ROBERT TIRRELL, 170 acs., New Kent Co., St. Stephen's Par., N. side of Mattapony Riv., 20 Apr. 1682, p. 122. Beg. at Major Wm. Wyatt; by an old Tobacco house; by Ford's line to a br. of Mastecoque Cr; to John Keyes line; by Indian Grave Br; crossing the King's Road, &c. Trans. of 4 pers: Robert Stanton, Wm. Stanton, James Lina, Tho. Shedwell.

MR. HENERY WYATT, 649 acs., New Kent Co., 20 Apr. 1682, p. 123. Beg. at mouth of a br. of Chickahominy maine Sw; upon land of Edmond Grosse; to W. side Elder Sw; by Piny Island Slash, &c. Trans. of 13 pers: John Medos, Antho. Rocke, Wm. Garner, Wm. Tarton, Jean Moor, Rice Hues, Edwd. Bumpos, Charles Scott, Robt. Steward, Wm. Smart, Eliz. Round, Robt. Burrell, Martin Middleton.

MR. THOMAS HARWOOD & THOMAS PLATT, 256 acs., Yorke Co., New Poquoson Par., 20 Apr. 1682, p. 123. On E. side of Denbigh Path, neer Robert Calvert; adj. Mr. Miles Carey, &c. Trans. of 6 pers: Susanna Howre, Tho. Slater, Mathew Late, Mary Lear, Eliz. Plackett, Richd. Johnson.

CAPT. JOHN WALLOP, *alias,* WADLOW, 2350 acs., Accomack Co., called *Wallop's Neck*, on S. & E. sides of Gingoteag Cr., 20 Apr. 1682, p. 123. Running neer head of the Cedar Br; downe the maine channell, towards Gingoteag Inlett; ot the narrows which goes into the *Flatts against Percimons Esson,* (?), &c. Part of 3050 acs. granted him 20 Apr. 1670.

WM. EDMONDS & JOHN WILLIAMS, 888 A., 2 R., 16 P., Chas. City Co., S. side James Riv., in Jordans Parish; 20 Apr. 1682, p. 124. Beg. at Major Povtries on the reedy br; to Bland's Neck; through the Round Pond; to the delightfull meadow; &c. Trans. of 18 pers: Fra. Linsley, Gilbert Hay, Geo. Burge, Wm. Turpin, Wm. Brown, Thomas Manning, Nicho. Whitmore,

Priscilla Chenye, Susanna Bridge, James Blamore, Xpher Addison, John Allett, Jean Booth, Sander Hempsteed, Rice Pritchett, Ellinor Madard, Mary Herbert, Mary Phillips.

WILLIAM PEAWDE, 1000 acs., James City Co., on SW side of Chickohominy Riv., 20 Apr. 1682, p. 124. Beg. in the mouth of *Mattahancks Necke;* to Webb's Run; to Nickedewans Path; along Toakins Br; to Mr. Ham's line; to Nickedewas Run; to a small Indian Feild in the bottom of *Muskout,* &c. Due in right of survivorship, sd. land having been granted sd. Peawde & George Sanders, 11 Feb. 1663, &c.

JOHN GILES, 1100 acs., Is. of Wight Co., or Nanzemond Co., upon Black Water; toward head of Chawen or Chawanock River; includ. an old Indian Feild called *Mountsack;* 20 Apr. 1682, p. 125. Granted to Thomas Woodward, Junr., 17 Apr. 1667; deserted; & granted sd. Giles by order, &c., & due for trans. of 22 pers: John Cordwell, Thomas Hobbs, Mary Bridges, James Wilson, Martha Malleyes, Nicholas Holmes, Priscilla Morgan, Jane Darby, Marke Tomlyn; 13 due, by 2 Clerkes certificates, whose names are not mentioned.

EVAN JONES, 148 acs., New Kent Co., S. side of Warranny Sw., 20 Apr. 1682, p. 125. SW of Mr. Hancock's land; on a br. of Ware Cr., & adj. Mr. Martin Baker & Coll. Wm. Hockaday. Trans. of 3 pers.* 3 Rights due, &c.

MR. FRANCIS GOWER, 420 acs., Rappa. Co., S. side Rappa. River; on SE side of Hoskins Cr., 20 Apr. 1682, p. 125. Beg. below Richard Gregorie's (Gregory) landing; adj. Mr. Thomas Games (or Gaines) below his house, by the Creek Marsh, &c. 140 acs. granted Mr. James Williamson 14 Nov. 1653; 280 acs. newly taken & due him for trans. of 6 pers: Alice Woolfe, William Reyton, Mary Hudson, An Barklett, William James, John Codon.

ROBERT HUGHES, 855 acs., New Kent Co., 20 Apr. 1682, p. 126. On N. side of the N. br. of Chickahominy Riv; down the br. dividing this from Col. Thomas Claibourne, &c. Trans. of 18 pers: Rees Hughes, Junr., Benj. Stroad, John Hiccoces (?), William Norris, Richd. White, Eliz. Hughes, John Kistell, George Swallow, Sarah Butterfeild, Edwd. Pittiway, James Hambleton, John Anderson, John Strong, Katherine Hyett, Richd. Thomas, Richd. Milton, Anthony Grant, Richd. Lumly.

MR. JOHN RICHARDS, 1676 acs., New Kent Co., St. Stephen's Par., 20 Apr. 1682, p. 126. Beg. at Bestland, nigh head of Robins' Br; on N. side of Contrary Br; along Edmond Bines; Mr. William Shirley; & Sir Grey Skipwith; up the Dragon Sw; to Col. Claibourne, &c. 900 acs. granted to George Morris & John Pigg, 24 June 1662; 776 acs. newly taken, & due for trans. of 16 pers: Alexdr. Day, Wm. Grigg, Wm. Hall, Xpher. Persons, Alice Andrews, Ann Ayres, Edward Traylor, Wm. Clarke, Nicholas Jarsey, William Spiltmore, Clement Bragg, John Baker, Roger Bradshaw, Jean Macana, Wm. Thestill; & Black Nan.

HUGH LAWRENCE, 90 acs., New Kent Co., St. Stephen's Par., 20 Apr. 1682, p. 127. Beg. at Mr. Gabriel Hill's cor., by Exoll's Sw; by path to Mr. John Richards, &c. Trans. of 2 pers: John Ridall, John Sanders.

MATTHEW KEMP, ESQR., 450 acs., Middlesex Co., 20 Apr. 1682, p. 127. Being escheat land of Elizabeth Bonner, dec'd; inquisition under Matthew Kemp, Sub-Escheator, &c; now granted by order, &c.

COL. WILLIAM BIRD, 4250 acs., Henrico Co., 20 Apr. 1682, p. 127. Being land which John Zouch, Esqr., died seized of & which was found to escheat, as by inquisition under William Bird, Esqr., Esch'r. &c. Granted to Abell Gower, who assigned to sd. Bird.

CAPT. BRYAN SMITH, 200 acs., New Kent Co., 20 Apr. 1682, p. 127. Land which William Cooke died seized of & which was found to escheat, as by iinquisition under William Leigh, Depty. Esch'r., &c.

JOHN KEEN, 270 acs., New Kent Co., 20 Apr. 1682, p. 128. Land which Margarett Basby, *alias* Gingell, died seized of & which was found to escheat as by inquisition under William Leigh, &c.

ISRAEL SHEPHARD, 350 acs., Nanzemond Co., 20 Apr. 1682, p. 128. Land which Nicholas Akerland died seized of & which was found to escheat, as by inquisition under John Lear, Depty. Esch'r. Granted to Roger Jones, who assigned to sd. Shephard.

WILLIAM HOLDERBY, 200 acs., New Kent Co., 20 Apr. 1682, p. 128. Land which Edward Markham died seized of & which was found to escheat as by inquisition under William Leigh, Depty. Esch'r. &c.

JOHN MORRIS, 750 acs., New Kent Co., 20 Apr. 1682, p. 128. Land which Mary Horsendine, *alias* Morris, died seized of & which was found to escheat, as by inquisition, under William Leigh, Depty. Esch'r., &c.

ANTHONY ARMSTEAD, Gent., 50 acs., Elizabeth City Co., 20 Apr. 1682, p. 129. Part of 150 acs. which John Powell died seized of & which was found to escheat, as by inquisition under Matthew Kemp, Esqr., Esch'r. &c.

JOHN TILLEY, 50 acs., Eliz. City Co., 20 Apr. 1682, p. 129. Part of 150 acs. which John Powell died seized of & which was found, &c. (As above.)

JOHN SYMONS, 50 acs., Eliz. City Co., 20 Apr. 1682, p. 129. Part of 150 acs. which John Powell died seized of & which was found, &c. (As above.)

JOHN CUSTIS, ESQR., 850 acs., Accomack Co., att Anduis (?), 20 Apr. 1682, p. 129. Land which Devourax Browne, Gent., died seized of, being part of 8150 acs., which was found to escheat, by inquisition under Col. John Stringer, Esch'r. &c.

MAJOR FRANCIS POYTRIES, 750 acs., Chas. City Co., 20 Apr. 1682, p.

130. Land which Thomas Morgan died seized of & which was found to escheat, by inquisition under Henery Hartwell, Depty. Esch'r., &c.

CAPT. JAMES BISSE, 103 acs., Chas. City Co., Wyanoke Parish; N. side of James Riv., 20 Apr. 1682, p. 130. Along the meadow belonging to Kittewan Cr; to the back landing; to the lower codd; to Persimond Island Sw; deviding sd. Bisse & Mr. James Lawrence. 60 acs. bought by Col. Thomas Stegg of Ferdinando Ashton, & sold to Andrew Meldram, who sould to sd. Bisse; 43 acs. for transs. of: Richard Armson.

HENERY COPELAND, 400 acs., Up. Par. of Nanzemond Co., neer *Sommerton*, 20 Apr. 1682, p. 130. Adj. his father's line, near a br. of the Indian Grave Sw., & adj. William Moore. Trans. of 8 pers: Henery Copeland Junr., Thomas Giles, Richard Cocke, John King, Morgan Fluellin, Peter "From bamberry", John Hanner, Mary Cromwell.

WILLIAM BOALDWINNE, 275 acs., Low. Par. of Surry Co., about the heads of the branches of the 1st br. of the main Black Water; 20 Apr. 1682, p. 131. Beg. att Arthur Davies (Davis) cor. into a Poquoson towards Capt. Baker; near Mr. George Hardie; to Capt. England; &c. Surveyed for Capt. John Gutheridge, who assigned to sd. Boaldwine, & due for trans. of 6 pers: John Arkells, Edward Keeling, Nicholas Downman, Morgan Bryan, Mary Earle; Joan a Negro.

JOHN ALFORD, WM. STONE & WM. MILLINGTON, 410 acs., New Kent Co., S. side Yorke Riv., 20 Apr. 1682, p. 131. Beg. Col. Hammon, in the slashes of *Coskockahick*; to Mr. Napier, below the mountaines, in sight of Wm. Peaslie's plantation; &c. Trans. of 9 pers: Tho. Murdah, Sanders Elly, Tho. Horton, Judith Jones, Frances Mandy, Hen. Browne, Tho. Hart, Tho. Harding, Wm. Kendal.

MATTHEW MORGAN, 202 acs., New Kent Co., S. side Yorke Riv., on branches of Skimmino; 20 Apr. 1682, p. ... Beg. in a br. deviding part of this from land of Moses Davies; to forke of a sw. deviding this & land of Wm. Cox; to the old path near the Mill, &c. 136 acs. due him by grant of an escheat, 24 Feb. 1675; the residue, being overplus, due for trans. of 2 pers: Tho. Walker, Jon. Drinkwater.

MR. ARGOLL BLACKSTONE, 389 acs., in the Co. & Par. of Yorke; 20 Apr. 1682, p. 132. Beg. on N. side of Cheeseman's Cr. 350 acs. granted to Mr. Jon. Chew, 18 Feb. 1638 & made over to sd. Blackstone; 39 acs. for trans. of: Wm. Harris.

JOHN ASHER, 226 acs., New Kent Co., 20 Apr. 1682, p. 132. Beg. at David Crafford upon N. branches of Chickahominy Sw; to John Dickeson; to Capt. Underhill; by run of Powhitt Sw., &c. Trans. of 5 pers: Wm. Alsop, Richd. Darall, Edwad. Broxam, Jon. Shepheard, George Binks (or Birks).

WILLIAM MAYO, of Is. of W. Co., 220 acs., in sd. Co., on Chewan River; 20 Apr. 1682, p. 132. Beg. at Thomas Mann's cor., to Giles Linscott; &c. Trans. of 5 pers: Wm. Oldis, Damaris Oldis, Alexander Fleming, John Barnes, Wm. Freeman.

JOHN BRYAN, of Nanzemond Co., 470 acs., on head brs. of the S. br. of Nanzemond (Riv.), 20 Apr. 1682, p. 133. Beg. near Robert Johnson; & Thomas Mason; &c. 150 acs. part of 350 acs. granted him 8 Oct. 1672; the remainder, being wast land adj., due for trans. of 7 pers: Jos. Vincent, Tho. Hunt, Bryan Ronorke, Jon. Sugar, Wm. Goodman, And. Browne, Dennis Reathdon.

HODGES COUNCILL, of Is. of W. Co., 320 acs., in sd. Co., on Chewan River, 20 Apr. 1682, p. 133. Beg. at Thomas Mann's cor; adj. Joseph Vick, &c. Trans. of 7 pers.* Note: Rights due by certificate from the Clerk of Is. of Wight, whose names are not mentioned.

THOMAS WALER, 420 acs., in Low. Par. of Surry Co., on the Black Water

... Aug. 1682, p. 133. Beg. at Allen Warren, by Mr. Robert Coufeild (or Cnfeild); to John Binham; &c. Trans. of 9 pers: Tho. Taylor, Rebecca Jones, Ann Cooke, James Jones, Mary Macdanell, Tho. Cooke, Lawrence Derrick, Wm. Sneath, John Frost.

MR. JOHN BASHEAR, 235 acs., Surry Co., near head of Up. Chipoakes Cr., 20 Apr. 1682, p. 134. Part of 900 acs. granted Mr. Edward Travis & —— Johnson, & this part by Johnson sold to Mr. George Steevens, from whom it descended to sd. Brashear, as marrying Mary, dau. of Col. Robert Pitt & heir at law to sd. Steevens. Sd. land adj. the orphans of Richd. Rogers, by Burchen Sw. Cr; Mr. Benjamin Harrison's line; to Richard Hide; &c.

PETER VASSER, of Is. of W. Co., 233 acs., in sd. Co., on E. side of the 3rd Sw. of the main Black Water; 20 Apr. 1682, p. 134. Adj. William Richardson; John Clark, &c. 200 acs. granted Mr. Danll. Boucher 24 May 1664 & conveyed to sd. Vasser 10 Dec. 1666; residue being waste adj., due for trans. of: Symon Wheeler.

WM. MURFEY, 200 acs., 20 Apr. 1682, p. 135. Betwixt Jacob Dardon & Robert Hookes, a mi. from the maine sw. of the W. br. of Nanzemond; by Francis Bridle, bet. William Smelly & old Powell; near Edward Perkins, &c. Trans. of 4 pers: James Osborne, Thomas Parren, Vincent Bradshaw, Richd. Haines.

JOHN MACLOODE, 270 acs., Low. Par. of Surry Co., on W. side of the 3rd Sw. of the maine Black Water; 20 Apr. 1682, p. 135. Betwixt Nicholas Sessum & Mr. Richard Jordan, Senr; adj. Phillip Hainsford, Charles Williams; Richard Jordan, Junr; & John Binham; &c. Trans. of 6 pers: Elinor Grant, Katherine Snelley, James Morton, Eze. Street, Eliz. Graves, Edwd. Sugg.

CHARLES SAVAGE, 570 acs., Low. Par. of Surry Co., on Black Water brs., 20 Apr. 1682, p. 136. Betwixt Major Marriot's land, in possession of Mr.

Samll. Thompson, & Nicho. Sessums'
land; &c. Trans. of 12 pers: Miles
Cooke, Tristram Southel, Abell Hatcher,
Margt. Wms. (Williams), Eliz. Scott,
Margery Goffe, Danll. Sweet, Tho.
Boytes (or Baytes), Orrel Mechanister,
Phillis Gary, Richd. Lane, Tho. Page.

THO. POWELL, 480 acs., Is. of W.
Co., on brs. of the W. br. of Nanzemond (Riv.), 20 Apr. 1682, p. 136.
400 acs. being ½ of patt. to Wm. Hunt,
14 Dec. 1653, & conveyed to sd. Powell
13 Feb. in the same year; betwixt sd.
Powell & Richd. Hutchins; adj. Wm.
Smelly; & Mrs. Denson, &c. 80 acs.,
being waste adj., due for trans. of 2
pers: Wm. Dawson, Richd. Greenhil.

JACOB DARDON, 435 acs., Is. of
W. Co., on SW side of the main Sw.
of the W. br. of Nanzemond (Riv.);
20 Apr. 1682, p. 137. 200 acs. being
½ of patt. of Robert Hookes & Wm.
Bream, which sd. Bream conveyed to
Stephen Dardon, late of sd. Co., who,
by will dated 19 Feb. 1679, bequeathed
to sd. Jacob. The residue being de-
serted by sd. Stephen, was granted sd.
Jacob by order, &c; adj. Mr. John
Nevell (or Neuell); Francis Bridle &
Robert Hooke. Trans. of 5 pers:
Alexander Cammell, Peter Colgrave,
John Haman, Ann Sharah, Peter Sturkey
(or Starkey).

ROBERT SAVAGE, 265 acs; (Co.
not given); 20 Apr. 1682, p. 137. Near
land of Charles Savage; beg. at Mr.
Samll. Thompson, &c. Trans. of 6 pers:
Roger Dines, John Foster, Richd. Broad,
Gilbert Messenger, Joshua Hinde, David
Johnson.

SAMUELL SIGNELL, 455 acs., York
Co., New Poquoson Par. in the Oake
Sw., 20 Apr. 1682, p. 138. Beg. near
the watering place att head of the
Damms; &c. 250 acs. granted to Wm.
Hays, Gent., 1 Sept. 1658 & due sd.
Signell as marrying sd. Hayes' daugh-
ter; 205 acs. for trans. of 5 pers:
Danll. O'Graham, Teage O'fahee, Ann
Spilman, Daniel Curtis, Richard Arm-
strong.

JOHN WANPOOLE, 216 acs., Chas.
City Co., 20 Apr. 1682, p. 138. On N.
side of the W. br. of Up. Chipoakes
Cr; adj. Wm. Heath. Surveyed for
Thomas Steevens, & due sd. Wanpoole
in right of his wife Sarah, dau. of sd.
Steevens, as likewise for trans. of 5
pers: An Wilcocks, Mary Bankes, Han-
nah Hemstead, Orelius Scriven (or
Scriver), John Thomas.

MR. WM. BUSH, 390 acs., Is. of W.
Co., on heads of brs. of Currawaugh
Sw., 20 Apr. 1682, p. 139. Beg. at
Robert Johnson in the County line; by
Thomas Mann, &c. Imp. of 8 pers:
Arthur Taylor, Tho. Lock, James Petter-
son, Phill. Jones, Danll. Bayly, Richd.
Emerson, Samll. Dunston, John Simpson.

ROBT. COOPER, 200 acs., Low.
Norf. Co., 20 Apr. 1682, p. 139. Which
land Francis Skipper died seized of &
was found to escheat, by inquisition
under Wm. Randolph, Depty. Esch'r.,
&c.

CAPT. WM. ROBINSON, all that
tract of land on the E. br. of Eliz.
River, in Low. Norf. Co., called Fausitt's
land, which Matthew Fausitt died
seized of, & which was found to escheat
as by inquisition under Wm. Randolph,
Depty. Esch'r., &c., & granted sd.
Robinson by order, &c. 20 Apr. 1682,
p. 139.

HENERY CREECH, 200 acs., Low.
Norf. Co., 20 Apr. 1682, p. 140.
Escheated from John Lownes, dec'd., by
inquisition under William Randolph,
Depty. Esch'r., &c.

JOHN JOLLIFFE, 867 acs., Low.
Norf. Co., at head of the Broad Cr., of
the W. br. of Eliz. Riv., 20 Apr. 1682,
p. 140. Adj. Thomas Cottle; James
Murray; &c. 267 acs. granted him 18
Oct. 1664; 200 acs. granted Jno. Jolliffe,
Senr. 13 Jan. 1661; 400 acs. for trans.
of 8 pers: Jno. May, Tho. Nutt, Her-
bert Spring, James Coppin, Andrew
Street, Rich. Heath, Tho. Dulana, James
Aust.

PATRICK WHITE, 323 acs., Low.
Norf. Co., at N. end of Knot's Island,

in *Corretuck,* 20 Apr. 1682, p. 140. Trans. of 7 pers: Jno. Ferrill, Richard Grant (or Grunt), Augustine Frowne, Michael Jones, Jno. Salmon, Bacerius (?) Chappell, Alice Stafford.

RICHARD WHICKER, 300 acs. Low. Norf. Co., on Knott's Is., in *Corretuck,* 20 Apr. 1682, p. 141. Adj. Patrick White; S. along the bay; to land of John Legatt, &c. Trans. of 6 pers: Herbert Jones, Cornelius Okely, Jno. Portlock, Wm. Smith, Alice Baker; Jane a servt. mayd.

RACHEL CORNELIUS, 300 acs., Low. Norf. Co., in Knot's Is., in *Corretuck,* 20 Apr. 1682, p. 141. Adj. William White; Jno. Vandemore; &c. Trans. of 6 pers: Richard Lee, James (or Jane) Davison. Elizab. Scott, Michaell Scott, Jno. Hunter, Jno. Trindall (or Findall).

MR. WILLIAM WHITE, 300 acs., Low. Norf. Co., in Knot's Is., in *Corretuck;* being his seated plantation; 20 Apr. 1682, p. 141. Adj. Rachel Cornelius. Trans. of 6 pers: Katherine Helter, Wm. O'Naught, Tho. Cope, Wm. Blaides, Hen. Hunt, Blandman Risder.

MR. PATRICK WHITE, 900 acs., Low. Norf. Co., at the S'wd. end of Knot's Island, in *Corretuck,* 20 Apr. 1682, p. 142. Beg. at King's point; SE on maine bay of Corretuck, a br. of same deviding this & land of Vandemore; including Crow Island SE from his plantation on Knot's Is. Trans. of 18 pers: Susan Stewart, Francis Stewart, Jno. Machall, Rich. Morrison, Rich. Millett, Agnes Nicholls, Jno. Carlisle (?), Gilb. Crider, Tho. Jacobs, Cha. Clerke, Jennett Carway, Wm. Hartwell, Fra. Kirkman, Wm. Bradly, Hen. Hartwell, Xpian. Wilson, Wm. Hinderson, Wm. Birney.

MR. EVAN JONES, 600 acs., called Hoskins' Is., Low. Norf. Co., in *Corretuck,* 20 Apr. 1682, p. 142. E. upon Bellisses Bay & land of Mr. Patrick White; beg. neare the half way point; W. upon Corretuck Bay; &c. Trans. of 12 pers: Jane Risder, Joan Hodges, Joan Williams, Mary Pool, Robt. Rose,

Tho. Collier, Jon. Farmer, Richd. Farmer, Alex. Broomley, John Dye, Tho. Thorogood, Richd. Gayney.

JOHN LEGATT, 400 acs., Low. Norf. Co., in Knot's Is., in *Corretuck,* 20 Apr. 1682, p. 142. Adj. Richard Whicker, &c. Trans. of 8 pers: Richd. Gardner, Joan Williams, Miles Gray, Robt. Wright, Eliz. Johnson, Jon. Knight, Jon. Mackmarry, Richard Davy.

SAMUEL WINGATE, 100 acs., Low. Norf. Co., at head of the W. br. of Eliz. Riv., 20 Apr. 1682, p. 143. Adj. Thomas Cottle; Jno. Jolliffee; Jno. Grigman; & Andrew Taylor. Part of patt. granted to Edward Wingate, dec'd., 27 Sept. 1661, & due sd. Samuel as heir at law.

WM. BURTON, 1150 acs., being all Cedar Island, Accomack Co., 20 Apr. 1682, p. 143. E. by the sea; S. by inlett parting this from Feekes' Is., &c. 500 acs. granted him by former patt; & 650 acs. for trans. of 13 pers: Tho. Jenkins, Fra. Crosson, Griffith Evan, Danll. Evan, Fra. Smith, Geo. Davis, John How, John Resha, Eliz. Brown, Martha Short, Matthew Harby, John Draper, Richd. Street.

JNO. CHERRY, 490 acs., Low. Norf. Co., upon Deep Cr., 20 Apr. 1682, p. 143. Adj. John Slough; Thomas Richason; &c. 350 acs. granted Richard Yates (Yeates) 11 Mar. 1664, who sold to sd. Cherry; 140 acs. for trans. of: Henry Sealey, 3 several times.

GEORGE BULLOCK, 300 acs., called *Bullocks Ridge,* Low. Norf. Co., on N'wd. part of Knot's Is., in *Corretuck;* 20 Apr. 1682, p. 144. Down a Cr. & marshes deviding this from lands of Jno. Legatt & Richard Whicker; &c. Trans. of 6 pers: Richd. Stones, Jon. Fillamore, Tho. Tuckey, Tho. Hapson, Doro. Greenwood, Rice Price.

CHRISTOPHER BUSTIAN, 660 acs., Low. Norf. Co., in the S. br. of Eliz. Riv., 20 Apr. 1682, p. 144. Adj. land of Markham; now in possession of George Valentine; to Capt. Carver, &c. 450 acs. granted to John Yates, who sold to James Warner, who assigned to sd. Bustian; 210 acs. for trans. of 4 pers: Tho. Muskett; Rob. Calderwood 3 times.

JOHN CORPERUE, 650 acs., Low. Norf. Co., 20 Apr. 1682, p. 144. 500 acs. beg. by Ridgford Sw. on head of the S. br. of Eliz. Riv., at the Beare Springs; &c., granted him 14 July 1673; 150 acs. adj. sd. land, & due for trans. of 3 pers: Mary Lloyd, Jno. Hopkins; Thomas a Negro.

ANNE HARDING, *alias* Emperour, 249 acs., Low. Norf. Co., on N. side of the Broad Cr., 20 Apr. 1682, p. 145. 140 acs. part of 740 acs. granted Thomas Harding, dec'd., 20 Oct. 1661; beg. at mouth of the Cr. coming up to the house; neare Thomas Cooper; by William Porten, Arthur Moseley, Edward Wilder & Samuell Roberts, who were appointed by the court to divide the land betwixt the two sisters, as by said division & order more plainly may appeare, &c. 109 acs. granted to Richard Hargrave, Junr., 5 June 1678 & assigned to sd. Anne; beg. in Cockroft's line, neare Alexander Gwyn; to line of Harding's orphans, &c.

MARY HOLLOWELL, 400 acs., Low. Norf. Co., towards head of the W. br. of Eliz. Riv., 20 Apr. 1682, p. 145. 300 acs. beg. on line of Peter Rigglesworth; which land was granted to Mary Capps 16 Mar. 1663 & due sd. Mary Hollowell, her dau. & sole heiresse; 100 acs. adj. sd. tract; & land of Tho. Cottle, &c; due for trans. of: Arthur Spoure (or Spourl), twice.

JEAN LOVELL, 17 acs., Low. Norf. Co., on S. side of the W. br. of Eliz. Riv., being the povnts adjacent to her land of Rigglesworth's pattent: beg. at the br. opposite to Granger's Gutt; to Horner's corner; &c. 20 Apr. 1682, p. 146. Trans. of: Arthur Spoar (?).

MATTHEW CASWELL, 300 acs., Low. Norf. Co; on S. side of Deep Cr; on S. Br. of Eliz. Riv., 20 Apr. 1682, p. 146. Running to mouth of Manning's Cr: to lands of Lakes & Etheridge; to land of Haswell; &c. Granted

to Richard Batchelor 27 Sept. 1665, who, with his wife, assigned to sd. Caswell.

JOHN GISBORNE, 200 acs., Low. Norf. Co., Lynhaven Par; upon N. brs. of Corretuck, 20 Apr. 1682, p. 146. Beg. at John Sivill; adj. Dennis Dulley & John White; & upon a pocoson bet. this & Newton's land, called Morris' kidge. Trans. of 4 pers: Frances Matthews, Edwd. Hind; & 2 Negroes.

LUCY KEELING, dau. of Thorowgood Keeling, dec'd., 300 acs., Low. Norf. Co; Lynhaven Par., 20 Apr. 1682, p. 146. Beg. on a poynt on the Dildoe Br; to br. dividing this & Jno. Johnson; &c. Bequeathed by sd. Keeling to sd. Lucy, to be possessed with the same after the death of his wife Lucy, (now Lucy Haies.) etc. Trans. of 6 pers: Abraham Easter, Jno. Rose, Richard Cock, Margaret Woollingham, Elizab. Sixworth, Robt. Calderwood.

THOMAS CANNON, 250 acs., Low. Norf. Co., in Lynhaven, 20 Apr. 1682, p. 147. Beg. at land of Lucy Keeling; adj. Jno. Johnson; & Mr. William Cornix. Trans. of 5 pers: Tho. Brinson, Joyce his wife, Thomas Brinson, Junr., Jno. Brinson, Mathew Brinson.

MICHAEL MACOY, 115 acs., Low. Norf. Co; at head of King's Cr., a br. of the E. br. of Eliz. River; 20 Apr. 1682, p. 147. Adj. David Murray; land that was Corperue's; Wm. Whithurst; & Richard Nicolls. 50 acs. sold to him by Richard King 16 May 1665; 50 acs. by Humphry Smith & Michael Claree 9 Jan. 1667; 15 acs. for trans. of: Arthur Spoure (?).

DENNIS AISHLEY & EDWARD OUTLAW, 556 acs., Low. Norf. Co; at head of the W. br. of Eliz. Riv., 20 Apr. 1682, p. 148. At head of Robert Capps' land; neare Thomas Cottle; by Capps', now Hollowell's land, to John Freeman; &c. 300 acs. granted to Thomas Dyer 9 Apr. 1662, & assigned to the abovenamed by Francis Thelaball & Sarah his wife, dau. & heiresse of sd. Dyer; 256 acs. for trans. of 5 pers: Jno. Dorey (or Dovey), Elizabeth

Michell, Edwd. Outlaw, twice; Rob. Calderwood.

CHARLES GRUNDIE, 75 acs., Low. Norf. Co; on N. side of the mouth of Daniel Tanner's Cr., called Sandy Point; 20 Apr. 1682, p. 148. Beg. by the Cr; to the *Careening place,* &c. Trans. of 2 pers: George Hudson; & Hannah a Negro.

THOMAS HUBY, 300 acs., Low. Norf. Co; towards head of Symons' Cr., in W. br. of Eliz. Riv., 20 Apr. 1682, p. 148. Adj. land of one Cranes (?). Said land sold to him by Robert Bowers, Senr.

CAPT. JOHN WALLOP *alias* WAD-LOW, 1800 acs., Accomack Co., 24 Apr. 1682, p. 149. 1450 acs. being all Keekotank Is. *alias* Accocomson Is., the next S. Is. to Gingoteag Is; & is part of 1550 acs. granted him 9 Oct. 1672; 350 acs. adj. the marshes of Kekotank Is., at the N. entrance into the W. narrows, next to land of Mr. Thomas Rideing & Col. John Stringer, on the main land near *Accocomson,* &c; which is due for Imp. of 7 pers: Rachel Hosted, Tho. Wheeler, Tho. Wortlee, William Dixon, James a Taylor; Besse a Negro; Harry Hadson.

THOMAS WARD, 350 acs., Is. of Wight Co., 24 Apr. 1682, p. 149. Escheated from Peter Hayes, dec'd., as by inquisition under Wm. Randolph, Depty. Esch'r., &c.

GEORGE SMITH, 60 acs., Low. Norf. Co., 20 Apr. 1682, p. 150. Escheat land of Deborah Jones, dec'd., as by inquisition under Wm. Randolph, Depty. Esch'r., &c.

MR. HEN. BATES & JAMES THWEAT, 673 A., 2 R., 6 P., Chas. City Co; Parish of Jordanes; on S. side James Riv., 20 Apr. 1682, p. 150. Beg. at Mr. Jon. Wingame; along Mr. William Edmonds; crossing the gr. Sw., to Mr. Edward Adington, &c. Trans. of 14 pers: Law. Fleming, Faith Sprigwell, Barbary Young, Geo. Hatton, Richd. Longwell, Eliz. Kendall, Robt. Evans, Eusebius King, Timoth. Allen,

Charles Clay; & Jack, Cophace & Tango, Negroes.

ROBERT SYMMONS (Symons), 300 acs., Low. Norf. Co; in the N. part from *Corretuck,* 20 Apr. 1682, p. 151. Beg. at Peter Malbone; downe the seaside to the *little wash;* includ. Cedar Is., which he purchased of Jno. Brookes' on the W'wd. side of sd. land. Trans. of 6 pers: Richd. Merchant, Peter Russell, Geo. Holmes, John Boss, Tho. Jones, Sarah Cooper.

HENRY HOLLOWELL, 118 acs., Low. Norf. Co; on N. side of the W. br. of Eliz. Riv., 20 Apr. 1682, p. 151. At head of his father's land; adj. Murraie's line; alongst Slawter's line, &c. Trans. of 3 pers: Henry Creech, his wife, Stephen Coleman.

JOSEPH HOLLOWELL & BENJAMIN HOLLOWELL, 200 acs., Low. Norf. Co; on N. side of the W. br. of Eliz. River, 20 Apr. 1682, p. 151. Beg. at their father's corner; adj. Henry Hollowell; on Slauter's line; neare Carter's land; to William Powell's old pattent; to Jno. Allott's line; to Thomas Hollowell, Senr., &c. Trans. of 4 pers: Wm. England, Eliz. Kenton, James Clerk, Robert Dyer.

MR. JNO. MOOR & MR. THOMAS SKERINGTON, (Skerrington) (or Skevington), 1350 acs., N'ly. from Corretuck, 20 Apr. 1682, p. 152. Beg. neare Robert Symmons' at the entrance of the *little Wash;* neare Curretuck Inlett; along Curretuck River; on Curretuck Bay & a cr. devideing the sand banks & the *great Wash;* &c. Trans. of 27 pers: Richd. Fletcher, James Moker, Stephen Joyes, Samll. Floyd, Jon. Jefferies, Geo. Morris, Jeffery Thomas, Ephraim Tomkins, Geo. Blyth, James South, Wm. Worth. Tho. Loth, James Irish, Tho. Leeth, Edmd. Price, James Black, Tobias Trotter, Esay Jarvis, James Scott, Wm. Jones, Edmd. Scott, Eliz. Symonds, Mary Jones, Hannah Moor, James Edwards.

JOHN JAMES, 1350 acs., Low. Norf. Co; Lynhaven Par., 20 Apr. 1682, p. 152. 1000 acs. beg. neare a runn; to a

Sw. parting this & the long ridge; to Richard Bonney; &c; granted to John James 27 Sept. 1680; 350 acs. beg. at his old corner; to Carver's (&) Brinson's quarter; to Francis Jones; &c; trans. of 7 pers: Wm. Scarlet, James Ware, Jane Watson, Gilbert Cornwell, Jon. Brown, John Carter, Margaret Brown.

CAPT. JOHN WALLOPP *alias* WADLOW, 1800 acs., Accomack Co., 20 Apr. 1682, p. 153. 1450 acs. being all Kickotanck Is. *alias* Accocomson Is., the next S. island to Gingoteag Is; being part of 1550 acs. granted him 9 Oct. 1672. 350 acs. is sunken marshes adj; beg. at the N. entrance to the Western Narrows next to Mr. Thomas Riding & Col. John Stringer, on the maine land neare *Accocomson;* &c. Imp. of 7 pers.*

JOHN GRIGMAN (Grignan), 61 A., 1 R., 8 P., being part of a devident of Samuell Wingall; beg. at the broad Cr., &c. 20 Apr. 1682, p. 154. Part of 200 acs. granted Edward Wingate 27 Sept. 1661.

WILLIAM CLAIBORNE (Claibourne), sonn of Col. William Clayborne, Junr., dec'd., & THOMAS CLAIBORNE, sonn & heir apparent of Mr. Thomas Claiborne, 545 acs., New Kent Co. 20 Apr. 1682, p. 154. Beg. in the forke of Chichahominy Riv. where the Sw. ends, &c. Trans. of 11 pers: Tho. Bell, Robert Bowles, John Ireland, Richd. Pearson, Corn. Bushy (or Busby), Margaret Bright, Richd. Ely, Micha. Wardrope, Mary Poll, Ann Hicks, And. Hall.

MR. WILLIAM LEIGH, 370 acs., New Kent Co., St. Stephen's Par., on N. side of Mattapony Riv., 20 Apr. 1682, p. 155. Behind land formerly Mr. Richard Barnhowse, now in the tenure of Mr. John Starke; beg. in Mostequokee (Mustecoque) Sw; to Appostecoque Sw; by Mr. Richard Tunstall to Mr. John Starke; nigh a Huckleberry slash; by Major William Wyatt, &c. Granted to Peter Ford in a patt. of 500 acs., 24 Mar. 1655, who made over to sd. Leigh.

RICHARD HUTCHINS, JUNR., 226 acs., Is. of Wight Co., on brs. of the Black Water, 20 Apr. 1682, p. 155. Beg. at John Watkins' line; adj. Phillipp Wrayford; by William Powell; &c. Imp. of 5 pers: Samuel Dunston, John Simpson, James Long, Robert Orrel, Mary Newton.

CHARLES MAN, 22 acs., Is. of Wight Co., on NE side of Currawaugh Sw., 20 Apr. 1682, p. 156. Beg. at corner of his father, Thomas Man; to Col. Bridges' line; &c. Trans. of: Ann Wood.

THOMAS UNDERWOOD, 400 acs., Is. of Wight Co., on Black Water brs., 20 Apr. 1682, p. 156. Beg. at Mr. Richard Lovegrove; &c. Trans. of 8 pers: Sarah Mosse, Jon. Alwood (or Atwood), Tho. Turner, Moses Wms. (Williams), John Green, Christian Peirce, Roger Banister, Wm. Browne.

MR. HENRY BATTS & MR. JAMES THWAITE, 673 A., 2 R., 6 P., Chas. City Co., Par. of Jordans, on S. side of James River, 20 Apr. 1682, p. 156. Beg. upon line of Mr. William Winingham (Winingame), to Mr. William Edmunds: crossing the gr. Swamp; by Mr. Edward Addenton (Adenton); &c. Trans. of 14 pers.*

WILLIAM TAYLOR, JUNR., & ELIAS TAYLOR, 200 acs., Accomack Co.. on SE side of the narrowes, neer the main land of *Accocomson,* 20 Apr. 1682, p. 157. SW by Assawan Bay, NE by Accocomson Bay; &c. Trans. of 4 pers: Uriah Cannan, Jno. Billett (or Billott), Tarloe Cary, Grace Cannan.

JOHN CORLEW, 128 acs., Warwick Co., 20 Apr. 1682, p. 157. Beg. on the Broad Ridge; adj. Gerrard Ridley; to the Hollybush Sw; to Samuell Chappell; &c. Imp. of 3 pers: Thomas Brampton, John Glifford, Frances Williams.

JOSHUA NAYLOR, 150 acs., on Deep Creek, adj. George Cookley; 20 Apr. 1682, p. 157. Granted to Dr. Richard Hall 13 Jan. 1652; renewed by order, &c; & bequeathed to sd. Naylor.

JOHN THORNTON (Thorneton), 390 acs., Is. of Wight Co., 20 Apr. 1682, p. 158. On head brs. of the W. br. of Nanzemund Riv; beg. at Mr. John Nevell (or Neuell) & Jacob Durden's (Druden) cor; to William West; to William Powell; & John Moore; to Francis Bridle, &c. Imp. of 8 pers: Wm. Browne, Antho. Norman, Aledander Mason, Danll. Norman, Richd. Pageant, Danll. Worton, James Lodge, John Clarke.

JOHN SELLAWAY, 250 acs., Is. of Wight Co., on brs. of Indian Cr. Sw., 20 Apr. 1682, p. 158. Betwixt Mr. Richard Lovegrove; Isaac Reekes; John Moore's; & his own land; to Mr. Edmd. Godwin; to Hugh Sanders; by Robert Cooper, &c. Trans. of 5 pers: Wm. Bisley, James Pederott, Robert Cooper, Deborah Bowler, James Perey.

ROBERT CAUFEILD, of Surry Co., 2250 acs., Low. Par. of sd. Co., 29 Apr. 1682, p. 159. Beg. at Allen Warren, by the maine Black Water; to Cyprus Sw; &c. 635 acs. granted George Blow 9 Aug. 1664, renewed & confirmed to his son Richard 4 Oct. 1675, who sold to sd. Caufeild 7 May 1678; 338 acs. granted to Matthias Marriott & Thomas Hart 14 Aug. 1672; deserted, & granted sd. Caufeild by order, &c. 1277 acs. for trans. of 26 pers: Robt. Coufeild, Tho. Browne, Wm. Dawson, James Peterson, Samll. Dunston, Mary Newton, John Green, Fra. Rownan, Jacob an Indian, Richd. Greenhill, Phill. Jones, John Simpson, Ann Wood, Roger Bannister, Wm. Rownan, Arthur Taylor, Danll. Bayly, James Loring, Sarah Moss, Jon. Cary, Tho. Page, Tho. Lock, Richd. Emerson, Robt. Orrell, Tho. Turner; James a Negro.

COL. JOHN CUSTIS, 3700 acs., in Pocomoke, Accornacke Co., 20 Apr. 1682, p. 160. Part of 8150 acs. which Debourax Browne dyed seized of, & was found to escheate as by inquisition under John Stringer, Esch'r., &c.

FRANCIS BOND, 100 acs., Low. Norf. Co., Lynhaven Par., 20 Apr. 1682, p. 160. Adj. Capt. William Carver's land called Brinson's quarter; a runn dividing this & land of Richard Bonney; into the Cyprus Sw., &c. Trans. or: 2 Negroes: King & Ann.

GAWEN GAWIN, 1000 acs., New Kent Co., on S. side of Totopottomoys Cr., 20 Apr. 1682, p. 160. Adj. Cornelius Dabney; &c. Granted to John Davis 27 Feb. 1666; deserted; & granted sd. Gawin by order, &c. Trans. of 20 pers: John Bryor, Corne. Degar, Mary Lemon, Jon. Wallington, Tho. Fonger, Cathe. Hubberd, John Trabowt (or Traboret), Jon. Jackson, Geo. Taylor, John Pope, Samll. Walton, Jacb. Lindsey, Tho. Barrow, Bess ——, Margaret Cheney, Mary Denham, And. Hill, Samll. Thomas, Danll. Shalton, Mariah ——.

FRANCIS JOND, 400 acs., Low. Norf. Co., 20 Apr. 1682, p. 161. Beg. on a reedy & the Negro Swamp; to the Cyprus Sw; to the Piney Sw; &c. Granted to Edmund Moore 9 Oct. 1675; deserted; & granted sd. Bond by order, &c. Trans. of 8 pers: Tho. White, Jon. Strange, Tho. Richason, Jon. Barnes, Xpher, Mede, Dan. Munrow, Mary Mohun, Beatrice Walkelate.

ARCHIBALD BROMLEY, 400 acs., Gloster Co., Kingston Par., on N. side of Horne Harbour, 20 Apr. 1682, p. 161. Running to S. side of Winter Harbour, &c. Trans. of 8 pers: Mary Bennet, Wm. Henderson, Jon. Taylor, Porteus, Jon. Bennet, Wm. Henderson, Jon. Taylor, John Ayres, Ellinor Gill, Hen. Peters, Tho. Bowler.

JAMES ATWOOD, 700 acs., Middlesex Co., upon Dragon Sw., betwixt the White Oake Sw. & Bryery Br., 20 Apr. 1682, p. 162. Beg. at Thomas Corwell; to Mr. Henry Niccolas; to Robert Aldin; to Thomas Cordwell; &c. Granted to Mr. John Lyndsey 10 June 1674, deserted, & now granted by order &c. Trans. of 14 pers: Barnaby Johnson, James Peirson, Tho. Hurt (or Hart), Ellinor Hart, Jane Salmon, Roger Pidlers, Edwd. Phillips, John Walker, Edwd. Weight, Wm. Griffin, Tho. Middleton, Wm. Angood, Hen. Wilcox, Katherine Burris.

THOMAS BOSWELL, 1100 acs., Gloster Co., Abbington Par., upon Yorke Riiver side & Timber Neck Cr., 20 Apr. 1682, p. 162. Beg. at mouth of sd. Cr; to 100 acs. sold to Mr. Booker; includ. all the islands to sd. Creek's mouth. 1000 acs. granted Richd. Richards 2 Aug. 1645, & descended to Hugh Richards, who assigned to Thomas Wilson & Richard Jones; by Wilson assigned to sd. Jones, from whom it descended to Cadwallader Jones, who conveyed to sd. Boswell, 19 Mar. 1679; 100 acs., being overplus, due for trans. of 2 pers: Wm. Morton, Joseph Thompson.

THOMAS BLANTON, 200 acs., Rappa. Co., on the maine Pocoson & brs. of Jelson's Cr., 20 Apr. 1682, p. 163. Beg. at the mouth of Beech Sw; to Major Robert Beverley; to Francis Graves; &c. Imp. of 4 pers: Ann Edwards, Grace Davies, John Elam, Richard Leather.

ABRAHAM BRADLEY, 150 acs., Gloster Co., Abbington Par., 6 May 1682, p. 163. Beg. at Daniell Langham; to Major Lawrence Smith; to Thomas & Jeffrey Graves neer the road side; by Robert Coleman; &c. Granted to Thomas Sowell 5 June 1675; deserted; & now enjoyed by order, &c. Trans. of 3 pers: Jeremiah Rawlins, Robert Smith, John Purvis.

HENERY ARMSTRONG, 198 A., 1 R., 16 P., Chas. City Co., Par. of Martin Brandon, on NW side of Up. Chipoaks Cr., on S. side of James River, 29 Apr. 1682, p. 164. Beg. upon the Cr; along line of Wm. Short; crossing the Cold Spring; to Mr. Nicho. Perry; &c. Imp. of 4 pers: James Cann, Richd. Atkinson, Eliz. Shaply, Hen. White.

MR. JOHN MOOR, 490 acs., Is. of W. Co., on brs. of Indian Cr. Sw; 20 Apr. 1682, p. 164. Adj. Mr. Pitt; Mr. Lovegrove; & Isaac Reekes. 300 acs. due him by former pattent; & 190 acs. for Imp. of 4 pers: Wm. Joy, Eliz. Fowler, Ann Woodford, Dorothy Banks.

THOMAS BLUNT & RICHARD WASHINGTON, 330 acs., Up. Par. of

Surry Co; ½ mi. from the main Black Water; 29 Apr. 1682, p. 165. Beg. at Richard Parker. Trans. of 7 pers: Rose Aldridge, Mary Trott, Giles Harman, Tho. Porter, Richd. Hawkins, John Knight, Joseph Townly.

THOMAS MANDUE, 320 acs., Is. of W. Co., on brs. of the Black Water, 20 Apr. 1682, p. 165. Beg. at George Perce's land, in possession of Phillip Wrayford; to Mathew Strictland; to the Coblers line; &c. Trans. of 7 pers: Tho. Parker, Richd. Stanly, Christopher Ellis, Samll. Bott, John Phillips, Jeter Moore, Tho. Anderson.

ROBERT HOOKES, 200 acs., on SW side of the main Sw. of the W. br. of Nanzemond; being halfe of patt. granted his father & Wm. Bream; 20 Apr. 1682, p. 165. Beg. by sd. Sw., bet. sd. Hookes & Wm. Wilkins; &c.

JOHN PERRY, 320 acs., in the Up. Par. of Nanzemond; near Humphry Griffin; 24 Apr. 1682, p. 166. Trans. of 7 pers: Walter Price, Morris Irish, John Larrum, Rowld. Williams, Richd. Bennet, Samll. Woodward, Ould Alex (or Alce ?).

RICHARD SLAUGHTER, 600 acs., at the head of Bennett's Creek, 24 Apr. 1682, p. 166. Adj. Thomas Akerland; Col. Edward Carter; &c. 450 acs. part of 600 acs. granted Richard Slaughter, Senr., his father, 3 June 1656; & renewed to be sealed 30 Oct. 1662; 150 acs., being overplus now added, due for trans. of 3 pers: Tho. Martin, Izarael Shepherd, Hen. Williams.

CHARLES DRURY, 41 acs., Nanzemond Co., Chuckatuck Parish, 24 Apr. 1682, p. 167. Beg. by his house, to Col. (alias Major) Lear's Cr; up by Nanzemond Riv; includ. islands & marsh within the bounds, &c. Granted to sd. Drury 30 Oct. 1662, in a patt. for 50 acs.

JOHN HOLLAND, 760 acs., in Nanzemond Up. Par., 20 Apr. 1682, p. 167. Beg. at a white oake of Walter Bazeley, being the beg. tree mentioned in Michael Gill's, alias Hill's, pattent;

to John Carr; by Foster's old line; to a Poquoson near head of the Dirty Br; below Francis Sanders' house; &c. 400 acs. granted to Michael Gill, *alias* Hill, 18 Feb. 1664, which after severall sales, &c., became due to sd. Holland; 360 acs., being overplus, due for trans. of 8 pers: Jon. Johnson, Ann Magges, Eliz. Harvy, Jon. Blast, Clause Cowse, Jon. Hoborough, Thomas Jones, Hester Howse.

FRANCIS SPEIGHT, 500 acs., Up. Par. of Nanzemond Co., on S. side of the Beech Sw., 24 Apr. 1682, p. 168. Along Sommerton Cr., to a little beyond the Indian Path that now is; &c. Trans. of 10 pers: Eliza. White, Jon. Harris, Walter Price, Wm. Booker, Hum. Green, Edwd. Harris, Richd. Catach, Jane Catach, Tho. Frost, Richd. Jones.

WM. COPHELD & JON. GRANDBERRY, 220 acs., in Low. Par. of Nanzemond; att head of Bennett's Creek, 24 Apr. 1682, p. 168. Beg. at Robert Peal; towards Col. Carter; &c. Trans. of 5 pers: Dorothy Wooten, Jon. Merry, Jon. Swancott, Jon. Green, James Scott.

JAMES LOCKARTE (Lockharte), 160 acs., in the Low. Par. of Nanzemond; at head of Bennet's Creek, 20 Apr. 1682, p. 168. Beg. at Wm. Cophell & John Grandberry at a place called *Holy hill;* nigh Robert Murrah & Col. Carter; &c. Trans. of 4 pers: John Temple, John Darling, Ra. French, Danll. Smith.

EPAPHRODITUS BENTON, 500 acs., in the Up. Par. of Nanzemond; upon the Cross Sw. of Barbacue, 24 Apr. 1682, p. 169. Beg. at Thomas Duke; to head of the Dogwood Neck; &c. Trans. of 10 pers: Danll. Maclood, Robt. Whittle, Eliz. Millard, Math. Keely, Stephen Powell, John Walby, Tho. Warner, Elinor Megorth, Elinor Merihurst, Bridgett Colfelt.

JONATHAN ROBINSON, in right of Ann his wife, the dau. of James Foster, dec'd; 242 acs., on head of the southern br. of Nanzemond (Riv.), 24 Apr. 1682, p. 169. Beg. at John Holland; adj. Charles Roades; by markt trees deviding this "from James Howards his wife's part", to line of James Foster; &c. Part of 800 acs. granted James Foster & Andrew Bonny 27 Sept. 1661.

JONATHAN ROBINSON, 175 acs., in the Up. Par. of Nanzemond; att head of the southern branch; 24 Apr. 1682, p. 169. Beg. about 4 poles from Henry Plumpton; by James Foster; by John Holland; to Michael Gill, *alias* Hill; by Richard Sanders; nigh Jon. Wallis, *alias* Makallam's; &c. Trans. of 4 pers: Eliz. Arrowsmith, Eliza. Marlin, Jos. Lockhart, David Clatchey.

JAMES HAYWARD ,in right of Elizabeth his wife, *Grandchild* of James Foster, dec'd; 242 acs., att head of the S. br. of Nanzemond, 24 Apr. 1682, p. 170. Beg. at cor. of Mr. Achelley; to Jonathan Robinson "his wife's parte"; to line of sd. Foster; joining with Henry Plumpton; &c. Part of 800 acs. granted sd. Foster & Adry Bonny 27 Sept. 1661.

LEWIS WILLIAMS, 100 acs., in the S. br. of Nanzemond (Riv.), 24 Apr. 1682, p. 170. Beg. at land Richard Peirce now lives on; near the Cyprus Gutt; to the Oister bank landing; to the Marish landing; &c. Trans. of 2 pers: Rowland Williams, Elizabeth Sidney.

DANIEL HIND, 850 acs., in Up. Par. of Nanzemond, 24 Apr. 1682, p. 170. Beg. nigh Tucker's Quarter att the head of Capt. Booth's line; &c. Trans. of 17 pers: Thomas Baker, Mary George, Abraham Evans, Wm. Browne, Mary Woodderd, Eliz. Sutton, Tho. Snow, Phillip Bardoe, John Bennett, Samll. Daines, Samll. Absolon, Fran. Yden (Asdan ?), Wm. Gwin, Tho. English, Eliza. Holman, Margaret Matthews, Robert Bach.

WM. EASON, 270 acs., in the Up. Par. of Nanzemond, 24 Apr. 1682, p. 171. Beg. in line of Francis Spight; to Fra. Cambridge; to Thomas Cowler (or Cowlen); to Col. Blake; &c. Trans. of 6 pers: Tho. Everard, Alex. Frissell,

Jon. Richards, James Crefre (or Cresre), George Gluddall, Robert Wethell.

THOMAS DUKE, 350 acs., in the Up. Par. of Nanzemond, att the Cross Sw. of Barbecue, 24 Apr. 1682, p. 171. Trans. of 7 pers: Mary Croft, Sarah Stiles, Geo. Walker. Arthur Holder, Peter Blein, Thomas Pryer; Matthew a Negro.

JOHN HARRIS, 200 acs., in the Up. Par. of Nanzemond, adj. land he lives on; 24 Apr. 1682, p. 171. Beg. in sight of Wm. Breames' house; through a place called *Hell;* to Mr. Danll. Hinds; to Jeremiah Orlie; by Col. Blake; &c. Trans. of 4 Negroes: Francisco, Richd., Ned, & Mary.

JOHN BATTLE, 580 acs., in the Up. Par. of Nanzemond, att a place called *Kill Many Swamp;* 24 Apr. 1682, p. 172. Trans. of 12 pers: Robt. Hubberd, Samll. Merrit, Wm. Morgan, Richd. Harrington, Tho. Skinner, David Hollingsworth, Joan Stiles, Mary Bates, Susan Meriday; Toney, Isabel, Bastian, Negroes.

MR. WM. COVINGTON, 300 acs., Rappa. Co., upon branches of Pyanketancke River, adj. land he liveth on; 24 Apr. 1682, p. 172. Beg. by the Horse (Path ?), in sight of his plantation; to Mr. Thomas Watkins; on S. side the Path to Paine's bridge; by Wm. Richards' path; &c. Imp. of 6 pers: Katherine Butler, Michael Raftus, Eliza. Holland, Katherine Clayton, Robert Burton, Margaret Smith.

JOHN LANE, 76 acs., New Kent Co., upon SE side of Mattapony Riv., & SSW side of Assatians Swamp; 20 Apr. 1682, p. 173. Beg. at a br. of sd. Sw., cor. to his seat of land purchased of Thomas Sanders, running to a markt tree called by the name of the *Hornes* standing by Mr. Ralph Green's quarter Path; ½ mi. up some to Robert Fothergall's (Fothergill) land; &c. Granted him by deed by George Dilliard, 20 Sept. 1679 & acknowledged, by sd. Dilliard & his wife.

WM. CUSTIS, Gent., of Accomack Co., 1350 acs., on the Seaboard side in sd. Co., 20 Apr. 1682, p. 173. 1200 acs. being part of 2400 acs. granted Col. Edmund Scarburgh 20 Oct. 1664 & conveyed to sd. Custis 16 Sept. 1665; lying N. upon little Nuswaddox, *alias* Middle, Cr; S. to Watchapregue *alias* Nicowomson & by some called little Matompkin Cr; 150 acs. being salt water marsh adj; & due for trans. of 3 pers: Wm. Baker, Tho. Edrington, Dennis Cox.

RICHD. REYNOLDS, 450 acs., Is. of W. Co., 20 Apr. 1682, p. 174. Land which Ambrose Bennet died seized of & was found to escheat, as by inquisition under Wm. Randolph, Depty. Esch'r., &c.

MRS. MARY WADE, 463 acs., James City Co., on a br. of Tiascun (Sw.), 20 Apr. 1682, p. 174. Which 463 acs., together with 100 acs. belonging to Joseph Preston, begins att Grimes' old line; to Capt. Hen. Duke; to mouth of Preston's spring br; by Esqr. Bray's plantation; along Mr. Burnell; down Warrany Run; &c. Granted to Mr. Thomas Hampton 8 Mar. 1658 for 400 acs., & by him (Preston's 100 acs. excepted), assigned to sd. Mary Wade, by the name of Duke, 30 Nov. 1670; further due for trans. of 4 pers: Fra. Heyne, Robert Griffith, Robt. Cannon, Morris Mosely.

DANIEL LONG, 60 acs., Is. of W. Co., 20 Apr. 1682, p. 174. Which land John Upton died seized of & was found to escheat, as by inquisition under Wm. Randolph, Depty. Esch'r., &c.

ELIAS OSBOURN (Osborn), 50 acs., Chas. City Co., 20 Apr. 1682, p. 175. Which land Jane Osbourn died seized of & was found to escheat, as by inquisition under Henry Hartwell, Depty. Esch'r., &c.

THOMAS BLANTON, 200 acs., Rappa. Co., on the main Poquoson, & brs. of Gilson's Cr., 20 Apr. 1682, p. 175. Beg. att mouth of Beech Sw; to Major Robert Beverley; to Francis Graves; &c. Imp. of 4 pers: Cha. Morgan, Wm. Lake, Edwd. Dowset, Tho. Mackall.

WM. LANGLEY, sonn & heir to William Langley, 200 acs. Low. Norf. Co., att head of the Indian Towne Br., of Daniel Tanner's Cr; 22 Nov. 1682, p. 175. Granted sd. Langley, dec'd., 16 Apr. 1653, & due for trans. of 4 pers: Robert Harper, Jon. Owen, Mary Owen, Teage Shone.

ROBERT PRIDDY, 150 acs., 22 Sept. 1682, p. 175. 50 acs. lying on Tassatiams Cr., adj. Mr. Henery Biggs & his own land; 100 acs. on Arracaico Cr. & Mattapony River; adj. Mr. Ambrose Clare & Bartholomew Ramsey. Trans. of 3 pers: John Harth, Edwd. Powel, Thomas Ward.

JOHN LAWRENCE, 942 acs., Low. Norf. Co., 22 Sept. 1682, p. 176. Beg. at point of a neck by a Cyprus Sw; towards the salt Ponds, &c. Surveyed for John Lawrence, & due the abovesaid John, his orphant, by order &c; & likewise for trans. of 19 pers: Gilbert Deacon, Jon. Bagly, Danll. Grimlet, Jon. Walter, Jos. Bourne, Eliz. Davies, Nehemiah Lynch, Jon. Norris, Geo. Burcher, Tho. Wells, Tho. Pool, Arthur Holden, Richd. Delabere, Danll. Ruze, Nicho. Larcum, Alexander Somers, Tho. Pinkard, Nicho. Chapman, Enoch Hutchinson.

CAPT. JOHN HATTON, 100 acs., Low. Norf. Co; 22 Sept. 1682, p. 176. Being the moiety of 200 acs., which John Debar died seized of, & was found to escheat by inquisition under Wm. Randolph, Depty. Esch'r., &c.

GEORGE PEAS & NICHOLAS WHITMORE, 388 A., 37 P., Chas. City Co., in Westover Par., on W. side of the Black Water maine Sw. & on S. side of James River, 22 Sept. 1682, p. 176. Trans. of 8 pers: Dorothy Westwray, Xpher. Corbyn, Wm. Andrick, Jon. Price, E. Ruffe, Martha Phillips, Jon. Pimet (or Pirret), Tho. Moor.

JOHN KERNEY, 100 acs., Low. Norf. Co., 22 Sept. 1682, p. 177. Being the moiety of 200 acs. which John Debar died seized of & was found to escheat as by inquisition under Wm. Randolph, Depty. Esch'r., &c. Granted to Wm. Kerney by order, &c., & due sd. John as his sonn & heir.

JOHN ALFORD & WILLIAM MILLINGTON, 350 acs., New Kent Co., S. side of York River, 22 Sept. 1682, p. 177. Being the remainder of land pattented by Col. Hammond, joining to sd. Hammond's land called Fort Royall; beg. at Mr. Napier's corner; along Mr. Walter Huckstep; by the Deep Br; &c. Trans. of 7 pers: Wm. Reynolds, John Morrow, Eliz. Story, Josep. Good, Tho. Fry, Joseph Start, Tho. Driver.

JOSEPH VICK, 320 acs., 22 Sept. 1682, p. 177. Beg. by Chewan River, neer the Indians Spring; & adj. land of Hodges Councill (Councell); &c. Trans. of 7 pers: Antho. Nash, Step. Fox, Richd. Lane, Wm. Hunt, Tho. Wilson, Jno. Davis, John Hamond.

MR. JOHN SMITH, 78 acs., in York Co. & Parish, 22 Sept. 1682, p. 178. Beg. neer plantation of Joan Worley; to head of a br. of Cheeseman's Cr; &c. Trans. of 2 pers: Ann Green, John Webster.

MR. THOMAS CLAIBOURNE, 545 acs., New Kent Co., 22 Sept. 1652, p. 178. Beg. at mouth of the forke of Chickahominy Riv., where the Sw. ends; &c. Trans. of 11 pers: Jos. Browne, Henry "a Distiller", John Barton, John Miller, Ellinor Rule, Ellinor Parke, John Lawrence; Toby, Doll, Samboy, Jenny, Negroes.

COL. JOHN WEST, 3000 acs., on N. side of Mattapony River, on the upper side of Dr. Moodie's land; 22 Sept. 1682, p. 178. Granted to Mr. Leonard Chamberlaine 1 Apr. 1671; deserted; & granted sd. West by order, &c. Trans. of 60 pers: Edwd. Phillips, Isaac Calcock, Sarah Rowling, John Foller, Jon Chapman, John Batts; Indian Nan; Jack; Joseph, Dilsey, Jasper, Maria, Tony, Grashear, Simon, Joseph, Jack, Sambo, Judith, Grace, Hannah, Kate, Samson, Tom, Maria, Besse,

James, King, Sam., Ned, Nick, Will.,
Oliver, Timothy, Fuller, Gybsye, Beck,
Doll, Susan, Mary, Titus, Tingo, Bur-
rows, George, Mullatto, Stephen, Jasper,
Harry, Billy, Frank, Cosh, Silver, Trans-
port, Barbados, Peter, Dick, Tab, Betty,
Mary, Giles, Negroes.

JOHN ALFORD & GREGORY
BARNET (Barnett), 150 acs.; New
Kent Co., on S. side of York River "and
is reputed Coll. Hammonds land call'd
by the name of *Nantacooke Necke*"; 22
Sept. 1682, p. 179. Beg. at sd. Ham-
mond's by Nantacooke Cr., to the forke
of same where it meets with Stone's
Sw., &c. Trans. of 3 pers: Edwd.
Dickins, John Hilton, Susanna Bedford.

MR. NICHOLAS WARE, 300 acs.,
New Kent Co., on N. side of Mattapony
River, 22 Sept. 1682, p. 179. Adj. land
of Jeremiah Rawlins, dec'd; Mr. Ed-
ward Cardingbrook; over the Indian
Cabin Meadow; by br. of Tassatians Cr.,
by John Ware & Griffin Lewis; &c.
Trans. of 6 pers: Alice Peyton, Xpher.
Clerk, Symon Blackwell, John Edwards,
Wm. Lucas, John Price.

THOMAS DRUE, 390 acs., Surry Co.,
neer head of Lawnes Cr., 22 Sept. 1682,
p. 179. 300 acs. part granted to Robert
Warren 9 Aug. 1649, & assigned to
Richd. Blunt 2 Apr. 1652 & by Thomas,
son & heir of sd. Richard, sold to sd.
Drue 1 Mar. 1677; 90 acs. being wast
land adj; the whole beg. in Capt.
Baker's line, neer Coolmer's Feild;
along Edward Drue, Walter Tayler,
John Drue, &c. Trans. of 2 pers:
Moses Rely, Samll. Milner.

MR. THO. MERREY, 186 acs., Warwick Co; S'ly. upon James River, 22
Sept. 1682, p. 190. Sd. land now in
possession of sd. Merrey & Mr. Richard Hatton; beg. at Capt. John Langhorne's tree, in a *swatch* by the river;
on the *Chappel* land; &c. 100 acs.
conveyed by Robert Newman to one
Powell, 9 Nov. 1630, & by Benjamin
& Wm. Powel, his sons, made over to
Thomas Glascocke, who assigned to sd.
Merrey 25 Sept. 1674; 86 acs. for trans.
of 2 pers: John Edes, John Johnson.

THOMAS MANN, 300 acs., Is. of
W. Co., 22 Sept. 1682, p. 180. Beg. in
a cove by Chewan River; &c. Trans. of
6 pers: Richd. Carter, Giles Thorn-
berry, Ann Downes, Eliz. Croomer, Joan
Littleton, Thomas Lacy.

MOSES DAVIS, 300 acs., New Kent
Co., on brs. of Chickahominy Sw., 22
Sept. 1682, p. 180. Beg. at Mr. Matt.
Hubberd's where Edmond Grose's line
by mistake intersects; to Phill. Freeman; to Thomas Landown; &c. Trans.
of 6 pers: John Hall, Isabella Dorbe,
Jude Walker, Susanna Hansman, Penelope West, Joseph Land.

MR. RICHARD BUCKNER, 500 acs.,
Rappa. Co., 22 Sept. 1682, p. 181.
Which land John Patterson (Paterson)
died seized of, haveing been purchased
of John Prosser, of sd. county, 10 Aug.
1670; found to escheat, by inquisition
under Col. Isaac Allerton, Esch'r.
Genr'l., & granted to Mr. John Buckner,
who assigned to his sonn, the sd. Richard; part of 4892 acs., known as the
Golden Vally; beg. next to *Manzinzin,*
being Mr. John Paine's mile's end, upon
S. side & in the freshes of Rappa. Riv.,
&c.

JARVIS DIX, 132 acs., Chas. City
Co., Bristoll Par., S. side of Appamattax
Riv., 22 Sept. 1682, p. 181. Beg. at the
Citty Cr. mouth; along Wm. Gower's
line; neer Mrs. Gillam's line; to cor. of
Barker & Leden; &c. Trans. of 3
Negroes: Guy, George, Thomas.

THOMAS BOWRY, 120 acs., James
City Co., S. side of Chickahominy Riv.,
in the fork of Arropor Sw., 22 Sept.
1682, p. 181. Beg. at Mr. Travis' cor.
on the head of sd. Sw., &c. Trans. of
3 pers: Wm. Hawly, John Wilby.

MR. THOMAS FOSTER, 138 acs.,
New Kent Co., 22 Sept. 1682, p. 182.
Adj. Gabriel Mitchell & Nicholas Ware,
&c. Trans. of 3 pers: John Caruthers,
John Dickson, John Hollioake.

COL. JOHN CUSTIS, 850 acs., Accomack Co., at the Deep Creeke, 22 Sept.
1682, p. 182. Which land Devorax
Brown died seized of, being part of

3600 acs., which was found to escheat, by inquisition under Col. John Stringer, Esch'r. of the Eastern Shore, &c.

JOHN DRAKE, 100 acs., Is. of W. Co., on SW side of Currawaugh Sw., 22 Sept. 1682, p. 182. Beg. at mouth of a br. deviding it from Thomas Man; to land of Hodges Councill, to Tho. Parnell; by Col. Bridger's land; &c. Trans. of 2 pers: Richd. Foot, Tho. Wiltshire.

MR. WILLIAM THOMPSON, Clerk, 460 acs., Surry Co., 22 Sept. 1682, p. 182. Beg. in a Gr. Cyprus Sw; along Mr. Meriwether's line; &c. Granted to Anthony Spiltimber 14 May 1666; deserted; & granted sd. Thompson 2 Apr. 1674, by order &c; due for trans. of 10 Negroes: Jack, Ned, Tony, Besse, Maria, Tom, Sam, Echo, Oby, Ann.

JOHN HICKS, 183 acs., James City Co., 22 Sept. 1682, p. 183. Beg. on S. side of the S. swamp against the mouth of Preston's Spring Br; to Capt. Duke; neer the Quarter Sw; along land of the Orphants of Mr. Collins, &c. Trans. of 4 pers: Hen. Roberts, Fra. Davies, Jon. Smith, Ralph Bassel.

RICHARD BENNET, 630 acs., Low. Par. of Surry Co., on W. side of Pokatink Sw., 22 Sept. 1682, p. 183. Beg. at Mr. Francis Mason; by Mr. Wm. Edwards; to Hollybush Sw., &c. Trans. of 13 pers: Elizabeth Peek, Richard Phillips, Mary Bryant, Elizabeth Halfepenny, Ann Webb, Richd. Lux, Andrew Cary, Tho. Smith, James Pyles, Priscilla Floyd, Tho. Harris, Wm. Beale, Joan Phillips.

HENERY FRANCIS, 580 acs., Up. Par. of Surry Co., on SW side of the Birchen Sw., 22 Sept. 1682, p. 183. Beg. at Mr. John Brashear; to Mr. Harrison; by a Cart Path; adj. Wm. Carpenter; Mr. Wm. Symons, &c. 150 acs. granted him 24 Oct. 1675; 430 for trans. of 9 pers: Tho. Martin, Jasper Lines, Moses Loyd, Wm. Ingle, David Johnson, Joshua Hiinde; Gilbert, Jack, Tony, Negroes.

ROWLAND BULKLEY, 330 acs., neer Currawaugh Sw., 22 Sept. 1682, p.

184. Beg. at Giles Linscott, neer Col. Bridger's line; &c. Trans. of 7 pers: John Carter, James Ellis, James Sharp, John Stephenson, Titus, Turner, Jacob Emerson, Tho. Watson.

EDWARD CALLEY, 150 acs., York Co. & Par., 22 Sept. 1682, p. 184. Beg. at the mouth of a br. out of the N. side of Cheeseman's Cr., &c. 100 acs. granted John Floyne, who dying without heires, was escheated by James Williams, 1 Oct. 1662; 50 acs. purchased by sd. Williams of Samuel Tucker, & is due for trans. of: Margaret Feild.

THOMAS LANE, 400 acs., Low. Par. of Surry Co., bet. brs. of Suncken Marsh Mill & Pokatink Sw., 22 Sept. 1682, p. 184. Beg. at Wm. Gray; by Mr. Thomas Binns; & neer a br. dividing this & land of Mr. Robert Ruffin. Trans. of 8 pers: Tho. Whitehand, Wm. Henchman, Wm. Moulsworth, Martin Baxter, Wm. Twig, John Fitzgerald, Patricius Christian, John Fludd.

COL. JOHN CUSTIS, 4600 acs., Accomack Co., 22 Sept. 1682, p. 185. On head or E. part of 2000 acs. in the bottom of Jolles Neck, pattented by Col. Edmund Scarburgh, dec'd; adj. Crooked Cr; Back Cr; & a freshwater br. thereof by some called Euemu's (?) Br; to *Oken Hall* land; 3700 acs. granted Devorax Browne 16 May 1672, & since his death found to escheat, by inquisition under Col. John Stringer, Esch'r. Genr'l., & since granted sd. Custis, &c; 900 acs. upon survey found to be wast land, granted for trans. of 18 pers: Richd. Smith, Dor. Slaughter, Margt. Allen, Geo. Daw, Fra. Rowles, Eliz. Bond, Sam. Lucas, Geo. Butcher, Tho. Newton, Tho. Buffeild, Phill. Gardner, Tho. Blacklock, Robt. Max, Jon. Jackson, Gab. Powel, Elinor Glover, Richd. Jones, Matt. Pipping.

CAPT. JOHN WALLOP, *alias* Wadlow, 350 acs., Accomack Co., 22 Sept. 1682, p. 185. Adj. his devdt. of Kekotanck Island; beg. at the N. entrance into the W. narrowes, next to land of Mr. Rideing & Col. John Stringer, whiich are on the main land neer *Acco-*

comson; &c. Trans. of 7 pers: Step. Cotton, Richd. Pickering, Sanders Wilson, Tho. Hogg, Matt. Wardell, Xpher. Donoh, Richd. Conner.

JAMES WATKINS, 100 acs., Surry Co., neer head of Up. Chipoakes Cr., 22 Sept. 1682, p. 186. Adj. Mr. Robert Moseley unto the Common Cart Path, to Mr. Stephens' Mill & upon John Barrow; in breadth 200 acs. & length 50 acs. Conveyed from Thomas Stephens to sd. Watkins, 21 Feb. 1669.

WM. ANDERSON, 90 acs., New Kent Co., 22 Sept. 1682, p. 186. Beg. by his fence; to Rappahannock Path; by Rappa. Road; to Mr. Wm. Lines; &c. Trans. of 2 pers: Jean Bennet, Wm. Leonard.

JOHN ROISTER, 633 acs., Chas. City Co., Westover Par., on N. side of Hern Cr. & N. side of James River, 22 Sept. 1682, p. 186. upon main br. of sd. Cr; cross Deep Br; to Mr. Thomas Cock's line; &c. Trans. of 13 pers: Lawrence, Dick, Cesar, Guy, Abbot; Geo. Cooke; 1 child, Maria, Agbo, Besse, Cetta, Chitta, Assa.

SAME. 97 acs., on E. side of Chimidges Cr., N. side James Riv., in same Co. & Parish; same date, p. 187. Beg. at Cuthbert Williamson; to Mrs. Bland's; crossing Tuskey Br., &c. Trans. of 2 Negroes: Hannibal, & Mary.

MR. ROBERT CHAMBERLAINE, 320 acs., New Kent Co., St. Stephen's Par., on N. side of Mattapony Riv & upon brs. of Horecock Creek, 22 Sept. 1682, p. 187. Beg. in the auntient bounds of land formerly belonging to John Maddison, dec'd; to land of Wm. Moor, dec'd; to land of Arnoll, dec'd; &c. Granted to Col. Robert Abrahall & John Pigg 10 July 1658, & by sd. Pigg sold to Richard Morley, from whom it escheated by inquisition under Wm. Leigh, Depty. Esch'r., &c.

MR. EDWARD ADCOCK, 500 acs., Rappa. Co., on S. side Rappa. River, 22 Sept. 1682, p. 187. Beg. at Beaver Damme Sw; along Mr. Henery Smith; by a slash to land of Mr. Bowler, formerly Col. Goodrich's; by a foot path; &c. Trans. of 10 pers: Jon. Pryor, Dan. Baker, Wm. Fisher, Jon. Wyse, Wm. Smith, Geo. Smiith, Matt. Bennet, Wm. Clerke, Richd. Smith, Jon. Symons.

WILLIAM BASSET & JAMES AUSTIN, 1100 acs., New Kent Co., on S. side & in the freshes of York Riv., 22 Sept. 1682, p. 188. Beg. at the mouth of Brandy Br. where it falls into a main br. of Chickahominy Sw., called the Beaver Damm Sw., &c. Trans. of 22 pers: Richd. Lee, James Rath, Grace Holmes, Robt. Smart, Robt. Smart, Junr., Wm. Heatrell (?), Tho. Haward, Wm. Bush, Wm. Barber, Wm. Forbush, Robt. Roe, Richd. Savings, Tho. Leborn, Eliz. Leborn, Mary Davis, Nicho. Olles, John Potiffe (?), Roger Ward, John Daverdon (?), Hannah Hull, Robt. Taylor, Eliz. Carter.

MR. THO. HARWAR, 647 acs., Rappa. Co., 22 Sept. 1682, p. 188. On back of Capt. Henry Smith; beg. at Randolph Curtis; by Lacie's fence, &c. 398 acs. purchased of sd. Smith, to whom it was granted 24 Sept. 1674; 79 acs. granted to Henery Woodnot & Thomas Smith 17 Nov. 1670; 150 acs. due for trans. of 3 Negroes: Tony, Cushton, Doll.

MICHAEL TUCKER & LYONEL MORRIS, 2000 acs., New Kent Co., 22 Sept. 1682, p. 189. Beg. on a Ridge bet. Chickahominy Sw. & Black Cr., in line of Mr. Matthew Hubberd; to David Crafford (Craford); to Goosberry Sw; to Mr. Henery Wyat; upon Edmund Grose; &c. Trans. of 40 pers: Jon. Symons, Jon. Monday, Jon. Fowler, Jon. Skinner, Jon. Johnson, Jon. Aggor, Ma. Finch, Jon. Morehead, Eliz. Hatly, Eliz. Pye, Dan Murray; Occome, Tony, Duke, Robin, Ufoler, Acquera, Ambe, Aura, Angora, Ay, Ottome, Moccafunke, Eare, Messon, Margaretta, Monque, Unto, Ogombe, Werrye, Ascone, Ottonco, Tubune, Taborsha, Janna, Tary, Janara, Tomora, Sango, Croila, Negroes.

JOHN BARKER, 240 acs., Up. Par. of Surry Co., on N. side of the Otterdam Sw., 22 Sept. 1682, p. 189. Betwixt Mr. Benjamin Harrison & Mr. Jordan, &c. Trans. of 5 pers: Fra. Everit, Isabella Smith, Tho. Jackson; Joan & Betty, Negroes.

MR. BENJAMIN HARRISON, 450 acs., Surry Co., on head of the brs. of the S. run of Up. Chipoaks Cr., 22 Sept. 1682, p. 190. Beg. on E. side of the up. Bridge br; cor. of land he purchased of Mr. Barker; &c. Trans. of 9 pers: Wm. Edwards, Wm. Avery, Wm. Browne, Wm. Gay, Danll. Sadler, Matthias Peach, Eliz. Carrington, John Woodle, Mary Stanly.

NICHOLAS BARNES, 140 acs., New Kent Co., S. side of York River, upon Chickahominy main Sw., 22 Sept. 1682, p. 190. Beg. at the mouth of Pynye Br., cor. of Mr. Henery Wyat; to White Oake Br., neer Capt. Underhill's Island; adj. John Dickeson; to S. side of Elder Br; &c. Trans. of 3 pers: Tho. Brown, Ann Brown, David Thompson.

THOMAS HARPER, 550 acs., Rappa. Co., on branches of Piscataway Cr., 22 Sept. 1682, p. 191. Beg. at Col. Goodrich, by an Indian Path; a br. deviding this from 1000 acs. granted sd. Harper & James Vaughan, dec'd., &c. Trans. of 11 pers: James Griffin. Hen. Deane, Mary Ridwell, John Willman, Eliza. Meuse, Tho. Barker, Hen. Rig, James Rigley, Wm. Fleetwood, Alce (or Alex) Blackstone, Eliz. Smith.

DAVID SMITH, 470 acs., New Kent Co., S. side of York Riv., 22 Sept. 1682, p. 191. Beg. at Mr. Dabney's land, sold to sd. Smith; by *Apponin* (?), a cor. of John Fleming; by Powhitt Path; to John Sexton; by Mattedegun Cr; to Mr. George Gill; &c. Trans. of 10 Negroes: Jurne, Ronno, Wingoe, Elloren, Corle, Marrom, Rondello, Jehar, Angoe, Wortello.

MR. THOMAS JORDAN, 265 acs., Up. Par. of Surry Co., on branches of Cyprus Sw., 22 Sept. 1682, p. 191. Beg. at John Rogers' land, &c. Trans. of 6 pers: Wm. Seaward, Edwd. Armstrong, Eliz. & Alex. Armstrong, Guy Worlock, Howell Rice.

LEWIS WALDIN & GEORGE MARTIN, 160 acs., New Kent Co., upon brs. of Arracoicoe Cr., 22 Sept. 1682, p. 192. Beg. at Mr. Samll. Clayton; cross the Rowleing Path; to Capt. Lane; to Capt. Wm. Jones; &c. Trans. of 4 pers: John Daniel, Edmund Buriall, Winnifred Pradock, John Mackmellon.

SAME. 460 acs; same Co., date & page. Bet. Mr. John Robinson, land of Samll. Patridge, dec'd. & Capt. John Lane; beg. by Middlesex Path; &c. Trans. of 10 pers: Thomas Cooper, Mary Lord, Ann Piper, Thomas Swaine, Edwd. Dudson, Thomas Poles, Peter, John, (& ?) James Overstreet, Wm. Corne.

THOMAS CURITTON, 150 acs., Chas. City Co., Westover Par., on S. side of James River, 22 Sept. 1682, p. 192. Beg. on S. side of the Dry bottom run, along James Mountford; to Mr. Warradine; to head of Woolfe Slash; nigh the King's Road, &c. Trans. of 3 pers: Samll. Marshall, Robt. Bittern, Reginald Anderson.

JOHN ROBINSON, 1252 acs., New Kent Co., upon Dragon Sw., 22 Sept. 1682, p. 193. Beg. at Thomas Landford; over brs. of Arracaicoe; by the Mill Path; by Middlesex Path, to Thomas Perrie; &c. 638 acs. purchased of Mr. Samuel Patridge, dec'd., who purchased of Mr. Edward Roe; 614 acs. for transs. of 13 pers: Robt. Castle, Thomas Bretaigne, Wm. Roberts, John Harris, Hugo Hunt, Anthony Drew, Daniel Dew, Thomas Henchman, Walter Waters, Arthur Sturman, John Robinson, Eliz. Richmond, Benjamin Wilson.

CAPT. ISAAC FOXCRAFT, 250 acs., N'ampton Co., 22 Sept. 1682, p. 193. N. & W. upon Nuswattox Cr; & S. upon 1000 acs. of Capt. Stephen Charleton; &c. Trans. of 5 pers: Christopher Thomas, John Brent, Joseph Belbore, John Bowler, Tho. Stephens.

THOMAS MULFORD, 200 acs., Up. Par. of Nanzemond, 22 Sept. 1682, p. 193. Trans. of 4 pers: Lorenzo Gunsalvo, Sarah Gunsalvo, Thomas Gunsalvo, & Peter Jones.

MR. THOMAS HARPER, 100 acs., Rappa Co; on the main Poquoson of Piiscataway Cr., 22 Sept. 1682, p. 194. Beg. at Robert Clements; by James Vaughan; to Mr. Francis Browne; & adj. land of Clements, dec'd; &c. Trans. of 3 pers: Nicholas Hagly, Henery Smith; & Bess a Negro.

JOHN ACKISS (Ackis), 113 A., 1 R., 6 P., Low. Norf. Co., Linhaven Par; called the Piny Thicketts; on S. side of Lyons Quarter Runn; 22 Sept. 1682, p. 194. Granted to David Murrow, the younger, 15 Mar. 1675; deserted; & due sd. Ackiss for Imp. of 3 pers: John Hanning, John Hokins, John America.

ROBERT HARPER, the Younger, 220 A., 1 R., 24 P., Low. Norf. Co., Linhaven Par., towards head of Linhaven River, on the W. side, called the Ashin Sw; 22 Sept. 1682, p. 195. Beg. at Renatus Lands near line; &c. Granted Robert Harper, the Elder, 9 Oct. 1675; deserted; & now due sd. Robert, his son, for Imp. of 5 pers: Rebecca George, John Scott, Sarah Turner als. Joanes, Robert Gourdon, Robert Rany.

FRANCIS SHIPP (Ship), 142 acs., Low. Norf. Co., 22 Sept. 1682, p. 195. Adj. Owin Willys; by the Green Sea; &c. Granted to Richard Stanly 5 June 1678, deserted, & now due for Imp. of 3 pers: Steephen Cossins, Katherine Whelpley, Margaret Richardson.

BENJAMIN AYRES & JOHN STOKELEY, 175 acs., of sand hills & marshes, called Hobson's Choice, Accomack Co., on S. side of Assawoman Inlet, by the Seaboard side; 20 Nov. 1682, p. 195. Trans. of 4 pers: Jon. Pope, Robt. Richards, Jean Pue, John Jones.

ISRAEL SHEPHERD & JOHN GRIMES, Churchwardens of the Low. Par. of Nanzemond; in behalfe of sd. Parish; 230 acs., for a Gleabe; 20 Nov. 1682, p. 196. Beg. by Brown's Br; to the Gleab Cr; to Edward Olliver; cor. of John Murfrey near his dwelling house; &c. Due the abovenamed & their successors by virtue of an order of the Gov'r. & Council, dated in April last, &c.

COL. JOHN LEAR, 900 acs., in Up. Par. of Nanzemond; at Plumpton Park, alias Orapeak; 20 Nov. 1682, p. 196. Beg. at a gr. White Marsh in line of Henery Plumpton, to mouth of Orapeak Gr. Swamp; to head of Pott Quarter Sw., &c. Trans. of 18 pers: And. Beech (?), 4 times; Tho. Andrews, Jon. Griffin, Jon. Freeman, Tho. Harding, Addam Rable, Luke Neale, Tomsin Tarner (or Tanner), Mary Price, Samll. Clarke, Wal. Noak, Jon. Wharton, Phillip Powell, Micha. Thomas, James Knight.

RICHARD MINSHEW & MERCY, his wife, 22 acs., Up. Par. of Nanzemond, in the Southern Br., 20 Nov. 1682, p. 197. Beg. at land formerly Silvester Baker's, neer dwelling house of sd. Minshew; to John Small; &c. Trans. of: John Macdannel.

MICHAEL BRINCKLY (Brinkly), 200 acs., Up. Par. of Nanzemond, 20 Nov. 1682, p. 197. Beg. nigh the Cyprus Sw; down the Gr. Swamp; &c. Trans. of 4 pers: Bridget Knight, Geo. Tucker, Hen. Long, Wm. Horse.

BENJAMIN STRATTON, 300 acs., N'ampton Co., on the Ridge, 20 Nov. 1682, p. 197. On Dun Br; adj. Farmer Jones; George Traveller & Major Wm. Waters. Due as son & heir of Thomas Stratton, to whom it was granted 27 Nov. 1657.

SAME. 247 acs; same Co. & date, p. 298. Called Aquasta Neck; W. upon the Old plantation & creek; N. on John Dennis, S. on Henery Charleton; &c. Granted his father, 5 Oct. 1654, & due (as above), etc.

LT. COL. ISAAC ALLERTON, 2172 acs., Rappa. Co., on S. side & in the freshes of the river, 20 Nov. 1682, p. 198. Beg. at John Bowsey; by br. of Nasaponnecks; &c. Granted to John

Burton & John Austin 5 Nov. 1673, & found to escheat, by inquisition under Lt. Col. Isaac Allerton, Esch'r. Genr'l. of the County, &c.

WM. RANDOLPH & ROBERT BOLLING (Bolding), Gent., 623 A., 14 P., Chas. City Co; Bristoll Par., S. side of Appamattox Riv., att Waughrick Sw., 20 Nov. 1682, p. 199. Beg. at Hugh Lee; to the Great Meadow; up the main Sw; &c. Trans. of 13 pers: Job. ——, Tho. Lyborne, Peter Prout, Jane Borar, Robt. Beazley, Jon. Witt, Lydia Sawyer, Edwd. Gower, Tho. Glover, Lyon Britton, Tho. Jones, Richd. Brown, Jon. Harrold.

MR. GEORGE GILL, 5000 acs., New Kent Co., S. side Pamunkey Riv., upon brs. of Crump's Cr., 20 Nov. 1682, p. 199. Beg. in line of Moses Davis & John Rea; &c. Trans. of 100 pers: Tho. Bin, Richd. Jones, Robt. Wilson, Jon. Andrel, Robert Kinsman, Hen. Long, Mary Acter, Jon. Williams, Sarah Puton, Robt. Flacker, An. Warford (or Wazford), Tho. Alford, Wm. Caneax (or Canear ?), Tho. Holman, Richd. Jewel, James Norway, Mance Huset, David Long, John Perton, Richd. Collins, Hen. Webb, Ann Dozet, Tho. Hull, Elliner Pain, Tho. Watson, Wm. Cohane, Tho. Max, Mary Bractor, Wm. Sewdal, Richd. Cramp, Mary Tenster, An Collen, Tho. Baxter, Jno. Weeden, Tho. Langster, Jon. Carter, James Bayman, Sarah Williams, Tho. Wilson, Richd. Morris, Sarah Narde, Mary Bartloe, Mich. Dane, Mary Banister, Tho. Jones, Ann Dean, Jon. Armstead, Jon. Baxter, Tho. Newel, Wm. Wilson. Susanna Damuns, Samll. Meer, Tho. Walker, Jon. Smith, Edwd. Iling (Hing), Phill. Wyat, Tho. Lane, Jar. Hews, Jon. Strange, Jon. Watkins, Ann Johnson, Tho. Pate, Jon. Hull, Mary Crisp, Ellinor Falleen, James Brickland, Jon. Pew (or Pece), Tho. Pickell, Jon. Bisety, Mary Butler, An. Webel, Tho. Twewil (or Twerril), Abra. Peirce, Tho. Proctor, Jos. Cox, Tho. Barel, Wm. Seth, Fra. Haswel, Edwd. Wyat, Adam Jaz, Jon. Napster, Mary King, Eliz. Banister, Jon. Buget (or Bugel), Mary Stepster, An. Webster, Jane Windsor, Edwd. Lacy, Tho. Merchant,

Hen. Flint, Jon. Underhil, Sarah Britlen, Edwd. Long, Tho. Longman, Tho. Godfrey, James Watson, Edwd. Crump, Richd. Hewson, Mary Jones, Jon. Rossell.

WM. PUCKET & THO. PUCKET, 757 acs., Henrico Co., Bristol Par., N. side of Appamatox Riv; 20 Nov. 1682, p. 200. The first 500 acs. next above Mr. Wm. Baugh, on Peirce's Toile Cr; 300 acs. whereof beg. on sd. Cr., at the Spring Bottom; to the Ashen Sw; along line of Mr. Wm. Walthal; &c; 257 acs. adj. Richard Womeck; & John Pucket; &c. 500 acs. granted John Pucket 27 Jan. 1665, & bequeathed to his 2 sons: Wm. & Thomas; 257 for trans. of 6 pers: Jone White, Alce ——, Patrick Foster, Robt. Tovey (or Povey), John Edwards, Gil. Pucket.

MR. MILFS CARY, 1590 acs., Warwick Co., 20 Nov. 1682, p. 201. Beg. in Farmers Feild, on Back Cr. Run; by Clayborne Neck Damms; on Mr. Hen. Cary, neer Poquoson Mill Path; neer the Otway Sw; neer N. side of Oken Sw; to John Lewis, by main br. of Potash Run; on Capt. John Matthews, to Col. Cole's; to *Labour and Vaine Feild;* on land of Thomas Cary, in possession of his mother Mrs. Ann Cary; neer the Dead Cow branch; neer Druit's old feild; to Magpye Sw; to thicket parting Hartlie's old feild from Brown's, &c. 750 acs. being part of 1050 acs. granted Zachary Cripps, dec'd., 10 Sept. 1645, & by his son Zachary sold to Col. Miles Carey, dec'd., who bequeuathed to his son Miles in fee simple; 840 acs. for trans. of 17 pers: Jon. Jennings, Wm. Walker, Wm. Tuffs, Ann Parker, Robt. Morris, Wm. Jackson, Alexander Farrel, James Williams, Andw. Berry, Jane Griffith, Tho. Senior, Tho. Pond, Jane Abbot, James Joyner, Fra. Gregory, Ja. Kirke, Wm. Richards.

MR. WILLIAM LINES, 230 acs., New Kent Co; on a br. of Poropotanck Cr; 20 Nov. 1682, p. 202. Beg. by William Henderson's fence; by Rappa. Path; to land of Davis; to Mr. Samuel Huckstep; by Wolfe Pit Br., adj. Col. John Lewis; to Mr. Hen. Fox, &c. 200

acs. granted George Austin & Arthur Nash, being the moiety of 400 acs., dated 8 June 1658; 30 acs. for trans. of Robert Feild.

JOHN PARISH, 390 A., 3 R., 26 P., Chas. City Co., Wyanoke Par., on N. side of James Riv., 20 Nov. 1682, p. 203. Beg. in forke of the Old Tree Run; to Richd. Bradford; on Fishing Run, &c. Trans. of 8 pers: Jane Hyme, Jon. Goodman, Joan Johnson, Danll. Cooksey, Wm. White, Richd. Wright, Wm. Powel, Mary Warren.

RALPH BURTON, 200 acs., James City Co., on N. side of Chickahominy Riv., 20 Nov. 1682, p. 203. Beg. in Mr. Dancie's line; down Black Sw., to Mr. Thomas Tinslie's line; down Moses' Run, &c. Purchased from John Williams, son & heir of Richard Williams, to whom 750 acs. was granted 3 Feb. 1651.

EDMOND BOWRING, son & heire of John Bowring, of Linhaven, in Low. Norf. Co; 800 acs. at head of Linhaven River; 22 Nov. 1682, p. 204. Surveyed by Col. John Custice for Sewell Gaskins & John Bowring; ordered by the Genr'l. Court to be pattented for sd. Edmond. Trans. of 16 pers: Tho. Ardington, Geo. Spel, Wm. Cowdry, Jon. Lawrence, Andrw. Rayne, Tho. Preston, Jon. Stephens, Jon. Lyon, Jon. Cradock, Reb. Melson (or Molson), Tho. Palliser (or Tallifer), Jane Goss, Jon. Short, Jon. Hart, Eli. Fletcher, Jon, Taylor.

JOHN FEREBEE, 450 acs.. Low. Norf. Co., at head of Deep Cr., on Southern Br. of Eliz. Riv., 22 Nov. 1682, p. 204. 400 acs. on a povnt, by Bowman's run; adj. Edward Browne, &c; granted to Mr. Richard Jones 23 Oct. 1673, & by severall assignments due sd. Ferebee; 50 acs. upon Deep Cr. & Duke Etheridge's Cr., adj. Yates' land & Marmaduke Etheridge. Trans. of: Ann Webb.

MR. HENRY SPRATT, 1136 acs., Low. Norf. Co., Lynhaven Par., 22 Nov. 1682, p. 205. 351 acs. beg. at Henry Smith, upon the Cypruss Sw; to

Edmund Moore, &c; granted sd. Spratt 15 Mar. 1675/6; 300 acs. on the Broad run; granted Henry Smith 3 Oct. 1671, & sold to Robert Fountaine, who sold to sd. Spratt; 485 acs. adj. sd. Smith & John Bowrin; granted to John Ferebee 27 Sept. 1680, & sold to Mr. George Newton, who sold to sd. Spratt.

JOHN KEELINGE, 2137 acs., Low. Norf. Co., Lynhaven Par., 22 Nov. 1682, p. 206. 700 acs. beg. on Oliver Vanhick's Cr; towards head of the main br. of Lynhaven Riv; granted to Thomas Keelinge 25 Oct. 1651; 100 acs. neer the Bever Dam; granted sd. Thomas as above; 537 acs. beg. in his old survey; neare Thorowgood Keeling; adj. Lt. Thomas Keeling, dec'd., by the road path; to a Marsh neare the Bridge; granted sd. John, 9 Oct. 1675; 800 acs. near Lucy Keeling; adj. Thomas Cannon; & Cornix's line; on the Western Sw; taking in the Beech Ridge to the Broad Run, neare land of Mr. Henry Spratt, to Mr. Anthony Lawson, & by a line trees marked by agreement betwixt sd. Keeling's father & Lawson, dated 15 June 1677. Trans. of 16 Negroes: Abraham, Wm., Sarah, Rebeca, Francis, Morgan, Robt., Matthew, Margaret, Ned, Jack, Tony, George, Cornelius, Daniel, & Derrick.

EDWARD WILLIAMS, 300 acss., Low. Norf. Co., 22 Nov. 1682, p. 207. On Puzzell Poynt Cr; neare William Powell's house; 68 acs. of which is waste land adj., taken by vertue of an order, &c. Granted to Mr. Wm. Daines (or Davies), 25 Mar. 1662, & sold to Nicho. & Robt. Jordan, who sold to sd. Williams.

JOHN BRIGHT, 140 acs., Low. Norf Co., on E. side of the S. Br. of Eliz. Riv., 22 Nov. 1682, p. 207. Beg. by the little Cr; adj. William Etheridge, &c. Trans. of 3 pers: James Jackson, Elizabeth his wife, Joseph Jackson.

MR. JAMES LAMMOND, 500 acs., Low. Norf. Co., Lynhaven Par., 22 Nov. 1682, p. 208. Beg. at his own land; to the Saltpond Cr; to Edward Owld's land, &c. 200 acs, part granted

Dennis Dalley 1 Oct. 1672, & by severall assignments. due sd: Lammond; 300 acs. for trans. of 6 pers: Robert Orrell, Mary Newton, Ann Wood, Sarah Mosse, Thomas Turner. Jno. Green.

THOMAS BENSON, 277 acs., Low. Norf. Co., Lynhaven Par., 22 Nov. 1682, p. 208. 100 acs. granted him 9 Oct. 1675; 177 acs. adj. Griffin's land; neare Jno. Jeams, &c. Trans. of 4 pers: Phillip Suffer (or Susser), Jno, Weeden; Sambo & Robin Negroes.

JOHN ALLOTT, 206 acs., Low. Norf. Co; at head of a br. of the W. br. of Eliz. Riv., 22 Nov. 1682, p. 209. Granted to Robt. Grimes 5 Jan. 1656; assigned to Nicholas Chapman, who assigned to Robert Allott, & now due sd John as heir at law.

MR. RICHARD MOORE (Moor), 148 acs., called the *Dam Necks*, Low. Norf. Co., 22 Nov. 1682, p. 209. Beg. at David Murray, Junr; along the Cyprus Sw., to the lower Dams, &c. Pattented by Warren Godfrey; deserted, &c. Trans. of 3 pers: John Caster; Simon & Ann Indians.

WILLIAM BOULTON, 106 acs., Low. Norf. Co., on the S. side & at head of the W. br. of Eliz. Riv., 22 Nov. 1682, p. 210. Adj. Jean & Grace Johnson; & land that was Edward Outlaw's. Part of 300 acs. granted Thomas Horne 27 Sept. 1665 & that part that did belong to Elizabeth Richason, dau. of sd. Horne & one of the co-heires, by her & her husband, Thomas Richason, sold to Thomas Lovell, who assigned to William Boulton, dec'd; due the above William as son & heir.

JEAN JOHNSON & GRACE JOHNSON, 100 acs., on the S. side & towards head of the W. br. of Eliz. Riv., 22 Nov. 1682, p. 210. Adj. Thomas Tucker & Wm. Boulton. Part of 300 acs. granted to Thomas Horne 27 Sept. 1665, & that part that did belong to Johannah Llewelling, dau. of sd. Horne & one of the co-heirs, by her & her husband, Abel Llewelling, sould to Jno. Johnson, Cooper, & now due the above-named, his daughters, as Coheirs.

THOMAS TUCKER, 100 acs., Low. Norf. Co., on the S side & towards head of the W. br. of Eliz. Riv., 22 Nov. 1682, p. 210. Adj. land of Rigglesworth, now in possession of Jno. Jolliffe, & Jean & Grace Johnson. Part of 300 acs. granted to Thomas Horne 27 Sept. 1665, & that part that did belong to Mary Fanshaw, his dau. & one of the coheirs, by her & her husband, Thomas Fanshaw, sold to Thomas Tucker, & due the abovenamed, his son & heir.

DERMAN MICHEEL, 150 acs., Low. Norf. Co., on N. brs. of Curretuck, 22 Nov. 1682, p. 211. Adj. Peter Crashlee. Trans. of 3 pers: Elizabeth Garrett, Robert Steevens; & Banee a Negro.

MR. THO. MERREDITH (Meredeth), Senr., 523 acs., New Kent Co., S. side of York Riv., 29 Nov. 1682, p. 211. Beg. at mouth of Hammons Cr., & is the land pattented by Col. Hammond by the name of the *Royall Fort; crossing* Mackdannell's Path; to the river below the *Hollowing Place* over against *Pamamack Town;* to *Rockahook Landing;* crossing the Spring Br., &c. Trans. of 11 Negroes: Robin, Jack, Titus, Julian, Besse, Kate, Harry, James, Ned, George, & Joan.

MR. JOHN BUCKNER & MAJOR HENRY WHITEING, 2673 acs., Gloster Co., 22 Dec. 1682, p. 212. Beg. on S. side of a cr. parting land of Mr. Abraham Iveson & Henry Rawlins; to Jno. Reade's old feild; through Cow Cr. Sw; to the mouth of Back Cr., &c. 2400 acs. granted Mr. Edward Dawber 28 Nov. 1642; conveyed to Mr. Richard Young, & due the abovenamed as purchasers of Mr. Samll. Young, his heire at law; 273 acs. found within, &c., due for trans. of 6 pers: Robt. Ellyson, Jon. Walton, Wm. Morgan, Danll. Whitby, Jon. Lirgson, Joan Cole.

EDMUND BORAM, Orphant, 364 acs., Gloster Co., Kingston Par., 22 Dec. 1682, p. 212. On S. side of Horne Harbour Cr. &c. Granted to Mrs. Winefred Morrison 26 Jan. 1651; assigned to Mr. Richard Huull; granted him 24 Nov. 1655; & assigned to sd. Boram, who renewed the same, &c.

MR. CHARLES FOSSON, 90 acs., of Marsh Land in Mattapony River; beg. at the marsh below the *old Stoor;* to Hartquake (Heartquakue) Cr., by the heyland, &c; 22 Dec. 1682, p. 213. Trans. of 2 pers: John Hewes, John Canon.

MR. JNO. LYLLIE, 234 acs., bet. Garden Cr. & Millford Haven, in Gloster Co., 22 Dec. 1682, p. 213. Adj. Mr. Edmd. Forrest; Mr. George Billops; Jno. Calles; & sd. Billops' old devdt., &c. Trans. of 5 pers: Xpher. Trow, Sarah Sparrow, Joan Godden, Isaac Hopkins; Sutton a Negro.

MR. MATHEW WHITTFIELD, 650 acs., Low. Norf. Co., at-head of the S. br. of Eliz. Riv; in the woods called *Sandy Hutton;* 22 Dec. 1682, p. 213. Trans. of 13 pers: Hen. Pate, Ann Hardin, Robt. Cock, Wm. Jolly, Jon. Jolly, Eliz. Pate, Jon. Wittv, Ann Mattocks, Robt. Jermin, Susan Knott, Elder Atkin, Ann Smith, Jon. Boggus.

MR. RICHARD THREADER, 31 acs., New Kent Co., N. side of Mattapony Riv., 22 Dec. 1682, p. 214. Beg. in Hartquake Sw., by Dr. Mathew Jenings, &c. Trans. of: Tho. White.

WILLIAM HOGGEN, 15 acs., Gloster Co., Kingston Par., 22 Dec. 1682, p. 214. Beg. at Mr. Gregg, neare head of a br. of Winter Harbour Cr; to Jno. Deggs' land, &c. Trans. of: Michael Thompson.

RICHARD BILLOPS, 92 acs., Gloster Co., Kingston Par., 22 Nov. 1682, p. 214. Beg. at his own land; adj. Morris Mackashanock, &c. Trans. of 2 pers: Susanna Emlyn, Eliz. Ostler.

WM. MORGAN, 50 acs., Gloster Co., Kingston Par., 22 Dec. 1682, p. 214. Adj. Walter Morgan's land, &c. Granted to Wm. Morgan, dec'd, & due the above Wm. as son & heire.

THOMAS SPENCER, 220 acs., New Kent Co., 22 Nov. 1682, p. 215. Beg. att Will Rogers'; to Mr. Biggs'; to the *Silk Grass Meadow;* to Mr. Nicholas Ware, &c. Trans. of 5 pers: Tho. Spencer; Millicent Spencer 4 times.

JOHN PEADE, Orphant of Mr. George Peade, 370 acs., Gloster Co., Kingston Par., on S. side Winter Harbour Cr., 22 Dec. 1682, p. 215. 150 acs. granted to Jno. Peade, father of George Peade, 21 Sept. 1652; & renewed by sd. George, 25 Sept. 1671; 220 acs. for trans. of 5 pers: Tho. Powel, Tho. Walker, Wm. Davis, John Beymon (or Begmon), John Corbyn.

THO. BUSBY, 475 acs., Surry Co., on NW side of the S. run of Up. Chippoaks Cr., 22 Dec. 1682, p. 216. Beg. in Mr. Benj. Harrison's line; by Heath Br., &c. Trans. of 10 pers: Jon. Williams, Eliz. Hobson, Robt. Atkins, Tho. Broadway, Eliz. Bond, Jon. Harris, Geo. Sheeres, Jon. Handle, Robt. West, Wm. West.

MR. JOHN EVANS, 557 acs., Chas. City Co., Bristoll Par., S. side of *Hapomatucke* (Appomattox) Riv., 22 Dec. 1682, p. 216. Beg. neare Major Gen. Wood; up the Southern run; crossing the maine Ready Br; & the Black Water, &c. Trans. of 12 pers: Mary West, Hen. West, Adam Miles, Margt. Turner, Nicho. Porter, Jon. Midleton, Tho. Stacy, Jon. Smith, Matt. Wilson, Eliz. Porter, Robt. Woodby, James Tanner.

THO. WOTTON & HENRY HAYWOOD, 178 acs., York Co., in New Poquoson Par; on the Oaken Swamp; 22 Dec. 1682, p. 217. Trans. of 4 pers: Wm. Samson, Geo. Fisher, Tho. Jackson, David Ketch.

MR. THO. ALLAMBY, 184 acs., Eliz. City Co., 22 Dec. 1682, p. 217. Beg. att a Figg Tree on James River; upon land of Robert Combes; & Mary Elcock (?). 100 acs. granted to Wm. Brooks, *alias* Morgan, 6 May 1620; 50 granted Wm. Cole 6 Dec. "next following," & by severall conveyances both came to the possession & seizin of Florentine Paine, dec'd, who gave same to his 2 sons, viz: 100 acs. to Florentine, & 50 acs. to Wm., who conveyed the same, in fee, to sd. Alamby; 34 acs. for trans. of Eliz. Wyn.

MR. THOMAS CHEESMAN, 370 acs., Warwick Co., 22 Dec. 1682, p.

218. Adj. his own, Robert Everett; & Mr. Carie's (Cary's) line. Trans. of 8 pers: Jon. Clerk, Tho. Maddin, Nicho. Dewes, Reb. Checke, Tho. Burton, Ralph Williams, Ann Checke, Ann Savage .

JOHN BARTLETT, 50 acs., Gloster Co., Kingston Par., 22 Dec. 1682, p. 218. Adj. Wm. Morgan. Granted to Wm. Morgan, but since his death the pattent is lost; the same being assigned by his heire to Jno. Bartlet.

ROBT. CULLY & RALPH ARM-STEAD, 63 acs., Gloster Co., on E. side of the Eastermost river, 22 Dec. 1682, p. 219. At head of land sd. Cully bought of Mr. Mann. Trans. of 2 pers: Wm. Bastable, Mary Winter.

MR. THO. JONES, 257 acs., New Kent Co., N. side Mattapony Riv., 22 Dec. 1682, p. 219. Beg. on the King's Road; adj. Gabriel Michell; to Tassatians maine Sw., &c. Granted by a former pattent.

MR. JOHN WELLS, 255 acs., Warwick Co., on W. side of Warwick River, 22 Nov. 1682, p. 219. Beg. in head of a br. of Queene Hive Cr; to land of Emanuell Wells, &c. Said land, pattented by Mr. Tho. Ikins, who died intestate & leaveing no heirs, was escheated by sd. Wells.

WALTER MORGAN, 201 acs., Gloster Co., Kingston Par., 22 Dec. 1682, p. 220. Beg. on W. side, at mouth of Peper Cr. 150 acs. part granted to Wm. Morgan, dec'd., & since his decease the patt. is lost; 51 acs. now taken; due sd. Morgan as Heire, &c.

MORRIS MACKASHANOCK, 140 acs., Gloster Co., Kingston Par., 22 Dec. 1682, p. 220. Beg. on E. side of Peach poynt Cr., which runs into Millford Haven; to br. dividing this from land of Richard Billops, &c. 40 acs. bought of Mr. George Billops, dec'd; 100 acs. for trans. of 2 pers: Wm. Morton, Tho. Halliar.

MR. EMANUELL WELLS, 159 acs., Warwick Co., on W. side of Warwick

River, 22 Dec. 1682, p. 220. Beg. at Jno. Wells; along the road to Mulbery Island; to cr. parting this & land of Mr. Anthony Haynes, &c. Sd. land pattented by Mr. Tho. Ikins (?), who dyed intestate & leaveing no heires was escheated by sd. Wells, &c.

MR. JOHN DEAN, 285 acs., in James City Co. & New Kent Co., 22 Dec. 1682, p. 221. Beg. at Dought's Spring; by Rickahack Path; to Farthing's Spring; to Arrow Reed Sw., &c. Purchased of Jno. Smyth & Jno. Williamson for 350 acs., & now surveyed, &c.

CHARLES GOSS, 275 acs., James City Co., on N. side of Moses Cr., 22 Dec. 1682, p. 222. Beg. at lower side of Kerbie's Cr. a little above the mouth, along Henry Young; & Thomas Bobby's land, &c. Said land formerly belonged to Eddy (?) Goss, & since found to escheat, as by inquisition under Henry Hartwell, Depty. Esch'r., &c.

MR. EDWARD LASSELL, 335 acs., Gloster Co., Kingston Par., 22 Dec. 1682, p. 222. Adj. Mr. Richard Billops; Mr. George Billops; Jno. Calles (or Colle's); Marke Foster; & Morris Mackashanock. Trans. of 7 pers: Edwd. Lassel, Junr., Moses Baker, James Sanderling, Ann his wife, Hen. Dawson, Jon. Duffy, Xpher. Starton.

CAPT. WM. SMYTH, Marriner, 527 acs., New Kent Co., 22 Dec. 1682, p. 223. Adj. his own land, & beg. within the plantation, &c. Trans. of 11 pers: Edwd. Owin, Richd. Boxwell, Samll. Birch, Joseph Wiltshire, Joseph Tanner, John Tidford, Mary Savage, Ann Mitchell, Wm. Bartlet, Robt. Tuck, Paul Caesar.

MR. SANDS KNOWLES, 230 acs., Glostei Co., Kingston Par., 22 Dec. 1682, p. 223. Beg. by the path to the head of the Eastermost River, &c. Trans. of 5 pers: Richard Phillips, Samll. Southworke, Margery Watkins, Isaac Sterlinge, Wm. Wood.

MR. WM. BALL & MR. JOHN PRICE, 350 acs., Rappa. Co., 22 Dec,

1682, p. 224. Adj. lands of Mr. Thomas Edmondson, Williamson & Hudson, dec'd; beg. at George Turner & Richard Jones, dec'd; to Thomas Williams, &c. Trans. of 7 pers: John Drapton, Ann Allen, Eliz. Baxter, Wm. Perrey, Sam. Baggot, Wm. Hartwell, Peter Wood.

MR. EDWARD ATCOCK, of Rappa. Co., 500 acs., in sd. Co., on S. side Rappa. Riv., 22 Dec. 1682, p.·224. Behind land of Mr. Henry Smyth; beg. in Bever Dam Sw; to Mr. Bowler's, formerly Col. Goodrich's land; by a foot path, &c. 350 acs., part granted Mr. Will. Hoskins, 8 Apr. 1668; & 150 acs. for trans. of 3 pers.*

MR. JOHN PIGG, 440 acs., Rappa. Co., 22 Dec. 1682, p. 225. Adj. Wm. Young, on Ralphs Cr. 240 acs. granted to Robt. Young 20 Sept. 1661, & renewed in Wm. Young's name 19 Mar. 1677/8; 200 acs. for trans. of 4 pers: John Barker, Tho. Goose, Wm. Seaman, Tho. Short.

JOHN HOLLOWAY, 237 acs., New Kent Co., S. side of York Riv., 22 Dec. 1682, p. 225. Beg. by the Mattoone Cr., a little below a br. called the Deep Bottome, &c; to fork of a Huckleberry Slash; up the Mattoone sunken ground, by the Mattoone lower landing, &c. Pattented by Maj. Gen. Hammond by the name of the *Royall Fort*. Trans. of 5 pers: Wm. Ball 4 times, Hugh Davids (or Davies).

MR. JOHN WELLS, 200 acs., Rappa. Co., S. side the river, bet. Hodgkins & Jelson's Creeks; by the King's Road; to Richd. Nighingale's fence, &c. Granted to Col. Tho. Gudrich (Goodrich), 29 Oct. 1666, & assigned to sd. Wells.

MR. USEBIAS KING, 731 A., 1 R., 30 P., Henrico Co., in Bristoll Par; N. side of Appamattux Riv., & on N. side of the maine Swift Creek; 22 Dec. 1682, p. 226. Trans. of 5 pers: Richd. Ball, Wm. Butler, Joan Butler, Wm. Perkins, Jon. Joanes. The rest being granted by patt. dated 1 Oct. 1674.

RICHARD JONES, JUNR., 232 acs., Low. Norf. Co., 22 Nov. 1682, p. 227. Beg. at Allexander Foreman, by the Cypress Sw; intersecting Gravelly Neck Run; to Bear Garden Sw; on the Eastern Ranges; adj. Mr. Jones, Senr; including all the Bear Garden Ridges, &c. Trans. of 3 pers: Sarah Lee, Jatience Martin, Nicho. Jackson.

MR. JNO. BARNESS (Barnes) & GEORGE PARKER, 350 acs., Accomack Co. on Rack Ileland, by some called the beaches; 22 Dec. 1682, p. 228. N. upon Gargaphya Inlett, S. upon Gr. Mattompkin Inlett, E. upon the Seaboard, & W. upon Salt water & Sunken Marshes. Trans. of 7 pers: Fran. Jackson, Wm. Sparrow, Eliz. Blag (or Blay), Judith Sewel, Tho. Cole, Richard Franklin.

WM. MOSELY, 40 acs., Rappa. Co., S. side the River; on S. or lower side of the mouth of Occupacon Cr; 22 Dec. 1682, p. 228. Beg. at Mr. Henry White near line of Tho. Moss, dec'd; to a small Sw. next above *the Church;* by the Church road, &c. Trans. of: Mary Dibbin.

MR. EDWARD TRAVIS, 550 acs., in James Citty Iland; on James River, att Back Poynt; to mouth of Pasmore Cr; to Cocket's Neck fork; to Pitch & Tarr Sw; to head of Harman's Cr; to back river, &c; including 12 acs. of Mr. Holliday. 326 acs. by pattent 10 Feb. 1663 relateing to a patt. dated 10 Mar. 1653; 150 acs. by purchase from Jno. Seinior, 5 Nov. 1654; 12 acs. purchased from Jno. Crumpe (?) 4 Dec. 1654; 15 acs. from Jno. Johnson 8 Aug. 1659; 70 acs. from Mrs. Susanna Chiles 7 Aug. 1672 & 12 acs. from Wm. Champion 15 Nov. 1677.

MR. BALDWIN SHEPPARD, 360 acs., Eliz. Citty Co; near head of Harris' Cr., 22 Nov. 1682, p. 229. Through Swampy ground, formerly called the White Marsh; adj. Humphry Tabb, &c. 250 acs. granted Thomas Norman 11 Apr. 1636 & after severall assignments came to Jno., the father of sd. Baldwin; 110 acs. for trans. of 3 pers: Joseph Bennet, Ann Shepherd, Tho. Meddars.

MR. EDWD. MUMFORD, 25 acs., being an Island in York Riv., Gloster Co., in Abbington Par; adj. his island called Oak Island; & with other small islands adj. included; 22 Nov. 1682, p. 230. Trans. of: Jon. Badworth.

LT. COL. ANTHONY LAWSON, 300 acs., Low. Norf. Co., in Eliz. River, 22 Nov. 1682, p. 230. Granted to Lt. Col. Thomas Lambert, who sold to Robert Davis, from whom it escheated, by inquisition dated 16 May 1666 under Col. Miles Carey, Esch'r. Genr'l; granted to William Carver, from whom it descended to his son Richard, who sold to sd. Lawson, 7 Dec. 1681.

CAPT. EDMOND CRASK, 650 acs., Rappa. Co., 22 Nov. 1682, p. 231. On S. side the river, adjacent to plantation called *Button's Range*, by vertue of a grant from Hon. Nicho. Spencer, Esq., Secretary, 23 June 1681, being part of patt. for 3650 acs. to Mr. Tho. Button, dec'd., dated 19 June 1666; beg. at SE line of sd. grand pattent, on N. side of path from the Range to Chickahominie Path; over branches of Occupacon (Cr.); by sd. Range house, cutting the maine run of Gilson's (Cr.), &c. Granted to Tho. Button & since his death found to escheat, by inquisition under Col. Isaac Allerton, Esch'r. Genr'l; &c.

By Thomas, Lord Culpeper.

JOHN BARNARD (Bernard), son & heire of Richard Bernard, 280 acs., New Kent Co., S. side of York River, 2 Apr. 1683, p. 231. Beg. upon 200 acs. granted to Col. Robt. Abrahall, 13 Apr. 1657; adj. Mr. Thomas Holmes; over Broache's Sw., upon land of Thomas Meredith; along Thomas Cunketon, &c. Trans. of 6 Negroes: Charles, Ned, Stephens, Besse, Jack, Susanna.

THOMAS MITCHELL, Planter, of New Kent Co., 2436 acs., in sd. Co., being the land he lives on; 28 Feb. 1682/3, p. 232. Beg. at Mr. Robert Jarrett, by Westover Path; by an Indian field, to line tree in the bounds of the County line, neere a br. of Skimino; by Mr. Lancelett Bathurst's fence; by

Towwink Sw., by the Rotten Br; by the horse roade, &c. Part of sd. land granted to him 15 Jan. 1662, & the other part granted to John Lewis & sd. Mitchell by patt. the same day, which sd. Lewis sold his title to sd. Mitchell & acknowledged same in the Co. Ct. of New Kent, 28 Feb. 1672.

ROBERT PEYTON, Gent., of Glocester Co., 150 acs., in sd. Co., in Kingston Par., 28 Feb. 1682/3, p. 233. Beg. at head of land formerly belonging to Mr. Edmund Welsh, dec'd., on N. side of Blackwater Cr; to Mr. Tabb; to land of Humpherey Tomkins, dec'd., &c. Trans. of 3 pers: Augustine Caudle, Thomas Roe, Jeffrey Hardle.

MR. HENRY HARTWELL, 900 acs., called *Ashleys*, Chas. City Co., 12 Mar. 1682/3, p. 234. Which land Dorithy Drew dyed seized of & was found to escheate, by inquisition under Mr. Henry Hartwell, Depty. Esch'r., &c.

MR. DAVID CRAFFORD, 1316 acs., New Kent Co., S. side York Riv., known as *Esoquan Plantation;* 12 Mar. 1682/3, p. 234. Beg. at the mouth of small a sw., dividing this from land of Sir Phillip Honiewood (Honywood); adj. Moses Davies; neere the horse Roade, to John Sleeman (or Fleeman) & Thomas Glass; to James Turner, &c. Granted to Mrs. Hannah Clark, & since her decease found to escheate, by inquisition under Mr. Mark Warkman, Depty. Esch'r.; 17 Sept. 1680, &c; granted to Mr. John Langstone, who assigned to Mr. William Taylo, 28 Oct. 1681, who assigned to sd. Crafford, 28 July 1682.

MARK WARKMAN (Warkeman), Gent., 200 acs., New Kent Co., 12 Mar. 1682/3, p. 235. Which land Robert Atkin dyed seized of, & was found to escheate, by inquisition under Mr. William Leigh, Depty. Esch'r., &c.

MR. GEORGE MORRIS, 750 acs., Rappa. Co., on brs. of Mr. Perrie's Cr., 16 Apr. 1683, p. 236. Beg. at Mr. Perrie's cor., nigh land of Baxter; to Evan Davis'; by Hodges' land, to the Rowling Path; by land of Evan Davis, dec'd; by William Hudson; cross the King's Road; to William Ball & John Price; to Mr. Thomas Edmundson; & land of Clayton & Perry, &c. Trans. of 15 pers: Hannah Howard, Edwd. Hunstone, Richd. Davis, Hum. Davis, Jon. Hunter, Jon. Roberts, Mary Evans, Mary Woodrell, John Lee, Jon. Martin, Jon. Hooke, Richd. White, Jon. Hogg, Tho. Maple, Richd. Bartlet.

BRIGMAN (Bridgman) JOYNER, 300 acs., Is. of Wight Co., -6 Apr. 1683, p. 236. Between Kinsale Sw. & the maine Blackwater; beg. at Hodges Councell; to Thomas Man, &c. Trans. of 6 pers: James Tyler, Mary Rhodes, David Otley, Roger Potter, Robert Mallet, Robert Wade.

MR. THOMAS WOOD (Woods), 400 acs., Rappa. Co., on branches of Pascataway Cr., 16 Apr. 1683, p. 237. Beg. at his house; adj. Mr. Joseph Goodrich; Francis Brown; his own plantation; Mr. Thomas Edmundson; Richard Jones & George Turner; & George Keffield. Trans. of 8 pers: Eliz. Ward, Tho. Parker, Jane Roper, Geo. Mosse, Tho. Dissey, Jane Evans, Jon. Okelly, Edwd. Cooke.

MR. RICHARD WILLIAMSON, 307 acs., Chas. City Co., S. side James River, in Wayonoake Par; att the Otter Dams; 16 Apr. 1683, p. 237. Along John Harris; to Otter Dam maine Sw., &c. Trans. of 7 pers: Jon. Goldin, Edmd. Reeves, Robert Bourne, Wm. Galel, Wm. Peck, Arthur Peirce, John Moor.

MR. THOMAS PLUNKETT, 582 acs., New Kent Co., St. Stephen's Par., 16 Apr. 1683, p. 238. Beg. at land of Richard Gizage; by Richason's line; by Chescurack (?) Path; by Nich. Abbot; to William Burch, &c. 500 acs. granted Tymothy Carter, 5 June 1678; 80 acs. for trans. of 2 pers: Cha. Walker, Mary Walker.

MR. TYMOTHY ELLIS, 35 acs., New Kent Co., on N. side of York River, 16 Apr. 1683, p. 238. Beg. at Hayses' Cr., by plantation of Mr. John King; to land of Orphanes of Mr.

Cant; to Mr. Masters; including a small island, &c. Trans. of: John Rasly.

JOHN SELLAWAY, 650 acs., Is. of Wight Co., neere head of br. of the Blackwater, 16 Apr. 1683, p. 239. Beg. at Thomas Underwood; by George Perce's line; to Capt. Aplewhaite; on John Williams; to Mr. Richard Lovegrove, &c. Trans. of 13 pers: James Davis, Tho. Reding, Roger Gibbs, Wm. Gibbs, Wm. Rogers, Ed. Darcy, Mary Crusty, Eliz. Smith, Mary Codin, Jane Walker, Margaret Blaton (or Beaton), John Needham, Tho. Copping.

MR. DAVID HURD, 300 acs., New Kent Co., S. side York River, 16 Apr. 1683, p. 240. Beg. by this landing; upon Richard Barnhouse; neere head of Ostin's Cr., &c. Purchased of Richard Austin, 28 Apr. 1664.

WILLIAM MAYO, 366 acs., Is. of Wight Co; on S. side of Kinsale Sw., 16 Apr. 1683, p. 240. Adj. Richard Boothe; Hodges Councell; & Joseph Vick; to mouth of the Bever Dam Sw., &c. Trans. of 8 pers: Wilmot Allingo, Mary Holmsley, Eliz. Holt, Mary Blander, Richd. Needham, Mary Manes, Kathe. Bridge, Phillip Russell.

ANTHONY NORTH, 200 acs., Rappa. Co., 16 Apr. 1683, p. 241. Granted to John Green, dec'd., & escheated, by inquisition under Major John Weyr, Depty. Esch'r., 5 May 1669; granted to William Lane, 11 Oct. 1670, who conveyed to sd. North.

MR. STEPHEN BEMBRIDGE & THOMAS ST. JOHN, 110 acs., Rappa. Co., 16 Apr. 1683, p. 241. Adj. land of Col. Wm. Clayborne, dec'd; beg. at fence of sd. St. John; down Wm. Coventon's br; to maine Sw. of Pianketank; to said St. John's plantation; through his corne field, &c. Trans. of 3 pers: Clemt. Corbell, Agnes Corbell, Gabriell Corbel.

MR. GEORGE MORRIS, 450 acs., Rappa. Co., on both sides of a br. of Pianketank River, 16 Apr. 1683, p. 242. Beg. at William Hudson, by Cabbin Br; adj. Mr. Thomas Watkins;

Stephen Benbridge; & land of Thomas Williams, dec'd. Trans. of 9 pers: David Miles, And. Scot, Hugh Peircy, Jon. Allen. Richd. Grimes, Robt. Peck, Tho. Powel; Tomboy & Maria Negroes.

MR. ROBERT FLAKE, 400 acs., Low. Par. of Surry Co., neere the Great Pocoson; 16 Apr. 1683, p. 242. Beg. ½ mi. from Pokatink Sw., bet. Col. Lear, Philip Huniford and Young —— Sumner; by Major Arthur Allen; & Joseph Rogers, &c. Trans. of 8 pers: Tho. Hatton, Geo. Hickson, Jos. Chizell, Tho. Cook, Ralph Bricks (or Bircks), Jo. Parker, Danll. Cooper, Wm. Cole.

MR. JOSEPH RING, 250 acs., Warwick Co., on E. side of Kith's Cr., 16 Apr. 1683, p. 243. Beg. att mouth of a br. running up to *Jacob's Well*, &c. 144 acs. pattented by Mr. Hurd; 106 acs. for trans. of 2 pers: Ed. Foster, Jon. Walker.

MR. JOSHUAH STORY & MR. WILLIAM MORRIS, 5000 acs., New Kent Co., on Mattopony River, 16 Apr. 1683, p. 243. Above land of sd. Morris, beg. at John Pigg & land of Thomas Hall, dec'd., &c. Trans. of 100 pers: Wm. Swift, Rose - Skinner, An Legg, Reb. Broughton, Tho. Nichols, Matt. Mariner, Jon. Gostrey, Tho. Bush, Jos. Cobb, Mary Clements, Kathe. Furnifold, Ann Wadskin, Ann Hodskin, Noah Bareford, Jos. Newman, Hen. Smith. Margt. Goldsmith, Jane Painter, Jon. Lyal, Alex. Right, Richd. Wakefeild, Robt. Beard, Jon. Tayler, Nich. Turk, Hen. Morehouse, Isa. Ashton, Sam. Bolton, Tho. Jackson; Wm., Murrea, Bridget, Peter, great Tom, little Tom, Judeth, Kate, Butcher, Barebones, Jack, Tony, Besse, Maria, Tippin, Tanks, Sam, Sambo, Samson, Simon, Brashear, Ned, Dick, George, Clem, King, James, Stephen, Rowland, Hugh, Tinker, Xpher., Silvester, Joyce, Hannah. Tab., Susan, Maria, Tanks, Nanny, Roger, Judith, Nich, Jasper, Hicks, Lylly, Cully, Morgan, Hoggen, Shepherd, Morris, Cowboy, Evan, Dudly, Francis, Goss, Robin, Bob, Wm., America, Angela, Guinney, Guiana, David, Closh, Basket, Dampier, Pigg, Burton, Gill—Negroes.

THOMAS WALTER, 400 acs., James City Co., 16 Apr. 1683, p. 244. Beg. 2 chains off of Poplar Spring br; to Hitchcock's line; along Mason's line; to br. of Webb's Sw., &c. Trans. of 8 pers: Jo. Reynolds, Timothy Pell, Wm. Hardin, Tho. Antell, Rob. Titterton, Robt. Dale, Wm. Clerke, Law. Baker.

MAJOR JOHN STITH, 236 A., 2 R., 16 P., Chas. City Co., Westopher Par., on S. side of James River; 16 Apr. 1683, p. 244. Beg. on E. side of the Northerne br; along western br. of Herring Cr., &c. Trans. of 5 pers: Alice Roomes, Roger Bell, Isaac Maskew, Mary Brown, Hen. Cheeseman.

(MR. HERY (Henry ?) FOX, son & heir of Mr. John Fox, dec'd., 300 acs., New Kent & Gloster Co.'s; 16 Apr. 1683, p. 245. Beg. at Mr. Wm. Anderson's fence; nigh Col. John Lewis' Quarter, up the maine Sw., to a br. dividing this & land of Mr. Wm. Lynes. 200 acs. purchased by sd. John of Mr. Thomas Hankes, having been granted to sd. Hankes & Jno. Garrett; 100 acs. for trans. of 2 pers: Robert Seale, Tho. Lee.

JOHN MADISON (Maddison) & RICHARD OWEN, 100 acs., New Kent Co., St. Stephen's Par., 16 Apr. 1683, p. 245. Beg. on land of Edwd. Estham; to Jacob Fleepo; to Mantepike Path, by the Indian Path & sd. Mr. Hansford; by Cattail br., to the Spring br. & joyning his own land, &c. Trans. of 2 pers: Robt. Dart, Tho. Watkins.

JOHN MADISON (Maddison), JUNR., 430 acs., New Kent Co., St. Stephen's Par., on N. side of Mattopany River, 16 Apr. 1683, p. 246. Running through the old Feild land; to N. side of the Spring br., crossing the Road, to Robt. Bagbie's; on land of John Miles; to Mr. Chamberlaine, &c. 300 acs. granted John Madison, Senr., 18 Mar. 1662; 130 acs. newly taken & due for trans. of 3 pers: Nich. Parsons, Jos. Ridge, Robert Wheeldon (or Wheedon).

JOHN HARRIS, 250 acs., Charles City Co., Wayenoake Par., S. side

James River, 16 Apr. 1683, p. 246. Beg. by the Otter Dams maine Sw., &c. Trans. of 5 pers: Hugh Carty, Tho. Holder, Robt. Barnes, Robt. Huet, Edmd. Taylor.

JOSEPH ROGERS, 1025 acs., Low. Par. of Surry Co., comonly called *Pokotink,* 16 Apr. 1683, p. 247. Beg. on E. side of Pokatink Sw; adj. Mr. William Newsam; down Corner Sw; & a run of Holybush Sw., &c. 850 acs. granted to Capt. Cockerham & Mr. Charles Borham 14 May 1666, & by sd. Borham, who became possest of the whole by survivourship, sold to sd. Rogers; the remainder being wast land within the bounds; & due for trans. of 4 pers: Richd. Johnson, Peter Edwards, Robert Jones, Jane Bently.

MR. STEPHEN BEMBRIDGE, 2315 acs., in New Kent & Rappa. Co.s; 16 Apr. 1683, p. 247. Beg. at Col. Clayborne on S. side of Bestland Sw; to Rappa. Roade; to land of Jones & Turner; on Williams', & Mr. Watkins' land, &c. Trans. of 47 pers: Tho. Goodry, Tho. Short, Wm. Jennings, Peter Forth, James Crosse, Mary Gilbert, Susan Thorne, Jon. Savage, Wm. Henchman, Sarah Smith, Rebecca Hodges, Tho. Green, Edwd. Davenport, Wm. Connier, Edwd. Taylor, Kathe. Tomlyn, Ann Leech, Robt. Hastings, Mary Ely, Tho. Herbert, David Purcel, Dorothy Garner, Ann Blyth, Eliz. Roberts, Tho. Wharton, Phillip Yorke, John Phillips, Peter West; (an) Indian, Tho. Biggs, Margaret Harland, John Watson, John Richardson, James Abb, Edwd. Macon, Edwd. Scruffe. Samll. Morgan, James Strahan, Francis Nicholas, Sarah Style, Richd. Tunstall, Tho. Kelligrew; 5 Negroes.

MR. GEORGE MORRIS, 5000 acs., New Kent & Rappa. Co.'s; 16 Apr. 1683, p. 248. 3000 acs. granted him 8 May 1674. Beg. at Col. Goodridge's, by Tuckahow Sw; by Portobago Path; to lands of Bagby; Burnell; Henry Pigg; & Mr. Richd. Whitehead; by Mattopany Br., &c. Trans. of 40 pers: Jonathan Marrow, Mary Marrow, Doughty Brown, Geo. Wilson, Hannah Lee, David Lynsey, Ann Marrei, Joshua

Esto, Ann Moor, Senr., Ann Moor, Junr., Dan. Lisle, Jon. Carr, Eliz. Parry, Mary Harris, Ed. Harding, Ann Murral, Mary Barbinton, Wm. May, Robt. Smart, Tho. Stephens, Wm. Roberts, Edwd. Braybrook, Cha. Perry, Richd. Wilson, Walter Price, Robt. Monday, Wm. Sydney, Jos. Lucas, James King, Margt. Hawkins, Jon. Padey, Richd. Keyes, Tho. Talbot, Alice Hobbs, Antho. Moor, Mary Guy, Jon. Fry, Jon. Williams, Jon. Peace, Tho. Reekes.

ROBERT MEREDITH, 217 acs., New Kent Co., S. side of York River, 16 Apr. 1683, p. 249. Beg. at Thomas Meredudd, Senr., & Thomas Dunketon; crossing the Brick House Road; by Brushes Sw; to Gabriell Wilson's Spring Br; &c. Trans. of 5 pers: Mary Willis, Tho. Bell, Geo. Devar, Law. York, Richd. Steele.

MR. JOSEPH TANNER & MR. RICHARD WAMOCKE, 206 A., 1 R., & 20 P., Henrico Co., in Bristoll Par., on N. side of Appomattock Riv., 16 Apr. 1683, p. 250. Beg. at Major Wm. Harris, to the *Holy Ground Slash;* to maine br. of Ashen Sw; &c. Trans. of 5 pers: Tho. Bayes, Richd. Perrot, David Salisbury, Tho. White, Hen. Boyce.

WILLIAM WARD, 50 acs., Nansimund Co., 16 Apr. 1683, p. 251. Escheated from John Ewins, by inquisition under William Alford, Deuty. Esch'r., 18 Nov. 1671; &c.

MRS. LYDIA NOWELL, 357 acs., James City Co., N. side James River, 16 Apr. 1683, p. 251. Near John Edloe on W. side of Woolfe's Plantation; on Ellibris' line; including Plantation called Foreman's; sd. land purchased 27 Sept. 1655 by William Fry, Gent., of Rice Hoe, Gent., for 252 acs; the residue for trans. of 3 pers: Hen. Bowser, Sam. Eldridge, John Rosse.

JAMES BRYAN, 315 acs., Is. of Wight Co., bet. Kinsale Sw. & the maine Blackwater; 16 Apr. 1683, p. 252. Beg. at William Mayo's cor. in Richard Booth's line; to Hodges Councill; &

Bridgman Joyner, &c. Trans. of 7 pers:
John Curtis, Ellen Burton, James Wilson, James Grandee, Wm. Mason, Tho.
Waldon, Sarah Briggs.

MR. JONAS LISCOMB, 432 A., 1
R., 7 P., Chas. Citty Co; Westopher
Par; S. side of James Riv., 16 Apr.
1683, p. 252. Adj. Major John Stith.
Trans. of 9 pers: Jon. Tucker, Margt.
Jones, Edwd. Cooke, Danll. Parker, Tho.
Scafe, Hen. Pott, Tho. Lylly, John
Simpson, Tho. Rockwell.

WILLIAM BLAKE, 550 acs., New
Kent Co., 16 Apr. 1683, p. 253. Beg.
below the Plantation in line of William
Richardson, by the Tymber Br; to
Tymothy Carter, to Mr. Bird; to Col.
Johnson; to Mr. Holmes; & Buford's
land; &c. Trans. of 11 pers: Richd.
Paine, Dameras Watney, Eliz. Picket,
Jon. Cassick, Robt. Parker, Jon. Hancock, Robt. Glover, Phill. Cole, Ann
Found, Eliz. Alexander, Ann Paine.

SAMUELL BLOMEFIELD (Bloomfeild), JOHN DANGERFIELD, WILLIAM MOSELY, BRYAN WARD, &
WILLIAM BENDERY, 2359 acs., bet.
Rappa. River & head or run of Mattopany Riv., 22 Nov. 1682, p. 254. (By
Sir Henry Chicheley.) E. upon Path
from Portobaco Indian Towne to Chickahominy Indian Towne, W. upon a great
tract of Major Robert Beverley's, &c.
Trans. of 47 pers: Jon. Sherman, Robt.
Baker, Jon. Rowly, Susan West, Mary
Godfry, David Tobdell, Sus. Ripley,
Luke Raven, Joan Swift, Tho. Joyner,
Wm. Marcum, Geo. Bayman, Jon.
Sands, Nich. Watts, Ja. Jones, Samll.
Carter, Mary Wood, Jane Sharp, Tho.
Vintner, Susan Colt, Ema. Harris, Tho.
Gold, Jo. Harper, Robt. Read, Wm.
Waters, Fra. Farmer, Jos. Marlar,
Joyce Davies, Wm. Jacobs, Mary Wilson, Jon. Poor, Ja. Mann, Eras. Perry,
Mary Smith, Wm. Cocke, Geo. Holmes,
Wm. Jones, Jon. Farmer, Wm. Towne,
Mary Williams, Wm. Wallis, Mary
Salter, Jon. Edwardson, Wm. Simpson.
Tho. Turner, Wm. Batem, Alexander
Monk.

JOHN STALLENGE & ELIAS
STALLENGE, 280 acs., of land & white

marish, Up. Par. of Nanzimund Co., att
.. .. the White Marish, 16
Apr. 1683, p. 255. Beg. Adj. Capt.
Boothe; Robert Reddick; & land of
John Ellis, now said Booth's; being
overplus within their bounds of a patt.
to William Wright, 18 Mar. 1662.
Trans. of 6 pers: John Serjeant, James
Johnson, Tho. Symons, Tho. Busby,
Tho. Barwick, Jon. Meekes.

JOSEPH BOOTH, 400 acs., Up. Par.
of Nanzimund Co., 16 Apr. 1683, p.
255. Beg. by maine run of Cypress Sw;
Adj. Mathew Spivey; & Mr. John Chilcott. Trans. of 8 pers: Tho. Bauldwin,
Jacob Hewes, Tho. Watson, Mary Tunstall, Martha Dell, Wm. Serjeant, Wm.
Anderson, Henery Dennis.

ROBERT BREWER, 300 acs., Up.
Par. of Nanzemund, att King-Sale, 16
Apr. 1683, p. 256. Beg. in the County
line; to William Collings; & William
Gatling, &c. Trans. of 6 pers: Jon.
Hall, Eliz. Hull, Eliz. Holland, Fra.
Sorrel, Jon. Sorrel, Geo. Watson.

JOHN HOLLAND, 200 acs., Up.
Par. of Nanzimund County, att King
Sale. 16 Apr. 1683, p. 256. Beg. at
William Gatling, a cor. of George
Corps, &c. Trans. of 4 pers.* (Marginal note: Recorded in folio 267.)

JOHN BRINKLY, 250 acs., Up.
Par. of Nansimund Co., att Chivey
Chase, 16 Apr. 1683, p. 257. Beg. att
mouth of a br. of Mossey Sw; by the
Gr. Swamp, &c. Trans. of 5 pers: Wm.
Tuffy, Wm. Brewer, Geo. Andrews,
Jon. Beard, Wm. Parker.

JOHN SUMNER & JOHN STALLENGE, 1000 acs., Up. Par. of Nansimund Co.. att Orapeak, 16 Apr. 1683,
p. 257. Beg. by the ridge of Orapeak
Sw., &c. Trans. of 20 pers: James
Williams, Job Lane, Barth. Lownes,
Arth. Upshot, Robt. Bradly, Doro. Perkins. Tho. Melford, Jon. Little, Mary
Fisher, Jane Jolly, Peter Peterson,
David Warren, Tho. Offeild, Roger
Beach, Tho. Rogers, Emlyn Taylor, Jane
Dunkin, Walter Wood, Phillip Cox,
Edwd. Norman.

HENERY PLUMTON (Plumpton), 100 acs., Up. Par. of Nansimund, 16 Apr. 1683, p. 258. Beg. by Oropeak Gr. Sw; cor. of Col. John Lear; to the White Oake Neck. Trans. of 2 pers: Tho. Lewis, Ann Custis.

ROBERT BLANSHARD, 100 acs., Up. Par. of Nanzimund, att *Jerico*, 16 Apr. 1683, p. 259. Adj. Col. Dew; &c. Trans. of 2 pers: Alice Thomas, Ann Hues.

MATHEW SPIVY (Spivey), 200 acs., Up. Par. of Nansimund, 16 Apr. 1683, p. 259. Beg. nigh the Cypress Sw., corner of his brother George Spivey, to a br. called Hawkins' hole, &c. Trans. of 4 Negroes: Henery, Joan, Bess, Overseer.

THOMAS PARKER, 150 acs., Up Par. of Nansimund, 16 Apr. 1683, p. 259. Beg. at Col. Thomas Dew, att the mouth of Craeny Cr., issueing out of the southern br; including *Rackoone Island*. Trans. of 3 pers: Richard Thomas, John Ross, Ann Perkins.

HUGH GAHAN, 400 acs., Up. Par. of Nansimund, 16 Apr. 1683, p. 260. Beg. at James Griffin, nigh the Cypress Sw., on the S. side, by the maine run, &c. Trans. of 8 pers: Hum. Pope, Eliz. Norton, Isaac Berkeley, Ann Clerk, Richd. Higdon, Tho. Brown, Samll. Green, Richd. Taylor.

FRANCIS SANDERS, 600 acs., Up. Par. of Nansimund, att *King Sale*, 16 Apr. 1683, p. 260. Beg. at Thomas Titus & Nicholas Dixon; to Reedy Br; crossing Cabbin Sw; adj. Jonathan Robinson & Richard Thomas. Trans. of 12 pers: Cha. Colket, Jos. Bennet, Jon. Coffer, Jon. Butler, Robt. Owen, Edwd. Pickery, Jon. Walker, Tho. Ross, Margart. Clerk, Richd. Hiill, Joan Hill, Tho. Hill.

FRANCIS PARKER, 20 acs., Up. Par. of Nansimund, 16 Apr. 1683, p. 261. In the line of *Hood's Neck*, in possession of sd. Parker; to the Cross Swamp Pattent, granted to his father Richard Parker, Sr; adj. *Jerico*, now belonging to Col. Thomas Dew. Trans. of: Wm. Foot.

JOHN CHILCOTT, 200 acs., Up. Par. of Nansimund, 16 Apr. 1683, p. 261. Adj. Joseph Booth; & his own land; nigh the Cyprus Run. Trans. of 4 pers: Roger Norman, Ann Phillips, Edwd. Massey, Hen. Coplin.

CHARLES ROADES (Rhodes), 322 acs., Up. Par. of Nansimund, towards head of the Southerne Br., 16 Apr. 1683, p. 262. To mouth of the Bever Dam Br; adj. John Winborne, &c. 270 acs. part of 800 acs. granted James Foster & Adrian Bonny, 27 Sept. 1661; & by sd. Bonny conveyed to James Sever, who surrendered to sd. Roades; 45 acs. for trans. of: Cha. Perches.

JAMES GRIFFIN, 400 acs., Up. Par. of Nansimund Co., 16 Apr. 1683, p. 262. Beg. at Michaell Brinkley, nigh S. side of the Cypress Sw., &c. Trans. of 8 pers: John Ellis, Robt. Frank, Law. Tomkins, Tho. Webb, Joyce Axell, Wm. Butler, Robt. Cockerell, Tho. Wilkinson.

WILLIAM BYRD, 450 acs., Up. Par. of Nansimund Co., att *Summerton*, 16 Apr. 1683, p. 263. Beg. at Knuckles Sw. Trans. of 9 pers: Danll. Lyss, Tho. Moor, Wm. West, Rac. Hailes, Richd. Huffe, Jon. Gayle, Tho. Butler, Hen. Vincent, Ellen Brown.

JOHN VADDY, 250 acs., N'umberland Co., 3 Apr. 1651, p. 264. N. upon Vaddies Cr., S. upon William Vincent & E. upon the Bay. Trans. of 5 pers.* Recorded in the Secretaries office 16 Apr. 1683. *(By Sir William Berkeley.)*

EDWARD ELLERBY, 100 acs., James City Co., 16 Apr. 1683, p. 264. From James Riv., along line of Mrs. Nowell, &c. Part of 600 acs. granted William Haveat, 20 Oct. 1661, who bequeathed to William Strong, 26 Aug. 1663, who sold sd. 100 acs. to Stephen Butts, 8 Oct. 1675, who sold to sd. Ellerby, 17 Sept. 1677.

JOHN DOBY, 362 acs., James City Co., 16 Apr. 1683, p. 265. From James Riv., along Edward Ellerby; to Drinkard's line; to head of a little creeke at *Mount Sinai Bridge;* & down same to the River. Part of 600 acs. granted to William Haveat 20 Oct. 1661, who by will dated 26 Aug. 1663 bequeathed to William. Strong, who on 30 Jan. 1677 sold 100 acs. to sd. Doby, & by will bequeathed 50 acs. more to sd. Doby; 212 acs. sd. Strong by will, dated 28 Aug. 1675, gave to William & Hester Thomas, who on 1st Aug. 1676 assigned to sd. Doby.

WILLIAM HUNT, 675 acs., James City Co., 16 Apr. 1683, p. 265. Beg. at head of Aroroper Sw., *alias* the head of the lower br. thereof; neere Oaken Sw; on S. side Ridge Field; to Pease Hills, Lucy Stratton, Judeth Beach, to Mr. Edward Travis 27 Feb. 1643; by him deserted, & granted by order, to sd. Hunt; trans. of 14 pers: Tho. Lund, Jon. Watson, Maurice Smith, Wm. Hills, Lucy Stratton, Judeth Beach, Tho. Reeve, Richd. Paine, Dam. Watnye, Ell. Pickett, Hen. Dunnham, Jon. Cassick, Robt. Parker, Jon. Hancock.

COL. WILLIAM KENDOLL (Kendall), 300 acs., N'ampton Co., 16 Apr. 1683, p. 266. Granted to Edward Drew, dec'd., & found to escheat, by inquisition under Col. John Stringer, Esch'r. Genr'l., 2 Nov. 1680, &c.

CORNELIUS REYNOLDS, 300 acs., Rappa. Co., in the freshes & on S. side of the River, 16 Apr. 1683, p. 267. Granted to John Godfrey, dec'd., & found to escheate, by inquisition under Col. Isaac Allerton, Esch'r. Genr'l., 14 Dec. 1681, the moyety whereof was sold to sd. Godfrey 6 May 1674 by Richard Perkinson, assignee of John Dolton, who possessed sd. land by will of Thomas Farrill; the other moyety sold to Godfrey by Dolton, the legatee of sd. Farrill, assignee of John Speed, 8 Apr. 1674, as by the severall deeds will appear, &c.

MR. LANCELOT BATHURST, 1300 acs., New Kent Co., S. side of York River in the Narrowes, & on N. side of Chickahominy maine Sw., 16 Apr. 1683, p. 267. Adj. Mr. Thomas Michell; Mr. Newell; land of Mr. Bur-

rell, now Col. Pate's &c. 1250 acs. purchased of Mr. Jonathan Newell, 5 Apr. 1670; 50 acs. for trans. of: Mary Ludwell.

COL. RICHARD JOHNSON & MR. JOHN PIGG, 1150 acs., New Kent Co; N. side the freshes of Mattopany River, 16 Apr. 1683, p. 268. Beg. at the mouth of Holly Poynt Cr; adj. land of Robert Bagby; William Herendon; & Mr. Richard Whitehead; by an Indian field, &c. Trans. of 23 pers: Antho. Stevens, Jon. Jones, Tho. Towers, Wm. Draper, Jo. Brown, Fra. Cooper, Wm. Cooke, Alice Swan, Fra. Bennet, Wm. Sawyer, Robt. Draper, Antho. Gunnel, Jon. West, Ma. Wright, Jon. Smith, Jon. Price, Tho. Williams, Jam. Smart, Jon. Eastland, Tho. Davis, Edwd. Travers, Wm. Richards, Tho. Jones.

COL. WILLIAM STEVENS & COL. DANNIELL JENIFER, 200 acs., Accomack Co., on S. end of Assateeg Island, 16 Apr. 1683, p. 269. Bounded NW by Assateeg, *alias* Mattopany, Inlett, N. along the Seaboard to the extent of Va. & Maryland bounds. Trans. of 4 pers: John Free, Hen. Parker, Richd. St. Loo, Jon. Perkins.

COL. DANNIELL JENIFER, 220 acs., Accomack Co; being sand hills & marishes, by some called the beeches; 16 Apr. 1683, p. 269. Beg. at George Parker & John Barnes, from S. side of Garaphia Inlett, to N. side of Assawoman Inlett; S. on land of Benjamin Eyre & John Stokeley, &c. Trans. of 5 pers: Samll. Castor, Jam. Thompson, Richd. Read, Jon. Flash, Tho. Howell.

MR. PETER BAINTON, 200 acs., Is. of Wight Co., 16 Apr. 1683, p. 270. Being land Mrs. Elizabeth Boucher, dyed seized of; escheated by inquisition under William Randolph, Depty. Esch'r., 1 July 1682, &c.

MR. DANNIELL HIGGDON, 518 A., 1 R., 16 P., Chas. City Co; Westover Par; S. side James River; 16 Apr. 1683, p. 270. From Major Francis Poytherys (Poytheris), upon the middle southern Br; on Mr. Warradine; crossing Hollow Bush Br., & Medow Br; to

William Edmunds, &c. Trans. of 11 pers: Mary Hilliard, Mary Whiting, Ann Dawes, Kath. Stone, Edwd. Chiswell, James Smith, Geo. Horne, Tho. Murrow, Tho. Jarvis, Jon. Mayden, Benjamin a Negro.

JOHN BAXTER, 517 A. 2 R. 28 P., Chas. City Co; Westover Par; N. side of James River, 16 Apr. 1683, p. 271. Beg. on N. side of Herring Cr., in line of Esqr. Place; to Madam Bland, &c. Trans. of 11 pers: Jon. Hagman, Jon. Darby, Eliz. Holland. Kath. Keating, Richd. White, Danll. Kelly, Phill, Eson, Arth. Bryant, Jon. Rich, Jon. Overton, Wm. Williams.

THOMAS DORBY, 65 acs. New Kent Co., Straton Major Par., on Arakeco (Arrokieco) Sw., 16 Apr. 1683, p. 271. Beg. at Symons' land; by the old Road, joyning to Sheere's land; to Capt. Jones', &c. Trans. of 2 pers: Theodorus Bran, Tho. Smith.

WILLIAM WILKINS, 265 A., 1 R., Chas. City Co., Westover Par., on S. side of James Riv., 16 Apr. 1683, p. 272. Beg. at Richard Cairlile; crossing the Mill Path; to Hangman's Neck, to head of Bridge Cr; on Bland's Path; to Alexander Davison's land, &c. Trans. of 6 pers: Robert Hurd. Wm. Thomas, Ann Cooper, Mary Phillips, John Yeo, Edwd. Spicer.

ROBERT ANDERSON, 727 acs., New Kent Co., 16 Apr. 1683, p. 273. On N. side of Chickahominy Sw., in the head of Holly Bush Br., cor. of Thomas Glass; to mouth of Meyry Br., &c. Trans. of 15 pers: Peter Ludwell, Jon. Goring, Tho. Duke, Ion. Steward, Tho. Gray, Ra. Carr, Hen. Chown, Hen. Bill, Edwd. May, Step. Elphidge, John Charles, Jon. Curle, Edwd. Nott, Robt. Staller, Law. Marsh.

MR. JOHN HOBBS. 381 A., 3 R., 20 P., Chas .City Co., Wayonoake Par., S. side of James River, 16 Apr. 1683, p. 273. Beg. at the Pouns (or Ponns) main run, belonging to land of Benia. Foster; crossing Swift's Br: to Morris Rose; on the maine Sw; to forke of the Cattailes & Poll Run; &c. Trans. of 8

pers: Sarah Guy, Hen. Vernon, Wm. Hilson, Richd. Prince, Susanna Wilnutt, Jane Hopkins, Robt. Crimly, Robt. Berry.

MR. DANNIELL HIGDON, & MR. ROGER REESE, 265 A., 1 R., 13 P., Chas. City Co., Westover Par., S. side of James River, 16 Apr. 1683, p. 274. Adj. Richard Pace; crossing King's field Br. & the Long Poynt Br; to John Williamson: crossing Black Water Path, & the Scotch Br., to Col. Edward Hill, &c. Trans. of 6 pers: Robert Hix, Phillip Row, Robt. Slye, Mary Cooper, Ann Dawes, Ren. Crickett.

MR. GEORGE BILLOPS. 750 acs., Gloster Co., on N. side of Garden Cr., 16 Apr. 1683, p. 275. Adj. John Calles (or Colles); neere Edward Forrest, &c. 500 acs. granted to George Billops, dec'd., viz: 27 Jan. 1663 & 9 Apr. 1674; 250 acs. for trans. of 5 pers: Tho. Glew, Richd. Martin, Richd. Hodges, Mary Partan, Wm. Wallis.

MR. GEORGE MORRIS, 1100 acs., New Kent Co., St. Stephen's Par., being the devd't. he lives upon, 16 Apr. 1683, p. 276. Beg. by the *Church Road;* to Mr. Leftwich's land; by John Pigg, to land of Rogers; by Mr. Broach, to land formerly Robert Florrie's; by Woolfe Pitt Br., joyning Col. Robert Abrahall, to the King's Roade; by James Quarles; over Mattepeke Path, adj. John Hill, to the Hodg house Br; by John Page, & Edward Estham, &c. 860 acs. granted him 29 Apr. 1668; 240 acs. for trans. of 5 pers: Eliz. Palmer, Darke Celebrand, Ann Thompson, Ann Smith, Richd. Faulkner.

EDWARD WILDER, 200 acs., on E. br. of Tanner's Cr., Low. Norf. Co., 16 Apr. 1683, p. 277. Beg. at Samuell Roberts'; to Richard Hartwell; to head of br. running into the old Bever Dam; neere path to Alexander Gwynn, &c. Trans. of 4 pers: Roger Hodges twice, Dorothy Godfrey, John Graham.

JOHN HOLLAND. 200 acs., Up. Par. of Nansimund Co., att *King Sale,* 16 Apr. 1683, p. 277. Beg. at William Gattling, cor. to George Corpes; &c.

Trans. of 4 pers: David Campbell, Hum. Baldwin, Eliz. Cooper, Jon. Taylor.

EVAN BAKER, *alias* Belange, & ROBERT MANN, 89 A., 8 P., Henrico Co., Bristol Par; on S. side of James River, & on N. side of Swift Cr., 16 Apr. 1683, p. 278. Adj. Mr. Henery Randolph. Trans. of 2 pers: Nicho. Phillipis, Tho. Ward.

JOHN SMITHER, 890 acs., Glocester Co., upon the Bay, bet. the mouth of Garden Cr. & mouth of Winter Harbour, 16 Apr. 1683, p. 278. Trans. of 18 pers: Mary Squire, Ursula Paine, Hum. Eldridge, Mary Stiles, Geo. Ridly, Wm. Blenkister, Hen. Williams, Eliz. Tindall, Tho. Combs, Richd. Leighton, Ma. Clinker; Tom. Betty, Ann, Tom, Gilbert, Negroes.

JOHN DEGGS, 1425 acs., Gloster Co., on S. side of Garden Cr., 16 Apr. 1683, p. 279. Beg. neere head of a Bever Dam parting this from land of Mathew Gale; to John Garnett; on head of Sandy Br; to land of Mr. Hampton, dec'd, &c. Granted to him 26 Sept. 1678.

JOHN PIGGOTT, 200 acs., being a seated Plantation, scittituated on *Cowen Gock* in Curretuck, in the S. br. of Low. Norfolk Co., 16 Apr. 1683, p. 279. Beg. on a bay; towards mouth of Sanders' Cr., &c. Trans. of 4 pers: Edwd. Court, John Smith, James Morgan, Martha Elford.

THOMAS COTTEN, 335 acs., Up. Par. of Surry Co., on NE side of the Otter Dam Sw., 16 Apr. 1683, p. 280. Adj. Mr. John Barker, neere his Cart path, &c. Trans. of 7 pers: Archibald Allen, Eliz. Stokeley, Abra. Hath. Jon. Smith, Tho. Brewer, Hen. Hunt, Tho. Owen.

JOHN PAGE, ESQR., one of his Majestie's Councill, 330 acs., in the Middle Plantation, York Co., 16 Apr. 1683, p. 280. 280 acs. Beg. in the Trench where the old pales stood on N. side of the Roade that leads through the Middle Plantation towards James Citty; to land of William Dyer, &c.

100 acs. bought of Col. George Reade 25 June 1655; 190 bought of William Newman, formerly belonging to George Lake, dec'd; 150 acs. of sd. 190 acs. escheated to his most Sacred Majesty the 6 May 1682, but by survey now made found to be but 280 acs., including 10 acs. of Mr. William Sherwood & Thomas Robley; 280 acs. due sd. Page, viz: 100 acs. granted to Lewis Burwell & Lucy his wife, 13 Oct. 1652, being purchased by Maj. George Read of William Bernard, Esqr., & *Lycy* his wife, heire to Capt. Robert Higginson, 28 Nov. 1653, & by sd. Read sold to sd. Page, 25 June 1655; 100 acs. purchased by Thomas Lucas & Thomas Gregory of Capt. Richard Popeley 1 Feb. 1641; by them sold to Thomas Heath; assigned to George Lake & George Wyat 29 Jan. 1643; 400 acs. likewise purchased by sd. Lake & Wyat of sd. Popeley 12 Apr. 1642, & then the sd. 500 acs. equally divided bet. sd. Lake & Wyat; the sd. halfe granted to sd. Lake 4 Oct. 1645, 100 acs. of which he sold to John Meekes 28 Oct. 1646, who sold to Nicholas Harryson 22 Nov. 1651, who assigned to William Newman 19 May 1652, who assigned to Henry Walker 17 Jan. 1652, who sold 50 acs. part to John Moler (or Maler) in June 1654, now in the tenure of William Dyer, & reassigned to sd. Newman 5 Sept. 1657, who sold about 10 acs. of sd. 100 acs. to William Plumtree, now in possession of Mr. William Sherwood & Mr. Thomas Robley; 190 acs., sold by sd. Newman & Priscilla, his wife, to sd. John Page 20 Jan. 1669; but sd. George Lake dying without heire or will, 150 acs. was found to escheate, & granted sd. Page; which sales of 50 acs. by Walker to Maler, & about 10 acs. to William Plumtree, being excepted, there ought of right and should have been 290 acs. to sd. Page, but upon an exact survey is found but 280 acs., including in the same the land sold to Plumtree, now in possession of William Sherwood & Thomas Robley (or Rabley), & also 50 acs. part of 200 granted to Lewis Burwell & wife, 13 Oct. 1652, lying & being without the *old Pallisado*, att Middle Plantation; bounded NW upon

Peter Efford, now in possession of Edward Malyn; along the run of a Swamp, & SE upon the *Pallisado;* purchased by Maj. George Reade of William Bernard & Lucy, his wife, heire, etc; & sold to John Dickinson 24 Sept. 1655, who assigned to Abraham Spencer, 10 Dec. 1655 & by Thomas Spencer, his son & heire, sold to sd. Page 4 Nov. 1657.

MR. ROBERT BIRD (Byrd), 330 acs., New Kent Co., St. Steven's Par., 16 Apr. 1683, p. 282. Adj. land of Mr. Thomas Holmes, dec'd; & Tymothy Carter; by the back Road; &c. Trans. of 7 pers: Gilford Slingsby, Symon Turpin, Eliz. Parry, Eliz. Serjeant; Edw., Ann & Mall, Negroes.

MR. GEORGE BURGE, 500 acs., New Kent Co., Stratton Major Par., upon Peanketank Sw., 16 Apr. 1683, p. 283. Adj. David Bram (or Brain). Trans. of 10 pers: Edwd. Weath, Matt. Roan, Jeffery Marsh, Jon. Blake, Richd. Snow, Roger Iron, Jacob Clackford, Paul Emerson, Jon. Thompson, John Freeman.

MR. WILLIAM COVINGTON, 90 acs., Rappa. Co., 16 Apr. 1683, p. 283. Adj. land he lives on, & beg. by the fence & (the) King's Roade; adj. Thomas Watkins; & Stephen Bembridge, &c. Trans. of 2 pers: John Heyward, Sarah Arnsley (or Amsley).

MR. WILLIAM SAYER, 550 acs., New Kent Co., N. side of Mattopony River, 16 Apr. 1683, p. 284. Beg. at Mr. Nicholas Ware's Path; by John Tayler; to Meade's cor; adj. Mr. Hall; Mr. Robt. Hill; & Mr. Henry Biggs; by Chiscake Path, to Mr. Light; crossing Bridge Br., to Mr. Nicholas Ware, &c. Trans. of 11 pers: Tho. Owen, John Awbry, Peter Guard, Tho. Street, Wm. Sheldon, Jon. Jones, Richd. West, Jon. Dawes, James Allet, Wm. Wright, Doro. Churchill. (Note: Marginal notation gives this as *SAWYER*).

MR. GEORGE MAJOR, 250 acs., New Kent Co., N. side York River, 16 Apr. 1683, p. 284. Adj. land he lives upon; by Mr. Graye's Plantation; to head of a br. of Papeteco Cr., adj. Mr.

Coate; to Ralph Emery, &c. (*Note:* The following names appear under this record:) Tho. Purser, Ann Lucas, Jon. Landers, Jeremiah ——, Tho. Wickham.

MR. EDWARD THOMAS, 350 acs., on S. side of Rappa. Co., 16 Apr. 1683, p. 285. Adj. Mr. Jones & Jackman; down path of Mr. Marish, &c. Granted to William Price, 6 May 1664, deserted, & granted sd. Thomas, by order, &c. Trans. of 7 pers: John Austin, Sarah Breedon, Wm. Jolly, Hen. Mansley, Tho. Vintner, Peter Hudson, Matthew Hixon.

MR. ALEXANDER DAVISON, 220 acs., Chas. Citty Co., Westover Par., on S. side of James River, 16 Apr. 1683, p. 285. Beg. at Mr. John Drayton, Junr; crossing Bland's path; to Mr. William Wilkison; to Richard Carrill, &c. Trans. of 5 pers: Edwd. Byrd, Jon. Kellum, Xpher Yeomans, Eliz. Phillips, Sisley Brookes.

CAPT. WM. ROBISON, 350 acs., called *Porters Ridges;* Low. Norf. Co; from head of the E. br. of Eliz. Riv., 16 Apr. 1683, p. 286. Beg. in the Ashen Swamp, &c. Part of 3000 acs. taken up by John Porter in 1673, deserted, & granted sd. Robison, by order, 19 Apr. 1681, & confirmed, 19 Apr. 1682. Trans. of 7 pers: Tho. Cox, Jon. Jones, Peter Clause, Samll. Bainton, Wm. Bernard, John Ellis, Eliz. Atkinson. (Marginal note gives this as *ROBINSON*).

ABRAHAM BRADLEY, 61 acs., Gloster Co., Abington Par., 16 Apr. 1683, p. 286. Beg. on E. side of the Roade to Tindall's poynt; to land of Christopher Abbott, dec'd., &c. Trans. of 2 pers: Robt. Barnham, Phill. Packet. (Marginal notation gives this as *BROADLY*).

GEORGE BILLOPS, 86 acs., Glocester Co., Kingstone Par., 16 Apr. 1683, p. 287. Adj. Richard Billops. Granted to George Billops, dec'd., 18 Mar. 1662.

JOHN PRICE & WILLIAM BALL, 1000 acs., Rappa. Co., towards head of Piscattaway Cr., 16 Apr. 1683, p. 287.

Beg. at Thomas Harper, by a small island, by the maine br; to Col. Goodrich; by an Indian path; over the Moyry Br., &c. Trans. of 20 pers: James Whettam, Jane Griffin, Danll. Neech, Jon. Watford, Jon. Poor, James Man, Wm. Cock, Jon. Gibson, Wm. Young, Susan Haynes, Tho. Buck, Morgan Watkins, Eliz. Wastcoat, Jon. Harris, Robt. Edge, James Orland, Tho. Orrell, Richd. Butler, Richd. Bulkly, Hugh Young.

MRS. ELIZABETH SMITH, 400 acs., St. Stephen's Parish; upon brs. of Aquintinoco Cr., 16 Apr. 1683, p. 288. Beg. in sight of her old Plantation; by Chescake Path; to Mr. John Broach, &c. Trans. of 8 pers: Peter Lotchard, Mary Jones, John Bradock, Edwd. Pate, Temple Whitfeild, Jon. Grimes.

PETER STARLING, 300 acs., Glocester Co., towards head of Horne Harbour Cr., on the N. side, 16 Apr. 1683, p. 288. 150 acs. formerly taken & 150 acs. for trans. of 3 pers: John Munnypenny, Patrick Nash, Toby Butler.

JOHN GARNETT, 260 acs., Gloster Co., S. side of Garden Cr., 16 Apr. 1683, p. 289. Beg. at a br. parting this from land of John Smither; to John Deggs', &c. 180 acs. purchased of Humpherey Toy, 15 June 1676; 80 acs. for trans. of 2 pers: Eliz. Tindal, Tho. Combs.

THOMAS MORRELL, 150 acs., Gloster Co., Abington Par., 16 Apr. 1683, p. 289. Beg. on N. side of the maine run falling into the head of Seaverne River about, 18 po. above the Spring belonging to his Dwelling house; along Maj. Lewis Burwell, neere the maine Roade, parting this & land of Mr. Benjamin Clements; neere a Bridge over the Swamp to Maj. Lawrence Smith, &c. Part of 300 acs. conveyed by William Boulding to Rachell, his then wife, for life, & to Morgan Lewis, his heirs, &c., for ever, 14 Mar. 1670; sd. Lewis by will, dated 6 Jan. 1675, bequeathed to sd. Rachell, for her to enjoy & dispose of as she should think fitt; by vertue of which bequest sd. Rachell had a good estate in fee simple;

by whom it was sold to sd. Morrell 11 May 1681.

MR. BENJAMIN CLEMENTS, 150 acs., Glocester Co., Abington Par., 16 Apr. 1683, p. 290. On E. side of the Roade that goes under the hills in Maj. Burwell's (Burrwell-Burrell) line, parting this & land of Thomas Morrell, &c. Part of 300 acs. conveyed by William Boulding to Rachell, his then wife, &c. (Note: As in abstract just preceding.) Conveyed by sd. Rachell, 22 Oct. 1680, * * * "Give to the said Benjamin Clements for his life & after his decease to Anne Clements, daughter of the said Benjamin and her heires for ever." (Marginal note: Vide Postea).

(Note: Page 291. Repetition of above record.

COL. ISAAC ALLERTON, 2172 acs., Rappa. Co., on the S. side & in the freshes thereof. 16 Apr. 1683, p. 292. Beg. at John Bowsey; by br. of Nusapommacks, &c. Granted to John Burton & John Austin, 5 Nov. 1673; found to escheat, by inquisition under Isaac Allerton, Esqr., Esch'r. Genr'l., 14 Dec. 1681, & granted by order, &c.

MR. EDWARD CHILTON, 2 A., 17 chs., in James Citty. 16 Apr. 1683, p. 292. Adj. Col. Phillip Ludwell; along an old ditch; down James Riv. bank, to stake neer the brick fort, &c. Trans. of: Peter Gibson.

PETER GLENISTER, 80 acs., York Co., 16 Apr. 1683, p. 292. Land Sarah Wilkinson, alias Glenister, died seized of, & was found to escheate by inquisition under Edmund Jenings, Depty. Esch'r., &c.

MR. THOMAS PARKER & MR. JAMES BAGNOLL, 470 acs., Low. Par. of Is. of Wight Co., on W. side of Tapsters (alias the Long Ponds) Cr., 29 May 1683, p. 293. 50 acs. granted to Peter Mountague 25 Feb. 1638, & after severall assignments conveyed to Thomas Parker, whose Widdow the above sd. Thomas interrmaryed; 380 acs. joyning, granted to Thomas Parker, dec'd., 18 Mar. 1650; 40 acs, within the bounds, &c. Which parcells descended to Dorithy & Sarah, daughters of sd. Thomas Parker, the eldest whereof, being marryed & of full age, did together with her husband sell & convey their rights to their Father in Law Thomas Parker abovesaid; the younger being lately marryed to James Bagnoll abovesaid; the whole bounded, viz: Beg. at mouth of Taptsters Cr., a little above Garrett's poynt &c; to a br. of the Ballasting Marsh Cr; to Wm. Smith, &c, 40 acs. for trans. of: Francisco, a Negro.

TYMOTHY CARTER, 700 acs., New Kent Co., on N. side of Mattopany River, 29 May 1683, p. 293. Beg. in sight of his house; by Richardson's line; by Blake's path; to Davis' Ridge Path; on Chiescake Path; to Mr. Holmes' Path; to Maj. Wyatt, &c. Granted sd. Carter in a pattent for 1000 acs., 1 June 1678, & now resurveyed.

THOMAS JOYNER, JUNR., 290 acs., on branches of the Western Br. of Nanzemond (Riv.); 29 May 1683, p. 294. Beg. at Mr. William Bodie's (Boddy) corner, in Mr. Coleman's line; to a maine br. of Elme Swamp; to Jno. Gardner; by sd. Garner's lines, &c. Trans. of 6 pers: Eliz. Thomas, Tho. Edwards, Rebecca Bayly, Symon Wright, Fra. Bristow, Jno. Charles.

BENJAMIN AYRES & JOHN STOKELEY, 175 acs., called Hobson's Choice, Accomack Co., on N. end of a Sandy beach, on S. side of Assowemen Inlett, on the Seaboard side; 29 May 1683, p. 295. Trans. of 4 pers: Fra. Salter, Tho. Edes, Jer. Thorne, Ger. Byham.

RICHARD THREDDOR (Threader), 105 acs., New Kent Co., on N. side of Mattopany Riv., 29 May 1683, p. 295. Beg. at a br. of Indian Cabbin Br., dividing this & land of Nicholas Ware; to Jeremiah Rawlins, over Tassasion Sw; to John Garrett; & Mr. Cardenbrooke, on the Iron Rock Br., &c. Trans. of 3 pers: Jon. Fowler, Tho. Fay, James Frier.

MR. HUGH WILLIAMS & MR. THOMAS JONES, JUNR., 350 acs., on N. side of Mattopany Riv., 29 May 1683, p. 296. Beg. on a poynt by Silke Grass Meadow &c; on Cornelius Vaughan's Rowling Path, to George Martin; on line of Greene; to Richard Durwood; to Mr. Williams' house, &c. Trans. of 7 pers: Robt. Worsley, Hugh Jefferies, Ber. Stilt, Hen. Seares (or Scanes), James Hukes, Jon. Webber, Peter Jackson.

DAVID PHILLIPS, 85 acs., Up. Par. of Surry Co., 29 May 1683, p. 296. Adj. Mr. Benjamin Harryson; Thomas Battle; John Battle; Thomas Hux; William Knott; & land of Hux & Syddaway, &c. Trans. of 2 pers: Hen. Warner, Arthur Slater.

GEORGE LOVEDAY, 100 acs., Surry Co., on brs. of Up. Chippoakes Cr., 29 May 1683, p. 297. Adj Mr. Busbie; the land he lives on; Trans. of 2 pers: Fra. Spencer, Wm. Reeves.

EDWARD GRANTHAM, 300 acs., Up. Par. of Surry Co., on brs. of the Cypress Sw., 29 May 1683, p. 297. Beg. at Mr. Thomas Jordan, in the head line of Grantham's land, purchased of John Rogers, &c. Trans. of 6 pers: Isabel Huberd, Jon. Bincks, Tho. Peel, Jon. Anderson, Jon. Walker, Timo. Jackson.

HOPTKIN HOWELL, 110 acs., Low. Par. of Is. of Wight Co., on brs. of Chuckatuck, 29 May 1683, p. 298. Beg. at the Beaver Dammns; by Mr. Rutter; & Thomas Jordan's land, &c. Trans. of 3 pers: Tho. Hayward, Eliz. Conway; Mary a Negro.

ROBERT ANDREWS, 140 acs. Up. Par. of Surry Co; on SW side of the Cypress Sw; adj. Thomas Andrews; 29 May 1683, p. 298. Trans. of 3 pers: Peter French, Richd. Palmer, Jon. Newham.

ANTHONY DOUGHTING, 151 acs., Middlesex Co., 29 May 1683, p. 299. Beg. close to Mr. Abraham Weekes; on Mr. Rice Jones at head of the Green Br; to Jamaica line; along Mr. Randall Segar, &c. Trans. of 3 pers: Peter Dean, John Hoper, Hannah Combes.

THOMAS GIBBINS, 400 acs., Up. Par. of Surry Co., neere head of the brs. of Cypress Sw., 29 May 1683, p. 299. Adj. Owen Mirick, & Mr. Thomas Jordan; down a great Reedy Br., &c. Trans. of 8 pers: Cha. Briscot, Wm. Dennis, Teague Row, Jon. Collins, Tho. Boswell, Richd. Salt (or Satt), Robt. Downer, Wm. Thompson.

NATHANIEL BACON, ESQR., 3-3/8 acs., in *James City,* 29 May 1683, p. 300. Beg. at E. cor. of Lawrence's old ditch, on a br. of Piitch & Tarr Sw; neere end of a little rising or ridge, &c. Being part of land belonging to Richard Lawrence, who being guilty of high treason against his Majesty, not daring to abide a legal tryal, fled for (from ?) the same, whereby all his goods, chattels, lands & tenements became forfeited to his Majesty.

Note: Page 301 left blank.

By Nicholas Spencer, Esqr., President, &c.

MOSES DAVIES, 1000 acs., New Kent Co., S. side of York Riv., on Chickahominy Maine Sw., 20 Sept. 1683, p. 302. Adj. Mr. Robert Anderson; a little below mouth of the Moyry Branch, &c. Trans. of 20 pers: Jon. Harwell, Ann Thrush, Ann Thorne, James Bayly, Alex. Murfrey (or Murfey), Natha. Jones, Pearce Morrice, Abigail How, Wm. Harvy, James Bishop, Tho. Willis, James Clare (or Claw), Andw. Dudding, Tho. Parke, Jon. Bradock, Peter Lotchard, Temple Whitfeild, Jon. Bryan, Kath. Whitfeild, Nicho. Harvey.

MR. THOMAS ANDERSON, 400 acs., Chas. City Co., Westopher Par., on S. side of James Riv., 20 Sept. 1683. p. 303. Beg. at Capt. Robert Lacy (or Lucy); crossing Cattaile maine Br; & Mr. Wallice's path, &c. Trans. of 8 pers: Eliz. Kish, Valen. Taylor, Tho. Barrow, Wm. Sheffeild, Tho. Barret, Wm. Stock, Jon. Stewart, Joseph Fells.

MOSES DAVIES & JOHN REE, 2100 acs., New Kent Co., St. Peter's Par., S. side of York Riv., on both sides of Cromps (Crumps) Cr., 20 Sept.

1683, p. 304. Beg. at sd. Ree's land; to the *Woodyard;* adj. Mr. Hubbard, & Mr. Whitcheare, &c. Trans. of 42 pers: Ja. Filline, Mary Hall, Joan Davis, Hono. Linsey, Hono. Swillivan, Timo. Isall, Jon. Stevens, Tho. Prescot, Jon. Chilcock, Jon. Lyon, Tho. Babister, Reb. Molson, Joan Guy, Ann Phipps, Jon. Tayler, Jon. Short, Jon. Smith, Jon. Holliday, Tho. Young, Jon. Brocas, Jon. Holley, Abig. Mills, Mary Coffin (or Costin), Marg. Isham, Wm. Watts, Mary Hull, Marg. Delton, Sarah Cane, Jane Gittin, Wm. Grant, Wm. Travis, Richd. Perry, Roger Sheely, Morris Plummer, Eliz. Vincent, Robt. Knight, David Mahone, Timo. Ives, Jon. Scot, Danll. Guerdon, Matt. Henderson, Ellen Westgate.

MR. PHILLIP HOWARD, 300 acs., Nansimund Co., 20 Sept. 1683, p. 305. Adj. Richard Slaughter; & John Jolly. Granted James Monroe 14 Apr. 1670, deserted ,& granted sd. Howard by order, &c. Trans. of 6 pers: Jon. Capel, Morris Williams, Jon. Speine, Junr., Wm. Walker, Tho. Jelly, Mary Smith.

MR. HENRY HARMAN (Harmon) & MR. JOHN BUSHOP (Bishop), 168 A., 3 R., 23 P., Chas. City Co., Wayencake Par., on S. side of James Riv., 20 Sept. 1683, p. 305. Adj. Isaac Bayts;* John Hobbs; Mr. William Wilkins; Jacob Bayley; Mr. Richd. Warren; &c. Trans. of 4 pers: James Brown, Ed. Cooper, Peregrine Fry. (*Note: The name of Isaac Bayts appears to have been written *Bayley* & altered).

MR. WILLIAM NEWMAN, 234 acs., Low. Norf. Co., 20 Sept. 1683, p. 306. Adj. Abraham Ellett; Richard Jones; & John Williamson. 184 acs. granted him 9 Oct. 1675; 50 acs. for trans. of: Richd. Peacock.

JOHN SYMMONS, JUNR., 400 acs., New Kent Co., St. Stephen's Par, 20 Sept. 1683, p. 307. Beg. at Col. William Clayborne's land called *Bestland;* to Giles Rogers; over the King's Roade; to land on which "this Orphanes father lived on which this land boundeth." Trans. of 8 pers: James Staples,

Mar. Wright, Geo. Dally, Mary Tanner, Jon .Ball, Abig. Hoe, Wm. Harp, Geo. Delves (or Delues).

EDWARD HOOKER, 87 acs., James City Co., 20 Sept. 1683, p. 307. Beg. at. the *Hotwater land;* to Mr. Sanderson's mill pond; to mouth of Jones' Sw; to Browne's poynt, &c. Due sd. *Hooper* for trans. of 2 pers: Paul Kinsey, Jon. Kinsey.

MR. THOMAS SKEVINGTON, 1356 acs., N'ly. from Currctuk; 20 Sept. 1683, p. 308. Beg. neere Robert Symons, att the entrance of the little Wash; to Curretuck Inlett; along Curretuck River; on Curretuck Bay; round & including the Great Wash. Granted Mr. John Moore & sd. Skevington 20 Apr. 1682 & due him in right of survivourship.

MR. ROBERT BYRD, 700 acs., New Kent Co., St. Stephen's Par., 20 Sept. 1683, p. 308. Beg. at land of Mr. Thomas Holmes dec'd; to Holly Branch; on Exoll's Sw; to mouth of Sorrell's B; adj. Gabriell Hill; on the *Church Path;* to Wm. Watt, &c. Trans. of 14 pers: Eliz. Pye, Mary Murrah, Doro. Loyd, Jon. Jacob, Susanna Hart, Geo. Johnson, Wm. Wilson, Eliz. Boston, Hannah Blackwell, Richd. Moor, Ed. Moor, Dennis Archer, Ann Gray, Wm. Butler.

ANDREW TAYLER, 200 acs., Low. Norf. Co., 20 Sept. 1683, p. 309. Granted Thomas Weel, dec'd., & escheated, by inquisition under William Randolph, Depty. Esch'r. &c.

JAMES DAVIS, 141 acs., Nansimund (Co.), on Chuckatuck Cr., 20 Sept. 1683, p. 310. Adj. *his brother* Thomas Davis; Thomas Cutchin; & Wm. Thompson. Being 1/3 of land his father Major Thomas Davis dyed seized of, who devised to sd. James.

JOHN PORTER, Senr., 500 acs., Low. Norf. Co., 20 Sept. 1683, p. 310. Land which Mary Fenwick, *alias* Porter, dyed seized of, & found to cscheat by inquisition under John Fereby, Sub-Esch'r., &c.

WILLIAM JOYNER, 520 acs., Low. Par. of Is. of Wight Co., 20 Sept. 1683, p. 311. Neere heads of the Cypress branches; beg. at Humpherey Marshall; cor. of Mr. Hardy & Capt. Applewhaite; to William West, &c. Trans. of 11 pers: Wm. Morgan, Danll. Whitbye, Eliz. Pate, Robt. Jermin, Susanna Knot, Ann Hardin, Ruth Harding, Richd. Johnson, Jon. Hutchins, Alex. Morgan, Joan Cole.

COL. ROBERT ABRAHALL, 600 acs., New Kent Co., S. side of York Riv., upon brs. of Chickahominy Sw., 20 Sept. 1683, p. 311. Beg. on W. side of *Rumley Mash,* a br. of sd. Sw., dividing this from land of John Williams; by Westopher Path; in sight or Price's house, & of Tonye's (?) Plantation; to Mr. Peter Butts, &c. Purchased of Josias Pickett ,by assignment of part of pattent from Thomas Brereton, 13 Oct. 1671, & escheated by inquisition under Wm. Leigh, Depty Esch'r., &c.

THOMAS DUNKETON, 161½ acs., on S. side of York River, 20 Sept. 1683, p. 312. Adj. Mr. Jno. Broach, in the forke of Mashemeeds Cr; by the Brickhouse Path; to Mr. Thomas Merodyth, &c. 50 acs. granted Thomas Dunketon, his father, 18 Nov. 1683; the rest purchased of Richard Barnhouse.

MALACHY THRUSTON, 69 acs., Low. Norf. Co; on the Fresh Ponds; 20 Sept. 1683, p. 313. Granted to Hugh Forgison 26 Sept. 1674, deserted; condemned 27 Sept. 1679 in the Genr'l. Court, & granted to John Fereby, 27 Sept. 1679; deserted, & now due sd. Thruston for trans. of 2 pers: Ann Mattocks, Walter Bruce.

ROBERT GRIFFITH, 200 acs., Nanzemond Co., 20 Sept. 1683, p. 314. Land Anthony Wells, dyed seized of, & was found to escheate, by inquisition under William Randolph, Depty. Esch'r. &c.

MR. DAVID CONDON, 114 acs., York Co., 20 Sept. 1683, p. 314. Land James Elcock, dyed seized of, & was found to escheate, by inquisition under Edmund Jenings, Depty. Esch'r. &c.

SAME. 300 acs., New Kent Co., same date & page. Land James Elcock dyed seized of, & was found to escheate, by inquisition under William Leigh, Depty. Esch'r., &c.

MR. HENRY WILLIAMSON, 420 acs., Rappa. Co., S. side of Rappa. Riv., 20 Sept. 1683, p. 315. Adj. Col. Richd. Lee & Anthony Jackman; running to head of 2 brs. of Hudson's Sw., &c. Granted George Marsh 19 Aug. 1664, deserted, &c. Trans. of 9 pers: Robert Newman, Arthur Grice, Hum. Thorne, Geo. Thomas, Richd. Flower, Jon. Stephens, Jonathan Tayler; Doll & Besse Negroes.

FRANCIS BROWNE, 1100 acs., Rappa. Co., on S. side of Puscation, alias Cox's, Cr; 20 Sept. 1683, p. 316. Granted him 9 June 1658.

JOHN PARKES, 964 acs., New Kent Co., St. Peter's Par., S. side of York River in the Narrowes, 20 Sept. 1683, p. 317. Beg. at mouth of Black Cr., on NW side; to mouth of a br. called the Littlehouse Runn, dividing this from land of Lt. Col. George Lyddall; up Boards Sw; by the Rowling Path; to Jones' Run, &c. 750 acs. purchased of George Chapman 28 Apr. 1662; 214 acs. for trans. of 5 pers: Wm. Chapman, Jon. & Mary Branch, Mary Robinson, Samll. Bell.

NICHOLAS COCKE, 346 acs., Middlesex Co., adj. Jamaica Land; 20 Sept. 1683, p. 318. Adj. John Jadwin. neere path from Jamaica to the Town: by Mr. Cock's, &c. Granted to Major Beverley & Mr. Henry Hartwell, 25 Sept. 1679, deserted, & now granted by order, &c. Trans. of 7 pers: Vincent Stanford, John Wilkinson, Ann Pettit, Mary Branch. Ed. Toogood, David Griffin, David Williams.

MR. JAMES BAUGH, 119 A., 1 R., 30 P., Henrico Co., Bristoll Par., on N. side of Appomattock Riv., 20 Sept. 1683, p. 318. Beg. at Thomas Burton; crossing the Mill Path & Cobb's Slash, to Robert Russell: along George Freeman, &c. Trans. of 3 pers: Peter Hamlin, Jon. Humphrews, Fra. Brester.

ABRAHAM WEEKES, 950 acs., Lancaster Co; on NE side of the Gr. swamp on the head of Peanketank River & about 6 mi. from Rappa. River; 20 Sept. 1683, p. 319. Crossing the Bryery Br., to head of the Green Br., &c. 700 acs. granted Thomas Willis 31 Aug. 1664, & by deed to sd. Weekes, 21 Oct. 1667; 250 acs. for trans. of 5 pers: Arthur Bagnal, Jon. Jarvis, Marm. Loyd, Arthur Dennis, Jon. Ramp.

MR. JOHN DANGERFIELD, 680 acs., Rappa. Co., on S. side of Rappa. Riv., 20 Sept. 1683, p. 320. Beg. on Cooper's poynt; to Mr. Reeves; on br. of Tucker's Cr; adj. Mr. Benja. Goodrich, & Mr. Robert Thomlin; by a br. dividing this & sd. Thomlyn; by Mr. Anthony North; to Gilson's Cr., &c. 560 acs. granted Mr. Bartholomew Hoskins, being part of 1350 acs., 1 Jan. 1645; & 64 acs. granted Mr. John Dangerfield 4 Apr. 1667; all of which parcells granted sd. Dangerfield 28 Sept. 1681; 60 acs. for trans. of 2 pers: Lewis Shepherd, Robt. Parry.

MR. JOHN JOY, 220 acs., New Kent Co., St. Stephen's Par., 20 Sept. 1683, p. 321. Adj. John Pigg; by the Foot Path, &c. Trans. of 5 pers: Jon. Chickens, Tho. Kemp, David Watson, Jon. Blake, Tho. Rider.

MR. JOHN & RICHARD WYATT, 650 acs., New Kent Co., N. side Mattopany Riv., 20 Sept. 1683, p. 321. Beg. att Christopher Carleton in Mr. Richard Tunstall's line, to Tymothey Carter; on Mr. William Fleming; to Wm. Henderson; on Mostecouque Sw; to Appostecoque Sw. 640 acs. granted Col. Robert Abrahall 19 Mar. 1660; & granted Maj. Wm. Wyatt, 24 May 1654; 10 acs. for trans. of: Morgan Rosier.

SARAH ALLEN, 700 acs., New Kent Co., S. side of York River & SE side of Ware Cr., 20 Sept. 1683, p. 322. Beg. at Cowpen Swamp; adj. Adam Symms (Simms); by Arrow Reed Sw; to Thomas Porthmouth (Parchmoth); & John Corker, &c. 200 acs. granted to Col. Thomas Ballard, 24 Sept. 1661, & assigned to John Boatwright, 21 Oct.

1670. 500 acs. for trans. of 10 pers:
Richd. Tirrel, Tho. Elsford, Israel Hard-
man, Dorothy Gilson, Tho. Knight, Fra.
Cole; Robt. Tirrel 4 times.

Att a Court held at James Citty Apr.
25 1688; Present: Nath. Bacon, Esqr.,
President & Councill: For as much as
it appears to this Court that by a mistake in the year 1683 the then Cl. of
the Sec. Office had in a pattent granted
to Sarah Allen, instead of Sarah entered
Jane, it is ordered that the sd. mistake
be amended in the Record by the present
Clerk of the Sec. Office. Test, R. Beverley, by W. Edwards, Cl. Genr. Ct. Page
322.

COL. EDWARD HILL, 2717 acs.,
in New Kent & Rappa. Co.'s; on brs.
of Mattopany & Piscadaway Cr.. 20 Sept.
1683, p. 323. Beg. at the Indian Path
from *Mattopany Town* that was att the
head of Piscadaway Cr. unto a *new
town* now planted by those Indians on
Mattopany River; to head of the Doctors Branch; crossing Richards path; to
Capt. Thomas Brereton; &c. Pattented
by Col. Thomas Goodrich, 5 Oct. 1672
containing 2200 acs., & lost for want
of seating; granted sd. Hill; &c. Trans.
of 55 pers: Alice May, Smll. Dobson,
Hum. Smith, Nicho. Watson, Wm.
Robinson, Zach. Foster, Hen. Copeley,
Jon. Briggs, Jane Catesby, Jon. Stubb,
Mary Franklin, Jon. Lee, Anth. Tayler,
Margt. Murfey, Tho. Woodham, Roger
Stilwell, Wm. Mace, Jon. Brice, Ja.
Francis, Nicho. Pritchard, Nicho. Tho-
mas, Bryan Moor, Wm. Morrice. Eliz.
Fenton, Jane Clay, Joseph Stowel, Jon.
Jackson, Jon. Lace, Micha. Lovet, Abra.
Griffin, Jon. Pride. Jon. Machin, Jon.
Drinke. Hen. Vassel, Robt. Tard. James
Fox, Tho .Abbot, Richd. Carrot. Mary
Reed, Tho. Jones, Margt. Weel, Jon.
Morely, Griffith Jones, David Jones,
James Wilson, Tho. Bavly, Margt.
Allen, Barth. Bell, Jon. Evered, Jon.
Newman, Tho. Hagg, Wm. Hague, Jon.
Burch (or Bunch), Tho. Prior, Wm.
Watts.

MAJ. GENR'LL. JOHN CUSTIS,
1400 acs., on Mackone Island, N'ampton Co., 20 Sept. 1683, p. 324. Trans.
of 28 pers: Edward Greene, Idia.

Franklin, Eliz. Grimes, Wenifred Broth-
ers, Mar. Rogers, Susanna Wynn, Eliz.
Sackler, Robt. Grice, Jeremy Barrow,
George Signett, Tho. Portous, Humph.
Evans, Tho. Sorry, Jno. Staples, Wm.
Beard, Jon. Beard, Tho. Stowt, Hen.
Meares, Fra. Withers, Tho. Lock,
Nicho. Middleton, Anth. Rockwood,
Marg. Walton, Tho. Bourcher, Jon.
Kitchin, Ellen Rogers, Richd. Smith,
Hen. Lee.

JOHN EASTERLY & ROBERT
CLIFFORD, 320 acs., New Kent Co.,
22 Sept. 1683, p. 325. Adj. Mr. Lockey,
upon Howcock Sw; beg. at Richard
Morley, &c. Granted to John Maddison
4 July 1664 & sold to Isaac Collier; by
him deserted, & now granted by order,
&c. Trans. of 7 pers: Jon. Roper,
Owen Kelley, Nicho. Britton, Walter
English, James Jones, Jon. Gerald,
Arthur Price.

COL. RICHARD JOHNSON, 150
acs., Rappa. Co., on maine Sw. of Piscataway Cr., 20 Sept. 1683, p. 326.
Adj. Thomas Harper & Robert Clements. Granted to James Baugham, 27
Feb. 1665/6, deserted, & granted to
Thomas Batts; assigned to James
Baugham, Junr., who deserted; granted
to sd. Johnson by order &c., 16 Apr.
1680. Trans. of 3 pers: Garret Hamon,
Jon. Canady, Jon. Davis.

MR. JNO. LEWIS, JUNR., 250 acs.,
New Kent Co., 20 Sept. 1683, p. 326.
Granted to Charles Hawley 7 Apr.
1674, & which he dyed seized of; escheated by inquisition under William
Leigh, Depty. Esch'r., 25 July 1681, &
now granted by order, &c.

MAIOR ROBERT PEYTON, 1000
acs., New Kent Co; St. Peter's Par.,
20 Sept. 1683, p. 327. Beg. at path of
William Ricketts, formerly an Indian
Path, to Mr. Brereton; by an Indian
Path; crossing the Ridge Path to Toma-
ticon (?) Sw., &c. 900 acs. granted to
Phillip Watkins. Thomas Watkins, &
sd. Ricketts, 6 Mar. 1673; & 100 acs.
granted sd. Phillip & Thomas, & sold
to Thomas Sewell & John Tubbs, 27
June, 1674, who sold to John Ascough,
6 Nov. 1674, & by him conveyed to sd.

Peyton & his heires forever, 10 Apr. 1680.

WILLIAM BRISCOE, 12 acs., James Citty *and* County, 20 Sept. 1683, p. 328. Land which William Pen dyed seized of & was found to escheate, by inquisition under Col. John Page, Esch'r., &c.

LEIUETENANT ABRAHAM JONES, 1217 acs., Chas. City Co; Bristoll Par., on S. side of Appomattox Riv., 20 Nov. 1683, p. 328. Beg. at lower side of Maj. Genll. Wood's *Indian Town lands;* neer br. of Rohowick; to a peninsula made by the main run of the Southerne Sw; to sd. Wood's *Fort lands, &c.* Trans. of 25 pers: Geo. West, Rich. Rice, Richd. Jones, Jon. Price, Step. Hall, Anne Hall, Jon. Moor, Eliz. Moor, Giles Cook, Gilbert May, Hen. Price, James Badcock, Tho. Peacock, Joan Dickson, Mary Thomas, Peter Thompson, Geo. Littlegood, Step. Buck, Ed. Herbert, Alice Smith, Tho. Floyd, Wm. Jones, Richd. West, Geo. South, Dennis Coniers.

CAPT. HENERY APPLEWHAITE, 902 acs., Is. of Wight Co; bet. main Sw. of Kingsale & the Beaver Dammes Br., 20 Nov. 1683, p. 329. Beg. by the main Sw., William Collins' corner, &c. Granted Matthew Strickland, 26 Sept. 1678, deserted; & granted to Edward Chilton, who conveyed to sd. Applewhaite, &c. Trans. of 18 pers: Hen. Pecket, Arthur Covington, Ja. Harris, Wm. Richards, Eliz. Boyer, Amb. Parke, Nicho. Lawrence, Anth. Barwell, Bar. Crosse, Mar. Fryer, Ben. Chandler, Jon. Cornelius, Hen. Lawrence, Edmd. Potter; Jack, Besse, Tony, & Mingoe—Negroes.

GEORGE WRIGHT & THO. WRIGHT, 100 acs., or there-bouts, in Is. of Wight Co., 20 Nov. 1683, p. 320. Land which Capt. Joñ. Upton died seized of, & was found to escheat, by inquisition under John Jenings, Depty. Esch'r., 13 June 1674; granted to Tho. Wright, dec'd., their father.

JAMES JONES, 734 A., 3 R., 24 P., Chas. City Co; Wyanoke Par., on S. side of James Riv., att a place known

as *the Devil's Woodyard,* 20 Nov. 1683, p. 329. Crossing the piny slash, to John Hobbs; & the Cattailes, & Pole Run to Cherry Br; along Mr. William Harrison; &c. Trans. of 15 pers: Matthew Holmes, James Mungor, Hen. Bond, Wm. Prescot, Fra. Bradly, Walter Hill, Jon. Felton, Wm. Noble, Jon. Long, Jon. Baker, Jon. Warden, Jon. Joyce, Tho. Jones, Tho. Crop, Richd. Stalye.

MR. FRANCIS BURNALL (Burnal), 2531 acs., New Kent Co., S. side of York Riv., in the Narrowes, 20 Nov. 1683, p. 330. Beg. in the *Poplar Neck;* adj. Mr. Flood; neere Broughton's line, crossing a br. called the White Marsh; to William Russell's fence, in a line of Mr. John Griffith; by Tankes Queenes Cr. Run; to Mr. William Blake, &c. 2350 acs. part granted his Father 1 Apr. 1661; the residue being surplus, &c., due for trans. of 5 pers: Roger Minshall, Wm. Chub, Wm. Weaver, Collin Mackine, Eliz. Rogers.

MR. JOHN WILLIAMS, 842 A., 2 R., 25 P., Chas. City Co; Westopher Par., on S. side of James Riv., & on N. side of the Blackwater maine Sw., 20 Nov. 1683, p. 331. Beg. at Mr. Daniell Higdon; to Wm. Edmunds, on a br. to the head of the *old Towne;* crossing head of Tanner's Br; to Col. Edwd. Hill; crossing Scotch Br; & Blackwater Path, to Richard Pace, &c. Trans. of 17 pers: Richd. Havet, Geo. Adams, Sarah Hitmore, Tho. Pattison, Antho. Box, Jona. Elizer, Bartho. Swinbourne, Silvester Atkins, Roger Fosset, James Rowland, Ann Turner, Geo. Archer, Hugh James, Jon. Nowel, Susan Mills, Jane Mills, Jane Long.

MR. BENJA. FOSTER, 833 acs., Chas. City Co; Wayonoake Par., on S. side of James Riv., 20 Nov. 1683, p. 332. Beg. at the *White Medow;* along Thomas Chapell; to Mr. Pawl Williams; Ward's Cr; to the Mill Path; crossing Poles Runn; to James Jones; on Cherry Br; to Capt. Archer; to Col. Edward Hill, &c. Trans. of 17 pers: Richd. Gardner, Ed. Sadler, Ed. Cranage, Xpher. Hammond, Wm. Spockford, Tho. Kirk, Tho. White, Isa. Ablesone, Tho. Sayer, Wm. Denson, Ed. Hartwel,

Richd. Gant, Ed. Butler, Fra. Barley, Natha. Carter, Hen. Symonds, Wm. Seldome.

COL. ARTHUR SMITH, 1100 acs. in the Low. Par. of Wight Co; on S. side of Currewaugh Sw., 20 Nov. 1683, p. 333. Beg. at land taken by him & Limescott; to Robt. Lawrence, Junr; on Hodges Councill; to Col. Joseph Bridger, &c. Granted Thomas Parnell, 20 Apr. 1680, deserted, & now granted by order, &c; trans. of 22 pers: Richd. Burgesse, Richd. Groves, Ed. North, Richd. Dean, Hen. Thompson, Jon. Gee, Rob. Medle, Jon. Seward, Jon. Williams, Ed. Brantley, Wm. Fry, Antho. Matthews, Gersyon Gromwel, Jon. Lippet, Phill. Plumly, Bar. Farthing, Eli. Willis, Edmd. Pullam, Tho. Lawly, Tho. Somersale, John Humphry, Jon. Meader.

MRS. ELIZABETH TERRELL & THOMAS CORRELL, 720 acs., New Kent Co., S. side of York Riv., on brs. of Chickahominy Sw., 20 Nov. 1683, p. 333. By Westover Path; to Col. Robt. Abrahall, formerly Brereton's; by poynt Dexter (Poindexter ?) path; to Mr. Boothe; on Thomas Mishell & Mr. Robert Jarrett; to Samuell Wever, &c. 470 acs. by purchase from William Jackman & Edward Morris by 2 deeds, viz: 30 Aug. 1673 & 28 June 1678, respectively; 250 acs. found within, &c. Trans. of 5 pers: Wm. Thorne, Wm. Dotson, Richd. Stephens, Thomas Kerby, Alice Rice.

CAPT. HENRY APPLEWAITE (Applewhaite), 1313 acs., Is. of W. Co; on the maine br. of King Sale; 20 Nov. 1683, p. 334. Granted to William Collins 20 Nov. 1679, deserted, & now granted by order, &c. Trans. of 27 pers: Wm. Everidge, Jon. Wall, Nicho. Pledge, Robt. Currant, Tho. Cooper, Cha. Maxney, Richd. Jennings, Oliver Dennington, Nicho. Oliver, Wm. Dormon, Teage Dormon, Jon. Bullock, Eliz. Curtis, Isa. Stubbs, Hester Patheridge, Edwd. Sparshot, Maudlin Cane, Robt. Honywood, Jer. Haly, Jer. Watts, Jon. Graine, Eliz. Flinton, Hen. Hayes, Elias Ivy (or Guy), Jane Hay, Robt. Newton, Robt. Muxford.

MAJ. FRANCIS POYTHERES (Poythries), 1252 A., 2 R., 30 P., Chas. City Co; in the Parish of Jordans; on S. side of James River, 20 Nov. 1683, p. 335. Beg. at Sampson Ellis, crossing the Gr. Sw; to southern Br; & br. of Horne Br; to Mr. Henry Batt; on Mr. John Woodley & James Mumford; to the Dry Bottome Runn, &c. Trans. of 25 pers: Sarah Henley, Eliz. Hayes, Wm. Sage, Symon Rouse, Jon. Flud, Jon. Conway, Morgan Welch, Roger Horner, Richd. Thornbury, Tho. Wood, Jone Graneley, Wm. Wood, John Lawrence, Jon. Cole, Jon. Rubye, Jon. Auerine (or Averine), Jon. Cooper, Jos. Marsh, Geo .Bell, Geo. Crosland, Wm. Arnold, Wm. Sarson, David Haynes, Richd. Hind, Eli. Brown.

ADAM MORRIS, 200 acs., Chas. City Co; S. side of Appamattuck Riv; Bristoll Par., att *Mounkeys Neck,* 20 Nov. 1683, p. 336. Beg. att Thomas Lowe; crossing the maine Mounkeys Neck Sw., &c. Trans. of 4 pers: Richd. Bruce, Tho. Toolye, Jon. White, Barth. Horton.

WILLIAM COLE, ESQR., one of his Majestie's Councill of State, 618 acs., in the Co. & Parish of York, 20 Nov. 1683, p. 336. Beg. on W. side of Beech Br., out of the S. side of Wormeley's Cr., parting this & land of Capt. Ralph Wormeley, Esqr; along Mr. Tho. Cheesman; to the *Church* old field, &c. 500 acs. purchased by Robert Kinsey about 30 years since, viz: 100 acs. of Col. George Ludlow; 250 acs. of Hugh Allen; 100 acs. of Richard Glover; & 50 acs. of John Pouncey; which descended to his *brother* & heire Hugh Kinsey, who sold to Henry Gooch, 14 Oct. 1656, who sold to Jonathan Newell, merchant, 3 Mar. 1664, after whose death sd. land came to David Newell, his bro. & heire, who sold to William Cole, Esqr., 28 Nov. 1679; & also Capt. John Tiplady & Elizabeth, his wife, who was the relict of sd. Jonathan Newell, by deed dated 14 Apr. 1681 assigned their right to sd. Cole; 180 acs. for trans. of 3 pers: Wm. East, Jon. Cook, Richd. Hewes.

COLL. EDWARD HILL, 980½ acs.,
Chas. City Co., Westover Par., on S.
side of James River, 20 Nov. 1683, p.
338. 600 acs. part bounded as in a
pattent to James Warradine, 13 Oct.
1652, who deserted, &c; 380½ acs. adj;
beginning at lands of Byears (?), on
N. side of the gr. Road; to Mr. Francis
Poytheris; on Roger Tilman; James
Binford; Robert Abernathy; & Wallice,
&c. Due, viz: 600 acs. by order of the
Genrll. Court att James Citty 28 Nov.
1682 & for importation of 12 pers; the remainder for imp. of 8 pers: Dor.
Bradly, Fra. Finch, Jon. Flood, Jon.
Wright, Fra. Shelton, Wm. Gage, Geo.
Hilliard, Tho. Bramstone.

PETER WYCKE & JOHN LENEARE
(Lanier), 1482 A., 3 R. 24 P., Chas.
City Co; Westover Par., on S. side of
James Riv., 20 Nov. 1683, p. 339. Beg.
at cor. dividing Wm. Pebbles (Peebles)
& Thomas Chappell; crossing head of
Bedlow Br., a br. of the Otter Dams;
James Jones' path; & a round pond; to
John Harris' land; crossing Henry
Weyck's path; the Piny Slash; Birchen
Sw; & the reedy Sw., &c. Trans. of 34
pers: Howel James, Jon. Gosal, Margt.
Sinckler, Tho. Bagwell, Jone Bagwel,
Wm. Wayder, Walter Collins, Bevis
Bulmer, Jon. Weaver, Wm. Gill, Bryan
Smith, Jon. Lumpton, Jon. Pasmore,
Mary Pasmore, Tho. Jent, Tho. Jennings, Alex. Maly, Oliver Symonds,
Walter Chiles, Hen. Tutton (or Sutton),
Jon. Sherrey, Jon. Shaw, Sarah Cole,
Wm. Hayward, Ellen Hayward, Jon.
Kendal, James Hews, Xpher. Branch,
Jon. Gibson, Jon. Matham.

THOMAS WILKINSON, 554 acs.,
whereon he now dwells; James Citty
Co., on S. side of Moses Cr., 20 Nov.
1683, p. 340. From head of the W'most br. of Ware gutt to Halie's cor;
along Phillipps' line; to Hawkes Nest
gutt, &c. Being part of a devdt. formerly held by Griffin Dickinson; trans. of
11 pers: Wm. Butler, Wm. Tossel (or
Possel), Jane Baxter, Robt. Rigby, Jon.
Allam, Robt. Martin, Walter Brooks,
Tho. Mitchel, Ben. Caryl, Eliz. Caryl,
Hen. Caryl.

JOSEPH CHASE, 368 acs., Low.
Norf. Co., in Corratuck; upon a bay
making into the North River, 20 Nov.
1683, p. 340. Trans. of 8 pers: Timothy Swindle, Rosamond Delacon (?),
Edward Rutledge, Giles Mathews, Jno.
Jones, Ann Jones, Francis Bestock (or
Bostock), George Williams.

MR. JOHN EDWARDS, 354 acs.,
Low. Norf. Co; bet. E. & S. branches
of Eliz. River, 20 Nov. 1683, p. 341.
200 acs. adj. Thomas Alexander; &
James Henson; granted sd. Edwards 5
June 1678; 154 acs. adj., & land of
William Whithurst, &c. Trans. of 3
pers: Bryan Omery, Rose Murphry, Jno.
Pearce.

JOHN WHITHURST, 400 acs., Low.
Norf. Co., at the 3 runs of the Easterne
Ridges, 20 Nov. 1683, p. 341. Beg. at
William Nicholls. Granted to James
Whithurst 23 Oct. 1673, deserted, &
now due for trans. of 8 pers: Richard
Hill, twice; Jane, his wife twice; Thomas Blackbird, Edward Stowell, William Stafford & his wife.

BENJAMIN CUMMINGS, 300 acs.,
Low. Norf. Co., neare the Blackwater,
in Corretuck; 20 Nov. 1683, p. 342.
Beg. by a Landing upon Arthur Steevens' Cr; to a br. dividing this & land of
Thomas Walker; to Cypresse Sw., &c.
Trans. of 6 pers: Thomas Munds,
Samuell Emmare, Joseph Yates, Thomas
Johnson, Powell Pullson, Eliz. Bennester.

EDWARD HEWES, 440 acs., Low.
Norf. Co., at head of Broad Cr., on W.
side of the S. br. of Eliz. River; 20
Nov. 1683, p. 342. Adj. Peter Poyner,
&c. Trans. of 9 pers: Ann Peterson,
Richd. Reek, Ja. Whitehead, Wm. Hill,
Ed. Camelin, Ed. Ellis, Eliz. Talley,
Hum. Williams, Jon. Darson.

THOMAS GRIFFIN, 177 acs., Low.
Norf. Co., on N. branches of Curretuck,
20 Nov. 1683, p. 342. Adj. Mr. Basnett & Thomas Smith. Trans. of 4 pers:
Len Jackson, Tho. Griffen, Alex. Morly
(or Morey), Jon. Groves.

WILLIAM OWEN, 434 acs., Low.
Norf. Co; at head of Julyan's Cr., on

West side of the S. br. of Eliz. River; 20 Nov. 1683, p. 343. Beg. in a pocoson at Nash & Taylor's cor; adj. land he bought of Theodore Taylor, &c; 70 acs. part being a neck, on side of sd. Creek, sold by Richard Taylor to sd. Theodore, who sold to sd. Owen, & is part of a pattent granted to Thomas Nash & Richard Taylor, 6 Nov. 1665. 364 acs. for transs. of 8 pers: Anthony Power, John Folkes, James Whitter, Mary Lott, Walter Dreu (?), Richard Chapman, Jeane Hewes, Henry Gilbert.

JOHN COOPER, 150 acs., Low. Norf. Co; S. side of Tanner's Creek, 20 Nov. 1683, p. 343. Beg. in Mellysan's line; to Marriner Jones; adj. Jno. Williams; & William Cooper, Senr; & Peyton's land. Trans. of 3 pers: Thomas Hone (or Thone), Christopher Salter; & Zona a Negro woman.

MARTHA ROUSE, 100 acs., Low. Long Thicketts; 20 Nov. 1683, p. 344. Trans. of 2 pers: Jno. Porter, Thomas Welch.

JOB KEMPE, 265 acs., Low. Norf. Co; Lynhaven Par., 20 Nov. 1683, p. 344. 200 acs. at a path from the E. br. of Eliz. River to the North Riv; granted to William Edwards 3 Oct. 1671, & after severall assignments due sd. Kempe. 65 acs. adj. James Kempe; & Col. Mason; by the Aishen Sw., &c. Trans. of 2 pers: Benjamin Robinson, Elizabeth Robinson.

DAVID MURRAY, SENR., 777 acs., Low. Norf. Co; on S. side of the E. br. of Eliz. Riv., 20 Nov. 1683, p. 345. 600 acs. adj. William Whithurst; granted to sd. Murray, 29 Oct. 1669; 177 acs. beg. by the Road, Mr. Hill's corner; to Michael Macoy's; by the Sw. &c; trans. of 4 pers: Nathaniell Macklamahan, 3 times, & Gilbert Hamilton.

MR. THOMAS GORDONE, 454 acs., Low. Norf. Co., in Knott's Island, in Corretuck, called the Gordian Knott. 20 Nov. 1683, p. 345. Beg. at Mr. Patrick White; to mouth of a cr. parting this & land of Rachel Cornelius, &c. Sd. land seated by Lt. Col. Thomas Lambert & given to his nephew John Vander-

mulen, who conveyed to sd. Gordone. Trans. of 9 pers: Thomas Gordone twice, Jean Gordone, Wm. Makenzev, Jno. Wood, Geo. Ward, Ann Sympson, Sarah Phillips. Elizabeth Kerre.

JOHN PRESCOTT, 95 acs., Low. Norf. Co; on E. side of the S. br. of Eliz. Riv., 20 Nov. 1683, p. 346. Beg. on Cormorant poynt; adj. John Biggs; & his own land, &c. Trans. of 2 pers: James Matthewes, William Goldstone.

MICHAEL JONES, 200 acs., Low. Norf. Co; in Knot's Island, in Corretuck, 20 Nov. 1683, p. 346. Adj. John Legatt; on the Gr. Swamp; along William White's line; to Bullock's &c. Trans. of 4 pers: Richard Bray, 4 times.

JOSIAS MORRIS, 250 acs., Low. Norf. Co; in Corretuck, 20 Nov. 1683, p. 346. Beg. by Nomenys Cr; adj. Thomas Morris; neare road to Mr. Henry Spratt; &c. Trans. of 5 pers: Tho. Cromey, Robt. Powel, Nicho. Meador, Jon. Bayly, Edm. Edwards.

THOMAS MORRIS, 200 acs., Low. Norf. Co., 20 Nov. 1683, p. 347. Beg on S. side of the mouth of Nomeny's Cr., on Corretuck Bay; &c. Renewal of former pattent.

JOHN WOODARD & HENRY WOODARD, Orphans of Francis Woodard, 150 acs., Low. Norf. Co; Lynhaven Par., 20 Nov. 1683, p. 347. Beg. at Lt. Col. Adam Thorowgood, neare Lynhaven River; to head of the reedy br; adj. Joseph Lake; into the Poplar Neck, &c. 100 acs. of which given by will of Owen Hayes to sd. Francis, who gave by will to the above-named; 50 acs. purchased by sd. Woodard of Bennony Burrowes.

JOSEPH LAKE, 150 acs., Low. Norf. Co; Lynhaven Par., 20 Nov. 1683, p. 347. Beg. at head of the reedy br; to Lt. Col. Adam Thorowgood; to a br. neare Cott's old field; into the Poplar Neck; to land of the Orphans of Woodard, &c. 100 acs. given him by will of Owen Haies; & 50 acs. purchased of Bennony Burroughs.

CAPT. WILLIAM ROBINSON, 70 acs., Low. Norf. Co; Lynhaven Par., 20 Nov. 1683, p. 348. Beg. at his own land; to William Hancox; by Capt. Thomas Jicesim, Ivy, &c. Trans. of 2 pers: Elizabeth Thompson, John Showland.

LAWRENCE SAWCER. 28 A., 1 R., 1 P., Low. Norf. Co; Lynhaven Par., 20 Nov. 1683, p. 348. Beg. towards the head of a br. of Broad Cr; adj. William Martin & Robert Young. Granted to Mary Jouslen (?), 15 Mar. 1675/6, deserted; & now due for trans. of: John Trever.

MR. LANCELOTT BATTERS (Bathurst) & MR. EDWARD CHILTON, 850 acs., New Kent Co; on SW side of Yorke River; on E. side of a br. of Black Cr; 29 Nov. 1683, p. 349. Granted to Maj. Genll. Hammond, 1 May 1661; deserted, & now granted by order, &c. Trans. of 17 pers: Geo. Chanon, Tho. Butler, An. Street, Richd. Flant, Wm. Patterson, Jon. Cole, Tho. Hart, Mould Snackson, Mich. Ison, Tobi. Horton, Gyles Tayler, Jon. Tayler, Hen. Killey, Jos. Faryc, An. Farye, Ed. Hutchinson, Richd. Sudd.

SAME. 600 acs; same Co., date & page. Bet. Col. Hammond's lower cr. & Pouncey Cr; on Nick's field. Granted to Col. Mannering Hammond, 11 Nov. 1658, deserted, & now due by order, &c. Trans. of 12 pers: Jon. Lewis, Tho. Goulding, Jon. Smyth, Tho. Grindal, Jon. Turner, Fra. Webster, Tho. Bolton, Geo. Barler, Ann Edmunds, Tho. Edwards, Wm. Allen, Wm. Hackney.

WILLIAM STAPLES, 200 acs., Nanzemond Co; 29 Nov. 1683, p. 350. Land which George Basse died seized of, & found to escheat, by inquisition under Wm. Randolph, Depty. Esch'r., &c.

JOHN SOANE, 457 acs., by *supposition* in James Citty & Chas. Citty Counties; 20 Nov. 1683, p. 350. Adj. Joseph Fry; W. by Dockman's Runn; on lands of John Hix; Mr. Bromfield; Jerry Ham. Granted to Curtis Land, 20 Apr. 1667, deserted, & granted by order, to John Wright & Cornelius Loften, 18 Nov. 1674; deserted, & now granted by order, &c. Trans. of 10 pers: Wm. Tayler, Wm. Reynolds, Wm. Coyt, Roger Adderson, Nicho. Williams, Anth. Obrey (?), Tho. Wood, Geo. Griffin, Tho. Wormewel, Capel Glaskine.

By Francis, Lord Howard

THOMAS RUSSELL, 70 acs., Low. Norf. Co; on the N. branches of *Curretuck;* 20 Apr. 1684, p. 350. Beg. on the Green Br; a marsh dividing this, Thomas Griffin; & land of Mr. Basnett. Granted to Sarah Russell, 15 Mar. 1675/6.

MR. JOHN FORREST, 520 acs., Gloster Co; Kingston Par., on N. side of Garden Cr., 20 Apr. 1684, p. 351. Beg. near head of Mr. Lillie's Cr; to head of the green Br., the dividing line between sd. John & Edmund Forrest, according to their father's will; near mouth of sd. Creek parting this & land of Mr. Thomas Cheesman, &c. 350 acs. granted Mr. Henery Forrest 15 Sept. 1658; 170 acs. for trans. of 4 pers: Wm. Brewer, Hen. Jones, Richd. Sternal, Jon. Hackley.

ANNE BORAM, 95 acs., Gloster Co; Kingston Par., 20 Apr. 1684, p. 351. Beg. on W. side of a small cr. out of the S. side of Horne Harbour Cr., adj. Edmund Boram; Ralph Armsted; &c. Renewal of her patent dated 20 Dec. 1667.

MR. JACOB BARNES, 215 acs., Low. Norf. Co; at head of the S. br. of Eliz. Riv., called *Barnes' Neck,* 20 Apr. 1684, p. 352. Beg. in the Gum Sw; & adj. Mr. Mathew Whitfield. Trans. of 5 pers: Jon. Wells, Cobb Howel, Xpher. Nugent, Ed. Broughton, Wm. Hunt.

COL. RICHARD DUDLEY, 704 acs., Gloster Co; Kingston Par., on Blackwater Cr., & on E. side of the North Riv., 20 Apr. 1684, p. 352. Beg. at mouth of Piny Poynt Cr; adj. Mr. Presson; Mr. James Ransome; a little above the Dividing Cr., &c. 492 acs. granted him 24 Sept. 1659, & renewed 18 Mar. 1662; 212 acs. for trans. of 5 pers: Wm. Matthews, Cha. Clarke, Ed. Clarke, James Clarke, Ann Cage.

MR. ROBERT READ, 350 acs., in York & Warwick Co.'s; 20 Apr. 1684, p. 353. Adj. Mr. Thomas Cheesman; on head br. of Black Sw; Capt. John Martin; & William Cole, Esqr. Trans. of 7 pers: Robt. Cope, Geo. Seaton, An. Drake, James Holding, Tho. Bramer, Richd. Miller, Marg. Miller.

MR. THOMAS DYAR, 100 acs., Gloster Co; Kingston Par; on W. side of Dyar's Cr; 20 Apr. 1684, p. 353. Granted to John Gundry 13 Aug. 1650, & sold to sd. Dyar.

JAMES SYMMONS, SENR., 255 acs., Low. Norf. Co; Eliz. Riv. Par., on Tanner's Cr. Precincts, 20 Apr. 1684, p. 354. Beg. at Buskin's poynt, at mouth of Gater's Cr; crossing a br. of Queen Graves Cr., &c. 50 acs. granted William Johnson, 10 Mar. 1653; 50 acs. granted John Marshall 16 Apr. 1653; both of which tracts were assigned to Symmons; 100 acs. to sd. Symmons by pattent, 23 Mar. 1663; 55 acs. for trans. of 2 pers: Wm. Lambdin, Martha Lambdin.

JOHN CORBETT, 400 acs., Gloster Co; Kingston Par., 20 Apr. 1684, p. 354. Beg. at head of Ducking Pond Cr., dividing this & land of Isaac Plumer & Thomas Plumer; adj. Ralph Armsted; & Thomas Dyar. Trans. of 8 pers: John Moye, Wm. Martin, Tho. Thorne, Xpher. Wyn, Wm. Tyton, Jon. Copeland, Richd. Ball, Jon. Wayne.

EDWARD DOCKER, 210 acs., Middlesex Co., 20 Apr. 1684, p. 355. 50 acs. adj. Danniell Long; & Randolph Seagor; on Bryary Br., by Long's house, &c; 160 acs. adj. Nicholas West: sd. Seagor, by the maine Road; John Bewford; Mr. Henry Nicholls; & by sd. Docker's plantation, in sight of his house, &c. The sd. 50 acs. granted to Mr. Robert Beverley 5 June 1678, &

assigned to sd. Docker, 13 Dec. 1679; 160 acs. for trans. of 4 pers: Capt., & Moll, Negroes; Charles, & Elizabeth.

THOMAS ALLOMAINE, 52 acs., Gloster Co., Kingston Par., 20 Apr. 1684, p. 355. Adj. Mr. William Elliott; William Lewis; & Lt. Col. Jno. Armstead. Trans. of 2 pers: Amery Waine, Mary Arckland.

COL. RICHARD DUDLEY, 281 acs., Gloster Co., Kingston Par., on *Gwin's (Gwyn's) Ridge;* 20 Apr. 1684, p. 356. Near Lawrence Parrott (Perrott). 250 acs. granted him 20 Dec. 1667; 31 acs. for trans. of: Geo. Arkland.

MR. EVAN BELLANGE, 83 Acs., 1 R., 32 P., Henrico Co., Bristoll Par., on N. side of Appamattock Riv., 20 Apr. 1684, p. 356. Adj. land of Mr. Thomas Wells, in possession of Richard Holmes, on Cobb's Slash; by Robt. Russell, &c. 47 A., 2 R., 20 P., purchased of sd. Russell; 5 A., 2 R. of James Aken, Senr; the residue being King's land & taken altogether within this survey. Trans. of: Wm. Watts.

JOHN BANISTER, 650 acs., called *New Poynt Comfort Neck;* E. on New Poynt Comfort Cr., W. on Mobjack Bay, S. on John Gundrey, &c; 20 Apr. 1684, p. 357. Granted to William Worleigh, 13 Aug. 1650, & assigned to sd. Banister 2 Feb. 1653.

MR. HENERY AWBERY, 189 acs., on S. side of Rappa. Riv., at mouth of Occupation Cr., 20 Apr. 1684, p. 357. Beg. at William Moseley's, by a br. next & above *the Church;* along land he purchased of Henery White; adj. Robert Cardin, &c. Trans. of 4 pers: Cheney Ellerly, Nicho. Clark, Robt. Tod, Abra. English.

MR. WILLIAM HURST, 300 acs., Gloster Co., Abingtcn Par., 20 Apr. 1684, p. 357. Adj. land of Mr. John Robins, dec'd; Col. Augustine Warner, dec'd; land belonging to the *free schoole,* &c. Trans. of 6 pers: Jeffery Powers, Nicho. Dale & uxor, Nicho. Cossin (or Coffin), Tho. Burbage, Xpher. Young.

MR. EDMUND FORREST, 505 acs., Gloster Co., Kingston Par., 20 Apr. 1684, p. 358. Adj. Mr. John Lilly; & Mr. George Billops; down Holly Bush Br., to Garden Cr; to Mr. John Forrest, according to intent & meaning of the last well of *their* father, Mr. Henry Forrest, &c. 350 acs. granted sd. Henry 15 Sept. 1658; & 155 acs. for trans. of 4 pers: Avice Turkly, An Matthéws, Alice Croxon, Wm. Antherson (or Archerson).

WILLIAM CHEYNEY & THOMAS STILL, 245 acs., Middlesex Co., S. side of Rappa. Riv., 20 Apr. 1684, p. 358. Beg. on the Island line, by Maj. Beverley's line; to, Mr. Mountegue; by Mr. Randall Seagor's old field in sight of his house; to W. br. of Mr. Parrett's Cr., &c. Trans. of 5 pers: Benja. Fletcher, Sarah Reinolds, Cormuch (?) Castloe, James Pierce, Walter White.

JOHN MEGSOM, 433 acs., Gloster Co., Abington Par., near head of Cedar Bush Cr., 20 Apr. 1684, p. 359. Adj. Mr. John Mann, Maj. Lewis Burwell; Lawrence Smith; & Capt. Richard Booker. 125 acs. bought by William Megsom, dec'd., of Francis Wheeler, dec'd., 4 Sept. 1652; 300 acs. sold by Maj. Lewis Burwell, dec'd., unto Mathew Hawkins, of Queene's Creeke, 17 Nov. 1651, who sold to sd. Wheeler 1 Sept. 1652, who sold to sd. Megsom 4 Sept. 1652; 8 acs. for trans. of: Andw. Robinson.

MR. JOHN CORBETT, 300 acs., upon the Island of New Poynt Comfort Cr., in Gloster Co., 20 Apr. 1684, p. 359. Beg. at mouth of a cr., running through the marishes into Dyar's Cr., bet. the island & maine land; down Mobjack Bay, &c. Trans. of 6 pers: Richd. Cooke, Fra. Bick, Richd. Bick, Alice Watkins, Alice Johnson, Eliz. Johnson.

JOSEPH FIRTH, 150 acs., York Co., 20 Apr. 1684, p. 360. Being land Hannah Brumfield, *alias* Price, dyed seized of, & found to escheate, by inquisition under Hon. John Page, Esqr., Esch'r. of sd. Co., &c.

JOHN DORMER, 350 acs., Jas. City Co., 20 Apr. 1684, p. 360. Being land which Mary Burney, *als.* Dormer, dyed seized of, & escheated by inquisition under Hon. John Page, &c.

MR. EDMUND GWYN, 200 acs., Gloster Co., 20 Apr. 1684, p. 360. Land which Thomas Breeman dyed seized of, & found to escheate, by inquisition under Mr. Francis Page, Depty. Esch'r., &c.

PETER GLENISTER, 546 acs., James City Co., 20 Apr. 1684, p. 361. Granted to Margaret Barrett, & escheated, by inquisition under Mr. Edward Chilton, Depty. Esch'r., &c.

CHARLES JONES, 650 acs., Gloster Co., 20 Apr. 1684, p. 361. Land which Joane Careless dyed seized of, & found to escheate, by inquisition under Mr. Francis Page, Depty. Esch'r., &c.

MR. ANTHONY HAYNES, 700 acs., Warwick Co., 20 Nov. 1684, p. 361. Granted to Thomas Newell, dec'd., & found to escheate, by inquisition under Richard Awborne, Depty. Esch'r., &c.

HONORABLE WILLIAM BYRD, Esqr., 300 acs., Henrico Co., upon the river, 20 Apr. 1684, p. 362. Land which William Light dyed seized of, & found to escheate as by inquisition under Mr. William Randolph, Depty. Esch'r., &c.

MR. HENRY GAULER, 418 acs., Jas. City Co., N. side of James Riv. & S. side of the run of Moses Cr., 20 Apr. 1684, p. 362. Adj. land of Moses; & Mr. Bishop, &c. Granted to Isaac Coates 20 Apr. 1680, deserted, & granted sd. Gauler by order, &c., 20 Sept. 1683, & for trans. of 9 pers: Hen. Snow, Nicho. Barnet, Ed. Bland, Matt. Brisse, Jon. Bell, Hercules Messenger, Tho. Street, Wm. Higgensorr, Rose Hill.

MR. BENJAMIN HARRYSON (Harrison), 620 acs., Surry Co., 20 Apr. 1684, p. 363. Beg. near Mr. Wm.

Symmons' cart path; bet. sd. Symmons, Mr. Allen & William Scarbrough, &c. Granted to Thomas Sorresby 10 July 1680, deserted, & granted sd. Harrison by order, &c., 27 Nov. 1683. Trans. of 13 pers: Matthew Beaver, Leo. Clarket (or Clacket), Isa. Sanders, Margt. Wignol, Melchi. Lawrence, Susan Clare, Jon. Cane, Ed. Langford, David MackWilliam, James Tayler, Wm. Dorman, Lazarus Thomas, Richd. Goodman. Marginal Note: The patt. made void. Harryson to have the Rts. by order of Gen. Ct. The first 5 rts. (rights) used for Jno. Barker's patt. Folio 695.

MR. MALACHY THRUSTON, 69 acs., Low. Norf. Co., 20 Apr. 1684, p. 363. Beg. on the fresh ponds, &c. Granted to Mr. John Ferebee 29 Sept. 1679, deserted, & granted sd. Thruston by order, &c., 20 Sept. 1683. Trans. of 2 pers: Wm. Hayes, Nicho. Troton.

JAMES PETERS, 750 acs., Up. Par. of Nanzimond Co., neare the Cross Sw. out of *Burboyne;* to a White Marsh, &c; 20 Apr. 1684, p. 364. Granted to Humpherey Griffin, 24 Feb. 1675/6, deserted, & granted sd. Griffin by order, &c. 23 Apr. 1683. Trans. of 15 pers: Tho. Deering, Patrick Wishart, Jon. Davis, Robt. Arnol, Jon. Ireland, Jane Ireland, Tho. Reaves (or Reanes), Jon. Rochester, Ed. Morgan, Ellen Edwards, Jon. Sater, Jane Sater, Tho. Hale, Xpher. Burston, Tho. Rouse.

MR. JOHN FEREBEE, 148 acs., called the *Dam Necks,* Low. Norf. Co., 20 Apr. 1684, p. 364. Adj. David Murray, Junr; along the Cyprus Sw; to the lower dams, &c. Granted to Warren Godfrey 19 Oct. 1677, & since granted sd. Ferebee by order &c. 1 Dec. 1682. Trans. of 3 pers: Wm. Blesbery (or Plesbery), Richd. Tisby, Tho. Medideth.

MR. BENJAMIN GOODRICH, 930 acs., on S. side of Rappa. Riv., neere 1350 acs. taken up by Bartholomew Hoskins; 20 Apr. 1684, p. 365. 600 acs. beg. on Hoskins' Cr., parallel to John Gillett; granted to Lt. Col. Thomas Goodrich, 18 Sept. 1663; 330 acs.

below mouth of Tickner's Cr; by land of Reeves, &c; 200 acs. part granted Clement Thrush, who sold to Col. Thomas Goodrich, 14 Apr. 1656; 800 acs. due as heire of his father, the sd. Thomas; 130 acs. newly taken, due for trans. of 3 pers: Francis Meredith, Tho. Meades, Robt. Meades.

MR. HUMPHEREY BROWNING, 192 acs., Jas. City Co., 20 Apr. 1684, p. 366. On S. side of Jones' Sw. in the little neck; along his land purchased of Thomas Meekins; to N. side of Corne Sw; on Jones' Sw; to the Mill pond, &c. Trans. of 4 pers: Wm. Goldsmith, Wm. Rice, Edwd. Windet, Wm. Johnson.

RICHARD PILAND (Pyland), 580 acs., in Up. Par. of Surry Co., on NW side of Pigeon Sw., 20 Oct. 1684, p. 366. Beg. at Mr. Samll. Plaw's line where it crosses sd. Sw; to Syon Hill's line; by George Williams; Mr. Thompson; Babbs' land; to John Collins, &c. Trans. of 12 pers: Walter Ashton, James Jefferson, Wm. Ward, Tho. Sheild, Richd. Williams, Jon. Williams, Jon .Jones, Jon. Holmes, Jon. Squire, Jon. Robert, Jon. Massey, Ed. Hill.

MR. THOMAS WARREN, 280 acs., Up. Par. of Surry Co., about 1½ mi. above Ware Neck Mill; 20 Apr. 1684, p. 367. 120 acs. part of 290 acs. granted his father, Mr. Thomas Warren, dec'd., 3 July 1648; 90 acs. being wast land adj; beg. on E. side of a gr. Sw., bet. sd. Warren & Robert House; neer Syon Hill's corner; to a br. dividing this & land of Peter de Berry, &c. Trans. of 2 pers: Danll. Gardner, Barbary Heale.

THOMAS SMITH, 200 acs., Up. Par. of Surry Co., bet. the Cypress Sw. of *John chokuck Sw,* 20 Apr. 1684, p. 367. Beg. at land of Richard Jordan, Junr., &c. Trans. of 4 pers: Morris Bowen, Wm. Milton, An Tatem, Mary Tatem.

NICHOLAS SESSUMS, 1050 acs., Surry Co., on SE side of Pigeon Sw., 20 Apr. 1684, p. 368. 550 acs. granted him by patt; & 500 acs. being wast land adj; betwixt Mr. William Edwards & Richard Blow; on land of Maj. Marriot, now in possession of Samll. Thompson, &c. Trans. of 11 pers: Jon. Woodliffe, Jon. Smith, Hen. Stephens, Eli. Wells, Rowld. Grayne, Nicho. Cliffe, Hen. Bentley, Wm. Rawley, Robt. Holman, Martha Flud, Jon. Parker.

RICHARD SMITH, 230 acs., Surry Co., on SE side of Pidgeon Sw., 20 Apr. 1684, p. 368. Adj. Mr. Merriwether & Joseph Wall. Trans. of 5 pers: Robt. Fent, Fran. Downes, Danll. Arrye, Sarah Keeling (or Reeling), Jon. Dale.

· JOHN COLLINS, 950 acs., Surry Co; on NW side of Pidgeon Sw., 20 Apr. 1684, p. 369. 220 acs. part of 248 acs. granted Maj. Samll. Swan, 18 Dec. 1668, who assigned to Roger Williams, 4 May 1680, who sold to Collins, 19 Jan. 1681; 730 acs. adj. same; Mr. William Thompson; & Babbs' land; a br. dividing this & Mr. Merriwether; down the Cypress Sw., &c. Trans. of 15 pers: Richd. Fulborne, Jean George, Hugh Davis, Wm. Parsons, Tho. Jones, Elliner Claydon, Tho. Osborne, Ralph Long, Esther Williams, Francis Biggs, Tho. Head, John Evans (?), Jeffery Evans, Richd. Reynolds, Jon. Arnice.

RICHARD JORDAN, Junr., 260 acs., Up. Par. of Surry Co., on NE side of John Checokuck Sw; being part of Mr. Owens' devident, &c; 20 Apr. 1684, p. 369. Trans. of 6 pers: Mary Hoskins, Jon. Avery, Jon. Cooke, Geo. Miller, Tho. Bernard.

MR. WILLIAM THOMPSON, 150 acs., Surry Co., on N. side of the head of Graye's Cr., 20 Apr. 1684, p. 370. 140 acs. part of 400 acs. granted Christopher Lawson; 10 acs. being a neck, below the Horse Bridge bet. sd. 140 acs. & land of Luke Meazell; adj. Mathew Merriott; a sw. dividing it from land of John Whittson. Trans. of 3 pers: Richd. Budnye, Wm. Metcalfe, Joseph Cox.

MR. SAMLL. PLAW, 240 acs., Surry Co., on both sides of Pigeon Sw., 20 Apr. 1684, p. 370. Beg. att Syon Hill's corner; adj. Mr. Wm. Edwards, & Mr. Pettaway. Trans. of 5 pers: Jon. James, Hercules Price, Doro. Jeffery, Crowder Joyce, Robt. Halsey.

JOHN COKER, 400 acs., Low. Par. of Surry Co., on SW side of Cypress Sw., adj. Mr. Merryweather, 20 Apr. 1684, p. 371. Trans. of 8 pers: Fran. Vicaris, Martin Church, Jon. Say, Ed. Lincoln, Tho. Peirce, Wm. Nayler, Hen. Smith, Robt. Braxton.

MR. HENERY BAKER, 350 acs., Surry Co., on SW side of John chokehocunt Sw., 20 Apr. 1684, p. 371. 150 acs. being part of Capt. Corker's devdt., purchased of George Branch, Junr., adj. the remainder; on the Cypress Sw., &c. Trans. of 3 pers: Hen. Carter, Robt. Ward, Nicho. Keyton.

MR. THOMAS JORDAN, 235 acs., Up. Par. of Surry Co., 20 Apr. 1684, p. 372. About 3/4 of a mi. from Capt. Corker, in Claye's Br; adj. Capt. Potter; & Luce Corker. Trans. of 5 pers.✷

RICHARD BLOW, 210 acs., Surry Co., 20 Apr. 1684, p. 372. On SE side of Pigeon Sw., 1/2 mi. above Mr. Merriwether; a br. dividing same from Richard Smith; & adj. Nicholas Sessums. Trans. of 5 pers.*

COL. WM. BROWN & MR. WM. FOREMAN, 550 acs., Surry Co., bet. Cypress Sw. & the maine Blackwater Sw., adj. Mr. Warren; 20 Apr. 1684, p. 372. Trans. of 11 pers.*

JOSEPH WALL, 900 acs., Surry Co., on NE side of Cypress Sw., adj. Mr. Wm. Thompson; 20 Apr. 1684, p. 373. Trans. of 18 pers.*

MR. ARTHUR JORDAN, 240 acs., Up. Par. of Surry Co., on SE side of Stony Run, 20 Apr. 1684, p. 373. 150 acs. granted him. 23 Apr. 1678; 90 acs. being wast land adj. Trans. of 2 pers.✷

GEORGE & RIVER JORDAN, 200 acs., Up. Par. of Surry Co: bet. lands of Mr. Arthur Jordan & Mr. Christopher Foster. 20 Apr. 1684, p. 374. Trans. of 4 pers.*

JOHN PARSONS, JUNR., 290 acs., Low. Par. of Surry Co., 20 Apr. 1684, p. 374. On heads of the Blackwater branches; adj. Thomas Lane, Mr. Robert Ruffin; Mr. Bins; & Mr. Richard Bennett. Trans. of 6 pers.*

JOHN BRETT, JUNR., 720 acs., Up. Par. of Surry Co; 20 Apr. 1684, p. 375. On both sides of Cypress Sw., adj. Mr. Thomas Jordan & Edward Grantham. Trans. of 15 pers.*

CHRISTOPHER WADE, 92 acs., Low. Par. of Isle of Wight Co: bet. Mr. Coleman & Mr. Jno. Nevill; 20 Apr. 1684, p. 375. Trans. of 2 pers.*

JAMES GARDNER, 200 acs., Low. Par. of Is. of Wight Co; on heads of the brs. of the W. br. of Nanzemond; adj. Christopher Wade & Mr. Coleman; 20 Apr. 1684, p. 375. Trans. of 4 pers.*

WILLIAM BALDWIN & JOHN DUCE, 2600 acs., Up. Par. of Surry Co., on SW side of Cypress Sw., at mouth of Tyase's Br; adj. Robert Andrews & Capt. Corker; 20 Apr. 1684, p. 376. Trans. of 52 pers.*

JOHN PARSONS, JUNR., 740 acs., Surry Co., on SW side of Johnchecohunk (Johnchohocunk) Sw., near Mr. Owens; 20 Apr. 1684, p. 376. Trans. of 15 pers.*

EDWARD PETTAWAY, 480 acs., Surry Co; on W. side of the Green Sw., 20 Apr. 1684, p. 377. Adj. John Clark; Owens' line; John Clemens; Syon Hill; Mr. Samll. Plaw; Mr. William Edwards; & Mr. Bins. Trans. of 9 pers.*

JOHN CLARK, 410 acs., Low Par. of Surry So; on E. side of the Green Sw., adj. Thomas Lane; Mr. Bins; Mr. Owens; & Mr. William Gray. 20 Apr. 1684, p. 377. Trans. of 9 pers.*

MR. ROBERT COLEMAN, 530 acs., on W. side of a reedy marsh, a br. of Chuckatuck; 20 Apr. 1684, p. 378. 400 acs. granted to Richard & Miles Lewis, 29 Jan. 1667, who sold to sd. Coleman; adj. land of Jeremiah Rutter; & land of John Turner. Trans. of 3 pers.*

MR. JOHN NEVELL, 92 acs., in Low. Par. of Is. of Wight Co; adj. Mr. Robert Coleman; & Christopher Wade; 20 Apr. 1684, p. 378. Trans. of 2 pers.*

MR. CHRISTOPHER HOLLYMAN, 1020 acs., in the Up. Par. of Isle of Wight Co., 20 Apr. 1684, p. 378. Beg. in an island by the maine Blackwater side, adj. William Gualtney. 600 acs. granted John Brown, 1 Mar. 1666, who sold to sd. Hollyman 3 Feb. 1668; 420 being wast land adj., due for trans. of 9 pers.*

JAMES & JOHN BAUGHAN, 900 acs., Rappa. Co., 20 Apr. 1684, p. 379. Adj. James Fullerton; & Rich. Grigory; by the horse path; to Col. Goodrich; Mr. Henery Awbery; & land of Ball & Price. Trans. of 18 pers.*

MR. GEORGE MORRIS, 400 acs., New Kent Co; St. Steven's Par., on either side the horse path from Dragon Sw. to Pascataway; 20 Apr. 1684, p. 380. Adj. Wm. Drumright (or Dumright), & Mathew York; John Symonds; Mr. Collier; Mr. Lockie, & the land John Bowles purchased of Col. Robert Abrahall, formerly the land of Wm. More. Trans. of 8 pers.*

MR. RICHARD ROY, 97 acs., New Kent (Co.); neare Mr. Graye's plantation; adj. Ashwell Batten; Mr. Coates' cleare ground; & Mr. George Major. 20 Apr. 1684, p. 380. Importation of 2 pers.*

JOHN GRIFFIN, 420 acs., New Kent Co; S. side of Yorke Riv., 20 Apr. 1684, p. 381. Beg. by the Image Field; adj. Mr. John Woodington, near Wm. Russell's fence; to N. side the maine Roade; bounded by land of Mr. Hope (now the Countie's) & land of Cox. Granted to Gearrett Robert Ellyson, 20 Apr. 1680, who sold to sd. Griffen, 2 Jan. 1681.

MR. JOHN SMITH, 748 acs., Chas. Citty Co; on Warrick Sw., 26 Apr. 1684, p. 381. Crossing Henry Witche's path; the Notaway Path; & Tonotara Path; to Hugh Lee, &c. Trans. of 15 pers.*

RICE GRIFFIN, 197 acs., James Citty Co; on S. side of Peasehill Cr. Sw., on the Ridge Path to Tinseley's line; to Alcock's corner; on *Potters field* land; &c; 26 Apr. 1684, p. 382. Trans. of 4 pers.*

RICHARD PALMER, 223 acs., in the Co. & Par. of York; 26 Apr. 1684, p. 382. Formerly pattented by Mr. Edward Palmer, dec'd., & "the pattent not found but supposed to be burnt in his dwelling house"; adj. Argoll Blackstone; to head of Back Cr., &c. Trans. of 5 pers.*

MALACHY THRUSTON, 180 acs., Low. Norf. Co; Linhaven Par; adj. John & Job Kemp; 26 Apr. 1684, p. 383. Granted to James Kemp 23 Apr. 1681, deserted, & granted sd. Thruston by order, &c. Trans. of 4 pers: James Porter, Senr., James Porter, Junr., Jean Porter, Martha Porter.

MR. CHRISTOPHER LEWIS, 700 acs., New Kent Co; St. Stephen's Par; in a great fork of Pyanketank Sw; by Axell's Sw., &c; 21 Apr. 1684, p. 383. 500 acs. part purchased of Lt. Col. Thomas Clayborne. 200 acs. for trans. of 4 pers.*

DANNIELL WARKEMAN, 288 A., 3 R., 3 P., Chas. City Co; Weyonoake Par; on S. side of Chichahominy River, 21 Apr. 1684, p. 384. Beg. by Dockman's Runn, along the Wading Place Path, &c. Trans. of 6 pers: James Littlewood, James Holman, Francis Chitty, Mary Fowke, Mary Cooke, Alice Long.

JAMES STRATLES, 240 acs., Jas. City Co., 21 Apr. 1684, p. 385. On E.

side of the Iron Mine hill meadow on Wetherall's line; to Powhatan Sw., down a slash to Long Meadowe Run; to Sir William Berkeley's line of *hotwater land,* &c. 200 acs. granted him 14 Apr. 1659, renewed, & alsoe graunted him 10 Jan. 1661; 40 acs. for trans. of: Jerimiah Mathews.

MR. JOHN SMITH, 716 acs., Rappa. Co; on S. side of the River; adj. Capt. Thomas Hawkins, above the falls; 21 Apr. 1684, p. 385. Granted Maj. Lawrence Smith & Mr. Anthony Buckner, 17 Mar. 1672/3, deserted, & now granted by order, &c. Trans. of 15 pers.*

MR. AUGUSTINE SMITH & MR. WILLIAM SMITH, 6500 acs., in Rappa. & New Kent Co.'s; adj. 4600 acs. of Capt. Lawrence Smith; by the Bever damms, neere head of the Reedy Br., &c. 21 Apr. 1684, p. 386. Granted to Capt. Lawrence Smith & Capt. Robert Beverley, 16 Nov. 1674, deserted, & now granted by order &c. Trans. of 92 pers.*

ROBERT BARLOW, 62 acs., Gloster Co; Abington Par; adj. land of Christopher Abbott, dec'd; crossing a marsh, to the Roade to Tyndall's poynt, &c; 26 Apr. 1684, p. 386. Trans. of 2 pers.*

JOHN PIGGOTT, 374 acs., Henrico Co; Bristoll Par; on S. side of Swift Cr; adj. Mr. Chandler; Mr. Francis Eps; & Tho. Webster; 21 Apr. 1684, p. 387. Trans. of 8 pers: Tho. Ruck, Tho. Sprouting, Kath. Daniel, Anne Turberveild, Wm. Pratt, Richd. Dobbs.

FRANCIS LEADBETER, 548 A., 32 P., Chas. City Co; Bristoll Par; on S. side of Appamatock River, att *Worrockhock;* 26 Apr. 1684, p. 387. Beg. on Hugh Lee; crossing Alder Br; & Worrockhock maine Br., &c. Trans. of 11 pers.*

JOHN SPEIGHT (Spight), 300 acs., Nanzemond Co., 21 Apr. 1684, p. 388. Granted to Francis Spight, his father, 17 Mar. 1654/5; renewed 3 Apr. 1662, & given by will to sd. John.

MR. JOHN SOANES, 710 acs., Jas. City Co., onW. side of Chickahominy Riv., 21 Apr. 1684, p. 388. Beg. at Thomas Walters, neere Webb's runn, on upper side of Poplar Spring Br; along Mr. Cowles; to br. of Hogpen Meadow; to Pease hill Cr; on the ridge path, to Potters field (*als.* of Mr. Hunt's land); to Thomas Bowrey, &c. Trans. of 14 pers.*

JAMES PETERS, 750 acs., Up. Par. of Nanzemond; nigh Cross Sw. out of *Barbicu* (Sw.); 21 Apr. 1684, p .389. Granted to Humpherey Griffin 24 Feb. 1675, deserted, & now granted by order, &c. Trans. of 15 pers.*

WILLIAM GREENFIELD, 119 acs., Henrico Co; Bristoll Par; on N. side of Swifts Cr; adj. William Bevin; Mr. Henry Randolph; & Robert Man. Trans. of 3 pers.* 26 Apr. 1684, p. 389.

WILLIAM LEIGH, 920 acs., New Kent Co; N. side of Mattapany Riv; adj. Tho. Hall & John Pigg's 3831 acs; & Robert Bagby & Wm. Hernden's 1800 acs; &c; 1 May 1684, p. 390. Said land taken up by John Pigg, who assigned to John Burnell & Edwd. Pigg, by them deserted, & now due by order, &c. Trans. of 19 pers.*

LT. COL. ANTHONY LAWSON, 1206 acs., Low.- Norf. Co; Linhaven Par; on both sides of Linhaven River, 1 May 1684, p. 390. Adj. land taken by Capt. Keeling in the name of his son John; along line agreed upon by sd. Keeling & Lawson, 15 June 1677; along Bowring's line; to corner formerly Mosier's, now Spratt's; to mouth of a cr. out of the beaver damms, near *London Bridge,* &c. 600 acs. granted to John Ladd, 27 May 1673, who sold to sd. Lawson; 606 acs. for trans. of 12 pers.*

BRYAN OQUIN, 550 acs., Up. Par. of Nanzemund; on S. side of the Cypress Sw., adj. land formerly Hugh Gauhan's, now in possession of Robert Reddock; Wm. Speight; & the maine runn of Barbicue Sw., &c; 26 Apr. 1684, p. 391. Trans. of 11 pers.*

ZACHARIAH CHAPPELL, 175 acs., Warwick Co; Denbigh Par; adj. Capt. John Langhorne; James Cathon; Mr. Samll. Ranshaw; Mr. Mumford; & land of the heir of Edward James, &c; 26 Apr. 1684, p. 391. Trans. of 4 pers.*

LT. COL. THOMAS MILNER, 12 acs., of marsh, Nanzemond Co; at the mouth of a cr. next below *Troublesome Poynt;* & adj. his own land; 26 Apr. 1684, p. 392. Trans. of 1 per.*

WALTER PRICE & THOMAS DYAS, 400 acs., Up. Par. of Nanzemond Co; nigh runn of Barbicue Sw; by Winborne's corner; to Chilcott's line, &c; 26 Apr. 1684, p. 392. Trans. of 8 pers.*

JOHN BOYCE, 200 acs., in the Up. Par. of Nanzemond; adj. Epaphraditus Benton; 26 Apr. 1684, p. 392. Trans. of 4 pers.*

MR. WILLIAM CHICHESTER, 400 acs., Low. Norf. Co; Lynhaven Par., on W. side of the Cyprus Sw., 26 Apr. 1684, p. 393. Adj. Francis Bond; on N. side of Parsimond Runn, neare the horse bridge. Trans. of 8 pers.*

AUGUSTINE COBHAM, 66 acs., James City Co., on upper side of Pease hill Cr; adj. *Potters feild devident.* 26 Apr. 1684, p. 393. Marginal note: 76 acres. Trans. of 2 pers.*

MR. WILLIAM BODDIE (Boddy), 3350 acs., Low. Par. of Is. of Wight Co; on both sides of the 2 gr. Swamps of the Cypress, & the W. br. of Nanzemond Riv; 26 Apr. 1684, p. 394. Adj. Edmund Palmer; Mr. Wm. Bressey; Mr. Coleman; & Thomas Joyner's corne field. Trans. of 67 pers.*

MR. JAMES TULLAGH (Tullaugh), 270 acs., Low. Par. of Is. of Wight Co; about a mile from William West's plantation; 26 Apr. 1684, p. 395. Adj. Mrs. Hardy; Mr. Fulgham, his own land purchased of Mr. William Brescie (or Bressie). Trans. of 6 pers.*

MR. THOMAS CLAYTON, 5800 acs., Accomack Co; called *Gengoteage;*

being the next Island to the N'wd. of Kekotank, *als.* Occocomson, Is; 26 Apr. 1684, p. 395. Granted Lt. Col. Danniell Jenifer, 27 Mar. 1677, deserted, & now granted by order, &c. Trans. of 116 pers.*

MR. QUINTILLIAN GOTHRICK, 200 acs., Eliz. City Co; on E. side of Hampton Riv; adj. John Spinkes; & land of —— Dolby; 26 Apr. 1684, p. 396. Part of 350 acs. granted Col. Charles Morryson, 20 July 1669, & lately purchased by Gothrick from sd. Morryson & Robert Bright.

MR. THOMAS PITT, 150 acs., Is. of Wight Co; 26 Apr. 1684, p. 396. Land William Lynch dyed seized of, & was found to escheate, by inquisition under William Randolph, Depty. Esch'r., &c.

GYLES WAKEFIELD, 100 acs., Nanzemond Co; in Chuckatuck Par., 26 May 1684, p. 397. Land Anne Tatem dyed seized of, & was found to escheate, by inquisition under William Randolph, Dep't'y. Esch'r., &c.

DANIELL HIND, 250 acs., Up. Par. of Nanzemond; adj. his own, Capt. Booth, & —— Lassitor's land; 26 Apr. 1684, p. 397. Trans. of 5 pers.*

JOHN WRIGHT & THOMAS CARRILL (Carrell), 102 acs., upon the Ridge, in the Co. & Par. of York; adj. Gozion Delong (or Delory); 26 Apr. 1684, p. 397. Pattented by Col. Richd. Lee, who sold to the above named.

MR. GEORGE NEWTON & RICHARD CHURCH, 1000 acs., Low. Norf. Co; in the S. br. of Eliz. River, att head of Cyprus Cr. or Pussel poynt Cr; adj. Peter Saxton; 26 Apr. 1684; p. 398. Granted Capt. Francis Emperor, Hugh Gale & Edward Morgan, 18 Feb. 1653, deserted, &c. Importation of 20 pers.*

MR. JAMES HALEY (Hayly), 593 acs., Jas. City Co., 26 Apr. 1684, p. 398. 493 acs. adj. Jones, att lower end of long thickett; adj. Ellerbies; Dobye's; Wolfe's; Lewis'; & Phillips' lines; 100 acs. beg. by the Cow (or Rowling)

path; cross James Town Road; along Mr. Phillips' line, to Mr. Freeman's; &c. 493 acs. granted 24 Mar. 1656, & renewed 18 Mar. 1672, to John Shell, for 300 acs; 100 acs. being part of 300 acs. granted to Griffith Dickinson, 5 Jan. 1656, who assigned to sd. Shell, 11 Apr. 1656, who sold both parcells to Lawrence Ash, 10 Mar. 1675, who sold to sd. Haley, 6 Apr. 1676. Trans. of 4 pers.* Marginal note: 993 acres.

EDWARD LAND & ROBERT LAND, Orphans of Renatus Land; 250 acs., Low. Norf. Co; in Lynhaven Par: near the gr. Cyprus Sw; by the horse bridge, on Persimond Runn; 21 Oct. 1684, p. 399. Trans. of 5 pers: Renatius Land, Ann Lewet (or Lewer), Edward Fallett, Eliza. Copeland; & Toby a Negro.

MR. GODFREY SPRUELL, 348 acs., Jas. City Co; which together with 100 acs. belonging to Hester Jones, begins by his plantation; on long thickett, etc; 21 Oct. 1684, p. 399. Trans. of 7 pers.*

JOHN PROSSER, 408 acs., Rappa. Co., on S. side the River, upon head of Golden naile Cr; & running to head of a br. of Mazensen; 21 Oct. 1684, p. 400. Trans. of 8 pers.*

MR. RICHARD LITTLEPAGE, 871 acs., New Kent Co., on S. side of York Riv., & upon N. side of Chickahominy maine Sw., 21 Oct. 1684, p. 400. Adj. Moses Davies; & Mr. Henery Wyatt's path, in line of Mr. William Basset & Mr. James Oustin. Trans. of 18 pers: Tho. Stevens, Richd. Elsom, Wm. Betham, Tho. Smith, Wm. Johnson, Joan Fuller, Joseph Cox, Wm. Cole, Alex. Richason, Ann Bland, Mary Clarke, James Wade, Wm. Hollingworth, Tho. Russell, Alex. Fleming, Ann Townsend; & 2 Negroes.

SAMUELL WARD, 1453¾ acs., on Rappa. River; on NW side of Occupation Cr., upon Popoman; adj. land of Wm. Gobson; dec'd; & Wm. Bowler. 21 Oct. 1684, p. 401. Trans. of 3 pers.*

JOHN BAUGHAN, 500 acs., New Kent Co; St. Stevens Par., on S. side of

York Riv., bet. branches of Black Cr. & Mattedequin Cr; 21 Oct. 1684, p. 401. Near Wm. Pullam; crossing Horsley's path; adj. Mr. James Woody's land, formerly Wm. Stone's; to James More (Moore). 300 acs. purchased of George Thomas & Samuell Right, 7 Sept. 1670; 200 acs. being surplus, & due for trans. of 4 pers.*

MR. JOHN WILLIS, 1150 acs., Middlesex Co., 21 Oct. 1684, p. 402. Beg. in sight of Thomas Tuggle's plantation; adj. Edmund Mickleburrough, John Nash; Middleton's plantation; his own plantation; Mr. Henry Thatcher, on head of the Indian Cabbin Br. at 2 springs; & Robert Williamson, &c. 600 acs. granted Thomas Willis, his father, & Robert Middleton, 15 Sept. 1658; Middleton assigned to sd. Willis; & due sd. John his son; 500 acs. for trans. of 11 pers: Sarah Tompson, Samuel Acton, Edwd. Fletcher, Bath. Penn, & Mary Goodman; Negroes: Jack, Nell, Quow, Cromwell, George, Mathew, Joe, Tome, Burrows, Mingo, Jacob, Peter, Robin, Sueseny, Jasper.

WILLIAM BATES, 704 acs., Rappa Co., S. side the River, 21 Oct. 1684, p. 403. Adj. Robert Nossey's (Moss ?) & Stokes' lands; Robert Mayfield; & George Marke; near the back road; by Butcher's line, &c. Part of patt. to Nicholas Willard dated 24 Jan. 1665; &c. Trans. of 14 pers.*

MR. SAMUELL CHAPPELL, 125½ acs., Warwick Co; in Harwood's Neck Reeds; 21 Oct. 1684, p. 403. Trans. of 3 pers.*

MR. WILLIAM YOUNG, 998 acs., Rappa. Co., 21 Oct. 1684, p. 404. Near Maj. Mottrom; ENE upon Rappa. Riv; by a gr. Hucklberry Sw., parting this & land of David Allison, & Capt. Josias Pickas' plantation; &c. 450 acs. granted Mr. Henery Soanes, 3 Sept. 1652 & assigned to Sir Henery Chicheley, who assigned to Robert Parr & sd. Young, 20 Jan. 1670; & now resurveyed; residue for trans. of 11 pers: Henry Gostin (or Goslin), Robert Polling, Ralph Sheppard, John Acres, Margarett Curtis, Edward Watson, Symon Smith, John

Greene, Jon. Potts, Eliza Marloe, Wm. Young, James Berkely, Alex. Westerton, Elianor Oliver, Thomas Hedgcock, Peter Hannah, Lewis Burow, Martha Sadler, Margery Symons, Mary Young.

MR. DAVID SMITH, 650 acs., New Kent Co; S. side of York Riv., 21 Oct. 1684, p. 405. Beg. at land he purchased of Mr. Cornelius Dabney; near Apponin Br; adj. Mr. John Fleming; & John Sexton; on Mattedequin Cr., & Mr. George Gills' land, now Robert Harmon's, &c. 470 acs. by former pattent, & the rest added. Trans. of 4 pers.*

SAMUELL GENTREY, 300 acs. New Kent Co; S. side York River; bet. head brs. of same & brs. of Tottapottamoys Cr., 21 Oct. 1684, p. 405. Adj. Col. John Page, Esqr; Edward Houchin & Nicholas Gentrey. Trans. of 6 pers: John Morris, Francis Middlton, Hen. Tully, Elizabeth Ody, Mar. Gardner, 2.

MR. JOSEPH GOODRICH, WM. BALL & JOHN PRICE, 629 acs., Rappa. Co., 21 Oct. 1684, p. 406. Adj. Thomas Harper; Col. Hill; the Indian path; John Jones; & Wilson's path, &c. Trans. of 13 pers: Eliz. Joy (or Ivy), Rich. Birch. Note: 11 rights by certificate.

MR. RICHARD WILLIS, 1340 acs., Middlesex Co., 21 Oct. 1684, p. 406. Adj. land of Richard Lewis & John Welsh, dec'd; along the maine swamp; by the Mill damms; by Mr. Curtis' plantation, &c. Trans. of 27 pers: John James, John White, Wm. Bamton, Tho. Brulfe, Rich. Sike, Alex. Mackdonnell, Rich. Gill, Rich. Serjeant, Owen Jones, Wm. Wildsmith, Kath. Wills, Susanna Wills, Dorothy Wills, Rachell Alderbury, Sarah Lee, an English boy, Randall Smith, Henry Freeman, Geo. Williams, Jane Pullen; 7 Negroes: Absolon, Sampson, Nero, Hewson, Maria, Nan, Besse.

WILLIAM HARRINGTON, 250 acs., Chas. City Co., 21 Oct. 1684, p. 407. Adj. lands of Capt. Thomas Busby; & Joshuah Meacham; down the Myery Meadow, &c. Trans. of 5 pers.*

MR. ROBT. THOMAS, 10 acs., Up. Par. of Is. of Wight Co; bet. Mr. Wm. Lewer & John Murray; 21 Oct. 1684, p. 407. Trans. of 1 per.*

MR. WILLIAM THOMPSON, 150 acs., near *Southwark Church,* in Surry Co., 21 Oct. 1684, p. 408. Beg. att Maj. Samll. Swan, bet. David Andrews & Luke Meazell; to William Foreman; & Col. Browne, &c. Trans. of 3 pers.*

MR. WILLIAM EDWARDS, 920 acs., Surry Co., on SE side of Pidgeon Sw., 21 Oct. 1684, p. 408. Adj. Mr. Samuell Plaw; Edwd. Pettaway; Mr. Thomas Binns; & Nicholas Sessum. Trans. of 19 pers.*

MAJOR FRANCIS SAYER, 610 acs., Low. Norf. Co., 21 Oct. 1684, p. 409. 550 acs. bet. the S. & E .brs. of Eliz. River, beg. on W. side of Smuggs' hole Cr; by the horse bridge br; 150 acs. of which granted to William Ranshaw, 24 Sept. 1636, who sold to Thomas Sayer, dec'd., who bequeathed to his son Trustram, & after his decease recovered by sd. Francis, by order of Assembly; 300 acs. granted Thomas Meeres, 17 May 1637, who sold to sd. Thomas Sayer, who bequeathed to sd. Francis; 100 acs. being wast land, now surveyed with the former; 60 acs. being severall necks or poynts, on S. side of Horse Bridge br; near Richard Yates, &c. Trans. of 4 pers.*

WILLIAM BALL & JOHN PRICE, 290 acs., Rappa. Co., 21 Oct. 1684, p. 410. Adj. Francis Brown, Thomas Harper, & Nimcock Indian Road. Trans. of 6 pers: Robt. Porter, Thomas Clayton, John Johnson, Eliz. Simpson, Humphry Rooks, Rich. Scott.

CAPT. WM. ROBINSON, 350 acs., Low. Norf. Co., att head of the E. br. of Eliz. River, 21 Oct. 1684, p. 410. Adj. Francis Shipp; on the Cyprus Sw. Granted by virtue of an order of Generall Court, 1 May 1684, & due for trans. of 7 pers.*

WILLIAM BAYLEY & JOHN LAWSON, 93 acs., in the Co. & Par.

of York; upon a br. of the Back Cr; adj. Capt. Ralph Wormeley, Esqr. 21 Oct. 1684, p. 411. Trans. of 2 pers: Joseph Foard, Henry Ruddle.

GEORGE IVY, 550 acs., Low. Norf. Co., 21 Oct. 1684, p. 411. 50 acs called *Julians Neck;* adj. Danniell Tanner, upon N. side of sd. Tanner's Cr; granted to John White, 10 July 1639, & by Josiah Crouch, son & heire of Wm. Crouch, assigned to sd. Ivy, 2 Nov. 1682; 500 acs. on N. side of sd. Cr; adj. Col. Lemuell Mason; bought of sd. Josiah Crouch, 23 Oct. 1682, & ack. in Low. Norf. Co. Ct., by Mr. Thomas Bridge, Atty. of sd. Josiah.

THOMAS CORBELL, 100 acs., Nanzimond Co., 21 Oct. 1684, p. 412. Late in the tenure of Mindart Deeds, which land Thomas Corbell, Junr., dyed seized of, & was found to escheate by inquisition under William Randolph, Depty. Esch'r., &c.

JAMES MURROE (Murhoe), 60 acs., Nanzemond Co., 21 Oct. 1684, p. 412 Land which Austin Gillet dyed seized of; escheated by inquisition under William Randolph, Depty. Esch'r., etc.

JAMES HOWARD, 300 acs., Up. Par. of Nanzemond; att head of Capt. John Mason in the W'n. branch; 21 Oct. 1684, p. 412. Adj. Richard Sanders; land of Michaell Hill, now Francis Sanders; John Wallis, & Thomas Gornigam (or Goringam). Granted to Richard Sandders, 10 July 1680, deserted, & now granted by order, &c. Trans. of 6 pers.*

HENRY VAUGHAN, 375 acs., Rappa. Co.; 21 Oct. 1684, p. 413. Adj. Maj. Georg Morris, James Vaughan, & Thomas Gaines; on br. of Hoskins Cr. Trans. of 8 pers: Francis Marriner, Robert Boone, Daniell Fenner, Alice Thomas, Rich. Draper, Mary Whaly, Wm. Parkes, Wm. Prior.

GRACE LEWIS, Orphan, of Midlesex Co., 646 acs., 21 Oct. 1684, p. 413. By a br. of Sunderland, *als.* Copeland, Cr; adj. Mr. Robert Chuning; John Blewford, & Mr. Robert Price. Trans. of 13 pers.*

JOHN GREGORY, 1200 acs., Rappa. Co., on S. side of Rappa. Riv., on E. side of Hodgskins' Cr., 21 Oct. 1684, p, 414. A branch dividing this from land of Mr. James Williamson. 600 acs. granted Wm. Johnson, 10 Mar. 1653, who assigned to sd. Gregory; 600 acs. for trans. of 12 pers.* Renewal of patent granted him 22 Oct. 1663.

MAJ. FRANCIS SAYER, 1000 acs., Low. Norf. Co., 21 Oct. 1684, p. 415. W. from the Mill land, at head of Puzzle Cr., on S. Br. of Eliz. River. Granted to Bartholomew Ingobrickson, John Prescot, Thomas Blanch, & Nicholas & Robert Jordan, 29 Sept. 1664, deserted, & now granted by order, &c. Trans. of 20 pers: Arthur Trott, Oliver Atkins, Miles East, Nehemiah Gold, Mary Edgerton, Wm. Blew, Jone Woolerton, Roger Grimes, Morgan Evans, James Halser, Joall Hindley (or Hundley), John Hoyle, Jane Lawry, Jno. Stapleton, Nich. Hollis, Robt. Weilding, Ralph Hedger, Abraham Leekes, Sarah Dicks, Barbary Hollis.

BRYAN MOORE & JOHN COCK-LEN, 200 acs., York Co., 21 Oct. 1684, p. 416. Land which Bryan Canady dyed seized of; found to escheate by inquisition under Edmund Jenings, Depty. Esch'r., &c.

EVAN GRIFFIN, 170 acs., Up. Par. of Nanzemond Co., 21 Oct. 1684, p. 416. Adj. Wm. Poope, & John Spight. Trans. of 4 pers: Tho. Hinton, Joseph Lane, John Ager, Danll. Maple.

JOHN MUNGOE, 100 acs., on SE side of Hutchison's Cr., in lower part of Waresquiock Bay, 21 Oct. 1684, p. 417. Adj. Mr. James Day; at head of Polentines Sw; & Mr. Thomas Taberrer. Granted to Gyles Jones 14 Dec. 1619, who sold to Justinian Cooper, 19 Oct.. 1628 (?), who sold to Wassell Weblin & George Fadding, 29 Sept. 1629, & by sd. Fadding, the surviving tenant, sold to Robert Sabine, 25 Feb. 1630, who sold to Christopher Reinolds, 21 Dec. 1634, who sold to Peter Hull, 1 May 1639, who sold to John Mungoe, 9 Feb. 1663, who bequeathed to his son,

the sd. John; further due for trans. of 2 pers.*

MR. ROBERT BYRD, 200 acs., New Kent Co., 21 Oct. 1684, p. 417. Land Michaell Robinson dyed seized of; found to escheate by inquisition under Mathew Page, Depty. Esch'r., &c.

MR. EDWARD CHILTON & MR. WILLIAM LEIGH, 500 acs., New Kent Co; N. side of Mattapany Riv., on Assanamyscocke Br; 21 Oct. 1684, p. 418. Adj. land supposed to be surveyed by George Chapman, &c. Granted to John Poteete, 10 May 1668, after whose decease John Hethershall, who married his widdow, escheated the land in that sd. *Potteete* was an alien; & afterwards Phillip Watkins purchased sd. Hethershall's right to same; sd. Phillip, & Elizabeth, his wife, sold to Thomas Seawell, 10 Jan. 1675; who deserted; & sd. land now granted by order, &c, Trans. of 10 pers.*

CASON MOORE, 50 acs., Low. Norf. Co., Lynhaven Par., neare the Cyprus Sw., & adj. his land called *Bear Quarter;* 21 Oct. 1684, p. 418. Trans. of: Jno. Cannady.

MAJOR JOHN NICHOLLS, 500 acs., Low. Norf. Co., in the W. br. of Eliz. River, 21 Oct. 1684, p. 419. Adj. Mr. Thomas Brown. 400 acs. granted to Benjam. Firby, 1 Oct. 1661, who sold to sd. Nicholls; 100 acs. granted to Wm.. Memox & Demetree Murreene, 14 Dec. 1653; sold to Samuell Crane, & by Thomas Crane, his sole heire, sold to sd. Nicholls.

MOSES SPRING, 200 acs., Low. Norf. Co., at head of the W. br. of Eliz. Riv., adj. Freeman's line; 21 Oct. 1684, p. 419. Trans. of 4 pers.*

MAJOR JOHN NICHOLLS, 350 acs., Low. Norf. Co., upon the N. runn of Deep Cr., bet. W. & S. brs. of Eliz. Riv; adj. Slough's line; 21 Oct. 1684, p. 420. Granted to Richard Batchelor, for a greater quantity, 15 Mar. 1675 & by him ordered to be disposed of; his Executrix sold to sd. Nicholls.

WILLIAM EDWARDS, 300 acs., Low. Norf. Co., Lynhaven Par; bet. the Horse Bridge Run & the Cypress Br., 21 Oct. 1684, p. 420. Trans. of 6 pers.*

WILLIAM CAPPS, 500 acs., Low. Norf. Co., in the N. brs. of Curretuck; neere forke of Nonnyes (?) Cr; & adj. land of Josias Morris; 21 Oct. 1684, p. 421. Trans. of 10 pers: Jno. May, Tho. Hurst, Herbert Sprig, James Coppin, Ann Street, Richd. Heath, Tho. Dalmer, James Ost (?); Maria & George, Negroes.

THOMAS HERMANSON, 1300 acs., N'ampton Co., 21 Oct. 1684, p. 421. Being a neck or island, E'ly. by Machepongo River, W. by a cr. of same & by Cattaile brs., &c. Renewal of patt. dated 12 June 1654.

MR. EDWARD MOSELEY, 1130 acs., Low. Norf. Co., on N. side of the E. br. of Eliz. Riv., 21 Oct. 1684, p. 422. 800 acs. beg. by the maine br., to W. side of Hoskins' Cr., &c; granted Mr. Bartholomew Hoskins, 1 Jan. 1645; assigned to Mr. Thomas Todd, who sold to Mr. William Moseley, & due sd. Edward as heire at law; 330 acs. adj. Wm. Hancox; Col. Lawson; Chapman's corner; Wm. Martin; & Capt. Plomer Bray, formerly land of Arthur Mosely. Trans. of 7 pers.*

THOMAS GOODACRE, 125 acs., Low. Norf. Co., in Linhaven, 21 Oct. 1684, p. 423. Land Wm. East dyed seized of, & was found to escheate by inquisition under John Ferebee, Depty. Esch'r., &c.

THOMAS FENWICK, 300 acs., Low. Norf. Co; att the Path from the E. br. of Eliz. River, 21 Oct. 1684, p. 423. Granted Jane Bowlton, 15 Mar. 1675, deserted, & now granted by order, &c. Trans. of 7 pers.*

THOMAS WILLOUGHBY, 200 acs., Low. Norf. Co., from the W. br. of Eliz. River, 21 Oct. 1684, p. 424. Adj. lands of Ashley; Outlawe; & Freeman; in the pocoson of the Beech Ridge Runn, &c. Trans. of 4 pers.*

ROBERT TUCKER, 50 acs., Low. Norf. Co., on N E side of the maine run of Deepe Cr; beg. at "old Slough's & young Slough's" cor., &c; 21 Oct. 1684, p. 424. Trans. of: Walter Drove.

WILLIAM TRUNTOE (or Gruntoe), 550 acs., Low. Norf. Co., Lynhaven Par., 21 Oct. 1684, p. 425. Beg. in line of Beare Quarter; to Cypress Sw; to Wm. Woodhouse, &c. Trans. of 11 pers: Kath. Richmond; & 10 Negroes: Jack, Jenny, Doll, George, Dick, Susan, Will, James, Ned, Hannah.

JASPER LANE, 640 acs., in Corretuck, neere mouth of the northwest river; 21 Oct. 1684, p. 425. Neare land of Doctor Finckley; adj. Emanuel Pitcher (or Pilcher); to Draper's Cr; &c. Which land since surveyed, the sd. Lane hath sold to Capt. Jno. Gybbs, & is due for trans. of 13 pers.*

DANIELL FRIZELL, 200 acs., Low. Norf., Co. in Lynhaven Par., towards the north river; neare Lane's (or Land's) land; on Cypresse Sw; & Bever Dam Sw; 21 Oct. 1684, p. 426. Trans. of 4 pers.*

MR. THOMAS JACKSON, 100 acs., called the good land, in Low. Norf. Co; on a marsh on Corretuck Bay; 21 Oct. 1684, p. 426. Granted to Robt. Simmonds, 9 Oct. 1675, deserted, & granted 20 Apr. 1682 to Lt. Col. Antho. Lawson, who sold to sd. Jackson. Trans. of 2 pers.*

MR. ROBT. RICHMOND, 600 acs., Low. Norf. Co., Lynhaven Par., on W. side of the Cypress Sw; & S. side of Bowrins River; 21 Oct. 1684, p. 426. Trans. of 12 pers: Jno. Ely, 4 times; Ann & Quack, Negroes; & 2 Negroes 4 times.

ROBERT SMITH, 530 acs., Low. Norf. Co., Lynhaven Par., on W. side & towards head of Lynhaven River; 21 Oct. 1684, p. 427. Beg. at cor. formerly Jno. Ladd's, now belonging to the Orphans of Owen Grady; adj. Col. Lawson, on Bowrin's line; Robert Harper; & Francis Land; &c. 200 acs. granted

Richard Smith, 20 Oct. 1661, & due the above named Robt., his heir at law; 330 acs. for trans. of 7 pers: David Kelley; Oubay, Nanny, Frank, Typpin, Tom, Tony.

WILLIAM MOORE, 200 acs., Low. Norf. Co., Lynhaven Par; beg. at Mr. Spratt; to head of a little run into the reedy swamp; on *Bear Quarter*, &c; 21 Oct. 1684, p. 428. Trans. of 4 Negroes: Samson, Besse, Jack, Sam.

RICHARD BONNEY, 504 acs., Low. Norf. Co., Lynhaven Par; adj. Jno. Brooks; Thomas Smith; & Jno. Jeams; 21 Oct. 1684, p. 428. Trans. of 10 pers: Nan, Will, Jack, Tom, Rose, Frank, Moll, Tom, Wm., Sym., George, Purle.

JOHN MOY, 250 acs., Low. Norf. Co., Lynhaven Par; called the *Brushy Ridge;* near the Poplar Branch; & the Horse Bridge run Swamp; 21 Oct. 1684, p. 429. Trans. of 5 pers: Timo. Hara; & a boy sold Mr. Jones; Jno. Corbett, Lewis Purvein, Wm. Vaughan.

MAJOR JOHN NICHOLLS, JOHN JOHNSON, & THOMAS WILLSON, 300 acs., Low. Norf. Co., betwixt W. & S. brs. of Eliz. Riv., 21 Oct. 1684, p. 429. Trans. of 6 pers: Marriott, Peter, 2 Negroes; Tho. Berry. (*Note:* Lack of punctuation makes it impossible to determine the number of headrights listed).

EDWARD BROWNE, 1400 acs., Low. Norf. Co; upon head of Deepe Cr; neare mouth of Bowman's Run; 21 Oct. 1684, p. 429. 1200 acs. granted Edward Browne & Richard Starnell, 20 Mar. 1663, the whole since become due to sd. Browne; 200 acs. for trans. of 4 pers.*

MR. THOMAS HODGIS, 707 acs., Low. Norf. Co., on N. side of the W. br. of Eliz. Riv., 21 Oct. 1684, p. 430. A branch dividing this & land of Richard Powell; adj. Thomas Hollowell; & John Bowles; on Langworth's Creek; 600 acs. granted Jonathan Langworh, 6 Dec. 1638; assigned to Osmond Col-

chester & Walter Michell, 3 Oct. 1640, who gave letter of Atty. to Mathew Phillips, who sold to John Watkins, who gave by will to his wife Frances, & his son John, & by their consent sold to James Frisby, who bequeathed to his son James, who sold to said Hodgis; 107 acs. for trans. of 2 pers: Wm. Ward; Best, a Negro.

THOMAS FENWICK, 2650 acs., Low. Norf. Co; where the Ashen Sw. joynes the Cypress Sw., intersecting Godfreese Runn; adj. Francis Shipp; James Whithurst; & Capt. Wm. Robinson; & including the antient bounds of a survey made by John Wallop, 3 May 1673; &c; part of 3000 acs. granted Mr. John Porter, 28 Oct. 1673, deserted, & due sd. Fenwick by grant of the Gen'll. Court in Apr. 1682, & now confirmed; importation of 53 pers.*

MRS. MARY SWANN, *als.* Randall, 1 acre at *Weare Neck*, in Southwarke Par., Surry Co., 21 Oct. 1684, p. 432. Land Robert Babb died seized of & was found to escheate, by inquisition under William Byrd, Esqr., Esch'r., 2 Feb. 1680, &c. Being part of patt. long since graunted to Mr. Corker, & now in possession of Mr. Samuell Thompson; beg. at the edge of the Mill pond very neare Weare Neck Mill, &c; about a yard without the SE end of Weare Neck howse; to the Conduitt of the Mill; & including said Mill.

JEREMIAH LANDY (or Lundy), 1600 acs., New Kent Co., on the SE side of Yorke Riv; on brs. of Mattedequin Creeke; 20 Apr. 1685, p. 432. Beg. at William Owens' spring br; to Mr. David Crafford; & Mr. Watson's land; on Little Cr; &c. Trans. of 32 pers.*

MR. WILLIAM PORTER, Senr., 315 acs., Henrico Co., Verina Par; on S. side of James River; adj. John Wadson; & Henry Watkins (Wadkins); 20 Apr. 1685, p. 433. Trans. of 7 pers.*

HENRY PIGG & JOHN PIGG, Junr., 790 acs., New Kent Co., in the freshes of Mattapony River; 20 Apr.

1685, p. 434. Adj. Col. Robert Abrahall; John Joy; & land of Mody; by the *Mongyes old landing,* &c. Trans. of 16 pers.*

WILLIAM PORTER, JUNR., MR. NICHOLAS AMOSS & MR. RICHARD FERRES, 459 acs., Henrico Co., in Verina Par; N. side of the White Oake Sw., 20 Apr. 1685, p. 435. Adj. Mr. Thomas Cock, crossing Bares Hill Branch; & New Kent path, &c. Trans. of 10 pers.*

MR. PASCO DUNN, 146 acs., at a place called *ridge of land;* Eliz. City Co., 20 Apr. 1685, p. 435. Beg. neare the maine swamp; to Mr. Thomas Curle; by path to sd. Dunn's howse, &c. Trans. of 3 pers.*

MR. RICHARD DAVIS, 166 acs., New Kent Co., in Stratton Major Par; on a br. of Arracaico Cr., 20 Apr. 1685, p. 436. Beg. at Mr. Thomas Foster; to John Smith's feild below his dwelling howse; through the lane bet. sd. Smith & John Sorrow's plantations; to William Anderson's cor., in Rappahanock Roade; to Mr. Samuell Huckley, &c. Trans. of 4 pers.*

JOHN ECKHOLLS & WILLIAM MORRIS, 350 acs., New Kent Co., St. Stephen's Par., 20 Apr. 1685, p. 436. Behind land formerly of Mr. Giles Moody; by Barrow's old howse, &c. Trans. of 7 pers.*

DAVID MURRAY, SENR., 10 acs., adj. his own land; Low. Norf. Co., in Lynhaven Par; on S. side of the E. br. of Eliz. Riv., 20 Apr. 1685, p. 437. Adj. King's land; & land of the Orphans of Macoy, &c. Trans. of 1 pers.*

OWEN DAVIS, 76 acs., Yorke Co., in the New Poquoson Par., 20 Apr. 1685, p. 438. Adj. land of David Lewis, &c. Trans. of 2 pers.*

CLEMENT HAIDON, 277 acs., James City Co; whereon he dwells in Martin's Hundred; 20 Apr. 1685, p. 438. Beg. in James River; along Mr. John Grice; down Skiffs Cr., &c. 100

acs. granted him, 26 Nov. 1663; 177 acs. for trans. of 4 pers.*

MR. JOHN ASCOUGH, 1400 acs., in New Kent (Co.), on SE side of Mattapony Cr. run; *part whereon the Mattapony & Morratico Indians formerly lived;* by the King's Road; to Capt. William Smith, Marriner; by the Towne branch, &c; 20 Apr. 1685, p. 439. Trans. of 28 pers.*

MR. ROBERT RUFFIN, 2250 acs., Surry Co., in Lawnes Cr. Par., 20 Apr. 1685, p. 439. About ¼ mi. S. of road from Augustine Huniccutt's to Sunken Marsh Mill, cor. of Joseph Rogers' 500 acs: by Mr. William Newsome; to sd. Rogers' *Pokatinck land,* by Bowling Green Sw; & Holly Bush Sw; to 917 ac. patt. of Mr. Georg Watkins, dated 1 Mar. 1666, now in possession of sd. Ruffin; &c. Trans. of 55 pers: Jno. Waddy, Tho. Carrill, Jane Bell, Wm. Butler, Walter Handam, Ellin Jones, Ed. Millington, Wm. Davis, Isabell Jones, Ed. Moss, James Collier, Owen Evans, Jno. Murry, Xpher. Anderson, Joseph Kelley, Jno. Treby (?), Terry Carter, Ed. Fen (?), Ed. Dyer, James Tayler, Charles Dyas, Jeremy Jones, John Debue, Wm. Frost, Adam Caster (or Carter), John Bush, Robt. Minor, Abraham Willis, Ellin Adams, Robt. Elliot, Ed. Fen, Joseph Jones, Wm. Hunter, Gesper Kelly, Fra. Ellis, Paul Peters, Wm. Evans, Ellin Carter, Edwin Kerby, Geo. Foster, Fra. Collins, Eliza. Jenkins, Edwd. Baptist; 1 Negro.

ANTHONY MATHEWS, 640 acs., Is. of Wight Co., 20 Apr. 1685, p. 440. Beg. on head of Cannages (or Carmages) (?) Sw., adj. Edward Palmer; & Palin's line, &c. Granted sd. Mathews 1 Feb. 1664.

JOHN & THOMAS HARRIS, 365 acs., Up. Par. of Is. of Wight Co; on N. side of the Ashen Sw., near the head & on W. side of Seaward's Cr., 20 Apr. 1685, p. 441. 250 acs. part granted Nathaniell Loyd, 20 Nov. 1637 & conveyed to said Harris' father, by Capt. Francis Hobbs & his wife, who was the relict & Admx. of sd. Loyd, 13 Jan.

1659; & among other lands found to escheate; granted to Honble. Col. Joseph Bridger, 22 July 1678, who sold to sd. John & Thomas Harris, the 6 Feb. following, to be equally divided according to their father's will, dated last day of Mar. 1672; 115 acs. being wast land; & the whole beg. by a marsh neare the head of Seaward's Cr; neare Col. Bacon, &c; due for trans. of 3 pers.*

JOHN CLEMENT (Clements), 42 acs., Surry Co., on E. side of a maine br. of Crouches Cr; adj. his own & Owens' line; 20 Apr. 1685, p. 441. Trans. of 1 pers.*

MR. THOMAS COOZENS, 71 acs., Yorke Co., in New Poquoson Par., at head of a br. of Footeball Quarter Creeke; adj. land of Thomas Kerbee, dec'd. &c; 20 Apr. 1685, p. 442. Trans. of 2 pers.*

DAVID LEWIS, 217 acs., on N. side of the damms parting Yorke & Warwick Counties; 20 Apr. 1685, p. 442. Near land of Owen Davis; by the Mill roade, cor. to Samuell Singnell, &c. 99 acs. purchased by David Lewis, dec'd; 118 for trans. of 3 pers.*

CAPT. JOHN TIPLADY, 345 acs. in the Co. & Par. of Yorke, 20 Apr. 1685, p. 443. Adj. Mr. Thomas Cheeseman; on W. side of Roade to the Poquoson Mill; & adj. land formerly Mr. Watkins', &c. 200 acs. granted Christopher Stoakes, 14 Aug. 1637, & afterwards sold to Mr. John Tiplady by Georg Holmes, 14 Nov. 1640; 145 acs. for trans. of 3 pers.*

THOMAS LILBURNE, 106 acs., Yorke Co., in New Poquoson Par; adj. Mr. Samuell Singnall; 20 Apr. 1685, p. 444. Trans. of 2 pers.* (Note: First written *John* Lilburne.)

MR. JOHN CARVER, 340 acs., Glocester Co., in Pettsoe Par., on S. side of the maine runn of the Draggon Swamp, 20 Apr. 1685, p. 444. Adj. Charles Roane; Robert Shackleford at the mouth of Spring Br., & Thomas Amies, &c. 245 acs. part of 700 acs.

purchased of Mr. Richard Wilson & Sarah, his wife, sister & heire to Mr. Samuell Partridge, 5 July 1678; 95 acs. for trans. of 2 pers.*

ISAAC VADIN, 300 acs., in the upper parts of James City Co., 20 Apr. 1685, p. 445. 300 acs. from Davis' corner on Tyascunn Sw; to Hopkins' feild, &c; being half of 600 acs. sd. Isaac & John Vadin purchased of Robert Crawley, 1 Sept. 1679, whoe purchased same of John Dormer & William Thomas, 2 Apr. 1672, being part of 1100 acs. granted to William Dormer, dec'd., 5 June 1656, who, by will dated 7 Jan. 1659, bequeathed to John & Rebecca Dormer.

MR. ROBERT FLAKE, 170 acs., Par. of Is. of Wight Co., bet. lands of Mr. Tooke, Capt. England, Thomas Blake & Edward Brantley; adj. Mr. Newman & neare the *danceing place,* &c; 20 Apr. 1685, p. 446. Trans. of 4 pers.*

JOHN WILLIAMS & JOHN BROWNE, 1200 acs., amongst diverse black water brs., in Low. Par. of Surry Co., 20 Apr. 1685, p. 447. Adj. Nicholas Sessums; Robert Savage; Charles Savage; Richard Lane; Mr. Cawfeild; Joseph Wall; Richard Smith; & Richard Blow, &c. Trans. of 24 pers.*

WILLIAM HOLLEMAN, 132 acs., Up. Par. of Isle of Wight Co., 20 Apr. 1685, p. 448. About a mi. S. of Mr. Robt. Flake's Mill; bet. his father, Mr. Christopher Holleman, & William Goaldney. Trans. of 3 pers: Robt. Owen, John Edwards, Ann Ward.

MR. WM. THOMPSON, 200 acs., on S. side of Daniell Tanner's Cr., Low. Norf. Co., 20 Apr. 1685, p. 448. Trans. of 4 pers.*

JOHN FEREBEE, 500 acs., Low. Norf. Co., upon Deepe Cr. & Mill Cr. runn; 20 Apr. 1685, p. 449. Adj. Edward Browne, Duke Etheridge's Cr; & land formerly Yates, now sd. Etheridges' & Lakes. 450 acs. granted him, 22 Nov. 1682; 50 acs. for trans. of 1 pers.*

THOMAS WALKER, 300 acs., Low. Norf. Co., bet. the Northwest River & the Black Water, being his seated plantation, called *the Hoult;* adj. Benjamin Cummings; the Landing, &c. Trans. of 6 pers.*

JOHN STEWARD, SENR., 670 acs., Henrico Co., Bristoll Par., on N. side of Appamattock Riv., at the Ashen Swamp, 20 Apr. 1685, p. 450. Adj. Willm. Puckett; Willm. Wallters; & Charles Fetherston. 600 A., 3 R., 32 P. granted him, 16 Mar. 1672; residue for imp. of 2 pers.*

MR. RICHARD WHITEHEAD, 180 acs., Glocester Co; in Abbington Par., & Ware Par., adj. Gill's land; & Mr. Thomas Cheeseman; 20 Apr. 1685, p. 451. Trans. of 4 pers.*

WILLIAM & JOHN PRICE, 550 acs., Glocester Co., Ware Par; about ½ mi. E. of the Indian Road; 20 Apr. 1681, p. 451. 366 acs. granted to John Benson, 10 Apr. 1667; 184 acs. for trans. of 4 pers.*

PETER BUTLER, 40 acs., Nanzemund Co., at the head of Chuckatuck Cr; adj. lines of Rye; & Scott; 20 Apr. 1685, p. 452. Trans. of 1 pers.*

WILLIAM HOWELL, 300 acs., Up. Par. of Nanzemund; upon the short Sw. of Sumerton Cr., 20 Apr. 1685, p. 452. Trans. of 6 pers.*

THOMAS JERNIGAN, SENR., 330 acs., at *Sumerton* in the Up. Par. of Nanzemund; 20 Apr. 1685, p. 452. Beg. by Sumerton Sw., adj. Johnson; & land of William Moore. Trans. of 7 pers.*

JAMES COLE, 200 acs., at *Sumerton*, in the Up. Par. of Nanzemund, on Knuckels Sw., 20 Apr. 1685, p. 453. Trans. of 4 pers.*

RICHARD WATRIDGE, 100 acs., Low. Par. of Nanzemund; adj. Robert Peele's 50 acs; William Coffeild; John Granbury; & Mr. James Lockhart; 20 Apr. 1685, p. 453. Trans. of 2 pers.*

THOMAS OSBORNE, 85 acs., Henrico Co., Varina Par., on S. side of James Riv., 20 Apr. 1685, p. 454. Beg. at land known as Proctor's & Ruth; on Osborne's antient patt. belonging to *Coxendale,* to the Redwater; to Thomas Jefferson, &c. Trans. of 2 pers: Peter Merritt, Mary Hossman.

LEMON CHILDRES, 406 acs., Henrico Co., Varina Par., on N. side of James Riv., on Grindon's run; adj. Mr. John Pleasants; & Edward Mathews; 20 Apr. 1685, p. 454. Trans. of 9 pers: Job ——, Thomas Lyborne, Peter Prout, John Leyden, Wm. Howse, Jon. Harris.

WILLIAM CLARKE, 124 acs., Henrico Co., 20 Apr. 1685, p. 455. Granted to Gilbert Deacon, dec'd, & found to escheate, by inquisition under Henry Randolph, Depty. Esch'r. 22 Mar. 1672, &c.

JOHN MURFREY, JUNR., in right of Susanna, his wife, 650 acs., Up. Par. of Nanzemund Co., at head of Dumplin Island Cr., 20 Apr. 1685, p. 455. Beg. opposite Capt. Jossy's howse; adj. lands of Peirce; Murdah & Sanders; on the maine swamp; to the horse road, &c. Granted Samuell Stephens, 20 June 1639 for 2000 acs., & after severall surrenders, becoming due to the Orphants of Thomas Francis, was pattented in their names, 20 Oct. 1665, but misbounded & this being the proper right of sd. Susannah, one of sd. orphans.

CHRISTOPHER BERRIMAN, 1250 acs., New Kent Co., S .side of Yorke Riv., bet. brs. of Mattedequin Cr. & Chichahominy Sw., 20 Apr. 1685, p. 456. Adj. Mr. Watson; & Mr. Landye's; crossing Pickanockey Path, to br. of sd. swamp called Powhitt Sw; adj. John Asher; & William Owen. Trans. of 25 pers.*

THOMAS SALLY, 100 acs., Low. Norf. Co., on S. side of the E. br. of Eliz. Riv., & adj. Henry Nicholls; 20 Apr. 1685, p. 457. Granted John Cartwright, 27 Sept. 1665, deserted, & now granted by order, &c. Trans. of 2 pers.*

MATHEW GODFREY, 75 acs., Low. Norf. Co., called *Caedar Island;* S'ly. from Long Island; E. on the seaboard; & W. on Curratuck Bay; 20 Apr. 1685, p. 457. Granted Robert Symons, 26 Sept. 1674, deserted, & granted by order, &c. Trans. of 2 pers.*

CAPT. FRANCIS PAGE, a devident called *Pampertike;* 1000 acs., New Kent Co., N. side Pamunkey Riv., in *Pamunkey Neck,* 20 Apr. 1685, p. 457. Beg. at mouth of Goddins Cr. or Sw., below Goddin's Island; along same 1½ mi; to Pampertike Cr., dividing this & land of Mr. William Woodward. Sd. land purchased by one Booth of the Queen of Pamunkey, after whose decease it was granted to his son Robert Booth, by Order of Assembly 25 Apr. 1679, who assigned to Mr. Marke Warkman, who assigned to sd. Page.

MALACHI THRUESTON (Thruston), 905 acs., Low. Norf. Co., towards the S., above head of the E. br. of Eliz. River, 20 Apr. 1685, p. 458. Land William Havercomb dyed seized of, & was found to escheate by inquisition under John Ferrebee, Depty. Esch'r., &c.

JAMES LAMOUNT, 582 acs., in *Lynhaven,* Low. Norf. Co., 20 Apr. 1685, p. 458. Land John Lawrance dyed seized of, & was found to escheate by inquisition under John Ferrebee, Depty. Esch'r., &c.

JOHN JONES, 167 acs., of wast or King's land, Rappa. Co., 20 Apr. 1685, p. 459. Beg. in the forke of Greene Sw; to Thomas Toseley; along Hudson's Br., to Mr. Henry Williamson, &c. Trans. of 4 pers.*

JOHN HALLOWES, 2400 acs., on S. side of Potomacke River, from mouth of Conawoman Cr., to Conawoman Bay; on Nomany Bay; adj. Mr. Speake; 28 July 1662, p. 459. *(By Francis Moryson, Capt. Genrll. of Va.)* Renewal of his patt. dated 11 Sept. 1653.

OWEN DAVIS, 18 acs., Warwicke Co., at head of the old Poquoson Damms; adj. Mr. Mumford's new devidend; & Gerrard Ridley's land; 20 Apr. 1685, p. 460. Trans. of 1 pers.*

ABRAHAM EVANS, 300 acs., adj. Mr. John Barker; 20 Apr. 1685, p. 460. Trans. of 6 pers.* (Location not given).

MR. EDWARD MUMFORD, 148 acs., Warwick Co., near head of the old Poquoson Damms; adj. land of James Turner, in possession of Owen Davis; & Gerrard Ridley; 20 Apr. 1685, p. 461. Trans. of 3 pers.*

JOHN POWERS & JOHN DAVIS, 128 acs., Warwick Co., neare the Oaken Sw; adj. Mr. Thomas Merrie's new devdt; & land of Capt. Langhorne; on the Bryery Swamp; 20 Apr. 1685, p. 461. Trans. of 3 pers.*

JOHN VODIN (Vadin), 300 acs., Jas. City Co., on N. side of Chichahominy Riv., 20 Apr. 1685, p. 462. Beg. at Esqr. Diggs, (als. Proson's), at head of Browne's Br; to Ravenett's Run; to Hopkins' feild, &c. Being ½ of 600 acs. purchased by John & Isaac Vodin of Robert Crawly, 1 Sept. 1679, whoe purchased of John Dormer & William Thomas, 2 Apr. 1672, & being the midlemost part of 1100 acs. granted to William Dormer, dec'd., 5 June 1656, whoe, by will dated 7 Jan. 1659, bequeathed to John & Rebecca Dormer.

EDWARD BOYKIN, 525 acs., betweene the 3rd Sw. & the maine Blackwater; adj. Mr. Williamson; & Mr. Thomas Moore; 20 Apr. 1685, p. 462. Trans. of 11 pers.*

WILLIAM ROGERS & JOSHUA PROCTER, 900 acs., Up. Par. of Surry Co., bet. John Chehockan (Swamp ?) & the maine Blackwater, 20 Apr. 1685, p. 463. Adj. John Collins, Thomas Smith, in Mr. Warren's line; Mr. Owens; & Capt. Corker. Trans. of 18 pers.*

CAPT. ROGER POTTER, 380 acs., Up. Par. of Surry Co., in Clay's (Cloy's) Br; adj. Mr. Thomas Jordan; & Mr. Owens; 20 Apr. 1685, p. 463. Trans. of 8 pers.*

JOHN COKER, 1450 acs., Low. Par. of Sury Co; in the Cypress Sw. & the maine Blackwater, 20 Apr. 1685, p. 464. 400 acs. by a former patt; & 1050 acs. adj; beg. at Mr. Merriweather, & adj. Col. Browne & William Foreman. Trans. of 21 pers.*

RICHARD WASHINGTON, 200 acs., by the maine Blackwater, neare mouth of a large branch, &c; 20 Apr. 1685, p. 464. Trans. of 4 pers.*

JOHN PROCTER, 250 acs., Up. Par. of Is. of Wight Co., bet. the 3rd Sw. & the maine Blackwater; adj. Doctor Williamson; Mr. Thomas Moore; & Edward Boykin; 20 Apr. 1685, p. 465. Trans. of 5 pers: Geo. Resse, Wm. Peirce, Jon. Farch (?), Jon. Barker.

ELIZABETH KEELING, 350 acs., Low. Norf. Co., towards the N. brs. of Corretucke; 20 Apr. 1685, p. 465. Beg. at Mr. Henry Woodhowse; on the Easterne Sw; neare parting of the road to Nominyes Cr. & *Marchepungo*, &c. Trans. of 7 pers.*

JOHN SCOTT, 100 acs., Chas. City Co., 20 Apr. 1685, p. 466. Granted to John Smith, dec'd., & found to escheate, by inquisition under Col. John Page, Esch'r., &c.

HONBLE. WILLIAM COLE, ESQR., one of his Majesties Councell of State; 1431 acs; viz: 1217 acs. in Warwick Co., & 216 acs. in Eliz. City Co., comonly called *Newports News;* 20 Apr. 1685, p. 466. Being all that can bee found upon an exact survey 2500 acs., granted to Daniell Gookin, Esqr., except 250 acs. made over by sd. Gookin whoe, with John Gookin, conveyed sd. 1431 acs. to John Chandler, whoe conveyed to Capt. Benidict Stafford, from whom same escheated, by inquisition under John Page, Esqr., Esch'r. Genrll. of sd. Counties, &c; granted sd. Cole & Capt. Roger Jones, whoe made over to sd. Cole.

SAMUELL JERKINS & ROBERT JERKINS, 200 acs., Surry Co., on E. side of Gray's Cr., 20 Apr. 1685, p. 467. Granted Thomas Zaines, dec'd.,

& found to escheate by inquisition under Mr. William Randolph, Depty. Esch'r., &c.

RICHARD ALLEN, 53 acs., Midlesex Co; adj. John Nash; & Grace Lewis; 20 Apr. 1685, p. 467. Trans. of 1 pers.*

HENRY SYMONDS, 400 acs., being his seated plantation, Low. Norf. Co., on the Blackwater River running into Curretucke; adj. John Vaughan; 20 Apr. 1685, p. 468. Trans. of 8 pers.*

MR. PETER FEILD, 240 acs., Henrico Co., Bristoll Par., S. side of the maine br. of Swift Creek; on a br. of Symons' Run; adj. Mr. Francis Epps; 20 Apr. 1685, p. 468. Trans. of 5 pers.*

HERCULES FLOOD, 296 acs., Chas. City Co., in the Parish of Jordans; S. side of James Riv., nigh the Blackwater; adj. his own; & land of Mr. Henry Batt; 20 Apr. 1685, p. 469. Trans. of 6 pers.*

MR. RICHARD PARRETT, SENR.; 170 acs., Midlesex Co., adj. his own land; 20 Apr. 1685, p. 469. Trans. of 4 pers.*

MR. THOMAS CHEWNING, 920 acs., Midlesex Co., 20 Apr. 1685, p. 470. Beg. where Burnham's, *als*. Sunderland, Cr. devides into 2 brs; up the SW br; to Copeland's Cr; to Thomas Pattison, now John Nash's land; to Richard Lewis; & by Edward Dockers, &c. 240 acs. granted to Henry Nichols, last of June 1653; sold to Georg Johnson, who sold to Robert Chewning; 370 acs. granted said Chewning, 8 Feb. 1658, & renewed 16 Dec. 1663; 370 acs. for trans. of 8 pers.*

THOMAS GAINES, 28 acs., Rappa. Co; by a marsh of Hoskins' Creek; 20 Apr. 1685, p. 470. Trans. of 1 pers.*

MR. ROBERT PRICE, 17 acs., Midlesex Co; adj. Thomas Chewning; his own; & land of Grace Lewis; on NW side of a br. of Copeland's Cr; on land of Richard Allen; & Nash; 20 Apr. 1685, p. 471. Trans. of 1 pers.*

MR. RICHARD WILLIS, of Midlesex, 300 acs., in the Draggon Sw; on Thomas Kidd; to the White Oak Sw., &c; 20 Apr. 1685, p. 471. Granted to Thomas Willis, his father, 22 Oct. 1661, & renewed last of Aug. 1664. Trans. of 6 pers.*

ROBERT WILLIAMSON, 389 acs., Midlesex Co., 20 Apr. 1685, p. 472. Beg. at Mr. Burnham's cor., at head of Sunderland Cr; to Col. Cuthberd Potter, by Mickleborrow bridge; by Thomas Fugle's quarter; to Mr. John Willis; to Mr. Henry Thacker. 200 acs. granted Richard Lewis, 10 Jan. 1658, & renewed 27 Jan. 1663; 189 acs. for trans. of 4 pers.*

―――― CAPELL, Orphant, of Rappa. Co., 333 acs., upon Piscattaway Cr., 20 Apr. 1685, p. 473. Beg. at land formerly Daniell Batts', now Robert King's; to Thomas Greene, just over a valley by Richard Holt's howse; to the White Oak Sw., &c. 250 acs. granted ―――― Capell, 4 Oct. 1653, then by order, &c., granted to Elizabeth Capell 24 Mar. 1661, & the last patt. dated 26 Mar. 1664; 83 acs. for trans. of 2 pers.*

MR. ROBERT KAE, 1 acre, in Surry Co., 20 Apr. 1685, p. 473. Granted to Edward Bushell, dec'd., & found to escheate, by inquisition under Mr. William Randolph, Depty. Esch'r., &c.

MICHAELL WEYBORNE (Weybourne), 1150 acs., Low. Norf. Co., 20 Apr. 1685, p. 474. 500 acs. viz: 200 acs. on N. side of the W. br. of Eliz. Riv., called Clark's Cr; 350 acs. by the branch side; 350 acs. beg. at Thomas Wright; by Broad Cr; 50 acs., called Starlings point, in sd. W. branch, bet. Mr. Hatton & sd. Wright; 200 acs. in the S. br. of sd. river, in Pussell point Cr. 550 acs. granted Richard Starnell, the elder, 10 June 1651; 350 acs. granted him, 11 Jan. 1652; as also 50 acs; (no date); 200 acs. granted him, 20 Apr. 1653; who bequeathed to Richard Starling, the younger, his son & heire; who dying without issue, the land came to Elizabeth & Ann Starling the only daughters of Richard, the elder, &c;

Joseph Newton marrying with Ann, & Dennis Morris marrying Elizabeth, did, by deed dated 16 Mar. 1670, sell sd. Weyborne the sd. land.

MR. WILLIAM SYMONDS, son & heire of Mr. William Symonds, dec'd., 800 acs., Up. Par. of Surry Co., on the Burchen Sw., one of the maine brs. of Up. Chippoakes Cr; 20 Apr. 1685, p. 475. 600 acs. granted sd. Symonds, dec'd., 8 Apr. 1650; 200 acs. within sd. bounds; beg. neare Bland's path; & due for trans. of 4 pers.*

RICHARD CHAMBERS, 200 acs., Low. Norf. Co., on N. side of a br. of the W. br. of Eliz. Riv., called Clark's Cr., 20 Apr. 1685, p. 476. Granted Thomas Goadby, 2 Mar. 1647, who assigned to Robert Loveday during his life, & after his decease Ann Goadby, by vertue of a letter of Attv. from her husband Thomas Goadby, by deed of guift, made over sd. land to Sarah Loveday, during her naturall life & after her decease to sd. Richard Chambers & Dorothy, his wife, 15 June 1652.

THOMAS TOOLEY, 200 acs., Low. Norf. Co., on NW side of Cyprus Sw., bet. the northwest river & the Blackwater; a swamp dividing this from Benjamin Cummings; & John Elkes; 20 Apr. 1685, p. 476. Trans. of 4 pers.*

FRANCIS JONES, 230 acs., Low. Norf. Co., on W. side of the North river, bet. the northwest river & the Blackwater; neare head of Arthur's Cr; adj. Peter Capell; on the Landing point, &c; 20 Apr. 1685, p. 477. Trans. of 5 pers.*

JOHN VAUGHAN, 300 acs., in Corrotucke precincts, Low. Norf. Co., on N. side of the Blackwater river; adj. Henry Southen (Southern); & on Hachilah Swamp; 20 Apr. 1685, p. 477. Trans. of 6 pers.*

HENRYP DALE, 300 acs., neare head of Paradise Cr. in Low. Norf. Co; adj. Peter Poyner; & Edward Hewes; 20 Apr. 1685, p. 478. Trans. of 6 pers.*

HENRY MILLS, 500 acs., Up. Par. of Nanzemund, upon Sarum Swamp; 20 Apr. 1685, p. 478. Trans. of 10 pers.*

JOHN PRESCOTT, 800 acs., called *Ludlow;* Low. Norf. Co., on the br. of the Northwest river of Curretuck; 4 Nov. 1685, p. 479. Beg. by the Indian Landing; to Hollowell's line, by a br. of the White Oake Sw., &c. Trans. of 16 pers.*

MR. MORGAN JONES, 150 acs., Low. Norf. Co; towards the North river; by the gr. Cyprus branch, &c; 4 Nov. 1685, p. 479. Trans. of 3 pers: James Williams, Roger Goding, David Fowler.

PATRICK GILLMORE, 244 acs., New Kent Co., in Stratton Major Par., 4 Nov. 1685, p. 480. Beg. on Arracaico Cr., a small way above Mr. Gough's Mill; by the Mill Path, in Capt. Pridier (or Pride's) line; by Sanders' line, &c. Trans. of 5 pers.*

MR. RICHARD HOULT (Holt), 620 acs., Rappa. Co., upon Piscattaway Cr. maine pocoson; being the devident hee formerly lived on; 4 Nov. 1685, p. 480. Beg. at King's Sw. below Piscattaway Mill; adj. Oliver Seager; by the horse path, to Thomas Gaines & John Moraine, &c. 400 acs. granted to William Danby; 220 acs. granted sd. Hoult, 25 Oct. 1669.

JOHN GIBBS, 80 acs., Warwick Co., 4 Nov. 1685, p. 481. Beg. above his corne feild, close to the Black Swamp on the W. side; & neare the opening of the bushy ponds; along Mr. Thomas Cheesman, &c. Trans. of 2 pers.*

JOHN TURNER, 134 acs., James City Co., 4 Nov. 1685, p. 481. From *Chichahominy Gate* along Mr. Freeman's land; to the ferry path; to head of Cross Cr. bottome, along Godian's land; along Winters land; to forke of the ferry path, & Freeman's, *als.* Chichahominy, path; to George Harvie's land, includ. Pyney board Swamp. Trans. of 3 pers: John Turner, John Grinfeild, William Watson.

STEPHEN GILL, 2369 acs., Glocester Co., on W. side of Roswell Cr., 4 Nov. 1686, p. 482. Beg. at land formerly belonging to Mr. Minnfree (or Minnifree), now Mr. John Man's; to E. side of Claybanke Cr; on Mr. William Hansford; to Mr. Thomas Cheesman; to br. above Creed's Spring, &c. Granted to Stephen Gill, dec'd., 18 Nov. 1642.

HUMPHRY PERKINS, 300 acs., Rappa. Co., 4 Nov. 1685, p. 483. Granted to Thomas Williams, dec'd., & found to escheate, by inquisition under Col. Isaac Allerton, &c.

MR. TULLY ROBINSON, 100 acs., Low. Norf. Co., Lynhaven Par., on S. side of the E. br. of Eliz. River, 4 Nov. 1685, p. 483. Adj. lands of Nichols, Emperor & Soucies (or Soncies ?) Cr. Trans. of 2 pers.*

MR. TULLY ROBINSON & MR. JAMES KEMP, 350 acs., Low. Norf. Co., Lynhaven Par., towards the North river; adj. Thomas Fenwick; 4 Nov. 1685, p. 484. Trans. of 7 pers.*

JAMES THELOBALL, 380 acs., Low. Norf. Co., Lynhaven Par; adj. *Woolfe's Neck,* & land of Henry Hawkins; (date blank), p. 484. Granted him, 15 Oct. 1651.

MR. WALTER SHIPLY (Shipley), 746 acs., Chas. City Co., Westover Par., on N. side of James Riv., 4 Nov. 1685, p. 485. Beg. at Jno. Roach; along Mr. Tho. Cocke; on W. side of Giles' path, &c. Trans. of 15 pers.*

MR. DAVID CRAFFORD, 1300 acs., New Kent Co., in St. Peter's Par., 4 Nov. 1685, p. 486. Beg. on S. side of Yorke Riv., at Asseskuin Run; to the Wading place where the gr. rosde crosseth, &c. Granted to Hannah Clarke, 10 Feb. 1652, & by her death found to escheate; then granted to John Langston, 28 Sept. 1681, who made over to William Tayloe, 28 Oct. 1681, who made over to sd. Crafford, 28 July 1682; & by reason of severall encroachments by some younger patentees, the sd. land now surveyed & plainly markt out, & settled in the presence of the Neighbourhood, &c.

SAME. 277 acs., in the upper part of New Kent Co., in —— parish; on S. side of York Riv; same date & page. Trans. of 6 pers.*

RICHARD SLAUGHTER, 65 acs., in Low. Par. of Nanzemond; adj. Robert Murrow; 4 Nov. 1685, p. 487. Trans. of 2 pers: John Leigh, James Murray.

JOHN BROTHERS, 400 acs., at a place called the *Beare Garden;* in the Up. Par. of Nanzamund, on S. side of the Mossie Sw., 4 Nov. 1685, p. 487. Trans. of 8 pers: John Barlow, Margarett Stancock, John Wasell, Joseph Demort, Tho. Wilkins, Mary Loader, Agnes Temple, James Temple.

CHARLES ROWNTREE (Rountree), 350 acs., in the Up. Par. of Nanzamund, 4 Nov. 1685, p. 487. Beg. at Michael Brinckly, by the Scypresse Sw. Trans. of 7 pers: Willm. Hunter, Nicho. Hunter, Joane Hunter, Rebecka Hunter, Charles Rountree, Robert Rountree, John Sayer.

MR. THOMAS TILLY, 220 acs., Nanzimund Co., 4 Nov. 1685, p. 487. Adj. Col. Edward Carter, William Twise, Thomas Addison & Richard Russell. Granted to Thomas Carter, 20 Sept. 1661, deserted, & granted to Col. Edward Carter, 1 Sept. 1665, & by him deserted; now granted by order, &c; trans. of 5 pers. *

JAMES JONES, 364 acs., Chas. City Co., in Westover Par; S. side of James Riv., 4 Nov. 1685, p. 488. Beg. on E. side the Mill Path; adj. Capt. Archer; Thomas Chappell; & Col. Edward Hill; &c. 141 acs. granted to Thomas Tanner 27 Nov. 1657, & assigned to sd. Jones; 223 acs., being the King's land, due for trans. of 5 pers.*

MR. HENRY BUTT, 1600 acs., Low. Norf. Co; in the Northwest Riv. of Corretucke, called the *Damm Necks,* 4 Nov. 1685, p. 488. Beg. by the Cyprus Sw; adj. land of Hollowell, &c. Trans. of 32 pers.*

MR. JOHN ASHBORNE, 90½ acs., Gloster Co; on W. side of the meane swampe running into the head of Ware River; 4 Nov. 1685, p. 488. Adj. Mr. Francis Taliaferoe; on NE side of Purtan Path. Trans. of 2 pers.*

JOHN ELLES, 464 acs., Chas. City Co., Bristoll Par., on S. side of Appamattuck Riv., 4 Nov. 1685, p. 489. Beg. at Mr. Abraham Wood Jones; to the maine river, &c. Trans. of 10 pers.*

MR. THOMAS BRANCH, JUNR., 760 acs., Henrico Co., in Varina Par., on S. side of James Riv., 4 Nov. 1685, p. 489. Beg. at Mr. Abell Gower; crossing Myry Run; & the Deepe Bottome; to John Clarke; to Mr. Thomas Branch, Senr., &c. Trans. of 16 pers.*

COL. ARTHUR SMYTH, 500 acs., in the Low. Par. of Is. of Wight Co., 4 Nov. 1685, p. 489. Adj. James Tullagh, Mr. Hardy, Matt Tomlin, Col. Smyth & Mr. Bressie. Trans. of 10 pers.*

MR. WILLIAM LEIGH, 400 acs., New Kent Co., in St. Stephen's Par., 4 Nov. 1685, p. 490. Beg. at Ashawaymankecacke maine run; adj. land formerly George Chapman's; to John Atkins; to Mr. Thomas Kemp & Mr. Samuell Clayton; to land of Mr. John Wood, dec'd., &c. Granted to John Poteet, 10 May 1668, after whose decease John Hethersall, who marryed his widdow, escheated sd. land in that sd. Poteet was an alien; Philip Watkins purchased sd. Hethersall's right, & sd. Watkins & Elizabeth, his wife, sold to Thomas Seawell, 10 Jan. 1675; sd. land being deserted, was granted by order, to Edward Chilton & William Leigh, 22 Oct. 1684; Chilton conveyed his right to Robert Smyth, who sold to sd. Leigh, 18 Apr. 1685.

JAMES SMYTH, 67 acs., Chas. City Co., in Weynoake Par., on S. side of James Riv; 4 Nov. 1685, p. 490. Adj. James Jones; John Hobbs; & Capt. Archer; down Pyney Slash, &c. Trans. of 2 pers.

MR. DAVID WHITFORD, 460 acs., Low. Norf. Co; towards head of Sympson's Cr., W'ly. out of the North River;

20 Apr. 1686, p. 491. Beg. by the Cyprus Sw., &c. Trans. of 9 pers: Jno. Jones, James Landy, Wm. Prior, Ann Denson, Wm. Fidler, Jacob Evans, Rebecca Morris, Jane Dennis, Wm. Gally.

COL. WILLIAM KENDALL, 200 acs., Accomack Co., at head of Mesango Cr; adj. Robert Johnson; 20 Apr. 1686, p. 491. Granted to German Gilliott, 9 Nov. 1666, deserted, & now granted by order, &c. Imp. of 4 pers: Abraham Reed, Robt. Cook, Wm. Bendon, Roger Roberts.

JAMES CASON, 450 acs., Low. Norf. Co., Lynhaven Par; towards the North Riv., 20 Apr. 1686, p. 491. Beg. by the Cyprus Br., by the Horse Bridge Run, cor. of William Edwards; adj. John Moye; by the Reedy Br., &c. Trans. of 9 pers: Charles Adams, Wm. Senior, Adam Jones, Rachell Foster, Isabell Fletcher, Robt. Car, Robt. (?) Jones, Wm. Evans, Roger Mayler.

HENRY HENLANE, 1000 acs., Low. Norf. Co; from head of the S. br. of Eliz. Riv., 20 Apr. 1686, p. 492. Beg. by the Cyprus Sw., cor of John Gamon; by Richford Sw; towards the Green Sea, &c. Trans. of 20 pers: Tho. Henly, Edwd. Dennis, Richd. Peircon, Abigail How, Tho. Adams, Susan Ree, Rice Jones, Ann Parks, Abraham Hamlin, Tho. Arthur, Wm. Perry, Wm. Gosnell, Jno. Farmer, Wm. Weeks, Tabitha Hart, John Adams, Tho. Dodson, Jno. Palmer, Jenkin Davice, Mary Linton.

SAMUELL ROBERTS, 800 acs., Low. Norf. Co; on the E. br. of Tanner's Cr., 20 Apr. 1686, p. 492. 500 acs., beg. on a point neare Queene Graves Cr; to the maine Sw., &c; granted to Jasper Hodgkinson, 16 Apr. 1653, & by severall assignments due sd. Roberts; 300 acs. adj. land of George Ashall called Wolfes Neck. 200 acs. granted to Robert Moody (or Woody), who sold to Jasper Hodgkinson; 100 acs. for trans. of 2 pers: Mathew Morris, Luke Morris.

ADAM MEKEELE, 600 acs., Accomack Co., at Pokamock; on land formerly Morrice Liston's (or Lifton's); adj. William Benton; Mr. Henry Smyth; Mr. Ambrose White; & William Benston; 20 Apr. 1686, p. 493. Granted to Mr. John Washbourne, 30 Apr. 1679, deserted, & granted sd. Mekeele by order, &c. Trans. of 12 pers: Peter Smith, Wm. Worrall, Jno. Sewell, Anne Bryant, Jno. Hanset, & his son, Tho. Dickson, Martin Cole, Amy Morris, Eliza. Bonden, Gilbert Finch, Richd. Sutton.

JOHN ELKS, 300 acs., Low. Norf. Co; betwixt the Northwest Riv. & the Black Water; 20 Apr. 1686, p. 493. Beg. at Peter Capell; to the Cyprus Sw., &c. Trans. of 6 pers: Jone Cornix, Martha Cornix, Wm. & Tho. Cornix, Tho. Lucas, Wm. Herne.

GEORGE BALLENTINE, 150 acs., Low. Norf. Co; on W. side of the S. br. of Eliz. Riv., 20 Apr. 1686, p. 493. Beg. at Christopher Bustian & John Markham; to Paradise Cr., &c. Trans. of 3 pers: Tho. Maw, Richd. Dobbins, John Edgscomb.

HENRY SOUTHEN, 400 acs., Low. Norf. Co; on N. side of the Black Water Riv., 20 Apr. 1686, p. 494. Beg. at Thomas Tooly; abr. dividing this from Harris' land, &c. Trans. of 8 pers: Peter Adams, Jno. Fen, Wm. Spight, Eliza. Spight, Robt. Williams, Edward Robins, James Cobb, Ellin Allen.

JOHN GAMON, 800 acs., Low. Norf. Co; bet. the Cyprus & Richford (Ridgford) Swamps; towards head of the S. br. of Eliz. Riv., 20 Apr. 1686, p. 494. 500 acs. granted him, 4 Nov. 1673; 300., now taken & surveyed with the former; for trans. of 6 pers: Owen Edwards, Richd. Dublin, Adam Fryer, Rebecca Ewin, Cob. Peters; Negro Jack.

HUMPHREY CLARK, 300 acs., Is. of Wight Co., 4 Nov. 1685, p. 495. Granted to Capt. John Upton, dec'd., & found to escheate, by inquisition under Capt. Willm. Randolph, Depty. Esch'r., &c.

COL. WILLIAM KENDALL, 400 acs., in N'ampton & Accomack Co.'s; 20 Apr. 1686, p. 495. Adj. Thomas Bell, the land formerly William Roberts', now Robert Foster's; Thomas Browne; land of Lt. Col. John Tillne, now in possession of John Mackeel, Junr., & land formerly Daniell Quillan's. Granted Mr. Thomas Kendall, 3 Oct. 1678, deserted, & now granted sd. Col. Kendall by order, &c., for trans. of 8 pers: Richd. Davis, Hannah Howard, Edward Huntstone, Jno. Hunter, John Holmes, Tho. Daniell, Mary Rossey, Tho. Lessen.

JOSEPH LAKE, 350 acs., Low. Norf. Co., Lynhaven Par; at head of the fresh pond in *Dam Neck:* 20 Apr. 1686, p. 495. Granted to William Brock, 3 Oct. 1671, deserted, & now granted, &c. Trans. of 7 pers: Tho. Flood, Tho. Stoke, Wm. Jones, Alice Smith, John Russell, Margaret Wilton, Sarah Hennell.

By his Excellency

In pursuance of the Act of Assembly made at James Citty the 8 June in the 32nd yeare of the Reigne of our Soveraigne Lord King Charles the Second of ever blessed memory and in the yeare of our Lord 1680 and by the authority thereof, and the power therein granted I Francis Lord Howard, Baron of Effingham, his Maj'ties. Lieut. & Governor Generall of Virginia, doe by this publique Instrument under my hand and the Broad Seale of this Collony of Virginia pronounce publish and declare DAVID DAVIDSON borne in Holland, professing theProtestant Religion, and first having taken the Oath of Allegiance and paid the fees therein mentioned, according to the tenor of the said Act, to be fully and compleatly naturalize him, the said David Davidson, giving and granting unto him and his heires for ever all and singular the priviledges Immunityes and Rights of the Inhabitants of this Collony of Virga. and that as fully and amply to all intents and purposes whatsoever as if he the said David Davidson had been borne within his Maj'ties. Dominion and as other his Maj'ties. naturall borne Subjects whatsoever have ought or doe in any sort enjoy, Any former Law Act usuage or Custome to the Contrary notwithstanding. Given under my hand and the Seale of the Collony this one and Twentyeth day of Aprill Anno Dom. 1686. Effingham. Page 496.

EDWARD WILDER, 109 acs., Low. Norf. Co., 20 Apr. 1686, p. 496. Beg. in Cockroft's line; neare Alexander Gwin; to line of Harding's Orphants, &c. Granted to Richard Hargrove, Junr., 5 June 1678, deserted, & now granted by order &c. Trans. of 2 pers: James & John Dudley.

WILLIAM VAUGHAN, 72 acs., Low. Norf. Co; Eliz. River Par., 20 Apr. 1686, p. 497. Adj. John Ashborne. Granted to John Elder, 18 May 1677, deserted, & now granted by order, &c. Trans. of 2 pers: John Stooper, Edward Moore.

THOMAS TERREY, 1000 acs., New Kent Co., on N. side of Mattopony Riv., 27 Apr. 1686, p. 497. Adj. Mr. Thomas Hall & John Pigg. Granted to William Hernden & Robert Bayly, 18 Feb.

1673/4, deserted, & now granted by order &c. Trans. of 20 pers: Richd. West, Jno. Brown, Sarah Lentell, Joseph Wellman, Eliza. Hunt, Anne Leige, Jno. Dance, Jacob Johnson, Henry Fasnell, Jno. Wilson, Abraham Sinckler, Wm. Moss, Sarah Allyson, Rebecca Bradshaw, Fra. Chambers, Morgan Williams, Sarah Allyson, Robt. Paddyson, Wm. Burrows, Margaret Gibson.

RICHARD BENNETT, 430 acs., Jas. City Co., on E. side of Chickahominy Riv., adj. Pagan Creek, 27 Apr. 1686, p. 498. Beg. at crosse Cr: on Winter's; & Warberton's lines; & Pagan Cr. swamp. 250 acs. granted Thomas Young, 5 Jan. 1658, renewed 18 Mar. 1662, & made over to Andrew Godian, 6 June 1679, from whom it escheated, by inquisition under Col. John Page,

Esch'r. Genrll., & now granted by order &c. Trans. of 4 pers: John Elcock, Thomas Griffin, David Lacy, Wm. Knowles.

COL. WILLIAM BYRD & MARY, his wife, 1086 acs., Chas. City Co., in Wynoake Par., 27 Apr. 1686, p. 500. Beg. on the river, on W. side of the 2nd gutt above Horsemenden's Cr., through the swamp; neare the gr. Road; to Robert Nicholson; by Merryman's Gutt, &c. 150 acs. granted John Merryman, 10 May 1638; & conveyed to Henry Cantrell; 800 acs. granted sd. Cantrell, 10 Jan. 1640; which tracts by sundry meane conveyances are come to sd. William & Mary; 136 acs. found within sd. bounds. Trans. of 3 pers: Mary Harwood, Henry Loyd, Wm. Morgan.

CAPT. WILLIAM CUSTIS, 800 acs., on Feak's Island; Accomack Co., 27 Apr. 1686, p. 500. E. by the Sea, N. by Matomkin Inlett, S. by Machapungo Inlett; beg. W. of the N. end of Herne Island, &c. Trans. of 16 pers: James Wallfleet, Thomas Lozengy, Jane Seily, Thomas Smith, Crispian Morris, Mary Sewill, Joseph Johnson, Anne Heath, Mary Williams, Jone Wilford, Tho. Dun, Thomas Wenham, Abraham Morgan, Wm. Lewis, Jno. Knowles, David Lassell.

GEORGE SPIVEY, 800 acs., Up. Par. of Nansamond Co., 27 Apr. 1686, p. 501. Beg. at Mr. James Petter's (or Potter's) land, in possession of Robert & Francis Roundtree; to Hawkins' Hole; by Cyprus Sw; &c. 400 acs. granted him 23 Apr. 1681; 400 acs. for trans. of 8 pers: Richd. Crook, Tho. Sanders, Jon. Doyley, Wm. Gannock, Wm. Wright, Samll. White, Ed. Heath, Wm. Bayley.

CAPT. WM. KNOTT, 1050 acs., Low. Norf. Co; from head of the S. Br; 27 Apr. 1686, p. 501. Beg. by a gr. Cyprus Sw., cor. of Jacob Barnes; to Sylvester's lyne; to mouth of Gum Sw., &c. Trans. of 25 pers: James Draper, John Almond, Richd. Wing, Roger Griffith, Tho. Jones, Geo. Laddell, James Jenkins, Tho. Stipfield, Rowlan Walter, Geo. Burry, Tho. Robbins, James Johnson, Richd. Williams, John Kirby, Ed. Dawkins, Adam Wood, Jacob Konner; 3 Negroes.

RICHARD SKEATE, 100 acs., Up. Par. of Nanzemond Co; at the mouth of a br. of Orapeake Sw., 27 Apr. 1686, p. 502. Trans. of 2 pers: Jeremiah Edcock, Adam Monk.

THOMAS HARRALL, 140 acs., Up. Par. of Nansamond Co., 27 Apr. 1686, p. 502. Adj. land formerly belonging to Mr. James Petters, & now sd. Harrall's, &c. Trans. of 3 pers: Jacob Adams, Ellin Williams, Adam Miller.

MICHAELL THOMAS & JAMES KNIGHT, 450 acs., Up. Par. of Nansamond Co; at mouth of a br. of Orapeake Sw., 27 Apr. 1686, p. 502. Trans. of 9 pers: Tho. Conroe, Cock Cromwell, Wm. Mandor.

JOHN WALLIS, 250 acs., Up. Par. of Nansamond Co., 27 Apr. 1686, p. 503. Beg. at Mr. Henry Plumton, on the southerne br; neare Jonathan Robinson; & Richard Sanders; to Jernagan's cor., &c. Imp. of 5 pers: Fra. Smith, Mary Field, Jno. Whittiker, Richd. Reeves, James Johnson.

GEORGE LAWRANCE, 830 acs., Up. Par. of Nansamond, on the Black Water; adj. Coleman's corner; 27 Apr. 1686, p. 503. Trans. of 17 pers: James Draper, Jno. Oblord, Oniment (?) Darry, Antho. Libb, Robt. Parrior (or Panior), Jno. Macken, Hen. Sylvester, Richd. Miller, Roger Griffin, Robt. Blays, Ann Waterson, Ann Byan, Richd. Ward, Tho. Sanders, Wm. Wright, Wm. Bayly, Wm. Gayny.

PETER CAPEL, 200 acs., Low. Norf. Co., on W. side of the North River; adj. Francis Jones; & land of Elks; 27 Apr. 1686, p. 503. Trans. of 4 pers: James Fryers, Wm. Gayny, Tho. Smith, Mary Sewell.

SUSANNA WEST, MARGARET WEST & MARY WEST, Relict, &

Orphans of William West; 250 acs., Low. Norf. Co; on NE side of the North River; 27 Apr. 1686, p. 504. Trans. of 5 pers: Edwd. Court, James Smith, Jno. Morgan, Richd. West, John Dawes.

CHARLES EDWARDS, 150 acs., Low. Norf. Co., Lynhaven Par; from the E. br. of Eliz. River; adj. land of Oliver; on the pocoson of Horse Bridge Run, &c; 27 Apr. 1686, p. 504. Trans. of 3 pers: James Aylet, Wm. Wright, Tho. Awbery.

CORNELIUS ELLIS, 250 acs., Low. Norf. Co; on E. side of the S. br. of Eliz. River, 27 Apr. 1686, p. 504. Beg. at Thomas Alexander, & Marmaduke Marrington; to Mr. Edwards; to line of Wm. Whithurst, now Dochartie's; through Fadding Sw., to land of Seaborne, now Whiddon's; to land of Morton, in possession of sd. Ellis. Trans. of 5 pers: Tho. Street, Wm. Sheldon, Thomas Jones, Jno. Baker, George Easy.

BENJAMIN HOLLOWELL, 1030 acs., Low. Norf. Co., towards the Northwest River of Corretuck; & S. the W. pocoson into the White Oake Swamp; adj. land of Butts; 27 Apr. 1686, p. 505. Trans. of 21 pers: Jno. Freeman, Ralph Bromfield, Jno. Thompson, Sarah Alinsley, Anne Corbitt, Isaac Whitsor, Hen. Mosely, Mary Kine, Jno. Walpoole, Priscilla Fips, Eliza. Phillips, Danll. Dormon, Jno. Kellum, Ed. Byrd, Robt. Blinkinson, Dorithy Churchhill, Richd. Welds, Xpher. Yeomans, Cicily Brooks, Jno. Proctor.

JAMES JACKSON, 400 acs., Low. Norf. Co; on E. side of Tanner's Cr., 27 Apr. 1686, p. 506. Adj. lands of Symmons; Macoy; Peyton; & Warden; on Gater's Creek. 200 acs. granted him 10 Sept. 1680; 200 acs. for trans. of 4 pers: Jonah Price, Anne Delfe, James Hill, Michaell Lewis.

MR. JOHN WOODHOUSE, 357 acs., Low. Norf. Co., Lynhaven Par., 27 Apr. 1686, p. 506. Beg. on Woodhouse's Bay; crossing Brock's gutt, to

Mr. Edward Attwood, crossing a cove of Gregorie's Cr., neare Lewis Purveine; to Wm. Okeham; crossing Causon's Cr., &c. Trans. of 7 pers: Ed. Weath, Mathew Roane, Francis Ureton (or Oreton), Benja. Augre, Jacob Blackford (or Clackford), Ed. Court, Thomas Owen.

THEODORE TAYLOR, 264 acs., Low. Norf. Co., towards head of the S. br. of Eliz. Riv; by Richford Swamp; adj. Henry Platt; 27 Apr. 1686, p. 507. Trans. of 6 pers: Roger Irons, Wm. Brent, Richd. Snow, Fra. Vincent, Robt. Bish, James Orton.

JOHN WHARTON, 450 acs., Low. Norf. Co: on head of the Black Water Riv; on a br. of Hachilah Swamp; adj. Henry Simmons; 27 Apr. 1686, p. 507. Trans. of 9 pers: Anne Fish, Silas Cole, James Wells, Robt. Perrin, Wm. Ashton, Jno. Reed, Ellin Owen, Kath. Davis, Jno. Harris.

THO. SCOT (Scott), 100 acs., Low. Norf. Co., 27 Apr. 1686, p. 508. Granted to John Singleton & found to escheate, by inquisition under John Ferrebee, Depty. Esch'r., &c.

SAMUELL BRIDGWATER, 333 acs., Henrico Co., Virina Parish; on N. side of James Riv., 27 Apr. 1686, p. 508. Beg. at Gillies' land, crossing Gillies' Cr., &c. Imp. of 7 pers: Phillip Elon (?), Arthur Bryant, Jno. Rich, Kath. Kalin, Jno. Hayman, Danll. Flinch, Jno. Darby, Eliza. Holly.

MR. ABELL GOWER & MR. EDWARD STRATTON, 487 acs., Henrico Co., 27 Apr. 1686, p. 508. Granted to George Browning, dec'd., & found to escheate, by inquisition under William Byrd, Esqr., Eschr. Genrll., &c.

WILLIAM CARPENTER, 450 acs., Up. Par. of Surry Co., bet. brs. of Burchen Sw. & Cyprus Sw., 27 Apr. 1686, p. 509. Bet. Jeremy (Jeremiah) Ellis & Owen Merrick, in Mr. Wm. Symmons' line; adj. John Brett; Mr. Thomas Jordan; & Thomas Gibson. Trans. of 9 pers: Henry Dever (?) James Kirkum, Humph. Griffin, Tho.

White, Ed. Joyner, Robt. Hadd (or Hudd), Wm. Thomas, Mary Phillips, Tho. Smith.

JOHN TURNER, 340 acs., 27 Apr. 1686, p. 509. 87 acs. being part of 1200 acs. granted Mr. John Seward, 15 Apr. 1648; 253 acs. being waste adj; beg. at a br. dividing this & Mathew Tomlin; adj. Wm. Westray; Mrs. Hardy; & Thomas Harris. Trans. of 7 pers: James Cox, Wm. Richards, Wm. Jud, Mary Hall, Ellis Carter, Wm. Jarvis, Henry James.

MATHEW TOMLIN, 1227 acs., Low. Par. of Is. of Wight Co., on brs. of the Blackwater, 27 Apr. 1686, p. 510. 781 acs. being part of 1200 acs. granted Mr. John Seward, 15 Apr. 1648; 446 being waste adj; beg. at a br. dividing land of John Turner from his daughter Marie's; by Wm. Westray; adj. Mary Turner; & Thomas Harris; to the bottome of *Pig neck,* &c. Trans. of 9 pers: Wm. Lee, Jno. Andrews, Jane Arnold, Alex. Dale, Watkin White, Alex. Jones, Ed. Rider, Math. Jones, Ellin Adlin.

NICHOLAS WYATT, 115 acs., neer his dwelling house, in *Mercht.* Brandon Parish; 27 Apr. 1686, p. 510. Bet. Capt. Wyat & Elizabeth Wheeler, Orphan; on Ralph Ratchell; on Mr. Walles (?) land; &c. Trans. of 3 pers: Cadwallader Mackerry, James Hollis, Wm. Bourne.

THOMAS HARRIS, 240 acs., 27 Apr. 1686, p. 511. Adj. Mathew Tomlin; Mrs. Hardy; William Westray; & John Turner. Trans. of 5 pers: Jno. Martin, Edward Foulks, Ed. Gooch, Mary Powell, Alex. Hinch (or Flinch.)

JOHN COLLINS, 1550 acs., Up. Par. of Surry Co., bet. Cyprus Sw. & maine Blackwater, 27 Apr. 1686, p. 511. Adj. Col. Brown; Wm. Foreman, near Mr. Warren's line; Mr. Merywether; John Coker; Mr. Henry Baker; & Capt. Corker, &c. Trans. of 31 pers: Alex. Pully, Fra. Kelly, Robt. Carter, Jos. Frith, Susan Mortin, Gostin Pullin, Fra. Pott, Wm. Savin, James Temple, Jno. Irish, Nicho. Corman, Samll. Spark, Jno. Duke, James Kenny, Ellin

Abrells, Wm. Eyers, Adam James, Ellin Williams, Owen Filkin, Elliza. Flecter, Jacob Obendict, Caleb Cockrahin, Sarah Williams, Silas Chapman, Ed. Cooper, Ed. Thompson, Ellin Owen, Anne Terrill, Paul Peters, Cath. Cordridge, Ed. Barret, Abra. Evans.

MR. JOHN TERRY, 750 acs., Chas. City Co., bet. Chipoakes & Wards Crs; 27 Apr. 1686, p. 512. Adj. Francis Ree, John Reekes, Mr. Good & Henery Armstrong; on Brains' line; the land in possession of Edward Green & belonging to an Orphan of Wm. Short; by the Road, to Mr. Richard Clark; by John Wilkinson; to Capt. Wyatt, &c. Trans. of 15 pers: Wm. Wilson, Jno. Johnson, Richd. Webster, Wm. Jones, Jeremiah Jones, Susan Wyn, James Fry, Wm. Mott, Mary Weet, Joane Trefry, Wm. Adams; 3 Negroes.

WILLIAM TOWNSEND, SENR., 162 A., 46 Chs., 8 Primes, in York & Warwick Counties, 27 Apr. 1686, p. 513. Beg. by Warwick Mill horse path; to Mr. Robert Hubbart; near the White Marsh; by Mr. Thomas Hansford, &c. Trans. of 3 pers.*

MAJOR HENRY WHITEING & MR. JOHN BUCKNER, 280 acs., Gloster Co., in Ware Par., upon WNW side of North Riv., 30 Oct. 1686, p. 513. Beg. at Edward Dauber's patt. of 2400 acs., dated 28 Nov. 1642, on S. side of a cr. in the N'most river in Mobjack Bay, dividing Dauber & George Levitt, &c.

MR. JOSEPH HAILE, 1000 acs., New Kent Co., in the freshes of Mattopony Riv., 30 Oct. 1686, p. 514. Beg. at the path from Wm. Rickett's house to the *Indian Town;* to Capt. Wm. Smith, Marriner, from his house to his Landing, to land where John Barrow liveth, formerly John Pigg's; to N. side of the Ridge Path dividing this & land of Mr. James Taylor; along Watkins & Ricketts, to Major Payton, &c. Trans. of 20 pers.*

GILBERT CHANEY, 50 acs., Jas. City Co., on W. side of Chichahominy Riv., 27 Apr. 1686, p. 515. Beg. in

Mr. Cowles' line; to Peashill Cr; through Bassett's field, &c. Trans. of 1 pers.*

WILLIAM PEAWD, 400 acs., in the up. part of Jas. City Co., on W. side of Chickahominy Riv., 30 Oct. 1686, p. 515. From Capt. Duke's cor. in Gwin's line, to a br. of Webb's run; to Walters Br; on Womsley's line, to NE side of Nicketewances Path, over Mason's & Bradford's paths; down a br. of Toroham Run, to Gwin's cor., &c. 150 acs. granted him by patt. for 1000 acs., 11 Feb. 1663; 250 acs. being surplusage within. Trans. of 5 pers.*

MR. FRANCIS DANCY, 287 acs., Jas. City Co., on W. side of Chickahominy Riv; & on N. side the Black Sw; adj. Tinsley's cor; 30 Oct. 1686, p. 516. Trans. of 6 pers.*

GARNETT CORBITT, 323 acs., Warwick Co., neer head of Deep Cr., 30 Oct. 1686, p. 516. Beg. neer a Cart Path; on Gerrard Ridley; Ed. Mumford; & Owen Davis; neer Finch's Dams; along Samll. Singnall; to Mr. Samll. Ranshaw; & Mr. Corlie, &c. 350 acs. found to escheate for want of heirs of Peter Evans, by inquisition under Honble. John Page, Esch'r; 23 acs. found within, & due for trans. of 1 pers.*

ROBERT BLACKEY, 23 acs., Middlesex Co., on a br. of Draggon Sw; adj. Thomas Kidd; Wm. Kidd; Mr. Henry Thacker; & Richard Willis; 30 Oct. 1686, p. 517. Trans. of 1 pers.*

MR. WM. NORWOOD, 70 acs., Warwick Co., in Denby Par., 30 Oct. 1686, p. 517. Beg. on NW side of the Church Br., cor. of Mr. Robert Browne; adj. land of Doctor Hall, in possession of the Widdow Naylor; to Rushy Br; on Mr. Argoll Ranshaw's line, now Thomas Edson's; along Mrs. Rice's line, &c. Trans. of 2 pers.*

WILLIAM STAFFORD, 99 acs., Low. Norf Co., Lynhaven Par; adj. John Akle's line; 30 Oct. 1686, p. 518. Trans. of 2 pers.*

MR. JOHN BUCKNER & MAJ. HENRY WHITEING, 2400 acs., on S. side of a cr. on the northermost river of Mockjeck Bay, dividing this & land of George Levitt; 30 Oct. 1686, p. 518. Granted to Edmund Dawber, 28 Nov. 1642, deserted, & granted Mr. Henry Wareing, by order, & assigned to the above, 16 Oct. 1686; trans. of 48 pers.*

RICHARD TUNSTALL, JUNR., 400 acs., New Kent Co., St. Stephen's Par., in Mattopany freshes, 30 Oct. 1686, p. 519. Beg. at Capt. Wm. Smith on the Town Br; to land of Price & Ball; by Col. Goodrich, & an Indian Path, &c. Trans. of 8 pers.*

EDWARD TUNSTALL, 750 acs., New Kent Co., St. Stephen's Par., 30 Oct. 1686, p. 519. Beg. at Mr. Ascough; by the Horse Path; to Wm. Nickolls; Capt. Smith & Thomas Wright. Trans. of 15 pers.*

MR. JAMES TAYLER, 950 acs. New Kent Co., which he lives upon; in the freshes of Mattopony Riv., 30 Oct. 1686, p. 520. Adj. George Weston; land of Bagby; John Joy; & the Ridge Path; over Torropin Sw., to land of Thomas White. 200 acs. purchased of Thomas Reinolds, 3 Dec. 1675; 100 acs. of Joseph Haile, 26 Mar. 1680; & 400 acs. of George Brooks, 30 Oct. 1682, which 3 parcels are part of 1000 acs. granted Maj. Martin Palmer & Mr. George Chapman; the residue for trans. of 5 pers.*

MR. JAMES MORRIS, 750 acs., Gloster Co., on W. side of the North Riv. in Mobjack Bay, 30 Oct. 1686, p. 520. Beg. at a place called the loane Pine; adj. Mr. Thomas Boswell; on the Back Cr., &c. 670 acs. granted Mr. Thomas Curtis, 20 Sept. 1652; 80 acs. for trans. of 2 pers: John Easterfield, James Huzzy.

JOHN POWELL, 272 acs., Low. Norf. Co., on NW side of the W. br. of Eliz. Riv., at head of Langley's Cr; 30 Oct. 1686, p. 521. 130 acs. neer Carter's land; granted to Wm. Powell, 5 June 1678 & assigned to sd. John; 142 acs. for trans. of 3 pers.*

THOMAS RUSSELL, 450 acs., Low. Norf. Co; from head of the S. br. of Elizabeth Riv; beg. at Hollowell's land; by the White Oake Sw; &c; 30 Oct. 1686, p. 522. Trans. of 9 pers.*

PHILLIP HUNDLEY, JUNR., 89 acs., Gloster Co., on N. side of Pudding Cr; & adj. the *Gleab Land;* 30 Oct. 1686, p. 522. Trans. of 2 pers.*

ROGER BRYAN, 350 acs., Low. Norf. Co., on S. side of the W. br. of Eliz. Riv., 30 Oct. 1686, p. 523. Adj. Thomas Smith, Bowers' land; *alias* Bramble's; lands of Sparrow; & Bowman. Trans. of 7 pers: Martha Millington, Sarah Pollard, James Hardy, Susan Paine, Gilbert Hay, Margery Davis, Jno. Bell.

JOHN EVANS, 460 acs., Up. Par. of Nanzemond Co., 30 Oct. 1686, p. 523. Beg. by the S. branch; adj. lands of Richard Guid's (?); Thomas Cowling; John Barefield; & Daniell Mackloud. Trans. of 10 pers.*

JOHN BURK, 191 acs., Middlesex Co., 30 Oct. 1686, p. 524. Beg. att Thomas Obrissell, neer head of the Green Br; to the maine Sw. of Sunderland Cr., *alias* Burnham's Cr; above Col. Cuthbert Potter's Mill house; to Mr. Richard Willis. Trans. of 4 pers.*

MR. JOHN REVELL, 450 acs., on Herne Island, Accomack Co; on W. side of the S. end of Fecksip's Island; 30 Oct. 1686, p. 524. Trans. of 9 pers.*

MR. AUGUSTINE SCARBROUGH, 722 acs., Middlesex Co., 30 Oct. 1686, p. 525. Beg. at Mr. George Kibble, on N. side of Bob's Br; to Maj. Genr'l. Robert Smith, neer sd. Smith's (Quarter) plantation; to S. side of Peankettank Roade; down the Green branch. &c. Trans. of 15 pers.*

MR. JOHN STARK, Merchant, 484 acs., New Kent Co., St. Stephen's Par., 30 Oct. 1686, p. 525. Beg. by his Landing; to Apostequick Sw., adj. land formerly Col. Abrahall's, to Mattopony River. 200 acs. granted to Mr. Richard Barnhouse, Senr., dec'd., & upon petition of his son & heire, Richard, obtained order to survey the same, which was effected by Col. John Lewis & George Morris, Surveyor, in presence of a Jury, 10 May 1673; which he sold to sd. Stark, to whom it was confirmed by order, &c., in a suit between sd. Stark & Maj. Wm. Wyatt. 284 acs. for trans. of 6 pers.*

CAPT. WILLIAM WHITTINGTON, 1300 acs., Accomack Co., being a neck or island; E. & W. upon Matchapungo River, &c; 16 Oct. 1685, p. 526. Granted Mr. Thomas Harmonson, 12 June 1654, assigned to James Nevell to whom it was granted, 26 Mar. 1662, deserted, & now granted by order &c. Trans. of 26 pers.*

THOMAS SANDERS, 165 acs., Up. Par. of Nanzemond Co., 30 Oct. 1686, p. 526. Adj. Gresham Cophell; & Wm. Sanders; By Dumplin Island Cr; down Nanzemond River, to mouth of Hollyday's Cr. 100 acs. part of 200 acs. granted to Epaphraditus Lawson, 1 Nov. 1637, which, after severall surrenders & descents, is in possession of sd. Sanders; 65 acs. for trans. of 2 pers: Richard Bonner, Charles Hoggett.

ROBERT & FRANCIS ROUNDTREE (Rountree), 490 acs., Up. Par. of Nanzemond Co., by the maine run of Cypress Sw., 30 Oct. 1686, p. 527. 400 acs. granted Mr. James Peters, 10 Nov. 1678, & now in possession of sd. Roundtrees'; 90 acs. added, for trans. of 2 pers: Thomas Roundtree, Elizabeth Roundtree.

WILLIAM SANDERS, 165 acs., Up. Par. of Nanzemond Co., 30 Oct. 1686, p. 527. Beg. on Dumpling Is. Creek, cor. of Capt. Jossy; to Thomas Sanders, &c. 100 acs. part of patt. granted to Epaphraditus Lawson, 1 Nov. 1637, which, after severall surrenders, is in fee possest by sd. Sanders; 65 acs. for trans. of 2 pers: Wm. Nickolls, John Read.

HENRY HEARNE, 133 acs., in the Up. Par. of Nanzemond, in Is. of Wight

Co; bet. Symon Symonds & land of Anthony Branch, dec'd; 30 Oct. 1636, p. 528. Granted sd. Branch, 22 Apr. 1670, deserted, & now due trans. of 3 pers: James Doughty, his wife, & James Doughty, Junr.

ANN HOOD, 250 acs., in the Up. Par. of Nanzemond Co., 30 Oct. 1686, p. 528. Adj. Gresham Cophell; Thomas Mansfield; & Capt. Jossy's fence. through the maine swamp; by lands of Murfrey, & Oliver, *alias* Carter's; &c. Granted to Peircivall Champion, 23 Aug. 1638.

JOHN HUDNELL, in right of his wife Mary, & THOMAS HASWEEL, in the right of Elizabeth, his wyfe, 90 acs., in the Low. Par. of Nanzemond Co; beg. in Knott's line; 30 Oct. 1686, p. 528. Part of patt. granted to Anthony Wells, which after severall sales, &c. descended in fee to sd. Mary & Elizabeth, daughters of Robert Haile.

MR. STEPHEN BEMBRIDGE, of Rappa. Co., & MR. RICHARD TUNSTALL, of New Kent, 8500 acs., in New Kent Co., in the freshes of Mattopany; 30 Oct. 1686. p. 529. . Adj Robert Bagby, William Herendon, Capt. Josuah Story, & William Morris; nigh Portobacco path, &c. Trans. of 170 pers.*

JOHN WARDEN, 100 acs., Low. Norf. Co., in Tanner's Cr., 30 Oct. 1686, p. 530. Bet. 2 creeks parting this from land of James Symons, & James Jackson; E. on Gater's Cr. Trans. of 2 pers.*

MR. STEPHEN BEMBRIDGE, of Rappa. Co., 330 acs., in New Kent Co., upon brs. of Horecock Cr., 30 Oct. 1686, p. 530. Adj. Col. Goodrich, John Jones' plantation; lands of Ball & Price; Mr. Brereton, & Turner's line. Trans. of 7 pers.*

ELIZABETH RIVER PARISH, 100 acs., for a *Gleahe,* 30 Oct. 1686, p. 531. In sd. parish, on E. side of sd. river; beg. on a poynt on S. side of the mouth of Ellett's Cr; neer Nicholas Wise's line. &c. Trans. of 2 pers.*

NICHOLAS WYATT, son & heire of Anthony Wyatt, Gent., late of the parish of Jordans in Chas. City Co; all that plantation known by the name of *Chaplins.* being 361 acs; on S. side of James Riv; 30 Oct. 1686, p. 531. Beg. in line of land now or late Col. Edward Hill's that runs into Mason's; along Mason's Cr., to Bickers' Cr. mouth, &c. Due as eldest son & heire of sd. Anthony, who dyed lately seized of same & had been many yeares in his possession, & by reason of burning of the house of sd. Anthony, the pattent which was granted to one Chaplin was lost; & the originall for the like accident of fireing, or otherwise, of the Secretarie's Office not att this day to be found amongst the records.

JOHN MURDEN, 498 acs., Low. Norf. Co; bet. the S. & E. brs. of Eliz. Riv; 30 Oct. 1686, p. 532. Beg. at Henry Butt's, by line drawn by agreement bet. them, to a pocoson of the Green Sea; along Thomas Butt, &c. 250 acs. granted to Warren Godfrey & Isaac Barrington, 23 Oct. 1673, & assigned to sd. Murden; residue for trans. of 5 pers.*

COL. JOHN ARMSTEAD & MR. JOHN GWIN, 202½ acs., Gloster Co., in Kingston Par., 30 Oct. 1686, p. 532. Beg. on E. side of a br. neer a *Chappell,* in line of land taken up by Col. Hugh Gwin, dec'd., who sold to Mr. William Armestead, dec'd; to land of Mr. William Elliott, Senr; to Thomas Allamaine; to Gwin's Dams, &c. Trans. of 5 pers.*

COL. JOHN ARMSTEAD, 130 acs., Gloster Co., in Kingston Par; adj. whereon he lives; 30 Oct. 1686, p. 533. Adj. George Seaton & William Elliott; on E. side of a br. not farr from *the Chappell;* &c. Trans. of 3 pers.*

MR. FRANCIS PETTIT, 400 acs., N'ampton Co., 30 Oct. 1686, p. 533. Granted Mrs. Anne Wilcox, dec'd., & found to escheate, by inquisition under Col. John Stringer, Esch'r., &c.

MR. ROBT. HANCOCK, 600 acs., Henrico Co., Virina Par., on S. side of James Riv; 30 Oct. 1686, p. 534. Beg. at his own land & a bottome of the Cattaile run, &c. Trans. of 12 pers.*

FRANCIS CATER, 622 acs., Henrico Co., in Virina Par., on S. side of James Riv., 30 Oct. 1686, p. 534. Beg. at Mr. Robt. Hancock; to Tymothy Allen, &c. Trans. of 13 pers.*

MR. ROBERT BOWLING (Bolling) & MR. DANNIELL NONALEY, 347 acs., Chas. City Co., Bristoll Par., on S. side of Appamatok River; 30 Oct. 1686, p. 535. Beg. at Mr. Robt. Bowlin's land. Trans. of 7 pers.*

MR. EDWARD BIRTCHETT, 230 acs., Chas. City Co., in Bristoll Par., on N. side of the maine Blackwater, 30 Oct. 1686, p. 535. Adj. Mr. Robt. Tucker. Trans. of 5 pers: Edmund Vickary, James King, Wm. Cooper, Richard Newman, Thomas Morris.

MR. SAMUELL TATUM, 803 acs., Chas. City Co., in Bristoll Par., att a place known by the name of *Warrockhock*, 30 Oct. 1686, p. 536. Beg. at John Smith, to Mr. Henry Batt; crossing the 2nd Sw., to land of Hugh Lee, &c. Trans. of 17 pers.*

LT. COL. DANNIELL JENIFER, 220 acs., Accomack Co; being sand hills & marshes, by some called the Beeches; 3 Nov. 1686, p. 536. Beg. at George Parker & John Barnes, from S. side of Garaphia Inlett to N. side of Assowmen Inlet; adj. Benjamin Eyres & John Stokeley. Granted to him 16 Apr. 1683, deserted, & granted to Mr. Wm. Sherwood, by order, 25 Oct. 1686; & on 2 Nov. 1686 sd. Sherwood assigned to sd. Jenifer. Trans. of 5 pers.*

SAME. 170 acs., same Co. & date; p. 537. Called *Hobson's Choice* on S. side of Assowomen Inlett. Granted to Benjamin Eyres & John Stokeley, 29 May 1683, deserted, & now granted by order, &c. Trans. of 4 pers.*

SAME. 200 acs., same Co., date & page. On S. end of Assateag Island; W. & N. by Assateage, *alias* Mattopany, Inlet; running to the extent of the Virga. & Maryland bounds. Granted Col. William Stevens & sd. Jenifer, 16 Apr. 1683, deserted, & granted to Mr. Wm. Sherwood by order, 25 Oct. 1686, & assigned to sd. Jenifer, 2 Nov. 1686. Trans. of 4 pers.*

MR. WM. ANDERSON, 200 acs. N'ampton Co., part on the marsh bet. *Pocomoke* & *Messango*, & is the 2 neerest Humocks to the W. end of St. George's Island; 3 Nov. 1686, p. 538. Granted to John Parker, 29 Mar. 1672, deserted, & now granted by order, &c. Trans. of 4 pers.*

MAJ. SAMUELL SWAN, 960 acs., in Low. Norf. Co; on E. side of brs. of the North River of Coratock, 3 Nov. 1686, p. 538. Beg. in a gr. Siprus Sw. Granted Mr. William Drommund, 5 Mar. 1672/3, deserted, & now granted by order, &c. Trans. of 20 pers.*

SAMUELL THOMPSON (Tompson), 350 acs., Surry Co., 3 Nov. 1686, p. 539. Granted to William Mills, dec'd., & found to escheat, by inquisition under Maj. Samll. Swan, Depty. Esch'r., &c.

MR. JOHN TOTON, 100 acs., York Co., 1 Feb. 1686/7, p. 539. Granted to John Merry, dec'd., & found to escheat, by inquisition under John Page, Esqr., Esch'r. Genrll., &c.

CAPT. RICHARD BOOKER, 740 acs., Glocester Co., 1 Feb. 1686/7, p. 540. Granted to John Sigismund Cleverous, dec'd., & found to escheate, by inquisition under Francis Page, Depty. Esch'r., &c.

MR. EDWARD ALCOCK, 142 acs., Rappa. Co., 1 Feb. 1686/7, p. 540. Granted to Randolph Petter, dec'd., & found to escheate, by inquisition under Col. Isaac Allerton, Esch'r., &c.

HENRY WOODNOT, 214 acs., Rappa. Co., 1 Feb. 1686/7, p. 540. Granted to Francis Thedford, dec'd., & found to escheate, by inquisition under Col. Isaac Allerton, Esch'r., &c.

SAME. 300 acs., same Co. & date, p. 341. Granted to John Standford, dec'd., & found, &c. (as above.)

MR. EDWARD ADCOCK, 150 acs., Rappa. Co., 1 Feb. 1686/7, p. 541. Granted to Richard Spurling, dec'd., & found to escheate, by inquisition under Col. Isaac Allerton, Esch'r., &c.

WALTER RUTTER, 150 acs., Low. Par. of Is. of Wight Co., bet. Col. Bridger, Col. Pitt & Thomas Poole, 30 Oct. 1686, p. 542. Being all that could be found in a patt. of 350 acs. to Mr. Richard Izard, 20 Jan. 1661; the remainder being within elder grants, & by sd. Izard's will, dated 2 May 1669, given to his daughters Mary & Martha; Mary dying without issue & before division was made, the whole fell to Martha now wyfe of sd. Rutter; beg. at Col. Bridger's cor. of Seward's land, neer the fishponds, neer Thomas Stanton, (*alias* Poole's) cor., to Turky Hill; & Rutter's own land, &c.

FRANCIS REE, 330 acs., on NW side of Up. Chipoakes Cr., bet. his & land of Mr. John Terry; 30 Oct. 1686, p. 542. Trans. of 7 pers: Wm. Wilkins, Sarah Daniell, Jane Web, Jno. Evans, Wm. Tyler, Tho. Davis, Wm. Field.

MR. HENRY GAULER, 400 acs., on the Blackwater, called *Rownam*, Chas. City Co., Bristoll Par., 30 Oct. 1686, p. 543. Granted to Hugh Lee, 20 Apr. 1680, deserted, & now granted by order, &c. Trans. of 8 pers: Wm. Jones, Jane Rhodes, Hanah Ellis, Jeremy Johnson, Jonas Kieth, Wm. Canter, Susan Herd, Jane Willis.

SAME. 265 A., 1 R., 13 P., same Co., Westover Par., p. 543. S. side James Riv; beg. on the lower King's field Br; by Richd. Pace; crossing up. King's field Br. & the long point Br., to John Williamson, crossing Scotch Br., on Col. Edward Hill, &c. Granted to Mr. Danll. Higdon & Mr. Roger Reece, 16 Apr. 1683. deserted. & now granted by order, &c. Trans. of 6 pers: Tho. Charles, Griffin Paul, Phebe Jones, Tho. Williams, Jno. Wyn, Alice Pierce.

MR. WILLIAM THOMPSON & MR. EDWARD CHILTON, 1160 acs., Up. Par. of Surry Co; bet. branches of Gray's Cr. & Pigeon & Cypress Swamps; 30 Oct. 1686, p. 544. Beg. on W. side of a br. of Besses Sw., cor. of George Williams; to Peter Duberry; to Wm. Ellett's corne field, &c. Trans. of 24 pers: Grace Jenkins, Wm. Powell, Watkin Edwards, Jno. Toy, Tymo. Field, Jonathan Ward, Xpher. Wood, Peter Reed, Phillip Coniers, Jno. James, Wm. Edwards, Abigail House, Sarah Jones, Richd. Moody, Alex. Pitts, Wm. Rely (or Kely), Charles Goss, Nicho. Fleming, Peter Butts, Wm. Clark, Jno. Foord, Wm. Lane, Sarah Lane, Rose Hyde, Steven Bayly.

ROBERT WILLIAMSON, 500 acs., Up. Par. of Isle of Wight Co., on W. side of the 3rd Sw. of the Blackwater; adj. his own & land of James Adkinson; 30 Oct. 1686, p. 544. Trans. of 10 pers.*

MR. JOHN NEVILL, 246 acs., Low. Par. of Is. of Wight Co., on the W. br. of Nanzemond Riv; opposite Thomas Oglthorp's house; & adj. Christopher Wade; 30 Oct. 1686, p. 545. Trans. of 5 pers: Peter Morgan, James Kerryman (or Kenyman), Ellinor Dobson, Xpher. Ellyson, Henry Kerby.

MR. GEORGE BLIGHTON, 1010 acs., Chas. City Co., 16 Nov. 1686, p. 545. Beg. in Westrop's line; neer an old Indian field; to the Southern Run, &c. 778 acs. granted to Edward Richards, 26 Sept. 1674, deserted, & granted sd. Blighton by order, &c; 232 acs. newly taken. Trans. of 21 pers.*

MRS. SARAH WILLIAMS, 750 acs., Chas. City Co., 1 Feb. 1686/7, p. 546. Granted to Edward Richards, dec'd., & escheated by inquisition under Capt. Francis Page, Depty. Esch'r., &c.

MR. GEORGE NICHOLAS HACK, 700 acs., Accomack Co., bet. heads of Assawomen Brs. & Messango; 20 Apr. 1687, p. 546. Adj. Col. Danll. Jenifer, John Stokeley, & Nicholas Michelhop. Granted to Griffin Savage, 25 Oct. 1673;

who assigned to Howell Gladding, 23 Apr. 1679, who assigned to sd. Hack, 26 Mar. 1684; for a further assurance, sd. Gladding & his wvfe, Alice, conveyed to sd. Hack, 25 Mar. 1684.

HONBLE. WILLIAM BYRD, Esqr., 5075 acs., Henrico Co., on S. side of James Riv; 20 Apr. 1687, p. 547. Beg. a little below John Stower's ditch; along Mr. Jno. Good; over Powetan Branch; to Powhite Creek; to Reedy Cr; to the late *Garryson house*, including Harwood, My Lords, Price's Folly, & Willow Islands; to cor. of the Orphants of Edw. Lane; to land late belonging to William Elam; against middle of & includ. Edward's 'Island; 1762 acs. due by severall conveyances; 3313 acs. adjacent for trans. of 67 pers. *Note:* "Sixty seven Rights by Mr. Edwd. Chilton's Cert. dated the 30th of Aprill 1686 for Eighty Rts." *Marginal notation:* "a mistake there being noe occasion for them." (The following names appear:) James Adams, Tho. Beast, Joseph Louther, Tho. Watts, James Edmonds, Margt. Bradshaw, Hanah Sarten, Margt. North, James Beck, Senr., James Beck, Junr., Wm. Pope, Luke Shaw, Ann Bennett, Jane Welch, Tho. Swift, Wm. Harryson, James Douglas, John Jordan, Hen. Walters, James Donns. Phillip Pursell, Irish Teige.

SAME. 956 acs., same Co., & date; p. 548. N. side of James Riv; beg. at mouth of Shaccoe Cr; down the river 250 po. to Gillie's Run, the division line bet. this & Gylly Groomamarin; N. to Pickinoky Road; to Shacko Cr., &c. 500 acs. included in a patt. to Honble. Thomas Stegg, Esqr., & from him *derived* to sd. Col. Byrd; the residue adj., included in the bounds, & due for trans. of 10 pers: Kath. Witchell, James Sands (?), Welch Davy, Walter Squire, Wm. Gold, James Darlow; Calle, Diana, Nan & Bess, Negroes.

SAME. 1820 acs., same Co. & date, p. 549. In Virina Parish, on S. side of James Riv. 300 acs. purchased of Wm. Gyles, 29 Mar. 1683; the residue being King's land; beg. at a cor. in Grindon's Run belonging to land of Peter Lee; to

Henry Sherman, to Edward Deally; crossing the maine br. of Falling Cr., nigh Seth Ward, to mouth of the Spring Run; &c. Trans. of 31 pers: Andrew, Simbo, Besse, Guy, Kove, Lilly, Mingo, Nanne, Jack, Bess; Tho. Swift, Wm. Harrysin, Jam. Douglass, Jno. Jordan, Hen. Walters, James Donnes (or Deanes), Phill. Purcell, Irish Teague; & 13 more by Mr. Chilton's Certif., 30 Apr. 1686.

THOMAS EDMUNDSON, 600 acs., Rappa. Co; adj. Francis Brown; 20 Apr. 1687, p. 550. Beg. by Mr. Perries Sw; over the King's Road; by Mr. Joseph Goodrich's path; to line of Turner & Jones; on line of Paine, &c. 513 acs. granted (him) 27 Sept. 1667; 87 acs. for trans. of 2 pers: David Bathurtson, Francis Berry.

MRS. JONE YATES, 400 acs., Low. Norf. Co., in the S. br. of Eliz. Riv., 20 Apr. 1687, p. 550. Beg. neer Ware Neck Point; to the Horse Bridge Cr; to Ethridge's Cr. dividing this & land of Johannah Yates, now in possession of Jno. Whiddon. 300 ac. granted Thomas Willoughby, 28 Feb. 1636, who sold to John Yates, & left to Richard Yates, as heir at law, who bequeathed to sd. Joane, his wyfe, dureing her life & after her decease to her dau. Faith Yates, & to the heires of her body forever; but in default of such issue, to the rest of his daughters & the heires of their bodyes; 100 acs. now taken with new rights & surveyed with the 300 acs; & due for trans. of 2 pers.*

SAMUELL NEWMAN, 559 acs., Henrico Co., Bristoll Par., on S. side of Swift Cr., & adj. Mr. Eusebius King; crossing Parsimon Br; 20 Apr. 1687, p. 551. Trans. of 12 pers: Eliz. Carter, Samll. Poope, Rich. Meyne (or Megue), Jno. Hardin, Margt. Myhill, Edwd. Stratton, Senr., Edwd. Stratton, Junr., Cha. Fetherston, Tho. Risbye, Hen. Brassell, Mary Johnson.

JACOB BARNES, *"liver in the Isle of Wight County,"* 250 acs., in Low. Norf. Co; from head of the S. br. of Eliz. Riv., 20 Apr. 1687, p. 552. Beg.

at John Corporice; by the Cypress Sw; to Sylvester's line, &c. Trans. of 5 pers: Richd. Page, David Magason, Fran. Hobson, Emma Henton, John Thomas.

MR. ROBERT HARMON, 1220 acs., New Kent Co., on S. side & in the freshes of York Riv., 20 Apr. 1687, p. 552. Beg. at the mouth of Honywood's Sw; opposite Pampatick Cr., a br. dividing this & land of Maj. Joseph Croashow (Croshaw), now Blackwell's; in sight of John Gunton's plantation, &c.

843 acs. purchased from William Crump, 30 June 1668; 383 being surplus; trans. of 8 pers: Giles Gameston, Francis Crippin, Eliz. Norman, Sarah Chrispin, Joseph Millard, Jno. Shoare, Hen. Barton, Tho. Wood.

MR. CHARLES GOODRICH, 550 acs., Chas. City Co., Westover Par; on S. side of James Riv., 20 Apr. 1687, p. 553. Adj. Danll. Higgdon; Wm. Edmunds; John Williams; & Maj. Poytheres. Trans. of 11 pers.*

GEORGE PACE, 600 acs., Chas. City Co., Westover Par; on S. side of James Riv., nigh the Blackwater, 20 Apr. 1687, p. 554. Beg. at John Williams; crossing the Blackwater Path; & the Reedy Br., to Capt. Lucie's line, &c. Trans. of 12 pers.*

EDWARD JONES, 533 acs., 20 Apr. 1687, p. 554. Upon Pruit (Pruett), & Fields' line; upon Amond's Creek; to Bayly's land, &c. (No county given). Trans. of 11 pers.*

JOHN EVANS, 125 acs., Rappa. Co., S. side of Rappa. Riv., on brs. of Hoskins' Cr; adj. John Medors; & James Tayler; on the Rowling Path, &c; 20 Apr. 1687, p. 555. Trans. of 3 pers: Robt. Coles, Robt. Studwell, Mary Bryan.

JOHN KEMBROW, Planter, 575 acs., in the up. parts of New Kent Co., on S. side Pomunky Riv., 20 Apr. 1687, p. 556. Beg. at land now, or late, Stephen Tarleton's; crossing Matchump Cr; to Col. Ludwell; & Col. Bacon; &c.

Trans. of 12 pers: Jno. Kimbro, Mary Kimbro, Jno. Russell, Tho. Madoes, Ann Flipperman, Vell Heden, Sarah Blackman, Rich. Poole, Jno. Jones, Wm. Williams. Note: 2 Rts. wanting and Col. Bacon promised the sd. 2 Rts.

MR. THOMAS COCK, JUNR., 671 acs., Henrico Co., Virina Par., on N. side of James Riv., 20 Apr. 1687, p. 556. Adj. Mr. Robert Burton & Mr. John Davis; crossing the Round about Br; to Edward Hacker, etc. Trans. of 14 pers: Sarah Carter, Anne Nobbs, Jno. Robinson, Grace Savage, David Williams, Peter Dangerfield, Jno. Watts, Hen. Hicks, Jno. Cuddy, Jno. Smith, Richd. Clark, Tho. Carey, Margaret Swin, Roger Dorman.

MR. THOMAS COCK, 296 A., 3 R., 19 P., Henrico Co., N. side of James Riv., 20 Apr. 1687, p. 557. Adj. his own, & land of Mr. John Watson; neer Cedar Br; neer New Kent Roade, &c. Granted to Thomas Wells, 3 Jan. 1677, deserted, & now granted by order, &c. Trans. of 6 pers.*

JOHN MEDOR, 640 acs., Rappa. Co; S. side Rappa. Riv., on Beverdam Sw., at the head of Hoskins' Cr., 20 Apr. 1687, p. 558. Beg. on S. side of the old Beverdam Sw., neer an Indian Path; to a small island, &c. 450 acs. granted Thomas Browning, 30 Nov. 1657; assigned to John Cook, 4 May 1659; assigned to Thomas Medors, 7 Aug. 1659; & granted him 9 Apr. 1664; 190 acs. for trans. of 4 pers: Jno. Chambers, Joseph Calloway, Robert Duell, Jno. Warrener.

MR. DAVID CRAFFORD, 196 acs., New Kent Co; on S. side of Pomunky Riv., 20 Apr. 1687, p. 558. Beg. at Thomas Glass, neer George Phillips' Plantation; to head of a br. of Assaquint Run; to Andrew Davis; bounded by his own, & lands of Samll. Waddy, & Mr. Bassett, or Honnywood's, &c. Trans. of 4 pers.*

LT. COL. THOMAS WALKER, of Gloster Co., 2600 acs., New Kent Co; in St. Stephen's Par., on N. side of

Mattapony Riv., 20 Apr. 1687, p. 559. Beg. at a cr., or run, called Potapannica; to Tornacorecon Sw., &c. 2300 acs. granted Edward Diggs, Esqr., 1 June 1653, deserted, & granted sd. Walker by order, 26 Feb. 1665; 300 acs., surplus, for trans. of 6 pers: James Golden, Jno. Venager, his wife & child, Jno. Temple, Samll. Odwin.

JOHN BAYLY, 736 acs., Henrico Co., Virina Par; N. side of James Riv., 20 Apr. 1687, p. 560. Beg. at Henry Pruett & John Field; to Gylles Cr; on Samuell Bridgwater, &c. Trans. of 15 pers.* Note: 15 rts. being parte of a certificate for 20 rights granted by Mr. Edwd. Chilton, 23 July 1686 to Walter Shipley.

MR. SAMUELL BRIDGWATER, 404 acs., Henrico Co., Virina Par; N. side of James Riv., 20 Apr. 1687, p. 560. Adj. line of Esqr. Place. Trans. of 9 pers: Isaac Sheffeild, Jno. Williams, Isaac Jones, Wm. Smith, Tho. Smith, Rachel Young, Alice Wingfeild, Tho. Stephens, Jno. Evans.

RICHARD BLAND, 1254 acs., Henrico Co., Bristoll Par; on N. side of Swift Cr., 20 Apr. 1687, p. 561. From the S. side of Hatcher's Run towards sd. Cr. 600 acs. granted Xpher. Robinson & John Sturdivant, 23 Feb. 1652, deserted, & granted to Mr. Henry Randolph, dec'd., by order, &c; 654 acs. adj., & included in one pattent, & granted to sd. Randolph 27 Nov. 1671, which was lapsed for want of seating, & now granted sd. Bland for trans. of 26 pers: James Aror, Jone Jeffreys, Richd. Winter, Adam Cockrahm, Abell Jones, Eliza. Willis, Jeremiah Cater, Edwin Keith, James Edwards, Evan Williams, Canter (or Carter) Williams, Mary Baaghan, Conon Danger, Jonathan Jenifer, Wm. James, Ed. Kenny, Trevor Williams, Geo. Day, Person Gezin, Joseph Adams, Ellin Dircett, Jone Daniell, Kath. Thomas, Ellis Welch; Jeffrey & Tony, Negroes.

GILLY GROOMEREN, 539 acs., Henrico Co., Verina Par; S. side of Chickahominy Sw., 20 Apr. 1687, p.

562. Beg. on the Cattaile Br., in line of Mr. Henry Wyat (Wyett); to head of Holey Br; to Lionell Morris, &c. Trans. of 11 pers: Jno. Smith, Avis Colling, Hen. Hicks, Anne Colling, Jno. Besle, Margt. Swaine, Roger Morris, Edwd. Richards, Tho. Cary, Tho. Charles, Henry Brodsha, Jno. Caddy, Xpher. Peckington; Maria a Negro.

JAMES LYLE, 156 acs., Henrico Co., Verina Par; on S. side of Chickahominy Riv; 20 Apr. 1687, p. 562. Adj. Francis Warren; on Ufnom Cr; &c. Trans. of —— pers.*

COL. DANIELL JENIFER, 3500 acs., on Assateag Island; Accomack Co; N. on *supposed* bounds bet. Va. & Maryland; 20 Apr. 1687, p. 563. Trans. of 70 pers.* *Note:* 60 rts. due by certificate granted by Mr. Edwd. Chilton 5 Nov. 1686; & 10 rts. parte of certif. granted by him, 8 May 1682.

ISAAC METCALFE, 100 acs., being all Sandy Island; Accomack Co; bet. Cedar Is. & Feckis Is., 20 Apr. 1687. p. 563. Trans of 2 pers.* *Note:* 2 rts. due by assignment of Col. Danll. Jenifer, being parte of certificate granted him 2 May 1682.

CAPT. JAMES BISS, 150 acs., Chas. City Co., 20 Apr. 1687, p. 564. Granted to Mr. Arthur Harwood, dec'd., & escheated by inquisition under Capt. Francis Page, Depty. Esch'r., &c.

MR. EDWIN THACKER, 1563 acs., Rappa. Co; S. side Rappa. Riv., bet. the maine Sw. of Piscataway Cr. & maine Sw. of Hoskins Cr., *but touching on neither;* 20 Apr. 1687, p. 564. Beg. on S. side the Rowling Path, adj. 5100 acs. granted Mr. Henry Awbery, 19 May 1677; along line of Vaughan; to James Tayler; on Jno. Evans; to John Medor, &c. Trans. of 32 pers: Robt. Bennet, Robt. Heading, Geo. Bullock, Samll. Coleham, Hugh Piper, James Grinvill, Jno. Billing, Mark Silly, Wm. Courtney, Tho. Hoblin, Jno. Dernam, Jno. Burgess, James Wry, Jno. Clarfield, Ridgby North, Peter Courtney, Richd. Prideaux, Charles Grill, Jonathan Lars, Richd.

Arundell, Jonas Rashley, Francis Buller, Jno. Elliott, Wm. Seawen, Wm. Cotten, Jno. Speckott, Humph. Noy, Tho. Robinson, Arthur Spry, Walter Kendall (or Hendall), Richd. Gibbs, Adam Ellis.

WILLIAM TIGNER, 750 acs., in Middlesex, formerly Lancaster, Co; S. side of Rappa. Riv., on E. side of Troublesome point Cr; adj. his own & *Tigner's Neck;* 20 Apr. 1687, p. 565. Granted to William Tigner, 4 Nov. 1656 & due, viz: 550 acs. granted to Richard Axome & Thomas Godwin, 22 May 1650 & purchased by Tigner; 200 acs. granted James Bonner, 15 Sept. 1651, & assigned to sd. Tigner.

MR. THOMAS PITT, 550 acs., Is. of Wight Co., 20 Apr. 1687, p. 566. Granted to Dorithy Sparks, dec'd. & found to escheate by inquisition under Maj. Samuell Swan, Depty. Eschr., &c.

HENERY GASKING, 100 acs., N'ampton Co., 20 Apr. 1687, p. 566. Granted to William Ganey, dec'd., & found to escheate by inquisition under Col. John Stringer, Esch'r., &c.

WILLIAM GASKING, 550 acs., N'ampton Co., 20 Apr. 1687, & page 566. Granted William Ganey, dec'd., escheated, &c., as above.

COL. PHILLIP LIGHTFOOT, 269 acs., Gloster Co., in Ware & Petsoe Parishes; 20 Apr. 1687, p. 567. Beg. at Col. John Cheesman, by Mr. William Hansford's path; in sight of Walter Gracewitt's plantation, & Robert Spinks' old feild; along John Burton; by Jonathan's Pond, &c. Trans. of 6 pers.*

MR. FRANCIS PETTITT, 150 acs., N'ampton Co., 20 Apr. 1687, p. 567. Granted to Edward Harrington, dec'd., & escheated by inquisition under Col. John Stringer, Esch'r., &c.

AMBROSE BENNET, 750 acs., Is. of Wight Co; upon the Lower Bay Cr., 8 Apr. 1641, p. 568. *(By Sir Francis Wyatt.)* Including a small island; a br. dividing this & land of Capt. Jno. Up-

ton; adj. Mr. Christopher Reinolds, &c. 350 acs. by assignment of patt. from Charles Barcraft, dated 10 Feb. 1637; 50 acs. by assignment of patt. from John Tayler, dated 22 ——— 1637; 350 acs. granted sd. Bennet 8 May 1638; 50 acs. for trans. of 1 pers.* Recorded 29 June 1687. Test: W E, Cl. G. Ct.

RALPH PEE, a parcell of land in Nanzemond Co., 20 Apr. 1687, p. 568. Granted to Henry Wilkenson, & conveyed to Joseph Exell, father to Elizabeth Green, dec'd., from whom it escheated by inquisition under Maj. Samuell Swan, Depty. Esch'r., &c.

MR. ROBERT RUFFIN, 422 acs., Surry Co., 20 Apr. 1687, p. 569. Granted to Mr. George Watkins; 105 acs. being part of patt. granted him 19 Oct. 1670; 317 acs. granted him 1 Mar. 1666, & escheated by inquisition under Capt. Wm. Randolph, Depty. Esch'r., &c.

MR. HENRY PRUETT & JOHN FIELD, 440 acs., Henrico Co., Virina Par; on N. side of James Riv., 20 Apr. 1687, p. 569. Beg. at Thomas Field's cor., on Almond's Cr; along Samll. Bridgwater; to Esqr. Place's line, &c. Trans. of 9 pers: Thomas Stephens, Wm. Gowry, Jno. Sampson, Wm. Cosby, Eliza. Gryer, Jane Ferne, Jno. Hubort, Anne Street, Porter Cranny.

MICHAELL TURPIN, 215 acs., Henrico Co., Virina Par; N. side James Riv., 20 Apr. 1687, p. 570. Beg. at Thomas Tayler; to maine br. of the Roundabout, in the fork; to Nicholas Perkins, &c. Trans. of 5 pers.*

THOMAS ILIFF, 300 acs., Low. Norf. Co., Lynhaven Par; towards the North River landing, upon a Cyprus Sw; adj. Morgan Jones; 20 Apr. 1687, p. 570. Trans. of 6 pers: Abraham Patch, Martha Patch, Simon Patch, Anne Patch, & 2 Indians.

MR. THOMAS SCOTT, 307 acs., Low. Norf. Co., Lynhaven Par., 20 Apr. 1687, p. 571. Adj. lands of Rouse; & Wm. Stafford. 100 acs. granted Martha

Rouse, 20 Sept. 1683, & sold to sd. Scott; 207 acs. for trans. of 5 pers; Thomas Scot, Thomas Scott; Sambo, Jno. & Maria, Negroes.

PETER CARTWRIGHT, 358 acs., Low. Norf. Co., on E. side of the S. br. of Eliz. Riv., 20 Apr. 1687, p. 571. Adj. Cornelius Ellis; John Whiddon; Mrs. Yates; Mr. Sayer; & by the Road to Doghartie's land formerly William Whithurst's; &c. Trans. of 7 pers: Peter Knight, Wm. Winston, Mary Barry, Edwd. Hayly, Jno. James, Eliza. Conniers, Jone Price.

MR. WILLIAM MALLORY, 3740 acs., New Kent Co., in *Pomunky Neck,* 20 Apr. 1687, p. 572. Surveyed by Col. Wm. Clayborne, ddec'd., for Capt. Roger Malory; beg. on Aquinton maine Sw. Run; to Nathaniell Barker's plantation; by the Ferry Path; by Mr. Woodward's path; crossing Nickattawance Sw; by George Slauter's plantation, in sight of Thomas Peaswhite (?) his plantation; to cor. of John Tabott & Mr. Samll. Ousteen, nigh the Ridge Path; to Mr. Randall; to land where Mr. Henry Maize liveth, &c. Trans. of 75 pers: Wm. Noble, Ja. Pye, Jer. Wilks, Est. Jones, Ad. Foster, Xpher. Milt, Jane Downes, Eliz. Adams, Jone Plant, Wm. Plant, Ed. Evans, 3 times; Wm. Long, Xpher. Jenkins, Elis or Eliz.) Hughes, Mary Winton, Eliza. Kelly, Richd. Downes, Abra. Reed, Wm. Coltman, Su. Crask, Ja. Kidd, 5 times; Ri. Hall, Wm. Lee, Chas. Rode, Ed. Price, Xpher. Ferrill, Ad. Jones, Evan Williams, John Colby, Wm. North, Ed. Fry, Abi (Abr.) Wells, Stephen Price, Roger Fleming, Wm. Hague, Richd. Dunbar, Mary Snow, Robt. Cotton, Wm. Allen, Jno. Deg, Ste. Tarleton, Moses James, Wm. James, Jno. Reed, Jno. Lee, Hugh Williams, Xpher. Thomas, Jno. Bell, Wm. Pullin, Hen. Snow, Ed. Row (?), Jno. Deines, Wm. Kelly, Kath. James, Roger Richards, Wm. James, Eliner Jeffreys, Adam Keines, Wm. Knot, Paul Cobb; Kate, Doll, Sue, Mingo, Tony, Ebel, Fly, Jeffrey: Negroes.

MR. BENJAMIN HARRYSON, 330 acs., adj. land whereon he lives; Up.

Par. of Surry Co., 20 Apr. 1687, p. 573. Above Thomas Cotton's br; on the easterne Spring Br., &c. Trans. of 7 pers: John Foord, Lancelot Plummer, Robt. Relph, Charles Alden, Phillip Poope, Jeffrey Pittman, Jno. Cricchell (or Crinkell).

JOHN SUMMERELL, 420 acs., Low. Par. of Is. of Wight Co; on brs. of the Blackwater; bet. lands of Gyles Limscot; Thomas Man, Wm. Mayo, Richard Booth, Bridgman Joyner & James Bryan; 20 Apr. 1687, p. 574. Trans. of 9 pers: Godfrey Davis, Simon Collier, Hugh Edwards, James Peacock, Tho. Blyth, Wm. Nash, James Hayes, Jno. Read, Jno. Howell.

JAMES ADKINSON, 216 acs., Up. Par. of Is. of Wight Co., on W. side of the 3rd Sw. of the Blackwater; 20 Apr. 1687, p. 574. Beg. ½ mi. from sd. Sw. in his *brother Thomas'* line; to the Doctors Br; cor. of John Sorjoarner's land; &c. Trans. of 5 pers: Andrew Bodkin, Wm. Kearne, Nicho. Haul, Richard Yeomons, Tho. Farmer.

JOHN REEKS, 320 acs., Chas. City Co., on NW side of Up. Chipoakes Cr; adj. Doctor Terry & Mr. John Good; 20 Apr. 1687, p. 575. Trans. of 7 pers: JohnKeys, Tho. Scot, Hen Clark, Alex. Snart (or Suart), Jno. Wednell, David Pikes, Ralph Haynes.

MR. EDWARD BAYLY, 220 acs., Up. Par. of Surry Co., on N. side of the Cyprus Sw., 20 Apr. 1687, p. 575. Adj. Mr. Christopher Foster; near Francis Soresby, on the middle Marsh.; by the White Marsh; to his own land, formerly Lt. Col. George Jordan's, &c. Trans. of 5 pers: David Scot, Luke Robinson.

HENRY HART, 285 acs., Surry Co; bet. 2 maine brs. of Crouche's Cr., 20 Apr. 1687, p. 576. 100 acs. part of 350 acs. granted to Henry Hart, his *Grandfather,* by the name of Piney Point, in 1635; 185 acs. adj; beg. on W. side of the Round Island Sw., cor. of Mr. Edward Pettaway; adj. Samll. Judkins & Mr. Edwards. Trans. of 4 pers: Henry

Reinold, Lettice Powell, Stephen Hartley, Kath. Langford.

MR. THOMAS MOORE, 1150 acs., Up. Par. of Is. of Wight Co., on the maine Blackwater Sw; adj. Mr. Christopher Holeman; 20 Apr. 1687, p. 576. Trans. of 23 pers: Jno. Chapman, Sarah Turner, Joseph Cheeseman, James White, Tobias Appleford, Tho. Rolfe, Jno. Carr, Wm. Redcross, Sarah Tanner, Tho. Battell, Jno. Rogers, Jone Rogers, Rich. Rogers, Tho. Short, Robert Webb, Tobias Stannup, Jane Ayres, Wm. Rutherford, Jone Mickleburrough, Roger Whitby, John Roberts, Rebecca Thompson Hester Brookes.

MR. THOMAS HUNT, JOHN FLOYD, EDMUND B I B B I E & GEORGE CLARK, 3350 acs., called *Hog Island* alias *Shooting Beach,* in N'ampton & Accomack Counties, 20 Apr. 1687, p. 577. S. on inlett bet. this & Prout's Is., N. on inlet bet. this & Feakes' Is., &c. 2200 acs. granted them 28 Sept. 1681; 1150 acs. adj., due for trans. of 23 pers: Jno. Henson, Wm. Seamour, Isaac Curtis, Jno. Blake, Rose Kelly, Tho. Walker, Wm. Aplugh, Geo. Clark, Mary Berry, Jasper Ellet, James Carpenter, Moor FitzGerald, Anne Ward, Jane Cassell, Susan Hyde, Ellinor Higbet, Richd. Morton, Hen. Sutton, Wm. Priston, Jno. Harris, Hen. Davis, Wm. Burdall, Anne Burrell.

JOHN POWELL & JOHN WARREN, 650 acs., on Rack Island, N'ampton Co., 20 Apr. 1687, p. 578. S. on inlet bet. this & Smith's Is; & N. on inlet bet. this & Prout's Is. Trans. of 13 pers: Wm. Smith, Jonathan Tatley, Hen. Allen, Fra. Burwell (or Barwell-, Abrah. Peuler (or Penler), Wm. Story, Anne Ewer, Agnes Powell, Jno. Price, Robt. Thompson, Wm. Batts, Edwd. Lacy.

JOHN FLOYD, 400 acs., on Prout's Is., N'ampton Co., 20 Apr. 1687, p. 578. The next island S. of Hog Is., & S. on inlet between this & Rack Is. Trans. of 8 pers: Wm. Tayler, Jane Moody, Tho. Adams, Richd. Pencomb, Henry Green, Eliza. Howard, Viven Staten (?), Jno. Donogh.

MR. SAMUELL SINGNALL, of York Co., in New Pocoson Par; 166 acs., adj. Mr. Henry Howard; by Denbye Roade; adj. Thomas Wooten; John Sandever; Isaac Collyer; William Wise; & Mathew Hubbert's plantation; 20 Apr. 1687, p. 579. Trans. of 4 pers: Joseph Potter, Mary Bley, Math. Hubbert, Mary Jones.

MR. THOMAS BOSWELL (Bozwell), 1100 acs., Gloster Co., Ware Par; on Ware River; adj. Maj. Robert Bristow; 20 Apr. 1687, p. 580. 972 acs. by patt., 8 Oct. 1656, & renewed 28 Jan. 1662; 128 acs. being overplus adj. trans. of 3 pers: John Penride, Richd. Twine, Jno. Sadler.

MR. SAMUELL DAWSON, 150 acs., Gloster Co., Ware Par; adj. Mr. Burch & Mr. Willis; 20 Apr. 1687, p. 580. 100 acs. by purchase, & 50 acs. for trans. of: Anne Potter.

THOMAS WILLIAMS, 175 acs., Middlesex Co; adj. land of Mr. Wadding or Col. Jno. Armsted; up Barbekue Cr., &c; 20 Apr. 1687, p. 581. 150 acs. granted to John Bell, 26 Feb. 1653 & sold to sd. Williams; 25 acs. overplus adj., for trans. of: Mary Lucas.

THOMAS THOMPSON, 140 acs., Middlesex Co., 20 Apr. 1687, p. 581. Adj. Wm. Beawmont, Thomas Williams, & Valentine Wallais; on the Shell branch, etc. Trans. of 3 pers: Jno. Baskerfield, Wm. Omry, Jno. Joseph.

MR. OSWALD CARY, (Carey), 460 acs., Middlesex Co., upon Pianketank Riv., 20 Apr. 1687, p. 582. Beg. att a Mulbery tree How ordered to be planted at SE cor. of *Timber Neck land,* now belonging to Ralph Wormeley, Esqr; adj. Mr. George Reeves; Thomas Hixon, Mr. Augustine Cant; & Andrew Williams. 250 acs. granted Capt. Wm. Brocas, 2 Feb. 1653; 210 acs. found to be King's land adj., & due for trans. of 5 pers: Thomas Evans, Wm. Ball, Jno. Head, Jno. Kiff, Eliza Ball.

JOHN SANDFORD, 94 acs., Middlesex Co., upon head of Miller's Cr.

20 Apr. 1687, p. 582. Adj. Mr. Kilby, on Cattaile Br; Mr. Kemp; & land of Miller. Trans. of 2 pers: Thomas Reynolds, Wm. Knibbs.

MR. THOMAS WYN (Wynn), 280 acs., Chas. City Co., in the Par. of Jordans; on S. side of James Riv., 20 Apr. 1687, p. 583. Adj. Mr. Joshua Wynn; on Balles Cr; to Mr. Adenton's line; on Mr. Poytheres; to Mr. Batts; &c. Trans. of 6 pers: Francis Hughes, Jno. Light, Wm. Gawrv, Edwd. Hughes, Jane Strangler, Wm. Forrest.

MR. ROBERT COLVERT, 375 acs. York Co., in New Pocoson Par.. 21 Oct. 1687, p. 383. 300 acs. pattented by Mr. Wm. Colvert, his father, 26 Jan. 1663; 75 acs. now taken, beg. at *the lone pine;* & adj. Mr. Henry Howard. Trans. of 2 pers.*

MR. THOMAS COCK, 721 acs., Low. Norf. Co., in Lynhaven Par: adj. lands of Land; Frizell; & Mr. West, on the pocoson side of West's Cr; 21 Oct. 1687, p. 584. Trans. of *15 pers:* Martha Wheeler, Samll. Smith, Walter Cock, 7 times; Edmund Cobbs, Thomas Cock.

CAPT. SAMUELL BLOMFIELD, 780 acs., Rappa. Co., on S. side of Rappa. Riv; adj. Thomas Wilkinson; 21 Oct. 1687, p. 584. Trans. of 16 pers: Ralph Creed, Grace his wife; Ellza, Magdalen & Jone. his daughters; Tho. Cary, Tho. Wall, Senr.. Tho. Wall, Junr.. Mary Sanders. Walter Clark, Ellis Waters, Tho. Johnson. Eliza. Morgan. John Jones, Lenard Ray.

MRS. ALICE HARLOW. 550 acs., Warwick Co; NE on Warwick Riv: SW on James Riv; on SE side of *the Common land.* NW on Mr. Jno. Brewer: from Bullen's point; passing house of Christopher Muschamp; including Poole's Island; 21 Oct. ——. p. 585. 200 acs. granted Anthony Elliott. 10 June 1643; 300 acs. granted Capt. Thomas Bernard, 24 Sept. 1645 & by Mr. John Harlow bequeathed to sd. Alice. his wyfe, & her heires.

MR. PHILLIP FISHER, 150 acs., being all Burnt Wood Island; Accomack Co; in Cheseapeak Bay, bet. mouth of Muddy Cr. & mouth af Messango Cr; 21 Oct. 1687, p. 585. Trans. of 3 pers: Wm. Hanson, Isaac Jones, John Dowman.

WILLIAM KIDD, 420 acs., Middlesex Co; on brs. of Burnham's Cr. & White Oake Sw., 21 Oct. 1687, p. 586. Beg. at Mr. Henry Thacker, neer br. of Draggon Sw., by 3 Springs; to Thomas Pattison, & Robert Chowning; by Mickleburrough's path; to Mr. Jno. Willis; to W. side of the maine Roade. Said land included within bounds of patt. to Robert Middleton, 16 Jan. 1658; granted to Thomas Kidd, his father, 15 Oct. 1663, for 250 acs; 170 acs. being overplus, &c. Trans. of 5 pers: Tho. Chowning, Svmon Nusum, Mary Colson, Alice Bornort.

MR. THOMAS HARRWOOD, 49 acs., York Co., in New Pocoson Par; at Pyny point, on New Pocoson River; up Oyster Cr., *alias* Laford's Cr., to mouth of Hayles Br; 21 Oct. 1687, p. 586. Trans. of: Francis Sudley.

JOHN SMITHER & MOTTROM WRIGHT, 395 acs., Gloster Co., 21 Oct. 1687, p. 587. Beg. by *"the five Shill. Dogwood;"* along John Deggs', in sight of Wright's plantation; to John Andrews' Sw., on N. side of *Winter Harbour;* to James Foster & Wm. Smitt's cor; through Wright's cornefield; to *little* John Andrews, plantation, *alias* Wright's; to Sw. of Muddy Run Br. Trans. of 8 pers.*

MR. HENRY SINGLETON, 155 acs., Gloster Co; bet. his own & patt. of his *brother,* Samuell; on Mobjack Bay; by Robt. Galles plantation; to Wm. Morgan; by Walter Morgan & John Martin; &c; 21 Oct. 1687, p. 588. Trans. of 3 pers: Edwd. Davis, Tho. Lewis, Mathew Brown, Anne Mathews.

JOHN BURTON, 31 acs., Gloster Co., in Petso Par; 21 Oct. 1687, p. 588. Beg. at Mr. Wm. Hansford & Mr. Ralph Green; to Mr. Benjamin Forcett-

& Mr. Wm. Haward; by the maine Roade to his plantation. Trans. of: Wm. Peircen.

JOHN ROBINSON, 351 acs., New Kent Co; on N. side of Chickahominy Sw; adj. Wm. Bassett & James Austen; on Beaver Dam Sw; 21 Oct. 1687, p. 589. Trans. of 8 pers: Jno. Ellis, Ed. Brenton, Wm. Harris, Jno. Charles, Wm. Okley, Eliza. Jones, James Harris, Jno. Moody.

JOHN PARKER, of *Mattopany*, 200 acs., in Accomack Co; neere mouth of Matchatank & Onancock Creeks; beg. at mouth of Pipemakers Cr; 21 Oct. 1687, p. 589. Trans. of 4 pers: Eliza. Morgan, Jno. Langsdaile, Ben. Eyres, Jno. Fox.

FRANCIS REDFORD, 775 acs., Henrico Co; N. side of James Riv., 21 Oct. 1687, p. 590. Beg. on N. side of one of the windings of a gr. slash or Sw. called the *Roundabout*, in Robert Sharp's line; to Tayler's cor; to sd. Redford's house; to land of Baker, &c. 630 acs. by patt., 1 July 1672, which was grounded on 2 former pattents, which lines enterfereing with adj. lands are now rectified; 145 acs. adj. due for Imp. of 3 pers: Susan Dale, Geo. Walker, Richd. Franklin.

MR. THOMAS CHRISTIAN, 1080 acs., Chas. City Co., Wayonoake Par; on S. side of Store's (or Stones) Run; adj. James Callum; along Bromfield's long br; crossing mouth of Black Gutt to Chickahominy Riv; 21 Oct. 1687. p. 591. 420 acs. purchased of Cornelius Loften, as appears by order dated 1 May 1684; 425 acs. for trans. of 9 pers: Roger Minshall, Wm. Club, Wm. Weaver. Thomas Collins, Adam Loftus, David Kennady, David Morgan, James Adam, Tho. Jones.

MR. JAMES MOORE, 420 acs., New Kent Co., in Stratton Major Par., 21 Oct. 1687, p. 592. On Mattassop maine Run or Sw; to mouth of Persimon Tree Br. Being surplus within bounds of patt. to Mr. Richard Major, Senr., dec'd., dated last of June 1656, & by

Richard, Junr., his son & heire, made over to sd. Moore, by an obligation, 21 June 1686. Trans. of 9 pers: Robert Burgess, Tho. Holmes, Grace Parker, Richard Roberts, Arnold Johnson, Jane Whitby, Thomas Mitchell, Wm. Ruffin, Jno. Johnson.

CAPT. WILLIAM CUSTIS, 36 acs., being all Coony Island, *alias* Cods Calfe Pasture; in Accomack Co; NW of the SW end of Cedar Island; 21 Oct. 1687, p. 592. Trans. of: James Burrell.

CHARLES LOVELL & ANDREW DAVIS, 1120 acs., New Kent Co., neer Chickahominy Sw., 21 Oct. 1687, p. 593. Beg. at land of John Guntin (Gunting) now Mr. Langsdale's; to Wm. Owen, on John Dickenson, to W. br. of Alder Sw; to Henry Wyat; up Goodlyhole Sw., to Mr. David Crafford, &c. Trans. of 23 pers: Edwd. Thomas, James Minge, Susan Bass, Hannah Bass, Eliza. Bass, Eliza. Bull, Alex. Bass, Tho. Hay, Ed. Jones, Ellin Gardner; Maria, Agbo, Bess, Setta, Chitta, Assa, Haniball, Mary, James, Mingo, a Negro boy, Cook, & a Child.

WILLIAM WINSTON, 266 acs., whereon he lives; part of patt. to Mr. Moses Davis; adj. John Lewis' plantation; Mr. Crafford; & land of George Phillips; 21 Oct. 1687, p. 594. Including land he purchased of Mr. David Crafford.

MR. HENRY HARTWELL, 1960 acs., Surry Co; bet. Gray's Cr. & Crouche's Cr., upon James Riv., 20 Apr. 1687, p. 595. Adj. Mr. Joseph Malden's 200 acs., formerly land of Jno. Twy, dec'd; Mr. Samll. Thompson, formerly Wm. Mills, dec'd; to Gilbert's landing; to Smith's Fort Landing; to Fishing Point; to Rockholepoint; on Lightwood Tree Sw; &c. Escheated by inquisition under Maj. Samll. Swan, Depty. Esch'r., &c. Trans. of 40 pers.* *Note:* 40 rts. by Mr. Edwd. Chilton's certificate dated 17 Sept. 1686.

JAMES TAYLER, 480 acs., Rappa. Co; adj. Mr. Henry Awbery, neer the Roade path to Piscaticon Cr; 21, Oct.

1687, p. 596. Granted to sd. Awbery, 3 Sept. 1669, deserted, & now granted by order, &c. Trans. of 10 pers: James Effells, Ratchell Pickles, Robert Downing, Anthony Humphreys, Sarah Fellows, Abra. Redcross, James Aliff, Robt. More, Thomas Jones; & Nando, a Negro.

MR. JOHN EVERETT, 162 A., 2 R., Henrico Co., on N. side of James Riv; Adj. Capt. John Knowles, on Cornelius Run; 21 Oct. 1687, p. 596. Granted to Rebecca Gyles, 26 Sept. 1678, deserted, & now granted by order, &c. Trans. of 4 pers: Alex. Robins, James Dudly, Jane Morgrove, Walter Allen.

CHARLES HAYES (Hay), 179 acs., named *Griffin's point;* on E. side of the North Riv; Low. Norf. Co., 21 Oct. 1687, p. 597. Adj. Col. Mason & Mr. Fowler. Granted to John Griffin, 9 Oct. 1675, deserted, & now granted by order, &c. Trans. of 4 pers: Jno. Williams, James Thredder, Wm. Montjoy, Alice Hayes.

MR. JOHN SOANE, 66 acs., Jas. City Co; on up. side of Pease hill Cr; beg. at Pease hill run at *Potters field devident;* 21 Oct. 1687, p. 597. Granted to Augustine Cobham, deserted, & now granted by order, &c. Trans. of 2 pers: James Harris, Wm. Lendell.

MR. LANCELOT BATHURST, 5000 acs., New Kent Co; S. side of Pomunky Riv., upon brs. of Crump's Cr., 21 Oct. 1687, p. 598. Adj. Moses Davis & Jno. Rea. Granted to George Gill, 20 Nov. 1682, deserted, & now granted by order, &c. Trans. of 100 pers: Jno. Price, Jno. Gunton, Jno. Kirkam, Wm. Dowers (?), Mary Capell, Dorcas Deane, Tho. Medston, Wm. Parker, Phill. Doell, Hen. Martin, Wm. Hansford, Jno. Deane, Wm. Ewder, James Crow, Adam Far, Wm. Fen, James Karr, Ed. Jeffreys, Wm. Winnick, Wm. Tanbret, Jno. Winit, Penelope Symonds, Tho. Hobson, Dorithy Greenwood, Rice Price, Frances Mathews, Ed. Hind, Robt. Johnson, Fra. Bayly, Hubbert Hansford. Eliza. Yates, Anne Rosmos. Wm. Eaton, Joshua Jones, Wm. Kenion, Adam Keele, Rebecca James, Wm. Firell, Ed. James,

Edmd. Conder, Kath. Symonds, Wm. Major, James Tayler, Roger Williams, Tobyas Jeffreys, Jno. Prator, Jno. White, Jno. Barker, Jno. Rackerses, Jno. Wistorly, Jos. Osborne, Jos. Billetor, Wm. Ford, Wm. Jordan, Wm. Bortlet, Lazarus Kemy, Eliza. Digby, Jone Hipdich, Edwd. Dabson, Susanah Cosbrook, Eliza. Digby, Jno. Powell, James Meeze (or Meere), Jno. Maddin, Ellin Jones, Abrah. Wicket, Dorithy James, David Condon, Peter Wilkins, James Scot, Wm. Seawell, Ed. Watts, Sarah James, Roger Kembrough, Stephen Penton (?), Wm. Winston, Charles Kemp, Gilbert Rawlins, Wm. Knight, Ralph Poe, Caleb Waggroft, Jarvis Peters, Xpher. Thomas & wyfe Elinor, Mildred Jones, Abrah. Duke, George Nickolls, Peter Ferne, Anne Davis, Jone Winter, Wm. Keith, Rebecca Macon, Xpher. Williams, Adam Jones, John Spauk (or Spank), Howell James, Wilmott Keith; & 3 Negroes.

RALPH WORMELEY, ESQR., 1500 acs., in the freshes & on S. side of Rappa. Riv., 21 Oct. 1687, p. 599. Granted to Henry Berry, who sold to John Barrow, 14 Mar. 1662, & confirmed by patt. 12 Oct. 1670; sold to George Jones, dec'd, of Rappa. Co., & escheated by inquisition under Col. Isaac Allerton, Esch'r. Genrll., &c; now granted by order, &c.

MR. JOHN LUKE, 400 acs., N'ampton Co., 21 Oct. 1687, p. 599. Granted to William Gayney & found to escheate by inquisition under Col. John Stringer, Esch'r. &c.

GEORGE WILLIAMS, 150 acs., adj. land he lives on; in Up. Par. of Surry Co; adj. Thomas Warren, Peter Deberry, & Richard Piland; 21 Oct. 1687, p. 600. Trans. of 3 pers: Robt. Austin, Jer. White, Ja. Richards.

MR. JAMES BLAIRE, Clerk, 453 acs., on N. side of James Riv., bet. E. br. & the maine br. of Cornelius Run; adj. Mr. Hatcher's line; Beauchamp's path, &c; 21 Oct. 1687, p. 600. 350 acs. granted to Mr. Benjamin Hatcher & Mr. John Milner, 30 May 1679, deserted, & now granted by order, &c;

103 acs. adj., for trans. of: James Urwin 10 times.

MR. ROBERT WOODSON, MR. RICHARD FERRES (FERRIS), MR. GILES CARTER, WM. FERRIS & ROGER CUMMINS, 1780 acs., Henrico Co., Verina Par; N. side of James Riv., at the White Oak Swamp; 21 Oct. 1687, p. 601. Beg. nigh Barr hill Br; crossing Deep Run; to John Wadson, &c. Trans. of 36 pers: Jno. Strong, Jno. Hicksoe, Geo. Swallow, Edmund Yernsher, Moses Reest, Patrick Robertson, Jno. Worth, Antho. Gant, Wm. Norris, Hanah Ellit, Hanah Deane, Danll. Walker, Tho. Adcock, Tho. Clark, Ed. Davehill, Eliza. Phips, Joane Wilks, Benja. Clarke, Jno. Marsh, Tho. Elliott, Mary Smith, Jno. Mole, Richd. Smith, Jno. Jackson, Jno. Finch, Cha. Lockey, Jno. Gower, Jonathan Cocks, Phill. Marshall, Mary Allen, Jno. Holmes, Elinor Bushell, Kath. Price, Cornelius Orts; Frank & Kate, Negroes.

MR. ROBT. WOODSON, SENR., MR. JOHN WOODSON, SENR., WM. LEWIS & THOMAS CHARLES, 470 acs., Henrico Co., Verina Par; on N. side of James Riv; 21 Oct. 1687, p. 602. Beg. neere the Colls. (Collonel's) Path *so called;* to Philemon Childers, on W. br. of the Deep Run; by Richard Ferres' line; & along Solomon Knibbs' line. Trans. of 10 pers: James Hayes, Roger Ingram, Wm. Bates, Ellinor Harris, James Wilcox, Rice Jones, Adam Tayler, Susan Hoyle, Rebecca Davis, Jane Adcock.

MR. ROBERT CURTIS, in right of his now wyfe Mary, 242 acs., York Co., in New Pocoson Par., on S. side of Cheesman's Cr; on head of Ling's Cr: 21 Oct. 1687, p. 602. Part of land conveyed by Col. John Cheesman, dec'd., to his br. Edmund, who bequeathed to Mary, dau. of sd. Cheesman, now wyfe to sd. Curtis.

MR. JOHN MOORING, 697 acs., Surry Co., 21 Oct. 1687, p. 603. Beg. at River Jordan's cor., along Thomas Jordan; crossing Reedy Br., to Thomas Gibbons' cor., &c. Trans. of 14 pers:

John Mooring, 2, his wyfe, Charles & John White, John Isaac, Tho. Fisher, Jno. Giddins, Jno. Broomwood, Eliza. Jenings, Jno. Attwood, John Oneale, Tho. James; Andrew, a Negro.

MR. RICHARD GREGORY, 850 acs., New Kent Co; N. side of Mattopany., 20 Apr. 1687, p. 604. Beg. at Mr. Watkins; to Mr. Richard Davis; on head of Brewerton's Br., &c. Granted to Phillip Watkins, Thomas Watkins & Wm. Ricketts, 6 Mar. 1673/4, deserted, & granted to Joshuah Story, 26 Apr. 1680, deserted; & now granted by order, &c. Trans. of 17 pers.*

MR. THO. WRIGHT, 300 acs., New Kent Co., in the freshes of Mattopany; beg. at Mr. John Ascough, on E. side of the Roade to William Morris' house; along Capt. Wm. Smith, &c; 21 Oct. 1687, p. 605. Trans. of 6 pers: Ed. Clark, Phillip Allman, Mary Swan, Sarah Clark, Wm. Allerton, Mary Burks (?).

JOSHUAH STAPP, 277 acs., Henrico Co., Verina Par; on N. side of James Riv., beginning on Shockhow Creek; 21 Oct. 1687, p. 605. Trans. of 6 pers: Thomas Ellis, Wm. Pulman, Elinor Thacket, Mary Shans, Edwd. Dennis, Ellin Jones.

JAMES DOUGHTY, 180 acs., on N. side of the Black Sw., in the Up. Par. of Nansemond; beg. at the mouth of Mamtopps Cabbin Branch; 21 Oct. 1667, p. 606. Trans. of 4 pers: Robt. Thomason, James Sanders, Jere. Whitby, Jane Robins.

EPAPHRODITUS BENTON, 200 acs., in Up. Par. of Nansamond; on the Cross Sw., 21 Oct. 1687, p. 606. Trans. of 4 pers: Sarah Moody, Jno. Travers, James Robins; Kate a Negro.

GRESHAM COPHELL, 360 acs., in Up. Par. of Nansamond; neare head of Holliday's Cr; by Elwood's land; neare head of the Gleab Cr. & by Nansamond River, &c; 21 Oct. 1687, p. 606. 200 acs. granted to his father, 20 July 1640; 160 acs. overplus, due for trans. of 4 pers: Robt. Evans, James Denton, Samll. Reade, Jone Avery.

THOMAS GOUGHF (Gough), 350 acs., at *Summerton;* in the Up. Par. of Nansamond; adj. John Odium; 21 Oct. 1687, p. 607. 200 acs. granted Thomas Brooks, 2 June 1673 & now in possession of sd. Goughf; 150 acs. overplus, due for trans. of 3 pers: James Rachelson, Robert Wood, Thomas Todd.

WILLIAM HOWELL, 550 acs., at *Summerton;* in the Up. Par. of Nansamond; at mouth of the Back Sw., adj. John Nash; 21 Oct. 1687, p. 607. Trans. of 11 pers: James Johnson, Jno. Thomas, Ralph Weston (or Waters), Jno. Ratcliffe, James Thornhill, Andrew Rider, Thomas Dodson, Richard Wheelehouse, Ann James, Thomas Roberts, Sarah Butler.

SAMUELL WATSON, 180 acs., at *Summerton;* in the Up. Par. of Nansamond; at the Black Sw., adj. Wm. Howell; 21 Oct. 1687, p. 608. Trans. of 4 pers: James Moony, Sarah Howard, Patrick Jolliffe, Abraham Moore.

SAMPSON MERIDITH, 440 acs., in the Up. Par. of Nansamond; on the Back Sw., adj. Thomas Jernagan; 21 Oct. 1687, p. 608. Trans. of 9 pers: James Jaquis, Tho. Roberts, Sarah Nelson, Abraham James, Robt. Wilde, James Huby; Sam, Kate & Bess, Negroes.

PETER FEBUS, JUNR., 200 acs., at *Saram;* in the Up. Par. of Nansamond; on Saram Sw; 21 Oct. 1687, p. 609. Trans. of 4 pers: Samll. Richardson, Wm. James, Sarah Rubtrtson; & Kate a Negro.

JOHN NASH, 400 acs., at *Summerton,* in the Up. Par. of Nansamond; adj. Richard Green; on the Bryery Br; & Summerton Sw; 21 Oct. 1687, p. 609. Trans. of 8 pers: Wm. Jones, Tho. Harris, Robert Thompson, Jane Ayres, Sarah Welch, James Bennet, Jonas Reeves, Jno. Bagnall.

MR. PETER FIELD, 483 acs., Henrico Co; on S. side of Swift, Cr., above

Mr. Francis Epes; 21 Oct. 1687, p. 610. Imp. of 10 pers: James Faulchon, (?), Wm. Evans, Edwd. Pargeter, Owen Mackinro, Danll. Mathews, Mary Levet; Tony, Pompey, Mingo, Doll, Negroes.

SAMUELL FOWLER, JUNR., 750 acs., Henrico Co., in Varina Par; N. side of Appamattock Riv; at the Ashen Swamp; 21 Oct. 1687, p. 611. Beg. at Willm. Ligon & Richd. Ligon; along Mr. Robert Hancock, to Powhatan Path, &c. Imp. of 15 pers: Samli. Fowler, & his wyfe, Samll. Fowler, Junr., Eliza. Fowler, Wm. Jacob, Rebecca Jones, Adam Williams, Robert Fisher, Wm. Roe, Xpher. Chant, Roger Demox, Wm. Griffin, Rachell Harris, Wm. Daines, Eliza. Rogers.

JOHN SMITH, of Rappa. Co., 634 acs., according to bounds of patt. granted him 19 Nov. 1663 for 473 acs; the bounds includ. 161 acs. more than expressed in sd. patt; beg. at a br. dividing this & land of James Merritt; by Mr. Andrew Gilson; by Gonges path; to land he lives on; 21 Oct. 1687, p. 612. Trans. of 4 pers: Tho. Hamond, Barth. Meriat, John Pemble, John Jeffreys.

ARTHUR OWNBEE, of Rappa. Co., 78 acs., on S. side the river; cor. to the Orphts. of Tymothy Bell, on N. side of Coleman's Cr., nigh Wm. Veale; & land of Maj. Hawkins; 21 Oct. 1687, p. 612. Trans. of 2 pers: Geo. Smith & Teague, an Irish boy.

THOMAS BLANTON, 266 acs., Rappa. Co; on the maine Pocoson, & brs. of Jelson's Cr., 21 Apr. 1687, p. 613. At the head of Beach Cr., in line of Francis Graves, cor. to his own 200 acs., ranted 20 Apr. 1682; along Henry Tandy; to Maj. Robt. Beverley, &c. Trans. of 6 pers: Dorby, an Irish boy; Jno. Grove, Susan Kinsman, Anne Cumber, Eliza. Richards, Xtian. Sherbrooke.

MR. THO. PITT, 550 acs., Is. of Wight Co., 20 Apr. 1687, p. 614. Part of 750 acs. granted to John Sparks, 3 June 1635, which escheated from Dorithy Sparks, his dau. & heiress, by inquisition under Maj. Samuell Swan, Depty. Esch'r., &c.

CAPT. EDMUND BACON, 243 acs. in the up. part of New Kent Co., next below *North Wales devident,* on Pomunky River; 21 Oct. 1687, p. 614. Trans. of 5 pers: Tho. Bacon, Anne Lyddall, Kath. Davis, Nathl. Smith, George Pargetor.

MAJOR CHARLES SCARBURGH, 30 acs., Accomack Co; called Scarburgh's Winter Island; on N. side of the mouth of Pungateage Cr; 21 Oct. 1687, p. 615. Trans. of: Rowland Pew.

HUGH MONTGOMERY, 250 acs. Low. Norf. Co., in Eliz. River Par; upon Tanner's Cr., 21 Oct. 1687, p. 615. 200 acs. upon Capt. Thomas Fulcher & adj. Robert Woody; 50 acs. adj., & upon Sandy point. Granted to Lawrence Phillips, who bequeathed to his son William, who sold to Edward Weilder (Wilder), who sold to John Wood, who bequeathed to sd. Montgomery.

WALTER CLOTWORTHY, 1075 A., 25½ P., upon the run & brs. of Branch's brook & the back of Col. Wm. Byrd's land at Falling Creek; 21 Oct. 1687, p. 616. Trans. of 22 pers: John Champion, Willm. Ellis, Jane Willis, Tho. Guanto, Wm. Aldus, John Crabb, Francis Crabb, James Amos, Francis Crabb, Samll. Temple, Anne How, John Clements, Tho. Goulebirg, John Elson, Richd. Cook, Robt. Spicer, Will A'dis (Aldis ?), Samll. Swanson, Eliza. Askew, Robert Jarmin, Theod. Bland; & Jack a Negro. (Marginal Note: "posted thus far and Seale charged thus far.")

HUGH BAWDEN, 160 acs., New Kent Co; on brs. of Arraicacoe Cr., 20 Apr. 1687, p. 617. Beg. at Mr. Samuell Clayton; crosse the Rowling Path, to Capt. Lane; on Lewis Waldin; to Capt. William Jones. Granted to Lewes Walden & George Martyn, 22 Sept. 1682, deserted, & now granted by order, &c. Trans. of 4 pers: Florentine Paine, Jno. Greenfield, Robt. Gilford, Grace Lovell.

MR. RICHARD GREGORY, 460 acs., New Kent Co; bet. Mr. John Robinson, the land of Samuell Patridge, dec'd. & Capt. John Lane; beg. at Middlesex Path; 21 Oct. 1687, p. 617. Granted to Lewis Waldin & George Martyn, 22 Sept. 1682, deserted, & now due by order, &c. Trans. of 10 pers.*

PETER KEMPE, 638 acs., Gloster Co; S. side of Poyanketanke Riv., bet. Allen's Cr. & Wadeing Cr; neare head of the Sw. supposed to be the Indian Lyne, parting this & land of Thomas Amee; 21 Oct. 1687, p. 618. Leased to Col. Mathew Kempe, Esqr., dec'd., under the hands of the King of Cheesecake & his great men, 16 Oct. 1671 & recorded in Gloster Ct; surveyed by Lawrence Smyth by order of the Gov'r. & Counsell held at *Greene Spring,* 22 May 1683. Trans. of 13 pers: Wm. Newton, Tho. Mugg, Robt. Newhouse (or Merrhouse), David Davis; Tony, Murrah, Patch, Robin, Goliah, Will, George, Samboy, Betty, Negroes.

HUGH BAWDEN, 590 acs., New Kent Co., in St. Stephen's Par., 21 Oct. 1687, p. 619. Adj. land that was John Robert's; beg. at Sawyer's cor; down the Miery Br; up Timber Br; to Burford's cor; to Wells & Read's lynes, &c. Granted to Bartholomew Ramsey, 20 Apr. 1680, deserted, & now granted by order, &c. Trans. of 12 pers: Margt. Haseldine, Fra. Smith, Jno. Buker, Rich. Ford, Wm. Betts, Robt. Casleton, Fra. Roberts, Tho. Taylor, Wm. Todd, Tho. Herbert, Jno. Hilliard, Mark Metherock.

SAME. 400 acs., same Co., Parish, date & page. Beg. at Col. William Clayborne's land called *Best Land;* to Gyles Rogers; over the King's Roade, & adj. land on which formerly John Symons' father lived. Granted to John Symmons, 20 Sept. 1683, deserted, & granted to William Morris by order; & assigned to sd. Bawden. Trans. of 8 pers: Tho. Newman, Susanna Newman, Ann Jones, Robert Mason, Fra. Holland, Eliz. Cook, Jno. Barnes, Michll. Dunington.

SAME. 134 acs., same Co. & date, p. 620. Beg. at forke of a br. of Exall Br. Granted to Gabriell Hill, 29 Nov. 1665, deserted, & now granted by order, &c. Trans. of 3 pers: Wm. Browne, Stephen Reade, Rich. Paget.

SAME. 629 acs., in Rappa. Co; same date & page. Beg. at Mr. Joseph Goodrich, by Thomas Harper's lyne, on head of Mossy Br; on Col. Hill's land; by the Indian Path; along lyne supposed to be John Jones', by Wilson's Path, &c. Granted to Mr. Joseph Goodrich, William Ball & John Price 21 Oct. 1684, deserted, & now granted by order &c., for trans. of 13 pers: Wm. Renolds, Ann Renolds, Wm. Jones, James Harry, Tho. Williams, Wm. Roberts, Ann Mason, Robt. Harrison, Rich. Evans, Tho. Steede, Joan Smith, Ann Palmer, Rob. Redliffe.

ROBERT HARRIS, 135 acs., in Yorke Co. & Par., 21 Oct. 1687, p. 621. Beg. on a br. of Brockas Sw; along land now or late of Bryan Kenady; of Maj. Bauldry; & of Edward Baptist, &c. Trans. of 3 pers: James Ely, Samll. Robins, Mary Elsmore.

WILLIAM WALLAIS (Wallice), 280 acs., Middlesex Co., 21 Oct. 1687, p. 621. Adj. William Beaumont, Patricke Miller, Rowland Mackrorie, & near the dwelling house of Valentine Wallais, his dec'd. father; by Holly Bush Cr., &c. Trans. of 6 pers: Anne Wallis, twice; Jane Wallis, Edward Allen, Anne Parker, Wm. Willis.

PHILLIP MAY & THOMAS POTTS (or Petts), of Glocester Co., 376 acs., in Rappa. Co; on brs. Gelson's run & Hoskins (Cr.), 21 Oct. 1687, p. 622. Beg. at an Indian Path ¾ of a mile from John Roberts, &c. Trans. of 8 pers: Wm. Byfield, Wm. Braggart, John Roberts, Jane Rolland (or Roeland), Tho. Leery (or Leevy), Geo. Salter, Jane Midmore, Eliza. Adkins, Jno. Dixon.

RICHARD HILL & WILLIAM BAYLY, 264 acs., Warwick Co; neer head of the Black Sw., adj. Capt.

Martin; Mr. Robt. Read; & Mr. Thomas Cheesman, 21 Oct. 1687, p. 622. Trans. of 6 pers: Jno. Meade, Susan Meade, Mary Meade, Paul Meade, Tho. Sykes, Edmund Bellison.

MR. THOMAS PALLISSER, 421 acs., Gloster Co., Kingston Par; S. side of Pyanketank Riv., 21 Oct. 1687, p. 623. Beg. at land of Mr. Gilbert Metcalfe, dec'd; adj. George Curtis; Col. Kemp; John Waters; land of Mr. William Elliott, dec'd., neer a great path upon the Ridge; to Col. John Armestead, &c. Trans. of 9 pers.* Note: 9 persons of a certificate granted Mr. Palliser by Mr. Ed. Chilton dated —— Nov. 1684 was made use of to this pattent.

MARTHA HARDING, sister and heire of JOHN BULLEN & now wife of William Harding; 333 acs. in Rappa. Co., upon Piscataway Cr., 21 Oct. 1687, p. 624. Beg. at land formerly Daniell Batts, now Robert King's; to Thomas Greene, by Richard Holt's house, &c. 250 acs. granted unto John Bullen, as sonne & heire of Rebecca Capell, 26 Mar. 1664; 83 acs. for trans. of 2 pers.*

JOHN WALKER, 560 acs., New Kent Co; on N. side of Matapany Riv., 21 Oct. 1687, p. 624. Beg. at Lt. Col. Thomas Walker; to Mr. John Starke in Jones' Meadow, on John Adkins; close to William & Thomas Camp's land; adj. Sylvester Alsworth, & Robert Spencer; on Tommacorican maine Sw. &c. Trans. of 12 pers: Samuell Acton, John Jones, Richd. Sick, Alexander Mackdonell, Richd. Gill, Richard Sargeant, Owen Jones, Wm. Wildsmith, Kath. Willis, Susanah Willis, Dorithy Willis, Rachell Aldberry.

JAMES TAYLOR, of New Kent Co., 744 acs., Rappa. Co; S. side of Rappa. Riv., 21 Oct. 1687, p. 625. 480 acs. granted to Mr. Henry Abery, who sold to Mr. Robert Bishopp, who bequeathed to John Gregory, who gave to his sister Mary, now wife of sd. James Taylor; sd. land in danger of being lost was petitioned for by sd. Taylor the 1st day of the last Genrll. Court—15 Apr. 1687 —& granted by the Gov'r. &c; beg. by the Indian Path alias Mr. Abrey's path;

to forke of Gregory's Cr; on Richard Gregory's lyne, in sight of John Gatewood's plantation; to the Rowleing Roade &c. 246 acs. for trans. of 5 pers: James Tayler, Hannah Martin, Robert Jones, Ursula Collis, Hannah Collier.

JNO. PORTLOCKE, 490 acs., Low. Norf. Co., on E. side of the S. br. of Eliz. Riv; on N. side of Gater's Cr.. 21 Oct. 1687, p. 625. Adj. Marmaduke Marrington. 200 acs. granted Jno. Manning, 25 Oct. 1648, & by severall deeds came due to Mathew Shippe, who assigned to sd. Portlocke, with 290 acs. more; 200 acs. by survey dated 24 Nov. 1685, beg. at Gater's Cr; to Hollowing Point Cr; to Cornelius Ellis, &c; trans. of 6 pers: Jonah Flowers, Robert Lasingby (or Lazingby), Oliver Barbican, Timothy Rowland, Robt. Whaley, Tho. Mercer.

JOHN ALEXANDER, 400 acs., Low. Norf. Co; on N. side of a br. of the S. br. of Eliz. Riv., called Gater's Cr., 21 Oct. 1687, p. 626. Granted Thomas Alexander, 27 Sept. 1665, & due sd. John as sonn & heir.

MR. JOHN GODFREE (Godfrey), 2650 acs., Low. Norf. Co; on brs. of Cypresse Sw., at head of Northwest River; adj. Henry Butts; a br. dividing this & James Willson; on the Green Sea, &c; 21 Oct. 1687, p. 627. Trans. of 53 pers: Margaret Malins, Edward Mostee, James Heyton, Jno. Long, Sarah Carter, Judith Smith (?), Richd. Dicks, Jno. Washford, Edger (?) Glascock, Thomas Standard, Miles Fortescue, Abigall Barnhouse, James Scott, Timo. Campion, Wm. Bolton, Jno. Davis, Wm. Appleyard, Francis Argoe, Tho. Rogers, Jno. Woodard, Elizabeth Duck, Jno. Bush, Tho. Boys, Herbert Powell, Jno. Mauriss (or Mauriff), Jno. Amory, Katherine Mathews, Nathan Abiram, Ben. Browne, Wm. Heafield, Tho. Cooper, Tho. Smith, Jone Bryant, Tho. Morley, Eliz. Taylor, Martha Wont, Tho. Billington; Besse, George, Maria, Guy, Bash, Gambo, Black Will, Black Harry, Tom, Tony, Tom, Besse, Franck, Toby, Nan, Gage—Negroes.

ALICE PETERS, 698 acs., Low. Norf. Co., 21 Oct. 1687, p. 628. Granted to Alice Peters, wyfe of Symon Peters, 12 June 1676, & found to escheate by inquisition under Phillip Howard, Depty. Esch'r., &c.

MR. WM. LEAKE, 114 acs. Rappa. Co., neer Piscaticon Cr., 21 Oct. 1687, p. 628. Beg. at James Baughan, on Clay patch Br; by plantation of the Widdow Baughan; adj. Mr. Samll. Perry; his own, & land of John Jones. Trans. of 3 pers: James Ellerly, Grace James, John Hugate.

MILES & RICHARD LEWIS**, 400 acs., Nanzeond Co., in Chuckatuck Par., 29 Jan. 1667, p. 629. (By Sir Wm. Berkeley.) Adj. lands of Thomas Jorden; & Jeremy Rutter; on the White Marsh. Trans. of 8 pers.* (Record incomplete). Phill. Ludwell, Clk. Recorded by order of the Genll. Court dated 19 Oct. 1687 Test W. Edwards, Cl. Gen. Ct. Phill. Ludwell, Clk. Sec. Office. (**Probably sons of Richard Lewis, dec'd.).

DANIELL LANE, 300 acs., Low. Norf. Co., in Corrotuck precinques; on E. side of the North River; 21 Oct. 1687, p. 629. Adj. Richard Draper; & Capt. John Gibbs. Trans. of 6 pers: George Purle, Wm. Oneale, Jno. Pennistone, Jane Lloyd; Ned, & Mall, Indians.

MR. PATRICK WHITE, 400 acs., Low. Norf. Co., on N. side of a gr. Cypresse Sw. of Sympson's Cr; adj. Evan Jones; 21 Oct. 1687, p. 630. Trans. of 8 pers: Sambo, Boke, Hannah, Will, Maria, Besse, Negroes.

MR. EVAN JONES, 200 acs., Low. Norf. Co., on NE side of a gr. Cypresse Sw. of Sympson's Cr; 21 Oct. 1687, p. 630. Trans. of 4 pers.*

CAPT. JOHN GIBBS, Esqr., 3100 acs., Low. Norf. Co; in Corretuck precincts; being his seated plantation; 21 Oct. 1687, p. 630. Beg. at land he bought of Jasper Lane; to mouth of the N. W. river; including Sampson's

Island, SW from his house; to mouth of the Reedy Br., dividing this & land of Capt. Willoughby, now in the tenure of Christopher Marchant; to John Elks; & Capell's cor; to Francis Jones, &c. 640 acs. granted to Jasper Lane, 21 Oct. 1684 & assigned to sd. Gibbs; 2460 acs. for trans. of 49 pers: Dan. Lane, Jno. Wood, Tho. George, Jno. Neale, Jno. Russell, Jno. Russell, Junr., Hester Lane, Hannah Russell, Jasper Lane, Elizab. Lane, Sarah Lane, Margaret Lane, Francis Nash, Eliza. Nash, Mary Nicholson, Thomas Love (?), Capt. Jno. Gibbs, Madam Eliz. Gibbs, Mr. Jno. Gibbs, Junr., Mr. Henry Gibbs, Miss Gibbs, Mrs. Sarah Bond, Mrs. Cradock, Senr., Eliz. Cradock, Junr., George Wolfe, Eliz. Wolfe, —— Williams, —— Williams, Jno. Tyler, Geo. Warlington, Batt. Shephard, Sarah Shephard, Steven Vincent, Wm. Paul, Joseph Fox, Jno. Barber, William Sedgley, Jno. Paine, Tho. Brothwayt, Jno. Read, Mathew Prier, Jno. White, Jacob Field, Jno. Buck, Elizabeth Love, Alice Parker & her child, Ann Aldridge, Ann Russell.

RICHARD DRAPER, 300 acs., Low. Norf. Co., in *Corrotuck Precinques:* on E. side of the North Riv; adj. Robert Swayne; & Daniell Lane; 21 Oct. 1687, p. 631. Trans. of 6 pers.*

HENRY SOUTHEN, 241 acs., Low. Norf. Co., in *Corretuck Precinaues;* N. from the Blackwater; adj. Whittford & Hea (?) (Heath ?); 21 Oct. 1687, p. 631. Trans. of 5 pers.*

JAMES HEATH, 550 acs., Low. Norf. Co., in *Corretuck Precinques;* on E. side of the North Riv; adj. Joseph Chase; on the Back Bay; 21 Oct. 1687, p. 631. Trans. of 11 pers: Wm. Harris, Jno. English, Mary Neale, Patrick Pollick, Anne Harris, James Hollvday, Martin Cob, Matthew Madder, Mary Britt, Elizabeth Glascott, Rachel Rewings (?).

CAPT. JOHN GIBBS, ESQR., 300 acs. Low. Norf. Co., in *Corrotuck Precincts:* being a seated plantation he purchased of *Black Charles:* adj. James Heath; neare the Back Bay; adj. Mr.

Thomas Jackson & Daniell Lane; 21 Oct. 1687, p. 632. Trans. of 6 pers: Elizabeth Avery, & Barbary Seward; Tony, Peter, Maria, Robin, Negroes.

HENRY BEACHER, 372 acs., Yow. Norf. Co., in *Corrotuck Precincts;* 21 Oct. 1687, p. 632. Beg. neare the Pocoson of the North Riv; to Henry Southen; to Thomas Tooly, neare Blackwater River. Trans. of 7 pers: Richard Bray 4 times; Nell, Sarah, James— Negroes.

DANIELL CAINE, 137 acs., Low. Norf. Co., in *Corrotuck Precincts;* called *Long Acre;* N. of the Black Water; adj. Whittford & Southen; 21 Oct. 1687, p. 632. Trans. of 3 pers.* *Note:* 3 Rts. out of certificate granted Jno. Ferrebee, for 50 Rts. by Mr. Edwd. Chilton, dated May 29, 1686.

ROBERT SWAINE, 300 acs., Low. Norf. Co., in *Corrotuck Precincts;* adj. Richard Draper, the North River & crossing Bonden's (or Bouden's) Cr; 21 Oct. 1687, p. 632. Trans. of 6 pers: Mordecai Bouden (or Bonden), Thomas Tooley & his wife, Tho. Tooley, Junr., Jno. Tooley, Elizabeth Tooley.

THOMAS TAYLOR, Planter, 1053 acs., Henrico Co., at *Harahadocks* (Harahadox): N. side of James Riv., 21 Oct. 1687, p. 633. Beg. on the river, a little below the Orchard; by land now, or late, John Cox's; along path to 4 Mi. Cr; over the Roundabout Sw; to land now or late Francis Redford's; to Burton & Taylor's river land; to Harahadox Cr. mouth, at the river, &c. 631 acs. due Thomas Taylor (the *uncle,* late dec'd.) by patt., 23 Sept. & descended to the abovenamed Thomas; 422 acs. lying parte within & parte contiguous to sd. 631 acs; due the *Nephew* Thomas for trans. of 9 pers: George, Dick; Thomas Lawrence; Ctsar, Guy, Abasse; George Cooke; one child Maria. *Marginal Note:* "Fees & Seale Charged."

WILLIAM WHITTINGTON, 250 acs., Chas. City Co., Bristoll Par; on S. side of the N'most Black Water; 23

Apr. 1688, p. 633. Adj. John Golightly; & Isaack Colson. Trans. of 5 pers: James Tuthill, Geo. Bass, Xpher. Adeer, Math. Roope, Tho. Gotham.

STEPHEN BENBRIDGE, of Rappa. Co., & MR. THOMAS TODD, of Gloucester Co., 333 acs., in New Kent Co., 23 Apr. 1688, p. 634. Beg. close to the Indian Path; by Goodrich's lyne over a br. of the maine br. of Mattapany Run; to the Indians' Land; by Stephen West, &c. Trans. of 7 pers: James Hays, Edwd. Mosier, Jno. Hide, Rebecka Caves (or Canes); Jack & Tony, Negroes.

STEPHEN BENBRIDGE, 238 acs., New Kent Co., 23 Apr. 1688, p. 634. Beg. at Mr. Joseph Goodrich & John Coleman on a Br. of Assaway Mansecock Sw; to *good ground* supposed to belong to Mr. Brereton; close to the Broad Br., &c. Trans. of 5 pers.*

MR. JOHN HESTERLEY & MOSES GODING, joyntly, 350 acs., New Kent Co., on N. side of Mattapony Riv., 23 Apr. 1688, p. 634. Granted to John Pigg about 23 yrs. since, by him sold, & since lapsed, & now again taken; beg. at Mr. Edward Lockey; by Drumrite's branches; to hill in sight of William Gandy's Plantation; by br. of Horecock Sw., &c. Trans. of 7 pers: Robt. Ridge, Jno. Wood, Charles Copper, Moses Vilet (?), Isaac Stone, Margaret Jenkins, Robt. Glascock.

MR. BENJAMIN ARNOLD, 1754 acs., New Kent Co; N. side of Mattapony Riv., 23 Apr. 1688, p. 635. 1050 acs. granted to Capt —— Taylow, & sold to Anthony Arnold, dec'd; 704 acs. beg. below the Mill Cr. as near the river as could be; in sight of William Nicholls' Plantation; by John Pigg; in sight of Daniel Coleman's Plantation, to Peck's Hill, by William & Thomas Campe; over the Mill Cr; &c. Trans. of 15 pers: Jack, Nell, Quow, Cromwell, George, Mathew, Joe, Tom, Barows, Mingo, Jack, Peter, Robin, Sue, Jenny, Jasper.

JOHN ECKHOLLS, 321 acs., New Kent Co., on N. side of Mattapony Riv.,

23 Apr. 1688, p. 635. Beg. by Capt. William Smyth's Landing path; along Moody's lyne; to the White Oake Sw; to John Joy by an Indian Path; by John Dunklev, &c. Trans. of 7 pers: Samuell Randoll, John London, John Courteney, Thomas Gardener, William Smithson, Deborah Marshall, Daniell Newman.

ROBERT ROSE, 185 acs. Low. Norf., Co; neare head of the Clerkes Cr., a br. of the W. Br. of Eliz. Riv; 23 Apr. 1688, p. 636. Beg. neare the path in the lyne of White's patt; up the maine Roade on Browne's land; to Capt. John Hatton, & adj. 200 acs. he purchased of John White, &c. Trans. of 4 pers: Thomas Whitlock, Thomas Morgasa, Robt. Penn, Richard Newell.

JAMES ALLEN (Allyn), 230 acs., Is. of Wight Co., on W. side of Beavor Dam Sw., 23 Apr. 1688, p. 636. Trans. of 5 pers: Jno. Smith, Robert Withers, Luke Dunfeild, Jno. Hinshaw, Tho. Herbertson.

ROBERT THOMPSON, 390 acs., Henrico Co; S. side of James Riv., bet. Branch's Brooke & Spring Run; 23 Apr. 1688, p. 636. Trans. of 8 pers: Jeremiah Williams, Edwd. Streeter, Wm. Fry, James Alley, Ellin Mayre, Patrick James, Wm. Marsh, Ester Flint.

SYMON STUBLEFEELD, Junr., 188 acs., Gloster Co., Ware Par., 23 Apr. 1688, p. 637. Beg. by the Roade to the *Court House,* at head of land of William Roe, dec'd; along the *Gleab land,* to Mr. Richard Whitehead, by Mr. Thomas Cheeseman to land formerly James Whitlock's. Trans. of 4 pers: John White, William Brinton (?), Thomas Brush, & Jasper a Negro.

HENRY PEWE (Pew), 411 acs., on N. side of James Riv., bet. the brs. & maine run of 4 Mi. Cr., 23 Apr. 1688, p. 637. Beg. by a slash of Lemman's Br; over Beauchamp's Path, &c. Trans. of 9 pers: Wm. Sanders, John Paine, Otho. Hughes, Wm. James, Rebecca Hughes, Edward Sanders, John Emerson, Wm. Floyd, John Edger.

MR. HENRY NICHOLLS, Junr., 55 acs., Middlesex Co; adj. Mr. Randolph

Seger; John Blewford; Mr. Henry Nicholls, Senr; & Mr. Robert Chowning; 23 Apr. 1688, p. 637. Trans. of 2 pers: Rich. Balbie, Jno. Ralph.

HUGH BAWDEN, 727 acs., New Kent Co., 21 Oct. 1687, p. 638. 661 acs. on a br. of Dragon Sw; 66 acs. by Gabriell Hill's house; adj. land sd. Hill purchased of James Cole & now liveth upon. Granted sd. Hill, 29 Nov. 1665, deserted, & now granted by order, &c. Trans. of 15 pers: Jno. Newman, Robt. Owen, Jno. Edmonds, Ann Hart, James Welch, Sarah Clifthell, Jno. Roberts, Alex. Dodman, Math. Holmes, Edwd. Richards, Ruth Hoskins, Mary Ricketts, Hen. Alllen, Robert Mason, Edmond Poole.

MR. JOHN WOODSON, Senr., 1850 acs., Henrico Co., Verina Par; S. side of Chickahominy Riv; 23 Apr. 1688, p. 639. Trans. of 37 pers: Robert Jarret, Tho. Stephens, Jose. Hughs, Edwd. Petto (or Petts), James Gold, Robert Bearge, Edwd. Cowed, Jno. Grumball, Jno. Tayler, Martha Tayler, Danll. Frignale, Sarah Arnell, Jane Farham, Jane Cox, Eliz. Thompson, Jno. Cook, Wm. Bininham, (?), Robert Jones, Jno. Cole, Rich. Crawley, Jno. Bromeley, Lewis Hales, Henry Lidgold, Jno. Brothers, Edwd. Morris, Jane Greene, Savell Covell, Robert Jarret, Abraham Renols, Jane Renolls, James Bigford, Adam Randall, Jer. Griffin, Jane Relfe.

MR. JNO. SKEEARE, 153 acs., Middlesex Co; in the forke of a br. of the Greene Sw., neare Henry Wood, Esqr; adj. Jno. Bourk, & Mr. Richard Willis, &c; 23 Apr. 1688, p. 639. Trans. of 4 pers: Wm. Smith, Ed. Hatcher, Jane Darnell, Wm. Foulks.

MR. WM. DOWNING, 322 acs., Middlesex Co., 23 Apr. 1688, p. 640. Beg. by the Indian Path to the Dragon Sw; to Tho. Williams' plantation; by land of the Orphants of David Allison; neare the Bridge Road; by run of the Blockhouse Br; to Thomas Minns (or Mum's) Plantation. Trans. of 7 pers: Ezeky Chambers, Tho. Whiteing, Judeth Smallwood, Tho. Golding, Wm. Fuller, Ann Page, Mary Plower.

SAMUEL SINGNELL (Singall), 30 acs., Yorke Co; on N. side of New Pocoson Riv., on S. side of a gutt out of the W. side of Oystershell Cr., adj. Jno. Clarke; 23 Apr. 1688, p. 640. Trans. of: Edward Potter.

MR. GEORGE CRAFORD (Crawford), 70 acs., Low. Norf. Co; in the N. brs. of Curretick; 23 Apr. 1688, p. 641. Beg. on the Green Br; a marsh dividing this; Tho. Griffin; & land of Mr. Bassnet. Granted to Thomas Russell, 20 Apr. 1684, deserted, & now granted by order, &c. Trans. of 2 pers: James Bromely, Wm. Harris.

MR. THO. JACKSON, 335 acs., Low. Norf. Co., in *Corrotuck Precincts*; 23 Apr. 1688, p. 641. Beg. at cor. of Heath & Capt. Jno. Gibbs; to Goodland Cr. &c. 100 acs. granted him, 21 Oct. 1684; 235 acs. for trans. of 5 pers: Tho. Jackson 4 times; & Will a Negro.

RICHARD SILVESTER, 300 acs., Low. Norf. Co; towards head of the S. br. of Eliz. Riv; 23 Apr. 1688, p. 642. Beg. at land he bought of Whittfield; to land of Barnes, now John Smith's, & adj. on lands of Tayler, Platt, Costen & Jno. Corporue. Trans. of 6 pers: Richd. Silvester, Isaac Bernop, Hannah his wyfe, Isaac Bernip, John Johnson, John Collah.

JOHN SMITH, 350 acs., Low. Norf. Co; on head of the S. br. of Eliz. River, 23 Apr. 1688, p. 642. Beg. at Richard Silvester; to land formerly Barnes'; into the Green Sea, &c. Trans. of 7 pers: John Roberts, James Hobbs, Toby Scot, Joane Atlas, Sarah Turner, Joane Elsby, Wm. Thomas.

MR. WILLIAM BASSETT, 2048 acs., New Kent Co., in St. Peter's Par; on S. side of Pamunky River; adj. Col. Bacon; 23 Apr. 1688, p. 643. Granted to Capt. Wm. Bassett, his father, 29 Apr. 1687; trans. of 41 pers.*

MARY, ELIZABETH & ANNE HOWARD, daughters of Mr. Thomas

Howard, dec'd; 180 acs., Gloster Co., in Petsoe Par., 23 Apr. 1688, p. 643. Beg. neer head of a branch called little Ease; adj. land of Mr. Wm. Howard, dec'd. 88 acs. t°ken by Mr. Ralph Green & sold to sd. Thomas, 8 Nov. 1673; 92 acs. for trans. of 2 pers: John Williams, Jane Porter.

MR. WILLIAM POOLE, JUNR., 1170 acs., Middlesex Co., 23 Apr. 1688, p. 644. Beg. on SSE side of Tigner's Cr; crossing Bever Dam Cr; neer the Green Sw; by sd. Poole's Quarter Plantation. 650 acs. granted to Wm. Tignor, 26 Feb. 1653; 250 acs. granted Mr. Wm. Leach, 17 July 1665; 270 acs. for trans. of 6 pers: John Denny, Richard Duncumb, Edwd. Sealinger, Thomas Redley, Mary Bryan, Margaret Atkins.

To the GENTLEMEN OF THE VESTRY & PARISHIONERS OF THE PARISH OF CHRIST CHURCH, 426 acs., Middlesex Co., in sd. Parish; 23 Apr. 1688, p. 644. 398 acs. part sold & made over to sd. Vestrymen & Parishioners by Mr. Richard Robinson & Anne, his wyfe, for a Gleabe, 6 Sept. 1673. Beg. at Nimcock, alias Rosegill, Cr., by a path to the King's Road, &c; 28 acs. added to sd. Gleab for the Minister; adj. Mr. John Cant, &c. Said 28 acs. due for trans. of: John Ambrose.

MR. THOMAS TODD, of Gloster Co., 2828 acs., in New Kent Co., on N. side of Mattopony Riv., 23 Apr. 1688, p. 645. Adj. Mr. Giles Moody, on the White Oake Swamp, &c. Granted to Col. John West, 22 Sept. 1682; assigned to Col. Thomas Claybourne, 28 Apr. 1683, who assigned to sd. Todd the same day.

MR. JOSHUAH STORY, 400 acs., New Kent Co; St. Stephen's Par; on either side of the Horse Path from the Draggon (Sw.) to Piscattoway; 23 Apr. 1688, p. 646. Beg. at land Wm. Drumwright & Mathew York now liveth (on); adj. Jno. Symonds; Mr. Collier; Mr. Lockie; & land John Bowles, purchased of Col. Robert Abrahall, formerly the land of Wm. Moore. Granted to Maj. George Morris, 20 Apr. 1684,

deserted, & now granted by order &c. Trans. of 8 pers.*

GEORGE PARKER, 250 acs., Accomack Co., neer Mattomkin; E. from the Root Branch where Gargatha Path crosses it, &c; 23 Apr. 1688, p. 647. Granted to Maj. Edmund Bowman, 21 Sept. 1674, deserted, & now granted by order &c., for trans. of 5 pers: Eliza. Morgan, Jno. Longsdale, Benja. Eyres, Jno. Fox, Richd. Hayes.

RICHARD GARRETSON, 268 acs., Accomack Co., neer Matchepungo; bet. Capt. Fra. Potts' 1500 acs., surveyed by Col. Edmund Scarburgh, & a line made since by order, &c; adj. Edward Hutchins & William Wouldhave; 23 Apr. 1688, p. 647. Granted Col. William Kendoll, 8 Apr. 1674, deserted, & now granted by order &c. Trans. of 6 pers: Tho. James, Roger Rely, Jno. Moss, Job. Jaquis, Sarah Neuton, Hester Bayly.

JABEZ BIGG, 95 acs., Low. Norf. Co; E. side of the S. br. of Eliz. Riv., on Cormorant Poynt; adj. John Bigg; & Prescott's land; 23 Apr. 1688, p. 648. Granted John Prescott, 20 Nov. 1683, deserted, & now due by order, for Imp. of 2 pers: Andrew Bell, James Jones. Note: Marginal notation gives this as 500 acres.

MR. WILLIAM EDWARDS, 480 acs., 23 Apr. 1688, p. 648. On W. side of Greene Sw., cor. of John Clarke, in Owens' lyne; adj. John Clements; Syon Hill; Mr. Samuell Plaw; & Mr. Bins, &c. Granted Edward Pettaway, 20 Apr. 1684, deserted, & now granted by order, &c. Trans. of 10 pers: Wm. Robins, James Moore, Antho. Evarard, Thomas Cooke, James Willice, Sarah Evans, Robt. Felps, James Edwell, Jane Richards; & Will, a Negro.

SAME. 290 acs., Lower Par. of Surry Co; on heads of Blackwater Brs; adj. Thomas Lane; a br. dividing this & land of Mr. Robt. Ruffin; adj. Mr. Bins; & Mr. Rich'd. Bennett; 23 Apr. 1688, p. 648. Granted John Parsons, 20 Apr. 1684, & now granted by order, &c.

Trans. of 6 pers: Samll. Holton, Tho. Woodby, Jno. James, Wm. Randolph, Richd. Wilks; & Jone, a Negro.

MR. THOMAS TOSELEY, 594 acs., Middlesex Co., 23 Apr. 1688, p. 649. Beg. at John Furwell; by Rice Jones' path; to his own plantation; to Mr. Edward Thomas; on Jno. Furwell's line; to the maine Roade. 507 acs. granted John Richines & George Hooper; deserted, & granted Mr. Edward Thomas, in Nov. 1678, who sold to sd. Toseley, 21 June 1680; 27 acs. for trans. of 2 pers.*

MR. JOHN FURWELL (or Farwell), 593 acs., Middlesex Co; adj. John Jadwin; & Wm. Blayse; on the maine Roade; to Mr. Maurice Cock & land of Doods Minor (?); 23 Apr. 1688, p. 650. Granted to John Richins & George Hooper; deserted, & granted to Mr. Edward Thomas, in Nov. 1678, who sold to Mr. Thomas Toseley, 21 June 1680, & by him sold to sd. Furwell.

MR. DUELL PEAD, Minister, 296 acs., Rappa. Co; on S. side Rappa. Riv., 23 Apr. 1688, p. 650. 206 acs. part of 300 acs. granted John Bibby, 4 Oct. 1655, & bought by sd. Pead of Richard Bush, who married the dau. of sd. Bibby; 90 acs. beg. at mouth of Piscataway Cr; & adj. sd. Bush. Trans. of 2 pers: John Cresswell, Keriah (or Keziah) Osbourne.

JOHN JOHNSON, 400 acs., Low. Norf. Co; on S. side of the W. br. of Eliz. Riv; beg. neare mouth of Goose Cr., neare the deep br; to Gallberry Sw; adj. Mr. Jno. Nicholls; 23 Apr. 1688, p. 651. 300 acs. granted Mr. Jno. Hill, 29 May 1649, who sold to Wm. Nicholls, who sold to sd. Johnson; 100 acs. for trans. of 2 pers: John Whitehall & Thomas Kelly.

MR. EDWARD MOSELEY, 490 acs., Low. Norf. Co; at E. br. of Eliz. Riv., neare Broad Cr; adj. Mr. Wm. Moseley; Wm. Hancox; Mr. Fowler; Robert Young; & Wm. Martin; 23 Apr. 1688, p. 652. Granted Anthony Lawson, 23 Oct. 1673, deserted, & now condemned

in the Genrl. Court; & due for trans. of 10 pers: David Morgan, Allen French, James Mason, Nicho., Prior, David Hare, Thomas Davis; Quoby, Maria, Changy, & James, Negroes.

MR. ANTHONY DOWTEN, 700 acs., Middlesex Co., 23 Apr. 1688, p. 652. Beg. at Mr. Maurice Cook's land calledd Jamaico Land; adj. Mrs. Jane Jones, Thomas Toseley; & Hooper's land. Trans. of 14 pers: Ed. Clark, James Sheares, James Bartlett, Jno. Reed, James Clark, Robt. Dyer, Robt. Conon, Nicho. Roberts, Nicho. Haslebourne, Samll. Stepkee, Mary Brint, Rachell Packet, Wm. Netherto; & 1 Negro.

MR. EDWARD THOMAS, 714 acs., Rappa. Co., on S. side of Rappa. Riv., 23 Apr. 1688, p. 653. 350 acs. granted him 16 Apr. 1683; 364 acs. now taken, beg. by the maine Roade; adj. Rice Jones; Thomas Toseley; Mr. Williamson; & Doctor Deputie's plantation. Trans. of 8 pers: James Gale, Hen. West, Jno. Richards, Antho. Bell, James Morgan, Hen. Kerby, Edward Tayler, Eliza. Shaten (or Straten).

RICHARD LEAGHTON (Layghton), 638 acs., Rappa. Co., on S. side the river, 23 Apr. 1688, p. 654. Adj. Edward Moseley & Nicholas Francklyn; by Occupacon Run, to Edward Rouzee; on John Williams, to Cooke & Ingram, &c. Trans. of 13 pers: Wm. Jervas, Hen. Smith, Jno. Lyndell, Jos. Mansfield, Tho. Jenkinson, Richd. Jones, James Cambleton, Henry Morgan, Wm. Morgan, Robt. Andrews, Robt. Meredith, James Wood, Jno. Brown.

HENRY ALLEY, 390 acs., Chas. City Co., in Bristoll Par., on N. main br. of Black Water, 23 Apr. 1688, p. 654. Beg. at Willm. Vaughan; to Henry Crowder, crossing Fockes' Br; to John Evans, to Mr. Richd. Jones. Trans. of 8 pers: Anne Collings, Avis Collings, John Besle, Roger Norris, Edwd. Richards, Tho. Charles, Henry Bradshaw; & Maria a Negro.

WILLIAM DODSON & JAMES FRANKLING (Franklyn), 360 acs.,

Henrico Co., Bristoll Par; on N. side the gr. branch of Swift Cr., 23 Apr. 1688, p. 655. Trans. of 8 Negroes: George, Mingo, Guy, Huba, Gosse, Maria, Crosse, Nedd.

COL. LEM. MASON, MR. THOMAS JARVIS & MR. THOMAS WILLOUGHBY, 2600 acs., at *Corrotuck;* Low. Norf. Co., comonly called *White's Island;* bounded E. with Corrotuck Bay bet. the inletts of Roanoake & Curretuck, N. with Cowinjock Bay, &c; 23 Apr. 1688, p. 655. Trans. of 52 pers: Jos. Fungall, Dorathy Wagstaff, James Ranger, Jno. Ratliffe, Jane Meeres, Abraham Willis, Teige West, Margt. Hockis, Jane Tayler, Jno. Richards, Wm. Meade, Ja. Galard, Owen Macgrough, Mary Henshaw, Ja. Turner, Rich. Wells, Samll. Tucker, Richd. Board, Evan Mongan, Humphry Fitchet, Jabez Rhoode, Robt. Tooker, Hen. Sheilds, Jane Moore, Samll. Floyd, Robt. Elsby, Jno. Reade, Ralph Creede, Sarah James, Robt. Wood, Jno. Phillipps, Robt. Brookes, James Pagan, Peter King, Sarah Hunt, Tho. Maples, Andrew Moore, Ja. Curtis, Robt. Fellows, Ab. Bateman, Robt. Bird, James Peters, Abigall Ware; Tony, Jack, Will, Mingo, Kate, Doll, Robin, Dick, Kate, Negroes.

CHARLES HANSFORD, 180 acs., Yorke Co; except such part as shall be found to be sold out of the same; 23 Apr. 1688, p. 656. Purchased by James Harris of Joseph Croshaw, 24 Mar. 1653, & escheated from Thomas Broad, late of York Co., son of Edward Brood, who purchased of sd. Harris, as by inquisition under John Page, Esqr., Esch'r., &c.

SAMUEL MOODY, 82 acs., Chas. City Co., in Wynoak Par., on N. side of James Riv., 26 Apr. 1688, p. 656. Beg. at the edge of Wynoak Marsh; along line of Robt. Evans, dec'd., to S. edge of the Sw. made by Kitawan Cr., &c. Due him as son & heyre of Thomas Moody, which sd. Samuell in 1663, being an infant, by his Guardian, Francis Redford, amongst other inhabitants of Wynoak, had an order dated at James Citty, 16 Sept. 1663, enabling them to patent their severall parcells whereof they were possessed, &c.

THOMAS BUSBY & MARY, his wife, dau. & heyre of Simon Simons; 539 acs., Chas. City Co., in Winoak & Westover Parishes; on S. side of James Riv., 26 Apr. 1688, p. 657. Beg. at head of Reedy Bottom Br. of Powell's Cr; crossing a br. of Flowerdy Hundred Cr., to lands now, or late, William Harryson's; John Hobbs; & John Poythres. Said land due, viz: 359 acs. within bounds of land reputed (& possessed by) Simon Simons, the *Grandfather* of said Mary; 150 acs. deserted land of James Ward, dec'd., by order &c; & 30 acs. of wast land adj. Imp. of 11 pers: Jno. Rogers, Francis Pott, John Lake, Andrew Cob, Patrick Johnson, Thomas Leech, Anthony Holder, Robert Long, Jeffry Conar, Adam Strong, Roger Gras.

CHARLES FLEMING, Planter, 1079 acs., New Kent Co., St. Peeter's Par; bet. Matadequnn & Totopotamoys Crks., 18 Apr. 1688, p. 658. Adj. land of John Fleming, de'cd; Mr. Daulany; David Smith, John Sexton, Mr. Bouth; Samuell Woddy; James Tate; Mr. Crawford; Geo. Phillips; & Charles Lovell; on Whiting's Swamp. Imp. of 22 pers: Mary Gardner, Margery Day, Francesco Merceir, Mary Goose, Henry Hetford, Richd. Leoberson, Alice Adkinson, Grace Deacon, Eliz. Waterson, Jane Tompson, Eliz. ——, John Davis, Caleb Currie, Martha Mason, Jno. Morris, Francis Midleton, Henry Tutty (or Tully), Eliz. Ody, Martin Gardner 5 times; 4 rights more certifyed by Mr. Hartwell, late Clk. of this office.

JOHN SANDFORD, 1517 acs., neer *Curratuck;* Low. Norf. Co., 23 Apr. 1688, p. 659. Beg. at Josiah Morriss, nee Bouden's Damms; by Rattle Snake Ridge, &c. Trans. of 31 pers: Fra. Dun, Margt. Mortley, Tho. Evans, James Shepherd, Nicho. Dugras, Jno. Guiden, Beneden Lewis, Math. Davis, Mary Button, Eliza. Valent, Wm. Cowpen, Tho. Mondien (?), Jno. Gun, Tymo. Holmes, Jno. Graves, Wm. Harris, James Jones, Cad. Kiddy, Ralph James, Ellin Owen, Jone Ellis, Mathew

Cooper, Edwin Fryzer, Foulk Mitton, George Reeves, Hancock Terry, Walter Fyler, Jacob Trutton, Hen. Galley.

EDMUND LOKIS, 640 acs., att *Curratuck;* Low. Norf. Co., 23 Apr. 1688, p. 659. Trans. of 13 pers: Will. Fairset, Jno. Nickolls, Anne Rogers, Jno. Amy, Xpher. Servt., (Servant ?), James Boyce, Alex. Chandler, Richd. Rogers, Eliza. Wynne, Ellinor Catlet, Jeremiah Connyers, Wm. Tandy, Jabez Curtis.

CAPT. ROGER MALLORY, 2514 acs., New Kent Co., St. John's Par; on S. side of Mattopany Riv., 30 Apr. 1688, p. 660. Beg. at mouth of a br. below the Cliffs Landing; up the maine Roade, to mouth of Little Cr., &c. Granted him by former patt. *& in the late troubles casually lost.* Trans. of 51 pers: James Harris, Tully Jones, Eliza. Atkins, Jacob Gerord, Ellinor Green, Dorithy Whitby, Pompey Honywood, Xpher. Carter, Darby Wilson, Alex. Fanwell; 41 rights by certificate from Mr. Richd. Awborne, 25 June 1670.

JOSEPH GREGORY, 500 acs., upon a br. of Cow Cr. in Ware River, in Mobjack Bay; ——— 1652, p. 661. Granted by virtue of an Act of Assembly, 25 Apr. 1652, requiring the Gov'r. & Secretary to sign all patents & shall be accounted authentick until a Colony Seale shall be provided, &c; & in the name of the *Keepers of the Liberties of England,* &c. Adj. Richard Daving; & Henry Peasley. Trans. of 10 pers.* Signed by: Richn. Bennet & Wm. Claybourne, Secty. *(Record incomplete.)*

ANTHONY GREGORY, son & heire of Joseph Gregory; 500 acs., upon a br. of Cow Cr., in Ware Riv., in Mobjack Bay; 30 Apr. 1688, p. 662. Adj. Richard Daving; & Henry Peasley. Granted to Joseph Gregory, his father, 6 ——— 1652; trans. of 10 pers: Robt. Manhood, Hugh Mackartine, Tho. Parsons, Wm. Hulk, Wm. Burbridge, Richd. Mishures, Ione Goodhand, John Ashford; Jack & Robins, Negroes.

EDWARD JONES, 89 acs., Low. Norf. Co., in *Curratuck Precints;* neer

the Goodland Cr; adj. Mr. Sandford & Danll. Lane; 23 Apr. 1688, p. 662. Trans. of 2 pers:Stephen Potter, Wm. Lewis.

MR. HENRY AWBERY, 1200 acs., Rappa. Co; on S. side the river, upon the maine pocoson of Hoskins Cr., 30 May 1688, p. 663. Granted Mr. Thomas Goldman, 4 Apr. 1667, deserted, & now granted by order, &c. Trans. of 20 pers: James Jones, Ralph Todd, Jane Mercer, Jno. Robins, Ralph Breniss, Abraham Richardson, Jno. Thomas, Alex. Hinton, James Bruton, Sarah Newton, Jno. Ives, Abraham Reede, Jno. Tandy, Robt. Elliot, James Scott, Margt. Ellis Robt. Spoyles, Ralph Seayres, Isaac Hitchcock, Ruth Hutchins, Wm. Ives, James Alto (or *Also*), Ann Pott, Jno. Emerby.

WM. VAUGHAN, 220 acs., Low. Norf. Co., in *Tanner's Creek Precincts;* 23 Apr. 1688, p. 664. Adj. Jno. Elder; Wm. Langley; land of Col. Mason, now Francis Thelaball's; & the Landing Poynt. 100 acs. granted Hugh Purdie, dec'd., & by deed from Hugh Purdie, the younger, to sd. Vaughan; 72 acs. granted sd. Vaughan, 20 Apr. 1686; & 48 acs. for trans. of: Henry Emperor.

HENRY LEE, 350 acs. York Co., in Hampton Par; adj. Francis Morgan; Mr. Lee & Wm. Sawyer's plantation by the Creek; 23 Apr. 1688, p. 665. 150 acs. granted to Henry Lee, his father. 22 Mar. 1670, & due him as son & heire.

HOPKIN HOWELL & MARY HOWELL, Orphants of Hopkin Howell; 200 acs., Is. of Wight Co., 23 Apr. 1688, p. 665. Granted Peter Johnson, 23 May 1642, & escheated by inquisition under Wm. Randolph, Depty. Esch'r., 16 June 1681 & granted to sd. Howell, dec'd., who by will, dated 9 Mar. 1686, bequeathed to his sd. son & dau. Marginal note: "Fees & Seale charged."

MR. THOMAS PEREN, 140 acs., Henrico Co., in Verina Par., on N. side of James Riv., 20 Oct. 1688, p. 666. Adj. Mr. Richard Peren; & Abraham Bayly; on Cornelius' Creek; to Wm.

Giles (Gyles) ; & Thomas Bayly. Trans. of 3 pers: Thomas Mortin (or Martin), Jonathan Bayly, Wm. Jesop.

MR. NICHOLAS MARSH, 528 acs., Henrico Co., in Verina Par., on N. side of James Riv., 20 Oct. 1688, p. 666. Adj. Mr. John Pleasants, on the head of Barrow; crossing Sampson's Slash; to Isaac Creswell; on Cornelius' Cr; to Henry Trent, &c. Trans. of 11 pers: Edwd. Richardson, Rich. Martin, Tho. Hill; "8 more out of Cert. Randolph."

MR. ABRAHAM BAYLY, 142 acs., Henrico Co., in Verina Par., on N. side of James Riv., called *Mount Peloin* (or *Pelom*); —— of Oct. 1688, p. 667. Beg. nigh the goeing over of Cornelius' Cr; to Mr. Burton; on head of Holly Br. Trans. of 3 pers: Jno. Good, Mary & Frank ——.

MR. THOMAS COCK, SENR., 1650 acs., Henrico Co., in Verina Par; S. side of Chickahominy maine Sw., adj. Mr. Jno. Woodson; 20 Oct. 1688, p. 668. Trans. of 33 pers: Jno. Smith, Anne Collins, Avis Collins, Jno. Bess, Roger Norris, Edwd. Richards, Tho. Charles, Humphrey Bradshaw, Mary Godfrey, Tho. Mitchell, Robt. Green, Humph. Smith, Lambert Tye, Martin Gardner, Danll. Jordan, Edwd. Richardson, Richd. Martin, Tho. Hill, Roger Dormer, Wm. Lambort (?), Roger Holden, Wm. Banks, Henry Henderson, Danll. Cock, Mary Clifford, Susanna Turner, Nicholas Prior, Robt. Cook, Wm. Soane, Job ——, Tho. Liburne, Peter Brant; Maria a Negro.

NATHANIELL ROBERTS & JOSHUAH PROCTOR, 566 acs., Surry Co; —— day of Oct. 1688, p. 669. Beg. at land granted sd. Proctor & John Rogers; by Robt. Warren; to Mr. Richard Washington, &c. Trans. of 12 pers: Jno. Davis, Alex. Evans, Jane Reuby (?), Andrew Crow. 8 rights by Rowld. Davies for Ed. Chilton's certificate to Jos. Malden & assigned to Maj. Samll. Swan, 21 May 1687, being part of a certificate for 20 rts.

THOMAS BAGE, 290 acs., Up. Par. of Surry Co; adj. Francis Sowersby; Mr.

Nicholas Merrywether & Danll. Regan; 20 Oct. 1688, p. 669. Trans. of 6 pers.* 6 rts. by Mr. Ed. Chilton's certif., 19 Oct. 1686. *(Note:* Index to Sury Co. patents lists this name as *Page.)*

THOMAS TYAS, 500 acs., Surry Co;, in Southwark Par; on E. side of the head of the maine br. of Mr. Jno. Barker's reedy swamp; 20 Oct. 1688, p. 670. Trans. of 10 pers: Alice Potter, Robt. Jenkins, James Elps (?), Kath. Robins, Peter le force, Anne Willis, Thomas Williams, Izabella Johnson; Arthur Davis, Eliza. Stephens.

THOMAS BENTLEY, JUNR., 300 acs., Surry Co; adj. Mr. Benja. Harryson; 20 Oct. 1688, p. 670. Trans. of 6 pers: Jno. Bagot, Susanah Skilton, Jno. Brown, Wm. Loe, Kate & Jno. Crane.

MR. WALTER COTTON & THOMAS COTTON, 314 acs., Up. Par. of Surry Co; Adj Mr. John Barker & sd. Thomas Cotton; 20 Oct. 1688, p. 670. Trans. of 7 pers: Jno. Bolton, Jno. Elmy, Hester Bradstock, Charles Trevor, Jno. Moss, Alice Ems, Howell Waters.

JOHN KING, 117 acs., in Up. Par. of Surry Co., on W. side of the Deep Sw; adj. Robert Burgess; & Thomas Sowersby; 20 Oct. 1688, p. 671. Trans. of 3 pers: Wm. Nance (?), Fra. Kirkman, Robt. Slye.

FRANCIS DAVIS, 100 acs., in Is. of Wight Co; adj. Robert Lawrence, Junr; Giles Lemscott; John Somerlin; & Richard Booth; 20 Oct. 1688, p. 672. Trans. of 2 pers: Thomas Brown, Jno. Cortee.

WM. BALDWIN, 67 acs., Up. Par. of Is. of Wight Co; adj. Jno. Harris; 20 Oct. 1688, p. 672. Trans. of 2 pers: Mary an Indian; Lan, a Negro.

MRS. HESTER BRIDGER & MR. JAMES TULLAH, 243 acs., Is. of Wight Co., 20 Oct. 1688, p. 673. Adj. Thomas Poole; neer the gr. Freshett, along Mr. Thomas Jordan's line; to

Jeremiah Rutter. Trans. of 5 pers: Eliza. Maycock, Mary Young, Mary Butler, Samll. Canadee; Will a Negro.

JOHN BROWN, 600 acs., Is. of Wight Co., on S. side of Kingsaile Sw; 20 Oct. 1688, p. 673. Trans. of 12 pers: Robt. Glover, Lawrence Story, Jno. Rugles, Joseph Baskervill, Jno. Carren, Hugh Nelton, Hen. Cox, Tho. Toyres; Phill. & Eliza, Negroes.

PETER BUTLER, JAMES BUTLER, the younger, & JOHN BUTLER, 678 acs., Is. of Wight Co; adj. Wm. Collins, John White; & Hodge Councell; 20 Oct. 1688, p. 674. Trans. of 14 pers: Tho. Tucker, James Jonesing, Wm. Rutt, Jno. Flood, James Massangin, Jno. Furbee, Edmund Ketle, Jno. White, James Menton, Donker (?) Frissell, Danll. Gray, Hugh Merriack (or Mernack), Jno. Pruet, Wm. Pruet.

MR. WILLIAM HUNTER, 80 acs., Low. Norf. Co., in Lynhaven Par; upon Little Cr; adj. Mr. Thorogood, neer the Road to Fowler's plantation; to land formerly Robert Hayes'; 20 Oct. 1688, p. 674. Part of 97 acs. granted to Henry Snaile, dec'd., 23 Aug. 1652, who sold to Joseph Birch, & by his coheires & their husbands assignments comes due to sd. Hunter; trans. of 2 pers: Mathew Young, Thomas Young.

CHARLES EGERTON, 400 acs., Low. Norf. Co., in the Up. Par. of Lynhaven; adj. land formerly David Murraie's; & upon patent of the *Dam Necks;* 20 Oct. 1688, p. 675. Trans. of 8 pers: Charles Egerton, Rachell Johnson, Capt. Richard Jordan, 3 times; Henry Hormon, twice; James Carter.

JAMES JOUSLIN, 300 acs., Low. Norf. Co., in Lynhaven Par; from the E. br. towards the North River; adj. Wm. Edwards by the Horse Bridge Run; & on the Gr. Cyprus Br; 20 Oct. 1688, p. 676. Trans. of 6 pers: Wm. Kerre, Elinor West (or Nest), Mary Butcher; Judith, Nancy, & Nick, Negroes.

MR. ARGALL THOROUGOOD (Thorogood), 700 acs., Low. Norf. Co.,

in Lynhaven Par; neer head of Bennett's Cr., parting this & land of Wm. Smith; 20 Oct. 1688, p. 676. 200 acs. part of 400 acs. granted Lt. Col. Adam Thorogood, dec'd., 19 Oct. 1642; 150 acs. granted to Xpher. Burroughs, 7 Nov. 1651 & by Benoni, his son & heire, sold to sd. Adam, 10 May 1667; 350 acs. for trans. of 7 pers: Thomas Bridge, 4 times; Hester, his wyfe, David Dunkan & Eliza. Singule (or Singale).

MR. JOHN RICHASON, 918 acs., Low. Norf. Co., towards *Matchepongo;* 20 Oct. 1688, p. 677. Beg. by the Easterne pocoson; neer land of Col. Mason; & into the pocoson of the North River. Trans. of 19 pers: James a Cooper; Michll. a Shoemaker; Tom Brown, Henry Nailer, Jno. Clansey, Tho. Bushell, Nathll. Plowman, Tom & Evan, 2 Brothers; Jno. Robinson, Geo. Michell, Jno. Smith, Senr., Jno. Smith, Junr., Wm. Hudson, Tho. Wraye, Tho. Freeman, Grae (or Grue ?) Tudman, Eliza. Smith, Francis Stacy.

MICHAELL FENTRIS, 150 acs., Low. Norf. Co., in Lynhaven Par; adj. Capt. Wm. Crafford; & James Whitehurst; 20 Oct. 1688, p. 678. Trans. of 3 pers: John James, Abraham Bates, Jane Boswell.

MR. SAMLL. RANSHAW, 132 acs., in the Oaken Swamp; Warwick Co., in Denbigh Par., 20 Oct. 1688, p. 678. Beg. neer *Shotbolt,* cor. of Capt. Mathews; to Thomas Wooton; his own, & land of Jno. Lewis, &c. Trans. of 3 pers: Joan Self, Paul & James, Negroes.

THOMAS COX, 79 acs., York Co., in New Pocoson Par; adj. John Lilbourne & Owen Davis; 20 Oct. 1688, p. 679. Trans. of 2 pers: Richard Lawes; Tabitha a Negro.

SAMUELL SINGNALL, 30 acs., York Co; on W. side of Ouster Cr., issuing out of the N. side of New Pocoson River; on S. side of a gutt parting this & land of Jno. Clark; 20 Oct. 1688, p. 680. Trans. of: Phillip Pilgrim.

MR. ROBERT READ, in right of his wyfe, M. ry, dau. to Mr. Jno. Lilly; 305 of acs., in York Co., & Par; beg. on S. side of the Back Cr., on W. side of Gwin's Cr; to br. of Cheesman's Cr., parting this & land of Mrs. Joane Worldley; along Thomas Wooton, to land of Argall Blackstone, dec'd; to land of Richard Palmer, dec'd; 20 Oct. 1688, p. 680. 100 acs. granted Jno. Congdon, 17 Dec. 1640, & assigned to Edward Mallson, 1 Feb. 1643, & due sd. John Lilly as marrying with the heiress of sd. Mallson; 125 acs. granted Robert Lendall & George Pennerell, 29 Oct. 1651 & by sd. Lendall sett over to sd. Malson, with consent of sd. Pennerell, 17 Dec. 1656; 120 acs. now taken, due for trans. of 3 Negroes.

EDWARD EASTHAM & JOHN PAGE, 48 acs., New Kent Co; N. side of Mattopony Riv; adj. sd. Page's plantation; Maj. Morris in the Hoghouse Br; & land of Edward Eastham; 20 Oct. 1688, p. 681. Trans. of: Jno. Alsop (or Absop).

ROBERT JONES, of New Kent Co., in St. Stephen's Par; 455 acs., on N. side of Mattopany Riv; 20 Oct. 1688, p. 682. 250 acs. part granted him, 23 Apr. 1681; 205 acs. on the Weesockan Br; adj. Col. Robt. Abrahall; Mr. Tho. Seawell, Senr; & Mr. John Stark; to a Hucklebery pond or slash belonging to sd. Jones, Stark, & Mr. John Walker; to Col. Thomas Walker, &c; due for trans. of 5 pers: Wm. Byrd, Jone Watkins, Roger Rogers, Tho. Grant, Sarah Thompson.

JAMES TAYLER, 350 acs., New Kent Co., in St. Stephen's Par; 20 Oct. 1688, p. 683. Behind land formerly of Mr. Giles Moody; by Barrow's old house, &c. Granted to John Eckolls & Wm. Morris, 20 Apr. 1685, deserted, & now granted by order, &c. Trans. of 7 pers: John Jones, Wm. Kitto, Jeffrey James, Cadwalader Hackle, Anne Eden, Eliza. Foster, Jno. Charles.

MR. CHARLES ROANE, of Gloster Co., 797 acs., in New Kent & Gloster Co.s; 20 Oct. 1688, p. 684. 500 acs. bought of Edward Row & Samuell Partridge, being part of 5380 acs. granted Col. Cuthbert Potter, 20 June 1659, who sold to sd. Row & Patridge; 297 acs. beg. by Hanks' Folly Branch, in sight of sd. Roane's & Hanks' old plantations; by the maine Dragon Sw; to George Martin (or Mortin) & Jno. Kelly's plantation. Trans. of 6 pers: Wm. Walton, Howell Davis, David Williams, Phillip Aldman, Jane Whitehaire, James Squires.

MR. MOTROM WRIGHT, 1000 acs., Gloster Co., Kingstone Par; on N. side of Winter Harbour Cr., 20 Oct. 1688, p. 685. Adj. land formerly belonging to Mr. Robert Greggs; Jno. Deggs, & Jno. Gardner; along a line parting this & land of John Smither, which was run by & with the consent of sd. Wright, in behalfe of his wyfe, to be a perpetuall bound betwixt them & their heires forever; to old dwelling house where sd. Greggs lived, &c. 400 acs. pattented by Richd. Ripley, 29 Jan. 1652; sold to Charles Sallet, & by Symon Sallet, his heire, sold to George Thompson, 16 Oct. 1657, who sold to sd. Greggs 23 Nov. 1657, & escheated by him in 1666; 370 acs. granted sd. Gregs & Edward Wyat, 19 Apr. 1662; the moyety made over to sd. Greggs by Wyat, 27 Oct. 1663; 230 acs. pattented by sd. Greggs, wherein is inserted 250 acs., 18 Mar. 1662. Due sd. Wright in right of his wyfe Ruth, dau. to sd Greggs, who bequeathed sd. 1000 acs. to her.

MR. HENRY WOODNUT, 1062 acs., Rappa. Co; on S. side of Rappa. Riv., 20 Oct. 1688, p. 686. 750 acs. pattented by Jno. Sharp & Nicholas Cox, & conveyed to sd. Woodnutt; 312 acs. beg. in sight of Richd. Brooks' plantation by the maine Roade; along Randall Curtis; by br. of Tizway Sw; to Mr. Edward Adcock; by the Beverddam Sw; to Esqr. Tho. Bowler; in sight of James Creswell's plantation, to John Sharp, alias Harwar's, line; in sight of Woodnutt's Quarter; by Thomas Hinds' plantation. Trans. of 7 pers: Charles Lathan, Charles Methin, Wm. Estnan, Ann Stanton, Jno. River, Tho. Atkinson, James Seco.

JOHN BURRUS & THO. COFFIN, 200 acs., on Rogues Island, in N'ampton Co; on W. side of the S. end of Hog Iland; 20 Oct. 1688, p. 688. Trans. of 4 pers.*

JOHN DICKENSON, 930 acs., Gloster Co., 20 Oct. 1688, p. 688. Granted to Mary Dickenson, *alias* Titterton, dec'd., & escheated by inquisition under Capt. Francis Page, Depty. Esch'r., &c.

MR. HENRY GAULER, 1091 acs; on back of land purchased by Henry Corbyn, Esqr., & another taken by sd. Corbyn, dec'd; crossing the maine br. of Ware Cr; a gr. br. of Passatink Cr; by a valley called *Solomon's Garden*, &c; 20 Oct. 1688, p. 689. Granted to Mr. Abraham Weeks & Mr. Hugh Williams, 26 Sept. 1680, deserted, & now granted by order, &c. Trans. of 22 pers: James Johnson, Ed. Hughes, Wm. Cortlet, Alex. Jenings, Michll. Jones, Wm. Byfield, Ed. Streater, James Collins, Tho. Oliver, Ed. Horton, Cornel. Atkins. Wm. Field, Ann Eden, Wm. Foster, Wm. Denis, Jno. Wheeler, Edwd. Foules (or Stoutes), Jane Evans, Richd. Pirete (?), Ed. James, Jone Yates, Ed. Fielding.

MR. JOHN FERREBY, 1000 acs., Low. Norf. Co; E'ly. from the *Mill land devident*, at head of Puzzle Cr., in the S. br. of Eliz. Riv; 20 Oct. 1688, p. 690. Granted to Maj. Francis Sawyer, 21 Oct. 1684, deserted, & now granted by order, &c. Trans. of 20 pers.*

ROGER WILLIAMS, 150 acs., Surry Co., neer *Southwark Church;* 20 Oct. 1688, p. 690. Beg. at Maj. Samll. Swan; bet. David Andrews & Luke Meazell; adj. Wm. Foreman, & Col. Brown. Granted Mr. Wm. Thompson, 21 Oct. 1684, deserted, & now granted by order &c. Trans. of 3 pers: Evan James, Jno. Jordan, Ellis Owen.

RICHARD JORDAN, 200 acs., in Up. Par. of Surry Co; bet. Cypress Sw. & Johnchounk Sw; adj. Richard Jordan, Junr; 20 Oct. 1688, p. 691. Granted Thomas Smith, 20 Apr. 1684, deserted, & now granted by order &c. Trans. of

4 pers: Jno. Mole, James Rendall; Toby & Dick Negroes.

ALEXANDER MACKENNY, 296 A., 3 R., 19 P., Henrico Co; N. side of James Riv; adj. Mr. Tho. Cock. & Mr. Jno. Watson; neer Cedar Br. falling into White Oake Br; neer New Kent Road; along line of Walton; 20 Oct. 1688, p. 691. Granted Thomas Wells, 3 Jan. 1677, deserted, & now granted by order, &c. Trans. of 6 pers.* 6 Rts. from a certificate granted by Mr. E. Chilton to Mr. Lanct. Bathurst, 7 Apr. 1687.

WM. SCARBROUGH & PHILLIP TORBSEY, 264 acs., Middlesex Co., 20 Oct. 1688, p. 692. Beg. at Mr. Robt. Smith, on N. side of Bobbs Br. of Peanketank Riv; up Little Dam Sw; to Mr. Jno. Cant, &c. Trans. of 6 pers: Abrah. James, Tymo. Worldley, Wm. Collins, Abrah. Williams, Ed. Jackson, James Bryant.

MR. JOHN GODARD, 696 acs., Low. Norf. Co., in *Curretuck;* at the forke of Boudens (or Bonden's) Cr; neer land of Necomoues (?); by Jno. Sandford; neer Richd. Drapier, & Swaine's land, &c; 20 Oct. 1688, p. 692. Trans. of 14 pers: Selleny (?) Miller, Jno. Byan, Martha White (?), Mary Fitzpatrick, Eliza. Clark, Judith Clark, David Ward, Jone Rea, Martha Jenkins, Robt. Jones, Hanah Clark, Wm. Barsley, Jno. Vaughan, Tho. Morris.

MR. ROBERT YARD & MR. JOHN WATERS, 900 acs., on S. side of Rappa. River; on the point of an island; adj. Mr. John Cox; in a marsh at mouth of Lawson's Cr; 25 Oct. 1688, p. 693. Granted to Epaphraditus Lawson, 22 May 1650, which became the estate of Robert Paine as marrying the dau. of sd. Lawson; which land was deserted, & now granted by order &c. Trans. of 18 pers: Tho. Adams, James Robins, Judeth Morgan, James Bissett, Richd. Jones, Jane Richardson, Sarah Jones, Wm. Young, Jno. Ellis, Jno. Peugh, Richd. Jones, James Rookins, Abraham Bates, Sarah Huberd, Jno. Shrowsberry, Jno. Relfe, Jane Brooks, Ratchell Jones.

ROBERT GAIMES, 186 acs., in Rappa. Co; 7 or 8 mi. back on S. side the river; adj. Maj. Robt. Beverley in line of Button, by br. of Occupation (Cr.); to land of Beverley & Morris, in a br. of Gilson's (Cr.) &c; 20 Oct. 1688, p. 693. Trans. of 4 pers: James Covill, Xto. Sally, Hen. Jenkins, Wm. Clark.

JOHN RICHARDSON, 100 acs., Low. Norf. Co., in Lynhaven Par; neer the Beverdams; 25 Oct. 1688, p. 694. Granted Thomas Keeling, 25 Oct. 1651, deserted, & now due for trans. of 2 pers: Jno. Graves, Abraham Richardson. Note: "Fees charged."

RALPH WORMELY, ESQR., 300 acs., New Kent Co., 25 Oct. 1688, p. 694. Granted to Richard Pierce, & escheated by inquisition under Christopher Wormely, Esqr., Esch'r. of sd. county, &c. Note: Fees not to be charged, given to Thacker by Mr. Secret. (Secretary).

Note: Began to charge fees in Aprll. Court 1689 at the following patt:

MR. JAMES WILLSON, 1083 acs., Low. Norf. Co; on brs. of Cyprus Sw., running into the head of the Northwest Riv. of Corrotuck; 20 Oct. 1688, p. 694. Trans. of 22 pers: James Bess, (or Boss), An. Hodge, Jacob Grey, Andrew Roberts, Robert Payne, Philip James, Ralph Anderson, William Robins, Robert Pee, Abraham Cannon, Vincent Good, Rebecka Rogers, Wm. Ellerby, Sarah Newton; Toby, Joane, Doll, Will, Jack, Humphry, Ned, Oneale, Negroes.

By Nathanial Bacon, Esqr., President of his Majestie's Council of State of Virginia.

MR. JOHN BARKER, 244 acs., Up. Par. of Surry Co; adj. Mr. Benjamin Harrison, & Thomas Cotten; 20 Apr. 1689, p. 695. Trans. of 5 pers: Math. Beaver, Leo. Clacket (or Clarket), Isa. Sanders, Margt. Wignoll, Melchi. Lawrance.

JOHN SOJOURNER, 162 acs., Is. of Wight Co., 20 Apr. 1689, p. 695. Adj. land he bought of Mr. Robert Williamson; cor. of James Atkinson; by the

Doctor's Branch, to Edward Boykins, &c. Trans. of 4 pers: Thomas Yates, Robert James, Jane Fellowes, Abraham Dugard.

JOHN CREEKEMAN, 100 acs., Low. Norf. Co., towards head of the Northwest River, 20 Apr. 1689, p. 695. Trans. of 2 pers: John Ives, James Wells.

THOMAS MILLER, 800 acs., Low. Norf. Co., in Corrotuck Precincts; on N. side of the Northwest River; beg. on the Mossey Point; up the Indian Creeke, &c; 20 Apr. 1689, p. 696. Trans. of 16 pers.* Note: Rights by Mr. Edward Chilton's Certificate, dated 1 Oct. 1685, being due.

JAMES WILLSON, Boatwright, 73 acs., Low. Norf. Co; in the S. br. of Eliz. Riv., adj. land he bought of William Peyton; crossing mouth of Kitts Creek, &c; 20 Apr. 1689, p. 696. Trans. of 2 pers: Robert Sandford; & Jane an Indian.

OWEN WILLEY, 253 acs., called the New Discovery, in Lynhaven Par; S'ly. from the Easterne Br., in Low. Norf. Co., 20 Apr. 1688, p. 696. Adj. land of Tully Emperour; including Pillitory Ridge, as in the former pattent. 200 acs. granted Evan Williams, 24 Nov. 1659; renewed 18 Mar. 1662; who bequeathed to his 2 daughters: Elizabeth, who married Warren Godfrey, & Eleanor, who married sd. Willey; & by consent of sd. Godfrey, sd. 200 acs. is pattented in the name of sd. Willey; 53 acs. which layes upon each sisters' division now taken, &c. Trans. of 2 pers: Robert Ellis, Wm. Rogers.

WILLIAM DYER, 1000 acs., Low. Norf. Co., in Lynhaven Par., 20 Apr. 1689, p. 697. Beg. on the Broad Bay, to corner, formerly of Mr. Cornix; &c. 800 acs. granted 22 Aug. 1647, to William Lucas & by assignments due, viz: 100 acs. to John Johnson, dec'd., now in possession of William Bassnett, who married the heyresse; 200 acs. unto Edward Cooper, dec'd., which was sold by William Dyer, dec'd., & now in possession of his son, Edward Cooper;

500 acs. sd. William Dyer willed to his son William; 200 acs. now taken & due for trans. of 4 pers: Jno. Calling (or Colling), Jno. Newbery; Kate & Bess, Negroes .

JOHN IVES, 483 acs., Low. Norf. Co; in the S. br. of Eliz. River, upon Puzzell Point Cr., 20 Apr. 1689, p. 697. 200 acs. adj. Edward Williams; granted 7 Apr. 1663, to Francis Fleetwood, who solod to sd. Ives; 283 acs. adj. lands of Lake; Duke Ethridge; Edward Williams; & William Powell; trans. of: Francis Lake, 4 times; Sampsy & Elmore, Negroes.

MR. TULLY EMPEROUR, 400 acs., Low. Norf. Co., Lynhaven Par; S'ly. from head of the E. br. of Eliz. River; 20 Apr. 1689, p. 698. Beg. neare Rogers' land; adj. his own; & land of Evan Williams. 300 acs. granted Richard King, 1 Nov. 1669, & by severall assignments due sd. Emperour; 100 acs. for tran of 2 pers: James Wells, Robert Bray.

JAMES DYER, 491 acs., Rappa. Co., in South Farnham Par; S. side of Rappa. Riv; being (the) King's land; 20 Apr. 1689, p. 698. Beg. at head of Yorkers Sw., by John Sharpe; by the maine Roade; to Richard Symmons & Mr. Williamson. Trans. of 10 pers: Thomas Banks, Martha Holyman, Mary Athy, Xpr. Hall, Fra. Robinson, Thomas Powell, Jonathan Whitehead, Mary Blackman, Rowland Jones.

RICHARD BUSH, 793 acs., Rappa. Co; S. side of Rappa. Riv., on Piscataway Cr., 20 Apr. 1689, p. 698. 550 acs. granted John Bibby, 13 Feb. 1661. Trans. of 5 pers: Edwd. Fisher, Anne Barnes, Timo. Kogan, Jno. Mechanly, Jno. Mosely.

LANCASTER LOVETT, 300 acs., Low. Norf. Co., in Lynhaven Par; from the head of Lynhaven River; 20 Apr. 1689, p. 699. Adj. land of Bowrin; the Gr. Cyprus Sw; & mouth of Bowrin's River. Trans. of 6 pers: Thomas Taylor, Senr., Thomas Taylor, Junr., John Taylor, Mary Taylor; Peter & Abigail, Negroes.

PETER DE BERRY, 100 acs., Surry Co., at head of Smith's Fort, 20 Oct. 1688, p. 699. (By Francis, Lord Howard). Which land was sold by Thomas Warren to Thomas Reynolds, 10 Feb. 1657, who, with his wife, assigned to sd. De Berry, 6 Mar. 1664; escheated by inquisition under Capt. Wm. Randolph, Depty. Esch'r., 28 Sept. 1683, & now granted by order, &c.

THO. VICCARS (Viccaris), Clerk, 2359 acs., bet. Rappa. Riv. & the head or run of Mattapany River; E. upon path from Portobacco Indyan Town to Chickahomany Indyan Town; W. upon a great tract of land of Maj. Robert Beverley; &c. Granted to Samll. Bloomfeild, John Dangerfeild, Wm. Mosely, Bryan Ward & Wm. Bendery, 22 Nov. 1682, & now granted by order &c. (Note: Name of Governor & date omitted.) Note: "This patt. not signed for that the time in which pattents ought to issue after the obtaineing the Grant was Expired." Page 700.

MR. HENRY HARTWELL, 2 A., 1 R., 24½ P. in James Citty; 20 Apr. 1689, p. 701. Beg. at the bank of the river, by the trench which faceth 2 of the E. bastions of an old ruined Turf Fort; on land, now or late, of Mr. Sherwood; on land, now or late, of Holder; to land, now or late of, Tho. Rabley; on N. side of an old ditch, to land late of James Alsop, &c. ½ acre granted Mr. Wm. May, 20 May 1661, who bequeathed to Mr. Nicholas Merryweather, who sold to Mr. Wm. White, 6 Feb. 1677, who dying without heirs, the land escheated by inquisition under John Page, Esq., Esch'r., & now granted by order, &c; ½ acre purchased of Col. John Custis, 29 Sept. 1683; the remainder being waste adj., granted by order, &c., for trans. of 1 pers.*

RICHARD SMITH, 200 acs., Low. Norf. Co., Linhaven Par; adj. land formerly Sarah Russell's; crossing the Green Br; to Basnett's land; 20 Apr. 1689, p. 702. Trans. of 4 pers: Adam Ellis, James Thorpe, Roger Newsum, Ann Edmonson.

MR. JOSHUA STOREY & MR. JOHN GWINN (Gwynn), 2500 acs., 20 Apr. 1689, p. 702. Part of 6000 acs. granted Mr. John Pate & Robert Beverley, 15 July 1669; adj. same & on the gr. run or Sw. of Mattapany Riv., &c. Granted to Walter & Margaret Keeble, son & dau. of Geo. Keeble, dec'd., 14 Jan. 1673, deserted, & now granted by order, &c. Trans. of 50 pers.*

SAMUEL GREEN, of Rappa. Co., 180 acs., on S. side of Rappa. Riv., & N. side of Dragon Sw; adj. Tho. Crow; William Cheyney; Thomas Hines; & land of Bredgarr; 20 Apr. 1689, p. 703. Said land bought by sd. Greene & Charles Chair of Hen. Creaton; being part of 220 acs. granted to Tho. Paddinson. Trans. of 4 pers: Robt. Thompson, Ab. Saxton, Edwd. the Shoemaker, Richd. Person.

MR. FRANCIS CLEMENTS, 450 acs., Surry Co., in Southwark Par., 20 Apr. 1689, p. 703. Adj. Mr. Arthur Jordan; Wm .Creed; & land of River Jordan. Trans. of 9 pers: Fra. Clements, Caleb Dowhunt, Tom Possum; Rose, Wm., Jone, Betty, Jack, Franck.

THOMAS BRANTON, 33 acs., Warwick Co., in the Oaken Swamp; 20 Apr. 1689, p. 704. Adj. Capt. Miles Cary; Mr. Tho. Harwood; Thomas Platt; & John Lewis; on Howard & Wootton's line; to Calvert's land. Trans. of: John Chandler. *Note:* "This patt. to be charged in York."

RALPH WALLIS, 1000 acs., Low. Norf. Co; from head of the S. Br. of Eliz. Riv; beg. at Capt. Knott's land; 20 Apr. 1689, p. 705. Trans. of 20 pers: James Gates, Ralph Ratchell, Abrah. Jones, Morgan Roads, Arthur Petkin (or Perkin), Jno. James, Robt. Rolfe, Tho. Grimes, Jane Alvary, Tho. Udall, Sarah Ellis, Theop. Tooke, James Elfe, Robt. Bleamount, James Egerton, Eliz. Ellerby, Robt. Tooker, Wm. Russell, Ann Jones, Robt. Ayres.

CAPT. HUGH CAMPBELL, 400 acs., Low. Norf. Co; being a neck whose point shoots against the up. landing of the North River; 20 Apr. 1689, p. 705.

Granted Mathew Ship, 27 May 1673, deserted, & now granted by order, &c. Trans. of 8 pers.*

ARTHUR EGERTON, 150 acs., Low. Norf. Co; towards the North Riv; beg. by the gr. Cyprus Branch; 20 Apr. 1689, p. 705. Granted Morgan Jones, 4 Nov. 1685; assigned to Mr. Charles Egerton; deserted, & now granted by order, &c. Trans. of 3 pers: Jno. Reeves, Tho. Richards, Jane Ellis.

HENDRICK WEEDICK, 225 acs., Low. Norf. Co; in the S. br. of Eliz. Riv., 20 Apr. 1689, p. 706. Sexton died seized of, & was found to escheat by inquisition under Edward Moseley, Depty. Esch'r., & now granted, &c.

DANIELL NEECH, 200 acs., Accomack Co; at head of Messango Cr; adj. Robt. Johnson; (date blank), p. 706. Granted to German Gilliot, 9 Nov. 1666; deserted, & granted to Col. Wm. Kendal, 4 Nov. 1685; deserted, & now granted by order, &c. Trans. of 4 pers: Nath. Oak, Michael Underhill, Peter Donellee, Nath. Teff (or Toff.)

RALPH WORMELEY, ESQR., 83 acs., Gloster Co; (date blank), p. 707. Purchased of Hen. Thacker, as by deed dated 14 Feb. 1655 to Sarah Williams als. Holdgate, & recorded in sd. Court, from whom it escheated, by inquisition under Francis Page, Depty. Esch'r., & now granted &c.

ROGER TILMAN, 1060 acs., Chas. City Co., in Bristoll Par; on S. side of Appamattock Riv., at a place known by the name of *Moncus-a-Neck;* 20 Apr. 1689, p. 707. Beg. at mouth of a gr. branch, nigh Thomas Loe; crossing Moncus-a-Neak main creek; a Beaver pond; & gravelly run, &c. Trans. of 22 pers.*

JAMES THWEAT, SENR., 125 acs., Chas. City Co., in Bristoll Par; on S. side of Appamattock Riv; adj. Mr. Henry Batte; & Edward Birchett; 20 Apr. 1689, p. 708. Trans. of 3 pers.*

JOHN LUCAS, 300 acs., Warwick Co., in Mulberry Par., 20 Apr. 1689,

p. 709. Purchased of Mr. Robt. Bullock, 15 Oct. 1673, & by "the sd. Alsop" bequeathed in 1675 to Elinor, his wife, & found to escheate from Eliner Alsop, *als.,* Lucas as by inquisition under John Page, Esch'r., &c. 17 Mar. 1672; since granted, &c.

REYNARD ANDERSON, 328 acs., Chas. City Co., in Bristol Par; on S. side of the 1st Black Water Sw; 20 Apr. 1689, p. 709. Trans. of 7 pers.* *Note:* Fee & seale to be ch'd. to Mr. Minns.

JEREMIAH LUNDY (or Landy), 361 acs., New Kent Co., in Blissland Par; on S. side of the W'n. br. of Ware Cr; 20 Apr. 1689, p. 710. Trans. of 8 pers.* *Note:* Same as above.

MR. HENRY RANDOLPH, 1000 acs., on N. side of Swift Cr; in Bristoll Par; next to Mr. Willm. Walthall, & on N. side of Appamattock Riv; above the Falls; 16 Feb. 1662, p. 710. (*By Sir Wm. Berkeley*). 850 acs. granted to Mr. Willm. Hatcher, deserted, & granted sd. Randolph by order of Court in 1655; 150 acs. for trans. of 3 pers.* Signed: William Berkeley; Tho. Ludwell, Secr'y; Test: Fra. Kirkman.

FRANCIS CRANE, 600 acs., New Kent Co; on N. side of Mattapony Riv., upon brs. of Ashunwaymanscott (?) Swamp; adj. Capt. Thomas Brereton, to whom it was granted, 14 Aug. 1669; deserted, & now granted by order, &c; 20 Apr. 1689, p. 712. Trans. of 12 pers: Jno. Robins, Henry Speeres, Jane Rooks, Abrah. Jones, Roger Myhill, Sarah Ree, Joan Roberts, Kath. James; Tom, Ned, Kate, Doll, Negroes.

COLEMAN BROUGH, 50 acs., Eliz. City Co., 20 Apr. 1689, p. 712. Bequeathed, by will dated 26 Sept. 1664, by Wm. Brafeild (Brayfeild) to his son Wm., & found to escheat by inquisition under Antho. Armistead, Depty. Esch'r., 7 May 1687, & now granted, &c.

PETER LETHERBURY, 1000 acs., Accomack Co., 20 Apr. 1689, p. 713. Adj. Willm. Benston, his own & land of Jenkins. Granted to Capt. Jno. West, 14 Jan. 1671/2, deserted, & now granted by order, &c. Imp. of 20 pers.* *Note:* The rts. due by certificate of E. Chilton, Cl., for 44 rts. to Col. Jno. West, proved according to order (of) Genll. Court.

DANIEL JOHNSON, 391 acs., Henrico Co., in Varina Par; N. side of James Riv., 20 Apr. 1689, p. 713. Adj. Joshua Stapp; crossing br. of Shacko Cr; & Pequoucky (or Peynoucky ?) Path; to Robt. Green's path, &c. Trans. of 8 pers: Jno. Sandford, Robt. Elliot, Jno. Sampson, Abrah. Holder, Wm. Ranger, Jno. Overton, Sarah Overton, Wm. Bishop.

JAMES MUMFORT, 50¼ acs., Chas. City Co., in Westopher Par; S. side of James Riv; adj. Mr. John Woodlef (Woodlief) & Maj. Francis Poythess; 20 Apr. 1689, p. 714. Imp. of 1 pers.*

CHRISTOPHER KELLBEE (Killbee), 590 acs., Middlesex Co., 20 Apr. 1689, p. 714. Granted to Charles Hill, 6 Mar. 1655 & renewed 26 Jan. 1663. Beg. at John Niccols *als.* Tigner's (or Pigner's) land; along line of Deal's; to Wm. Churchill, Gent; by br. of Beners (?) Cr., &c. Imp. of 12 pers.* *Note:* "The clause of being due by Importation of twelve p'sons. is a mistake, it being old patented land that did not want Rights. W. Edwards, Cl. Genll. Cou."

JOHN CUSTIS, Esqr., 458 acs., N'ampton Co., 20 Apr. 1689, p. 715. Granted to Richd. Whitmarsh, & escheated by inquisition under Jno. Stringer, Esch'r., & now granted, &c.

JOB HOWES, about 300 acs., in *Pamonky Neck,* in New Kent Co., 24 Apr. 1689, p. 716. Purchased of Georg Chapman, as by deed to Mr. John York, dated 19 Jan. 1682, & recorded in sd. Co. Beg. at sd. Chapman's old field, adj. Thom. Baker; John Hollins, Col. John West; & Joseph Norment; on the Spring Br. Escheated from sd. York, by inquisition under Christopher Wormeley, Esqr., Esch'r., & now granted, &c. *Signed:* Nathll. Bacon, P.

GEORGE NICHO. HACK, 350 acs., Accomack Co., 20 Apr. 1689, p. 716. Land Mrs. Anne Boat died seized of & escheated by inquisition under John Stringer, Esch'r. &c; & now granted, &c.

THOMAS CARDWELL, Planter, 550 acs., Henricoe Co., in Varina Par; N. side of James Riv., 20 Apr. 1689, p. 716. Beg. at Samuell Bridgewater, on N. br. of Gilley's Cr., &c. Trans. of 11 pers.*

MRS. ALICE STANFORD, Widdow, 1400 acs., Surry Co., 25 Apr. 1689, p. 717. Granted to William Ewen, 8 July 1648, 400 acs. of which was granted sd. Ewen, 15 Sept. 1619 & 1000 acs.

granted him, —— Jan. 1621; escheated by inquisition under Saml. Swan, Sub. Esch'r., 27 Nov. 1686, & now granted, &c.

MR. HUGH CAMPBELL, 500 acs., Surry Co; 20 Oct. 1688, p. 718. On SE side of Pigeon Sw; adj. Nicholas Sessums' old land, a br. dividing this, Richd. Blow, & land of W. Edwards. Granted to sd. Sessums, 20 Apr. 1684, deserted, & now granted by order, &c. Trans. of 10 pers: James Eccolls, Ralph Strattles, Robt. Jones, Sarah Whitford. Abraham Douglas, Tho. Metsall, Richd. Janison, Mary Janison, Samll. Warton, Jeremiah Eggerton. (By Francis, Lord Howard).

PATENT BOOK NO. 8

By Nathaniel Bacon, President of Council, &c.

GILLEY GRUMEREN, 481 acs., Henrico Co., Verina Parish; 20 Oct. 1689, p. 1. N. side of James Riv., nigh Chickahaminy Sw; beg. at his former survey. Importation of 10 pers.*

THOMAS COCK, Senr., 816 acs., Henrico Co., Verina Parish; (date blank), p. 1. S. side Chickahaminy main Sw; beg. at land known as *Oposum*, in possession of Jno. Baxter; crossing a br. of Oposom, to Mr. Bland's corner, along Mr. Richard Cock, &c. Imp. of 17 pers: Jane Borar, Robt. Beasley, Jno. Witt, Joane White, Alex ——, Patrick Foster, Robt. Povey, Jno. Edwards, Gill. Fuckett, Tho. Mathews, Hen. Baltamore, Fra. Cleavely, Hugh Davis, Jno. Herbert, Eliza. Harrison, Negro Nell, Benetta Clame (or Claine).

ROBERT BEVERLEY, 988 acs., Henrico Co., Verina Par., 20 Oct. 1689, p. 2. N. side of James Riv., above the falls; beg. by a great point of rocks just above the *old Powhite feilds*, &c., crossing branches falling into Chickahaminy Sw; on Westham Cr., nigh a great Beaver pond, &c. Imp. of 20 pers: Jno. Butterfeild, Will. Hitchins, Jno. Dixon, Anne Davis, Jane Jackson, Joan Sanders, Reece (?) Williams, Julius Deeds, Vere Boswell, Amy Boswell, Peter Williams, James Jackson, Anne Swanley; & 6 Negroes: Tom, Mingo, Sambo, Santo, Toney, Bess.

EDMUND JENNINGS, Esqr., 6513 acs., N. side of James Riv., about 12 or 14 mi. above the foot of the falls; 20 Oct. 1689, p. 2. Part of which was taken up by one Ramsey & Groves; by them lapsed, for which sd. Jennings hath the Governor's grant; the rest being King's land; beg. at Tuckahoe Cr., where it forks into the river; to the Horse Pen Br., which is supposed to be the upper side of Westham, &c. Imp.

of 131 pers: Jno. Bell, Tho. Ray, Geo. Phillips, Anne Elder, Benja. Haeles, Jno. Start, Wm. Bayts, Sarah Hughs, Deborah Short, Geo. Stone, Darcy Hughs, Jno. Duncomb, Hen. Hall, Margart. Roe, Timo. Briess (?), Mathew Hall, David Mansfeild, Geo. Harvey, Tho. Hull, Jno. Lackerman, Tho. Loyd, Jno. Fairface, Anne Hulett, Wm. Halchard, Henry Willis, Fra. Eaton, Tho. Payton, Jno. Burley, Isaac Hill, Eliza. Hambleton, Jane Bull, Hen. Mitchell, Hump. Moody, Tho. Pall, Jno. Ashby, Geo. Morley, Wm. Creede, Walter Waters, Dennis Millford, Hugh Nanny, Abell Windsor, Rebecca Breedon, Jno. Story, Hen. Hopkins, Jno. Pardoe (or Bardoe), Sarah Hatten, Oliver Stone, Owen Parker, Jno. Wooden, Alice Allen, Tho. Marston, Richd. Dixon, Edward Dover, Samll. Hunt, Sudeavor Austine, Bartho. Savage, Geo. Sherne, Edwd. Fowler, Richd. Batts, Josh. Henley, Stapleton Ubank, Gawen Wilson, Tho. Brothwaite, Jno. Kingstone, Wm. Woodward, Owen Micraugh, Eliza. Harrison, Fra. Inch, An. Ruggles, Susan Hollaway, Eliza. Venis, Tho. Mitchell, Robt. Greene, Humphry Smith Lambert Tye, Martin Gardner, Danll. Jordan, Jno. Greene, James Hormell (or Horsnell), Jno. Ayres, Christian Peirson, Jone Roberts, Grace Jones, Tho. Morris, Richd. Rogers, Jno. Welsh, Robert Williamson, Honor Peach, Wm. Grace, John Wiseman, Robert Owen, Jone Owen, Wm. Owen, Abraham Johnson, Wm. Reade, Sarah Rookeings, Jno. Turner, Ja. Wilson, Owen Tunstall, Rich. Heathfeild, Jno. Banister, James Powell, Walter Thompson, Jonas Roberts, Jno. Westoby, Tho. White, Jno. Lambart, Hester Lambert; & 23 Negroes.

ROBERT OWEN, 743 acs., Surry Co., 20 Oct. 1689, p. 3. On S. E. side of *Jno. Chehocon* Swamp; 648 acs. part granted Mr. Barth. Owen, 14 May 1673, & due sd. Robert, as son & heir; & 95 acs. for imp. of 2 pers: Jno. Sharp, & Henry Wych.

CAPT. ROGER POTTER, 268 acs., Surry Co., 20 Oct. 1689, p. 4. Beg. at Robt. Owen's on S.W. of *Jno. Chehocon* Sw; on Capt. Corker's line; &c. 100 acs. bought of Richd. Tyas; & 168 for imp. of 4 pers: Harry, Guy, Tom, & Frank.

RICHARD JORDAN, 568 acs., Surry Co., 20 Oct. 1689, p. 4. Adj. Robt. Owen's; & Nath. Roberts; by John Chehocon Sw., & his own land. 200 acs. by his patent, 20 Oct. 1688; & 368 acs. for imp. of 8 pers: Abraham Red-Cross, Jno. Harry, Joan Bates, Jno. Hayes, Jno. Elliott, Sarah Moore, Robt. Ellis, Jane Mitchell.

ABRAHAM EVENS, 472 acs., Surry Co., 20 Oct. 1689, p. 5. Adj. his own & along land of Richard Washington. Imp. of 10 pers: Morgan James, Wm. Hughs, Ralph Spratt, Jno. Richards, Wm. Jones; Dick, Jone, Harry, Bucka, Kate.

THOMAS HUNT, 150 acs., Surry Co., 20 Oct. 1689, p. 5. Adj. Abraham Evens. Imp. of 3 pers: Tho. Hunt, Sarah Hunt, Anne James.

WILLIAM RAY, 314 acs., Surry Co., 20 Oct. 1689, p. 5. Adj. land of Richard Washington. Imp. of 7 pers: Robert Morris, James Echols, Sarah Jones, Anne Roberts; Sambo, Dick, & Toney.

WILLIAM LUCAS, 213 acs., Surry Co., 20 Oct. 1689, p. 6. Adj. his own; Barth. Figures; Benja. Harrison; & Wm. Carpenter. Imp. of 5 pers: Wm. Ratchell, Abraham James, Sarah Knott, Jno. Jones, Abell Gower.

NATH DENNIS, 140 acs., Surry Co., 20 Oct. 1689, p. 6. Adj. Benja. Harrison; & Wm. Lucas. Imp. of 3 pers: James Wagstaff, Ralph Jones, Abraham Roberts.

JOHN RAWLINS, 455 acs., Surry Co., 20 Oct. 1689, p. 6. In Jno. Chehocons Sw., adj. Richd. Jordan, &c. Imp. of 10 pers: Edward & Hanah Greenwood, Samll. Parker, Geo. Procter, Robt. Foster, Samll. Wilcox, Eliza. Floyd, Sarah Tonnsell, Josep. Richason, Wm. Gardner.

SAMUELL THOMPSON, 278 acs., Surry Co., 20 Oct. 1689, p. 7. Adj. Mr. Wm. Thompson, Mr. Edward Chilton, Wm. Grey, Danll. Regan, & Mr. Nicho. Merriwether, &c. Imp. of 6 pers: Jno. Rawlins, Wm. Hunt, Jane Ellison, Tho. Snow, Roger James, Jno. Hulins.

JETHROE BARKER, 261 acs., Surry Co., 20 Oct. 1689, p. 7. Beg. at Edward Gunell, on S.W. side of Otterdam Sw. Imp. of 6 pers: Sarah Newton, Jno. Ellerby, James Boyes, Jno. Roberts, Jethroe Rookins, Samll. Read.

JAMES BRYAN, 762 acs., Isle of Wight Co., 20 Oct. 1689, p. 8. Beg. by the Black Water Riv; to Jos. Vick's; along James Allen; &c. Trans. of 16 pers: Hen. Sandford, Andr. Relfe, Tho. Moore, Robt. Mann, Ada. Wallop, Jno. Jaquis, Robt. Horn, Mary Brookes, Jacob Johnson, Tho. Cary, Sampson Duke, (or Duce), Richd. Hide, Jno. Samon; Betty, Jack, & Mingo, Negroes.

FRANCES COPELAND, 380 acs., Up. Parish of Nansemond, near the White Marsh, at place called the middle Pacoson; 20 Oct. 1689, p. 8. Beg. at Dan'l. Hind; S.W. to the meadows of Hawkins' Hole, &c. Imp. of 8 pers: Eliza. Brayley, Jno. Low, Jno. Kerks, Eliza. Arrowsmith, Eliza. Marling, Jos. Lockheart, David Chitchley (or Clutchley), Rowland Williams.

JAMES KELLEY & USLEY YELLOTT, 350 acs., Up. Par. Nansemond Co., 20 Oct. 1689, p. 8. On W. side of a br. of Orapeak Sw., dividing this & land of Henry Plumton, along Jno. Sumners' line, &c. Imp. of 7 pers: Jno. Emberly, Wm. Wood, James Sanders, Abraham Bates, Jno. Phillips, Anne Phillips, Sarah Marshall.

WILLIAM SEAUELL, 80 acs., Low. Par. Nansemond, 20 Oct. 1689, p. 9. Beg. at land whereon Col. Edwrd Carter formerly lived; by his own, to land of Joseph Holloway; & Jno. Powell. Imp. of 2 pers: Jno. RedCross, James More.

THOMAS JERNAGAN, Junr., 300 acs., at *Summerton*, Up. Par. of Nansemond; on the Back Sw; 20 Oct. 1689, p. 9. Imp. of 6 pers: Joan Harwell, Jno. Nottingham, Margaret Grady, Wm. Sandiford, Abraham Jolly, Robt. Crane.

JOHN POWELL, 90 acs., Up. Par. Nansemond, at a place called *Orapeak;* 20 Oct. 1689, p. 10. Adj. Col. Jno. Lear; & Jno. Brothers. Imp. of 2 pers: Sarah Brookes, Jno. Blanker.

RICHARD & JOHN SANDERS, 350 acs., in the Western Br., in the Up. Par. Nansemond, 20 Oct. 1689, p. 10. Beg. at Tho. Mason; to Jno. Reynolds', *alias* Mulford's. pattent: to edge of ground cleared by Wm. Byrd; by land of Henry Plumpton ;& James Foster. *alias* More's land. 300 acs. granted Thomas Davis, 11 Mar. 1664, & now in possession of sd. John & Richard; 50 acs. for imp. of: Jno. Grimes.

MR. JAMES LOCKHEART, 338 acs., Low. Par. Nansemond, 20 Oct. 1689, p. 11. Beg. at John Grandbury (Grandberry), in the main sw: by Cofeild's line; adj. Robt. Murray: Richd. Slaughter; & Col. Edward Carter. 160 acs. granted him, 20 Apr. 1682; 178 acs. for imp. of *2 pers:* Jno. Temple, Jno. Darling, Ralph French, Danll. Smith.

HENRY PLUMPTON, 620 acs., on the Wn. Br., in the Up. Par. Nansemond Co., 20 Oct. 1689, p. 11. Beg. at Micha. Brinkley's land; to Wm. Moore's ancient pattent of 300 acs; to James Foster's. *alias* Moor's. land. 500 acs. granted him, 5 Apr. 1664; 120 acs. for imp. of 3 pers: Sarah Jones, Anne Meazle, Tobias Corbett.

ROBERT LASISTER (Lassister), 440 acs., Up. Par. of Nansemond, 20 Oct. 1689, p. 12. Beg. at the White Marsh, near Joseph Booth's Orchard; crossing Mattapocoon pocoson; to land sd. Lassiter purchased of Danll. Hind; to Robt. & Fra. Roundtree; to the main sw., &c. 400 acs. granted him, 8 Oct. 1672; 40 acs. for imp. of: Jno. Presley.

MATHEW BRINSON, 338 acs., Lynhaven Par., Low. Norf. Co., 20 Oct. 1689, p. 13. Adj. Jno. James; & Edmd. Moore; through the Greenland Sw., &c. Imp. of 7 pers: Samll. Whitehead; Richard, Pheebe, Mary, Eliza., & Pheebe Farrington; Andrew Lawther.

JAMES DAUGE, 1034 acs., Low. Par. of Lynhaven. Low. Norf. Co., 20 Oct. 1689, p. 13. 250 acs. beg. in Richd. Bonnie's line; to his own; & land of Jno. James; on the Cyprus Run; to Wm. Gruntoe; to survey of Brinson's Quarter, &c. 784 acs. granted Capt. Wm. Carver, 9 Oct. 1675 & by severall assignments due sd. Dauge; 250 acs. for imp. of 5 pers: James Dauge 3 times; Margaret Dauge, & James Bell.

RALPH WALLACE, 250 acs., Low. Norf. Co; towards head of the S. Br. of Eliz. Riv; 20 Oct. 1689, p. 14. Beg. near land of Walter Coston (or Cotton); & upon Richford Sw. Granted Henry Platt, 27 Sept. 1680 by him deserted, & granted by order, &c. Imp. of 5 pers.*

CAPT. HUGH CAMPBELL, 215 acs., Low. Norf. Co; at head of the S. br. of Eliz. Riv., called Barnes' Neck; 20 Oct. 1689, p. 14. Adj. Mr. Mathew Whitfeild; on the Gum Sw; &c. Granted Jacob Barnes, 20 Apr. 1684, deserted, & now granted by order &c. Imp. of 5 pers.*

THOMAS SCOTT. 150 acs., in the Western Br. of Eliz. Riv., 20 Oct. 1689, p. 14. Beg. at land of Capt. Jno. Sipsey & adj. Richd. Pinner. Granted to Xper. Rivers, 11 Mar. 1653, deserted, & granted sd. Scott by order, &c. Imp. of: James Singleton, 3 times.

SAME. 150 acs., in Eliz. River, bet. the 2 main brs. of Church Cr., 20 Oct. 1689, p. 15. Bounded from Timber Neck Sw., parallel to the Great Sw., &c. Granted to Richd. Pinner, 20 Apr.

1653, deserted, & granted sd. Scott by order, &c. Imp. of: James Singleton, 3 times.

RICHARD SHEWELL, 115 acs., Eliz. City Co; near a place called *Ridge of Land;* 20 Oct. 1689, p. 15. Beg. at Mr. Pasco Dunn; on land of Powers & Davies in Warwick Co., &c. Imp. of 3 pers.*

MR. JOHN BROACH, 342 acs., of (the) King's land, in New Kent Co., St. Stephen's Par; on N. side of Mattapony Riv., 20 Oct. 1689, p. 15. Beg. by Col. Abrahall's house; by Claud Dennis' Church path; on Mantipike Sw. Imp. of 7 pers: Robt. Sadler, Samll. Ward, Richd. Harrard, Rowling Peirce, Tho. Hobbs, Richd. Hugging, Mary Barwick.

MR. JAMES TAYLOR & JOHN NEAL, both of New Kent Co; 209 acs., of King's land; in sd. Co., in St. Stephen's Par; on N. side of Mattapony Riv., 20 Oct. 1689, p. 16. Beg. below James Taylor's plantation, along John Neel's line, to Col. Tho. Walker; on Robert Jones; to Tho. White's &c. Imp. of 5 pers: Tho. Grimstone, Hugh Jones, Tho. Allen, Tho. Davis, Anne Brooking.

MR. ROBT. PRIOR (Pryor), 309 acs., Gloster Co., Ware Parish, 20 Oct. 1689, p. 16. Near head of a br. of Crany Cr; adj. Mr. Rigault; Xper. Greenaway; & Tho. Wisdome. 92 acs. granted Tho. Jefferson, 1 Apr. 1668, deserted, & granted by order to Robert Collis, who assigned to sd. Pryor, 21 Apr. 1689; 217 acs. now taken; & all due for Imp. of 7 pers: Jno. Savory, Phillip Macaskin (?), Mary Dowsy, Richd. Right; Tom, Toby, & Dick Negroes.

CHRISTOPHER GREENAWAY, 445 acs., Gloster Co., Ware Par., 20 Oct. 1689, p. 17. Beg. in Rigault's line, in Peaches Sw; adj. land of John Waller, dec'd. &c. 370 acs. granted Christopher Greenway, dec'd., 28 Oct. 1665; 75 acs. due for Imp. of 2 pers: Abraham Stanton, Grace Holmes.

AUGUSTINE HORTH, 441 acs., of land *and water*, Gloster Co., Ware Par.,

20 Oct. 1689, p. 17. Beg. on W'wd. side of the North River, & including the 5 pine Islands; adj. James Morris, &c. 350 acs. granted Wm. Dudley, 20 Sept. 1652, & assigned to sd. Horth, who took a pattent in his own name, 31 Dec. 1662. Said land now surveyed by order, &c; 91 acs. for Imp. of 2 pers: Math. Hudson, Eliz. Desermacox (?).

MR. HENRY JEFFS, 143 acs., Gloster Co., Ware Par., 20 Oct. 1689, p. 18. Beg. at land of Peter Starling, dec'd; along his own, & land of one Goodson; to Cooley's line, &c. Imp. of 3 pers: Robert Davies, Eliza. Allen, Mary Piercy.

MR. THOMAS TODD, 300 acs., on N. side of a Cr. near Horn Harbor; 20 Oct. 1689, p. 18. Adj. land of Mrs. Morrison, &c. Granted to Jno. Needler, 10 Mar. 1652, deserted, & granted sd. Todd by order, &c. Imp. of 6 pers.*

GEORGE BLAKE, 227 acs., Middlesex Co., 20 Oct. 1689, p. 19. Beg. at his own, & adj. Wm. Scarburgh & Philli. Torbsey (?); & land of Mr. Robt. Smith, dec'd; along the main Road, &c. Imp. of 5 pers: Duke Hornsby, Dor. Hales, Elinor Banbridge, Hen. Bedford, Jno. Moss.

MR. JAMES CURTIS, 360 acs., Middlesex Co., on NW side of Nimcock Cr., 20 Oct. 1689, p. 19. Beg. at Cedar point; adj. Ralph Wormley, Esqr; &c. 273 acs. granted Abraham Moon, 19 Oct. 1653, & conveyed to Arthur Dunn, 6 Nov. 1653; Imp. of 2 pers: Jos. Talling, Richd. Thaxton.

JOHN WEBSTER, 189 acs., of King's land, Rappa. Co., on S. side of Rappa. River, & on brs. of Piscataway Cr., 20 Oct. 1689, p. 20. Adj. Thomas Bowler, Esq; by Brown's Sw., &c. Imp. of 4 pers: Jno. Shuller (or Shutter), Aaron Perry, Jane England, Ralph Randall.

ARTHUR HODGES, Orphan, 253 acs., of King's land, Rappa. Co., on S. side of Rappa. Riv; in South Farnam Parish; 20 Oct. 1689, p. 20. Beg. by the Plantation side; to Thomas Cooper; along Samll. Perry's line; by Wm. Young's Rowling Road; on Gleab Sw; to Evan Davis, &c. Imp. of 6 pers: Thomas Platt, Jno. Martin, Wm. Leigh, Jno. Steppings, Jno. Hall, Jno. Hall, Jno. Pilgrim.

EVAN DAVIS, 1035 acs., Rappa. Co., S. Farnam Parish; on S. side Rappa. Riv., 20 Oct. 1689, p. 21. 861 acs. granted Evan Davis, his father, 21 May 1666; 174 acs. now taken, beg. at an oake deviding this from land of his *brother*** Arthur Hodges; by the mill Road; along Wm. Hudson; to Thomas Dayes' plantation; by Edward Hudson; to the Glebe Sw. &c. (Note: **It is assumed *"and"* has been omitted in the above immediately preceding the name of Arthur Hodges.) Imp. of 4 pers: Andrew Smith, Richd. Woodsoll, Mary Caswell, Mary Blayton.

COL. ARTHUR SMITH, 310 acs., Is. of Wight Co., 20 Oct. 1689, p. 22. On W. side of the Cyprus (Sw.); beg. at Wm. Oldis, bet. a Cart path & small pocoson; adj. line of Body &c. Granted to Wm. Oldis 30 Oct. 1662, & conveyed to Wm. Blith, 1 May 1665; deserted, & granted sd. Smith by order. &c. Trans. of 7 pers: James Wells, Tho. Maples, Giles Yates, Margt. Emerson, Geo. Pettus, Ruth Jarvis, Ann Young.

THOMAS TAYLER & THO. EDWARDS, 1000 acs., Low. Norf. Co., at head of the S. Br. of Eliz. Riv., 20 Oct. 1689, p. 22. Beg. by the Cyprus Sw., cor. of Jno. Gamon; by Richford Sw; towards the Greene Sea, &c. Granted Henry Henlain, 20 Apr. 1686, deserted, & granted the abovenamed by order, &c. Trans. of 20 pers: Adam Yeomans, Jno. Chapman, James Elfe, Sarah Newton, Jno. Richmond, Jane Richmond, Wm. Ellerby, Dorothy Meadows, Richard Evans, Jane Bates, John Turner, Isabella Plaw, Lawrance Thomas, Tho. Battison, James Elmore, Jno. Richardson, Sarah Jacob, Robert Paine, Abraham Skidmore, Thomas Ellerby.

MR. HENRY WARING, 500 acs., New Kent Co., Stratton Major Par.,

upon Pianketank Sw., 20 Oct. 1689, p. 23. Adj. David Bram's land, &c. Granted to Mr. George Burge, 16 Apr. 1683, deserted, & granted sd. Waring by order, &c. Imp. of 10 pers: James Nicholson, Jno. Richards, Israel Sheppard, James Welch, Andrew Neech (or Welch), James Rogers, Sarah Ellis, An. Jordan, Moses Roper, Anselm Bayly.

WILLIAM HOOD, 600 acs., Up. Par. of Nanzemond, at *Summerton;* on the Knuckles Sw., 20 Oct. 1689, p. 24. Imp. of 1 2pers.*

MR. THOMAS TAYLOR & MR. THOMAS EDWARDS, 1000 acs. Low. Norf. Co., 20 Oct. 1689, p. 24. (*Note:* Repetition of abstract second above. The adj. land owner is given as Samon instead of Gamon).

MR. JOHN GILLOM, 261 acs. in Chas. Citty Co., Bristoll Par., on S. side of Appamattuck Riv., 20 Oct. 1689, p. 25. Beg. at a point of Rocks; & adj. Hugh Leaden's land. Imp. of 6 pers.*

THOMAS TINSLEY, 111 acs., Rappa. Co., on S. side & in the freshes of the river; 20 Oct. 1689, p. 25. Beg. at James Scott, att foot of *Mount Clapham* hitt (hill ?); to James Coghill; crossing br. of Portobago, &c. Imp. of 3 pers: Eliz. Symonds, Mary Dicks, Charles Harbert.

WILLIAM JONES, 62 acs., Rappa. Co., on S. side the river; adj. Tobias Ingram; 20 Oct. 1689, p. 26. Imp. of 2 pers: Ellis Bradshaw, Richd. Davis.

JOHN WHITEHURST, 50 acs., 20 Oct. 1689, p. 26. Being on the N. end of a patent for 100 acs. granted to William Rogers, of Low. Norf. Co., from whom it escheated, by inquisition under Edward Moseley, Depty. Esch'r., & now granted, &c.

OWEN DAUGHEARTY, 170 acs., Low. Norf. Co., 20 Oct. 1689, p. 26. Granted to Nicholas Robinson, & escheated by inquisition under Edward Moseley, Dep'ty. Esch'r., &c.

JAMES MOORE, 573 acs., Henrico Co., in Verina Par., on the S. side of

Chickahomony main Sw; on Uffnum brook; 21 Apr. 1690, p. 27. Adj. James Lisle (Lile); Fra. Warren; & Mrs. Izard. Imp. of 12 pers: Mary Godfrey, Humph. Smith, Danll. Jordan, Thomas Hill, Tho. Michell, Lambert Tye, Edw. Richardson, Robt. Greene, Martin Gardner, Richd. Martin, Fra. Hayes, John Cole.

JOHN WADSON, 480 acs., Henrico Co., Verina Par; on S. side of Chicka- hominy Sw: adj. Mr. Tho. Cock; & on a br. of Gilley's Creek; 21 Apr. 1690, p. 28. Trans. of 10 pers: John New- ton, James Echolls, Samll. Newby, Sarah Orton, Alex. Richardson, James Relfe, John Ashton; Jone, Robin & Tom, Negroes.

WILLIAM PORTER & DANIELL PRICE, 440 acs., Henrico Co., Verina Par: on N. side of James River, nigh Chickahomony Sw., 21 Apr. 1690. p. 29. Adj. Lionell Morris; & Gilley Grummeren; crossing a br. of Gilley's Cr., &c. Imp. of 9 pers: John Byrd, Ellen Browne, Antho. Bourn (?), John Worth, James Sanders, Jno. Partridge, Jane Sykes, Wm. Parrott, Jane Price.

JOHN PARKER, of Mattabany. 200 acs., on an island on the N. side of the mouth of Pungoteag Cr., in Acco- mack Co; 21 Apr. 1690, p. 30. Trans. of 4 pers: Eliz. Morgan. John Langs- dole, Ben. Eyres, John Foxe.

JAMES MUIRE, Orphan of James Muire: 93 acs. of King's land, in New Kent Co., in Straton Major Par., on N. side of York River: by sw. side of Matusup Cr. & by Solly Bush Branch; 21 Apr. 1690, p. 30. Imp. of 2 pers: James Long, Eliza. Gooding. (Note: Name of Gov'r. left blank.)

MR. ROBERT BOWLING (Boll- ing), 166 acs., in the Co. of Happa- matuck River. & is known by the name of the Parsons old house; 21 Apr. 1690, p. 31. 100 acs. granted Mr. Wm. Farrer, 1 Dec. 1620; 66 acs. being King's Land; beg. between Puddle Dock Cr. & the river; to John Gillum's (Gillom) land; &c. Imp. of 2 pers: Peter Wielden. Danll. Lambert. (Note:

There is some doubt as to whether the scribe intended to leave the name of the county blank or called it County of Happamatuck River.)

ALEXANDER MEKENEY (Mac- kenny), 640 acs., Henrico Co., in Verina Par., on N. side of James Riv., 21 Apr. 1690, p. 31. Beg. at Samll. Bridgewater on Gilley's Cr; to Josha. Step; & Danll. Jonson. Imp. of 13 pers: Jno. Richards, James Redman, Antho .Cornish, Tho. Andrews, Jane Andrews, Wm. Hunter, Jno. Short, Robert Prideman; Tony, Sambo, Dick, Hector, Franck, Negroes.

JOHN WALLIS, JUNR., 35 acs., Low. Norf. Co; at head of Cedar Island Cr., in the S. Br. of Eliz. Riv; adj. land of Poyner; John Wallis, Senr; & Ed- ward Davis; 21 Apr. 1690, p. 32. Imp. of: Antho. Buckner.

THO. BELL, WM. BELL, & ROBT. BELL, 150 acs., on Sandy Island, in Accomack Co., 21 Apr. 1690, p. 32. Imp. of 3 pers: Mary Farrell, Rose Turrell, Judith Irish.

RICHARD SHEWELL, 115 acs., Eliz. City Co; neare a place called Ridge of Land; adj. Mr. Pasco Dunn; land of Potoer's (?) & Davis in Warwick County; 21 Apr. 1690, p. 33. Imp. of 3 pers: Hen. Morgan, Thomas Harvey, Edith Francklin.

JOSEPH MUMFORD, of Gloster Co., 410 acs., in Warwick Co., 21 Apr. 1690. p. 33. Beg. upon the Old Poko- son Damms, by the Graves & butting on land of John Brown; Zach. Chap- pell; & Mr. Ranshaw; to Harwood's Neck reeds; to Sam'l. Chappell; neare Mr. Corlie; & on James Russell, &c. 340 acs. part of 650 acs. granted Robt. Newman, 10 Mar. 1638, which after severall assignments came to Richard Watkins, & descended to Joseph, his son; & from him to Mary his dau. & sole heir, & late wife of sd. Mumford, at whose request the land was surveyed, she being now a widdo & desires a patt. of the whole may be (issued) to Joseph Mumford, her son & heire apparent; 70 acs. for imp. of 2 pers: Mary Downer, Christian Golte.

MR. ROGER HOUSDEN, 300 acs., in *Corrotuck Precincts;* Low. Norf. Co; neare Henry Beacher's line; 21 Apr. 1690, p. 34. Imp. of 6 pers: John Allain (or Allam), Wm. Miles, Sarah Kirby, Jno. Overton, Andrew Kirk; Sambo a Negro.

JOHN BIGGE (Bigg), SENR., 1200 acs., Low. Norf. Co., on E. side of the S .Br. of Eliz. Riv., on the *Cormorant poynt;* 21 Apr. 1690, p. 34. Adj. land of Prescott; Danll. Macoy; by the old Roade, to John Bright (formerly Hall's line) ; along Mr. Allderson; to Costen's corner. 450 acs. granted him, 28 Apr. 1665; 750 being wast within sd. bounds, &c. Imp. of 15 pers: Jno. Chambers, Abigail hore (?), Mary Wilkins, Wm. Casell, Martha Havers (?), Mark Gilbert. Jno. Humphryes, Wm. Edwards, Ja. Gregory, Jno. Taylor, Xpr. Parcivall, Hum. Palmer, Jno. Ford, Jno. Barnard, Math. Hutchins.

MR. JOHN SCOTT, 748 acs., Chas. City Co., in Bristoll Par., on S. side of Warreck maine Sw., 21 Apr. 1690 ,p. 35. Imp. of 15 pers: Jno. Roberts. James Vaughan, Mary Vaughan, Tho. Jaquis, Jno. Nicchols, Tho. Voss, Sarah Newton, Doroth. Turner, Abrah. Read, Tho. Collins, Jno. Meadowes. Wm. Holsworth, Ja. Cook, Eliza. Willis, Jer. Watts.

MR. WM. BANKS, of New Kent Co., in St. Stephen's Par., 1079 acs., on N. side of Mattapany River, in sd. county; called & anciently knowne by the name of *Mantipike Land;* 21 Apr. 1690. p. 36. 750 acs. granted Edward Diggs, Esqr., 18 Apr. 1653, who assigned to Mr. Adam Holland, who assigned to sd. Banks; & by a resurvey, by Maj. Geo. Morris, it appears to contain 379 acs. more than in the pattent expressed together with some King's Land, upon which sd. Banks entered rights, according to law, & took out a new patt. for the whole, 20 Mar. 1660; beg. at mouth of a cr. devidine this & land of Col. Robt. Abrahall; &c.

MR. JAMES BLAIR. MR. JEREMIAH BROWNE. & MR. NICHOLAS BULLENTUN (Bulenting). 130 acs.,

bounding on their plantations, in Henrico Co., in Verina Par; on N. side of James Riv., over against *Neck a Land;* 21 Apr. 1690, p. 37. Beg. at the *Gleabe Land,* to mouth of 2 Mi Cr., &c. Imp. of: James Irwin (or Urwin), 3 times.

CAPT. JOHN LANE, of New Kent Co., in Straton Major Par., on N. side of Mattapony Riv; 140 acs., adj. Mr. Green, now Mr. Robt. Peyton's land; Geo. Martin; Geo. Dillard; & Mr. Edward & John Lewis; along the *Flaxmans* Roade, &c; 21 Apr. 1690, p. 37. Imp. of 3 pers: Jno. Collins, Rebecca Blake, Grace Feeld.

MAJOR THOMAS CHAMBERLIN (Chamberlain), 856 acs., Chas. City Co., in Bristoll Par; on S. side of Apamatuck Riv., at a place called *Rehoweck;* 21 Apr. 1690, p. 38. Beg. at Mr. Abraham Jones; by Wm. Jones; on Otterdam Run; on the W. br. of Rehoweck; to former survey of Rehoweck, &c. Imp. of 18 pers.* *Note:* 18 rights by Mr. Jno. Soan, as he is assignee of Wm. Hunt. Certified by E. Chilton, Cl.

MR. MALLACHY THRUSTON, 100 acs., Low. Norf. Co., 21 Apr. 1690, p. 39. Granted to Francis Plumer & escheated, by inquisition under Honble. Jno. Lear, Esqr., Esch'r., & now granted, &c.

MR. ROBT. YARD & MR. JOHN WATERS, 179 acs., Rappa. Co., on S. side of Rappa. Riv., 21 Apr. 1690, p. 39. Adj. Mrs. Eliz. Cox & Leonard Chamberlin: by Hoskins Cr; to Thomas Pettis; & Thomas Green; down Piscataway Cr; to Mr. John Cox, & plantation of Henry White. Imp. of 4 pers.* *Note:* W. Edwards' cert. to Coll. Potter.

JOHN MEADOR, 50 acs., Rappa. Co., on S .side of Rappa. Riv., 21 Apr. 1690, p. 40. Adj. his own; & land of Mr. Henry Awbrey; on the maine Sw. of Hoskins' Cr., &c. Imp. of: Jno. Chambers.

MR. THOMAS WELLBOURNE (Welburn), 550 acs., Accomack Co;

SE from the Marsh of Muskeeta Point; 21 Apr. 1690, p. 40. Trans. of 11 pers: Eliza. Poole, Jo. Thorn, Reb. Hallawell, Jno. Irish, Anne Fish, Gellian Connar, Jos. Mathews, Step. Barrett (or Barnett), Eliza. Walker, Wm .Adams, Jno. Denny.

DUGWELL FERSON, 63 acs., Middlesex Co; by W. br. of Parrett's Cr; adj. land of Mr. William Cheaney; 21 Apr. 1690, p. 41. Imp. of 2 pers: Joseph Calloway, Robt. Duell.

MRS. ELIZ. CARTER, Executrix of Col. Edward Carter; 764 acs., Nansamond Co., 21 Apr. 1690, p. 41. Beg. at Bullock's Cr., by Capt. Thomas Burbage; to John Grimes', *als.* Parrott's, line, &c. 614 acs. granted sd. Burbage, 1 Jan. 1649, & is in possession of sd. Eliz. as Ex'ix; 150 acs. found within the bounds. Imp. of 3 pers.*

MR. WM. EDWARDS, 73½ perches of land, in *James Citty,* 21 Apr. 1690, p. 42. From Joseph Copeland, on James River, to land of Honble. Nathaniel Bacon, Esqr., &c. Imp. of: Jno. Roberts.

MR. EDWARD & MR. JOHN LEWIS, 352 acs., on brs. of Assatiame Sw., on N. side of Mattapony Riv., 21 Apr. 1690, p. 42. Adj. plantation of George Dillard; down the Cross Br; up the E. br. of Tassatiames Sw. to the Coole Spring Br; to Cornelius Vaughan; on the Indian Cabin br; to Nich. King's spring br. Imp. of 8 pers: Danll. Hay, Jno. Butler, Jno. Lewis, Roger Haye, Anne Hay, Eliza. Lovell, Wm. Morgan, Samll. Holding.

MR. MARTIN KEY, 489 acs., New Kent Co., in St. John's Par., 21 Apr. 1681, p. 43. Given to him by his *Grandfather* Maj. Martin Palmer & Mr. John Humes, by deed of guift; which was surplus land within Capt. Joseph Croshawe's pattent, & granted to Mr. George Chapman, who conveyed to sd. Palmer & Humes; beg. by Woodward's Road; along John Fore, & sd. Key, to the maine Sw. of Cohoacke; cor. of the *Gleab Land,* &c.

ELIZABETH MARSTON, 349½ acs., James City Co; (*date blank*); p. 43. Granted to Wm. Wigg, who sold to Wm. Elcorne, 29 Mar. 1657, from whom it escheated by inquisition under Maj. Saml. Weldon, Depty. Esch'r., & granted to John Marston, who bequeathed to sd. Eliza.

WILLIAM WISE, 106 acs., York Co., in the New Poquoson Par; adj. Mr. Samll. Singnall; 21 Apr. 1690, p. 44. Granted Thomas Lilburn, 26 Apr. 1685, deserted, & now granted by order, &c. Imp. of 3 pers: Wm. Wise, Wm. Garro (?), Ja. Mathews.

JOHN WHITE, 100 acs., in the Up. Par. of Nansamond Co., 21 Apr. 1690, p. 44. Granted to James Welch, from whom it escheated by inquisition under Honble. Jno. Lear, Esqr., Esch'r., & now granted, &c.

JAMES MURRAY, 50 acs., called *the Rich Neck;* in Nansamond Co., 21 Apr. 1690, p. 44. Escheated from Nicho. Ackerland by inquisition under Honble. Jno. Lear, Esqr., &c.

WM. HILLIARD, 250 acs., Low. Norf. Co., in Linhaven Par., 21 Apr. 1690, p. 45. Lately Joel Martin's & now in possession of sd. Hilliard; escheated from Thomas Allen by inquisition under Honble. John Lear, Esqr., Esch'r., & now granted, &c.

MR. JOHN LYDDALL, 2248 acs., New Kent Co., in St. John's Par., 21 Apr. 1690, p. 45. Beg. on S. side of Black Cr., at mouth of the S. Br., about 35 po. below the new mill; adj. land, now or late, of Mr. Napier, &c. 1600 acs. granted to Capt. Geo. Lyddal, deserted, & granted to Mr. John Langston, 11 Mar. 1672/3, but never pattented & deserted; & granted to sd. John Lyddall by order, &c; 648 acs. being waste. Imp. of 45 pers: Tho. Dickson, Simon Burlington, Jno. Husse, Jno. Harris, Roger Norton, Richd. Lewis, Edwd. Hooke, Tho. Welch, Wm. Gates, Mich. Tirpin, Geo. Williams, Richd. Almond, Joice Mathews, Jno. Jones, Mary Warrell, Danll. Latre (or Latne), Tho. Cave, James Coran, Eliza. Sweeting,

Francis Young, Jno. Vord, Mich. Tenison, Edwd. Skryme, Jno. Rowland, Stephen Pullen, Robt. Owles (or Owgles), Susan Opton, Jno. Milkham, Wm. Nortrop, Tho. Stevenson, Henry Woodstock, Wm. Dove, Ja. Collison, Tho. Hodson, Mary Winington, Wm. Wood, Andrew Francklin, Ja. Role, Jno. Dawson, Mary Sherman, Antho. Boddy, Ambrose Bamblet, Ann Feild, Rich. Orgever, Jno. Willis.

JOHN SCOTT (or Stott), 206 A., 1 R., 20 P., Henrico Co., in Bristoll Par., on N. side of Appomattock Riv., 21 Apr. 1690, p. 46. Beg. at Maj. Wm. Harris; on the Holy Ground Slash; down maine br. of the Ashen Sw; to Richard Waymock (Wamock). Granted Mr. Joseph Tanner & Mr. Richard Waymock, 16 Apr. 1683, deserted, & now granted by order, &c. Imp. of 5 pers.*

WM. OWEN, 484 acs., Low. Norf. Co; on Julian's Cr., on W. side of the S. br. of Eliz. Riv., 21 Apr. 1690, p. 46. 364 acs. beg. at Nash & Taylor's cor; & adj. land he bought of Theodore Taylor; 70 acs. being a neck of land on N. side of sd. Cr., & sold by Richard Tayler to sd. Theodore, who sold to sd. Owen; being part of patt. granted Tho. Nash & Richard Tayler, 6 Nov. 1665; sd. 434 acs. granted sd. Owen, 20 Nov. 1683; 50 acs. adj. land of Wallis; & due for Imporation of himself.

MR. HENRY RANDOLPH, 520 acs., Henrico Co., on S. side of Swift Cr., above the 2nd br; adj. Samll. Newman; 21 Apr. 1690, p. 47. Imp. of 11 pers: Tho. Town, Wm. Crouch, Jno. Williams, Wm. White, Wm. Partlow. 6 by Mr. Chilton's cert. to Jno. Soan.

NICHOLAS COPELAND, 145¾ acs., on S. side of Rappa. Riv., on NW side of Occupation Cr. upon *Popoman:* 21 Apr. 1690, p. 48. Beg. at land of Wm. Gibson, dec'd., to Popoman (Sw.); to Mr. Bowler, &c. Granted to Samll. Ward, 21 Oct. 1684, deserted, & now granted by order, &c. Imp. of 3 pers: Nicho. Post, Eliza. Baly, Val. Lane.

CAPT. HUGH CAMPBELL, 1050 acs., Low. Norf. Co; from head of the

S. Br; 21 Apr. 1690, p. 48. Beg. by a grate Scypris Sw., adj. Jacob Barnes; & Silvester's line, &c. Granted Capt. Wm. Knot, 27 Apr. 1686, deserted, & now granted by order, &c. Trans. of 21 pers: Wm. Bell, Junr., Wm. Cotton, Tho. Fenston, Jno. Corkerill, Tho. Taylor, Tho. White, Hump. Mold, Robt. Bond, Jno. Potts, Nich. Filmore, Jno. Niccolson, Tho. Barren, Tho. Walker, Edwd. Bier, Tho. Workman, Tho. Gunston, Jno. Whittaker, Sybill Arnold, Mary Hudson, Richd. Timberneck, Ja. Gibson.

ALEXANDER FOREMAN, 288 acs., Low. Norf. Co; from the S. brs. of Eliz. Riv; adj. his own land & Gilliam's Neck Sw; 21 Apr. 1691, p. 49. Imp. of 6 pers: Edward Burn, Richd. Overton, Jno. Niccholson, Fra. Flear, Martha Short (?) & Coffe a Negro.

EDWARD HEWES, 17 Acs., Low. Norf. Co; toward head of Parradise Cr. on the N. side; adj. Capt. Crafford; Bustian's (or Bastian's) land; & George Vallentine; 21 Apr. 1690, p. 50. Trans. of: Hugh Wilson.

THEODORE TAYLOR, 212 acs., Low. Norf. Co; S. from head of the S. Br. of Eliz. Riv; adj. his own land, neare head of Richford Swamp; 21 Apr. 1690, p. 50. Imp. of 5 pers: Edwd. Farnfeild, Jno. Atkinson, Reb. Lewcey, Robt. Taylor; & a Negro.

JOHN WOODSON, SENR., 1324 acs., Henrico Co., in Verina Par., on S. side of Chickahomony Sw., 21 Apr. 1690, p. 50. Beg. at his land neare New Kent Road; to the falls; down a br. of White Oake Sw; to Mr. Cock; down Bare Sw., &c. Imp. of 27 pers: Robt. Martin, Alice Hill, Fra. Sink, Diane Seares, Tho. Langdell, Danll. Horton, Richd. Stiball, Fra. Whitwell, Tho. Devin, Robt. Hall, Jno. Lauthorp, Jno. Louth, Eliz. Clifton, Anne Scofeild, Ser. Somerscales, Kath. Gerrulld, Tho. Elder, Wm. Leigh, Josh. Lowder, Tho. Kagen, Eliza. Yowell, Ann Kees, Eliza. Hoton, Jno. Wade, Tho. Briscom (?), Tho. Welch (?), Wm. Selbe.

ALEXANDER MACKENNY, 790 acs., New Kent Co; in the freshes of Mattapony Riv; (date blank), p. 51. Beg. at Robert Abrahall; adj. John Joy, & Moody's land, by Mongye's old Landing, &c. Granted to Hen. Pigg & John Pigg, Junr., 20 Apr. 1685, deserted, & granted to Hugh Bawden, 30 Apr. 1688, but not pattented; now granted by order, &c. Imp. of 16 pers.* *Note:* "Not signed."

SAME. 167 acs., Rappa. Co., 21 Apr. 1690, p. 52. Beg. in the fork of the Green Sw; adj. Thomas Toseley; on Hudson's br; to Mr. Henry Woodson; & Mr. Williamson. Granted to Jno. Jones, 20 Apr. 1685, deserted, & granted to Hugh Bawden, 30 Apr. 1688, but not pattented; now granted by order, &c. Imp. of 4 pers: Jno. Turner, Abraham Wood, Sarah Marshall, Jno. Jones.

MR. JOHN SOAN, 82 acs., James (City) Co; W. side of Chickahominy Riv., near Webb's Run & adj. his own land; 21 Apr. 1690, p. 53. Imp. of 2 pers: Robt. Smallpage, Jno. Ingerton.

JEREMIAH BENSKIN, 780 acs., on S. side of James Riv., above land of Honble. Wm. Byrd, Esqr., at a place called *Powhite Swamp;* 21 Apr. 1690, p. 53. Beg. at a white oak hard by 4 beeches makeing Powhite Island; up Powhite Cr; towards upper end of sd. Island & comprehending same within the bounds. Imp. of 16 pers: Robert Warwick, Samll. Smith, Jno. Edwards, Tho. Andrews, Tho. Adams, Tho. Amry, Ja. Armestrong, Robert Carrige, Robert Taylor, James Richason. Tho. Rouse, Sarah Heath, Robert Perrot; Sambo, Robert, & Dick, Negroes.

JOHN JONES, Orphant son & heire of Rice Jones. Junr; 1780 acs., Middlesex Co., 21 Apr. 1690, p. 54. Beg. at cor. of *the Jamaico Land,* formerly one Haward's; to the Green Br; by the Dragon Sw., &c. 1000 acs. granted

John Apleton, 15 May 1661, who sold to Henry Ward, Marriner, & acknowledged in Lancaster Ct., 11 Nov. 1663, who sold to Rice Jones, Senr., 10 May

1664; resurveyed & found to contain 1300 acs., which was granted him, 8 Nov. 1667; 400 acs., being overplush was granted to him, & now due sd: John for trans. of 10 pers: Richard Anderson, Sarah Salmon, Daniell Ashpoole, Jane Warde, Robert Reppitt, Hincent (Vincent ?), DeLoppo, John Warrine, Sarah Rawleigh, Patrick Reney, Peter Blomwell.

MR. THOMAS WYNNE (Winn), 659 acs., on Black Water, 21 Apr. 1690, p. 55. Adj. John Wallice, dec'd; Herculus Flood; & Maj. Fra. Poythris, dec'd; on the Gr. Swamp; to mouth of Bland's Br; to land of John Williams, dec'd., &c. Imp. of 14 pers: Wm. Luck, Robert Wood, Sarah Willoughby, Jane Moore, Tho. Rosse, James Isham, Robert Shaw, Robert Willis, Sarah Shelly, Tho. Winter, Robt. Wallis, Robert Hill, Jno. Moss, Abraham Wood.

NICHOLAS ROBINSON & NICHOLAS DARRELL, 289 acs., on Black Water, 21 Apr. 1690, p. 55. Beg. at land of Mr. Ja. Wallice, dec'd; cross the 2nd Sw. to the Hoggpen Br; on the Ashen Br; to Hugh Lee, Senr., &c. Imp. of 6 pers: Jno. White, Sarah James, Richd. Wheelehouse, Robt. Middleton, Jno. Farmouth, Ruth Tunstall.

COL. EDWARD HILL, RICHARD LIGON, HUGH LIGON, & SAMUEL NEWMAN, 292 acs., Henrico Co., in Bristoll Par; N. side of Swift Cr; adj. Henry Walthall; 21 Apr. 1690, p. 56. Imp. of 6 pers.*

THOMAS HARMANSON (Hermanson), SENR., 1800 acs. N'ampton Co., 21 Apr. 1690, p. 56. Granted to Phillip Taylor, 19 Dec. 1643, for 1000 acs., & by Thomas Taylor, his son & heire, sold to Maj. William Andrews, who sold to said Hermanson. Beg. as neare as can be to sd. Taylor's pattent; on N. of Broad Cr. &c; 800 acs. contayned within sd. bounds; adj. John Savage, &c; granted sd. Hermanson, 17 Apr. 1667.

HERCULES FLOOD (Fludd), 1254 acs., upon Black Water, on E. side of the Ready Br., 21 Apr. 1690, p. 57.

Adj. William Harris, Adam Taplie, Capt. Henry Batts, *Mrs.* Frances Poithress; & Major Fran. Poithris; on the Long Meadow, adj. the Ealeroot Levell; &c. Imp. o f 26 pers: Tho. Hay, Edwd. Willoughby, Jane Isham, Jno. Nowell, Jane Nowell, Wm. Nowell, Henry Nowell, Jervis Hay, James Lock, Tho. Rudder, Robt. Allin, Wm. Rudder, Joan Scarlett, Robert Whaley, Jervis Wrack, Robt. Lock, Sarah Ridley, Dorothy Rooke, Wm. Long, Robert Mallard, Robt. Smith, Robert Joy, Sarah Moat, Robert Croe, Adam Holt, Richd. Gaines.

MR. PETER FIELD, 130 acs., Henrico Co., Bristoll Par; S. side of the gr. Br. of Swift Cr; adj. his own land; & crossing the White Oak Br; 19 Apr. 1690, p. 59. Trans. of 3 pers: James Drisdell, Edwd. Kennion, Jno. Smith.

SAME. 690 acs; same Co., Parish, date, & page. Adj. his own; land of Willm. Dodson; & Capt. Fra. Epes; on S. side of Swift Cr. & on the S. br. of the 2nd great br. Trans. of 14 pers: Alexdr. Ayr, Wm. Simmons, Robt. Nelson, Jno. Barnes, Marm. Beckweth, Bridget Freer, Eliza. Bell, Owen Mackenrow, Mary Levit, Danll. Martin (?); Tony, Mingo, Doll, Pompy, Negroes.

MR. HEN. RANDOLPH, MR. JAMES COCKE (Cock), JOHN GOLIGHTLY, & SOLOMON CROOK, 647 acs., Chas. City Co., in Bristoll Par; at a place known as the Second Swamp; 19 Apr. 1690, p. 60. Beg. at John Sturdevant. Imp. of 13 pers: Wm. West, Jno. West, Jno. Baxter, Mary Pedinn (or Pedum), Robt. T:, Thomas Woolls, Mary Wools, Paul Vaudin, Clare Vaudin (or Vandin), Anne Wells, Peter Prior, Robt. Man, James Miller.

JOHN DEANE & WILLIAM CLAPHAM, 1050 acs., Rappa. Co; on S. & in the freshes of the River, about 2 mi. from *Potobacco Towne;* beg. at James Coghill; crossing Potobacco run, &c; 21 Apr. 1690, p. 60. Trans. of 21 pers: Arthur Spicer, Augt. Wingfeild, Hannah Greene, Eliza. Simpson, Thomas Fairchild, Samll. Jaquis, Robt. Tayler,

Tho. Towling, Tho. Mason, Hannah Scrivener, Jno. Davies, Mary Rowland, Eliza. Miscn, Jno. Turner, Robert Johnson, Sarah Nubee, Law. Jarrett, Jane Rookeings, Rebecca Turner, Abell Atkinson, Jno. Sampson.

MR. JOHN BROADNAX, 1129 acs., on S. side of James Riv; on back of land of Honble. Wm. Byrd, Esqr., at the falls of James Riv; beg. by a piny Br. or slash; cross the Ochaneche Path, &c; 21 Apr. 1690, p. 61. Imp. of 23 pers: James Nicholson, Robert Harmon, Abraham Charnock, Sarah Charnock; Robt. Evans, Wm. Sims, Jane Roberts, Sarah Newton, Robert Savage, Dorothy Tunstall, Wm. Avery, Jone Evans, Abraham Ridley, Hannah Emerson, Jno. Salem, Richd. Hood, Jno. Richardson, Hezekiah Talbott, Wm. Oxly, Sarah Smith, Tho. Willis, Richd. Crow, Ruth Goslin.

CAPT. JOAKIM PAGETT, 129 acs., called *Crany Island;* Low. Norf. Co., 21 Apr. 1690, p. 61. N'ly. with James River, E'ly. with Eliz. Riv., S'ly. with Craney Br., dividing this & land of Capt. Jno. Sibsey, in possession of Lewis Conner, & W'ly with an isthmus; &c. 50 acs. granted sd. Sibsey, 26 Mar. 1649, & by severall deeds due sd. Pagett; 79 acs. within the bounds, due for Imp. of 2 pers: Jno. Roberts, Andrew Chadock.

LYDIA NOWELL, Widdow, 1752 acs., James City Co., 15 Apr. 1690, p. 61. Said land granted to Wm. Fry, viz: 750 acs., 17 Apr. 1653; 252 acs., 6 Feb. 1655; & 750 acs., 29 Apr. 1656; which lands escheated for want of heirs of Joseph Fry, his son & heire, by inquisition under C. Wormley, Esqr., Esch'r., & now granted, &c.

CHRISTOPHER WORMLY (Wormeley), Esqr., 800 acs., in Middlesex Co., formerly Lancaster; a mile from the river, 21 Apr. 1690, p. 62. Beg. by the *Church* Path from Col. Antho. Elliott's house; by sd. path from Col. Smith's house, &c. Granted to Leu't. Col. Anthony Elliott, 26 Feb. 1661, deserted, & now granted by order, &c. Imp. of 16 pers: Jno. Smith, Ja. Tutnell, Robert Cuningham, Jno. Cross, Sarah Cross, Robert Palmer, Wm. Witherington, Jane Roberts, Ann Finch, Tho. Felps, Adam Eland, Geo. Knott, Su. Tilley, Jno. Elliott, Wm. Rogers, Joan Sibbs.

MR. HUGH OWEN, 220 acs., Rappa. Co., on S. side the river; on brs. of Occupace (Cr.), 21 Apr. 1690, p. 62. Adj. Wm. Mosely; Coghill's line; & Wm. Grey; on the maine swamp, &c. Granted Richard Good, 29 Sept. 1674, deserted, & granted to Mr. Thomas Viccaris, 30 Oct. 1685, but never patented; now granted, &c. Imp. of 5 pers: Jno. Tuden, Hen. Crabb, Sarah Crabb, Wm. Smiter, Jno. Flint.

THOMAS DUDLEIGH & WM. ELLIOTT, 722 acs., Middlesex Co., 21 Apr. 1690, p. 63. Beg. at Mr. George Keeble, on N. side of Bob's Br; to Maj. Genll. Robt. Smith, near Smith's (Quarter) plantation; to S. side of Pianketank Road; down the Green Br., &c. Granted to Augustine Scarburgh, 30 Oct. 1686, deserted, & now granted by order, &c. Imp. of 15 pers: Jno. Fryer, Wm. Jerruld, Wm. Miller, Tho. Dillon, Jacob Johnson, Sarah Penington, David ——, Eliza. Crocker, Eliza. Collings, Honor Rider, Welkin (?) Ball, Jos. Bontell, Wm. Cotter, Wm. Bracey, Edwd. Congdon.

COL. JOHN WEST, 200 acs., Accomack Co; bet. his land at Pungoteague Cr. on the S., & land formerly belonging to one Price, at *Machotank,* on the N; 21 Apr. 1690, p. 64. Imp. of 4 pers.* *Note:* 4 by Mr. Chilton's Cert. 22 Apr. 1685.

JOHN WADE, 34 acs., James City Co; bet. Rockahock Path, Arrow Reed Path, & Arrow Reed Branch; 21 Apr. 1690, p. 64. Imp. of: Wm. Cheesman.

WM. MOSELY, JUNR., 514 acs., Low. Norf. Co., in Linnhaven Par., 21 Apr. 1690, p. 64. Beg. at Piney Point; to Geo. Poole & Holland's pattent; adj. Lancaster Lovet; by main br. of Bennett's Cr. 400 acs. granted to Mr. Richd. Poole, 18 Mar. 1662, & due sd. Mosely as marrying his sole heiress;

114 acs. for Imp. of 3 pers: Jack, Hector, Tom.

THOMAS RICHARDSON, 290 acs., Low. Norf. Co; on Goose Cr., in the Southern Br. precincts; adj. Roger Hodges; & land of Nash & Taylor; being sd. Richardson's seated plantation & Henry Dale's. 21 Apr. 1690, p. 65. Trans. of 6 pers: Joseph Greenaway, Rachell Field, Peter Steale, Wm. Bragg, Charles Bagley; & Cushee, a Negro.

THOMAS BOBBY, Planter, 750 acs., Jas. City Co., on W. side of Chickahomony Riv., 23 Apr. 1690, p. 65. 500 acs. adj. land formerly Humphry England's, & land formerly Thomas Warden's; 250 acs. by the old Cart way; adj. Richard Williams, Jno. Williams & David Phillips. Granted Wm. Fry, 29 Apr. 1656; descended to his son Joseph, who died without will or heir; escheated, & granted to Lydia Nowel, Widdow, 15th of this instant Apr., & she by deed, recorded in the Genrll. Court the 19th of this Apr., released & confirmed to sd. Bobby.

HENRY SOAN, Gent., 1500 acs., in the upper part of Jas. City Co., on W. side of Chickahomony River, 23 Apr. 1690, p. 66. Beg. by mouth of a little neck or feild, called now Walnutt feild; over Strawberry Hill Run to Williams' land, &c. 750 acs. granted to Wm. Fry, 7 Apr. 1653, & descended to his son Joseph, who died without will or heir, whereby it escheated, & was granted to Lydia Nowell, Widdow, 15th of this Apr., who by deed, 19 of this Apr., assigned to sd. Soan & his heirs forever; 750 acs. for trans. of 15 pers: Tho. Parker, Andrew Broadhurst, Jno. Wheately, Robert Seech, Sarah Roberts, Ambross Edwards, James Turner, Tho. Sherard, Adam Holt, Wm. Ives, Jno. Elsmore, Eliza. Jarrett; Tom, Jack & Dick, Negroes.

MR. PATRICK WHITE, 1554 acs., in *Corotuck* & Knott's Island, in Low. Norf. Co., 21 Apr. 1690, p. 67. 900 acs. at S. end of the Island, on King's point; SE on the main Bay of Corotuck, to mouth of a creek dividing this land & Vandermore's; including Crow Island

SE from his plantation on Knott's Island; granted him, 20 Apr. 1682; 454 acs. adj. his own, & running to cr. dividing it from land of Rachel Cornelius; sd. land seated by Lieut. Col. Thomas Lambert & given to his *nephew* Jno. Vandermulen, who sold to *said* Gordon, & granted to Mr. Thomas Gordon, 20 Nov. 1683, who sold to Capt. Thomas Russell, 13 May 1685, who assigned to sd. White, 9 Feb. 1687/8; 200 acs. adj. land he bought of sd. Russell; cor. of Richd. Jones, & on the creek, which the road bridge goes over; Trans. of 4 pers: Jack, Toney, Sampson, Hector.

MICHAEL FENTRIS, 270 acs., Low. Norf. Co., in Lynhaven Par., 21 Apr. 1690, p. 68. 150 acs. part adj. Capt. Wm. Crawford; & James Whithurst; granted him, 20 Oct. 1688; 120 acs. adj. his own; & land of William Nicholls. Imp. of 3 pers: Mary Butcher; Judyth & Nan, Negroes.

JOHN SHURLEY, 450 acs., Low. Norf. Co., in Lynhaven Par., 21 Apr. 1690, p. 68. 300 acs. adj. John Porter & Humphry Belt; granted to Tho. Cartwright, 21 Ju. 1664, who sold to sd. Shurley; 150 acs. adj. Capt. Robinson, etc. Imp. of 3 pers: Richard Carver; Nick & David, Negroes.

MR. WILLIAM PORTEN, 248 acs., Low. Norf. Co., on N. side of the E. br. of Eliz. River, 21 Apr. 1690, p. 69. Beg. neare mouth of the back creeke, a cor. of the *Towne* bounds, crossing sd. creek to the *Glebe Land;* adj. Adams' land; 150 acs. part of 200 acs. granted Nicholas Wise, 18 Mar. 1662, who sold to sd. Porten; 98 acs. for trans. of: Thomas Mason, Gent., twice.

WILLIAM WHITEHURST & RICHARD WHITEHURST, 1150 acs., Low. Norf. Co., in the Indian Creeke; 21 Apr. 1690, p. 69. 1000 acs. granted sd. William, 6 Nov. 1665; 150 acs. due them for Imp. of 3 pers: John Dunbar, Mary Battson, John Moore.

JAMES KEMP, 600 acs., Low. Norf. Co; at head of the E. Br. of Eliz. Riv., in Lynhaven Par., 21 Apr. 1690, p.

70. Adj. Mr. Jno. Porter; Job Kemp; Matthew Pallett; Mr. Thorowgood; & Mr. Ivie's land. Granted George Kempe, dec'd., 20 Oct. 1661, 200 acs. of which he assigned to Col. Lemuel Mason, 16 June 1666; 400 acs. due sd. James as heire to his father.

HENRY NICHOLAS, 380 acs., in Lynhaven Par., Low. Norf. Co., 21 Apr. 1690, p. 70. 300 acs. granted Henry Nicholas, dec'd., 30 Oct. 1669, & due the above named as heir at law; 80 acs. for Imp. of 2 pers: Thomas Richason; Tugg, a Negro.

MR. PATRICK WHITE, 400 acs., in *Corrotuck Precincts,* Low. Norf. Co; 21 Apr. 1690, p. 71. On NW side of Sympson's Cr. Swamp; adj. Evan Jones; & land of the Orphan of Almond; &c. Granted sd. White 21 Oct. 1687, & is now plainly marked & bounded.

MR. JAMES COCK, JOHN BUTLER, & WM. LOW, 1684 acs., Chas. City Co., at a place known as *Moncuseneck;* 21 Apr. 1690, p. 71. Beg. at Jno. Evans & Roger Tillman; crossing Cattail Br; & upper Nottaway Path; to Moncuseneck main Sw. Imp. of 34 pers: Wm. Barker, Joan Barker, Benja. Lucas, Robt. Case, James Brown, Jane Palmer, Samll. Ward, Jane Pepper, Alice Cockin, Nath. Goldin, Phill. Turner, Mary Read, Mary Lowman, Jno. Jones, Richd. Rogers, Wm. Cocken, Isak Mokeland, Robt. Boukley, Margt. Ballingslee (?), An. Phips, Mary Bennet, Eliza. Lucas, Tho. Wilkinson, Tho. Smith, Hen. Clench, Andr. More, Jer. Brookes, Mary Clapham, Elinor Ford, Jno. Knight, Tho. Butler, Eliz. Wats, Margt. Robinson, Cha. Machartee.

JOSEPH PERRY, 50 acs., called the *Ragged Island,* in *Corrotuck;* Low. Norf. Co; adj. Cedar Island; 21 Apr. 1690, p. 72. Imp. of: William Flear.

HENRY DALE & EDWARD HEWES, 800 acs., Low. Norf. Co; on W. side of the S. Br. of Eliz. Riv; 21 Apr. 1690, p. 72. Adj. Edward Hewes'; Crawford; Brackett; Muns; sd. Dale; Wm. Owens; John Joyce; Bunting; Thomas Green; & land of Wingfield. Imp. of 16 pers: Wm. Odeon, 16 times

GEORGE POOLE, 300 acs., Low. Norf. Co., in Lynhaven Par., 21 Apr. 1690, p. 72. Adj. lands of Mr. Wm. Moseley; Poole & Pallett; Smith; & Harper; crossing the Aishen Sw., to Lancaster Lovett, &c. Imp. of 6 pers: William Seeds, Margery Protherer; Tom, Maria, Ned & John, Negroes.

THOMAS WILLSON, 246 acs., Low. Norf. Co; in the W. Br. of Eliz. Riv., 21 Apr. 1690, p. 73. Beg. at John Johnson, on S. side of Goose Cr; to the Gaulberry Sw; to br. dividing this from lands of Ivie's & Defnall's. 150 acs. granted him, 20 Sept. 1661; 96 acs. for Imp. of 2 pers.*

MATTHEW PALLETT, 368 acs., Low. Norf. Co., in Lynhaven Par; upon head of Bennett's Cr., 21 Apr. 1690, p. 73. 168 acs. beg. near John Kemp; in Grace Holland's line; to land of Mr. Argall Thorowgood, now sd. Pallett's; to James Kemp. 200 acs., part of 750 acs. granted sd. Argall Thorowgood & his division of 140 acs; & 60 acs. part of Francis Thorowgood's division sold, viz: 40 acs. out of Argall's, & 60 out of Frank's, to Richard Lyster, who assigned to sd. Pallett; 100 acs., remaining of Argall's, sold to sd. Pallett; 168 acs. for Imp. of 4 pers: Tho. Finckley, Nicholas Finckley, Katherine Finckley, Ann Finckley.

JOHN FEREBEE, 1200 acs., Low. Norf. Co., in Corrotuck Precincts; on SE side of Sympson's Cr. Swamp; adj. Whitford's land & Charles Heas (?), &c; 21 Apr. 1690, p. 73. Imp. of 24 pers.*

EMANUEL WILLS, 153 acs., Warwick Co., (date blank), p. 74. Beg. at an oak on W. side of Warwick River, parting this from land of Thomas Pierce; along George Harwood; to land of Brewar; to Mr. James Pawley; &c. 100 acs. pattented by Mr. Thomas Iken, who dying intestate & leaving no heires, the land escheated, &c; 53 acs. for Imp. of 2 pers: Joan Tope, Eliza. Baker.

JOHN HERBERT, 1215 acs., Chas. City Co., in Bristoll Par., att or near Moncosaneak, 21 Apr. 1690, p. 74.

Beg. at land, now or late, of Roger Tillman, on W. side of Hatcher's Run; through Moncasaneak mayn Sw., &c. Imp. of 25 pers: Miles Hockley, Ja. Webster, Richd. Bossington, Jno. Lovelock, Tho. Steele, Ann Mathews, Jno. Deering, Andrew Jeffers, Tho. Lockley, Jno. Lockley, Mary Lockley, James Durant, Abraham Elmore, Jno. Sampson, Andrew Wray, Susanna Elsby, Dorothy Howard, Adam Roe, Emanuel Robins, Rich. Pembrooke, Will. Mills, Sarah Mills, Tom, Sambo, Moll Negroes.

SAME. 2870 acs; same Co. & Par., & date; on S. side of Apamatock Riv; p. 75. Beg. at John Ellis' land; crossing Powhipanock Mayn Branch, &c. Trans. of 58 pers: Wm. Jeffreys, Abraham Jackson, Timo. White, Bernard Moore, Mary Feild, Jaquis Johnson, Peter Elliott, Edward Hinton, Andrew Beale, Ja. Watson, Edwd. Cary, Robert Haines, Wm. Jarret, Tho. Yates, Nath. Carter, Richd. Harwood, Millescent Baker, Mary Clayton, Joan Wilson (or Wilton), Eliza. Greene, David Andrews, Edwd. Peirson, Ambros Page, Hen. Wootton, Tho. Pirkins, Randall Crayford, Hannah Hall, Ja. Parker. Note: 30 Rights by Mr. Edwd. Chilton's Certificate to Mr. David Crafford, May 2, 1685.

JOHN EVANS, 818 acs., Chas. City Co., in Bristoll Par; 21 Apr. 1690, p. 75. Adj. his patt. of 557 acs., granted 22 Nov. 1682; beg. on E. side of the Southern run, &c. Trans. of 17 pers: Ja. Appleby, Peter Feake (or Flake), Antho. Tarkin, Wm. Weaver, Andrew Corby, Susanna Hall, Jno. Roper, James Thornton, Adam Rugsbye, Tho. Hamillton, Robert Ellis, Jno. Carver, Joan Relfe, Anth. Hux, Jane More; Grace & Judah, Negroes.

HENRY KING & THOMAS PARHAM, 824 acs., Chas. City Co., in Bristoll Par., att or near Moncosaneak, 21 Apr. 1690, p. 76. To be equally divided. Beg. on land, now or late, of Roger Tyllman; down Cow Br., to Low's land; to Moncasaneak main run, &c. Imp. of 17 pers: Jno. Turner, Robert Rookeley, Jane Rookeley, Ann

Jones, David Morgan, Sarah Wharton, Jno. Newbee, Robert Creede, Geo. Hewlett, Tho. Dickenson, Adam Earley, Robert Savage, Jane Hughes, Wm. Morgan, Jno. Turner, James Ashton; & Guy, a Negro.

HENRY WALL, 275 acs., Chas. City Co., in Bristoll Par., att or near *Rahowick;* 21 Apr. 1690, p. 76. Beg. at land, now or late, of Maj. Chamberlin; to line late of Col. Wood, now, or late, sd. Chamberlin's, &c. Trans. of 6 Negroes: Harry, Sambo, Ruth, Tom, Moll, Ned.

NICHOLAS OVERBEE, the younger, 323 acs., Chas. City Co., in Bristoll Par., att or near *Rahowick;* 21 Apr. 1690, p. 77. Beg. at land, now or late, of Col. Wood, cor. of land late of Abraham Jones; to Henry Wall, &c. Trans. of 7 pers: Jno. Pawlet, Antho. Ragsdale, Sarah Howes, Robert Wilson, James Holmes, Tho. Gilson, Ruth Wigmore.

THOMAS CHAPELL, 904 acs., Chas. City Co., 21 Apr. 1690, p. 77. Adj. Robt. Bollin. Trans. of 19 pers: Jno. Throgmorton, Aron Wood, Jane Wood, Wm. Egerton, Ja. Bellamy, Tho. Maples, Sarah White, Tho. Harmon (or Hannon), Jno. Wharton, Rebecca Edwards, Abrah. Doughtye, Adam Wells, Tho. Ramsey, Jane Emerson, Rogert Holt, Jno. Welch, Robt. Sanders; Tom & Dick, Negroes.

MATHEW MARKS, 556 acs., Chas. City Co., in Martin Brandon Par., 21 Apr. 1690, p. 77. Beg. neer Ward's Run, by land late of Edward Richards; by Mr. Blighton; &c. Trans. of 12 pers: Tho. Wells, Robt. Wood, Jane Whitby, Jno. Sampson, Adam Good, Wm. Wright, Rich. Lewis, Edwd. More, Walter Long, Wm. Webster, Diana & Robin, Negroes.

ADAM TAPLY & WILLIAM HARRYSON, 1068 acs., Chas. City Co., in Jordan's Par; on S. side of James River, 21 Apr. 1690, p. 78. Beg. at Maj. Poythres; neer Aroccock Path; & neer Nich. Whitmore. Trans. of 22 pers: Elfrid Snow, Tho. Oxly, Ja. Allin, Geo.

Rudder, Antho. Scarlett, Ja. Lewis, Robert White, Edwd. Hutchison. Jno. Whiting, Wm. Rosse (or Roffe), Sarah Moore, Tho. Osborne, Tho. Randall, Ruth Everett, Rich. Isham, Geo. Nelson, Robt. Wells, Andrew Isham, Jno. Willoughby, Robert Norton, Joshua Royston, Richard Mallard.

JOHN UNDERHILL, 2317 acs., New Kent Co., in St. Peter's Par., 21 Apr. 1690, p. 78. Beg. at his own land; adj. Edward Johnson; on Powhite Swamp; to Beavour Dam Br; on Pickanock Path; adj. Bassett & Austin; down Brandy Br., &c. Trans. of 47 pers: James Trewe, Jno. Jordan, Phillip Wright, Jervis Salmond, Fra. Plumond, Fra. Fisher, Wm. Rades, Em. Upton, Sarah Waight, Tho. Carier, Jno. Card, Stephen Rogers, Charles Smart, Jno. Symes, Jno. Mehewe (or McHewe), Rich. Hollis, Eliza. Tatler, Tho. Jones, Jno. Tayler, Wm. Griffin, Saml. Pigg, Robert Hall, George Cole, Jno. ——, Tho. Sawyer, Roger Phillips; & 20 Negroes.

PHILLIP LIGHTFOOT, ESQR., 525 acs., New Kent Co; comonly called the *Doctors Field;* on the Draggon Sw., 28 Apr. 1690, p. 79. WHEREAS Anthony Arnold, late of New Kent Co; did purchase of one John Pigg, 525 acs. comonly called the *Doctors Field,* on the Draggon Sw., being the moyety of 1050 acs. granted sd. Pigg & Jno. Maddison, 4 July 1664; to be held by sd. Arnold & his heirs for ever, as by deed dated 24 Feb. 1664, & recorded in sd. County Court; by vertue whereof sd. Arnold was seized in his demesne as of fee of & in the sd. 525 acs., & being so seized sd. Arnold comitted Rebellion & high treason & was legally convicted & executed, & legally attainted by Act of Assembly, 8 June 1680, whereby all his estate, both reall & personall, became forfeited to his Majesty; and Whereas Phillip Lightfoot, Esqr., hath made composition for the said land & paid what by the Charter, Law & custome of Virginia is required in such cases, Know yee, &c.

Petition of sd. Lightfoot to President & Council, 19 Oct. 1689, p. 79. Composition paid Mr. Auditor Byrd, &c.

LT. COL. ANTHONY ELLIOTT. 800 acs., Lancaster Co; a mile from the River; 26 Feb. 1661, p. 80. Beg. by the *Church* Path from his house; to the *Church* path from Col. Smith's house, &c. Trans. of 16 pers.* *(By Francis Morryson, Esqr.)*

ELIZA. WALLIS & MARY WALLIS, daughters & coheirs of James Wallis; 567½ acs., Chas. City Co., 21 Apr. 1690, p. 80. Granted to Joseph Johnson, 14 Sept. 1642, who assigned to Jno. Banister, 7 June 1645, who bequeathed to his wife by will, dated 12 Oct. 1660, but in case she married in Virginia then the same to come to John Judseth (?); escheated from the wife of sd. Banister by inquisition under Francis Page, Depty. Esch'r., 3 Dec. 1685; & now granted, &c.

By Francis Nicholson, Esqr., Lieut. Governor.

THO. CHARLES, an island containing 115 acs., James City Co; over Chickahominy Riv., opposite land he now dwells upon; bounded S.W'ly. by the uper Gulph of sd. river, &c; 23 Oct. 1690, p. 81. Imp. of 3 pers: Mrs. Eliza. Perry, Mrs. Joanna Low, Wm. Downs.

MR. GEO. HUNT, 200 acs., in the Up. Par. of James City Co., 23 Oct. 1690, p. 81. From Tho. Wood's, on W. side of Long Thickett; to Phillips' line; along Halie's line, &c. Imp. of 4 pers: Jno. Hubbert, Geo. Read, Gabriel Allen, Mary Taylor.

JOHN BRIM, 200 acs., Middlesex Co., 23 Oct. 1690, p. 81. 105 acs. beg. at Hooper's Neck Land, now Mr. Morris Cocks'; to land of Dodes Minor, (?); 95 acs. beg. at sd Neck; to *Jamaco Land;* to Nich. Pain, on E. side of the Reedy Br; to Thackwell's Neck, &c. Imp. of 4 pers: Robt. Glenn, Jno. Streate, Tho. Falmer, Geo. Turner.

JOHN HOWARD, 172 perches in *James Citty;* from NE cor. of the *Church* Yard along the rayles thereof; to Honble. Nathl. Bacon, Esqr; along the old Great Road, &c. *(date blank),* p. 82. Note: "The Governor wou'd not sign this patent of John Howard." W. Edwards, Cl. Gen. Cou. Test: Danll. Chesley.

MR. JAMES BARRET, 418 acs., on N. side of James Riv., & S. side of the run of Moses Creek; 23 Oct. 1690, p. 82. Granted Mr. Hen. Gauler, 20 Apr. 1684, who assigned to Isaac Coats, from whom it escheated by inquisition under Cr. Wormley, Esqr., Esch'r, & now granted, &c.

WM. SHERWOOD, Gent., 150 acs. in *James Citty Island;* 23 Oct. 1690, p. 83. Granted Richd. James, 5 June 1657, & descended to Richard, his son, from whom it escheated by inquisition under Col. Chr. Wormley, Esch'r, &c.

MR. JOHN WOODSON, JUNR., 1385 acs., Henrico Co., in Varina Par; N. side of James Riv., 23 Oct. 1690, p. 83. Beg. at land of Henry Pue; crossing the main br. of 4 Mi. Cr; on Cornelius' Cr; to Mr. Bleare (?); down the main road; &c. Trans. of 28 pers: Cha. Scarburgh 2, Wm. West, Wm. Boldry, Jno. Evans, Jno. Eves (or Ever), Jno. Newell, Bridget Clare, Tho. Jones, Jno. Jones, Kath. Newjant, Hen. Wheeler, Hump. Jones, Susan Jones, Ed. Morris, Richd. Hayes, Eliza. Frank (or Funk), Geo. Wilson, Jonas Terrey, Sarah Jones, her 2 children; Dick, Mary Jno., Jone, Tom, Masun, Negroes.

MR. CHARLES DOUGLAS, 435 acs., Henrico Co., in Verina Par; S. side of James Riv., & N. side of Falling Cr; crossing Grindall's Run; 23 Oct. 1690, p. 84. Imp. of 9 pers: Tho. Evans, Robert Elmore, Jno. Richardson, Tho. Ives, Jno. Lather, Richd. Prescott, James Elton, Robt. White, Tho. Lovejoy.

JNO. WOODSON, JUNR., 732 acs; upon brs. of Chickahomony Sw. at a place called *Half Sink;* upon Stoney Point; 23 Oct. 1690, p. 84. Imp. of 15 pers.*

MR. JOHN PLEASANTS. 2625 acs., Henrico Co., in Verina Par; N. side of James Riv., 23 Oct. 1690, p. 85. Adj. Edwd. Mathews; Philmon Childers; & Robert Woodson; down W. br. of Deep Run, to Richard Ferrell; on the White Oak Sw; to br. of 4 Mi. Cr. Imp. of 53 pers: Abraham Blagg 8; Jno. Buckley, 2; Tho. Hilton, Eliza. Long, Herbert Duncumb, Jno. Wright, his wife & child; Wm. Thomas, Jno. Feuray, Sarah Audry, Timo. Hair, Jno. Belson, Isaac (a) french boy, Owen Macdarmott, Wm. Penquit, Jno. Chainys, Mary Swillifant, Tho. Kelley, Honor Kelley, her son & daughter; Gilbert Wright, his wife & 5 children; Eliza. (&) Cultis 2 children (?), Wm. Browning, Sarah Spencer, Honor Berk, Senr. (?); Mary ——, Jack a Negro, Debora an Indian.

HENRY TALLEY, 350 acs., Chas. City Co., in Bristoll Par; S. side of Appamattux Riv; 23 Oct. 1690, p. 86. Beg. at a great Rock, on the Otter Damm Br; along line of Wm. Jones; crossing the Ockenechy Path, &c. Imp. of 7 pers: Sambo, Jack, Kate, Harry, Franck, Judy, Dick.

RICHARD LIGON, SAMUEL TATOM & WM. TEMPELL, 1022 acs., Chas City Co., in Bristoll Par; S. side of Appamattuck Riv., at *Warreek Swamp;* (date blank); p. 86. Adj. Jno. Ledbetter; & Jno. Scott; crossing Warreck Br., &c. Imp. of 21 pers.* *Note:* "The Governor refused to sign the above patent for that part of it laid on the South side the main Black Water Swamp." *Note:* Never Issued.

LUKE MIZLE (Meazell), 150 acs., Surry Co., 23 Oct. 1690, p. 87. Granted to John Newman, & escheated by inquisition under Jno. Lear, Esqr., Esch'r., &c.

JOHN VINCENT, 287 acs., Surry Co., 23 Oct. 1690, p. 87. Adj. Fran. Sorsby, & Mr. Fra. Clements, &c. Imp. of 6 pers.* Note: 6 Rights being part of a certificate for 20 Negroes imported in the Shipp *Two Friends* in Sept. 1686, the sd. Certificate being granted Mr. Benja. Harrison by the Court of Surry Co., 3 May 1687.

Whereas JOHN WHITSON, of Surry Co., purchased of Richard Welbeck 200 acs. in sd. county, near head of Greye's Cr., 14 Sept. 1672, to be held by him & his heirs forever; & whereas sd. Whitson was seized in his demesne as of fee of & in sd. 200 acs., & being so seized committed rebellion & high treason & was for the same legally convicted & executed & also legally attainted, as appears by Act of Assembly of 1680, whereby all his estate both real & personal became forfeited to his Majesty; & whereas WM. WRAY, & MARY, his wife, the only dau. of sd. Whitson, hath made composition for sd. land & payed what by the Charter, Law & Custome of Virga. is required in such cases; know yee, therefore, &c. give & grant unto sd. Wm. Wray & *Martha*, his wife, all the aforesd. 200 acs., &c. 23 Oct. 1690, p. 88.

MR. RICHARD WASHINGTON, 772 acs., Surry Co., 23 Oct. 1690, p. 88. Beg. by the main Black Water; adj. Joshua Proctor & Natha. Roberts; Wm. Wray's; & Richard Parker; 200 acs. granted him, 20 Apr. 1685; 572 acs. for Imp. of 12 pers: Jno. Scot, Tho. Roberts, Wm. Woodhouse, Jone Phillips, Richd. Vincent, Jno. James; Sambo, Dick, Tom, Mingo, Jack, Mary Negroes.

JOHN WILKINSON, 189 acs., Surry Co., 23 Oct. 1690, p. 89. Adj. Edward Greene; Capt. Tho. Busbie; Timo. Essell; Richd. Atkins; & Peter Baglie. Imp. of 4 pers: Jno. Turner; Robin, Grace, Judy, Negroes.

RICHARD ATKINS & PETER BAGLEY, 274 acs., Surry Co., 23 Oct. 1690, p. 90. Beg. at mouth of a br. of Heathe's Sw; along Timo. Essell; to Mr. Benja. Harrison; up the E. Spring Br., &c. Imp. of 6 pers: Jno. Temple, Rose Thorne, Thomas Waters, Andrew Atkinson, Jno. Hodges.

JAMES CORLEE, 187 acs., Is. of Wight Co; adj. Isaac Rix; 23 Oct. 1690, p. 90. Imp. of 4 Negroes: Kate, Moll, Judy, Nan.

MR. WM. SCOTT, 54 acs., Is. of Wight Co; adj. Mr. John More; Mr. Thomas Pitts; & a line formerly John Garwood's; 23 Oct. 1690, p. 91. Imp. of 2 pers: Robt. Richardson, Jno. Thornton.

MR. ROBT. KING, 168 acs., Is. of Wight Co; on W. side of a gr. marsh; adj. Tho. Parker; 23 Oct. 1690, p. 91. 150 acs. by conveyance from Mr. Tho. Norsworthy, 12 July 1670; 18 acs. for imp. of: Kingsmill Miniard.

HODGES COUNCELL, the younger, & THO. MAN, 200 acs., Is. of Wight Co; beg. at Jno. Brown's cor., on Kingsale Swamp; 23 Oct. 1690, p. 92. Imp. of 4 pers: Thomas White, Jno. Waterhouse, Robt. Brian, Jno. Barnard.

SAMUEL FURMENT (Ferment), 100 acs., Nancimond Co., in Chuckatuck Par; on W. side of ChuckaTuck Cr; 23 Oct. 1690, p. 92. Adj. Henry Bradley; & John Camble. Imp. of 2 pers: Jno. Knight, Wm. Brookes.

THOMAS PARKER, JUNR., 240 acs., in the Up. Par. of Nansimond Co., near a place called *Kingsale;* 23 Oct. 1690, p. 92. Adj. James Collins; Edward Thelwell; Nicholas Perrot; Thomas Parker, Senr; & a line said to be Osborne's. Imp. of 5 pers: Jno. Colledge, Edwd. Doswell, Timo. Donho (?), Danl. Ball.

BARTH. WILLIAMSON, 584 acs., Low. Norf. Co., Linhaven Par., 23 Oct. 1690, p. 93. Beg. at land surveyed for the Widdow West & her 2 daughters, now in possession of Capt. Jno. Gibbs; crossing Knowell's Br; to Pocoson of the North River; to land of Mr. Wm. West, &c. Imp. of 12 pers: Jno. Macon, Jno. Dauson, Edmd. Garret, Wm. Bennet, Anne Whitesides; Peter, David, Tom, Hector, Jack, Hannah, Sue, Negroes.

MATHEW PALLET, 100 acs., Low. Norf. Co., in Linhaven Par., called the *Burnt Reeds;* adj. land of James Kemp; 23 Oct. 1690, p. 94. Imp. of 2 pers: Eliza. Jordan, Sarah Smith.

MR. EVAN JONES, 93 acs., Low. Norf. Co; on Knot's Island, in *Corotuck;* adj. Geo. Bullock; & Wm. White; 23 Oct. 1690, p. 94. Imp. of 2 pers: Jno. Morson, Timo. Collender.

MICHAEL FENTRIS, 59 acs., Low. Norf. Co., in Linhaven Par., 23 Oct. 1690, p. 95. Adj. William Nichols, Evan Williams, Tully Emperour, Wm. Rogers, Henry Nichols & his own land. Imp. of 2 pers: Wm. Kerl, Ellinor Nest (or West).

JOHN WILBORE, 150 acs., Low. Norf. Co; S'ly. from the Indian Creek; adj. land that was Corperue's; David Murray; & on land Whitehurst sold to Richd. Stanley. Trans. of 3 pers: Jno. Cook, Nath. Hatton, Lawrence Bridger.

MR. JOHN TOWNLY, 0 acs., of marshes, islands, & points; in New Kent Co., on Poropotank Creek; adj. land formerly Mr. Jno. Harwell's; & plantation of Saml. Leviston; 30 Oct. 1690, p. 96. Imp. of 2 pers: Jno. Townly, Robt. Grice.

CAPT. JALOB LUMPKIN (Lumpking), 741 acs., of (the) King's land, in New Kent Co; N. side of Mattapony Riv. & on brs. of the main Dragon Sw., 23 Oct. 1690, p. 96. Beg. at Richard Williams' old feild; to Maj. Morris' best land Quarter; over br. of Axell Sw; by Wm. Drumwright's path; by sd. Williams' Tobo. (Tobacco) house, &c. Imp. of 15 pers: Wm. Knight, Wm. Archer, Tho. Brown, Roven Swanson, Jane Warden, Blesen Clark, Math. Lumkin, Fra. Loe, Jno. Grey, Jacob Lumkin; 2 Negroes. *Note:* 3, Col. Potter.

THOMAS TURNER, 17 acs., New Kent Co., Stratton Major Par; on NE side of Mattapony Riv; beg. by Harcourt Cr; along line of Phineas Gibson, now said Turner's, down little Harcourt Sw; down little Harquep Sw., &c; 23 Oct. 1690, p. 97. Imp. of: Tho. Hodgkins.

MR. JOHN CHILES, 345 acs., in New Kent Co., 23 Oct. 1690, p. 97.

Beg. at Mr. Whitehair, on Crump's Cr; to fork of a br of Mathumps Cr; adj Capt Bassett, &c Granted to Mary Pyron, 24 Feb 1675/6, deserted, & now granted by order, &c. Imp. of 8 pers.*

MR. EDWARD GRESHAM, SENR., 641 acs., New Kent Co., in St. Stephen's Par; N. side of Mattapony Riv; NE side of the Axel Swamp; & on Helican Swamp; 23 Oct. 1690, p. 98. 500 acs. granted him, 18 Mar. 1662; upon resurvey 141 acs. found to be overplus. Imp. of 3 pers.*

MR. RICHARD BARNARD, 1090 acs., Gloster Co., in Petso Par., 23 Oct. 1690, p. 98. Beg. in the middle of the main Roade, near Mr. Hansford's Mill; to land of Mr. Pritchet, dec'd; adj. his own; Joseph Coleman; & land of Mr. Thornton. 900 acs. granted Mrs. Anne Bernard, 27 Nov. 1661; 190 acs. now taken. Imp. of 4 pers: Andr. Teddar, Wm. Harpur, Elias Roy, Mary Ball.

LAWRENCE PERROT, 340 acs., Gloster Co., in Kingston Par; joyning *Gwynn's Ridge;* 23 Oct. 1690, p. 99. Beg. at Col. Jno. Armisted; to Mr. Roberts; by the *Peaso patch* joyning the sd. Ridge; & land of Col. Richard Dudley. 137 acs. granted him, 26 Sept. 1678; 203 acs. for Imp. of 5 pers: Jno. Acorne, Abraham Buckley, Edwd. Davies, James Bradick, Jno. Williams.

MR. WM. EDWARDS, 1626 acs., Henrico Co., in Verina Par; N. side of James Riv., 23 Oct. 1690, p. 99. Beg. at Mr. Henry Weyat; to Gilly Grumeren; on br. of Ufnam Brook; to James More; & James Lisle; on br. of Horse Swamp; to line of Francis Warren, &c. Imp. of 33 pers.*

WILLIAM EDWARDS, 80 acs., in Surry Co; bet. lands of Ralph Creed & Col. Jordan; & adj. land of Woodhouse; 23 Oct. 1690, p. 101. Granted to Fra. Sowerby, 1 Mar. 1666, deserted, & now granted by order, for Imp. of 2 pers.*

MR. JOHN EDWARDS, 950 acs., Surry Co; on NW side of Pigeon Swamp; (date blank), p. 101. Adj.

Mr. Wm. Thompson; & Babbs' land; a br. dividing this & Mr. Meriwether; to a run of the Cyprus Sw., &c. Granted to Jno. Collins, 20 Apr. 1684, deserted, & now granted by order, &c. Imp. of 19 pers.* *Note:* "Entered by mistake, and there is no such patent."

JOHN CUSTIS, ESQR., 458 acs., N'ampton Co., 23 Oct. 1690, p. 102. Granted to Richard Whitemarsh, from whom it escheated by inquisition under Col. Jno. Stringer, Esch'r., 25 Nov. 1687, & now due, &c.

JOHN JAMESON, 89 acs., on N. side of James River, 23 Oct. 1690, p. 102. Beg. at Wm. Bartue; up the gr. piney slash; to Robt. Bartue; to br. of the Roundabout; to his own land, &c. Imp. of 2 pers: Tho. Robins, Jno. Temple.

GEORGE MARR, 2100 acs., New Kent Co., in St. Peter's Par; on S. side of York River & upon both sides of Crump's Cr., 23 Oct. 1690, p. 103. Beg. at Jno. Ree; to the *Woodyard;* to Mr. Hubbert & Mr. Whitehair's land, &c. Granted to Moses Davies & John Ree, 20 Sept. 1683, deserted, & now granted by order, &c. Imp. of 42 pers: Wm. Arnock, James Argoll, Ben. Clark, Jno. Moles, Mary Jones, Jone Davies, Tho. Grandsell, Jos. Day, Wm. Forbush, Tho. Arnold, Richd. Wheeler, Tho. English, Richd. Martin, Ja. Cobb, Susan Shepard, Hen. Chinn, Jno. Foulkes, Hen. Madocks, Wm. Haies, Math. Fones, Jno. Rice, Richd. Dale, Jonas Jones, Wm. Prosier, Jane James, Ann Tolison, Anne Veater, Anne Browne, Jno. Downham, Wm. Butwell, Tristam Eastons, Luke Mancias (?), Merrick Edwards, Robt. Samson, Merlin, Cant, Jos. Baker, Fra. Rippingto; Sam, Tom, Dick, Will, Tom, Negroes.

ROBERT ANDERSON, JUNR., 1200 acs., New Kent Co; S. side of York Riv., on brs. of Mathumps Cr. & Crump's Cr., 23 Oct. 1690, p. 103. Assigned to Jno. Wray by John Webb, who entered same with Col. Wm. Claybourne then Surveyor who died before finishing the survey, & by sd. Wray deserted; & granted sd. Anderson by order, &c. Beg. in James Pyron's line where Jno. Langworthy's line cuts same; adj. Stephen Tarton (Tarleton) & Fleman's land; &c. Trans. of 24 pers: Hugh Bethel, Jno. Acum (?), Edwd. & Mary Carter, Richd. Parker, Jno. Parker, Jno. Hair, Wm. Minum, Wm. Large, Tho. Dalty, Jos. Greenaway, Rachel Feilding, Jos. Shrimp, Lala, Wafen, Saml. Whitson, Rebecca Feild, Fra. Broughton, Fra. Broughton, Richd. Thompson, Peter Steel, Wm. Bragger, Cha. Baggely; Mingo & Peter, Negroes.

CAPT. ROGER JONES, 357 acs., Chas. City Co., in Bristoll Par; S. side of Appamattox Riv., 23 Oct. 1690, p. 104. Adj. Mr. Robt. Bolling. Granted Mr. Robt. Bolling & Mr. Danl. Nonaley, deserted, & now granted by order, &c. Trans. of 7 pers: Jno. Johnson; Sambo, Nick, Guy, Tony, Wafra, Sim, Negroes.

CHARLES FLEMING, 1000 acs., New Kent Co; adj. Andr. Davies, on brs. of Machumps Cr; 23 Oct. 1690, p. 105. Granted Jno. Fleming & Andr. Davies, 20 Apr. 1680, deserted, & granted sd. Fleming by order, &c. Imp. of 20 pers: Jno. Jackson, Mary Succofeild, Wm. Cooper, Jno. Pierson, Susan Alden, Abraham Vintner, Wm. Jones, James Jarret, Mark Anthony, Samll. Powel, Susa. Stainer, Phill. Dove (or Dow), Piersey Vellin, —— Kellion, Tho. Carr, Hen. Ellis, Dorthy Jones, Sar. Closby, Eliza. Dewick, Phill. Spillman.

SAME. 1000 acs; county & date; page 106. On S. side of Tottapotamoy Cr., adj. Cornelius Debony, &c. Granted to Jno. Davies, 27 Feb. 1666, deserted, & granted sd. Fleming by order, &c. Imp. of 20 pers: Susan Ecock, Wm. Hamson, Jno. Weyman, Hen. Abbot, Hen. Collins, Robt. Edwards, Wm. Marchant, Jno. Murrow, Ellinor Driver, Tho. Morgan, Eliza. Sanders, Saml. Flaner, Nicho. Howard, Freeman Wooliff, Math. Taylor, Richd. Morris, Robt. Perkins, Jno. Webster, Duke Rothmill, Phill. Smith.

MR. ROBT. BOLLING, 400 acs., on the Black Water, called *Rownam;* Chas. City Co., in Bristoll Par.; 23 Oct. 1690,

p. 106. 400 acs. granted Hugh Lee, 20 Apr. 1680, deserted, & granted to Mr. Hen. Gauler, 30 Oct. 1686, deserted, & now granted sd. Bolling by order, &c. Imp. of 8 pers: Jno. Sanders, Tho. Robins, Eliz. White, Robt. Holmes, Lucy Festervill, Jno. Richardson, Rebecca Branch; Tony a Negro.

ROBT. ANDERSON, JUNR., 727 acs., New Kent Co; N. side of Chickahominy Sw., 23 Oct. 1690, p. 107. Beg. at a br. of said Sw. called Holly Bush Br., cor. of Thomas Glass, &c. Granted Robt. Anderson, 16 Apr. 1683, deserted, & now granted Robt. Anderson Junr., by order, &c. Imp. of 15 pers: Wm. Hair, Saml. Prichard, Jno. Manor Duck, Tho. Greenvill, Tho. Collins, Jno. Julius, Tho. Deeds, Vere Boswell, Jno. Ougan (?), Saml. Mathumps, Jno. Stanup, Mary Mansell, Wm. Howles, Jno. Howles.

WILLIAM EDWARDS, GENT., 736 acs., James City Co., 23 Oct. 1690, p. 108. 200 acs. on brs. of Warany Cr., on the Burchen Sw., in Sir Jno. Ayton's line; along the horse path, to the Timber Sw. &c; 536 acs. adj. William Elcomb; near Mr. Sorrell's path; near an Indian feild; adj. lands of Mr. Burwell, &c. Granted Mr. Hen. Hartwell, 30 May 1679, deserted, & granted Mr. Edward Chilton, 20 Nov. 1682, deserted, & now granted by order &c. Imp. of 15 pers.*

MR. SAMUEL TAYLOR, 600 acs., Accomack Co; by Jengoteague Island; 23 Oct. 1690, p. 109. Imp. of 12 pers: Thom. Cuff, Edmd. Allet, Richd. Sanders, Wm. Jones, Ann Salmon, Lanct. Jacques, Anne Harcey, Jane Lacy, Edwd. Knight, Obed. Bromkin, Saml. Fichman, Jos. Ash.

PETER MASSEY, 855 acs., New Kent Co., 23 Oct. 1690, p. 109. Beg. on N. side of the mouth of the N'most br. of Chickahomony Riv. where the swamp ends, to br. dividing this & land of Col. Thomas Claybourn. Granted Robert Hughs, 20 Apr. 1682, deserted, & now granted by order, &c. Imp. of 18 pers: Jno. Worth, Jno. Evans, Moses Rest, Eliza. Surrage, Jno. Car-

pinter, Alice Jones, Tho. Barnes, Abra.
Tooker, Peter Johnson, Wm. Thompson; Jeffry, Frank, Cate, Frank, Bess,
Nan, Cecill, Mingo, Negroes.

MR. SAMUEL TAYLOR, 300 acs.,
known as *Georges Island*, in Accomack
Co., on the Seaboard side within Gingoteague Inlett; 23 Oct. 1690, p. 110.
Imp. of 6 pers: Wm. Ketchein, Isaac
Englesdon, Hen. Newans (?), Samll.
Taylor, Tho. Jenkins, Ellinor Ballard.

JOHN MORRIS & JOHN READ,
550 acs., being a marshy island, in Accomack Co; SE from the marsh of
Musketo Point at *Gingoteague;* divided
from same & Wallop's Marsh by a saltwater creek; 23 Oct. 1690, p. 110. Imp.
of 11 pers: Jno. Wilkinson, Saml. Taylor, Tho. Jenkins, Ellinor Ballard;
Adam, Sware, Toney, Rose, Sarah,
London, Shambo, Negroes.

JOHN CANNON, 158 acs., Henrico
Co; N. side of James River; adj. John
Pledge, on the 4 Mi. Creek; 23 Oct.
1690, p. 111. Imp. of 4 pers: John
Brodnax 3 times, & Anthony Bourn.

MR. JOHN BANISTER, 1730 acs.,
Chas. City Co; in Bristoll Par., S. side
of Apomatock Riv., at a place known as
Hatcher's Run; running to a great parcell of Rocks, &c; 23 Oct. 1690, p. 111.
Imp. of 35 pers: Phillis Millington,
John Spell, Anne Berry, Sarah Pollard,
John Alee, Antho. Hacket, Gewen
Berry, Wm. Tayloe, Wm. Brown, Jno.
Thomas, Giles Waters, Elizabeth Hollis,
William Standback, Humphry Hix,
Francis Hill, Mary Drew, Sanders
Bruce, Martha Occondon (?), Wm.
Price, Tho. Gent, Robt. Aston (or
Acton), Jno. Ellis, Jno. Eggerton, William Southaway, Hester Vaughan, Francis Goard, Wm. Price, Jno. Davies,
Nich. Dison, Wm. Davies, Elinor
Vaughan, Gabriel Arthur, Saml. Buxton; Abraham & Jenny, Negroes.

BENJAMIN EGGLESTON, 595 acs.,
James City Co., 23 Oct. 1690, p. 112.
Beg. in Mr. Brumfeild's line, near br.
of Chickahomony Riv., called the great
run, where Francis Storey liveth; by
Shaddock's Br; cor. of Mr. David

Newal (Newell), &c. Granted to Will.
Broadribb, 6 Sept. 1665, deserted, &
now granted by order, &c. Imp. of 12
pers: Edwd. Houchin, Tho. Day, Tho.
Coney, Anth. Corbin, Wm. Herton,
And. Yewren, Price Corbin, Mill. Maybey, Diana Jones, Jno. Lever, Nath.
Newman, Anne Hussey (or Hastey).

WM. MOSELEY, 230 acs., in Rappa.
Co; on S. side the river; 23 Oct. 1690,
p. 113. Beg. about ½ mi. below mouth
of Occupation Cr., cor. to Wm. Bendry;
to Hen. White, to Mr. Hen. Awbrey;
to mouth of sd. Creek above the *Church,*
&c. 40 acs. granted him, 22 Oct. 1682;
104 acs. parte sould by Hen. White to
Tho. Parker, 6 Apr. 1683, who assigned
to sd. Moseley; 86 acs now taken & adj.
said parcells; Imp. of 5 pers: James
White, Jno. White.

WM. BENDRY, 500 acs., (as marrying Elizabeth the dau. of Tho. Moss)
Rappa. Co; on S. side the River; 23
Oct. 1690, p. 114. Formerly belonging
to Augustin Bleydenburgh, an alien,
who sould to sd. Moss, & by reason of
being an alien & neither naturalized nor
denizied he could make no title in fee
to sd. Moss for that his lands must
escheat to his most Excellent Majesty;
sd. land granted to sd. Moss, by way
of escheat. 6 Oct. 1675. Including 125
acs. than expressed in patent to sd.
Moss, dated 20 Feb. 1662. Imp. of 10
pers., whose names are in this *& the
other records:* Elizabeth Crow, Thomas
Bradburn, Elizabeth Bowell.

CORNELIAS NOWELL, 390 acs., in
Rappa. (Co); S. side the River, on brs.
of Occapaccon Run; 23 Oct. 1690, p.
114. Beg. at Mr. Tho. Page; along
Mr. Tho. Vicaris; to Maj. Tho. Hawkins, &c. Imp. of 8 pers: Judith Price,
Jno. Daniel, Alexander Robins, Edmond
Buriall (or Bariall), Alexander Robins,
Winifrith Padrock, Jno. Mackmillion,
Tho. Cooper.

BRIAN WARDE, 299½ acs., in
Rappa. (Co.); S. side the river, on brs.
of Occupaccon & Mattapony Path; adj.
Mr. Tho. Button; & Nicho. Copeland;
23 Oct. 1690, p. 115. Imp. of 6 pers:

Mary Lord, Ann Piper, Mary Sheperd, Thomas Swann, Edward Dudson, Tho. Poles.

JNO. AMIS, 47 acs., in Rappa. (Co.); on S. side the river, 23 Oct. 1690, p. 115. Beg. on Jno. Meader's Cr; along Jno. Gray; to Wm. Clapham; crossing part of the old feild, &c. Imp. of: Peter John.

THOMAS PARKER, 37 acs., in Rappa. (Co.); on S. side the river; adj. Wm. Harper; Lodowick Rowzee; & Wm. Spicer, (now Richd. Mathews'), &c; 23 Oct. 1690, p. 115. Imp. of: Tho. Cotten.

JOHN WOOD, 29 acs., in Rappa. (Co.); on S. side the river; beg. at Thomas Powell; nigh land of Button, &c; 23 Oct. 1690, p. 116. Imp. of: James Overstreet.

SARAH FREEMAN, relict of David Freeman; 250 acs., Low. Norf. Co; in Lynhaven Par; adj. Jno. Jeames (James); & land of Mr. Attwood, &c; 23 Oct. 1690, p. 116. Imp. of 5 pers: Joseph, a Shoemaker; Michael Collins, Tabitha Brisco, Elizabeth, a newhand; Stercy, a Turke.

ADAM HAYES, 661 acs., Low. Norf. Co., in Lynhaven Par., 23 Oct. 1690, p. 116. Beg. at Mr. Henry Woodhouse, in the Gr. Swamp; cor. to Mr. Cornix; neare the *Thunderbolt pine;* to Thomas Brock; to pattent of Greenland, &c. Imp. of 14 pers: James Russell, Rob. Warmouth, Rob. Ozzell, Mary Newton, Ann Wood, Tho. Turner, Jno. Green, Roger Bannister, Jno. Attwood, Moses Williams, Christ. Peircy, Wm. Browne, Alex. Mason, Rich. Pageant. *Note:* 12 by Capt. Campbell.

MR. JOHN GODDARD, 300 acs., Low. Norf. Co., in Lynhaven Par; adj. Lancaster Lovett; & land, formerly Bowrin's, now Spratt's; &c; 23 Oct. 1690, p. 117. Imp. of 6 pers: William Carey, 3 times; Rowland Lewis; Mingo, & Maria, Negroes.

THOMAS WILLOUGHBY, GENT., 3200 acs., Low. Norf. Co., 23 Oct.

1690, p. 117. Beg. at head of Col. Mason's Cr; on the damms to a cr. out of Chesapeac Bay neare a point opposite Hog Island; neare his house on James River; including land his father, Lt. Col. Thomas Willoughby, sold to Jno. Elder, as alsoe what the sayd Willoughby disposed of to Jno. Gooscott; 2900 acs. granted Capt. Tho. Willoughby, 18 Mar. 1662; 300 acs. due him for Imp. of 6 pers.* *Note:* 6 by Rowland Davies Cert. to Col. Danl. Jenifer 29 Apr. 1687.

MR. HENRY WALTHALL, 326 acs., Henrico Co., in Bristoll Par; on N. side of Swift Cr; on Poplar Br; 23 Oct. 1690, p. 118. Imp. of 7 pers: Wm. Dodson, Geo. Middleton, Sarah Crowther, John Mackdaniell, John Machell, Eliza. Carr, Mary Frankin.

PETER CRASHLEY, 166 acs., Low. Norf. Co., in Lynhaven Par; adj. Richard Bonnie; 23 Oct. 1690, p. 118. Imp. of: Jno. Booth, 4 times.

JAMES PURDIE (Purdy), 662 acs., Low. Norf. Co., in Lynhaven Par., 23 Oct. 1690, p. 119. Beg. at Betty Keeling; to Mr. Henry Woodhouse; to the pocoson of West's Cr; to Bonnie's Turky Quarter, &c. Imp. of 14 pers: Jno. Dixon, twice, Jno. Clarke, twice, Francis Chelton, Jno. Booth, twice; Besse, Sharper, Nan, Joan, Tom, Watt, Kate, Negroes.

JAMES PEETERS (Peters), 695 acs., Low. Norf. Co., in Low. Lynhaven Par., 23 Oct. 1690, p. 119. Beg. at Thomas Griffin, now Newton's cor; neare Wm. Walston, to Pyny Island side crossing the Swan ponds, to *old* Walston's Island, &c; 50 acs. called Piney Island, granted to Thomas Griffin, & sold to Joseph Walstone, dec'd., & since due William Walstone, & by him to James Peters & Henry Walstone; 645 acs. for Imp. of 13 pers: Richard Ashall, Thomas Reynolds, Richard Davis, Alex. Jemson, Elizabeth Lane, Robt. Smith, & 3 Negroes: Lucas, Peter(Annshue. *Note:* 4 from Campbell's Cert.

NICHOLAS MANNING, 267 acs., Low. Norf. Co., S'ly. from the W. br.

of Eliz. River; adj. lands of Ward;
Bruce; & Jno. Joyce; 23 Oct. 1690, p.
120. Imp. of 6 pers: Wm. Dundas, 5
times; Geo. Hutson.

WILLIAM WHYDDON (Whid-
den), 150 acs., Low. Norf. Co; S'ly.
from Puzzle Poynt Cr., in the S. br. of
Eliz. River; 23 Oct. 1690, p. 120. Beg.
at Bustian & Nasworthy's lines; to
Jacob Smith (Smyth); on Thomas
Mercer, &c. Imp. of 3 pers: Augustine Whyddon, Edward Pedley, Ann
Frend.

RALPH WORMLEY, ESQR., 300
acs., New Kent Co., 23 Oct. 1690, p.
120. Formerly land of Richard Peirce,
as by deed in sd. county from Francis
Izzard, 29 Feb. 1682, from whom it
escheated by inquisition under William
Leigh, Depty. Esch'r., & now granted,
&c.

WILLIAM OVERTON & JOHN
LYDALL, 837 acs., New Kent Co., in
St. Peter's Par; above the main fork of
Pamunky River, next above land of
Johnathan Newell & Ambros Clare, late
in the tenure of Samuel Ousteen; 23
Oct. 1690, p. 121. To be qually divided
between them. Imp. of: Benj. Felton,
Ja. Johnson, Richd. Horn, Gabr. Bick-
erin, Tho. Bradley, Jno. Davies, Jno.
Hester, Ja. Bowlin, Jos. Sperie, Jno.
Jaquis, Sus. Allie, Tho. Webb, Robt.
Broughton, Jno. Carter, Jos. Hasted, Ja.
Newton, Robt. Horsefeild.

ROBERT NAPIER, 190 acs., New
Kent Co., in St. Peter's Par; beg. on his
own land; to fork of the *tanhous* deep
Sw; on land late of Mark Warkman;
to line late of Hukestep, &c; 23 Oct.
1690, p. 121. *Note:* 4 (rights) by
Rowland Davies' Cert. to Robt. Bouth,
6 Aug. 1683.

WILLIAM WINSTON, 1079 acs.,
New Kent Co., in St. Peter's Par., 23
Oct. 1690, p. 121. Beg. at land, now
or late, of Francis Burnell; to line, now
or late, of Tarleton; along line of John
Kimbrough, &c. Imp. of: Jno. Webb,
Hen. Clark, Ja. Wodson, Jno. Rogers,
Tho. Shaw; Harry, Sambo, Guy, Mingo,
Dick, Peter, Kate, Doll, Moll, Will,

Tony, Jacob & Harry, Negroes. *Note:*
4 (rights) by R. Davies to R. Bouth,
6 Aug. 1683.

THOMAS BATT & JOHN BEVILL,
400 acs., Henrico Co; on Apamatock
River; & N. towards *Conjurers Feild,*
23 Oct. 1690, p. 122. By inquisition
taken at *Varina,* in sd. county, 28 Aug.
1689, under James Minge, Depty.
Esch'r., it was found that sd. 400 acs.
did escheat, &c. And Whereas Thomas
Bott & Thomas *Batt,* the present pos-
sessors of same, have made composition
according to law, i. e. Thomas Bott for
270 acs. & Thomas *Batt* for 130 acs; &
whereas sd. Bott by deed recorded in
sd. Co. Court, 2 June 1690 did grant
his right, &c. to John Bevill, &c.

HENRY WADKINS, 60 acs., Hen-
rico Co., in Varina Par; N. side of
James Riv., 23 Oct. 1690, p. 122. Adj.
his own; Tho. Wales; & land of Madam
Bland; on run of Turkey Island Cr.
Imp. of 2 pers: Robt. Fellows, Jno.
Trotman.

MR. EDWARD HOLLOWAY 819
acs., Chas. City Co; S. side of James
Riv., 23 Oct. 1690, p. 123. 250 acs.
granted William Arrenton, beg. in the
Mirey Meadow; adj. Joshua Meacham,
&c; 569 acs. for Imp. of 12 pers: Jno.
Daniell, Tho. Lambert, Robt. Elton,
James Nicholls, Adam Bush, Sarah
Bush, Wm. Roberts, Jno. Welsh, Abrah.
Rethden, Jone Phillips, Tho. Maples,
Jno. Sanders.

CAPT. HENRY DUKE, 1000 acs.,
James City Co; S. side of Chickahomony
River; 23 Oct. 1690, p. 123. Granted
to Thomas Towner, from whom it escheated by inquisition under Chr.
Wormley, Esqr., Esch'r., & now granted,
&c.

MARTIN ELAM, 900 acs., Henrico
Co., in Varina Par; on S. side of James
Riv., & on Proctor's Branch, 23 Oct.
1690, p. 124. Adj. Fowler's line; &
lands of Francis Kater; Henry Hatcher;
& Robt. Hancock. Imp. of 18 pers:
Anne Wapping, Robt. Turland, Jno.
Cole, Isabel Baccus, Sara. Audry, Doro-
thy Heart, Kath. Laugton (or Langton),

Martin Elam, Timo. Hare, Tho. Chetham, Mary Glue, Jno. Fail, Wm. Thomas, Wm. Chambers, Tho. Cutler, Saml. Brown, Jno. Feuray; Debora an Indian.

JOHN STOWERS & JOHN GOOD, 888, acs., Henrico Co., Verina Par; S. side of James Riv., 23 Oct. 1690, p. 124. Through a gr. piney slash; to John Good; to Col. Wm. Byrd, &c. Trans. of 18 pers: Eliza. Hood, Eliza. Minifry, Wm. Gold, Martha & Jno. Good, Jno. Belson, Isaac (a) french boy, Owen Mackdumot, Wm. Penquit, John Champ; Abrah., Martha, Jno., Robin, Sire, Joe, Grace, Jupiter, Maria, Tom, Negroes.

SAMUEL JOURDAN, Gent., an Ancient Planter, 450 acs., Chas. City Co., 10 Dec. 1620, p. 125. (Note: See Vol. 1, p. 228, for full copy.)

MAJ. ARTHUR ALLEN, 200 acs., by the main Black Water; 28 Apr. 1691, p. 127. Granted to Richard Washington, 20 Apr. 1685, deserted, & now granted by order, &c. Imp. of 4 pers: Fra. Sumners two children, Ann Donn, & Jno. Browne.

WM. BRECEY, JUNR., 720 acs., on both side of the Cyprus Sw., in the Up. Par. of Surry Co., 28 Apr. 1691, p. 127. Beg. at Jordan's cor; adj. Edward Grantham, &c. Granted Jno. Brett, Junr., 20 Apr. 1684, deserted, & now granted by order, &c. Imp. of 15 pers: Hugh Williams, Edward Bradborne, Jno. Dobe, Jno. Dobbs, Benja. Carver, Jane Middleton, Saml. Sayres, Rebecca Nowell, Saml. Wright, Thomas Derby, Thomas Lashington (or Luskington), thrice, James Broadnax, Grace Harper.

WILLIAM FOWLER, 100 acs., Is. of Wight Co; SW side of Carrawaugh Sw., 28 Apr. 1691, p. 128. Beg. at a br. dividing this & Thomas Man; adj. Hodges Councill; Tho. Tarwell (or Farwell); & Col. Bridgers. Granted John Drake, 22 Sept. 1682, deserted, & now granted by order, &c. Imp. of 2 pers: Francis Sumner, & his wife.

COL. DANIELL JENIFER, 200 acs., Accomack Co; S. side of the narrowes near the main land of Accocomson; SW upon Assawan Bay, &c; 28 Apr. 1691, p. 129. Granted Wm. Taylor, Junr., & Elias Taylor, 20 Apr. 1682, deserted, & now granted by order &c. Imp. of 4 pers: James Argo, Jno. Richard, Tho. Edwards, Robert Jeffs.

WM. WINSTON & JNO. ENGELBRECHT, 800 acs., New Kent Co; on lower side of Mattadecun Cr; adj. Jno. Geraway; 28 Apr. 1691, p. 129. Granted Jno. Pouncy, 9 June 1666, deserted, & now granted by order, &c. Imp. of 16 pers: Wm. Hudcheson, Jno. Tainter, Wm. Cabourne, Richard Penduake, Samll. Powell, Jno. Clark, Elliner Driver, Eliza. Allen, Susana Stainer, Eliza. Barefoot, Danll. Veares, Wm. Winson, Sarah Winson, Jno. Price, Sarah Price, Jno. Ellison.

HUGH OWEN, 2359 acs., bet. Rappa. Riv. & the head or run of Mattapony Riv; E. upon a path from Portobacco Indian Town to Chickahominy Indian Town; W. on a gr. tract of Maj. Robert Beverley, &c; 28 Apr. 1691, p. 130. Granted Samll. Broomfeild, Jno. Dangerfeild, Wm. Moseley, Bryan Ward & Wm. Pendry, 22 Nov. 1682, deserted, & granted to Tho. Vicaris, 16 Apr. 1686; not patented, & now granted by order, &c. Imp. of 47 pers: Wm. Winneger, Chr. Wollock, Lydia Nicholson, Jno. Addams, Wm. Swinsen, Jno. Ward, Sarah Ward, Eliza. Ward, Antho. Allerton, Mary Whiskin, Sarah Davis, Jno. Triscott, Jno. Samper, David Nunquam, Wm. Iddem, (Nunquam), Tho. Siquis, Sarah Volens, Jno. Sadome; Toney, Salem, Mingo, Kent, Audo, Shambo, Macon, Will, Nat, Tom, Sawney, York, Hull, Manky, Dick, Jack, Negroes.

JOSHUA STOREY, 7440 acs., New Kent Co; N. side of Mattapony Riv; above the forke where the great run comes into Morocosick Cr; 28 Apr. 1691, p. 131. Part of 10,050 acs. granted Lt. Col. John Smith, Mr. Jno. Buckner, Mr. Phillip Lightfoot, Mr. Thomas Royston, & Mr. Jno. Lewis, 25 Feb. 1673/4; due sd. Storey by order, &c., 17 Oct. 1688, for trans. of 149 pers:

Andr. Lovejoy, Jno. Stockings, Mary Vale, Mary Direferes, Antho. Yaring, Tho. Twisdell, Esther Turke, Mary Thomas, Richd. Marchant, Peter Russell, Geo. Holmes, John Ross, Tho. Jones, Sarah Cooper, Wm. England, Eliza. Kenton, James Clark, Robert Dyer, Richd. Fletcher, James Moker, Stephen Joyes, Samll. Floyd, John Jeffreys, Geo. Moore, Jeffry Thomas, Ephraim Tomkins, Geo. Blythe, James South, Wm. Worth, Tho. Loth, James Irish, Tho. Leeth, Edmd. Price, James Black, Tobias Trotter, Esau Jarvis, James Scot, Wm. Jones, Edmd. Scott, Eliza. Simonds, Mary Jones, Hanah Moore, James Edwards, Wm. Scarlit, James Ware, James Watson, Gilbert Cornwall, John Brown, John Carter, Margt. Brown, Jno. Caruthers, John Dixon, John Hallihawk, John Titford, Wm. Edwards, Antho. Leay, Joseph Tanner, Joseph Thomas, John Bernard, John Ford, Magalen Hutchins, Julian Woodland, Mary Bodrich, William Hardy, Tho. Wright, Ralph Lauson (or Lanson), John Read, Tho. Johnson, Tho. Martin, Danl. Filcher, Tho. Bright, Edwd. Scrymshire, Robert Wateman, Margt. Hillman, Saml. Upter, Jane Hammond, Mary Middleton, John Maires, Wm. Brown, John Gills, Eliza. Westifer, Wm. Barset, Eliza. Lasly, Robt. Deynes, John Wood, Cha. Hare, Mary Strong, John Wilmore, Sarah Brown, Joseph Milner, Tho. Brooks, Mary Ridway, Margt. Brown, Peter Willington, Math. Davison, Edward Love, Hen. Love, James Bradly, Eliza. Prince, Alex. North, Eliza. Page, Wm. Morris, Sarah Marsh, Alice Hart, Wm. Carraday, Tho. Ambros, Wm. Richardson, John Ashton, Roger Jones, Richard Sargant, John Simonds, Robt. Wells, Jno. Chichester, Cha. Price, Tho. Davies, John Ward, James Smith, Jacob Stringer, Anne Trowle, Eliza. Crowder, Eliza. Beard, Alice Coffe, Bridget Croft, Ralph Shepard, William Nicholas, Cha. Petty, Edward Bockman, James Lard, Peter Chesrim, Robert Forsay, Tho. Robinson, John Oliphant, John Betty, Eliza. Pierce, Tho. Curtis, Richard Creed, John Clark, Wm. Brookes, Jno. Knight, Edward Gibson, Isaac Gibson, Richd. Timberlake, Mary Hodgeson,

Sybill Arnold, John Whittaker, Tho. Gunston, Christopher Warkman, Edmd. Reeves, Neger ——.

GEORGE MARR, 1000 acs. New Kent Co; S. side of York Riv., on Chickahominy main Sw; adj. Mr. Robert Anderson; 28 Apr. 1691, p. 134. Granted Moses Davis, 20 Sept. 1683, deserted, & now granted by order, &c. Trans. of 20 pers: Wm. Barker, Benja. Lucas, Robert Case, James Brown, Jno. Palmer, Jno. Peters, Alice Cocking, Wm. Cocking, Nath. Golding, Phillip Turner, Mary Read, Mary Lowman, Jno. Jones, Samll. Ward, Richard Rogers, Robert Burkley, Issabella Mackland, Margarett Billingsee, Ann Phillips, Mary Bennett.

LAWRENCE BATHURST, 5000 acs., New Kent Co; S. side of Pamunky Riv., on a br. of Crump's Cr; 28 Apr. 1691, p. 135. Beg. at Moses Davis & John Rea, &c. Granted Mr. Lancelot. Bathurst, 15 Apr. 1687, deserted, & now granted by order, &c. Trans. of 100 pers.* Note: 100 rights, save 6, by order of Genll. Court, 26 Oct. 1689: Jno. Scot, Robert Scott; Tom, Harry, Dick & Hector.

ALLEXANDER NEWMAN, 580 acs., on S. side of Rappa. Co., about 3 mi. from the river; near run of Occupace Cr., adj. Cornelius Nowell & Vall. Allen; E'wd. of Chickahominy Run path, towards *Portobacco Town;* 28 Apr. 1690, p. 136. Granted Rawleigh Travers, 12 Sept. 1668, & by Rawleigh, his son ***** & since granted sd. Newman by order, &c. Trans. of 12 pers: Wm. Labin, Peter Richards, Robert Wigg, Katherine Kelk, Thomas Tomson, Robt. Dale, Tho. Fletcher, Isabella Hay, Jno. Hedley, Jane Bradon, Eliza. Lee, Cicely Maycup.

WILLIAM CLIFTON, as marrying Eliza., sole heire to Jno. Rabley; 1650 acs. called *Boar Quarter,* in the low. part of York Co; formerly in the tenure of Henry Webb; 28 Apr. 1691, p. 137. Beg. on upper side of the mouth of Back River, at lower side of the mouth of Thoroughfare Cr., lying NW by N ½ Wly. one mile from *Old Point Comfort,* &c. Due by order &c., as aforesaid.

JOSHUA STOREY, GENT., 4270 acs., New Kent Co; N. side of Mattapony Riv; adj. land of Robert Beverley, dec'd; & Keible's old line; on Morocosick Cr; 28 Apr. 1691, p. 138. Part of 6000 acs. gran'd Mr. John Pate & Mr. Robert Beverley, 5 July 1669; Due by order, &c., for trans. of 80 pers: Daniel Skandon, Dennis Skandon, Edmd. Flagherty, John Verdon, Mighall Raftery, John Mapler, Tho. Foster, Fillis Foster, Alice Foster, Mary Foster, Priscilla Stoneman, Priscilla Stoneman, Junr., Wm. Downman, Geo. Worley, Eliza. Silvester, John Nicholson, Matthias Lipps, Cha. Wane, Nicholas Lockler, John Cooper, Tho. Barker, John Cooley, James Goldin, John Vineger, his wife & child; John Temple, Samll. Oldwyn, William Marshall, Antho. Potts, David Clark, Eliza. Roberts, John Poope, Grace ——, John Walker, Tho. Morgan, William Clark, William Roose (or Reese), Wm. Copney, Joan Woolley, Jno. Holland Richd. Sproose, Wm. Hall, Mary Gold, Fra. Blackley, James Franey, Morgan Powell, Bridget Hollen, Fra. Knefton, Richard Smith; Sorrow, Jack, Indians; Sarrow, Ross, Betty, Will, Mary, & Eliza. Negroes; Susana Soanes, Tho. Green, William Eubank, Edward Hudson, Thomas Workman, William Turner, Rice Thomas, Thomas Swan, Lance. Patrick, Nicho. Weeks, Stephen Hix, Cornelius Taylor, Samll. Taylor, Anne Chillingworth, Samuel Payne, Henry Heath, William Wood, Stephen Gooding, John May, Grace Feild, Rebecka Block, John Collings, Joshua Story, Mary Edwards, Charles King, Moses Fox, William Budd, Timothy Johnson.

DOCTOR WALTER WHITAKER, 150 acs., Middlesex Co., 28 Apr. 1691, p. 139. Granted to Joseph Smith, from whom it escheated by inquisition under Christopher Wormeley, Esqr., Depty. Esch'r., &c.

MR. WM. LEIGH, 400 acs., New Kent Co., in St. Stephen's Par; on brs. of Herocock Swamp, upon the Road to *Piscattaway;* 28 Apr. 1691, p. 139. Granted Col. Phillip Ludwell, 22 Oct. 1673, & assigned to Walter Caradine, Senr., 13 Nov. 1673, who died in Feb.

1675, & sd. land descended to his son Walter, from whom it escheated by inquisition under Mr. William Leigh, Depty. Esch'r., &c.

MR. RICHARD GRIGORY, 400 acs., New Kent Co., 28 Apr. 1691, p. 140. Granted to William Canhoe, Clerk, from who it escheated by inquisition under Christopher Wormeley, Esqr., Esch'r., &c.

JNO ARMISTEAD, ESQR., 80 acs., Gloster Co., in Kingstone Par; S. side of a br. of the North River; adj. his own, land of John Sares, dec'd., & Poundell's line; 28 Apr. 1691, p. 141. Imp. of 2 pers: Jno. Turnball, Jno. Hues.

ST. STEPHEN'S PARISH in New Kent Co., 312 acs., for a *Gleab;* 28 Apr. 1691, p. 141. Part of patent granted to Jno. Maddison, Jno. Pigg & Richard Evans in 1661 for 685 acs; after a devision, sd. Maddison sold his part to the Parish; beg. in sight of Mr. John Starke's plantation, bet. sd. Stark & the *Gleab,* along Cheescake Path, to Mr. George Godard, by the maine Quintanockack Sw; through Wm. Watts' plantation, just by Watts' Grave (?); by Col. Abrahall, &c.

SAMUEL NORRINGTON, in right of his wife Hannah; 540 acs; Gloster Co., in Pettsoe Par., 28 Apr. 1691, p. 142. On E. side of Poropotanck Cr., &c. 120 acs. granted to Olliver Greene, 24 July 1653, who assigned to Mr. Edward Corderoy, who assigned to his *brother* William, who gave to Jno., son of sd. Edward; 200 acs. formerly called *Tapses' Neck,* being part of patent granted to Samll. Sallis & Robert Taliaferoe for 750 acs., dated 1 Oct. 1652, & by them sold to one Taps, who sold to Richard Croshaw, who sold to William & Edward Corderop; by the death of Wm., it fell to Edward, at whose death it descended to Jno., his son & heir, who, upon contract of marriage, with Hanah Jones, by deed dated 20 Oct. 1682, conveyd sd. land to her & her heires as Relict of sd. Corderoy; 220 acs. due sd. Norrington for Imp. of 4 pers: Samll. Nicholls, Jno. Staples, Barbary Newman, Jno. Cosby.

JOHN HALL, 45 acs., Warwick Co., in the Oaken Swamp; adj. Mr. Samuel Ransha; the Widdow Corbit; Jno. Sandifer; & Thomas Wootton; 28 Apr. 1691, p. 144. Trans. of 1 pers.* 1 Right by Edwd. Chilton's Certificate to Col. Tho. Milner, 20 Oct. 1685.

WILLIAM FLEMING, 600 acs., Gloster Co., in Pettsoe Par., 28 Apr. 1691, p. 144. Beg. over against Capt. Lightfoot's plantation; adj. land of Wm. Cooke & William Prechett, both dec'd; Joseph Cooleman; & land of Francis Iremonger; along W. side of path to *Purton,* & on land of Mr. Pryor, dec'd., &c. 200 acs. granted to Edward Williams, viz: 100 acs., 20 July 1642, & 100 acs. in 1651; & by Edward Williams, lawfull son & heir to sd. Edward, dec'd., & Abigall Davis, relict of sd. Edward, & now wife of Richard Davis, of *Dorssettsheire* in the province of *Maryland* sold, to sd. Fleming, 4 Sept. 1685; 200 acs. granted to Francis Iremonger, 21 Aug. 1665, who sold to Mathew Miller, Marriner, who sold to sd. Fleming, 21 Mar. 1685; 200 acs. now taken, for trans. of 4 pers: Wm. Butcher, Jeffery Phillips, Eliza. Standley, Jno. Rosse.

WILLIAM BROADRIBB, 416 acs., in James Citty Co., on Powehatan Sw., 28 Apr. 1691, p. 146. Beg. on E. side of sd. Swamp where the old Bridge was; to line of Honble. Xo. (Christopher) Wormeley, Esqr; by br. of Drinking Sw; down his mill stream, &c. Trans. of 9 pers.*

GILBERT ELAM, SENR., GILBERT ELAM, JUNR., & EDWARD WARD, 2015 acs., Henrico Co., in Varina Par; on Fallen (or Faller) Cr. maine br; 28 Apr. 1691, p. 147. Trans. of 41 pers: Jno. Drake, Jno. Colbourne, Hannah Smith, Geo. Dodson, Jno. Jenings, Antho. Hick, Wm. Stark, Jno. Potter, Robert Frost, Mary Simpson, Jno. Knowles, Abra. Flood, Jno. Gardner, James White, Tho. Wats, Tho. Elliot, Teague Collaine, Jno. Lawrence, Anne Doughty, James Harris, Jno. Porter,

Tho. Livesay, Jno. Waltasse, Jno. Redliffe, Sarah Meares, Wm. Thomas, Jno. Ellison, Wm. Wetherford, James Amys, Jno. Richardson, James Turner, Jno. Whitby, Wm. Ellis, Eliza. Revis, Dorothy Turner, Hester James, Richd. Whitby, Edwd. Wood; Danl., Bess, Tawney, Negroes.

WILLIAM COLLAINE, JUNR., 140 acs., Gloster Co., in Pettsoe Par; adj. his father, William Collaine; & Gill's land; 28 Apr. 1691, p. 148. Trans. of 3 pers: James Rice, Jno. Sop, Tho. Grant.

WILLIAM & RICHARD VAGHAN, 281 acs., Chas. City Co., in Bristoll Par; on W. side of Moncuse Neck maine Sw; adj. Thomas Low; on Hatcher's Run; (date blank); p. 149. Trans. of 6 pers: Jno. Bull, Eliza. Pain; Dick, Tom, Nan, Petro, Negroes. *Note:* "Not signed, Mr. Ligon the Surveyor, saying he believed it was upon or over the Line betweene the English & Indians."

WILLIAM BAYLY, 93 acs., James City Co., 28 Apr. 1691, p. 149. On E. side of Porohatan (or Powhatan) Swamp, where was formerly a bridg; along Mr. Broadribb; to Honble. Christr. Wormeley, Esqr; to Porehatan Cr., &c. 50 acs. from his father, —— Bayly dec'd., who purchased from Rt. Honble. Wm. Berkeley, dec'd; 43 acs. for trans. of: Eliza. Shepherd.

JOSHUA STOREY, GENT., 11,620 acs., New Kent Co; on N. side of Mattapony Riv., 28 Apr. 1691, p. 150. Beg. against an island, cor. to 5000 acs. granted sd. Storey & William Morris; to land granted Lt. Col. Jno. Smith, Mr. Jno. Buckner, Mr. Phillip Lightfoot, Mr. Thomas Royston, & Mr. Jno. Lewis; crossing Morocosick Cr., &c. Trans. 232 pers: Jno. Hill, Walter Jno. Johnson, Perygreen Try (or Fry), Richd. Baker, Hatton Trever, Anne Woollet, Saml. Brothers, Richd. Williams, Anne Spicer, Richd. Booker, Tho. Dale, Jone Jenkins, Eliz. Duck, Jno. Barlow, Robt. Barlow, Edward Dare, Mary Popper, Wm. Ogle, Anne Stokes, Edwards, Alex. Scott, Corn. Macone,

Danl. Fisher, Wm. Oliver, Tho. Knight, John Magoon, Saml. Mechan, Robt. Clark, Corn. Akee, Dav. Strahan, Sarah Brothers, Richd. Hobbs, Ja. Clay, Tho. Smith, Richd. Price, Eliz. Dobson, Richd. Griffith, Fra. & Alice Pember, Tho. Roberts, Jno. Laythen, Margt. Davis, Jno. Sturgis, Jno. Abot, Eliza. Oliver, Alice Douglas, Stephen Binns, Wm. Pate, Robt. Thompson, Jno. Burton, Tho. Whaler, —— Hudson, Jane Chapfeild, Eliza. Kidley, Robt. Ashley, Jno. More, Mary Davis, Duke Dennis, Tho. Ashby, Anne Bridges, Hen. Morgan, Jno. Ray, Richd. Marct. (Marchant ?), Peter Russell, Geo. Holmes, John Ross, Tho. Jones, Sarah Cooper, Wm. England, Eliz. Kenton, Ja. Clark, Robert Dyer, Richd. Fletcher, Ja. Moker, Step. Joyes, Saml. Floyd, Jno. Jeffrey, George Mores, Jeffrey Thomas, Eph. Tomkins, Geo. Blith, James South, Tho. Johnson, Jeffr. Tarnton (?), Jno. Saker, Jno. Jones, Wm. Sims, Ja. Parker, Edmd. Price, Ja. Black, Tobias Trotter, Esau Jarvis, Tho. Jeffs, Wm. Scot, Edmd. Spratt, Mich. Maxfeild, Jno. Donkley, Robt. Bushell, Mary Worley, Jno. Woods, Mary Faris (?), Robt. Fenley, Mary Feather, Tho. Faith, Jno. Candey (?), Jno. Ellot, Margt. Pain (?), Geo. Keeble, Richd. Langley, Richard Willis, Matt. Miller, Jno. Jones, Ja. Harris, Tho. Tanner, Tho. Cooke, James Brown, Edwd. Paine, Jno. Douger (?), Tho. Foreskins, Tho. Fairchild, Eliz. Browning, Ja. Cables, Dennis Quanden, Edwd. Flaget, Jno. Weeden, Michael Lastley, Jno. Mayler, Hen. Foster, Jno. Mackabine, Tho. Goodwin, George Worley, Eliza. Seldwick, Jno. Nicholson, Hugh Mayes, Andrew Cresley, Al. Leister, Jane Baker, Isaac Sweet, Jno. Wilkock, Phil. Phillips, Sarah Walker, Jone Stedmond, Kath. Hugo, Joseph Hide, Wm. Simcock, Jno. Gough, Wm. Gough, Ra. Gough, Rebecca Gough, Eliz. Rich, Eliza. Finch, Susan Bell, Jno. Rider, Mary Alsop, James Lewis, Michael Rice, Anne Gosling, Jonathan Fisher, Tho. Rowland, Wm. Terry, Alice Reed, Mary Ponyard, Jno. Jenkinson, David Williams, Mary Rose, Ellinor Hogsfletch, Jno. Caruthers, Jno. Dixon, Jno. Hallyhawk, Jno. Titford (or Tilford), Wm. Edwards, Anth.

Leay (or Seav), Joseph Tanner, Joseph Thomas, Jno. Townley, Robt. Gayne (?), Mary Swann, Wm. Price, Phillida Seawell, Saml. Nichols, Jno. Caisby, Jno. Hayes, Bard. Newman, Robt. Watson, Jno. Staple, Ja. Flint, Nichol. Lee, Eliz. Rigbey, Eliz. Bullock, Jno. Palmer, Jno. Taylor, Jno. Prince (or Prime), Mary Godfrey, Andr. Lovejoy, Jno. Stockins, Mary Vail, Mary Diarfers, Anth. Ayring, Tho. Twisdell, Hester Turk, Mary Thomas, Richd. Lee, James Ralph, Grace Holmes, Robt. Smart, Robt. Smart, Junr., Wm. Heasel, Tho. Howard, Wm. Bass, Wm. Baker, Wm. Forbs; Pr. (?) Beverley Neger; James, Cate, Tom, Bess, Primus, Secundus, Mary, Nanny & 2 (other) Negroes.

JOHN BLACKBORNE, 211 acs., Chas. City Co., in Westopher Par., on N. side of James Riv; adj. John Royster; & Jonas Liscomb; 28 Apr. 1691, p. 152. Trans. of 5 pers: Diana Brigan, Tho. Goodman, Stephen Nowell, Richd. Yarnall, Elianor Thompson.

MR. RICHARD KENNON, CAPT. FRANCIS EPES, MR. JOSEPH ROYALL, & MR. GEORGE ARCHER, 2827 acs. Henrico Co., in Bristoll Par; on N. side of Appamatock Riv., (date blank); p. 153. Beg. at mouth of a gr. Creek; to the main river on *Wortapock, &c.* Trans. of 57 Negroes, not named, out of a Cert. to Mr. Richard Kennon, proved in Henrico Co. Ct., 1 Apr. 1690. *Note:* "Not signed."

ABRAHAM EVANS, 190 acs., Up. Par. of Surry Co; bet. his own, land of Mr. Jno. Barker & Thomas Hunt; 28 Apr. 1691, p. 154. Imp. of 4 pers: Jno. Jones, Adam Robinson, Jno. Turner, William Ekerbye.

NICHOLAS SESSUMS, 260 acs., Up. Par. of Surry Co; bet. lands of Mr. Meriwether, Richard Smith & Joseph Wall; ½ mi. from the Pigeon Swamp; adj. Mr. Thompson; 28 Apr. 1691, p. 155. Imp. of 6 pers: James Whitley, Thomas Judkins, William Chandler, Susanna Chandler, Robert Welch.

RICHARD BULLOCK, 160 acs., Up. Par. of Surry Co; near head of Savidge's

Run; 28 Apr. 1691, p. 155. Beg. in line deviding Surry & Chas. Citty Counties, near Wm. Short; along br. from Hickinses' meadow, &c. Imp. of 4 pers: Honor Thomas, Jane Webb; Hector & Ned, Negroes.

JOHN STUART, 275 acs., Up. Par. of Surry Co; S. side the Otterdam Sw., adj. Jethro Barker; 28 Apr. 1691, p. 156. Imp. of 6 Negroes: Tony, Robin, Jone, Kate, Bess, Symon.

PHILLIP JONES, 189 acs., Henrico Co., in Bristoll Par; S. side of Swift Cr; adj. Mr. Richard Kennon, crossing the gr. branch of Old Town Cr., to Thomas Webester, &c; 28 Apr. 1691, p. 157. Trans. of 4 pers: Mingo, Toney, Sambo, Guy.

MR. RICHARD COCKE (Cock), 270 acs., Henrico Co., in Verina Par., 28 Apr. 1691, p. 157. Beg. at the hedgrow deviding *Bremow* & the patent of *Curles;* crossing the main cr. of Curles Swamp, down the main river, &c. Trans. of 6 pers: John Hammon, Mary Suewell; Pomp, Tom, Will, Sue, Negroes.

SAMUEL MOODEY, 36 acs. in *Weynoak*, Chas. City Co., in Weynoak Par., 28 Apr. 1691, p. 158. Adj. Mr. James Lawrence; along Kittawan Sw., to a gutt parting this & Mr. David Jones; on Kittawan Cr; along Mr. Harwood's line, &c. Trans. of 2 pers: Susan Dale, John Morton. *Note:* Not signed; being stopt by order of Court.

JOHN GUTHRY, 200 acs., Gloster Co; S. side of Kings Cr., near *Poropotank;* 28 Apr. 1691, p. 158. Granted Humphry Dennis, 6 July 1654, deserted, & now granted by order, &c. Trans. of 4 pers: William Thomas, Jno. Humphreys, Jane Humphreys, Sarah Johnson.

MR. HENRY WAREING (Waring), 152 acs., Gloster Co., in Kingstone Par; adj. Edmond Roberts; & Charles Joanes; near Gwin's Ridge; 28 Apr. 1691, p. 159. Trans. of 4 pers: Henry Waring, Richd. Cordell, Grace Small.

GEORGE TRUET, JUNR., son of Henry Truet, dec'd; 100 acs., Accomack

Co; on an island to the W. of Hobson's Choice Island; 28 Apr. 1691, p. 159. Imp. of 2 pers: Katherine Singleton, Hope Taylor.

WILLIAM GLOVER, 217 acs., Henrico Co; N. side of James Riv., 28 Apr. 1691, p. 160. Adj. John Davis & Robert Burton; N. on the Miry Sw; adj. Wm. Ballue; & land of Abraham Bayley. Imp. of 6 pers: James Urwin 3 times; Tho. Jeffreys, Jane Snell (or Suell).

GEORGE POOLE, 230 acs., Low. Norf. Co., in Lynhaven Par., 28 Apr. 1691, p. 160. Adj. Mathew Pallett; & Wm. Moseley. Part of 600 acs. granted John Martin & Lancaster, Lovett 21 Oct. 1651, who assigned to John Pearse, from whom it escheated by inquisition under Col. John Leare, Esqr., Esch'r., &c.

THOMAS VICARIS (Viccaris), 600 acs., Rappa. Co; on S. side & in the freshes of the river; 28 Apr. 1691, p. 161. Beg. 3 mi. from the river, near Mattapony Path, cor. of Christopher Blackborne & William Gray; to Occupason Run; to Henry Jarman; & Thomas Page; &c. Granted to James Coghill, 16 Apr. 1667, deserted, & now granted &c. Trans. of 12 pers: Jno. Turner, Sarah Evans, Wm. West, Jno. Thruston, James Elam, Sarah Johnson, James Ellison, Wm. Wetherton, Jno. Ashton, Jno. Myles, Aron Sparrow, James Willowby, Andrew Edwards.

MICHAEL MUSGRAVE, 500 acs., Middlesex Co., 28 Apr. 1691, p. 162. Granted to Mr. Thomas Borne, viz: 250 acs., 20 Dec. 1649, & 250 acs., 16 Sept. 1651; found to escheat from Anthony Crisp by inquisition under Christopher Wormeley, Esqr., Esch'r. & now granted, &c.

ISAAC HAGGAMAN, 200 acs., N'ampton Co., 28 Apr. 1691, p. 162. Escheated from William Ganey by inquisition under John Stringer, Esch'r., 9 Apr. 1687; granted to Isaac & John Haggaman, which sd. John is since dead, & sd. Isaac remaines his onely heir; now granted, &c.

JOHN MORRIS, 300 acs., on an island; Accomack Co., near Oyster Cr; bet. Jengoteag & Assateag Islands; 28 Apr. 1691, p. 162. Trans. of 6 pers: Tho. Morris, John Daniel, John Dale, Richard Hall, Tho. White, William Booker.

MR. JOHN CHILES, 900 acs., New Kent Co; S. side & in the freshes of York Riv., above *Mehixon,* 28 Apr. 1691, p. 163. Part of 2700 acs. granted Mr. William Crump, Mr. Charles Edmonds & Mr. Robert Whitehair, 3 Nov. 1688, & in devision fell to sd. Whitehair, from whom it escheated by inquisition under Mr. William Leigh, Depty. Esch'r., & is now granted, &c.

FRANCIS COSTIN, 75 acs., N'ampton Co; on head of Thomas Mac-Mellon's 300 acs. at *Goggs;* 28 Apr. 1691, p. 164. Imp. of 2 Indians: Terah & Bettee.

JOHN CUSTIS, ESQR., 2600 acs., being all Smith's Island; in N'ampton Co; including all the long sandy beach, &c; 28 Apr. 1691, p. 164. Trans. of 52 pers: James Davis, Thomas Townsin, Fra. Hackny, Susan Dutch, John Middleton, Wm. Cripps, Tho. Locker, Jno. Turner, Sarah Brooks, Chris. Tod, Jno. Pickells, Jno. Cotterall, Lancelt. Errington, Tho. Potts, Edwd. Dickinson, Robt. Merriefild, Jno. Storer, Wm. Lester, Tho. Bird, Richd. Blagrove, Geo. Hart, Antho. Dorelin (or Dowlin), Fra. Williams, Thim. Morgan, Wm. Mattox, Tho. Fillpot, Robt. Cocks, Francis Wood, Jno. Flint, Tho. Malloburn, Wm. Weblow, Hen. Crouthers, Robt. Sims, Jno. Herring, Hen. Packson, Tho. Lewis, Geo. Proverb, Jno. Willson, Edward Floyde, Hen. Nicklors, Ann Peirce, Jane Made, Margaret Raget, Ellinor Darcy, Jahell Wells, Ellinor Carty, Jane Rider, Jone Kahalon, Jno. Neale, Stephen Miles, Wm. Meredith, Alexr. Turner.

JAMES HALL, SENR., 157 acs., Chas. City Co., in Bristoll Par; adj. Mr. Robert Bowling; & Samuel Woodard; 28 Apr. 1691, p. 165. Trans. of 4 pers: Cook, 1 child, Marya, Agbe.

JOHN SMITH, son & heir of Jacob Smith, 200 acs., in *Diggs' Hundred,* Chas. City Co; W. upon Turkey Island Cr; & adj. land of Thomas Oggs; 28 Apr. 1691, p. 165. Granted Joseph Royall, 4 May 1638, who sold to Edward Martinn, 22 May 1643, who assigned to sd. Jacob Smith, 1 Dec. 1643.

RICHARD BLAND, 593 A., 42 P., Chas. City Co., 28 Apr. 1691, p. 166. Beg. at Locust Point in Mason's Neck; a sw. parting this & land of Mr. John Hardiman; to land of Morgan Jones & *old mayns;* along sd. run till it brancheth out towards the *bloody Spring,* sd. run parting this & John Wallice; by the *old maynes* feild; land of Mr. George Wodlief; to James River, under the *Church hill;* along Mason's Cr. &c. 388 acs. due him by will of Theodorick Bland, who purchased of Benjamin Sidway & Mary, his wife, 3 Aug. 1658; 200 acs. by the same gift of his *sd. father in sd. will,* who purchased same of Anthony Wyat, 3 Feb. 1668; the remainder due for Imp. of: Wm. Snape.

GEORGE CLARKE, son of George Clarke, Gent., dec'd; 100 acs., N'ampton Co., 28 Apr. 1691, p. 166. N. on James Jackson, W. on the maine bay, & S. on the *Gleab land.* Granted to George, son of George Clark, dec'd., 1 July 1653, & now renewed to abovesaid George Clarke, the *Grandson.*

MR. MATHEW HUBBERD, 1500 acs., in up. part of Jas. City Co; on NE side of the head of Chickahominy Riv; taking in all that can bee found of patent to Mr. Robert Huberd, dec'd., for 2400 acs; 28 Apr. 1691, p. 167. From Ravenett's Run on Mr. Marston's line; to up. Landing of Long Neck; along Williams' lines, &c. "Due said Mathew Huberd as Cozen German and heir at Law to Robert Huberd deced., who was son and heir of the abovementioned Robert Huberd unto whome the sd. patent of twenty four hundred acres of land was granted the 2d day of June 1657."

MR. WILLIAM KENDALL & MAJ. JOHN ROBINS, 1500 acs., N'ampton

Co., called Jingoteague Island; NE on the Maryland line; 28 Apr. 1691, p. 168. Granted to Col. Danl. Jenifer, 1 Apr. 1671, deserted, & granted by order, &c. Imp. of 30 pers.*

WILLIAM COLE, ESQR., 280 acs. Warwick Co; at head of Talbot's Cr; 28 Apr. 1691, p. 168. On Harwood's Neck; on S. side of a br. of Stokes' Cr; by Samuel Chappell's house & tobacco house, &c. 250 acs. granted John Williams, 26 Sept. 1645, & purchased by sd. Cole of John, son & heir of the patentee; 30 acs., over plus, for imp. of: Tom, a Negro.

MR. HENRY RANDOLPH, 5650 acs., Henrico Co; on N. side of Swift Cr; 28 Apr. 1691, p. 169. From head of the Little Cr. being the 1st br. of the Back Cr., through Steward's Field; on Fetherstone's line; up N. side of Hatcher's Run, to Timsbury dividend; near John Steward's plantation; near Mr. Pride's plantation; by Mr. Eusebius King; to low. side of Parsimmon Br., by Swift Cr; against the Dividing Falls, being Bevins' cor; to Tho. Totty's land; by Mrs. Judith Randolph; down the Sawmill div'dt; to below mouth of the 2nd run into Swift Cr., above the Mills; including all islands, &c. 1000 acs. granted his father, Mr. Hen. Randolph, dec'd, 16 Feb. 1662; 1254 acs. granted Mr. Richd. Bland, 20 Apr. 1687, & conveyed to sd. Randolph, 1st of Aug. following; 731 A., 1 R., 30 P. granted Mr. Eusebius King, 22 Dec. 1682, includ. a patent granted sd. King, 1 Oct. 1674, deserted, & granted sd. Randolph by order, &c; which with 2665 acs. is due for trans. of 68 pers: Mary Swillifant, Thomas & Honora, Kitty, her son, Gilbt. Wright, his wife & 2 children; Eliza. Coultis, Willm. Browning, Sarah Spencer, Hen. Beck, Senr., Hen. Beck, Junr., Hugh Morphy; Tony, Amy, Toby, Nocky, James, Will, Mary, Negroes; 7 by Mr. Edward Chilton's Cert. to Col. Tho. Milner, 20 Oct. 1685; Jno. Chandler, Andrew Robinson, Jno. Fiveash, Robert Turbervill, Jno. Rose, Sarah Rose, Robert Rose, Jno. Thomas, Wm. Withers, Dorothy Turner, Abigall Meeres, Ralph Johnson, Robt. Phillipps, Ann Phillipps, John Flowers, Richd.

Swett, Thomas Lewis, Hen. White, Honor Heath; Hector, Cuba, Florence, Tom, Nan, Harry, Dick, Mingo, Robin, Peter, Will, Jack, Andrew, Kate, Doll, Roger, Sambo, Bess, Tom, Judy, Tony, Negroes.

CAPT. WM. RANDOLPH, 400 acs., Henrico Co; crossing Mr. Branch's brook, &c; 20 Oct. 1691, p. 171. Granted Abell Gower, 7 Nov. 1673, deserted, & now granted by order, &c. Imp. of 8 pers: John Peterson, David Price, Tho. Crimberton, Nich. May, Wm. Gessop, Andrew Martyn, Samll. Courser, John Gates.

MR. JOHN WILSON, SENR., 148 acs., Henrico Co., in Bristoll Par., on the Old Towne Cr., 20 Oct. 1691, p. 171. Adj. Mr. Phillip Jones; Mr. George Worsham; Mr. Pickett's cornfeild; & Mr. Tho. Webster. Imp. of 3 pers.*

MR. JOHN WORSHAM, MR. EDWARD STRATON (Stratton), & MR. ABRAHAM WOMACK, 879 acs., in Henrico Co., Verina Par; N. side of Swift Cr., 20 Oct. 1691, p. 172. Beg. at mouth of Cold Water Run. Imp. of 18 pers: Richard Lewis, Judith Lewis, Sarah Somerseal, Clemens Proveer, John Stewart, Wm. Migettoe, James Butlidge, John Bull, Eliza. Pain; Dick, Tom, Nan, Peter Negroes; 5 Negroes by Cert. granted Mr. Rich. Kennon, for 70 Negroes by Hen. Co. Ct., 1 Apr. 1690.

MR. WILLIAM CLARKE (Clark), 81 acs., Henrico Co., Verina Par; S. side of James River; adj. Edward Straton; Mr. Elam; & Timothy Allen. Imp. of: William Clark, twice.

MR. JOHN PLEASANTS, 1221 acs., Henrico Co., Verina Par; N. side of James Riv., 20 Oct. 1691, p. 173. Beg. at mouth of West Ham Creek & mouth of a br. of Tuckahow Cr., &c. Imp. of 25 pers: Wm. Randolph, George Lynn, William Dod, Mary Lynn, Kath. Mathers, Mary Madden, Allanson Clarke, Charles Rumbold, Winefred Conner, Jane Sawkins, John Sawkins, Bartho. Fowler, Wm. Oake; Will, Tom, Tony,

Eastham, Coney, Yamon, Davy, Scipio, Haniball, Toby Sambo.

MR. HENRY BATT, 700 acs., Chas. City Co; on brs. of Baylie's Cr; 20 Oct. 1691, p. 173. Adj. James Warendine's land called *High Peake,* now in occupation of Mr. Wm. Ditty & Robert Langram., Granted Mr. Wm. Batt, 22 Apr. 1670, deserted, & now granted by order, &c; Imp. of 14 pers: Wm. Sharpe, Thomas Bushell, Mary (&) Anne, his children; John Sawer, Dorothy White, Anth. Morly, Tho. Bucher, Math. Huret (or Haret), Samll. Anderson, Phill. Trott, Wm. Young, Antho. Wood, Tho. Sturt.

WM. KNOTT, 216 acs., Chas. City Co; N. side of the W. br. of Up. Chipoakes Cr.; adj. William Heath; 20 Oct. 1691, p. 174. Granted John Wanpoole, 20 Apr. 1682, deserted, & now granted for Imp. of 5 pers: Hester Downes, Wm. Grea, Wm. Bently, Mary Parlett, Jno. Underwood.

MAJ. ARTHUR ALLEN, 170 acs., Up. Par. of Is. of Wight Co., 20 Oct. 1691, p. 174. Adj. Thomas Blake; Mr. Tooke; Mr. Newman; Capt. England; Edward Brantley; & neare the *Danceing Place.* Granted Mr. Robert Flake, 20 Apr. 1685, deserted, & now granted by order, &c. Imp. of 4 pers: Jno. Greenwood, Robert Spather, Hester Malder, Tho. Horswell.

SAME. 525 acs., bet. the 3rd Sw. & the maine Black Water; adj. Mr. Williamson & Mr. Tho. More; 20 Oct. 1691, p. 175. Granted Edward Boykin, 20 Apr. 1685, deserted, & now granted, &c. Imp. of 11 pers: Eliza. Idens, Tho. Idens, Wm. Russell, George Burnham, Rebecca Bantell, Ann Mungall, Math. Wills, Wm. Clelos (?), Nath. Pill, Richd. Turner, Mary Newgant.

WILLIAM CHAMBERS, 1150 acs., Up. Par. of Is. of Wight Co; on the maine Black Water Sw; adj. Mr. Christopher Holman; 20 Oct. 1691, p. 175. Granted Tho. More, 20 Apr. 1687, deserted, & now granted by order &c. Imp. of 23 pers: Tho. Robert, Adam Morgan, Peter Hargrove, John Hargrove, Grace Hargrove, Robert Nelson, Jno. Turner, Rachell Meers, Alice Phillips, Symon Hatton, Dorothy Meade, Jno. Stamp, Robert Wells, Abra. Johnson, Richd. Bayley, Sarah Mountjoy, Abigall Thorne, Peter Harrison; Tom, Sambo, Mingo, Judy, Kate, Negroes.

MR. HENRY POPE, 187 acs., Is. of Wight Co; adj. John Williams, Richd. Lovegrove, John Sellway & Henry Sanders; 20 Oct. 1691, p. 176. Imp. of 4 pers: Wm. Marchant, John Lidard, John Watts, Barth. Palmer.

MR. WM. MAYO, 170 acs., Is. of Wight Co; adj. John Izing; Gyles Lymscott; John Lawrence; & Col. Bridger; along the main Black Water; 20 Oct. 1691, p. 175. Imp. of 4 pers: John Vates, Owen Burne, Wm. Calfe Mary Nickell.

THOMAS BIZELL, 170 acs., at *Kinosayle,* in the Up. Par. of Nansamond Co; adj. Francis Sanders, on S. side of Queens Graves Sw; 20 Oct. 1691, p. 177. Imp. of 4 pers: Tho. Peters, Nath. Pile, Fra. Peirce, James Pellen.

THOMAS DAVIS, 500 acs., at *Kingsayle,* in the Up. Par. of Nansamond; S. side of Kingsale Sw., opposite William Collings; on line bet. James Haward & James Moore; 20 Oct. 1691, p. 177. Being half of patent granted to Tho. Titus & Nicho. Dixson, 1 Oct. 1672, which 500 acs. is now in the right of sd. Davis.

WM. COLLINS, 100 acs., at *Kingsayle,* in Up. Par. of Nansamond; adj. Tho. Davis; from W. side of Capt. John's Br. to run of Kingsayle Sw; 20 Oct. 1691, p. 177. Imp. of 2 pers: John Robinson, Robert Redman.

JAMES HAWARD, 500 acs., at *King Sayle,* in Up. Par. of Nansamond; on King Sayle Sw; adj. Thomas Davis; 20 Oct. 1691, p. 178. Being halfe of patent granted Thomas Titus & Nicho. Dixson, 1 Oct. 1672, which, after severall surrenders & decents, is now of right & in possession of sd. Haward, as marrying one of the daughters of sd. Titus.

MATHEW PALLETT, 370 acs., Pr. Anne Co., in Lynhaven Par., 20 Oct. 1691, p. 178. Part of 600 acs. granted John Martin & Lancaster Lovett, 21 Oct. 1651, who assigned to John Peirce, from whom it eschc.ted, by inquisition under John Lear, Esqr., Esch'r., &c., 21 Dec. 1689, & now granted by order, &c. Beg. on Piney Point; adj. lands of George Poole; & Mr. William Mosely.

RICHARD WILKINSON, 100 acs., Nansamond Co., 20 Oct. 1691, p. 179. Escheated from Andrew Burton & Tho. Tatum, by inquisition under William Randolph, Depty. Esch'r., &c., 21 Aug. 1685, & now granted by order, &c.

GEORGE NASWORTHY, 400 acs., Norfolk Co., (date blank) 1691, p. 179. Escheated from Christopher Williams by inquisition under John Lear, Esqr., Esch'r, &c.

DENNIS MECARTEE, 250 acs., on the Easterne Shore of Lynhaven; at time of survey in Low. Norf. Co., but now in Pr. Ann Co., 20 Oct. 1691, p. 179. Beg. by the Swd. Bay; by William Capps; &c. 150 acs. granted John Stratton, 27 Mar. 1651, who conveyed to Hugh Wood, from whom it escheated as by patent dated 26 Nov. 1663, to William Capps, who bequeathed to his son, Henry Capps, who exchanged with Edmund Moore, for lands in the woods; by Moore conveyed to sd. Mecartee, 21 Sept. 1675; 100 acs. for Imp. of 2 Negroes: Isaac & Harry.

MR. HENRY WOODHOUSE, 400 acs., in Lynhaven Par; in Low. Norf. at time of survey, but now Pr. Anne Co., 20 Oct. 1691, p. 180. Beg. at his old land called the Quarter; adj. lands of Gisborn; Dallis; Sprat; & William Capps. Imp. of 8 pers: Saml. Fullerton, John Macoy, Jos. Smith, Eliza. Davis, Tho. Browne; black Jack, Mingo, Sarah.

SAME. 1288 acs; same location, date & page. Adj. lands of Mr. William Cornix; Mr. Spratt's (formerly Smith's);

& John Keeling. Imp. of 26 pers: John Laberart, John Kirson, John Deronseaux, Wm. Scott, Paul Micable, Robt. Grimes, Walter Grimes, James Elliott, Ann Gould, Jasper M'trisad (?), Fra. Bennett, John Scotchmon, Edward Loyde, Alice Loyde, Alice Paine, Dona Requmm, Donack Millivance, Patrick Scott, Ferdinando Batt, Ann Seapes, —— Trowell, Edward Deane, Richd. Mosbee, John Buble, Math. Fisher, Nich. Broadway.

JAMES MOHUN, 100 acs., on S. br. of Eliz. Riv., in Low. Norf. at time of survey, but now Norfolk Co., 20 Oct. 1691, p. 181. Beg. at John Bustian's Landing, on E. side of Kitts Cr., deviding this from Willson's; to Jacob Smith's Cr; & on land of Nasworthy. Imp. of: Nath. Maclainihan (or Maclannhan), twice.

THOMAS FRANCKLIN, 228 acs., in Lynhaven Par; at time of survey in Low. Norf. Co., but now Pr. Anne Co; adj. lands of Dalley (Dallie), & Gisborne. Imp. of 5 pers: Doll & Jane, Indians; Tom, Combo, & Will, Negroes.

PETER CRASHLEY, 602 acs., in Lynhaven Par; at time of survey in Low. Norf. Co., but now Pr. Anne Co., 20 Oct. 1691, p. 182. By Indian Snare Creek; on Meeres' Damms; adj. land of Dyer; & John Woodhouse. 520 acs. granted Edward Cannon & Thomas Allen, 11 Mar. 1652; by assignment became wholly due to sd. Allen, long since dead; due sd. Crashley as marrying Sarah Gaskins, heiresse to sd. Allen; surveyed by order, in presence of a jury, &c., & 82 acs. found within the bounds; due for Imp. of 2 Negroes: Peter & Betty.

JOSEPH MILLER, 796 acs., on br. of Symson's Cr. Cyprus Swamp; adj. lands of Patrick White; & John Aldrage; 20 Oct. 1691, p. 183. Imp. of 16 pers.* Note: 6 by Paul Hilman's cert. to John Biggs, 23 Dec. 1685; 4 Prescott, 1 Oct. 1685, & 4 by sd. Chilton's cert. to Wm. Maund, of same date.

by Mr. Edward Chilton's cert. to Jno.

JOHN SMITH, 300 acs., on the damms of Sympson's Cr. Sw; in *Currotuck precincts;* at time of survey in Low. Norf., but now Norfolk Co; adj. Capt. Russell; 20 Oct. 1691, p. 183. Imp. of 6 pers: Richard Wickins, Roger Ellett, Danll. Russell. John Quick, Charles Quick, Tho. Tickley.

JOHN ALDRAGE (Aldrige), 82 acs., on W. side of Sympson's Cr. Cyprus Swamp; in Low. Norf. Co. at time of survey, but now Norf. Co; adj. Patrick White; 20 Oct. 1691, p. 183. Imp. of 2 pers: John Phillpott, Henry Moore.

GEORGE BALLINTINE, JUNR., 400 acs., from head of Julian's Cr., on W. side of the E. br. of Eliz. Riv; at time of survey in Low. Norf., but now in Norf. Co; adj. William Owens, & land of Hewes & Dale; 20 Oct. 1691, p. 184. Imp. of 8 pers: Abgo, Bess, Setta, Chitta, Negroes; 4 by cert. signed by Rowlandd Davis, 10 July 1688.

RICHARD CAPPS, 390 acs., in Low. Par. of Lynhaven; at time of survey in Low. Norf. Co., but now Pr. Anne Co; S. side of the Indian Landing Land; adj. Peter Mackbones, & Robert Symmons; 20 Oct. 1691, p. 184. Imp. of 8 Indians: Dick, Bess, Jacob, Harry, Wm., Gust, Lighting, Sobriety.

JOEL MARTIN, 1500 acs., on a Cyprus Sw. of the uper Indian Cr. of the north west river; in *Corrotuck Precincts;* at time of survey in Low. Norf., but now in Norf. Co; adj. Malder's land; 20 Oct. 1691, p. 185. Imp. of 30 pers: Mary Watts, Eliza. Cheslett, Thomas Strickland, Thomas Barker, Edward Pettway, John Handson, Thomas Walker, James Carpinter, Ellinor Highlett, John Harris, Isaac Curtis, Wm. Seamer, Wm. Alphugh, Morris Fitz Gerald, Richard Moorton, Henry Davis, George Clarke, Ann Ward, Henry Sutton, Wm. Burdell, John Polake, Mary Parry, John Cassell, Abraham Jewell, Roger Lyle; Jack & Harry, Indians; Jack, Harry, & Christian, Negroes.

THOMAS BODMAN, 200 acs., in Lynhaven Par; at time of survey in Low.

Norf., but now Pr. Anne Co: beg. by a Cyprus Sw; rounding the Cape. &c; 20 Oct. 1691, p. 185. Imp. of 4 pers: Jane, Katherine, Charles, Wm. Lawther.

MR. WM. MAUND, 400 acs., at time of survey in Low. Norf., but now Norf. Co: adj. John Hanbury; E'ly. along the Green Sea, &c; 20 Oct. 1691, p. 186. Imp. of 8 pers.* Due by Mr. Edwd. Chilton's cert., 1 Oct. 1685.

CAPT. THOMAS RUSSELL. 300 acs., from head of the S. br. of Eliz. River; adj. his own land; 20 Oct. 1691, p. 186. Imp. of 6 pers: Capt. Thomas Russell, Samll. Russell. Wm. Drew. John Heler, Corbett Benson, Roger Heler.

ANN, wife of GEORGE JACKSON, & SARAH RANSHA, 220 acs. in Harwood's Neck, Warwick Co., 20 Oct. 1691, p. 186. Beg. at head of Talbot's Cr; to land of Col. Cole, now in the occupation of John Chitty; to br. of Stoke's Cr; by Deep Cr., near Stamp's Landing, &c. 150 acs. due be decent from their father, Argall Ransha, & is part of patent to Thomas Ransha for 300 acs., 25 Aug. 1642; 70 acs. due them for Imp. of 2 pers.* 2 rights by Mr. Chilton's cert., 20 Oct. 1685.

CAPT. MILES CARY, 122½ acs., Warwick Co: adj. his own land; & Harwood's Neck reeds, &c; 20 Oct. 1691, p. 187. Granted Mr. Samll. Chappell, 21 Oct. 1684, deserted, & now granted by order, &c. Imp. of 3 pers.* 3 Rights by Mr. Edward Chilton's cert., 20 Oct. 1685, to Col. Tho. Milner.

MR. WILLIAM HUNT, 215 acs. Jas. City Co; on James River below mouth of Little Cr., adj. John Clarke; along Wood's & Rumball's lines, &c; 20 Oct. 1691, p. 187. Part of a greater parcell purchased by Wm. Hunt, his father, of Rice Hoe, 3 Dec. 1656.

MR. HENRY RANDOLPH, 66 acs., Jas. City Co; on uper side of Pease Hill Cr., 20 Oct. 1690, p. 187. Beg. at Pease Run, on *Potters feild devident* of land, &c. Imp. of 2 pers: James Varney, Robt. Clarke.

MR. ANTHONY ROBINSON. 33 acs. in Pequoson Par., Yorke Co; adj. his own, & land of Robert Kerby; 20 Oct. 1691, p. 188. Imp. of: Peter Willdon.

MR. ARMINGER WADE, 165 acs. in New Poquoson Par., Yorke Co., 20 Oct. 1691, p. 188. Adj. Robert Kirby; & Mr. Cousens; down Robins' Cr. on W. side, to line supposed of Oldis' patent; to Wm. Taverner; on land reputed to be Mr. Parsons'; by Anthony Robinson, &c. Imp. of 4 pers: Arminger Wade & his wife, Arminger Wade, his son, & Thomas Horton.

MR. ROBERT BIRD, 134 acs. in King & Queen Co., formerly New Kent Co; beg. at a forke of Exoll's branch, &c; (date blank) 1691, p. 188. Granted to Gabriel Hill, 29 Nov. 1665, deserted, & now granted by order, &c. Imp of 3 pers: Eliz. Heath; & 2 Negroes.

SAME. Same Co., 20 Oct. 1691, p. 189. Beg. at a forke of Exoll Swamp, about ½ mi. above Gabriel Hill, &c. Granted to Shurley Mordit, 20 Oct. 1665, & now granted, &c. Imp. of 2 Negroes.*

JOHN PERRY, 321 acs., King & Queen Co; on head br. of Assatians Sw; adj. Robert Hill; & Wm. Rogers; 20 Oct. 1691, p. 189. Granted Henry Bigg, 30 May 1679, deserted, & now granted by order &c. Imp. of 7 pers: Edward Letts, Arthur Letts, John Letts, Eliza. Letts, Alexr. Chrisum, Cha. Foreget, Rich. Bagwell.

ROBERT NASH, 333 acs., 20 Oct. 1691, p. 190 (County blank). Beg. close to the Indian Path; adj. Mr. Goodrich, just over a small br. of one of the maine brs. of Mattapony Runn; cor. to the Indians' Land, & Stephen West, &c. Granted Stephen Benbridge, of Rappa. Co., & Mr. Tho. Todd, of Glocester Co., deserted, & now granted by order, &c. Imp. of 7 pers: Jesper Taylor, Jno. Hamlin, Tho. Elff, Ashby Chase, Jane Weeds, Claret Emmitt, John Toward.

MR. WM. TODD, 238 acs., King & Queen Co., 20 Oct. 1691, p. 190.

Adj. Mr. Joseph Goodrich & John Coleman, on a br. of Assaway Mansecock Sw; on good ground supposed to belong to Mr. Brereton; on run of the Broad Br., &c. Granted Stephen Benbridge, 23 Apr. 1688, deserted, & now granted by order &c. Imp. of 5 pers: John Collier, Thomas Harris; Hager. Jane, Doll, Negroes.

WM. CARDWELL & WM. FENNEY, 499 acs., at time of survey in New Kent Co., on N. side of Mattapony Riv., but now in King & Queen Co., 20 Oct. 1691, p. 191. Granted Wm. Sawyer, 16 Apr. 1683 for 550 acs., but no more found; sold to Mr. Benja. Clements & Mr. James Cawdle. who sold to the above named; beg. by Powlcatt Br; by Thomas Meade; by Thomas Browne's, just over the Bridge Br; by Thomas Maconees (?); along Eapharim Rove's; to Mr. Henry Biggs; by Mr. Bird's Road; down Ingram's Meadow; to George Light; to Nicholas Ware, &c.

JOSEPH WILSHEARE, 48 acs., at time of survey in New Kent, on N. side of Mattapony River, but now King & Qu. Co; by run of Anscomansca Sw., to land of Brewerturne; on Scandall's line, &c; 21 Oct. 1691, p. 191. Imp. of: Charles Clayton.

MR. CHARLES ROANE, 164 acs., Glocester Co., in Pettsoe Par; adj. his own, & land of Wm. Brookin; 20 Oct. 1690, p. 192. Imp. of 4 pers: Robt. Croper, Jno. Crump (or Cramp), Wm. Oakeley, Mary Willde.

SAME. 278 acs; same Co., parish, date, & page. On N. side of Cole's Br. of the main Sw. of Poropotanck Cr; cor. of Col. Richard Lee; along main roade to the Dragon Bridge; to Wm. Brookin, &c; Imp. of 6 pers: Wm. Shaw, Judeth Butler, Mary Grant, John Hanks (or Hauks); Tom & Dick, Negroes.

WM. BROOKIN & ROBERT NETLES, 270 acs., Glocester Co., in Pettsoe Par; adj. their own & land formerly belonging to Robert Collis; 20

Oct. 1691, p. 193. Imp. of 6 pers: Wm. Hargrove, Dorothy Hargrove, Geo. Warner, Fra. Prince, Ralph Lisney, Tho. Higden.

MR. WM. BROOKIN, 517 acs., Glocester Co., in Pettsoe Par., 20 Oct. 1691, p. 193. Near head of a main br. of Poropotanck Cr., &c. 450 acs. granted Thomas Hancks, 8 Apr. 1663, who sold to Owen Kelley, 18 July 1665, who sold to Robert Collis, 17 May 1677, who assigned to sd. Brookin, 20 Jan. 1689; 67 acs. for Imp. of 2 pers: Edward Shepheard, Eliza. Pert.

MR. WM. HEYWARD, 150 acs., Glocester Co., in Pettsoe Par., 20 Oct. 1691, p. 194. Beg. at his own land; along Mr. Edward Porties; to br. of a Sw. of Capahosack Cr; by a White Marsh, &c. Imp. of 4 pers: Richard Jackson, Wm. Heagarth, Wm. Widdon, John Driver.

MR. JOHN BAKER, 40 acs., Glocester Co., in Kingstone Par; S. side of a br. of Winter Harbour Cr., adj. his own land; 20 Oct. 1691, p. 194. Imp. of 1 pers.*

MR. THOMAS VICARIS, Clerk, 150 acs., Glocester Co., in Pettsoe Par., 20 Oct. 1691, p. 195. Beg. at Mr. Faucett; by Rappa. Path; to Mr. Lee & Mr. Wm. Thornton; to James Faucett; crossing Bull Head Swamp, &c. Imp. of 3 pers: David Goosetree, Mary Grey, John Nitingall (or Witingall).

WM. HALL, 220 acs., Glocester Co., in Pettsoe Par., 20 Oct. 1691, p. 195. Adj. Mr. Haines; & Rich. Lee, Esqr., near the main Road; on Mr. Brookin & Dudley's line. Imp. of 5 pers: Margaret Younge, John Young, Edmond Day, Geo. Proud, Christian Boros.

THOMAS HASLEDOOD, 244 acs., Middlesex Co., 20 Oct. 1691, p. 196. Beg. at Parrott's Cr., at 300 acs. of David Fox, now Mr. George Haslewood's; to 200 acs. granted Oliver Segar & Francis Browne; by Mr. Wm. Cheaney; to Dugwill Ferson, &c. 200 acs. granted John Phillips, 2 Sept. 1652; 44 acs. for Imp. of: Francis Werry.

EDWARD WILLIAMS, 70 acs., Middlesex Co., 20 Oct. 1691, p. 196. Adj. Mr. Wm. Downing, by the Dragon Sw; & Mr. John Wortham, &c. Imp. of 2 pers: John Eateman, Hump. Mayo.

JOHN MILLER, 352 acs., Middlesex Co., 20 Oct. 1691, p. 197. Beg on SE side of Doles Cr; to line of Bonner, now John Man's, &c. Granted to him, 20 Dec. 1667.

THO. PETTICE, 93 acs., Rappa. Co., on S. side of Rappa. River, 20 Oct. 1691, p. 197. Beg. by Hosking's Cr., cor. of land of Mr. Robt. Yard & Mr. Jno. Waters; by the White Oak Swamp, &c. Imp. of 2 negroes: Mingo, Bess.

EDWARD THOMAS, GENT., 450 acs., Rappa. Co., 20 Oct. 1691, p. 198. Beg. at land of John Jones, Orphan, by the Dragon Sw., in an old feild below mouth of a great branch; by John Masey's line, &c. 290 acs. granted Rice Jones, 19 Sept. 1664; 95 acs. part of patent to Anthony Jackman, dated 21 Sept. 1664; 65 acs. for Imp. of 2 pers: Mary Ongley, Ann Harwood.

JOHN HARPER, 1150 acs., Rappa. Co., on S. side of Rappa. River, 20 Oct. 1691, p. 198. Beg. by the maine pocoson of Pescattaway Cr., below a gr. White Marsh; by the Bridge Sw; along Col. Edward Hill, to John Price; including 2 small islands, &c. 500 acs. granted to James Boughan & Tho. Harper, 8 Oct. 1672; 600 acs. being overplus; due for Imp. of 13 pers: Richard Wright, John Faine (?), Ellinor Edwards, Wm. Markes, William Dobson, Wm. Copeland, Isaac Jones, Martin Pettus, Hen. Clegg, Geo. Massey, Fra. Keen, Robt. Rogers, William Willis.

MR. JOHN BREDGER & MR. RICHARD HANEY, 1428 acs., Rappa. Co., on S. side of Rappa. River, 20 Oct. 1691, p. 199. Beg. in Anthony Jackson's line, now Richard Grinsted's, by the maine road at Mr. Williamson's path; up the Dragon Sw. to mouth of the Yorker Br., &c. 750 acs. granted Geo. March, Gent., 9 Nov. 1659, & since by patent the 24 Mar. 1662; 428

acs. granted Richard Bredgar, 19 Sept. 1664; 222 acs. being overplus, & 28 acs. now taken, due for Imp. of 5 pers: Eliza. Free, Eliza. Browne, Katherine &c., Henry, Richard Perrott, Junr.

JOHN WILLIS, JUNR., 150 acs., on Woodmans Island, Accomack Co; near Jengoteag Island; 20 Oct. 1691, p. 200. Imp. of 3 pers: Deborah, Lathum, Homidees.

SAME. 250 acs., called Wild Catt Island; same Co., date & page. At N. end of Jengoteag Is. & S. from Ragged point, on Assateage Is. Imp. of 5 pers: Joseph Robinson, Wm. Nicholson, Alice Adkinson, John Procter, Fra. Nicholson.

RICHARD NOTINGHAM, BENJA. NOTINGHAM & THOMAS COWDRY, 200 acs., on Rogues Island, in N'ampton Co; on W. side of the S. end of Hogg Island; 20 Oct. 1690, p. 201. Imp. of 4 pers: Owen Monion, Dune Monion, Margt. Monion (or Morion); Jack a Negro.

CAPT. WM. HUNT, 159 acs., Chas. City Co., in Weynoake Par., on N. side of James Riv., & known as *Fer Neck;* (Note: It is assumed the above is an abbreviation for *Ferry* Neck.) 20 Oct. 1691, p. 202. Beg. at land formerly belonging to Mr. David Jones, on the 2nd bottom of the up. back Cr; to Doby's point; up Jones' Cr; to the main Road to Chickahominy Ferry. Imp. of 4 pers: Andrew Parker, Chris. Read, Tho. Sisson; Mingo a Negro.

CHARLES COLTHORP, son of Mr. James Colthorp, dec'd; 165 acs., Yorke Co., in New Pocoson Par., 20 Oct. 1691, p. 202. Imp. of 4 pers: Samll. Phillpon, Walter Barne, Timo. Haggarth, Joan Morris.

CAPT. HUGH CAMPBELL, 250 acs., from head of the S. br. of Eliz. Riv., in Low. Norf. Co. at time of the grant, but now Norf. Co., 20 Oct. 1691, p. 203. Adj. John Corperue, & Selvester's line. Granted Jacob Barnes, 20 Apr. 1687, deserted, & now granted by order &c. Imp. of 5 pers: Jno. Little-

ton, James Wood, Ralph Burton, Adam Simpson, Sarah Rookeings.

SAME. 372 acs., in *Currotuck Precincts;* in Low. Norf. at time of grant, but now in Pr. Anne Co; same date, & page. Adj. Hen. Southen; & Tho. Tooly; on a pocoson of the Black Water River & of the North River. Granted Hen. Beacher, 21 Oct. 1687, & now by order, &c. Imp. of 8 pers: Jno. Norcoate, Ja. Searle, Abra. Watts, Jane Watts, Robert Rust; Dick, Sam, Jack, Negroes.

MR. WM. EDWARDS, 410 acs., Low. Par. of Surry Co; on E. side of the Green Sw., 20 Oct. 1691, p. 204. Beg. at Thomas Kane's cor., in Mr. Thomas Bins' line; adj. Mr. Owens; Mr. Wm. Gray; & Thomas Lane. Granted John Clarke, 20 Apr. 1684, deserted, & now granted by order, &c. Imp. of 9 pers: Tho. Dyar, Lewis Street, Rich. Holman, Tho. Harris, Robt. Johnson, Wm. Burley, Wm. Hussey, Wm. Williams, Jno. Cannon.

MR. JOHN BUCKNER, SENR., of Glocester Co., 3125 acs., in the freshes & on S. side of Rappa. River, on maine brs. of Pewmansend, brs. of Goulden Vale & brs. of Passating; 20 Oct. 1691, p. 204. Adj. land of sd. Buckner, Mr. Bryan & Mr. Royston. Imp. of 63 pers: Richd. Phillips, Hen. Wilkison, Robt. Perriot, Wm. Eure, Hannah Allen, Wm. Bennett, Tho. Buttler, John Jason, Richd. Read, Jno. Willis, Samll. Hope, Roger Allen, Grace Collins, Phill. May, Gammer Harris, Danll. Richmand, Grace Myford, Eliza. Brown, Affrica Floyd, Xtr. Feilding, John Hind, Thomas Holt, Rice *App* Williams, George Clough, Izabell &: Samuell Smith, Robert Stevenson, 3 times; Jack, Sam, Abbigall, Tom, Aqua, Sampson, Ton, Moll, Judieth, Izabell, Mingo, Sambo, Kate, Sampson, Jack, Peter, Roger, Symon, Great Charles, Marya, Nick, Moll & Hom, Negroes.

RICHARD GLASSCOCK, 335 acs., Glocester Co., in Kingston Par., 20 Oct. 1691, p. 206. Adj. Mr. Richard Billops; George Billops' 100 acs; John Colles;

Marke Foster; & Morris Mackachacock. Granted Mr. Edward Cassell, 22 Dec. 1682, deserted, & now granted by order, &c. Imp. of 7 pers: Francis Right, John King, Mary Browne, Tho. Jones, Luke Barkins (or Burkins), Ann Noades, Andrew Reward.

CHRISMAS RAYE, son of Chrismas Raye, dec'd; 91 acs., Yorke Co., in New Pocoson Par; on N. side of a cr. parting this & land of Thomas Nutting; adj. Peter Starkey; 20 Oct. 1691, p. 206. Imp. of 2 pers.*

JOHN BIGG, JUNR., 137 acs. called *Long Acre;* to the N. of the Black Water, in *Currituck Precincts;* formerly Low. Norf., but now Pr. Anne Co; adj. lines of Whitford's & Southen's; on the Western Sw; 20 Oct. 1691, p. 207. Granted Daniell Cane, 21 Oct. 1687, deserted, & now granted by order, &c. Trans. of 3 negroes: Tom, Dick, Bess.

JOHN CLERKE, (Clark), of Rappa. Co., 104 acs., in King & Queen Co; on N. side of Mattopony Riv., 20 Oct. 1691, p. 207. Adj. land granted Mr. Jos. Goodrich, Wm. Ball & John Price; Col. Edward Hill; & land of Brewerturne. Imp. of 3 pers: Jane Stuard, Richd. Borkinshan, Peter Rockford.

EDWIN THACKER, 210 acs., Middlesex Co., on N. side of Peanketanck Riv., 24 Oct. 1691, p. 208. Beg. at Mr. Geo. Keible; to the Green Glead Br., &c. Granted Geo. Keible, 29 Jan. 1663. deserted, & now granted by order, &c. Imp. of 5 pers: Wm. Oliver, Wm. Rose, Chris. Harrum, Daniel Trigg, Margaret Heal.

MR. JOHN BLAND, 108 acs., in King & Queen Co., 20 Oct. 1691, p. 208. Imp. of 3 pers: Giles King, Jno. Stamford, & his wife.

JOHN SALMOND, 61 acs., Rappa. Co., on S. side of the River, 20 Oct. 1691, p. 208. Beg. a br. of Occupacon Run; to land of Col. John Cattlett, dec'd; along Mr. Thomas Button; & adj. Thomas Powell. Imp. of 2 pers: Bartholomew Vawter, Mary Burkett.

WILLIAM COLLINS & TIMOTHY CONIERS, 620 acs., King & Queen Co., 20 Oct. 1691, p. 209. Beg. neer Geo. Dillard's plantation; to mouth of Coole Spring Br; nigh Cornelious Vaughan; to Tasatine maine Sw; on Nicholas King's Spring Br. 350 acs. granted Mr. Edward & John Lewis, 21 Apr. 1690, who conveyed to the abovenamed, 30 Mar. 1691; 268 acs. being overplush. Imp. of 6 pers: Wm. Marrow, Edmd. Lambert, Ann Lambert, Ann Lambert, Jno. Mackdogle, Tho. Brewer.

MR. RICHARD GRIGORY (Griggory), of K. & Q. Co., 40 acs. in Rappa. Co., on S. side the River; beg. by Pescataway Cr; along Robert Halsey; to his own; land of Robt. Young; 20 Oct. 1691, p. 210. Imp. of: Barbados Mary.

WILLIAM BRISCOE, 153 acs., Middlesex Co., 20 Oct. 1691, p. 210. Beg. in a br. of the Green Sw., neer land of Hen. Wood, Esqr; adj. John Bourk; & Mr. Richd. Willis. Granted to John Sceare, 23 Apr. 1688, deserted, & now granted by order &c. Imp. of 4 pers: John Deadye (or Deadge), Abraham Buckley, Edw. Davis, James Bradick.

CHRISTOPHER ADDISON, 265 A., 1 R., 13 P., Chas. City Co., in Westopher Par; S. side of James Riv., 20 Oct. 1691, p. 211. Beg. on the lower King's feild Br; along Richard Pace; up Long point Br; to John Williamson, crossing Black Water Path, & Scotch Br., to Col. Edward Hill, &c. Granted Danll. Higdon & Roger Reese, 16 Apr. 1683, deserted, & granted to Mr. Henry Gauler, 15 Oct. 1686, who never patented the same; now granted by order &c. Imp. of 6 pers: John Nicholls, Judeth Francklin, Tho. Walkman, Hen. Jeffs, Sa. Stephens, Robert Roye.

MR. THOMAS MARSTON, 1300 acs., Jas. City Co., on NE side of Chickahominy Riv., 20 Oct. 1691, p. 211. Above the fork of Chessnutt Run, to (Indian *alias*) New Invasion (?) Sw; to (Indian *alias*) Barbadoes Sw. Run, &c. Granted Richard Williams for 800 acs., the last of Oct. 1653, & joyned to 750 acs., 24 Jan. 1655, on opposite side of the river; & being all deserted; this part was granted to sd. Marston by order &c., for Imp. of 26 pers: Math. Pyle, Fra. Peirce, James Pollin, Jno. Robinson, Robt. Redman, Jno. Smith, Richd. Smith, Rich. Symons, Samll. Shelfeild, Tho. Huby, Alex. Schofeild, Jno. Gosslin. Wm. Stilling. Rich. Toms, Tho. Walldrum, Edward Wright, James Welsh, Jno. Cutler, Toby Smith, James Turner, Andrew Coleby, Jno. Smith, Robt. Snead, Sa. Nicholls; Guy & Sambo, Negroes.

MAJ. LAWRANCE SMITH (Smyth), 1200 acs., Gloster Co., in Abbington Par., 20 Oct. 1691, p. 212. S. side of Severne Riv. neare the head, along land of Col. Augustin Warner, dec'd; to Mr. Robert Bryan; along Vallentine Layne & Thomas Graves, to Abraham Broadley; neer dwelling house of William Graves; to land of Mr. Thomas Graves, dec'd; to Gillion White, near house of Robert Earbrough; to Jerimie Hoult, SE side of a Sw. of Timber Neck Cr; to land of Mr. Peters, dec'd; to Capt. Richd. Booker; along Mr. John Meggson; to Maj. Lewis Burwell; crossing the Church Path; &c. 882 granted sd. Smyth, viz: 807 acs. 18 Mar. 1666; 75 acs. 15 Mar. 1668; 318 acs. now taken, for Imp. of 7 pers: Eliza. Long, Robt. Colles, Eliza. Day, Tho. Fanch, Rich. Hust, Tho. Phipps, Hen. Cluthero.

MR. WILLIAM EDWARDS, 750 acs., Surry Co., 20 Oct. 1691, p. 213. Beg. on E. side of the river, adj. George Jordan; to swamp deviding this from plantation whereon Capt. Thomas Flood formerly lived, &c. 150 acs. part of a greater dev'dt. granted Col. John Flood & by Thomas Flood, his lawfull heir, sold to Ralph Creed, & by David Andrews & Mary his wife, to whom sd. Creed gave same by will, sold to sd. Edwards; which 150 acs., with the remaining 600 acs., was granted to sd. Creed, 14 Mar. 1666; 600 acs. being deserted, is now granted by order, &c. Imp. of 12 pers: Jno. Smith, Edw. Andrews, Addam Armstrong, Samll. Carrid, Eliazer Taylor; 7 Negroes: Antho., Cobarro, Kebo, Doll, Robin, Kate & Mingo.

RALPH WORMELEY, ESQR., a parcell of land, bee it more or less, in York Co., 20 Oct. 1691, p. 214. Granted Thomas Creaton & escheated by inquisition under Christopher Wormeley, Esqr., Esch'r., &c., 4 Feb. 1687/8, & since granted, &c.

JOHN LEAR, ESQR., & REBECCA, his wife, 180 acs., Eliz. City Co; bet. Hapton Riv. & Back Riv; on Deep Cr; 20 Oct. 1691, p. 214. Being the bounds of 350 acs. late of Col. Leonard Yeo, now in the tenure of sd. Lear, in right of his wife; adj. land of Henry Royall, formerly John Robins'; & lines of Bright, & John Naylor. Imp. of 4 pers.*

MR. ROBERT LEE, 542 acs., Gloster Co., 23 Dec. 1662, p. 215. Adj. Mr. Thornton, Col. Lee's Horse Path & sd. Lee's plantation. 200 acs. granted Col. Richard Lee, 17 May 1655, who sold to sd. Robt. Lee; 342 acs. for trans. of 7 pers.* *Note:* Recorded in pursuance to an order of the Genll. Ct., 27 Oct. 1691. Test: Miles Cary, C. Genll. Cor. *(By Sir William Berkeley.)*

MR. THO. OSBORN, Senr., 1113 acs. Henrico Co., in Varina Par; S. side of James River, known *now* by the name of *Coxendale*, but the patent for 1000 acs., dated 6 Feb. 1637, known by the name of *Fearing;* 29 Apr. 1692, p. 215. Upon re-survey found to contain 1113 acs; beg. at mouth of Proctor's Cr., to mouth of the Redwater, &c. 1000 acs. granted Capt. Tho. Osborn, his father, as above mentioned; 113 acs. due for Imp. of 3 pers: Mary Norman, William Buckston; Tom a Negro.

MR. ABRAHAM WOMACK, SENR., 269 acs., Henrico Co., 19 Apr. 1692, p. 216. 200 acs. purchased of Gilbert Deikon; the residue being King's land; beg. on line of Gilbert Elam, deviding this from Wm. Clark; adj. Edward Stratton; Hugh Ligon; the Granerey road; & Thomas Shipey. Imp. of 2 pers: Tom & Sue.

FRANCIS MAYBURY, 440 acs., Henrico Co., in Bristoll Par; on N. side of Swift Cr., 29 Apr. 1692, p. 216.

Beg. at land formerly Mr. King's, but now Mr. Henry Randolph's; on Samll. Newman; to Mr. Willm. Pride, &c. Imp. of 9 pers: Elinor Buckley, Mary Watson, Fra. Burnham, Mary Burnham, Mary Butler, her child, Margt. Querk, Margt. —— at Jno. Oneal's; Susanna Symonds.

MR. PHILIP JONES, 1238 A., 2 R., 36 P., Henrico Co; on S. side of Swift Cr., 29 Apr. 1692, p. 217. Granted Bartho. Chandler, 27 Nov. 1671, from whom it escheated by inquisition under Willm. Byrd, Esqr., Esch'r., 26 May 1686, & now granted, &c.

THO. WEBSTER, 900 acs., Henrico Co., in Bristoll Par; N. side of Appamattock Riv., 29 Apr. 1692, p. 217. 754 A., 1 R., 3 P. granted 28 Oct. 1673; 146 acs. being King's land within the bounds; beg. nigh head of the *Old Town* Land; adj. Tho. Bott's cor; Mr. Archer; & Godfrey Fowler; crossing Old Town Run, to Mr. Philip Jones; down Old Town Cr., to John Wilson; & John Bevill. Imp. of 3 pers: Julian Jarrett (or Jarrell), Eliza. Beamont, Edmd. Reade.

CAPT. JAMES BISS, 138 acs., in low. end of *Weynoake;* Chas. City Co., in Weynoak Par., 29 Apr. 1692, p. 218. Adj. his own, & land of James Lawrence; through the Marsh Sw., to mouth of Piney Is. gutt; down Kittawan Cr; up James River, &c; including 5 acs. at foot of 60 acs. sold by William Justice to Capt. Perry, who sold to sd. Biss; on line of Samll. Moody, bought of Peter Evans, &c. Imp. of 3 pers: Richard Wells, James Braithwitt; & Pendor, a Negro.

MR. SOLOMON CROOKE, 89 acs., Chas. City Co., in Bristoll Par; adj. Robert Burdges; Mr. Coleman; Baley's meadow; & land of Hugh Lee; 29 Apr. 1692, p. 218. Imp. of 2 pers: Timothy Redding, Eliz. Clark.

MR. WM. FOREMAN, 240 acs., Surry Co., in Southwark Par., near the *Church;* 29 Apr. 1692, p. 219. Adj. Mr. John Watkins; Mr. Wm. Edwards,

Col. Brown; Mr. Wm. Thompson; & Chris. Lawson. Imp. of 5 pers: Capt. Wm. Brown, Mary Brown, Thomas an Irishman, Sarah Wilson, Francis Meddowe.

MAJ. ARTHUR ALLEN, 1000 acs., Surry Co., in Lawnes Cr. Par; on both sides the 2nd Sw., 29 Apr. 1692, p. 219. Adj. land lately belonging to Capt. Lawrence Baker, dec'd; his own, Mr. Robt. Flake; John Pittford; Mr. Wm. Newsome; Charles Jarrett; & land Mr. Robert Canfield purchased of Joseph Rogers. Imp. of 20 pers: Jno. Dawson, Leond. Shelden, William Peirce, Fran. Fetherston, James Pierce, Hump. Larcy, Ellenor Duke, Wm. Mallerory, Jno. Woodson, Wm. Watson, Ca. Jones, Phill. Barawayes, Jona. Burrows, Wm. Bugg, Jno. Boiston, Nath. Dodson, Wm. Terry, Henry Burgen, Wm. Blayer, Hen. Baddison.

JOHN RAWLINS, 220 acs., Up. Par. of Surry Co., 29 Apr. 1692, p. 220. Adj. Richard Washington, Abraham Evans, & Tho. Hunt. Imp. of 5 pers: John Hill, Peter Michell, Jos. Petty, Rich. Green, Wm. Preston.

JOHN BROWNE, 220 acs., Low. Par. of Is. of Wight Co; S. side of Kingsale Sw; adj. lands of Jonathan Robinson; 29 Apr. 1692, p. 220. Imp. of 5 pers: James Amy, Richd. Burden, Ph. Bowey, Richd. Caper (?), Tho. Craforth.

OWEN DANIELL, 175 acs., in Is. of Wight & Nansemond Counties; on brs. of Kingsale Sw; adj. Jonathan Robinson; on the Halfe Moon Swamp. 29 Apr. 1692, p. 220. Imp. of 4 pers: Phillip Johnson, Wm. Peterfeild, James Johnson, Henry Johnson.

MR. CHRISTOPHER ROBINSON, of Middlesex Co., 959 acs. in the freshes of Rappa. Co., on S. side the river, 29 Apr. 1692, p. 221. Beg. at head of *Uzenzen;* adj. his own land; & Mr. John Buckner; crossing Moons Mount Sw; by a br. of Passating; by Esqr. Corbin, to land formerly Moon's, now his own; &c. Imp. of 20 pers: Edward

Docker, Thomas Bond, Edward ——, Mrs. Mary Potter, Hester Bustoe, Jno. Blanket, Ann Deliske, Elinor Hutson, Francis Knitter, Christopher Hale, Jno. Lee, Andrew Vincent, Edward Poole, Richd. Batting, Richd. Broome, Sarah Mould, Rowland Jones, the Bricklayer, & another bought of Mr. Richards; (&) Stephen Rudnell.

BRIDGEMAN JOYNER, 600 acs., Is. of Wight Co., neer Kingsale Swamp; along James Brian & run of the maine Black Water Sw; 29 Apr. 1692, p. 222. Imp. of 12 pers: Bridgman Joyner, Elizabeth Jones, Jno. Edmond, Thomas Wright, William Walker, Phillip Rafford, Jno. Edmondson, Mary Wilkinson, Jno. Edwards, Owen Ellis, Derick Stone, Black Moll.

JOHN JOHNSON, 250 acs., Is. of Wight Co., 29 Apr. 1692, p. 222. Adj. James Brian & Bridgman Joyner; James Allen & William Mayo; on Beavor Damm Sw; & Kingsale Sw. Imp. of 5 negroes: Hanah, Robin, Kate, Peter, Lewis.

JOHN CORPOROE, 400 acs., Norf. Co; on brs. of Sympson's Cr. Cyprus Sw; 29 Apr. 1692, p. 223. Imp. of 8 pers: Jno. Bucknell, Eliz. Williams, Vall. Smith, Abraham Smith, Jno. Folconer, Tho. Rolston, Robt. Haynes, Jno. Clay.

DANIELL MACOY, 82 acs., Norf. Co; E. side of the S. br. of Eliz. River, 29 Apr. 1692, p. 223. By patent granted his father Daniel Macoy, 23 Oct. 1673, & in his possession as heir, &c; beg. on N. side of Little Cr; adj. Jon. Ross; Edmond Creekman (or Cheekman); Moses Prescott; & Jon. Bright.

JOHN ROSS, 125 acs., Norf. Co; upon S. side of Clarke's Cr., out of the E. side of the S. br. of Eliz. River; 29 Apr. 1692, p. 224. Granted to Thrustrum Norsworthy, 19 Aug. 1650, who assigned to Lewis Vandermule, who sold to Alexander Ross, & now in possession of sd. John, as his son & heir, who escheated the same.

MAJ. FRANCIS SAYER, 147 acs., Norf. Co., 29 Apr. 1692, p. 224. Part of patent for 660 acs. to John Yates, who assigned to James Warnner, who assigned to Christopher Buston, Senr; renewed in the name of Xtopher. Buston, Junr., 20 Apr. 1682; which 147 acs. sd. Christopher, Senr., assigned to Robert Digby, & by Jon. Digby, his son & heire, assigned to John Ives, who sold to sd. Sayer. Beg. nigh land of Jon. Markham, &c.

WILLIAM MILLER, 760 acs., Norf. Co; near Sympson's Cr. Cyprus Sw., on head of the S. br. of Eliz. Riv; cor. to Joseph Miller; & Patrick White; 29 Apr. 1692, p. 225. Imp. of 16 pers: Martha Hunt, Judieth Wilson, Rebecca Marshall, Jane Cooper, Easter Ashton, Tho. Bedon, Alice Thornby, Tho. Glover, Tho. Francklin, Kath. Fillia (?), Tho. Jones, Mary Andrews, Fra. Harrinton, Eliz. Branch, Jno. Smith, Samll. Hall.

CAPT. HUGH CAMPBELL, 730 acs., Norf. Co., 29 Apr. 1692, p. 226. Adj. Patrick White; & Evan Jones; on the Cyprus Sw; by Mount Pleasent Run. Said land being formerly in a difference betwixt Ralph Wallis & Wm. Ravenning, & by order, &c., the right in Wallis, by reason of his rights entered according to law, & since by another order, ordered the survey to sd. Campbell, because sd. Wallis was indebted to him for a considerable sum of tobacco & other reasons. Imp. of 15 pers: Tho. Davis, Jonas Williams, Roger Murry, Alex. Worth, Jno. Keniford (or Reniford), Hugh Conway, Ambrose Hariat, William Dethinge, Richd. Martinge, William Daw, James Maddock, Tho. Davis, Eliz. Tucker, Jas. Williams, Jno. Cootes (or Cookes).

SAME. 200 acs. at head of Julians Cr., a br. of the S. br. of Eliz. River; same date & page. Granted Mr. Edmond Bowman, 9 Mar. 1653, deserted, & granted Alexander Champbell, 21 Apr. 1691, who assigned to sd. Campbell, to whom it is due for Imp. of 4 pers: David Thomas, Tristram Acnetly, Wm. Johnson, Mary House.

FRANCIS BOND, 872 acs., Pr. Ann Co., 29 Apr. 1692, p. 227. Beg. at Robert Richmond; on a run deviding this & Richard Whitehurst; adj. land of Chicester; along Cyprus Sw; by Bowrin's River, &c. 400 acs. granted him, 8 Apr. 1682; 474 acs. for Imp. of 10 pers: Fra. Bond twice, Evan Jones, an English servt. twice; Moll, Doll, Tony, Sambo, James, Otto, Negroes.

CHRISTOPHER COPELAND, 220 acs., Eliz. City Co; 29 Apr. 1692, p. 228. On W. side of Harris' Cr; adj. Needham's old line; Daniell Ferguson; & neer his own dwelling house, &c. Part of 2000 acs. granted Samll. Stephens, 23 Sept. 1637 & after severall assignments came to Wm. Lunier (or Limner), who bequeathed to sd. Xpher.

JACOB WALKER & GEORGE WALKER, the younger, 125 acs., Eliz. City Co; adj. Kiteley's orchard; by a br. of John's, *alias* Hook's, Cr. to the mouth falling into James River; 29 Apr. 1692, p. 229. 100 acs. granted Capt. Fra. Hookes, 9 Aug. 1637; 25 acs. being part of the 50 acs. devised to Mr. Thomas Oldis, 29 Sept. 1642, & the whole devised by Thomas Oldis, the *Grandson* of sd. Thomas, to the abovenamed Jacob & George.

HENRY COPELAND, 220 acs., Eliz. City Co; on W. side of Harris' Cr; adj. Henry Dunn, Daniel Ferguson, & land of his *uncle* Chris. Copeland; 29 Apr. 1692, p. 229. Part. of 2000 acs. granted Samll. Stephens, 3 Sept. 1637, & after severall assignments came to Wm. Lunier (or Limner), dec'd., who bequeathed to William Copeland, dec'd., father of sd. Henry, who now on devision prayeth a patent.

MR. JOHN PERSONS, 650 acs., Yorke Co., in New Pocoson Par., 29 Apr. 1692, p. 230. Beg. at a gutt parting this & Arminger Wade; on Brice's pond; adj. *Boar Quarter;* down Long Cr., to Back Cr., neer the back river. &c. 400 acs. bought of Thomas Ouldis, 17 Dec. 1663, who purchased of George Downes, who patented it in 1633; 250 acs. for Imp. of 5 pers: Hen. Freeman,

Math. Hooper, Ann Crundell (or Crandell), Tho. Carter, Jno. Wood.

HENERICK FORSON VANDEAVORATT, 504 acs., Yorke Co., in New Pocoson Par., 29 Apr. 1692, p. 230. On S. side the New Pocoson Riv; adj. Henry Heyward; Owen Davis; land formerly Mr. Rookesbee's; & the *Gleab* land. 270 acs. bought by sd. *Henryck Forson* of Xpher. Garlington, 1 Nov. 1675, recorded in sd. court 24 Feb. 1679/80; 214 acs. granted *sd. Forson,* 14 Nov. 1666; 20 acs. for trans. of 1 per.*

WILLIAM NANCE, 520 acs., Jas. City Co., on S. side of Chickahominy Riv., 29 Apr. 1692, p. 231. Beg. next above plantation whereon John Randall dwells, along Gregory Wells; to Ashes feild; to Mr. Bobby's land; to Lofftin's cor; to & including Nance's Neck. 150 acs. due as marryinge the daughter & one of the coheires of Grace Tinsly, who was sister & one of the coheires of Richard Peirce; being part of 600 acs. granted sd. Peirce, 12 Sept. 1636; 370 acs. being surplusage of sd. Nance's survey, & due for Imp. of 8 pers: Ann Keser, Wm. Kent, Wm. ——, Kath. Davis, Eliz. Grover, Berrebe Farmer, Nich. Prior.

JAMES HOOD, of Jas. City Co., 232 acs., in said Co; on E. br. of Morgan's Sw; 29 Apr. 1692, p. 232. Imp. of 5 pers: Robt. Bradly, Hanah Bradly, Eliz. Jennett, Jno. Buberry, Nath. Timberell.

ADAM FERGUSON, 120 acs., Pr. Anne Co; on W. side of the north River Sw; adj. lands of Beecher, & Tho. Tuly; 29 Apr. 1692, p. 233. Imp. of: Dorotheus Vincent, 3 times.

JAMES BARRETT, 305 acs., James City Co., called *Peashill;* on E. side of Peas hill Cr; on Bruer's line, to Chickahominy River Marsh; 29 Apr. 1692, p. 233. Due as son & heir of Capt. Wm. Barrett, the former proprietor of sd. *Peas hill,* but by reason of defaceing (?) of the records the title appears not; further due for Imp. of 7 pers: Ellinor Keeney, Sibella Wood, Jno. Sorrelll.

Ann Blewet, Jno. Finch, Clement Loo; & Prancer, a Negro.

GEORGE ALVES, 653 acs., New Kent Co., in St. Peter's Par., 29 Apr. 1692, p. 234. Beg. at land, now or late, of William Bassett & James Astin; to Beaver Dam Sw: to land, now or late, of Charles Turner; & land, now or late, of Littlepage. Imp. of 14 pers.*

ROBERT BEVERLEY, son of Maj. Robert Beverley, dec'd; 200 acs. Glocester Co; E. side of Poropotank Cr; adj. William Ginsey, & Mr. John Pate; 29 Apr. 1692, p. 234. Granted to Michael Crafton, deserted, & granted to sd. Pate, & deserted; then to John Oakham, 22 Mar. 1665, deserted, & granted sd. Maj. Beverley by order, & joyned in patent with 720 acs., 24 Oct. 1673, but not seated, & now again granted to Robert Beverley, by order, &c. Imp. of 4 pers: Jno. Drake; Danll., Bess, & Tony, Negroes.

THOMAS HICKMAN, 428 acs., Rappa. Co; S. side of Rappa. Riv., & N. side of a gr. swamp of Peanketank Riv; adj. Anthony Jackman; & Mr. George Marsh; 29 Apr. 1692, p. 235. Granted Richard Bredgar, 19 Sept. 1664 deserted, & now granted by order, &c. Imp. of 9 pers: Ralph Wheeler, Tabitha Garatson, Margaret Garetson, Derrick Garetson, Desire Garetson, Phillip Farrar, Henry Gauler, Catherine Gauler, Watkin Thomas.

MR. WM. KENDALL, 2725 acs., Accomack Co; including Piney Island; on NE end of & being halfe of Jengoteage Island; NE on marshes of Wild Catt Is., SE by Assateag Inlett & from the mouth of a gutt of Sheepshead Cr. to NW side of Piney Is., &c; 29 Apr. 1692, p. 235. Imp. of 36 pers.*

JOHN WALLOP, alias WADLOW, 2500 acs., being all of Kecotanck Island; Accomack Co; SW on Assawomen Inlett, NE on Jengoteag Inlet; 29 Apr. 1692, p. 236. 1800 acs. part due by rights of his patent dated 20 Apr. 1682; 700 acs. for Imp. of 14 pers: Chris. Thompson, twice; Tho. Tarretts, Jane Brown, Tho. Tally, Rich, Kessly, Hen.

Flowers, Jno. Munrow, Jno. Currin, Fra. Hilly, Nich. Backman (?), Thomas Cocks, Jno. Bissbe, Tho. Warrins.

JOHN STITH, JUNR., 595 acs., Jas. City Co., 29 Apr. 1692, p. 237. Beg. in Mr. Brumfeild's line near the Gt. Run, a br. of Chickahominy Riv., where Francis Story liveth; down Shadocks Br; to Mr. David Newell. First taken by Mr. David Newill, 3 Sept. 1664, who assigned to Capt. Wm. Broadribb, 22 Aug. 1665, sd. Newill haveing never patented sd. land; deserted, & granted sd. Stith by order, &c. Imp. of 12 pers: Jno. Hair, Jno. Johnson; Guy, Will, Clay, Pheby, Cesar, Tony, Sue, Meriah, Hector, Pompy, Negroes.

CAPT. WM. HUNT, 908 acs., Chas. City Co., in Wynoak Par; at head of the N. br. of Moses (Mosses) Run; 29 Apr. 1692, p. 238. On head of Peas-hill Sw., deviding this & land, now or late, of Thomas Cole; on Queen Cr. run, *otherwise called* Old Tree Run; to land, now or late, of Mr. Harwood, &c. 300 acs. granted Wm. Benard, 18 Apr. 1688, who assigned to sd. Hunt; 608 acs. for Imp. of 13 pers: Wm. Alford, Wm. Ledfores, Wm. Briscow, Wm. Newby, Wm. Rawlins, Wm. Gibbons, John Man, Geo. Simons, Margaret Woodburn, Jonah Banister & Mary his wife, Jno. Lapage, Cha. Springer.

SAME. 610 acs., Jas. City Co; same date & page. Beg. at Moses' Run; along Travis' line, to N. side of the Oaken Sw., to a White (alias Long) Meadow; on Mr. Cowles' line, &c. Purchased of Edmond Brewer, 5 Dec. 1681 for 300 acs., more or less. Imp. of 7 pers: John Green, John Arnold, Tho. Brown, John Coates *or* Catt (?), Joseph Renshaw, Mary Woodbone, John Thomason.

BENJA. HOLLOWELL, 1150 acs., Norf. Co; W. side of the up. Indian Cr. of the northwest river; 29 Apr. 1692, p. 239. Beg. at Joseph Hollowell; to the Cyprus Sw; along land of Prescott, &c. Imp. of 23 pers.* *Note:* 23 rights of a certif. from Mr. Edw. Chilton.

JOSEPH HOLLOWELL, 1750 acs., Norf. Co; W. side of the up. Indian Cr. & Cyprus Sw. upon the northwest river; 29 Apr. 1692, p. 240. Adj. Benja. Hollowell; Capt. Russell; & land of Prescott. Imp. of 35 pers: Jno. Horson, Timo. Callender, Eliz. Miller, Anth. Blackman, Robt. Woodle (or Woodbe), James Tander, Wm. Ralph, James Portis, Robt. Aylett, Mary Hutchins, Lewis Mac —— (?), & his mate, Marke Junger, Wm. Oden, 12 times; Peter, Harry, Jack, Meriah; Mingo; Hannah, Robin, Kate, Negroes.

CAPT. JOHN STITH, JUNR., 471½ acs., Chas. City Co., 29 Apr. 1692, p. 240. Granted James Warradine, 8 July 1647, & escheated by inquisition under Peter Perry, Depty. of Christopher Wormeley, Esqr., Esch'r., & now granted, &c.

HENRY NEWMAN, 300 acs. Pr. Anne Co., 29 Apr. 1692, p. 241. Adj. Mr. Godard; & Col. Mason. Imp. of 6 pers: Henry Newman, his wife Magdalen, his sonn Henry, his servt. Jno. Dally, Robt. Paraford, Edward Hughes.

MRS. REBECCA POYTHRES, 1000 acs., Chas. City Co., 29 Apr. 1692, p. 241. Late in the tenure of Edwd. Ardington, dec'd., by vertue of his own right & fee therein; found to escheat by inquisition under Peter Perry, Depty. of Christopher Wormeley, Esqr., Esch'r., &c.

MR. GILES WEBB, 132 acs., Henrico Co; on N. side of James Riv., bet. Honble. Willm. Byrd, Esqr., & Mr. Robt. Beverley; 29 Apr. 1692, p. 242. Beg. at an heap of Great Rocks on up. side of sd. Byrd's land, &c. Imp. of 3 pers: Richd. Griffin; Robin & Jane, Negroes.

SAME. 344 acs., same location, date & page. In Varina Parish; on the middle run bet. Colson's & the Deep bottom; on Mr. Francis Reeves; Henry Trent; on head of Barrow-land; cor. of Mr. Pleasants. Imp. of 7 pers: Anne Hughes, John Elderkin, Edwd. Tustin (or Tuffin); Robin, Tom, Betty, Jenny, Negroes.

MAJ. JOHN ROBINS, 200 acs., Accomack Co; at head of Mesango Cr; adj. Robert Johnson; 29 Apr. 1692, p. 242. Granted to German Gilliott, 9 Nov. 1666, deserted, & granted Col. Wm. Kendall, 4 Nov. 1685, deserted, & granted to Daniell Neech, 20 Apr. 1689, deserted, & now granted by order, &c. Imp. of 4 pers: John Chapman, Benja. Cox, Tho. Webb, Eliz. Lewin.

SAME. 2765 acs; same Co., & date, p. 243. 2725 acs. being ½ of Jengoteag Island; SW on Jengoteag Inlett, SE on the main sea, Assateag Inlett & Sheepshead Cr. Sd. island granted to Mr. Tho. Clayton, 6 Apr. 1684, & by Wm. Clayton, of Leverpoole, Merchant, oldest bro. & heir, sold to Wm. Kendall, Merchant, of N'ampton Co., 31 Aug. 1687, & by Wm. Kendall, his son & heir, sold the moyety to sd. Robins, 12 Sept. 1691; 40 acs., being a marshy Island on NW side of the SW end of sd. island; due for imp. of 1 pers.*

RALPH JACKSON, JOSEPH MADDOX & JOHN DUGLES (Dowgles), 784 acs., Chas. City Co., in Bristoll Par., 29 Apr. 1692, p. 244. Beg. on a br. of Moncuseneck maine Cr., crossing Wildcatt fall down, &c. Imp. of 16 pers: Geo. Hatton, Rich. Longwell, Eliz. Kendall; Pompy & Guy. 11 Rights by Cert. from Mr. Wm. Edwards, Clk., 1689.

HUGH LEE, SENR., & JOHN BARLOR, 530 acs., Chas. City Co., in Jordan's Par., 29 Apr. 1692, p. 244. Adj. sd. Lee; & land of John Smith; crossing the 2nd Swamp, &c. Imp. of 11 pers: James Cutthill, Geo. Bass, Xtopher. Adgar, Mathew Rope (or Roye), Tho. Goten, Rich. Bass, Geo. Packar, Jno. Borrow, Robt. Heath, Jno. Crump, Mary Hamson.

By Sir Edmond Andros, Knight, Gov'r.

RICE HUGHES, 436 acs., New Kent Co., in St. Peter's Par., 29 Apr. 1693, p. 245. Beg. at land, now or late, of George Polegreen; Atkins; Littlepage, & Underhill; on Bever dam Sw., &c. Imp. of 9 pers: John Greenhaugh, Susanna Greenhaugh, Joseph Moreys (or Moneys), Tho. Braddy John Martyn, Andrew Parker, Xpher. Read, Thomas Sisoms; Mingo, a Negro.

MR. WM. WILSON, 1000 acs., Low. Norf. Co; W'ly. from the Mill Land devd't., at head of Puzle Cr., in the S. br. of Eliz. River; 29 Apr. 1693, p. 246. Granted Mr. John Ferrebe, 20 Oct. 1688, who obtained grant thereof as deserted from Maj. Fran. Sawyer, who patented the same 21 Oct. 1684; deserted & now granted by order, &c. Imp. of 21 pers.* *Note:* Did not pass the Seal, there being no such county. R. B., Cl. Sec. Off.

WILLIAM CHAMBERS, 50 acs. called *Bay Tree Neck,* Surry Co., in Lawnes Cr. Par., 29 Apr. 1693, p. 247. Which land Wm. Batt dyed seized of, as appears by will of Wm. Carter proved in sd. court 8 Mar. 1664; escheated by inquisition under Capt. Wm. Randolph, Depty. Esch'r., & since granted, &c.

MR. THOMAS COCKE, 250 acs., Low. Norf. Co., p. 247. (Note: Name of Gov'r. & date omitted). Which land Wm. Wilson dyed seized of, & escheated by inquisition under John Lear, Esqr., Esch'r., & now granted, &c. *Note:* Did not pass the Seal, there being no such county. R. B. (Robt. Beverley) Cl. Sec. Off.

SAMPSON MEREDITH, 200 acs., Nansemond Co., on the Indian Cr., 29 Apr. 1693, p. 247. Which land belonged to Lewis Perrot an alien, & escheated as by inquisition under John Lear, Esqr., Esch'r., & now granted, &c.

MR. DANIEL PARK (Parke), 74 acs., York Co; on up. side of Queens Cr., 29 Apr. 1693, p. 248. Being all the marsh from the Oyster Shell Landing to land, now or late, of Robt. Clarke. Granted to Daniel Parke, Esqr., but patent thereof not found, & is confirmed to the abovenamed by order, &c. Imp. of 2 pers.*

MR. ROBERT PRIOR, 92 acs., Gloster Co; on N. side of Craney Cr. Swamp; 29 Apr. 1693, p. 248. Granted

Robert Jefferson, 1 Apr. 1668, from whom it escheated by inquisition under Mr. Wm. Todd, Depty. Esch'r., & now granted, &c.

JOHN WILLIAMS, of K. & Q. Co., 410 acs., near Poropotank Cr., on N. side of York River, 29 Apr. 1693, p. 248. Adj. Mr. Roger Shakleford, John Major & John Levistone; 250 acs. patented by Thomas Bell, 29 June 1659, & assigned to Andrew Cotton, but the patent not being renewed, sd. land lapsed, & now taken as King's land; 160 acs. being overplus; beg. at head of Bennet's Cr. just below the Bridge; by the *Church* Road; in sight of White Horne's plantation, &c. Imp. of 9 pers.*

THOMAS PARKER, 30 acs., Rappa. Co; S. side the river, on a br. of Occupation Cr., 29 Apr. 1693, p. 249. Adj. lands of Wm. Harper; & Robt. Gullock. Imp. of 1 pers.*

MR. JAMES WILSON, 600 acs., Norf. Co; on brs. of the northwest river; 29 Apr., 1693, p. 250. On E. side of the Cyprus Sw., & crossing same to the Green Sea, &c. Imp. of 12 pers: Alice, Hannah, Welsh Jack, Wm. Chambers, Margaret, Thomas Chambers, Gilbt. Wilson, Saml. Neal, Fenley, Jno. Newton, John Fulford, & Mary Williamson.

PETER CARTWRIGHT, 1050 acs., Norf. Co; on brs. of Simpson's Cr. Cyprus Swamp; adj. Joseph Miller; & Jno. Corporoe, &c; 29 Apr. 1693, p. 251. Imp. of 21 pers.*

JOSEPH BOOTH, 37 acs., in Up. Par. of Nansemond Co., at the White Marsh; 29 Apr. 1693, p. 251. Adj. lands of Robt. Lassister; & Capt. Jossy (or Jessy); & his own Orchard. Imp. of: John Swinson.

JOSEPH HALLOWELL (Hollowell), 97 acs., Norf. Co; in a fork of the North West River Cyprus Sw; adj. John Godfrey; 29 Apr. 1693, p. 252. Imp. of 2 pers: John Mills, John Man.

JOHN CAMBLE, 150 acs., Nansemond Co; on NW side of Chuckey

Tuck Cr., 29 Apr. 1693, p. 252. Adj. Thomas Jordan, nigh E. side of Cross Cr; through an old feild to land of Samuel Ferment, &c. 100 acs. granted Peter Mountague, 3 Nov. 1647, which after several sales & descents is in possession of sd. Camble; 50 acs. overplus due for Imp. of: James Ross.

WM. JONES, 550 acs., in the Up. Par. of Nansemond; at a place called *Orapeake;* 29 Apr. 1693, p. 253. On S. side of Orapeake Sw., to mouth of Loosing Sw; by a great White Marsh. Imp. of 11 pers: John Smith, Richd. Smith, Nicho. Simmons; 8 by cert. signed (by) Hen. Hartwell, Cl.

MR. JOHN WILLIAMS, 818 acs., Jas. City Co., 1692, p. 253. On NE side of Moses Cr; a little above the old Landing. Due as son & heir of Richd. Williams, viz: 550 acs. part of 755 acs. granted sd. Richard, 3 Feb. 1651; 100 acs. part of 1330 acs. assigned to sd. Richard by Wm. Strong, 7 Apr. 1655; 133 acs. surplus for Imp. of 3 pers.* *Note:* Did not pass the Seal, not being any such county. R. B., Cl. Sec. Off.

WM. HESLETT & WM. BALLANCE, 730 acs., Norf. Co; S. side of the North West River; on S. side of the Ash Branch; crossing the Cyprus Swamp, &c; 29 Apr. 1693, p. 254. Imp. of 15 *pers:* Daniel Jones, Robert Thorne, John Bowste, John Wright, Peter Story.

HENRY PRICE & MR. FRANCIS TALIAFERRO, both of Rappa. Co., 806 acs., in said Co; S. side of the river, on the maine run of Pewmansend; p. 255. Adj. Capt. John Catlett; Prosser; Mr. John Buckner, & Mr. Robt. Bryan. Imp. of 17 pers.* *Note:* Did not pass the Seal, not being any such county.

HENRY BRADLEY, 450 acs., named *Rainsworth;* Nansemond Co; W. side of the head of Chuckeytuck Cr., near Peter Butler's house; by the Cooper's Br; & E. of Jacob Butler's house NE to the Foot Bridge; 29 Apr. 1693, p. 255. 350 acs. granted to Humphry Scowne, by 2 patents dated 28 May 1638; & granted Henry Bradley,

(Grandfather of the now Henry) with the addition of 100 acs., 21 Dec. 1643; & after several descents is now in possession of sd. Henry.

MR. JAMES WILSON, 120 acs., Low. Norf. Co; towards head of the S'wd. Cr. of the S. br. of Eliz. Riv; adj. his own land; to mouth of Gilliam Neck Run, &c; p. 256. Imp. of 3 pers: Mary West Coat, Willis Willson, Willis Willson. *Note:* Did not pass Seal not being any such county. R.B., Cl. Sec. Off.

WILLIAM SHERWOOD, GENT., 3000 acs., New Kent Co; on both sides of Totopotomoys Cr., adj. Mr. John Page; 29 Apr. 1693, p. 257. Granted William Phillips, 25 Sept. 1679; deserted, & now granted by order, &c. Imp. of 60 pers.*

ROBERT COUCH, 77 acs., Gloster Co; adj. Abraham Ivesonn; 29 Apr. 1693, p. 258. Imp. of 2 pers: Thomas Cloutsom, John Trevillian.

GEORGE POOLE, 350 acs., Pr. Anne Co; on W. shore of Linhaven River, near head of Bennet's Cr., 29 Apr. 1693, p. 258. Adj. Mathew Pawlet; James Kemp; Edmund Boring; & Robert Smith. Imp. of 7 pers: Richd. Bingly, Will. Fow, Mary West, Mary Eutell, Richd. Hamblin; Asme & Anna, Negroes.

JOHN CREEKMAN, EDMOND CREEKMAN. & ROGER HODGES, 1920 acs., Norf. Co; S. side of the Northwest River; on W. side of Pipe Ridge Branch; 29 Apr. 1693, p. 259. Imp. of 39 pers.*

THOMAS COCKE (Cock), JUNR., 528 acs., Henrico Co., in Viriña Par; on N. side of James Riv., 29 Apr. 1693, p. 260. Beg. at Mr. John Pleasants, on the bank of Barrow; crossing Sampson's Slash; to Isaac Creswell; up Cornelious' Cr; to Henry Trent, &c. Granted Nicholas Marsh, 20 Oct. 1688, deserted, & now granted by order, &c. Imp. of 11 pers: John James, Tho. Williams, William Johns, Joseph Thomas, John

Thomas, Simon Edwards, Arthur Robins, John Robins, Thomas Roberts, William Richards, Oliver Richards.

MR. LEMUEL MASON, JUNR., of Norf. Co., 184 acs., in Pr. Anne Co; SE side of the North River, commonly called Matchepango; 29 Apr. 1693, p. 261. Beg. on N. side of a ridge called Rattle Snake Island. Imp. of 4 pers: Lemuel Mason; Jack, Missi, & Sambo, Negroes.

THOMAS RICE, 35 acs., Gloster Co., in Kingston Par; adj. Edward Boram; Mark Thomas; & Mr. John Man; 29 Apr. 1693, p. 261. Imp. of: Edward Jenkins.

WILLIAM COLLAINE, JUNR., 97 acs., Gloster Co., in Pettsoe Par; adj. his own, & land of Mr. Haines; 29 Apr. 1693, p. 262. Imp. of 2 pers: Gillian Clare; Tony, a Negro.

EDWARD DAVIS, 400 acs., Gloster Co., in Kingstone Par., 29 Apr. 1693, p. 262. Beg. at head of Ducking Pond Cr., dividing this, land of Isaac Plumer, & Thomas Plumer; adj. Ralph Armistead; & Thomas Dyer. Granted John Corbett, 26 Apr. 1684, deserted, & now granted by order, &c. Imp. of 8 pers: Richard Smith, George Walter, Hen. Green. Fran. Weesell, Richd. Harford, William Attwood, Abrah. Roane, Humphry Hunt.

HEZEKIAH RHODES (Rohdes), 410 acs., Middlesex Co., 29 Apr. 1693, p. 263. Adj. William Hackny; Sir William Skipwith; & Capt. Mathew Kemp; on a br. of Bonner's Cr; by Killbee's land, &c. 350 acs. granted Wm. Frissall, 20 Dec. 1667; 60 acs. overplush, due for Imp. of 2 pers: Daniel Mathews; Pompey a Negro.

JOHN MAGUFFEY, 77 acs., Essex Co., 29 Apr. 1693, p. 264. Beg. in a br. of Gibson's Cr., cor. of Mr. Edmond Paggit, & Tandy's land. Imp. of 2 pers: Thomas Washford, Wm. George.

CORNELIOUS VAUGHAN, 288 acs., King & Qu. Co., 29 Apr. 1693, p. 264. Beg. near head of the Gr. Meadow, &c. 150 acs. granted to John Derwood, who conveyed to Cornelious Mathews, 28 Aug. 1673; 131 acs. being overplush within sd. patent & deed, & 7 acs., now taken. Imp. of 3 pers: Thomas Booth, Nicholas Smith, Thomas Hill.

JOHN BROOKES, 189 acs., Essex Co., 29 Apr. 1693, p. 265. Adj. Thomas Williams; up Dragon Sw; to Thomas Day; by Evan Davis; to mouth of the Dry Branch, &c. 95 acs. granted John Pigg, 10 June 1675, being half of sd. patent; granted to Edward Adcock, 1 Feb. 1686, who assigned to sd. Brookes, 10 Jan. 1688; the residue for Imp. of 2 pers: John Spragg, Wm. Gardner.

WILLIAM TODD, 500 acs., K & Q. Co., in Stratton Major Par; upon Peanketank Sw., 29 Apr. 1693, p. 266. Adj. David Bram (or Brain). Granted George Burge, 16 Apr. 1683, deserted, & granted to Henry Waring, 20 Oct. 1689, deserted, & now granted by order, &c. Imp. of 10 pers: Henry Gibbons, John Belmaine, Richard Williams, Edward Hughes, John Barker, Jane Dyton, William Blomfeild, Dorothy Oliver, George Flood, Samuel Pomeroy.

CAPT. JOSHUA STORY, 300 acs., K. & Q. Co; on a gr. run of Morocosick Cr., adj. his 7440 ac. patent; & land of Maj. Robert Beverly; 29 Apr. 1693, p. 266. Imp. of 6 pers: Richard Anderson, Roger Cooly, Thomas Rice, Menelcius Ager (?), (or Eger), William Bracy, Edward Conigon.

RICHARD TURBERFEILD, 200 acs., Chas. City Co; S. side of Appamattuck Riv., in Bristoll Par., at Monkey's Neck; 29 Apr. 1693, p. 267. Beg. at Thomas Lowe; crossing the maine Monkeys Neck Sw., &c. Granted Adam Morris, 20 Nov. 1683, deserted, & now granted by order, &c. Imp. of 4 pers: John Jones, William Canter, Richard Wheeler, Abraham Ducket.

THOMAS VICARIS, Clerk, 81 acs., Gloster Co., in Petsoe Par; adj. land of Mr. William Pritchet & William Cook, dec'd; 29 Apr. 1693, p. 267. Imp. of 2 pers: John Camel, John Wornam.

CAPT. JOSHUA STOREY, MR. JAMES TAYLOR, & MR. JONATHAN FISHER, 9150 acs., K. & Q. Co., on N. side of Mattapony River; by a br. of Morocosick Cr; 29 Apr. 1693, p. 268. Imp. of 185 pers: Charles Scarburgh, John Jones, Humphry Jones, Susana Jones, Edward Morris, Henry Wheeler, Cath. Newjant, Will. West, Wm. Baldry, John Evans, Richard Hailes, Jonas Terry, Sarah Jones, George Wilson. John Newell; Isaac French 6 times; Mary, John & Thomas Sullivant; Thomas & Honora Kelly & 5 children; Gilbert Wingfeild, his wife & 5 children; Elizabeth Coltis, William Browning, John Child, Elinor Candy, Debora Thomas, William Feuray, John Audrey, Sarah Hare, Timothy Belson, Owen Penquit, Wm. Champe, Honora Morphy, Hugh Borry. Ellinor Watson, Mary Burnham, Fran. Burnham, John & Mary Butter & 3 children, Margt. Queek, Wm. Oneal, Rachel Oneale, their 7 children; Dick, Mary. John, Jone, Tom, Mafuca, Humphry, Ned. Sue, Tony, Franck, Bess, Betty, Jonah, Sarah, Hiccory, Tapsco, Mingo, Peter, Harry, Nedd, Gingo, Susan, Ellick, Herb, Hector, Helen, June, Vulcan, Sampson, Cyclops, Priapus, Lymtum, Jenkin, Hagar—Negroes; & 79 Negroes. (Unnamed).

THOMAS WEBB, 206 acs., Pr. Anne Co., 29 Apr. 1693, p. 269. A cove deviding this from land of Richard Caps; up a cr. to James Peters' land, &c. Imp. of 5 pers.*

THOMAS VICARIES (Viccaris), 360 acs., K. & Q. Co., 29 Apr. 1693, p. 269. Beg. at a cr. of Poropotank Cr; by Mr. Richard Anderson; down Hayes' Cr: to Timothy Ellis; along John Major's line; to John Williams, &c. Imp. of 8 pers: Phillip Thomas, Wm. Sowell. James Blackly, Fra. Simpson, Joseph Topping, Chr. Pearce, Fra. Coles, Wm. Bradshaw.

MARTYN ELAM, 17 A., 2 R., Henrico Co., in Varina Par; S. side of James River; adj. his own, land of

Thomas Wells; & Edward Stratton; 29 Apr. 1693, p. 270. Imp. of: Edward Banks.

GEORGE TANKERSLY, 713 acs., Gloster Co., in Kingstone Par., 29 Apr. 1693, p. 270. Beg. on W. side of Gwyn's pond, on S. side of Peanketank Riv; to Queens Cr. mouth, &c. 500 acs. granted Col. John Armistead, 25 Sept. 1679; 100 acs. purchased by sd. Armistead of severall men; & the whole purchased of him, by sd. Tankersley, 14 Feb. 1689; 113 acs. for Imp. of 3 Negroes: Harry, Rose, Sampson.

MR. ARTHUR SPICER, 2750 acs., in the freshes of Rappa. Co., now Essex Co; S. side the river, about 2 mi. up Pwomasend Cr., 29 Apr. 1693, p. 271. Beg. on E. side of a run; over several paths to Nanzatico; by William White; to Mr. Robert Payne; neare maine run of Portobago Cr., &c. Granted Alexander Fleming, 17 Apr. 1667, deserted, & now granted by order, &c. Imp. of 55 pers: Valentine May, Michal Basset, Thomas King, Richard Goldin, Susana Gobett, Margaret Griffs, David Purvis, Richd. Monjoy, Fra. George, Hen. Lash, Jos. Strange, Kath. Yeatts (or Yealls), Peter Dallee, Ann Crumshare, John Spence, John Collerell (or Cotterell), Richd. North, John Bryand, John Hasell, John Persefull, Anne Grines, Edmd. Whoden, Hen. Williams, Fra. Jenings, Jonath. Bathow, Eliza. Chambers, Mary Putty, Anne Jack, John Thomas, Anne Joy, David Rome, Jno. Spiers. John Wilkison, Jno. Wilcock, John Creek, Edmd. Colleny, Hen. Dier, Ja. Daniel, Joan Woodward, Margt. Nichols, Wm. Harris, Antho. Hales, Geo. Benford. Cha. Collingford, Math. Ellis, Cha. Wyndam, Tho. York, Geo. Pierson, Joan Woodward, Margt. Nichols, Debora Mumford, Isabell Collier.

THOMAS ROYSTOAN (Roystone) 1616 acs., Gloster Co., in Pettsoe Par., 29 Apr. 1693, p. 272. Beg. at land of Col. Augustine Warner, dec'd; along William Collaine; by Rappahanock Path; to John Wheystoan; to land of Col. John Pate, dec'd; by Rappa. Roade.

to Lorraine's land; along Jeremy Darrell (or Darvell), &c. 270 acs. granted him, 18 Mar. 1662; 608 acs. granted him, 6 Feb. 1667; 500 acs. by joynt patent to sd. Roystoane & Mr. Jno. Buckner for 1000 acs., 12 Oct. 1669; 238 acs. now taken, due for Imp. of 5 Negroes.*

RICHARD MARCHANT (Merchant), 84 acs., Gloster Co., in Kingstone Par; adj. Mr. Long & Thomas Puttman; 29 Apr. 1693, p. 273. Imp. of 2 pers: William Oakly, Susana Mann.

WILLIAM YARDLEY, 164 acs., in Up. Par. of Nanzemond; adj. James Collings, & Francis Wells; 29 Apr. 1693, p. 273. Granted James Collings, 20 July 1671, deserted, & now granted by order, &c. Imp. of 4 pers: John Mackadam, William Hickman, Richard Skemell, William Brooker.

JOHN AMIS, 500 acs., Essex Co., on brs. of Cockelshell Cr., 29 Apr. 1693, p. 274. On a br. of Portobago, in line of Dean & Clapham; on land of James Coghill, &c. Imp. of 10 pers: Daniel Mackey, Elias Wilson, Edward Prime, David Clark, John Murdon, John Jones, Thomas Taylor, Thomas Markam, Thomas Moore, John Moore.

EDWARD CANNON, 46 acs., Pr. Anne Co; on the Eastern Shore of Linhaven River; on S. side of the Reedy Br., cor. of patent granted Thomas Allen & Edward Cannon, dec'd; up Wolfe Snare Creek, &c; 29 Apr. 1693, p. 274. Imp. of: Robert Russell.

NICHOLAS BRUCE, 180 acs., in the *Tarrascoe Neck;* in Chuckeytuck Par., inNansemond Co., 29 Apr. 1693, p. 275. Beg. on E. side of the Hole Cr., by Mount Lawsons Bay & Chuckeytuck Cr. to Carter's Neck Cr., parting this & land of John Copeland; to the Up. Wadeing place poynt; a br. parting this & land of Mathew Whitfeild. Part of 700 acs. purchased by Mr. Walter Bruce of Epaphroditus Lawson, 18 Nov. 1651, out of patent of 1400 acs. granted sd. Lawson, 15 Feb. 1640, which 180 acs. was bequeathed to sd. Nicholas by sd. Walter, & confirmed to him by a deed from his *brother* Abraham Bruce, 18 Dec. 1688.

BENONY BURROUGHS, 150 acs., Pr. Anne Co; neare the N. brs. of Currituck, 29 Apr. 1693, p. 275. Adj. Peter Crashley. Granted Darmon Michael, 22 Nov. 1682, deserted, & now granted by order, &c. Imp. of 3 pers: Edward Oswell, Timothy Dunhow, Daniel Rawles.

THOMAS BOBBY, 862 acs., (whereon he lives) in Jas. City Co., 29 Apr. 1693, p. 276. From Gregory Wells, on Chickahomany Riv. marsh, along lands of Nance & Loftin; to Mr. John Williams & Mr. Isaac Williams; by Mr. Davey's land; & Henshaw's plantation to br. of Beaver Damm Cr. 750 acs. granted him 23 Apr. 1690. 112 acs. for Imp. of 3 pers: Eliza. Clark, Amy, & Nero.

RICHARD BUTT, of Norf. Co., 160 acs., in the Southern Br. precincts of Eliza. River; 29 Apr. 1693, p. 277. Beg. in the cut of the Round Sw., cor. of his own & land of Henry Butt; adj. John Murden; & Thomas Butts; down the Burchen Sw., &c. Imp. of 4 pers: Richard Adams, Sumer Harlzed, William Peterson, Edward Willis.

ROBERT BIRD, GENT., 225 acs., K. & Q. Co., 29 Apr. 1693, p. 277. 200 acs. beg. at Timothy Carter; by Cheescake Path; by sd. Bird's Roade, to James Parks; on Holmes' line, &c; 25 acs. beg. in Holmes' line, &c. Imp. of 5 pers: Aneas, Dido, Guy, Cablabar, Marina.

CAPT. WM. CARY, 256 acs., Yorke Co., in New Poquoson Par., 29 Apr. 1693, p. 278. Beg. on E. side of Denbigh Path neare land of Robert Calvert; to Mr. Miles Cary, &c. Granted Mr. Thomas Harwood & Thomas Platt, 20 Apr. 1682, deserted, & now granted by order, &c. Imp. of 6 pers: Robert Symons, Hannah Owen, John Brazier, Thomas Hill, Daniel Abbott, Old Thomas.

JOHN CHILCOT, 220 acs., Low. Par. of Nanzemond; at head of Bennet's

Cr; adj. Robert Peale; & towards land
of Col. Carter; 29 Apr. 1693, p. 279.
Granted Wm. Coepheld & John Grandberry, 24 Apr. 1682, deserted, & now
granted by order, &c. Imp. of 5 pers:
Thomas Hinton, John Ager, Joseph
Lane, Daniel Maple, John Colledge.

WILLIAM COOK, 250 acs., Up. Par.
of Is. of Wight Co; bet. the 3rd Sw.
& the maine Black Water, 29 Apr. 1693,
p. 279. Adj. Doctor Williamson; Mr.
Thomas More (Moore); & Edward
Boykin, &c. Granted John Proctor, 20
Apr. 1685, deserted, & now granted by
order, &c. Imp. of 5 pers.*

THOMAS CHEESMAN, 253 acs.,
Yorke Co., in New Pocoson Par; adj.
Lawrence Platt; Henry Wattkins; &
land of Capt. John Tiplady, dec'd; his
own & land of Col. John Cheesman,
dec'd; on N. E. side of Cod Run; 29
Apr. 1693, p. 300. Imp. of 6 pers:
John Lane, Mary Jones, Richard Awbrey, Wm. Hickman, John Garret, Tho.
Plumpket. (Note: Error in pagination.)

STEPHEN COCK, of Henrico Co.,
1040 acs. in Jas. & Chas. City Co.s; on
SW side of the head of Chickahomany
Riv., 29 Apr. 1693, p. 300. Below the
Wadeing place; on Strawberry Hill
Run; through James Collaine's corne-
field, &c. Granted to Richard Williams
togeather with 800 (acs.) more for 750
acs., 24 Jan. 1655; & for want of
seating, granted to sd. Cock by order,
&c. Imp. of 21 pers: Edward Elleston,
Wm. Davies, James Willis, John Suill-
man (Sullivan ?), Jane Tucker, Tho.
Michell, Joseph Bucher, Eliza. Skips,
Wm. Stephens, Rachell Baker, Hen.
Richardson, James Oglevy, Richd.
Brookes, John Goram, John Leasam,
Roger Bolt, John Butt; & 4 Negroes.

HUGH CAMPBELL, GENT., 160
acs., Low. Par. of Nansemond, at head
of Bennet's Cr., 29 Apr. 1693, p. 301.
Beg. at Wm. Cophell & John Grandberry, at a place called Holly Hill; nigh
Robert Murray & Col. Carter, &c.
Granted James Lockheart, 20 Apr.
1682, deserted, & now granted by order,

&c. Imp. of 4 pers: John Goose, John
Kemble, John Damrell, Richard Evans.

OWIN DAVIS, 193 acs., York Co.,
in New Poquoson Par., 29 Apr. 1693,
p. 301. Adj. David Lewis; Henderick
Vandevorick; land formerly of Mr.
Merrie; Thomas Lilborn; neare the Mill
path. 76 acs. granted him, 20 Apr.
1685; 117 acs. for Imp. of 3 pers:
Richard Smith, George Walter, Henry
Green.

CAPT. JOHN HATTON, 200 acs.,
Norf. Co; on NW side of the W. br.
of Eliz. Riv., & on E. side of Clarke's
Cr. 29 Apr. 1693, p. 302. Granted
Richard Sterling, 10 June 1657, who
sould 150 acs. to Gideon Tillison, who
sold to John Hatton, dec'd., & now in
possession of the abovenamed John, as
his heire at law; 50 acs. sould to
Michael Weighbourn & patented in his
own name, 20 Apr. 1685, & by him
sould to sd. Hatton.

RICE HUES (Hughs), 627 acs., New
Kent Co., in St. Peter's Par; on the
Beaver damms, a br. of Chickahomany
Sw; along land, now or late, of Alvey;
adj. land of Napier; 29 Apr. 1693, p.
303. Granted to Charles Turner, deserted, & granted sd. Hues (interalia)
by order, &c. Imp. of 13 pers.*

LT. COL. ANTHONY LAWSON,
60 acs., Norf. Co., in Linhaven Par; in
the Little Cr., 29 Apr. 1693, p. 303.
Escheated from George Mason by inquisition under William Porten (or
Porteis), Depty. Esch'r., 22 Sept. 1688,
& now granted by order, &c.

RICHARD LIGON & JAMES
EAKENS, JUNR., 285 acs., Henrico
Co., in Bristoll Par; at Swift Cr., 29
Apr. 1693, p. 304. Beg. at mouth of
Poplar Br; on head of Proctor's; to Mr.
John Wortham & Edward Stratton; &c.
Imp. of 6 pers: Marmaduke Woodum,
Robert Flynt, Samuel Polly, Richard
Collins, Anthony Fisher, William Tho-
satt (or Fossatt).

MR. EDWARD MOSELY, 800 acs.,
Norf. Co; in the E. br. of Eliz. Riv.,

29 Apr. 1693, p. 305. Granted Mr. William Moseley, & escheated by inquisition under Col. John Leare, Esch'r., & now granted, &c.

ROBERT NAPIER, 753 acs., New Kent Co., in St. Peter's Par., 29 Apr. 1693, p. 305. Adj. George Pargiter, & land, now or late, of Doctor Phillips. Part of 2400 acs. granted to Charles Turner, deserted, & granted (interalia) to sd. Napier, by order, &c. Imp. of 16 pers.*

GEORGE PARGITER, 635 acs., New Kent Co., in St. Peter's Par., 20 Apr. 1693, p. 306. Adj. land, now or late, of William Phillips. Part of 2400 acs. granted Charles Turner, 21 Apr. 1681, deserted, & now granted (interalia) sd. Pargiter, for Imp. of 13 pers.*

HENRY SLADE, 330 acs., Pr. Anne Co; on NE side of the Northwest River; 29 Apr. 1693, p. 306. Imp. of 7 pers: Lemuel Mason, Mary Davies, Thomas More, Joseph Blunt, Francis Loyd, Frances Evans, Mary Ross.

MATHEW WHITFEILD, 240 acs., Nansemond Co., in Chuckeytucke Par., 29 Apr. 1693, p. 307. Beg. at the Hole Cr., by Mount Lawson's Bay; to Little Ware Poynt; by an old Cart Roade, to John Copeland; down Carter's Neck Cr; to the Up. Wadeing Place Poynt, &c. Part of 700 acs. purchased by Mr. Walter Bruce of Ephaphroditus Lawson, 18 Nov. 1651, out of Lawson's patent of 1400 acs., dated 15 Feb. 1640; which 700 acs. descended to Abram, son of Walter Bruce, from whom sd. Whitfield purchased 15 Dec. 1686.

THOMAS WALKE, 194 acs., Norf. Co; at head of the S. Br. of Eliz. Riv., 29 Apr. 1693, p. 308. Adj. John Corporue; John Dixon; & Joseph Mulders; neare the Bridge Foot (Fort ?); by Ridgeford Sw., &c. 60 acs. part of 200 acs. granted Richard Jones, Senr., 15 Mar. 1675, who sold to William Maund; the whole 200 acs. sold in parcells to severall others & from them till it comes due unto sd. Walke; 134 acs. for Imp. of 3 pers.*

MR. ROBERT THOMPSON, 1230 acs., 29 Apr. 1693, p. 309. 390 acs. granted him, 23 Apr. 1688; in Henrico Co., in Varina Par; on S. side of James Riv., nigh Falling Creek; adj. Mr. Ward; nigh Branch's Brooke; on Mr. Gower's line; to Walter Clatworthy, &c. 390 acs. granted him 23 Apr. 1688; 688 acs. for Imp. of 17 pers: Edward Wise, Thomas Stanhop, Anne Hewett, Wm. Blast, Simon Ligon, Cornelious More, John Rockford, Fra. Mathews, John Day, Mary Spencer, Eliza. Turner, Wm. (or Vin.) Powell, Edward Hughs, John Alexander, John Mayne, William Holly, Jeffry Adams.

WILLIAM PRIDE, 1278 acs., Henrico Co., in Bristoll Par., 29 Apr. 1693, p. 310. Adj. John Stuard; Mr. Henry Randolph; on the Ashen Swamp, &c. Imp. of 26 pers: William Pride, Jane his wife, Thomas Mansell, Esther Mansell, Anne Mansell, Maccabees Mansell, Eliza. Mansell, Richard Tidmarsh, Meriall Mansell, Thomas Starkey, John Rothbourne, Anne Richson, Powell Evans, Catherine Fry.

HENRY SLADE, SENR., 1078 acs., being his seated plantation; Norf. Co., in *Currotucke Precincts;* upon the lower Indian Cr. of the Northwest River, 29 Apr. 1693, p. 311. Beg. neare Black Water roade; along SE side of sd. Creek to the mouth; to Mossy point; by path to Hector's Damms; to mouth of Cyprus Br; &c. Imp. of 22 pers: Hen. Avery, Will. Burett, Wm. Rundell, Evan Rundell, Wm. Price, Mary Wheeler, Robert Paine, Thomas Hubert, Susana White, Mary James Lewis Servant, Hester Hardiman, Isaac Showard, William Mosse, Peter Proby, 4 times; Hanah, Mariah, Peter, Indians; Francis a Negro.

JOHN WILKINSON, 100 acs., Surry Co; on head of the brs. of Up. Chippoaks Cr., 29 Apr. 1693, p. 312. Beg. near land George Loveday lives on; by Mr. Busbie's line, &c. Granted George Loveday, 29 May 1683, deserted, & now granted by order, &c. Imp. of 2 pers: William Barker, Benjamin Lucas.

ANTHONY SEALE, 220 acs., Essex Co; on upper side of Pewmansend Run; adj. John Gosse; & Capt. John Cattlett; 29 Apr. 1693, p. 312. Imp. of 5 pers: Sanders Mackoulas (or Mackenlas), Thomas Jones, John Wood, Thurnock Mackloud, Mackono Cloud.

JOHN WARDEN, 200 acs., Norf. Co; on N. side of Eliz. River, 29 Apr. 1693, p. 313. Part of 250 acs. granted Abraham Ellet, dec'd., 25 Mar. 1664, who bequeathed said land & plantation to his wife Ailce, who by deed of gift, 5 May 1687, as alsoe by her will, dated 15 Mar. 1688, assigned the above to said Warden. Beg. at Mr. Porteen; cross Ellet's Cr; to Jones' line, at head of Madely branch, &c.

WILLIAM WINSTON, 769 acs., New Kent Co., in St. Peter's Par., 29 Apr. 1693, p. 314. Beg. at land, now or late, of Doctor Phillips; along Pargiter's line; down a S. br. of Totopotomy Cr., &c. Part of 2400 acs. granted Charles Turner, who deserted, & granted (interalia) to sd. Winston, by order, &c. Imp. of 16 pers.*

PHILLIP LUDWELL, ESQR., 1½ acs; adj. to the ruins of his 3 Brick houses between the State House and Country House in *James City;* beg neare Pitch & Tarr Swamp 8 cheynes of the Eastmost end of the said houses & runing by said end S. 2 degrees W'ly 16 chs., thence N. 88 degs. W'ly 3¾ chs., N. 2 degs E'ly 16 chs. by the other end of the said houses; S. 88 degs. E'ly 3¾ chs. to beg; 20 Apr. 1694, p. 315. Imp. of: David Thompson.

WILLIAM LOW, 674 acs., Chas. City Co., in Bristoll Par; on S. side of Appomatox Riv., at a place comonly called *Moncusaneck;* crossing the 1st & 2nd branches & Persimon Br., to Moncusaneck maine Swamp, &c; 20 Apr. 1694, p. 315. Granted to Thomas Lowe, his father, 20 Apr. 1682, deserted, & now granted by order, &c. Imp. of 14 pers.*

NICHOLAS SMITH, 150 acs., in Up. Par. of Surry Co; adj. land George Williams lives on; 20 Apr. 1694, p.

316. Adj. Thomas Warren, & Peter Deberry; Richard Pyland; & Sion Hill, &c. Granted to sd. Williams, 21 Oct. 1687, deserted, & now granted &c. Imp. of 3 pers: Harry, Dick, Moll.

MR. THOMAS JONES & MR. CORNELIOUS VAUGHAN, 420 acs., K. & Q. Co., 20 Apr. 1694, p. 317. Adj. George Martin, & land formerly taken by sd. Jones & Hugh Williams. Imp. of 9 pers.*

JAMES TAYLOR, 134 acs., K. & Q. Co., 20 Apr. 1694, p. 317. Beg. in a fork of a br. of Axall branch, &c. Granted Gabriel Hill, 29 Nov. 1665, deserted, & granted to Hugh Baldwin, 21 Oct. 1687, deserted, & now granted by order, &c., for Imp. of 3 pers: Simon Edwards, Mary Edwards, Hugh Malden.

MR. ZACHERY LEWIS, 500 acs., K. & Q. Co., 20 Apr. 1694, p. 318. Beg. neare the Draggon Swamp; along land granted to Thomas Clayborne, now belonging to Mr. Christopher Lewis, &c. Granted to Domingo Maderes & James Johnson, 8 Apr. 1668, deserted, & now granted by order, &c. Imp. of 10 pers: James Coleburn, Richard Smith, William Cook, John Pool, Wm. Sterling, Dorcas Lewis, Lydia Harvey, Eliza. Gooding, Hanah Comes, Sarah Davis.

WILLIAM BEAMOUNT, 800 acs., Middlesex Co; on Peanketank River; 20 Apr. 1694, p. 319. Granted to Perigrime Bland, 10 Aug. 1642, & granted to Hope Bland, his daughter & heir, 19 Jan. 1650 for 1000 acs., but being exactly surveyed but 800 acs. found, &c. Due sd. Beamount for Imp. of 16 pers.*

GEORGE DILLARD, 139 acs., K. & Q. Co., 20 Apr. 1694, p. 320. Adj. William Collins; along Hugh Chinn's (?); to mouth of Cross Br., &c. Imp. of 3 pers: Thomas Miles, Nathan Palmer, Tho. Ashton.

JOHN HOWARD, 172 perches, *James City,* 20 Apr. 1694, p. 320. From NE cor. of the Church Yard, along the railes thereof, to Honble. Nathaniel Bacon, Esqr., to the gr. old Road, &c. Trans. of: John Lever.

HENRY DUKE, GENT., 736 acs., Jas. City Co., 20 Apr. 1694, p. 321. 200 acs. on brs. of Warrony Cr; & the Birchin Sw., in Sir John Ayton's line; on the horse path; to Timber Sw., &c; 536 acs. adj. William Elcome (or Elcore); neare Mr. Sorrell's path; neare an Indian Field; adj. sd. Ayton & Mr. Burnell (or Burrell), &c. Granted Mr. Henry Hartwell, 30 May 1679, deserted, & granted Mr. Edward Chilton, 20 Nov. 1682, deserted, & granted Mr. William Edwards, 16 Apr. 1690, & patented 23 Oct. 1690, deserted, & now granted by order, &c. Imp. of 15 pers: Tho. Capwell, Richd. Stubbs, Susan Ally, Cath. Dunahow; Jack, Judith; 3 by cert. of E. Chilton, Cl. S. off; Toney, Franck, Tony, Crocky, Bess, Betty, Negroes.

CAPT. HENRY DUKE, 90 acs., Jas. City Co., 20 Apr. 1694, p. 322. From his cor. on Tiascunn Swamp, allong land he purchased of William Manning; down Warrony Cr. to Tiascun Bridge, &c. Trans. of 2 negroes: Daniel, & Murreah.

MR. EDWARD WADE, 83 acs., Jas. City Co., 20 Apr. 1694, p. 323. From John Hixe's cor. on a br. of Warrany Sw; along land formerly Mr. Collins'; along Gammase foy (?) land; to Rockahock path, along Warrany Land, &c. Imp. of 2 Negroes.*

HENRY THOMSON (Thompson), 10 acs., Jas. City Co., 20 Apr. 1694, p. 323. Beg. at the crossing of Rockahock and Hotwater Road; to Hotwater Devident of land, &c. Imp. of 1 Negro.*

JOHN YOUNG, 376 acs., Jas. City Co., 20 Apr. 1694, p. 324. Beg. at Mr. Robert Sorrell & Mathew Collins; near a br. of Warrany; on W. side of old Rockahock Path, &c. Granted James Bray & Thomas Hancock, 18 Apr. 1671, deserted, & now granted by order, &c. Imp. of 8 pers: James Pollard, Thomas Graves, Tho. Falk, Jane Falk, John Jones, Samuel Jones, Marry Sorrell, Sarah Hannot.

WILLIAM COLLINS, 443 acs., Nansimond Co; on W. side of the Queen's Graves Sw., 20 Apr. 1694, p. 325. Adj. Francis Sanders; & Thomas Bissell (Bizell). Imp. of 9 pers: Fra. Hattaway, John Steeva (?), Robert Whittaker, Mary Wolly, Jane Tostoby; Ilaff, Turke, Sarro, Doll, Negroes.

JOHN WRIGHT, 600 acs., Up. Par. of Nansemond Co., 20 Apr. 1694, p. 325. Adj. Mr. Thomas Francis, & his own land. Granted to William Harrison, deserted, & now granted by order, &c. Imp. of 12 pers: Jeffrey, Mingo, Manuel, Robin, Dego, Jone, Tom, Sambo, Malaback, Croco, Coshue, Caite.

WILLIAM BIRD, 234 acs., on both sides of Peters' Br., in Sumerton, in the Up. Par. of Nansimond; 20 Apr. 1694, p. 326. Adj. John Keyton. Imp. of 5 pers: Henry Adams, Peter Cossens, Christopher Berryman, Sarah Brookes, Francis Cleveland.

JOHN WALLIS, 370 acs., in the Up. Par. of Nansemond; on E. side of the Back Sw. of Sumerton, 20 Apr. 1694, p. 327. Adj. Sampson Meredah, &c. Imp. of 8 pers: Richard Scriver, John Halford, Samll. Butler, William Hack, William James, Sarah Cary, Alice Cary; Clodpate, a Negro.

MR. NATHAN KING, 635 acs., Up. Par. of Nansemond Co., 20 Apr. 1694, p. 327. Beg. at John Taylor & Ballard's land; to N. side of Durty Swamp, to Battle's land; nigh Drury's line; along old Mr. King's line; to Brady's line; & Keyton's land, &c. Imp. of 13 pers: Timothy Love, Robert Clark, Thomas Atkins, Richard Watkins, Mary Lenford, William Jones, Edward Davis, Sarah Taylor; Salto, Tambo, Nan, Cis, Cate, Negroes.

SAME. 65 acs., same Co. & date; p. 328. Between Black Water & Sumerton Cr; down Black Water River, & Choan (Riv.) &c. Imp. of 2 pers: Tho. Banks, William Cunningham.

JOHN BRYAN, of Is. of Wight Co., 750 acs., on NW side of Sumerton Sw., in Nansemond Co., 20 Apr. 1694, p.

329. Adj. Michael King; & Cardugcan's land. Imp. of 15 pers: Deborah Mountford, Isabell Collier, Elizabeth Flowrence, Thomas Barnford, John Buttler, William Wilkinson; & 9 Negroes.

JOHN COPELAND, 207 acs., Up. Par. of Nansemond Co; on S. side of the back Sw. of Sumerton, 20 Apr. 1694, p. 330. Adj. John Wallis, &c. Imp. of 5 pers: William Hillyard, David Cannon, Arthur Adams, Fran. Parsley, Elizabeth Griffin.

JOHN MOLTON, 200 acs., Up. Par. of Nansemond Co; on S. side of the Beech Sw., 20 Apr. 1694, p. 330. Beg. on E. side of the Long Br., cor. of John Davies. Imp. of 4 pers: William Syer, John Quarke, John Hatton, Mary Hatton.

WILLIAM KING & MICHAEL KING, JUNR.; 840 acs., Up. Par. of Nansemond Co., 20 Apr. 1694, p. 331. Beg. at Nathan King, neare Battle's cleare ground, cross Battle's Br; to William Jones; nigh Peirce's line; on Drury's land to George's markt trees, &c. Imp. of 17 pers: Henry Stevens, Henry Castle, Edward Edwards, John Clayton, Thomas Andrews, Charles Best, William Woodby, Robert Whittaker, Jane his wife, Sarah Gutry, Rachel Haryson, Cath. Tabley; & 5 Negroes.

BENJAMIN ROGERS, 350 acs., Up. Par. of Nansemond Co; on S. side of Summerton Cr., 20 Apr. 1694, p. 332. Beg. at Ballard's cor. on S. side of the pequoson of sd. Cr., neare the Beech Sw., &c. Imp. of 7 pers: Henry Peirce, Edward Roberty, Marg. Dodsworth, Susanah Scotchman, John Elrington; Alla & Ovid, Negroes.

JAMES COLE, 519 acs., Up. Par. of Nansemond Co; adj. Mr. Baker's Land at *Buckland*, on SE side of Saram Sw., 20 Apr. 1694, p. 333. Imp. of 11 pers: Tho. Jones, Mary Whitehead, John Bratt, Hannah his wife, Peter & John, their children, Wm. Dews, Hump. Nicholls; Mingo, Peter, Gugana, Negroes.

JOHN DAVIE, 250 acs., Up. Par. of Nansemond Co; on S. side of the Beechen Sw. of Sumerton Cr., & on the Long Branch of same; 20 Apr. 1694, p. 333. Imp. of 5 pers: Gawin Lewis, James Tree; Hannah, Tony, Jerom, Negroes.

JOSEPH BALLARD, ELISHA BALLARD, 550 acs., Up. Par. of Nansemond Co; S. side of Sumerton Cr. & on N. side of Beech Sw; 20 Apr. 1694, p. 334. Imp. of 11 pers: John Guttridge, William Green, Joseph Sairs, Sarah Kirk, Abel Kerk, Jane White, Alex. Maggregory, Elizabeth his wife; Jno, Jupiter, Tom, Negroes.

ROBERT YATES, 150 acs., Up. Par. of Nansemond Co; E'ly. from the Meadow Sw; cor. to Bream's patent; 20 Apr. 1694, p. 335. Imp. of 3 pers: Henry Baker, John Leason, Mary Powell.

CATHERINE LANGSTONE, Widdow of John Langstone; 380 acs., Nansemond Co; on the Cyprus brs. of Sarum Cr; 20 Apr. 1694, p. 335. Imp. of 8 pers: Simon White, Wm. Wildsmith, Hanah Wildsmith, Thomas Gillett, John Lewis, Wm. Lewis; Tony, & Mingo, Negroes.

JOHN BUTLER, Taylor, 230 acs., Up. Par. of Nansemond Co., called *Maids Town*, on E. side of the Knotty Pine Sw; next to *Buckland;* 20 Apr. 1694, p. 336. Imp. of 5 pers: John Pollet, David Thomas, Hannah Thomas; Harry, Jack, Sarah, Negroes.

CHARLES SCOT, 160 acs., Up. Par. of Nansemond Co; on SW side of br. of Sarum Sw., 20 Apr. 1694, p. 336. Imp. of 4 pers: Richard Brooks, Rebecca Brookes, Edward Dance, Eliza. his wife.

SAME. 300 acs.; same co., & date; p. 337. On NW side of Knotty Pine Sw., running out of Sarum Sw; adj. Peter Phebus. Imp. of 6 pers: William Parteridge, William Lobb, Tho. Stripling, Jane his wife; Santo & Dolodero, Negroes.

HENRY HACKLEY, 210 acs., Up. Par. of Nansemond Co; on SW side of Saram Sw., adj. Mr. Mills' land; 20 Apr. 1694, p. 338. Imp. of 5 pers: John Billingly, Edwd. Schrimshire, Jno. Schrimshire, Hannah Cutting; Sambo a Negro.

RICHARD BAREFIELD, 90 acs., Up. Par. of Nansemond Co; on W. side of a br. of Saram Sw; 20 Apr. 1694, p. 338. Imp. of 2 pers: William Parker, Charles Smith.

MR JOHN WRIGHT, 450 acs., Up. Par. of Nansemond Co; E. side of Saram Cr. & N. side of Bennet's Cr; 20 Apr. 1694, p. 339. Adj. James Cole, &c. Imp. of 9 pers: Thomas Johnson, Sarah Nicholson, Robert Brookes, Richard Barlow, William Smith, Nathan Tinny, Elizabeth his wife, Jane & Elizabeth, his children.

PETER PHEBUS, 250 acs., Up. Par. of Nansemond Co; on E. side of a br. of Saram maine Sw., adj. Richard Barefield; 20 Apr. 1694, p. 340. Imp. of 5 pers: Tho. Lott, Tho. Redfera, John, & Hannah, his children, John Bines.

MR. JOHN KEYTON, 15 acs., Up. Par. of Nansemond Co; in a forke made by Sumerton Sw. & the Knuccles Sw.; adj. his own land; 20 Apr. 1694, p. 340. Imp. of: John Gorram.

WILLIAM EDWARDS, 96 acs., Up. Par. of Nansemond Co; on SW side of Knuccles Sw. out of Sumerton Sw; adj. Mr. Wright & James Cole; 20 Apr. 1694, p. 341. Imp. of 2 pers: Thomas Graves, Thomas Belvin.

JOHN LEE, 960 acs., Up. Par. of Nansemond Co; on E. side of Sumerton Cr., 20 Apr. 1694, p. 341. Beg. on a small island on E. side of said Cr; to NE side of the Cyprus Sw., &c. Imp. of 20 pers: Dennit Abney, Mary Emerson, Hannah Haines, Elizabeth Evans, Cath. Jones. Rachell Redfera, Alice Godale, Thomas Godale, Geo. Lawrence, Walter Wright, William Knowles, Adam Broach, John Watts, John Saterwhite; Pallas, Attkena, Jupiter, Vulcan, Mars, Negroes.

CHARLES RHODES (Rodes). 267 acs., Nansemond Co., in Kingsale; on W. side of Capt. Johns' Swamp; 20 Apr. 1694, p. 342. Adj. James Howard; Davies' line; William Collins; & his own land. Imp. of 6 pers: John Lanham, John Mase, John Bayley. John Ingell, John Kenedye, Wilks Chirme.

ROBERT CARR, 297 acs., Nansemond Co; on a br. of Wickham Sw., 20 Apr. 1694, p. 343. Adj. Col. Milner & Capt. Lear: & Mr. Baker's line. Imp. of 6 pers: Edward Harienes (?), Richard Sandders. Susana Garland, John Littlewood, Elizabeth Littlewood, Rachell Littlewood.

ROBERT SIMS (Syms), 250 acs., Nansemond Co; in Kingsale; on W. side of Capt. Johns' Sw; adj. Charles Rhodes & Robert Bissell (Bizell). Imp. of 5 pers: George Sammons, Thomas Pulling; Dick, Sambo, Harry, Negroes.

RICHARD TAYLOR, 293 acs., Nansemond Co; on head brs. of Kingsale Sw; adj. Robert Brewer; & John Gatling; 20 Apr. 1694, p. 344. Imp of 6 pers: Nicholas Rochester, Thomas Dewrent, Dennis Cornell, Arthur King, Rebecka Lawfull, Jane Lawfull.

MICHAEL KING, JUNR., 84 acs., Nansemond Co., 20 Apr. 1694, p. 345, Adj. a tract called King Stone, taken up by old Mr. King; & land of John Bryan. Imp. of 2 pers: William Wren, Henry Michael.

JOHN HOLLAND, Planter, 500 acs., Nansemond Co; on E. side of Capt. Johns' Sw; adj. his own; & land of William Gatling; 20 Apr. 1694, p. 346. Imp. of 10 pers: William Walker, Thomas Bee, Hen. Pickerell, Wm. Garland, Anne Garland, Thomas Moore, Sarah Earle, Tho. Turner, William Smith, Hannah Smith.

THOMAS BISSELL, 208 acs., Nansemond Co; on head brs. of Wickham Sw; adj. land of Col. Milner, Capt. Lear, & Robert Carr; 20 Apr. 1694, p. 346. Imp. of 5 pers: John Dawson, Leonard Shelden, William Pierce, Francis Theterston. Benja. Lucas. (Note: First written Robert.)

MR. RICHARD REYNOLDS, of Is. of Wight Co., 720 acs., Nansemond Co; on Cabbin Branch; 20 Apr. 1694, p. 347. Imp. of 15 pers: Mary Lawrence, Richard Ansly (or Ausly), Robert Brewer, Thomas Hill, Geo. Brooks, Tho. Hinson, W'm. Farmer, Tho. Loyd, Joyce Wilson, Mary Biss, Dorothy Sexton, Tho. Giles & his wife. Patrick Wall, William Parker.

JOHN FRISSALL, 327 acs., Nansemond Co., in the Terrascoe Necks; on a cr. of Mount Lawson's Bay parting this & land of Daniel Sanborne; near house of Christopher Best; adj. Robert Laurance; John Copeland; & Mathew Whitfield; by an old Cart Road; to Little Ware Point; 20 Apr. 1694, p. 347. Part of 700 acs. purchased by Mr. Walter Bruce of Epaphroditus Lawson, 18 Nov. 1651, out of Lawson's patent for 1400 acs. granted 15 Feb. 1640; which descended to his son Abraham Bruce, from whom sd. Frissall purchased, 12 Oct. 1691; 50 acs. now added. Imp. of: Robert Brock.

JAMES THELAB9LL, of Norf. Co., 423 acs. in Little Creeke precincts; 20 Apr. 1694, p. 349. Adj. Wolfe's Neck, which was granted to James Thelabell, dec'd., 15 Oct. 1651 & renewed 4 Nov. 1685, & in his life tyme set over to his son Francis, 23 Feb. 1685/6, on S. side of Wolfes Neck Br., &c.

JAMES WISHEART (Wishart), 145 acs., in Little Cr. precincts; Norf. Co., 20 Apr. 1694, p. 349. Granted to James Wisheart, dec'd., 8 Aug. 1673 & due the abovenamed as his son & heir at law. Adj. Richard Williams; Charles Griffen; & James Thelabell.

CHARLES GRIFFEN, of Norf. Co., 208 acs. in sd. Co; at head of Little Cr; adj. Huggins' land; Lemuel Holmes; Richard Williams; & James Thelabell; 20 Apr. 1694, p. 350. Granted to Charles Egerton, 20 Sept. 1661, & assigned to Edward Holmes & William Olifant, who sold to Thomas Reynolds, who sold to Robert Blake, & by Arthur Blake, his son & heir, sold to John Snayl; by him sold to Elizabeth Preston & her heirs forever. 14 June 1684; Benjamin Hargrove & sd. Elizabeth, his wife, by deed of gift, 18 Mar. 1688/9, gave to their son-in-law, the abovenamed Charles Griffen & Elizabeth, his wife, & to to the heires of their two bodys lawfully begotten for ever.

HUGH MACKDANIEL, 28 acs., Norf. Co; bet. Tanner's Cr. & Broad Cr; adj. Harden's patent on S. side of the maine Road & run; adj. land he bought of Michael Wilder, & Gwynn's land; 20 Apr. 1694, p. 351. Imp. of: John Cutting.

RICHARD SILVESTER, 130 acs., Norf. Co., on brs. of Simpson's Cr. Cyprus Swamp, E. of his plantation; adj. Peter Cartwright; 20 Apr. 1694, p. 352. Trans. of 3 pers: Henry Tibbet, Wm. Tilsey, Humphry Beck.

GILES COLLINS, 40 Acs., 2 R., Norf. Co., on NE side of Piney Neck Damms in Little Cr. precincts; adj. James Wisheart, Thorowgood & his own land; 20 Apr. 1694, p. 352. Trans. of: George Paine.

RICHARD SMITH, 150 acs., Norf. Co., on E. side of the S. br. of Eliz. River; adj. patent of 400 acs. he lives on; neare the Horse Bridge Br; & adj. the Widdow Yates' land; 20 Apr. 1694, p. 353. Granted to Richard Yates 13 Mar. 1667 & included in a patent of 400 acs., by him deserted, & sd. 150 acs. included in a patent of 610 acs. to Maj. Francis Sayer 21 Oct. 1684, deserted, & now granted by order &c., for trans. of 3 pers: Jno. Green, Ebenezer Sandford, Simon Richason.

MR. JAMES WILSON, 120 acs., Norf. Co; towards head of the S'wd. creek of the S. br. of Eliz. River; to mouth of Gillham Neck Run, &c; 20 Apr. 1694, p. 354. Imp. of 3 pers: Mary Westcate, Willis Wilson, twice.

EDWARD CREEKMAN, WILLIAM HESLETT & HENRY DALE, 2000 acs., Norf. Co; SW side of the Northwest River; cor. of John Creekman, Edmond Creekman, & Roger Hodges; 20 Apr. 1694, p. 354. Imp. of 40 pers:

Phill. & Sarah Stephenson, Tho. Long, Nicholas Reed, Jno. Demintner, Mildred May, Oliver Druit, Hugh Bradwell, Nicho. Chadwell, Jno. Chadwell, Tho. Chalis, Nich. Buckston, Anne Williams, Mary Odway, Duncomb Belamore, Maurice Skinner, Elinor Green, John Moble, Mary Edwards, Grace Watkins, Adam Green, Hen. Mildbay, Martha Newman, Jno. Curtis, Tho. Barefoot, Anne Underwood, Fra. Gaston, Edward Stephens, Eliz. Hunt, Mary Stone, Ralph James, Humphry Ballens, James Jaquis, Alex. Dowty, Wm. Roberts, James Allane, Jer. White, Robert Gillores (or Gillows ?), Richard Herd, James Wickliff.

NATHANIEL MACKLENAHAN, Gent., 45 acs., Pr. Anne Co; on the western shore of Linhaven Riv., 20 Apr. 1694, p. 355. Adj. Adam Thorowgood; land escheated by Doctor Finkley, now in possession of Dennis Maccarty; Keeling's land; William Grant, & Mr. Porteen's. Imp. of: John Evahs.

THOMAS TURTON, 91 acs., Pr. Anne Co., in Linhaven Par; neare head of Basnet's Cr., & adj. a place called the *Bare garden;* 20 Apr. 1694, p. 356. Beg. at Richard Bony (Bonny), cor. of Thomas Smith; on Thomas English & John James. Imp. of 2 pers: Richard Monday, Mary Jones.

CAPT. HUGH CAMPBELL, 300 acs., Pr. Anne Co., in Linhaven Par; towards the North River Landing; 20 Apr. 1694, p. 356. Adj. Morgan Jones. Granted Thomas Iliff, 20 Apr. 1687, deserted, & now granted by order, &c. Imp. of 6 pers: John Knight, William Brooks, John Clarke, Richard Creede, Thomas Curtis, Elizabeth Peirce.

FRANCIS BOND, 250 acs., Pr. Anne Co; on NE side of the North River; 20 Apr. 1694, p. 357. Granted to Susanna, Margaret, & Mary West, 27 Apr. 1687, deserted, & now granted by order, &c. Imp. of 5 pers: Jane Craddock, Tho. Robinson, Robert Forsay, Peter Chessum, Ja. Lard.

HOPKIN HOWELL, son of Hopkin Howell, dec'd; 100 acs., on N. side the Damms or head of Newtown haven River, Is. of Wight Co., 20 Apr. 1694, p. 358. Being halfe of patent granted to Peter Johnson, 23 May 1642, & escheated by inquisition under William Randolph, Depty. Esch'r., &c., 16 June 1681; then granted to Hopkin & John Howell, who made a devision thereof in their life tyme, &c. Further due by order & judgement of the Genrll. Court, &c.

JOHN EDLOE, 1611 acs., New Kent Co., in St. Peter's Par; upon head of the brs. of Black Creek, 20 Apr. 1694, p. 358. Imp. of 33 pers: William Watlin (or Wallin), Eliza. Sparrow, Robert Comes, Jno. Swingfeild, Robert Dixon, Pilgrim Jones, Jno. Buffoon, Saml. Dryon, Cath. Smith, Wm. Banks, Mary Fletcher, Sarah Stokes, James Gentleman, Geo. Seaward, Edward German, Timothy Davies, Giles Linscot, Mary Tight, Mary Pearce, Lawrence Emerson, Jno. Emerson, Toby Emerson; Jack, Will, Guy, Robbin, Toby, Cuffy, Negroes.

MR. GIDEON MACON, 155 acs., New Kent Co., in St. Peter's Par; being the island on NE side of the maine runn of Chicohamony Sw., at the Wadeing Place, neare Meraday's plantation; 20 Apr. 1694, p. 359. Imp. of 4 pers: Catherine Clease, Cha. Langley, Cha. Downes, Geo. Downing.

WILLIAM MOSS, 231 acs., New Kent Co., 20 Apr. 1694, p. 360. Adj. land, now or late, of John Tandy; lands of Robert Jarrett; William Cromp; & Richard Barnes. Imp. of 5 pers: Thomas Ward, Hanah Nichols, Jonathan Fisher, Moses Crawford, Margaret Bock (or Bork).

CORNELIOUS NOWELL, 220 acs., Essex Co; S. side of Rappa. Riv., on brs. of Occupatia, 20 Apr. 1694, p. 360. Adj. William Moseley; William Grey, &c. Granted to Hugh Owen 21 Apr. 1690, deserted, & now granted by order, &c. Imp. of 5 pers.*

THOMAS WOOD, JOHN WOOD & THOMAS WOOD, JUNR., 900 acs., Essex Co., 20 Apr. 1694, p. 361. Adj.

James Fullerton; Richard Gregory; the Horse path; Col. Goodrich & Mr. Henry Awbrey; & on land of Ball & Price. Granted James & John Boughan, 20 Apr. 1684, deserted, & now granted by order, &c. Imp. of 16 pers.*

ISAAC FLOWER, 56 acs., Essex Co; on brs. of Martin Johnson's Creek; 20 Apr. 1694, p. 362. Adj. Timothy Pell; Capt. Francis Slaughter; & William Gibson. Imp. of 2 pers: Roger Morgan, Richard Tandy.

CAPT. JOHN BATTAILE & MR. FRANCIS MERIWETHER, 560 acs., in the freshes of Essex Co; about 2 mi. from the river; neare a br. of Cochill Cr., issuing into Mr. Lucas' Cr; by Mr. Beth. Gilson; neare Mr. Robert Payne; 20 Apr. 1694, p. 363. Granted Capt. Alexander Fleming, 4 Sept. 1667, deserted, & now granted by order, &c. Imp. of 12 pers.* Note: 12 rights unnamed in Cert. signed by M. Cary, Cl. Gen. Ct.

MR. FRANCIS MERIWETHER, 299½ acs., Essex Co; S. side of Rappa. Riv., about 6 mi. into the woods, upon br. of Occupatia & Mattapony Path; adj. Mr. Thomas Button; & Richard Copeland; 20 Apr. 1694, p. 364. Granted Bryan Ward, 23 Oct. 1690, deserted, & now granted by order, &c. Imp. of 6 pers.* Note: 6 rights unnamed in Cert. signed by M. Cary, Cl. Gen. Ct.

ARTHUR ALLEN, 150 acs., at head Parker's Cr; adj. Silvester Blake (?); 20 Apr. 1694, p. 365. Granted John Blake, Esqr., 30 Oct. 1662, deserted, & now granted by order, &c. Imp. of 3 pers: Bernard Sikes, Senr., Bernard Sikes, Junr., Eliz. Sikes.

MR. JOHN KING, 44 acs., Surry Co; bet. his own & land formerly of James Elson, dec'd; adj. Wm. Rookins; NW on Up. Chippoaks Cr; 20 Apr. 1694, p. 365. Imp. of: Michl. Gill.

WILLIAM BALDWIN, 100 acs., Up. Par. of Surry Co; NE side of Clay's Branch; adj. Roger Delk, Capt. Robert Randall; & his own land; 20 Apr. 1694,

p. 366. Imp. of 2 pers: Wm. Tully, Jno. Phoenix.

MR. JOHN WATKINS (Wattkins), 966 acs., Surry Co., in Southwark Par; adj. Christopher Lawson; & the Horse Bridge Swamp; 20 Apr. 1694, p. 366. 850 acs. granted John Watkins, dec'd., & descended to the abovenamed John, as eldest sonn & heir; 116 acs. now taken. Imp. of 3 pers: Thomas' Morris, Robert Penny, Richard Shutwell.

FRANCIS LEDBETER, JOHN LEDBETER & WILLIAM JONES, 300 acs., Chas. City Co., in Bristoll Par; beg. in forke of Warwick maine Sw; 20 Apr. 1694, p. 367. Imp. of 6 pers.*

GEORGE PASSMORE, 93 acs., Chas. City Co., in Jurden's Par., 20 Apr. 1694, p. 368. Adj. William Jones; Mr. Henry Batts; & John Wallice. Imp. of 2 pers: Catherine Clark, Jane Furbush.

THOMAS PARRAM, 70 acs., Chas. City Co; N. side of Black Water Sw; adj. James Thweat, John Clay; & Henry King; 20 Apr. 1694, p. 368. Imp. of 2 pers: Jno. Kelsey, Wm. Anderson.

ROBERT HICKES (Hicks), 600 acs. Chas. City Co., in Bristoll Parish; S. side of Appamatuck River, 20 Apr. 1694, p. 369. Beg. at John Evans; to Mr. James Cock; crossing the 2nd Sw., &c. Trans. of 12 pers: Roger Jones, Richard Griffith, Geo. Clayton, Jno. Prichard, Tho. Miller, Fra. City, Jno. Wright, Richard Bates, Jno. Binley, Wm. Kerney, Eliza. Clark, Wm. Drudge.

JOHN HAMBLIN, 265 acs., 1 Rood, Chas. City Co., in Westopher Par; S. side of James River, 20 Apr. 1694, p. 370. Beg. at Richard Carlisle; crossing the Mill Path, to Hangmans Neck; on head of Bridge's Cr; along Wilkins' line; to Bland's path; on Alexander Davison, &c. Granted William Wilkins, 16 Apr. 1683, deserted, & now granted, by order &c. Imp. of 6 pers.*

THOMAS CHAPPELL, 423 acs., Chas. City Co; on S. side of James Riv., 20 Apr. 1694, p. 371. Beg. on the Otterdamm Sw; adj. Thomas Smith; &

Thomas Blunt. Trans. of 9 Negroes: Buck, Doe, Santall, Mingo, Gerald, Moreton, Sarah, Abell, Sue.

SAMUEL KNIBB, 82 acs., Henrico Co., in Varina Par; in *Burmoedy Hundred Neck;* 20 Apr. 1694, p. 372. Part of 150 acs. granted John Howell, 10 June 1639, who assigned to John Morgan & his heires, 18 Oct. 1644; Morgan died having one onely daughter Jane, who intermarried with Samuel Knibb, by whom she had Samuel, who entered said land; & bequeathed same to his son Samuel. Beg. at the maine river next (to) *Shirly Hundred,* through the Sw. to Capt. Royall; to a great grape vine; adj. Richard Dewe's; Mr. Elam's; & Mr. Bowman's lands. Imp. of 2 pers.*

MR. FRANCIS MACKENNY, 180 acs., Accomack Co; adj. his own land; SW by the salt water of a Cr. from Matchotanck Cr; towards Pungoteague Cr., & is comonly called the *Streights;* 20 Apr. 1694, p. 373. Imp. of 4 pers: Fra. Mackenny, Wm. Boggs, Henry Alen, Eliza. Clayton.

FRANCES PEALE (Peal), 700 acs., at Occumpson; Accomack Co., 20 Apr. 1694, p. 373. Escheated from Thomas Riding, dec'd., by inquisition under John Custis, Junr., Esch'r. &c; now granted sd. Frances, who hath paid *her* composition, &c.

JOHN DARDEN, 300 acs., Nansemond Co., 20 Apr. 1694, p. 374. Escheated from Stephen Darden, dec'd., by inquisition under Thomas Milner, Esch'r., &c.

THOMAS THROP & Martha, his wife, 350 acs., Is. of Wight Co., 20 Apr. 1694, p. 374. Escheated from William Lewer, dec'd., by inquisition under John Lear, Esqr., Esch'r., &c.

MR. JOHN WILSON, SENR., 828 acs., Henrico Co., in Bristoll Par; S. side of Swift Cr., 20 Apr. 1694, p. 375. Beg. on Simon's Run, parting the lands of Capt. Field & Capt. Epes; on main br. of Old Town Cr; to Phillip Jones; & Mr. Richard Kennon. Imp. of 17

pers: Henry Smith, Robert Randall twice, Horrace Young, Margaret Davis, Izabell Domson (or Donison), Phebe Jeweller, Mary Kingtone, Elizabeth Williams, John Bayly, John Page, John Mills, Tho. Garton, Anne Bates, Xtopr. Bass; Mann, a Negro.

RICHARD BOOKER, 180 acs., Glocester Co., 20 Apr. 1694, p. 376. Escheated from Nicholas Baldwin, by inquisition under Henry Whiteing, Esqr., Esch'r., &c.

JOHN MACKENNY, 450 acs., Is. of Wight & Nansemond Counties, 20 Apr. 1694, p. 377. Escheated from Michael Mackenny, Henry Gay & John Plummer, dec'd., by inquisition under Col. Thomas Milner, Esch'r., &c.

JOHN KING, 100 acs., Surry Co., 20 Apr. 1694, p. 377. Escheated from James Nelson, by inquisition under John Lear, Esqr., Esch'r., &c.

EDWARD MOSELEY, 800 acs., Norf. Co., 20 Apr. 1694, p. 378. Escheated from William Moseley, dec'd., by inquisition under John Lear, Esqr., Esch'r, &c.

EDWARD CHILTON, ESQR., 850 acs., New Kent Co., 20 Apr. 1694, p. 378. Escheated from Maj. Generall Hammond, dec'd., by inquisition under Henry Hartwell, Esqr., Esch'r., &c.

WALTER CLATWORTHY, 341 acs., Henrico Co., in Verina Par; adj. Robert Thompson; crossing Branch's brook, &c; 20 Apr. 1694, p. 379. Imp. of 7 Negroes,* by the *Frienddship.*

JOHN HOWELL, son of John Howell, dec'd; 100 acs., Is. of Wight Co; S. side of the damms, or head, of Newtown haven River; 20 Apr. 1694, p. 379. Being ½ of patent granted to Peter Johnson, 23 May 1642, from whom it escheated by inquisition under William Randolph, Depty. Esch'r., 16 June 1681; then granted to Hopkin & John Howell, who made a devision thereof in their life tyme, & sd. 100 acs. being the lott of sd. dec'd. John;

further due the abovenamed by order & judgement of the Genrll. Ct., 15 Apr. 1691.

JOHN SANDERS & ROBERT ROBERTS, 7½ acs. of marsh land, on E. side of King's Cr; adj. 50 acs. belonging to them in right of their wives Sarah & Mary; 20 Apr. 1694, p. 380. Imp. of 1 pers.*

SAMUEL GOOD, 888 acs., Henrico Co., in Verina Par; S. side of James River; 20 Apr. 1694, p. 380. Beg. neare a gr. Piney Slash; adj. John Good; & Col. William Byrd. Granted to John Stowers & John Good, deserted, & now granted by order, &c. Imp. of 18 pers.*

SEAMORE POWELL, 282 acs., York & Warwick Counties; adj. to Lodge Land, now belonging to Mr. Hill; 20 Apr. 1694, p. 381. Beg. on S. side of Brocas Sw; adj. Owen Morris; land belonging to "old Charles"; Maj. Harwood; land of Wade; & land of Brocas, dec'd. 130 acs. granted William Major, 20 Nov. 1678, who sold to Seamore Powell, 1 Feb. 1686; 152 acs. now taken. Trans. of 4 pers: Robert Collis, Wm. Lane, David Robinson, Tho. Stradling.

MR. JOSEPH WHITE, 800 acs., Yorke Co., in Bruton Par; on St. Andrew's Cr; 20 Apr. 1694, p. 382. From the Mill Path at a place called the *Three Trees,* at head of Axfield's Br; up mouth of Back Cr., to br. of Horsington Sw; adj. Mrs. Baskervile & Mrs. Jones; & Col. Jening's Mill Pond; up Adcock's Br; & along Mr. Graves' line. Due the abovenamed as son & heir of Henry White & Mary, his wife, to whom it was assigned by Joseph Croshaw, 22 Mar. 1659 for 500 acs; 300 acs. surplus, for Imp. of 6 Negroes: Africa, Jack, Lopears, Robin Hood, Jack, Tom.

WILLIAM SHERWOOD, GENT., 308 acs., in *James City & James City Island;* 20 Apr. 1694, p. 384. On James Riv., at head of a br. of Pitch & Tarr Sw., next above the *State House;* a ditch divideing his land & land formerly

of Thomas Woodhouse; to 3½ acs. he purchased of John Page, Esqr., 6 Feb. 1681; neare John Fitchett; to 1 acre he purchased of David Newell; towards dwelling house of Henry Hartwell, Esqr; to the Orchard of James Chidleigh & Ann his wife; along Mr. Travis' line, to S. side of said Sw; to Pinney Point; to land formerly of Richard James; through the Back River marsh; to Sandy Bay; to a persimon tree under *Blockhouse hill,* &c. Due, viz: 3½ acs. as above; 133 A., 35.9 chs., granted to John Knowles, 6 May 1665; who conveyed to Jonathan Newell, 28 Apr. 1668; & purchased of David Newell, bro. &heir at law, & the creditors of sd. Jonathan; 28½ acs. granted John Baldwin, 4 Oct. 1656, who bequeathed to John Fulcher who conveyed to sd. Sherwood & his heirs forever, 22 Oct. 1677; the remainder of sd. 308 acs. granted Richard James, 5 June 1657, from whom it escheated, & granted to sd. Sherwood, 23 Oct. 1690.

CAPT RICHARD HALE (Haile) of Essex Co; 720 acs. bet. Rappa. & Mattapony Rivers; 26 Oct. 1694, p. 386. Beg. at Goldman's land, in line of Robins, by an old Indian path; to land of Maj. Robert Beverley, dec'd. 450 acs. granted Theophilus Whale & Daniel Swellivant, 23 Sept. 1674; 270 acs. overplush, due for Imp. of 6 Negroes.*

MR. MAURICE COCK, 58 acs., Middlesex Co., 26 Oct. 1694, p. 387. Beg. at 1200 acs. granted Col. Cuthbert Potter, (known as Potter's quarter devident), in line of 3000 acs. granted to William Dudley; along land of Mr. John Shepard, dec'd., &c. Imp. of 2 pers.*

SAME. 275 acs., Essex Co., 26 Oct. 1694, p. 387. Beg. at the White Oak Marsh, a br. of Dragon Sw. Included in bounds of 1200 acs. granted Richard Bredgar, Robert Hill, & John Mayhew, 20 Mar. 1665/6, but it does not appear that rights was entered; due sd. Cock for Imp. of 6 pers.*

EDWARD HILL, ESQR., 445 acs., Chas. City Co., Westopher Par; on N. side of James Riv., adj. the Cattails &

N. br. of Herin Cr; 26 Oct. 1694, p. 388. Beg. at John Roatch; down the W. br; to Maj. Stith; &c. Imp. of 7 pers: Anne Newton, Mary Blackbeard; 7 Negroes.

RICHARD CLARK & RICHARD WATHEN, 950 acs., Chas. City Co., 26 Oct. 1694, p. 389. Escheated from Capt. Richard Bond, dec'd., by inquisition under Francis Page, Depty. Esch'r., 3 Dec. 1684; now granted by order, &c.

JOHN PARKS, 450 acs., New Kent Co., 26 Oct. 1694, p. 390. Escheated from Elinor Thomas, dec'd., by inquisition under Mathew Page, Depty. Esch'r., 30 Aug. 1684; now granted, &c.

TO THE VESTRY BELONGING TO KINGSTONE PARISH IN GLO-CESTER CO; 40 acs. on N. side of Puddin Cr; adj. the *Gleab Land* of sd. parish; & land of Phillip Hunly, Junr; 26 Oct. 1694, p. 390. Imp. of: Thomas Cornish.

ROBERT BEVERLEY, 6500 acs., Essex Co., & K. & Q. Co; formerly Rappa., & New Kent Counties; adj. 4600 acs. of Capt. Lawrence Smith; beg. by the Beavor Damms; 26 Oct. 1694, p. 391. Granted Capt. Lawrence Smith & Capt. Robert Beverley, 16 Nov. 1674, deserted, & now granted by order, &c. Imp. of 130 pers: Edward Baley, Jno. Wright, Jos. Babb, Robt. Kellet, Antho. Hales, Wm. Harris, Charles Colliford, Geo. Benford, Math. Tenny, Cha. Windam, Tho. York, Theo. Peirson, Joan Woodard, Margt. Nichols, Debora Munford, Isab. Collier, Eliza. Florence, Tho. Banford, Jno. Butler, Wm. Wilkeson, Edwd. Benn, Mary Ball, Math. Dean, Wm. Jemson, Geo. Calleton, Nicho. Arnold, Anne Armestead, Saml. Tharwell, Tho. Brown, Richd. Merchant, Peter Russell, Geo. Hoomes, Jno. Boss, Sarah Cooper, Tho. Jones, Wm. England, Mary James, Mary Penyard, Jno. Fox, Anne Faring, Tho. Burton, Jno. Hardinan, Richd. Lockman, James Walk, Eliza. Putman, Hanah Selby, Sarah Clerk, Wm. Coleman, Joyce Bayley, Jno. Gwyn, Jno. Powel, Richd. Folks, Joan Wharton, Wm. Seaborne, Den. Mackarte, Jno. Hampton, Jos. Hill, Tho.

Gooding, Ralph Doby, Jno. Barker; & 70 Negroes: Lawrence, Sarah, Nanny, Salvo, Jack, Cromwell, Charles, Papa, Mingo, Lawrence, Harry, Bess, Absalom, Jack, Moll, Gambo, Joseph, George, Sarah, George, Roger, Peter, Beck, Nagar, Betty, Paul, Sue, Ructon, Peg, Andrew, Cecill, James, Jeffrey, Abell, Kate, James, Jack, Gomar, Rack, Robin, Sam, Frank, Tony, Billy, Margt., Marcelles, Kell, Joakim, Willoby, Scipio. Elah, Hodae, Beck, Joan, Marina, Brisk, Racham, Nadar, Will, Adam, Nan. Selam, Robin, Nora, Cis, Lydie, Hanah, Will, Nurse.

EDWARD COLLINS, son & heir of Thomas Collins; 422 acs. New Kent Co., Blisland Par., 26 Oct. 1694, p. 392. Beg. on N. side of the main Br. of Skimmino Sw., to mouth of Crooked Sw; to land, now or late, of Thomas Biggins, &c. 250 acs. being the moiety of patent granted to Robert Wyld & Phillip Chesley; sold by Daniel Wyld, son & heir of Robert, & sd. Chesley, to Thomas Collins & Thomas Biggins; 172 acs. for Imp. of 4 Negroes: Sambo. Jack, Taylor, Bess.

MR. THOMAS CHRISTIAN, Sen., 193 acs., Chas. City Co., in Westopher Par; on S. side of Chickahomony Sw; adj. land of Baxter, on the W. br. of Oposom maine br; & land of Walltall Shipley, &c; 26 Oct. 1694, p. 393. Imp. of 4 pers.*

CAPT. JOHN BATTAILE & MR. FRANCIS MERIWETHER, 1091 acs., 26 Oct. 1694, p. 393. Adj. land of Henry Corbyn, Esqr., dec'd; on main br. of Ware Cr; crossing a gr. branch of Passatink Cr; to a hill by a valley called *Solomon's Garden*. Granted Mr. Abraham Weeks & Mr. Hugh Williams, 26 Sept. 1680, deserted, & granted Henry Gauler, 20 Oct. 1688, deserted, & now granted by order &c. Imp. of 22 pers: Peter Little, Eliz. Webster, Alice Barrow, Mary Martin, Mary Whitehead, Nicho. Allies, Jno. Stafford, Jno. Bliss, Tho. Rogers, Thomas Threashly, Tho. Herbert, Jno. Russell, Geo. Neste, Mary Neste, John Loe, Nathanl. Pendleton, Phill. Pendleton,

Eliza. Wayte, Edmd. Craske, Martha Craske, John Craske, Ellen Crak (Craske ?).

MAJOR LEWIS BURWELL, of Gloster Co., 1200 acs., York Co., at *Kiskeyack;* E. on Kings Cr., towards Capt. John West; W. on Queens Cr; N. on the maine river called Pamunkey Riv; 26 Oct. 1694, p. 394. Late in possession of Elizabeth, late wife of Honble. Nathaniel Bacon, Esqr., dec'd., from whom it escheated by inquisition under Edward Hill, Esqr., Esch'r. &c., 9 Dec. 1691 & a judgement of the Genrll. Ct., 26 Oct. 1693; now granted, &c. Surveyed by Col. Lawrence Smith.

MR. JOHN BRODNAX (Broadnax), 435 acs., Henrico Co., in Varina Par; S. side of James Riv. & N. side of Falling Cr; crossing Grindall's run; 26 Oct. 1694, p. 394. Granted Mr. Charles Douglas, 23 Oct. 1690, deserted, & now granted by order, &c. Imp. of 9 pers: Jno. Morris, Eliza. Morris, Cha. Foster, Jno. Toby, Fra. Adams, Sarah Dillon, Jno. Carlisle, Sarah his wife; Dick a Negro.

ELIZABETH BRACKETT, Widdow of Mark Bracket; 150 acs., James City Co., 26 Oct. 1694, p. 395. Escheated from Mark Bracket, by inquisition under Henry Hartwell, Esqr., Esch'r., & now granted, &c.

RICHARD PUGH, 100 acs., Low. Par. of Is. of Wight Co., 26 Oct. 1694, p. 396. Adj. Col. Milner & Owen Daniell's land. Trans. of 2 pers: James Taylor, Jno. Campbell.

THOMAS SMITH, 300 acs., Surry Co; N. side of Otterdam Sw; adj. Jethro. Barker; 26 Oct. 1694, p. 396. Imp. of 6 pers: Edward Wats, Wm. Donkeley, Sarah Sawney, Sarah Chessum; Mingo & Pedro, Negroes.

LEONARD HENLY, 360 acs., James City Co; N. side of Merriman's Sw; from Cattaile Meadow, along line of Pettus, &c; 26 Oct. 1694, p. 397. 175 acs. due as heir of his father, Reynold Henly, to whom it was sold 15 Dec. 1661, by Thomas Holliday; 185 acs.

within. Imp. of 4 Negroes "by the *two friends".*

MR. ROBERT THOMAS, 569½ acs., Essex Co; in the freshes thereof, & on main brs. of Snow & Weir Creeks; nigh land of Hugh William & Prosser; 26 Oct. 1694, p. 397. Imp. of 12 pers: Antho. Dolby, Richd. Bannell, Will. Reynolds, Lewis Rice, James Harper. Wm. Robinson, Knight Richeson. Geo. Kerkup, Rebecca Gregory, Anne Jeffrey. Alice Child, Margt. Clark.

COL. ANTHONY LAWSON, of Norf. Co; 1078 acs., Pr. Anne Co., in Currotuck Bay, 26 Oct. 1694, p. 398. 850 acs. part of 1680 acs. granted John Sandford, 27 Feb. 1680, who sold to Peter Smith. 16 May 1683 who sold to Lawson, 15 May 1690; beg. ' nigh Thomas Morris & John Sandford; on W. side of the long br., &c. 228 acs. due for Imp. of 5 pers: Wm. Griffin. Henry Kent, Eliza. Jinon (?), Fra. Andrews; Jack a slave.

MR. CHARLES BROWN, 920 acs., Essex Co; on brs. of Occupation Run & Cockelshell Cr., 26 Oct. 1694, p. 399. Beg. at Mr. Richard Robinson & Mrs. Beth. Gilson; crossing an Indian Path, &c. Imp. of 19 pers: Jno. Cole, Jno. Wale, Saml. Ascough, Edward Howard, Tho. Monday, Abigl. Hancock, Wm. Colston, Margt. Pritchet, Grace Redland, Richd. Russell, Chr. Wilson. Tho. Bollington, Martha Bonsey (or Bousey), David Jones, Margt. Williams, Wm. Abbot, Wm. Whaley, Christian Price, Wm. Fennel (or Fennee).

ELIZABETH DAVIS, 550 acs., Nansemond Co., 26 Oct. 1694, p. 399. Escheated from Thomas Davis, dec'd., by inquisition under John Lear, Esqr., Esch'r., & now granted, &c.

ROBERT BEVERLEY, 3 A., 1 R., 6 P., in *James City;* at S. end of the ditch dividing this from W. side of land late of Lawrence, (or) Col. Bacon at the Road; N. 36-2/5 po., to Pitch & Tarr Sw., to the maine Cart Road, &c; 26 Oct. 1694, p. 409. Imp. of: Isabella Mackland.

WILLIAM GOUGH, 70 acs., K. & Q. Co; adj. Ashwell Battin, in Capt. Chamberlain's line; on Arrakiako Sw., &c; 26 Oct. 1694, p. 409. Granted to John Goffe, 18 May 1661, deserted, & now granted for Imp. of 2 pers.*

THOMAS EVANS, of K. & Q. Co; 220 acs., Glocester Co., 26 Oct. 1694, p. 401. Escheated from John Kelly, dec'd., by inquisition under Peter Beverley, Depty. Esch'r., &c.

ROBERT KING, 124 acs., Low. Par. of Is. of Wight Co; adj. his own, & land of Maj. Burwell; 26 Oct. 1694, p. 401. Imp. of 3 pers Thomas Ellet, Alice Griffin; Kisarr, a Negro.

HENRY PRICE & MR. FRANCIS TALIAFERO, 806 acs., Essex Co; on S. side of the maine run of Pewmansend; 26 Oct. 1694, p. 402. Beg. at Capt. John Catlett; by a Ridge Path; along line of Prosser; to Mr. John Buckner; & Mr. Robert Bryant. Imp. of 17 pers: Richard Care, Jno. Peake, Wm. Sewer, Henry Crump, Arth. Muram, Cha. Ramsey, Moses Groom, Susan Place, Robt. Place, Thomas Montly, Ardery Peilham, Eliza. Champon, Sarah Bradley, Susan Champley, Mary Beckley, Roger Tarkley, Jno. Jones.

CAPT. HUGH CAMPBELL, 1000 acs., Norf. Co., 26 Oct. 1694, p. 403. Beg. at the Cyprus Sw., cor. of John Sammon; by Richford Sw; towards the Green Sea; to the cod of sd. Swamp, to end of an Occult line, &c. Granted Henry Henlane, 20 Apr. 1686, deserted, & granted Mr. Thomas Taylor & Mr. Thomas Edwards, 20 Oct. 1689, deserted, & now granted by order, &c. Imp. of 20 pers: Henry Glover, Jno. Drocut (or Dreuit), Anne Sleed, Jno. Colte, Peter Johnson, Edward ———, Jno. Willis, John Hanson, Tho. Walker, Ja. Carpenter, Ell Higlet, Jno. Harris, Isaac Curtis, Wm. Seamor, Wm. Ap-Hugh, Morris Fitzgerrald, Richd. Moreton, Henry Davies, George Clarke, Anne Ward.

CAPT. ANTHONY ARMISTEAD. 150 acs., Eliz. City Co; adj. his land at the Mill; Mr. Pascho Curle; Mr. John Archer; Capt. Henry Jenkins; & Mr. Thomas Curle; 21 Apr. 1695, p. 404. Imp. of 3 pers: Amalaca, Will, Barrow.

CAPT. WILLIAM SOANE, 130 acs., Henrico Co., in Verina Par; N. side of James Riv., over against Neck of Land; upon plantations of Mr. James Blair, Mr. Jeremiah Brown, & Mr. Nicholas Bullington (Bullenton); beg. at the Gleab Land, to mouth of 2 Mi. Cr., &c; 26 Apr. 1695, p. 404. Granted sd. Blair, Brown, & Bullenton, 20 Apr. 1690, deserted, & now granted for Imp. of 3 pers: Zarue, Huchin, Dinah.

CAPT. MATHEW KEMP, 180 acs., Middlesex Co; on N. side of George Keible; & along land of ——— Moore; 21 Apr. 1695, p. 405. Part of 390 acs. granted sd. Keible, 29 Jan. 1663, deserted, & now granted, by order &c. Imp. of 4 pers: Edward Hoomes, Tho. Collinworth, Joseph Smith, Michael Smith.

JOHN ARCHER, 375 acs., Eliz. City Co; adj. Mr. Pascho Curle; Capt. Henry Jenkins; Capt. Anthony Armistead; land of Capt. Thomas Alomby, dec'd., & Mr. Preston; 21 Apr. 1695, p. 406. Imp. of 8 pers: Jer. Beck, Jno. Hickman, Jno. Lewis, Raleigh Willis, Wm. Took; Peter, Tony, Cate.

MR. WALTER BAYLY, 106 acs., Eliz. City Co; on S. side of Back Riv., 21 Apr. 1695, p. 406. Beg. at a br. parting this from Eaton's Freeschool Land; along the Church Road; to br. parting this & land of Major William Wilson, &c. 83 acs. part of 200 acs. granted John Robins, 1 Apr. 1639, & purchased by sd. Bayly of Robert Armstrong, as marrying Jane, the eldest dau. & co-heir of Christopher Robins, son & heir of sd. John Robins; 23 Acs. for Imp. of: William Lowry.

CAPT. JOHN STYTH, 595 acs., James City Co., 21 Apr. 1695, p. 407. On S. side of Chicohamony Riv., beg. at Mr. Brumfeild, near the gr. run of sd. river, where Francis Story liveth; by Shaddock's br., to Mr. David Neviell, &c. Granted William Broadribb, 6

Sept. 1665, deserted, & granted Benjamin Eggleston, 23 Oct. 1690, deserted. & now granted by order, &c. Imp. of 12 pers: Richard Smith, Wm. Cheil. Antho. Wellman, Robert Davies, Antho. Comens, Tho. Powell, Ruth Williams, Andr. Barren, Edwd. Haskins, Jno. Barloe, Jno. Chandler, Danll. Raven.

WILLIAM RANDOLPH, ESQR., 1221 acs., Henrico Co., in Verina Par; N. side of James Riv., above Westham Cr., 21 Apr. 1695, p. 408. Beg. at mouth of sd. Cr. & mouth of a br. of Tuckahoe Cr; &c. Granted Mr. John Pleasants, 20 Oct. 1691, deserted, & now granted by order, &c. Imp. 25 pers: Tom, Jack, James, Abram, Davy, Scipio, Haniball, George, Harry, Jupiter, Mingo, Will, Conde, Nan, Moll, Hannah, Winny, Tony, Effy, Sam, Ned, Giles, Sambo, Moses, Manuell.

EDWIN THACKER & JAMES BAUGHAN, 550 acs., Essex Co., formerly Rappa. Co; on brs. of Gibson's Cr., adj. Capt. Beverley, Elick Robins & Theo. Whale (Wale); 21 Apr. 1695, p. 409. Granted John Masters, 8 Apr. 1674, deserted, & now granted by order, &c. Imp. of 11 pers: James Hose, Anne Simpson, Wm. Bruse, Augt. Smallwell, William Sebin, Danl. Clark, Eliza. Evans, Phill. Wheeler, William Prest, James Jones, Cerverses Peterson.

EDWIN THACKER, GENT., 210 acs., Middlesex Co; on N. side of Peyanketank Riv., 29 Apr. 1695, p. 410. Beg. at 700 acs. of Mr. George Keible; to the Green Glade Br., &c. Granted to sd. Keible, 29 Jan. 1663, deserted, & granted sd. Thacker 24 Oct. 1691, deserted, & granted to John Everitt, 24 Oct. 1694, who assigned to sd. Thacker, 3 Dec. 1694; now granted by order, &c. Imp. of 5 pers.* 4 Negroes by Capt. Wm. Daniels' certif.

CAPT. HENRY BATT, 700 acs., Chas. City Co; upon brs. & towards S. side of the head of Bayley's Cr; adj. land of James Waradin, called *High Peake*, now in the occupation of Mr. William Ditty & Robert Langman; 24 Apr. 1695, p. 411. Granted Robert West, 2 Aug. 1652, deserted, & now

granted by order, &c. Imp. of 14 pers: Michael Maxfeild, Jno. Donklin, Robt. Bushell, Marey Worley, Mary Wood, Mary Fans (or Faus), Robert Fenly, Mary Tedder, Jno. Kenedey, Jno. Ellett, Margt. Pain, Geo. Keeble, Richd. Langly, Richd. Wallis.

SAME. 270 acs., same Co., date, & page. In Bristoll Par., on S. side of Appamattock Riv; being all the wast lands bet. Christopher Woodward on the river, & land called Bayley's on the head of Mr. John Mays, & James Hall; adj. Henry Newcomb; near plantation called Hafford's; over Hafford's run, to the King's road, &c. Part of 870 acs. granted Samll. Woodward, 20 Apr. 1680, deserted, &c. Imp. of 6 pers: Math. Miller, Jno. Jones, James Harris, Tho. Stanner, Tho. Cook, James Brown.

ADAM HEATH, 386 acs., Surry Co; S. side of James Riv., on SW side of Up. Chipoakes Cr; adj. George Burcher; 21 Apr. 1695, p. 412. Granted John Barrow, 3 May 1653, deserted, & now granted by order, &c. Imp. of 8 pers: Yarrow, Atha, Sybill, Ned, Sissa, Sambo, Tony, Doll.

MAJ. PETER BEVERLEY, 4500 acs., K. & Q. Co; on N. side of Mattapony Riv., 21 Apr. 1695, p. 413. Adj. Col. Lawrence Smith, &c. Imp. of 90 pers.*

JAMES TAYLOR, 500 acs., K. & Q. Co., 21 Apr. 1695, p. 414. On brs. of Aquintanaco Sw; beg. at Capt. William Claybourn; adj. his own, & land of Anthony Haines. Granted Lt. Col. Robert Abrahall, 1 May 1661, deserted, & now granted by order, &c. Imp. of 10 pers: Antho. Savine, Jno. Leekman, Jno. Stone, Wm. Peirce, Alice Hughs, John Rickman, Jeffry Tindall, Sarah Dows, Adam Keeling; Thrumball, a Negro.

CAPT. HUGH CAMPBELL, 1311 acs., Is. of Wight Co., 21 Apr. 1695, p. 415. Escheated from Giles Linscott, dec'd., by inquisition under John Lear, Esqr., Esch'r., &c.

SAME. 300 acs.. same Co., date, & page. *"Heretofore recorded Nansemond County"*; on E. side of the NW br. of Nansemond Riv. Granted John Landman, 9 Apr. 1648. deserted, & now granted by order, &c. Imp. of 6 pers: Charles. James & Richard Hawley; Quoby, Sambo, Dido, Negroes.

MR. GEORGE ARCHER, 1536 acs.. Henrico Co., in Bristoll Par; on N. side of Appamattock Riv., 21 Apr. 1695, p. 416. Beg. at Mr. Thomas Batts; crossing the gr. branch of the Old Town Cr., &c. Imp. of 31 pers: Thomas Peters, Jno. Medcalf, Tho. Anderson, Tho. Towns, Walter Steirs, Geo. Garwood. Isaac Gilly, Anne Gilly, Wm. Wheeler, Richard Feild, Wm. Willis. Jeffrey Johnson, Adam Jones, Wm. Jenings, Fentris Wodland (or Woeland), Anne Pierce, Wm. Gaylard, Rebecka Stapleton, Wm. Oldis, Edwd. Roe, Cath. Stoner, Wm. Bage (or Page). Edward Thomas, Tho. Prichard.

MR. WILLIAM WILSON. 1000 acs., Norf. Co; W. from the Mill Land at head of Purle (or Puzle) Cr., in the S. br. of Eliz. River; 21 Apr. 1695, p. 417. Granted Mr. John Ferrebec, 20 Oct. 1688, who obtained a grant thereof as deserted from Maj. Francis Sawyer, who pattented same 21 Oct. 1684; deserted, & granted sd. Wilson by order, &c. Imp. of 20 pers.*

SAMUEL TAYLOR JUNR., & MARY TAYLOR, 600 acs., Accomack Co., 21 Apr. 1695, p. 417. SE on channel bet. Jengotegue Is., & 600 acs. of marshy land; to Jengotegue Cr., &c. Granted Samuel Taylor, their father, 20 Oct. 1690, deserted, & now granted by order, &c. Imp. of 12 pers: John Booker, Edward Johnson, Andr. Dickinson, Henry Cope, Eliza. Speer, Tobias Wrack, Alice Timberlake, Henry Allen, Cath. Ruth, Mary Sanderson, Tho. Wilson, William Booker.

CAPT. JOHN CUSTIS, 250 acs., on Wild Catt Is., Accomack Co; at N. end of Jengotegue Is., S. from Raged Point, on Assateag Is; 21 Apr. 1695, p. 418. Granted John Willis, Junr., 20 Oct. 1691, deserted, & now granted by order,

&c. Imp. of 5 pers: Fran. Armitage, David Englishman, George Green, Eliza. Read, Eliza. Knott.

CAPT. WILLIAM BASSETT, 1086 acs.. New Kent Co., in Blisland Par; 21 Apr. 1695, p. 419. On Pamunkey River from the new dwelling house of sd. Bassett, to mouth of sd. river & to his house called the *Brick House where the County Court was formerly held;* to cr. dividing his from lands, now or late. of Job Howes. Imp. of 22 pers: Wm. Bassett, Robt. Merritt, Wm. Overton, Wm. Kemp, Richd. Box, Hen. Barber, John Hog, Jno. Dring, Richard Widing. Wm. Sparing, Wm. Russell. Edward Roberts, John the Seaman, Eliza. Hughs. Sarah Smith. John Clark. James Douglas, Charles Davidson, Henry Gibson. Antho. Savery, Antho. Lambert, Sarah Davis.

CAPT. JOHN BATTAILE, 600 acs.. on S. side of Rappa. Riv., opposite the lower part of *Nansimond Town:* NW on Best's Cr., SE on Cedar Cr; 21 Apr. 1695, p. 419. Granted John Gillett, 21 Apr. 1657, & due Thomas Button, Gent., as marrying the relict of sd. Gillett, as by patent dated 18 Mar. 1662; deserted, & now granted by order, &c. Imp. of 12 pers: James Galt. James Monghan (or Moughan) Henry Wist, Henry Kerby, John Richards. Edward Taylor, Anth. Bell, Eliza. Shorten, Mary Ougley, Anne Harwood, Peter Duty, Cath. Fortemore.

RANDOLL LOVETT, 100 acs., Pr. Anne Co; S. of the head of E. br. of Eliz. Riv; adj. Havacomb's patent; & James Kemp's; along Purdy's line, &c; 21 Apr. 1695, p. 420. Imp. of 2 pers: William Hill, William Thomas.

WILLIAM SUMNER, 110 acs., Nansemond Co; on W. side of the S. br. of Nansemond Riv., 21 Apr. 1695, p. 421. 78 acs. part of 300 acs. granted William Brooks, 6 Jan. 1642, who sold to Abraham Pitt, who sold to John Ridding, who sold to John Sumner, 8 Apr. 1656; bequeathed to his eldest son John & to his *heires Male,* but in case of his son's decease or want of such heires, then he did give sd. 78 acs. to his youngest son, the aforesaid William, & to his heires, as by his will dated 7 March 1670; sd. John being dead without children, sd. William is now in possession; 32 acs., the remainder, is a poynt bet. his own & the S. br. of said river; adj. Hampton's land; & on Aires' Creek. Imp. of: Thomas Walker.

RICHARD PUGH, 100 acs., Low. Par. of Is. of Wight Co; adj. Col. Milner & Owen Daniell; 21 Apr. 1695, p. 422. Trans. of 2 pers: Sarah Wilson, Frances Medowes.

MR. ROBERT COLEMAN, 80 acs., Low. Par. of Is. of Wight Co., 21 Apr. 1695, p. 422. Adj. Thomas Jordan; & Giles Driver. Trans. of 2 pers: William Shepard, Anne Thompson.

MR. RALPH STANNUP, 95 acs., New Kent Co., in Blisland Par; in a forke bet. 2 gr. branches of Taskanas Cr., 21 Apr. 1695, p. 423. Imp. of 2 pers: Daniel Reynalls, William Owen.

CAPT. JOHN THOROWGOOD (Thurrogood), 340 acs., Pr. Anne Co; by his house; 21 Apr. 1695, p. 423. Imp. of 7 pers: Tho. Churchyard, Wm. Nutto, Alice Nutto, Jno. Heningstall, Tho. Bradhurst, Wm. Hill, Howell Window.

JOHN RICHASON & MATHEW BRINSON, 128 acs., Pr. Anne Co; 21 Apr. 1695, p. 424. Beg. in Bever house Neck, by a br. dividing this & land of Anne Keeling, dau. of Adam Keeling, dec'd; on the pequoson dividing this & land of Thomas Brock, &c. Imp. of 3 Negroes: Itho, Rachell, Dibna.

EDWARD HOLMES & JOHN RICE, 382 acs., Up. Par. of Nansemond Co; on N. side of Bennett's Cr., 21 Apr. 1695, p. 424. Beg. at William Spight, Junr. on N. side of the Mirey Br; down N. side of Holmes' Br., &c. Trans. of 8 pers: Fra. Green, Geo. Reed, Jno. Knott, David Armitage, Tho. King; Gore, Bridget, Harry, Negroes.

EDWARD GUTHREY (Guthry), 600 acs., K. & Q. Co., 21 Apr. 1695, p. 425. 300 acs. upon lalnd of Edward Simpson; adj. Ashwall Battin or Leonard Chamberlaine; on head of Pepeticoe Cr; 300 acs. by sd. Simpson; &c. Granted sd. Simpson, 4 Dec. 1654 under the usurpation of Oliver Cromwell, & now renewed; & due for Imp. of 12 pers: Jonathan Acum, Wm. & Susana Hair, Emd. & Edward Carter, Richard Parker, Wm. Minnen, Tho. Large, Wm. Dally, Saml. Whitson, Rebecka Feild, Mala. Wafon.

WILLIAM SPIGHT, JUNR., 520 acs., Up. Par. of Nansemond Co; E. side of Bennet's Cr; S. side of Spight's Br; down N. side of Mirry Br., &c; 21 Apr. 1695, p. 426. Imp. of 11 pers: Jno. Roberts, Rachell Puchin, Andr. More, Joan Jeffreys, Saml. Stegall, Michael Dean, Antho. Cole, Sarah Stanprick, John Doolittle, Simon Jokes, Tho. Long.

MR. HENRY HILL, 733 acs., Henrico Co., in Bristoll Par; 21 Apr. 1695, p. 426. Beg. on the 1st gr. br. of Swift Cr., &c. Imp. of 15 pers: John Sogery, Rose Towerson, Fra. Ridley, Jane Sorrell, Margt. Phillipson, Tho. Shurley, Jane Sorrell, Joan Smitter Robert Bright, Jno. Rigsby; Negroes: James, Buck, Toney, Mingo, Dinah.

ALEXANDER CAMBELL (CAMPBELL), 195 acs., K. & Q. Co., in Stratton Major Par; beg. at John Garrett, by the Ridge Path; to Rogers' corner, &c; 21 Apr. 1695, p. 427. Granted Richard Threder, 28 Sept. 1681, deserted, & now granted by order, &c. Imp. of 4 Negroes: Jack, Robin, Peg, Cate.

OWEN DANIELL, 130 acs., in Is. of Wight & Nansemond Counties; beg. at Col. Milner's cor. by maine run of King Saile Sw; to maine run of the Black Water Sw; to mouth of Wickum Sw., &c; 21 Apr. 1695, p. 428. Trans. of 3 pers: Wm. Brown, Mary Brown; & Nick, a Negro.

MR. THOMAS COCKE (Cock), 250 acs., Norf. Co., 21 Apr. 1695, p. 428. Escheated from William Wilson, dec'd., by inquisition under John Lear, Esqr., Esch'r., 21 Dec. 1689, &c.

WILLIAM HALL, 278 acs., Glocester Co., in Petsoe Par., 21 Apr. 1695, p. 429. On N side of Cole's Br. near forke which falls into the maine Sw. that runs into Poropotank Cr; to Col. Lee's cor; by the maine road to the Dragon Bridge; to William Brookin's land, &c. Granted Charles Roane, 20 Oct. 1691, deserted, & now granted by order, &c. Imp. of 6 pers: John Bayley, Jno. Dashwood, Tho. Greenwood, Joseph Ranson, Patrick Ferguson.

JAMES MINGE, 2317 acs., New Kent Co., in St. Peter's Par., 21 Apr. 1695, p. 430. Beg. at his own land, cor. of Edward Johnson; down Powhite Sw; to Beavor Damm Br; to Pickanock Path; on Bassett & Asting's line; down Braidy Br., &c. Granted John Underhill, 21 Apr. 1690, deserted, & now granted by order, &c. Imp. of 47 pers: Pr. Goldsmith, Tho. Mires, Saml. Man, Mary Wilson, James Butler, Wm. Walter, Richard Farr, Michael Irish, Nath. Hickambottom, Saml. Chappell, Gideon Peltier, Mary Goslin, Jno. Allen, Edwd. Woodsworth, Mary Wright, Wm. Read, Ellin Wench, Hen. Fisher, Edwd. Wilson, Will. Smith, Tho. Mims, Hump. Osborne, Jno. Chest, Jno. Bechem, Jno. Bellet, Jno. Ward, Antho. Ballard, Tho. Cobb, Alice Strange, Eliz. Davies, Nath. Onely, Habbk. Book, Wm. Hudson, Wm. Taylor, Richd. Seaman; Jack, Mingo, Mary, Growey, Surrat, Dick, Kate, Tom, Kate, George, Peter, Jane.

WILLIAM HUNTER, Weaver, 200 acs., Up. Par. of Nansemond Co; E. side of the maine Cypruss Sw. of Bennet's Cr; on S. side of the Further Br. of Oysterlong Neck, &c; 21 Apr. 1695, p. 431. Imp. of 4 pers: Alla, Harry, Shambo, Ned.

ROBERT HALSEY, 100 acs., Essex Co., 21 Apr. 1695, p. 431. Escheated from John Hawkins, dec'd., by inquisition under Abraham Clunis, Deputy Esch'r., &c.

THOMAS GAINES, 100 acs., Essex Co., 21 Apr. 1695, p. 432. Escheated from William Larke, dec'd., by inquisi-

tion under Isaac Allerton, Esqr., 9 Sept. 1680, &c.

JAMES BLAISE, 167 acs., Essex Co., 21 Apr. 1695, p. 432. Escheated from Richard Easterby, dec'd., by inquisition under Peter Beverley, Deputy Esch'r., &c.

WILLIAM EDWARDS, 200 acs., Up. Par. of Nansemond Co; on N. side of Davies Mare Br. & SW side of Bennett's Cr; beg. near mouth of Baytree Br; 21 Apr. 1695, p. 433. Imp. of 4 pers: Shannon, Anty, Ruth, Tulie.

ALEXANDER YOUNG, of Yorke Co; 188 acs. in James City Co., near Wilmington lower Church; adj. James Hood; 21 Apr. 1695, p. 433. Purchased from John Major, 8 Apr. 1689, to whom it was bequeathed by Robert Morgan, son & heire of William Morgan, to whom with other lands it was granted, &c. Note: This patent hath a mistake in it & is therefore recorded in the next leaf according to the Originall. R.B.,C.G.C. (Robert Beverley, Cl. Gen. Court.)

MR. DANIELL PUGH, 1134 acs., Up. Par. of Nansemond Co; called Dogwood Neck; on W. side of Bennett's Cr; 21 Apr. 1695, p. 434. Imp. of 23 pers: Jacob Ulseley, Wm. Harrison, Edward Williams, Antho. Laramore, William Trewman, Henry Hobbs, William Truely, Jno. Welsh, Mary Arley, Peter Coward, Eliza. Murfrey, Tho. Halsey, Anne Halsey, Robt. Taliaferro, Benja. Hall, Jno. Edmunds, David Jones, John Motley, John Nutts, Eliza. Humphrys, William Batten, William Stanley, Tho. Jackson.

ALEXANDER YOUNG, of Yorke Co., 188 acs., James City Co., near Wilmington Lower Church; from James Wood's cor; along Morgan's land; along Fishe's land, &c. Note: Same as abstract second above.)

JOHN HARRIS & JOHN LARKUM (Lurkum), 888 acs., Up. Par. of Nansemond Co; S. side of the Loosing Sw. & W. side of the maine desert; 21 Apr.

1695, p. 435. Beg. on said Sw. near the Southward road; to the Vineyard Poynt, &c. Imp. of 18 pers: Luke Redman, Arthur Cavenah, Robert Dresdale, Sarah Hutchins, Anne Sumeraell, Faith Anderson, Homer Daniel, Susan Okeele; 10 Negroes.

MR. LEWIS CONNER, Merchant, of Norf. Co., & MR. JOHN KEYTON, Merchant, of Nansemond Co., 1280 acs., Up. Par. of Nansemond Co; in the *Mehering Camp Neck,* on S. side of Bennett's Cr; 21 Apr. 1695, p. 436. Beg. on W. side of the maine Cyprus Sw; down the Deep Sw., &c. Imp. of 26 pers: Jno. Lemon, Robert Arppe, Jno. Presley, Jno. Wall, Alice Meers, Jno. Meers, Saml. Booth, Richd. Garley, Tho. Bayley, Robt. Uslerwood, Jane Knight, Will. Cagan, Honora Shallbe, Cha. Gallock, Nicho. Reston, Wm. Price, Fra. Taylor; Daniel, Betty, Jack, Nan, Jenny, Silvester, Guy, Judy, Adam.

WILLIAM CAPPS, 123 acs., Pr. Anne Co; on the Pinny Sw., NW'ly. from the Salt Ponds on the E. Shoar of Linhaven River, 21 Apr. 1695, p. 437. Adj. James Lemond; & his own land. Imp. of 3 pers: Anna, Cate, Hagar.

FRANCIS BENTON, 108 acs., Up. Par. of Nansemond Co; on NW side of the S. br. of Nansemond River, beg. at mouth of Powell's Cr; on Widow Hill's land, &c; 21 Apr. 1695, p. 438. Imp. of 3 pers: Andrew Brasseur, Richd. Jossey, John Lovegrove.

EDWARD DAVIS, 600 acs., Pr. Anne Co; S. of the E. br. of Eliz. River; beg. at Alexander Lisbon & line of Havacomb's patent; 21 Apr. 1695, p. 438. Imp. of 12 pers: Abraham Iveson, Peter Knight, Jno. Smith, David Cant; 8 Negroes.*

ALEXANDER LISBON, 200 acs., Pr. Anne Co; S. of the head of the E. br. of Eliz. River, 21 Apr. 1695, p. 439. Adj. Col. Lawson; Mr. Moseley's; & Havacomb's patent; on run parting this & Mr. Robinson's land, &c. Imp. of 4 pers: John Godwin, John Booth; & 2 Negroes.

JOHN CARRAWAY, SENR., of Norf. Co; 100 acs., Pr. Anne Co; S. of the head of the E. br. of Eliz. River; beg. at Randoll Lovett & line of Havacomb's patent; to John Kemp, &c; 21 Apr. 1695, p. 439. Imp. of 2 pers: Johnson Reding, Anne Reding.

JAMES COLE, SENR., 50 acs., Up. Par. of Nansemond Co; in the great Sw., on E. side of Nansemond River; adj. Mr. Wright & Murfry's land, &c; 21 Apr. 1695, p. 440. Imp. of: Thomas Mark.

JOHN BONNER, 346 acs., Chas. City Co., in Weynoake Par; S. side of James River; beg. at Joseph Meatchamp; on Mr. Wallis' line; along Edward Hollaway, &c. Imp. of 7 pers.*

GEORGE PASSMORE, 220 acs., Chas. City Co; on S. side of James River; adj. Mr. Robert Thucker; William Jones; Mr. Batts; Robert Burtchild, & Col. William Byrd, Esqr; 21 Apr. 1695, p. 441. Imp. of 5 pers.*

JOHN MURFREY, 80 acs., Up. Par. of Nansemond Co; in the Gr. Sw., on E. side of Nansemond River; beg. at his own & Mr. Wright's land; 21 Apr. 1695, p. 442. Imp. of 2 pers: James Spear, Tho. Lear.

JEREMIAH ARLINE, JUNR., 36 acs., Up. Par. of Nansemond Co; on SE side of Blake's Mill Run; beg. at cor. of Jeremiah Arline, Senr; on Mr. Blake's line, &c; 21 Apr. 1695, p. 442. Imp. of: Jane Thomas.

ROBERT VAUGHAN, 243 acs., Pr. Anne Co; on E. side of the North River, by the Landing, cor. of land he lives on; adj. Col. Mason's land at *Matchepongo;* & Lemuel Mason's land; 21 Apr. 1695, p. 443. Imp. of 5 pers: Guy, Tony, Mingo, Sarah, Poll.

INDEX

A NOTE TO THE USER

PERSONAL NAMES. The user of this index should be as imaginative in his pursuit of a surname as a seventeenth-century clerk might have been in his spelling. Variant spellings of personal names in the abstracts appear unchanged in the index. The indexer has not presumed to decide, for example, whether the John Abbot mentioned on page 115 is the same person as the Jno. Abot mentioned on page 362. Titles of military rank, which may have changed during the subjects' lifetimes, have been omitted from the index when both the given name and the title are present in the abstracts. Thus, under the entry *Abrahall* the three page numbers for the subentry *Col.* indicate that in each of those locations no given name appears in the abstract. In such cases the user is allowed to decide for himself whether the Çol. Abrahall mentioned in a 1691 patent on page 360 is the same Robert Abrahall who had patented land in 1654, according to a patent abstracted on page 30. Researchers interested in groups within the population may also consult the subject headings INDIANS and NEGROES.

PLACE-NAMES. Minor variant spellings of place-names and variant abbreviations of geographical terms have not been retained in the index; for example, the index entry *Accomack* does not show that in a patent on page 133 the word is spelled *Accamack*, nor does the subject entry *Counties, Accomack*, reflect other variations in spelling that may appear in the abstracts. Again, the user should remember that colonial clerks were recording names for which there were no standard English spellings and that the index consolidates only the obvious variant spellings of place-names. No attempt is made to indicate the best or most frequent spellings of place-names used during the late seventeenth century. Researchers may consult the following subject headings that appear in the index in capital letters:

BAYS	LANDINGS	PONDS
BRANCHES	MARSHES	QUARTERS
BRIDGES	MEADOWS	RIDGES
BROOKS	MILLS	RIVERS
COUNTIES	NECKS	ROADS
CREEKS	PARISHES	RUNS
DAMS	PATHS	SHIPS
FIELDS	PLANTATIONS	SLASHES
GUTS	POCOSINS	SPRINGS
INLETS	POINTS	SWAMPS
ISLANDS		VALLEYS

ALPHABETIZING. Main entries in this index are arranged in letter-by-letter alphabetical order.

INDEX

Thomas, 294; Wm., 2, 5, 6, 13; Xpher, 229
Additt, Samll., 170
Addlstone, Antho., 138
Adeer, Xpher, 320
Adenton, Mr., 311
Adgar, Xtopher, 378
Adington, Edward, 235
A'dis, Will, 316
Adison, Alexdr., 159
Adkings, Robt., 156
Adkins, Eliza., 317; James, 18; John, 317; Lewis, 42, 43; Mary, 219; Michaell, 134; Nic., 85; Ralph, 148; Robert, 118; Robt., 98; Wm., 111
Adkinson, Alice, 324, 371; James, 304, 309; Mathew, 209; Richd., 139, Thomas, 309
Adkis, John, 180
Adleston, Jno., 69
Adley, Rog., 148
Adlin, Ellin., 299
Adly, Xtopher, 93
Adolphus, Will, 18; Wm., 18
Adookhart, Jno., 187
Adough, Sebastian, 85
Adwell, Geo., 204; Mathias, 3
Africa, a Negro, 394
Agard, Charles, 10, 128
Agbe, 364
Agbo, 170, 244, 312
Ager, John, 284, 384; Menelcius, 381
Agg, Wm., 59
Aggor, Jon, 244
Agnewes, Wm., 164
Agnis, a Negro, 181
Agore, Charles, 119
Aheron, Morris, 184
Ainsly, Jno., 23
Aire, Katherine, 49
Aires, Will, 14; Wm., 41; land of, 123
Aishley, Dennis, 234
Akee, Corn, 362
Aken, James, 274
Akerland, Nicholas, 230; Thomas, 238
Akeron, Morris, 184
Akerson, Daniel, 153
Akin, Ann, 143; James, 126
Alaman, Wm., 165
Alanson, Antho., 174
Alarine, Wm., 135
Albane, Rich., 76
Albert, Jo., 184
Albin, Roger, 156
Albon, Jno., 135
Albots, Math., 137
Alce, Ould, 238

Alcock, Edward, 303; Tho., 72
Alcock's corner, 279
Aldage, Robt., 101
Aldberry, Rachell, 317
Alden, Cha., 217; Charles, 309; Susan, 354
Alder, Ja., 134; Jane, 165, Wm., 5
Alderbury, Rachell, 282
Alderly, Thomas, 112
Aldgie, Alce, 78
Aldin, Robert, 237; Robt., 149, 152
Aldman, Phillip, 328
Aldrage, John, 367, 368
Aldree, Tho., 150
Aldridge, Ann, 319; Jeremy, 58; Jno., 50; Mary, 58, 199; Rich., 108; Rose, 228, 238; Tho., 191; Wm., 50
Aldrig, Mary, 183
Aldrige, Joseph, 84; Mary, 157
Aldrith, Wm., 170
Aldus, Wm., 316
Aldwick, Peter, 173
Aldwith, Fra., 170; Wm., 170
Aldworth, Wm., 119
Aleberry, Lewis, 10
Alee, John, 355
Alees, Geo., 220
Alen, Henry, 393
Alepp, Alice, 135
Alester, Marke, 14
Aleworth, Mr., 105; Wm., 68
Alex, Ould, 238
Alexander, Eliz., 257; Jno., 16, 42, 61; John, 79, 200, 318, 385; Robt., 35; Thomas, 173, 182, 271, 298, 318; Wm., 57, 132, 149
Alford, Henry, 224; Jno., 152; John, 230, 241, 242; Tho., 147, 154, 247; William, 86, 110, 256; Willm., 86; Wm., 20, 27, 50, 63, 89, 97, 109, 110, 134, 137, 141, 377
Alfred, Tho., 103; Winifred, 18, 122
Algood, Edward, 214
Alice, 379
Aliff, James, 313
Alinsley, Sarah, 298
Alla, 401; a Negro, 388
Allain, John, 341
Allam, Jno., 40; John, 341; Jon., 271
Allamaine, Thomas, 302
Allaman, Hen., 146
Allamby, Tho., 250
Allan, Wm., 91, 105, 197
Allane, James, 391
Allderson, Mr., 341
Allem, Jacob, 138
Allen, Abraham, 92; Alex., 196; Alexr., 158; Alice, 335; Ann, 252;

And., an Irishmen, 158
Andersen, Geo., 121
Anderson, Alexander, 38, 80; Amy,
29, 106; An., 8; Daniel, 168; David,
34, 35, 53, 76, 134, 160; Ed., 29;
Edward, 8; Edwd., 106; Ellinor,
117; Faith, 402; Geo., 121, 133;
George, 27; Inghambred, 154;
James, 59; John, 229; Jon., 264;
Mary, 65; Peter, 182; Phill., 134;
Ralph, 330; Reginald, 245; Rey-
nard, 333; Richard, 344, 381, 282;
Rob., 77; Robert, 260, 265, 353,
359; Robt., 6, 75, 208, 354; Saᵐll.,
203, 366; Sar., 208; Tho., 47, 238,
399; Thomas, 265; William, 287;
Willm., 54; Wm., 102, 150, 174,
176, 244, 255, 257, 303, 392,
Xpher., 287
Anderton, Dan., 149; George, 121
Andrel, Jon., 247
Andrew, 305; a Negro, 314, 365, 395;
Ed., 139; Gutt, 39; Jno., 79; Wm.,
3
Andrewes, Andrew, 183; Cornelius,
135; David, 91; Grace, 18; Jane,
138; Jno., 59; Mary, 54, 138; Tho.,
138; Wm., 80, 108, 198
Andrews, Alice, 178, 229; David, 283,
329, 348, 373; Edw., 373; Edwd.,
185, 190; Fra., 396; Geo., 47, 257;
James, 155; Jane, 340; Jno., 193,
299; John, 183, 311; Mary, 181,
373, 375; Robert, 264, 278; Robt.,
323; Samll., 193; Tho., 246, 340,
344; Thomas, 264, 388; William,
183, 344; Wm., 215, 218
Andrewson, Eliz., 126
Andrick, Wm., 241
Andros, Edmond, 378
Anduis, 230
Andwell, Wm., 226
Aneas, 383
Angela, a Negro, 255
Angell, Audrey, 48; **Mary,** 40; **Ra.,**
188; Rich., 65; Richd., 142; Uriah,
28; Wm., 28
Angelo, a Negro, 150
Angett, Wm., 75
Angoe, a Negro, 245
Angood, Wm., 237
Angora, a Negro, 244
Anguis, Patrick, 168
Anington, An., 189
Anmors, Tho., 59
Ann, 210, 213; an Indian, 249; a
Negro, 140; 237, 243, 261, 262,
285; Escott, 123

Anna, 402; a Negro, 380
Annacoston Indian Towne, 21
Anne, a Negroe, 27
Annis, Jno., 221; Step., 91
Annshue, a Negro, 356
Anny, Eliz., 173
Ansell, Mary, 38
Anselle, Jno., 226
Anser, William, 183
Ansly, Richard, 390
Anson, Wm., 189
Answorth, Ralph, 145
Antell, Tho., 255
Antherson, Wm., 275
Antho., a Negro, 185, 225, 373
Anthony, Mark, 354
Anto., a boy, 109
Anty., 401
Anvill, Alexander, 215
Any, Marg., 198
Anzer, Wm., 162
Ap-Hugh, Wm., 397
Apleby, Jno., 189
Apleton, John, 344
Aplewhaite, Capt., 254
Aplugh, Wm., 310
Apostecoake, mouth of, 30
Appleby, Ja., 348
Appleford, Tobias, 310
Appleton, Jno., 66; John, 25; Rachell,
91; Tho., 93
Applewaight, Hen., 198
Applewaite, Henry, 270
Applewhaite, Capt., 266; Henery, 269;
Henry, 151, 184, 227; Mr., 184
Appleyard, Wm., 318
Appomatock, 35
Appomatock Indian Towne, 92, 137,
146
Apponin, 245
Appowell, How., 166
Apslands, Tho., 98
Aqua, a Negro, 371
Aquakick, an Indian town, 21
Aquintenockco, 30
Arahall, Robt., 30
Arbery, Ja., 204
Arbrey, Jane, 103
Arcadia, 24, 119
Arch, Mary, 195; Robt., 195
Archbold, Geo., 183
Archer, Ambrose, 68, 154; Capt., 269,
294; Dennis, 266; Edwd., 210; Eliz.,
175, 226; Esop, 48; Fra., 96; Geo.,
66, 91, 135, 269; George, 137, 362,
399; Henry, 40; Jno., 43; John,
397; Jon., 180; Mr., 374; Rich.,
136; Richd., 188; Tho., 38; Wil-

Rich., 369; Roger, 189; Tho., 21, 271
Bagworth, Jno., 96
Bailey, John, 109; [Mr.?], 163; Rich., 121; Richard, 121; Richd., 169; Thomas, 109
Bailie, Richd., 132
Baily, Ja., 164; Rich., 111; Richard, 120; Richd., 160
Bainbridg, Ellen, 112
Baines, Fran., 195; Giles, 179
Bainton, Hen., 136; Lewis, 18; Peter, 259; Samll., 262
Bakehouse, Eliz., 20
Baker, Abr., 212; Alice, 233; Ann, 138; Capt., 20, 101, 141, 230, 242; Charles, 100, 180; Dan., 244; Daniell, 109; Danll., 149; Dor., 173; Eliz., 43, 75; Eliza., 348; Evan, 261; Geo., 36, 47, 80; Henery, 277; Henry, 299, 388; Herc., 165; Ja., 188; James, 178; Jane, 16, 362; Jno., 15, 17, 43, 52, 65, 79, 80, 88, 90, 111, 298; John, 229, 374; Jon., 225, 269; Jos., 353; Joseph, 32, 59, 123; Judith, 80; Law., 43, 255; Lawrence, 43, 186, 374; Mar., 150; Martin, 227, 229; Mary, 16, 121, 179, 212, 215; Math., 87; Millescent, 348; Moses, 87, 177, 251; Mr., 388, 389; Murcy, 172; Nich., 5; Rachell, 384; Rich., 191; Richard, 172; Richd., 135, 361; Robert, 112; Robt., 58, 65, 257; Samll., 8, 93; Silvester, 172, 221, 246; Stephen, 5; Tho., 91, 115, 129; Thom., 333; Thomas, 239; Wm., 4, 31, 91, 104, 111, 115, 138, 165, 189, 192, 210, 240, 362; land of, 312.
Bakers, 61
Bakorne, Rich., 40
Balaer, Eliz., 156
Balam, Bridget, 82; Charles, 57; James, 45
Balbie, Rich., 321
Balcott, Jeff., 10
Bald, Mary, 190
Balding, An., 220
Baldrin, Nich., 125
Baldry, Wm., 115, 144, 382
Baldwin, Hugh, 386; Hum., 261; Jeffry, 114; Jno., 118; John, 394; Jonath., 78; Nich., 111, 146; Nicholas, 393; William, 278, 392; Wm., 326
Baldwinne, Niccolas, 73
Baldwyn, John, 222

Baley, Edward, 395; George, 34; meadow of, 374
Ball, Alphonso, 3, 159; Antho., 138; Arth., 170; Barth., 268; Danl., 352; Eliz., 194; Eliza., 310; Han., 184; Hanah, 20; Hen., 32; Isaac, 2, 89; Isaak, 6, 13; Isack, 5; Jno., 58; Jon., 266; Joseph, 27; Lewis, 22; Mary, 353, 395; Peter, 10, 114, 145; Richd., 252, 274; Robt., 175; Tho., 58; Tymothy, 8, 29, 104; Welkin, 346; Will., 20; William, 20, 254, 262, 283, 317; Wm., 20, 49, 85, 132, 152, 163, 184, 195, 251, 252, 282, 310, 372; land of, 278, 300, 302, 392
Ballad, Wm., 141
Ballance, Wm., 380
Ballard, Antho., 401; Besheba, 130; Elisha, 388; Ellinor, 355; Jno., 130, 172; John, 151; Joseph, 130, 388; Mr., 73, 96; Robt., 101; Tho., 128, 163; Thomas, 5, 208, 267; cor. of, 388; land of, 387
Ballenden, Georg., 212
Ballens, Humphry, 391
Ballentine, Geo., 12; George, 295
Balley, Susan, 215
Ballicorne, Ja., 146
Ballingslee, Margt., 347
Ballintine, George, 368
Balliott, land of, 68
Ballitoune, Ja., 146
Ballow, Wm., 208
Ballows, the, 208
Balls, Rcbec., 97
Ballue, Wm., 363
Ballum, Edwd., 88; Ja., 7
Balms, Symon, 15
Balono, Symon, 15
Balt, Rebecca, 153
Baltamore, Hen., 335
Baltropp, Wm., 61
Baly, Eliza., 343
Bamblet, Ambrose, 343
Bames, Giles, 179
Bamfeild, Jane, 10
Bamly, Tho., 191
Bamton, William, 218; Wm., 282
Banbridge, Elinor, 338
Banckes, Andr., 129; Eliz., 70; John, 24
Bancroft, Alice, 39, 54, 112; Geo., 111; Wm., 4
Bandall, Wm., 45
Bandermull, Lewis, 132
Bando, a Negro, 195
Bandy, Eliz., 50

Blissard, Amy, 159
Blissed, Robt., 139
Blith, Geo., 362; Tho., 217; Wm., 339
Block, Rebecka, 360
Blockhouse hill, 394
Blomefield, Samuell, 257
Blomfeild, William, 381
Blomfield, Samuell, 311
Blomwell, Peter, 344
Bloomfeild, Samll., 257, 331
Blore, Mathew, 114
Blossom, Wm., 155
Blow, Geo., 165; George, 13, 237;
    Richard, 165, 199, 237, 277, 288;
    Richd., 334; land of, 71
Blowd, Jos., 181
Blowe, Geo., 71; George, 112;
    land of, 186
Blowes, Tho., 40
Blows, cor. pine of, 199
Bloxam, Jno., 154
Blue, Wm., 23
Blumfeild, Eliz., 189; William, 183
Blundall, Jane, 50
Blunden, Hen., 136
Blunt, Edwd., 142; Elidey, 109; Ja.,
    193; Jno., 139; Jos., 194; Joseph,
    385; Mary, 32; Richd., 242; Tho.,
    42; Thomas, 97, 238, 242, 393
Blurry, Mary, 21
Bly, Chr., 198; Christo., 198
Blyth, Ann, 256; Geo., 235; Tho., 309
Blythe, Geo., 359; land of, 164
Boadman, Phill., 50
Boaldwinne, William, 230
Boales, Jno., 153
Boalton, Wm., 169
Boane, Thomas, 49
Boar Quarter, 376
Board, David, 208; Eliz., 226;
    Richd., 324
Boat, Anne, 334
Boate, Ann, 158
Boateright, Eliz., 138
Boaterite, Mr., 166
Boates, Nich., 98
Boatwright, John, 267
Boaz, Jane, 99; Xpofer., 99
Bob, a Negro, 255
Bobbett, Will., 134
Bobblett, Xper., 165
Bobby, Mr., 376; Thomas, 222, 251,
    346, 383
Bobett, Wm., 146
Bock, Margaret, 391
Bockanoctun, 10
Bockatenoctum, 11
Bockman, Edward, 359; Edwd., 145

Bocock, Jno., 22
Boddie, William, 280
Boddy, Antho., 343
Bodie, Mr., 123; William, 264;
    Wm., 151
Bodin, Mary, 182
Bodkin, Andrew, 309
Bodman, 368
Bodrich, Mary, 359
Bodurda, Thomas, 113
Body, Jane, 190; line of, 339
Bodye, Mr., 164
Boeman, Edmd., 158; Edmund, 151,
    158; Tho., 220
Bogan, Wm., 24
Bogas, Robert, 42
Boggs, Wm., 393
Boggus, Jon., 250
Bohannan, Dunken, 160; Dunkin, 161
Boharry, Wm., 53
Bohomini, Propter, 164
Bohonno, Dunkin, 29, 189
Bohono, Dunkin, 29
Boiston, Jno., 374
Boke, a Negro, 318
Boker, Kath., 171
Bolding, Robert, 247
Boldry, Wm., 350
Boles, Ja., 107
Bolfe, Oliver, 38
Bollin, Robt., 349
Bolling, Robert, 247, 303, 340, 364;
    Robt., 354
Bollington, Tho., 396
Bolt, Jane, 101; Roger, 384
Bolter, Wm., 77
Bolton, Ad., 144; Jno., 29, 326; Mary,
    92; Ralph, 143; Sam., 255; Tho.,
    273; Thomas, 4; Wm., 318
Bomly, Ann, 136
Bompas, Edward, 42
Bomps, Margt., 205
Bonam, Saml., 66; Samll., 84
Bond, Eliz., 243, 250; Francis, 237,
    280, 376, 391; Hen., 269; James,
    10; Jno., 65; Nicho., 28; Phill., 57;
    Richard, 395; Robt., 343; Samuell,
    224; Sarah, 319; Tho., 54, 113;
    Thomas, 375; Will., 123; Wm., 135
Bonden, Eliza., 295; Mordecai, 319
Boner, Steph., 153
Bones, Tho., 50
Bonfeild, Amos, 157
Bongee, John, 63
Bonison, Honor, 63
Bonne, Rich., 128
Bonnell, Mary Jone, 213
Bonner, Elizabeth, 229; James, 28,

Bougee, John, 63
Bough, Jennett, 143; Mary, 143;
Rebecka, 92
Boughan, James, 14, 370, 392; Jno.,
170; John, 392
Boughton, Richard, 178
Boukley, Robt., 347
Boulding, Rachell, 263; William, 263
Boulton, Jane, 174; Jno., 169; William, 249; Wm., 169, 174, 249
Bourcher, Tho., 268
Bourer, Wm., 11
Bourk, Jno., 321; John, 372
Bourn, Antho., 340; Anthony, 355
Bourne, David, 160; Edw., 14; Edwd.,
145; Ja., 115; Jeffery, 104; Jos.,
241; Robert, 254; William, 79;
Wm., 299
Bours, Tho., 50
Bourrough, Benony, 99
Bousey, Martha, 396
Bousser, Oliver, 180
Bouten, Peeter, 108
Bouth, Mr., 324; Robt., 357
Bouthen, Jno., 110
Bow, Math., 172; Richd., 399
Boward, Pet., 213
Boway, Phill., 191
Bowcher, Jno., 25
Bowden, Tho., 177
Bowell, Amos, 114; Elizabeth, 355
Bowen, Jno., 8, 34; Morris, 276
Bower, An., 226; Edwd., 226;
Sarah, 60
Bowers, Robert, 185, 235; Robt., 132,
185; land of, 301
Bowes, Mary, 20, 27, 51; Tho., 27
Bowey, Ph., 374
Bowin, Jno., 188; Walkin., 64
Bowle, Dorothy, 108
Bowler, Ann, 99; Deborah, 237; Esqr.,
187; John, 13, 245; Mr., 166, 244,
252, 343; Tho., 154, 237, 328;
Thomas, 109, 167, 338; Wm., 281
Bowles, Ja., 99; Jno., 96; John, 278,
286, 322; Jon., 181; Phill., 134, 144;
Robert, 236; Tho., 20; Wm., 81
Bowleware, Wm., 90
Bowlin, Ja., 357; James, 92; Mrs.,
215; Robt., 146, 303; William, 36;
Wm., 42
Bowling, Robert, 303, 340, 364;
Simon, 194
Bowlton, Jane, 285
Bowly, Mr., 188
Bowman, Edmond, 33, 375; Edmund,
94, 183, 211, 322; Edwd., 149;

John, 108; Mr., 393; Robert, 24;
Robt., 24, 59, 73, 91, 107; land
of, 301
Bowne, John, 81
Bowney, Eliz., 91
Bowre, Jno., 6
Bowrey, Thomas, 280
Bowrin, John, 174, 214, 248; land of,
331, 356; line of, 285
Bowring, Edmond, 248; John, 248;
line of, 280
Bowry, Thomas, 242
Bowser, Hen., 50, 256
Bowsey, Jno., 138; John, 139, 246, 263
Bowste, John, 380
Bowtell, Margarett, 215
Bowthen, Jno., 94
Bowzee, Jno., 139; John, 159
Box, Antho., 269
Boxwell, Richd., 251
Boy, Jo., 178
Boyce, Elinor, 170; Fra., 94; Hen.,
256; James, 325; Jno., 160; John,
280
Boyd, Hugh, 35; Ja., 162
Boydon, Jno., 90
Boyer, Eliz., 269; Fran., 85; Jno., 191;
Tom., 152
Boyes, James, 336; Wm., 23
Boykin, Edward, 290, 291, 366, 384
Boykins, Edward, 330
Boys, Tho., 318
Boyse, Fra., 144; Lewis, 159;
Samll., 144
Boyston, Jno., 191; Robt., 135
Boyter, Tim., 210
Boytes, Tho., 232
Brace, Robert, 104; Robt., 154, 156
Bracewell, Parson, 150; Robert, 79,
175; Robt., 175
Bracey, Elizabeth, 119; Robert, 119;
Wm., 346
Bracket, Mark, 396
Brackett, Elizabeth, 396; [Mr.], 347;
Wm., 213
Brackwell, Tho., 111
Bractor, Mary, 247
Bracy, William, 381
Bradberry, Ja., 150
Bradbery, James, 8
Bradborne, Edward, 358; Tho., 138
Bradburn, Thomas, 355
Bradburye, James, 41
Braddy, Tho., 379
Bradford, Ann, 150; Jno., 47, 110,
111; Mary, 47, 195; Mr., 184;
Nath., 196; Nathanael, 23; Nathaniel, 118, 204; Nathll., 159;

171, 359; Tho., 217, 245, 258, 352, 377, 395; Thomas, 284, 326; Tom, 327; Wm., 85, 228, 277, 355, 359, 374, 400
Brown's old feild, 247
Browne, Abra., 143; Alex., 13, 81; And., 231; Ann, 87, 123, 154; Anne, 353; Ben., 318; Betty, 153; Col., 283, 291; Danl., 62; David, 53, 82; Debourax, 237; Devereaux, 104; Devereux, 109; Devorax, 97, 243; Devourax, 230; Dorothy, 30, 48, 54; Ed., 13; Edward, 173, 248, 286, 288; Edwd., 176; Eliz., 37, 62, 113; Eliza., 225, 371; Ellen, 340; Ellenor, 28; Fra., 166, 201; Francis, 14, 246, 267, 370; Geo., 166; Hen., 38, 95, 230; Henry, 65; James, 13, 81, 138; Jane, 128; Jeremiah, 341; Jno., 2, 4, 6, 14, 62, 70, 88, 93, 128, 146, 148, 150, 154, 358; John, 40, 49, 74, 112, 125, 192, 288, 374; Jos., 241; Katherin, 111; Lawr., 225; Marge., 172; Marmaduke, 146; Mary, 114, 116, 145, 146, 372; Math., 98; Mathew, 155; Moll, 134; Mr., 119; Nath., 37, 73; Nich., 50; Original, 94; Originall, 181; Phillip, 72, 168; Ra., 205; Rachell, 119, 133; Ralph, 215; Raulph, 92; Rebecca, 90; Richard, 117; Robert, 300; Robt., 9; Roger, 67; Samll., 164, 174; Sara, 175; Sus., 219; Tabitha, 155; Tho., 32, 51, 91, 115, 124, 142, 143, 154, 156, 171, 174, 175, 186, 190, 237, 367; Thomas, 49, 296, 369; Tobias, 98, 118, 133; William, 181, 183, 200, 222; Willm., 61; Wm., 16, 22, 53, 75, 79, 113, 129, 134, 154, 176, 236, 237, 239, 245, 317, 356; Xpofer., 82; land of, 320
Browneing, Geo., 44, 134; George, 25, 44; John, 52; Marg., 134, 167; Margaret, 44
Brownen, Jno., 32
Browning, Eliz., 362; Eliza., 86; Geo., 204; George, 153, 218, 298; Humpherey, 276; Tho., 86, 174; Thomas, 104, 211, 306; William, 382; Willm., 365; Wm., 351
Brownlow, Rich., 23
Browsgrove, Jno., 157
Broxam, Edwad., 231
Broxo, Robt., 193
Bruce, Abraham, 383, 390; Abram, 385; Alex., 81; Alexr., 112, 115; Christian, 169; Hen., 62; James,

18; Mary, 101; Nicholas, 383; Richd., 270; Robt., 43; Sanders, 355; Thom., 76; Walter, 266, 383, 385, 390; Wm., 59; land of, 357
Brue, Alexr., 13
Bruch, John, 215
Bruer, line of, 376
Bruerton, Jno., 193
Bruester, Rich., 215
Brulfe, Tho., 282
Brumfeild, Mr., 355, 377, 397; Tho., 37, 123
Brumfield, Hannah, 275
Brumidge, Eliz., 34
Brumley, Isaak, 13
Brumly, Isaac, 2; Isaak, 6; Isack, 5
Brumwell, Wm., 90
Brundell, Jno., 111
Brunridge, Eliz., 34
Bruse, Ann, 152; Arthur, 152; Sanders, 211; Will., 74; Wm., 398
Brush, Harbert, 115; Jno., 193; Robt., 78; Tho., 170; Thomas, 320; Wm., 18
Brussells, Mary, 93
Bruster, Ann, 75; Jno., 149; Rich., 92, 205; Richd., 150
Bruton, James, 325; Jno., 17; John, 34, 46, 84
Brutons, Hen., 73
Bry, Hen., 160
Bryan, Cha., 170; Charles, 89, 111, 129; Ed., 35; Geo., 165; James, 256, 309, 336; John, 216, 231, 387, 389; Jon., 265; Mary, 192, 306, 322; Morgan, 114, 230; Mr., 371; Robert, 110, 373; Robt., 14, 149, 192, 380; Roger, 301; Tho., 76; Wm., 157
Bryand, John, 382
Bryant, Anne, 295; Arth., 260; Arthur, 298; Eliz., 138; Fran., 189; Henry, 88; James, 48, 329; Jno., 75; John, 113, 157; Jone, 318; Mary, 243; Nora, 227; Robert, 397; Will., 16; Wm., 22
Bryar, George, 22
Bryce, Wm., 27
Bryden, Mary, 28
Brydon, Jno., 90
Bryer, Geo., 46; Giles, 149
Bryerley, Robt., 192
Brynn, Robert, 110; Willm., 61; Wm., 61
Bryon, Robt., 58
Bryor, John, 237
Buberry, Jno., 376
Buble, John, 367

Burfeild, ——, 127
Burford, Jno., 155; William, 223; Wm., 38; corner of, 206, 316
Burgaine, Hen., 191
Burgained, Jno., 134
Burgalle, Joell, 136
Burgamed, Jno., 134
Burge, Geo., 228; George, 262, 339, 381
Burgen, Henry, 374
Burger, Tho., 161
Burges, Jno., 147; Mary, 42; Mr., 203; Robt., 146, 208
Burgess, Francis, 11; Jno., 307, Robert, 312, 326; Robt., 136
Burgesse, Ann, 78; Richd., 270; Robert, 11; Robt., 173
Burgeste, Robt., 173
Burgh, George, 201; Wm., 54, 210
Burgis, Jno., 70; Samll., 191; Tho., 62
Burgiss, Amos, 194
Burhle, Wm., 124
Buriall, Edmond, 355; Edmund, 245
Burk, Cicely, 155; John, 301; Mary, 155; Wm., 170
Burke, Jno., 95; Phillip, 114; Richard, 179; Rickett, 68
Burkeley, Eliz., 76
Burket, Nich., 84
Burketan, James, 66
Burkett, Henery, 116; Jno., 84; Mary, 372
Burkins, Luke, 372
Burkitt, Wm., 219
Burkley, Robert, 359
Burks, Mary, 314; Wm., 166
Burkum, Roger, 24
Burlace, Nic., 139; Nich., 94
Burland, Nich., 94
Burley, Jno., 335; Wm., 371
Burlington, Mary, 184, 227; Simon, 342
Burlinton, An., 219
Burlison, Ann, 219
Burly, Robert, 80; William, 180
Burn, Edward, 343
Burnall, Francis, 269
Burne, Owen, 366; Randall, 102
Burnell, Elizabeth, 81; Francis, 27, 87, 357; Jno., 142; John, 280; Mr., 44, 170, 200, 240, 387; land of, 256
Burnet, Robert, 151
Burnett, Eliz., 60, 74, 151; Jno., 82, 152, 155, 163; Tho., 127, 189; Wm., 222
Burnett's land, 151
Burney, Mary, 275
Burnham, Fra., 374; Fran., 382;

George, 366; Jno., 130; John, 155; Major, 175; Mary, 374, 382; Mr., 292
Burnt Reeds, 352
Burnum, Jno., 92
Burny, Willi., 183
Buroughs, Robt., 171; Wm., 134
Burow, Lewis, 282
Burr, Ed., 35; Rivers, 92, 130; Wm., 35
Burrage, Jac., 91; John, 134
Burras, Nich., 148
Burrell, Anne, 310; Elinor, 135; James, 312; Mr., 259, 387; Robt., 228
Burridge, Tho., 132
Burris, Katherine, 237
Burroug, Benony, 99
Burrough, Christopher, 99; Enock, 103
Burroughs, Benoni, 327; Benony, 383; Tho., 92; Xpher., 327
Burrow, Modling, 131
Burrowes, Bennony, 272; Wm., 44
Burrows, a Negro, 242, 282; Benony, 83; Jona., 374; Wm., 296
Burrs, Robt., 75
Burrus, John, 329
Burry, Geo., 297
Burson, Ana., 62; Edwd., 142
Burst, Wm., 105
Burston, Cha., 121; Xpher., 276
Burt, Jone, 9; Nicholas, 25
Burtchild, Robert, 402
Burte, Ri., 50
Burthenhod, Nath., 101
Burthwell, Jno., 48
Burtock, An., 171
Burton, a Negro, 255; Andrew, 367; Ben., 57; Eliz., 67; Ellen, 50, 257; Isabell, 145; James, 84; Jno., 47, 138, 193, 362; John, 81, 117, 123, 246-247, 263, 308, 311; Margarett, 48; Mr., 319, 326; Nic., 85; Percivall, 76; Ralph, 248, 371; Rich., 47; Robert, 240, 306, 363; Samll., 14; Tho., 35, 98, 139, 251, 395; Thomas, 210, 267; William, 227; Wm., 58, 155, 233; ——, 201
Burts, Ralph, 49, 104
Burtt, Jno., 34
Burwell, Eliz., 13; Fra., 310; Lewis, 43, 215, 261, 263, 275, 373, 396; Lucy, 261; Maj., 397; Mr., 12, 49, 354
Burwicke, Abrm., 129
Busbie, Capt., 228; Mr., 264, 385; Tho., 351
Busby, Corn., 236; Jno., 52, 89, 149; John, 180; Mary, 324; Robt., 69;

C

Roger, 5, 19, 47; Samll., 73, 157, 257; Samuell, 183; Sar., 144, 197; Sarax, 165; Sarah, 23, 125, 165, 306, 318; Terry, 287; Tho., 24, 210, 376; Thomas, 294; Timo., 186; Timothy, 383; Tym., 95; Tymothey, 276; Tymothy, 254, 257, 262, 264; William, 195; Wm., 19, 41, 134, 143, 196, 379; Xpher., 325; land of, 185, 235, 300. 302
Cartright, Tho., 131
Cartwright, Fra., 35; John, 289; Peter, 309, 379, 390; Tho., 347
Carty, Ellinor, 364; Hugh, 256
Carusey, Jno., 94
Carusue, Jno., 139
Caruthers, Jno., 359, 362; John, 242
Carvell, Cornelius, 226
Carver, Benja., 358; Capt., 233; Eliz., 131; Jno., 86, 201, 348; John, 192, 288; Jon., 196; Mary, 86; Phebe, 130; Richard, 253, 347; Rose, 131; Samll., 196; Samuell, 183; Tho., 69; William, 237, 253; Wm., 101, 131, 169, 337; quarter of, 236
Carvett, Mary, 169
Carway, Jennett, 233
Carwright, Tho., 155
Cary, Alice, 387; Andrew, 243; Ann, 247; Edwd., 348; Eliz., 30; Fran., 92; Hen., 247; Henry, 220; Ja., 161; Joane, 24; John, 68; Jon., 237; M., 392; Miles, 2, 9, 63, 84, 100, 220, 247, 332, 368, 373, 383; Myles, 9, 11; Oswald, 310; Richd., 161; Robt., 60; Sarah, 387; Tarloe, 236; Tho., 14, 165, 307, 311, 336; Thomas, 247; Wm., 93, 383
Caryl, Ben., 271; Eliz., 271; Hen., 271
Case, Jane, 184; Robert, 359; Robt., 347; Wm., 148
Casell, Wm., 341
Caser, 170
Casleton, Robt., 316
Cason, Abra., 191; James, 295
Cassell, Edward, 372; Jane, 310; John, 368; Pat., 188
Cassick, Jon., 257, 259
Cassinett, Jno., 84
Castell, Hen., 89, 149
Castellin, Jno., 106
Caster, Adam, 287; Jno., 164; John, 249
Castle, Henry, 388; Robt., 245; Tho., 9, 165
Castloe, Cormuch, 275
Castor, Samll., 259
Caswell, Mary, 339; Matthew, 234

Catach, Jane, 239; Richd., 239
Catalina, a Negro, 214
Catch, Ja., 216
Cate, 397, 402; an Indian, 131; a Negro, 175, 355, 362, 387, 400
Cater, Francis, 303; Jeremiah, 307
Caterch, Jno., 191
Caters, Col., 194
Catesby, Edwyn, 86; Jane, 268
Catford, Jonathan, 29; Walter, 40
Catherwood, Tho., 148
Cathom, James, 224
Cathome, James, 223, 224
Cathon, James, 280
Catle, Robt., 191
Catlet, Ellinor, 325
Catlett, Jno., 2, 4, 5, 19, 25; John, 20, 380, 397; Nich., 101
Catling, John, 389
Catlock, Jno., 209
Catt, John, 377
Cattailes, the, 170, 269
Cattaile br. forke, 203
Cattle, Ja., 122
Cattlett, Col., 75; Jno., 43; John, 372, 386; Niccolas, 157; Nicholas, 82, 116
Catton, Wm., 225
Cattrickle, Jno., 191
Catwell, Francis, 1
Caudle, Augustine, 253
Caufeild, Robert, 237
Causey, Tho., 54
Causins, Stephen, 183
Causon, Wm., 27
Cautancean, Jacob, 4; John, 4; Wm., 4
Cauthorn, Aurelia, 153; Richard, 153
Cauthorne, Ann, 153
Cave, David, 68; John, 26; Tho., 342
Cavenah, Arthur, 402
Caves, Rebecka, 320
Cavine, Detman, 162
Cawdle, James, 369
Cawdwell, John, 129
Cawfeild, Francis, 21; Mr., 288
Cawfield, Ben., 68
Cawsey, Wm., 27
Cecill, a Negro, 355, 395
Ceely, Rich., 6, 123; Thomas, 3
Celebrand, Darke, 260
Celie, Tho., 140
Cell, Mary, 60
Cellby, Fra., 189
Cely, Tho., 128; Tobyas, 93
Cencer, Mary, 50
Cennett, Edw., 40
Cerly, Jno., 9

Clarket, Leo, 276, 330
Clarketon, Jno., 69
Clarkson, Oliver, 111
Clason, Alice, 106
Classe, Tho., 191
Clatan, Mary, 55
Clatchey, David, 239
Clator, Mercy, 65
Clatworthy, Walter, 385, 393
Claughton, James, 67, 82, 101;
   Nich., 100
Clause, Peter, 262
Clavator, Wm., 150
Clave, Pet., 198
Clavell, Wm., 109, 149
Claw, James, 74, 265; William, 29
Clawson, Andrew, 61; James, 90
Clawton, James, 90
Clay, a Negro, 377; Cha., 191;
   Charles, 235; Fra., 53; Francis, 4,
   20; Hen., 97; Ja., 362; Jane, 268;
   Jno., 12, 61, 375; John, 392; Rich.,
   149; Richd., 153; Symon, 193;
   Wm., 80
Clayborne, Capt., 38; Coll., 3, 256;
   Elizabeth, 52; Jno., 62; Leonard,
   27, 92; Mr., 32; Tho., 42; Thomas,
   279, 386; William, 218, 236, 265,
   316; Wm., 6, 27, 46, 51, 62, 70,
   132, 184, 254, 309
Claybourn, Thomas, 354; William, 398
Claybourne, Thomas, 322; Wm., 325,
   353
Clayden, Hum., 222
Claydon, Elliner, 277; Joane, 31, 47
Clayton, Andrew, 142; Charles, 369;
   Eliz., 47; Eliza., 393; Geo., 392;
   John, 388; Katherine, 240; Mary,
   348; Roger, 13, 14; Samll., 245;
   Samuell, 294, 316; Tho., 378;
   Thomas, 280, 283; Wm., 378; land
   of, 254
Cleare, Ambros, 78; Jno., 168
Clearke, Henry, 134
Clease, Catherine, 391
Cleaton, Jer., 164; Jeremia, 42
Cleavely, Fra., 335
Cleavers, William, 147; Wm., 156
Clecke, Elizab., 120
Cleed, Tho., 164
Cleer, Jno., 167
Cleere, Tho., 146
Cleft, William, 181
Clefton, Rich., 204; Wm., 164
Clegg, Hen., 370
Clelos, Wm., 366
Clem, a Negro, 255
Clemance, Jno., 170

Clemens, Br., 216; Jno., 13; John, 278
Clement, Edwd., 227; John, 288;
   Sara, 92
Clements, Ann, 263; Benja., 369;
   Benjamin, 263; Fra., 351; Francis,
   332; Jeremy, 122; John, 225, 316,
   322; Mary, 255; Robert, 246, 268;
   Robt., 214; Samll., 219; Tho., 189;
   Willm., 99; Wm., 158
Clemonds, Robt., 14
Clemons, Jno., 16
Clench, Hen., 347
Clengsen, Jno., 136
Clent, Wm., 184
Clerk, Ann, 258; James, 235; Jo., 164;
   Jon., 251; Margart., 258; Sarah,
   395; Xpher., 242
Clerke, Cha., 233; Curby, 139; Elizab.,
   120; Henry, 155; Jno., 155, 165,
   171, 177; Joane, 155; John, 372;
   Judith, 39; Richd., 165; Samll.,
   147; Wm., 244, 255
Cleveat, Wm., 155
Cleveland, Francis, 387
Cleverdon, Jane, 127
Cleverly, Xpofer., 87
Cleverous, John Sigismund, 303
Cleyborne, William, 179
Cleybourne, Leonard, 111; Wm., 108
Cleymond, Darby, 74; Penelope, 74
Cliaverley, Constant, 106
Cliffe, Nicho., 277; Thomas, 137
Clifford, Ann, 154; James, 68; Mary,
   326; Ralfe, 146; Ralph, 73, 111;
   Robert, 268
Clifthell, Sarah, 321
Clifton, Eliz., 343; Eliza., 359; Fra.,
   90; Ja., 194; James, 180; Robt.,
   90; Tho., 156; Thomas, 108; Wil-
   liam, 359; Wm., 189
Clinch, Jonas, 191
Clinker, Ma., 261; Tho., 77
Clodpate, a Negro, 387
Cloid, Robt., 222
Clood, Tho., 164
Clopton, Wm., 139, 143
Closby, Sar., 354
Closh, a Negro, 255
Clotworthy, Walter, 316
Cloud, Jno., 203; Mackono, 386;
   Mary, 43
Clough, George, 371
Cloutsom, Thomas, 380
Clowes, Martha, 23
Club, Wm., 312
Clubb, Antho., 184
Clunis, Abraham, 401
Clutchley, David, 336

295; Martyn, 67; Mary, 55, 93; Math., 21; Mathew, 16; Phill., 257; Ralph, 138, 159; Rebec., 66; Richd., 145; Robt., 188; Sarah, 271; Silas, 298; Tho., 62, 110, 139, 252; Thomas, 112, 377; Will., 178; William, 177, 270, 274, 291, 365; Wm., 250, 255, 281
Colebeck, Tho., 35
Colebrook, Samll., 37
Coleburn, James, 386
Coleburne, Wm., 115
Coleby, Andrew, 373
Coleham, Samll., 307
Coleman, Daniel, 320; Ja., 126; Jno., 170; John, 320, 369; Joseph, 353; Mary, 201; Mr., 161, 264, 278, 280, 374; Ric., 138; Rich., 26; Richard, 22, 67, 199; Richd., 69, 198; Robert, 49, 208, 211, 238, 278, 400; Robt., 10, 12, 37, 46, 72, 82, 87, 124, 160, 161, 164; Steph., 226; Stephen, 235; Tho., 9, 66; Willm., 67; Wm., 67, 103, 395; ———, 9; corner of, 297; cor. tree of, 179; land of, 7, 18
Coleman's field, 18
Coles, Edward, 51, 195; Fra., 382; Robt., 306
Coleson, head of, 140
Coleston, Jno., 66
Colesy, Eliz., 12
Colfelt, Bridgett, 239
Colgrane, Peter, 53
Colgrave, Peter, 53, 232
Colket, Cha., 258
Coll, Jno., 48
Collah, John, 321
Collaine, James, 384; Teague, 361; William, 361, 381, 382
Collavine, Wm., 103
Collawn, Wm., 93
Colle, Jno., 195; Robt., 150; Tho., 18
Colledge, Jno., 352; John, 384; Ruth, 109
Collen, An., 247; Ellenor, 114; Mary, 226
Collender, Timo., 352
Colleny, Edmd., 382
Collerell, John, 382
Colles, Jno., 251; John, 31, 260, 371; Robt., 373; Sarah, 27; Tho., 27, 215; Thomas, 21, 26, 27
Collet, John, 77; Robert, 24
Collett, Fra., 82; Henry, 13, 65; Jno., 79; John, 122
Collhart, Wil., 158
Collier, Eliz., 40; Hannah, 318; Isaac,

268; Isab., 395; Isabell, 382, 388; Issabell, 121; James, 287; Jno., 191, 192; John, 369; Mr., 278, 322; Robert, 42; Simon, 217, 309; Tho., 115, 233; William, 193; Wm., 107
Colliford, Charles, 395
Colling, Anne, 307; Avis, 307; Jno., 331; Tho., 142
Collingford, Cha., 382
Collings, Anne, 323; Avis, 323; Eliz., 123; Eliza., 346; James, 383; Jane, 24; John, 360; William, 257, 366
Collingwood, Robert, 74, 79
Collins, Amy, 90; Anne, 30, 326; Avis, 326; Edward, 395; Fra., 287; Giles, 14, 168, 178, 390; Grace, 371; Hen., 354; James, 11, 61, 95, 209, 329, 352; Jno., 5, 8, 12, 19, 40, 57, 116, 136, 209, 218, 341, 353; John, 47, 121, 276, 277, 290, 299; Jon., 265; Math., 151; Mathew, 94, 387; Michael, 356; Mr., 243, 387; Rich., 97; Richard, 124, 384; Richd., 153, 247; Robt., 85; Susan, 79; Tho., 32, 39, 67, 107, 125, 163, 193, 341, 354; Thomas, 69, 72, 312, 395; Timothy, 112; Walter, 271; William, 210, 221, 269, 270, 372, 386, 387, 389; Wm., 48, 141, 183, 187, 204, 221, 327, 329, 366
Collinworth, Tho., 397
Collis, James, 31; Jno., 60; John, 113, 190; Nich., 84; Robert, 338, 369, 370, 394; Robt., 188; Ursula, 318
Collison, Ja., 122, 343; Jno., 103
Collit, Rich., 203
Collomb, Mary. 160
Colls, Robt., 103
Colly, Tho., 90
Collyer, Isaac, 310
Colman, Rich., 74; Richard, 79, 81
Colona, Owen, 106
Colonan, Ogen., 106
Colson, Isaack, 320; Mary, 311; [Mr.], 378; line of, 208
Colston, Jno., 212; Wm., 396
Colstreame, James, 26
Colt, Eliza., 23; Jno., 61; Susan, 257; Wm., 90
Colte, Jno., 397
Colthorp, Charles, 371; James, 371
Colticoate, Mr., 188
Coltis, Elizabeth, 382
Coltman, Wm., 309
Colton, Mary, 112
Coltrop, Cha., 188; Hen., 188
Coltwit, Wm., 196
Colvert, Robert, 311; Wm., 311

157, 166, 176, 189, 191, 203, 270, 318, 355; Thomas, 182, 234, 245, 339; William, 185, 272; Wm., 82, 107, 129, 177, 184, 303, 354
Coops, Jno., 5
Coote, Nicho., 31
Cootes, Jno., 375
Coozens, Thomas, 288
Cope, Henry, 399; Robt., 274; Tho., 233
Copeland, Christopher, 376; Eliza., 281; Frances, 336; Henery, 230; Henry, 376; John, 113, 383, 385, 388, 390; Jon., 274; Joseph, 342; Mar., 67; Nicho., 355; Nicholas, 155, 343; Richard, 392; William, 376; Willm., 85; Wm., 70, 155, 370; Xper., 157
Copeley, Hen., 268
Copeman, Jno., 48; Wm., 17, 36, 47
Coper, Jno., 226
Cophace, a Negro, 235
Copheld, Wm., 239
Cophell, Gresham, 301, 302, 314; Wm., 239, 384
Copin, Abra., 190, 195
Coplestone, Jno., 115
Coplin, Hen., 258
Copney, Wm., 360
Coppage, Wm., 2, 19
Copper, Charles, 320
Coppin, James, 232, 285; William, 167
Copping, Tho., 254
Copres, Jno., 145
Copse, John, 113
Copton, Joseph, 90
Coran, James, 342
Corbel, Gabriell, 254
Corbell, Agnes, 254; Clemt., 254; Henry, 91; Thomas, 283
Corben, Nic., 92
Corbett, Ja., 216; Jno., 286; John, 274, 275, 381; Rice, 138; Saml., 2; Tho., 86; Tobias, 337
Corbill, Hen., 15
Corbin, Anth., 355; Ed., 198; Esqr., 374; Henry, 21, 33; Price, 355; Rich., 17, 22; Richard, 16
Corbit, Jno., 206; the Widow, 361
Corbitt, Anne, 298; Garnett, 300
Corbutt, Helie, 164; Wm., 206
Corby, Andrew, 348
Corbyn, Col., 105; Hen., 123, 128; Henry, 26, 32, 55, 64, 73, 98, 109, 155, 212, 329, 395; John, 250; Xpher., 241
Cord, Rich., 14; Richard, 13
Cordell, Richd., 363

Cordenbracke, Edwd., 147
Cordenbrook, Mr., 208
Corderoy, Barbara, 92; Edward, 21, 360; Jno., 360; William, 360
Corderoye, Wm., 41
Cordewell, Tho., 150
Cordin, Robt., 204
Cordridge, Cath., 299; Wm., 168
Cordwell, Jno., 96; John, 229; Tho., 149, 152; Thomas, 185, 226, 237
Core, Mary, 4; Rich., 54
Corey, Deborah, 141; John, 141
Corker, Ann, 68; Capt., 55, 277, 278, 290, 299, 336; John, 69, 267; Luce, 277; Mr., 125, 286; Wm., 69, 95
Corkerill, Jno., 343
Corkers, Capt., 13
Corle, a Negro, 245
Corlee, James, 351
Corlew, John, 236
Corley, Rich., 170
Corlie, Mr., 300, 340
Corlile, Sym., 125
Corman, Nicho., 299
Cornall, Margarett, 171
Corne, Jno., 103; Wm., 245
Cornehill, Peter, 47
Cornelius, a Negro, 248; Charles, 168; Jon., 269; Noah, 135; Nora, 129; Rachael, 233; Rachel, 272, 347
Cornell, Dennis, 389; Eliz., 171; Marth., 101
Cornick, Edw., 156
Cornicks, Wm., 168
Cornish, Antho., 340; Joseph, 73; Thomas, 395; Wm., 100, 101
Cornith, Edward, 147; Edwd., 155
Cornix, Jone, 295; Martha, 295; Mr., 330, 356; Symon, 126; Tho., 295; William, 98, 234, 367; Wm., 126, 295; land of, 214, 248
Cornwall, Gilbert, 359; Jno., 207; Nich., 86
Cornway, Jennet, 102
Cornwell, Gilbert, 236; Peter, 35
Corperhew, Jno., 172
Corperue, John, 234, 371; land of, 352
Corpes, Georg., 222; George, 260
Corporew, John, 57
Corporice, John, 306
Corporoe, Jno., 379; John, 375
Corporue, Jno., 321; John, 385
Corporyon, John, 129
Corprew, John, 129
Corps, George, 257
Correll, Thomas, 270
Corroff, James, 60
Corross, James, 60

359, 369, 371, 372, 373, 376, 379, 383, 384, 394, 396, 401
County line, the, 216, 221, 232, 257
Courser, Samll., 365
Court, Ed., 298; Edwd., 261, 298; James, 10; Jno., 220; John Paybridg, 182; Joseph, 13; William, 179
Courte, Wm., 90
Courteney, John, 320
Courthouse, 75, 117, 320
Courtin, Phillip, 81
Courtine, Phillip, 81
Courtman, Georg., 179
Courtmell, George, 100; Phebe, 100
Courtney, Geo., 36; Hugh, 94, 140; Miles, 115; Peter, 307; Wm., 307
Courts, William, 200
Coury, Franc., 111; Hannah, 124
Couse, Clause, 40
Cousens, Mr., 369
Cousins, Stephen, 183
Cove, Oyster, 214
Covell, Savell, 321
Coventon, William, 86; Wm., 254
Coventry, Jane, 46
Covill, James, 330
Covington, Arthur, 269; William, 262; Wm., 85, 240
Cowan, Edwd., 207; Patrick, 207
Coward, Jane, 106; Peter, 401; Richd., 106; Tho., 172
Cowboy, a Negro, 255
Cowcombe, Will, 50
Cowden, Dorothy, 99
Cowdrip, Ann, 159; Eliza., 159
Cowdry, Thomas, 371; Wm., 248
Cowed, Edwd., 321
Cowell, Eliz., 14
Cowen Gock, 261
Cowes, Hanna, 175
Cowler, Thomas, 239
Cowles, Edmd., 3; Edmond, 103; Mr., 280, 300, 377
Cowling, Tho., 49, 130; Thomas, 301
Cowpen, Wm., 324
Cowpens, 123, 124
Cowse, Clause, 239
Cowthorne, Ann, 143
Cowting, Thomas, 151
Cox, Benja., 378; Cha., 160; Charles, 68; Dennis, 240; Edwd., 30; Eliz., 341; Fra., 85; Fran., 31; Geo., 226; Gilb., 191; Hen., 206, 327; Henery, 153; James, 299; Jane, 220, 321; Jno., 12, 15, 146, 184, 329; John, 117, 120, 319, 341; Jos., 247; Joseph, 22, 277, 281; Mary, 153, 175; Mr., 166; Nich., 52, 89, 92,

166; Nicholas, 165, 328; Nickolas, 166; Phillip, 257; Ralph, 151; Richard, 86, 101; Richd., 155, 156; Samll., 49, 121, 133; Sus., 158; Tho., 8, 27, 50, 128, 160, 197, 219, 262; Thomas, 327; Timo., 198; Vincent, 20; Wm., 67, 146, 165, 166, 206, 227, 231; land of, 279
Coxe, Richard, 3
Coxendale, 44, 289, 373
Coxon, Cha., 191
Coxson, Geo., 203
Coy, Jane, 14
Coyt, Wm., 273
Crab, Fra., 170
Crabb, Francis, 316; Hen., 346; Jno., 170; John, 112, 316; Osman, 172; Sarah, 346; Tho., 159
Crabtree, Jno., 196; Samll., 30
Cracherly, Jno., 118, 126
Crackrell, Ellinor, 147
Craddock, Jane, 391; Jno., 189; Martin, 219; Tho., 176; Wm., 85
Cradock, Eliz., 319; Jno., 96; Jon., 248; Mrs., 319; Robert, 117
Crafford, Anthony, 85; Capt., 343; David, 25, 170, 171, 231, 244, 253, 286, 293, 294, 306, 312, 348; Wm., 200, 327
Crafft, Bridgett, 143
Craford, David, 111, 112; George, 321; Tho., 191; Tobias, 53
Craforth, Tho., 374
Crafton, Alexr., 115; Michael, 377; Michaell, 24, 140; Tho., 110
Crafts, Gilb., 191
Crage, Terlock, 98
Cragoe, Ja., 146
Crainby, Roger, 112
Craine, Francis, 77, 132, 195; Jno., 93; Wm., 201
Crains Ehancing, 221
Crak, Ellen, 396
Crame, Jno., 93
Cramer, Eliz., 129
Cramp, Jno., 369; Richd., 247
Crampton, Arthur, 151
Cranage, Ed., 269
Crandell, Ann, 376; Tho., 179
Crane, Francis, 203, 333; Jno., 106, 326; Kate, 326; Rich., 74, 226; Robt., 16, 337; Samuell, 284; Thomas, 284; Wm., 109, 149
Cranes, Jno., 85; land of, 235
Cranidge, Will., 149
Crank, Alice, 122
Cranny, Porter, 308
Crasby, Josua., 85

Crisp, Anthony, 363; Edmd., 195; Mary, 247
Crispe, Tho., 23
Crispin, Eliz., 175
Crissell, Edw., 74
Critchell, Jno., 217
Critchett, Jno., 50
Criton, Jno., 152
Crittendon, Richd., 148
Croach, Geo., 61; Wm., 79
Croashow, Joseph, 306
Crock, John, 26; Wm., 217
Crocker, Eliza., 346; James, 11
Crocky, a Negro, 387
Croco, 387
Croe, Robert, 345
Croft, Bridget, 359; Mary, 240; Symon, 19
Croftes, Jno., 139
Crofts, James, 64; Wm., 18
Croila, a Negro, 244
Croiton, Jno., 10
Croker, Geo., 167
Cromey, Tho., 272
Cromp, William, 391
Crompton, Jno., 14; Thos., 134
Cromwell, 320
Cromwell, a Negro, 282, 395
Cromwell, Cock, 297; Jno., 58; Mary, 230; Oliver, 400
Croney, Jno., 127
Cronley, Wm., 103
Crook, Richd., 297; Solomon, 345
Crooke, Hugh, 128; Solomon, 374
Croome, Edw., 10
Croomer, Eliz., 242
Croop, Walter, 39
Crop, Edward, 40; Tho., 269
Croper, Robt., 369
Crosdell, Ann, 222
Crosfield, Joseph, 24
Croshaw, Joseph, 44, 54, 75, 145, 227, 324, 394; Major, 74; Richard, 360
Croshawe, Joseph, 342
Crosland, Geo., 270; Jno., 198; Luce, 35
Cross, Ann, 225; Jono., 346; Jon., 181; Robt., 115; Sarah, 346; Tho., 5; Winifred, 132; Wm., 5
Cross Cr. bottome, 293
Cross Swamp Pattent, 258
Crosse, a Negro, 324
Crosse, Amy, 139; Bar., 269; Catherine, 123; Cha., 164; Charles, 108; Ja., 184; James, 256; Jno., 173; Jone, 112; Mary, 41, 172; Nath., 151; Peter, 220; Tho., 22; Wm., 52, 92

Crosse Sw. Pattent, 221
Crossland, Jonas, 184
Crosson, Fra., 233; Francis, 227
Crossr, Bridgett, 143
Crostell, Tho., 191
Crostie, Wm., 159
Croston, Jno., 10
Crouch, Ann, 146, 148; Anne, 73; Eliz., 62; Josiah, 283; Wm., 177, 283, 343
Crouche, land of, 187
Crouthers, Hen., 364
Crow, Andrew, 326; Elizabeth, 355; James, 313; Julyan, 33; Peter, 96; Richd., 345; Tho., 138, 203, 332; Thomas, 200
Crowch, Ann, 159
Crowcher, Jno., 94
Crowder, Eliz., 143; Eliza., 359; Henry, 323; Jno., 206; Robt., 35; Wm., 134
Crowe, Tho., 167
Crowg, Jno., 127
Crowther, Henry, 208; Sarah, 356
Crox, Math., 193
Croxcroft, corner of, 203
Croxon, Alice, 275
Croy, Winifred, 132
Crueden, John, 110
Crues, Tho., 39
Crumbe, Wm., 45
Crump, Edwd., 247; Elizabeth, 76; Ellen, 139; Geo., 187; Henry, 397; Jno., 369, 378; John, 76; Stephen, 223; William, 223, 306, 364; Wm., 61
Crumpe, Jno., 252
Crumpton, Arthur, 151; Robt., 136
Crumshare, Ann, 382
Crundell, Ann, 376
Crusty, Mary, 254
Cuba, a Negro, 365
Cubb, Jane, 50; Tho., 67
Cubbige, Jno., 185
Cube, Bab., 33; Frank, 33
Cuddy, Eliz., 91; Jno., 306
Cudrin, Grace, 126
Cuenin, Grace, 126; Uriah, 126
Cuff, Tho., 138; Thom., 354
Cuffy, a Negro, 391
Cugley, Daniell, 116
Cullam, Ann, 111
Cullen, Tho., 55, 61, 159; Thomas, 55
Culliford, Robt., 23
Cullin, Jno., 142; Tho., 142
Culling, Math., 184; Culling, Matt., 227
Cullis, Jno., 60

164, 193, 201, 250, 287; corner of, 288; land of, 247, 340

Davise, Wm., 189

Davison, Alexander, 260, 262, 392; Cha., 115; Charles, 13, 81; James, 104, 233; Jane, 102, 204, 233; Jennet, 112; Jone, 204; Math., 359; Robt., 174; Wm., 114

Davoratt, Jno., 40

Davy, 366, 398; Jno., 10; Richard, 233; Tho., 120; Welch, 305

Davyd, George, 78

Davyes, Geo., 32

Davyis, Jno., 64

Davys, Dorothy, 96; Edwd., 55; Elizabeth, 38; Evan, 100; Hen., 77, 79; Jane, 72; Kath., 30; Lewis, 97; Moses, 72; Rich., 82, 99; Rose, 28; Rowland, 91; Tho., 34; Wm., 88

Daw, Barth., 40; Geo., 243; William, 375

Dawber, Edmund, 300; Edward, 249

Dawby, Jno., 175; Wm., 123

Dawes, Ann, 260; John, 298; Jon., 262

Dawfeild, Mary, 34

Dawham, Tho., 191

Dawker, Wm., 89

Dawkes, Jno., 98; Peter, 177

Dawkiins, Thomas, 192

Dawkins, Anne, 220; Ed., 297; Tho., 32, 118, 133, 174, 204, 219; Thomas, 201, 220

Dawling, Teague, 228

Dawloop, Rich., 126; Richard, 118

Dawly, Jno., 175

Daws, Ja., 208; Jno., 208

Dawsey, James, 107

Dawson, Fra., 64; Geo., 1, 35, 138; Gilbert, 193; Hen., 251; Jno., 65, 85, 191, 343, 374; John, 389; Robt., 107; Samuell, 310; William, 116; Wm., 27, 143, 232, 237

Day, Alexdr., 229; Edmond, 370; Eli., 19; Eliza., 145, 373; Elizab., 113; Ellinor, 2; Geo., 104, 222, 307; James, 56, 95, 217, 284; Jane, 35; Jno., 42, 111, 152, 163, 166; John, 39, 385; Jos., 353; Lewis, 163; Margery, 324; Mary, 79; Rich., 50, 67; Robt., 154, 181; Tho., 355; Thomas, 181, 381; Ursala, 94; Wm., 85

Dayes, Thomas, 339

Dayly, Bryan, 135

Daymard, Tho., 127

Daynes, Killman, 38

Dayves, Jno., 79

Deacon, Gilbert, 241, 289; Grace, 324;

Tho., 43, 100, 167; Thomas, 80

Deacons, Ed., 29; Edw., 49; Edwd., 104

Dead Man's Stake, 25

Deadge, John, 372

Deadman, Tho., 212

Deadye, John, 372

Deal, line of, 333

Deale, Roger, 205

Deally, Edward, 305

Deame, Tho., 225

Dean, Ann, 247; Jno., 42; John, 251; Math., 395; Michael, 400; Peter, 264; Richd., 270; line of, 383

Deane, Charles, 110; Dorcas, 313; Edward, 367; Hanah, 314; Hen., 245; Jno., 18, 153, 213, 313; John, 7, 100, 345; Peter, 167, 175; Ralph, 180; Tho., 128, 214

Deanes, James, 305

Deaprise, Rich., 101

Deare, Jno., 97

Deareing, Tho., 193

Dearelove, Richd., 134, 144

Dearing, Jno., 79, 135; John, 120

Deason, Ed., 8; Mrs., 232

Deavorack, Van, 12

Deb., 210

Debany, Cornelius, 20, 42

Debar, Jno., 31; John, 241

de Berry, Peter, 276, 313, 331, 386

Debins, Symon, 150

Debnam, John, 201; Wm., 49, 202

Debony, Cornelius, 354

Debora, an Indian, 351, 358

Deborah, 371

Debue, John, 287

Decart, Jno., 75

Deckan, Jno., 127

Deckson, Jano., 123

Decone, Alice, 120

Dedman, James, 111; Mr., 28; Susa., 64

Dee, Margery, 114

Deeds, Julius, 335; Mindart, 283; Tho., 354

Deep Bottome, 125, 252, 294, 378

Deer, Tho., 141

Deere, Ann, 151

Deereing, Osmond, 67

Deering, Jno., 348; Tho., 276

Deerling, Edmd., 144

Deerton, Richd., 146

Deffant, Jno., 190

Defnall, William, 176; land of, 348

Deford, Stephen, 175

Deg, Jno., 309

Degar, Corne., 237

Dernam, Jno., 307
Deronseaux, John, 367
De Rouse, Jno., 42
Derrell, Bridgett, 112; Jno., 85;
John, 137
Derrick, a Negro, 248
Derrick, Hen., 105; James, 75; Law-
rence, 231; Peter, 65, 80; Robt.,
55; Thomas, 194; Wm., 93
Derwood, John, 381
Desermacox, Eliz., 338
Deserson, Zach., 189
Deshasero, Peter, 218
Deston, Tho., 43
Deswell, Stephen, 27
Dethinge, William, 375
Devar, Geo., 256
Devenham, Jno., 123
Devenport, Ann, 122
Dever, Henry, 298
Deverett, Jno., 221
Devil's Woodyard, 269
Devin, Tho., 343
Devorett, Jno., 20
Devy, Jno., 91
Dew, Col., 258; Daniel, 245; Jno.,
100; Jo., 67; Jonath., 90; Tho., 142;
Thomas, 83, 258; Wm., 193
Dewe, Richard, 393; Thomas, 221
Dewell, Phillip, 61
Dewes, Nicho., 251; Tho., 20
Dewick, Eliza., 354
Dewrent, Thomas, 389
Dews, Wm., 388
Dewson, Rowland, 69
Dey, Xtopher., 106
Deynes, Robt., 359
Diammond, Geo., 151
Diamond, Geo., 139; John, 79
Diana, a Negro, 305, 349
Diarfers, Mary, 362
Dibald, Peter, 94
Dibbin, Mary, 252
Dibble, Nath., 61
Dibdell, John, 125
Dible, Hen., 191
Dibna, a Negro, 400
Dica, a Negro, 194
Diccot, Edwd., 156
Dicer, Tho., 175
Dick——, 170, 213, 244, 319, 336,
351, 359, 386, 401
Dick, an Indian, 368
Dick, a Negro, 71, 144, 153, 242, 255,
285, 324, 329, 338, 340, 344, 346,
349, 350, 351, 353, 357, 358, 361,
365, 369, 371, 372, 382, 389, 396
Dick, Jno., 84; John, 111; Steph., 193

Dickason, Ed., 139; Jno., 104
Dicke, Jerm., 150
Dicken, Xper., 156
Dickens, Xtophr., 93
Dickenson, John, 312, 329; Mary, 329;
Tho., 349; Walter, 7
Dickes, Jer., 154
Dickeson, Jeremiah, 163; Jno., 80;
John, 220, 231, 245; Mary, 171;
Rich., 96
Dickins, Christo., plantation of, 195;
Christopher, 190; Christopr., 215;
Danll., 18; Edwd., 242; Mr., line
of, 190, 192; Rachell, 105; Tho.,
20; plantation of, 190
Dickinson, Andr., 399; Edwd., 364;
Griffin, 271; Griffith, 281; John, 262
Dicks, Isaac, 127; Jno., 189; Mary,
339; Rich., 176; Richard, 182;
Richd., 318; Sarah, 284; Tho., 215
Dickson, Joan, 269; John, 242; Nico.,
217; Sus., 206; Tho., 295, 242;
Xper., 156
Didley, Jacob, 152, 155
Dido, 383; a Negro, 399; Sar., 148
Dier, Hen., 382
Digby, Edwd., 55; Eliza., 313; Jon.,
375; Robert, 375; Wm., 191, 193
Diggs, Edward, 53, 102, 227, 307, 341;
Edwd., 188; Esqr., 290; Mary, 154;
Mr., 202-203, 219, 222
Digory, Jno., 9
Dike, Elinor, 129; Ralph, 8, 107
Diligence, a Negro, 113
Dilke, Clemt., 158
Dill, Mary, 76
Dillard, Geo., 341, 372; George, 342,
386
Dilliard, George, 240
Dillin, Tho., 103
Dilling, Peirce, 105
Dillon, Sarah, 396; Tho., 346
Dilsey, a Negro, 241
Dilyard, Jno., 77
Dimer, Nicho., 185
Dimes, Nicho., 185
Dimgoe, a Negro, 116
Dimwell, Mary, 82
Dinah, 397; a Negro, 400
Dines, Roger, 232; Samll., 172
Dinot, Edwd., 156
Dinto, Tho., 136
Dinton, Tho., 119
Dios, Tho., 5
Dircett, Ellin, 307
Direferes, Mary, 359
Dirham, Moses, 123
Disford, Anne, 28

Dunington, Michll., 316
Dunkan, David, 327
Dunken, Peter, 16, 22, 60
Dunkeston, Tho., 219
Dunketon, Thomas, 256, 266
Dunkin, Jane, 257; Jno., 57; Peter, 84
Dunkley, Jno., 30; John, 320
Dunn, And., 145; Andrew, 116;
    Arthur, 338; Grace, 132; Henry,
    376; Jno., 50, 159; John, 129;
    Joseph, 17; Mary, 219; Pasco, 287,
    338, 340; Roger, 192; Thomas, 180;
    Wm., 130
Dunn, 117
Dunnell, Mary, 82
Dunnham, Hen., 259
Dunning, Hen., 57; Mary, 57; Saml.,
    57; Tho., 33
Dunston, Jno., 91; Mr., 151, 220;
    Robt., 132; Samll., 232, 237;
    Samuel, 236
Dunstone, Thomas, 93
Dunton, Tho., 66, 105; Thomas, 117
Dunwell, Mary, 74
Duram, Mary, 55
Durant, George, 78; Henry, 22, 85;
    James, 74, 82, 348
Durden, Jacob, 237; Stephen, 53, 64
Durham, Mary, 144; Sar., 219;
    Wm., 148
During, Mary, 165
Durkin, Annie, 85
Durley, Jno., 39
Durman, Jno., 135
Durrant, Wm., 138
Durrett, Jno., 4
Durring, Jacob, 81
Durwood, John, 42, 218; Richard, 264
Dutch, Susan, 364
Dutch body, a, 129
Dutcheley, Edward, 83
Dutchman, Isaac, 154
Duthkaies, Charles, 72
Duttenfield, Ann, 195
Dutton, Andrew, 219; Anne, 29;
    Saml., 82; Samll., 46; Tho., 16,
    17, 19, 22, 36, 40, 47, 138
Duty, Peter, 399
Dver, Jno., 30
Dyall, Tho., 85
Dyamood, Robt., 85
Dyar, Tho., 371; Thomas, 274
Dyas, Charles, 287; Peter, 101; Tho.,
    79; Thomas, 16, 22, 280
Dybly, Jno., 165
Dye, 103; Elizabeth, 103; John, 127,
    233; Margaret, 103; Martin, 3, 5,
    47; Sarah, 103

Dyell, Agnes, 88
Dyer, Ed., 287; Edwd., 57; Eliz., 134;
    Geo., 36, 47; Grace, 53; James, 331;
    Jno., 185, 190; Jos., 178; Mary, 73;
    Math., 191; Phill., 175; Robert, 235,
    359, 362; Robt., 174, 323; Tho.,
    91, 190; Thomas, 234, 381; Will.,
    178; William, 261, 330; Willm., 85;
    Wm., 70, 73, 156; land of, 367
Dyers, Samll., 7
Dylera, Jane, 162
Dymon, Ann, field of, 97
Dynars, Tho., 164
Dyos, Peter, 120
Dyton, Jane, 381
Dyway, Is., 221

E

Eabank, Wm., 209
Eabury, Edwd., 94
Eadall, Jon., 73
Eagerly, Wm., 86
Eagle, Joane, 178
Eagres, Geo., 109, 149
Eakens, James, 384
Ealeroot Levell, 345
Eamman, James, 114
Eanig, Jno., 176
Eanks, Ellen, 53
Earbrough, Robert, 373
Eare, a Negro, 244
Earle, Jno., 99; Mary, 230; Rich., 71;
    Sarah, 389
Earley, Adam, 349
Eason, Jane, 59; Tristram, 59;
    Wm., 239
East, Henry, 21, 128; Jacob, 21;
    Joane, 4; Miles, 23, 284; Peter, 120;
    Thomas, 223; Will., 133; Wm., 39,
    270, 285
Easter, Abraham, 234
Easterby, Richard, 401
Easterfield, John, 300
Easterly, John, 268
Eastern Ranges, 252
Easterne Ridges, 3 Runns of, 132
Eastern Shore of Va., 108, 243
Eastfeild, Tho., 56
Eastham, 366; Edward, 218, 328
Eastland, Jon., 259
Easton, Tristram, 123; Tristrum, 82
Eastons, Tristam, 353
Eastwood, Richard, 185
Easy, George, 298

Eggerton, Cha., 203; Jeremiah, 334; Jno., 355
Eggleston, Benjamin, 355, 398; Mary, 31
Eglestone, Edwd., 30; Tho., 149; Jo., 166
Eglstone, Hugh, 135
Eire, Danll., 156; Tho., 156
Eitcharbett, William, 37
Ekerbye, William, 362
Ekins, James, 114
Elah, a Negro, 395
Elam, Eliza., 59; Gilbert, 59, 154, 361, 373; James, 363; John, 238; Martha, 59; Martin, 59, 91, 107, 134, 357, 358; Martyn, 382; Mr., 365, 393; Robt., 59; William, 305; Wm., 175
Eland, Adam, 346
Elben, Wm., 114
Elbury, Tho., 205
Elcock, James, 266, 267; John, 297; Mary, 250
Elcom, Wm., 170
Elcomb, William, 354
Elcombe, William, 200
Elcome, William, 387; Wm., 44
Elcones, William, 179
Elcore, William, 387
Elcorne, Wm., 342
Elder, Anne, 335; Ja., 184; Jno., 325, 356; John, 181, 296; Tho., 343; William, 118
Elderkin, John, 378
Eldish, Jno., 126
Eldred, Rach., 138
Eldridge, Hum., 261; Sam., 256; Saml., 50; Sy., 57; Tho., 95, 118, 142
Eldrige, Tho., 178
Eldritt, Za., 189
Eldy, Pers., 216
Eleatherell, Rich., 219
Elerfeild, Lydia, 11
Elestree, Roger, 10
Elett, Jasper, 105
Elfe, James, 332, 339
Elff, Tho., 369
Elford, Martha, 261
Elgar, Tho., 27
Eliot, Thom., 126
Eliott, Jno., 176; Ralph, 160; Sampson, 160; Simon, 93
Elis, Wm., 131
Eliston, Tho., 159
Eliza, 351; a woeman, 146; a Negro, 327, 360
Elizabeth, 274, 356

Elizer, Jona., 269
Elkes, John, 292
Elkin, Jno., 138; Ralph, 138
Elkinson, Jno., 70
Elks, John, 295, 319; land of, 297
Ellam, Tho., 216
Ellen, a Negro, 114; Christian, 153; Christr., 204
Ellerbies, [Mr.], 281
Ellerby, Edward, 258; Eliz., 332; Jno., 336; Thomas, 339; Wm., 330, 339
Ellerly, Cheney, 274; James, 318
Elles, John, 294; Jone, 152
Elleston, Edward, 384
Ellet, Abraham, 386; Ailce, 386; Jasper, 310; Peter, 59-60; Thomas, 397
Ellett, Abrah., 168; Abraham, 129, 169, 265; Fra., 78; Jaspar, 135; Jasper, 86; Jno., 398; Martha, 135; Rich., 84; Roger, 368; Tho., 37; Wm., 304
Ellibris, line of, 256
Ellick, a Negro, 382
Ellin, Jane, 138; John, 37; Wm., 144
Ellinor, an Irish wench, 51
Elliot, Antho., 160; Anthony, 132, 163; Col., 160; Giles, 155; Humphry, 92; Math., 162; Robt., 160, 287, 325, 333; Tho., 163, 164, 227, 361; Wm., 132, 160, 163, 197
Elliott, Abigall, 166; Alice, 138; Anth., 71, 86; Antho., 64; Anthony, 121, 138, 311, 345, 350; Capt., 26; Col., 61; Edward, 11; Henry, 47; Ja., 146; James, 367; Jno., 171, 308, 336, 346; John, 1; Lt. Coll., 54; Mary, 195; Mr., quarter of, 72; Peter, 348; Rich., 85; Robert, 121, 138; Robt., 147; Susan, 57, 128, 216; Tho., 314; William, 121, 274, 302, 317; Wm., 57, 117, 161, 163, 190, 197, 210, 346
Ellis, Adam, 308, 331; Alice, 132; Ann, 124; Christopher, 238; Cornelius, 155, 298, 309, 318; Ed., 271; Edward, 58; Edwd., 56, 204; Fra., 287; Griffin, 155; Hanah, 304; Hen., 111, 354; Henry, 73, 146; Isaac, 209; James, 100, 243; Jane, 332; Jeremy, 298; Jeremiah, 298; Jno., 89, 94, 103, 150, 151, 155, 312, 329, 355; Jo., 178; John, 113, 257, 258, 262, 348; Jone, 348; Margt., 325; Mary, 228; Math., 382; Nic., 103; Nich., 116, 150; Nicholas, 91; Owen, 375; Phill., 116, 145; Ralph, 78; Rich., 90;

Jacob, 159; Robt., 43; Tho., 46
Fowle, Ellenor, 58
Fowler, Antho., 115; Arthur, 111;
Bartho., 365; Beata., 92; David,
293; Edwd., 335; Eliz., 66, 79, 238;
Eliza., 315; Geo., 99, 100, 132, 202;
George, 169, 217; Godfrey, 374;
Jno., 35, 92, 136, 146; John, 23;
Jon., 226, 244, 264; Joseph, 27;
Ma., 204; Mr., 131, 168, 313, 323;
Robt., 11, 33; Roger, 53; Samll.,
315; Samuell, 315; Tho., 103; Wil-
liam, 358; Wm., 33; line of, 357
Fowler's plantation, 327
Fowles, Robert, 85
Fowlet, Ann, 123
Fownding, Ed., 4; Rich., 4
Fownes, Jno., 65
Fox, Capt., 195; David, 20, 31, 36,
195, 370; Fra., 160; Hen., 247;
Hery, 255; James, 268; Jno., 27, 78,
113, 191, 312, 322, 395; John, 44,
54, 111, 116, 146, 255; Jon., 73;
Joseph, 319; Lawrence, 86; Marie,
126; Mihill, 123; Moses, 360; Rich.,
39; Slash, 59; Step., 241; Tho.,
116; Wm., 31, 208
Foxcreep, Wm., 103
Foxcraft, Danl., 68; Danll., 106; Isaac,
158, 245
Foxcroft, Antho., 35; Daniell, 81;
Danll., 35
Foxe, John, 340
Foxell, Fra., 150
Foxhall, Jno., 70, 72; John, 26, 100,
181; Marth., 70; Mary, 70; Rich.,
56; Sara, 70
Foxland, Jno., 107
Foxon, Eliz., 179
Fra., a Negro, 226
Fraime, Diana, 19
Frale, Robt., 118
Frame, Arthur, 124, 141
Frampitt, Tho., 8
Fran., a Frenchlad, 170
Frances, Nath., 58
Francesco, a Turke, 6
Francis, Alice, 182; Capt., 193;
Ezekiel, 21; Ezekiell, 16; Henery,
243; Henry, 171; Ja., 268; Jno., 50,
206; a Negro, 248, 255, 385, Tho.,
173; Robt., 68, 105, 135; Samll.,
5; Sara, 101; Thomas, 289, 387
Francisco, a Negro, 240, 264;
a Turk, 106
Franciscoe, a Negro, 172
Francisoys, Eliz., 88
Franck, 332, 340, 351; a Negro, 115,

318, 382, 387; Robt., 178
Franckland, Robt., 123
Franckleyn, Tho., 191
Francklin, Andrew, 343; Ann, 6;
Edith, 340; Jno., 193; Judeth, 372;
Peter, 2, 6, 13; Tho., 375; Thomas,
367
Francklyn, Jdia., 109; Nicholas, 323
Frane, Marrian, 67
Franey, James, 360
Frank, 286, 336; Eliza., 350; Foster,
58; a Negro, 102, 200, 242, 314,
355, 395; Robt., 258
Franke, Devereli, 35; Eliz., 144;
Han., 197
Frankin, Mary, 356
Franklin, Idia, 268; Jno., 138, 193;
Josias, 67; Lidia, 149; Mary, 138,
268; Peter, 5; Richard, 252; Richd.,
219, 312; Wm., 138, 193
Frankling, James, 323; Jno., 156;
Joane, 158; Margarett, 73
Franklyn, Jno., 39; Symom, 53
Franklynn, Tho., 160
Frank's, 348
Franks, Saml., 67
Franks quarter, 213
Fransham, Jno., 102
Fraviles, Wm., 112
Fravills, William, 137
Frawlin, Ann, 111, 146; Anne, 73
Frayer, Eliz., 113; John, 113
Frazell, Jno., 159
Freake, Mr., 181; Thomas, 24
Freborne, Peter, 48
Free, Eliza., 371; John, 259
Free schoole, land belonging to, 274
Freech, Wm., 85
Freegrave, Jno., 67
Freeke, Wm., 1
Freele, Margt., 152
Freeman, David, 169, 356; George,
267; Hen., 376; Henry, 282; Jno.,
154, 176, 217, 298; John, 176, 234,
262; Jon., 246; Mr., 281, 293;
Nath., 20; Nich. Kirby, 143; Phill.,
242; Phillip, 112, 150; Sarah, 356;
Susan, 93; Tho., 327; Tymothy, 51;
Wm., 92, 130, 144, 148, 157, 231;
land of, 285; line of, 284
Freeme, Jno., 62
Freer, Bridget, 345
Frees, Wm., 29
Freeze, Benock, 158; Jno., 158
Fregott, Rich., 124
Freind, Jno., 107
Freland, Robt., 170
Freman, Ed., 21; Rich., 67

G

Gaant, Tho., 132
Gable, Edward, 9
Gabree, Jno., 135
Gaffer, Jno., 32
Gage, a Negro, 318
Gage, Henry, 157; John, 49; Mary, 2, 4, 6, 70, 167; Wm., 271
Gagecome, Thomas, 25
Gahan, Hugh, 258
Gaile, Jno., 159; Step., 156
Gailer, Wm., 145
Gaimes, Robert, 330
Gaineford, Jno., 92
Gainerell. James, 137
Gaines, Danill, 74; Danll., 35, 167; James, 2, 46; Jno., 94; Richd., 345; Robt., 139; Tho., 74; Thomas, 14, 229, 283, 291, 293, 401
Galard, Ja., 324
Galattby, Ben., 30
Gale, Eliz., 144, 197; Hugh, 281; James, 323; Jno., 138; John, 2; Margt., 197; Mary, 192; Math., 197; Mathew, 261; Thomas, 209
Galel, Wm., 254
Gales, Ann, 154; Tho., 145
Gall, Jno., 5
Gallamore, Jno., 144
Galle, Tho., 53
Galles, Robt., 311
Galley, Hen., 325
Gallis, Chas., 201
Gallock. Cha., 402
Gally, Wm., 295
Galopper, Jno., 103
Galt, James, 399
Gambo. a Negro, 318, 395
Gamerell. James, 137
Games. Thomas, 229
Gameston, Giles, 306
Gammase foy land. 387
Gammon. Jno., 140; John, 137
Gamon, Jno., 339; John, 295; Tho., 116
Gandy, Abralom, 109; Cha., 136; Tho., 38: William, 320
Ganey, William, 308, 363
Gannell, Edward. 62
Gannock, Wm., 297
Gant, Antho., 314; Richd., 270
Gante, Mary, 198
Gapin, William, 78; Wm., 122
Gappin, William, 171
Garatson, Tabitha, 377

Gardener, Thomas, 320
Gardiner, Adren, 138; Giles, 73; John, 116; Martin, 48; Tho., 54
Gardnar, John, 153
Gardner, Alex., 31; Alice, 160; Anth., 12; Danll., 276; Ellin, 312; Giles, 64; Hen., 132; James, 278; Jno., 27, 175, 264, 328, 361; Lucas, 66; Mar., 282; Martin, 324, 326, 335, 340; Mary, 55, 227, 324; Phill., 243; Richd., 156, 233, 269; Ringing, 223; Tho., 57, 189; Wm., 67, 155, 336, 381
Gareford, Nath., 90
Garetson, Derrick, 377; Desire, 377; Margaret, 377
Garey, John, 222; Stepli, 193
Garey, land of, 193
Gargaphya, 106, 108, 155
Gargrave, Mary, 219
Gariand, Peter, 72
Garill, Jno., 211
Garland. Anne, 389; Bethel, 92; Bethell, 52; Eliz., 79, 131; Hump., 94; James, 56; Peter, 215; Susana, 389; Wm., 18, 122, 389
Garley, Richd., 402
Garlin, Wm., 149
Garlington, Christopher, 100; Xpher., 376
Garner, Dorothy, 256; Jno., 164; Wm., 228
Garnett, John, 261, 263; Jonathan, 127; Tho., 58, 149
Garnygan, Thomas, 210
Garr, Edw., 40
Garrard, Tho., 157
Garratt, Antho., 34; James, 135; Thomas, 36
Garraway, Jno., 6; John, 77
Garret, Edmd., 352; Elizabeth, 79; John, 384
Garretson, Richard, 322
Garrett, Elizabeth, 249; Ja., 204; Jno., 6, 55, 89, 165, 171, 205, 255; John, 223, 264, 400; Mary, 39; Robert, 58; Rowland, 116; Tho., 17, 47; Thomas, 89; Wm., 18, 28, 32, 169
Garrett, orphans of, 125
Garro, Wm., 342
Garry, Christopher, 154
Garryson house, 305
Garton, Eliz., 125; Jno., 21; Tho., 393
Gartricke, Mary, 90
Garwood, Geo., 399; John, 205, 352; Thomas, 112
Gardford. Nath., 90
Gary, Phillis, 232

Wm., 254
Gibson, And., 138; Anna, 189; Antho.,
193; Edward, 359; Hen., 162;
Henry, 399; Isaac, 359; Isaak, 14;
Ja., 343; Jno., 43, 121, 132, 139;
John, 31, 83, 195; Jon., 121, 263,
271; Joshua, 32; Margaret, 296;
Martha, 149; Peter, 76, 263;
Phineas, 352; Symond, 163; Tho.,
70, 79; Thomas, 298; William, 392;
Wm., 71, 343
Giddins, Jno., 314
Giddons, Tho., 178
Gifford, Sarah, 138
Gilam, Jno., 143
Gilbert, a Dutchman, 71
Gilbert, a Negro, 243, 261
Gilbert, Eliz., 7, 8, 73, 142; Fra., 100;
Geo., 59; Henry, 272; Jno., 33, 193;
Mark, 341; Mary, 256; Rich., 193;
Tho., 88; Wm., 1, 4, 5
Gilbert Platt, 12
Gilder, Jno., 14
Gildimore, Mary, 84
Giles, 398
Giles, a Negro, 242
Giles, Eliz., 139; Elizab., 12; John,
229; Nathanll., 124; Tho., 13, 145,
390; Thomas, 230; William, 224;
Wm., 76, 325-326
Gilford, Robt., 316
Gilfred, Ja., 217
Gill, a Negro, 255
Gill, Andrew, 55, 95; Capt., 117;
Edward, 228; Ellinor, 237; Geo.,
70, 151, 197; George, 219, 226, 245,
247, 313; Ja., 192; John, 74;
Leonard, 179; Mary, 42; Michael,
alias Hill, 238, 239; Michl., 392;
Pet., 55; Peter, 30, 93; Rich., 282;
Richd., 317; Stephen, 49, 293; Will.,
155; Wm., 271; ——, 163
Gill's corner, 41
Gill's land, 60, 289, 361
Gilla, 170
Gillam, Fra., 103; Jno., 25; John, 125
Gilles, Edwd., 206; Thomas, 14
Gillet, Austin, 283
Gillett, Jno., 143; John, 30, 32, 276,
399; Robert, 41; Thomas, 388;
Wm., 84
Gilliam, Mrs., 242
Gillies, land of, 298
Gillifer, Sara, 30
Gilline, Nich., 131
Gilling, Rich., 220
Gillins, George, 3
Gilliot, German, 6, 332; Germon, 6;

Jerman, 81; Tho., 6
Gilliott, German, 295, 378; Germane,
135; Sarah, 6
Gillman, land of, 170
Gillmore, Patrick, 293
Gillom, John, 339
Gillores, Robert, 391
Gillott, German, 32
Gillows, Robert, 391
Gills, Edmd., 219; George, 282;
John, 359
Gillson, Mrs. Bethlm., 46
Gillum, John, 340
Gilly, Anne, 399; Edwd., 165;
Isaac, 399
Gilman, Elizab., 107
Gilron, Tho., 191
Gilson, Andrew, 5, 64, 121, 152, 178,
315; Behethlem, 19; Beth., 47, 48,
392, 396; Bethl., 138; Bethlehem,
87; Dorothy, 268; Jno., 58; Tho.,
349; Thomas, 87
Gilsonn, Andrew, 193
Gimbalson, Robt., 177
Gingell, Margarett, 230
Gingo, a Negro, 382
Gingoteag, 104, 107, 115, 118, 119,
120, 126, 182, 215, 355
Gingoteag Accocomson, 154
Ginhorne, Jane, 164
Ginsey, William, 140, 377; Wm., 192
Ginsye's corner, 41
Gipson, Mary, 113; Sam., 67
Girling, Jno., 23, 170
Gisbone, Jno., 213
Gisborn, land of, 367
Gisborne, John, 234
Gissell, Mary, 32
Giszard, Richard, 206
Gittes, Edwd., 160
Gittin, Jane, 265
Gitting, Rich., 220
Gittins, Alex., 213; Tho., 68
Givor, Wm., 160
Gizage, Richard, 254
Gizage's line, 186
Gladding, Alice, 305; Howell, 305
Gladwin, George, 4
Glagdon, Jno., 127
Glandfeild, Joane, 130
Glanfeild, Jone, 93-94
Glantin, Jno., 143
Glas, Mary, 15
Glascock, Deborah, 83; Edger, 318;
Robert, 83; Robt., 320; Thomas,
181
Glascocke, Edgar, 23; Mr., 38;
Thomas, 242

Guiana, a Negro, 255
Guid's, Richard, 301
Guiden, Jno., 324
Guildford, Eliz., 13; Eliza., 65
Guin, Jno., 177
Guinney, a Negro, 255
Guiton, Jno., 133
Gulin, Wm., 188
Gull, Sampson, 91
Gullack, James, 100
Gulley, Anne, 39
Gullington, Christopher, 12
Gullock, Leonard, 139; Robt., 379
Gulls, Tho., 207
Gully, Sam., 10; Tho., 80
Gultumnee, Jno., 166
Gumstead, a Negro, 94
Gun, Her., 214; Jno., 324; Roger, 97
Gundivile, Anne, 93
Gundrey, John, 274
Gundry, Hanna, 96; Jno., 63; John, 274
Gundwile, Anne, 93
Gunell, Edward, 336
Gunn, Hum., 204; Robt., 83; Roger, 153; Wm., 62
Gunnel, Antho., 259
Gunnell, Edwd., 94; Geo., 94
Gunsalvo, Lorenzo, 245-246; Sarah, 246; Thomas, 246
Gunson, John, 37, 113
Gunston, Tho., 212, 343, 359
Gunt, Geo., 58
Gunter, Jno., 150
Guntin, John, 312
Gunton, Jno., 313; John, 306
Guonshott, Jasper, 185
Gurgrave, Mary, 219
Gurnett, Peter, 106; Tho., 58
Gurr, Edw., 40
Gurton, Eliz., 125
Gussiso, Rosse, 135
Gust, an Indian, 368
Gutheridge, Ellenor, 145; John, 202, 230
Guthrey, Edward, 400
Guthry, John, 363
Gutry, Sarah, 388
GUTS:
   Beaver Dam Gut, 151; Black Gutt, 312
   Cyprus Gutt, 239
   Granger's Gutt, 234
   Hawkes Nest gutt, 271; Hoggpen Neck gutt, 140; Horner's gutt, 168
   Jackson's Gutt, 116
   Merryman's Gutt, 297

   Piney Is. gutt, 374
   Selevants gutt, 8
   Wilcock's gutt, 183; Williams' gutt, 196
Gutteridge, Tho., 116
Guttridg, Elianor, 114
Guttridge, John, 388; Lt. Coll., 41
Guy, 170, 244, 305, 319, 336, 363, 378, 383, 402
Guy, a Negro, 185, 242, 318, 324, 349, 354, 357, 373, 377, 391
Guy, Ann, 141; Elias, 270; Joan, 265; Mary, 256; Sarah, 260; Wm., 191
Guydon, Jno., 169
Guyor, Wm., 160
Guysick, Rich., 28
Guyton, Jno., 133, 140, 161, 162
Gwill, Ran., 20
Gwilliams, Rich., 95
Gwillin, Alice, 156
Gwillins, Georg, 171
Gwin, Alexander, 296; Hugh, 302; Joan, 7; John, 302; Wm., 12, 239; line of, 300
Gwinn, Edmund, 179; John, 332; Wm., 172
Gwyn, Alex., 114, 179; Alexander, 182, 218, 234; Ann, 186; Anne, 29; Edmund, 275; Griffin, 132; Humphrey, 197; Jno., 395; Mary, 76; Tho., 68; land of, 189
Gwynn, Alexander, 214, 260; Hugh, 38; Hum., 189, 190; Joyce, 190; Tho., 220; Wm., 110; land of, 390
Gybbs, Jno., 285
Gybsye, a Negro, 242
Gyles, Rebecca, 187, 313; Wm., 175, 305
Gyllett, James, 139
Gyllie, Edwd., 143
Gyton, John, 124; Wm., 111
Gytont's, Jno., 133

H

Habeard, Jno., 35; Wm., 35
Habeck, Digby, 191
Haberd, Willm., 45
Haborne, Robt., 203
Hack, Ann, 8, 158; Geo., 158; George, 8; George Nicho., 334; George Nicholas, 304; Nicholas, 8; Peter, 8, 158; William, 387
Hacker, Edward, 306; Fra., 106; Jon., 225; Mr. ——, 79; Peter, 115, 149;

Haverfinch, Thomas, 112
Haverly, Jno., 107
Havers, Martha, 341
Havet, Richd., 269
Havours, Tho., 108
Haward, Eliz., 167; James, 366; Tho., 244; William, 37; Wm., 134, 312; house of, 37; land of, 25, 344
Hawboro, Zupere, 107
Hawford, Jno., 143; land of, 171
Hawgood, Fra., 74, 82
Hawke, Richard, 9
Hawker, Ferdinand, 104
Hawkes, Thomas, 94
Hawkins, Capt., 139; Edward, 38; Henry, 293; Jeff., 102; Jno., 4, 156, 176, 200; John, 142, 221, 401; Maj., 315; Margt., 256; Mathew, 275; Mr., 41; Rich., 99; Richard, 228; Richd., 227, 238; Tho., 39, 86, 115, 123, 355; Thomas, 20, 86, 107, 120, 166, 279; Thos., 86; Wm., 39, 193
Hawkins' hole, 258, 297, 336
Hawle, Henry, 81
Hawley, Anth., 58; Charles, 268, 399; Hen., 48, 63; Henry, 135; James, 36, 40, 46, 69, 399; Richard, 399; Wm., 143
Hawly, Charles, 145, 199; Henry, 144; Ja. 157; Wm., 242
Hawman, Sarah, 169
Hawsone, Geo., 160
Hawthorn, Hum., 104
Hay, Anne, 342; Danll., 342; Gilbert, 228, 301; Isabella, 359; Jane, 270; Jervis, 345; Jno., 196; Tho., 312, 345
Hayard, Tho., 222
Hayden, Gideon, 23
Haydens, Jane, 175
Haydon, Francis, 1, 52; Wm., 50
Haye, Roger, 342; Tho., 170
Hayes, Adam, 356; Addam, 126; Alice, 313; Charles, 313; Edward, 112; Edwd., 89; Eliz., 270; Fra., 340; Hen., 191, 270; Ja., 186; James, 309, 314; Jane, 124; Jno., 336, 362; John, 154; Mary, 143; Nathaniell, 126; Owen, 272; Patrick, 106; Pattrick, 106; Peter, 205, 235; Ric., 139; Richd., 144, 322, 350; Robert, 126, 327; Robt., 127, 191; Wm., 276
Hayles, 178; Samll., 84; Tho., 175
Hayls, Fra., 188
Hayly, Edwd., 309; Hugh, 206; James, 220; Wm., 213
Hayman, Jno., 85, 298; John, 23

Haynes, Anth., 70; Anthony, 130, 251, 275; David, 270; Geo., 73, 157, 163, 185; Hump., 40; Mary, 39, 94; Ralph, 309; Robt., 84, 375; Susan, 263; Sy., 67; Tho., 71, 194; Thomas, 56, 125, 193; Thos., 194; Wm., 57
Hays, James, 320; Wm., 232
Hayter, Charity, 100
Hayward, Elizabeth, 239; Ellen, 271; Henry, 187; James, 239; Jno., 149; John, 89; Roger, 150; Sam., 19; Tho., 142, 203, 264; Wm., 58, 271
Haywood, Henry, 250
Hazleworth, Bryan, 77
Hea, [Mr.?], 319
Heabeard, Jno., 65; John, 76; Rich., 5; Richard, 65, 76, 85; Will., 76; Wm., 65
Heaberd, Richard, 1; Richd., 84
Heabert, Wm., 34
Head, Jno., 23, 310; Kath., 55; Tho., 277
Heading, Robt., 307
Heady, Tho., 176
Heafield, Wm., 318
Heaford, Jno., 94
Heagarth, Wm., 370
Heal, Geo., 194; Margaret, 372
Heale, Barbary, 276; George, 11, 89; Math., 68; Nicholas, 66; Robt., 80
Heanes, Jno., 107
Heapes, Hen., 167
Heard, Edw., 71; Joseph, 127; Mary, 127; Morris, 166; Walter, 125
Hearing, Sam., 152
Hearle, Edward, 9; Francis, 9; Tho., 10
Hearne, Barthew., 108; Geo., 36, 41, 50; Henry, 111, 301; Wm., 140
Heart, And., 138; Dorothy, 357; James, 139; Tho., 119
Heas, Charles, 348
Heasard, Jno., 94
Heasel, Wm., 362
Heasell, Wm., 219
Heates, Ja., 150
Heath, Adam, 398; Anne, 297; Ben., 210; Ed., 297; Edwd., 145; Eliz., 369; Hen., 209; Henry, 360; Honor, 365; James, 319; Jno., 156, 164; Margt., 99; [Mr.?], 319; Rich., 232; Richd., 285; Robt., 23, 378; Sarah, 344; Stephen, 145; Tho., 23; Thomas, 261; Willi., 74; William, 366; Wm., 8, 165, 232; cor. of, 321
Heathcock, Tho., 115
Heathfeild, Rich., 335

72; Symon, 162; Tho., 9, 199, 313;
Thomas, 52, 69; Wm., 33, 67, 146
Hobson's Choice, 246, 264, 303
Hockady, John, 122; Lt. Col., 122;
Wm., 229
Hocker, En., 193; Isaac, 154; Isack,
152; Mary, 154; Susanna, 154;
Tho., 111
Hockett, Robert, 81
Hockis, Margt., 324
Hockley, Hen., 96; Miles, 348
Hockly, Jno., 33
Hocknott, Tho., 193
Hodae, a Negro, 395
Hodeins, Rich., 191
Hodge, Abra., 188; An., 330; Ann, 66;
Jno., 214; Mathew, 66; Robert, 140,
214; Robt., 214; Roger, 67; Wm.,
140
Hodges, Ann, 91; Arthur, 338, 339;
Hen., 123; Jno., 351; Joan, 233;
Mary, 91; Rebecca, 256; Richd.,
260; Roger, 260, 346, 380, 390;
land of, 253
Hodgeson, Mary, 359
Hodgis, Rger., 213; Thomas, 286
Hodgkins, Tho., 352; William, 94;
land of, 162
Hodgkinson, Jasper, 295
Hodgskins, Antho., 196; James, 23
Hodgskins, land of, 30
Hodgson, Onah, 35; Will., 48; Wm.,
35, 45, 47
Hodgston, Jno., 150
Hodkin, Richd., 152
Hodkins, Abra., 175; Kath., 11
Hodsden, Robt., 150
Hodskin, Ann, 255
Hodson, Tho., 207, 343; Willm., 45
Hodvn, Jno., 204
Hodwood, Sarah, 179
Hoe, Abig., 266; Jos., 192; Rice, 55,
95, 256, 368; Wm., 64
Hoell, Cho., 164
Hoer, An., 170
Hog, John, 399; Thomas, 81
Hogg, Andr., 96; James, 153; Jno.,
115; Jon., 254; Robt., 14; Tho.,
244
Hoggard, 62
Hoggard, Anthony, 26
Hoggen, a Negro, 255
Hoggen, William, 250
Hoggerd, Antho., 84
Hoggett, Charles, 301
Hoggs, Tho., 40
Hogpen bottom, 129
Hogsdon, Richd., 160

Hogsfletch, Ellinor, 362
Hogshead, Jno., 98, 155
Hogson, Math., 16; Mathew, 20
Hohen, Joane, 178
Hoile, John, 23
Hokins, John, 183, 246
Holbrooke, Joan, 24; Saml., 24
Holburd, Antho., 16
Holden, Ann, 171; Arthur, 241; Jno.,
186; Robert, 151; Roger, 326; Wm.,
175
Holder, Abrah., 333; Anthony, 324;
Arthur, 172, 240; Caleb, 133, 197;
Clemt., 84; Eliz., 197, [Mr.?], 331;
Richard, 122; Tho., 75, 216, 256;
Thomas, 172, 216
Holderby, William, 230
Holdersbye, Jno., 82
Holdfast, Mary, 149; Tho., 155
Holdgate, Sarah, 332; see also Wil-
liams, Sarah
Holding, James, 274; Rich., 5, 19, 47;
Samll., 342
Holdip, Ed., 35
Holdman, Tho., 127
Holeman, Christopher, 310
Holesteed, Wm., 106
Holford, Anne, 35; Tho., 35
Holladay, John, 53; Susa., 17; Susan,
47; Xpian., 88
Hollady, Susan, 36
Holland, Adam, 341; Bar., 217;
Daniel, 101; Danl., 100; Edw., 44;
Eliz., 257, 260; Eliza., 240; Fra.,
316; Fran., 5, 19, 47; Grace, 348;
James, 65; Jno., 8, 85, 100, 157,
360; John, 238, 239, 257, 389;
Jone, 74; Margery, 179; Mr., 169;
Rich., 10, 22, 87, 136; Richard, 16,
119, 183; Richd., 65; patent of,
346
Hollaway, Edward, 402; J., 149;
Tho., 171
Hollowaye, Mr., 105
Holleman, Christop., 77; Christopher,
288; William, 288
Hollen, Bridget, 360
Holley, Jon., 265; William, 110
Holliday, Jno., 213; Jon., 265; Mr.,
252; Thomas, 396; Wm., 160, 213
Hollings, Tho., 94, 102-103, 150
Hollingsby, Jeffrey, 22
Hollingsworth, David, 240
Hollingworth, Cha., 135; Wm., 281
Hollins, John, 333; Tho., 91, 116,
204; Thomas, 148
Hollinsby, Eliz., 175
Hollioke, John, 242

Jo., 178; Joha., 145; Jonathan, 116; Margery, 74; Mary, 87; Ra., 67; Ralp., 42; Ralph, 90; Rich., 16, 22; Rob., 193; Sarah, 42; Tho., 33, 92, 130, 160, 189; Wm., 27, 105; field of, 288, 290
Hopp, Tho., 124
Hopper, John, 69
Hopton, Wal., 210
Hopwell, Stephen, 36
Hopwood, Tho., 107
Horchings, Richd., 141
Hords, Fra., 150
Hore, Abigail, 341
Horecraft, Tho., 130
Horecroft, Tho., 93
Horgott, Mar., 141
Hormell, James, 335
Horman, Henry, 327
Horn, Richd., 357; Robt., 336
Hornar, Roger, 270
Hornbuckle, Hen., 155
Horne, Eliz., 43; Geo., 260; George, 182; Mary, 43; Jno., 38; Thomas, 249; Wm., 34
Horne Harbor, 28, 189, 237, 338
Horne tree, 219
Horneing, Robt., 204, 216
Horner, Ann, 81; Edwd., 81; corner of, 234
Hornes standing, 240
Hornesby, Duke, 54
Hornsby, Duke, 112, 338
Horpu, Marke, 216
Horrid, Saml., 45
Horrod, Jno., 56
Horse, Wm., 246
Horsefeild, Robt., 357
Horseley, Roland, 111; Stephen, 174; Tho., 209
Horsely, Rowland, 129
Horseman, Jno., 23; John, 26
Horsendine, Mary, 230
Horsey, Wm., 115
Horsfall, Grace, 35; Judith, 35; Rich., 35
Horsham, Isa., 130
Horsington, Jno., 23; Robert, 51; Sw., 394
Horsley, Robt., 198
Horsly, Row., 170; Wm., 184
Horsnell, James, 335
Horson, Hause, 151; Jno., 378
Horswell, Tho., 366
Horth, Augustine, 64, 71, 338
Horton, Barth., 270; Danll., 194, 343; Ed., 5, 329; Edw., 47; Edward, 19; James, 8; Jno., 61; Pat., 18;

Patriack, 9; Tho., 230; Thomas, 369; Tobi., 273; Walter, 10; Wm., 14, 21, 22, 34, 42, 45, 46
Horty, Israel, 207
Hose, James, 398
Hoshton, Rich., 10
Hoskins, Antho., 199; Anthony, 204; Barth., 99; Bartholomew, 267, 276, 285; Edwd., 206; Elizabeth, 48; Henry, 106; Jno., 22, 68, 205, 206; John, 180; Mary, 277; Mr., 60; Peter, 68; Ruth, 321; Samll., 126; Tho., 90; Will., 252; William, 41, 115
Hoskins' pocoson, 153
Hosock, Jno., 167
Hossman, Mary, 289
Hosted, Rachel, 235
Hoton, Eliza., 343; Tho., 12
Hotting, Wm., 146
Hotwater land, 266
Hotwater Devident, 387
Hotwaters, devdt. called, 206
Houchin, Edward, 282; Edwd., 355
Houge, Jno., 212
Hough, Fra., 175
Houghton, Dorcas, 20
Houlden, Samuell, 218
Hoult, Jerimie, 373; Rich., 74; Richard, 293; Richd., 166
Hoult, the plantation, 289
Houndson, Richd., 209
House, Abigail, 304; Ann, 33, 98, 184; Hester, 129; James, 19; Mary, 37, 375; Robert, 276; Robt., 80, 225; Rowland, 22; Warren, 276
Houseden, Wm., 193
Houseford, Wm., 30
Houseing, Mr., 66; Robert, 26
Houson, Hugh, 155
How, Abigail, 265, 295; Anne, 316; Danl., 67; Jno., 4; John, 227, 233; Lidia, 171; Lydia, 32; Mary, 182; Nath., 155; Nathall., 155; Nathaniell, 147; Phillip, 155; Rich., 136; Wm., 216
Howard, Anne, 321; Barbara, 106; Benjamin, 58; Dorothy, 348; Edward, 32, 396; Eliz., 219; Eliza., 310; Elizab., 167; Elizabeth, 321; Elth., 196; Francis, Lord, 273, 331, 334; George, 24; Hannah, 254, 296; Henry, 310, 311; Ja., 175; James, 283, 389; Jno., 159; Joane, 67, 125; John, 350, 386; Jon., 118; Math., 191; Mr., 62; Nicho., 354; Phil., 10; Phillip, 13, 218, 265, 318;

Mathew, 13, 14; Otho., 320; Rebecca, 320; Rees, 229; Rice, 49, 378; Robert 223, 229; Thomas, 3; Wm., 21
Hughill, Jno., 67; Mihill, 90
Hugnlett, Jno., 43
Hughs, Alice, 87, 398; Darcy, 335; Edward, 385; Eliz., 399; Jose., 321; Robert, 354; Sarah, 335; Wm., 336
Hugnson, Hugh, 159
Hugill, Michaell, 8; Mihill, 75; Miles, 41, 86
Hugo, Kath., 362
Huhr, Jon., 181
Hukes, James, 264
Hukestep, line of, 357
Hulett, Anne, 335; John, 197; Joseph, 68
Hulford, Jno., 19
Hulins, Jno., 336
Hull, a Negro, 358
Hull, Alexr., 103; Ed., 150; Eliz., 257; Geo., 111; Hannah, 244; Jno., 7, 8, 9, 18, 40, 46, 50, 83, 195; John, 46, 75, 83; Jon., 247; Mary, 265; Peter, 38, 202, 284; Rich., 63; Richd., 151; Robt., 89, 149; Robert, 80; Sarah, 20, 27, 138; Tho., 1, 4, 247, 335
Hulling, Sarah, 128
Hullings, Abra., 65
Hulk, Wm., 325
Humble, Jno., 48
Hume, John, 75, 145, 199, 227
Humen, Jno., 53
Humes, John, 123, 342
Humford, Phillip, 129
Humfrey, Mary, 108
Humfry, James, 75; Wm., 79
Humfryes, Robt., 79
Humpheres, Mary, 42
Humphrews, Jon., 267
Humphreys, Anthony, 313; Jane, 363; Jno., 363; Jos., 144
Humphries, Jno., 4; Wm., 141
Humphry, a Negro, 330, 382
Humphry, Alice, 43; Hanna, 91; Jane, 216; John, 270; Tho., 141
Humphryes, Jno., 341
Humphrys, Eliza., 401; Georg, 182; Peter, 128; Tho., 149; William, 218
Humstead, Margerett, 160
Humston, Edward, 16
Hundley, Joall, 284; Phillip, 214, 301
HUNDREDS:
Bermuda Hundred, 59
Diggs Hundred, 364
Shirley Hundred, 40, 52, 393

Hungars, 66, 105
Hungarth, Edmd., 22
Hungers, 121
Huniccutt, Augustine, 287
Hunicut, Austin, 19
Huniford, Philip, 255; Wm., 20, 188; land of, 17
Hunington, Rich., 94
Hunley, Phill., new line of, 190; Phillip, 112, 118, 124; Wm., 54
Hunlock, John, 215; Tho., 150
Hunlocke, Tho., 92
Hunly, Phill., 190; Phillip, 395
Hunniferd, Phill., 32
Hunson, Thomas, 190
Hunstead, Mich., 214
Hunstone, Edwd., 254
Hunt, Anne, 93; Eliz., 182, 391; Eliza., 296; Fra., 227; Francis, 42; Geo., 67, 87, 350; Godfrey, 39, 54, 78; Godfry, 207; Hen., 76, 94, 144, 216, 233, 261; Hugo, 245; Hum., 150; Humphry, 381; James, 9, 18; Jane, 183; Jno., 89, 92, 149; Martha, 189, 375; Mary, 18, 30; Mr., 280; Nathll., 23; Nico., 138; Peter, 74; Rich., 74, 102; Robt., 19, 36, 47, 49, 152, 155; Samll., 203, 335; Sarah, 324, 336; Seth, 83; Stephen, 128; Tho., 59, 65, 79, 84, 231, 336, 374; Thomas, 12, 225, 310, 336, 362; Thos., 65; William, 259, 368; Wm., 71, 102, 189, 198, 232, 241, 273, 336, 341, 371, 377; Xper., 150
Hunter, Ja., 67; Jno., 102, 233, 296; Joane, 294; Jon., 183, 254; Margtt., 211; Mary, 122; Nicho., 294; Rebecka, 294; Tho., 28, 53; William, 327, 401; Willm., 294; Wm., 152, 287, 340
Huntley, Joab, 23
Huntly, Edw., 125; Edwd., 67; James, 11
Hunton, Alexd., 58; Rebecka, 105
Huntstone, Edward, 296
Huntt, Geo., 125
Hurd, Anth., 58; David, 254; Mr., 255; Nathaniell, 78; Robert, 260
Hurdings, Wm., 134
Huret, Math., 366
Hurke, Wm., 203
Hurle, Augustine, 65
Hurlock, Tho., 205
Hurlstone, Tho., 187
Hurly, Eliz., 220
Hurst, Em., 203; Hen., 103; James, 203; Michll., 159; Tho., 285;

I

K

Kae, Robert, 210, 227, 292
Kagen, Tho., 343
Kahalon, Jon., 364
Kakett, Rich., 40
Kalin, Kath., 298
Kane, Thomas, 371
Kanere, Jane, 135
Kanie, Roger, 154
Kant, Walter, 220
Karr, Abra., 169; James, 313
Karre, Eliza., 225; Wm., 225
Karrington, Kather., 112
Kate, 336, 351, 401
Kate, a Negro, 147, 241, 249, 255, 309, 314, 315, 324, 331, 333, 351, 356, 357, 363, 365, 366, 371, 373, 375, 378, 395
Kately, Katherine, 37
Kater, Ann, 123; Francis, 357
Kates, Eliz., 178; Jno., 120
Kath., a Negro, 186
Kath, Cat., 184
Kathericke, Rich., 25
Katherin, a Negro. 114
Katherin, Jno., 148
Katherine, James, 180
Kave, 305
Kay, Abraham, 35
Kea, Jno., 123
Keale, Dudly, 99
Kearne, Wm., 309
Keate, Jo., 40
Keating, Kath., 260
Keble, Eliz., 212
Kebo, a Negro, 185, 373
Keck, Jno., 111
Keddickes, James, 43
Kee, Rich., 2
Keeble, Geo., 332, 362, 398; George, 346; Margaret, 332; Walter, 332; Xpher., 27
Keebles, Joseph, 104; Xtopher., 104
Keele, Adam, 313
Keeling, Adam, 226, 398, 400; Ann, 84; Anne, 400; Betty, 356; Capt., 280; Ed., 210; Edward, 230; Elizabeth, 291; John, 169, 280, 367; Lucy, 234, 248; Sarah, 277; Tho., 169, Thomas, 177, 226, 248, 330; Thorowgood, 169, 234, 248; land of, 391
Keelinge, John, 248; Thomas, 248
Keely, Edwd., 148; Math., 239; Rich., 219

Keen, Anth., 80; Fra., 370; John, 230; Wm., 192
Keene, Jno., 226; Rich., 14
Keeney, Ellinor, 376
Keeper, Jno., 135; Symond, 216
Keepers Lodge, 156
Kees, Ann, 343
Keffield, George, 254
Keible, Geo., 372; George, 8, 397, 398; Xropr., 8; line of, 360
Keines, Adam, 309
Keith, Edwin, 307; Wilmott, 313; Wm., 313
Kele, Mathew, 118
Kelham, Wm., 57
Kelk, Ambrose, 111; Geo., 111; Jno., 111; Katherine, 359
Kell, a Negro, 395
Kellam, Jno., 68; Richard, 118, 119, 120; Wm., 131
Kellbee, Christopher, 333
Kellegrew, Jno., 11
Kellet, Robt., 395
Kellett, Richard, 113
Kelley, Arthur, 155; David, 286; Honor, 351; James, 336; Jno., 89; John, 38; Joseph, 287; Key, 32; Owen, 268, 370; Tho., 351
Kellick, Wm., 164
Kellie, John, line of, 192
Kelligrew, Tho., 256
Kellion, ——, 354
Kellum, Jno., 298; Jon., 262; Rich., 127; Richard, 11, 23
Kelly, Danll., 260; Edm., 128; Edwd., 2; Eliza., 309; Fra., 299; Gesper, 287; Honora, 382; Jno., 149, 328; John, 397; Rich., 128; Rose, 310; Thomas, 323, 382; Wm., 309
Kelsey, Jno., 392
Kely, Tho., 19; Wm., 304
Kemble, John, 384
Kembrough, Roger, 313
Kembrow, John, 306
Kemp, Alexr., 191; Ann, 141; Charles, 313; Col., 197, 317; Edmd., 117; Edmond, 45; Elizth., 203; Eusc., 20; Eusebius, 16; Geo., 115, 132; Hanah, 178; James, 152, 279, 293, 347, 348, 352, 380, 399; Jno., 87, 152, 184, 218; Job, 218, 279, 347; John, 11, 154, 187, 279, 348, 402; Math., 193; Mathew, 161, 202, 224, 381, 397; Matthew, 229, 230; Mr., 72, 311; Richard, 169; Robert, 98; Robt., 45; Tho., 267; Thomas, 294; Wm., 399

Jon., 233; Judith, 21; Ma., 162; Mary, 9; Mr., 222; Peter, 37, 44, 72, 86, 122, 147, 217, 309, 402; Rebecka, 95; Rich., 73, 111; Richard, 168; Richd., 146; Robt., 14, 178, 265; Sar., 197; Tho., 28, 160, 268, 362; Wm., 107, 138, 203, 313, 352
Knighton, George, 227; Henry, 116
Knipe, Bartho., 206
Knishman, Alexr., 106
Knitt, Wm., 197
Knitter, Fra., 54; Franc., 113; Francis, 375
Knot, Susanna, 266; Wm., 309, 343
Knott, Capt., 332; Eliza., 399; George, 346; Jno., 9, 400; Sarah, 336; Susan, 250; Tho., 120; William, 264; Wm., 175, 198, 297, 366; line of, 302
Knowles, Eliz., 199; Henry, 25; Jane, 129; Jno., 70, 93, 160, 187, 297, 361; John, 123, 223, 313, 394; Mary, 159; Rich., 52, 220; Sands, 251; Sara, 67; Thirstrum, 35; William, 389; Wm., 397; land of, 164
Knox, land formerly of, 220
Knoxe, land of, 163, 174
Knoxes, ——, 164
Knt., Jno., 135; Jona., 203; Peter, 40; Wm., 107
Koell, Tho., 160
Kogan, Timo., 331
Konner, Jacob, 297
Koone, Jno., 155
Kreven, Wm., 135
Krewe, Robt., 116
Kub, Will, 136
Kule, Patrick, 136
Kyte, Cath., 165; Patrick, 136; Tho., 175

L

Laberatt, John, 367
Labin, Wm., 359
Labor, Nathll., 105
Labor in Vayne, 29
Labour and Vaine Feild, 247
Lace, Jon., 268
Lacey, Wm., 111
Lachett, Tho., 191
Lacie, fence of, 244
Lack, Tho., 138
Lackerman, Jno., 335

Lackland, Michael, 119; Miles, 10; Nich., 128
Lacy, Ann, 193; David, 297; Edwd., 151, 247, 310; Fra., 169, 188; Jane, 354; Jno., 88, 89, 166, 190; John, 38; Robert, 265; Thomas, 242; Wm., 32
Lacye, Jno., 38
Lad, Jno., 126
Ladbroke, Richd., 156
Ladd, Ed., 134; Jno., 285; John, 126, 280
Laddell, Geo., 297
Lading, Danll., 2, 93
Ladrick, Jno., 92
Laeke, James, 16
La: feavour, Marke, 225
Lafeeter, Pet. Jno., 186
Lafull, Jno., 209
Laine, Robert, 186; Robt., 71; Wm., 34
Laipero, Peter, 50
Laird, Katherine, 135
Lake, Alice, 35; Francis, 331; George, 261; John, 324; Jos., 214; Joseph, 272, 296; Rich., 125; Robt., 142; Tho., 35; Wm., 241
Lake, land of, 331
Lakes, land of, 234, 288
Lamb, Tho., 226
Lambart, Jno., 335
Lambdin, Martha, 274; Wm., 274
Lambe, a Negro, 38; Joseph, 91; Wm., 160
Lambeck, Jno., 216
Lambemott, Will., 78
Lamber, Jno., 165
Lambert, 99
Lambert, Ann, 194, 372; Antho., 399; Barsheba, 145; Bathsheba, 113; Danll., 340; Ed., 87; Edmd., 372; Hen., 48; Hester, 335; Lt. Col., 60; Margery, 35; Mary, 208; Mr., 127; Paul, 150; Richd., 198; Sarah, 138; Tho., 23, 99, 114, 132, 138, 188, 357; Thomas, 253, 272, 347; Will, 50; Will., 123; Wm., 8, 104, 197; land of, 218
Lambethson, Lambeth, 31
Lambo, Robt., 143
Lamboe, a Negro, 142
Lambort, Wm., 326
Lameham, Alice, 143
Lammerton, Robert, 228
Lammond, James, 248
Lamount, James, 290
Lampart, Jno., 20
Lampert, William, 154; Wm., 90

Lanton, Henry, 24
Lantthorpe, Jno., 199
Lany, Ann, 193
Lapage, Jno., 377
Lapthorne, Peter, 127
Laramore, Antho., 401
Larby, Hen., 219
Larcum, Nicho., 241
Larcy, Hump., 374
Lard, Ja., 391; James, 359
Larding, Ellen, 178
Lardoys, Jean, 106
Lardy, Sampson, 217
Larford, Thomas, 80
Large, Tho., 400; Wm., 354
Larke, William, 401
Larkey, Hum., 191
Larkin, Edward, 4
Larkum, John, 401
Larrett, Eliz., 189
Larrum, John, 238
Larthrop, Thomas, 7
Lash, Hen., 382
Lasher, Eliz., 92; Eliza., 145
Lashington, Thomas, 358
Lasingby, Robert, 318; Tho., 126
Lasister, Robert, 337
Laske, James, 16
Lasley, Elizabeth, 113
Lasly, Eliza., 359
Lassel, Edwd., 251
Lassell, David, 297; Edward, 251
Lassers, Jane, 88
Lassingby, Roger, 7
Lassister, Robert, 113
Lassiter, Robt., 379
Lassitor, —, 281
Lastley, Michael, 362
Late, Mathew, 228
Lateby, And., 184
Lately, And., 184
Latham, Margt., 60
Lathan, Charles, 328
Lather, Antho., 104; Jno., 350
Lathum, 371
Latimore, Hugh, 130
Latmer, Willi., 183
Latne, Danll., 342
Latnett, Wm., 189
Latom, Wm., 102
Latre, Danll., 342
Latten, Wm., 130
Latterell, James, 104
Lauder, Alice, 156
Lauderell, Edgar, 126
Laughton, Leonard, 37
Laugton, Kath., 357
Laurance, Capt., 114; Robert, 390

Laurence, 170; Giles, 12; Jane, 175;
    Wm., 150
Laury, Dahl., 60
Lauson, Ralph, 359
Lauthorp, Jno., 343
Law, Abra., 136; Jno., 60; John, 24
Lawes, Abra., 32; Jno., 98, 106;
    Richard, 327
Lawfull, Jane, 389; Rebecka, 389
Lawler, Nicholas, 81
Lawly, Tho., 270
Lawne, John, 181
Lawrance, Georg, 209; George, 297;
    Jno., 198; John, 209, 290; Melchi.,
    330; Robt., 128
Lawrans, John, 60
Lawrenc, Wm., 191
Lawrence, 244
Lawrence, a Negro, 395
Lawrence, Elizabeth, 88; Geo., 389;
    Hen., 269; Henry, 88; Herbt., 198;
    Hugh, 229; Jacob, 195; James, 55,
    230, 363, 374; Jno., 72, 86, 99, 222,
    361; John, 270, 366; Jon., 248;
    John, 187, 205, 241; Katherine,
    110; Mary, 76, 184, 227; Mary,
    390; Melchi., 276; Mich., 100;
    Nicho., 269; Rich., 52, 67; Richard,
    22, 265; Robert, 206, 326; Robt.,
    20, 68, 88, 183, 205, 216, 270; Tho.,
    93; Thomas, 319; Willm., 25; Wm.,
    82, 98, 176, 220; old ditch of, 265
Lawrens, Henry, 60
Lawrenson, Tho., 67
Lawrett, Jno., 102
Lawrey, Jeane, 23
Lawry, Jane, 284
Laws, Jonathan, 307
Lawson, Ann, 54; Antho., 217, 285;
    Anthony, 131, 214, 248, 253, 280,
    323, 384, 396; Chris., 374; Chris-
    topher, 277, 392; Col., 285, 402;
    Eliz., 6, 54; Epa., 46; Epaphd.,
    193; Epaphraditus, 301, 329;
    Epaphroditus, 2, 82, 383, 390;
    Ephaphroditus, 5, 385; Jno., 54,
    101; John, 283; Rich., 5; Richard,
    4; Row., 67; Rowland, 71
Lawsons land, 7
Lawther, Andrew, 337; Charles, 368;
    Jane, 368; Katherine, 368; Wm.,
    368
Lawthern, Owen, 7
Lawton, Robt., 93
Lay, Elizabeth, 28
Laycock, Jno., 12
Layler, Nicholas, 105, 133, 135

M

Magregory, James, 93
Magrey, Allen, 212
Magrock, Danl., 98
Maguffey, John, 381
Mahanes, Mary, 136
Mahaxeenes, 144
Mahen, Jno., 10
Mahone, David, 265
Mahoon, Patrick, 57
Maide, Ann, 4; John, 18
Maidestard, Thomas, 87
Maids Town, 388
Maidstaird, Tho., 45
Maies, John, 134; Wm., **37**
Mailer, Andrew, 13
Mainard, Cha., 45
Maine, John, 191; Tho., 27; Wm., **191**
Mainerd, Samll., 203
Maire, Herman, 131
Maires, John, 359
Maise, Jno., 146
Maize, Henry, 309; Katherine, 108
Major, Geo., 44; George, 262, 278;
  Jno., 11, 67; John, 379, 382, 401;
  Richard, 312; Richd., 44; Will., 11;
  William, 194, 394; Wm., 80, 90,
  194, 313
Makeady, Walter, 208
Makean, Mary, 135
Makeley, Hen., 47
Makellow, James, 112
MaKenzey, Wm., 272
Makenzie, Wm., 225
Makepeace, Rich., 219
Makerby, Ja., 216
Makevary, Gilb., 92
Makhane, David, 135
Makins, Marke, 88
Malaback, 387
Malary, Peter, 164
Malbone, Peter, 153, 235
Malby, Ann, 117
Malden, Francis, 118; Hugh, 386;
  Jos., 326; Joseph, 312
Malder, Hester, 366; land of, 368
Maldin, Francis, 79; Rowld., 115
Male, Eliza., 104; John, 119;
  Jonathan, 142
Maler, John, 261
Malins, Margaret, 318
Mall, a Negro, 262; an Indian, 318
Mallace, Wm., 76
Mallages, Mar., 96
Mallard, Eliz., 49-50; Richard, 349;
  Robert, 345; Tho., 60; Wm., 88
Mallary, Eliz., 35
Mallerory, Wm., 374
Mallers, Wm., 93

Mallery, Diana, 135; Nath., 35;
  Phillip, 35
Mallet, Robert, 254
Mallett, Georg, 180
Malleyes, Martha, 229
Malloburn, Tho., 364
Malloone, Rich., 161
Mallory, Capt., 74, 75; Roger, 35,
  227, 325; Susanah, 134; Tho., 35,
  58, 134, 144; William, 309; Wm.,
  35, 191
Mallson, Edward, 328
Malory, Roger, 309
Malum, Jno., 48; Robt., 115
Maly, Alex., 271
Malyn, Edward, 262
Mampry, Tho., 201
Man, An., 81; Ann, 48; Anna, 135;
  Arnold, 85; Charles, 236; James,
  19, 188, 263; Jno., 107, 151; John,
  293, 370, 377, 379, 381; Robert,
  280; Robt., 345; Saml., 401; Tho.,
  352; Thomas, 236, 243, 254, 309,
  358; Will., 10; William, 215
Manaclith, El., 141
Mancias, Luke, 353
Manders, Weilkes, 52
Mandor, Wm., 297
Mandue, Thomas, 238
Mandy, Arthur, 206; Frances, 230;
  Jno., 150; Wm., 210
Manell, a Negro, 189
Manering, Benj., 191; Hen., 211
Manes, Mary, 254
Manford, Charles, 42
Manhood, Robt., 325
Maning, Jno., 29, 106; John, 56;
  Mary, 16
Manington, Walter, 3, 156
Maninton, Jos., 189
Manky, a Negro, 358
Manlow, Marke, 197
Manly, Edwd., 226; Overton, 103;
  Thomas, 10
Mann, a Negro, 393
Mann, Arra., 211; Ja., 257; John, 275;
  Mr., 251; Robert, 261; Robt., 336;
  Samll., 187; Susana, 383; Tho., 70,
  165; Thomas, 85, 231, 232, 242
Mannell, Jno., 85
Mannering, Stephen, 115
Manning, Ja., 184; Jno., 8, 318; John,
  56, 213; Mary, 21; Nicholas, 356;
  Thomas, 228; William, 387
Manniton, Jos., 189
Manns, Tho., 110
Manoikin, run of water, 45
Manor, Jno., 216

Mars, a Negro, 389
Marsall, Peter, 149
Marsh, And., 191; Elizabeth, 118;
Geo., 37; George, 97, 267, 377;
Jeffery, 262; Jno., 88, 314; Jos.,
270; Law., 260; Nicholas, 326, 380;
Paul, 118; Richd., 92; Sara, 146;
Sarah, 73, 111, 359; Susan, 137;
Tho., 170; Walter, 164; Wm., 73,
146, 320
Marsh land, 250
MARSHES:
    Bedlam Marsh, 56; Browne's
        Marshes, 112
    Chickahominy River Marsh, 376;
        Creek Marsh, 229
    Garden Cr. Marsh, 214; great
        marsh, 56; gr. white marsh, 23,
        95, 105, 246
    Little Marsh, 171; Lower Sunken
        Marsh, 207
    Middle Marsh, 171, 309
    Needham's Marsh, 99, 127
    Reedy Marsh, 171; Reedy White
        marsh, 194; Rumney Marsh
    Somerton Marsh, 60; Sunken
        Marsh, 41, 82, 122, 252
    Towne Marsh, 113
    Wallop's Marsh, 355; Warner's
        Marsh, 163; White Marsh, 13,
        49, 88, 122, 156, 167, 171, 224,
        252, 257, 269, 276, 299, 309,
        318, 336, 337, 370, 379, 380;
        White Oak Marsh, 394; Wynoak
        Marsh, 324
Marshall, Andrew, 33; Ann, 60; Cha.,
85; Deborah, 320; Ed., 204; Ester,
92; Geo., 52; Humpherey, 266;
Humphry, 87; Jno., 87, 152; John,
26, 227, 274; Mary 85; Mr., 7;
Peter, 39, 150; Phill., 314; Rebecca,
375; Robert, 38; Roger, 84; Samll.,
245; Sarah, 336, 344; Susanna, 138;
Tho., 6, 194; William, 360; Wm.,
128, 191; —, 173
Marson, Dennis, 219; Edward, 123
Marston, Elizabeth, 342; Jno., 15;
Joane, 165; John, 33, 342; Mr.,
364; Roger, 59; Tho., 335; Thomas,
372; Thomas, 58
Marsy, ——, 116
Marteaw, Capt., 7
Martha, a Negro, 155, 358
Martin, And., 167; Andrew, 168;
Alex., 174; Anne, 181; Antho., 106;
Capt., 317; Danll., 345; David, 167;
Eliz., 219; Fra., 136; Francis, 59,
108; Geo., 184, 341; George, 20,

218, 245, 264, 328, 386; Godfrey,
10; Hannah, 318; Hen., 313; Henry,
178; Hugh, 139, 166; James, 85,
179, 225; Jatience, 252; Jno., 29,
158, 177, 196, 299, 339; Joel, 342,
368; John, 76, 83, 154, 274, 311,
363, 367; Jon., 254; Margarett, 135;
Mary, 36, 120, 395; Nic., 92; Peter,
136; Rich., 74, 326; Richard, 112;
Richd., 115, 260, 340, 353; Robt.,
47, 136, 194, 271, 343; Sar., 207;
Sara, 188; Solom., 160; Sus., 162;
Susan, 183; Th., 208; Tho., 141,
188, 238, 243, 359; Thomas, 140,
326; Willi., 178; William, 273;
Wm., 131, 174, 274, 285, 323
Martin's Hundred, 287
Martinge, Richd., 375
Martinn, Edward, 364
Marty, Mary, 47, 85
Martyn, Andrew, 365; Ann, 75;
Arrable, 99; George, 316; Hen., 32,
41, 68; James, 54, 64; Jno., 48,
83; John, 83, 379; Mary, 142;
Peter, 56; Robt., 56; Susan, 57;
Wm., 40, 60
Marvell, Sus., 166
Marven, Anne, 114; Grace, 103
Mary, 105, 123, 195, 312, 401
Mary, a Negro, 114, 136, 144, 172,
225, 226, 240, 242, 244, 264, 350,
351, 360, 362, 365, 382
Mary, an Indian, 326
Mary, Antho., 142; Barbados, 113, 372
Mary Gold, The, 167
Marya, 364
Marya, a Negro, 371
Marygold, Amy, 72
Maryland, 80; province of, 361; lyne
of, 67, 109, 365; see also, Virginia
Mase, John, 389
Masease, Charles, 81
Maselin, Henry, 119
Masey, John, 370
Mash, Tho., 100
Mashell, Ja., 221
Masingam, Ja., 164
Maskell, Ja., 221
Maskew, Isaac, 255
Maslin, Henry, 10
Mason, Aledander, 237; Alex., 356;
Ann, 317; Chas., 134; Col., 100,
168, 272, 313, 325, 327, 378, 402;
Edwd., 205; Eliz., 71, 75; Eliza.,
180; Emanuel, 32; Fra., 187, 195,
207; Fran., 13; Francis, 14, 15, 243;
George, 384; Han., 193; Henry, 42;
Ja., 216; James, 129, 206, 323;

James, 33, 111, 312, 322, 339, 366; Jane, 324, 344; Jeffry, 58; Jeter, 238; Jno., 1, 16, 21, 27, 35, 50, 51, 55, 94, 118, 130, 157, 162, 173, 199; John, 22, 26, 126, 143, 182, 216, 237, 266, 347, 383; Jona., 216; Joseph, 64; Lambert, 117, 133, 163, 204; Marmad., 111; Marmaduke, 73; Martin, 104, 106; Martyn, 68; Morgan, 132; Nice., 141; Nich., 102, 122; Richard, 91, 123, 249; Robt., 192; Samll., 156, 158; Sar., 199; Sarah, 157, 182, 336, 349; Theod., 134; Tho., 68, 76, 107, 115, 137, 194, 211, 218, 336; Thomas, 24, 77, 80, 112, 179, 290, 291, 310, 383, 389; Will, 8; William, 80, 113, 230, 286, 289; Wm., 30, 39, 96, 104, 142, 144, 162, 189, 191, 322, 337; ——, 397
Mooring, John, 314
Moorton, Richard, 368
Mophatts, Jno., 51
Moraine, John, 74, 293
Morant, Ja., 203
Moraticon, 53
Morcott, Jonath., 42
Mordant, Lestrange, 5
Mordaunt, Le Strange, 91
Morden, Wm., 150
Mordit, Shurley, 369
Mordy, Tho., 217
More, 196; And., 165; Andr., 347, 400; Cornelious, 385; Danll., 141; Edwd., 349; Eliz., 141; George More's line, 145; James, 165, 197, 282, 337, 353; Jane, 348; Jno., 138, 165, 362; John, 177, 352; Lambert, 141; Mar., 125; Marmaduke, 146; Robt., 313; Susan, 139; Tho., 112, 141, 366; Thomas, 384, 385; Wm., 278
Morecock, Wm., 95-96
Morecraft, Randall, 143
Morefeild, Tho., 109
Morehead, Jon., 244; Morgan, 148
Morehouse, Hen., 255
Morley, Jon., 268
Moreman, Tho., 74
Mores, George, 362
Moreton, a Negro, 393; Richd., 397
Morey, Alex., 271
Moreys, Joseph, 378
Morfeild, Jno., 159, 162, 165, 205
Morgan, a Negro, 248, 255; Abraham, 297; Adam, 366; Alex., 266; Alice, 64, 135; Allice, 105; Ann, 43, 85; Cha., 176, 240-241; David, 182,

312, 323, 349; Ed., 276; Edmond, 12; Edward, 281; Eliz., 59, 340; Eliza., 312, 322; Eliza, 311; Fra., 37; Francis, 95, 325; Geo., 94; Hen., 58, 85, 340, 362; Henry, 56, 115, 323; Howel, 94; Howell, 144; Hugh, 193; Isaac, 115; James, 261, 323; Jane, 393; Jno., 32, 57, 94, 144, 173, 197, 298; John, 28, 195, 393; Jon., 226; Judeth, 329; Marke, 177; Mary, 43, 193; Mathew, 170; Matt., 225; Matthew, 230; O., 205; Owen, 169; Pat, 192, 203; Patria, 19; Patriack, 5; Patriak, 47; Peter, 304; Priscilla, 229; Prist., 96; Rees, 181; Robert, 401; Roger, 120, 392; Rowland, 20, 126, 133; Samll., 256; Thim., 364; Tho., 17, 36, 40, 47, 68, 149, 154, 166, 354, 360; Thomas, 29, 154, 230; Walter, 27, 28, 250, 251, 311; Waltron, 20; Willi., 181; William, 6, 218, 401; Wm., 28, 52, 85, 88, 90, 147, 156, 159, 162, 165, 187, 204, 205, 240, 249, 250, 251, 266, 297, 311, 323, 342, 349; ——, 116
Morgane, Jone, 213
Morganhoragon, Hugh, 154
Morgasa, Thomas, 320
Morgrove, Jane, 313
Morice, Thomas, 14
Mories, Jno., 8
Morion, Margt., 371
Morkeday, John, 216
Morland, Rich., 144
Morle, Jno., 186
Morley, Geo., 335; Joseph, 24; Margarett, 224; Rich., 62, 100; Richard, 244, 268; Tho., 59, 318; Wm., 222
Morline, Xper., 143
Morly, Alex., 271; Anth., 366; Jer., 79; Rebecka, 133
Morlyn, Wm., 215
Morman, Rich., 213
Morphy, Honora., 382; Hugh, 365
Morpus, Jno., 148
Morraw, Edwd., 210
Morray, Alex., 112
Morrell, Jno., 35; Thomas, 263
Morrice, Corn., 158; Geo., 143, 150; Mr., 143; Pierce, 265; Wm., 268
Morrill, James, 128
Morrine, Jno., 149
Morris, a Negro, 255
Morris, Abraham, 42; Adam, 270, 381; Amy, 295; Andrew, 69; Crispian, 297; Davd., 195; Denis, 173;

Elo., 225
Neste, Geo., 395; Mary, 395
Nesum, Symon, 39
Netherby, Wm., 143
Netherland, Robert, 177
Netherto, Wm., 323
Netherton, Rich., 180; Wm., 39, 54, 112
Netles, Robert, 369
Nettle, George, 110; John, 44; Mary, 150; land of, 174
Neuton, Sarah, 322
Nevell, James, 301; Jno., 160, 161; John, 87, 232, 237, 278; Peter, 182
Nevett, An., 188; Hugh, 101; James, 139
Neviell, David, 397
Nevill, Jno., 278; John, 304; Peter, 58
New, James, 210; Richard, 222; Tho., 175; Wm., 88
New Discovery, The, tract called, 180, 330
New Towne, 222
Newal, David, 355
Newans, Hen., 355
Newarder, Edwd., 164
Newardo, Geo., 164
Newark, Jno., 111
Newbee, Jno., 349
Newberry, Edwd., 58; Jo., 67
Newbery, Jno., 331; Tho., 162
Newby, Edwd., 151, 227; Samll., 340; Wm., 377
Newcock, Tho., 90
Newcomb, Henry, 206, 398
Newcombe, Henry, 211
Newcome, Doroth., 159
Newel, Tho., 247
Newell, David, 125, 223, 270, 377, 394; Jno., 37, 144, 350; John, 382; Johnathan, 357; Jonathan, 26, 27, 54, 223, 259, 270, 394; Mary, 76, 180; Mr., 259; Richard, 320; Thomas, 275; Wm., 226
Newet, Elizabeth, 117
Newett, Wm., 117
Newgant, Mary, 366
Newham, Jon., 264
Newhouse, Robt., 316; Tho., 47, 58, 74; Thomas, 82
Newington, Jeffry, 23
Newis, Margaret, 35
Newitt, James, 115
Newjant, Cath., 382; Kath., 350
Newjat, Kath., 144
Newland, Wm., 206
Newly, Edwd., 227

Newman, Alexander, 187; Allexander, 359; Barbary, 361; Bard, 362; Daniell, 320; Hannah, 4; Henry, 378; Jno., 16, 37, 72, 187, 191, 193, 321; John, 188, 351; Jon., 268; Jos., 255; Josep., 206; Magdalen, 378; Martha, 391; Mary, 83, 171; Mr., 64, 130, 288, 366; Nath., 355; Nicholas, 106; Phill., 88; Priscilla, 261; Rebecca, 86; Rich., 166; Richard, 303; Robert, 100, 242, 267; Robt., 340; Samll., 343, 374; Samuel, 344; Samuell, 305; Sara, 87; Sarah, 60, 94; Susanna, 180, 316; Tho., 316; William, 261, 265; Wm., 87, 138, 166, 168; Zach., 128; land of, 189
Newmar, Jno., 191
Neworth, Wm., 109
Newport, Antho., 115; Wm., 99
Newport News, 291
Newsam, William, 256; Wm., 186, 187, 188
Newsom, Tho., 138
Newsome, William, 287; Wm., 67, 374
Newsum, Roger, 331
Newton, Ann, 292; Anne, 395; Edwd., 30, 210; Elinor, 226; Elizth., 202; George, 248, 281; Hen., 79, 192; Henry, 120; Ja., 160, 357; Jno., 134, 379; John, 340; Joseph, 9, 173, 292; Mary, 93, 236, 237, 249, 356; Rich., 170-171; Robert, 38, 54; Robt., 270; Sara, 186; Sarah, 325, 330, 336, 339, 341, 345; Tho., 243; Thomas, 11; Wm., 73, 316; cor of, 356; land of, 234
Newty, Eliz., 160
Nexford, Rowland, 24
Nibbs, Jno., 62
Niblett, Richd., 135
Nicapouckes, 90
Nicchols, Jno., 341
Niccholson, Jno., 343
Niccolas, Henry, 237
Niccoles, Jane, 107
Niccoll, Agnes, 102
Niccolls, Hen., 149; Henry, 185; John, 119; Julan, 212; Rich., 208; Richd., 206; William, 114; Wm., 212
Niccols, John, als. Tigner, 333; Rebecca, 220
Niccolson, Jno., 343
Nich, a Negro, 255
Nicho., Capt., 173
Nicholas, Edwd., 141; Francis, 256; Henry, 76, 347; James, 87; Jno.,

Orly, Tho., 94; Tho., 144
Orme, Wm., 175
Orphants Br., 175
Orrel, Robert, 236
Orrell, Alexdr., 150; Robert, 249;
Robt., 237; Tho., 263
Orthar, Simon, 22
Orton, James, 298; Mich., 15;
Sarah, 340
Orts, Cornelius, 314
Orvin, Arch., 81
Orum, Aug., 13
Ory, Tho., 147
Osborn, Tho., 373
Osborne, Edward, 111; Edwd., 73,
146; Elias, 38, 109; Hump., 401;
James, 231; Jno., 54; John, 38, 113,
181; Jos., 313; Joseph, 38; Margtt.,
189; Morgan, 47; Morgan, 17, 36;
Oswald, 116; Oswell, 92; Richd.,
212; Tho., 138, 277, 349; Thomas,
289; Wm., 38; line of, 352
Osbourn, Elias, 240; Jane, 240
Osbourne, Keriah (or Keziah), 323;
Oswall, 103
Osburn, Eliz., 92
Osburne, Tho., 136
Osey, Franc., 111
Osmotherly, Wm., 51
Ost, James, 285
Ostler, Eliz., 250; Volen, 139
Oswell, Edward, 383
Oswillan, Teige, 186
Otey, Elizabeth, 219
Other, Tho., 68
Otley, David, 254
Otly, Tho., 217
Otter, Rich., 69
Otterham, Jno., 216
Otto, a Negro, 376
Ottome, a Negro, 244
Ottonco, a Negro, 244
Oubay, 286
Oudeland, Elizabeth, 7
Oude lant, Cornelius, 2, 3, 7
Oudelant, Mrs., 12
Ougan, Jno., 354
Oughnom Brook, 203
Ought, Wm., 135
Ougley, Mary, 399
Ouglived, Jno., 114
Ould, Wm., 4, 14
Ouldcastle, James, 10
Ouldis, Thomas, 376
Oulds, Edward, 168
Ousman, Jno., 219
Ousteen, Samll., 309; Samuel, 357
Oustin, James, 281; Sam., 128

Outhery, James, 99
Outlaw, Edward, 234, 249;
Edwd., 235
Outlawe, land of, 285
Outrell, Geo., 118, 126
Ovell, Elin, 164
Overbee, Nich., 211; Nicholas, 349
Overbury, Jno., 143; Wm., 105
Overdell, Margaret, 70
Overed, Wm., 91
Overedd, Wm., 5
Overill, Tho., 62
Overing, Andrew, 44
Overman, Edwd., 129
Oversea, Tho., 115
Overseer, a Negro, 258
Overstreet, James, 245, 356; John, 53
Overton, Eliz., 219; Francis, 81; Jno.,
333, 341; Jon., 260; Richd., 343;
Roger, 38, 148; Sarah, 333; Tho.,
35; William, 218, 357; Wm., 219,
399
Ovid, a Negro, 388
Owen, Ann, 33; Barth., 336; Bartho.,
125; Charles, 62; David, 191; Edw.,
74; Ellin, 298, 299, 324; Ellis, 329;
Evan, 123; Hannah, 383; Hugh, 27,
51, 68, 346, 358, 391; Jno., 27, 42,
51, 95, 204, 205; Johna., 156; Jon.,
241; Jone, 335; Mary, 136, 222,
241; Rich., 62, 194; Richard, 255;
Richd., 143; Robert, 335; Robt., 56,
72, 222, 258, 288, 321, 336; Sarah,
181; Tho., 261, 262; Thomas, 298;
William, 111, 220, 271, 289, 400;
Willm., 54; Wm., 54, 129, 159, 170,
312, 335, 343
Owens, Mr., 277, 278, 290, 371;
Nicholas, 192; Thomas, 168; Wil-
liam, 182, 368; Wm., 170, 171, 347;
line of, 288, 322
Ower, Edwd., 87; Eliz., 87; Jno., 87;
Marth., 87; Math., Junr., 87
Overy, Tho., 138
Owgles, Robt., 343
Owin, Edwd., 251; Hugh, 21; Jno.,
21; John, 188; Sara, 127; Will., 77
Owld, Edward, 168, 214, 248
Owles, Robt., 343
Ownbee, Arthur, 315
Owneley, Richd., 228
Ownes, Wm., 213
Oxbrow, Jno., 111
Oxford, Elizth., 201; Joane, 23
Oxley, Edgar, 126; Rowld., 22
Oxly, Jno., 189; Tho., 349; Wm., 345
Oxwich, Natha., 95
Oyden, Jno., 93

88; Thed., 3; Wm., 319
Paulett, Wm., 32, 207
Paulin, Jno., 160
Paulle, land of, 56
Paully, John, 217
Paveat, Jno., 206
Pavy, Jno., 215
Pawell, Tho., 46
Pawer, Katherine, 140
Pawle's land, 56
Pawlet, Jno., 349; Mathew, 380
Pawlett, Ellis, 111; Robt., 57;
    Tho., 226
Pawley, James, 348
Pawlyes, Doctor, 101
Pawting, Thomas, 81
Paydon, Antho., 152
Payne, Anne, 38; Eldred, 58; Jo., 84;
    Jon., 64; Nichol., 27; Robert, 35,
    40, 87, 330, 382, 392; Samuel, 360;
    Will., 173; Wm., 14, 111, 112, 209
Payton, Major, 299; Robert, 219;
    Tho., 335
Peace, Jon., 256
Peach, Honor, 335; Matthias, 245;
    Tho., 70; Willm., 38; Wm., 21, 39,
    70
Peachy, Samll., 143; Samuell, 94
Peacock, Eliz., 9, 157, 182; Ja., 217;
    James, 309; Jno., 151; Margaret,
    55; Margt., 97; Richd., 205-206,
    265; Tho., 269
Pead, Duell, 323; George, 59; Jno.,
    168; John, 59; Tho., 40; Tom., 156
Peade, George, 250; Jno., 250;
    John, 250
Peake, Jno., 397; Rich., 36; Robt.,
    166; Tho., 65, 75
Peakock, Eliz., 199
Peal, Malag., 192; Robert, 239
Peale, Frances, 393; Mary, 105; Mr.,
    181; Robert, 384
Pearce, Chr., 382; Geo., 150; Jno.,
    271; Mary, 391; Tho., 156; Thomas,
    196
Peare, Jno., 21; John, 128, 181
Peareman, Wm., 40
Pearepoint, Wm., 23
Peares, Peter, 111
Pearie, Tho., 156
Pearman, Danll., 85; Mary, 86
Pearse, Jno., 128, 136, 208; John, 363
Pearson, Jno., 159; Richd., 236;
    Tho., 219
Peartree, Phillip, 107
Peas, George, 241
Pease Hills, 249, 376
Peasely, Jno., 145

Peasley, Henry, 325
Peaslie, Wm., 230
Peasly, Mich., 219; William, 1;
    Wm., 1
Peaso patch, 353
Peasock, Ed., 211
Peaswhite, Thomas, 309
Peather, Jno., 88
Peawd, William, 300
Peawde, William, 229
Pebbles, Wm., 271
Peble, William, 82
Pebles, William, 74; Wm., 47
Pece, Jon., 247
Peck, 62; And., 162; Danll., 41; Hen.,
    121; Ralph, 138; Robert, 26; Robt.,
    26, 255; Tho., 186, 188; Thomas,
    225; Wm., 254
Peck's Hill, 320
Pecke, Hen., 135; Tho., 135
Pecke's land, 142
Pecket, Hen., 269
Peckett, Edwd., 73; Tob., 219
Peckington, Xpher., 307
Peckitt, Edwd., 142
Peckstone, Wm., 103
Pecort, Danll., 213; Tho., 213
Pedarmis, Wm., 94
Pede, Hen., 85
Pederott, James, 237
Pedinn, Mary, 345
Pedley, Edward, 357
Pedro, a Negro, 57, 396
Pedum, Mary, 345
Pee, Ralph, 308; Robert, 330
Peed, Geo., 189
Peek, Elizabeth, 243
Peeke, John, 79
Peel, Robert, 196; Tho., 264
Peelam, Mary, 136
Peele, Hump., 84; Robert, 196, 289;
    Robt., 196
Peely, Ti., 219
Peese, Rich., 191
Peeters, Henry, 8; James, 172, 356;
    Jno., 8; Robt., 196; Symond, 184;
    Tho., 191; Wm., 116
Peets, Ed., 40
Peg, a Negro, 395, 400
Pege, Ann, 104
Pegg, 213
Pegg, a Negro, 220
Peike, Chris, 134; John, 46
Peilham, Ardery, 397
Peirce, Abra., 247; Ann, 364; Arthur,
    42, 254; Christian, 236; Elizabeth,
    56, 391; Fra., 191, 366, 373;
    Francis, 21, 27; Geo., 128; George,

POCOSINS:
Poquoson, 3, 5, 14, 29, 41, 46, 116, 221, 238, 240, 246, 400
Easterne pocoson, 327
gr. Poquoson, 127, 202, 221, 255; gr. arrowhead pocoson, 95, 113, 159
Mattapocoon pocoson, 337
Pascataway Pocoson, 113, 114; Piscattaway Cr. maine pocoson, 293
Rappahannock Poquoson, 225
Poe, Jno., 57; Ralph, 313
Poeland, Jno., 151
POINTS:
Back Poynt, 252; Black Poynt, 112; Black Walnutt point, 199; Block Howse Hill point, 222; bloofe poynt, 121; Blunt poynt, 47; Browne's poynt, 266; Bullen's point, 311; Buskin's poynt, 274
Cedar point, 338; Church poynt, 108; Cooper's point, 45, 224, 267; Cormorant poynt, 272, 322, 341
Doby's point, 371; Dry Poynt, 42
Ewe tree Poynt, 139
Fishing point, 201, 312
Garrett's poynt, 264; Griffin's Points, 168, 313
half way point, 233; Herring poynt, 40; Hogpen point, 195; Hollowing point, 133
Indian Cabin point, 163; Iron point, 55
King's point, 233, 346
landing point, 113, 292, 325; Light wood poynt, 20; Little Ware Poynt, 385, 390; Locust Point, 364; Lodge point, 175; Long point, 203, 207
Mirtle Pt., 215; Mossey Point, 330, 385; Motte's poynt, 78; Muskeeta Point, 342; Musketo point, 87, 355
old womins poynt, 44; Orchard point, 203; Oystershell poynt, 111, 218
Persimon point, 199; Peyney point, 48; Pigg Poynt, 19, 175, 221; Piney Point, 309, 311, 346, 367, 394; Pollington's poynt, 38; Powell's point, 193; Prescott's point, 173
Quiruck poynt, 3
Ragged Point, 371, 399; Rigbye's point, 214; Road point, 173; Roule's point, 173; Rumney Marsh Point, 199
Sandy point, 122, 235, 316; Starlings

point, 292; stony point, 136, 350
Tindall's point, 152, 155, 160, 201, 262, 279; Troublesome poynt, 118, 280; Turtle poynt, 39
Upper Wadeing place poynt, 383, 385
Vineyard Poynt, 402
Ware Point, 71; Ware Neck Point, 305
Poithress, Frances, 345
Poithris, Fran., 345
Pokatinck land, 287
Pokotink, 256
Polake, John, 368
Poland, Hanah, 13; John, 140
Polchill, Jno., 23
Poldon, Tho., 49
Pole, Mary, 211
Polegreen, George, 378
Polentine, Nicho., 142
Poles, Tho., 356; Thomas, 245
Poll, 402; Mary, 236
Pollard, Amos, 68; Anne, 35; Geo., 149; James, 387; Phill., 191; Robert, 25, 42, 62; Robt., 35; Samll., 188; Sarah, 301, 355; Tho., 35
Pollet, John, 388
Pollick, Patrick, 319
Pollin, James, 373
Polling, Robert, 282
Pollintine, Jno., 198
Polly, Samuel, 384
Pomeroy, Samuel, 381
Pomfrett, Tho., 177
Pomp, a Negro, 363
Pompey, a Negro, 315, 381
Pomprett, Robt., 142
Pompy, 378
Pompy, a Negro, 345, 377
Pomroy, Florence, 99; Fra., 99; Hugh, 11; Sam., 183
Poncey, Sam., 135
Pond, Margarett, 224; Robt., 23; Stephen, 182; Tho., 247
PONDS:
Beavor pond, 99; Brice's pond, 376
Cattaile pond, 68
Fresh Ponds, 266
gr. pond, 82; Gwynn's Ponds, 201, 382
Hollybush pond, 21; hucklebury pond, a, 55
Col, Jening's Mill Pond, 394; Jonathan's Pond, 308; Jones' pond, 174
Long pond, the, 220
Margerty Bay Pond, 80; Mill pond, 276, 286

Q

S

Jon., 121; Wm., 148, 220
Snelly, Kath., 217
Snerly, Wm., 4
Snip, Wm., 19
Snitton, Wm., 27
Snoell, Ann, 114
Snoswell, Su., 40
Snousing, Edwd., 164
Snout, Esk., 217
Snow, Elfrid, 349; Eliz., 4; Hen., 275, 309; Jno., 33, 160, 213; John, 29; Marth., 197; Mary, 309; Richd., 262, 298; Tho., 129, 239, 336; Wm., 188
Snowden, Wm., 83
Snowe, Ann, 172; Hannah, 168; James, 169
Snuggs, Edwd., 217
So. Key, 142
Soames, Henry, 108
Soan, Henry, 346; Jno., 341, 343; John, 344
Soane, Henry, 70; John, 273, 313; Mary, 5; William, 397; Wm., 326
Soanes, Henery, 282; John, 280; Susana, 360; Thomas, 30; William, 206
Sobriety, an Indian, 368
Sogery, John, 400
Sojourner, John, 330
Solday, Edwd., 142
Solder, Jno., 210
Solders, Edwd., 148
Solomon, 102
Solomons garden, valley called, 32, 212, 329, 395
Somerlin, John, 326
Somerly, Jno., 79
Somers, Alexander, 241; Henry, 111; Jno., 75; John, 208; Math., 86
Somersale, Tho., 270
Somerscales, Ser., 343
Somerseal, Sarah, 365
Somersett, Tho., 9
Somerton, 39, 172, 221, 230, 258, 289, 315, 337, 339, 387, 388
Sommefeild, Will., 153
Sommerfeild, David, 21
Sommerhill, An., 169
Sommers, Mary, 112
Soones, George, 34
Sop, Jno., 49, 361
Sope, Eliz., 147, 155, 156
Sore, Tho., 66
Soresby, Francis, 309; Thomas, 210
Sorjoarner, John, 309
Sorre, Tho., 109, 149
Sorrel, Fra., 257; Jon., 257

Sorrell, Jane, 400; Jno., 35, 376; Jon., 181; Mary, 387; Richd., 203; Robert, 387; Samll., 166; Tho., 165; Wm., 166
Sorresby, Thomas, 276
Sorrill, Rob., 94
Sorrow, an Indian, 360
Sorrow, John, 287
Sorry, Tho., 268
Sorsby, Fran., 351
Soruter, Ja., 115; James, 13, 81
Sosbie, Tho., 138
Sotherby, Leo, 43
Sothersby, Fra., 95
Souch, Peter, 167
South, Edwd., 10; Geo., 269; James, 23, 235, 359, 362; Peter, 167, 207; Robt., 193, 199
South Key, 172
Southaway, William, 355
Southcott, Wm., 17, 36, 47
Southel, Tristram, 232
Southen, Hen., 371; Henry, 292, 295, 319; line of, 372
Southerby, Robert, 116
Southerland, Geo., 164; John, 51
Southern, Richd., 95
Southern Br. precincts, 346, 383
Southerne, Henry, 168
Southfeild, Magl., 23
Southscott, Capt., 129
Southwark Church, 283, 329
Southwarke, 93
Southwell, Th., 217
Southworke, Samll., 251
Sowell, Jno., 58; Thomas, 238; Wm., 382
Sowerby, Fra., 353; Francis, 17, 31; Hen., 104
Sowerbye, Francis, 17
Sowersby, Francis, 110, 326; Robt., 27; Thomas, 326
Spackford, Wm., 269
Spaine, Jo., 178; Jon., 265
Spaines, Ann, 191
Spank, John, 313
Sparing, Wm., 399
Spark, Samll., 299
Sparke, Jno., 102; Jonathan, 24; Nich., 212
Sparkes, Gartreed, 18; James, 163; Jno., 45, 67, 115; Richd., 146; Roger, 191; Saml., 29
Sparks, Antho., 91; Dorithy, 308, 315; John, 315; Sarah, 77
Sparrow, Aron, 363; Edwd., 193; Eliza., 391; Hen., 40; Jno., 95; Mary, 76; Mr., 58; Sarah, 250;

Stever, David, 94
Stevers, Alexr., 216
Steward, Cha., 152; Edwd., 150; Eliz., 192; Ja., 145, 164; Jno., 15, 141, 213; John, 289, 365; Jon., 260; Kath., 226; Robt., 228; Sarah, 226; Walter, 171; Will, 81; Wm., 13
Stewarde, Gra., 164
Stewarder, Edwd., 164
Stewart, Francis, 232; John, 365; Jon., 265; Susan, 232
Stewer, Jno., 106
Stiball, Rich., 194; Richd., 343
Stiff, Peter, 85
Stigins, Samll., 210
Stile, Geo., 68; Perryes, 2; Wm., 61
Stiles, Edw., 126; Eliz., 152; Joan, 240; John, 78; Mary, 261; Sara, 172; Sarah, 240
Still, Jno., 68; Thomas, 275
Stillen, Wm., 191
Stilling, Wm., 373
Stilt, Bar., 264
Stilwell, Roger, 268
Stinton, Alexr., 184; Jno., 219; Rich., 219; Wm., 144
Stipfield, Tho., 297
Stirke, Wm., 10
Stith, Jno., 3, 165; John, 163, 255, 257, 377, 378; Maj., 395; Wm., 48, 175
Stoakeley, John, 177
Stoakely, Fra., 177
Stoakes, Christopher, 288; Dorothy, 160; Jane, 70, 210, 217; Mary, 21; Mr., 201; Will, 10
Stoaks, An., 47
Stock, Ann, 125; James, 77; Jno., 52; Mary, 203; Richard, 220; Robt., 175; Wm., 200, 265
Stocken, Geo., 219
Stockett, Doro., 170
Stockings, Jno., 359
Stockins, Jno., 362
Stockley, Jno., 66; John, 68
Stockley's land, 133
Stockly, Jno., 135
Stockman, Hen., 78
Stocks, Margt., 113; Robt., 35
Stoell, Wm., 197
Stoke, Nich., 75; Tho., 296
Stokeley, Eliz., 261; Jno., 117; John, 81, 99, 105, 246, 259, 264, 303, 304
Stoker, Robt., 84
Stokes, Anne, 361; Arthur, 110; Jone, 188; Sarah, 391; Wm., 212; land of, 282

Stoling, Wm., 6
Stone, Ben., 80; Capt., 65, 121; Derick, 375; Geo., 84, 335; Isaac, 320; Isaak, 53, 64; Jeffry, 40; Jno., 30, 167, 173, 197, 398; Judeth, 17; Judith, 5, 11, 47, 48; Kath., 260; Mary, 391; Oliver, 335; Peter, 217; Richd., 199; Thomas, 8; Willm., 54; Wm., 54, 103, 121, 230, 282
Stoneman, Priscilla, 360
Stoner, Cath., 399; Hen., 84; Jno., 110, 115
Stones, Richd., 233
Stooper, John, 296
Store, Jno., 66
Store point devident, 28
Storer, Jno., 364
Storey, Francis, 355; Jos., 209; Joshua, 332, 358, 360, 361, 382; Samll., 111
Stork, Wm., 200
Storke, Tho., 16, 22; Wm., 16
Storken, Geo., 219
Storey, Wm., 165
Story, Alex., 87; Eliz., 241; Francis, 377, 397; Jno., 187, 335; Joshua, 209, 215, 360, 381; Joshuah, 255, 314, 322; Josuah, 302; Lawrence, 327; Mary, 35; Peter, 380; Tho., 27; Thomas, 116; Wm., 310
Storyie, John, 121
Stott, Bryan, 82; John, 343
Stotwell, Mary, 10
Stout, Peter, 18, 122
Stoute, Tho., 85
Stoutes, Edwd., 329
Stover, Jno., 110
Stowe, Judith, 48
Stowel, Joseph, 268
Stowell, Edward, 271
Stower, John, 305; Peter, 115
Stowers, John, 358, 394
Stowker, John, 78
Stowt, Tho., 268
Stowverd, Cha., 155
Stradling, Geo., 143; Ja., 123; Tho., 394
Strahan, James, 256
Straid, Francis, 8
Strainge, Phillip, 110
Stramford, Rich., 6
Strang, Wm., 50
Strange, Alice, 401; Ann, 210; Anth., 175; Eliz., 123; Hum., 220; Jon., 237, 247; Jos., 382; Petr., 57; Tho., 90, 107, 135, 187
Strangler, Jane, 311

liam, 292; Wm., 98, 187
Symons, Anthony, 182; Edmond, 181; Fra., 90, 164; Francis, 193; James, 214, 302; Jno., 92, 103, 143; John, 127, 226, 230, 316; Jon., 244; Margery, 282; Mary, 181; Rich., 373; Richard, 177; Robert, 266, 290, 383; Roger, 13, 14, 145; Symond, 79; Tho., 144, 257; Wm., 155, 243; land of, 260
Symons' oake, 178
Symoonds, Symon, 11
Sympson, Ann, 272; Jno., 101
Syms, Isaak, 88; James, 45, 96; Jeremy, 72; Saml., 101
Symson, Jno., 135; Jo., 81; John, 82; Timothy, 79
Synn, Wm., 102
Synock, Fra., 194
Syra, Ann, 160
Syrott, Henry, 110
Syuch, Richd., 156

T

T——, Robt., 345; Wm., 138
Tab, a Negro, 19, 242, 255
Tabb, Humphry, 252; Mr., 253; Tho., 74, 177, 201, 202, 204; Thomas, 110
Tabbutt, Wm., 147
Taberer, James, 209; Mr., 38; Tho., 217
Taberrer, Thomas, 202, 284
Tabitha, a Negro, 327
Tabley, Cath., 388
Tabor, Wm., 144
Taborsha, a Negro, 244
Tabott, John, 309
Tacker, Geo., 141
Tackfeild, Samll., 135
Taffy, 213
Tagger, John, 35
Tailor, Eliza., 23
Tainter, Jno., 358
Talbot, Tho., 256
Talbott, Emanuel, 73; Hezekiah, 345; Ja., 58; John, 27, 128; Mary, 15; Rebecca, 73; Samll., 219; Wm., 88
Talbutt, Wm., 41
Talcoate, Fra., 67
Taliafer, Robt., 123
Taliafero, Francis, 397; Robt., 123
Taliaferoe, Francis, 294; Robert, 360
Taliaferro, Francis, 380; Mr., 149; Robt., 401

Talifro, Mr., 21
Talke, Samll., 143
Taller, Ann, 84
Talley, Eliz., 271; Henry, 351
Talliafero, Robt., 93
Talliaferro, land of, 138
Tallifer, Tho., 248
Talliferoe, Mr., 39, 90; Robt., 32
Talling, Jo., 54; Jos., 338; Joseph, 113
Talliser, Tho., 161
Tallman, Mich., 134
Tallon, Jno., 170
Tally, Fra., 128; Hen., 91; Tho., 377
Talye, Tho., 128
Tam, Eliz., 128
Tambo, a Negro, 387
Tampin, Tho., 49
Tanbret, Wm., 313
Tander, James, 378
Tandy, Henry, 315; Jno., 325; John, 391; Richard, 392; Wm., 325; land of, 381
Tandys, Henry, 126
Tanges, Mr., 147
Tango, a Negro, 235
Tankard, John, 215
Tankersly, George, 382
Tanks, a Negro, 255
Tannar, Edwd., 136; Joseph, 136; Martha, 136; Mary, 136
Tanner, Alice, 84; Barnard, 155; Cornelius, 129; Danniell, 283; James, 250; Jno., 10, 24, 86, 119, 136; John, 126; Joseph, 107, 117, 251, 256, 343, 359, 362; Mary, 266; Tho., 362; Thomas, 294; Tomsin, 246; Wm., 14, 25, 169, 210; Orphants of, 141
Tanner's Creek Precincts, 325
Tanners, Danll., 56
Tanry, Wm., 166
Taplie, Adam, 345
Taply, Adam, 349
Tapper, Jno., 155
Tappin, Arrhur, 154; Arthur, 74; Jno., 84; Rebecca, 21, 71
Taps, Mr., 360
Tapsco, a Negro, 382
Tarbett, Alice, 197
Tard, Robt., 268
Tarett, Henry, 5
Tarkin, Antho., 348
Tarkely, Roger, 397
Tarleton, Mr., 223; Roger, 150, 204; Ste., 309; Stephen, 306; line of, 357
Tarner, Tomsin, 246
Tarnton, Jeffr., 362

Thrueston, Malachi, 290
Thrumball, a Negro, 398
Thrush, Ann, 265; Clement, 64, 276; Clemt., 3
Thruson, Ann, 62, 76
Thruston, Jno., 212, 363; Malachy, 110, 266, 276, 279; Mallachy, 341; Robt., 149
Thucker, Robert, 402
Thunder bolt pine, 214, 356
Thurloe, Tho., 103
Thurrell, Tho., 184
Thursby, Edmond, 111
Thursell, Thomas, 227
Thurston, Peter, 29; Robt., 29, 89; Samll., 118; Tho., 67, 89
Thurstone, Wm., 93
Thurlow, Eliz., 86
Thurwell, Sam., 179
Thwait, Mary, 93; Robt., 135
Thwaite, James, 236
Thweat, James, 72, 235, 332, 392; Wm., 102, 124
Thweate, James, 72, 123, 124, 137
Tibalts, Robt., 204
Tibbalds, Wm., 150
Tibbet, Henry, 390
Tibbo, Wm., 85
Tibbs, Wm., 85, 93
Tibolts, Robt., 74
Tickener, Wm., 138
Tickley, Tho., 368
Tickner, Mat., 50
Ticknor, Francis, 138; Moses, 138; Simon, 30
Tidborne, Richard, 182
Tiddin, James, 227
Tider, Robert, 24
Tidford, John, 251
Tidmarsh, Richard, 385
Tigg, Jonath., 115
Tight, Mary, 391
Tigner, John, 333; William, 308
Tignoll, William, 195
Tignor, Willm., 69; Wm., 157, 322
Tilbury, Wm., 103
Tilby, Stephen, 106
Tiler, Mary, 197
Tilford, Jno., 362
Till, Danll., 48; Geo., 149
Tiller, Tho., 40
Tillery, Jno., 152, 176
Tillett, Jno., 78; John, 189
Tilley, John, 230; Su., 346; Thomas, 221
Tillison, Gideon, 384
Tillitt, John, 189
Tillman, Roger, 347, 348

Tillne, Jno., 154, 156; John, 296
Tillney, Jno., 11
Tillison, Isaak, 28
Tilly, Anthony, orphan of, 177; Thomas, 294
Tilman, Roger, 271, 332
Tilne, Jno., 158
Tilney, Anth., 76; Hen., 207; John, 48, 80, 85, 86, 108; Major, 68
Tilsey, Wm., 390
Tilson, Jno., 21; John, 120
Tilt, Wm., 35
Timber neck land, 208, 310
Timberell, Nath., 376
Timberlake, Alice, 399; Richd., 359
Timberneck, Richd., 343
Timbusbery, 188
Timothy, a Negro, 242
Timple, Katharine, 8
Timsbury divident, 365
Tindal, Eliz., 263
Tindall, Eliz., 96, 261; Henry, 180; Jeffry, 398; Tho., 207
Tingey, John, 67
Tingo, a Negro, 242
Tinker, a Negro, 255
Tinny, Elizabeth, 389; Jane, 389; Nathan, 389
Tinseley, line of, 279
Tinsley, Thomas, 108, 339; cor. of, 300
Tinslie, Thomas, 248
Tinsly, Grace, 376
Tinting, Mary, 181
Tiplady, Elizabeth, 270; John, 270, 288, 384; Mr., 194
Tippett, Wm., 33
Tippin, a Negro, 255
Tirpin, Mich., 342
Tirrel, Richd., 268; Robt., 268
Tirrell, Hen., 42; John, 117; Richmond, 96; Robert, 40, 228; Robt., 42; Wm., 42
Tirry, John, 182
Tisby, Richd., 276
Tistaile, Jno., 150
Tite, Mary, 148
Titele, Susan, 37
Titerton, Edward, 179
Titford, Jno., 362; John, 359
Titibury, Richd., 213
Title, Steph., 39
Titterton, Edwd., 171; Mary, 179, 329; Rob., 255
Titus, a Negro, 242, 249
Titus, Tho., 217, 366; Thomas, 114, 258, 366
Tiverton, Robt., 4
Tobdell, David, 257

Elizabeth, 81
Turk, Hester, 362; Nich., 255
Turke, a Negro, 387
Turke, Esther, 359
Turkey, Tho., 76
Turkinton, Jno., 85
Turkly, Avice, 275
Turky Hill, 304
Turland, Robt., 357
Turley, Fra., 184; Francis, 227; Jno.,
    72; Jone, 226
Turly, Georg, 179
Turnagen, Mary, 198
Turnball, Jno., 360
Turner, Abra., 202; Abraham, 165;
    Ad., 160; Alexr., 364; Ann, 269;
    Archib., 103; Cha., 219; Charles,
    16, 219, 377, 384, 385, 386; David,
    8, 107; Doroth., 341; Dorothy, 361,
    365; Ed., 47, 49; Edward, 19, 36;
    Eliz., 193; Eliza., 385; Geo., 143,
    166, 350; George, 114, 206, 252,
    254; Hen., 143, 203; Henry, 220;
    Ja., 58, 164, 189, 324; James, 6,
    74, 225, 253, 290, 346, 361, 373;
    Jas., 197; Jno., 65, 138, 151, 165,
    335, 344, 345, 348, 349, 351, 362,
    363, 364, 366; John, 53, 78, 184,
    278, 293, 299, 339; Jon., 273; Jona.,
    138; Jonat., 139; Marey, 40; Margt.,
    250; Marie, 299; Mary, 32, 95, 164,
    299; Peter, 93, 216; Phill., 347;
    Phillip, 359; Rebecca, 345; Rich.,
    64, 138; Richd., 366; Sara, 154;
    Sarah, 138, 245, 310, 321; Susan,
    139; Susanna, 326; Tho., 76, 96,
    150, 205, 215, 236, 237, 257, 356,
    389; Thomas, 249, 352; Titus, 243;
    William, 180, 360; Wm., 3, 24, 67,
    105, 111, 154, 209; land of, 201,
    256; line of, 302. 305
Turner's corner, 170
Turney, Hen., 203; Mr., 17;
    Richard, 17
Turnor, Sarah, 109
Turnwood, Jno., 116
Turpin, Math., 191; Michaell, 308;
    Symon, 262; Tho., 179; Thomas,
    179; Wm., 228
Turrell, Rose, 340
Turreton, Robt., 144
Turrett, Jno., 22
Turrill, Tho., 10
Turrnor, Tho., 92
Turtle, Robt., 143
Turton, Robt., 219; Thomas, 391
Turtons, Timothy, 93
Turtyn, Tho., 93

Turvon, Robt., 134
Turwyn, Jno., 58
Tusan, Claus, 159
Tustin, Edwd., 378
Tutherfeild, Ann, 102
Tuthill, James, 320
Tutin, Anne, 35
Tutnell, Ja., 345-346
Tutte, Jno., 176
Tuttle, Jno., 132
Tutton, Hen., 271
Tutty, Henry, 324
Tuty, Jno., 149
Twewil, Tho., 247
Twiford, Trist, 103
Twig, Wm., 243
Twigar, Lucy, 173
Twill, Sar., 207
Twine, Richd., 310
Twiner, Tho., 214
Twinson, Rich., 169
Twisdell, Tho., 359, 362
Twise, William, 294
Twist, Elizabeth, 169
Twy, Jno., 312; Thomas, 92
Twye, Jno., 30
Twyford, John, 74; Wm., 87
Twyney, John, 38
Twynny, John, 73
Tyas, Richd., 336; Thomas, 326
Tybaulds, Robt., 208
Tydy, Ed., 85
Tye, Lambert, 326, 335, 340;
    Richd., 25
Tyford, Wm., 166
Tyler, Ann, 195; Edith, 87; Henry,
    84; James, 254; Jane, 85; Jno., 13,
    14, 145, 319; Nich., 136; Wm., 304
Tylney, Major, 112
Tyman, Hen., 121
Tymson, Wm., 155
Tyne, Rog., 76
Typpin, 286
Tyre, Charles, 140; Hen., 165
Tyrrell, Wm., 96
Tyton, Wm., 274

U

Ubank, Stapleton, 335
Uble, John, 168
Udall, Mr., 152; Tho., 332
Ufoler, a Negro, 244
Uggins, Wm., 111
Ulseley, Jacob, 401

W

Martha, 226; Mary, 188, 222, 282, 327; Mathew, 327; Nich., 210; Rachel, 307; Rich., 75, 82, 92, 189; Richard, 249; Robert, 94, 115, 120, 174, 273, 323; Robt., 66, 67, 101, 131, 160, 181, 252, 372; Samll. 249; Tho., 265; Thomas, 296, 327; Vincent, 26, 62; Walter, 207; Will, 1, 153; William, 181, 282; Wm., 62, 104, 148, 150, 187, 252, 263, 282, 329, 366; Xpher., 274; land of, 64

Younge, James, 130; Joane, 112; Margaret, 370; Minion, 26; Richard, 227; Sarah, 28; Wm., 127

Youngman, Geo., 127; George, 119; Robt., 127

Yowell, Eliza., 343; Tho., 60, 86

Z

Zaines, Thomas, 291
Zambo, a Negro, 214
Zarve, 397
Zona, a Negro, 272
Zouch, John, 229
Zouche, Sir John, 24